Understanding Society

Understanding Society

An Introduction to Sociology

Caroline Hodges Persell

New York University

HARPER & ROW, PUBLISHERS, New York
Cambridge, Philadelphia, San Francisco,
London, Mexico City, São Paulo, Sydney

To Albert and Katherine
with love and appreciation for starting my inquiry

Sponsoring Editor: Alan McClare
Development Editor: Ann Torbert
Project Editor: Brigitte Pelner
Designer: T. R. Funderburk
Production Manager: Jeanie Berke
Photo Researcher: Mira Schachne
Compositor: York Graphic Services, Inc.
Printer and Binder: R. R. Donnelley & Sons Company
Art Studio: Vantage Art, Inc.
Color Inserts: A Good Thing, Inc.
Cover Photo: Chris Den Blaker

UNDERSTANDING SOCIETY: An Introduction to Sociology

Library of Congress Cataloging in Publication Data

Persell, Caroline Hodges.
Understanding society.

Bibliography: p.
Includes index.
1. Sociology. I. Title.
HM51.P45 1984 301 83-12953
ISBN 0-06-045133-5

Acknowledgments

Pages 6, 7: From *Migrants, Sharecroppers, Mountaineers,* Volume II of Children of Crisis, © 1967, 1968, 1969, 1971 by Robert Coles. Reprinted by permission of Little, Brown and Company in association with the Atlantic Monthly Press.

Pages 8, 9: From *Privileged Ones,* Volume V of Children of Crisis, © 1977 by Robert Coles. Reprinted by permission of Little, Brown and Company in association with the Atlantic Monthly Press.

Page 34: Quotation from "Why Public Schools Fail," *Newsweek,* April 20, 1981, p. 62, beginning with the words, "In the sweeping public verdict of 1981, the schools are failing," and ending with the words, "for parents who choose private education." Copyright © 1981, by Newsweek, Inc. All rights reserved. Reprinted by permission.

Page 37: Figure "The Continuous Circle of Science." From Walter L. Wallace, *The Logic of Science in Sociology,* 1971, p. 18. Reprinted by permission of Aldine Publishing Co.

Page 43: Relationship questions 1, 2, and 3 from Couples Survey, Male Questionnaire, University of Washington, Seattle. Reprinted by permission of Philip Blumstein and Pepper Schwartz.

Page 78: Quotation from Ronald W. Clark, *Einstein: The Life and Times,* published by Thomas E. Crowell, 1971, beginning with the words, "When Albert Einstein completed his university studies . . ." and ending with the words, "Einstein's major scientific insights occurred during his several years at the Patent Office."

Page 78: Adapted with permission of Macmillan Publishing Company, from *Networks and Places,* C. S. Fischer, Copyright, 1957, by The Free Press, a Corporation.

Pages 84–85: Excerpts from R. Ricklefs, "The Hidden Hurdle," the *Wall Street Journal,* September 19, 1979, front page. Reprinted by permission of the *Wall Street Journal,* copyright © Dow Jones & Company, Inc. 1979. All rights reserved.

Page 86: Quotation from R. Wallace and A. Wolf, *Contemporary Sociological Theory,* 1980, p. 248, beginning with the words, "During the rallies of the Free Speech Movement," and ending with the words, "Explain why the sixties was a period of campus turmoil." Reprinted by permission of Prentice-Hall, Inc.

Page 112: Excerpt from p. 469 of *American Society: A Sociological Interpretation,* 2d ed. Revised by R. M. Williams, Jr. Copyright © 1960 by Knopf. Reprinted by permission of Alfred A. Knopf, Inc.

Page 157: Excerpt from R. M. Kanter, *Men and Women of the Corporation,* 1977, p. 210, line 11, consisting of the symbols: "X X xx X X O X x X." Reprinted by permission of Basic Books.

Page 167: Figure (adapted) from M. T. Hannan and J. Freeman, "The Population Ecology of Organizations," *AJS* 82:5, 1977, p. 947. Reprinted by permission of The University of Chicago Press.

Page 170: Table 1 from J. Rothschild-Whitt, "The Collectivist Organization," *ASR,* Vol. 44, August 1979, p. 519. Reprinted by permission of the American Sociological Association.

Pages 171–173: Quotation from Zwerdling, *Workplace Democracy,* 1980, pp. 2–8, beginning with the words, "Forms of democracy at work" and ending with the words, "Workers in a self-managed firm have the actual voting power to *shape* the kind of workplace environment and work lives they want." (edited for length). Reprinted with permission.

Page 190: Reprinted with permission of Macmillan Publishing Company from *Social Theory and Social Structure,* Revised and Enlarged ed., R. K. Merton, "A Typology of Modes of Individual Adaptations," 1957, Free Press, p. 140.

Page 191: C. R. Shaw, *The Jack-Roller,* 1930, p. 54. Reprinted by permission of The University of Chicago Press.

Pages 206–207: Quotation from P. G. Zimbardo, "Pathology of Imprisonment," *Society* 9 (April), 1972, p. 8, beginning with the words, "At the end of only six days we had to close down" and ending with the words, "of their mounting hatred for the guards." Published by permission of Transaction, Inc. from *Society,* Vol. 9, Number 6. Copyright © 1972 by Transaction, Inc.

Page 229: Table entitled "Two Views of Stratification" from Arthur L. Stinchcombe, "Some Empirical Consequences of the Davis-Moore Theory of Stratification," *ASR,* 28 (October 1963), p. 808. Reprinted by permission of the American Sociological Association.

Page 241: Table 1 entitled "Distributions of Prestige Ratings, United States, 1947 and 1963," from R. Bendix and S. M. Lipset, *Class, Status, and Power,* 2d ed., 1966, pp. 324–325.

Page 244: Figure from E. O. Wright and L. Perrone, "Marxist Class Categories and Income Inequality," *ASR,* Vol. 42, February 1977, p. 34. Reprinted by permission of the American Sociological Association.

Page 280: Quotation from W. J. Wilson, *The Declining Significance of Race,* 1978, p. 2, beginning with the words "it is clearly evident," and ending with the words, "falling further behind the rest of society." Reprinted by permission of The University of Chicago Press and the author.

Page 282: Figure 1, page 655, from Bruce Campbell, "The Interaction of Race and Socioeconomic Status in the Development of Political Attitudes," pp. 651–658, *SSQ,* Vol. 60, no. 4, March 1980. Reprinted by permission of the University of Texas Press.

Page 283: Figure by Pettigrew from "American Indians, Blacks, Chicanos, and Puerto Ricans," *Daedalus,* Vol. 110, No. 2, 1981. Reproduced by permission of *Daedalus,* Journal of the American Academy of Arts and Sciences.

Page 285: Quotations from M. Gordon, *Assimilation in American Life,* 1964, p. 88, beginning with the words, "The desirability of maintaining English institutions," and ending with the words, "Standard in American life," and p. 115, beginning with the words, "as a totally new blend, culturally and biologically," and ending with the words, "Interaction into a distinctly new type." Reprinted by permission of Oxford University Press.

Page 299: Figure from Yankelovich, Skelly, and White survey, "Qualities considered important for men and for women," *Public Opinion,* December/January, 1980, p. 32.

Page 300: Figure from Yankelovich, Skelly, and White survey, "Percent of U.S. adults approving of married women working and percent of all women who work, 1938–1978," *Public Opinion,* December/January, 1980, p. 33.

Page 301: Passim to make chart from J. M. Nielson, *Sex in Society,* 1978, pp. 12–19. Reprinted by permission of Wadsworth Publishing Co., Inc.

Page 323: Figure on what kind of marriage is considered more satisfying, from CBS News/New York Times survey, from "The Modern Woman: How Far Has She Come?" *Public Opinion,* January/February, 1979, p. 37. Copyright © 1979 by The New York Times Company. Reprinted by permission.

Page 338: Data from Table 2.14, p. 56, Masnick and Bane, *The Nation's Families: 1960–1990.* Copyright © 1980, Joint Center for Urban Studies, MIT and Harvard University.

Page 339: Figure on percent of women who never married in different age groups, from C. Westoff, "Marriage and Fertility in the Developed Countries," *Scientific American,* December 1978, p. 55. Copyright © 1978 by Scientific American, Inc. All rights reserved.

Page 342: Figure 2.7 from Masnick and Bane, *The Nation's Families: 1960–1990,* p. 41.

Pages 351–353: Selected quotations from John F. Cuber and Peggy B. Harroff, *The Significant Americans,* 1965, pp. 43–65. Reprinted by permission of Holt, Rinehart and Winston.

Page 368: Data for chart from *Hammond Almanac,* 1981. Reprinted by permission of the Hammond Almanac, Inc.

Page 374: Excerpts from the Largest Multinational Corporations' list—July 5, 1982. Reprinted by permission of FORBES Magazine, July 5, 1982. Copyright © Forbes Inc. 1982.

Page 376: Table adapted from P. D. Montagna, *Occupations and Society,* 1977, p. 16. Reprinted by permission of John Wiley & Sons, Inc. Copyright © 1977 by John Wiley & Sons, Inc.

Page 386: Excerpts and chart from "Unemployment on the Rise," by James Kelly, p. 26, *Time* magazine (February 8), copyright © 1982 Time Inc. All rights reserved. Reprinted by permission from *Time.*

Page 390: Excerpts from S. Lohr, "How Tax Evasion Has Grown," the *New York Times,* March 15, 1981. Copyright © 1981 by The New York Times Company. Reprinted by permission.

Page 415: Data on voter participation in various countries, from K. P. Philips and P. H. Blackman, *Electoral Reform and Voter Participation,* 1975, pp. 98–99. American Enterprise Institute for Public Policy Research.

Page 416: "Indicators of Political Alienation, 1966–1977," *Public Opinion,* May/June, 1978, p. 23. American Enterprise Institute for Public Policy Research.

Page 440: Quotations from E. Ludwig and J. Santibanez (eds.), *The Chicanos: Mexican American Voices,* 1971, pp. 149–153, beginning with the words, "Barriology Exam," and ending with the words, "10. Lowered, channeled, chopped, primed all refer to what barrio art form?" plus answers to first ten questions. Reprinted by permission of Edward W. Ludwig.

Pages 442–443: Excerpts from Frazier and Sadker, *Sexism in School and Society,* 1973, pp. 99–100, from line 9, "Whenever an issue is too big" to "and subservience begins to come across," and p. 138, line 1, "Adjectives describing good" to "poised."

Page 452: Data estimating the number of members in the major religions of the world from F. H. Littell, "World Church Membership" in *Encyclopaedia Britannica Book of the Year,* 1981, p. 604. Reprinted with permission from the 1981 BRITANNICA BOOK OF THE YEAR copyright © 1981, Encyclopaedia Brittannica, Inc. Chicago, Ill.

Page 454: Map showing major distribution of Islam in the World, from G. M. Wickens, "Introduction to the Middle East," in R. M. Savory, ed., 1976, *Introduction to Islamic Civilization,* p. 2. Reprinted by permission of Cambridge University Press.

Page 482: Drawing and excerpt from S. Harris, "Fudging Data for Fun and Profit," *Time*, December 7, 1981, p. 83. Copyright © 1981 Time Inc. All rights reserved. Reprinted by permission from TIME and Frederic Golden.

Page 503: Quotation from R. Findley, "St. Helens: Mountain with a Death Wish." *National Geographic,* 159 (1), January 1981, pp. 17–18, beginning with the words, "Vancouver! Vancouver!" and ending with the words, "and closing the busy Columbia River to deep-draft ships" (edited for length).

Pages 504–505: Excerpt from E. P. Thompson, "A Letter to America." *The Nation,* January 24, 1981. Copyright © 1981 *Nation* magazine, The Nation Associates, Inc.

Pages 517–518: Excerpts from J. J. Fialka, "Ground Zero," the *Wall Street Journal,* April 16, 1982, front page ledger. Reprinted by permission of the *Wall Street Journal.,* copyright © Dow Jones & Company, Inc. 1982. All rights reserved.

Page 529: Data from Table 1 from D. M. Heer, *Society and Population,* 2d ed, 1975, p. 5. Reprinted by permission of Prentice-Hall, Inc. Copyright © 1975 by Prentice-Hall, Inc.

Page 529: Data from E. S. Deevey, Jr., "The Human Population," *Scientific American,* September 1960. Copyright © 1960 by Scientific American, Inc. All rights reserved.

Page 533: R. Reinhold, "China's Millions Are Still Hard to Count," the *New York Times,* November 26, 1978. Copyright © 1978 by The New York Times Company. Reprinted by permission.

Page 534: Figure 9 from P. A. Morrison, "Overview of Demographic Trends Shaping the Nation's Future," May 1978, p. 23. Reprinted by permission of The Rand Corporation.

Page 538: "How They Grow," *Time* magazine (November 6), p. 95. Copyright © 1978 Time Inc. All rights reserved. Reprinted by permission from TIME.

Pages 548–549: "Not So Merry Widowers," *Time* magazine (August 10), p. 45. Copyright © 1981 Time Inc. All rights reserved. Reprinted by permission from TIME.

Page 564: Figure on three theories of urban development, from C. D. Harris and E. L. Ullman, "The Nature of Cities," *The Annals,* Vol. 242, 1945, p. 17. Reprinted with permission of The American Academy of Political and Social Science. Copyright © 1945 The American Academy of Political and Social Science and the authors.

Page 566: Map noting 37th parallel and sunbelt from B. R. Rice, "Searching for the Sunbelt," *American Demographics,* 3 (3), 1981, p. 23. Reprinted by permission of American Demographics.

Page 569: Excerpt from E. Anderson, *A Place on the Corner,* 1978, pp. 58–60. Reprinted by permission of The University of Chicago Press and the author.

Page 573: Figure showing percentage of blacks who live in central cities and suburbs, 1960–1980, from L. Long and D. DeAre, "The Suburbanization of Blacks," *American Demographics* 3 (8): p. 19. Reprinted by permission of American Demographics.

Page 586: Quotation from S. Brownmiller, *Against Our Will,* 1975, p. 422, beginning with the words, "a sexual invasion of the body by force," and ending with the words, "a hostile, degrading act of violence." Reprinted by permission of Bantam Books.

Page 588: Reprinted with permission of Macmillan Publishing Company, from *Teenage Sexuality* by A. Hass, M.D. Copyright © 1977 by The Free Press, a division of Macmillan Publishing Company.

Page 592: Heterosexual-Homosexual Rating Scale from *Sexual Behavior in the Human Female,* A. C. Kinsey et al, 1953. Reproduced by permission of The Kinsey Institute for Research in Sex, Gender & Reproduction, Inc.

Page 608: ABC News-Harris Survey. Copyright © 1979. Reprinted by permission: Tribune Company Syndicate, Inc.

Page 612: Drawing from Loy, McPherson, Kenyon, *Sport and Social Systems.* Copyright © 1978. Addison-Wesley, Reading, Mass., p. 23. Reprinted with permission.

Page 622: Data from an article by F. Klein, "The Richest Oriole," the *Wall Street Journal.* Reprinted by permission of the *Wall Street Journal,* copyright © Dow Jones & Company, Inc. 1982. All rights reserved.

Color insert III-1: B. Quinn, H. Anderson, M. Bradley, P. Goetting, and P. Shriver, *Churches and Church Membership in the United States 1980.* Glenmary Research Center, Atlanta, Georgia, 1982. Copyright © 1982 by the National Council of the Churches of Christ in the U.S.A.

Color insert IV-1: Map, the U.S. population density, 1979, drawn by a computer for the ASPE X program. Reprinted by permission of Harvard Laboratory for Computer Graphics and Spatial Analysis, Harvard University.

PHOTO CREDITS

Page 2 © Chris Den Blaker / *Page 4* Corlett, DPI / *Page 7* © George W. Gardner, 1973 / *Page 9* © Heron, 1982, Woodfin Camp / *Page 13* © Spratt, Picture Group / *Page 20* Taylor, Sygma / *Page 22* © Joel Gordon, 1975 / *Page 28* © Druskis, Taurus / *Page 38* © Gordon, 1981, DPI / *Page 41* Franken, Stock, Boston / *Page 42* © Heyman, Archive Pictures / *Page 46* © Eagan, 1980, Woodfin Camp / *Page 54* © Aurness, 1980, Woodfin Camp / *Page 56* © Harbutt, Archive Pictures / *Page 61 (top)* Lee, Anthro-Photo; *(bottom)* DeVore, Anthro-Photo / *Page 65* Byrnett, Contact / *Page 76* © Freeman, Archive Pictures / *Page 79* Strickler, Monkmeyer / *Page 82* © Berndt, 1981, Stock, Boston / *Page 89* © Gazdar, 1982, Woodfin Camp / *Page 94* © Hankin, Stock, Boston / *Page 96* © Azzi, 1982, Woodfin Camp / *Page 99* © Azzi, 1983, Woodfin Camp / *Page 100* Anderson, Monkmeyer / *Page 104* © Heller, Picture Group / *Page 107 (top)* Reno, Jeroboam; *(bottom)* © Budnick, 1983, Woodfin Camp / *Page 120* © Hedman, Jeroboam / *Page 128 (top)* © Joel Gordon, 1978; *(bottom)* Vandermark, Stock, Boston / *Page 130* Vine, Leo deWys Inc. / *Page 132* Heyman, Archive Pictures / *Page 150* Delevingne, Stock, Boston / *Page 153* © Owens, Archive Pictures / *Page 154* Southwick, Stock, Boston / *Page 160* © Hoffman, Archive Pictures / *Page 163* © Bellak, Jeroboam / *Page 178* © Freedman, Archive Pictures / *Page 188* Culver / *Page 192* Laffont, Sygma / *Page 196* © Harbutt, 1968, Archive Pictures / *Page 206* © Lyon, 1970, Magnum / *Page 210* Hartmann, © Magnum / *Page 212* © Hofer, Archive Pictures / *Page 220 (top)* Kalvar, © Magnum; *(bottom)* Arnold, © Magnum / *Page 222* UPI / *Page 224* Marlow, Sygma / *Page 236* Reininger, DPI / *Page 240 (top)* Antman, Stock, Boston; *(bottom)* © Hopker, 1978, Woodfin Camp / *Page 247 (top)* © Owens, Archive Pictures; *(bottom left)* © Seitz, 1980, Woodfin Camp; *(bottom right)* Tannenbaum, Sygma / *Page 266* Smolan, Leo deWys Inc. / *Page 272* UPI / *Page 274* © Hofer, Archive Pictures / *Page 277* UPI / *Page 278* © Siteman, 1983, Taurus / *Page 279* UPI / *Page 291* Baldwin-Watriss © 1983, Woodfin Camp / *Page 293* © Hopker, 1978, Woodfin Camp / *Page 296* Reno, Jeroboam / *Page 307* Rose, Sygma / *Page 316 (top)* © Gardner, Stock, Boston; *(bottom)* Saxe, Picture Group / *Page 321* © Bronstein, Picture Group / *Page 328* © Berger, 1981, Woodfin Camp / *Page 333* © Berger, 1982, Woodfin Camp / *Page 335* Rosenthal, Stock, Boston / *Page 344* © Lawrence, Stock, Boston / *Page 360* © Preuss, 1976, Jeroboam / *Page 370* © Hrynewych, Picture Group / *Page 378* © Gelles, 1981, Stock, Boston / *Page 389* McElhinney, Archive Pictures / *Page 394* © Seitz, 1980, Woodfin Camp / *Page 399* © Hopker, 1981, Woodfin Camp / *Page 403* Bellerose, Stock, Boston / *Page 415* Franken, Stock, Boston / *Page 417* UPI / *Page 420* © Hrynewych, Picture Group / *Page 425* © Durskis, 1980, Taurus / *Page 428* © Kroll, Taurus / *Page 436* © Herwig, 1980, Stock, Boston / *Page 446* © Menzel, 1981, Stock, Boston / *Page 450* © Garrett, 1982, Woodfin Camp / *Page 457* Southwick, Stock, Boston / *Page 461* Grossman, Leo deWys Inc. / *Page 472* © Herwig, Stock, Boston / *Page 475* © Jacobson, Archive Pictures / *Page 485* © Wellman, Picture Group / *Page 488* Goldberg, Sygma / *Page 490* Wyman, Sygma / *Page 494* © Skoogfors, 1982, Woodfin Camp / *Page 496* © Godfrey, Archive Pictures / *Page 507* © Hamlin, 1978, Stock, Boston / *Page 510* Leinwand, Monkmeyer / *Page 518* © Pelaez, 1983, Contact / *Page 526* Delevingne, Stock, Boston / *Page 539* © Chris Den Blaker / *Page 547* Weisbrot, Stock, Boston / *Page 550* Southwick, Stock, Boston / *Page 554* © Adams, 1976, Contact / *Page 560* Hamlin, Stock, Boston / *Page 562* © Reininger, 1982, Contact / *Page 570* Menzel, Stock, Boston / *Page 576* Kelly, Archive Pictures / *Page 578* Vandermark, Stock, Boston / *Page 581* © Anderson, 1981, Woodfin Camp / *Page 582* © Heller, Picture Group / *Page 583* © Siteman, 1981, Taurus / *Page 600* © Aurness, 1979, Woodfin Camp / *Page 607* Prelutsky, Stock, Boston / *Page 609* © Chris Den Blaker / *Page 625* Heyman, Archive Pictures.

Color Portfolios

Page I-1 (top) Routh, DPI; *(bottom)* © Kroll, 1981, Taurus / *Page I-2 (top)* Austin, DPI; *(bottom)* © Schwartz, Int'l Stock Photo / *Page I-3 (top)* Rhodes, Taurus; *(bottom left)* © Choy, Peter Arnold; *(bottom right)* DPI / *Page I-4* Kaplan, DPI / *Page II-1* Blanche, DPI / *Page II-2 (top left)* © Dodge, DPI; *(bottom left)* Reeberg, DPI; *(right)* © Uzzell III, Woodfin Camp / *Page II-3 (top)* © Heron, 1980, Woodfin Camp; *(bottom)* Kirk, © Peter Arnold / *Page II-4 (top)* Schweikerdt, Image Bank; *(middle)* UPI; *(bottom)* UPI / *Page III-1 (top)* © Azzi, 1980, Woodfin Camp; *(bottom)* Gritscher, © Peter Arnold / *Page III-2 (left)* © Gazdar, Woodfin Camp; *(right)* Hill, Leo de Wys Inc. / *Page III-3 (top)* Kirkland, Leo deWys Inc.; *(bottom)* © Fischer/Visum 1981, Woodfin Camp / *Page III-4 (top)* © 1982, Smith, Image Bank; *(bottom)* © Caspary, Woodfin Camp / *Page IV-1 (left)* © Hall, Woodfin Camp; *(right)* © Hall, 1981, Woodfin Camp / *Page IV-2* © Heron, 1980, Woodfin Camp / *Page IV-3* © Zehnder, Peter Arnold / *Page IV-4 (left)* © Pfeffer, Peter Arnold; *(right)* © Grant, Int'l Stock Photo.

Contents in Brief

Contents

Preface

This book explores society and how it operates. My goal in *Understanding Society* is to illuminate the powerful social forces and patterns that impinge on students' lives and careers. As a result, students should be in a stronger position to pursue informed choices and actions.

Both classic and current sociological theories are used to examine the major aspects of social life. Each of the primary perspectives—interactionist, functionalist, and conflict—helps provide unique insights. Instructors can follow the chapter order or change it to suit the focus of their particular course. The result, I hope, is a text flexible enough to meet the varied needs of students and teachers.

The book is organized in six parts: one, theoretical orientations and research methods; two, core aspects of social life; three, the significance of social inequality; four, major institutions; five, social changes; and six, contemporary areas of inquiry.

Part One presents sociology's theoretical orientations and methods of gathering evidence. In Chapter 1, the reader meets two pairs of young people whose lives demonstrate the profound influence of social forces. Chapter 2 illustrates types of social research with recent studies, for example, Blumstein's and Schwartz's study of couples and their relationships.

Part Two, focusing on core aspects of social life, introduces various types of societies and the major concepts of status, role, and social institutions. In Chapter 3, the concept of social role is explored from two perspectives, functionalist and interactionist, and insights from both are synthesized into a richer understanding of this basic sociological concept than either approach alone can provide. Chapter 4 examines how social networks link individuals, organizations, and institutions, and how they may provide opportunities for individuals, including their importance for finding jobs. Chapter 5 analyzes culture as a human creation and as a social envelope that influences behavior, attitudes, and values, and Chapter 6 presents the critical process of socialization in terms that integrate structure and process. Chapter 7, "Groups and Organizations," contains a unique discussion of how the proportions of groups affect their dynamics. It also contrasts two major forms of organization: bureaucratic and democratic-collective. Competing explanations of deviance and crime are considered in Chapter 8.

Part Three treats the profound significance of various forms of social inequality based on class, race, caste, and age in Chapters 9–11. Chapter 12 examines gender from the perspective of social stratification as well as in terms of socialization.

Part Four surveys major social institutions, including the family (13), economy (14), politics (15), education (16), and religion (17), from the dual perspectives of what they do and how they are changing. Chapter 18 surveys the rise of modern science, resistance to change in the scientific community, and the critical relationship between science and society.

Part Five explores social changes. A chapter (19) on collective behavior, social movements, and social change shows how societies change. Chapter 20 considers the issues of population, ecology, and health, including the social sources of health and illness and the organization of health care systems. A final chapter (21) examines where people live, how urban living differs from suburban living, and theories of urban development and urban problems.

Part Six treats several topics that do not appear in most texts, sex and sexuality (22), and sport and leisure (23). These chapters illustrate the power of culture and socialization in shaping social behavior.

The book is generously illustrated with cartoons, graphs, summary charts, and photographs. There are stimulating boxed materials and instructive color graphics. Among the aids to student learning in each chapter are an opening outline, a list of key terms (defined in the Glossary), and a summary of major points. Class testing of the manuscript and the learning aids with students in the liberal arts, business, nursing, computer science, and the natural sciences helped identify their interests and excite their curiosity. A glossary of more than 400 key terms and concepts and a full bibliography and index appear at the end of the book.

Supplements

The text is well integrated with the *Instructor's Manual, Student Study Guide,* and *Test Bank.* The *Test Bank* contains 35 multiple-choice, 10 true-false, and 5 matching questions plus 3 to 5 essay questions for each of the 23 chapters. Every objective test question has been pre-tested in sociology classes. The questions cover major figures in the field, important concepts, and significant sociological insights and trends.

Eleen A. Baumann, Richard G. Mitchell, Jr., and I have worked closely together writing the *Instructor's Manual* and *Student Study Guide.* For each chapter of the text there is a corresponding chapter in the *Instructor's Manual* consisting of: (1) a Statement of the Goals of the Chapter; (2) a Chapter Outline; (3) Teaching Suggestions, including in-class exercises, out-of-class projects, community assistance for the teaching process, and a list of film/audio-visual aids; and (4) Supplemental Materials, including examples or materials that may be used in class discussions or lectures. The *Instructor's Manual* also contains visual aids that can be used with overhead projectors for classroom instruction, including copies of some of the key tables and figures in the text, which can be presented and discussed in the classroom.

The *Student Study Guide* is keyed to the text. For each chapter there is: (1) a brief summary of the chapter; (2) a section reviewing what students have learned in the chapter, including review questions and a chance to define major concepts; (3) a section of exercises in which students can apply what they have learned; and (4) a section testing what students have learned, consisting of 10 multiple-choice questions, 15 fill-in-the-blanks, and 5 to 10 matching questions, plus answers. A computer-assisted student study program reinforces the major material in the text. A special appendix to the *Student Study Guide* contains the work sheets for some of the exercises in the *Instructor's Manual.* The exercises in both supplements are designed to show how sociology can illuminate students' daily lives. We have successfully used most of these exercises with our own students.

I would like to thank my colleagues and students at New York University for their comments on chapters or their very helpful ideas and suggestions, especially Beverly Burris, Edward Chapel, Linda Cushman, Eliot Freidson, David Greenberg, Sharon Grosfeld, Floyd Hammack, Wolf Heydebrand, Hope Klapper, Edward Lehman, Marsha Lichtman, Debra Lombardo, Barbara O'Meara, Herbert Menzel, Mary Phillips, Susan Schapiro, Edwin Schur, Farrell Webb, Dennis Wrong, and all the Introduction to Sociology students who made comments on earlier drafts of this book.

Many knowledgeable sociologists in various specialities generously shared their insights with me and I am grateful to them.

Michael T. Aiken, University of Wisconsin, Madison
Howard Aldrich, Cornell University
Camilla Auger, Tasca Foundation
Pauline Bart, University of Illinois-Lincoln Medical School
Ivar Berg, Vanderbilt University
Charles Bidwell, University of Chicago
George W. Bohrnstedt, Indiana University
Charles M. Bonjean, University of Texas
Alvin Boskoff, Emory University
Elise M. Boulding, Dartmouth College
Wilbur B. Brookover, Michigan State University
Aaron V. Cicourel, University of California, San Diego
Arlene Kaplan Daniels, Northwestern University
Norman Denzin, University of Illinois, Urbana
Carolyn Etheridge, SUNY, Old Westbury
William A. Gamson, University of Michigan
Mark Granovetter, SUNY, Stony Brook
Andrew Greeley, University of Arizona
Michael T. Hannan, Stanford University
Roscoe C. Hinkle, Ohio State University
Arlie R. Hochschild, University of California, Berkeley
The Rev. William Johnstone, Episcopal Churchmen for South Africa
Rosabeth Moss Kanter, Yale University
Herbert Kelman, Harvard University
John C. Leggett, Livingston College
Nan Lin, SUNY, Albany
Seymour Martin Lipset, Stanford University
Lora J. Liss, Washington, D.C.
Judith Lorber, CUNY, Brooklyn
Karen Louis, University of Massachusetts, Boston
Raymond W. Mack, Northwestern University
Edward L. McDill, Johns Hopkins University
John W. Meyer, Stanford University
Stanley Milgram, Graduate Center, CUNY
John M. Mogey, Boston University
Charles B. Nam, Florida State University
Peter K. New, University of Toronto
Charles Perrow, SUNY, Stony Brook
Elizabeth Petras, University of Pennsylvania
Karen Polonko, University of Iowa
Barbara Reskin, University of Michigan
James Rosenbaum, Northwestern University
Morris Rosenberg, University of Maryland
Joyce Rothschild-Whitt, University of Louisville
Sheryl K. Ruzek, University of California Medical Center, San Francisco
John Scanzoni, University of North Carolina, Greensboro
Janet Ward Schofield, University of Pittsburgh
Rita J. Simon, University of Illinois, Urbana
Murray A. Straus, University of New Hampshire
Ann Swidler, Stanford University
Richard Travisano, University of Rhode Island
Ralph Turner, University of California, Los Angeles
Donald Van Houten, University of Oregon
Christy Visher, Indiana University
Charles F. Westoff, Princeton University
Everett K. Wilson, University of North Carolina, Chapel Hill
J. Milton Yinger, Oberlin College
Marjorie Zatz, Indiana University
Maurice Zeitlin, University of California, Los Angeles
Morris Zelditch, Stanford University

Numerous sociology teachers reviewed chapters of this manuscript or participated in groups that discussed my ideas for this book, and I appreciate their helpful suggestions.

Andrew D. Abbott, Rutgers University
Larry Adams, Texas Christian University
David Alcorn, Angelo State University
David T. Bailey, Sam Houston State University
Wilbur B. Brookover, Michigan State University
Brent T. Bruton, Iowa State University
Leonard Cargan, Wright State University
Richard Crester, California Polytechnic Institute
Kenneth W. Eckhardt, University of Delaware
David L. Ellison, Rensselaer Polytechnic Institute
William Feigelman, Nassau Community College
Hugh Floyd, University of New Orleans
Cheryl Townsend Gilkes, Boston University
Dee Ann Spencer Hall, Central Missouri State University
Julia G. Hall, Drexel University
Joan Huber, University of Illinois, Urbana
Butler A. Jones, Cleveland State University
Irwin H. Kantor, Middlesex Community College
Debra R. Kaufman, Northeastern University
Martin P. Levine, Bloomfield College
J. Robert Lilly, Northern Kentucky University
Anne R. Mahoney, University of Denver
Hiram Mariampolski, Yeshiva University
Hans O. Mauksch, University of Missouri, Columbia
Jerry B. Michel, Memphis State University
Peter B. Morrill, Bronx Community College
Karen A. Polonko, University of Iowa
Regina Robin, New York City Community College
Earl Rubington, Northeastern University
Marcia T. Segal, Indiana University Southeast
Richard A. Shaffer, California Polytechnic Institute, San Luis Obispo
Kenneth Smith, University of Miami
David Sternberg, John Jay College of Criminal Justice, City College of New York
Kenrick S. Thompson, Northern Michigan University
William Waegel, Villanova University
Theodore C. Wagenaar, Miami University (Ohio)
George Wallis, University of Georgia
Robert H. Walsh, Illinois State University, Normal
Thomas S. Weinberg, State University College, Buffalo
Kenneth R. Wilson, East Carolina University
David R. Zaret, Indiana University

A number of people at Harper & Row helped me immeasurably during the five years I spent researching, writing, and revising this book. Among them were: Dale Tharp, whose vision sparked my interest in writing the book; Ann Torbert, whose wit, care, and commentary encouraged my writing and rewriting efforts; Neale Sweet, whose sound judgment and advice were invaluable at several key junctures; Alan McClare, who remained cheerful even in the face of seemingly insurmountable problems; Brigitte Pelner, whose good humor and devotion to accuracy were unparalleled; Mira Schachne, whose energy and good ideas made the photo selection a pleasure; and T. R. Funderburk, whose patience and sense of proportion never wavered.

I want to express special appreciation to Shirley Diamond who did the fine index for this book and to Charlotte A. Fisher who typed the final draft of the manuscript. They inspired me with their interest in the project and their excellent work. Finally, I want to thank Karen Helsing and Pam Pozarny for helping to proofread and check the book with me.

C. H. P.

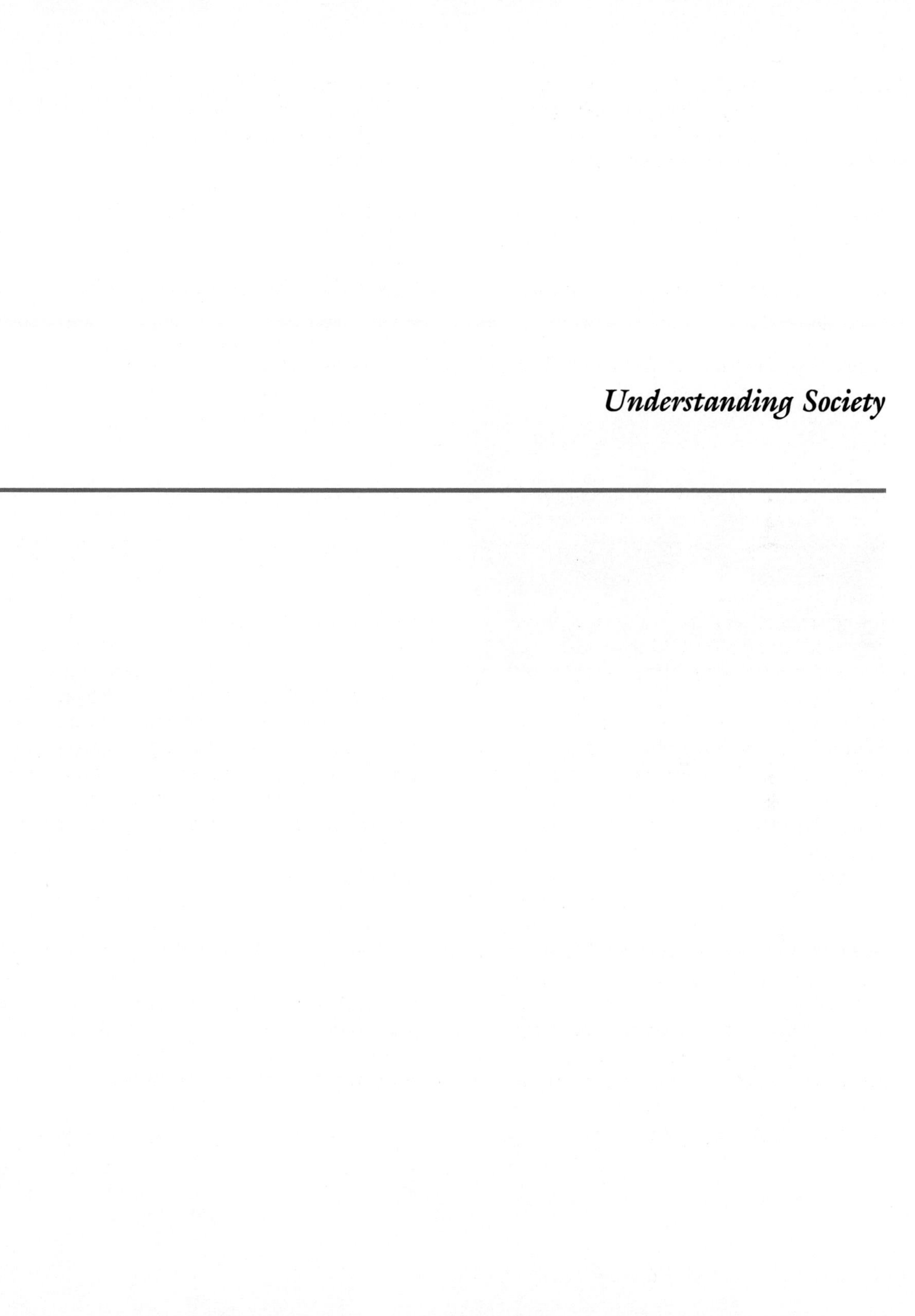

Understanding Society

Part One

Introduction

Chapter 1

An Introduction to Society and Sociology

What is the longest time you have been totally out of contact, in person or by phone, with another human being? For most of us, it is probably less than 24 hours. Although we think of ourselves as individuals, we long for contact with others. Indeed, we cannot survive or become fully human without that contact, since above all else humans are social beings. *Sociology* as a field of study explores the social *contexts* and social *processes* that influence our lives. It helps us understand the patterns that occur in the interactions of individuals with each other and with various social groups. Paradoxically, becoming aware of the forces that shape our lives and how they do so may make us freer to be who we want to be.

AN INVITATION TO THE SOCIOLOGICAL OUTLOOK

To get a glimpse of how social forces affect us, consider the lives of two very different pairs of young people: Albert and his wife are migrant workers; Alice and her twin brother Alex are heirs to a New Mexican fortune. They spoke to Robert Coles, a social psychiatrist, who has reported on their lives:

> Youth for Albert and his wife was a short-lived time; youth for them was working the way they had done for years as "children." . . . As Albert said, *"You stop, you die*—that's what we say when we need to remind ourselves about the kind of life we have ahead of us. And if we forget to remind ourselves, the crew leader won't; he won't forget to tell us the score.
>
> "He was the one, the crew leader was, who told me I should pick a girl and stay with her. . . .
>
> "I listened to his advice; I chose my girl, my wife. She is a good woman. She's always been good. She's nice to be with. She loves me. She tries to be a good mother. I love her. I'd die without her. We'll be moving on up to the next farm, and I'll feel sick. I put my head on her shoulder, and I feel better, all of a sudden; it's like there's been a miracle. She says I make her feel good. She says if it wasn't for me and the children, she'd have died a long time ago."
>
> By fifteen, all of [this] had happened to Albert; and by thirteen or fourteen other migrant youths are going through what he described. They are getting ready to surrender a certain exhilaration, a curiosity of mind, a kind of youthful intensity, an inclination to experiment and dream and speak out—and escape. . . .
>
> [Albert] tells how he once tried to break away from the crew leader, how he failed to do so. The sheriff came and arrested him for owing money, for disturbing the peace,

Migrant workers are individuals whose lives are influenced by larger social institutions such as the law and the economic system. Sociologists try to see the connections between individuals and such institutions, and to see the world through the eyes of various individuals including migrants.

for drinking too much, for possible thievery. . . . It was all faked, all trumped up, but the point was made, and he was quickly released—into the hands of his accuser and longtime "friend," the crew leader. He was at the time "about fourteen." . . .

"If I'd been able to, I would have started on a new life. I would have been my own man and said only what I believed. But maybe you can't have but one kind of life, at least here on this earth—especially if you're like us migrant people. I guess those few weeks, when we were dating and figuring out our plan to break away—I guess that was when we were young, when we could hope for a good break." . . .

His wife,[1] who is his age, remembers all of that. . . . "My children ask me questions about what we used to do and where we used to live, a lot of questions. I tell them it's always been the same. They stop asking you if you tell them that. If you let them go, let them ask more and more questions, you'll soon get sad; that's the trouble." (Coles, 1967: pp. 544–546)

Some growers, gas station attendants, and local residents describe the migrants as "animals." Sociologists and other social scientists like Coles who study human behavior do not simply accept other people's pictures of "reality." The sociological outlook requires us to go beyond these explanations and look for possible connections between individuals and larger social institutions such as the law and the economic system. It leads us to ask "What's really going on here?" In this case, Coles refused to accept the definition of migrant workers as "animals." Instead, he has shown us the world through the eyes of the mi-

[1]Coles does not mention Albert's wife's name in his book.

grants themselves. He does the same for two economically privileged young people, Alice and Alex, a girl and a boy who are twins.

> Their parents own a large and beautifully maintained ranch in the so-called North Valley of Albuquerque. . . . The mother collects antiques, the father is a prominent New Mexican . . . and his father . . . is one of the richest men in New Mexico. [Alice] knows that both her father and her grandfather have long been involved in various ways with Indians. The Pueblo people have land, and her family has an interest in land, a willingness to buy it, sell it, build on it, divide it up, display it, advertise it, promote its virtues, and, she knows, overlook (at the very least) its deficiencies. . . . Alex talks of his crusty grandfather's response to Pueblo life: "He said they are nice people, but they don't ever amount to much, because they've got no real *fight* in them. . . . [Alex] has asked his father whether he thinks the Indians actually suffer, and has been told no, they don't—or don't any more than others do. His father's strongly worded views have (but only tentatively) become his. Every once in a while Alexander has a moment or two of disagreement. . . . Not to his face, however; he tells Alice about his opinions, as against his father's. And she says yes, he ought to stick to his guns, even go speak up to their parents, let them know what one of their children thinks. He has not followed her suggestion, though.
>
> He explains why: "My father knows more about the Indians than the teacher. He says he talks to them face-to-face about business, and the teacher only gets her information from books. . . . Alice will probably ask to go to a public school one of these days, just because she likes to argue with Daddy. She tells him she thinks he's wrong sometimes! He smiles and says she's young and she will change her mind later on. She asked him last week what would happen if she *didn't* change her mind. He said nothing for a while, then he said she would, even if she thinks she won't. . . . [Alice] asked Daddy about Indians: would he mind if she married one? He said she wouldn't. She said yes, but what if she decided she wanted to. He told her to stop asking him a lot of silly questions. She got upset, because he was really angry with her, and she could tell. That's why I don't want to argue about the Indians with my parents or my grandfather. They think the Indians aren't the same as the white people, and we should stay away from them, just like they stay away from us. The teachers have a different opinion; they like the Indians. So does my best friend's father. He's a doctor, and he says the Indians have a lot of diseases, and they should go to the hospital, but they have no money, and the government is supposed to have doctors taking care of Indians, but there aren't enough doctors and it's bad to be born an Indian, because you might die very young. I told my mother what he said, and she said it's sad, but it can be the fault of an Indian mother: she doesn't keep a clean house, and she doesn't know the right food to feed her kids, so then they get sick. She said my grandfather is right when he says that the Lord helps the people who try to help themselves."
>
> The boy wonders whether Indians pray to the same God his parents ask him to beseech before going to sleep. His parents are Presbyterians, attend church with the children every Sunday, and encourage in them prayers at the table and upon retiring. . . . Alice will ask the Lord's "kindness" to descend to animals she loves—horses, dogs, cats, a bird—and to "the poor people." So will Alex. He even specifies who they are—"the Indians and the Spanish." . . . The parents say nothing, but the twins know that their concern for the

> impoverished or the socially and racially "different" is theirs alone at the table. The father has often commented upon how "different" Indians or Spanish-speaking people are. The differences, to him, go quite deep, have to do with what he calls "mentality" as well as social or historical experience, and are ultimately (he has argued) spiritual, hence derived from that hard to comprehend source (for children, certainly, and maybe for grown-ups as well): God's Will. . . .
>
> [Alice] says, "Daddy said he used to worry about the poor Indians and the poor Spanish people, but when you grow up you begin to realize that even if you gave away every penny you have, there would be no change in the world: the rich and the poor would still be there. . . . Maybe if the rich people gave some money to the poor people, Maria [their maid] would be better off. But Alex says he doesn't think they will give enough!" (Coles, 1977: pp. 182–205)

These two examples illustrate that people's personal identities are socially rooted. Albert notes the difficulties they face, "especially if you're like us migrant people." Alex and Alice struggle with the social identity their parents and grandfather try to impose: Are they really "different" from Indians and the Spanish, or not? If all human beings are alike, how can the great inequalities between them be justified? The identities of Alex and Alice are maintained by social relationships with their parents, as Albert's is with the crew leader. These people—parents and employers—mold the young people's lives through affection and through superior power and resources. Their power is rooted in larger social structures, so there is a crucial link between personal feelings and those structures.

These examples also reveal that people struggle to change their social confinements. Albert and his wife tried to run away. Although they failed, they made the attempt. They also have forged a loving, meaningful relationship with each other, even in the face of adversity. Alex and Alice actively question their parents' views of the world. They ponder how to improve the life of their maid, rather than assuming it should be the way it is. Thus, while bosses, parents, and others seek to define things in certain ways, individuals can resist those definitions to some extent. The sociological outlook stresses that we can play an active role in our lives even in the face of social influences.

Although most of us are neither as rich as Alice and Alex nor as poor as Albert and his wife, social forces work just as actively in our lives as in theirs. These forces touch us and shape us in various ways. How much we are influenced depends upon our other resources, social sup-

Privileged young people may grow up wondering why Indians or other poor people are less privileged than they are.

ports, and individual personalities. Sociology considers how society affects us as individuals. It also explores how we take parts of society into ourselves—how we may come to believe, to feel, to think, and to act in ways society promotes.

Social forces can be seen as a strong current in an ocean or river. Sometimes such currents are irresistibly strong, and no amount of effort can prevent someone from being pulled out to sea or over a waterfall. At other times, however, swimmers can counteract the force of the current. They can move diagonally across the current rather than directly against it. Or they can decide to flow with the current and use its force to carry them to a better position. Some swimmers are better equipped than others, through training or through natural strength. As a result, they may have a better chance than others to fight dangerous currents. The purpose of this comparison is to illustrate that as conscious, thinking beings, we can make some choices or exercise will even in the face of strong social currents. The idea

"I demand to know what hidden forces are impeding my progress and strewing my path with obstacles!"

SOURCE: Drawing by Sempé, © 1982, *The New Yorker Magazine, Inc.*

that we can shape events as well as be influenced by them is captured in the statement made by the archbishop of Canterbury at the wedding of Prince Charles and Lady Diana of Great Britain: "We help to shape this world and are not just its victims." Few people have the resources of that couple, but the message applies to us all—individuals working alone and together can try to carve out a degree of independent action, even in the face of social forces.

Clearly our personalities, styles of life, and the choices available to us would be totally different if we had been born Albert, Alice, Alex, Prince Charles, or Lady Diana instead of who we are. A major tool sociologists use to see the ways humans create and carry on varied social patterns is the *method of comparison*. We can compare our society or our subgroup within society with other societies or with other subgroups. This method helps determine analytically what factors lead to similarities or differences in behavior. For instance, students cheat more in some colleges than in others. Are the variations due to personality differences among the students, or to social and organizational variations? Sociologists seek to answer such questions by making careful comparisons. Comparing different groups or societies can also reveal how beliefs and ideas are related to social organization and may benefit some people in society more than others. The beliefs about Indians that Alice's and Alex's father holds may be bound up with how he uses their land, for instance.

The sociological outlook is fed by curiosity. Why, we wonder, are individuals and societies so varied? What social forces have shaped different existences? Our quest to understand society has an urgency and importance to it, for if we cannot understand the social world, we are more likely to be overwhelmed by it. Although we may survive without understanding the social world, our chances of influencing social processes are slim indeed. To understand society, we need careful observations and good theories about the way things occur.

The quest for understanding has practical as well as intellectual value. Sociology can help us to understand ourselves better, since it examines how the social world influences the way we think, feel, and act. It can also help with decision-making, both our own and that of larger organizations. Sociologists can gather systematic information from which to make a decision, provide insights into what is going on in a situation, and present alternatives. In many people the desire for understanding society is also sustained by the wish to change the way things are. Sociologists themselves differ on this issue. Some see understanding and change as intimately linked; others stress that analysis can occur without commitment to change. These different views are rooted in the values of the people holding them. Some people are unhappy with the way things are; others see no need to change them.

THE GROWTH OF SOCIOLOGY

THE SOCIAL SCIENCES

Sociology is not the only discipline that studies human behavior and societies. Neighboring disciplines share an interest in some aspect of the social world.

Sociology, economics, anthropology, history, political science, and psychology are neighboring disciplines. One of the characteristics they share is that each has a coherent base of knowledge which is grounded in theory and research. They also are marked by one or more distinctive methods of obtaining knowledge. Law, public administration, social medicine, social work, education, and business administration are closely related professional areas that draw upon the social sciences to deal with practical problems. They may also add to our knowledge of social life when they conduct systematic studies. Different historical origins and professional differences of opinion sometimes interfere with relationships among these fields. Despite their differences, however, these specialized subjects all deal with social behavior. All *social sciences,* as these disciplines are called, study human activity and communication, but each discipline separates out certain behaviors as its particular focus of study.

Economics

The field of economics considers activity relating to the production, distribution, and consumption of goods and services. In studying a factory, an economist tends to see the work force as a "supply of labor." Sociologists consider other aspects of the workers' social makeup that may influence the work situation. They see the work force comprised of individuals of various races, sexes, ages, and religions. Any or all of these factors may affect the work process.

Because goods and services may easily be counted and measured, economists have been able to use sophisticated mathematical and statistical analyses in their work. But the production, distribution, and consumption of goods and services also occurs within a social web, leaving additional areas for sociological inquiry. The surging demand for smaller cars was possible, for example, because of smaller family size. Thus the supply and price of oil operates within a social world to influence consumer choices. And while valuing the expertise of economists, sociologists can provide additional perspectives on economic life.

Political Science

The study of political science emerged after the development of economics and focused on political philosophy and the ideals of good government. In the twentieth century, political science has turned to the study of forms of government in the United States, Great Britain, France, the USSR, and elsewhere. In recent decades political scientists have come to use more numerical data, such as voting records or numbers of people holding certain attitudes. They have also begun to focus on actual political behaviors more than on political philosophies. Today the interests of political scientists and political sociologists overlap to a large degree—for example, in studies of voting behavior and public opinion formation.

Anthropology

Anthropology seeks to describe human variations, both physical and social, since humankind's earliest beginnings. It has a highly comparative, or cross-cultural, perspective. Traditionally, anthropologists have studied remote cultures; they have lived with tribal, exotic, and often preliterate societies that were isolated from the contemporary world. As such untouched societies disappear, anthropologists have begun to study social groups in industrial societies. Thus we begin to see ethnographies (detailed anthropological descriptions) of urban street gangs, peer culture in schools, the transmission of culture among immigrants, and gender-role behavior. These studies closely parallel many of the concerns of sociology.

History

The study of past societies has only recently attracted the attention of American sociologists, who previously left this field to historians. Some historians claim that history is a series of unique events which can only be described separately and which never form patterns or trends. They tend to see history as part of the humanities (along with literature, art, and music), rather than as a social science. Other historians provide comparisons across time or record disappearing styles of life; they resemble sociologists who study the past. A few historians borrow sociological methods for analyzing numerical data, and some sociologists include historical background in their studies of communities, class structures, or organizational change. A sociological study comparing social leadership in Boston and Philadelphia, for example, traces its historical roots to the colonial experience and even back to Europe (Baltzell, 1979).

Social workers provide a number of services to people in need, such as organizing classes for people in prison. Sociologists might study the causes of crime or evaluate the success of such rehabilitation programs in prisons.

Psychology

Psychology explores both the biological and the social origins of human behavior. Physiological psychology considers the physical processes that underlie thinking, feeling, and perceiving. *Social psychology* involves the scientific study of how individual behavior is socially influenced. Social psychologists focus on what happens inside individuals, including personality development, and how they are influenced by the groups, societies, and cultures to which they belong. Social psychology is well established in both psychology and sociology departments in universities all over the United States.

Social Work

The professional field of social work is frequently confused with sociology. Sociology is concerned with scientifically analyzing social relationships; its goal is to understand and explain those relationships. Social work, on the other hand, is directed toward helping people who have problems. These problems may stem from public friction or from private troubles. Social workers provide a wide variety of services to people in need. For example, among the many activities of social workers would be these: helping families of chronically ill children cope with their situation; administering public assistance to welfare mothers; counseling young people about their personal problems; and helping ex-convicts find jobs. Sociological understanding may assist social workers as they do their work, and sociologists often want their studies to help people.

The difference between the two lies in their primary concerns. One sociologist, Patricia Nash, described it this way: If a man staggered out of a bar and collapsed in a heap, a social worker would go over, try to help him up, and see that he had a place to spend the night. The sociologist would try to understand the social factors affecting alcohol use and abuse and the consequences resulting from alcohol abuse. The social worker provides immediate assistance to one individual; the sociologist might help numerous people in the long run by gaining insights into the roots and results of certain social behaviors. Similarly, sociology differs from other practical fields such as public administration, public health, education, and management, which draw on theories and research from sociology and other behavioral sciences to try to improve social policies and practices.

THE BIRTH OF SOCIOLOGY

The social sciences and the professional fields that apply them to practical problems developed in response to a series of social changes and trends that occurred in the seventeenth and eighteenth centuries in Europe. At that time, Europeans began exploring the world, and voyagers were returning from Asia, the Americas, Africa, and the South Seas with amazing stories of other societies and civilizations. Widely different social practices challenged the view that European life reflected the natural order of God. People began to think more critically about the European social world as the ways of newly discovered peoples became known. In the eighteenth and nineteenth centuries, science and technology were developing rapidly. James Watt invented the steam engine in 1769, and in 1865 Joseph Lister discovered that an antiseptic barrier could be placed between a wound and germs in the atmosphere to inhibit infection. These and other scientific developments spurred social changes and offered hope that scientific methods might help explain the social as well as the natural world.

In the late nineteenth century, social upheavals that forever changed the social order shook Western Europe. The old order was collapsing "under the twin blows of industrialism and revolutionary democracy" (Nisbet, 1966, p. 21). Mechanical industry was growing, and thousands of people were migrating to cities to work in the new factories. People once rooted to the land they farmed found themselves crowded into cities. The authority of the church, the village, and the family was being undermined by impersonal factory and city life.

Industrialization undermined the dignity of labor by pulling workers out of the protective order of family, village, and parish life and putting them into a commercial relationship. Property relations were also transformed, from a continuous personal relationship to land to the abstract ownership of shares that were impersonally bought and sold. Urban life expanded along with industrialism and was viewed with alarm by those who feared its ills and squalor, as well as by those who felt that losing the natural rhythms of country life would destroy European culture and morals. The factory and the machine were seen as additional negative features of industrialization, making people subject to extreme regimentation and turning their minds and hearts into machines (Nisbet, 1966).

Even more revolutionary than industrialization were the changes wrought by the French Revolution in 1789. That revolution changed the nature of property, the family, education, trade associations, and other social institutions. The state, for example, became infused with a kind of religious moralism. Two seemingly contradictory conditions resulted from these upheavals. The first was the rise of individualism with the separation of individuals from such communal structures as guilds, village communities, and churches. Second was the destruction of particular social relations, for example between monarch and subject or priest and parishioner, in favor of abstract social categories such as "the poor" or "the working class" (Nisbet, 1966). The social sciences emerged within this context, as early sociological thinkers struggled with the vast implications of industrial and political revolution.

THE FIRST SOCIOLOGISTS

COMTE AND SPENCER

Auguste Comte (1798–1857), a French philosopher, aimed to establish a new social science which he named "sociology," to be based on the methods of observation and reasoning that had been used so successfully in the natural sciences. Comte also believed that sociology would use the historical method to compare the consecutive states of humanity. He believed that social phenomena are subject to natural law and hoped that the scientific study of the social world would help to improve the human condition. Since he coined the word "sociology" and did a great deal to advance the discipline, Comte has been called the "father of sociology."

Herbert Spencer (1820–1903), an Englishman, contributed several key ideas to the developing science of sociology. Both he and Comte believed that the social world was patterned and could be understood through careful observation, but they differed with respect to how knowledge that comes from social science inquiry should be used. Comte believed social scientists should become a new kind of priestly class that would direct the course of society.

While believing in the value of studying society scientifically, Spencer stressed the complexity of social causes and the interconnection of various parts in society. He also saw social arrangements in biological terms. The oldest of nine children and the only one to survive into adulthood, he coined the term "survival of the fittest" to describe the evolutionary process he saw operating in social systems. He realized that human actions may have unanticipated consequences. Therefore, Spencer argued, society must not be tampered with by governments or reformers. Similar arguments are heard today. For example, U.S. legislators debate whether the government should provide health insurance or whether a free-market model of health care delivery should prevail. The issue of whether we understand society well enough to change it in a rational, planned way is still very much alive.

KARL MARX

Along with naturalist Charles Darwin and psychologist Sigmund Freud, Karl Marx (1818–1883) is undoubtedly one of the three most influential thinkers of the past century. He did not think of himself as a sociologist, but his sociological insights are profoundly important. Marx thought social scientists should not only describe the world, but also change it; his ideas have done both. Today about one-quarter of the world's population lives in societies that are officially linked to Marxist doctrines.

One of Marx's central contributions is the emphasis he placed on material conditions and how they affect social life. Marx wrote: "It is not the consciousness of men that determines their being, but, on the contrary, their social being determines their consciousness" (Marx and Engels, 1846). At the same time, Marx was aware that people made choices—for instance, when he said that we create our own history, but we do not make it in a vacuum. This statement suggests the operation of freedom within a social framework that sets limits. According to Marx, our ideas, feelings, and even the way we perceive reality are influenced by the social relations surrounding economic production. Whoever controls the means of production will also, to a considerable degree, control the ruling ideas of an era, Marx suggests. The organization of production also determines the class structure of a society. According to Marx, there is a built-in antagonism and conflict between classes, and history consists of the struggles between contending classes.

Marx also stressed that capitalism was riddled with contradictions which might prove to be its undoing. For example, as capitalists produced more and more, the market would not necessarily grow at the same rate. In the face of limited markets and increasing competition, capitalists would have to cut prices, driving the rate of profit down and leading to unemployment and economic depression. Such results could disenchant people with capitalism.

In the unequal class structure that exists in capitalist societies, all the major social institutions, including the state, religion, and political economy, are characterized by what Marx called *alienation*. For him, alienation referred to the creation, by humans, of something that turns back upon people as an alien power. For example, people create religions but then let religion dictate what they should or should not do. People establish a state, but then the state's power may limit what people can do. They begin to use money to facilitate exchanges of goods and services, but money soon becomes an end rather than a means. In these and other ways, people become alienated from their own creations.

EMILE DURKHEIM

If you approve of the existing social order and it is being seriously challenged from within, it is not surprising that your major preoccupation will be with social order, stability, cohesion, integration, authority, and regulation. This was the case with Emile Durkheim (1858–1917), who lived in France during the severe disorders of the Paris Commune and the Third Republic. For both Durkheim and Comte, writing about social change and social conflict must have been like trying to convey the joys of world travel while desperately seasick. Their intellectual problems were rooted in their views of the social problems of their day. Nevertheless, Durkheim's observations about society still have value today. He developed the notion that social features serve important social functions. *Functions* refer to the consequences of a thing for the operation of the whole social system, or for some part of the system. Certain religions, for instance, teach that a wife should "love, honor, and obey" her husband, thereby stating a view of ideal gender roles in the family that functions to stabilize the *patriarchal* (father-centered) *family*.

Durkheim was particularly interested in the social functions of group bonds, and he wondered about the factors that affect the cohesiveness of social groups. One of the forms of social "glue" that caught Durkheim's attention was religion, particularly the role of religious rituals in generating social bonds among group members. Such social bonds, Dukheim argued, are important explanations even for such seemingly personal actions as committing suicide, which cannot be explained simply by psychological or biological causes. Something happens—emerges—when people get together in groups or institutions that differs from what happens to lone individuals. Durkheim called these properties "social facts" and saw them as defining the unique subject matter of sociology.

GEORG SIMMEL

The German Georg Simmel (1858–1918) viewed society in yet a different way. Rather than seeing society as an organic whole, as a "thing" in itself, Simmel saw it as an intricate web of group affiliations. He felt that society was nothing more than all the individuals who compose it, although he stressed that people in different-sized groups—twosomes, threesomes, and larger groups—interact differently.

Like other early sociologists, Simmel believed we can discover underlying uniformities in social life. For example, the social processes of dominance and submission share certain similarities, whether they occur between parent and child, boss and worker, or king and subject. Simmel analyzed such processes as conflict and cooperation, intimacy and distance. He also studied social types, such as the stranger, the adventurer, the mediator, the renegade, the miser, and the spendthrift. Simmel's work helps to prime our own minds to see the social world in new ways.

MAX WEBER

Max Weber (1864–1920) was a German scholar whose interests ranged across religion, economics, cities, and music, among other topics. One of his major contributions was the effort to trace connections between religion and other institutions such as the economy. These ideas are discussed in Chapter 3. While seeking to identify patterns in human affairs, Weber also stressed the importance of the subjective meanings humans place on their actions. *Subjective meanings* are the values and meanings that individuals place on their life experiences. Because these meanings are not always the same, social action can be classified into four major types: goal-oriented action, value-oriented action, emotionally motivated action, and traditional action. The same action can be viewed in different ways by various people. Consider, for example, your going to college. You may be goal-oriented, in that you want to earn a degree that will help you to achieve other goals. You may be going to college because you value education; if so, your action is value-oriented. You may be going to school because someone you love (a parent, spouse, or friend) wants you to go, or you may love the process of going to school; in that case, you are emotionally motivated. Finally, if you are motivated by tradition, you may be in college because many generations of your family have attended college and you do not want to break that pattern. Weber believed virtually all human actions could be characterized as one or more of these four types.

Weber carried these types of action into his analysis of the types of authority that operate in the world. He saw three major types of authority: rational-legal, which is based on rationality and is goal-oriented; traditional, which is based on the weight of the past (the way things have always been done); and charismatic, which is based on the emotional appeal of a particular individual. Rational-legal authority tends to prevail in large bureaucratic organizations, while traditional authority appears in old, aristocratic families. Popular political figures and religious cult leaders are likely to have charismatic authority.

Although each of these first sociologists had some unique ideas, they may all be seen as responding to the economic, political, and moral turmoil of their times. On the one hand, the old tyrannies of church and king were undermined, granting more independence to individuals. On the other hand, the weakening of religious authority, the growing power of the state, the rupture of community bonds, the rise of unchecked individualism, and excessive rationality all helped to destroy the old order without creating a new one to take its place. Comte, Spencer, Marx, Durkheim, Weber, and Simmel all struggled with these issues, giving birth to sociology, the formal study of society, in the process.

Although its origins were European, sociology made big gains in the United States in the twentieth century. Many Americans who studied in Europe were introduced to the ideas of sociology, and a number of prominent American sociologists have made important contributions to its body of knowledge. These individuals and their ideas are introduced in this and subsequent chapters.

MAJOR SOCIOLOGICAL ORIENTATIONS

A *theoretical outlook* is a set of guiding ideas and questions that provides an overall approach to a subject. Several major theoretical outlooks exist in sociology today: they are functionalism, Weberian conflict theory, Marxian theory, and interpretive outlooks. Each of these directs attention to particular aspects of the social world. The existence of seemingly contradictory approaches is not unique to sociology. Even in the scientific field of physics, light appears in some ways to be a wave, yet at the microscopic level it behaves like a particle. Quantum theory puts these two views together into one coherent theory. To maximize our understanding of society we need the multiple views of society that coexisting outlooks provide, because the social world is easily as complex and varied as light. Since no single perspective adequately explains all of social life, there is no totally "right" outlook that makes the others completely "wrong."

THE FUNCTIONALIST PERSPECTIVE

By the 1940s, Harvard and Columbia universities had become especially important for American sociology. Returning from graduate study in Germany to teach at Harvard, Talcott Parsons (1902–1979) wove together a number of ideas from Durkheim, Weber, Marx, and others in his influential book, *The Structure of Social Action* (1937). Probably more than anyone else, Parsons shifted American sociology toward theory-building. He developed what has come to be called *structural-functional sociology,* a perspective that focuses on how the various parts of society fit together to maintain the equilibrium of the whole.

The functionalist outlook analyzes social phenomena in terms of their *functions* or consequences for other parts of society or for society as a whole. For example, a functionalist approach to sports in society might consider whether sports creates a sense of community among fans that helps to overcome the extreme individualism generated at work. Functionalists might also ask whether sport has taken the place of religion for many people as a way of forging social solidarity through shared rituals. These questions arise from the functionalist assumption that every part of society contributes to the functioning of the whole, thereby creating an *equilibrium,* or balance, in society. A change in any part creates a certain imbalance, which leads to changes in other parts of the system, and perhaps eventually to the reorganization of the entire system.

Functional analysts have trouble explaining the original source of change. In the case of sports, for example, functionalists do not suggest why sports changed from a local pastime to a national, highly organized system. Nor are functionalists especially concerned about the relative importance of various parts of society. A change in the organization of sports, for example, is not likely to have as many and as far-reaching consequences for society as a change in the organization of the family or a reorganization of the economy. Critics tend to see functionalism as concerned about the consequences of something for the entire society, rather than considering the possibility that some groups or classes may benefit more than others from a particular arrangement. In a related vein, functionalism has been attacked for its conservative bias, because it is concerned with order more than with change.

One of Parsons' students, Robert K. Merton, addresses some of these issues (1957). He suggests that all parts of a society may not be functional. Some may actually be dysfunctional at some level. A *dysfunction* is any consequence of a social system that disturbs or hinders the integration, adjustment, or stability of the system. For example, parents in developing nations may find that high birth rates are functional for their family as a means of providing support when they are old, but the same high rates may be dysfunctional for the society at large because of the demands they place on food, housing, education, and jobs. Finally, according to Merton, some features of a society may be dispensable or may have *functional equivalents.* For instance, modern singles may find that communal living arrangements offer a functional equivalent to (or substitute for) the family by providing companionship and affectional ties without families.

Merton also distinguishes between manifest and latent functions. *Manifest functions* refer to the intended functions of something. The manifest function of an automobile, for example, is transportation, to which there are a number of functional alternatives (depending on the distance to be traveled) such as walking, bicycle, moped, train, bus, and plane. The *latent functions* are the unintended and unrecognized consequences of a social thing or process. The latent functions of a car may be to impress other people, to display one's wealth, or to provide a place to be alone with someone we especially like.

A functionalist sociologist would be likely to ask: What are the consequences, both positive and negative, of what I am examining for the other institutions in society and for society as a whole? What are its latent (unintended) functions, as well as its manifest (intended) functions? What functional equivalents, if any, exist for this social arrangement? These questions provide helpful insights, but they run the risk of seeing society in static terms. Functionalists ask what are the functions *now,* rather than asking how this feature emerged, what alternatives were excluded along the way, and what groups or interests benefit from the way things are. In large, complex, societies, it is unlikely that a particular feature has the same consequences for everyone in society.

WEBERIAN CONFLICT THEORY

While the functionalist perspective sees society as being in equilibrium and held together by shared values, conflict theory emphasizes the role of conflict and unequal power in society. Drawing on the powerful insights of Max Weber, *Weberian conflict theorists* stress the importance of membership in different social groups—for example, groups based on race, occupational position, social status, and religion. They note that conflicts arise between and among groups divided along any and all these lines. As developed in the work of Randall Collins (1975), Lewis Coser (1956, 1967), Ralf Dahrendorf (1959), and Gerhard Lenski (1966), Weberian conflict theory assumes that humans strive to maximize their own interests, in competition with others trying to do the same thing, and that they use whatever

Macro sociological thinkers in the tradition of Marx and Weber stress that social behavior may often be influenced by economic activities and how they are socially arranged.

resources they possess in order to do so.

A Weberian might ask how various sports activities become membership badges in particular status groups, or how people use belonging to an elite country club to enhance social status.

MARXIAN THEORY

Marxian theorists stress the importance of class struggle centered around economic production. For them, class is the major basis for social conflict. Marxian conflict theorists stress that economic factors do not adequately explain the world, but that "ultimately" or "in the last analysis," the social arrangements flowing out of economic activities are major determinants of social behavior. The relative importance of economic and social characteristics can be studied. Weberian conflict theorists tend to see conflicts as universal and inevitable since they result from individuals trying to arrange things advantageously for themselves. For Marxians, conflicts result from historically unfolding contradictions. Conflict is not assumed to be inevitable, since it may be resolved at some future time.

Marxians would ask different kinds of questions about sports. They might ask what intensifies or cools economic conflicts between team owners and players, for instance. Or they might consider whether sports takes people's minds off their economic situation.

Weberian and Marxian theories suggest important ways of looking at the world. Weberian theory urges us to consider all the major social positions people occupy. Marxian theory recognizes that all positions may play a role, but that we should be especially attentive to the historical roots of a social situation, the underlying importance of economic arrangements and interests, and the possibility of contradictory trends. Both sets of theorists ask, "Who benefits from this situation at any given moment?" These perspectives reappear throughout this book because they provide important angles of vision for understanding society.

INTERPRETIVE PERSPECTIVES

Although different in many ways, functionalism and conflict theories share certain similarities. They both focus on structural features of entire societies—for instance, how economic production is organized or how social institutions such as religion and the family affect society and individuals. But as a number of important sociologists stress, social life also goes on between individuals, who interpret their worlds, their behavior, and the behavior of others in various ways. Interpretive sociologists urge us to take those meanings into account.

The need for both structural and interpretive perspectives is evident in the study of unemployment. Government agencies provide an official "unemployment rate," which is a structural measure of the phenomena. But the interpretations of individuals influence that figure. If someone is not looking for work, he or she is not counted as unemployed, even though not working. Also, people react differently to being out of work. Some get depressed and give up; others get angry and violent; still others move to a different state or change the type of work they will do. People vary in the way they define and react to a structural situation, and the interpretive perspective stresses these varied definitions and reactions.

In contrast to structural perspectives, the *interpretive perspective* focuses on how individuals make sense of—or interpret—their world and react to the symbolic meanings attached to social life. There are several variants within the interpretive perspective. These include symbolic interaction, exchange theory, and ethnomethodology. Each of these will be described briefly, but the one that is stressed here is symbolic interaction, because considerable work has been done in that tradition.

Symbolic Interaction

Human behavior differs from that of animals because it uses symbols and attaches meanings to those symbols; hence, it can be called *symbolic interaction*. Being pregnant, for example, is a biological reality. But how women react to pregnancy, how they feel about it, and what they do about it stem from the symbolic meanings they have learned to attach to that reality (Miller, 1978). Symbolic interaction was developed by George Herbert Mead (1863–1931), a philosopher at the University of Chicago, and Charles Horton Cooley (1864–1929) at the University of Michigan. Mead studied the emergence of a sense of self in individuals and the place of signs and symbols in social life.

According to Mead, the sense of self emerges fully through social interaction. At first, children have relationships with specific individuals. Later on they develop a sense of the "generalized other"—that is, they learn what other people in their social world are like and what they can expect from them in the way of thoughts, feelings, and actions. Individuals shape their own behaviors in light of what they know about others. Language and other symbols play a critical role in this process, as do games and other forms of play. Baseball, for instance, requires each player to be aware of all the other players in the game and to anticipate what they are likely to do under various conditions. Leaders, according to Mead, are those individuals who are best able to see things through the eyes of the other people in a situation. Mead's work had a major impact on American social thought and inspired the sociological orientation called *symbolic interactionism*.

Mead stressed that we learn meanings through interaction with others and then organize our lives around those socially created meanings. This feature of social life is readily apparent in the case of sexual behavior. Although some see sexual behavior as a biological or perhaps even instinctual process, there is a great deal of social and symbolic content to it. Masters and Johnson (1979) found that bisexuals acted like homosexuals when they were with homosexuals (for example, more communication than heterosexuals usually show) and like heterosexuals while making heterosexual love (for example, an assumption that the male should take the lead). To Masters and Johnson, these actions are clearly a result of "cultural influences"—bisexuals learn different cues for how heterosexuals and homosexuals make love. Clearly these differences in the same people reflect the socially learned, symbolic features of lovemaking.

A second major theme of symbolic interactionism is that society is most usefully viewed as consisting of people interacting with each other (Manis and Meltzer, 1978). This view emphasizes human society as being in process and always changing, rather than as something static and unchanging. At the same time, symbolic interactionists realize that individuals act within networks of other individuals and groups and know that not everyone is equally powerful.

Symbolic interactionism stresses the active role individuals play in guiding their own behavior. Because human beings have some capacity to select and interpret what aspects of their situation they will respond to, they can shape their course of action. Although they are not totally free agents, humans can try to modify the social influences and limitations they face.

The symbolic interaction approach has been criticized for having vague concepts that are difficult to research, for playing down unconscious or emotional factors, and for ignoring social structures. More recent work shows that the concepts can be clarified and that social organization can be studied from this perspective. Symbolic interactionism has also been criticized for its inability to explain specific behaviors. It cannot explain, for instance, why money is so important to some people but not to others, or why the incest taboo appears in widely dispersed cultures.

Erving Goffman developed a new perspective on symbolic interaction with his concept of social life as theater. He views humans as busy acting out complex displays designed to communicate images of self, define a situation, or demonstrate social membership. He sees us as actors playing different roles and managing the

People joining social groups often adopt the language, clothing, and behavior of the group. Symbolic interactionists focus attention on these aspects of social behavior. They also point to the symbolic meaning of various items. In this picture, the different belts signify various levels of skill in karate, one form of martial arts.

impressions we give others. Goffman analyzes "front stage" areas of social life, such as the living room of a house or apartment, and "backstage" areas, such as the kitchen, bedroom, or bathroom. This *dramaturgical analysis* raises questions about the roles people play, the props and staging areas needed to support those roles, and the kinds of behavior that are appropriate in the roles.

Unlike the functionalist focus on goal attainment, Goffman's work centers on affective behavior. People wish to belong to a particular social group, so they adopt the special handshakes, language, clothing, or behaviors of group members, if they can. In his early work, Goffman concentrated on individuals and their responses to institutional demands, to social values, or to being stigmatized—that is, negatively labeled and reacted to (1959, 1961, 1963). In his later work, Goffman studied systems of social interaction (1967, 1971). Goffman and symbolic interactionism will be discussed at greater length in Chapter 4.

Symbolic interactionists ask quite different questions about sports than do structural theorists. They might ask, for example, how do people define and interpret the sports they are playing or watching, and how do the meanings they attach to those activities affect their interactions with others? Do mountaineers stop climbing when they hear about someone who has a fatal accident, or do they interpret the situation in such a way that they can safely feel no such fate awaits them?

Exchange Theory

"There is no free lunch, even in social life," according to *exchange theorists* of social interaction. Everything we do and everything others do has its price, whether the currency is money, time, food, social approval, company, or prestige. People are viewed as active agents who choose which exchanges they wish to make. They weigh the costs and benefits of various social actions and rationally choose the one that is most attractive to them. According to this theory, exchange is a basic principle of social interaction that can explain behavior as diverse as the decision to get divorced, college dating patterns, and the origins of revolutions.

Exchange theorists recognize the exchange of intangibles like respect, affection, help, and acceptance, as well as the avoidance of pain, embarrassment, or rejection. The exchange of these social rewards and punishments can be quite subtle and unspoken, or it can be very explicit. Grandparents, for instance, may do a great deal for their grandchildren and expect little back. On the other hand, most grandparents hope and even assume that they will receive some love, affection, and gratitude in return. More explicit exchanges occurred in pioneer times. Barn-raisings brought everyone in an area together to build one family's barn, with the clear understanding that the one getting the barn would help the others later. Exchange theory represents an individualistic approach in social theory. The focus is on the behavior of specific individuals, and it assumes that people act for their own reasons to maximize what they value and minimize what they dislike. Therefore a person's actions can be determined by manipulating rewards. Exchange theory explains altruistic acts such as saving a drowning child or giving money to refugees in terms of the personal satisfaction and/or social esteem an individual receives for the action.

Exchange theory goes beyond explaining single acts of kindness to explain more complex social phenomena such as the rising divorce rate. Among the general explanations for divorce that have been offered are affluence, the women's movement, and changing moral values. Exchange theorists do not start by considering such abstract "factors," however. Their beginning assumption is that divorces start with individuals deciding whether or not they will stay married. The question then becomes, why are more people choosing divorce today than in the past? John Scanzoni (1972) suggests that women are more likely to choose divorce today because increased job openings for women, higher salaries, and a mobile population make divorce a more possible alternative for women than it was in the past. A 35-year-old woman in 1920 had few alternatives to a husband who drank and beat her. A similar woman today could find a job to support herself and any dependent children, and choose an alternative to marriage. The fact that not all women would weigh these factors in the same way does not destroy the value of exchange theory. What is important about this approach is that it examines social behavior in terms of how different people weigh the considerations they face and what choices they make.

Exchange theory would raise certain kinds of questions about sports. For example, it would suggest that athletes continue to participate in sports only as long as the rewards they receive outweigh the costs for them. If psychic and social rewards are included as well as financial ones, it goes a long way toward explaining why professional athletes continue to play after they have passed their prime, and often even when they are in great physical pain.

Exchange theory has been criticized on the grounds that it offers a "market model" of motivation; that is, people do something only in exchange for something else. But since much of what is exchanged is intangible, such as social esteem or personal satisfaction, the exchange differs from a purely economic one. Exchange theory shares a limitation of economic theories generally in that it has little capacity to explain why people have the beliefs, values, and tastes that they do. It simply takes those cultural and individual values as the starting point and asks how people with such values behave. As such, the theory does little to explain the origins of cultural norms and their variations. The strength of exchange theory seems to lie in explaining behavior in small group situations rather than in analyzing societal-level processes. Even Peter Blau, one of the foremost proponents of exchange theory, believes that the theory is mainly suited to analyzing "face-to-face relations and must be complemented by other theoretical principles that focus on complex structures" (Blau, 1968, p. 457).

Ethnomethodology

Social exchanges can occur only when people communicate successfully. How people make sense of the social world and share their views of it has been explored by a type of sociology called ethnomethodology.

Ethnomethodology is concerned with how people see, describe, and explain order in the world in which they live (Zimmerman and Wieder, 1970). It is the study of the methods used by individuals (called "ethnics") to communicate and make sense of their everyday lives as members of society (Garfinkel, 1967). Many ethnomethodologists focus on language and conversation, since they see these areas as central to interpreting life in society.

When two people see each other in the morning, for example, and one says, "Last night was wonderful," and the other says "Yes," these words mean much more to them, from their shared experiences and knowledge, than their simple literal content. The talk between them stands for, or indexes, much more than it actually says. This feature of language characterizes much, if not all, social interaction. It underlies communication between bosses and workers, parents and children, blacks and whites, males and females. For ethnomethodologists, the meaning of the interaction, in this case through words, can be explained only through knowledge of the context in which it occurs.

Carried to its extreme—where statements can be understood only within the contexts in which they occur—this position has pitfalls. It means we can never communicate something to someone who has not experienced it. Although this may be true in absolute terms, a central feature of the human condition is the continual struggle to try to communicate with others.

ASSESSMENT AND SYNTHESIS

You have just encountered four major theoretical approaches used in studying society: functionalist theory, Weberian conflict theory, Marxian theory, and various interpretive perspectives. Three basic features differentiate these orientations.

1. First, they differ in whether they focus primarily on social stability or on social conflict and change. Functionalists tend to stress shared values, which promote social stability, whereas conflict theorists probe power differences, which result in conflict and change. Interactionists emphasize the meanings individuals attach to events and the active role individuals can play in their own lives. Interactionists suggest that even when participants are unequal in power, they will negotiate over what definitions will prevail and how action will occur. Thus they direct attention to social processes and changes rather than social structures and stability. This relates to a second major difference.

2. The four approaches differ in terms of whether they are more interested in objective social structure or in the interpretations people place on their social experiences. Functionalists and Marxian theorists focus on objective structural characteristics of society, whereas Weberians and symbolic interactionists place more emphasis on subjective meanings.

3. A third distinguishing feature is the level of analysis each theory addresses. The social world can be conceptually divided into at least four different levels, as shown in Table 1.1.

The *micro level* includes how we feel about the

Table 1.1 Various Levels for Analyzing the Social World

I. Micro level, including the intrapsychic and the interpersonal levels	How we feel and what we think about the social world. How the social world affects us subjectively. How we interact with others. What meanings we attach to social actions.
II. Organizational level	Social life in larger groups and formal organizations.
III. Institutional level	The patterned activities that focus on meeting important social needs, such as obtaining food or raising children. How those institutions are related to each other or vary across societies or over time.
IV. Macro level	Entire societies as the unit of analysis. Comparisons across societies or over time.

social world and how it affects us subjectively. It also includes how we interact with others and the meanings we attach to the social actions of others. This level was richly explored by sociologists such as George Herbert Mead and others in his tradition. More recently, Rosabeth Moss Kanter (1977) linked this level to features of organizational structure in her study of how powerlessness within an organization affects the motivations of individuals. Other research found that working-class wives are more likely to value traits in their husband such as "he's a steady worker, he doesn't drink, he doesn't hit me," than are middle-class wives, who never mention those qualities when asked what they value most in their husbands (Rubin, 1976). In this instance, their subjective appraisal of what they value in their husbands seems highly linked to a class structure that unevenly distributes unemployment, alcoholism, and violence across families. The subjective feeling of satisfaction that one obtains from work also seems to be influenced by the nature of the class structure in which one labors (Sennett and Cobb, 1972). These studies all illustrate how subjective evaluations are influenced by organizational and other structural conditions.

The organizational level treats social life in larger groups and formal organizations, such as colleges or universities, corporations, or the military service. It considers how we behave in organizations and how organizational processes affect us.

The structure of higher education, for example, is affected by organizational size. The larger the university, the more likely it is to develop a "center" that handles critical public relations and financial dealings with outside organizations, and the more likely the disciplinary departments and faculty governing boards are to influence educational policy decisions (Boland, 1973). Such a situation affects both students and faculty. Functionalists, Weberian conflict theorists, and Marxian theorists have studied organizations.

More general than the organizational level is the institutional level. It focuses on social *institutions,* which consist of a cluster of patterned activities centered around meeting an important social need, such as obtaining food or raising children. Sociological studies at the institutional level examine the different ways that educational systems are organized in the United States, Great Britain, and France, for example, or consider different forms of family structure in industrial and tribal societies. Within a single society, it is possible to analyze how various social institutions are interrelated, the way Marxian theorists such as Bowles and Gintis (1976) have begun to analyze the links between education and the class structure. Colleges, universities, and other schools, for example, are all part of what we call the institution of education. Durkheim, Weber, and other functionalist analysts have conducted extensive institutional analyses.

Analysis at the macro level seeks to unearth the core features of an entire society by focusing on large-scale institutions, structures, and processes. Much of the work of Marx and Weber as well as that of Durkheim was concerned with macro-level analysis and comparisons between societies. Sociologists cannot conduct macro-level analysis successfully by examining one society alone at a single point in time. Rather, they need to compare a society at various points over time, or several whole societies with each other. A macro-level analysis was done by Ouchi (1981) in his comparison of the national cultures, management styles, and organizational productivity of Japan and the United States. He suggests that Japanese society is characterized by greater trust, subtlety, and intimacy than is American society, and that differences in national culture are reflected in management styles that emphasize lifelong employment rather than short-term employment, job rotation rather than specialization, slow evaluation and promotion practices rather than rapid evaluation and promotion, collective responsibility and decision-making rather than individual responsibility and decision-making, and a wholistic concern rather than an isolated concern with only one aspect of the organization.

Levels of analysis, the focus on objective or subjective social realities, and concerns about stability or change are some of the central themes that emerge from the major orientations in sociology. Table 1.2 summarizes the basic fea-

Table 1.2 Basic Features of the Four Theoretical Approaches

		Major Theorists	Emphasis on Stability or Change	Stress on Objective or Subjective	Level of Analysis
Structural Theories	Functionalist perspective	Comte Durkheim Parsons Merton	Stability	Objective	Organizational, institutional, macro
	Weberian conflict perspective	Weber Collins Coser Dahrendorf Lenski	Change	Objective (but subjective interpretations as well in Weber and Collins)	Organizational, institutional, macro (but micro as well in Collins)
	Marxian perspective	Marx Bowles Gintis	Change	Objective	Organizational, institutional, macro
Interpretive Perspectives	Symbolic interactionism	Mead Cooley Blumer Goffman	Change	Subjective interpretations	Micro (interpersonal and intrapsychic)
	Ethnomethodology	Garfinkel			
	Exchange theory	Homans Blau			

tures of the four major orientations. These varied themes can be brought together. The work of C. Wright Mills, for example, tried to integrate the analysis of social structures with the social psychology of individuals. He studied such topics as white collar workers, "the power elite," and the causes of war, and wanted other sociologists to assume the role of social critic and activist.

An integrated approach requires an awareness of all four levels of analysis, an alertness to power differences, and a sensitivity to both stability and change. It requires us to conceptualize social structure and understand how it can set limits or provide opportunities. At the same time, we need to deal with social definitions, processes, and changes. These are the diverse theoretical strands this book brings to bear on understanding society. Sociologists are becoming increasingly aware that their methodological "bag of tricks" needs to be as diverse as their theoretical one. No single perspective or method can capture the complexity and meaning of social life, but a composite approach, that stands on many legs, holds the greatest promise.

Summary

1. Sociology represents a blend of the imaginative and the scientific. It requires us to look at the social world with various lenses. The sociological enterprise is fueled by curiosity and personal urgency, and is guided by scientific criteria.

2. Sociology has practical value for us as we try to understand how the social world affects us and as we seek to make personal decisions.

3. Related social science fields—economics, anthropology, history, political science, and psychology—share some similarities with sociology, but also diverge in their central focus. Sociology differs from practical fields such as social work, public administration, public health, education, and management, which aim to apply knowledge from sociology and other social sciences to deal with important social issues.

4. Sociology developed in Western Europe in response to the scientific revolution, industrialization, and urbanization.

5. Early major sociological thinkers were Comte, Spencer, Marx, Durkheim, Simmel, and Weber. All of them were responding to the industrial, political, and moral turmoil of their times.

6. Four major sociological orientations exist today: functionalism, Weberian conflict theory, Marxian theory, and various interpretive outlooks. Each of them centers upon certain problems and issues, and each has unique contributions to make to our understanding of society. The most complete understanding of society requires us to draw on all four approaches.

Key Terms

alienation
conflict perspective
dramaturgical analysis
dysfunction
equilibrium
ethnomethodology
exchange theory
functional equivalent
functions
institution
interactionist perspective
interpretive perspective
latent function
macro level
manifest function
Marxian conflict theory
method of comparison
micro level
social psychology
social sciences
sociology
structural-functional perspective
subjective meanings
symbolic interaction
symbolic interactionism
theoretical outlook
Weberian conflict theory

Chapter 2

Doing Social Research

What happens to young men and women in the 10 years after they graduate from high school? This question is being probed by James Coleman and Carol B. Stocking of the National Opinion Research Center in Chicago. They have information on 58,000 students who were high school sophomores or seniors in 1980. About one-third of them will be tracked over a 10-year period. The study will address questions like the following: How many of the students got jobs? How did they get their jobs? Do they like them? How many of the students went on to college? Do they feel that the additional education made any difference in their lives? How many of the students married? How many have children? Does adult life meet their expectations? Do they believe that school prepared them for life?

Such a project interests the people being studied. It is also important for educators, employers, policy-makers, and parents because it deals with crucial issues in our society—the transition from school to work, and the feelings of a whole generation of students about that process.

Coleman and Stocking face the problems all social researchers face—how to grasp vibrant human issues with scientific procedures. Sociologists do not just sit in their armchairs and spin grand schemes; they go out in the world, observe, talk with people, and do systematic research to try to understand what is going on and why. This chapter considers some of the ways social researchers do their work. After reading it, you should have a better idea of how social scientists conduct their inquiries; you should be acquainted with a number of important research terms that will reappear in this book; and you should be aware of some of the ethical concerns that confront social researchers. You may also become more aware of your own reasoning processes.

SCIENCE VERSUS EVERYDAY KNOWLEDGE

Most social researchers make every effort to be scientific in the way they conduct their research. To understand better how they proceed, it is helpful to consider how scientific research differs from everyday knowledge. Our everyday knowledge-gathering strategies suffer from a number of weaknesses. We are not always the most careful observers. Considering your friends, for instance, can you say who is right- and left-handed? Do you know what color clothing your professor wore the last time you went to class? Unless we work consciously to observe and note behaviors or traits, there is much we can overlook. We also tend to "overgeneralize"—that is to draw conclusions about many based on only a few cases. Suppose you talk with 3 out of 300 student demonstrators on campus and all 3 say they are protesting the food in the dining room. It is tempting, but faulty, to infer that all 300 are demonstrating for the same reason.

Left to our own devices, we tend to overlook cases that run counter to our expectations. If you think all football players are politically conservative, you may ignore the ones who are not. Or if you notice some exceptions, you may conclude they are not really football players. Often there is an emotional stake in our beliefs about the world that causes us to resist evidence that challenges those beliefs. This tendency may lead to closing one's mind to new information—an "I've made up my mind, don't confuse me with the facts" approach. Research seeks to overcome some of these pitfalls of everyday inquiry.

Although some people complain that research is simply an expensive way of finding out what everyone already knew, the results sometimes contradict commonsense expectations. Consider the following statements of the "obvious."

1. Suicide is caused by psychological depression or other mental states. Social factors really have no effect on suicide.
2. Soldiers in units with high rates of promotion are more satisfied about their own chances for promotion than soldiers in units with very low promotion rates.
3. Men engaging in occasional homosexual acts in the bathroom of a public park belong to a highly visible homosexual subculture.
4. When a number of people observe an emergency, they are more likely to go to the aid of the victim than when only one person is a witness (the "safety in numbers" principle).
5. The more money school systems spend, the higher the achievement scores of their students. ("To get quality, you have to pay for it.")
6. Baseball is the American "national pastime." Attendance is higher at baseball games than at any other sports events.
7. Religious beliefs are less important to Americans than they are to Europeans. (Everyone knows Europeans are more traditional than Americans).

All these commonsense statements have been contradicted by careful research studies: (1) Durkheim (1897) presented compelling evidence that social integration strongly affects the rate of suicide among different social groups. (2) In a study of army units in World War II, soldiers were actually happier about their own promotion chances in units that had very low promotion rates, since they did not feel they had been passed over while less worthy people were promoted (Stouffer et al., 1949). (3) A study conducted by Laud Humphreys (1970) found that many of the men he observed engaging in homosexual acts in the bathroom of a public park were married, had children, and were model citizens in their communities; very few of them belonged to a homosexual subculture. (4) When witnessing an emergency, a single individual has been found more likely than several people together to help the victim, perhaps because he or she is the only one who can do so (Latané and Darley, 1970). (5) The amount of money spent by a school system does not directly filter down to the achievement test scores of its students (Coleman et al., 1966). (6) Whereas about 44 million people attended American baseball games in 1980, more than 75 million people attended horseraces (U.S. Bureau of the Census, 1981, p. 235). (7) Americans are actually much more likely than Europeans to say that their religious beliefs are "very important" to them. In 1975–1976, 56 percent of Americans felt that religion is very important, compared to 36 percent of Italians and 17 percent of Scandinavians (U.S. Department of Commerce, 1980, p. 523).

The existence of research findings that run counter to what we might expect suggests that we should pause before we say "everyone knows that. . . . " Instead, we should ask: "What evidence do we have for believing that to be true?" Social research is concerned with how evidence is gathered and evaluated.

SCIENCE AS A FORM OF KNOWING

A central feature of human existence is the desire to know and to understand the world. Knowledge is part of all human cultures, along with strategies for obtaining knowledge and for deciding whether or not something is true. In all cultures the major sources of knowledge are tradition, authority, and observation and reasoning. Cultures differ with respect to how much they emphasize each source. Science flourishes in societies that place relatively greater stress on observation and reasoning. Some societies see the natural and social worlds as caused, patterned, and open to human understanding through observation and logic. Others see the world as mysterious. One way these differences are reflected is in the ways cultures and individuals respond to unknowns. Sometimes they say "We don't know enough yet," as contrasted with "There are many things we will never understand." The former statement reflects a strong faith in science; the latter suggests a more limited view of science.

Social theory and research deals with what is and why it is that way in social life, not with what should be. "Should-be" issues are the concern of philosophy, religion, and ethics, although they invariably color the problems researchers wish to study and the ethical principles they follow in conducting their research. A carefully done research study could add to our understanding, for example, of the social causes and consequences of drug use. How you react to that knowledge depends on your own values. Sometimes personal, religious, or political concerns lead people to deny or ignore unappealing research results. This fact helps explain why research supporting key values or interests tends to be more widely accepted than research which opposes strong values and interests. It also suggests why some research may be utilized by policy-makers and other research may not be.

ASSUMPTIONS UNDERLYING SOCIAL THEORY AND RESEARCH

Social theory and research assume there are patterns in social life. This assumption is sometimes challenged on several grounds. First, there are always individual exceptions. For instance, while whites earn more than blacks in the United States in general, some individual blacks earn more than some individual whites. Theory and research generate knowledge about collections of individuals, not about lone individuals. In addition, they make these statements in terms of percentages or probabilities; that is, they say 5 percent of white households had incomes of less than $5,000 in 1979, compared to 18 percent of black households, a difference of 13 percent (Bureau of the Census, 1981, p. 435).

Sociology helps us understand the chances people have of being in certain situations and of behaving in certain ways. Sociologists can make strong statements about the approximate percentage of people who will behave in certain ways, even though they cannot say how *particular individuals* may act. Similarly, life insurance specialists can say with confidence that nonsmokers will live seven years longer than smokers, in general; they cannot say that any particular nonsmoker will live longer than any specific smoker. Generalizations and predictions are possible when they deal with large numbers of people, but not when they refer to single individuals. Sociological knowledge permits similar kinds of statements. We can say what percentage of people will behave in a certain way, if the social conditions around them do not change drastically, but we cannot predict how a specific individual will act. There is no inconsistency in recognizing a measure of choice available at the individual level, while finding patterned behaviors at the collective level. We can know the general tendencies about the sex, race, or class to which we belong and yet still hope that we as individuals will be an exception to general sociological trends.

The effort to achieve a scientific understanding of human behavior has also been criticized on the grounds that human affairs are extremely complex. Many factors—historical, social, psychological, economic, organizational, societal, and interpersonal—influence human behavior. How can any explanation or prediction take them all into account? No study or theory *can* include every factor, which is the reason sociologists cannot explain every possibility that may occur. But a study or theory can state that one factor is relatively more important than several others or that something will occur more frequently under one set of conditions than another. Although incomplete and imperfect, such statements are more accurate than uninformed guesses.

The accuracy of general statements in the social sciences depends on how observations are conducted. The social sciences do not consist simply of one person's opinion pitted against that of someone else. There are rules of evidence and inference that social scientists follow. Some evidence is better than other evidence; some conclusions are more supportable than others. The difference lies in the *methodology*—that is, in the rules, principles, and practices that guide the collection of evidence and the conclusions drawn from it.

Research differs from everyday inquiry in that researchers try to be conscious of what they are doing, how they are doing it, and what their biases are. *Bias* refers to the way the personal values and attitudes of scientists may influence their observations or conclusions. *Objectivity* refers to the efforts researchers make to minimize distortions in observation or interpretation due to personal or social values. Every research report has a section describing what procedures were followed in order to arrive at the results. That section should be explicit enough so that another researcher can duplicate the procedure. Researchers also point out the limitations of their work and highlight questions that remain. However, caution is sometimes lost when results are presented in the popular press. See Table 2.1 for a comparison between research and journalistic styles of presenting results. Finally, by publishing their work, researchers allow others to question the quality of their procedures, evidence, and conclusions. These practices help to keep inquiry open to new or better evidence.

THE USES OF RESEARCH

Social research has numerous applications, many of which depend on the ingenuity of the people using it. Leaders in education, business, labor, and government, for example, sometimes use existing or commissioned research to help them decide whether a school should be closed in a particular neighborhood; whether a university should be decentralized into mini-colleges; how teachers should be trained; where a new manufacturing plant should be located; what type of work organization will maximize productivity and minimize absenteeism; what new products should be developed; or how services can be most effectively distributed. Doctors, nurses, and other health professionals can gain from research showing ethnic differences in responses to pain and medication, or research linking social experience and disease (Brown, 1976). In writing this book, I have used a variety of research tools and strategies.[1] Individuals can use research to investigate schools to attend, careers to pursue, or places to live. Throughout this book I will suggest possible applications of the research and theories we will be considering. As you read the book, you might ask yourself—what are the implications of these ideas for my life, my family, my community, and my career?

[1]The research strategies used include depth interviews with students, teachers, and researchers; large-scale surveys of instructors; content analysis of research articles and books; social indicator analysis to uncover social trends in American and other societies; and field observation of social life in different states and countries. These types of methods will be described later in the chapter.

Table 2.1 Public versus Private Schools: Research Report and Journalistic Styles of Presenting Research Results and Policy Recommendations

Column A	Column B
Why Public Schools Fail	Public and Private Schools
In the sweeping public verdict of 1981, the schools are failing. In a NEWSWEEK Poll conducted by The Gallup Organization, nearly half the respondents say schools are doing a poor or only fair job—a verdict that would have been unthinkable just seven years ago, when two-thirds in a similar poll rated schools excellent or good. Fifty-nine percent believe teachers should be better trained; more than 60 percent want their children taught in a more orderly atmosphere; almost 70 percent call for more stress on academic basics. That public verdict is increasingly shared by professional educators. Last week, in a comprehensive study of public and private high schools made for the National Center for Education Statistics, sociologist James S. Coleman concluded that the private schools not only give better academic training, but are in some respects less segregated than public schools. He argued that there is a good case for public support in the form of tuition tax credits or vouchers for parents who choose private education.	When family background factors that predict achievement are controlled, students in both Catholic and other private schools are shown to achieve at a higher level than students in public schools. The difference at the sophomore level, which was greater for Catholic schools than for other private schools, ranged from about a fifth of the sophomore-senior gain to about two-thirds the size of that gain (i.e., from a little less than half a year's difference to something more than one year's difference). This evidence is subject to a caveat: despite extensive statistical controls on parental background, there may very well be other unmeasured factors in the self-selection into the private sector that are associated with higher achievement. . . . The greatest difference found in any aspect of school functioning between public and private schools was in the degree of discipline and order in the schools. The Catholic and other private schools appear somewhat different in their discipline and behavior profiles, with students in other private schools reporting more absences and class-cutting but also more homework, fewer fights among students, and greater teacher interest in students. However, in all these respects, both sectors showed greater discipline and order than the public schools.

SOURCES: *Newsweek,* April 20, 1981, p. 62; Coleman, Hoffer, and Kilgore, 1981, pp. xxiv, xxvi.
Note: The journalistic account (column A) which appeared in *Newsweek* takes the conclusions from the Coleman study and uses those conclusions to support the thesis of the headline article, "Why Public Schools Fail." It also reports Coleman's policy conclusion that a case can be made "for public support in the form of tuition tax credits or vouchers for parents who choose private education." Without more information, however, we cannot assess the evidence that is being used to justify that policy position.

The research report (excerpted in column B) by Coleman, Hoffer, and Kilgore (1981) immediately qualifies the conclusion that students in Catholic and other private schools achieve better by noting that other background characteristics which were not measured in their study might help to explain their higher achievement. They also describe some of the differences that occur within schools which may account for part of the variation in achievement, therefore suggesting the possibility that public schools with such features might have students who achieve as well as those in private schools. In addition, the report describes in much greater detail the sample studied and how data were gathered and analyzed. The research report gives us enough information to analyze critically what the study found and the policy proposals Coleman draws from them; we are not simply required to accept or reject them on face value.

TOOLS OF THE TRADE: DEFINITIONS AND PROCEDURES

Part of encountering any new field involves learning the names of some of the "tools of the trade," so that you know what people are talking about. If you are learning to work with wood, for example, it helps to know the difference between a claw hammer and a ball-peen hammer so that you will use the right one. In studying sociology, it is useful to know the unit of analysis in a study; sampling procedures; the difference between a descriptive and an explanatory study; what a hypothesis is; and how concepts, variables, operational measures, and relationships between variables are defined. (Additional tools of the trade are presented in the boxes throughout this chapter.)

A second step in exploring a new area involves learning something about the procedures people use to do their work. Certain procedures used in research are very powerful; they enhance our potency in everyday life as well as in social research. At the top of this list are rules for believing that one factor may have caused another one, and the steps in doing research.

SOME RESEARCH TERMS

Units of Analysis

One of the first things to know about research is the *unit of analysis*—that is, who or what is being studied. Social researchers often look at individuals—at their attitudes or behaviors. Sometimes the unit of analysis that interests us is something larger, like a social group or an organization. For example, studies have found that some hospitals have lower rates of infectious hepatitis among their patients than others (Titmuss, 1971, p. 146). While the rates were compiled by adding up the total number of individuals who caught the disease and dividing by the total number of people in the hospital, the unit of analysis was the hospital, and the research question was "Why should some hospitals have higher rates than others?" The explanation lay in the sources of blood used by different hospitals, rather than in the patients' medical histories. Teaching hospitals received blood for transfusions from volunteer donors, while some other hospitals were more likely to purchase blood from private blood banks that paid indi-

Mean, Median, Mode

Suppose you listed on a piece of paper all the grades you got last year in school. For illustrative purposes, assume you had the following 11 grades:

4.0	(A)	4.0	(A)
3.0	(B)	2.0	(C)
2.0	(C)	2.0	(C)
1.0	(D)	4.0	(A)
3.0	(B)	2.0	(C)
		1.0	(D)

You can see how even as few as 11 separate pieces of data get a bit cumbersome to present. So social researchers use a variety of statistics to summarize data and report general tendencies. There are three ways to present the central tendencies in a set of data.

The *mean,* or average, is computed by adding all the items and dividing by the number of figures. In this case the mean grade is 2.55 (or a low B). Many schools use the mean as your grade point average (GPA). The mean is most useful and least misleading when the range of figures is narrow. Otherwise, the average tends to obscure the lower and higher ends of the range. In the case of last year's grades, the range is fairly wide.

The *median* is the number that cuts a distribution of figures in half. In this list of 11 items, it is the sixth one, or 2.0 (C):

1.0, 1.0, 2.0, 2.0, 2.0, *2.0,* 3.0, 3.0, 4.0, 4.0, 4.0

The *mode* is the figure that occurs most often, in this case 2.0 (C).

All three of these summary statistics obscure the range of grades received. The *range* is the simplest way to indicate the extent of variation in a set of data. The range can be stated by reporting the lowest and highest examples, in this case 4.0 (A) and 1.0 (D). Someone with a 2.55 GPA based on the grades in this example may be quite a different type of student from someone with a similar GPA but a range of 3.0 (B) to 2.0 (C).

viduals to give blood. People selling their blood were more likely to have hepatitis than were people giving blood voluntarily. If the unit of analysis had been individuals who contracted hepatitis in the hospital, this research mystery might never have been solved. Looking at the hospitals as the unit of analysis raised new questions and supplied answers.

Units of analysis can also refer to families, ethnic groups, nation-states, or societies, when appropriate. Social artifacts such as books, TV shows, sculptures, songs, scientific inventions, and jokes could all be units of analysis for social research. Selecting from these units involves special methods of sampling.

Sampling Procedures

The special sampling procedures social researchers have developed are among their most powerful tools in the kit. Properly done, sampling permits conclusions about entire populations (of individuals, groups, organizations, or other aggregates) by studying only a few of them. The key lies in how those few are selected. A *population* is the total number of cases with a particular characteristic. Suppose you are interested in the sexual attitudes of American college students. Do you think you could walk out the door (wherever you are) and select the first 10 warm bodies you encountered, interview them, and draw accurate conclusions about the attitudes of all college students? Such a technique is likely to be very unrepresentative. To overcome this problem, researchers use random sampling.

In a *random sample,* every element (person, group, organization, or whatever) of the population must have an *equal* and *known* chance of being selected for inclusion in the sample. Whenever we hear about the findings of a research study, our first questions should be: Who was the population studied? How was the sample selected?

Descriptive and Explanatory Studies

There are two major types of research studies: descriptive and explanatory. In a *descriptive study,* the goal is to describe something, whether it is the behavior and values of a religious cult, the culture of an old age community, or the nature of a national population. Such studies help to outline the social world. *Explanatory studies* seek to explain why or how things happen the way they do in the social world. An explanatory study might seek to explain why crime rates are much lower in Switzerland than in the United States, West Germany, or Sweden, or why the birth rate declined in industrial nations in the 1960s and 1970s.

Hypotheses

A *hypothesis* is a tentative statement asserting a relationship between one factor and something else, based on theory, prior research, or general observation. A descriptive hypothesis is a tentative statement about the nature or frequency of a particular group or behavior. For instance, the statement that "premarital sexual relations are increasing" is a descriptive hypothesis that could be tested by comparing data on sexual relations today with data from an earlier time. An explanatory hypothesis tries to link behavior or a trait with another factor, as in the statement that "premarital sex is not related to marital happiness." Researchers try to design studies to test whether or not their hypotheses are true and to rule out *rival hypotheses* (that is, explanations that compete with the original hypothesis). They reason the way a detective does in trying to figure out who the murderer is. The data uncovered in a study may support the original hypothesis, refute it, support a rival hypothesis, or suggest conditions under which the hypothesis is supported. This method of reasoning goes beyond the testing of academic social science hypotheses. It is widely used by market researchers to test ideas for designing and selling new products or services, by political candidates seeking to understand public sentiments, and by policymakers developing new social programs.

One source of hypotheses for a research study may be social *theory,* which can be defined as a system of orienting ideas, concepts, and their

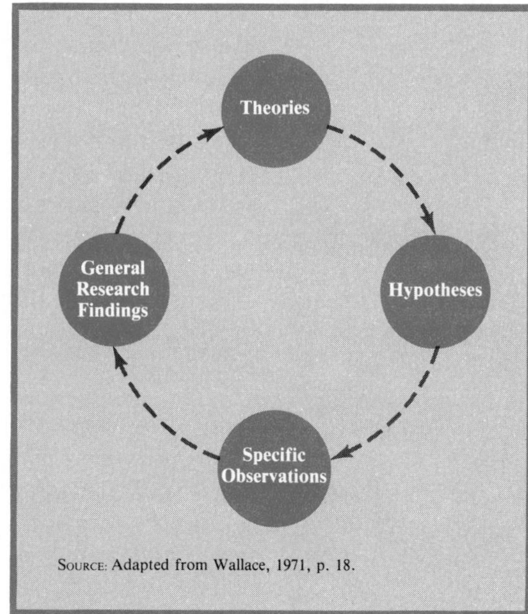

Figure 2.1 The Continuous Circle of Science

relationships that provide a way of organizing the observable world. The interplay between theory and research is shown in Figure 2.1. In this model, theories suggest hypotheses, which lead to observations, which produce research findings, which in turn may modify theories, generate new hypotheses, and so on. Scientists may step into this circle at any point and work to advance knowledge.

Concepts and Variables

Suppose you want to investigate the question of whether premarital sexual relations are related to marital happiness. One of the first steps in any research study is to define the concepts—in this case premarital sexual relations and marital happiness. A *concept* is a word or words that try to describe what is being studied. Researchers must decide what their major concepts include and do not include, what they are like and unlike. For instance, does the concept of premarital sex include kissing, hugging, touching, and oral sex, or only intercourse?

Most concepts allow us to characterize people or things (for example, as male or female, black or white). These characteristics, called *attributes,* can be logically grouped into sets called *variables*. Thus, the attributes of male and female may be grouped as the variable sex. Political party is a variable that may be defined by such attributes as Democratic, Republican, and other.

A variable must contain more than one attribute so that individual cases can be classified according to which attribute they possess. In the example above, the key variable of marital happiness needs to be defined so that it has more than one attribute. We would probably feel comfortable with at least three levels of marital happiness, say "high," "medium," and "low."

Operationalizing Variables

Variables are said to be *operationalized* when we define the procedures used to measure them. One procedure for measuring premarital sexual relations, for example, would be to observe people's behavior before they were married. In this case there are ethical and practical problems with using observation as a method of measurement. (Before or after marriage, most people do not want researchers under their beds studying their sexual behavior.) Researchers generally rely on interviews to measure private behaviors and feelings such as those relating to premarital sexual relations. So we say that the variable premarital sexual relations is *operationalized* in terms of one or more questions in an interview. The operationalization of complex variables like marital happiness requires a series of thoughtful questions, such as these:

1. Do you enjoy the time you spend with your spouse?
2. Do you generally agree about how you want to spend your time? Your money?
3. Do you find you usually agree with your spouse about the division of responsibilities in your marriage?
4. Do you feel your spouse loves and accepts you the way you are?

Sociologists are generally not able to study emotional and sexual intimacy through observational research. Instead, they rely on interviews or questionnaires to yield data about private behaviors and feelings.

5. Do you wish you had not gotten married?
6. Do you look at other people's marriages and wonder what it is that they have that you don't?
7. Do you and your spouse agree about whether or not you want to have children?

A procedure can be developed for scoring the replies to such questions, and using those replies people could be classified as "high," "medium," or "low" with respect to marital happiness.

Relationships Between Variables

If one variable is thought to cause another one, we call the first variable the *independent variable* and the second variable the *dependent variable,* because it is believed to depend on the independent one. Put differently, the independent variable is the hypothesized cause and the dependent variable is the hypothesized effect. In the example above, premarital sexual relations is the independent variable and marital happiness is the dependent variable.

In Table 2.2, fictional respondents have been grouped on the independent variable into those who did and those who did not have premarital sexual relations. The people in each of these categories were then classified as being high, medium, or low on the dependent variable, marital happiness. To analyze the results, we compare people with differing premarital sexual experience with respect to the same attribute on the dependent variable. Among those who had premarital sexual relations, 60 percent scored high

Table 2.2 A Positive Relationship Between Two Variables
(Fictional data)

		Did Respondent Engage In Premarital Sex?	
		Yes	No
Marital Happiness	High	60%	40%
	Medium	30	20
	Low	10	40

on the marital happiness scale, compared to 40 percent of those without premarital sexual experience.

The preceding sentences report the findings of a fictional study. (A real study would probably not show such a dramatic difference between people with and without premarital sexual relations.) How do we summarize and interpret these findings? We can say that in the fictional study more people with premarital sexual experience were likely to be happy in marriage than people without. We can also say that premarital sex and marital happiness are positively associated with each other, or that premarital sex and marital happiness are correlated. A *correlation* is an observed association between a change in the value of one variable and a change in the value of another variable.

RULES FOR INFERRING CAUSALITY

Although we can say that the two variables are correlated, we cannot say at this point that one *caused* the other. Correlation is only the first piece of evidence needed to decide that one factor caused the other one. We also need to know that the independent variable occurred *before* the dependent variable (a time order that is clear in our fictional example), and that no other factors might have caused the observed result. Many other factors such as emotional compatibility, similar social expectations, financial problems or security, and fidelity might also affect marital happiness. Without evidence ruling out such alternative explanations for the observed relationship between premarital sex and marital happiness, we cannot assume that premarital sex caused marital happiness. In any explanatory research study, one of the major problems is obtaining enough evidence of the right kinds so that we can conclude that one thing causes something else, not simply that it is related to it. Social researchers try to rule out alternative explanations by *controlling for* other factors that might be affecting the relationship. In our example, for instance, they would look for couples who were similar with respect to race, age, social background, emotional compatibility, financial situations, and so on, in an effort to hold those factors constant.

No matter how strong a correlation is, it is important to remember that it does not indicate causality unless time order and the elimination of alternative explanations are also present. We can sharpen our everyday thinking and our critical appraisal of causal claims made by others by asking whether all three of these criteria are being met.

Suppose, for example, you have a job, but you have not received a raise in three years. Can you infer that your boss is not pleased with your work? Applying the research orientation to everyday life suggests a number of questions: Do you have any direct indicators of how your boss feels about your work? Did anyone else where you work get a raise? What else might be affecting whether you get a raise (for example, is the boss making money)? What might the boss expect you to do if you do not get a raise? Can the boss replace you with someone as good for the same or less money? What kind of bargaining power do you and other employees have? There are many rival explanations for why you did not get a raise, only one of which consists of the boss's appraisal of your work. Thinking like a researcher can help you assess the evidence for inferring that one factor caused another.

The strongest way to rule out all rival explanations is to conduct a tightly controlled experiment where carefully chosen subjects are randomly assigned to two groups, only one of which experiences the independent variable while the other does not. In the example of premarital sex, it is quite unlikely that such an experiment would be ethically or practically possible. Happily, no experimenter has the power to assign us randomly to groups and then tell us that we must or must not have premarital sexual relations so that their effect on our later marital happiness can be studied. Many areas of sociological research share these ethical and practical constraints. In such situations, we can only try to approximate the logic of experimental designs by controlling for as many rival explanations as possible.

STEPS IN THE RESEARCH PROCESS

Although not all research studies follow the same pattern, it is possible to spell out the steps that occur frequently in the research process.

Defining the Problem

Defining the problem involves selecting a general topic for research, identifying a research question to be answered, and defining the concepts of interest. Individuals have personal research questions, just as social researchers have more general ones. You may wonder, for example, how you will get your first job. On a larger scale, sociologists might ask how people in general find jobs (see Granovetter, 1974).

Reviewing the Literature

The next step is to review the existing literature to determine what is already known about the problem. Prior work may offer general descriptions, raise key questions, discuss the strengths and limitations of measures that have already been tried, and suggest profitable lines of further research. More and more libraries offer computerized literature searches that speed up the review process.

Devising One or More Hypotheses

Ideally, in the effort to build knowledge, researchers form several competing hypotheses. Durkheim did this in his classic study of *Suicide* (1897). He considered the possibility that suicide rates varied as a result of heredity, climate, or social factors. He found social factors, such as the presence or absence of cohesion within a social group, to be the most important determinant of suicide.

Designing the Research

Researchers then decide on a design for the study that will allow them to exclude one or more of the hypotheses. *Research design* is the specific plan for selecting the unit of analysis, determining how the key variables will be measured, selecting a sample of cases, assessing sources of information, and obtaining data to test correlation, time order, and to rule out rival hypotheses.

Collecting the Data

Sociologists gather information in a variety of ways, depending on what they want to investigate and what is available. They may use field observations, interviews, written questionnaires, existing statistics, historical documents, content analysis, or artifactual data such as physical traces. Each of these methods will be discussed briefly in the next section.

Analyzing the Data

Once the data are collected, they need to be classified, and the proposed relationships need to be analyzed. Is a change in the independent variable indeed related to a change in the dependent variable? Can time order be established? Are alternative explanations ruled out?[2]

[2]The growing use of computers for social science research has greatly enlarged the statistical analyses that can be performed on data. Although it can speed up the process of data analysis and make complex computations feasible, the computer can do nothing to improve the quality of the data collected. Simply because data were analyzed by computer does not necessarily mean that a study is of high scientific quality. "Garbage in, garbage out" is the maxim that captures the inability of computers to improve on the material fed to them.

Social scientists are increasingly likely to use computers to analyze and organize their data. As a result, they may spend time examining and interpreting computer printouts.

Drawing Conclusions

Drawing conclusions involves trying to answer such questions as these: Which of the competing hypotheses are best supported by the evidence? Which are not? What limitations in the study should be considered when evaluating the results? What lines of further research does the study suggest? Of all the steps in the research process, the major one we have not yet considered is the issue of how data are collected.

DESIGNING STUDIES AND GATHERING DATA

Social researchers study and try to understand the social world. Either they seek to describe some feature of social life, or they try to analyze and explain interrelationships among social factors. Various types of data are available for both goals, and those data may be collected in different ways.

EXPERIMENTS

What happens when "normal" people are admitted to a mental institution? Are they immediately noticed by the professional staff as being out of place and so discharged? This research question was posed by D. L. Rosenhan in 1973, when he created a field experiment in which he and seven colleagues contrived to get themselves admitted to several mental hospitals. The individuals interviewed by hospital staff gave fictitious names, occupations, and employment histories, and they complained of hearing voices that said such things as "empty," "hollow," and "thud." Otherwise, they described major life events as they had actually occurred.

These life histories included relationships with parents and siblings, with spouses and children, with people at work and in school. None of the individuals had past or current behaviors that were pathological in any serious way (Rosenhan, 1973). Upon their entry into the psychiatric ward, they behaved as they normally did, speaking to staff and to patients and attempting to engage others in conversation. When asked by the staff how they were feeling, they said fine and reported that they were no longer experiencing symptoms. They responded to instructions from attendants and staff and spent their time participating in available activities and writing down their observations about the ward, its patients, and the staff. These pseudopatients were told by the researchers that they would have to get out of the hospital by their own devices, basically by convincing the staff that they were sane. They were highly motivated to do this, since they did not like hospital life. They not only behaved sanely, but tried to be paragons of cooperation. Nursing reports note that they were "friendly," "cooperative," and showed "no abnormal indications." Despite their sane behavior, the patients were in the hospitals for 7 to 52 days, with the average time being 19 days.

In a social experiment, the experimenter tries to see whether a change in the independent variable (in this case, the behavior of the pseudopatients) is related to a change in the dependent variable (the psychiatric diagnosis), while other conditions are held constant (the setting of mental hospitals). Rosenhan found that the setting and conditions of the mental hospital so outweighed the behavior of the patients once they were inside that it was difficult for behavioral changes to alter the diagnosis. Thus, this carefully conceived experiment was able to isolate the relative importance of patient behavior and situational context for psychiatric diagnosis, and to reveal that one (situational context) is much more important than the other (how patients behave).

Experiments allow researchers to observe actual behavior in response to a situation.

Experiments allow observation of actual behavior rather than relying upon people's statements about what they may or may not do. They permit alternative explanations to be controlled, and they unfold over time. Some experiments use a *control group;* that is, a group that is not exposed to the independent variable of interest but whose background and experience are otherwise like those of the *experimental group,* which is exposed to the independent variable. Hence experiments are strong methods for meeting the three criteria discussed above for inferring causality. They are limited by the practical and ethical restraints that exclude private, personal, and dangerous behavior from manipulation and observation. Another method—interviews—can help researchers to obtain information about private, personal, or taboo attitudes and behaviors.

INTERVIEWS AND SURVEYS

What kind of gender role behavior occurs between long-term partners in a relationship? Are there differences in the gender roles people assume when couples are straight (heterosexual) and gay (composed of two homosexual men or lesbian women)? These are some of the research questions posed by Pepper Schwartz and Phillip Blumstein, two sociologists at the University of

Washington. To investigate these and related issues, they conducted interviews with more than 600 people living in long-term relationships, and they mailed a written questionnaire to more than 10,000 people who agreed to participate in the study. (See Table 2.3 for a sample of some of the questions that were asked in this study.) While carefully protecting the identities of the individuals involved, the researchers collected background information on the respondents' education, occupations, incomes, and ethnicity, as well as considerable information about their relationships with their partners.

The use of interviews and questionnaires enabled them to ask everyone the same questions, so that comparisons could be made between long-term and short-term couples; between gay, lesbian, and straight couples; between couples with children and those without; and so forth. Practical and ethical considerations would have made it impossible to gather such data by observation, and other methods of data collection would have been equally inappropriate. Surveys are useful for describing the characteristics of large numbers of people in an efficient way. In this case, if only a few individuals had been studied, we might think that the results were unique to them and did not occur in the larger population. Surveys of carefully selected samples permit the accurate determination of rates of behavior or the frequency with which certain attitudes are held.

Table 2.3 Sample Questions from Blumstein and Schwartz Study of Couples and Their Relationships

	Extremely Satisfied							Not at All Satisfied	Does Not Apply to Our Situation
1. How satisfied are you with these parts of your relationship?									
a. Our moral and religious beliefs and practices	1	2	3	4	5	6	7 8	9	
b. How my partner's job affects our relationship	1	2	3	4	5	6	7 8	9	X
c. How we communicate	1	2	3	4	5	6	7 8	9	
d. How my job affects our relationship	1	2	3	4	5	6	7 8	9	X
e. My partner's attitudes about having children	1	2	3	4	5	6	7 8	9	
f. How the house is kept	1	2	3	4	5	6	7 8	9	
g. The amount of influence I have over the decisions we make	1	2	3	4	5	6	7 8	9	
h. Our social life	1	2	3	4	5	6	7 8	9	
i. The amount of money coming in	1	2	3	4	5	6	7 8	9	
j. How we express affection for each other	1	2	3	4	5	6	7 8	9	
k. How we manage our finances	1	2	3	4	5	6	7 8	9	
l. How we raise the children	1	2	3	4	5	6	7 8	9	X
m. Our sex life	1	2	3	4	5	6	7 8	9	
2. How satisfied are you with your relationship in general?	1	2	3	4	5	6	7 8	9	
3. How would your partner rate [his/]her satisfaction with your relationship in general?	1	2	3	4	5	6	7 8	9	

SOURCE: Couples Survey, Male Questionnaire, Philip Blumstein and Pepper Schwartz, Copyright © 1978.

"Would you say Attila is doing an excellent job, a good job, a fair job, or a poor job?"

SOURCE: Drawing by Chas. Addams, © 1982, *The New Yorker Magazine, Inc.*

Surveys work only when respondents are able and willing to report what they know, do, or feel. One of the limitations of survey research is the need to standardize the question wording and, in precoded versions, the allowable responses. This may lead to the problem of people not understanding what a standardized question means, or not finding the answer they want to give. Such limitations can be overcome by using open-ended or depth interviews before developing precoded response categories. Field research can also be used prior to designing a survey to get a better understanding of what is important to people and what meanings different words have for them, and a sense of how social processes unfold. Without depth interviews prior to designing a questionnaire, it is often impossible to know what questions to ask or how to ask them.

OBSERVATIONAL RESEARCH

Field research involves going where people are. It includes observation and sometimes *partici-*

pant observation, in which the researcher does observations while taking part in the activities of the social group being studied. In her study of how policewomen were accepted by others in the force, Martin (1980) worked as an auxiliary policewoman and actually went out on patrol with other officers. Social researchers can do fieldwork by being a complete participant or only an observer, or anywhere in between.

The ability to observe in field research can be enhanced by recording devices, just as the ability to listen in interviews can be aided by a tape recorder. Film, still photography, and videotape can add to the ability to record and later note (and code) specific behaviors. Videotape or film is particularly useful for studying interactions. For example, using film that could be studied frame-by-frame, Stern (1977) and others were able to observe in caregiver-child interactions whether the caregiver or the child moved first toward the other. To the unaided eye, the movement occurred so fast that it was impossible to unravel without the help of a tool to slow down the process.

Still photography provides a check on eye memory. It allows researchers to record cultural and social events precisely. These records can then be studied by people who were not present when they were taken. Cameras share the same limitations that affect all human observation. They are subject to bias or personal projection—in terms of what we select to "see" or "film," in terms of how we frame a picture, and in terms of what we juxtapose within a picture.

Another potential instance of bias arises when we present interviews on film or videotape. Do researchers select sympathetic and likable people to express certain views, or are the spokespersons unattractive or unsympathetic? Obviously in such techniques, social research borders on journalism and mass media. Similar problems arise in both: What is being included and what excluded? How representative are the people selected? How were they sampled?

OTHER SOURCES OF DATA

Existing Data and Government Documents

A major source of social statistics exists in government documents. The United States and many other governments spend millions of dollars each year gathering information from residents and private and state sources. World statistics are available through the United Nations *Demographic Yearbook,* which presents births, deaths, and other vital statistics for individual nations of the world.

Comparative Historical Methods

Making causal inferences requires the study of events over time and the comparison of cases that differ in certain key respects but are similar in other important ways. For some problems this is possible only by using historical materials. In her study of revolutions, Theda Skocpol (1979) utilized comparative historical analysis. This method is appropriate for developing explanations of large-scale historical phenomena of which only a few major cases exist (such as revolutions within entire nation-states). Skocpol's problem was to identify and validate the causes of social revolutions. Her strategy was to find a few cases that shared certain basic features. France, Russia, and China were similar in their old regimes, their revolutionary processes, and the revolutionary outcomes. All three revolutions occurred in wealthy and politically ambitious agricultural states, none of which had ever been the colony of another state. All three suddenly faced a military competitor that was more developed economically than itself. External problems combined with widespread peasant rebellions and competing political leaders. The result in each case was a centralized and bureaucratic nation-state with potential for considerable international power. The analysis of these three cases is an example of the method of agreement, where similar causal chains appear in several situations.

Unobtrusive measures like this graffiti on student lockers may reflect cultural themes and issues that concern the locker users.

Unobtrusive Measures: Physical Traces and Artifacts

Some of the methods mentioned so far are limited by the fact that when people know they are being studied, they may try to influence what is learned about them. One solution is to look for nonreactive measures—that is, indicators that do not change because they are being studied. For example, one could assess the amount of drinking that occurs on a "dry" college campus by counting the number of beer, wine, and liquor bottles in the trash rather than by asking people about their drinking behavior (Webb et al., 1966).

Content Analysis

How can we analyze the mass media? In her book *The Feminine Mystique* (1963), Betty Friedan systematically analyzed the content of fiction that appeared in women's magazines. After World War II, she found that the courageous and independent heroines of the 1920s and 1930s gave way to women who abandoned their ambitions to stay home and raise a family. Called *content analysis,* this method of research is used to describe and analyze in an objective and systematic way the content of literature, speeches, or media. It helps to identify cultural themes or trends. Alone it cannot tell us whether people think or behave differently as a result of reading certain stories, but it can measure the ideas that are in circulation.

The preceding discussion of various types of data and data collection suggests that each method has one or more limitations, as well as having particular strengths. Some of these strengths and limitations are summarized in Table 2.4.

ETHICAL ISSUES

Some of the ethical issues involved in social research have already been mentioned. People cannot and should not be endlessly manipulated by researchers seeking to control independent variables or alternative explanations. Certain ethical canons guide most social researchers. First, subjects should be told as much as possible about the nature of the study without jeopardizing the validity of the information to be gathered.

Having had the research study described to them, subjects should be asked for their consent to participate. Even when cooperation in research is voluntary, there should be no possibility of harm to the subjects being studied. This includes physical, psychological, and social harm. Any research is somewhat of an intrusion into the lives of individuals, and researchers need to be as sensitive and delicate as possible when making such intrusions. Potential discomfort to respondents must be weighed against likely scientific gains.

If respondents cannot be told everything in advance, there should be a careful "debriefing" session in which the purpose and value of the research is explained, so that the subjects do not feel used, humiliated, or otherwise abused. Particularly when their behavior has been embarrassing, it is important for them to feel that they

Table 2.4 Strengths and Limitations of Various Methods of Collecting Data

Method of Data Collection	Type of Data—Quantitative or Qualitative	Strengths	Limitations
Participant observation	Qualitative (nonnumerical)	Permits processes to be observed as they occur. Good for studying interactions. Helps get at the meanings of words and events for people. May show the range of possibilities that exist. Flexible; focus can shift as research progresses. Relatively inexpensive. Puts primary researcher in direct contact with people being studied.	Hard to tell how typical the observed people are. Difficult to repeat. Close ties between observer and observed may bias results.
Surveys and interviews	Either	Standard questions can be asked of randomly selected respondents, giving comparable and representative information about a large population. May be repeated by other researchers. May reveal information about private or illegal behavior that would not have been observed.	People must know the meaning of the questions they are answering. Only works when people are able and willing to report what they know, do, or feel. Generally an expensive method.
Existing data and government documents	Quantitative (numerical)	Collects data on nearly everyone in a population or on a carefully drawn, representative sample of the population. Less expensive than gathering data oneself.	Omits certain data such as religion. May not define and measure concepts the way researcher would like (the census defines a place as "urban" if it has more than 2500 people in it).
Comparative historical analysis	Qualitative	Useful for studying large-scale social processes that unfold over decades or centuries. May suggest the causes behind those processes.	Cases that can reasonably be compared may be rare and difficult to find. Requires a great deal of comparative historical knowledge.
Content analysis	Either	May provide a good measure of "real" culture compared to "ideal" culture. May catch cultural shifts over time, even when possible respondents are dead.	Tells only about symbolic behavior. Actual behavior may or may not conform to the symbolic portrayals. Does not reveal how the content of various cultural products affects the people exposed to it.
Physical traces and artifacts	Either	People do not know they are being studied; therefore they cannot try to influence the results.	Many behaviors and attitudes do not leave physical traces. High "dross rate"; a great deal of garbage must be sifted through to find something useful.

have not made complete fools of themselves, that others behave similarly under comparable conditions, and that their participation has contributed to scientific knowledge.

Should researchers always reveal their identities, especially when doing participant observation? There are certain groups that may not want researchers in their midst, such as reclusive religious cults, corporate boards, and certain criminal groups. There are ethical and practical dangers in clandestine research, however, and many people do not feel comfortable doing it. Many research topics can be studied without concealing one's identity as a researcher. The highest

Reading Tables

Sociologists are interested in data from a variety of sources. They often summarize these data in statistical form and present them in tables of numbers. Learning to read a table is like learning to drive a car with a stick shift: you never know when it might be really useful. And, there are similar procedures to follow each time you do it. The basics that are worth mastering are these:

1. *Read the title,* which tells what the table is about and how it is presented. Table 2.5, for instance, describes the median income of black and white families from 1947 to 1979, in 1979 constant dollars (that is, dollars adjusted for the rate of inflation).

2. *Read the headings* that group the data in relevant ways. In Table 2.5, separate columns distinguish whites from blacks and other races. The labels on the rows down the side indicate the relevant year.

3. *Note the source.* At the bottom of a decent table you should find the source of the data. You can then judge how much confidence you want to place in the table, and you can locate the original data if you want to check them further. In this case, the source is the Department of Commerce's Bureau of the Census, one of our best sources of descriptive data about the United States.

4. *Make comparisons.* For any given row (in this case year), compare the income of white and black and other races. That is, look at columns B and C in row 1. We can see that white families earned much more than black families in 1950. This difference is quantified in column D, where the table maker has computed a ratio of black to white family income. That number is obtained by dividing the annual median income of black families ($5,636) by the annual median income of white families ($10,388). The ratio tells us that in 1950, black families had a median income that was 54 percent of the median income of white families. By 1979, black families had a median income that was 60 percent of white families. Hence, the gap in median incomes between blacks and whites has narrowed somewhat over time, but has by no means disappeared.

This conclusion requires us to make several comparisons at the same time—one comparing whites and blacks (as summarized in the ratio), the other moving down the time rows to compare 1950 with 1979, and to note in passing whether there were any years when this trend did not appear.

In general terms, the rule for making comparisons in tables is to compare columns within rows, and then to compare rows within columns.

5. *Ask what is missing, or what you cannot tell from the table.* For example, in Table 2.5, were both parents working in the family? What might be the effects of age, geographical region, education, or other factors on this correlation between race and income over time? The table cannot answer these questions, but the probes suggest further data or research that is needed before we can say that race and income are causally related.

Table 2.5 Median Income of Families by Race: 1950–1979 (1979 constant dollars)

	Families			
	Col. A	Col. B	Col. C	Col. D
Year	Total	White	Black and Other Races	Ratio of Black and Other Races to White
1950	$10,008	$10,388	$ 5,636	.54
1955	11,976	12,505	6,896	.55
1960	13,774	14,301	7,917	.55
1965	16,005	16,681	9,186	.55
1970	18,444	19,134	12,180	.64
1971	18,433	19,127	12,033	.63
1972	19,287	20,038	12,329	.65
1973	19,684	20,572	12,407	.60
1974	18,990	19,735	12,626	.64
1975	18,502	19,242	12,571	.65
1976	19,073	19,811	12,522	.65
1977	19,176	20,051	12,148	.61
1978	19,626	20,436	13,077	.64
1979	19,661	20,502	12,380	.60

SOURCE: U.S. Department of Commerce, 1981a, p. 436.

ethical cost is that clandestine activity of any kind breaks down the threads of trust that hold the social fabric together. Every violation makes us more likely to wonder: Is somebody spying on us here? What will they do with what they learn? Who will see the results? How will these results affect us? These undercurrents do not improve trust in social relationships.

Social researchers must ask whether the same or similar results could have been obtained without deceiving people, without concealing the identity of the researchers. In many cases, the answer is yes. Where it is no, researchers must scrutinize the value of the research. In an interview or a written questionnaire, subjects can refuse to answer particular questions they find offensive. Of course, they should be informed of this right at the outset. The right to withhold consent is more difficult to exercise in experiments where one does not know in advance what is going to be asked.

Equal in importance to the rights of informed consent and freedom from harm is the right to have one's identity protected. Respondents should be informed that their replies will be kept anonymous (if there are no identifying features on their data sheets) or confidential (if they need to be contacted later in a follow-up study, say). Confidentiality can be protected by giving each respondent a code number, which is connected to his or her name only on one master list kept locked away in a file or safe. Especially when studying illegal activities, such as participation in prison riots, drug use, white collar crime, or prostitution, it is essential that the identity of respondents not be detectable, both for their sakes and in order for the research to be sound. If people are afraid they will be identified, they may be less than candid about their activities. Unlike doctors and lawyers, social scientists do not have a privileged relationship with respondents, and they can be subpoenaed to provide evidence in court that might be used against their respondents.

A final important ethical issue is who gets studied and who learns the results of the re-

"Could you go over that once again, Gene? Just in case any of us don't understand it."

SOURCE: Drawing by Weber, © 1979, *The New Yorker Magazine, Inc.*

Reading Graphs

In Figure 2.2., the same data that appear in Table 2.5 are presented in graphic form. Interpreting a graph involves the same initial steps as reading a table. First, read the title, identify the relevant headings, and note the source. Generally tendencies are more immediately apparent in a chart. We can tell at once that median incomes for everyone were generally rising between 1950 and 1979, although there were setbacks in certain years. While the general trends are more immediately apparent, and differences between black and white families are readily visible, the ratio number that was so useful in Table 2.5 is not presented directly. Instead, the ratio of black to white income must be sensed from the chart. We can look from the $0 point on the chart to the white family median income, and then see about where between these two points the black family median income falls. By doing that, we can estimate that black family income was slightly more than half that of white in 1950, and not quite two-thirds in 1979. Hence we can make a similar inference, but not in such a rigorously quantified form. Ultimately, the purpose for which we will use the data should determine the form in which it is presented. For communication purposes, graphic presentation is usually more effective and efficient than tabular material. Therefore, throughout most of this book, material will be presented graphically whenever possible.

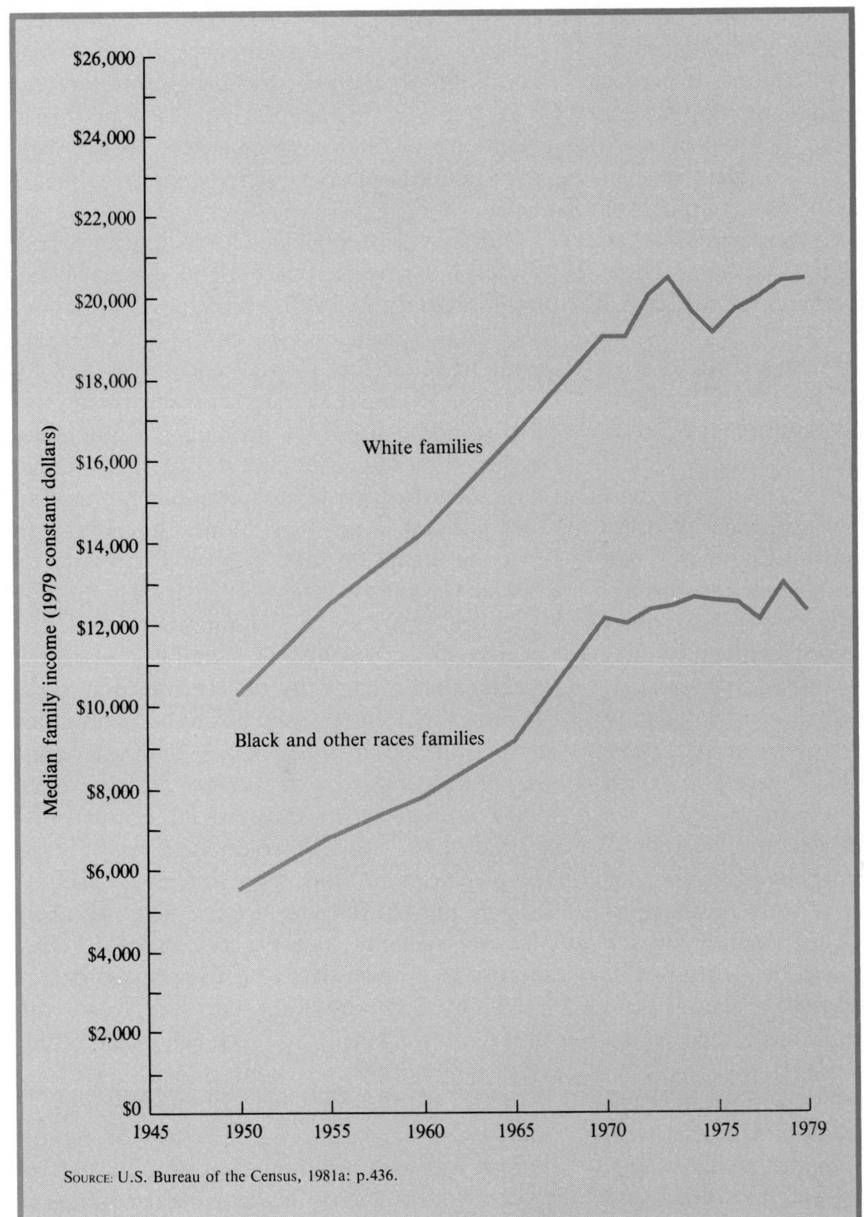

SOURCE: U.S. Bureau of the Census, 1981a: p.436.

Figure 2.2 Median Income of Families, by Race, 1950–1979

search. Traditionally, the poor and the powerless have been studied most frequently, usually with little or no gain for themselves. Hence, we know quite a bit about welfare mothers and children, for example, but rather little about wealthy parents and their children. In organizational research, management often commissions research on worker attitudes and behaviors, and only management sees the results. The more powerful are generally better at insulating themselves from researchers, with the result that we know much less about the rich than about the poor.

Ethics have practical implications. If people feel that they (or people like them) will get something out of the research, they will be more willing to participate in it. If they feel that they can trust researchers to tell them the purposes of the research and to protect their privacy, they will also be more willing to cooperate. These somewhat abstract ethical considerations leap to life in controversial studies.

Many research projects have provoked controversy over ethical issues, but one of the most prominent ones is Laud Humphreys' study *Tearoom Trade: Impersonal Sex in Public Places* (1970), about homosexual acts between strangers meeting in the public restrooms of parks (called "tearooms" by those meeting there). Initial research by Humphreys suggested the hypothesis that the men involved were very often family men who were accepted members of their community. They were not active homosexuals in any other sense. For these reasons, anonymity was very important to them. To avoid hassles with the police, participants always got a third person to serve as lookout (called the "watchqueen") at the door of the "tearoom." Humphreys took this role, and was thereby able to observe the behaviors directly. Testing his hypothesis required more information on the social background of participants. To get this, Humphreys quietly noted the car license plate numbers of participants and traced their names and addresses.

A year later, while conducting a social health survey of men in the community, Humphreys was able to add the tearoom men to his sample. He changed his appearance, style of dress, and the car he drove in the days he served as watchqueen and then called on them at home. He reports that none of the respondents recognized him or appeared upset by the interview. They were being treated as normal people, answering survey questions that might be asked of anyone. In this way Humphreys obtained information about their family backgrounds, socioeconomic status, personal health, social history, religious and employment background, social and political attitudes, friendships, and marital and social relationships. He discovered that many participants were married, living with their families, and were active community members.

While widely applauded for its ingenuity and success in lifting the veil of stigma that shrouded homosexuality in 1970, Humphreys' work was also roundly criticized for its use of deception, both to observe the sexual encounters and to gain background information on participants. In the second edition of his book, Humphreys agrees with this criticism, and says he should have identified himself as a researcher, even if it meant losing some observations. Others suggest that the deception may have been necessary to obtain the information needed to test the hypothesis. And, they add, Humphreys completely protected his respondents' identities. He kept a single master list with their names and code numbers in a safe deposit box a thousand miles away from the city where the research was done; he ultimately destroyed that list. He even once went to jail rather than reveal respondents' names. Less steadfast researchers might have been coerced into turning names over to the police. Some participants became nervous when the case made the local papers and called Humphreys in a panic that their lives would be ruined. Besides public exposure, they feared the threat of blackmail. So, even while protected, they suffered personal anguish.

This example raises many of the ethical issues noted above. Who gets the results of the research and who benefits? How are the subjects protected from harm? Under what conditions, if any, is deception justified in social research?

Ethical issues such as these suggest that social research need not be a dull, bloodless substitute for life. It stands astride real human and social concerns. This fact will become more apparent in the next chapter, which considers how various types of societies survive and change and how sociologists study social structure.

Summary

1. Science differs from other forms of knowledge in the way it stresses observation and reasoning. Science tries to improve upon everyday inquiry by being systematic and careful and by trying to link observations with more general statements (theories).

2. Social science assumes that social life is patterned and that these patterns occur in collections of individuals on a probability basis. Individual exceptions occur, and general statements rarely apply 100 percent of the time. Although it may be complex, the social behavior of collections of people can be described and understood.

3. Researchers following careful, conscious procedures sometimes make discoveries that contradict commonsense expectations. Such instances remind us to ask, "What evidence do we have for believing something to be the way someone suggests, and how was that evidence obtained?"

4. The careful, systematic nature of good research means that it is potentially useful in education, business, public policy-making, the courts, social services, and other fields.

5. The various "tools of the research trade" include units of analysis, sampling procedures, descriptive and explanatory studies, hypotheses, concepts and variables, operationalizing variables, relationships between variables, rules for inferring causality, and steps in the research process.

6. A variety of design and data-gathering techniques are used by social researchers. The primary ones are experiments, interviews and surveys, and observational research. Other sources of data include government documents, comparative historical methods, physical traces and artifacts, and content analysis. Each has certain strengths and certain limitations.

7. Research may affect the lives of the people studied, as revealed in a number of ethical issues. Human subjects have the right to informed consent, protection from harm, privacy, and the benefit of the knowledge gained from research.

Key Terms

attributes
bias
concept
content analysis
control group
controlling for
correlation
criteria for inferring causality
dependent variable
descriptive study
experimental group
explanatory study
hypothesis
independent variable
mean
median
methodology
mode
objectivity
operationalization
participant observation
population
random sample
range
research design
rival hypothesis
theory
unit of analysis
variable

Part Two

Core Aspects of Social Life

Chapter 3

Societies and Social Structures

Social life is not random; neither does it reflect the inflexible expression of a natural law. Instead, social life is patterned by the strategies a society employs to gather and produce food and by the social structures that develop around those strategies. What people eat, how tasks are assigned, the size of communities, the amount of inequality between individuals, and the importance of family ties are among the various features of social life that are influenced by food-gathering and food-producing strategies.

Since the focus of this book is society and how people interact with it, we begin this chapter by defining society. We will consider what needs societies have in order to survive, the major subsistence strategies they have adopted for meeting those needs, and some major theories that examine the "great transformation" from small, simple societies to complex, urban, industrial societies. After examining several types of societies, we will explore some key concepts sociologists use to analyze the social structure of a society.

Subsistence strategies and social structures affect our social life on a daily basis. The people we see and talk with and how we interact with them is affected by societal variations and by one's place in the social structure. But before we begin interacting with others, all of us are born into a preexisting society.

SOCIETIES

WHAT IS SOCIETY?

At what point does a cluster of people become a society? The first major feature of a society is that its people share a common heritage, called *culture,* consisting of customs, values, ideas, and artifacts. Culture, including language, distinguishes human societies from animal societies. Culture includes religious and other beliefs; strategies for obtaining food; tool use; and all the other symbolic and material creations resulting from human actions. In a society, this common cultural heritage is transmitted from one generation to the next. Part of what people in a society share are patterned ways of interacting: ways of raising children, forming families, dividing work, making love, greeting one another, and so on.

A *society,* then, is a group of people with a shared and somewhat distinct culture, who live in a defined territory, feel some unity as a group, and see themselves as distinct from other peoples. A society needs to be large enough to avoid being swallowed up by other societies. One test of a society is whether it could survive in a form close to its present one if all other societies in the world disappeared. A society, in short, is an independent collection of people who share a common heritage, common ways of interacting, and a set of institutions such as the family and religion.

SOCIETAL NEEDS

To survive, all societies must meet certain basic needs, which functionalists call *functional prerequisites*. They include these:

1. Subsistence needs. Living beings have physical needs—subsistence needs—for air, food, water, warmth, shelter, and sleep that must be met in order for them to survive. Among humans there are psychic needs as well, such as the need for affection, avoidance of excessive stress, and participation in a system of shared beliefs. Meeting subsistence needs usually requires some kind of work to hunt, gather, or produce food and shelter.

2. Distribution needs. The means of subsistence need to be distributed in some way among the members of a society. Very seldom does every member have equal access to the means of subsistence. If nothing else, the babies and young members of a society need others to provide them with an adequate food supply.

3. The need for biological reproduction. Individuals do not need to reproduce, but for a society to survive some of its members must reproduce.

4. The need to transmit culture. For a society to persist in its present form, there is a need to transmit existing culture—the customs, values, and ideas of the society—to new members in order for that culture to survive or continue.

5. The need for protection. Societal members need to avoid destroying one another, and a society as a whole needs protection from external threats, whether physical or social.

6. The need for communication. To meet all these needs, members must be able to communicate with one another.

How the needs of a society are met varies widely and seems to depend on a series of factors that may be grouped into physical environment or societal features. The physical environment includes climate and the variety of available resources (water, animals, plants, soil, sun, minerals, and metals). Physical environment will influence but not completely determine the subsistence strategies followed by a society. Societal features include a society's subsistence strategies, its social structure, culture, and material products, and the demographic features of the society—that is, the number of people, their age and sex, birth rates, and death rates. (*Demography* is the study of population trends.) These interrelated features shape much of social life in different societies.

SUBSISTENCE STRATEGIES[1]

Examining the subsistence strategies of various societies has intellectual and practical value. Intellectually, such an exploration illustrates how subsistence strategies may influence social structures and culture and gives us a sense of our history as a species. In practical terms, such an analysis helps us to understand societies today, for people still use these strategies to survive. The United States and other industrialized societies have been involved at various times in military, diplomatic, or trade activity with societies using subsistence strategies different from their own. For these reasons, it is valuable to survey some of these strategies.

About 30,000 years ago, people were seeking protection from the huge masses of ice that covered much of North America and Northern Europe. They lived in caves and depended on their abilities as hunters to supply themselves with food and clothing. As the glaciers retreated and people emerged from their caves, there was a gradual shifting away from the hunting mode of existence toward farming and stock raising. This shift, which began around 11,000 B.C., may have occurred because the numbers of large ani-

[1]The following discussion benefits from Lenski (1966) and Lenski and Lenski (1978).

mals were reduced by heavier hunting and the changing climate (Harris, 1979). The human population on earth then began to surge, from about 5 million in 8000 B.C. to about 86 million by 4000 B.C. (Deevey, 1960). By the time Jesus was born (A.D. 1) there were an estimated 200 to 300 million people on earth (United Nations, 1953).

During this time, farming evolved from the simple use of hoes and sticks, with no animals, to the more effective use of plows using animals to pull them. The use of animal labor increased the agricultural surplus, which in turn could support more people in closely settled groupings. The first cities arose. Agricultural surplus also permitted new social arrangements. As irrigation and agricultural techniques developed, social groupings grew larger and more complex, leading to the rise of large nation-states. The Industrial Revolution that has so shaped contemporary society as we know it began only 250 years ago. It has brought us to a world of assembly-line factories, nuclear bombs and power plants, supersonic jets, communications satellites, multinational corporations, and computerized banking.

Societies may be grouped according to the subsistence strategies they use. The key questions to ask about subsistence strategies are these: What is a group's food supply, and how is it obtained? The answers to those two questions determine whether a social group will settle down permanently or move from place to place; what size group can be maintained; the amount of warfare the group engages in; the kind of culture that develops; and the type of social structure that emerges. In the history of the human species, societies have been characterized by four major types of subsistence strategies. In their pure forms, these appear as hunting and gathering societies, horticultural societies, agrarian societies, and industrial societies. Considering each of these suggests how subsistence strategies are related to the types of authority and inequity that develop in a society, and to its culture, religion, and social interaction.

Hunting and Gathering Societies

The subsistence strategy used for the longest time in human history was that of hunting animals for meat and gathering berries, nuts, vegetables, and fruit for food. This strategy prevailed until only a few thousand years ago. Today, there are still a few hunting and gathering societies around, such as the bush people of Namibia (Southwest Africa) and the Tasaday who live in a rain forest in the Philippine Islands. Our knowledge of hunting and gathering societies is based on two major types of evidence: archeological remains of early humans and anthropological studies, called *ethnographies,* of remaining hunting and gathering groups.

With the exception of larger fishing societies, *hunting and gathering societies* typically are very small, with only about 40 people each (Murdock, 1967). They are almost always independent societies in their own right. Until 1970, for example, the Tasaday apparently had no contact with modern societies. Hunters and gatherers are generally nomads, since they tend to exhaust the supply of food in one area and then move on to another. Activities are divided by age and sex. In some tribes, reaching the age at which he can hunt with the men is a sign of adulthood for a boy. In most hunting and gathering societies, there is a sexual division of labor. Women do most of the gathering, and also are responsible for child care. Men do most of the hunting.

Hunting and gathering societies reveal a number of important connections between subsistence strategies and social structure. The major organizing institution is the system of family and kinship. In such societies, all individuals have relationships with others that are clearly defined in kinship terms. Virtually everyone is related in some way, and individuals need to know what that relationship is so they know how they should behave toward one another (Elkin, 1954). The kinship ties of the family encourage the practice of sharing food, which is especially important because of the uncertainty and variability that marks a hunting and gathering economy.

Hunting and gathering societies catch or find their food rather than producing it. As a result, they tend to contain no more than about 40 members, to be fairly mobile, and to have relatively small differences in social rank between individuals.

Because of their nomadic existence, members of hunting and gathering societies can accumulate few possessions or other types of wealth. The tendency not to accumulate a surplus is shown by the life of the Tasaday. The first outsiders to see the Tasaday brought knives as presents, which they laid out for the Tasaday to take. Each man took one, and there was one left over. They explained "Everyone has a knife now," so they did not need the extra one (Nance, 1975). Every man can provide for his own material needs and that of his family to about the same degree. Every man learns how to make his own weapons out of available materials and how to use them. No one has a monopoly over the means of production. As a result, the headman's position is based largely on respect and prestige rather than on superior wealth. It may be that he is the best hunter, has the best ideas about how to do things, has a talent for storytelling, or gives away more food and gifts to other villagers (Harris, 1979). These behaviors are likely to gain him respect, prestige, and influence. Nevertheless, there are no major differences in social rank between individuals.

Horticultural and Pastoral Societies

Horticultural societies are societies in which the cultivation of plants is the primary means of subsistence. In simple horticultural societies, people garden with hoes and sticks; in more complex horticultural societies, they use metal tools. Somewhere between 11,000 and 7000 B.C., hunters and gatherers began to shift to farming and animal raising. Even before this, they had been harvesting wild grains for food, as the name "gatherers" indicates. The shift from hunting and gathering strategies to simple gardening and animal raising enabled humans to produce food rather than simply to find it.

As a result, cultivators may be able to accumulate surpluses. The existence of a surplus food supply promotes trade and commerce, since the food stored by one group can be traded or sold to another group. Surpluses also permit increasing occupational specialization because they free people to do more than just find food. Plant cultivation also makes possible larger, more permanent settlements with denser populations, since there is less concern about overhunting in an area. Gardening societies can be as large as 150 to 200 inhabitants; occasional settlements as large as 2000 to 3000 people have been found—for example, in the Sudan region of Africa. The growth of food surplus and of population made possible by cultivation can also contribute to the growth of warfare. Conquest and exploitation of some groups by others may be more attractive and profitable if stored food can be seized.

In dry areas unsuited to farming, hunters began to raise sheep, goats, and cows for their milk, skins, and meat. Such *pastoral societies* still exist today in the Middle East and the drier regions of Africa. They are by necessity *nomadic*—that is, they move their residences from place to place. With the expansion of human and animal populations in a region, warfare increases as groups begin to compete over who will use the land for grazing. Although pastoral communities are fairly small, due to the limited number of herds an area can support, they are tied together into larger societies. The median size of herding communities is 55 people, but they may be grouped into societies of 2000 or more (Murdock, 1967). Their frequent travel, contact with others, and the need to band together to protect grazing territories probably account for the considerable degree of trading and political development pastoral societies show. The idea of a supreme being as a shepherd who takes an active interest in his flock emerged in a number of herding societies. So the means of subsistence influences even such "otherworldly" aspects of culture as religion.

A development that separated simple from advanced herding and gardening societies was metallurgy, the extraction of metals from ore. First, copper and then bronze were discovered by various simple farming societies. In the beginning, metals were used primarily for weapons, ornaments, and religious artifacts. The specialized knowledge and skill that was necessary to smelt and shape bronze meant that the processes of metalworking tended to be learned and controlled by a few specialists, who were sometimes thought to possess magical qualities. Because making bronze weapons was costly, such weapons tended to be monopolized by the wealthy. Since bronze weapons were sharper and more durable than stone weapons, societies with such weapons had an advantage in warfare against societies without them.

In the more advanced horticultural societies, there was more warfare and greater inequality. Wherever there were critical resources that could be monopolized, whether of metallurgy, irrigation facilities, or domestic animals, the concentration of wealth and power began to increase. The advantages that one generation possessed were now more likely to be transmitted to the next generation than had been the case in hunting and gathering societies. Rank came to be based less on personal skills, talents, or behaviors and more on control of technology and wealth.

Agrarian Societies

Agrarian societies are those in which large-scale cultivation takes place. They represent a giant leap forward from simple and even advanced horticultural strategies. The key tool that made this advance possible was the plow. Plowing turned over the soil regularly and brought up buried nutrients. For the first time, people could continue to use the same piece of land for a series of crops. With the use of plows, the scale and permanence of food-growing activities changed dramatically.

Then animal power began to be used to supplement human energy to pull plows. This change set the stage for the future development of additional nonhuman energy sources. The period in which the plow came into use, from about 4000 to 3000 B.C., was an extremely creative one, marked by the invention of the wheel for use in wagons and making pottery; by the harnessing of windpower to propel sailboats; and by the development of writing, numbers, and the calendar (Childe, 1964). Human productivity increased greatly as a result.

Technological development, and probably population pressures as well, fueled the production and distribution of an ever-greater agricultural surplus. This surplus, in turn, permitted a host of social changes. The total population expanded considerably. With improved grain production and transportation, cities developed, although most people still lived and worked on the land. Some of these had as many as 100,000 people by the time of the Roman Empire (first century B.C. to fourth century A.D.). Agricultural surplus and urban concentration allowed ever-greater division of labor and specialization. For example, there were a hundred or more occupational specialties—including tanners, innkeepers, fishermen, sailors, wooldressers, and spicers—in Paris and in Barcelona in the fourteenth century (Russell, 1972). Increasing specialization, in turn, was related to the growth of trade, the use of money as a medium of exchange, and the emergence of a new merchant class of traders and shopkeepers.

The existence of a large surplus created the possibility for one ruler to claim a good deal of it for himself and his followers in the form of taxes, tithes, rents, and offerings. All the large agricultural civilizations of history—ancient Egypt, Babylonia, Assyria, Persia, Greece, and Rome, old India, old China, and pre-Columbian Mexico and Peru—were governed by aristocracies that monopolized military force. A few rulers lived in great splendor. They wore special clothing for each occasion (with servants to care for each type of clothing) and ornaments made from precious metals and jewels. They engaged their own personal entertainers, such as jugglers and musicians. Under the sponsorship of wealthy rulers, architecture and the arts flourished. Such monuments as the Taj Mahal in India and the Egyptian temples and pyramids were built in agrarian societies.

Economic diversity was accompanied by growing institutional specialization. One notable shift involved the gradual separation of religion and kinship. In hunting and gathering societies, religion was closely tied to one's clan—that is, one's extended family. The great world religions, including Buddhism, Christianity, Hinduism, Islam, and Judaism, emerged in the major agrarian societies. They are called world religions because they claim to apply equally to all persons, regardless of family ties.[2] This shift meant that people in different clans might belong to the same religion. Religious beliefs were also transformed in the process, with numerous local deities being replaced by universal religions claiming that one deity ruled the entire world. The tendency to believe in a single deity may have reflected a greater awareness of the world that arose from trade and military contact with other lands and peoples.

The combination of rulers, military elites, and surplus is associated with greatly increased warfare and tendencies for empire building. Empires in Egypt, Rome, China, and elsewhere were claimed by societies with dominant military power. Once conquered, however, new territories posed organizational and administrative problems that rulers sought to handle with a growing number of state officials. The ability to read, write, and count was important for state officials so that they could collect taxes properly and communicate with the empire's home base. These skills were generally limited to the sons of the wealthy, since they were the only ones who could afford the time and the tutors needed to learn such skills.

In agrarian societies such as those of ancient Egypt (3100 B.C. to 1085 B.C.) and the Roman Empire, the class structure became increasingly complex. Besides the rulers and the ruled, there were a growing array of state officials and military commanders and a thriving class of merchants, who were often more wealthy than even high state officials. Greater complexity in the class structure was reflected in marriage practices. Increasingly, marriage took on political as well as economic significance, as parents tried to solidify their position in the social structure by making good matches for their children.

The era of agrarian revolution that began with a number of highly significant innovations, including the plow, the wheel, money, and writing, was followed, almost paradoxically, by a rather stagnant period in human affairs. The social anthropologist Vernon Childe (1951) suggests that this stagnation may have resulted from the structured social inequality in society. Rulers lost touch with the technology of their times, in part because of their scorn for physical labor. The producers, who had the knowledge to make innovations, knew that the benefits would be enjoyed by the rulers. They had little motivation to try to improve on the processes they were using. Industrialization, however, represented a dramatic return to innovation.

Industrialized Societies

Industrialization replaces human or animal energy and labor with machines and new energy sources such as water power, steam, electricity, and oil. The Industrial Revolution began in England in the mid-1700s. Hand spinning wheels and looms were replaced by increasingly efficient mechanical devices for spinning and weaving. By the 1850s, iron, steam, and machine technologies were applied successfully to transportation, and a national railroad network developed in England. It reduced the costs of shipping heavy commodities and facilitated trade. Similar advances were made in water transport.

The combined forces of industrialization and political revolution that shook Western Europe in the eighteenth and nineteenth centuries profoundly affected European social structures. The supreme authority of the church was shattered, and family structure was deeply wrenched by the increasing separation of family and work. Whereas the household was once the center of work for most families, industrialization greatly

[2] I am indebted to Zaret, 1981, for bringing this idea to my attention.

undermined its importance as a center of economic production. The massive size, weight, and cost of steam-powered spinning and weaving machines required that factories be built. Factories needed plentiful supplies of labor living nearby, so more and more factories were built in cities. Cities also sprang up around outlying factories when factory owners built cheap, substandard housing to attract workers.

These developments had their social and human costs, however. The growth of factories and urbanization created new social problems. Migrations to cities cut social ties with kin and village. Individuals who had been well integrated into a kinship and community group at home found themselves without the social support and social control such ties provide. Workers spent long hours under dismal and often dangerous working conditions, and they returned to equally dreary quarters at night. Sickness, drunkenness, crime, and vice were rampant. Any immediate benefits of technology and industrialization must have been all but invisible to those working in the factories and coal mines in the early years of the Industrial Revolution.

Once productive machinery was built and owned by a limited number of individuals, other individuals had only their labor to sell in the marketplace. They owned neither land nor the expensive machinery needed to produce cloth or anything else. Owners paid workers very low wages. In Britain, as in the United States later on, industrialization and capitalism went hand in hand. Over time, however, some of the gains came to be shared by workers as well as owners.

The period from 1900 to 1940 in both Europe and the United States witnessed the expansion of the automobile, electrical, oil, telephone, and chemical industries. During and after World War II the aviation industry expanded, which fanned aluminum production. Plastics, electronics (including computers), and nuclear technology also emerged during this time. By 1969, technical developments had reached the point where a passenger-carrying spacecraft could be launched from the earth, fly to the moon, and circle the moon while a smaller lunar module detached itself from the larger craft and landed on the moon, enabling two American astronauts to get out and walk around. From horse and wagon to lunar module in slightly over 300 years—such has been the speed and extent of the Industrial Revolution. Throughout this time, the division of labor became ever more specialized, with new occupations developing steadily. Technical innovations continued; the amount of knowledge and information exploded; and methods of transportation and communication improved.

Industrial societies actively produce food on a mass basis. A relatively small proportion of the population is involved in food production. Through mechanization and a high degree of specialization, food producers are often able to produce a surplus.

THE GREAT TRANSFORMATION

One theory of why the Industrial Revolution developed in England when it did was advanced by Max Weber. He suggested a possible link between what he called the Protestant ethic and the rise of capitalism (1904). Weber stressed that culture, in this case religion, contributed in a major way to the rise of capitalism. Capitalism requires that some portion of an economic surplus be saved and invested rather than consumed immediately. Weber argued that there was a certain compatibility between the religious teachings of Protestantism and the early growth of capitalism.

First, Protestant reformers saw work as noble. One's work in the world was a "calling," with religious significance. The Protestant view of work offered respect and legitimacy to craftspeople and merchants. Second, Protestants believed the world to be a rational and orderly place. Therefore, rational planning of one's life and work was a sensible approach. This "world view" facilitated both the development of science and the rational planning of business enterprises. Finally, Protestants practiced thrift and spent little on personal pleasures. These behaviors enabled individuals to accumulate capital that could be invested in business or trade.

Weber has been most severely criticized for failing to consider that economics might have influenced the development of religion: Protestantism might never have emerged if there had not been a merchant class receptive to it. Although Weber stressed the close relationship between capitalism and Protestantism, he was careful not to claim that Protestantism caused capitalism. Weber's importance lies in his explanation of how economic traditionalism was replaced by capitalism. In today's world, the virtues of hard work are encouraged by political ideologies like Marxism-Leninism in the Soviet Union and Maoism in China. These ideologies may serve as functional equivalents to Protestantism: "Like Protestantism, they uphold the virtue of the work ethic and extol the importance of service to a higher moral entity through labor, although for them this entity is the state whereas for the Protestants it was God" (Zaret, 1981).

All the major figures in sociology in its early years thought about the issue of the "great transformation" from simple, preliterate societies to massive, complex, industrial societies. The German sociologist Ferdinand Tonnies (1887) contrasted these two types. He used the term *gemeinschaft* (ge mine′ shaft) or *community,* to describe a small, traditional society where people have personal, face-to-face relationships with each other and where they value social relationships as ends in themselves. There people are committed to tradition and group values. The French sociologist Emile Durkheim (1893) felt that people in such a society share common tasks that develop similar values. Nearly everyone plants a crop, harvests it, marries, and has children. These similarities bind them together.

Tonnies characterized urban industrial society as a *gesellschaft* (ge zell′ shaft), or association. People in such societies have more impersonal, distant relationships with each other and tend to use social relationships as a means to an end. Individualism is valued more than group solidarity. More complex societies are held together by webs of trade among otherwise quite different individuals. The farmer and the transportation worker need each other, and both depend upon manufacturers and bankers.

To Weber, the dominant theme of the great transformation was the growing emphasis on rationality in all aspects of modern social life. He saw rationality as coming to replace tradition and personal qualities, whether in running an organization or making decisions. Karl Marx focused on the issues of class struggle and exploitation that accompanied the great transformation. He viewed different modes of production (ways of producing goods) as leading to specific types of social organization (for instance, feudalism or capitalism). The division of labor widens and fortifies inequalities between people, although those divisions do not go unchallenged according to Marx, who saw human history as the history of class struggles.

FEATURES OF SOCIAL STRUCTURE

RANK AND FUNCTIONAL DIFFERENTIATION

As we have seen, subsistence strategies and the great transformation affect a society's social structure. One of the major features of social structure is the amount of rank differentiation found in a society. *Rank differentiation* refers to the unequal evaluation of various positions in society. As the number of unequally ranked positions increases, there is usually a growing gap between leaders and followers. For example, a chief may have increasing power and privileges, and there may be growing numbers of subchiefs. The result may be that the chief has less contact with the rank and file members of the group.

The amount of functional differentiation in a society may also change. *Functional differentiation* refers to the increasing division of labor in society. As societies become more complex, more and more distinct occupations develop, such as hatmaker, pinmaker, watchmaker, baker, and so forth. Today the United States Census lists more than 33,000 occupations. In addition, the *division of labor* means that people become more specialized in what they do.[3] Functional differentiation also refers to institutional specialization at the societal level. In early societies, family role determined political and occupational roles. In more complex societies, family, politics, and religion become increasingly separate institutions. Thus, where once the institution of the family performed almost all social functions—education, religious rituals, economic activities, and governing and regulating functions—now a whole series of additional institutions evolve to deal with each of these functions (Parsons, 1966).

Does functional differentiation inevitably lead to rank differentiation? Sociologists do not agree on an answer. Some say that increased specialization invariably provides some people with inside information and a more central position in the production process, which in turn can be converted into greater power and privilege. Others question whether the process is inevitable. Even if some inequality occurs, how much there is may vary from one society to another. Functional differentiation in both the occupational and the institutional realms continues as societies become more industrialized. Each occupation, or institution, takes on an ever greater degree of specialization.

The increasing division of labor and institutional differentiation is related to yet another structural feature. Kin groups gradually become less important than they had been, especially with the transformations that accompany industrialization. Craft or occupational groups, religious groups, and voluntary associations such as clubs or civic groups become increasingly important sources of individual identity and social support.

In brief, functional and rank differentiation are two central features of social structure. Differences in these features are associated with different types of societies, as Table 3.1 indicates. In simple societies, functional differentiation is low; it is based on age and sex, and sometimes on kin group membership.[4] In such a society, functional position would be based almost entirely upon *ascribed status,* which includes characteristics, such as sex and age, that one is born with. Ascribed status does not depend on an individual's actions. In an agrarian society, posi-

[3]Some critics raise the interesting point that occupational differentiation and specialization may not be functional for everyone. Braverman (1974) stresses that "scientific management" promoted task specialization as a way of limiting the control of workers over the production process while increasing the control of owners and managers (Zaret, 1981).

[4]The word *simple* in this context refers to the degree of complexity in social structure.

Table 3.1 Major Social Differences in Simple, Agrarian, and Industrial Societies

	Type of Society		
	Simple	Agrarian	Industrial
Food Supply	May be irregular	Steady; usually surpluses	Steady; surpluses
Community Size	Small (40)	Wide variation; some towns and cities	Large; many towns and cities
Societal Size	Small (40)	More than 100,000	In the millions
Social Relationships	Face-to-face	Mostly face-to-face	Many impersonal ones
Culture	Similar; widely shared	Somewhat diverse	Very diverse
Functional Differentiation	Low	Medium	High
Basis for Functional Differentiation	Age and sex; sometimes kinship	Kinship, age, sex	Skills, knowledge, age, sex, family, kinship
Rank Differentiation	Low	High	Medium
Basis for Rank Differentiation	Wit, talent, ideas, age, sex, kinship, gift giving	Family, kinship, age, sex	Wealth, occupation, race, sex, kinship, education, talent, skills, age
Amount of Leisure for Most People	Quite high	Low	Medium
Social Change	Slow	Slow to medium	Rapid

SOURCES: Elkin, 1954; Lenski, 1966; Murdock, 1957; Nance, 1975.

tion in the occupational and status hierarchy would be almost entirely determined by family origins, also an ascribed characteristic. In industrial societies, where functional differentiation is high, occupational position is based to a somewhat greater degree upon *achieved* traits such as skill and knowledge, as well as being influenced by age, sex, race, and class.

Within the restrictions of age and sex, simple, agrarian, and industrial societies differ considerably with respect to amount of rank differentiation. Anthropological studies of existing simple societies suggest that they have less rank inequality than do industrial societies. The amount of inequality of wealth or political power was probably greatest in the large agrarian empires of history, such as those of Rome and Egypt, the Ottoman Empire, and that of nineteenth-century China. Industrial societies fall in between simple societies and agricultural empires with respect to amount of inequality. Some inequalities are based on talent, skill, or specialized training, although race, sex, and kinship may influence whose talent gets developed.

STATUSES AND ROLES

Functional and rank differentiation enable us to compare societal types on a macro level. Within this broad perspective, sociologists have several conceptual tools for looking at the social structure of a society. The *social structure* consists of the patterned and interrelated statuses and roles in a society. Subsistence strategies and functional and rank differentiation shape statuses and roles in a society.

An individual's positions within the system of social differentiation are called statuses. The term *status* refers to a socially defined position in society. Each position has certain prescribed rights, obligations, and expected behaviors that accompany it, although there is considerable variation in actual behaviors. The status of child, for example, is an identifiable social position in virtually every society, although the age limits vary widely. Occupants of that position have certain socially prescribed rights (such as to be fed), obligations (say, to obey one's elders), and expected behaviors (for instance, finding firewood and gathering berries or playing with companions). Various children may behave differently, even though they all occupy the same status. Individuals are born into some positions that are called *ascribed statuses*. These include their sex, race, nationality, and social class. Other statuses, such as baseball player, are *achieved* through an individual's own talents and efforts. Given the arrangement of statuses in a particular society, your location within various institutions of society largely determines *with whom* you will interact (in both personal and structural terms) and to a considerable degree the *form* that interaction will take.

Status: Position and Rank

The term status also connotes *rank*—that is, a position relative to other people in society. Someone is of higher or lower social status than someone else. In virtually all societies, children occupy an inferior status relative to adults, for instance. How is location in the functional and status systems of society determined? Family social status; parental occupation; neighborhood, school, and racial and religious group membership; age; and gender are major determinants of position in the social structure. These features interact with educational experiences to shape aspirations, occupational choices, and goals. Even in complex societies, one status may dominate. A *dominant status* is one that overshadows all others (Hughes, 1945). In the past, race was the dominant status of blacks in the United States. Even if they were doctors or lawyers, people responded to them first in terms of their race. The statuses of female and of child also tend to be dominant.

Role: Two Views

In sociology, the key concept of *role* is defined differently by functionalists and by interactionists. Rather than choosing one definition or the other as the "correct" one, we will bring both conceptions to bear on the social world in order to understand the different aspects of role behavior each explains.

For functionalists, roles are the culturally prescribed behaviors associated with particular social positions. Roles are normative in that they convey a sense of how people should behave in particular situations. These norms may be enforced by rewards or punishments. Roles also are socially patterned; role patterns are established by societal values, behaviors, and attitudes that influence how people with a given status are expected to behave. A wife in Saudi Arabia, for example, is expected to perform very different roles from those of a wife in Hollywood, California. When you become a college student, there are certain rights and duties associated with that status. These rights and duties are often reinforced by the role expectations held by others with whom you interact. Your professors, for instance, expect certain behaviors from you, and the college grants you certain rights. You yourself probably have certain expectations about how you should perform the roles attached to your particular position. Each status has a cluster of role partners and roles attached to it, each with a variety of expectations. Knowing what statuses people occupy helps sociologists predict how people are likely to behave.

To a functionalist, *role performance* refers to the way people perform the behaviors expected in certain roles. Sometimes role behavior is judged quite loosely, as Woody Allen noted when he said "showing up is eighty percent of life" (Rowes, 1979: 207). At other times, role performance is judged by exacting standards, as in microsurgery. Functionalists, then, stress that roles exist before individuals come along and fill them. Once role performers appear, roles impose their demands upon them. This conception of role leaves little room for individual freedom.

Interactionists do not accept a rigid and fixed conception of role. When they speak of role, they stress its interactive nature rather than a social role specified by society. The interactive role is an effort to mesh the demands of a social position with one's own personality and identity (McCall and Simmons, 1966). People directing traffic may fill that role like a robot or find ways to express their personalities and identities on the job. The interactionist approach stresses the different ways various individuals express themselves in a role, rather than looking at the common aspects of a role.

Our understanding of social roles is enhanced by using both functionalist and interactionist approaches. Social roles vary from those that are tightly patterned and prescribed to those that are much more flexible. When a priest, minister, or rabbi conducts a religious service, for example, certain attitudes and behaviors are usually expected. The functionalist view may better explain role behavior in this instance. The roles attached to the position of sports announcer, on the other hand, may allow a wider range of feelings, beliefs, and behaviors. The interactive view can explain the variation to be found among people occupying this role.

Role Expectations

In simple, relatively traditional societies, there may be a smaller range of possible role behaviors and less room for improvisation. In a society like ours, with many cultural patterns and practices and where considerable social change is occurring, roles associated with particular positions—for example, with being male or female, black or white, old or young—are not universally prescribed. Even in our diverse society, however, there are guidelines for how people should play their roles. These guidelines are called *role expectations.* Often these guidelines are not simply a single prescription, but rather an inventory of possible behaviors. There may even be competing prescriptions—for example, should mothers of small children work or stay home with the children? The existence of a range of possible role behaviors gives individuals room for choice. There may even be the chance to improvise new behaviors and add them to the inventory.

Flexibility and improvisation allow for greater individual freedom on the one hand, but may create personal and organizational strain on the other hand. Social changes begin to occur when groups of individuals create new recipes for role behavior. We have witnessed this, for example, in the broader inventory of role behaviors that has recently come to be attached to the status of wife in the United States.

Role expectations are like social recipes that enable us to cook up a number of social interactions with relative ease, rather than having to produce a newly created social behavior each time. Cultural habits in the form of role prescriptions mean that people can buy magazines, borrow library books, cross the street, get married, and do many other social acts without having first to lay down common ground rules and establish practices with all the other people in the situation.

The power of expectations is evident not only in people often behaving in ways that are expected, but also in the fact that they often feel

Table 3.2 **Likely Statuses and Role Partners of a College Student**

Status	Likely Role Partners
College student	Professors, deans, classmates, librarians, coaches, roommates, college staff members, friends
Daughter or son	Parents, siblings, aunts and uncles, cousins
Male or female	Members of the same and of the opposite sex
Catholic, Protestant, Jew, other	Clergy, members of the congregation, agnostics, atheists
White, black, Hispanic, other	Members of one's own ethnic group; members of other ethnic groups
Citizens of the United States or other country	Fellow citizens; other nationals
Employee	Boss; co-workers; perhaps customers or clients

the way occupants of that position are "supposed to feel," just as some actors and actresses feel the emotions of the characters they are playing (Hochschild, 1978). The fact that role expectations can affect behavior is illustrated by people who are suddenly elevated to leadership positions in civic organizations. They often say they used to be terrified of speaking in public, but that the demands of the role called forth capacities they did not know they had.

In your status as student, you have a *role set*—that is, a cluster of roles to play in relation to professors, other students, roommates, college staff members, friends, and so forth. You also occupy statuses besides that of student. You have one or more family statuses, a gender status (masculine or feminine), a racial status, a religious status, a nationality, and perhaps an occupational status. Table 3.2 shows some of the statuses and role partners of a "typical" college student.

Role Conflict and Strain

Role conflict refers to the incompatibility between two or more roles, either within a status (as when a parent is torn between playing with the children and cleaning house, for instance) or between statuses (as when your coach expects you to play in an away game and your professor requires you to take an exam at the same time). Role conflict tends to give the feeling of being pulled in many different directions at once. Role conflict is particularly acute in situations where there are no socially prescribed guidelines for resolution. Competing demands from various role partners about which status should dominate can also cause role conflict. Do you and your parents agree about when studying should take precedence over a family reunion, for example? The participants in most role relationships tend to feel that their expectations and demands are paramount and that they should receive priority. Even among professors, you may have noticed that each tends to assume you are taking only one course.

Sometimes a person may suffer from *role overload* or *role strain*. This description refers to the feeling that the various demands being made by one's social positions are more than a person can handle. You might experience role strain if you

"We ought to consider taking Freedley off crisis management."

SOURCE: Drawing by Stevenson, © 1981, *The New Yorker Magazine, Inc.*

have to plan your summer job hunt, your apartment is robbed, and you have final exams all in the same week. Role strain makes a person feel burdened by the weight of role demands, and often makes it difficult to set priorities among the demands or know what to do next.

Role Accumulation

The possibilities for role conflict and strain tend to increase as an individual occupies more statuses. Nevertheless, according to Sieber (1974), *role accumulation,*—that is, adding to one's statuses and roles, may be more gratifying than stressful, since it offers the possibility of greater privileges, status security, resources for status enhancement, role performance, personality enrichment, and ego gratification. If Sieber is right, his view helps to explain why women want to hold responsible jobs or take part in local and national affairs in addition to running a household and raising children. Despite the chances of more role conflict and strain, women value the chance to increase their resources (which may enhance their role performance as wives and mothers), gain privileges, and feel a greater sense of personal worth.

Drawing on symbolic interaction theory, Thoits (1983) formulates the concept of social isolation in terms of possessing few social statuses and roles. Using data from a New Haven, Connecticut, community survey, she tests her theoretical ideas and finds evidence to support the view that the more statuses and roles people have, the less likely they are to experience psychological distress.

All societies have rituals and rites of passage to mark the progression of young members from novices to full-fledged members of their society. Here an Apache girl is undergoing a puberty ceremony, indicating that she has moved from the status of girl to a woman in her tribe.

SOCIAL INSTITUTIONS

The survival of every society requires that it meet such basic needs as finding food and shelter, reproducing, protecting and rearing its young, preserving sufficient social order, and transmitting culture and values. Members of all societies develop ways of meeting these needs, and they tend to preserve the successful strategies they find. These strategies, which then become established and patterned, include social positions and the roles and norms associated with those statuses.

Sociologists call these patterned positions and responses institutions. An *institution* consists of statuses, roles, and norms centered around the task of meeting an important social need, such as producing and distributing food or rearing children. A particular institution such as the economy may involve individuals from different families, members of different religions, perhaps even persons of different nationalities, as well as members of labor unions, business organizations, consumer groups, and farm organizations. Despite the social differences individuals may have, an institution like the economy operates to regularize the thoughts and actions of people involved in fulfilling its functions. The institution of religion deals with the mysterious aspects of life through shared rituals and beliefs; the institution of the family channels sexual behavior, reproduction, and childrearing; political institutions address the use of power and force in society; the institution of education transmits cultural knowledge and skills to young people; the legal institution maintains social control and administers justice; and the military institution protects or extends a society's boundaries.

Institutions tend to change slowly. The social practices that become *institutionalized*—that is, well established—have been hallowed by tradition and custom for so long they seem "natural" to members of a society. They feel comfortable, familiar, predictable, and safe. Supports provided by custom and tradition make it difficult to change social institutions.

It is also difficult to change institutions because they are part of a complex web that binds various groups, values, and norms in society. A change in one institution, such as the economy, may have major implications for the family, education, and so forth. Analyzing institutional change or stability requires that we consider the relative power of various groups seeking or resisting change. It may be that resistance to institutional change is centered among the most powerful individuals and groups in society. They may be satisfied with the way existing institutions are operating and have no desire to change them. Marginal groups too sometimes fight hard to preserve institutions in their traditional forms. Some sociologists suggest, for example, that the economic marginality of the "moral majority" lies behind its efforts to stifle changes in institutions such as religion and the family (Greenberg and Bystryn, 1978). So resistance to change may go beyond the weight of shared custom and include the specific concerns of particular groups or classes in a society.

A major source of both continuity *and* change lies in the way individuals interact, forming networks, transmitting culture, preparing new members to join their groups, organizations, and societies, and exercising social control over people who do not conform. These issues are explored in the next five chapters.

Social structures, including functional specialization, rank inequalities, statuses, roles, and institutions, are affected by the subsistence strategies and demographic features of a society. Social structures, in turn, influence the culture and social interactions that develop in a society. Together, social structures and culture make up the *social forces* that confront individuals in a society. Sociologists seek to explain these social forces. They also believe that individuals do make choices and can carve out a realm of independent action, even in the face of social forces. Knowledge of social forces and processes helps us to steer a course through them.

Summary

1. A society is a group of people with a shared and somewhat distinct culture, who live in a defined territory, feel some unity, and see themselves as distinct from other peoples.

2. To survive, all societies need to meet certain basic needs, including physical subsistence, distribution, reproduction, protection, and communication. These needs can be met in a wide variety of forms, as the major types of subsistence strategies suggest. The major subsistence strategies found in human societies are hunting and gathering, horticultural, agrarian, and industrial.

3. The subsistence strategy employed by a society affects social institutions such as the family, shapes the type of authority and inequality that develops, and influences culture, religion, and social interaction.

4. Social structure refers to the patterned, interrelated, rather stable institutions, statuses, and roles in a society.

5. The concepts of status and role help us see how individuals are connected to abstract social structures. A social status is a socially defined position in society. It is usually accompanied by certain expectations and privileges. The term status also suggests a ranking of positions, with some people occupying positions with greater status, wealth, or power than others.

6. Each status is accompanied by certain roles. Interactionists stress the negotiable quality of roles; functionalists stress the way in which roles impose expectations on individuals. Both views capture an important aspect of social roles.

7. Social institutions consist of statuses, roles, and norms clustered around the task of meeting an important societal function, such as producing food and rearing children.

8. Subsistence strategies, social structures, and social roles do not eliminate the possibility of individual initiative, but they do influence how people feel and act in many situations. Sociology helps us to understand the interplay between our own creative possibilities and the social structures we encounter.

Key Terms

achieved status
agrarian societies
ascribed status
community
culture
demography
division of labor
dominant status
ethnography
functional differentiation
functional prerequisites
gemeinschaft
gesellschaft
horticultural societies
hunting and gathering societies
industrialized societies
institution
institutionalized
nomadic
pastoral societies
rank differentiation
role
role accumulation
role conflict
role expectations
role performance
role set
role strain
social forces
social structure
society
status

Chapter 4

Networks and Interactions

"When Albert Einstein completed his university studies in 1900, he could not obtain a job appropriate to his training, in part because he had so antagonized his professors that they would neither hire nor help him. After more than a year of searching and temporary employment, Einstein applied for a post at the Swiss Patent Office and was a few months later called to Zurich for an interview with the office director. In spite of an inadequate performance during the interview, Einstein was hired. As it turned out, the director was an intimate friend of the father of Marcel Grossman, a good friend and former classmate of Einstein. The appointment was no doubt a favor from the director to the Grossmans. Einstein's major scientific insights occurred during his several years at the Patent Office" (Clark, 1971, cited in Fischer et al., 1977, p. 19).

Einstein's job was a direct result of his informal network of social relationships. Being a genius was not enough to secure a position. The statuses we occupy generate social networks; social networks, in turn, may help us to gain certain positions.

In fact, growing evidence suggests that most people hear of their jobs through networks rather than through want-ads or agencies (Bolles, 1977; Granovetter, 1974). This is one important reason for knowing more about social networks and how they operate. In this chapter, we consider how networks form and how they operate, and we consider the nature of social interaction.

SOCIAL NETWORKS

NETWORKS DEFINED

A *social network* is a set of interdependent relations, or links, between individuals. Everyone belongs to some network, if only one based on family ties. Because networks create important social connections, they help to explain why people are not as isolated as early observers of urban industrial life thought. People linked in networks can be relatives; they can like or love each other; they can do things together, such as discuss finances, play tennis, or work together. The more links two people have, the stronger the bond between them. But the strength of that bond also depends on how often and how intensely they interact.

Some networks consist of social equals who have a symmetrical relationship. In a symmetrical relationship, the exchanges between members are relatively equal (Fischer et al., 1977, p. 36). Not all links are symmetrical, however. In a study of Christmas-card sending behavior, for example, Sheila Johnson (1971) found that almost everyone sent some cards to people above them in social status and fully expected not to receive a card in return. Most people have non-

Social networks begin forming very early, in our families, neighborhoods, and school groups. These networks transmit culture, provide access to ideas, and suggest what social futures lie ahead.

reciprocal, or asymmetrical, relations with certain individuals, often those of higher social status. In most cases in Johnson's study, the asymmetry of the relationship indicated the greater status of the receiver. In some cases, however, a person of higher status may send cards to related individuals of lower status. For example, the president of a college or a corporation may send everyone in the organization a card, not expecting one in return from most of them.

NETWORK FORMATION

A person's first social network is the one he or she is born into—usually immediate family and other relatives. Parents have social ties with people in the neighborhood, with people where they work, perhaps with people around the world, as well as in religious, fraternal, occupational, voluntary, or other associations. Other social links are forged as children grow up, with other children and adults in the neighborhood, with people in school, perhaps with people in a religious group, and so forth. Through the statuses individuals and their parents occupy, they have certain social, economic, informational, and other resources. To those are added the resources of people with whom individuals and their families form ties. By the time people go to work, they have added many contacts beyond the family members with whom they started. New ties form on the job and in careers. Social statuses such as race, sex, age, social class, and occupation affect the number and types of networks formed. Individuals may be linked with people who have useful information or

"Do you know how far this chap and I go back together? Since college! He was one of the first to notice I just might have a little something on the ball."

SOURCE: Drawing by Saxon, © 1982, *The New Yorker Magazine, Inc.*

other resources. In this way, networks can help individuals as they pursue their life goals.

HOW NETWORKS OPERATE

Social networks operate in a number of ways. People in a network can "put in a good word" for you even with persons who are strangers to you. They can transmit culture (values, norms, and styles of presenting yourself) and provide access to information, money, status, or power. A recent study found that young people obtained considerable help from their social ties, particularly when those ties were with people who had more status and experience than they did. Contact with these helpful links was not accidental, however. The occupational status of the "contact" was highly related to the education and career of the young person's father. Much more of the social status of the "tie" was explained by these parental characteristics than by the young person's talent or experience (Lin, Ensel, and Vaughn, 1981). This research suggests that the nature and operation of networks in social life is an important trail to follow into the forest where individual lives become connected to careers and social status.

Network theory has direct practical applications—for instance, as a valuable means of obtaining information about the world of work. A senior partner in a major New York law firm keeps a notebook with the names, addresses, telephone numbers, and other helpful information on the people in his network (including people he has just met). Thus, when he has a question, needs some information, or needs to know whom to call, he has leads in his notebook. The wisdom of this approach is upheld by Mark Granovetter's research on how people find jobs (1974). Most of the people he studied found their jobs through personal contacts; better-paying and more presitgious jobs were particularly likely to be obtained in this way. The existence and operation of networks is one of the ways individuals manage to survive in bureaucratic organizations and in large urban environments.

Social networks operate in a way that is seldom visible to the naked eye. People run into each other on the street, in their clubs, at a dinner party, or a convention; they telephone each other; or they correspond. If, for example, the subject matter of the contact is a job, it is likely that the job will not be visible to 80 percent or more of the people who would be interested in it (Crystal and Bolles, 1974). As that fact makes obvious, news about most job openings runs through networks, rather than in newspapers. Sometimes dubbed the "old boy" network, this system of connecting people with jobs is deplored by equal employment opportunity advocates. One of the features required under the Equal Opportunity Employment Act, for instance, is the public advertisement of available jobs. From the employers' point of view, however, the network system may be much more efficient. News travels faster that way; networks may provide more reliable information about candidates; and the chances of finding someone appropriate may be enhanced. Hence, networks often provide efficient channels of communication and effective methods of screening potential candidates for positions. (See the box on the "hidden hurdles" that may operate through social networks.)

Traditionally networks have been heavily used by "old boys"—that is, people in established positions who have school, military, social, or other connections. Women and minorities have usually been excluded. As more women and minorities form their own networks, however, and build bridges to existing networks of insiders, they will begin to benefit from these informal processes as well.

The pattern of links between people is such that, at least in the United States, most individuals are connected indirectly to everyone else. Do you doubt that statement? I did the first time I heard it. But some interesting experiments, called "small world studies," document it.

NETWORKS IN ACTION: SMALL WORLD STUDIES

If you were given the name of a total stranger living 1500 miles away, do you think you could get a document to him using only a chain of acquaintances? This was the problem Jeffrey Travers and Stanley Milgram (1969) set out to answer. They wanted to know how many people could establish contact with the "target" individual, and how many individuals the document had to go through to reach its target. The target individual was a Boston stockbroker. The senders were 296 volunteers—one a group of general residents from Nebraska, another a set of Nebraska blue-chip stockholders, and the third a set of general Boston residents who responded

The Hidden Hurdle

Social networks can put you in the running for a position, assuming you have the qualifications. They can assure that your candidacy is given a fair hearing. They can also provide helpful information about what employers are really looking for and what "turns them off." This information never appears in an ad. In the case described here, executive recruiting firms are serving as official, and paid, networks.

Networks can help you get in the door, but once you are in, a whole set of additional criteria appear. What is called "chemistry" in this article from The Wall Street Journal *really refers to personal and social style, which is a direct outgrowth of the social groups one belongs to, the family one comes from, one's prior social and cultural experiences, in combination with one's own personal talents and tendencies.*

Executive Recruiters Say Firms Tend to Hire 'Our Kind of Person'

Personal-Chemistry Factor Is Big When Candidates Seem Equally Qualified

Don't Carve an Artichoke

By ROGER RICKLEFS

The personnel executive was as good as hired. During a pro forma final-stage interview, the board chairman observed that the job might involve a relocation later. "That sounds fine," said the candidate, "but of course I'd have to check with Mommy."

"Mommy"? His wife.

"Let's skip this guy," the board chairman said after the interview to Frank B. Beaudine, the executive recruiter. "If he calls his wife 'Mommy,' he might think I'm 'Daddy.'" The chairman wanted a team of hard-hitting executives, and the Mommy talk suggested to him an executive hopelessly dependent on his wife, Mr. Beaudine says.

And that was goodbye to a $55,000-a-year job—not the only one ever lost over a single word. Corporations like to say that competence overwhelmingly decides who gets managerial jobs. But executive recruiters say subjective chemistry—deciding whether the candidate is "our kind of person"—often is far more important than the executives doing the hiring realize.

The Big Factor

. . .Chemistry counts more than ever these days, recruiters and executives say. Given today's operating styles and large staff bureaucracies, management involves more consultation and staff coordination than in years gone by, they note. This means the chemistry between the executive and his associates counts more heavily in getting the job done smoothly—and companies know it, personnel officials say.

Sifting Candidates

Of course, chemistry probably won't get an obvious bungler a good job, and where one candidate is clearly superior, it may play no role at all. But in the common situation where three or four candidates all could handle the job, executives often lean to people who share their personal values, manner of dressing and even personal habits, recruiters say.

For instance, Mr. Rozner cites a $55,000-a-year-pharmaceutical executive who landed a $90,000-a-year division presidency partly because he liked Victorian houses. The fact that both the company chairman and the executive loved the old houses, hated television and rarely allowed their children to watch TV suggested to the chairman a great similarity of values that would allow the two to work comfortably together, Mr. Rozner explains. . . .

Artichokes were the Waterloo of one company president seeking the $300,000-a-year presidency of another consumer-goods company. Though the executive was generally well polished, he revealed at dinner with the chairman a pitiable incompetence at handling the unfamiliar first course. At one point, he even tried carving the leaves with a knife and fork.

"The chairman said he just didn't want a guy who didn't know how to eat properly," says Robert A. Staub, president of Staub, Warmbold & Associates, New York recruiters. "I just couldn't believe it. I never did tell the guy the real reason he didn't get the job."

Recruiters say prejudice against Jews and ethnic groups still prevails in many companies, especially in smaller communities. "Sometimes, people never get beyond the names," one recruiter observes. Many recruiters privately concede that they usually go along with the client's prejudices without much protest.

Prejudice against divorced executives has declined, and junior-level management ranks have gained more diversity in recent years. But in most companies, senior management still is drawn from a remarkably narrow range of society, personnel officers note. In a survey of senior executives of the largest 750 companies, only eight of the 1,708 respondents were women and only three were black. Some 95% were married, but only 11% had been married more than once. Nearly 70% were Republicans, and 92% identified with "conservative or moderate" views on social issues, said the study, conducted by the University of California at Los Angeles and Korn/Ferry International, recruiters based in Los Angeles. . . .

Keys to Success

Given the increased attention to chemistry, the job that called for three interviews in the company five years ago often calls for five or six today, recruiters say. NCR Corp., Dayton, also has prospects meet with more prospective peers than in the past. "That's where the applicant will spend the majority of his time; jobs require more interaction than in the past," says William H. von Reichbauer, director of corporate recruitment.

SOURCE: *The Wall Street Journal,* September 19, 1979, pp. 1, 35.

to an ad for volunteers in a local paper. Participants were not paid or otherwise rewarded for being in the study.

The original volunteers were given the following information about the target person: his name, address, occupation and place of employment, his college and year of graduation, his military service dates, and his wife's maiden name and home town. They were asked to send the document directly to the target if they personally knew him on a first-name basis. If they did not, they were asked not to contact him directly, but to mail the document to a friend, relative, or acquaintance who "is more likely than you to know the target person" (Travers and Milgram, 1969: 184). Out of 296 initial volunteers, 217 actually sent the document on to someone else. Of those sent on, 64, or 29 percent, eventually reached the target person.

How many contacts were needed to link starters with targets? The mean number required was 5.2 links. The Boston group did it with fewer contacts than either Nebraska group, not surprisingly. Those moving the document through Boston business contacts reached the target sooner (through fewer links) than those

"Old boy" networks based on school, club, or occupational ties serve to refer people to jobs and pass along useful information of various kinds. Women and minorities have traditionally been excluded from such networks, a factor that has hampered their efforts to achieve equality. One of their responses has been to form their own self-help networks.

moving it through the target's home town of Sharon, Massachusetts. Senders got the document to the town readily, but it sometimes circulated around there before it hit the target's acquaintances. As chains converged on the target, senders used many of the same intermediaries. Twenty-five percent of all the documents reached the target through one intermediate, his neighbor. This fact suggests that chains converge on a few key individuals who have a substantial number of outside personal contacts.

Participants in the study tended to send the document on to individuals who were similar to themselves with respect to occupation, gender, and age. The social similarity of links in a network helps to explain how social inequalities are passed from one generation to the next. Middle-class parents, for example, may be more likely than lower-class parents to know someone who can help their teenagers get a job. In the small world studies, both senders and target were middle-class, a factor that undoubtedly helped them to make contact. Another small world study discovered that the number of intermediaries needed to link white and black senders and targets does not differ markedly from that needed to link white senders and targets, despite the need for racial crossover (Korte and Milgram, 1970).

The Travers and Milgram study and other small world studies have gone a long way toward documenting the existence of personal interconnections in a society of more than 200 million people. They show the existence of far-flung contacts among people. Because the people you know also know other people whom you do not know, there is a good chance you can reach a total stranger through a personal contact. In addition to linking people who may be able to help one another, social networks influence who people meet, who they marry, where they get jobs, what they know, where they live, and how they spend their leisure time. Networks forge the links between social institutions, statuses, organizations, and individuals. We cannot understand how society operates without a clear conception of networks, since they provide or prevent opportunities for social interaction.

SOCIAL INTERACTION

DEFINING SOCIAL INTERACTION

Ignoring someone you know, waving enthusiastically when a friend approaches, telephoning, borrowing a book, dancing, or buying a candy bar (from a person, not a machine) are a few examples of social interaction. Exchanges between heads of state, submitting architectural plans for zoning approval, cutting someone's hair, reserving a concert ticket, and having a job interview are also social interactions. *Social interaction* refers to the ways people behave in relation to one another, using language, gestures, and symbols.

Much of what we do each day involves social interactions, which can have profound significance or be quite trivial in their consequences. Even an act you may do alone, like reading this book, may well be done because of your social interactions with others. You may do it because you want to pass the course you are taking or because you want to learn about the social world in which you live, or both. Thus, even seemingly solitary acts may be rooted in a fabric of social interactions.

Many species of animals also interact socially. Human interaction appears to be unique, however, in the degree to which it uses complex symbols, including language. These symbols, especially language, can transcend time and space and allow people to communicate widely with one another. The term *symbolic interaction* is often used to refer to interactions that rely on shared symbols. A second unique feature of human interaction is that people attach symbolic meanings to virtually everything in their lives, although these meanings can vary widely. The same event (for example, being pregnant) can mean very different things to different people, as noted in Chapter 1. And the same meaning can be assigned through quite different procedures, as we will see later in the chapter in the discussion of who is declared "dead on arrival" at a hospital and who is not. Interaction is central to social life, and sociologists approach it in several distinct ways.

DIFFERING VIEWS OF SOCIAL INTERACTION

Functionalists stress that shared social standards shape social interaction: How you behave in your role as a son or daughter is largely prescribed by society and by other people. Certain forms of social interaction are considered "appropriate" and are expected in certain circumstances. The functionalist view of social interaction emphasizes its patterned and predictable nature. This view helps us to understand something about how social interaction is possible, even between strangers.

The functionalist view suggests there is one "right" way to interact socially. Some functionalists acknowledge that different ethnic groups or social classes may prescribe different behaviors, but hold that the element of prescription still exists and is imposed in some way on the individuals involved. It is this "straitjacket" aspect of cultural prescriptions that led Herbert Blumer and others to stress the creative side of social interaction. They developed the major theoretical approach called symbolic interactionism in response to the neglect they felt human action and social interaction were receiving in sociology. There are no prescribed social behaviors in many situations, suggests Blumer, particularly in such unusual situations as riots, panics, or wild celebrations. Social behaviors in such contexts therefore cannot be understood in terms of cultural prescriptions. Instead, we need to understand how people attach meaning to situations, and to their own and others' actions within them.

Functionalist and interactionist approaches lead sociologists to understand social interaction in different ways. For instance, Wallace and Wolf have compared and contrasted the behaviors of two sociologists at work:

> During the rallies of the Free Speech Movement at Berkeley (in the 1960s), [Herbert] Blumer could be observed mingling with the crowds, observing from an upper level window, and later talking at length with students involved. As a symbolic interactionist, his approach to explaining students' involvement was to find out how individuals perceived and interpreted events and how they had made the decision to become involved. An illuminating contrast can be found in the work of sociologists such as [Amitai] Etzioni, who are more concerned with "social structure." They approach such an event not by looking at individual decisions and actions that went into making up the Free Speech Movement, but by looking for general social phenomena that explain why the sixties was a period of campus turmoil. (Wallace and Wolf, 1980: p. 248)

Etzioni looked at social structural factors like the fact that young people constituted a larger proportion of the population than ever before or since. His approach suggests that certain societal conditions may result in greater or lesser amounts of student turmoil and reflects the interest of functionalists in explaining why patterned social behaviors occur. Blumer's microscopic scrutiny of how individuals behaved and the meaning of those behaviors for them helps to explain why certain individuals rather than others decided to get involved and what the consequences of certain symbolic meanings and behaviors were for the way they organized their actions.

FORMS OF SOCIAL INTERACTION

In keeping with their interest in finding and explaining patterned social behaviors, functionalists have identified and described several major forms of interaction, including cooperation, exchange, conflict, competition, negotiation, and coercion. Each type of interaction can be considered separately, even though they frequently blend together in social life.

Cooperation

Cooperation refers to a collaborative effort between people to achieve a common goal. It seems to arise most frequently when working with others can produce a desired end more effectively and efficiently than can working alone. Team sports illustrate this well. It is usually difficult for a single football, basketball, or volleyball player to create a winning team. Instead, a group effort is needed. In that process, individuals with special talents are an asset to the team if they can work well with other team members. Communities facing natural disasters like floods or earthquakes often respond to the threat with cooperative effort. In such events, individual effort cannot adequately meet the challenges at hand. Cooperation therefore seems most likely to arise when individuals assessing a situation conclude that their own chances of eating, surviving, or whatever will be greater if they work together than if they proceed alone. Cooperation also brings its own social rewards—a sense of sharing a challenge, adversity, or fun with others, a sense of caring about others, and of being cared for in return.

Exchange

Exchange represents a more formalized system of cooperation, in which individuals trade valued objects or sentiments. Exchange is commonly noted in economic activities, but it occurs also in love and friendship relationships. Social exchange usually involves intangibles such as respect, affection, acceptance, or help. Members of a family assist one another, knowing that they can count on the help of other members when they need it. Neighbors lend each other tools or watch each others' children. Work colleagues provide assistance in return for esteem. Although such social exchanges may not be strictly scored, the principles of exchange may still operate. Simmel, Blau, Homans, and Nisbet, four sociologists who have analyzed exchange processes, suggest that exchange creates and reinforces social bonds between individuals and groups. This is certainly true of economic exchange. Trade, for example, increases social contacts and ties between neighboring communities. Similarly, successful social exchanges increase social interactions. Everyday speech reflects the fact that people take this feature into account in sizing up other people—"They have nothing to offer me," or "They do a lot for me."

Conflict

Conflict involves direct struggle between individuals or groups over commonly valued resources or goals. It differs from cooperative interaction, where people work together to achieve a common goal or to make a mutually agreeable exchange. Conflict may involve a relatively insignificant object or quite important one. Conflict may arise between two children over one television set when they want to see different programs at the same time. It may arise between nations that seek exclusive fishing rights in the ocean or control over a piece of land.

Virtually all conflicts occur within certain ground rules that are shared by opponents. This is necessary, as Simmel (1905) pointed out, to ensure some basis for reaching a peaceful settlement at the end. Rather than fighting each other to the death, antagonists usually establish certain rules to mediate their conflicts and keep them from being destructive: "First I choose the show; then you get to choose the next one." Even armed conflicts are governed to some extent by certain norms: "You take care of our prisoners of war (especially officers), and we'll take care of yours."

Not only are conflicts accompanied by rules governing their conduct, but they may have positive sociological results as well, as Simmel (1905) and Coser (1956, 1967) have pointed out. Groups that have a common enemy are drawn closer together. Members of religious sects that were persecuted by other religious groups tended to band together more tightly within their group. Conflict can also clarify values and issues. Labor and management may not realize until they are in open conflict that their interests are essentially dissimilar. Similarly, the "right to life" versus "right to choice" conflict over abortion has brought that issue home to many Americans and required more thought about it than might have otherwise taken place.

Competition

Competition is a form of conflict in which there is fairly common agreement on the means that can be used to pursue an end. There are more rules and limits imposed on the interaction than in open conflict, and they are more strongly adhered to by the participants. At one extreme is the classic case of sports, where the rules are well known, clearly spelled out, and strictly enforced by presumably impartial referees or judges whose decisions are final. Everyone involved knows what constitutes a "win" or "loss." Other instances of competition could be winning a scholarship or being promoted in one's job.

Our society seems to produce a number of situations in which people must cooperate and compete at the same time. In trying out for the football team, hopefuls are expected to shine individually, but they are also supposed to be good team players who can cooperate with others, help others when needed (like block for them), and share their skills and ideas. Similarly, junior professors or young associates in a law firm are judged by their seniors in relation to one another. At the same time, they need the social support, help, and cooperation of their peers.

Negotiation

Negotiation is the process by which two or more parties in conflict or competition are able to arrive at a mutually satisfactory agreement. Negotiation is often necessary in order for other social processes to occur. People may negotiate the terms under which they agree to social exchange, social cooperation, or competition. College roommates, for example, often peacefully decide when their room will be used for entertaining and when for study; whether or not they will smoke in the room; and whether they will compete for members of the opposite sex or adopt a "hands off" attitude toward their roommate's friends. They do not usually sit down and say, "let's negotiate." Instead, they work out a way of getting along or they change rooms. When negotiations break down, conflict or coercion sometimes occurs.

Coercion

Coercion refers to the process of making someone do something, frequently through the use of social pressure, force, or threats of force. You may be surprised to see coercion described as a form of interaction, since at first glance it appears to be one-sided. Upon reflection, it becomes apparent that every act of coercion is at least partially determined by the expected reaction to it. In this sense there is a relationship between the coercer and the coerced. The relationship between master and slave, guard and prisoner, or sadist and masochist can be recognized as an interactive relationship, even though a very asymmetrical one.

Coercion often occurs through the use of physical force—the armed might of the police or a robber, or the greater size and strength of a parent carrying a child to bed. Coercion can involve the use of social sanctions such as ridicule, guilt, excommunication, withholding of love, or failure to grant recognition. When individuals claiming legitimate authority coerce others into doing their will, they usually cover the "iron fist" of coercion with some kind of "velvet glove," or ideology, that seeks to explain why the superior power and authority of the dominant person or group should be obeyed.

INTERACTIONAL CUES

Social interaction involves a mutual relationship between two or more people. It includes actions and responses between the interacting individuals. These actions and responses are communicated from one participant to another by means of various cues. A major medium of communication, of course, is language, but communication can also occur through facial expression, body movement, visual behavior, the use of space, the structuring of time, and speech features (such as tempo).

Language, both spoken and written, is undoubtedly one of the most important means of social interaction. It makes it possible to interact on a remote as well as a face-to-face basis. *Nonverbal communication,* including the use of visual and other symbols, supplements language. While much of the information conveyed nonverbally parallels that transmitted through language, nonverbal behaviors often add to the information obtained from verbal channels. They may reveal the underlying attitudes of a speaker, including feelings toward the person with whom he or she is interacting. Interactive cues appear in a speaker's tone of voice and speed of talking. Facial expressions and bodily movements also convey emotions, sometimes without a speaker's being aware of it. People answering questions in class, for example, may twist their hair, a gesture that has nothing to do with what they are saying but may reveal inner anxiety or self-consciousness. Folding the arms across the body may be a protective move to fend off attack and may contradict a verbal message of trust and openness (Ekman and Friesen, 1969).

Space may be used to indicate social closeness or distance. We move close to and touch people we like or love; we move away from people we dislike. The "unnatural" social closeness that occurs when strangers are pressed together on a crowded elevator or subway is handled by other strategies of avoidance. Even though their bodies may be in full contact, they tend to avoid making eye contact, they rarely talk, and in general they act as though the other people were not there. In this way, people neutralize the inappropriate closeness of strangers.

Time provides other clues about interaction. As Barry Schwartz (1975) has noted, "the distribution of waiting time coincides with the distribution of power," whether in a social relationship or a society. People receiving unemployment compensation wait on long lines to get their checks. Salespersons may wait a long time to see a prospective customer. Attorneys may make every effort not to keep prominent clients waiting. Beyond waiting, the amount of time a person spends with someone else is one nonverbal indicator of value and esteem for that person. This can produce problems if, as happens in many marriages, husbands and wives hold different expectations about how much time together is desirable. The quality of time also makes a difference. If you are always preoccupied when you see someone, that gives a negative impression of your regard for that person.

In addition to language, communication occurs through facial expressions and body language.

All these cues provide insights into the nature of the interactions between people. When sociologists analyze interactions, they often consider who initiates contact, how frequently people interact, how intensely they appear to feel about the interaction, and why they interact. Interactions vary in terms of whether they are based on face-to-face or on indirect contact. Considering these issues about a situation goes a long way toward beginning to understand its significance. Symbolic interactionists examine a number of dynamic features of social interaction.

APPLICATIONS OF THE SYMBOLIC INTERACTIONIST APPROACH

Symbolic interactionists have studied various aspects of social interaction, including micro-level analysis of impression management; studies showing how individuals reserve a part of themselves from the hold of organizations and institutions; and studies of how meanings are constructed in social situations. Symbolic interactionism is also useful for analyzing organizations and institutions.

IMPRESSION MANAGEMENT AND FACE-WORK

Some of the best-known work in the interactionist tradition is that done by Erving Goffman (1959, 1961, 1963a, 1967, 1971, 1974). Goffman analyzes factors from everyday life that might not ordinarily be apparent to people as they interact. He draws parallels, for instance, between the theater and the way individuals perform in their relationships with others. Because people draw inferences and make judgments about one another in their dealings, individuals may try to influence how others come to perceive them. Goffman calls this *impression management* and suggests that it characterizes many types of interactions. A host and hostess giving a party, for example, will try to make their home attractive before the guests arrive. Someone coming to the door may start to smile before the door is opened. Before the party, parents may give children elaborate instructions about how they are to behave. Even the food served may be selected with an eye to the impression it will create or reinforce.

Individuals vary considerably with respect to how much they calculate and try to control the impression they create and how spontaneous, sincere, or unaffected they are in their interactions with others. There is the possibility that part of their impression management is designed to convince others that they are "sincere" or "natural," so they may behave in a way the leads others to form this impression. Politicians and other people running for public office are particularly concerned about impression management. They may hire a publicist or an "image" specialist who will help them design and project an image that will gain support for them. Although the thought of an "image consultant" may seem somewhat silly, Goffman's work suggests that people serve as their own image managers to a more or less conscious degree in many aspects of their daily interactions.

One way impressions are managed in daily interactions is through what Goffman calls *facework*. He uses the word "face" to mean a favorable image a person presents to others; "facework" refers to the actions taken by individuals to make whatever they are doing consistent with the face they are presenting (1967, p. 12). Individuals try to present certain images to others, but the success of that presentation depends on others who either accept or reject that face. Because face can only be granted by others, it is a social attribute. Face "is only on loan . . . from society; it will be withdrawn unless [a person] conducts himself in a way that is worthy of it. Approved attributes and their relation to face make of every man his own jailer; this is a fundamental social constraint even though each man may like his cell" (Goffman, 1967, p. 10). This statement suggests that people may act to preserve the faces that go along with certain social positions. Teachers, for instance, may not always feel like acting in a dignified way, but may realize that if they do not, it may be difficult to reassert their authority and position at a later time. Individuals are always weighing how much they can do and still maintain their face. "Ordinarily," Goffman says, "maintenance of face is a condition of interaction, not its objective. . . . To study face-saving is to study the traffic rules of social interaction" (1967, p. 12).

One way face is maintained is by avoidance strategies. People avoid situations in which they may lose face. A quarrel between two neighbors or two family members, for example, may be reconciled by a go-between who can save the face of both parties by not having it appear as though either party had lost face by approaching the other one first. People often cooperate in interactions to help save each other's faces. Social mores, for instance, encourage men not to ask women for New Year's Eve dates too early in the year, thereby making it difficult to offer a graceful excuse for refusing (Goffman, 1967, p. 29).

RESERVING PART OF THE SELF

Goffman also suggests that individuals reserve a part of their selves from the hold of the institutions to which they belong. Goffman conducted a number of studies inside *total institutions*—that is, places where people spend 24 hours of every day, for an extended part of their lives, cut off from the rest of society, and tightly controlled by the people in charge. Based on his studies inside mental hospitals, he noted how patients in the hospital refused to assume completely the identity the hospital and its staff tried to impose on them. Sometimes they asserted their independence by refusing to play the role of the "good patient," by being incontinent or refusing to get out of their bathrobes for meals, for example. At other times they carved out little areas where they could be free from the surveillance of the staff—clumps of trees out on the grounds where they could smoke, little rooms in the basement where they could play poker, or an area with a sink and a radiator where one patient set up his own personal laundry to wash and dry clothes. In these and numerous other ways, even the patients in a total institution retained some independence and autonomy. They did not allow their entire identities to be controlled by the institution in which they were confined.

Individuals in totalitarian situations such as concentration camps devise similar strategies to try to neutralize the institution's efforts to monopolize their lives and identities. Psychologist Bruno Bettelheim describes how, when confined in a Nazi concentration camp, he tried to manage the situation by mentally "stepping back" from it and trying to analyze it very objectively (1971). In this way he could reaffirm in his own eyes his identity as an analyst of human behavior and he could resist the efforts of his captors to impose a degraded identity upon him.

A key element of the interactionist perspective is its focus on how individuals can reflect on themselves and their own actions, as well as on the behavior of others. We ask ourselves, "What do you suppose he means by that?" or "What am I trying to do here?" We do not need to act in a way that resembles a knee-jerk reflex; we can think about what is being done to us (by other people or by certain social patterns) and can choose among several courses of action. This capacity for self-reflection enables us to reserve a part of ourselves from the domination of social organizations and institutions to which we belong.

One of the ways people cooperate in protecting the self from potentially embarrassing situations is by the use of stage management and props to manage uncomfortable interactions. Goffman's dramaturgical analysis, which examines social interaction as though it were a series of scenes in a play, is useful for analyzing such situations.

Dramaturgical Analysis—The Pelvic Examination

No matter how liberated women become, a pelvic examination, especially the first one, can be an anxiety-provoking experience. In it women are asked to expose what may be the most private part of their bodies to a stranger, usually a male. A situation like this, which is potentially embarrassing or sexually suggestive, needs to be socially defined so that it seems as "normal" and comfortable as possible.

The social management of this interaction has been analyzed by James Henslin and Mae Briggs (1971), who drew on Briggs' observations of several thousand pelvic examinations that she legitimately attended as a practicing nurse. They applied Goffman's dramaturgical analysis, looking at the examination as a series of scenes in a play. The "prologue" to the play consists of the woman entering the doctor's waiting room, preparing to take on the role of patient. The first "scene" opens when she is called into the consulting room, where she meets the "character" of the competent doctor. He relates to her as another human being and inquires about her medical problems in a polite and professional manner. He may make notes in her file. If the patient needs a pelvic exam, the doctor mentions that he will do one, and then he leaves the room.

The second "scene" begins with the entrance of the nurse, who helps to stage the following scenes. Her role is to help the patient shed her identity as a woman and to create a new situation in which a depersonalized pelvis is to be clinically inspected. The nurse provides sympathy and support to the patient as she prepares for the experience, and she provides the "props" that help to stage the clinical setting, including a hospital gown or sheet that covers the patient's body. She suggests to the patient a place to leave the underwear and other clothes she has removed, so they will not be hanging in the doctor's view. By having the doctor out of the room during this preparation, any resemblance to a sexually suggestive striptease is eliminated, and the businesslike, clinical definition of the situation prevails. When the doctor returns, the patient has become a covered body lying on the examination table.

Doctor, nurse, and patient are all in the next scene. The nurse's presence underscores the clinical nature of the encounter. The sheet covering the patient's body down to her raised knees conveys the illusion that much of her body is covered. She may not be able to see the doctor's face as he sits on a low stool below her line of vision. He may raise one or two medical questions, but the patient can mentally disengage herself from the whole scene.

Emerson's (1980) use of Berger and Luckmann's *social construction of reality* approach shows how the special language of doctor-patient interactions helps to desexualize their encounter. That approach involves creating definitions of situations that appear to be natural. When speaking to a patient, the doctor refers to "the vagina" rather than "your vagina." The sexually charged statement "spread your legs" is replaced with the neutral instruction, "let your knees fall apart" (Emerson, 1970). In such ways as these, language contributes to the staging and sustaining of a medical rather than a sexual definition of the situation.

After the examination, the doctor departs. The nurse may stay on for a few moments to straighten up, and to welcome the patient back into her regular role again. They may talk, and the patient may comment on how glad she is that the exam is over. The nurse may then leave while the patient dresses and combs her hair. In the final scene, the patient meets with the doctor, perhaps in his book-lined office, where they return to more usual roles. The doctor treats her in the same professional and polite way that he did before, affirming that nothing unusual has happened and that he views her in the same way that he did before. They discuss her medical situation and agree on whatever course of medical action is to be followed. The patient then exits, returning to her roles in the outside world.

This analysis helps us to understand certain social situations in terms of the stage settings, props, and roles called into play to manage potentially embarrassing or ambiguous situations for the purpose of accomplishing some larger goal.

Defining the Situation—Dead on Arrival

Much of social action concerns defining situations, and social factors influence how situations are defined. Even something as apparently biological as death does not have a single simple meaning independent of the people involved.

In his research in the emergency room of a county hospital, David Sudnow (1967) found that patients who arrived at the hospital without a heartbeat or not breathing were treated differently by the attending staff, depending upon the patient's age and appearance. A person aged 20 or younger was not immediately pronounced "dead on arrival." Instead, a long time was spent listening for a heartbeat, inspecting the eyes, stimulating the heart, and giving oxygen and stimulative medications. All this was likely to occur before the patient was pronounced "dead." The older the person, Sudnow reported, the less thorough the examination given. Frequently these people were pronounced dead simply on the basis of a stethoscopic examination of the heart. But not only the age of a patient shaped the definition as death or not-yet-death: Social characteristics such as dress and whether or not alcohol could be smelled on the person also influenced how quickly a patient was pronounced dead (Sudnow, 1967, p. 104).

STUDYING SOCIAL SERVICES THROUGH SYMBOLIC INTERACTIONISM

So far we have seen how symbolic interactionism helps to illuminate impression management and face-work, how individuals reserve part of their selves from institutions, how a dramaturgical analysis can interpret a potentially awkward situation, and how the defining of someone as "dead on arrival" is influenced by social factors. Symbolic interactionism may also be usefully applied to an understanding of larger social institutions. In such social services as health care or social work, for example, various participants in the situation may challenge prevailing "meanings" that are assigned to the services provided, as Carole Joffe (1979) suggests. For instance, "traditional ways of giving birth . . . are under significant challenge, as natural childbirth enthusiasts, 'birth without violence,' and homebirth advocates confront the practices of obstetricians and hospital maternity ward personnel; at the other end of the life cycle, there are similar confrontations over the most appropriate organization of death, as a coalition of euthanasia, hospice, and 'death at home' advocates challenge traditional medical practices" (Joffe, 1979, p. 254).

Not only are the prevailing meaning of various processes being challenged and redefined, but the different participants in social service situations come with different personal, professional, and political agendas for what the social services "are" or should be. These different conceptions may erupt in conflicts—for example, between welfare workers and clients over appropriate client behavior in a welfare office, between doctors and counselors over whether an abortion should occur, among rape counselors over the advantages and disadvantages of working closely with the local police force, or between county health officials and free clinic staff members over the issues of recordkeeping and patient confidentiality (Joffe, 1979, p. 252). Individuals with different concerns do not always see a situation the same way, and thus they behave differently and try to negotiate new definitions of the situation that are more in keeping with their own perceptions.

Joffe goes one important step further in her application of symbolic interactionism to social services. She suggests that the negotiation of new and different meanings, and the institutionalization of certain practices rather than other ones, may actually transform the larger social order in important ways. As an example, she notes that certain social services, such as crisis centers for battered wives, abortion clinics, and changing adoptive practices for single individuals, may appear to some people to be eroding the foundation of the nuclear family. To others, these changes represent shifting conceptions of family structure and gender role behaviors within the family that may be desired by individuals who find traditional forms of family organization unsuitable. Thus the definitions that get negotiated within newly emerging social service organizations may serve in various ways to redefine family structures and roles in the larger society. By developing such lines of analysis, interactionists reveal how individual and group efforts at negotiation and redefinition may alter the nature and operation of major social institutions.

EVALUATION AND IMPLICATIONS

Social interaction, like social life, is both structured and created. Functionalists stress the structured aspects of social interaction. They believe that institutions, statuses, roles, and values impinge strongly on individuals, largely governing their actions, beliefs, and feelings. Blumer and

Symbolic interactionists focus on the way various participants in a social organization define key events or processes. Whether in business or a social agency, different participants may bring competing viewpoints into the formal and informal negotiations that shape the conduct of work.

other symbolic interactionists stress the creative role individuals play constructing their own conduct by interpreting, evaluating, defining, and planning their actions.

Fusing a structural and an interpretive approach requires us to acknowledge that social structures such as stratification, population features, and major social institutions like the family, religion, politics, and the economy restrict our behavior and at the same time provide opportunities. People face very different possibilities if they are born in the United States, in Poland, or in a hunting society in Australia. Even within the United States, people growing up in situations as different as those of Albert, Alex, and Alice, whom you met in Chapter 1, have different opportunities and obstacles resulting from where they are within the social structure.

Given the constraints and opportunities they face, people retain a capacity for self-reflection and for actively evaluating, interpreting, and defining their own actions. Individuals do not need to bob passively like corks on the waves of social forces; they can join or form groups pursuing a course they want to follow. In such groups they can work to strengthen or challenge various social definitions, institutions, and organizations. They can avoid groups whose nature or goals they dislike. Individuals can carve out freedom, choice, and initiative within the structural constraints they face. Sociology provides some powerful tools for doing this when we bring together the interactionist and structural approaches. The apparent paradox that social life is both structured and created now takes on meaning.

Summary

1. Status and role focus on the individual; social networks draw attention to the relationships between individuals. A network is the set of links, or connections, a person has with others. Our first links are with family members, and we gradually add links with other people. Small world studies suggest that most people could make direct personal contact with someone unknown to them through a chain of personal connections. Nevertheless, social factors affect networks by influencing who is in them and how the people in them interact. Networks provide people with information, introductions, influence, exposure to cultural styles, and access to power, money, or status.

2. Ultimately, it is individuals interacting with one another who create social life anew every day. Humans have the capacity to reflect on what they and others are doing, and to interpret those actions. Social interaction refers to the ways people behave in relation to one another.

3. Functionalists stress that interaction is patterned by the population, institutions, statuses, and roles in a society. In contrast, interactionists emphasize the creative aspects of social interaction.

4. Social interaction appears in a variety of forms, including cooperation, exchange, conflict, competition, negotiation, and coercion. Interactions occur through written or spoken communications and through nonverbal cues.

5. Symbolic interactionism has proved useful for analyzing impression management and face-work; the ways in which individuals reserve parts of their selves from institutions; the management of potentially awkward situations; the influence social characteristics have on certain decisions; and the negotiation of new meanings and new structures in social organizations and institutions.

6. Like all aspects of social life, social interaction is both structured and created. Social structures provide limits as well as possibilities for what we can do. At the same time, individuals actively evaluate, interpret, and try to define their own actions.

Key Terms

coercion
competition
conflict
cooperation
dramaturgical analysis
exchange
face-work
impression management
negotiation
nonverbal communication
social construction of reality
social interaction
social network
symbolic interaction
total institution

Chapter 5

Culture

Culture affects almost everything we do, think, and feel. It shapes our habits, behaviors, language, and interpersonal style. Often it does this in unknown ways—for example, by shaping our ideas about physical beauty. Culture affects what we take for granted and what we question. What is culture anyway?

DEFINING THE CONCEPT

Even a definition of culture depends upon culture (language, practice, history). In the German, Scandinavian, and Slavic language groups, the word "culture" tends to mean a particular way of life, whether of a people, a time period, or a group. But in Italian and French, the word refers more to art, learning, and a general process of human development (Williams, 1976, p. 81). Both meanings exist today as the word is used in English. It is helpful to distinguish so-called high culture (classical music, opera, ballet, art, literature, and so forth) from all processes and products of human activity. High culture is associated with class distinctions, and is sometimes put down with the affected pronunciation "culchah" (Williams, 1976). We will use the term *culture* in its more general social sense to mean the customs of a group or a society.

Culture has a certain durability. This does not mean it is unchanging; culture changes constantly. Indeed, it is like a living, breathing entity. Only the rate of change varies. But there is an important historical dimension to it that cannot be ignored. Culture has a certain coherence, although it may contain contradictions. Ruth Benedict, in her famous book *Patterns of Culture* (1934) referred to "cultural configurations." When people encounter a new culture, they can see, hear, feel, and otherwise sense the existence of a culture that differs from their own. When such changes are very dramatic, they say they experience "culture shock" from the jolt of so many unfamiliar activities.

It takes some time to adjust to the different tempo, social styles, food, and activities. Even experienced anthropologists who have made numerous trips to study other cultures report they feel culture shock when they return home. In the United States, visitors from the North to the South, or vice versa, also notice differences in tempo, politeness, languages, customs, and diet. Northerners may get impatient with the apparent slowness of southern service; southerners may be shocked by what seems like northern rudeness.

These examples suggest several important features of culture. First, we tend to take it for granted until we are confronted with differences or changes. Second, marked variations can exist, even within the same society or nation. These variations are sometimes referred to as *subcul-*

We all tend to take our own culture for granted until we are struck with sudden cultural changes or contrasts.

tures, meaning the cultures of distinguishable smaller groups (Williams, 1976: 82).

A subculture can share a number of the major features of the dominant culture within which it exists, as well as having certain unique features. A subculture is both part of a larger society and identifiably different from it—for instance, in language, customs, and values. Many ethnic groups—Japanese-Americans, Italian-Americans, and Jewish-Americans—may have subcultural identities that distinguish them from other ethnic groups in the United States. On the other hand, they are also members in various legal and cultural senses of the larger United States society.

Sociologists do not agree on how distinctive cultural patterns need to be in order to form a separate subculture. Although most would agree that various ethnic groups have distinctive subcultures, the term has also been used to refer to the social patterns of adolescent street gangs and rock musicians, and of various occupations and social classes. The anthropologist Charles Valentine (1971), suggests that many individuals are *bicultural*—that is, they are able to understand and function well in more than one cultural group. Black Americans, for instance, may enjoy the food, music, and speech of the Afro-American subculture, but also understand and function well in the white culture that predominates in the United States.

Although culture and society are intimately bound together, it is possible to separate them, at least conceptually. Society consists of people and their interactions. Culture is all the socially learned behaviors, beliefs, feelings, and values the members of a group or society experience. It includes customs and language. It affects how people interact, the meanings they place on different interactions, and how interactions are

These Swedish, Mexican, and Chinese countermen and the food they are serving reflect the existence of subcultures within the United States. Members of a subculture have a number of unique features, including their taste in food, yet they also share characteristics with the dominant culture in which they live.

organized. Society is like the actors in a play, and culture is like the script they follow (or do not follow in some cases). Culture provides tested techniques for dealing with various problems that arise in the course of finding food, water, shelter, sex, and ways of living together that minimize friction and maximize cooperation.

The capacity to create, transmit, and modify culture dramatically distinguishes humans from animals. Animals appear to depend upon instincts, imitative social learning, or trial and error for solving their survival problems.[1] Humans rely much more on cultural prescriptions. If culture distinguishes humans from animals, it is important to consider the similarities between us and animals, as well as the unique features of human life.

[1]Many insects and animals inherit instincts for behaving in certain ways. *Instincts* are genetically determined behaviors triggered by certain conditions and over which animals have little or no choice. Beavers, for example, have an instinctual response to cut down trees with their teeth. If, however, they cut through the trunk of a tree and it does not fall because its branches are caught in the branches of other trees, the beaver will start chewing all over again. Their instincts tell them to chew until the tree falls. For humans, culture and reasoning greatly outweigh instinctual bases for behavior.

HUMAN UNIQUENESS

Which biological traits do we share with other animals and which represent unique features? We are born and we die. Unlike humans, most animals appear to be unaware of the fate that awaits them. Humans, like our closest relatives the great apes, are a sociable species, preferring to live in groups rather than alone. We interact with one another often and enjoy being affectionate. We have unusually large brains, which have grown dramatically in size during the last 3 million years of evolution (Wilson, 1975a). The increasing size of the brain has meant ever-increasing intelligence for members of the species, leading to increasingly complex culture and technology. We have very useful hands that are strong, precise, and skillful. Having an opposing thumb means that we can grasp, grip, and manipulate in ways few other species can. This allows us to make and then to use all kinds of tools and implements.

Human feet, legs, and backs have evolved in such a way that we can walk and run easily in an upright position, something most animals are unable to do for any length of time. Human females can have sexual intercourse any time during the year, rather than being limited to a particular period of female "heat" or estrus. This year-round potential for sexual activity increases the chances that humans will form relatively lasting social-sexual relationships. These relationships are particularly important in view of the long period of human infant dependency. Human infants need care from others for a number of years to meet their physical needs and to learn their culture. Finally, along with our primate forebears, we are very talkative, and spend a lot of time calling, chattering, and chatting with each other.

The combination of large brains and useful hands has enabled humans to adapt to widely varying geographical locations. Humans live more widely and more densely than any other mammal species on earth. The inventions of our brains, hands, and tongues can be passed along to our descendants through cultural transmission. Each generation in turn will adapt or modify existing cultural forms and continue the never-ending process of cultural creation.

CULTURAL UNIVERSALS

All human societies appear to share certain cultural features. These are called *cultural universals* and include the use of language and other symbols, the existence of norms and values, and the tension between ethnocentrism (the attitude that one's own culture is superior to all others) and cultural relativism (the view that the customs and ideas of a society must be viewed within the context of that society).

COMMON CULTURAL ELEMENTS

After comparing 220 societies, anthropologist George Murdock identified cultural elements found in all of them. These universal elements include age grading, athletic sports, cooking, dancing, folklore, hospitality, hygiene, joking, mourning, personal names, and soul concepts. Although these cultural features exist in all the societies studied, their particular content varied widely. Every culture, for example, has symbols and language, but there are many different symbolic meanings and languages.

Symbols

More than any other animal, humans fill the physical and social world with symbolic meanings. A *symbol* is any object or sign that produces a shared social response. A piece of rock, an animal, the moon, a cross, a glance at another person, a piece of paper with the word "dollar" on it are all imbued with various meanings and sometimes mythical or magical qualities. The symbolic meaning placed upon something may be separated from its physical aspects (as the box entitled, "The Car Culture" indicates).

Symbols share several characteristics. First, they are socially developed. The sun may symbolize strength to you or to me, but unless that meaning is shared with others, it will not become a significant symbol. So, one feature of symbols is that they are socially shared. Black symbolizes mourning for many Americans, but New Guinea women paint themselves white to show grief. Symbols also may have more than one meaning. A stack of hundred-dollar bills can symbolize wealth, happiness, greed, materialism,

The Car Culture

Americans, perhaps more than any other society, and especially young Americans, value the freedom, privacy, and independence they feel in a car. Cars seem to represent a "coming of age" for American youth and have major cultural significance.

There are subcultural variations in the car culture, expressed in varied decorations and styling. Some people see their cars as extensions of themselves and their personalities. Cars may reflect what people value—bigness, flashiness, dependability, frugality, sportiness, and so forth. In a highly mobile society, a car is one of the few cultural "badges," besides one's dress and speech, seen by strangers. It may be used by others as a basis for classifying one's style, taste, values, affluence, and other traits. The same car will mean different things to different people. Thus, a car that appeals to young people may negatively impress older people. A car one subgroup considers impressive may strike another subgroup as wasteful. Some care about how smoothly a car runs; others value how long it lasts; and still others care most about how it looks. Many people, however, are unable to distinguish the amounts of prestige various cars confer (Felson, 1978).

Nevertheless, the cultural components of automobiles far surpass their economic necessities. Even in major urban areas with extensive rapid transit systems like New York or Chicago, the car culture flourishes. If transportation were the only consideration, any old car would do, and the less expensive the better. But most cars on the road are relatively new. Therefore, the economic needs of individuals do not appear to be a primary force. But another economic force may underlie and help to support the car culture. The automobile business is the biggest industry in America. In 1978, Americans spent $128 billion for autos and trucks and for parts and service. At that rate, about 16 percent of total retail sales in the United States go to the auto industry (McDowell, 1979). "The automobile industry, counting suppliers, is the nation's largest private-sector employer. Like a mighty economic river, its tributaries touch every state, sustaining three million workers" (Bracy, 1979, p. A21). Other major industries, including oil, steel, and rubber, are all directly related to automobile production and use. Hence the cultural prominence of cars may be rooted in economic configurations.

and a host of other things, depending on the meanings people attribute to it. So all meanings are not equally shared, and a variety of symbols can arise from an object like the stack of bills. There is a certain amount of cultural arbitrariness in the meanings assigned to particular symbols, and symbols may differ in time and place. The skirt, for instance, has traditionally symbolized femininity in Western cultures, although Scottish men proudly wear kilts without being considered feminine. Many women wear pants and are considered no less feminine, and the meaning of long hair on men has varied widely.

One of the features of a highly diverse society such as ours is that people share different symbolic universes. That is, the symbolic meaning your group agrees on for something may not be shared by other groups. Wearing jeans may symbolize that someone is unpretentious, unconcerned with displaying material success, desirous of comfort, unhappy doing laundry, and a host of other meanings you could supply. Designer jeans, however, introduced an element of status competition into casual dressing. In our society, there is less and less common meaning attached to cultural symbols. It used to be that driving a large car was a sign of success. But is it still? If you asked 20 different people, I expect that you would get 20 different responses. The size of one's car no longer means the same thing to everyone in our society.

Language

Of all the symbols humans use, language is the most highly developed. *Language* consists of spoken or written symbols combined into a system and governed by rules. It enables us to share with others our ideas, thoughts, experiences, discoveries, fears, plans, and desires. Written language extends our capacity to communicate through time and space. Without language, it would be difficult to transmit culture, and culture would develop exceedingly slowly. Language is a critical key to understanding any culture and any society. It is the secret to reaching beyond ourselves, which is the heart of our social existence. A person may be a superb athlete, mechanic, or cook, but teaching or talking about that skill requires language. Otherwise, learning can only come from imitating actions.

Yet the importance of language goes even further. Two American linguists, Edward Sapir and Benjamin Whorf, argue that language shapes the way people think and the way they view reality. If this is the case, it helps to explain why both the civil rights movement and the women's movement have been concerned about the use of language. Contrast the words "boy" and "man" with respect to what they say about a person's role and stature in society. Similarly, use of the words "girl" and "woman" has been important to the women's movement. Not only are roles and statuses reflected in language, but language seems to shape a person's identity and sense of self. Language concepts can erect mental fences around the conceptions of self available to us and to others. The concept of "old" as applied to people in our society, for example, has generally implied that "old" people do not want or need sex, despite recent research showing that they desire and enjoy sexual relations of all kinds (Starr and Weiner, 1980). And by excluding sex as part of the identity of an "old" person, older people and the people around them may not be able directly to address their sexual needs.

The Sapir-Whorf hypothesis that language characteristics influence thought has been extensively criticized. Some argue that culture shapes language. Others hold that the iron grip of language over all our thought categories has not been demonstrated. However, people tend to see natural objects, such as colors, in the terms language provides. An artist may have words for 14 shades of red, and "see" them accordingly, while the Jale of New Guinea name and "see" the world only in terms of warm and cold color categories. Even social perceptions seem to be shaped by language, as research on teachers' expectations for "gifted" and "slow" learners suggests. In short, language does in some ways shape how we see the world and makes it difficult, although not impossible, to experience the world in alternative ways. Becoming aware of how language may limit us is the first step toward breaking free of those limits.

Language also provides clues to what a culture considers important. Farmers have many words to describe various types of soil, reflecting its importance to them. Our culture has numerous slang words for money (including "bread," "dough," "jack," "simoleons," "kale," "greenbacks," "bucks," "bones," "wad," "shekels," and "do-re-mi"), suggesting the importance of money in our culture.

Language also identifies the members of a particular subculture. If you "know the language," whether of football, electronics, or human physiology, you are a long way toward being "in" in a group. If you do not know the language, you probably will not be accepted as part of the inner group, and also may not know what is going on. (This applies to sociology as well. You need to learn enough sociological "lingo" to pass the course you are taking.) Fi-

A shared special language is one of the identifying features of subculture members, such as these computer operators who handle foreign exchange transactions for a bank.

nally, language can obscure as well as clarify. For example, the phrase "nuclear events" refers to *accidents* in nuclear power plants, but plays down their importance and removes them from the realm of human responsibility.

NORMS

Suppose you were taking a seminar with 20 other students and you circulated a list with your names and telephone numbers on it. Then assume that several members of the seminar began receiving obscene phone calls, apparently from someone in the class. How would you feel if you received a call? Probably you would feel outraged. Your feelings would be intensified because the caller would be violating a social norm. A *norm* refers to shared rules about acceptable and unacceptable social behavior. In this case, the phone numbers were shared to advance the work of the seminar, not to aid obscene phone callers.

All societies have norms, although their content differs from one society to the next. In rural West Africa today, if a stranger knocks on the door in the middle of the night, the norm is to invite the person in and offer food and a place to sleep (even if only on the floor). In downtown Chicago, this would not be the normative response to a midnight caller. Norms provide guidelines about what is "acceptable" or appropriate behavior in a given situation. They go beyond suggesting what people *might* do, however, in that they also contain an aspect of what they *ought* to do. Quite often they come to believe that they *should* behave in a certain way. Probably most of us feel that we ought to avoid talking out loud to ourselves in a crowded public place.

Norms apply to more than behavior, however. Even emotions are saddled and bridled by norms, as Hochschild (1980) points out. We think to ourselves, "I ought to feel grateful for all they have done for me," or "I shouldn't have felt so angry," suggesting that we are comparing our feelings to a normative standard. These examples suggest that norms, like other features of culture, slip into people's minds in subtle ways. We may be unaware of how strongly norms weave together the fabric of social life. In an effort to unearth these normative threads, Harold Garfinkle had his students set out to disrupt the usual flow of social life. He asked them to do such things as go home for dinner with their parents and act as though they were a stranger visiting there for the first time: "Yes, thank you, Mrs. Jones, I would like to have some more lima beans." "Mr. Jones, how is your bowling team doing?" It took very little of this "bizarre" behavior for the parents to react: "What's wrong with you? Are you sick? Are you playing games with us? Why are you behaving this way?" Some became rather heated.

In another experiment, researchers Stanley

"Hi. We're Ted and Maggie Wilkins. The Chases couldn't make it tonight and asked us to fill their slot."

SOURCE: Drawing by Lorenz, © 1979, *The New Yorker Magazine, Inc.*

Milgram and John Sabini (1978) asked students to ride a crowded bus or subway during rush hour when there were no seats left. They were to approach a stranger and ask if they could please have his or her seat. This was such counter-normative behavior that many students found they could not do it. They simply felt "too awkward." It was easier for them to ask for the seat when they could give a reason: "I feel dizzy," or "I just got out of the hospital." Other passengers were more likely to give up their seats when presented with a "legitimate" reason. Otherwise, you can imagine the reactions the students received. Part of their discomfort in asking undoubtedly arose from anticipating those reactions. And that discomfort is a clue to the existence of a social norm.

Two kinds of norms can be identified, depending on the degree of conformity that is required. *Folkways* require less conformity; they are social customs to which people generally conform, but receive little pressure to do so. We are expected to wear matching socks (if we wear socks), to wear clothes without holes in them, to speak when introduced to someone, to shake hands when someone offers a hand, and to eat at least some of what is offered us when we are a guest at dinner. Violations of folkways do not usually arouse moral outrage. People who do not accept the social customs of the group may be considered odd or sloppy, but they are not likely to be arrested for their behavior.

Mores, on the other hand, are strongly held social norms. Their violation arouses a sense of moral outrage. A naked baby on an American beach may be violating a folkway (to some), but a naked man on anything except a nude beach is violating mores, and indeed is breaking the law in most communities. Violating mores excites strong public reaction, and usually involves legal sanctions as well, since most are written into formal law. When protestors against the Vietnam war burned their draft cards or carried the Vietcong flag, they not only provoked violent reactions, but many also were arrested.

A *taboo* is a strongly prohibited social practice. It is the strongest form of social norm. The most nearly universal rule in all known human cultures is the *incest taboo*—the prohibition of sexual intercourse between fathers and daughters, mothers and sons, and brothers and sisters. The wide appearance of this taboo suggests that it may have developed early in human evolution. Just because something is taboo, however, does not mean it never happens. Indeed, there is growing evidence that the incest taboo is violated fairly frequently (although no definitive statistics exist on how often incest occurs). The taboo nature of incest is evident in the fact that people do not practice it openly. Moreover, they are usually so embarrassed or ashamed that they are afraid to discuss what happened to them. The existence of such feelings signals the presence of a taboo behavior.

Social norms, folkways, and mores are supported by sanctions. A *sanction* is a reward or penalty directed at desired or undesired behavior. Negative sanctions include disapproving looks, negative gossip, social shunning, imprisonment, and the electric chair. Positive sanctions range from prizes such as the Nobel award, praise, applause, esteem, and financial rewards, to smiles. The effectiveness of a sanction depends on how the receiver feels about it and about the people giving it. Electrocution is fairly universal in its negative impact, whereas prizes may mean little or a great deal to the people winning them.

The type of sanction helps us to distinguish whether something is a folkway or a more. Violations of folkways usually receive only social sanctions, such as stares, snide remarks, or other signs of disapproval. Mores are usually backed up with legal sanctions. Taboos vary as to whether or not they have legal sanctions. Norms may be socially sanctioned, as in the case of norms about appropriate dress, or legally sanctioned, as in the case of norms against beating up people and stealing their money. Folkways, mores, and norms are rooted in social values.

How people choose to spend their leisure time is one indicator of their values.

VALUES

Norms are specific rules or guidelines that may be applied directly to everyday life. *Values* are strongly held general ideas people share about what is good or bad, desirable or undesirable. Values are more general than norms in that they do not prescribe specific behaviors for concrete situations. In fact, the same values may support a number of different—or even competing—norms. For example, parents who value their families may be torn between working hard in their occupations and spending more time at home. Both behaviors may be normative expressions of the underlying value of commitment to their families. Examples of values generally held in our society include freedom, justice, and individualism. The normative counterparts to these more general values are freedom of speech, equal justice before the law, and the right to privacy.

A society's values are important to understand because they influence the content of both norms and laws. How can we tell what we, our neighbors, or other societies value? Sociologist Robin Williams (1965) suggests a number of indicators of the choices people make that may point to their underlying values. Patterns of money expenditure, directions of interest (in literature, movies, music, and other arts), and direct statements all provide clues to what individuals, groups, or societies value. To these can be added time allocation (how much time people spend on various activities), as another indicator of how highly they value the activities or the goals those activities represent. Value statements may reflect what people see as *ideal,* while time or money expenditures may be better indicators of their *real* values.

In any given situation, more than one value may be operating. A desire for efficiency in business clashes with a growing value on humanizing the work setting. You may value friendship and also value getting your schoolwork done. Often these values compete for one's time and attention. Many societies experience tension and even conflict over competing values. Developing nations often experience conflict over preserving valued traditions and modernizing. Industrialized countries face conflicts between the values of equality and rewarding merit. Even when they have conflicting values, though, most societies have a tendency to see their own values as superior to those of other societies.

ETHNOCENTRISM

The tendency to see one's own culture as superior to all others is called *ethnocentrism.* At its most extreme, ethnocentrism involves taking one's own culture for granted and being unaware of the existence of any culture, values, behaviors, or beliefs besides one's own. In a somewhat less extreme form, it is the tendency to see one's culture as superior to all other cultures, even though one is aware that other cultures and societies exist. Ethnocentric people tend to judge all other cultures by the standards of their own, and to see them as inferior, unnatural, or wrong when they diverge. An American oil company executive, for instance, expressed disgust over the way Arab workers in the desert would stop working for an entire day if someone they knew came along. From the American's ethnocentric viewpoint, work was much more important than socializing. To the Arab, however, whose cultural values were shaped by centuries of dealing with the dangers of the desert, "a friend in the desert is much more important than work." Stress, hostility, or other features of social life may affect the degree of ethnocentrism a group expresses (LeVine and Campbell, 1972).

CULTURAL RELATIVISM

Cultural relativism is the opposite of ethnocentrism. Cultural relativists realize that no belief, practice, behavior, or custom is inherently good or bad, right or wrong. Instead, cultural practices are assessed in terms of how they work within a particular culture as a whole. Do various cultural practices contradict each other? Are the features of the culture highly integrated? What are the major cultural configurations of a particular society? How do they compare with those of other societies? These are some of the sociological questions we can ask about culture while maintaining cultural relativism.

Trying to understand a cultural practice from within the context of another culture does not mean that sociologists never make moral judgments about other cultures. In a society with numerous subcultures, for example, they may try to understand why some subcultures value large families while others prefer having no children. The sociologist may personally prefer one position, and even make a moral judgment about what he or she thinks is better. It is important, however, to try to separate one's analysis of the causes and consequences of a cultural feature from one's moral evaluation of it. By becoming aware of personally held values and norms, we can better understand how they affect our reactions to other cultures. Some people may find cultural practices that appeal to them in other societies—for example, the greater social cooperation shown by American Indian children or the sexual permissiveness of the Trobriand Islanders off New Guinea (Wax and Wax, 1971).

CULTURAL VARIATION

Within the general cultural similarities found in many societies, there are vast differences in what people eat, what they believe, and how they behave. The Dutch, Eskimos, and Japanese eat raw fish; Americans eat it cooked, if at all. The Chinese like dog meat but loathe cow milk; we like both cow milk and meat but do not eat dogs. Some tribes in Brazil love ants but are repulsed by venison; some Americans enjoy venison but are repelled by the thought of eating ants (Harris, 1974, p. 35). Clearly, while hunger is an underlying biological drive, the tastes people develop to satisfy hunger are culturally acquired.

Like eating habits, sexual preferences are culturally influenced. In an extensive survey of cross-cultural sexual practices, Ford and Beach (1951) found that societies ranged from permissive to restrictive in their treatment of sexuality. Restrictive societies try to keep children from learning anything about sex, and they check any spontaneous sexual activities. For example, the Ainaye (a technologically simple, peaceful, monogamous tribe in Brazil) and the Ashanti (a complex society in Ghana) forbid children to masturbate. By contrast, in permissive societies such as those in the Pacific Islands, both boys and girls freely engage in autoerotic and heterosexual play, including oral-genital contacts and imitative coitus (Katchadourian and Lunde, 1972).

Economic activities also vary. Some societies stress acquisition and the display of wealth (perhaps American society more than most). Others, such as the Kwakiutl Indians of the Pacific Northwest, made great ceremonies (called *potlatches*) of giving away their possessions to others. In some societies wealth is indicated by the number of wives a man can support or by how fat family members are. In other societies wealth is related to how slender family members are, or how hefty their bank accounts. Members of Chinese communes and of Israeli *kibbutzim* share valued tools, resources, and goods, with only a few personal possessions retained as private property. In other societies, virtually all property is privately owned.

Why do these vast differences in food preferences, sexual behavior, and economic activity occur? Three major explanations for cultural variation have been offered: the ecological view, the functionalist view, and the Marxian view.

THE ECOLOGICAL VIEW

The *ecological view* suggests that climate, food and water supplies, and the presence or absence of threatening enemies, influence the evolution of various cultural practices that help people adapt to the environment. More specifically, according to anthropologist Marvin Harris (1979), how people produce food and other necessities explains the origin and development of many cultural practices.

Harris examined the tribal custom of the potlatch in terms of its ecological significance (1974). The intent of a potlatch was to give away or even to destroy more wealth than one's rival could. The potlatch was a magnificent feast celebrating a major social event such as a marriage. A chief would display urns of food, copper pots, woven mats, smoked fish, whale oil, and anything else of value he had. Then he would press these lavish gifts on his guests, including rival chiefs. The more a chief could give away, the higher his prestige and the more obligated his guests and rivals were. The only way they could get out of his debt was by holding an even more magnificent potlatch themselves (Mauss, 1954).

These competitive feasts were practiced by the Kwakiutl Indians in the Pacific Northwest and by tribes in New Guinea and the Solomon Islands. To prepare for the potlatch, a chief and his supporters caught and dried extra fish and berries, and accumulated animal skins, blankets, fish oil, and other valuables. The wealth to be given away was arranged in neat piles and counted by official gift counters. Harris explains this status rivalry as serving the economic system by ensuring that a greater level of wealth was produced and distributed. He believes that when everyone had equal access to the means of subsistence, the competitive feasts helped keep the labor force from slacking off and being content with levels of productivity that offered no margin of safety for crises such as crop failures. In the absence of political institutions that could integrate separate villages into a viable economic framework, competitive feasting served to pool the productive efforts of a larger population than that of any single village. If one village had a poor year for fishing, its people could benefit from the better luck of another village. The competitive thrust of the feasts assured that food and other valuables would be transferred from richer to poorer villages (Harris, 1974).

Thus, an otherwise apparently bizarre custom becomes explainable in terms of how it raises productivity and distributes wealth. Like the functional explanation of cultural variation, the ecological approach runs the risk of concluding that whatever exists must be "right" because it is adaptive or functional for the society. But the sheer range of cultural alternatives suggests that a wide variety of "functional equivalents" can and do exist. Basic needs may be met in a wide variety of ways.

THE FUNCTIONALIST VIEW

Cultural variations have often been explained in terms of the different functions they serve in the society in which they are found. Basically, the functionalist approach assumes that society has a tendency to maintain a state of equilibrium and that various cultural elements play a role in restoring or maintaining the equilibrium. Early anthropologists such as A. R. Radcliffe-Brown and Bronislaw Malinowski found this view useful in understanding otherwise seemingly strange customs in the isolated societies they studied.

As Malinowski (1926) said, functionalist theory aims to explain social facts by their function in society; that is, by the way they work within the entire system of culture and the way they are related. Anthropologists developing functionalist ideas, however, tended to study nonliterate, tightly knit, rather small societies. It is questionable whether the concept of functional unity can be transferred to more complex, literate societies (Merton, 1957). Religion, for example, may be said to contribute to the functional unity of society by developing common values and ends. But when this function is transplanted from nonliterate, simple societies to literate, complex industrial societies, it tends to overlook the possibility that religion may serve to splinter and divide societies (Merton, 1957). Consider the deep religious conflict in Northern Ireland, conflicts between Christians and Muslims in Lebanon, and numerous other examples of religion serving as a basis for cultural and social division within a society. The functionalist view may suggest that some form of religion (or its functional equivalent) will exist in a society to deal with the universal problems of illness, death, and the hope for an afterlife. But the exact form religion takes may vary widely. The functionalist view is not able to explain, for instance, why religion takes such different forms.

THE MARXIAN VIEW

The Marxian approach to culture differs from functionalism in several important respects. First, Marxians suggest that functionalist sociologists stress the independent importance of culture too much. An extreme version of this view, *cultural determinism,* sees the nature of a society as determined by the ideas and values of the people living in it. This view ignores the origin of those ideas and their possible relation to forms of economic production. Beliefs are treated as far too independent of other aspects of society.

Marxians stress that culture may be created by dominant groups in society who use cultural ideas and values to advance their own interests. Far from being functional for all members of society, culture thus serves as a means of domination. Clearly, not all forms of culture fall into this category. It is not a matter of cultural domination, for instance, whether a red or a green light means stop, but only that the color be consistently and widely used. Nevertheless, while some cultural features are clearly a matter of convenience for all, it is important to consider the question raised by the Marxian perspective: Do certain groups favor particular beliefs or practices especially strongly? For example, the claim that Scholastic Aptitude Tests (SATs) reflect some kind of basic academic aptitude, rather than cultural and academic exposure, benefits the children of upper-middle-class families who do well on the tests, but does not help students with weaker academic backgrounds. Some cultural elements may be functional for all, while others clearly benefit some groups more than others.

Finally, functionalist and Marxian views differ in terms of how they explain cultural change. When functionalists consider cultural change at all, they tend to explain it by saying that it was functional for a society, say, to change its religious practices. But the question remains—why was it functional for a society to change at that time and why did religious beliefs take one form rather than another? Functionalist answers to these questions are not always convincing. Marxians suggest that cultural variations evolve as forms of economic production change. Within each form (slavery, feudalism, or capitalism, for example) variations arise through class conflict, internal contradictions, and adaptation. By indicating such mechanisms for change, this approach suggests how cultural changes might occur.

In short, both Marxian and ecological views suggest how and why cultural changes occur. Moreover, they both see change as an expected aspect of social life. Functionalism, on the other hand, tends to view cultural change as disruptive or dysfunctional for the social system. Hence functionalism seems better suited for analyzing how cultural components operate within a relatively static society than for analyzing cultural change.

AMERICAN CULTURE AND VALUES

Some of the variations discussed above demonstrate that known cultural patterns are not the only ones possible. Such contrasts may help us get a stronger sense of American culture. To characterize a culture, we can look at what people spend their time doing; how they spend their money; themes in their literature, art, and music; and what they talk about. All these features, when compared with other societies, help reveal the cultural center of a society. In the process, certain contradictions may come to light. For instance, Americans tend to be generous toward those in need, and yet they urge self-reliance.

One of the earliest studies of American society was conducted by the Frenchman Alexis de Tocqueville (1835). To him, one of the notable features of American life was the emphasis on equality between people. He observed that Americans do not like people who "put on airs" and try to seem better than others. They like people to be like themselves. The anthropologist Clyde Kluckhohn (1954) calls this tendency the "cult of the average man." It is reflected in the use of humor to sanction people who try to be what they are not and also in press stories that carry detailed descriptions of the problems of people in public life. This tendency may be related to the way we personalize issues and achievements, whether they are good or bad. We tend to blame inflation or recession on the president, making him personally responsible. Similarly, if someone gains great wealth, the media analyzes the person's character to see what propelled him or her to riches. Despite the emphasis on equality in American life, there is the countertendency to glorify, publicize, and even imitate. Americans are both attracted and repelled by nobility, celebrity, glamour, and the elite. The absence of nobility and the relative equality of position in America leads people to be "forever brooding over advantages they do not possess . . . and restless in the midst of abundance," suggests Tocqueville in his nineteenth-century observations of the American scene (1935, vol. II, chap. XIII).

Perhaps because of the absence of formally structured inequality in their heritage, Americans tend to avoid searching for structural explanations for either success or failure. This tendency is reflected in the remarkably consistent attitudes of young people in Muncie, Indiana, in 1924 and 1977. Muncie was first described in the famous *Middletown* study conducted by Robert and Helen Lynd in 1924 (published in 1929) and in a 1977 replication study by Theodore Caplow, Howard M. Bahr, and Bruce A. Chadwick. Both teams of investigators asked high school students whether they agreed or disagreed with the statement "It is entirely the fault of a man himself if he does not succeed." In both 1924 and 1977, exactly the same percentage of students (47 percent) agreed with that statement (Caplow and Bahr, 1979). This result suggests that nearly half the young people surveyed still believe in complete individual responsibility for success or failure; they discounted health, race, or social class background as factors.

Certain elements of stability may exist in other core American values noted by Williams (1965). He suggests the following central features of American culture:

> American culture is organized around the attempt at *active mastery* rather than *passive acceptance*. Into this dimension falls the low tolerance of frustration; . . . the positive encouragement of desire; the stress on power; the approval of ego-assertion, and so on.
>
> American culture tends to be interested in the *external world* of things and events . . . rather than in the *inner experience* of meaning and affect. Its genius is manipulative rather than contemplative.
>
> The American world-view tends to be *open* rather than *closed;* it emphasizes change, flux, movement; its central personality types are adaptive, accessible, outgoing and assimilative.
>
> In wide historical and comparative perspective, the culture places its primary faith in *rationalism* as opposed to *traditionalism;* it de-emphasizes the past, orients strongly to the future, does not accept things just because they have been done before.
>
> Closely related to the above is the dimension of *orderliness* rather than unsystematic *ad hoc* acceptance of transitory experience. (Williams, 1965, p. 460)

Williams' description is similar to that given by Kluckhohn, who saw American values as "faith in the rational, a need for moralistic rationalization, an optimistic conviction that rational effort counts, romantic individualism and the culture of the common man, high valuation of change . . . and the conscious quest for pleasure" (1954, p. 199).

By citing general or core tendencies, both these social scientists seem to have captured traits that existed at least between 1954 and 1965. By focusing on a longer time span and on more specific cultural values, other analysts have noted changes in American values during the past 50 years. These changes are summarized in Table 5.1. Some of these changing values may be reflected in students' changing concerns between 1970 and 1981 (Figure 5.1). They became less interested in keeping up with politics or with changing the political structure, and considerably more interested in being well off financially. The disenchantment with politics is paralleled in other realms as well. Several sociological explanations have been offered for the growing importance of financial success and the increased focus on self.

Americans have become obsessed with the self at the expense of public life, suggests Richard Sennett. He sees the source of this shift as lying in changes in capitalism, specifically the movements toward mass production and mass retailing; by a shift in religious beliefs away from an otherworldly focus to a center on this world; and the loss of boundaries between public and private life. As a result, Sennett believes that Americans have lost the capacity to work with relative strangers in the interests of larger social institutions (Sennett, 1974).

Daniel Bell echoes the theme of preoccupation with self. He sees the central principle of modern culture as being the "expression and remaking of the self in order to achieve self-realization and self-fulfillment" (1976, p. 13). Capitalism has developed a culture, he argues, that contradicts future capitalist development. By encouraging the push toward individualism that began in the eighteenth century, Western culture and capitalism have encouraged individual self-expression, self-indulgence, and anti-intellectual ways of knowing and experiencing the world. These tendencies run counter to the needs of capitalism for rationality, hierarchy, bureaucracy, efficiency, self-denial, and hard work. These sociologists suggest that cultural values are shifting in relatively short time periods, and much faster than they did in traditional societies. These changes in American culture, along with some of the variations that occur in other cultures, strongly suggest the plasticity of cultural forms.

Table 5.1 Changing American Values

	American Values, 1930s to 1950s	"New Breed" American Values, 1960s to 1980s
Content	Self-denial. Emphasis on work. Success as something to be achieved. Future planning, saving.	Focus on self, self-expression. Stress on leisure time off the job. Success as something to which one is entitled. Living for today, loss of confidence in the future.
Origins	Forged in the austerity of the Depression and the frugality of World War II.	Begun in the individualism sparked by the Industrial and French revolutions. Fanned by postwar prosperity, advertising, and the rapid inflation of the 1970s.
Indicators	High rates of saving, modest use of debt.	Shrinking savings, rising consumer debt, declining public participation in voting and public office-holding.

SOURCES: Bell (1976), Lasch (1979), Sennett (1974), Skelly (1978), Yankelovich (1978).

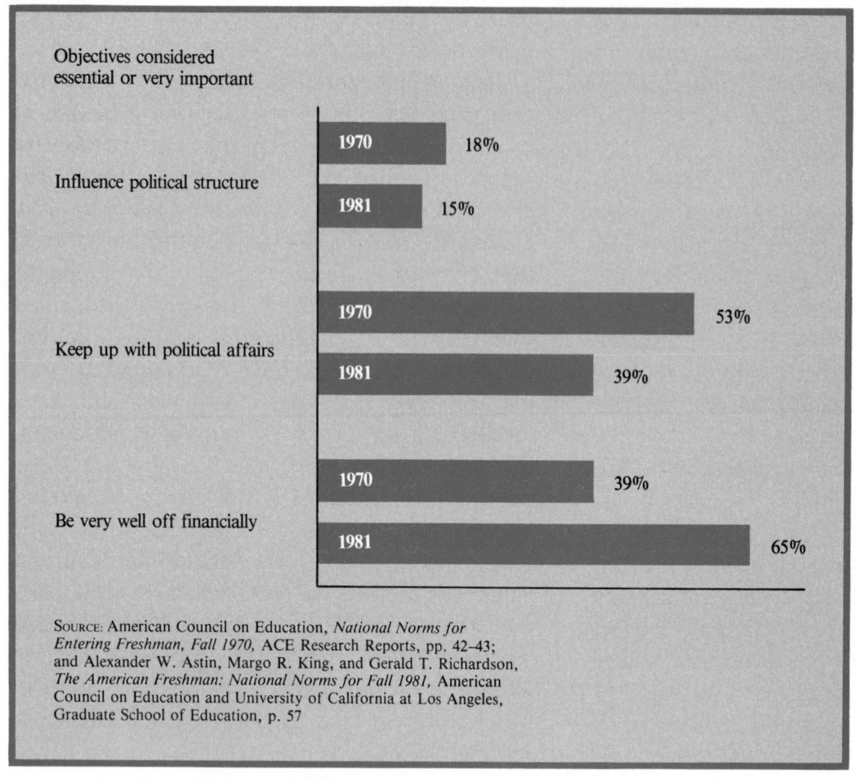

Figure 5.1 Changes in College Student Attitudes, 1970–1981

CULTURE, INDIVIDUALISM, AND CHANGE

ARE INDIVIDUALS TRAPPED BY CULTURE?

Anthropologists such as Kluckhohn (1954) stress the enormous power of culture over individuals. He suggests that if we understand a particular culture, we can predict many of the values and actions of people who share that culture. Does this insight mean we are somehow trapped by our culture and lose the chance for independent action? Clearly not. Culture influences us, but we also shape its direction. Culture provides us with valued strategies that have been developed by our ancestors. In this way, it may offer opportunities for action as well as limitations on what we can do. But individuals retain the capacity for self-reflection. They do not always accept traditions blindly. Recently observed changes in American values suggest that things need not always be the way they are now. Other factors also help to keep us from being prisoners of culture.

Cultural relativism suggests that ours is not the only way of doing something, nor is it necessarily the best way. Cultural diversity based on the existence of many subgroups, each of which possess somewhat different values and norms, helps to provide knowledge of alternatives and offers the possibility of finding a comfortable group or subculture. The existence of countercultures or social movements dedicated to encouraging cultural change indicates that cultural features may be changed by conscious actions.

SOURCES OF CULTURAL CHANGE

Cultures may remain relatively constant for long periods of time if their ecological and population context remains relatively stable and if they have little or no contact with other cultures. However, most societies in the "global village" that is now our world are bombarded with stimuli for cultural change. As a result, cultural changes stem from a variety of sources.

1. Invention. *Inventions* are new cultural creations, often produced by combining existing cultural elements in new ways. Inventions occur in all areas of material and cultural life, from the observation that corn grows better when dead fish are planted with it to the realization that representative government may work more effectively than dictatorship. While some people may enjoy invention for its own sake, without regard to its usefulness, the old maxim "necessity is the mother of invention" captures the conditions under which inventions often occur, are adopted, and spread. The rate of invention in industrial societies has taken off like a jet plane in the last century.

2. Discovery. Discovery involves uncovering something that existed but was unknown. The Pacific Coast Indians discovered the existence of copper, which had both ornamental and hunting value. Imagine when humans discovered fire for the first time, and realized what potential it contained.

3. Diffusion. When people of different cultures come into contact, useful inventions and discoveries are likely to be diffused—that is, spread from one to another group on a voluntary basis. The advantages of using fire, for example, or clay pots to hold water, could readily be seen by observers from other tribes, who could then adopt such techniques themselves.

4. Cultural imposition. Cultures may also be imposed by one group on another—as, for instance, when one society occupies or dominates another one. Systems of taxation, government, language, military service, and religion may then be required of people in the subjugated group.

5. Cultural revolution. Cultures may be imposed by some on others; they may also be resisted or opposed, as occurred in the Chinese cultural revolution or in the counterculture in the United States in the 1960s and 70s. Cultural revolution involves the repudiation of many existing cultural elements and the substitution of new ones. A *counterculture* is defined as "a set of norms and values of a group that sharply contradicts the dominant norms and values of the society of which that group is a part" (Yinger, 1977, p. 833). Various religious cults such as the Hare Krishna, drug-oriented groups, or political radicals may all develop a counterculture. Yinger believes that the changes in values and norms desired by countercultures cannot proceed far without parallel changes in social structure and character.

Cultural changes suggest that culture is not rigid, but bends or moves in response to human actions. Hence people help to shape their culture at the same time that it influences them.

SOCIOBIOLOGY

One of the most hotly debated issues in social thought is the degree to which human nature is shaped by culture or is biologically determined. This old "nature versus nurture" controversy took new form with the publication in 1975 of Edward O. Wilson's book *Sociobiology.* Wilson defines *sociobiology* as "the systematic study of the biological basis for human behavior" (1975a, p. 4). The goal of sociobiologists is to compare societies of animals and humans and to develop and test theories about the degree to which social behavior might be hereditary. Sociobiology is basically the application of Darwinian evolutionary theory to social behavior. Evolutionary theory suggests that individual organisms are selected to maximize their fitness (their ability to reproduce themselves) in a particular environment. This theory can explain a certain amount of behavior, but how can it explain altruism and self-sacrifice? Suppose a set of parents is killed defending their children from a saber-toothed tiger. This behavior, say sociobiologists, increases the chances that their genes will survive, because they have helped relatives who possess their genes to stay alive. One problem with sociobiology is that there are different levels at which behavior may be adaptive. An act may be adaptive for individuals, for their family or kin, for the group to which they belong, for the population, or for the species as a whole.

Sociobiology hypothesizes that the powerful emotion underlying altruism, which appears in all human (and some animal) societies, may have evolved genetically by preserving the genes of people willing to help their relatives. Even Wilson acknowledges, however, that the "intensity and form of altruistic acts are to a large extent culturally determined" (1975b, p. 41). In a similar vein, Wilson suggests that aggression is "an important and widespread organizing technique in human and animal societies" (1975b, p. 42). However, the human species exhibits an incredibly broad range of behavior, from peaceful to aggressive. A number of very peaceful societies have been discovered in the world, including the Tasaday of Mindanao, encountered in a dense Philippine rain forest (Nance, 1975), the Hopi Indians of the American Southwest, and the cooperative Arapesh discovered by Margaret Mead in the South Seas (1935). At the other end of the spectrum of human behavior are the dangerous Dobuan tribe discovered by Ruth Benedict (1934), the fierce Yanamamö tribe of Brazil (Chagnon, 1968), and the Nazi military machine in Germany during the 1940s.

Sociobiology suggests that humans have the genetic potential for a wide range of possible behaviors on a scale from very peaceful to very aggressive. But it does not claim that the particular notes played on this scale are genetically determined. Given this broad range of possible behaviors, the task for the social sciences is to identify the conditions under which peaceful behavior may be triggered and the conditions under which aggressive behavior is called forth. What role does culture play, for instance, in supporting or inhibiting peaceful or violent behavior?

Human forms of social organization vary much more than the social organization of any other primate species. Wilson believes that this great variation is due to the wide range of individual behavior and achievement, and suggests that perhaps "genes promoting flexibility in social behavior are strongly selected at the individual level" (Wilson 1975a, p. 549). Even if individuals were selected for their variability, however, "variation in social organization is only a possible but not a necessary consequence of this process . . . " (Wilson, 1975a, p. 549). Some evidence suggests that people are moderately likely to inherit tendencies to be fast- or slow-moving, good at sports, depressed, dominating, or schizophrenic (Parsons, 1967; Lerner, 1968). If these traits are somewhat inheritable, perhaps societies differ because they contain various numbers of individuals with particular traits. Although this hypothesis would strengthen sociobiology's claim to explaining cultural variations, there is little evidence to support it. Research on genes that specify enzymes, for example, reveals little genetic differentiation between nations and races (Sociobiology Study Group of Science for the People, 1976).

Culture rather than genetic differences may help a species or group adapt to a particular environment. Eskimos, for example, have developed certain cultural traditions that may help them to survive; these include such behaviors as always giving a stranger shelter for the night, and sometimes even offering their wives to visiting men (Birket-Smith, 1935). In warmer climates, such a cultural tradition is less necessary and tends not to occur. What was adaptive behavior at one time, however, may become worthless or even maladaptive in another time and place.

As sociobiologist David Barash suggests, humans live a split existence because of their dual nature as biological and cultural creatures. He suggests that "we are all time travelers, with one foot in our biological, evolutionary past and the other balanced precariously on our rampaging cultural present" (1977, p. 318). Clearly the extent to which human culture has developed suggests that humans possess a biologically evolved *capacity* for culture. But while biological evolution takes thousands of years to occur, cultural evolution moves at incredible speed. Major changes occur within a lifetime, and now they seem to occur even within decades. The uneven rate of change in culture and biology leads to some curious human situations.

Animals that are able to kill others of their species generally avoid doing so (Lorenz, 1952). Deer and antelope will lock horns to test their relative strengths against each other, but they will not use the sharp tines of their horns to kill each other. Rattlesnakes do not bite each other while fighting, and wolves seldom fight to the death. Barash suggests that animals which are biologically capable of killing each other seem to possess an inhibition against doing so. Animals without the biological capacity to kill each other easily generally lack inhibitions about doing so (1977). Humans are among those lacking such inhibitions to kill, although cultural evolution has now placed ample means of destruction at our disposal. In these examples, cultural changes have outstripped biological evolution, which suggests the potential for contradictions between culture and biology, rather than a biological determinism.

The lack of supporting evidence for Wilson's hypotheses and the concern that sociobiology tends to legitimate the status quo are criticisms leveled by the naturalist Stephen Jay Gould and the Sociobiology Study Group of Science for the People. Gould asserts that there is at the moment no direct evidence for genetic control of specific human social behavior (1976). It is not necessary to reject biological influences in our lives or to say that everything is environmental. Instead, Gould believes that human behavior can be understood in terms of biological potential. Thus, humans have a brain able to perform a full range of human behaviors, but predisposed toward none (Gould, 1976). The intense political and social reactions to sociobiology hinge on the way biological determinism may be used to defend, as biologically inevitable, existing social arrangements such as aggression, competition, domination of women by men, and racial and wealth hierarchies. "Why else," Gould suggests, "would a set of ideas so devoid of factual support gain such a consistently good press from established media throughout the centuries?" (1976).

On balance, sociobiology hypothesizes very general potentials and possible constraints on human social behavior. Human behavior is widely variable, but not infinitely plastic. Sociobiology amplifies the importance of identifying environmental and cultural factors that encourage or inhibit the expression of particular behaviors, such as altruism or aggression, and that may shape the form such behaviors take. Sociobiology does *not* suggest that certain genes directly determine particular behaviors. Nor does it suggest that whatever is in nature is either adaptive or "ought to be."

Human biological potential and limits are enclosed in many different cultural envelopes. Genes do not tell us how to plant corn, tell time, write letters, cook dinner, or do most of what we do. Much more than any other animals, humans can self-consciously modify their environment or adapt themselves to it. We can live in the desert, undersea, or in space without waiting for natural selection or mutation to modify our biological capacities. Truly it is culture that sets us apart from all other animals.

Summary

1. Even one's definition of culture varies by culture, ranging from the way of life of a group or society to their artistic products. In this book we use the first, more general definition. Culture includes material objects like tools, homes, and art, as well as nonmaterial elements such as norms, values, language, and other symbols.

2. Humans share sociability and communication with other primates but have much more highly developed brains, language capacity, and tool-using capabilities.

3. A number of common cultural features appear in all societies. These include the use of symbols and language, the existence of norms and values, and a tension between ethnocentrism and cultural relativism.

4. Language is one of the most important features of human society. It allows us to share ideas, plans, and feelings. Written language extends communication through time and space. Language may also limit perception of the world, but it is possible to overcome such limitations through conscious effort and analysis. Language provides clues to what a culture values and what it seeks to hide.

5. Norms are shared expectations about desirable and undesirable behavior and contain an "ought to" aspect that affects emotions as well as minds.

6. Values are more general ideas, also strongly held, about what is desirable and undesirable.

7. The tendency to see one's own culture, language, norms, and values as superior to others is called ethnocentrism. It may be accentuated by stress or hostility. Cultural relativism, on the other hand, means viewing cultural practices within the context of the culture in which they occur.

8. Cultural variations exist in food preferences, sexual practices, economic activities, and other social behaviors. Three explanations have been offered for these variations. The ecological view suggests that cultural differences emerge from population pressures or other environmental constraints. Functionalist theory explains social facts according to how they work within the integral system of culture. The Marxian view suggests that cultural variations emerge from changing systems of production, and benefit dominant groups more than subordinate groups.

9. American cultural values may include individualism, equality, active mastery, involvement with the external world, openness, rationality, and orderliness. Despite these core values, several social observers suggest that American values have changed in recent decades, moving away from self-denial, the "work ethic," and future planning toward a new focus on self, stress on leisure, and living for today rather than for the future.

10. Rapid social changes may help individuals avoid being trapped in their culture, since things need not always be the way they are. Sources of cultural change include invention, discovery, diffusion, cultural imposition, and cultural revolution.

11. The emerging field of sociobiology raises the question of how much of human behavior is genetically determined. Edward Wilson, a leading sociobiologist, suggests that biology provides humans with a wide range of potentialities, but that environment and culture are the keys to behavioral variations within this range. Critics of sociobiology are concerned that biological hypotheses that lack supporting evidence may be used to legitimate the status quo.

Key Terms

bicultural
counterculture
cultural determinism

cultural relativism
cultural universals
culture
diffusion
discovery
ecological view
ethnocentrism
folkways
ideal values
incest
incest taboo
instinct
invention
language
mores
norm
real values
sanction
sociobiology
subculture
symbol
taboo
values

Chapter 6

Socialization

What do childrearing, teaching someone a new game, orienting a new member of an organization, preparing someone who has been in sales work to become a manager, or acquainting an immigrant with the life and culture of a new society have in common? These widely diverse situations are all instances of socialization. *Socialization* refers to the preparation of newcomers to become members of an existing group. Viewed from the group's point of view, it is a process of member replacement.[1]

Socialization is a central process in social life. Its importance has not been overlooked by sociologists, but it is fascinating to see how their image of it has shifted over the last hundred years.[2] In the early years of American sociology, socialization was equated with civilization. The issue was one of taming fierce individualists so they would willingly cooperate with others on common endeavors. An unruly human nature was assumed to exist prior to an individual's encounter with society. This nature had to be shaped to conform to socially acceptable ways of behaving.

As time went on, however, socialization came to be seen more and more as the end result—that is, as a process of internalization. *Internalization* means taking social norms, roles, and values into one's own mind. Society was seen as the primary factor responsible for how individuals learned to think and behave. This view is evident in the work of functionalist Talcott Parsons, who gave no hint that the result of socialization might be uncertain or might vary from person to person. If people failed to play their expected roles or behaved strangely, functionalists explained this circumstance in terms of incomplete or inadequate socialization. Such people were said to be "unsocialized"—they had not yet learned what was expected of them. The trouble is, they might very well know what was expected, but simply be rejecting it. They might want to act one way, yet do something quite different. The possibility that individuals might have needs, desires, values, or behaviors different from those that society expected (or demanded) of them was not seriously considered by functionalists.

As Parsons used the term internalization, it referred to the tendency for individuals to affirm particular values and norms and to conform to them in their conduct. It was this view of internalization that Dennis Wrong (1961) deplored as presenting an "oversocialized" conception of human beings. It left no room for the "animal" or biological side of human existence, where motivational drives might conflict with the discipline of internalized social norms. Functionalists deny the presence in humans "of motivational forces bucking against the hold that social disci-

[1]I am grateful for Anne Rankin Mahoney's helpful comments on earlier drafts of this chapter.

[2]I am indebted to Wentworth (1980) for his excellent analysis of the changing conception of socialization through time.

pline has over them" (Wrong, 1961, p. 187). Individual drives do sometimes conflict with social expectations, however.

Undoubtedly as a reaction to the overly determined Parsonian view of socialization, a group of interpretive sociologists have reasserted the independence and significance of the individual. They reject Parsons' view of socialization as internalized values, norms, and habits, and they reject the notion of society as something out there (a given) that affects individuals the way Parsons suggested it did. The interpretive perspective sees socialization as an interactive process, rather than simply as the incorporation of society's values and norms by the individual. Individuals negotiate their definitions of the situation with others in the social situation. A couple, for example, may negotiate between themselves a conception of marriage that is sharply different from the view of marriage held by people in the larger society. The interpretive view offers an "undersocialized" view of human behavior, since it tends to minimize the importance of historical social structures and the deep internalization of social values and norms (Wentworth, 1980).

Both the functionalist and the interpretive views of socialization are incomplete. Each is relevant for understanding certain phenomena, but tends to ignore other important aspects of social life. Therefore, rather than trying to say which one is "better," a more useful step is to see how the helpful features of each can be combined into a more complete view of socialization. Wentworth (1980) proposes exactly such a synthesis. He suggests that an adequate view of socialization needs to leave room for free will and human autonomy, at the same time that it acknowledges the existence of patterned social structures and processes which influence individuals. The synthesis offered by Wentworth may help us to understand the socialization that occurs in families, schools, groups, sports teams, organizations, and societies. It may also explain why resocialization programs such as those designed to rehabilitate criminals, drug addicts, alcoholics, or sex offenders have relatively low rates of success.

Following Wentworth's lead, it is helpful to distinguish three major aspects of socialization:

1. The *context* in which it occurs.
2. The actual *content and processes* people use to socialize others.
3. The *results* arising from those contexts and processes.

The *context* sets the stage on which socialization occurs. Social context includes culture, language, and social structures such as the class, ethnic, and gender hierarchies of a society. Context also includes social and historical events, power and control in social life, and the people and institutions with whom individuals come in contact in the course of their socialization.

The *content and process* of socialization includes the structure of the socializing activity—how intense is it, how prolonged, who does it, how they do it, whether it is a total experience or only a partial process, how aware the individual is of alternatives, and how attractive those alternatives are. *Content* refers specifically to what is passed from member to novice. *Processes* are those interactions that convey to new members how they are to speak, behave, think, and even feel. The view of socialization as an interactive process stands in contrast to the deterministic views of how socialization occurs. Old and new members interact, and in the process exercise mutual influence on each other.

Outcomes may properly be defined as what happens later, after someone has been exposed to particular content and processes. New members may learn the behaviors, attitudes, and values that old members hoped they would learn. What do these include? First and foremost among humans is learning how to speak and how to apply the rules of language to creating new sentences. Like learning to play chess, learning a language involves being shown some of the ways vocabulary and grammar can be combined (like learning how the various pieces can be moved in a chess game), and then creating one's own combinations from those possibilities. Closely related to learning to use a language is gaining a sense of the rules underlying a society's culture. Even learning to walk in an upright position appears to be the result of socialization.

THE CONTEXT OF SOCIALIZATION

Socialization occurs within the context of biological, psychological, and social factors. Each of these offers possibilities and limitations that may influence socialization.

THE BIOLOGICAL CONTEXT

In the nineteenth century, people were strongly influenced by Charles Darwin's *On the Origin of Species* (1859), which suggested that humans were simply one animal among others. Since the behavior of animals was largely determined by inherited factors and instincts, the same was thought to be true of humans. Nineteenth-century psychologists developed long lists of human instincts such as greed and lust that were believed to be the basis for war, capitalism, and other human activities.

In this century, sociobiologists (see Chapter 5) suggest that some human capacities may be "wired into" our biological makeup. For example, even newborn babies seem to strive for maximum social interaction. They move their heads back and forth in burrowing or "rooting" motions looking for milk; they have powerfully grasping fingers that cling tightly to other human fingers or bodies; and they move so as to maximize human bodily contact. These facts suggest that infants are not "conditioned" by rewards to want human contact, but are born wanting it. Sociobiologists argue that traits which aid survival and reproduction (like learning not to eat things that induce vomiting) will survive, while others (like unusual whiteness in certain animals, which makes animals easier prey) will tend to die out. Although this evidence suggests that biological factors clearly play a role in development, it does not show that all human behavior is biologically determined. Biology sets the stage, on which a very broad range of human behavior occurs. Most, if not all, of the important differences between societies are due to social rather than biological factors.

Humans must satisfy certain biological needs for food, water, air, shelter, and warmth. They need to have the chance to develop certain minimal brain capacity in order to learn what is required for performing as a social being in society. However, the mental level that is required to learn these things may be much lower than many assume. A number of chimpanzees and gorillas have been taught to use sign language, and some apes have acquired large vocabularies of signs. There is considerable debate among the researchers in this area, however, about whether the apes have learned the rules of syntax and grammar that seem to lie behind the capacity to string words together in meaningful sentences. So-called mentally retarded children with tested IQ scores of 60 have been taught how to read, and virtually all biologically "normal" children can learn the language, customs, and behaviors of the culture they are exposed to.

As educators have become more aware of children with "learning disabilities," they have begun to wonder if some conditions, such as those labeled "dyslexia" (that is, the inability to grasp the meaning of something one reads) may not be due to incomplete development of certain nerve pathways in the brain that may scramble signals on the way to the brain, making it likely that children will "see" *b*s instead of *d*s, *g*s rather than *p*s, and so forth. If such problems are rooted in physical development, they are part of the biological context of socialization. They may interact in significant ways with psychological and social factors during socialization and have important impacts on the effects of socialization—for example, if children are labeled retarded or develop a sense of worthlessness because of their learning problems.

In short, biology provides rich potential for becoming human and may present general tendencies, such as the tendency to seek out social interaction or to use language, but it does little to determine the particular form such social development takes.

THE PSYCHOLOGICAL CONTEXT

Emotional States and the Unconscious

The primary factor in the psychological context of socialization is the psychological state of the person being socialized. Psychological states include feelings such as fear, anger, grief, love, happiness, or emotional deprivation. Strongly feeling one or more of these emotions might very well inhibit or promote socialization of a particular kind. Fear may make it difficult for young children to be socialized in school, while people in love may learn very quickly what makes their loved ones happy. Emotions can also influence how individuals perceive the content of socialization, whether in becoming a member of a family group or a religious sect. Knowing something about the feelings of the people involved (the psychological context) helps explain the results of the socialization process.

Freud's notion of the unconscious helps to describe the psychological setting in which socialization occurs. Sigmund Freud (1856–1939) was one of the most influential thinkers of this century. Freud changed the understanding of personality structure. He theorized that the human personality is heavily influenced by unconscious motives, that people often do not know why they behave the way they do. Early childhood experiences or conflicts, often repressed from consciousness, may shape feelings and actions in later life. Freud suggested that clues to unconscious motives can be found in slips of the tongue, in dreams, and in free associations about daily events. These clues can be explored and analyzed with the help of trained experts, through psychoanalysis, in an effort to increase awareness of unconscious motivations and perhaps reduce or control the effect they have on adult behavior, particularly neurotic behavior.

Cognitive Development Theories

A number of psychologists emphasize the series of stages through which humans progress. Although emotional concerns can be involved, these theorists focus on *cognitive* (intellectual) *development,* which occurs in a systematic, universal sequence, through a series of stages. The most influential theorist of intellectual development was the Swiss psychologist Jean Piaget. A sharp observer of children's development, Piaget stressed that children need to master the skills and operations of one stage of intellectual development before they are able to learn something at the next stage. He proposed four major stages: (1) sensorimotor, (2) preoperational, (3) concrete operations, and (4) formal operations.

Sensorimotor Stage (0 to 18 months of Life). The sensorimotor stage is the time prior to learning language, when children begin to use their senses and muscles. First they simply move their arms and legs for the fun of it. They spend a lot of time creeping, standing, and then walking. Around 1 year, they learn that if they want a toy resting on a blanket away from them, they can pull the blanket toward them to get the object. They also learn that even though something is out of sight, it still exists. It is a significant piece of knowledge that Mommy may be in the other room or out for a while, but she still exists.

Preoperational Stage (Ages 1½ to 7). Children in this stage use language. They can treat objects as symbols of other things; for example, they can treat a doll as though it were a baby. They learn to represent the outside world and their own feelings in language. Magical or fantasy explanations make sense to children at this time. For instance, they may believe that dreams fly in the window at night, that the moon follows them as they walk, or that moving things such as the current in a stream or kites flying in the wind are alive. At this stage children also have a very literal sense of justice. For example, they consider a child who breaks three plates while helping with the dishes more naughty than a child who breaks only one in a fit of rage. The intentions behind the action count for little at this age.

Concrete Operations Stage (Ages 7 to 12). By this age, children learn new general rules about their world. For example, they learn that length, mass, weight, and numbers remain constant even if shape or arrangement is changed. Children also learn that concepts such as *heavier* or *brighter* do not refer to absolute qualities, but to a relation between two or more objects.

The Stage of Formal Operations (Age 12). By this stage, young people can isolate the elements of a problem and systematically consider a variety of solutions. By adolescence, most young people become aware of their own thoughts and feelings and begin to reflect on them. As one youth remarked, "I began to think about my future, and then I began to wonder why I was spending so much time thinking about my future" (Mussen, Conger, Kagan, 1969: 455).

Even though Piaget and others agree that environment plays an important role in development, they have been criticized because they underemphasize its importance for thought processes. Piaget, however, stressed that development depends on vigorous interaction with the environment. Cognitive theorists like Piaget have also been criticized because they tend to think of children as rational little problem-solvers who never get angry, frightened, or worried. Finally, this perspective does little to explain individual variation in socialization. Despite these limitations, there is widespread acceptance of Piaget's general notion of developmental sequences. Indeed, it has been carried over into theories of moral development.

Theories of Moral Development

A man's wife is dying and only one drug exists that might save her. But the druggist who invented it wants 10 times what the drug cost him to make, and much more than the man can pay. The man raised half the money and asked the druggist to give him credit for the rest or else lower his price, but the druggist refused. Should the husband steal the drug to save his wife?

This is the kind of moral dilemma that Lawrence Kohlberg has presented to adolescents in various countries, to see how they make moral judgments. He believes there are universal ways that young people think about moral questions, and that as children mature they go through levels of development in their thinking about moral issues.

At the first level, individuals do not understand society's rules and expectations, nor do they feel that they had any part in creating those rules. They respond to rules because of the superior power of authorities and because they fear punishment or other negative consequences from breaking rules. Children under 9, some adolescents, and some adults who have committed crimes are at level 1.

Most adolescents and adults in all societies are at level 2. People at this level have internalized social rules and expectations. They respect the law as an entity, and feel loyalty toward the social order to which they belong. People never reach level 3 before the age of 20, and many people never achieve it. At this level, people accept society's rules not because they unquestioningly identify with the social group, but because they understand the general principles from which the rules are derived. They accept the law because they believe it protects individual rights. They also realize that it is possible to change social rules if such a change would be helpful to many people (Kohlberg, 1963, 1969, 1976, 1981; Rosen, 1980).

Gilligan (1977) has criticized Kohlberg for not including women's differing conceptions of morality in his scheme and hence for presenting a limited view of adulthood. Her research on the

SOURCE: Drawing by Woodman, © 1979, *The New Yorker Magazine, Inc.*

moral reasoning of women facing abortion decisions suggests that they move from a concern with survival, through an awareness of goodness, and finally to an understanding of the principle of nonviolence as the best means of resolving moral conflicts (Gilligan, 1977). Her work broadens the focus on moral development. She also reminds us to ask of all theories: On whom are they based? To whom do they apply?

THE SOCIAL CONTEXT

Social contexts influence individual development. Culture exists before the socialization of new members begins. Parents, for example, do not need to decide alone what they are going to teach their children; much of it they have themselves learned through socialization. Besides culture, individuals are affected by social and historical events and by a number of individuals who actively try to socialize them.

Social and Historical Events

Major social and historical events can be a force in socializing an entire generation. Such major events as the Great Depression of the 1930s, the Holocaust in Europe, or the civil rights movement in the United States may have profound implications for the behavior individuals learn. Elder (1974) compared children whose families were very poor during the 1930s with those whose families were more comfortable. Those suffering greater deprivations depended less upon formal education for their life achievements and more on effort and accomplishments outside of education. Their health as adults tended to be affected negatively by their economic hardships. Finally, they tended to value marriage and family more highly as a result of their economic deprivations (Elder, 1974). Thus, individuals who live in extraordinary times appear to be influenced by the historical events around them.

Parent–child interaction is a major process in the socialization of newcomers into membership in a social group.

Participants in Socialization

Obviously, parents and the immediate family of infants are important to their early care and development. Major changes in the family are increasing the importance of other infant caregivers as well. Teachers and schools transmit formal skills, knowledge, and social values. As infants mature, they have more and more contact with other children of their age, called peers. Inevitably, children are affected by the community and nation in which they are reared. Children in the United States today spend a great deal of time with the mass media. Radio, movies, and—most significantly—television have transformed the way we experience the world and what we know about it.

The Family. In rural societies children have most of their early social contact with the family. Today, however, the family's importance in the child's life is changing. The American family no longer necessarily conforms to the stereotype of a nuclear family with two parents and two or more dependent children. Fewer than one family in five consists of a working father, full-time homemaker mother, and at least one child. There are more and more single-parent families, and 52 percent of all mothers with children under 6 years old are working (U.S. Bureau of the Census, 1982a, p. 382). More and more children are receiving their early and primary care from someone other than their parents. Indeed, 57 percent of all 3- to 5-year-olds were in preschool programs in 1981, compared to only 29 percent in 1966 (U.S. Bureau of the Census, 1982a, p. 142). A 1982 study of day care facilities found that churches are the largest suppliers of childcare to American families. More than 25,000 different churches are involved in some type of childcare program. Altogether these programs were providing care to an estimated 1 million children (Austin, 1982). What are the effects on young children of having only one parent in the home? Of having the mother work? At least one study suggests that single parents with adequate financial and emotional support are able to raise their children quite effectively (Monaghan-Leckband, 1978).

Although most children growing up in America today will spend a great deal of time with people other than members of their families, this does not mean that the participation of families in socialization has ended. On the contrary, the family continues to be a major means of passing on the race, social class, ethnicity, religion, and social outlook of the family. As we saw in Chapter 1, in the case of Alex and Alice compared to Albert and his wife, family origin does a great deal to shape a child's social opportunities, resources, and experience. And as we will see in the next section, different social positions may be related to different socialization for children even when they live in the same society.

Schools. As societies become more complex and there is a greater division of labor, the family is less able to teach children everything they need to know to function effectively as adults in society. Therefore, most societies have established schools to teach youngsters certain skills. Schools teach values and attitudes as well. These values and attitudes include, for example, competitiveness or cooperation, conformity or innovation.

Schools try to impress upon children the importance of working for rewards determined by someone else, and they try to teach neatness, punctuality, orderliness, and respect for authority. Although more and more children are coming under the care of people who are not their relatives before they enter school, at school they meet these nonrelatives in a supervisory capacity. Unlike caregivers, teachers are often called upon to evaluate how well children perform a particular task or how much skill they have. Thus, children's relationships with adults move from nurture and behavioral concerns to performance of tasks and skills determined by others.

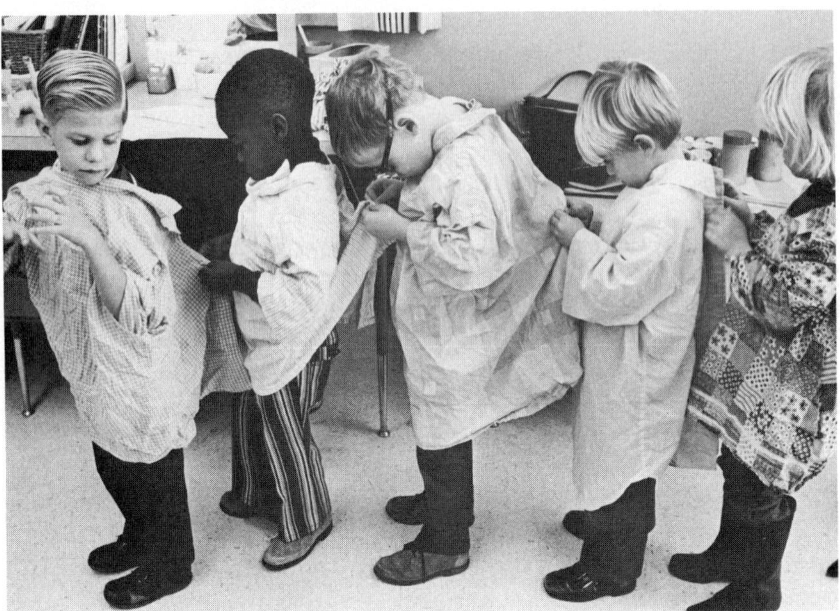

One's peers, that is, other children one's own age, are an important source of social interaction and socialization. Schools bring children together into age-segregated groups that may influence a child's development.

Peers. A *peer group* consists of friends and associates who are about the same age and social status. As children get older, going to school brings them into regular contact with other children of their age. As early as first and second grade, children form social groups. In these early peer groups, children learn to share toys and other desired resources (such as the teacher's attention). Peers also tend to reinforce certain behaviors that are stressed by parents and schools—for example, whether it is all right to hit someone else, what are acceptable behaviors for boys and girls, and how one talks about bathroom activities. As children move through school, the interests of peer groups may diverge more and more from what adults want. This seems to be particularly true of the United States, but it seems to have also been true of ancient Greek society and to be the case in certain socialist societies today. Youthful concerns may center on popular music and movies, sports, sex, or illegal activities. Parents and teachers, on the other hand, may wish that children were concentrating more on schoolwork, helping more at home, or at least "staying out of trouble." Peer groups can provide social rewards—praise, prestige, and attention—to individuals for doing things adults disapprove of. In that way, they may encourage young people to ignore the wishes of parents and other adults. Peers can also exert pressure on individuals to do things they may not really want to do.

In the Soviet Union, the peer group is used by authorities to reinforce the behaviors and attitudes desired by them. For example, if a child comes to school late, it is not only the teacher who notes this (perhaps by praising children who are on time), but the child's row in the classroom may be enlisted to urge the child to come to school on time (Bronfenbrenner, 1970). Peer sanctions (punishments) are particularly effective. In Israel, for instance, in a collective farm group a child who breaks a rule such as using a tractor when it is not allowed and damaging the machine in the process may be formally ostracized for some time. During this period, the other children will not speak to or play with the child. While effective in achieving social goals, the united effect of peer and official authority is more powerful and painful than official authority alone for the individual who does not conform. It leaves less room for individual resistance, because it tends to remove the friends of someone who does not conform as well as punish the action. In our society, some people deplore the excessive dominance of peer cultures, which can negate official authority nearly completely at times.

Community and Country. Every society tries to influence how young people grow up. Much of this influence is expressed through parents, schools, and peers, but it is worth considering for a moment how children get exposed to the political and economic ideas that are considered important for citizens of a particular country.

Children learn political information and attitudes rapidly during the elementary school years, particularly in the time between fourth and fifth grades (Hess and Torney, 1967). One of the first things they learn is that they belong to some kind of a political unit. Even very young children develop a sense of "we" in relation to their own country and learn to see other countries in terms of "they." Children also tend to believe that their own country and language are superior to others. This affectional bond may be the most critical socialization feature relating to the political life of the nation (Hess and Torney, 1967). The family helps provide this basic loyalty to country, but the school also shapes the political concepts that expand and develop children's early feelings of attachment. Political orientations develop early and reach nearly adult levels by the end of elementary school, but there are still some critical changes that occur at other points during the life cycle. High school students become more aware of differences between political parties and tend to become more active politically. In the first decade of adult life people modify their political orientations as they take on new occupational and family roles (Jennings and Niemi, 1968).

Although many people have studied the political socialization of children, only a few have examined economic socialization. One study that did considered how youngsters are socialized into capitalism. When third-graders were compared with twelfth-graders, the older students were found to hold more negative attitudes toward labor unions and more favorable attitudes toward business than did the younger children (Cummings and Taebel, 1978), suggesting that over time they developed attitudes that were more favorable toward capitalism, perhaps because of what they learned at school or at home.

Mass Media. The *mass media* include many forms of communication, such as books, magazines, radio, television, and movies, that reach large numbers of people without personal contact between senders and receivers. In the last few decades, children have been dramatically socialized by one source in particular, television. Studies have found that children spend more time watching TV than they spend in school.

It seems unbelievable that in 1945 the pollster George Gallup asked Americans, "Do you know what television is?" Now virtually every American home has at least one television set, and the average set is on almost 7 hours a day (Comstock et al., 1978). How has this transformation affected us, and particularly how does it affect children? Reports vary, but children in the fifth to eighth grades view an average of 4 to 6 hours daily (Lyle and Hoffman, 1972; B. S. Greenberg and Dervin, 1970). Most of the research on the effects of television has been on the cognitive and behavioral results of TV watching. The topic most often studied has been the influence of television on antisocial behavior, especially violence. Current research supports the view that seeing violence on television increases the chance that a child will be aggressive (Com-

Television has become a major agent of socialization in modern industrial societies, since most children spend more hours watching television than they spend in school. Social researchers have examined both the content and the experience of television viewing and suggest that large amounts of television interfere with a child's chances to develop social relationships, learn self-direction, and take initiative.

stock et al., 1978). No publicly available studies unambiguously relate changes in behavior (such as food habits or drug use) to exposure to television advertising (Comstock et al., 1978).

Recent research also suggests that young people obtain considerable political and social information from television, but that how they perceive the information depends largely on parental influence (Comstock et al., 1978). For example, during the Vietnam war, television was the most important source of public information about the war. Yet how young people felt about the war—whether they favored or opposed it—seemed to be influenced more by their parents than by the opinions presented on television. Those who opposed the war interpreted the news on TV as opposing the war, while those favoring it construed the news as favoring it (Comstock et al., 1978).

Most researchers studying the effects of television on children have focused on the content of the programs, and not on the total experience of television watching. They argue that there is too much violence and sex on children's programs, and that more good educational programs for children are needed. But Winn takes exception to this concern with content and points the finger at the experience itself. When people watch television, no matter what the program, they are still simply watching television rather than having any other experience. According to Winn, and many agree, children need to develop family relationships, the capacity for self-direction, and the basic skills of communication (reading, writing, and speaking); to discover their own strengths and limitations; and to learn the rules that keep social interaction alive. Television works against all these goals by putting children in a passive situation where they do not speak, interact, experiment, explore, or do anything else active because they are *watching* a small moving picture on a machine. These findings have major implications.

This research has led to a growing recognition of the importance of television as a medium of socialization, although clearly it is only one among a number of important influences on socialization.

SOCIAL POSITION AS PART OF THE CONTEXT

A social feature we have not yet mentioned is the ranking system operating in a society and the child's location in that ranking system. Whether social position is based on economic situation, race or ethnicity, social prestige, or some combination of these factors, a number of writers have suggested that position in the ranking system of society is an important feature of the context in which socialization occurs. Sociologists ask, for instance: Are middle-class children socialized differently from lower-class children? If so, why and how? Middle-class parents are slightly less likely to use physical punishment than are lower-class parents (Gecas, 1979). Middle-class parents appear to be more concerned about their children's intentions than with the negative consequences of their actions. Thus, if a child breaks a dish, a middle-class parent will be concerned with whether he or she did it "on purpose" or whether it was an accident; and the reaction will vary accordingly. Lower-class parents tend to react in about the same way whatever the intention of the child (Kohn, 1969).

These differences in parental response may stem from the life situations of people in different classes. Kohn (1969) and Pearlin (1971) stress that different parental experiences in the occupational world color the view of what children need to learn. Parents who are closely supervised on the job (more often blue collar workers) value conformity more than do less supervised parents (usually white collar workers). This relationship between the amount of supervision parents receive and what they value for their children appears to extend beyond the workplace to the general economic and political structure of a society. Cross-cultural studies show that members of agrarian and herding societies (where food can be accumulated and stored) tend to emphasize compliance in their socialization practices. In societies where food cannot be stored (as in hunting, gathering, or fishing economies), members more often stress individual achievement and self-reliance (Barry, Child, and Bacon, 1959).

Political structure may also be related to socialization practices. Autocratic states tend to have more "severe" socialization, show clear power and deference relationships, and stress obedience (Stephens, 1963). The Soviet Union, for example, works harder to socialize children to conformity than does the United States (Bronfenbrenner, 1970). By way of contrast, tribal societies that lack a centralized or autocratic political system allow children to be less obedient and less conforming (Stephens, 1963).

All these studies suggest that parents value different traits for their children, depending on the economic, political, and social situations they face. In general, when adults have more opportunities for self-determination, they value and try to develop greater self-reliance in their children (Ellis, Lee, and Petersen, 1978). All groups try to socialize their children as well as they can, but they stress different behaviors, depending on what they see as needed in their own situation. Just as different societies may see the need for different behaviors and skills in their children, subgroups within society may do the same thing. They try to prepare their children as well as possible for the society in which they are going to live.

THE CONTENT AND PROCESSES OF SOCIALIZATION

These examples show that certain features of social context, specifically the type of society in which one lives and one's position in the class structure, are related to the content of socialization—that is, to the kind of behavior that is preferred. These studies do not, however, show how people learn what is valued in their cultures. In this section we consider several theories about how people are socialized. These ideas include learning theory, social learning theory, the importance of interaction, and how a sense of self emerges through interaction. We then consider a number of case studies that show what happens when these processes are absent.

LEARNING THEORY

At one time, socialization was considered the same as learning theory. *Learning theory* suggests that specific human behaviors are learned or forgotten as a result of the rewards or punishments associated with them. The focal problem of socialization was how to teach children to become the "right" kind of adults. This approach stressed the importance of "nurture," or environment, for the development of human potentialities. Ivan Pavlov, a Russian psychologist, demonstrated in 1902 that even such an apparent instinct as salivating in response to food could be taught, or conditioned, by structured learning situations. Pavlov rang a bell when he fed his dogs in the laboratory, and soon they began to drool when they heard the bell even if there was no food around. This experiment demonstrated that biological behavior can be learned.

A major American learning theorist, James B. Watson, carried on this tradition. Watson argued that human behavior and personalities are completely flexible and can be shaped in any direction. He taught an 11-month-old boy to fear white rats and other furry white objects, such as Santa Claus's beard, by conditioning. Today, social learning theorists such as B. F. Skinner and other behaviorists continue Watson's tradition. *Behaviorism* is based on the belief that only things which can actually be observed should be studied. Basically behaviorists believe that humans and other animals learn things through a process called *conditioning*. Behavior that is rewarded gets reinforced because the action and the reward get associated with each other in the subjects' minds. Behavior that is not reinforced tends to get extinguished, or wiped out. Skinner stresses that rewards are much more effective conditioners than punishments; he was even able to teach pigeons to play ping-pong using this approach.

Applied to childrearing, learning theory takes the form of *behavior modification*. Children are praised or otherwise rewarded for desired behaviors; undesirable actions are ignored. Older children and adults can set up their own goals and systems of rewards in an effort to modify their own behavior—for example, to do their school work on time, to stop smoking, or to exercise regularly. The greatest controversy over this method surrounds the use of behavior modification by some people over others. Who, after all, has the right to decide *what* behaviors should be conditioned? This issue was vividly portrayed in Anthony Burgess's novel *A Clockwork Orange*, in which a young criminal's violent tendencies were conditioned out of him so effectively that when he was attacked by a group of thugs he was psychologically unable to defend himself. Aside from the moral issues surrounding this technique, there are questions about the effectiveness of behavior modification. Are people infinitely modifiable? Perhaps the processes of conditioning cannot completely determine the course of human learning and behavior.

Behaviorism has been modified by some social psychologists who have advanced a *social learning theory* (Bandura, 1969; Bandura and

Social stratification in the United States and many other countries around the world is related to income inequalities but goes much deeper. Stratification affects how people live, their self-concepts, their education and general socialization, the way they use media, and the degree of political involvement or alienation they feel.

Percent of families and unrelated persons at various income levels in the United States, 1981. Families include slightly more than two-thirds of the population; while about one-third are unrelated persons.

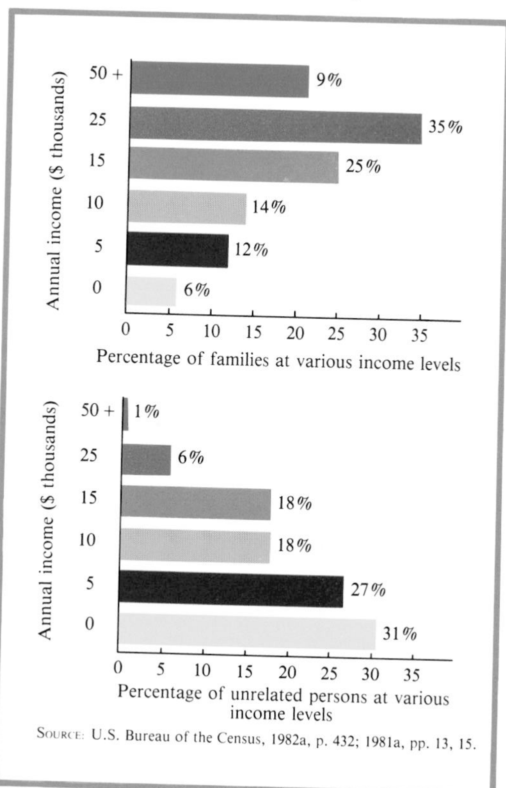

SOURCE: U.S. Bureau of the Census, 1982a, p. 432; 1981a, pp. 13, 15.

College enrollment in the United States by sex (in millions)

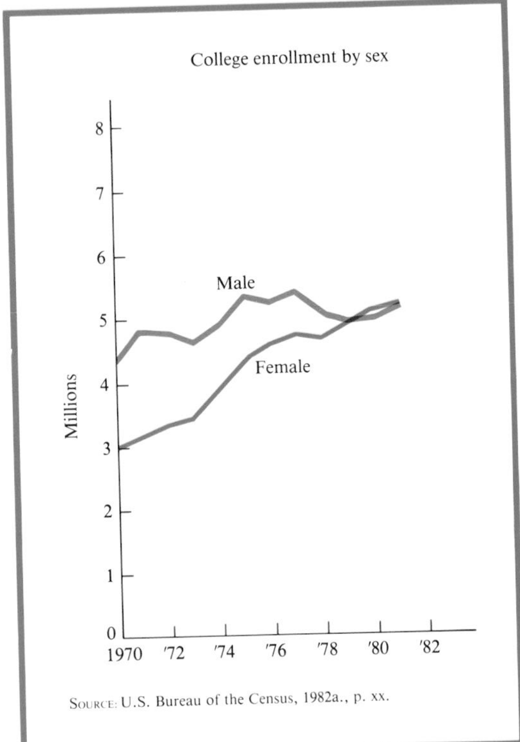

Communications in the United States

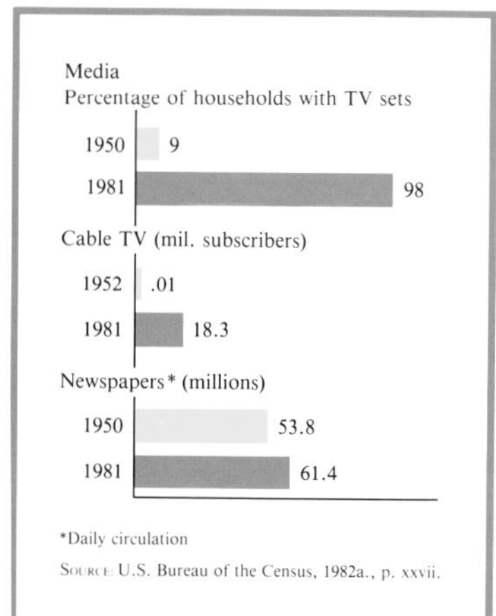

Walters, 1963). These psychologists study such human behaviors as aggression, sharing, and competitiveness, and are particularly interested in how children imitate or model the behavior they see in others. They argue that people learn through observation, even if they are not always rewarded. Observational learning is more likely to occur in some situations than in others. For example, children are more likely to imitate the behavior of someone who is more prestigious than that of someone who has less prestige (a sports star more than a bum); more likely to imitate someone like themselves (another child more than a cartoon animal); and more likely to imitate the behavior of models who are rewarded for their actions than that of those who are punished or not rewarded. Social learning theory stresses the vital role played by other people in the socialization process.

THE IMPORTANCE OF INTERACTION

A newborn child's fussiness, liveliness, or good spirits may affect how people respond to him or her. Whether such traits are genetic or learned, there is growing evidence that people caring for infants react to individual differences in babies (Freedman, 1974). The individual variations that caregivers react to in infants may be social as well as biological and learned. For example, race, class, or gender may influence caregiver reactions as much as crankiness, cuteness, health, or size. There also may be a complex interaction between social and biological traits. A high activity level, for example, may be viewed by some as desirable in a boy but not in a girl.

Infants, in turn, respond differently to similar treatments. This evidence underscores the importance of interaction between new and old members in the process of socialization. Recent observational studies suggest that babies may be born with certain innate tendencies that stimulate social interaction between infants and their caregivers. Babies learn early, or are born with, ways of inviting caregivers to play with them. By 3 months, if not before, infants are well equipped with various behaviors to engage and disengage their caregivers. These include gazing directly into caregivers' eyes, turning their heads or eyes to invite further interaction or to withdraw from it, smiling, and crying (Stern, 1977). In these ways, infants present caregivers with signals that enable them to modify their behaviors. Stern's findings suggest that caregivers are reinforced in the attention they offer infants, and therefore are motivated to spend more time interacting with them. They also suggest that infants play an active part in the process. Stern also indicates that infants learn something about sequencing of human interaction, and a sense of "taking turns" in social interaction that develops further as they get older.

MEAD'S VIEW OF THE SELF

How interactions affect socialization and development may be illuminated further through George Herbert Mead's concept of the self. Mead (1934) saw the self as composed of two parts, "I" and "me." The "I" portion of the self represents the spontaneous disposition or impulse to act. This part of the self allows for some innovation and creativity on the part of individuals, as well as for some freedom from control by others. The "I" acts when the individual takes the initiative in a situation. This part of the self allows individuals to act on their environment. The "me" portion of the self brings the influence of others into the individual's consciousness. This part of the self includes the views of self an individual learns from others, and it carries the thoughts, norms, and values that the major agents of socialization (family, school, peers, television, and so forth) present.

Another version of this idea was elaborated by Cooley (1902), who used the term *the looking-glass self* to describe how people become aware of who they are from the ideas others have about them. In his view, other people are like mirrors who reflect back to us what they think we are. Just as people get a sense of what they are like from an image in the mirror, so they get a sense of self as they see how others treat them and react to them.

This social nature, or what Mead calls the "me" portion of the self, develops as children grow up and learn to play multiple-person games that require them to take the role of the *generalized other*—that is, to be able to see how each player will behave toward each other player. Ultimately the generalized other expands to include the attitude of the whole community, which children come to be aware of. This process is continuous, and Mead saw the self as always emerging—that is, constantly developing and changing, rather than being static or fixed. This potential for change is due in part to the way Mead's self can *reflect on itself* and make choices.

The "I" and the "me" parts of one's self can interact with each other in what Mead calls "self-interaction." In this way individuals are able to have "internal conversations." What they think, feel, and wish to do interacts with what they know others wish or expect them to do. People can decide to give relatively greater weight to one rather than another of these demands, and they can make choices among the competing influences of self. They can weigh alternatives, take things into account, make choices, and organize themselves for action. In this way, Mead's conception of the self allows individuals to participate in their own socialization. They can even "rehearse" mentally for actions they plan to take in the future.

People frequently seem to prepare for certain life roles before they happen. Sociologists call this *anticipatory socialization* and see it as referring to the way people take on the attitudes, values, and behaviors of some status they expect to occupy in the future. One 5-year-old boy, for example, ran to watch his father barbecue dinner outside, saying: "I need to learn how to do this because when I grow up I'll need to do this for my family." This is a good example of modeling behavior, but the imitation is not immediate. Instead, there is the expectation that certain skills and behavior will be useful or desirable at some fairly distant time in the future. People may want to learn how to read a map or change a tire because someday it might be helpful. The intrinsic motivation for competence combines with an anticipation of what will be useful or fun in the future, stimulating people to internalize certain values or learn new skills.

CASE STUDIES OF SOCIALIZATION

Socialization contexts and processes inevitably affect the results that occur. Nowhere is this more apparent than in the cases of individuals who receive distorted or deprived childhood experiences. Of course it is unethical and illegal to perform experiments on infants or children that would deprive them of social contact from an early age. However, a number of "natural" experiments have occurred that indicate what happens when infants or children are denied social contact. Some instructive experiments showing the results of denying them contact with a caring adult have also been done with monkeys.

There are numerous reports from the Middle Ages onward about infants whose every physical need was met, and yet who failed to grow normally and often grew sick and died (Ross and McLaughlin, 1949; Spitz, 1945). Evidence suggests that to survive and become human, people need certain kinds of social as well as biological sustenance. This evidence comes from reports of what have been called feral, or untamed, children supposedly reared by wild animals; accounts of children kept isolated by their own families; studies of children raised in institutions; and experiments on the effects of isolation in monkeys.

Feral Children

While scientists do not agree on whether feral children ever lived or behaved in the ways reported, it is dramatic how many reports of children reared in the wild have surfaced. In an extensive review, Malson (1972) discovered more than 50 recorded cases. Early Greek and Roman myths add untold numbers of fictional stories. Most cases, Malson says, are myths or hoaxes, but not all. Consistent themes appear in the more reliable accounts: The children cannot speak, they walk on all fours, they eat strange (to us) food that varies according to the type of animal that raised them. A number of reports express surprise at the subjects' apparent lack of interest in sex, although the subjects were biologically mature. Also, the feral children showed no signs of laughing and smiling. In the more reliable reports, after they were found by other humans the children were sometimes able to learn simple language, to walk upright, to wear clothes, and to eat some different foods.

Why these children were abandoned and how long they lived in the wild is open to controversy. Skeptics suggest that the infants were abandoned because they were mentally defective, but some were left or lost at such an early age (as young as 18 months) that retardation seems an unlikely reason. The fact that the children learned something after they were found, even though they could not learn the full range of language, argues for their normal intelligence. Certain children had heavily calloused feet and elbows, suggesting that they had been in a "wild" condition for a considerable time. Also, in certain accounts the feral children had been glimpsed by residents of the area over a considerable time period. So, while some stories are undoubtedly contrived, other accounts of feral children are probably sound. They suggest that language, especially, requires considerable early and sustained human interaction to develop. Much of what people assume to be biologically "given," such as sexual drive, food preferences, and even walking upright, may very well depend on social learning for its development, focus, or form.

Effects of Early Childhood Isolation

Two cases of extreme childhood isolation in the United States were reported by Kingsley Davis (1940, 1947). Most children who are kept isolated eventually sicken and die, but there is the known case of a girl, named Anna, who did not. She was kept locked in the attic of her family's Pennsylvania farm because she was born illegitimately and her grandfather was unwilling to acknowledge her presence. The mother was unable to place Anna in a foster home, so she brought her home. Since Anna's grandfather was violently opposed to the child, her mother put her in an attic room, where she stayed. The girl was fed just enough to keep her alive, but she received no social play or affection. When she was discovered by a social worker six years later, Anna was unable to speak, sit up, walk, keep herself clean, or feed herself. She didn't laugh, smile, or seem to care about anything or anyone. The social workers assumed she was mentally retarded, deaf, or both. Placed in a special school, Anna learned to coordinate her body and to communicate. She could speak words and phrases. She also learned how to string beads, to build with blocks, to identify some colors, to wash her hands and brush her teeth, to play with dolls, and to help other children. She learned to walk and even to run clumsily before she died four and a half years later.

A second child, Isabelle, found about the same time as Anna, fared somewhat better. Like Anna, Isabelle was illegitimate and was about 6½ when discovered. Isabelle's grandfather kept her and her deaf-mute mother in a dark room most of the time. Unlike Anna, Isabelle had the advantage of interaction with another human being, but she could not learn conventional language. Instead, she and her mother developed a system of gestures for communicating with each other. When discovered, Isabelle reacted wildly to other people. Because she could utter only strange croaking sounds, she was first thought to be deaf. Specialists declared her feebleminded. Even so, a skilled team of psychologists and doctors began working intensively with her. Her learning began slowly, but suddenly she began racing through the stages of childhood learning that usually occur in the first six years. She went through the stages in the usual order, but far more rapidly. By the age of 8½, she had gone from being "feebleminded" to achieving an apparently normal level of development. She eventually entered school and took part in school activities as normally as other children. Her giant gains seem to have been due to the early interaction she had with her mother and to her skilled trainers. These cases suggest that communicative contact is the core of socialization (Davis, 1947, p. 205).

A third child, Genie, was found in 1970, and Susan Curtiss, a psychologist, worked closely with her for several years and wrote a book about her in 1977. Genie's father kept her locked in a room from the age of 20 months until age 13. Genie was harnessed naked to an infant's potty seat, and left for hours and days through the years. When she was remembered at night, she was put to bed in a home-made straitjacket. There were no radios or televisions in the house, people spoke in hushed tones, and the only language Genie heard was an occasional obscenity from her father. He hated noise, and if Genie made any sound her father would growl at her like a dog or beat her with a stick. As a result of her confinement, Genie could not walk and her eyes could not focus beyond the boundaries of her room. She was malnourished, incontinent, and salivated constantly.

Despite all this, Genie was alert, curious, and intensely eager for human contact. When frightened or frustrated she would erupt into silent frenzies of rage—flailing about, scratching, spitting, throwing objects, but never uttering a sound. Aside from not speaking, her lack of socialization was apparent in her behavior: She would urinate in unacceptable places, go up to someone in a store and take whatever she liked of theirs, and peer intently into the faces of strangers at close range. Although Curtiss worked with her for several years, Genie never developed language abilities beyond those of a 4-year-old, and she ended up being placed in an institution. Her mother has since sued Curtiss for disclosing confidential information for "prestige and profit" (Pines, 1981).

Such examples reveal that most of the behavior we think of as human does not arise directly from biology. Instead, it seems to depend upon the interplay between biological potential and social interaction and affection. Isabelle, although deprived in her early years, did receive affection and had contact with at least one other human. Hence, she could, in effect, catch up with other children her age. Isabelle shows that the developmental stages children are thought to go through are *situationally activated*—that is, they may not occur at the expected time unless certain things are happening in the infant's environment. Without those situational triggers, the development may not occur. These cases illustrate the complex interaction between "unfolding" human nature and the environment in which a child lives. What children need from their environment is further specified by cases of children raised in institutions.

Children Raised in Institutions

In two classic studies done in 1945 and 1946, Rene A. Spitz, a psychologist, compared infants raised in a foundling home (an institution for babies whose mothers could not support themselves and their children) with those cared for in the nursery of a penal institution for delinquent girls. If anything, Spitz suggests that the parents of the foundling home infants had social and intellectual backgrounds that were superior to those of the nursery children's parents. This difference was reflected in their early development at 2 to 4 months of age. Both institutions were clean, offered adequate food well prepared, dressed the children similarly, and offered comparable health care. In terms of physical provisions, they were similar.

The 45 babies in the foundling home were cared for by a head nurse and five assistant nurses. Although Spitz reported that the nurses loved the babies, each one had to divide her time among eight babies. As a result, the babies of the foundling home lacked human contact for most of the day. Much of the time there was little going on to attract the babies' attention. Their beds had sheets draped over the sides so that they could see only the ceiling of the room. A quarter of the babies died before they were 3 months old, apparently from lack of attention.

In contrast, the nursery was run by a head nurse with three assistants, but the care of the children fell to their own mothers, the young women in the penal institution. Each baby had the full-time care of his or her own mother. Moreover, Spitz indicates that caring for their babies was one of the few sources of solace for the otherwise heavily deprived inmates. So their babies received lavish attention and tenderness. All day long the nursery teemed with social activity. Despite the probably better hereditary background of the foundling children, Spitz suggests, the nursery children actually developed faster and further physically, emotionally, and socially. Good physical care is not sufficient for the healthy physical, emotional, intellectual, and social development of children. They also need social stimulation and sustained human warmth and contact. Similar effects have been found with young monkeys.

Even Monkeys Need Others

In a series of famous experiments, Harry F. Harlow and his associates explored what happens to monkeys raised in isolation or without mothers. He reared the monkeys under different sets of conditions: some only with other baby monkeys, some with terrycloth models of mothers, and some with chicken-wire mothers. All these monkeys developed serious problems as adults. Most of the mother-deprived monkeys could not play or otherwise interact with other monkeys, socially or sexually. Those few adult females who were successfully impregnated showed completely abnormal maternal behavior. They either avoided their infants completely or they beat them. The monkeys needed both a live mother *and* live peers to develop normally (Harlow, 1963; Seay, Alexander, and Harlow, 1964; Harlow and Harlow, 1965).

Harlow's work suggests that monkeys deprived of needed interpersonal socialization in their youth are unable to reproduce and nurture a new generation. Adequate socialization seems necessary for survival of the species. Of course, we need to be careful about generalizing from other primates to humans, but the fact that humans depend even more than monkeys on social learning suggests the importance of early social interaction. Together these strands of evidence weave a strong cloth to support the assertion that while human potential may be rooted in biological capacities, its full development requires key social experiences. Virtually all theories of human development assume that infants and children receive at least minimal social contact.

The need for social contact is consistent with the behaviorist position. Assuming such contact occurs, and an individual begins to develop a conception of self, the Meadian view of self becomes useful. People do "talk to themselves" about what they are doing and what will happen as a result of what they are doing. They can decide to make one choice rather than another. They can weigh the value of various alternatives. Such a situation does not seem likely until the minimal conditions for social development are met, as the cases described here make abundantly clear.

These cases are summarized in Table 6.1. In this brief form, very dramatic relationships appear between context, processes, and results. These patterns dramatize the social nature of socialization and suggest that outcomes depend heavily on social processes rather than solely on innate capacities.

Table 6.1 Socialization Case Studies in Terms of Context, Processes, and Results

Case	Context	Processes	Results
Anna	Nearly total isolation.	Little or negative contact with others.	Could not speak, sit up, walk, feed herself, laugh, smile, or wash at age 6. Uninterested in anything.
Isabelle	Locked in a darkened room with a deaf-mute mother.	No exposure to other people, culture, or society. Mother and child developed a system of signs for communicating.	At age 6, she had not learned to speak and she behaved wildly.
Genie	Nearly total confinement.	Punished for vocalizing. Very little stimulation.	Did not learn language beyond that of 4-year-old. Unsocialized. Could not walk.
Foundling Home Babies	Sterile hospital environment; one nurse for eight babies.	Little human contact. Physical needs were met, but babies received little play or attention.	Twenty-five percent died by their third month. Others were very slow to develop speech and motor skills.
Prison Nursery Babies	Early rearing in a prison ward; cared for by their own mothers.	Prison mothers lavished attention and tenderness on their babies.	Babies were curious, very vocal and active. Most walked at 10 months.
Harlow's Monkeys	Wire "mothers."	No bodily contact or touching.	Could not play or interact with other monkeys socially or sexually.
	Live mother and peers.	Much touching and playing.	Able to interact with others, to mate, and to rear their young.

THE RESULTS OF SOCIALIZATION

LANGUAGE ACQUISITION

Language acquisition is a critical part of the interaction that occurs during socialization. One of the results of socialization in virtually every society is that people learn to use the language of their group. The first words children learn are simply labels for persons, things, or actions—for example, "Daddy," "juice," "go," or "dog." Children also learn to describe or request things: "stove hot" or "want milk." At this stage, words serve basically as signs—that is, as names that substitute for things themselves. In the early stages of using language, children create sentences that are shorthand versions of adult sentences. For instance, "where is Mommy?" is often expressed as "where Mommy?"

In their second year, children begin to attach words to objects. Average 1-year-olds understand only about three words, but by age 2 vocabulary has swelled to nearly three hundred words. Children in the 1970s used longer clauses and sentences and had larger vocabularies than children in the 1940s. This change may be due to television, to the existence of nursery school, or to the general rise in the level of education in the population. Besides vocabulary, children also need to learn the rules of grammar that prevail in their language. It is not fully understood how they learn grammatical rules so early and how they can use these rules to generate totally new sentences. It does not seem to be the result of direct training, since parents seldom systematically reward correct grammar and punish incorrect forms. Nor does simple imitation explain the process, since children can create new sentences.

By the age of 6, the average child has a vocabulary of about 2500 words, assuming the child has interacted regularly with people in a social environment. By this time children have begun learning the symbolic uses of language, and they begin to make jokes and puns. They realize that words have various meanings and that these meanings are appropriate at different times. It may be all right to call a friend who knows it is a joke a "cuckoo-head," but not so nice to call a visiting stranger that name.

Learning to talk and learning to walk are two of the most difficult tasks the growing child must learn. Yet virtually all children succeed in doing both by the age of 5 or 6 unless they are physically impaired or isolated from human contact.

SENSE OF SELF AND PERSONALITY

Freud's Id, Ego, and Superego

In the social realm, Freud saw the individual and society as being at war. According to him, individuals are born with uncontrolled drives, especially for sex and aggression, and society seeks to repress or channel those drives into acceptable outlets. The dictates of society, particularly the Victorian era in which Freud lived, often shaped this suppression in such a heavy-handed way that people became neurotic.

In explaining the conflict that arises between self and society, Freud identified three concepts in the personality structure. The first is the *id*, the unconscious part consisting of instinctual impulses—for instance, aggressive or sexual impulses that seek immediate expression. Newborn babies and very young children are governed almost exclusively by the id. As children mature, a conscious part of the self emerges, which Freud called the *ego*. The ego strives to mediate between the impulses of the id and the rules of society. Parents are the major carriers of societal requirements; they teach their children what is expected and hope that children will internalize, or come to believe for themselves, the values of their society. The internal regulator that develops in most people is the third personality part proposed by Freud, which he called the *superego*. The superego upholds the norms of society. Freud felt that healthy individuals learned how to accommodate the inherently conflicting desires of the id and the socially prescribed restrictions on expressing those desires. That accommodation represented successful socialization, in Freud's view.

Locus of Self-Definition

Another way of assessing the results of socialization is by probing an individual's self-conceptions. A method for doing this was developed by Kuhn and McPartland (1954). They asked individuals to give 20 answers to the question "Who am I?" You might try doing this now, before you read further. Simply list on a piece of paper 20 words or phrases that describe who you are. When this question was asked of college students in 1957, most of them (51 percent) gave answers such as "I am a student," "I am an American," and so forth (Hartley, 1968). This type of reply described the self in terms of social roles. In its extreme form, the conception of the self as comprised only of all the social roles an individual plays denies the existence of any self separate from the performance of social roles. This view leads to an "oversocialized" view of behavior. Fewer students (31 percent) described themselves in terms of personal qualities such as "I am a happy person," "humorous," or "shy." Fewer still (2 percent) used physical descriptions ("I am blond"), or very general and vague replies like "I am a living person" which did nothing to distinguish the respondent from anyone else (16 percent).

When the same question was asked of college students 12 years later, in 1969, the results were dramatically different. The majority of students (68 percent) described themselves in terms of personal qualities. Whereas earlier students were more likely to say "I am a college student," the later group more often replied with a personal statement, such as "I am a concerned person" (Zurcher, 1977). This trend is consistent with data from national samples that have been collected and analyzed by Florence Skelly (1978). This shift alerted Zurcher (1977) and Turner (1976) to the possibility that the self might have shifted its point of primary anchor from an institutional to an impulse base. In this sense, the institutional base refers to social roles. In all these cases, it is important to note that one's self-identity is rooted in both the impulse and the institutional realms. What Turner, Zurcher, and others are remarking on is the relative importance of one in relation to the other.

Turner suggests several social reasons for these changes in the primary anchor of self that have little to do with the personality or character of the individual replying. First, group life may have shifted from being organized around economic production to being organized around economic consumption. This shift might enhance the development of an impulse-oriented conception of self. Another reason may be that people are losing confidence in the institutions in society; thus they may be less willing to locate a primary sense of self in those institutions. As Turner underscores, these two possible explanations are only tentative at this point.

Some of the same social changes that have produced the shifting locus of self noted by Turner and others may have produced the necessity for a mutable, or flexible, self. The mutable self refers to a sense of self that varies widely, depending on the context. According to Zurcher (1977), self is not rooted in just one mode, whether impulse, institution, or some other anchor. Instead, the concept of self has multiple anchors, and people are becoming increasingly able to move from one to another. Zurcher describes a man, James, who is able to enjoy the physical mode while running; the institutional mode in his work as a stockbroker and his volunteer activities as a boys' baseball team coach; and his cosmic self while practicing Zen meditation. Ultimately, the conditions of intense social change in which we live may produce more and more individuals who have their sense of self rooted in several modes rather than primarily in one. Zurcher believes that the development of mutable selves is beneficial both to those developing them and to the society in which they live.

EFFECTIVE SOCIALIZATION

All societies socialize new generations reasonably effectively. The only exceptions seem to occur when a society loses its physical means of sustenance. This happened in this century to the Ik tribe in Uganda when it was moved off its hunting lands and could not survive physically. Ik culture and socialization practices broke down, and Ik people tended to ignore their own children (Turnbull, 1973). Within any particular society, different families are more or less effective in getting their children to feel and act deeply committed to the values of their group. Why and how do such differences occur?

Certain conditions have been identified as leading to a greater likelihood that individuals will come to resemble their elders. Caretakers who are warm, nurturing, and loving are more likely to reinforce good behavior in children. Also, the withdrawal of approval is seen as more serious by children when they feel an adult loves and approves of them. Hence such withdrawal of love represents a more serious punishment. A warm, nurturing relationship makes children want to identify with the adults who care for them. When children identify with parents or other significant adults, they seek to be like them; they "take on," or internalize, the behaviors and attitudes of those adults. Children also are more likely to follow their parents' advice or commands if they see their parents as having authority in other areas of their life. If outsiders defer to their parents, if their parents seem to be in charge of their own lives in reasonably successful ways, and in general seem to know what they are doing, that helps to persuade young people that parental authority should be taken seriously. Several observers have noted that the combination of power and love is particularly influential in a child's life (Goode, 1977).

Consistency in the application of rules also helps children to follow them and to see them as fair. If an action is treated in the same way every time and if different children are treated the same way for doing something right or wrong, children are more likely to get a clear idea of what is expected of them. Of course, most adults are not 100 percent consistent, so the question becomes one of the relative consistency of different adults. In the application of rewards, some inconsistency tends to reinforce behaviors more effectively than being rewarded for something every time. Called *intermittent reinforcement* by psychologists, this phenomenon has daily applications. If children are sometimes praised or rewarded for particularly good behavior, they are more likely to keep doing it in the hope that this time they will be rewarded or praised. As they get older, they can usually go longer and longer between reinforcements.

Participation in the rule-making process also elicits greater commitment to those rules than does the imposition of rules. Youngsters on a ball team who agree to certain rules of play are very involved in maintaining and defending those rules, much more so than if a teacher or other adult tells them what the rules are. Children and adults who are told what the rules are are more likely to accept the rules if they are told why it is important to follow them. Even quite young children can be persuaded to do something (or not to do it) if they can be led to see what the likely outcome is, and if they value or detest that consequence.

One of the most hotly debated issues in childrearing is the effect of punishment on children. "Spare the rod and spoil the child" is a maxim from an earlier era. Today, there is little evidence to support the use of corporal punishment on children, but it is not clear that there is less physical harm done to youngsters. One study found that more than 80 percent of American parents had physically punished their children within the past year, and more than 60 percent had done so at least once a week, on the average. Among college students, 46 percent had been beaten or physically assaulted by a parent during their senior year of high school (Straus et al., 1979).

How do spanking and other forms of physical punishment affect children? In a systematic review of relevant evidence, Gilmartin (1979) reports many negative effects and virtually no positive ones. Children who are frequently spanked tend to become highly resentful and distrustful of authority; they are more likely to develop low self-images; they are more likely to fight and be aggressive at school and elsewhere; and they are very apt to beat their own children. Even more serious, violent criminals are more likely to have been frequently beaten and otherwise cruelly punished as children than are law-abiding citizens. Plus, such criminals seldom received any warmth or respect from their parents or guardians. The authorities in their lives were cruel, callous, hostile, or indifferent to them (Gilmartin, 1979). To the degree that physical punishment makes children nervous and tense, it impedes their ability to learn effectively. Children who are relaxed but alert learn and think better than tense ones. If children misbehave frequently, that should be taken as a sign of unfulfilled and unrecognized needs (Gilmartin, 1979, p. 23). Harsh physical punishment increases the social distance between adult and child and reduces the chance that they will interact on a mutually enjoyable basis. To be most effective, socialization requires mutual trust and respect.

SOCIALIZATION THROUGH THE LIFE COURSE

There is no special age at which people stop growing and being influenced by the social world. Although many earlier theorists tended to see development as ending in childhood, we now view the processes of socialization as continuing throughout the life course, although perhaps at a somewhat slower rate as people get older. We continue to be exposed to new ideas, people, and situations that may require us to learn and grow further. One such development may involve learning an occupational identity, as Becker (1964) and others have noted. Medical students, for instance, gradually begin to acquire the identity of doctor as they go through the rigors, despairs, exhilarations, and doubts of medical school. The intense, lengthy, and concentrated training helps to solidify that identity, as do the rewards and status that accompany it. Socialization is something that occurs throughout life, as Erik Erikson proposed.

THEORIES OF HUMAN DEVELOPMENT: ERIKSON

Erik Erikson was one of the first to suggest that human development continues past infancy. In *Childhood and Society* (1950), Erikson outlined eight stages of human development and described how each stage is marked by a crucial issue for the self in relation to the external world. These stages and issues are presented in Table 6.2. In infancy, for example, the tension is between trust and mistrust, and in adolescence the pull is between identity and identity confusion. Indeed, Erikson coined the term "identity crisis."

RESOCIALIZATION

It is helpful to distinguish between socialization for something new and *resocialization*. The former refers to such experiences as going to law school or being an apprentice or a management trainee. The latter refers to the process of socializing people away from a group or activity in which they are involved. Resocialization is the

Table 6.2 Erikson's Eight Stages of Human Life

Age	Developmental Crisis	What Happens
1. Infancy	Basic trust vs. mistrust	Even their own bodies are unpredictable for infants. Warm and consistent parenting fosters infants' feelings of trust and predictability.
2. Early childhood	Autonomy vs. shame and doubt	Muscular growth allows child to experiment with holding on and letting go. Early efforts at autonomy need to be protected from shame and doubt. Children should not be made to feel that their bodies, wishes, or actions are evil or dirty. A sense of self-control with no loss of self-esteem leads to good will and pride.
3. 4 to 5 years	Initiative vs. guilt	If children gain autonomy, they begin to extend their control into the world around them. They initiate actions, are ready to work cooperatively with others to plan and make things, and are ready to emulate ideal models. When initiative is prohibited rather than guided, it may produce excessive guilt.

Table 6.2 Erikson's Eight Stages of Human Life (Continued)

Age	Developmental Crisis	What Happens
4. School age (6 to 12)	Industry vs. inferiority	The desire for active mastery in stage 3 gets channeled into winning recognition by working and producing things. The child learns skills, tasks, a sense of industry, and the capacity to put work ahead of play. In all cultures children receive some systematic instruction at this stage, although not always in schools. The danger is that the child will feel inadequate and inferior. Socially this is a critical stage, since learning to work is so central to adult life. If children feel their worth as learners depends on their race, family background, or dress rather than on their will to learn, their identity as competent persons will suffer. Feelings of inferiority may lead to pulling away from the world of work or to overattachment to it, as in the case of "workaholics."
5. Adolescence	Identity vs. role confusion	Rapid body growth combined with choosing an adult occupation places a heavy burden on a youth's sense of identity. One result may be to overidentify with the heroes of cliques and crowds, or with rituals, creeds, and programs (such as certain religious or political cults) that clearly define good and evil. "Falling in love" may indicate the desire to clarify one's identity by seeing a diffused image reflected back in the eyes of another. (This is why conversation plays such a large part in young love.) In their efforts to focus their own identity and stave off role confusion, young people may exclude those whose race, religion, background, dress, or speech is different from their own.
6. Young adulthood	Intimacy vs. isolation	Having gained a sense of identity, the young adult is eager to build emotional ties with others. Avoiding such experiences leads to deep isolation.
7. Middle age	Generativity vs. stagnation	Generativity is the effort to help the next generation develop, although it also includes productivity and creativity. In this respect, the older generation needs the younger one as much as the younger one needs it. If adults do not feel needed, they tend to stagnate.
8. Old age	Ego integrity vs. despair	Ego integrity is the ripening of the fruit of the prior seven stages. It occurs when people accept the life they have lived. Despair and fear of death arise when people are dissatisfied with the life they have led and feel the time is too short to start another life. To bring it full circle, Erikson believes that "healthy children will not fear life if their elders have integrity enough not to fear death" (Erikson, 1950, p. 269).

Table 6.3 Socialization for Something New and Resocialization (or Rehabilitation)

Socialization for Something New	Resocialization
CONTEXT	
1. Involves socialization *toward* something (a new status, position, skill, or reward).	1. Involves socialization *away from* something (drug use, overeating, alcoholism, criminal or delinquent behavior).
2. This goal is usually chosen and desired by the individual.	2. This goal may not be desired or chosen by individuals, who may prefer their present behaviors.
3. Sometimes people pay the cost themselves.	3. Individuals seldom pay the cost themselves.
PROCESS	
4. The process may be interesting and enjoyable.	4. The process may be unpleasant or unbearable, physically, psychically, or socially.
5. The connection between the process and the end is clear to the participant.	5. The connection between the process and any desired end may be completely unclear to the participant.
RESULT	
6. The process succeeds at a fairly high rate.	6. The process fails more often than it succeeds.

goal of programs for alcoholics, drug addicts, delinquents, or criminals. Comparing socialization for something new with resocialization in terms of key differences in their social contexts and processes shows why they tend to have different results (see Table 6.3). The former involves some new, usually attractive goal valued and freely chosen by the individual, rather than simply the giving up of something that may be desired by the individual. The process of socialization for something new may itself be interesting or enjoyable; most resocialization processes are not. It is possible that these differences account for the widely different success rates in the two types of socialization.

SOCIALIZATION FOR DEATH

In many ways socialization for death resembles resocialization. It is not a goal actively sought by most people; it may be seen mainly as socialization away from something (life). Socialization for death has been made more difficult in our society by the way death and dying are treated. Socialization involves interactions that result in socially constructed meanings. But if people have limited interactions in a particular realm, it is difficult to develop socially shared meanings and a sense of how to behave.

This lack is vividly apparent in the way our society deals with death and dying. For quite a while in our culture, death was virtually a taboo topic. People didn't die, they "passed away." Death was considered too morbid to discuss. It also became unacceptable for people to die at home. Instead of dying comfortably in their own surroundings, people were relegated to hospitals and old age homes. The medical profession's definition of death tended to prevail. Because doctors and nurses are trained to save lives, and consider themselves successful when they do, death may represent failure to them. For them to be actively involved in preparing people for death suggests somehow that they have given up hope for the sick person. Part of being prepared to be a physician ideally involves being trained to deal with, and ultimately to accept, death, as Coombs and Powers (1975) indicate.

The "denial of death" as Ernest Becker (1973) has called it, begins at an early age in our society. Children under a certain age are not allowed into most hospitals, so they cannot see a sick or dying person. Sometimes they are even told "grandma went away" rather than what really happened. Yet when children are in a home where death has struck, when they join in the talk, fear, and grief, they may gain comfort from the shared responsibility and mourning. Gradually they may come to view death as part of life (Kubler-Ross, 1969). Communities that provide opportunities for people to witness death, talk about death and dying, and collectively prepare for it seem to socialize people rather successfully for impending death (Hochschild, 1973; Marshall, 1975).

A few communities have hospices, which offer an alternative to hospital or home care for the terminally ill patient. In such an institution it is understood that no heroic efforts will be made to prolong the patient's life (such as resuscitations, use of respirators, or endless operations), although comfort therapy (for example, pain medications and nutrients) will be provided. The aim is to make such an institution as comfortable and pleasant, and as unlike a hospital, as possible. Knowing that doctors would treat patients as they themselves would want to be treated set to rest many of the worries and fears of people in one retirement community (Marshall, 1975, p. 1139).

Using a facility like a hospice requires, of course, that patients be told how sick they are. Controversy surrounds the issue of how much patients should be told about their condition. Increased discussion of death and dying is one of several social changes that are occurring and that may help people prepare for death. A number of books, including Kubler-Ross's *On Death and Dying* (1969) and Ernest Becker's *Denial of Death* (1973), as well as articles, have promoted public discussion of death.

After interviewing hundreds of terminally ill patients over a number of years, Kubler-Ross, for instance, began to discern a pattern in their behavior. She noticed that individuals move through five distinct stages in response to their impending deaths. The first stage is one of denial, even for patients who suspect the worst and fight to hear the truth. They may retreat into a self-imposed isolation at this point. Second, patients get angry—at their relatives for being healthy, at nurses for being young, at doctors for doing nothing to help, or at God. After the rage has been expressed, patients enter a third phase in which they try to bargain for their lives. They promise they will mend their ways if only they are allowed to live. In the fourth stage, patients grieve for themselves. They often get quite depressed at this point. Patients who get through this stage often face death more calmly for having been through it. The fifth and final stage, reached by only some, is the acceptance of death. These stages offer psychological preparation for death. But without the social opportunities to share such experiences, individuals may miss the chance to be socialized for death.

After someone has died, there is wide variation in how the event is handled. A few people have private, nearly secret, burials; others have socially shared customs for dealing with death and the ensuing grief. Irish and Italian Catholics have "wakes," or vigils over the corpse before a burial. Jews engage in "sitting shivah." Both practices allow time and space for families and friends to gather to share their mourning and reaffirm their support for one another. This provides people with some preparation for death, as well as help in their time of loss.

Socialization toward death is something most people experience only once. The broader socialization processes that it illustrates, however, occur much more frequently in such life-giving experiences as learning to be a student, joining a team, preparing for parenthood, becoming a citizen, becoming a grandparent, and so forth. The process of being socialized continues throughout life, and individuals continue to play an active part in that process.

Summary

1. In the last hundred years, the view of socialization has changed from one of civilizing unruly individuals with a focus on the end result of internalization to an interpretive reaction that stresses individual responsibility for creating the social world.

2. Wentworth's synthesis combines aspects from each of these views. He offers a framework for analyzing socialization in terms of contexts, processes, and results.

3. Context consists of biological, psychological, and social factors. People need food, water, warmth, and shelter. Certain behaviors such as grasping, rooting, and sucking are evident at birth, before they could have been socially reinforced.

4. The psychological context of socialization includes emotional states, the unconscious mind, and stages of cognitive development. Piaget envisioned mental development occurring in systematic, universal sequences, through a series of stages. Kohlberg suggests that moral development unfolds through analogous stages.

5. The social context of socialization is influenced by historical and social events, by the major participants in the situation, and by one's position in the social hierarchies of society. Families, other caregivers, schools and teachers, peers, communities, nations, and the mass media all interact with growing individuals.

6. The process of socialization is an interactive one. Infants with certain innate temperaments or traits interact with their social world, and indeed even influence it. The social world and social stimuli, in turn, influence individual development and growth.

7. Mead and Cooley suggest a conception of the self that incorporates individual drives, desires, and initiatives (the "I" portion) with an internalization of social values, norms, and ideas the individual has learned from others (the "me" part of the self). These two parts can interact, and individuals can make choices among the competing alternatives available to them.

8. Both young people and adults anticipate positions they will occupy and begin thinking and behaving in ways they see as appropriate for their futures.

9. Case studies of extreme social deprivation suggest that infants do not develop into walking, talking, social beings without experiencing social interaction.

10. Learning to use the language of one's group is proof that socialization occurs. Children cannot learn to speak by themselves. They need to learn not only the objects and actions words represent, but also the underlying rules of grammar and syntax that permit those words to be strung together in ways that are meaningful to others.

11. Freud offers a theory of the self as composed of id, ego, and superego. The ego mediates between the impulses of the id and the demands of society.

12. The terms people use to describe their "selves" have shifted in recent decades away from social roles toward personal traits.

13. Effective socialization appears to depend on a reasonably secure food supply, caregivers who love and interact with infants and children, the perceived reasonableness of what is expected, and the encouragement of favored behaviors rather than excessive punishment of undesirable behavior.

14. Socialization continues through one's lifetime, as adults learn new roles. Erikson's theories of adult development reflect the interplay between psychological processes and social experiences.

15. Resocialization differs in a number of significant ways from socialization for something new. Such differences may explain why resocialization seems to have only limited results.

16. Socialization for death resembles resocialization in certain respects. Moreover, in the United States death is structured in ways that make it difficult for people to develop socially shared meanings and behaviors in relation to death. Several social changes including increased discussion and the existence of hospices contribute to successful socialization for death. Socialization toward death illustrates the processes of socialization that occur in life-giving experiences such as preparing for parenthood.

Key Terms

anticipatory socialization
behavior modification
behaviorism
cognitive development
concrete operations stage
conditioning
ego
formal operations stage
generalized other
id
intermittent reinforcement
internalization
learning theory
life course
looking-glass self
mass media
peer group
preoperational stage
resocialization
sensorimotor stage
social learning theory
socialization
superego

MELHA
HADJI
MELHA
HADJI
MELHA
HADJI
MELHA
MELHA
HADJI

Chapter 7

Groups and Organizations

Consider the people in *Hill Street Blues,* the television series. Part of this show's popularity is undoubtedly due to the engaging people in it. But another appealing feature is the fact that they are part of a group in which individuals know and care about each other. Almost everyone belongs to one or more groups and likes the sense of belonging that group membership gives. This chapter explores features of social groups and organizations of various kinds. *Groups* are collections of people who know each other and interact on the basis of common expectations. As a result, they tend to feel a sense of belonging and shared identity. Groups differ from *aggregates,* which are collections of people who do not know each other and who feel no sense of belonging together.

GROUPS

PRIMARY AND SECONDARY GROUPS

Primary groups are the first and most important groups to which people belong. They include families and close friends. Primary groups are characterized by frequent face-to-face interaction, by the commitment and emotional ties members feel for each other, and by their relative permanence. These early and usually rather intense group ties are critically important for the development of an individual's sense of identity.

In the nuclear family primary group, members see one another often; they remain members of the group even when some of them have moved away; they are intimate with one another; and they are committed to one another and to the group aside from any common tasks they may be trying to accomplish. Elementary school classmates, tentmates at an overnight camp, or members of a youth gang may all form primary groups. Like families, these groups have the capacity to offer affection and support, as well as inflict pain and anguish.

People often find it difficult to leave their primary groups. Soldiers, children, or tribespeople are not usually free to leave their platoons, families, or tribes. It may be difficult emotionally or legally for primary group members to break away. Because of bonds with primary groups and because so many parts of people's lives are involved with them, they usually have a profound influence on feelings, values, and behaviors. People may dislike and reject what they experience in primary groups or love it and seek to maintain it, but it is unlikely that they will be indifferent.

Secondary groups differ from primary groups in that they are less intimate. In addition, they tend to be more temporary, to have less face-to-face interaction, and to be bound more by common tasks. Your classmates in a large lecture course may become a secondary group. You probably do not see the other members every day; the group will probably disband when the

Most people belong to a primary group such as their family. Not everyone's family is as large as the extended family that turned out for this family reunion.

course is completed; and you are unlikely to get to know one another in a wide variety of situations the way you do family members. You share a common task, but you may have little else in common.

People who work together may form secondary groups, or they may become more involved with their co-workers and form primary groups. For most people, college alumni groups, union or professional associations, or consumer cooperatives are examples of secondary groups. Some of the differences between primary and secondary groups are summarized in Table 7.1. Groups often contain a mixture of primary and second-

Table 7.1 **Major Differences Between Primary and Secondary Groups**

	Primary Groups	Secondary Groups
Size	Relatively small (usually 10 or fewer).	May be several dozen or more
Interaction	Face-to-face.	Often indirect.
Type of involvement	Engages whole personality of individual members.	Engages only a limited part of a member's personality. Relates to a single status.
Social relations	Emotional.	Instrumental (that is, goal-oriented).
Frequency of interaction	Frequent.	Less frequent.
Length of relationship	Long-term.	Short-term.

Group identity may be enhanced by shared activities and special forms of dress.

ary group characteristics. Whether they act more like one or the other may depend on the surrounding social conditions. In a crisis such as a flood, blackout, or bombing raid, secondary groups tend to become more like primary groups. But once the external crisis lessens, they tend to drift back into secondary groups.

DISTINGUISHING FEATURES OF GROUPS

Although different in important ways, the members of primary and secondary groups share one or more social statuses in common. For instance, they are members of the same kinship group; they are neighbors; they belong to the same social class; they have the same racial or ethnic background; or they share a common activity. A common social status generates shared values and goals among the members of a group. Shared values and goals tend to emerge from frequent interaction. The members of a basketball team, for example, all share the status of being a team member. They share the goal of trying to win games. The more they interact, especially in the face of a common challenge, the more they feel like a team. This point represents the sense of common identity that distinguishes a group from an aggregate, a collection of unrelated individuals. It does not always work this way, however. Sometimes the more the individuals in an aggregate interact, the more aware they become of their different interests and values. In such a case, they may never form a group.

Group identity is enhanced by a clear sense of group boundaries that delineate members from nonmembers. Often this takes the form of a special form of dress (a football uniform, for example), or a badge (safety patrol), or a pin (as in a fraternity or sorority). Some fraternal groups develop special handshakes or greetings to separate members from nonmembers. Some groups require members to cut their social ties with nonmembers and physically to isolate themselves from others as well (for example, the Unification Church or the Jonestown cult).

When group members identify with the group as a whole, there is a tendency for them to see the world in terms of "in group" members and "out group" people, or "we" and "they." They may try to claim that all the "right" people belong to one clique or club and set themselves up as social judges to decide who can and cannot become a member. Such processes add the dimension of social ranking to group membership. Sometimes outgroup members may feel excluded and hurt by such boundaries. On a campus dominated by fraternities and sororities, for example, individuals may feel devastated if they are not pledged by the house they prefer. In other cases individuals do not care because they happily belong to a group of their own. The New Year's Day Rose Parade in Pasadena, California, for instance, is planned by a socially exclusive committee. Someone from Chicago, however, might not care at all about being on that committee.

Sociologists coined the term *reference group* for groups whose standards and opinions are important to us. We compare ourselves to members of reference groups and use them as yardsticks for our own attitudes and behaviors. A positive reference group, like a group of popular, smart athletes on campus, shows valued behaviors and attitudes. A negative reference group illustrates what people do not want to imitate—for instance, a group of drunken bums. Reference groups affect people as they assess themselves and their life situations. Factory workers who have been promoted may compare themselves with their friends who have not been promoted and feel satisfied, whereas junior managers (even if they have been promoted) may compare themselves with managers above them and be dissatisfied.

It is not always clear why individuals adopt one rather than another group as a reference group. Very often individuals belong to a number of groups that may have competing values and goals, thereby producing potential conflicts for the individual. A Catholic woman, for instance, may feel conflict over the issue of abortion—torn between her religious teachings and her concerns for independence and responsible parenthood. If she belongs to both a woman's group and a religious group, she may gradually be drawn more to the one whose view she favors. Although sociologists cannot always say why an individual adopts one rather than another reference group, they do know something about what features of groups influence individuals. One of the most important of these is group size.

THE EFFECTS OF GROUP SIZE

Group size directly affects the number and type of interactions that can occur within a group. For each person added to a group, the number of possible relationships in the group increases dramatically. With four people there are 25 possible relationships among individuals and various subgroups. With six people there are 301 possible relationships (Kephart, 1950). As the size of a group increases, the satisfaction of each individual member with the group tends to decrease. Dissatisfaction may grow because each member has less chance to participate. When groups increase from 5 to 12 members, they are less likely to reach consensus based on group discussion (Hare, 1976). While it is hard to get a family of 5 to agree on something, it is much more difficult to get a family of 12 to agree.

Dyads

Two-person groups, or *dyads,* have certain unique characteristics that are not shared by groups of other sizes. Consider the dyad of a couple. Either member can destroy the pair by withdrawing (Simmel, 1950). Because the dyad depends totally on the participation of both members, concern about its existence is accompanied by concern about its termination more than in groups of any other size. Larger groups can more easily survive the loss of one or more members without causing the group to dissolve. Even disagreement threatens the unity of a dyad. There is no majority in a dyad to which a member can appeal for fairness or justice. The only group standards of behavior that are binding are those shared by both members. Many of these unique features of a dyad change with the addition of even one member. A marital relationship changes, for instance, with the birth of a baby.

Triads

When a third person is added to a dyad, each individual in the newly formed group, called a *triad,* can act as an intermediary between the other two members. As such, the third one can serve to unite the two or to separate them. There is always the possibility that two of the three members of the triad will consider the third an intruder. A close union of two is generally disrupted by a spectator (Simmel, 1950). At the same time, the third person can mediate disputes between the other two. Triads, or triangles as they are popularly termed, contain the potential for the pairing of two members against one. Unless one member is consistently more powerful than the other two, coalitions are possible between A and B against C, between A and C against B, and between B and C against A. Triads are unstable because one of the members of the pair may join the single person. Two roommates out of three, for example, may be in agreement over how neat to keep their room, but one of them may unite with the lone person over what television show they want to watch. Such shifting usually prevents one member from being permanently excluded, which might lead him or her to leave the group altogether.

The power of these coalitions should not be underestimated. Even in the rather unbalanced power relation of a parent and two young children, a firm coalition between the children can diminish parental power. This coalition is most pronounced in the case of identical twins who have genetic and social bonds. Twin observers note a phenomenon called "twin solidarity," which takes the form of shared secrets, behaviors, and sometimes even language. An individual twin's first loyalty is often to the other twin rather than to a parent or older sibling. Coalitions between identical twins are difficult to separate.

In sum, dyads experience certain tensions no other groups do, and triads have a shifting nature because of the structural effects of group size. These features of group size operate independently of the personalities of the group members. In groups that exceed three people, two other features of size are worth noting: odd or even numbers and group proportions. Whether there is an odd or an even number of people in a group makes a difference, particularly if the group needs to reach a decision. In groups with an even number of people there is always the possibility of a deadlock, where the same number of people will support and oppose some idea or plan. Groups with an odd number contain the potential for one member to break a tie. Groups that are mandated to come up with decisions, such as the Supreme Court of the United States, have an odd number of members or a procedure for breaking ties.

THE EFFECTS OF GROUP PROPORTIONS

The relative proportion of different individuals in a group is a structural feature that affects what happens in them. A homogeneous group, for example, where most members are adults rather than children, males rather than females, or blacks rather than whites, differs from a group with a more balanced mixture of statuses. While Simmel's analysis of dyads and triads refers to absolute numbers, Kanter alerts us to the importance of relative proportions in a group. Suppose we symbolize people in the majority as Xs (whether they be males, whites, adults, or whatever), while those in the minority are signified by Os. Four types of groups can be formed, as shown in Figure 7.1. Homogeneous groups consist only of Xs. In skewed groups, Xs predominate. In tilted groups, with about one third Os to two thirds Xs, the minority members begin to be perceived as individuals; they can

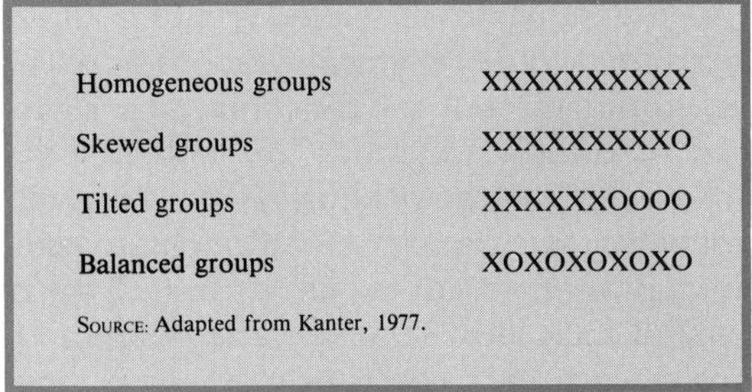

Homogeneous groups	XXXXXXXXXX
Skewed groups	XXXXXXXXXO
Tilted groups	XXXXXXOOOO
Balanced groups	XOXOXOXOXO

Source: Adapted from Kanter, 1977.

Figure 7.1 Four Types of Proportions That Occur in Groups

form alliances with other members, and their type will be noticed and distinguished from the majority type. Finally, when Xs and Os are about even, groups become balanced. The balance is reflected in the interests and activities (the culture) and the interaction of the group (Kanter, 1977).

Skewed groups are typical of many professional and organizational groups today that have recently begun to include women or ethnic minorities as "token" representatives of their social type. Because tokens are proportionately rare, they face certain unique problems of visibility, contrast, and fitting in (Kanter, 1977). Although tokens sometimes get ignored by the majority, more often their minority status makes them stand out. It is impossible, for instance, for tokens to keep a "low profile." They always get noticed. Being in the limelight can aid recognition and promotion, but it can also advertise a token's early mistakes. The presence of tokens may lead dominant members to exaggerate their culture, as in heightened sexual innuendos around token women. Tokens may also be stereotyped by dominant members. Women in a largely male organization, for example, tend to be categorized into one of the following familiar roles: mother, seductress, pet, or "iron maiden." Each of these stereotypes may make it difficult for token members of the group to exhibit fully appropriate behavior in their situation (Kanter, 1977).

GROUP PRESSURES AND CONFORMITY

Group pressures by a majority on a minority were observed by Asch (1952) in his famous experiments on conformity and resistance to group pressure. Asch called together groups of college students (usually 7 to 9 students) for what he called an experiment in visual perception. The group was shown two pictures of lines (see Figure 7.2). One card had a single standard line (line A) on it, the other had three lines—one the same length as the standard one, one longer, and one shorter. The experimenter went around the group, asking each individual to say which line was the same as line A. It sounds easy enough. There was unanimous agreement by the group the first two times the experimenter showed line A. But the third time, seven out of eight students called out line 2 as the one that matched line A. These seven students were in secret partnership with the experimenter, and they all spoke before the real subject of the experiment did.

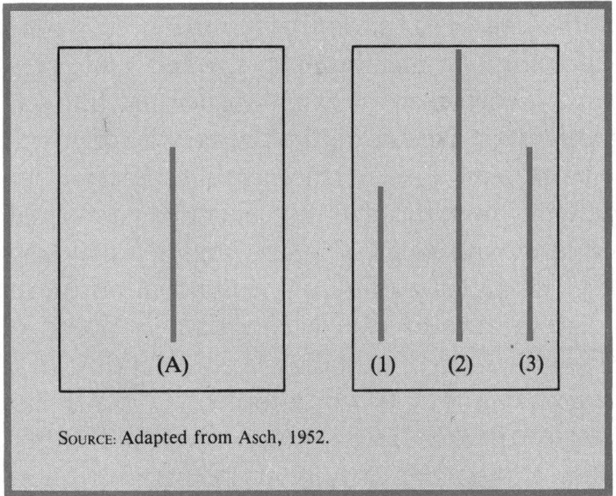

Source: Adapted from Asch, 1952.

Figure 7.2 Lines Shown to Subjects in the Asch Experiments *The subject was shown line A, and asked whether line 1, 2, or 3 most closely matched it in length. The secret partners of the experimenter chose line 2, which is longer, rather than line 3, which is the same length.*

How did individuals react to having direct evidence from their senses challenged by the other members of an experimental group? They got very upset. They wondered if their eyes were going bad, or the light was wrong, or if they were losing their minds. About a third of the subjects conformed to the opinion of the majority. Most of these individuals yielded to group pressures even though the group contradicted the evidence of their senses. Part of this *conformity* (that is, going along with the norms or behaviors of a group) occurred because the individuals represented a minority of one against a unanimous majority, a situation comparable to that of the single token analyzed by Kanter. Asch's experiments yield a number of other important results. It is notable that two-thirds of the subjects did not conform, although even those who were confident of their own perceptions still yearned to be in agreement with the group. When group size was reduced to just one other person (making a dyad), subjects almost never went along with the incorrect call of the other person, reinforcing Simmel's distinction between dyads and other groups.

In another variation, Asch introduced an additional group member who selected a different but also incorrect line as the proper match. Even though that person did not agree with the subject in the experiment, the fact that someone else differed from the majority liberated individual subjects, who then felt free to "call it as they saw it." The presence of even one noncomformist in a group breaks the chains of groupthink. *Groupthink* refers to the tendency of individuals to go along with the ideas or actions of a group because they feel a strong loyalty to it and do not want to disagree or raise uncomfortable questions. When President Kennedy and his advisors were considering the Bay of Pigs invasion of Cuba in 1961, for example, no one among the advisors opposed the plan publicly, although several people had strong personal reservations (Janis, 1973; Janis and Mann, 1979). No one wanted to appear weak or disloyal in front of the others.

One solution would be for groups to have individuals write down their questions or reservations anonymously and then bring them all up for discussion in the group. The work of Asch, Janis, and Mann shows how important it is for groups and societies to protect the rights of people who disagree with prevailing views. Even if many of their ideas seem silly, the presence of such independent thinkers frees other members of a group or a society to say what they think, thereby increasing the creative possibilities available to the group.

GROUP DYNAMICS

Division of Labor

Groups vary in terms of how much of their time they spend on task behavior—that is, behavior devoted to accomplishing a particular goal, and on socioemotional behavior—that is, managing tensions, building friendships within the group, or being mutually supportive. The roles played by individual members in a group also vary, with some serving more as socioemotional leaders and others more as task-oriented leaders. Certain individuals make the jokes, tease the other members of a group, and mediate conflicts between group members. They are called *expressive leaders* and they help to maintain the stability of the group. Others, called *instrumental leaders,* try to keep the group's attention and effort directed to the task at hand. They may say such things as "Let's see, what we have to do here is this," or "What do you think would be the best way for us to accomplish this?" Considerable research on group life suggests that both kinds of members and activities are needed in groups if they are to operate successfully.

Early work on the division of labor in small groups suggested that instrumental and expressive leadership roles are not usually played by the same person in a small group (Bales and Slater, 1953), in a family (Zeldich, 1955), or in a complex organization (Etzioni, 1965). However, other researchers concluded that expressive and instrumental roles need not be incompatible and may be integrated in the same person (Lewis, 1972). The possibility that expressive and instrumental roles could be played by one person is supported by a study done by Rees and Segal (1980) of two college football teams. They found that some players scored high on both types of leadership, suggesting that leadership roles may be integrated in the same person, at least in some groups. Groups differ with respect to how much attention they devote to task versus expressive activities. One place these differences occur is during decision-making.

Group Decision-Making

Recall a group decision you have observed, perhaps a family meeting to decide how to share the housekeeping tasks or a club meeting you attended. Every group tends to move through four stages as its members work to arrive at a decision (Bales and Strodbeck, 1951). First, members get oriented to the problem at hand. They gather information, share ideas, and suggest possible solutions. Second, the group debates and weighs available information and suggestions. Tension and conflict increase as a group approaches the third stage, which is actually making a decision about what to do. Different interests, values, goals, and emotional responses tend to surface at this point. After a decision has been made, the group becomes more relaxed again, members begin to joke and laugh, and group solidarity reappears, if only because members have shared a common trial and made a joint decision. The next time you decide something in a group, see if these four stages occur. Knowing that they are likely to happen can make you less anxious as a group moves into the phase characterized by conflict and anxiety.

Even if a group has no formal leader, certain individuals tend to assume leadership roles as groups work to arrive at a decision. As exchange theorist George Homans noted in his classic study *The Human Group* (1950), leaders tend to conform most closely to shared standards of behavior in a group. Conformity is related to greater status in a group. Leaders interact more with other group members than do people of lower status. Interaction, in turn, contributes to friendship between the members of a group, just as friendship tends to be associated with more interaction. Those who participate in pleasurable communal activities with group members tend to become committed to the group and its values. Competition or conflict between one group and another tends to enhance the cohesiveness of a group, as Simmel noted.

Commitment to a Group

Everyone who cares about and benefits from the existence of a group is concerned about members being committed to it. This includes ministers, business leaders and managers, scout leaders, founders of communes, club owners, and school administrators, for instance. Commitment of group members seems to depend on a balance between what group members want to give to a group and what the group expects or requires of them. Committed group members are loyal and involved; they have a sense of belonging and a feeling that the group is an extension of themselves and they are an extension of the group (Kanter, 1972). According to Kanter, "*Commitment* thus refers to the willingness of people to do what will help maintain the group because it provides what they need" (1972, 66). Committed athletic team members will help each other on and off the playing field. Many decisions will be made based on what is in the team's best interest, rather than just an individual's interest. Such commitment invariably strengthens a group and often enhances its task performance. Obviously, groups vary widely in terms of the commitment of their members.

Understanding some of these dynamics of group life puts us in a better position to grapple with a major feature of the social world today—life in organizations.

Some groups require considerably more commitment and conformity of their members than do other groups. These members of a Krishna commune in Virginia are engaged in a 5 A.M. prayer session. Everything about the situation suggests a high degree of commitment and conformity. Sociologists try to understand the social conditions which lead to greater or lesser commitment to a group by its members.

ORGANIZATIONS

Organizations are social groups deliberately formed to pursue certain goals. How many organizations have you encountered? You were probably born in a hospital; your birth certificate is on file in the records of the community where you were born; you have been inoculated in ways determined by health organizations; you go to school; you may have worked in an organization; you probably have applied for a driver's license; and you may belong to a religious organization. You can undoubtedly add to this list of encounters with formal organizations. In truth, it is becoming ever more difficult to do anything in our society without meeting one or more organizations. Beginning about 1875, the United States started becoming an "organization society," marked by large-scale bureaucracies in every social area (Presthus, 1962).

Three features of organizations have profound implications for our lives. First, fewer and fewer jobs exist outside of organizations. The number of self-employed workers continues to decline in the United States, having dropped from 11 percent of employed male workers in 1965 to 9 percent in 1981 (U.S. Bureau of the

Census, 1982a, p. 385). For females, the rate of self-employment has always been low. In the United States in 1965, only 5.8 percent of women were self-employed, and by 1981 only 5 percent were. These statistics mean that fewer people can work for themselves today than in the past. Second, organizational units are becoming ever larger. The number of government employees, for example, has grown from 2.6 million in 1920 to 16.3 million in 1980, mostly at the state and local levels (Serrin, 1981, pp. 1, 44). Third, these ever-larger organizations control a major share of the material and social resources of society. In 1980, the 200 largest manufacturing corporations owned 60 percent of all corporate assets, compared to 48 percent in 1950 (U.S. Bureau of the Census, 1981, p. 541). These figures point to one of the dominant trends in our society today—namely, the increasing centralization and concentration of power and resources in huge organizations. In fact, we are moving from a society that has organizations in it to an "organizational society" (Perrow, 1979a). It is virtually impossible to live in our society without being affected, on a daily basis, by large and powerful organizations. Therefore, it is imperative to know something about how these organizations are structured, how they work, and how they affect people.

Why has the importance of organizations grown so much in modern industrial society? Modern organizations did not exist in hunting and gathering societies. They began to take shape in horticultural societies. Organizations became important in agrarian societies because of the need to manage complex irrigation systems. Weber saw the growth of bureaucratic organizations as part of the growth of rationality in Western civilization. Marxian analysts stress the growth of bureaucratic organizations as useful instruments of control over an economic or agricultural surplus.

Huge gains in industrial and agricultural productivity in less than a century show the effectiveness of organizing work in a rational way. Between 1890 and 1960, for example, national output per worker increased nearly 200 percent in the United States and about 750 percent in Japan (*Encyclopaedia Britannica,* 1977, vol. 15, p. 30). Many organizational innovations introduced in the name of rationality and effectiveness, however, seem to serve mainly to centralize knowledge, control, and profits in the hands of managers and owners, as Marxians suggest. Whatever the reasons for the growth of modern organizations, their importance in our lives today is indisputable.

In this section we examine organizations from a number of vantage points. First, we consider types of social action and forms of organization, an approach that enables us to compare bureaucratic organizations, such as government agencies, corporations, or universities, with democratic-collective organizations, such as a legal aid or health clinic. Second, we examine bureaucratic organizations, including Weber's classic view of them, problems in them, additional features, and comparisons between bureaucratic and democratic-collective organizations. Third, we consider the tasks shared by all organizations, bureaucratic and democratic-collective.

TYPES OF SOCIAL ACTION AND MODES OF ORGANIZATION

Max Weber felt that all social action could be viewed in one of four ways, as:

1. Traditional action
2. Emotionally based action
3. Rational goal-oriented action
4. Value-oriented action

As Weber saw it, the first three forms of action correspond to particular types of authority, as shown in Table 7.2. The basis for authority could be traditional or affectual, charismatic, or rational-legal, depending on the type of action in which it was rooted. Specific authority types are often related to organizational types. Thus social action and authority based on tradition, loyalty,

Table 7.2 **Ideal Types of Social Action, Authority, and Organization**

Type of Social Action	Type of Authority	Type of Organization	Examples
Traditional or affectual	Traditional	Patrimonial administration	Feudal society
Value-oriented	Charismatic	Band of followers, collectivist-democratic	Religious cults, some political campaigns, free schools, free medical or legal clinics, media collectives, food co-ops
Instrumental-rational	Rational-legal	Formal bureaucracy	Army, government agencies, universities, hospitals, corporations

and duty are likely to coexist with a patrimonial administration, where positions are inherited from ancestors and the social order is maintained by the sanctity of tradition and loyalty. Many agrarian societies illustrate this type of social organization.

Traditional society was most likely to be challenged by *charismatic leaders* who appealed to the emotions of their followers through their personal and usually prophetic characteristics. *Charisma* refers to the exceptional mystical quality of personality that others see in a person. The organizational form of charismatic movements was based on loyalty to the individual leader; such groups have great difficulty staying organized when the leader dies. This form of action and organization occurs in religious cults with a strong prophetic leader or in some political movements. Gandhi, for example, was a charismatic religious and political leader for many East Indians seeking independence from Great Britain.

Value-oriented social action is marked by a belief in the value of an action for its own sake, regardless of its chances for success (Weber, 1925b, p. 24). Such action occurs when people act according to their convictions rather than primarily to achieve some aim. This action is typical of many rebels and revolutionaries. For example, Afghan soldiers who continued to fight the Soviet army after the invasion in 1980, members of the Irish Republican Army (IRA), Japanese pilots on suicide missions during World War II, and American Indians trying to retain their homelands all acted on the basis of deeply felt values.

Instrumental-rational action is based on authority believed to have been established in a way that is recognized as legal. Authority resides in the office rather than the person, so that who fills a position is less important than the rights and duties that accompany the office. Called a *bureaucracy,* this form of organization appears in most modern armies, government agencies, business corporations, and hospitals. The functions of the organization can presumably continue even when the occupants of various positions change. Thus, regularized, relatively predictable forms of action are possible.

BUREAUCRATIC ORGANIZATIONS

Formal organization refers to a consciously organized group aimed at pursuing certain values and goals. The most prevalent form of formal organization in modern society is the bureaucracy. Traditional, rational, and value-oriented action are all associated with types of formal organization. But in modern industrial society, the bureaucratic type like the telephone company or the Pentagon is the most common. Since individuals and society are strongly affected by bureaucratic organizations, we need to understand how they work. The ideas of Max Weber are helpful in this regard.

Max Weber was one of the first sociologists to study large bureaucratic organizations. He realized that bureaucracy was an efficient way to coordinate the efforts of large numbers of people but that it often operated without regard for the individuals involved.

Weber's View of Bureaucracy

Weber worked as a civil servant in the German government around the turn of the century, so he had a chance for firsthand observations of bureaucracy. He saw both strengths and limitations in bureaucratic organization. He believed that bureaucracy was technically superior to other forms of organization for coordinating the efforts of large numbers of people working toward specific goals. Bureaucratic organizations could do things with greater precision, speed, and financial efficiency than organizations based on tradition or charisma. Bureaucratic organizations were intended to operate "objectively"—that is, "according to calculable rules and without regard for persons," said Weber (1925a). This meant they sometimes had negative, dehumanizing effects on the individuals who worked in them. Indeed, Weber wondered how to "keep a portion of mankind free from this parcelling out of the soul" demanded by the bureaucratic way of life. Like most social scientists who study bureaucratic organizations, he was aware of their two-sided nature.

Weber developed an "ideal type" or model of bureaucracy. (An ideal type is a mental model of something in terms of its essential traits.) Actual organizations can be compared with this model. To him, there were six essential features to the model.

Division of Labor and Specialization. The total work to be done in an organization is divided up into smaller tasks. Each position is responsible for a limited number of these tasks and has no authority for doing other ones. Thus positions are highly specialized. In the university, for instance, professors do not change lightbulbs and the maintenance staff does not teach classes.

Hierarchy. Positions in a bureaucracy are arranged in order of rank—that is, in a hierarchy. People in lower positions are supervised by those in higher positions. Orders and directives are issued from the top down, through a specified chain of command. Those at the top have greater authority over more people and more activities than do those further down. Hierarchy is most visible in the military, but it also appears in corporations and government agencies. Formal authority is limited, however. Corporate bosses can say what time employees must be at work, but they cannot say what time they should go to bed.

Rules and Regulations. Formal, written rules govern almost all activities in a bureaucracy. Decisions are based on these rules. Explicit procedures are spelled out for all actions. As a result, the organization operates in an orderly, stable, and predictable way. For instance, once you have mastered college registration procedures, you can probably assume they will continue about the same way in the future.

Impartiality. Rules, procedures, and decisions are to be carried out in a rational, nonemotional way, without regard to personal feelings. Clients are viewed as cases; subordinates are thought of as replaceable. Relatives and friends are barred from being considered as job applicants or are treated the same way as everyone else.

Technical Qualifications. Occupants of positions are trained specialists. The more complicated the work becomes, the more it demands the "personally detached and strictly 'objective' expert" (Weber, 1925a). Advancement is based on merit and seniority. This ensures that competent people fill organizational positions and helps staff morale.

Records and Files. Bureaucratic organizations rely heavily on records and files. Originally kept in written form by scribes and then by typists and clerks, they are increasingly stored in computers. One of the transformations of modern bureaucracies has occurred in the way that records sometimes come to be regarded as "official secrets" of the organization. One recent legislative thrust in the United States has been to

"Each employee can have one plant or one poster. But they can't have both."

SOURCE: Drawing by Victor, © 1982, *The New Yorker Magazine, Inc.*

make some of these organizational records available to individuals through the Freedom of Information Act and credit information laws.

Although useful in suggesting what Weber thought bureaucratic organizations should be like, his "ideal type" is not reflected perfectly in the world of real organizations. Weber's analysis of bureaucracy looked basically at its positive functions for increasing the efficiency and goal attainment of the organization. Weber was well aware of the negative features of bureaucracy, but he did not analyze them as systematically as others have since.

Problems in Bureaucracies

Later observers of bureaucracy have noted a number of their negative features. These include incompetence, waste, and ritualism.

The Peter Principle. The *Peter principle* refers to a phenomenon observed by Laurence Peter (1969). Employees who perform well at one position may be promoted to a higher position. If they perform well in that position, they may be promoted again. They may continue to be promoted until they reach what Peter calls their "level of incompetence"—that is, a position in which they are unable to perform well. As a result, he feels many higher positions in organizations are increasingly staffed by incompetents.

Organizational Waste. Because there are many layers in a bureaucratic hierarchy, those at the top may be quite unaware of the ideas, problems, and feelings of those down below. *Organizational waste* of ideas, expertise, money, or materials may contribute to inefficiencies and mistakes. Other wasteful tendencies in bureaucracies were noted by C. Northcote Parkinson, who observed that work expands to fill the available time, a saying that has come to be called *Parkinson's law.* Someone whose job is answering letters may be able to write 20 good letters in a day. But if he or she has only three letters to write, Parkinson's law suggests that those three will take the whole day. Parkinson also noticed that having one or more assistants is a mark of organizational prestige. Officials gradually add assistants who need supervision. The assistants fill out forms and write memos and reports others must check on and file. Parkinson argues that much of this effort is wasteful.

Ritualism. *Organizational ritualism* occurs when people follow the rules and regulations in a bureaucracy so closely that they forget the purpose of the rules and regulations. Merton describes what he calls the "bureaucratic personality," a person who enforces the rules rigidly, perhaps out of excessive caution (1957). People more concerned with the letter of the law than its spirit can slow things down a great deal in an organization. For example, someone's doctoral diploma was delayed three weeks by one university until the clips holding the dissertation were replaced with a different binding.

Additional Features of Organizations

Additional significant organizational characteristics include the problem of oligarchy, the existence of informal as well as formal organizational structures, the relations between organizations and their environments, and the views of human nature associated with various views of organizations. All these features provide useful sociological insights for people who deal with or work in organizations.

Oligarchy. *Oligarchy* refers to the rule of the many by the few. As coined by Robert Michels (1911), the "iron law of oligarchy" states that in any organization, power tends to become concentrated in the hands of a small group of leaders, as those with the most time, energy, and ability take over. Once there, their power and prestige grow, since they have access to information and resources unavailable to nonleaders. This happens even in supposedly democratic organizations like political clubs or labor unions. The main interest of these leaders becomes one of preserving the organization and their own leadership in it rather than the interests of the members. Members feel they know less and so they look to the leaders for direction. The result of these tendencies is to make oligarchy inevitable.

Although Michels is correct that power in organizations is greater at the top of the hierarchy, there are usually some legal or political checks on how that power is exercised. There may be several groups contending for leadership in an organization, which may at least lead to a "circulation of elites." The United States Congress, for example, places considerable power in the hands of committee chairs and senior members. The defeat of the Democrats in the 1980 election resulted in some "circulation of elites" as members of the winning party took over those leadership positions.

Informal Structures within Formal Organizations. There are informal as well as formal structures of power in organizations. Bureaucratic organizations provide specific job descriptions and indicate lines of authority (often formalized in an organizational chart showing who reports to whom). But once people fill formal organizational slots, they form friendships and find ways to bend or ignore the rules; they develop personal ways of solving problems; and they cut through bureaucratic "red tape" when possible. These informal groups may also affect productivity.

In a classic study of men wiring telephone switchboards at a Western Electric Company plant in Chicago, Roethlisberger and Dickson (1939) found that whatever incentives the company offered to encourage productivity, the men had their own notion of what was a fair day's work: wiring about 6000 terminals. Anyone who did less was a "chiseler," but anyone who did more was condemned as a "ratebuster," "slave," or "speed-king." The latter were semi-playfully punched in the arm by the other workers, who felt they might cause layoffs or higher work requirements for the whole group. Informal rules affected more than productivity. To keep from getting too bored, the men sometimes did each other's tasks, although doing so was against company rules. They also worked very quickly in the morning but much more slowly in the afternoon. No members "squealed" to management about the shortcomings of any other group member. In these ways, the informal structure of the group operated independently of the formal organizational structure.

All formal organizations have informal lines of power, influence, and communication (the "grapevine"), and informal norms about missing work, tardiness, acceptable amounts of overtime, and practical divisions of labor. Functioning in a large organization, then, requires people to understand both the formal and the informal structures and rules. And just as there is an informal structure, there is also a context within which organizations must function.

Organizational Contexts. One way of looking at organizational contexts is to distinguish between open and closed systems. An *open system* depends on the environment to provide nourishment, raw materials, or resources, as well as to absorb products or wastes. There are degrees of openness in a system. A forest fire, for instance, is a fairly open system, being strongly affected in its course by available air, fuel, and water. A mechanical clock, on the other hand, is a relatively closed system once its spring has been wound. An isolated family or tribe living on an island without contact with other humans is in a relatively closed system, while a family that entertains foreign visitors is much more open. A system may accept passively what its environment offers (as in the case of the fire), or it may work actively to control its environment. Like humans, organizations that are better able to control their environments stand a better chance of surviving and thriving. For this reason, some business organizations become involved in the political affairs of the country in which they operate.

Rather than assuming just one kind of organizational structure, Lawrence and Lorsch

(1967) asked what kind of organizational structure is most useful for dealing with different environmental conditions. They suggested that flexible, humanistic structures may be best for dealing with highly uncertain tasks and environments. Uncertainty cannot be handled well through rigid rules.

In addition to varying their internal structure, organizations may relate to their environments as specialists or generalists (Hannan and Freeman, 1977). Figure 7.3 shows how specialist and generalist organizations relate to their environments. Population A, the generalist organizations, occupies a very broad position in the environment, but has not penetrated it very deeply. Population B, specialist organizations, concentrates on a narrow band of the environment, but with greater depth. In the popular music business, for example, a specialist recording company may concentrate on a particular type of music, like country western, in the hope that there will be both performers and buyers for it. The generalist music company may record a wide variety of music groups, as well as producing films, sound track recordings, and videotapes. The latter may not reach a highly specialized musical taste, but may be in a better position to retain its balance if the environment (that is, the music-buying public) changes. All organizations work out a relationship with their environments that is relatively specialized or relatively general. Sometimes an organization's survival depends on whether it has established the right relationship.

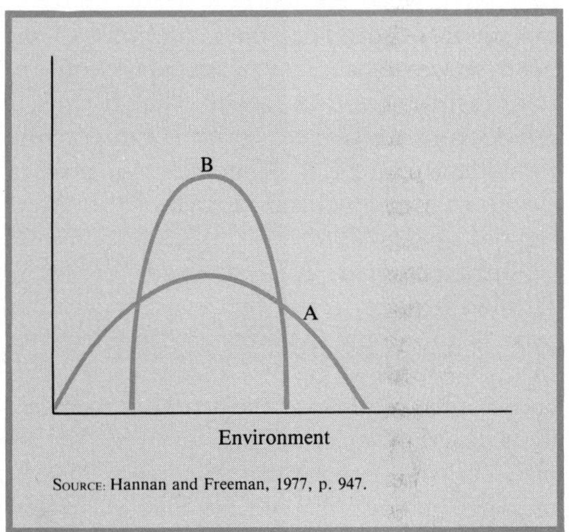

Source: Hannan and Freeman, 1977, p. 947.

Figure 7.3 How Specialist and Generalist Organizations Relate to Their Environments *The generalist organizations (A) occupy a broad band in the environment, but do not penetrate very deeply into the environment. The specialist organizations (B) occupy a narrower band, but attain greater penetration.*

Besides adapting to the environment as it is, organizations use a variety of strategies to manipulate or control uncertain and changing environments, so that they can be successful within them. *Multinational corporations,* for example, reduce their dependency on a single environment (whether for labor, raw materials, or markets) by locating in a number of nations. Such arrangements often lead to domination of the environment by the organization. (See Table 14.3 for a list of the top 50 multinational corporations.)

Another effort to control the environment occurs through vertical integration. *Vertical integration* involves an organization assuming control of one or more of its resources or outlets. For example, a photographic company may buy silver mines to ensure an adequate supply of the natural resource it needs (silver) at a predictable price, and it may own photography stores to sell its products. Even educational systems can have some degree of vertical integration. Primary schools may have "feeder" nursery schools which send them children, and they in turn may supply specific secondary schools with students. Oil companies use vertical integration to control the production, refining, and distribution of gasoline and related products.

Certain forms of vertical integration have been declared illegal because they destroy competition and lead to monopolies. *Monopoly* refers to the exclusive control of a particular industry, market, service, or commodity by a single organization. The United States began enacting antitrust laws in 1890 with the Sherman Anti-Trust Act. Such laws are designed to restrict business practices considered monopolistic or unfair. In recent years, major antitrust lawsuits were brought against International Business Machines (IBM) and American Telephone and Telegraph Company (AT&T) by the U.S. Department of Justice. The IBM case was dismissed in 1982 after more than 10 years of litigation, and in 1982 AT&T was ordered by the courts to separate itself from many of the regional companies it controlled.

Sometimes control is exercised by several large organizations, in which case it is called *oligopoly*. Monopoly and oligopoly eliminate competition in the marketplace. Particularly when a vital product like food or oil is controlled, it means that prices can rise far above production costs. But a monopoly greatly reduces organizational uncertainty.

Without monopoly, organizational uncertainty appears in the distribution and marketing of goods or services. Advertising, publicity, and sales forces are legally accepted ways organizations use to deal with such unknowns. Illegal ways have also been used, however. In the record business, for example, four big firms dominated the industry from 1948 to 1955. They were vertically integrated through long-term contracts with artists and producers; they owned the manufacturing facilities; and they controlled the system of distribution. But for a record to become popular, disc jockeys needed to feature it on the air. Since the big firms did not control all the radio stations, they used bribery (called "payola") to encourage disc jockeys to play their records (Perrow, 1979a). In other instances, companies have resorted to illegal price-fixing to ensure their share of the market and available profits.

Sometimes the environmental uncertainty organizations face goes beyond labor, raw materials, or markets to include the financial sphere in which they operate. The practice of interlocking directorates may be used to gain control over these broader environments. *Interlocking directorates* are boards of directors that control two or more separate organizations by overlapping membership. Thus, the key officers of a steel company may be on the board of a major bank, and several top bank executives may be on the steel company's board. The links between board members of major industrial corporations and financial institutions (banks) were noted by Levine, who discovered what he called "spheres of influence" among banks and corporations (1972). Morgan Bank, for instance, shares three directors with General Motors and General Electric; two directors with Ford, U.S. Steel, Bethlehem Steel, and Continental Oil; and one common director with Chrysler, Boeing, National Dairy, and Proctor and Gamble.

Common directors are one mechanism through which corporations tend to ensure financial support from banks, and banks in turn have the potential for influencing the policies that corporations pursue. The interlocking directorates between them tend to reduce uncertainties in the environments of each—corporations need to be assured of a steady source of capital for expanding their operations, and banks seek to enhance the success of the corporations that borrow their money. The existence of interlocking directorates contains the potential for influencing social, economic, and political events on a national and international scale.

Organizational Analysis and Views of Human Nature. How one analyzes organizations is not simply an empty academic exercise. Instead, the views owners and managers have about organizations and the people in them lead to competing styles of management. In one view, called *Theory X* by McGregor (1960), managers believe that people hate their jobs, want to avoid responsibility, resist change, and do not care about organizational needs. Theory X suggests that people work only when controlled through time clocks and rewards like bonuses or promotions. In contrast, *Theory Y* suggests that people are passive or irresponsible because of their experiences in organizations;

that, by nature, people have the desire to work, to be creative, and to take responsibility. Under this set of assumptions, control rests on self-direction. Management's task, in this view, is to organize things so that people can accomplish their own goals while furthering the organization's goals. Few managers totally accept either one of these theories, but tendencies toward one or the other may be identifiable in various organizations.

These competing views of human nature, along with various other human and contextual features of organizations, can be added to Weber's description of bureaucracy. For some people, however, features of bureaucracies such as oligarchy, informal organization, relations with their environments, and assumptions about human nature, as well as problems such as incompetence, waste, and ritualism, are not just intellectual shortcomings. Some people feel that bureaucracy runs counter to their humanistic values, as well as being inefficient. They have proposed nonbureaucratic ways of structuring organizations.

Comparing Bureaucratic and Democratic-Collective Organizations

Recent decades have witnessed the growth of so-called alternative organizations or *democratic-collective organizations,* such as alternative schools or worker-owned and -controlled firms.[1] Although relatively small in number, such organizations provide an important contrast with bureaucratic organizations. They show that bureaucracy is not necessarily inevitable, but that people can choose to organize their endeavors in alternative ways. And they point out some of the advantages and liabilities of various organizational forms.

Case studies of democratic-collective organizations permit comparisons between them and bureaucratic organizations. If you worked in a democratic-collective organization, you would spend considerable time discussing all major decisions the organization had to make. Such decisions might include who to hire, how to divide work assignments, and how to determine pay scales. You would spend much of your working day in meetings. You would also know a great deal about all phases of the organization's programs, problems, and policies, and you might perform a wide variety of tasks within the organization.

In a bureaucratic organization, your actions and behaviors would be shaped by established rules and procedures. You might work alone or with a few other people in a small group. Your tasks would be fairly narrowly defined and relatively specialized. You would not be involved in making decisions about all aspects of the organization's program. Indeed, you might know very little about areas outside your own. Ideas or new proposals would need to go through the "proper channels"—that is, be presented to your boss and perhaps your boss's boss in the organizational hierarchy. Only then might you be authorized to go ahead with innovations. You would probably spend less time in meetings and more time producing goods or services, or in writing or filing letters, memos, and reports. Table 7.3 compares seven features of democratic-collective organizations and bureaucracies. These features spotlight some of the major differences in organizational types.

1. One way of assessing democratic-collective and bureaucratic organizations is in terms of the tasks or activities they perform. Some tasks, such as making plastic garbage bags, are clear, predictable, routine, and repetitive. For such tasks, a bureaucratic structure may be the more efficient one. But nonroutine tasks, such as teaching children with learning disabilities or inventing new technologies, are more difficult to accomplish in a bureaucracy. Personnel in such organizations require more discretion and will depend more on experience or professional expertise than on rules for making decisions. Hence fewer activities can be covered by bureaucratic procedures.

[1]This discussion of democratic-collective organizations draws heavily on the work of Rothschild-Whit (1976, 1979).

Table 7.3 Features of Democratic-Collective Organizations and Bureaucracies

Organizational Feature	Democratic-Collective Organizations	Bureaucracies
Authority. The power to act, with that power seen as legitimate by other participants.	Place authority in collective as a whole. Decisions have authority when everyone participates in making them. Everyone has an equal voice.	Place authority in the position that individuals occupy. Often based on education or experience. Hierarchically organized.
Rules	Minimize the use of rules. (One free school had only one rule, "No dope in school.") Make decisions as they are needed.	Rely heavily upon codified, often written, rules. Use rules to guide many decisions. Most decisions are predictable.
Social control. Needed in some form in all organizations if they are to accomplish their goals.	Use personalistic or moral appeals to secure conformity. Try to recruit new members who share values of existing group members.	Use mainly three types of social control: direct supervision, standardized rules, and selecting people who are similar (Perrow, 1976).
Recruitment and advancement. On what basis are people hired and promoted?	Use friendship and shared social-political values. Advancement not an issue, since there is no hierarchy of positions.	Based on credentials and other rationalistic criteria.
Incentives. What rewards does the organization offer individuals?	A chance for individuals to fulfill their values and share a sense of community. Members also gain valuable experience and contacts (help in getting into law or medical school). May offer members considerable control over their work.	Stress financial incentives and promotion possibilities.
Social stratification. How are positions ranked in the organization?	Egalitarianism is a central value. Reflected in small variations in pay (Bernstein, 1976, pp. 20–21; Perry, 1978; Russell et al., 1977). Try to convey equality of status through dress, informal social relations, terms of address, and task sharing.	Organizational position is consistent with stratification by race, sex, age, education, and experience (three-quarters of all managers and administrators are white males). Compensation may range from $1.5 million per year for chief executive officer to $8,000 for clerks. Use prestige differences to support organizational hierarchy, through office size and decor, titles, executive bathrooms, and company cars.
Differentiation. How specialized is the division of labor?	Try to minimize it by keeping work roles as general as possible and by rotating jobs.	Stress maximum division of labor, with experts doing very narrow specialized tasks.

SOURCE: Adapted from Rothschild-Whitt (1976, 1979).

2. Bureaucratic organizations may limit the damage that a relatively incompetent person can do; democratic-collective organizations may find it more difficult to contain the havoc that one clearly unsuited person can wreak. On the other hand, a bureaucratic organization may also restrict the contribution that a particularly original or unorthodox individual can make.

3. One of the major social costs of democratic-collective organizations is the time it takes to make decisions. For instance, an alternative newspaper spent more than 15 hours in meetings to plan one systematic job rotation. As a result, less time remains to do the tasks of the organization. Although two-way communication seems to generate higher morale, more innovative ideas, and creative solutions to complex problems, it is undeniably slow (Leavitt, 1964).

This brief comparison of the advantages and disadvantages of democratic-collective and bureaucratic organizations assumes that pure models of both types are widespread. In fact, pure cases are rare. Many bureaucratic organizations are adopting some features of democratic-collective organizations, including two-way communication, task rotation, collective decision-making on some issues, and even partial worker ownership. It is important to realize, however, that ownership and control do not always go together. Some large corporations such as IBM, for example, enable workers to purchase the company's stock at a below-market price. But although employees may share in some of the profits this way, they do not have any more influence over how their work is organized. (See the box "Forms of Democracy at Work," for more discussion.)

Plants that have recently been bought by their

Forms of Democracy at Work

What does "democracy at work" really mean? [T]he *ways* in which [companies] are reshaping the workplace are dramatically different. In some cases, employees have gained limited powers over their day-to-day jobs while in other companies the workers have acquired enormous power to change the corporation. In still other companies, the workers have gained only the potential to acquire power—perhaps some day in the future. . . . [This selection presents] four of the major kinds of workplace changes which often get lumped together under the concept of "workplace democracy": humanization of work, labor-management committees, worker ownership and workers' self-management, or workers' control. . . .

Humanization of Work

To treat worker woes, a number of major corporations came up with a new kind of cure: social scientists in the field call it humanization of work. As corporate social scientists describe it, the main cause of worker alienation and boredom is the faulty design of jobs. Corporate managers have been preoccupied for decades with the technological design of the workplace—what kind of machines to use and how to arrange them on the shopfloor—and workers have been considered as living parts to plug into the production machine.

The problem, these corporate researchers say, is that managers have forgotten the *social* design of the workplace: how workers interact with management and with each other, and how they feel about their work. . . .

And so, major corporations across the country (more than 2,000 of them, according to some estimates) have been "humanizing" their white- and blue-collar factories. A General Motors factory abolished the traditional assembly line, and gave small worker teams the power to assemble entire mobile homes on their own; each worker would no longer be alienated by having to screw on an isolated assembly-line part.

[Under] the humanization of work projects . . . workers gain some power and autonomy over their jobs [but] they must exercise them within a larger framework which has been dictated by corporate management. At humanized enterprises, the traditional power relationship—management gives the orders, and employees do what they're told—remains essentially unchanged.

Corporations that have humanized the production process have made it clear that increasing worker contentment is not the workers are struggling with the problems of collective decision-making. Workers may lack specialized knowledge about markets and finance; managers may know little about manufacturing processes and machinery. Both may find it difficult to break out of past ways of organizing their work. Their problems are compounded because many plants that have been sold to workers in recent years had already begun to lose money before they were sold and were facing the prospect of being closed down. Often their equipment was obsolete, and the markets in which their products were sold had become more competitive. Such circumstances are not optimal conditions for the success of any organization, bureaucratic or worker-owned.

ORGANIZATIONAL TASKS

All organizations, whether democratic-collective or bureaucratic, need to perform certain tasks if they are to survive and flourish. How an organization fulfills those tasks, and the relative emphasis it places on each one, varies widely.

goal. Increasing worker satisfaction is merely the means to the corporation's primary goal, which is maximizing productivity and profits. The humanization of work experiments at Procter & Gamble have been so successful in boosting productivity, in fact, that corporate executives keep the projects secret, like the recipe for making Pringles New Fangled Potato Chips. . . .

Labor-Management Quality of Work Life Committees

As numerous corporations have been "humanizing" the workplace, joint committees of labor and management officials have begun launching similar experiments in unionized companies across the nation.

The unions and shopfloor workers take part with management in controlling and designing the changes under the quality of work life projects. "The *way* in which we do things is as important as *what* we do," participants in the Harman Industries labor-management project write. "This program of work improvement is not one which is designed by concerned managers, with the help of social scientists, and imposed on the plant," but "a *process* of democratic decision-making."

Labor-management quality of work life committees give employees more influence over the workplace than they had before. . . . [T]hey set in motion a process in which workers can learn to analyze their jobs, think critically about work, and join together with fellow workers to dream up shopfloor improvements and solve problems. But, like the humanization of work projects, they are not aimed at upsetting the traditional balance of power between management and the workers. . . .

Worker-Owned Companies

[The] fact that employees have purchased their workplace is a far cry from saying they control it; in fact, it doesn't necessarily mean the employees have any voice in making decisions at all. For there are markedly different kinds of worker ownership, and each one gives the workers access to varying degrees of power.

Workers can own their workplace by becoming members of a producer cooperative: witness the workers at the plywood factories in the Northwest or the farmworker ranches in California. In these co-ops, each worker owns one share and casts one vote in corporate affairs from electing the board of directors to voting on how to spend the profits. More than any other enterprises in the United States, these worker-owned enterprises are also worker-controlled.

But workers can also own their own enter-

1. All organizations must maintain their sources of support, whether sales and profits in an industrial corporation, clients in a clinic, or legislative allocations in a government-supported organization.

2. Organizations need to hire and keep staff members. Voluntary organizations need to attract volunteers; profit and not-for-profit organizations need to attract and hold employees. Rapid turnover is a major organizational problem, because introducing new members to an organization takes the time and energy of existing members. There is also the problem of continuity of effort, contacts, and knowledge. In a school with many new teachers, for example, teachers will not know the students' names, they may not understand the culture of the school, and they may not know the neighborhood. If only a few new teachers enter each year, veterans can orient them.

3. Organizations must prevent internal or external conflict from destroying them. Most organizations have norms against physical fighting among members. This may be from the

prises by buying common stock on the open market. That's how employees purchased the Vermont Asbestos Group, the Herkimer Library Bureau and Saratoga Knitting Mill. In these cases, the workers exert far less power over the company than workers do in the co-ops, because individuals outside the company can also buy stock. Furthermore, individuals can buy more than one share. The result: managers with high salaries, and financial resources to spare, buy more stocks and cast more votes than hourly workers on the production floor.

There is a third way in which workers have become owners of their firms, one which in practice has given them the least direct control of all—establishing an Employee Stock Ownership Plan, or ESOP. At companies such as South Bend Lathe, for instance, the corporation in effect gave its stocks to the employees, free of charge, by depositing them in an ESOP trust. But as South Bend Lathe and most other companies designed their ESOPs, the number of [shares] each employee receives is based on his or her salary—which means, again, that managers get far more shares than the workers tooling the machines on the shopfloor. South Bend Lathe also designed the ESOP so that workers won't have the power to cast the votes on most of their stock for at least a decade. . . .

Workers at such companies have the *potential* for controlling their workplace, some day in the future. But it will be years before the potential at these worker-owned firms can possibly be fulfilled.

Workers' Self-Management

The fourth major development in the American workplace is dramatically different; it stands the traditional corporate power structure on its head. Under workers' self-management, or workers' control, the management doesn't give the employees some expanded powers on the shopfloor—the rank and file workers control the entire corporation, period.

"Workers' control means that a firm's management should be accountable to its employees," write the editors of *Workers' Control.* "And it means conversely, that the workers—blue- and white-collar alike—should bear responsibility for running the enterprise's operations."

Advocates of workers' self-management argue that it is the only long-term solution to the crises of the workplace. . . . [Only] workers in a self-managed firm have the actual voting power to *shape* the kind of workplace environment and work lives they want.

SOURCE: Adapted from Zwerdling, *Workplace Democracy,* pp. 2–8.

value attached to nonviolence, but even in organizations dedicated to fighting and violence (for example, professional hockey teams or armies), there are rules about what constitutes permissible behavior. Organizational concerns in this area go beyond physical fighting, however, to include excessive verbal conflict, antagonisms, sabotage of work, excessive competition, or other behaviors the organization sees as injurious. Members of organizations are expected to comply with city, state, and federal laws that apply to their situation. Some universities, for example, have handbooks spelling out rules of conduct. In others, standards of permissible behavior are transmitted informally. Very often nothing is ever said directly; new members simply observe what is and is not done. Sometimes senior members will take newcomers "under their wings" and explain how things are done in that organization.

4. Organizations must try to achieve their goals to some extent. It is helpful to distinguish between the stated goals of an organization and its real goals (Etzioni, 1964). The stated goals are what the organization says in its annual report, publicity releases, brochures, advertising, and other public statements. An organization directs major resources and efforts toward its real goals. When they conflict with stated goals, the clear priority of real goals emerges (Etzioni, 1964, p. 7). Utility companies may state in their press releases that they value clean air very highly. Their real goal, however, may be to make a profit. Therefore, when they need to burn sulfur-filled coal rather than oil to continue making money, the stated goal of cleaner air loses out to the real goal of making money.

Does the incentive system in an organization support its major goals? If not, those goals may not be realized. A study of two employment agencies, for example, showed that one was placing many more people in jobs than the other (Blau, 1955). In the more successful agency the departmental group was rewarded for the total number placed, while in the less successful agency individual employment counselors were rewarded for the people they placed in jobs. In the latter organization, counselors hid information about jobs from one another, hoping to be the one to find someone to fill the slot. Sometimes this meant that a job remained open for weeks. Meanwhile the employer with the job to be filled got tired of waiting and hired someone without using the employment agency or just eliminated the job. In the other agency individual counselors cooperated by pooling job information, since they all benefited from an increased number of placements. Thus, the structure of the incentive system in an organization will affect individual behaviors within it.

When analyzing organizations, we can ask what are the real, underlying goals any behavior reveals? It is possible to discover that a behavior serves none of the goals of the larger organization, but only the many, and often competing, goals of individuals and small groups working within it. A number of scholars (for example, Simon, 1957, and Perrow, 1979b) caution against holding an overly rational view of organizational behavior. Organizations show a great deal of irrational, contradictory behavior, as Joseph Heller described so well in his novels *Catch 22* and *Something Happened,* or as the movie *Apocalypse Now* showed. (Perrow, 1979b).

Ultimately organizations cannot be understood in isolation from the people in them. Organizational and individual behaviors and goals may work in concert or at cross purposes, with varying results for both parties. For these reasons, it is important to analyze some of the ways organizations and individuals may be linked together.

LINKS BETWEEN ORGANIZATIONS AND THE PEOPLE IN THEM

Why is it that some organizations have high employee morale and productivity, while others do not? Why do people hate to work in some organizations and find others good places in which to work? There are many ways to analyze the links between individuals and organizations, but among the most helpful are the concepts of location, opportunity, and power as developed by Kanter (1977, 1979).

One's *location* with respect to having control over decision-making in an organization profoundly affects task performance. Kanter suggests that organizational location is more important for morale and job satisfaction than the task being performed. This was apparent in the reorganization of a Volvo automobile manufacturing plant. The structure of the work was changed from an assembly line where the workers had no communication or decision-making roles to a work group that was charged with building a car. The group organized a system of who would do what and when, and they talked with one another and decided how they would do the work. As a result, their morale was better, absenteeism was lower, and work quality and productivity was higher (Dickson, 1975).

The concept of *opportunity* also helps to explain the way people behave in organizations. This idea refers to the potential that a particular location contains for the expansion of work responsibilities and rewards. Jobs and job categories tend to be evaluated in terms of the prospects they contain for advancement, aside from the job content, grade level, or salary. In the organization Kanter studied, clerical jobs had low status because they led nowhere, whereas sales was attractive because people were promoted from it into management. Most people preferred line jobs rather than staff jobs because they offered longer and more varied chains of career opportunity (Kanter, 1977). Originating in the military, the term *line job* refers to those who actually do the fighting, selling, manufacturing, production, or whatever, as distinct from the *staff* that serves in an advisory or administrative capacity (for example, legal departments, accountants, clerical workers, data processing personnel, and so forth).

A particular location, then, can be assessed in terms of the opportunities it offers for advancement and mobility, for doing more important tasks, and for gaining responsibility. Hierarchical organizations affect individuals by making advancement within the hierarchy the measure of personal success or failure. In an organization where locations are assessed in terms of the opportunities they offer for advancement, it is not just how well you do your job that matters; the opportunities the job provides for advancement and how rapidly that advancement comes are also significant.

The relative opportunities of a position affect how involved people become in their work. This is especially evident in Kanter's comparison of organizational "movers" and those who were organizationally "stuck." "Movers" took on extra assignments and poured time, energy, and new ideas into their work. They sought to learn skills that would be useful in their journey upward in the company. They zeroed in on what was happening further up in the hierarchy (Kanter, 1977). Sudden promotion opportunities within an organizational hierarchy could accelerate an individual's aspirations, work commitment, and responsibility. The movers and others with opportunities within the organization tended to form task-oriented groups. If they had a grievance, they were likely to do something about it formally.

The organizationally "stuck" contrasted vividly with the movers. These were people on short career ladders and those who had no further career possibilities. They had reached a dead end in the organization. Structurally blocked from moving and lacking opportunity in a system where success was measured by mobility, they behaved in many ways opposite to the "fast trackers." They tended to see fewer chances to use their skills and indeed used fewer skills; they were less involved in their work and less attached to it. They invested their energies outside their jobs and dreamed of escaping. Individuals blocked from opportunities for advancement within the organization tended to form strong peer bonds. These peer groups were openly critical of organizational superiors. Kanter found that members of such closed peer groups experienced pressure to stay loyal to their co-workers. Leaving the group, even when they were promoted, was seen as "disloyal" (1977).

The reactions of individuals to open or blocked opportunities suggests the operation of a self-fulfilling prophecy—that is, what superiors expect to occur often happens. People in high-mobility tracks tend to develop commitment to their work, high ambitions, and an orientation toward their superiors that fuels future success. Those on low-mobility or blocked tracks tend to withdraw or become indifferent, thereby seeming to "prove" to their superiors that they are not able to handle opportunities (Kanter, 1977).

Just as the structure of opportunities within an organization appears to influence individuals, the structure of *power* can also shape their behavior. Power, suggests Kanter, refers not just to the capacity of one individual to dominate or control others. It also refers to the capacity to get things done or to mobilize resources. Organizational locations vary in terms of their productive power. Organizational sources of power include access to supply lines, information sources, and lines of support. The marketing and the finance divisions of most corporations are strong because they control the vital supplies of money and customers.

The amount of power in a position affects the way authority is exercised. Those in positions of authority who lack real power tend to become coercive, petty, rule-minded, and frequently oversupervise their subordinates. Since they have no real power to delegate, they are afraid to delegate anything (Kanter, 1977, 1979). This situation may apply to organizations as well as to individuals. Government agencies with little legislated power may operate in a particularly petty way. Kanter's concepts of location, opportunity, and power within organizations offer interesting examples of how structural features of organizations can affect the individuals working within them.

Summary

1. Primary groups, including family and close friends, are characterized by frequent face-to-face contact, by commitment and emotional ties among members, and by relative permanence.

2. As people get older, they join more secondary groups—a school class or a work group—which are more limited and task-oriented than primary groups.

3. Group members share a common social location; they tend to share values and goals; and they interact frequently. These characteristics may generate a sense of common identity.

4. Group boundaries may be strengthened by external conflict or by greater internal conformity.

5. Reference groups are groups whose standards or behaviors we accept or reject for our life situations.

6. Dyads (two-person groups) and triads (three-person groups) have unique characteristics resulting from their numbers.

7. Groups are affected by the relative proportion of individuals of different types they possess. Token minority members of a group face certain unique problems. Group size and unanimity affect the amount of pressure to conform felt by individuals in the group.

8. Organizations are growing in size and influence. There is very little we can do in society today without dealing with one or more organizations.

9. Weber's model of bureaucratic organizations stressed six distinctive features: division of labor and specialization, hierarchy, rules and regulations, impartiality, technical qualifications, and records and files.

10. Bureaucracy sometimes shows the negative features of incompetence, waste, and ritualism.

11. Organizations have the tendency to become oligarchical. They reveal patterns of informal social relations and standards, and many organizations depend heavily on their environment for success and survival. Assumptions about human nature may affect organizational structures and styles of management.

12. Bureaucratic and democratic-collective organizations differ with respect to their authority, rules, social control, recruitment and advancement, incentive structures, social stratification, and division of labor.

13. All organizations must maintain their sources of support, recruit and retain staff, avoid being destroyed by internal or external conflict, and achieve their goals, at least to some extent.

14. Some of the links between organizations and individuals can be explored by using the concepts of location, opportunity, and power.

Key Terms

aggregate
bureaucracy
charisma
charismatic leader
commitment
conformity
democratic-collective organization
dyad
expressive leader
formal organization
group
groupthink
instrumental leader
interlocking directorates
line job
monopoly
multinational corporation
oligarchy
oligopoly
open system
organization
organizational ritualism
Parkinson's law
Peter principle
primary group
reference group
secondary group
staff job
Theory X
Theory Y
triad
value-oriented action
vertical integration

29

Chapter 8

Deviance and Crime

What do burping after a meal, tattooing one's face, having intercourse with one's cousin, picking one's nose in public, and piercing one's ears have in common? They are all behaviors considered deviant in some societies but practiced widely by members of other societies. And they illustrate several key aspects of deviant behavior.

DEFINING DEVIANCE

Nothing is intrinsically deviant. The same personal characteristics or behavior can be considered deviant in one instance but not in another. The determining factor is whether a significant expectation or norm is being violated by the behavior or trait. Furthermore, other people or groups must see and react negatively to the behavior or trait. As Durkheim noted, an action does not offend society because it is deviant. Instead, it is deviant because it offends society.

Behaviors that offend society the most are ones that violate strongly held norms. There is a strongly held prohibition against child-molesting, for example. Not only is such action illegal, but it arouses moral indignation as well. Because different norms are considered more or less important by various societies and social groups, deviance is a matter of degree, rather than an "all-or-nothing" characteristic (Schur, 1979). Child-molesting may be considered quite deviant, while littering may be considered only mildly deviant.

Deviance is also relative to the time and place in which a particular behavior occurs. A drug user may be considered highly deviant by some people but not by others. A man who is considered a "Communist" by his conservative friends at the bank where he works may be considered a "reactionary conservative" by his friends at a liberal political club, although his politics remain unchanged in both situations. A guerrilla band may be viewed as a "liberation army" by some groups in a society and as dangerous terrorists by others. It is particularly important to stress the relative aspect of deviance in a pluralist society such as that of the United States. One group's definition of what is deviant may not be shared by other social groups. Take smoking as an example. It used to be that people who smoked did so wherever it was not expressly prohibited. In recent years, however, designated nonsmoking areas have appeared in airplanes, restaurants, and even some offices. As the health hazards for nonsmokers have been publicized, smokers have become more likely to ask others for permission to smoke. In short, smoking has moved from being thought a socially neutral behavior to a somewhat more deviant behavior. Similarly, a couple living together before marriage used to be considered "sinful" or "deviant" by many people, and in some parts of the country such an action may still be viewed this way. In other regions, however, such behavior is considered perfectly "normal."

These examples demonstrate that norms may be *ambiguous*. People may not know if what they or someone else is doing will arouse a negative reaction. Even within a group, there may be little agreement about whether or not a particular behavior violates a norm. Is smoking marijuana viewed as deviant? By whom? Is oral sex deviant, or jaywalking, "borrowing" someone's car to take it for a spin, beating a child, or cheating on an exam? Is a woman surgeon, a male nursery school teacher, a school superintendent who "flashes," or a college drug dealer a deviant? If you asked 100 college students around the country which of these activities and people they considered deviant, it is likely that you would receive a wide variety of responses.

One study asked a sample of respondents to name people or behaviors they considered deviant. The list of replies included homosexuals, prostitutes, drug addicts, radicals, and criminals; it also included liars, reckless drivers, atheists, Christians, suburbanites, the retired, priests, executives, divorcees, motorcycle gangs, smart-aleck students, and know-it-all professors (Simmons, 1969). This variation in responses suggests the relativity and ambiguity in defining behavior as deviant. It also suggests the inherently social nature of deviant behavior. An action will not be defined as deviant unless other people know about it and react negatively to it. This reaction generally includes the feeling that something should be done about the behavior, usually to change or to stop it (Erikson, 1966).

Finally, an important aspect of deviance is the fact that certain social groups have relatively greater power and resources to use in getting their own definition of deviance rather than some other definition to prevail, and perhaps even to be written into law. As Becker has suggested, middle-class definitions of marijuana use as deviant held sway through the 1940s and 1950s, and may have been in part a reaction to the use of marijuana by lower-class and minority subcultures. As we see later in this chapter, the definition of homosexuality as a sickness was successfully challenged in the 1970s, as gay rights groups mobilized political and intellectual resources to support their point of view. These examples illustrate some of the essential features of deviant behavior. Deviance is relative to time and place; it results from social and political processes; it depends on the existence of social organization and norms; and it provokes a negative response.

DEFINING AND MEASURING CRIME

A *crime* is a behavior that is prohibited by law. Although many crimes are considered deviant, not every crime is considered deviant by all groups. Smoking marijuana, for example, is a crime in many states, but it is not considered deviant by the Rastafarians, a religious sect from the island of Jamaica. And not all deviance is a crime. For instance, not wearing a shirt when it is 30° F outside or performing a sexual act with a plant might be considered deviant by many, but it is not illegal.

MEASURING CRIMINAL ACTIVITY

Federal law defines more than 2800 acts as crimes, and this number is swelled still further by state and local statutes. Literally thousands of activities have been defined as illegal. Eight of these are considered very serious crimes, and they are called "index offenses": rape, robbery, murder, aggravated assault, burglary, larceny (theft of $50 or more), arson, and auto theft. These index offenses are used by the Federal Bureau of Investigation to compute changes in the rate of serious crimes.

In the United States there is one property crime committed every 3 seconds, on the average, as the "crime clock" in Figure 8.1 indicates.

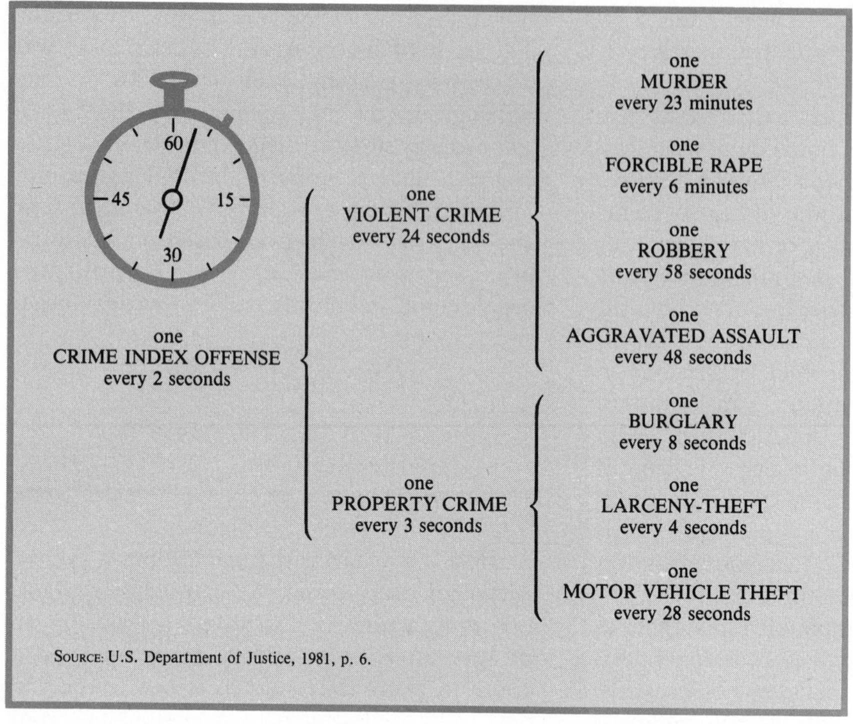

Figure 8.1 The Crime Clock, 1980 *The crime clock should be viewed with care. It is designed to convey the number of annual reported crimes by showing the relative frequency of occurrences of the index offenses. It does not imply a regularity in the commission of crimes; rather, it represents the annual ratio of crime to fixed time intervals.*

Moreover, the crime rate is increasing dramatically, as reflected in FBI data shown in Figure 8.2. Forcible rape was up 8 percent and robbery up nearly 18 percent in 1980, compared to 1979. These figures are compiled by the FBI using police reports from all over the country. The numbers may be low because not all crimes are reported. In an effort to measure unreported crimes, the government conducts surveys of the population in which it asks if a person has been the victim of a crime. These surveys give a crime rate based on reports by victims (see Table 8.1).

As is apparent from comparing the columns in Table 8.1, the rate of all crimes reported by victims is much higher than the rate based on FBI data. The rate of forcible rape and theft reported by victims, for example, is more than five times as high as the FBI rate (Ennis, 1967; Hindelang, 1976). Why do FBI figures and reports from victims differ so widely? People say

Table 8.1 Crime Rates per 100,000 Inhabitants, Based on FBI Data and Victim Reports

	FBI Rate	Reported by Victims
Forcible rape	36	167
Robbery	244	589
Aggravated assault	291	2,685
Burglary	1,668	8,591
Larceny-theft	3,156	11,985
Motor vehicle theft	495	1,750

SOURCES: U.S. Department of Justice, *FBI Uniform Crime Reports*, 1981, p. 38; Hindelang et al., *Sourcebook of Criminal Justice Statistics—1980,* 1981.

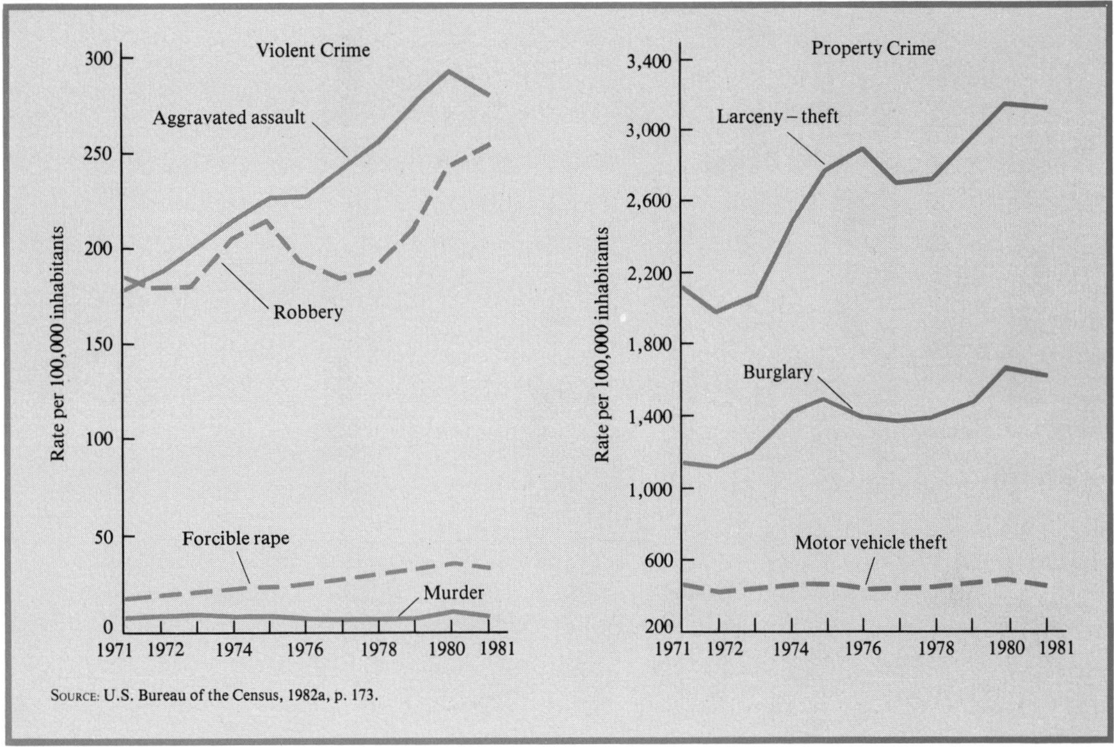

SOURCE: U.S. Bureau of the Census, 1982a, p. 173.

Figure 8.2 Selected Crime Rates: 1971 to 1981

they do not report crimes to the police because they think it will not do any good. Some say they do not want to get the offender in trouble or they fear revenge if they report the crime. (As far as rape is concerned, underreporting is associated with the fact that sexual abuse often occurs within families or that rape victims may be stigmatized.) These reasons may explain why some people do not report crimes to the police.

In 1980 the proportion of families victimized by crime fell slightly to 30 percent (from 32 percent in 1979), according to reports from victims. The proportion of violent crimes stayed the same, at about 6 percent. This relative stability flies in the face of FBI reports that the crime rate is skyrocketing. The FBI's figures for the same period show that the proportion of reported crimes rose 10 percent nationally in 1980, while violent crimes increased 13 percent.

Both victim reports and FBI data omit many crimes, however. First, they represent only efforts to count index offenses. Yet only a small portion of criminal acts are in the crime index. Second, surveys of victims fail to ask about crimes against business, such as burglaries or robberies. Third, what Edwin Schur (1965) calls "crime without victims," including gambling, homosexuality, and prostitution, is not included in these crime counts. Fourth, crime statistics do not include much of the substantial white collar crime that occurs.

White collar crimes committed by "respectable" individuals include embezzling money, evading taxes, stealing computer time or data, forging checks, or printing counterfeit money. At the corporate level, they include fraudulent advertising, price-fixing, illegal payoffs to politicians, unlawful monopolies, and disregard for

"Just between us, Don, are we ripping off the public?"
SOURCE: Drawing by Stevenson, © 1979, *The New Yorker Magazine, Inc.*

the health of consumers and the safety of products or wastes. Governments also commit white collar crimes when they spy on citizens, do unauthorized wiretapping, perform political assassinations, or deny due process. A considerable amount of white collar crime is concealed because it may occur while people practice their occupations. Some, such as mail order frauds or stock market manipulations, may go undetected even by the victims. For all these reasons, then, both FBI data and crimes reported by victims represent a serious undercount of criminal activity in the United States.

WHO COMMITS CRIMES?

The types of crimes people commit vary by the race, social class, age, and sex of offenders. White middle class males are more likely than lower-class males to commit such white collar crimes as forgery, embezzlement, computer theft, and such corporate crimes as price-fixing or illegal waste disposal. Arrest rates for these types of crimes are fairly low, however. Lower-class males are more likely than middle-class males to commit violent crimes and burglaries, according to official arrest rates as well as self-reports by offenders (Elliott and Ageton, 1980).

Arrest records show major differences by race, age, and sex, with blacks, persons under 20, and males arrested more frequently than whites, persons 20 or older, and females (see Table 8.2). Some sociologists argue that arrest and sentencing records show more about bias in the way the police and the courts process offenders than they show about who commits crimes.

Table 8.2 A Comparison of the Race, Age, Socioeconomic Status (SES), and Sex of Offenders

	Arrest Records: Official Criminal Behavior	Self-Report Data: Law-Violating Behavior	Victimization Studies: Perception of Victims
Race	Blacks are arrested proportionately more often than whites (Hindelang et al., 1981).	Frequency of law violations among black males is only slightly higher than it is among white males (Gold, 1970; Hirschi, 1969; Institute for Juvenile Research, 1972; Williams and Gold, 1972). However, male black youths are more likely than white youths to commit serious offenses, resulting in greater personal injury to others (Illinois Institute for Juvenile Research, 1972, pp. 23–24; Williams and Gold, 1972, p. 217; Gold and Reimer, 1974, p. 17).	Offenders are twice as likely to be perceived as black or of another minority than their proportion in the population would suggest (Hindelang, 1976, p. 455).
Age	Majority of arrests involve young persons under the age of 20. Young people are twice as likely to be arrested for index offenses than their proportion in population suggests (U.S. Department of Justice, *Uniform Crime Reports*).	Extent of juvenile lawbreaking is far greater than extent of official delinquency (Empey, 1978, p. 163). Same may be true of adults, but data are rare.	One-third of lone offenders and one-half of multiple offenders were perceived to be 12 to 20 years old (Hindelang, 1976, p. 453).
SES	Lower-class persons are more likely than middle-class persons to be arrested (Wolfgang et al., 1972).	Some studies suggest little or no correlation between social class and self-reported crimes (Akers, 1964; Hirschi, 1969; Nye et al., 1958; Tittle et al., 1978; Voss, 1966; Williams and Gold, 1972). When prior record and seriousness of offense are considered, lower-class persons report more numerous and more serious crimes than middle-class persons (Braithwaite, 1979, 1981; Elliot and Ageton, 1980, p. 80; Hardt, 1968; Smith, 1975).	Victims cannot tell the socioeconomic status of offenders.
Sex	Females are much less likely than males to be arrested.	Females generally report fewer offenses than males, but their offenses are similar to those of males (Hindelang, 1980; Jensen and Eve, 1976; Williams and Gold, 1972; Wise, 1967).	Lone offenders perceived to be female 4 percent of the time, and multiple offenders, 3 percent of the time (Hindelang, 1976, p. 456).

This position is supported by a number of studies that find little or no significant correlation between social class, for instance, and self-reported crimes (Akers, 1964; Hirschi, 1969; Nye et al., 1958; Tittle et al., 1978; Voss, 1966). Tittle and Villemez (1977) found that all social classes commit thefts, assaults, and use marijuana, with the middle classes more likely to gamble or cheat on their taxes than the highest or the lowest social classes. The nonexistence of differences in criminal behavior by race, age, and social class has recently been challenged, however.

Although there may well be biases in the way police and courts handle offenses, such biases do not explain completely the variations in criminal rates by race, social class, age, and sex. Instead, considerable research suggests that when the seriousness of an offense and prior record are taken into account, the possible role of class bias in the generation of official data is quite small (Braithwaite, 1979, 1981; Liska and Tausig, 1979; Hindelang et al., 1979; Terry, 1967; Hohenstein, 1969). With respect to race, whites comprise 86.5 percent of the population, but only 70 percent of those arrested in 1978 were white (Hindelang et al., 1980). Victim studies corroborate racial differences in official arrest records. In personal and business victimizations, offenders were twice as likely to be perceived as black or of other minority status than their proportion in the population would predict (Hindelang, 1976).

Once arrested, does race affect the types of criminal sentences people receive? Kleck (1981) performed a comprehensive assessment of research dealing with the effects of race on criminal sentencing and concluded that black homicide offenders were less likely than white offenders to receive a death sentence or be executed except in the South, where they faced considerable discrimination. Sentences for crimes other than murder also revealed no racial bias. When black defendants committed crimes against black victims, they tended to receive more lenient sentences than did white offenders. Kleck suggests that one explanation for these lighter sentences may be the devaluing of black victims by the criminal justice system.

Not all the literature agrees with Kleck's conclusion that sentencing is unbiased by race. Other work suggests that both occupation and race influence being held in jail before trial and length of prison sentence. The amount of bail that is set depends on the severity of the crime committed and the judge's estimate that the individual charged with a crime will appear in court for trial. An individual's ability to pay bail may depend on the amount of bail and on financial status. Laborers and nonwhites receive longer sentences than white collar workers and whites, even when prior arrests and seriousness of crimes are the same (Hagen, 1974, 1975; Lizotte, 1978). A number of factors besides race may influence the length of sentences people receive. These include the jurisdiction (federal or state, lower or superior court), the nature of the offense, and the race of the victim (Zatz, 1982).

The sex of an offender has no clear-cut relation to the sentences received. Instead, existing research shows mixed results by sex. A number of states give women longer or more indeterminate sentences than men for the same crimes (Temin, 1973). In other states, women offenders may get lighter sentences than men, except with regard to such status offenses as running away from home or promiscuity (Martin, 1982). There may also be an interaction between sex and type of offense; a woman who uses a gun, for example, may be sentenced more harshly than a man (Zatz, 1982).

Many studies challenging the relationship between race and social class depend on self-reports of offenders. One of the limitations of such studies is that middle-class youths report more of their offenses than do lower-class youths (Hardt, 1968; Smith, 1975; Braithwaite and Braithwaite, 1978). Another problem with self-report studies is that they lump respondents who report three or more offenses together with those who report dozens of offenses (Elliott and Ageton, 1980, p. 80). Virtually all youths report some delinquent activities on a self-report measure—for example, destroying property, lying to get into the movies, jumping on a bus without paying, failing to return extra change, making obscene phone calls, or skipping classes without an excuse. For most young people, though, these acts are neither very frequent nor very serious. When the frequency and seriousness of offenses are considered, those at the upper end of the scale on self-reports have the same social class and racial characteristics as those in police reports. Lower-class respondents report four times as many "predatory crimes against persons" and twice as many "predatory crimes against property" as do middle-class respondents (Elliott and Ageton, 1980).

With respect to sex, 84 percent of those arrested in 1978 were male and only 16 percent were female, a ratio of more than 4 to 1, although more than half the United States population is female (Hindelang et al., 1980). Self-reports of delinquent behavior, however, suggest that the ratio of males to females is only about 2 or 3 to 1. Females apparently commit more crimes than arrest records suggest. Moreover, the number of crimes committed by females appears to be rising in recent years, particularly with respect to larceny/theft, embezzlement, and fraud (Simon, 1979), perhaps because of increasing financial need or growing access to the financial resources of a business.

Finally, both official arrest records and self-reports show that crime rates drop dramatically with age. Arrests for property crimes and vandalism peak at age 15–16, drop in half in two to four years, and continue to decline rapidly thereafter. Arrests for assaulting another person (homicide, forcible rape, aggravated assault, robbery) reach their highest rates at age 19–21 and decline with age, although more slowly than property crimes do (Greenberg, 1977a).

As the rate of crime has been increasing, it is not surprising that people's fear of crime has grown. Crime is rated by urban residents as the most severe problem facing people. More than 70 percent of urban dwellers rated it as a severe problem, compared to 20 percent or less for suburban, small town, or rural dwellers. Crime was also perceived by more people as a serious problem than drugs, unemployment, or other problems.

EXPLANATIONS OF DEVIANCE AND CRIME

Deviance and crime have concerned social thinkers for a long time, and many explanations for why deviance and crime occur have been offered. There are physical and psychological explanations; the anomie theory of functionalists; differential association and labeling theory, which are influenced by the symbolic interactionist approach; Marxian explanations of crime; and economic and deterrence theories.

PHYSICAL AND PSYCHOLOGICAL EXPLANATIONS

For years, people have searched for biological reasons that might explain deviant or criminal behavior. The Italian physician Cesare Lombroso (1911) thought that people might be "born" criminals because of certain physical traits. While conducting an autopsy of a notorious Italian criminal, it occurred to Lombroso that the deviant's skull looked similar to that of an ape or a primitive human. He and his students examined the skulls of many criminals and found many with such traits. However, they did not examine the skulls of noncriminals, many of whom also had these physical traits. The British physician Charles Goring did perform such examinations and found few differences between criminals and ordinary citizens (Goring, 1913).

More recently, considerable attention has been focused on the possibility of a genetic explanation of criminal behavior—the XYY syndrome in males. The normal male has an XY chromosome pattern. Males with an extra Y

Early theories of deviance and crime suggested that certain inborn, physical traits led to lives of deviant behavior. Sociological theories suggest social conditions or processes that influence what gets defined as deviant or criminal and explain variations in rates of deviant or criminal behavior in different societies.

chromosome—the XYY pattern—were thought to be predisposed toward violence or deviance. However, as was the case with the skull theory, the research was done only on criminals. A Danish study found that a greater percentage of XYY men than XY men had been convicted of a criminal offense, but found little connection between the XYY pattern and aggressiveness (Witkin et al., 1976). XYY men tend to be unusual looking, often being taller than average and more likely to have acute cases of acne (Taylor, Walton, and Young, 1973). Their appearance may influence the way people react to them, which in turn may affect their behavior. Those with an extra Y chromosome are also often less intelligent than ordinary XY males, which might increase their chances of being caught for their criminal activity (Witkin et al., 1976).

Like physical attempts to explain deviance, psychological theories focus on the characteristics of individuals. In general, psychological theories suggest that the tendency to deviate is neither inherited nor inborn, but results from early socialization. At least three major psychological theories have been offered: psychoanalytic theory, frustration-aggression theory, and modeling theory.

Psychoanalytic Theory. This approach suggests that individuals have developed insufficient control over their aggressive, selfish, or antisocial impulses. While growing up, most children learn from loving parents to curb their antisocial tendencies or to direct them into socially acceptable channels such as sports or music. People who do not have such caring adults in their lives may fail to develop a conscience that guides and controls their impulses. The psychoanalytic theory seems to fit and explain some people's antisocial behavior, but not that of others. This theory says little, though, about how much love is needed; nor does it fully explain why various individuals react differently to the absence of love in their early lives.

Frustration-Aggression Theory. This theory suggests that when people are frustrated in their efforts to satisfy their needs for love or their sexual desires, they become aggressive.

This reaction sometimes leads to deviant behavior or crime, and sometimes it does not. Frustration-aggression theory is easy to apply after someone has committed a deviant or criminal act, but it tells us little about why some people react to being frustrated by becoming aggressive or criminal and others do not.

Modeling (or Social Learning) Theory. This approach suggests that when people see someone they admire performing an act that society defines as deviant or criminal, they pattern their own behavior after that person, who serves as a model (Bandura, 1969, 1977). In this view, learning to be a criminal is similar to learning to be a doctor, lawyer, or nurse. As Sutherland (1937) made clear in his book *The Professional Thief,* there is a period of apprenticeship, during which one learns the craft by watching and imitating the master. Through association with others, one gradually learns the values, attitudes, and skills that are needed to practice the trade. The aspirant faces various trials and examinations and gradually takes on the identity of the occupation. This theory assumes that to learn to be a thief, for example, one needs role models and mentors who can pass on the lore of the trade and can indicate whether someone has mastered it. If individuals have no contact with such people, they will have little chance to learn criminal behaviors and values or to be reinforced in them. Thus, the nature of one's social network plays an important role in determining who will become a criminal and who will not.

By emphasizing the identity of the criminal, however, this view does little to explain the occasional criminal acts of those who do not go on to become professional criminals. As we will see later in this chapter, a great deal of criminal behavior is performed by juveniles who appear to taper off or stop committing criminal acts as they get older. A good theory of criminal behavior should be able to explain these changes in criminal rates by age. By itself, modeling theory has not been very successful at explaining why some behaviors are copied but others are not, or why some individuals follow the lead of people around them while others do not.

The physical and psychological explanations of deviance may help explain why individuals perform certain acts that a society has labeled as deviant. They cannot explain different *rates* of deviance in various societies or social groups, if such differences exist, except by saying that societies with higher rates of deviance or crime have people with different physical traits or different psychological histories. In order to try to explain different rates of deviance or crime, we need sociological explanations. Several sociological theories—anomie theory, differential association, and labeling theory—address this question.

ANOMIE THEORY

Anomie theory was first proposed by Emile Durkheim (1893) to explain different rates of suicide among people with different religious and marital statuses. (Married persons and Catholics and Jews had the lowest rates, Protestants the highest.) Durkheim believed that human desires and aspirations, if unchecked by social values and norms, were virtually limitless. In social life, groups usually develop norms that regulate and set limits on human aspirations. But in times of revolution, extreme prosperity, or economic depression, the power of social norms breaks down and people are in the state of normlessness Durkheim called *anomie,* in which life lacks meaning. As a result, people become more aggressive or depressed, resulting in higher rates of homicide and suicide.

The American sociologist Robert K. Merton (1957) adapted Durkheim's concept of anomie to a theory of deviant behavior. He suggested that deviance occurs when there is a mismatch between the normative goals of a society—for example, being successful and wealthy—and the allowable means for achieving those goals—getting a good job, for instance. If the goal of success is held out to everyone, but only some people have access to legitimate means for achieving

Table 8.3 Merton's Types of Deviance

	Response to	
	Culturally Approved Goals	Culturally Approved Means
Conformist	Acceptance	Acceptance
Innovator	Acceptance	Rejection
Ritualist	Rejection	Acceptance
Retreatist	Rejection	Rejection
Rebel	Substitution of new goals	Substitution of new means

SOURCE: Merton, 1957, p. 140.

that goal, some people may become frustrated and deviate.

Merton notes five types of responses that people make to the culturally prescribed goals and means in a society. These are presented schematically in Table 8.3. *Conformists* accept both conventional ends and means, even though they may be only partially successful in achieving the ends. *Innovators* accept the social goals but reject the approved ways of achieving them. They substitute theft, drug selling, or prostitution as an alternative means of trying to achieve material goals. They may also reject approved ways of doing something and yet still try to stay within the law, as in "creative" accounting. *Ritualists* reject grandiose views of success but conform closely to prescribed means. Office bureaucrats embody ritualism when they religiously follow the rules of their organization but lose sight of its goals. *Retreatists* abandon both means and goals; they become drug addicts, alcoholics, or bums. *Rebels* reject culturally valued means and goals, and substitute their own goals and means. They may become political revolutionaries or live a modest life dedicated to religion or to serving other people. Although it is possible to measure what proportion of a society adopts one or another of these responses, we can say little about why particular individuals react in one or another way.

Applied to crime, anomie theory offers a direct explanation of theft and perhaps an indirect explanation for murder, rape, and vandalism, if the latter are assumed to arise at least in part out of frustration over failing to attain culturally valued goals. One application of this theory has been made by Messner (1978), who found that a measure of income inequality in 39 countries, including the United States, was associated with murder rates, whereas economic production, population, population density, and urbanization were not. He suggests industrial and industrializing nations have a certain commitment to the value of equality that is violated when income is very unequally distributed. The resulting discrepancy between social expectations about how income should be distributed and how it actually is, he argues, undermines respect for social rules. It is this breakdown in the normative order that he believes is reflected in the high murder rates of nations with great income inequality. Additionally, short-term economic fluctuations, as reflected in unemployment rates, may also be related to changing criminal behavior (Brenner, 1973). Unemployment rates are related to arrest rates in Canada (Greenberg, 1977b) and in the United States as well (Yaeger, 1979).

Anomie theory looks at deviance as a rational adaptation to the discrepancy between culturally approved goals and means. As Table 8.2 shows, lower-class individuals are more likely to report that they commit crimes and more likely to be arrested than middle-class individuals, findings consistent with Merton's anomie theory of criminal activity. The theory may thus explain certain types of deviance, especially theft and robbery, but it does little to explain many forms of insanity and a number of other acts that are often termed deviant.

DIFFERENTIAL ASSOCIATION

Another group of sociologists has focused on why one rather than another behavioral response is followed. These sociologists suggest that people learn responses from the people with whom they associate. People whose parents and friends are conformists, they suggest, are more likely to become conformists themselves; those surrounded by innovators or retreatists are more likely to choose one of those approaches. The theory of *differential association* attempts to explain how deviant behavior, including criminal activity, is transmitted from one generation to another and from one ethnic group to a new one that may replace it in an urban neighborhood. Yet everyone is surrounded by a number of different types of people, some who are retreatists, some who are innovators, ritualists, conformists, or rebels. Why does a person choose to model behavior after one rather than another type? Is it the appeal and attractiveness of the people, their apparent success, or their similarity to the observer?

The prestige of the person in the eyes of other people is relevant to the influence that person has (Sutherland and Cressey, 1978). This process is evident in Shaw's classic study, *The Jack-Roller* (1930). One youngster told Shaw:

> Stealing in the neighborhood was a common practice among the children and approved by the parents. Whenever the boys got together they talked about robbing and made more plans for stealing. I hardly knew any boys who did not go robbing. The little fellows went in for petty stealing, breaking into freight cars, and stealing junk. The older guys did big jobs like stick-ups, burglary, and stealing autos. The little fellows admired the "big shots" and longed for the day when they could get into the big racket. Fellows who had "done time" were big shots and looked up to and gave the little fellows tips on how to get by and pull off big jobs. (Shaw, 1930, p. 54)

Deviant or criminal behavior is learned, just like language, religion, or baseball, according to Edwin Sutherland (1937). He suggests that people who have an intense emotional relationship at an early age with individuals who hold favorable attitudes toward breaking the law are more likely to break the law themselves. Conversely, people who grow up surrounded by family and friends who do not favor breaking the law (or any other form of deviant behavior) are much less likely to be lawbreakers or deviants themselves.

David Matza (1969) suggests that becoming deviant is usefully understood in terms of the notion of "causal drift," which falls between free will and total determinism. Becoming deviant involves a person being converted to a particular way of life. Such a conversion involves several steps. First, people must be willing to try an action defined as deviant (say smoking marijuana), and they must actually try it. The next question is whether or not the experience serves to satisfy the people trying it. Does the experience fit with what they expected and wanted from it? If so, they may become converted. If not, they may walk away from the experience and decide not to try it again.

Although every deviant situation contains a dare that is intimidating, it would be a mistake, Matza suggests, to say that people convert to deviance simply because they cave in to pressure from others. The people offering a deviant experience may be attractive or admired for reasons that go beyond that experience. Their influence may be considered by individuals who may take group pressure into account. But they also consider the nature of the experience itself. Before deciding to convert, people consider themselves in relation to a particular activity. They may choose to say no and pass the joint on, or they may take another drag. In short, people form a picture of themselves that may or may not include certain deviant actions, and they act accordingly.

One's choice is shaped by the situation one is in and by the attractions of the experience itself, suggests Matza. But he seems to assume that all individuals are equally likely to find themselves in similar situations. His view contains no conception of social structure, in which some people are more likely to be exposed to certain opportunities than others. The theory of differential association begins to explain how deviant or criminal behavior is learned. It does not, however, suggest how the behavior originated, who gets exposed to it, or how it came to be defined as deviant. Indeed, both differential association and anomie theories assume that an understanding of what deviant behavior is is something that everyone agrees upon. Labeling theory challenges this assumption by stressing that deviance and crime are socially defined by various groups and are relative.

LABELING THEORY

In his book *The Outsiders* (1963), Howard Becker rejected the view of deviance as similar to sickness. Treating deviance as a sickness for which causes and cures can be found ignores the critical role played by power and politics in the definition of deviance. Deviance, according to Becker, is created when some groups are able to impose their definitions and rules on others. By making rules whose infraction constitutes deviant behavior, some social groups label particular people as outsiders. *Labeling theory,* then, describes the ability of some groups to impose a label of "deviant" on certain other members of society. It focuses attention on the process by which individuals are labeled as deviant rather than on the nature of their behavior.

Everyone behaves in ways that might be considered deviant, but most of us are not labeled as deviant because the behavior is invisible to others, is short-lived, or is unimportant. Such behavior is called *primary deviance.* Examples include such actions as running a red light, stealing a candy bar, flirting with one's cousin, or screaming obscenities out a car window at a stranger. If people do not notice or comment on such behavior, the persons doing it are not

The appearance and behavior of so-called "punk" groups may lead other social groups to label and treat them as deviant.

viewed as deviant by others, nor are they likely to see themselves as deviant. But if someone else discovers and makes such acts public, *secondary deviance* may occur: The behavior may be publicly labeled as deviant, the person may be treated as a deviant, and the person may possibly begin to see himself or herself as deviant.

Such labeling may involve a "degradation ceremony" (Garfinkel, 1956), in which a person is publicly accused, berated and punished, and forced to admit wrongdoing. The person gets labeled: "sinner," "queer," "crazy," "junkie," "slut." Sometimes called *stigmatization,* this process involves spoiling someone's identity by labeling him or her in a negative way. (Figure 8.3 shows how this process occurs.) The process has several parts. For example, suppose an individual exhibits a certain behavior, such as theft. Other people may feel threatened or displeased with that particular behavior, and they may begin to label that person or behavior in an effort to control what they find objectionable.

The police, for example, have ideas about "typical" juvenile behavior, and of who are "good kids" or "punks," partly depending on family background. Later actions by youngsters, the nature of their family life, their school adjustment, psychiatric evaluations, and other evidence are all weighed by juvenile authorities as they decide whether or not someone is delinquent (Cicourel, 1968). Groups vary with respect to how well they can resist official definitions. Middle-income families, for example, mobilize resources to fight the definitions law enforcement officials try to impose. These families are routinely able to generate or command resources for neutralizing or changing probation and court recommendations, particularly with respect to putting youngsters in detention centers. A juvenile justice official's relationship to juveniles influences the immediate disposition of their cases and has long-range career consequences for the youths. Having spent time in a juvenile facility or detention center is a serious negative feature of juveniles' records and may hurt their futures (Cicourel, 1968).

If police officers are in a position to impose their judgment on the situation, as teachers can sometimes impose the label of "stupid" on a child or psychiatrists can impose the label of "mentally ill" on an individual, then their social typing may lead to the label being accepted by others or by the individual. The accused may incorporate the label into his or her self-image and begin to behave accordingly. The person may then associate only with others who share the stigmatized identity, which leaves little chance to practice other forms of behavior. One feature of stigmatization is that it has a cumulative negative effect in a person's life, just as high social status can have a cumulative positive effect.

Thus, the process of labeling may produce *deviant careers*. Other people interpret the present and even the past behavior of stigmatized individuals in terms of their new identities. Someone caught cheating on a test is assumed not to have written the excellent paper turned in earlier. Sexual relations experienced with someone later labeled a prostitute may lose their former personal significance.

In addition, stigmatized individuals bear the pain and shame of being viewed solely in terms of the stigmatized trait or behavior. All other aspects of their personalities and behavior may be ignored by other people, making it difficult if not impossible for them to form normal social relationships with others. People with physical handicaps, for example, often report the experience of being stigmatized. People rush to help them when they fall, stare at their handicaps, or constantly bring up the topic in conversation. All these actions tend to stigmatize someone with a handicap and make it more difficult to have normal social relationships with others (Goffman, 1963).

At the interpersonal level, stigmatizing occurs when people engage in vicious gossip about someone, with or without regard to the facts in the situation. Stigmatizing processes continue when someone is avoided at the water fountain or the coffee shop, or is not invited to social

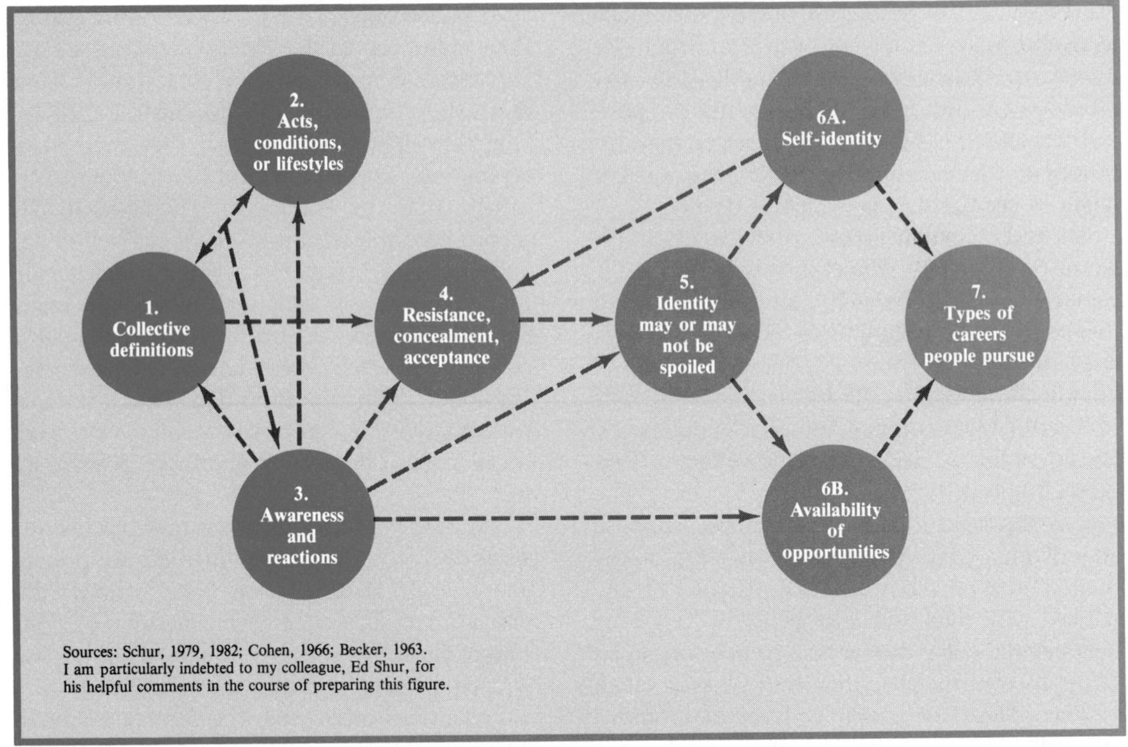

Figure 8.3 The Labeling Process *A series of processes is involved in labeling. Within each is a range of possible experiences, and each may have a variety of consequences.*

1. Collective definitions *are socially created with respect to a wide variety of acts, conditions, life-styles, or omissions. Collective definitions refer to the broad characterizations in a whole society of certain types of behavior or conditions (Schur, 1979). Some of these are defined as deviant to varying degrees. This is what Becker (1963) meant when he said groups create deviance by making rules, which may then be violated. Labeling theorists like Schur raise questions such as these: How are collective definitions made? What is the relative power of various groups in the process? What resources are mobilized in what ways in this process? Some collective definitions are formally stated as laws; others are negotiated more informally. Even laws, however, may be changed through political processes.*

2. *Individuals* perform acts, exhibit conditions, or pursue certain life-styles *(for example, stealing a candy bar, being handicapped, or living openly as a gay person) that may be defined to varying degrees as deviant if they are known to other people.*

3. *If other people become aware of certain behaviors or conditions they may react to them as deviant, through some formal means like a trial or informally through many small interpersonal expressions of revulsion or rejection. These reactions may help to create the collective definitions of something as relatively deviant, depending on where the boundaries get set. The relative power of the people who are reacting is an important factor in this process. Finally, the reactions of others may change the behaviors or life-styles of those being stigmatized.*

4. *The persons being labeled may try to resist or fend off the efforts to stigmatize them (for example, by trying to get the charges against them dropped, by concealing behaviors or conditions that might be stigmatized, or by trying to change the negative collective definitions of particular physical conditions or life-styles). Their success in changing collective definitions depends in part on their own rejection of those definitions and on their relative power. On the other hand, they may accept the collective definition of their behavior as deviant (as do some rapists or alcoholics when they decide to seek help).*

5. *Depending on the strength of the collective definitions and the capacity of those being labeled to resist being stigmatized, one's identity may be spoiled to a greater or lesser degree. Child molesters face much more social*

gatherings. At the organizational level, stigmatizing may occur when a bad evaluation is placed in a personnel file, when a person is fired, when a computer shows negative credit information, or when someone is required by organizational authorities to go for psychological counseling. At the societal level, someone who has been imprisoned, hospitalized for mental illness, dishonorably discharged from the armed services, treated for cancer, or who has worked for an unpopular political organization may find it difficult or impossible to obtain employment, housing, insurance, or credit.

The process is very close to that of *scapegoating,* whereby someone who is different or weaker is picked out and blamed for the problems of a larger group, regardless of the person's part in those problems. Hitler did this in the 1930s when he blamed the Jews for the structural social and economic problems Germany faced. Stigmatizing some individuals or behaviors may temporarily increase the cohesiveness of a group, but it also has several grave costs. First, it creates undeserved pain and suffering in the individuals who are stigmatized. Second, their contributions to the group are often lost because they are excluded or demoralized. Third, individuals in the larger group often cannot feel really secure, since they may be the next to be stigmatized. In addition, scapegoating involves misplaced grievance. Many problems have their roots in social structural causes that are difficult to pinpoint. It is easier to blame some weak yet visible group for these problems than to link them to structural causes. Archie Bunker, in the TV shows *All in the Family* and *Archie Bunker's Place,* deals with many of his problems by scapegoating minorities rather than by analyzing the structural sources of those problems.

Besides providing temporary emotional relief and unity to those doing the labeling, the process of stigmatization may unify and mobilize the stigmatized individuals. They may organize to change the way their behavior is defined. This struggle over whose definition will prevail has been called "the politics of deviance" (Schur, 1980), and is discussed in the next section.

The labeling explanation of crime suggests that crime rates may not vary much from one country to another or from one time to another. Instead, what changes is whether or not people define acts as crimes and how police depart-

---

consensus about the "deviantness" of their condition than do people who spray paint on public property. Conditions or behaviors differ with respect to how easily they may be concealed. Sadomasochists, for example, may be better able to conceal their predilections than transvestites; blind persons may be less able than epileptics to hide their condition.

6. The degree to which a person's identity is spoiled may affect that person internally and externally.

6A. Internally, people vary in the degree to which they accept or reject the stigmatized definition of themselves and incorporate it into their identities. Thus, for instance, they may see themselves as "nothing but a common thief," as a "pervert," or as a persecuted minority.

6B. Externally, being stigmatized may close off future opportunities for individuals (for example, for legal employment or for acceptance by people who have not been stigmatized, and so forth) (Cohen, 1966). Such a limitation of opportunities may make people who have been stigmatized more likely to pursue deviant careers. *A* deviant career *refers to the regular pursuit of activities that are regarded by individuals and by others as deviant.*

7. Self-identities and the availability of nonstigmatized opportunities may affect the degree to which individuals pursue relatively deviant or nondeviant careers (Cohen, 1966). For example, individuals may conclude, "there's nothing else I can do but be a full-time thief," or "I may be a dwarf, but I can still do worthwhile things with my life." Thus, individuals can be deviant in some ways without necessarily accepting a spoiled identity. In addition, deviant identities do not necessarily involve people on a full-time basis. Someone may be a reputable banker in the daytime and spend the evenings snorting cocaine. By concealing behavior that might be stigmatized, people may be able to pursue two careers, one that might be labeled by many as deviant and another that many people would not see as deviant. It is also possible that people might abandon behavior, life-styles, or conditions that are considered deviant.

ments and other officials record crimes. Unquestionably there are variations in crime statistics because of the way acts are defined and the way records are kept. Sometimes the murder rate in a country leaps from one year to the next when a new and more efficient set of public bureaucrats begins keeping records. Societies do vary with respect to what they consider to be crimes. Prostitution, for example, is legal in some societies. And even where it is illegal, the number of arrests made for prostitution may swing wildly, depending on the political pressure put on the police at any given time. It is important to realize that social factors influence the definitions of crimes, the number of people who are arrested for those crimes, and the care with which records are kept. But even a social constructionist would have trouble maintaining that all differences in crime rates can be explained by social factors.

The Nazi party tries to blame social problems on a group that is weaker or different from them, a process sociologists call scapegoating. Many others in the United States see the Nazi party as itself a deviant group.

CONFLICT AND MARXIAN EXPLANATIONS

The Politics of Deviance

A conflict perspective on deviance and crime emphasizes the relative power of different groups in a social situation and their capacity to impose rules and definitions on others. When, for example, is a particular behavior like drinking liquor or smoking pot defined as deviant or illegal, and when is it viewed as an "alternative life-style" that individuals are free to accept or reject? Formal and informal social power play major roles in this definitional process.

The social conflict surrounding the definition of behavior as deviant or not, legal or illegal, is well illustrated by the case of the gay rights movement. Members of this movement mobilized themselves politically in an effort to change the American Psychiatric Association's definition of homosexuality as a sickness and to change laws in many states that discriminate against homosexuals in hiring, housing, or credit. By openly challenging the label other groups in society were trying to pin on homosexuals, the gay rights movement has been rather successful. Behavior that had been considered sinful, criminal, perverse, or sick has come increasingly to be defined as a sexual variation or an alternative life-style. By the middle of the twentieth century, a growing body of social science literature was suggesting that a wide range of sexual practices fall within the range of "normative" human behavior. Moreover, the distinction began to be made between sexual behavior, on the one hand, and how that behavior is defined, on the other hand. In the 1960s, a growing number of publications and organizations grew up in response to efforts to gain equal rights for homosexuals. The term "homosexual" was increasingly replaced with the term "gay," which represents an alternative definition of a particular orientation and life-style (Conrad and Schneider, 1980; Spector, 1977; Teal, 1971).

A police raid on a gay bar in Greenwich Village in 1969 became one of the rallying points for the gay rights movement. When the police raided the bar, allegedly on the charge of a liquor license violation, the patrons resisted the attack with fists, bottles, and fire. A number of people were injured, and the police had to summon reinforcements. For the first time, the patrons of a gay bar refused to be harassed by police and society. The incident mobilized the gay community: there were public protests, demonstrations, and the organization of the gay rights movement. By 1972, more than a thousand local gay organizations existed in the United States, and by 1980, 26 states had decriminalized private consensual same-sex acts between adults (Conrad and Schneider, 1980).

Besides political and legal mobilization and change, removing the definition of a behavior as deviant requires changing the definitions used by public definers of behavior. This case involved modifying the way research and writings on same-sex behavior was classified in American libraries and changing the American Psychiatric Association's definition of homosexuality as sickness. In 1970 the American Library Association formed a Task Force on Homosexuality to remove the topic of homosexuality from its file location under "Sexual Perversion" (Spector and Kitsuse, 1977). After a heated political and scientific controversy within the American Psychiatric Association, that organization voted in 1973 to remove homosexuality as a psychiatric condition from the *Diagnostic and Statistical Manual.* People disturbed by their sexual orientation or wishing to change it are considered to have a "sexual orientation disturbance," and as such can receive psychiatric treatment for it. But anyone who accepts his or her preference for same-sex partnerships is no longer, according to the diagnostic manual, considered "sick."

Although the gay rights movement has made major gains in changing the way important groups in society define same-sex behavior, it has done less to change the way that preference is viewed in the larger society. About three-quarters of the general public in 1981 believed homosexuality to be morally wrong. More than two-thirds of the leaders in the news media, government, education, law, justice, and science viewed homosexuality or lesbianism as not morally wrong (*Wall Street Journal,* May 15, 1981). Gay rights activists have made some gains with respect to changing the legal and medical definitions that others place on their behavior, but they have not yet had the same success in changing what the general public thinks about that behavior.

This example suggests that the definition of something as deviant or illegal may depend quite heavily upon the social and political resources of groups favoring such a definition. Groups opposing such definitions may sometimes mobilize successfully. Thus, the definition of something as deviant may result from the social and political resources and strategies of contending groups. This theory would explain uneven rates of deviance in various societies in terms of which definitions prevailed in which societies.

Marxian Criminology

Some Marxian criminologists explain deviance and crime in terms of the relative powerlessness of different groups. They suggest that capitalism may produce conditions that generate deviant or criminal behavior. Some Marxian criminologists explain much of lower-class crime as a substitute for revolutionary activity. As such, criminals are actually rebels against a repressive capitalist system that uses the law, courts, prisons, mental institutions, and juvenile centers as weapons for controlling ever-larger numbers of rebellious members (Taylor, Walton, and Young, 1973). They see law as a tool of the powerful used to maintain social relations, especially class relations (Quinney, 1970, 1974; Chambliss, 1969).

Marxian criminology provides valuable insights into the place of law in capitalist societies, but it tends to overlook several important features of crime. There is, for example, considerable social agreement about the major crime categories. Most people, regardless of their social class background, are offended by and opposed to most instances of murder, rape, assault, armed robbery, breaking and entering, and arson. Moreover, ghetto residents and members of the working classes are among the most concerned in society about being victimized by crime (Greenberg, 1976), perhaps because they are the ones who are most likely to be victims.

ECONOMIC AND DETERRENCE THEORIES

Whatever the social conditions that encourage criminal acts and however people learn to do criminal activities, the possibility remains that criminals are sufficiently rational to respond to the certainty and severity of punishments imposed by law. Regardless, then, of what causes crime, one way to try to reduce it is to catch and punish offenders. A number of policy analysts argue that increasing the certainty and severity of punishment should lead to lower crime rates, when other things are equal (Becker, 1968; Sjoquist, 1971; Reynolds, 1971; Tullock, 1974; Van Den Haag, 1975).

Economic and deterrence theories of crime extend economists' analysis of choice in an effort to explain variations in crime rates. This approach suggests that people will commit crimes if they feel they will gain more by doing so than they would by using their time and resources in some other way (Becker, 1968). Some people become criminals and others do not because the costs and benefits differ. For example, burglars may believe that the economic or other benefits of stealing outweigh their feelings about committing an illegal act or their fears of being caught and punished. Sociologists who accept this economic explanation stress, in addition, that people have different costs and benefits depending on their locations in the social structure, their wealth, prior offenses, and the other opportunities available to them. As a result, not everyone has the same likelihood of committing crimes.

The general population tends to think about crime in terms that are compatible with economic and deterrence explanations. One-third of the respondents in a Gallup poll indicated that people commit crimes because of "the high cost of living or unemployment." The second most frequently mentioned reason also fits into a cost-benefit analysis. One-quarter of the respondents said that the "court system is too lenient," suggesting they believe that the costs of criminal activity are not high enough (cited in Flanagan et al., 1981, p. 192).

At the societal level, an economic explanation for crime indicates that the number of offenses depends upon the probability of conviction, the punishment if convicted, income available from legal and illegal activities, and an individual's willingness to commit an illegal act (Becker, 1968). The focus, then, is on the probabilities of being caught and the severity of punishment. Even murder is deterred by punishment, according to several research studies (Ehrlich, 1974, 1975, 1977). But one study of reported crime and arrest rates for 98 cities from 1964 to 1970 failed to show that a greater chance of being arrested reduced the rate of crime (Greenberg, Kessler, and Logan, 1977).

Despite the absence of a relationship between crime and arrest rates, Greenberg feels that this evidence does not invalidate deterrence effects on crime. These records show only arrests, not punishments. Moreover, numerous reports from former juvenile offenders, as well as introspection, point to the importance of punishment as a deterrent to crime. For example, if it were possible to steal $100,000 from a bank and be sure of never getting caught, many people would do so. Some people would not because they have internal controls against stealing, believing that it is deeply wrong. Others do not find stealing incompatible with their self-image and do not have deeply held feelings against doing it. Some of them are deterred from stealing, however, by the possibility of being caught and then embarrassed or punished. The punishment need not be a severe one to be a deterrent. In the Scandinavian countries, the Netherlands, and Switzerland, punishments are quite mild, yet those countries have very low rates of crime (Greenberg, 1981).

INTEGRATION AND EVALUATION

The potential of several of these theories of crime can be seen by applying them to the task of explaining variations in crime rates by age. Using a strand from anomie theory, Greenberg (1977a) argues that the structural position of juveniles in American society puts a great deal of pressure on them to realize highly valued immediate goals. Strong age segregation that makes youths particularly dependent on peers for approval and the rise of a clear "teenage market" for records, entertainment, clothes, makeup, cigarettes, alcohol, drugs, and other goods have combined to generate consumer "needs" in teenagers. When tastes were less expensive, parents or part-time employment could support such consumer desires. The growing costs of adolescent life-styles, along with the persistent decline in employment opportunities for young people, presents teenagers with a gap between the wish for activities and purchases and the legitimate means to pay for them.

Considerable qualitative evidence supports this explanation of teenage theft; money and goods are stolen because they are strongly desired. As teenagers grow older, their chances of getting jobs increase and their growing involvement in other instititutions such as the family and work may reduce their dependence on peers for self-esteem at the same time that it provides legal sources of income. Thus, anomie theory predicts a rapid decline in theft, which is what happens.

Schools may contribute to such delinquent acts as vandalism in that they shackle teen autonomy, publicly evaluate student performance, and sometimes humiliate students before their peers. Certain acts of seeming bravado may stem from anxieties over gender identity that are certainly not helped by the absence of paid employment and being humiliated in school. This explanatory strand draws on the insights of labeling theory.

A third explanatory strand stems from the growing seriousness of being caught, a form of deterrence theory. As offenders get older, their behavior is no longer so likely to be viewed as simply "childish pranks" by parents or police. Judges are likely to be more severe with older offenders, and the penalties may be harsher. Some former delinquents say they stopped committing crimes because they were unwilling to risk stiffer penalties as they grew older. By drawing on these several theoretical threads, Greenberg (1977a) has woven a composite theory that explains different types of criminal acts and fits the way criminal behavior declines with age.

When evaluating the various theoretical approaches to crime and deviance that have been presented here, we cannot conclude that some are "correct" and others are not. Instead, the different approaches allow us to consider somewhat different questions and address those questions several ways. Physical and psychological explanations, anomie theory, differential association, conflict, and Marxian views are all useful approaches to the question of who is relatively more likely to commit crimes. If we want to consider such questions as why crime rates vary at different times or in different societies, or why crime rates vary by age, then anomie, economic, conflict, Marxian, and labeling theory are all helpful viewpoints. Labeling theory is well suited to considering how acts, conditions, or life-styles are reacted to in ways that stigmatize them as deviant.

SOCIAL CONTROL AND LAW

SOCIAL CONTROL

Deviance and crime, like other social behaviors, are defined and shaped by the forms of social control in a society. *Social control* refers to the relatively patterned and systematic ways in which society guides and restrains individual behaviors so that people act in predictable and desired ways. An essential means of social control is socialization, through which growing children learn the values and norms of their social group. Once social rules are learned, many people conform to them out of habit. But sometimes individual desires clash with social expectations, and people behave in ways that violate social rules and values.

Society must then use other means to ensure conformity. Chief among these are *sanctions*—the rewards or punishments issued by individuals, organizations, or societies in an effort to secure conformity of behavior. Sanctions that are seen as rewards for desirable behavior are called *positive sanctions;* those that are meant to deter unwanted behavior are *negative sanctions.* At the interpersonal level, sanctions include smiles, scowls, praise, complaints, favors performed or withheld, and numerous other ways humans have devised for making life pleasurable or miserable for people they wish to influence. Organizations also have an extensive repertory of rewards and punishments. Higher organizational authorities can manipulate pay, hours worked, type of work done, size and location of someone's office, opportunities for promotion, and chances for internal and external acclaim or blame. Depending on how such elements are handled within the organization, they can serve as rewards or punishments. Clear negative sanctions include being disgraced within the organization or being fired.

Most societal rewards and sanctions are filtered through individuals or organizations. Certainly an organization's sanctioning power is enhanced by the amount of respect the society holds for the money, title, and power the organization does or does not confer upon individuals within it. Newscasters, for example, face stiff competition to attain anchor positions on the evening news. Because of the public recognition and high financial rewards the major networks can offer, the networks also hold considerable sanctioning power. Broadcasters are readily fired or demoted, thereby immediately losing all the advantages of their position. Through local, state, and federal laws, society can also exercise negative sanctions resulting in fines, arrests, or imprisonment for certain behaviors.

In primary groups and small communities, most social control is exercised *informally,* through the immediate responses of people whose reactions matter very much to an individual in the group. *Formally* applied sanctions are embedded in such institutional forms as the law or in procedures for granting awards. Table 8.4 offers examples of positive and negative formal and informal sanctions. All four types of sanctions operate in many social situations to ensure social control. Consider, for example, an individual teacher in a classroom who wants the students to be quiet or to do the assignment.

If social control is not formalized, the teacher has only personal charm, wit, smiles, scowls, or praise to draw on in exercising social control (Swidler, 1979). Many educators—and parents—feel that this is an insufficient and chancy basis for social control in the classroom; hence,

Table 8.4 Types of Social Sanctions and How They Are Administered

	Form of Administration	
Sanctions	Formal	Informal
Positive	Money, diplomas, medals, awards, prizes, promotions	Praise, admiration, approval, smiles, kisses, "pats on back"
Negative	Fines, imprisonment, banishment, death	Ridicule, ostracism, criticism, threats, name-calling ("weirdo," "fink," "nut")

more formal methods exist in most schools. Schools grant teachers the power to grade (including the power to flunk students), and authority to send pupils to the detention center or the principal's office. School systems have the formal authority (through law and accreditation organizations) to grant or withhold diplomas, certificates, degrees, and honors. These credentials have a certain value in the marketplace, and withholding them can have negative economic and status effects on individuals. In this way, using positive and negative formal and informal sanctions, one individual teacher is part of a larger system of social control.

Functionalists tend to define social control as the means and processes used by a group or a society to ensure that members conform to its expectations. This definition assumes that a society or group agrees on the expectations held for members—for example, that adultery is not only illegal but also a sin. A conflict view of social control suggests that groups with relatively greater power and legitimacy are most likely to get their power formalized. In a pluralistic society with many competing groups and interests, it is impossible for all views to be fully expressed in the law. So to some degree law and social control are arbitrary in such societies (Toby, 1974, 1981). This is evident, for instance, in statutes against loitering in certain neighborhoods.

In the interactionist view, social control emerges out of interactions between individuals rather than being something that exists, ready-made, in a situation, needing only to be exercised in various ways. Norms and rules are created or defined as they are applied (Schur, 1979), and we can only become aware of what those norms or rules are after we see how they have been applied. For example, in a study of mental illness, Yarrow et al. (1955) found that wives tended to "normalize" the erratic behavior of their husbands for quite a while before coming to the conclusion that their husands were mentally ill. When they "couldn't take it any longer," they concluded the behavior was not normal. As Schur (1979) suggests, the process of defining "mental disturbance" has at least two parts—the husband's behavior and the wife's reaction to that behavior. This example illustrates that rules and norms do not simply exist "out there," waiting for someone to come along and apply them. Instead, they emerge out of behaviors and the reactions to those behaviors.

Like rules and norms, social control emerges from an ongoing process of struggle and negotiation. Various participants bring unequal resources to bear in this process. Formal systems of social control include formal agents of social control. Every system of formal social control needs control agents. Becker (1963) distinguished two kinds of control agents: rule creators and rule enforcers. Rule creators such as lawmakers shape the rules, norms, or laws for a group, organization, or society. Rule enforcers like police officers try to keep people in line through various processes. In practice, however, the distinction between rule making and rule enforcement is a matter of degree rather than kind, as the interactionist approach reminds us.

In brief, functionalism points to the universality of social control in all societies, while the interactionist perspective emphasizes that rules are negotiated in social interactions. Conflict theory suggests that some groups may gain greater control over the negotiations that define what is to be socially controlled and how those definitions are enforced. All three outlooks contribute to our understanding of social control.

One of the major mechanisms of social control in modern societies is the law.

LAW AS A MEANS OF SOCIAL CONTROL

One of the central differences between modern industrial societies and simple tribal societies is the reliance of modern societies on law and formal legal systems to manage social processes that were once handled by tradition, the family, or tribal customs. This is true about what behavior is defined as deviant as well as about other social practices. An American returning from Upper Volta, in West Africa, remarked that he could leave his bicycle on the ground in a village and it would still be there a year later. Bicycles are valuable in Upper Volta, but tribal customs dictate what you may and may not do with something that belongs to someone else. In a pluralistic and highly complex society like ours, however, there is no one custom dictating how things should be done. Moreover, the binding quality of tradition works in a highly cohesive society where people see each other often on a face-to-face basis and can reward or sanction one another for their behavior. Tradition or personal honor is deeply undermined in a society where strangers do business and people have different goals, interests, and traditions. In a transitory, diverse, and highly complex society, growing reliance is placed on law rather than other methods to establish procedures, resolve disputes, and uphold rights and duties.

Law is a system of formalized rules established for the purpose of controlling or regulating social behavior. Even in a modern society, however, law is like an empty sack if it tries to stand up for a principle that is largely at odds with widely held mores and values. For example, in the 1920s the Prohibition Amendment did not stop people who wanted to drink from doing so, and today the national speed limit of 55 miles per hour is widely violated on many highways. Thus, the law is a social beast. Social processes and social relations shape the content of law, and the law at any given moment affects society and social life. (See the box on pages 204—205 for a summary of how functionalists and conflict theorists view the law.)

Law also touches on politics. Laws are enacted through political procedures, and they are interpreted and enforced by political authorities rather than purely according to custom. In modern societies, the body of law required to control and regulate social behavior consists of two types—criminal and civil.

Criminal law is concerned with wrongs

How Functionalists and Conflict Theorists View the Law

Law has tremendous potential to protect people and property. It also has the potential to oppress. Functional and conflict views of the law stress different sides of this double-edged blade.

Functionalists See the Law as Functioning:

1. To maintain public order, by defining crime and criminal activity and empowering agents to regulate it. Law may be called into play to settle disputes (such as broken contracts), marital disagreements, or differences over property boundaries. Law can take the place of screaming contests, fist fights, or murder.

2. To establish and uphold rights and duties. The law functions to interpret constitutional and other legal precedents for rights and duties. It also supports or denies an individual's rights or obligations in a particular situation. For example, there are laws that affirm a handicapped person's right to access to a public building and that state parents' obligations to support their children.

3. To establish procedures for doing certain things. The laws surrounding wills, for example, ensure the protection and disposal of property.

4. To confer legitimacy. The law operates to confer legitimacy on political leaders, on the heads of publicly chartered organizations such as universities, on religious leaders, and on corporate business leaders. Legal systems also operate as a major means of keeping records in a society. Births, deaths, marriages, citizenship—all these and other details of modern life need to be recorded in a legally binding and legitimate way.

5. To redistribute or innovate. Government agencies seek to use the legal system for social planning. Health care delivery, for instance, is affected by a system of laws that regulate what services are and are not covered by government medical insurance, by permissible fee schedules, and so forth.

6. To permit and protect certain rights and actions, such as First Amendment rights to freedom of religion, speech, assembly, or foreign travel.

7. To advance the interests of virtually all members or groups in a society. Stability and predictability, supported by law, facilitate the conduct of production, commerce, and education. Another benefit for the vast majority of citizens stems from laws that are designed expressly to limit the power of rulers. This was a major concern of those drafting the Constitution of the United States. They set up legal procedures enabling Congress to overrule or impeach the president, allowing the president to veto laws, and establishing the Supreme Court's right to declare laws unconstitutional.

Conflict Theorists Suggest That:

1. Law may operate to maintain a highly unjust or unequal social order.

2. The more powerful members of society may define the rights and duties that laws uphold in ways that benefit them. For example, doctors may influence legislation requiring influenza vaccine, and then benefit from the added business it gives them.

3. Some people may benefit more than others from particular procedures. Lawyers in the state legislature of New York have made the procedures surrounding wills complicated enough so that people cannot handle their relatives' estates themselves. The procedures in California are much simpler and make it possible for many people to handle the estates of their relatives.

4. More powerful classes or groups may influence who is defined as legitimate. Deciding on the criteria to be used to confer legitimacy is often the real point where power is exercised. What criteria determine who is to be granted state, federal, or local scholarship aid for college?

5. Who should be making social planning decisions? In the case of health care delivery, for example, it is obvious that older citizens who receive services, the medical profession, and taxpayers have different views of how social engineering should be conducted, or even if it should occur.

6. The legal system is inevitably bound up with a society's system of stratification (Schur, 1968). The most extreme cases of law being used in the interests of dominant groups occur in totalitarian societies such as Nazi Germany or South Africa today. There the ruling group shapes the legal system to serve its aims. But even in more democratic societies "law invariably reflects and influences the ordering of social strata within a society" (Schur, 1968, p. 88).

The functionalist and conflict views together show the law's potential for both oppression and protection. They alert us to the possibility that a legal system or particular set of laws may be more beneficial for some members of society than for others. To youths who like to hang out on street corners, antiloitering laws seem oppressive and discriminatory, while homeowners may see the same laws as their only way of controlling strangers who may be planning burglaries. One's actual (or hoped for) position in a society's system of privilege and property goes a long way toward explaining one's view of the law.

against society. It is enacted by recognized political authorities and prohibits or requires certain behaviors and provides specific punishment, administered by designated authorities, for violators. Criminal offenses may be grouped into three broad types: first, acts of physical violence such as murder, rape, and assault; second, infringements on property rights, including theft, fraud, and burglary; and third, a broad range of actions labeled crimes against health, morals, and public safety, including prostitution, gambling, pornography, drug use, drunkenness, and (in some areas) homosexuality. In a serious criminal case, the state initiates legal proceedings, often beginning with a police arrest. The rules of evidence are strict; a defendant must be found guilty "beyond a reasonable doubt"; and the court decides whether to acquit or convict the person charged. A crucial element in a criminal violation is the existence of criminal intent by the lawbreaker, who is thereby thought to deserve punishment, deterrence, or rehabilitation.

Civil law, which developed from Roman law, largely deals with private wrongs; that is, wrongs against the individual. Such actions as defamation of character, the invasion of privacy, selling defective goods, trespass, and negligence are violations of civil law. Civil cases are initiated by private citizens. The alleged wrongdoer receives a summons to appear in a civil court. The claim against him or her must be established by a "preponderance of the evidence," rather than the rule of "beyond a reasonable doubt." The court decision is termed a finding or a judgment, and violators are not usually punished. Instead, the victim is "made whole" (that is, compensated for any losses), or competing claims are resolved by further legal proceedings (Sykes, 1978).

The uniform commercial code is an example of a civil law that has been adopted in a number of states. This group of laws operates to standardize the law surrounding business practices such as the sale of goods, negotiable instruments such as checks, the loan of money, or documents of title such as a bill of sale.

PRISONS AS A FORM OF SOCIAL CONTROL

When law fails as a form of social control, prisons may be called on to perform that function. Prisons are designed to contain criminals so that they cannot harm more people and they are intended to punish wrongdoers. At the same time they are charged with treating or rehabilitating criminals so that they may return to society. An unintended result of prisons is that they may teach new criminal behaviors by providing contact between novices and hardened criminals.

Do Crimes Lead to Prison?

What happens when someone commits a

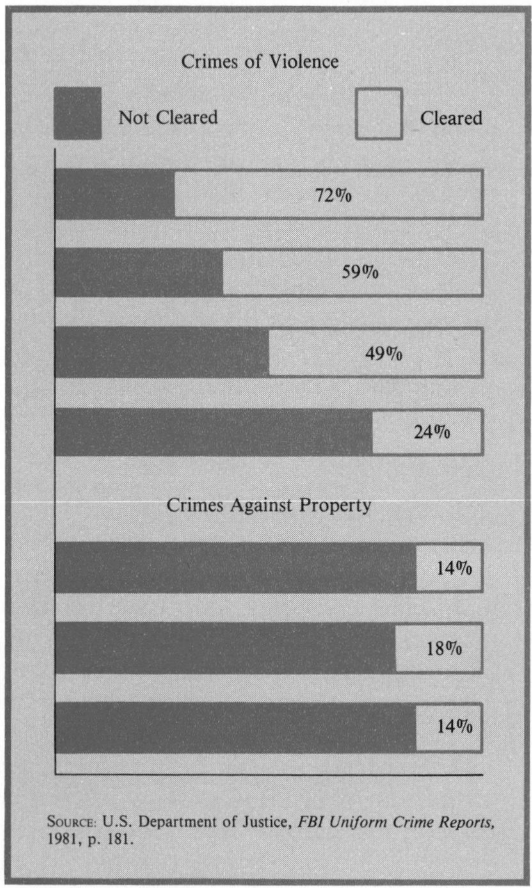

Figure 8.4 Crimes Cleared by Arrest, 1980

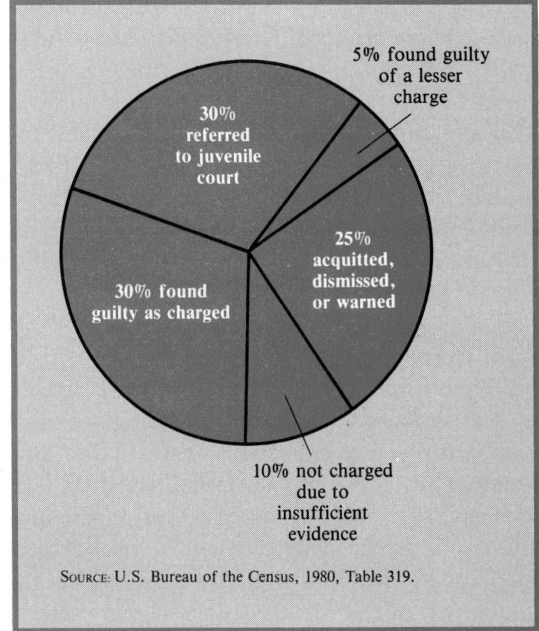

Source: U.S. Bureau of the Census, 1980, Table 319.

Figure 8.5 What Happens to People Arrested?

crime? Not all crimes are reported, as we have already seen. For those crimes that are reported, there is a wide variation in the percentage that result in arrests, as Figure 8.4 shows. Murder is most likely to result in the arrest of a suspect (in 73 percent of the cases), whereas motor vehicle theft is least likely to lead to arrest (only 14 percent of the cases).

Of those arrested, only about 30 percent are found guilty as charged, and another 5 percent are found guilty of a lesser offense. Another one-third of those arrested are referred to juvenile court, and about 10 percent are not charged because of insufficient evidence. The remainder of those arrested are acquitted, dismissed, or warned (U.S. Bureau of the Census, 1981a, Table 308). Figure 8.5 illustrates these data.

Arrested adults face a prosecutor who decides whether the evidence warrants prosecuting the case. The prosecutor may offer to "plea bargain" with the offenders—that is, to charge them with lesser offenses if they agree to plead guilty to the lesser charge. "Copping a plea," as it is known in the courts, was ruled legal by the Supreme Court in 1969. It reduces the overload faced by the courts and cuts the expense of a lengthy trial. People who cannot afford a lawyer to try the case are more likely to plea bargain. Those who insist on going to trial for the original offense face the threat of longer sentences, if they are found guilty, than those who plea bargain. The outcome of a trial can be acquittal for those found not guilty, or a suspended sentence, probation, or jail sentence for those found guilty. Some states have mandatory penalties for certain crimes; others leave the length of a prison sentence to the discretion of the judge.

Juveniles, those under the age of 18 in most states, are processed through a juvenile court. They may be acquitted, put on probation, returned to the care of their parents, placed in a foster or group home if the family situation is considered undesirable, placed in a community rehabilitation program, or sentenced to a juvenile correctional facility. Both adult and juvenile offenders may be released on parole after they have served some portion of their sentences.

In 1982 there were 394,380 people imprisoned in federal and state prisons in the United States, and nearly 200,000 more on parole (*New York Times,* 1982, p. A12). Public expenditures on the criminal justice system totaled nearly $26 billion in 1979 (U.S. Bureau of the Census, 1982a, p. 183). People get put in jail who have been arrested for a crime, are awaiting trial, and are unable to raise the money required for their bail. Given the delays in the court systems of many cities today, poor people who cannot raise bail may stay in jail for months awaiting trial, without ever having been convicted of committing a crime. The rest of the jailed population consists of people who have been arrested, tried, convicted, and sentenced to serve a jail term.

Effects of Prison on Guards and Prisoners

Sociologists sometimes suggest that treatment and custody are different goals that may govern prison life. But even when prison officials say their goal is treatment, such a statement may not always be taken at face value, since treatment programs can be used to achieve the aims of custody and control as well. Drugs, psychotherapy, and even lobotomies have been used to control prisoner militance, particularly when public attention prohibited the use of more obvious violence (Greenberg, 1977c; Speiglman, 1977).

Nearly 400,000 people are in federal and state prisons in the United States. Prisons are expected to perform a number of conflicting functions, including punishing prisoners for wrongdoings, preventing them from harming innocent people, and treating or rehabilitating convicts so they may return to society.

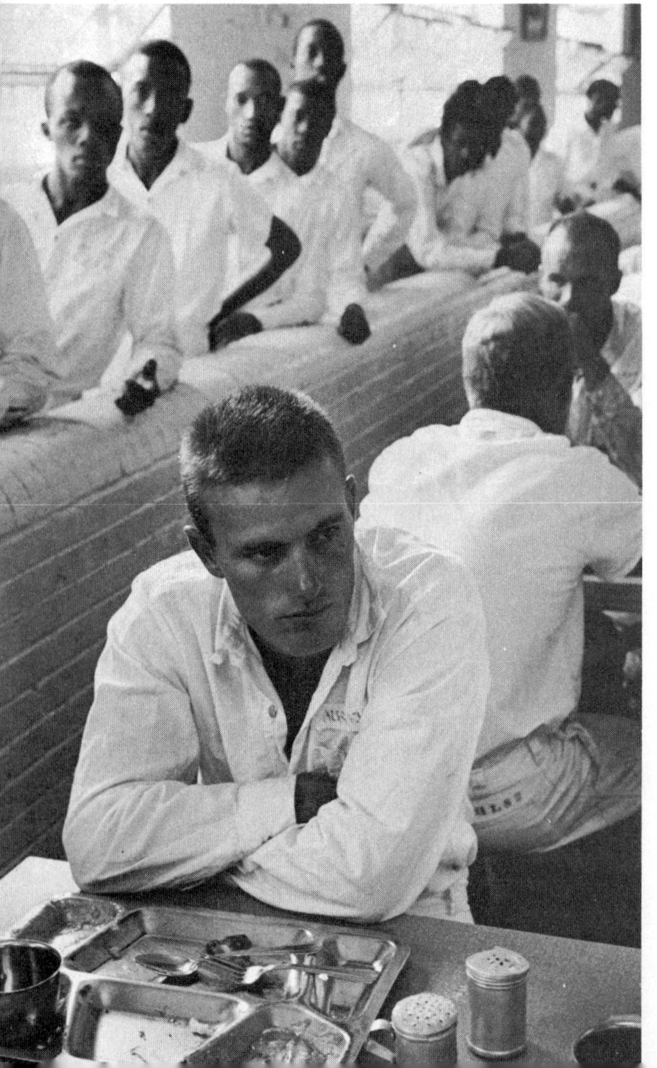

The potential abuse of power exists in any situation where power differences between participants are very large and where there is little chance for outsiders to know what is going on. This situation is pronounced in prisons, and reports of prisoners being murdered by guards, beaten, drugged, unlawfully put into solitary confinement, and not protected from attack or rape by other prisoners confirm the possibility that power can be abused in prisons.

The role of prison guard seems to call forth stern, harsh, or cruel actions, even from mild-mannered college students in an experimental situation. The social psychologist Philip Zimbardo (1972) simulated a prison in the basement of his office at Stanford University. He advertised for paid volunteers to participate in a study and screened more than 70 young men who applied for his experiment before selecting about two dozen for the study. Those selected were mature, stable, normal, intelligent college students from middle-class homes throughout the United States and Canada. By flipping a coin, Zimbardo assigned half of the volunteers to be prisoners and half to be guards. The guards made up their own rules, and were assigned to 8-hour, three-man shifts. The Palo Alto police arrested the "prisoners" at unexpected times and places, such as their homes, and brought them to jail, where they were stripped, deloused, put into uniforms, given numbers, and put into cells with two roommates. They were expected to stay there for two weeks.

The motivation of prisoners and guards alike had been the same—to make money (they were paid $15 per day). But the roles of prisoner and guard took over the values and personalities of the individuals involved and dehumanized them both. In Zimbardo's words:

> At the end of only six days we had to close down our mock prison because what we saw was frightening. It was no longer apparent to most of the subjects (or to us) where reality ended and their roles began. The majority had indeed become prisoners

> or guards, no longer able to clearly differentiate between role playing and self. There were dramatic changes in virtually every aspect of their behavior, thinking and feeling. In less than a week the experience of imprisonment undid (temporarily) a lifetime of learning; human values were suspended, self-concepts were challenged and the ugliest, most base, pathological side of human nature surfaced. We were horrified because we saw some boys (guards) treat others as if they were despicable animals, taking pleasure in cruelty, while other boys (prisoners) became servile, dehumanized robots who thought only of escape, of their own individual survival and of their mounting hatred for the guards. (Zimbardo, 1972, pp. 4–8)

Although the results of the study were startling, we should be careful about generalizing from Zimbardo's study. One problem in doing so is that the college students were new to the game of being a prison guard. In a real prison, a guard enters an existing structure that has been set up to be repressive. In such a situation, individual guards may not be required to be as tyrannical as they were in Zimbardo's experiment.

Because prisons are "total institutions" in the sense that Goffman uses the term, meaning a place where people conduct all aspects of their lives (sleep, work, relaxation) under the same authority, with the same group of other people, and on a tightly scheduled and regimented basis, individuals are cut off from the outside social world and lose most of their capacity to be self-determining. One result is that prisons tend to develop their own subcultures, although these subcultures are influenced by the wider society.

Racial hostilities that exist in the larger society may get acted out inside prison. Groups of inmates may form informal understandings with prison guards whereby certain inmates receive special privileges, such as extra rations of cigarettes or greater freedom of movement, in return for keeping things "under control" inside the prison (Barton and Anderson, 1966; McCleery, 1966). Inmate subculture forbids open cooperation with prison authorities and prohibits "squealing" or "ratting" to the authorities about anything. "Square Johns" are middle-class people who never become part of the criminal subculture; "right guys" avoid contact with prison officials and other inmates; "outlaws" disrupt life for inmates and guards alike; and "dings" behave inconsistently and tend to avoid others completely, according to Garabedian (1963).

Do Prisons Reduce Crime?

Prisons fail to accomplish most of the major goals society holds for them. Since so few crimes actually result in arrest, conviction, or sentencing, the goal of restraining crime by keeping people out of circulation is only partially realized. Few offenders actually mend their ways and follow the "straight and narrow" after they are released, partly because once someone is labeled as an ex-convict it becomes difficult to find a legitimate job. Moreover, many criminals learn new tricks in jail. Prisons are often called "schools for crime."

Numerous surveys of different correctional programs, including rehabilitation and treatment programs, suggest that most programs do not prevent people from returning to crime (Lipton et al., 1975; Martinson, 1974; Greenberg, 1977c). Some programs show modest success, particularly those that offer educational opportunities or vocational training. Existing rehabilitation programs rest on the assumption that individual behaviors are entirely responsible for crime and ignore the social effects of opportunity structures and differential association. Since prisons deal only with individuals and not with the social conditions that might cause or increase crime, and they do this with mixed purposes, it is not surprising that they do little to prevent repeat offenses. But although prisons may do little to prevent new offenses by former prisoners, their existence may serve as a deterrent to members of the larger society.

Summary

1. Deviance is socially defined and varies by time, place, and social group. Behavior that is defined as deviant violates strongly held social norms. Certain groups have more power than other groups to get their definitions of what is deviant accepted.

2. Crimes are acts that are prohibited by law. More than 2800 acts have been defined as crimes by federal law, but only eight are termed "index offenses": rape, robbery, murder, aggravated assault, burglary, larceny, auto theft, and arson.

3. Crime rates in the United States are high and have increased rapidly in recent years. Interviews with victims suggest that crime figures are even higher than the FBI statistics suggest.

4. White middle-class males are more likely to commit white collar crimes such as embezzling, tax evasion, price-fixing, or illegal waste disposal than are blacks or females. Lower-class and black males are more likely to commit violent crimes and burglaries than are middle-class whites or females. The way the police and the courts handle and record offenses explains part, but not all, of the variation in criminal rates by race, age, social class, and sex. Differences do exist, and they need to be explained by social theory.

5. Physical, psychological, sociological, and economic theories of deviance and crime have been offered. Physical theories suggest that something inborn in people, such as the XYY chromosome pattern, causes them to be deviant. Psychological theories suggest that tendencies to deviate result from early socialization. Social learning suggests that criminal or deviant behavior is learned like other forms of social behavior.

6. The four major sociological explanations are anomie theory, differential association, labeling theory, and conflict and Marxian theories.

7. Anomie theory suggests that when there is a tension between the goals a society holds out for individuals and the available means for achieving those goals, some people may become frustrated and deviate from either the goals or the acceptable means for achieving those goals.

8. The theory of differential association asserts that deviant or criminal behavior is learned by associating with people who have already been labeled as deviants or criminals.

9. Labeling theory challenges a relatively fixed view of deviance. Most people engage in a variety of unusual behaviors in their lives but are never labeled deviants either because no one observes the unusual behavior or because they choose to ignore it. The process of labeling a behavior as deviant may stigmatize individuals and stimulate further deviant behavior.

10. The politics of deviance refers to the way the differential power of various groups in society helps determine which social rules get imposed and on whom they are imposed. The struggle of the gay rights movement to change the definitions of deviance imposed on homosexuals by the American Psychiatric Association, the law, and the American Library Association reveal the political nature of these definitional conflicts over what is defined as deviant.

11. Marxian criminologists suggest that criminal behavior grows out of capitalist social relations, in which one class exploits the labor of another class.

12. Economic and deterrence theories grow out of the economic assumption that people will commit crimes if they feel they will gain more by doing so than they would by using their time and resources in some other way. In these theories, the certainty and severity of punishment are expected to influence criminal behavior.

13. The usefulness of several theories together is apparent in Greenberg's explanation of why youthful crime rates drop dramatically as youths reach their early twenties. The various theoretical views of crime and deviance provide useful approaches to various types of questions, including which individuals are most likely to commit crimes, why crime rates vary, and how particular acts or conditions are stigmatized.

14. Functionalism stresses the universality of social control in all societies. The interactionist perspective emphasizes how rules are negotiated in social interactions. Conflict theory suggests that some groups may have more control over the processes that define what is to be socially controlled and how such rules are enforced.

15. Law, socialization, and sanctions are some of the ways societies and social groups try to get their members to conform to social expectations. Positive sanctions like smiles and praise as well as negative sanctions such as scowls or scolds operate on the individual level. Organizations and legal entities can bestow rewards or punishments as well.

16. Modern industrial societies rely heavily on the law and legal systems rather than upon custom and tradition to define deviance, maintain public order, establish the rights and duties of members, set procedures, confer legitimacy, and resolve disputes.

17. Functionalists tend to focus on the purposes law serves for the whole society. Conflict theorists suggest that some interests might benefit more than others from particular legal arrangements. Each view captures part of the double-edged nature of law in society: Law can both oppress and protect individuals.

18. Less than half of all reported index crimes are cleared by arresting a suspect, and of those arrested only about 30 percent are found guilty as charged. The charge being leveled against someone may be reduced by the process of plea bargaining. As a result, most people are not brought to trial for the actual crimes that they commit.

19. Prisons are designed to contain criminals to prevent their harming other people; they are meant to punish wrongdoers; and they may be expected to treat or rehabilitate prisoners so they are fit to return to society.

20. Prison life takes its toll on prisoners, guards, and taxpayers. Zimbardo's experiment (1972) shows how even "normal" college students took on the roles of prisoners and guards in a very short time. There are nearly half a million people in federal, state, and local prisons in the United States. Public expenditures on the criminal justice system totaled nearly $26 billion in 1979.

21. Surveys of correctional programs suggest that such programs often do not prevent people from returning to crime. They may, however, serve as deterrents to people who might otherwise commit crimes.

Key Terms

anomie
anomie theory
civil law
crime
criminal law
deviance
deviant career
differential association
formal sanction
informal sanction
labeling theory
law
negative sanctions
positive sanctions
primary deviance
rebellion
retreatism
ritualism
sanction
scapegoating
secondary deviance
social control
stigmatization
white collar crime

Part Three

Social Inequality

Chapter 9

Social Stratification

What comes to mind when you think about patterned social inequalities? Fat cats and hungry cats? Expensive cars and waiting for a bus? Never having enough money to do what you want to do? Rich or poor, we have all experienced the effects of social stratification in our lives. Our personal tastes, leisure activities, friends, individual aspirations for life and work, health, life expectancy, where we live, work, and go to school are all directly influenced by social stratification. This statement holds true for most societies.

WHY IS STRATIFICATION IMPORTANT?

Social stratification is the fairly permanent ranking of positions in a society in terms of unequal power, prestige, or privileges. Stratification refers to patterned, or structured, social inequalities among whole categories of people, not just among individuals. *Social inequalities* refer to the unequal opportunities or rewards for people in different social positions. Stratification systems contain social inequalities, but the term stratification goes beyond inequality in several key respects. First, stratification refers to differences in social groupings; inequality refers to differences among individuals. Stratification is relatively permanent and may be handed down from one generation to another; inequalities are less likely to be passed from one individual to another. The proportion of the United States population that is poor, for example, remains fairly constant from one year to the next, even though each year some new individuals fall into poverty and some who were poor escape to a higher standard of living. Systems of stratification are relatively permanent because they are systematically linked with other important institutions in society, such as the economy, the family, religion, politics, or education.

The lives of Alice and Alex and Albert and his wife (in Chapter 1) illustrate the differences between stratification systems and inequality. These young people have individual differences in personality, appearance, and speech style, but those personal differences are not what cause their starkly different lives. Instead, they occupy positions in a system of social stratification based on wealth, power, and prestige that profoundly affect virtually every aspect of their lives—who they know; when, where, and how they start working; and what alternatives are open to them.

Social stratification affects the life chances of individuals in the various social groupings of a society. *Life chances* refer to individuals' odds for obtaining various opportunities in their society. Sociologists often use the term to include, for example, chances of earning a college degree, having a healthy and long life, getting a good job, or living in pleasant surroundings.

Societies around the world differ with respect to their systems of stratification. Western capitalist countries tend to have relatively greater equality with respect to political power and rights and fairly high levels of economic inequality. Many Communist countries reduce the degree of economic inequality, but have high concentrations of power in the hands of state and party officials.

Social stratification has led to revolutions, bloodless reforms, and other social changes. Sociologists focus on stratification both because of its potential for social tension and upheaval and because of the way stratification is related to so many other aspects of social life, from family size to test scores, schooling, political beliefs, mental and physical health, leisure pursuits, and life expectancy. The nature of social stratification in a society is one of its most significant features and one of the most important ones to understand.

The stratification system of our society affects the people with whom we associate, the social groups and networks to which we belong, and the kinds of interactions we have with people. Do we treat other people with respect, or do we expect them to treat us with special respect? Do we approach situations with confidence or with anxiety? To a large degree, these seemingly personal features of social life are affected by one's relative position in the stratification system. People high in the stratification system are more likely to know people who are also highly placed (or at least to have access to them through family or friends). Others will react to high-rank people with respect, deference, envy, or anger, but their reactions may be based on position, independent of personality. On the other hand, people at the bottom of the stratification system may be shunned, spurned, banned from certain places, treated more harshly by the legal system, or denied opportunities of many kinds, regardless of personal talents.

One's objective position in the system of stratification and how others respond to that position will affect how weak or powerful that person feels in the social world. People who feel powerless in a society will be less likely to support the norms of that society, since they have few opportunities within it. (We saw in Chapter 7 how powerlessness in an organization affects how people feel about it.) Individuals who occupy positions of power and importance, and see their importance reflected in the reactions of others to them, may be staunch supporters of the status quo, including its values, ideology, and mechanisms of social control (Huber and Form, 1973). Individuals who occupy similar positions in the stratification system will not necessarily behave and believe in the same way. However, there are patterns in the behavior of individuals who occupy similar positions, and sociologists are concerned with identifying and explaining those patterns.

Some systems of stratification, for example, caste systems, rest on social prestige differences. Class systems are rooted primarily in economic inequalities. A third form of stratification hinges on the amount of political and military power members possess. In this chapter we consider the three major roots of stratification—property, power, and status—and examine how these three sources are interrelated in the class society of Great Britain, the totalitarian regime of Nazi Germany, and the caste society of South Africa. Then we consider why stratification systems exist and how they are maintained. Despite their mechanisms for dominance, stratification systems do not go unchallenged. Every system contains contradictions and other potential for change, including competing ideas, status inconsistencies, and historical trends that make change possible.

THE ROOTS OF STRATIFICATION

Where social stratification exists, members of privileged groups (usually families) are generally able to transmit their positions of superior power and resources to others regardless of their personal qualities. For example, a wealthy family seeks to protect the wealth being given to inept family members by establishing trust arrangements and legal and financial advisors. Young people who want to become doctors but are not admitted to an American medical school may go to other countries to study medicine if their parents have the knowledge and money to help them do so. Systems of social stratification are firmly grounded in three major interrelated sources of inequality: property, power, and prestige.

PROPERTY

Property includes the ownership or control of productive resources, whether land, water, industrial equipment, ideas, or technology. The concept of *property* includes the rights and obligations a group or individual has in relation to an object, resource, or activity. Private property in the United States includes the right to occupy a home that you own, the right to dig for oil on your own land, and the right to receive available interest or dividends on money you have invested. Ownership of productive resources, rather than consumer goods or "collectibles" such as paintings or diamonds, constitutes socially significant property in the long run. People who own productive resources not only get whatever income those resources generate, but they also make decisions that may affect the lives of many other people. People owning real estate may decide where they will build an apartment building, to whom they will rent units, and how much they will charge (within legal and market limits). People owning a factory may decide to close it or to move it somewhere else, thus dramatically affecting the lives of people who work there. For these reasons, control of productive property has a much greater effect on other people than do inequalities of income or prestige. It is significant that in the United States, Canada, and Western Europe, inequalities of wealth are much greater than inequalities of income. (These differences are discussed further in the next chapter.)

Societies vary widely in terms of what property individuals own. Many societies, especially hunting and gathering societies, regard land as something no individual can "own." Instead, the right to use land for certain purposes is shared by the entire community. Social ranking begins to occur when surpluses are generated, and when some individuals own or control appreciably more productive resources than others. Those who own more gain higher rank.

POWER

Individuals and groups vary in terms of how much political or military power they possess. *Power* is the ability to get others to obey your commands. To be most effective, the exercise of power needs to be seen as *legitimate* by those affected; that is, they need to accept the authority of those exercising power and to feel that those with power have the right to exercise that power. Legitimate power (authority) is being exercised when the librarian asks to see your card when you check out a book. When a person with a gun asks for your wallet, that represents an illegitimate use of power.

Social ranking enters the picture when some individuals or groups have more military or political power, more influence, or more authority than others. In most modern industrial societies, the military power of individuals has been severely limited by the state. Although it is still possible for individuals to buy dynamite, machine guns, rifles, and handguns, it is certainly illegal for them to be used in most situations. So military power is more frequently used to compare nations than individuals. Political power is important to both individuals and groups. Their goal usually is to influence the selection, election, and behavior of important political figures. Groups seeking to change or to maintain the legal order seek to maximize their political power, and they differ widely with respect to how much political influence they have.

Power is the central basis for stratification in a totalitarian society, where there are few limits on the power of the state. The state extends its control to all features of social life, without regard for individual rights. The term *totalitarian* was coined to refer to political regimes that use every conceivable control mechanism, such as party machines, police, terror, torture, the destruction of all opposition, control of the mass media, and even youth groups that report on "disloyal" parents. Expensive and sophisticated technologies increase and concentrate the instruments of oppression available to nations today. These include electronic surveillance equipment, computerized data banks, physically and psychologically sophisticated methods of torture, and elaborate weaponry.

The importance of occupational and organizational power, rather than state power is stressed by the contemporary German sociologist Ralf Dahrendorf (1959). He underscores the importance of authority in the working world for determining one's position in society. Individuals with authority over large numbers of subordinates frequently have greater power, income, and prestige than individuals who do not have such authority.

PRESTIGE

Prestige refers to social recognition, respect, admiration, and deference. In different societies and even within different groups in the same society, prestige may be accorded to individuals for the possession or achievement of very different traits. In some circles in the United States, family and "breeding" are still considered more important for prestige than newly acquired wealth.

Weber (1920) touched on prestige differences when he used the term *status group* to describe people who share a social identity based on similar values and life-styles. Members of the same status group are likely to belong to the same clubs and associations, enjoy social activities together, and consider it appropriate to intermarry.

In American sociology, prestige has been studied using a variety of indicators and by using occupation alone. In a famous study of Newburyport, Massachusetts, researchers Warner, Meeker, and Eels described social prestige within the community. They suggested there were six classes based on social reputation, life-style, occupation, and wealth (1949). The six classes were upper-upper class, lower-upper class, upper-middle class, lower-middle class, upper-lower class, and lower-lower class. In Newburyport, the tiny upper-upper class was composed of rich families with old wealth, usually made at sea. The lower-upper class was wealthy families with new money made in shoes or textiles. They had less social prestige than the upper-upper class. The upper-middle class consisted of professionals and owners of smaller stores and businesses. They aspired to join upper-class prestige groups, but seldom succeeded. They worked actively in civic life, generally advancing the interests of the upper class. The top three classes made up about 13 percent of the population of that city.

The lower-middle class consisted of clerks, white collar workers, small tradespeople, and highly skilled workers. This group represented about 28 percent of the population. The upper-lower class consisted of "poor but honest workers" who made up 34 percent of the population. Lower-lower class members were alleged by others to be shiftless, improvident, and sexually promiscuous. Warner found them to be simply poor and lacking in ambition. Although Warner and his associates asserted the independent importance of prestige differences, the distinctions they observed were actually rooted in economic positions consolidated over generations (Rossides, 1976). This example reveals that prestige does not exist in a vacuum: It has economic and cultural sources.

The prestige of various occupations has also been studied. The prestige ranking of occupations is based on the income, educational level, nature of the work, clothing worn to work (particularly white collar versus blue collar), and social or political influence that an occupation commands (Hatt and North, 1947; Hodge, Siegel, and Rossi, 1966; Hodge, Treiman, and Rossi, 1966; and Treiman, 1977). Over the last two decades, Americans have been fairly consistent in the way that they ranked occupations, and these rankings are fairly constant in other industrialized and nonindustrialized societies as well (Hodge, Treiman, and Rossi, 1966; Treiman, 1977).

The three roots of stratification—property, power, and prestige—very often go together. Sometimes they do not, as in the case of sports figures or movie stars who may have high incomes and high prestige of a certain kind but little power, or federal judges who have considerable power and prestige but are not highly paid. And sometimes it is possible to distinguish one or another as the foundation for a particular stratification system.

THREE TYPES OF STRATIFICATION SYSTEMS

Certain types of societies have stratification systems based on one major source of ranking. Great Britain, for example, is mainly a class society based on property distinctions; Nazi Germany was stratified by power; the caste society of South Africa is an example of a society stratified by racial prestige. In a caste society, the law and police power are used to harden the boundaries between status groups. Differences in social prestige may therefore result in restricted human rights, freedoms, and opportunities for certain groups.

CLASS SYSTEMS—THE CASE OF GREAT BRITAIN

In a *class system,* stratification is based primarily on the unequal ownership and control of economic resources. One gains power, position, and prestige by controlling productive wealth. Generally it is difficult to pass along prestige or political power to a second generation without owning productive property. Popular rock singers, sports stars, or politicians occasionally get rich, but if their money is not invested in economically productive ways, their position will be neither influential nor lasting. If newly rich folk heroes spend their money on consumer goods—houses, Rolls Royces, fur bedspreads, and so on—they may change their life-styles but not their social class, because they have no control over productive resources.

The stratification of society along class lines is more apparent in Great Britain than in most other industrial societies. Political leaders are drawn almost exclusively from privileged families and upper-status occupations. Business leaders are drawn from even more privileged backgrounds (Putnam, 1976). Britain has a very small upper class comprised of families with "old wealth." The top 1 percent owns 25 percent of the nation's wealth; the richest 5 percent owns nearly 50 percent; and the wealthiest 10 percent owns more than 60 percent of the nation's riches (according to a 1980 Royal Commission report). The upper class retains many of the trappings of a feudal hierarchy, with earldoms, knighthoods, and peerages still bestowed upon people and reflected in titles of social address, such as Lady Bellamy or Sir Henry. Originally, English wealth was based on land ownership, but since the Industrial Revolution it has branched into industrial ownership as well. In addition to controlling the wealth and being addressed in distinctive ways, the upper class is notable for its accent and speech. In fact, differences in accent are a rather precise indication of social class membership in Britain.

"So long, Bill. This is my club. You can't come in."

SOURCE: Drawing by Weber, © 1979, *The New Yorker Magazine, Inc.*

Beneath the upper class, Britain has a small upper-middle class of professionals, a rather large lower-middle class of skilled white collar workers, and a big working class comprising more than half the total population. Taxes are very high on earned income, but differences in inherited wealth are profound. Income above about $35,000 a year is taxed at a rate of nearly 90 percent (compared to a top tax rate of 50 percent in the United States), and most of the

The highly stratified British class system influences virtually all aspects of social life. Political and economic power is concentrated heavily in the hands of upper-class families, even though more than half the population is working class.

deductions available to Americans do not exist for Britons.

Besides inherited wealth and accent, class divisions in Britain are maintained by a system of private boarding schools (called "public schools"). The children of the top 5 percent attend these exclusive and expensive schools, where they receive rigorous academic preparation for Oxford and Cambridge, the nation's two elite universities. The majority of public school graduates attend "Oxbridge," as it is called (Gathorne-Hardy, 1977, p. 450). They are virtually assured a high position in business, religion, the media, or political life upon graduation. Exclusive men's clubs keep members of the national elite in contact with one another, forming what has been dubbed "the establishment" or "the magic circle," a rather vivid example of social networks in operation. The magic circle is a closed circle to most outsiders, since rates of upward mobility in Britain are lower than in the United States (Treiman and Terrell, 1975; Covello, 1979).

STRATIFICATION BY POWER—NAZI GERMANY

Some systems of stratification are based primarily on political power and force. This becomes particularly apparent in an *autocracy,* where power is concentrated in a single ruler or group of leaders, who are willing to use force to maintain control. The contemporary and most complete form of autocracy is called *totalitarianism,* and it involves the use of state power to control and regulate all phases of life. Divergent views are treated as threats to the state, and conformity is enforced by propaganda, censorship, regimentation, and force. Stratification occurs in this system when rank, prestige, and material resources as well as political power are controlled by the state. Stratification by political power is evident to some degree in such state socialist countries as the Soviet Union, Poland, Hungary, and Czechoslovakia (Lenski, 1979). Nazi Germany under the rule of Adolf Hitler was perhaps the most extreme example of stratification by power.

Hitler was appointed chancellor of Germany in 1933. Through a series of maneuvers, he succeeded in obtaining the authority to issue decrees without the approval of the general legislative body or the president. He also appointed a Nazi party member to the cabinet position of minister of public enlightenment and propaganda. Having gained control of the state apparatus, Hitler proceeded to build an alliance with business leaders and the army. With the army's support, the offices of president and chancellor were merged, making Hitler supreme commander of the armed forces.

From 1934 to 1939, the Nazi totalitarian police state extended its power. Dissidents were controlled by the dreaded SS police and security system. Education, art, media, science, and religion were all required to conform to Nazi dictums. The compulsory Hitler Youth Movement aimed to indoctrinate the young. Although politically under Hitler's control, the army and the foreign service remained relatively independent until 1939. By attacking their private lives, Hitler succeeded in removing the commander in chief and the minister of defense. He also retired 16 senior generals, thereby gaining full control of the army. Individuals and groups, particularly Jews, were persecuted, arrested, had their property seized, and were imprisoned. Eventually millions were killed: Institutionalized inequality was taken to its outer limit.

CASTE SYSTEMS—THE CASE OF SOUTH AFRICA

Suppose the government told you where you could and could not live, that you could not vote in regional or national elections, that you could under no circumstances join a labor union, and that there were certain people whom you could not marry or have sexual relations with. That is exactly the situation of 18 million nonwhites in South Africa today, despite the fact that they comprise 83 percent of the total population. They live in the most complete caste system in the world.

Defining Caste

A *caste system* is a closed system of social stratification based on heredity that determines a person's occupation, prestige, residence, and social relationships. The term *caste* originally referred to religiously sanctioned social categories in India, where there was a priestly Brahmin caste at the top and an "untouchable" caste at the bottom of society, and a number of other castes in between. A caste system is established by law and custom and is supported by religious or other ideologies.

Because social contacts between members of different castes are prescribed and restricted, most caste systems require that one's caste be immediately visible. Racial or other physical differences often form an important basis for stigmatizing certain individuals as lower caste, and

Hitler used the power of the state to persecute, imprison, and kill millions of Jewish citizens. These men are being marched to a concentration camp by gestapo agents in Warsaw, Poland, March 27, 1940.

serve as boundary markers for caste groups. Caste systems, then, are very likely to be based on racial or ethnic differences. Besides the traditional caste system in India, caste systems of social stratification have developed in certain advanced horticultural and agrarian societies. In addition, features of a caste society were evident in the southern part of the United States during and after the period of slavery, when blacks were denied the right to vote or to use public facilities such as restaurants, and were required to use deferential terms of address such as "Sir," "Ma'am," "Mr.," and "Mrs." but were never addressed that way themselves. Similarly, native Americans were treated in castelike ways when they were barred from political participation and moved off their land. Since the caste system in South Africa is the most intact one in the world today, it is worth considering in more detail.

South Africa: A Case Study

The Republic of South Africa represents a contemporary caste system that is supported by the religious, legal, and police apparatus of that country. One of the notable features of South Africa is the fact that it has not always been a caste society. It is only within this century that nonwhites lost their rights to own property, vote, and obtain certain legal protections. South African history from 1910 to the present reflects the reaction of the early Dutch settlers, called Afrikaaners, to their economic situation, and their use of a racially based caste system to try to catch up with the more privileged British members of white society. Their strategy was to gain control of the state and its legal apparatus. Between 1924 and 1929, legislation was passed to protect white workers from African competition. Certain better-paying and more desirable jobs were simply reserved for whites.

In 1948 the Afrikaaner National Party won electoral control over the South African government. That election was fought over both racial and class issues. One of the issues was governmental policies for white supremacy. The "pass laws" (requiring Africans to have passes for being anywhere off their reserves), color bars to jobs, and the legal prohibition of African trade unions contributed greatly to the rapid growth of the white standard of living, while that of nonwhites remained effectively level for decades. During these years there was a policy to erode the rights of nonwhites. Multiracial political parties were outlawed in 1968. Under the separate development policy, nonwhites were denied national and provincial political participation in exchange for the establishment of their own separate political institutions. As opposition to white domination mounted, many nonwhites (the numbers are not even reported) were detained without trial, allegedly for violation of the pass laws. In the mid-1960s, 2.5 million Africans were arrested. In 1982, more than 200,000 people were arrested for violating residence and travel restrictions, a 90 percent increase since 1981. Many arrested persons died mysteriously in jail, with no adequate explanation.

Unequal rights are also apparent in education, which is free and compulsory for all whites aged 7 to 16, including free books and equipment. For nonwhites, education is neither free nor compulsory, and parents must pay for some books and equipment. The average per capita expenditure for primary and secondary education varies widely, with whites receiving more than ten times the average per capita expenditure of blacks in 1976–77. University enrollments are also unbalanced. Although whites comprise only 18 percent of the total population, they make up 80 percent of university enrollments. Africans, who constitute about 70 percent of the national population, represent only 9 percent of university students. The other 11 percent consists of "coloreds"—that is, East Indians and other nonwhites.

The vastly unequal distribution of income in South Africa is assured by job and geographical restrictions, the banning until very recently of any union representation, the absence of political and legal rights, and low pay. Whites earn nearly five times what Africans earn. In 1977, the average per capita income of whites was nearly $4000, while for blacks it was $880 (Gordon et al., 1979).

South Africa spends a great deal on police, justice, and prisons. Police activities are coordinated with military defense for any perceived antiguerrilla activities. Nearly $2 billion is spent on defense (Gordon et al., 1979). Nonwhites serve in the police and armed forces, but they are not allowed to carry guns.

Along with the economic, political, legal, and educational inequalities whites impose on blacks in South Africa, there is a religious and political ideology that attempts to legitimate that inequality. The Dutch Reformed Church supports the "policy of racial separation and guardianship of whites over the native" (Moodie, 1975, p. 261).

South Africa operates as a caste society, but it has strong elements of a class society, with whites owning and controlling all the major productive resources, including diamond, gold, and other mines, most of the land, and all the manufacturing concerns. Within the white population there are class divisions between those who own or control a great deal and those who control very little. Resentment over these class inequalities is undoubtedly reduced by the caste society, which enables whites to feel superior to nonwhites. There are few class divisions within the black population, since blacks do not own or control significant resources.

Particularly since whites are in such a minority in South Africa, they have used political, state, legal, police, and military means to retain social control and to advance the policy of racial separation called *apartheid*. They have also used the power of the state to influence the ideology and ideas that circulate within the society. There is close censorship of all publications appearing in the country. Religious leaders, authors, and other ideological trend-setters run the risk of being banned from the country if their views are

In South Africa today, the domination of whites over blacks is enforced by numerous laws, including those requiring blacks to carry identity papers at all times. Blacks are denied free education and access to many jobs, are allowed to live in only a few remote and undesirable areas, and may not interact socially with whites.

unacceptable to the authorities. Thus, in all realms—intellectual, religious, social, economic, and political—the South African state uses its resources, backed by its tremendous police and military apparatus, to enforce the policy of apartheid. In the way it uses state-sanctioned force, South Africa resembles Nazi Germany and other totalitarian societies.

WHY DOES STRATIFICATION EXIST?

Why do various systems of stratification exist? There are several competing explanations. Some suggest that people "get what they deserve"; others maintain that advantaged members of society use their superior power, wealth, and influence to maintain their privileged positions. The former include functionalists who stress that merit and achievement lead to social position; they consider occupational position, status, and sometimes earnings. The latter, who are conflict theorists, focus on unequal wealth, power, and control. Thus, functionalists and conflict theorists are examining different features of stratification.

FUNCTIONALIST EXPLANATIONS

Functionalists begin with the assumption that unstratified societies do not exist. Their first goal, therefore, is to explain why stratification is necessary in all social systems. They see stratification as necessary because all societies need to place and motivate individuals in social positions. If many people have the necessary talents and it is easy to fill a particular position, then it does not need to be heavily rewarded, even though it is functionally important. Sometimes talent is abundant, but a long and difficult training process scares people away. Davis and Moore (1945) feel, for example, that many people have the mental capacity to become doctors, but that the burdensome and expensive process of medical education would discourage most from even trying to be a doctor if that goal did not carry rewards equal to the sacrifice. Functionalist explanations are supported to a degree by cross-national research which finds that occupations are ranked very similarly in 60 industrial and agricultural countries (Treiman, 1977).

Because positions vary in their importance, attractiveness, and the talents or training they require, functionalists argue that a society "must have" rewards it can offer as incentives to lure people into vital positions. Rewards include unequal economic, symbolic, and esthetic benefits. University presidents, for instance, are paid more than professors; usually have large offices and ample secretarial help; and often have substantial travel and entertainment budgets, high prestige in the wider community, and a university house in which to live.

For functionalists, the rank of a position is determined by how important the position is for society and by the scarcity of people with the talent or skill for filling the position. In short, functionalists feel that stratification is "an unconsciously evolved device by which societies insure that the most important positions are conscientiously filled by the most qualified persons" (Davis and Moore, 1945). The functional view of stratification held sway over American sociology for nearly 20 years, despite the existence of vigorous arguments against it. Six major criticisms have been leveled against this view.

1. Rewards are not associated with importance. Although no fully objective measure of importance is possible, various observers note that rewards often are poorly correlated with jobs that appear to have societal importance. Sports or rock stars who earn six- or seven-figure salaries do not seem more important than garbage collectors. Similarly, people who inherit their wealth may do nothing socially important for society. Moreover, there is a connection between the amount of protection a group can gain for itself and the income of its members. Unionized auto workers earn much more than nonunion textile workers, but clothes are as important as cars. The reason doctors are scarce and highly paid is that medical school admissions are tightly limited. Other occupations restrict the number of practitioners by strict licensing practices that may or may not be relevant to performing well in the occupation. The most important and responsible positions in government, education, the judicial system, and religion are not nearly as highly rewarded as comparable positions in private industry. Are they really so much less important for society? Numerous discrepancies between rewards and social significance seriously undercut the functional argument.

2. The functionalist view justifies the status quo. Functional theories support the status quo because they suggest that the existing stratification system is necessary and indeed desirable (Simpson, 1956; Tumin, 1953; Dahrendorf, 1958). The view suggests that people who do important and difficult jobs deserve the rewards they get. Thus, the theory operates as an ideology that legitimates existing social inequalities and says they exist for the benefit of society as a whole.

3. Talent is only imperfectly utilized. Stratification may actually restrict the development of scarce talents, rather than being necessary to place people effectively in various positions. The assumption that stratification is based on functional criteria overlooks the existence of stratification by race, sex, social class, or inheritance. Such stratification limits the size of the pool that may be tapped as a source of talent. In this way, stratification may restrict rather than enhance the development of special talents.

4. Unequal rewards are not the only way to

motivate people. The extremes of inequality that exist in the United States are neither functional nor inevitable (Tumin, 1953). In worker cooperatives, people work hard for the same rewards or for very small differentials. Therefore, it remains an open question how much inequality is required to generate maximum effort. Some people work for pleasure, challenge, and excitement as well as for external rewards, so it is possible that individuals could be motivated more by intrinsic rewards than they currently are. Finally, how does the functional theory address the problem of motivating "the masses"? Can a society survive if they are not motivated? A vastly unequal system of rewards may not be productive for the many people who fill "unimportant" positions in society. People seeing others who work no harder than they do yet receive much greater rewards may become angry, withdrawn, unconcerned, or deliberately sabotage the work they are doing. Such a reaction is hardly functional for society in general.

5. The functionalist view fails to explain changes in rewards. The functional theory is unable to explain why certain positions may change with respect to the rewards they receive. Teachers' salaries went up during the 1970s, while there was a surplus of teachers. Clearly, other factors, such as unionization and strikes, operate to change the rewards particular positions receive.

6. The theory is not testable. Scientific theories need to be formulated in such a way that they can be proved or disproved. The functionalist theory does not meet this criterion because societal "importance" cannot be objectively measured. There is no scientific way to assess whether the most "important" positions are the ones that receive the greatest rewards.

CONFLICT THEORIES

Whereas functionalists see stratification as inevitable and necessary for the "good" of society, conflict theorists see it as resulting from the competition of various interest groups or classes. Groups use the power and resources they control to advance and protect their own positions in relation to other groups. Institutionalized inequality developed with the concept of private property, and the creation of an economic surplus along with a belief in private property set the conditions for some individuals or groups to obtain more wealth than others. First, through force or legitimating ideologies, some groups gained privileged positions. Once they had a relatively permanent material base, those positions could be passed along to their heirs. Inequalities of wealth arose and then became a resource that could be used to retain superior advantages. Conflict theories try to explain human behavior in terms of how individuals seek to realize their interests in a world marked by inequality, threats, and sometimes violence.

"Conflict theorists" is an umbrella term that includes a number of scholars who emphasize issues of conflict and dominance in stratification systems. Since Karl Marx and Max Weber approached stratification differently, their views are worth considering separately.

Marxian Theory

According to Marx and others using his ideas, stratification develops through the following steps:

1. When the economy produces a surplus that can be controlled by those who own the means of production, classes develop.
2. With their economic power, owners dominate those who do not own property.
3. Dominant groups use the state, religion, education, and ideas to legitimize the system that benefits them.
4. Those being exploited may be unaware, unorganized, or viciously suppressed. Therefore, conflict and resistance are controlled.

5. Potential contradictions may occur within the production process. Potential contradictions are forces that may undermine the development of capitalism. For example, bringing workers together in urban areas where they can recognize their common plight may intensify class conflict and change.

Marxian class theory has been criticized on several grounds. First, critics argue that societies reflect more than simply economic interests (Turner, 1974). The state, the military, or even the education system may sometimes operate independently of the economy. This is particularly true in the state socialist societies of Eastern Europe, where party leaders may become a new elite strata.

Second, the last step in Marx's theory has rarely occurred. Class conflict has not always led to revolutionary change, perhaps because Marx failed to predict the shift from individual capitalists to large corporations; underestimated the growth in size and importance of the middle class, which tends to buffer conflict between the upper and lower classes; and did not anticipate the rise of labor unions. Also, he failed to predict the enormous economic development that raised the living standard of middle- and working-class members alike.

These criticisms question Marx's theory of class conflict, but they should not persuade us to overlook the usefulness of a Marxian approach. As Zeitlin (1967) suggests, anyone wanting to understand a particular society should consider the economic order first, and see whether changes in it affect unemployment rates, the distribution of workers in the economy, or social relationships at work. The next step would be to try to identify the major economic classes and determine their objective economic interest, level of class consciousness, and extent of class conflict. How is the dominant class related to major social institutions? What coalitions develop between classes and political parties? How strong or powerless are the subordinate classes? Zeitlin concludes that questions like these make Marx's work very relevant to contemporary social inquiry.

Weberian Theory

Weber's explanation of social stratification differs from Marx's because Weber considered other sources of inequality and stratification besides economic ones. Stratification could also be based on status groups or on political and organizational power that might sometimes be independently based. It is important to stress that Weber shared Marx's view that property and market relations are extremely important. Weber, however, suggested that the state could have power that was independent of economic production, whereas Marx felt that the state was subordinate to the economy in capitalist societies.

Marx and Weber also differ with respect to the role of ideas in the social world. Marx wrote that in any era, the ruling ideas were the ideas of the ruling class. Writing within the Marxian tradition, for example, Karier (1973) suggests that the rise of intelligence testing in the 1920s reflected the interests of the corporate liberal state. It did this by helping to create a more orderly corporate state. Weber, on the other hand, felt that ideas could influence economic behavior, for instance in the way Protestantism encouraged people to save and invest their money. Although ideas cannot change the world on their own, they can encourage people to act. A particular interest group or stratum may have some vague feelings about the way the world is, and a set of ideas may come along that captures what they have been thinking. Thus, by creating a particular world image in someone's mind, ideas may help push action along one rather than another track. But despite such differences of emphasis in Marx and Weber, they share a number of ideas about how and why stratification exists.

Common Themes in Weber and Marx

Major themes shared by Marx and Weber include the following:[1]

1. Social stratification emerges as the result of the domination of one or more groups by other groups. This domination may be based on differing control over property, goods, and services, and the unequal market value of different occupations.
2. Because stratification is based on dominance and coercion, the potential for opposition, resistance, and hostility on the part of the subordinated groups is always present.
3. Members of the dominant class are faced with crucial problems of social control of the subordinate classes. A number of mechanisms, however, may be employed to keep the lower classes in line. (These methods are discussed in the next section of this chapter and in the next chapter.)

Criticisms of Conflict Theory

Conflict theory is open to several criticisms. Like functional theory, it is hard to test. The concepts of power, dominance, and coercion are difficult to measure. Two steps are needed to confirm conflict theory. First, the dominant class must be shown to play a major role in formulating actions and ideologies. Second, those actions and ideologies need to be shown to serve the interests of the dominant class but not the interests of other classes. Numerous studies of local school boards, for example, have documented that their members are overwhelmingly upper-class or upper-middle-class members of the community. But evidence has not been presented to show that they operate in their own interests rather than in the interests of the community "at large" (Charters, 1974).

Finally, conflict does not always result in change. Sometimes it contributes to social order by establishing relationships, reaffirming values, resolving disagreements, or reasserting power (Simmel, 1956; Coser, 1956). Children who were previously strangers, for instance, may fight over the use of a toy and later play happily together with it. They have established a relationship through conflict. In some instances, the relatively equal strength of two competing parties can serve as an effective deterrent to conflict. But their respective strengths may be detectable only through conflict.

Both functional and conflict theories have been modified but not demolished by their critics. The general themes in each have been compared by Stinchcomb, as shown in Table 9.1. This comparison provides a useful backdrop to the efforts that have been made to synthesize the two theories (Ossowski, 1963; van den Berghe, 1963; Williams, 1966; Horowitz, 1962; Lenski, 1966).

A SYNTHESIS

Perhaps the most complete attempt to synthesize the functionalist and conflict views of stratification is the one offered by Lenski (1966), who tried to explain both conflict and order in society. He began with the assumption that humans are selfish beings who need to live and cooperate socially with others. Forced to choose, most individuals will opt for their own or their group's self-interest rather than for the interests of all other humans, although they may try to hide this choice from themselves and others. Self-interest is particularly apparent with regard to the rewards and resources that are in relatively short supply—especially power and privileges. People will struggle for these scarce rewards. In that struggle, some people will be better endowed by their social locations, by resources they already control, and by their natural talents. The result is social inequality. Power, rather than need, usefulness, or merit is the primary source of major social inequalities. Some of these inequalities may be functional for soci-

[1]This and the next section draw heavily upon Vanfossen, 1979, pp. 43–46.

Table 9.1 Two Views of Social Stratification

The Functional View	The Conflict View
1. Stratification is universal, necessary, and inevitable.	1. Stratification may be universal without being necessary or inevitable.
2. Social organization (the social system) shapes the stratification system.	2. The stratification system shapes social organization (the social system).
3. Stratification arises from society's need for integration, coordination, and cohesion.	3. Stratification arises from group conquest, competition, and conflict.
4. Stratification facilitates the optimal functioning of society and the individual.	4. Stratification impedes the optimal functioning of society and the individual.
5. Stratification is an expression of commonly shared social values.	5. Stratification is an expression of the values of powerful groups.
6. Tasks and rewards are equitably allocated.	6. Tasks and rewards are inequitably allocated.
7. The economic dimension is subordinate to other dimensions of society.	7. The economic dimension is paramount in society.
8. Stratification systems generally change through evolutionary processes.	8. Stratification systems may change through revolutionary processes.

SOURCE: Arthur L. Stinchcombe, "Some Empirical Consequences of the Davis-Moore Theory of Stratification." *American Sociological Review,* 28 (October, 1963), p. 808. Reprinted by permission of the American Sociological Association.

ety—for example, giving the best hunter the best weapons—but inequalities tend to last long after they cease to be useful. The relative stability of the stratification system is explained, in Lenski's view, by the fact that humans are creatures of habit who are strongly influenced by custom and tradition.

An approach that combines both functional and conflict elements may explain many social inequalities. Treiman (1977) does this in his explanation of why occupations are ranked so similarly in many different societies. He suggests that the division of labor is functional for a society. Once such a division occurs, however, occupational groups are able to convert their command of scarce resources, such as skill and knowledge, economic power, and authority, into additional material and social advantages. They can do this because their control of scarce resources improves their market position and can be used to manipulate the system that allocates additional power and resources (Treiman, 1977). As a result, the more powerful occupations gain more prestige and privileges in all societies.

The most complete sociological answer to the question of why stratification exists involves an interplay between functional specialization and power. People perform certain roles in society, whether because of skill, training, or interest. They also tend to use the positions, power, and resources they control to maximize their own advantages. In this way inequalities widen and become relatively permanent systems of stratification. Such systems do not exist without human intervention, however. A number of institutions and social processes help to maintain systems of stratification, and sometimes internal conflicts lead to changes.

HOW ARE STRATIFICATION SYSTEMS MAINTAINED?

The mechanisms used to maintain stratification are most apparent in a country such as South Africa, but all stratification systems use a variety of social processes to maintain and re-create themselves. Crucial links with the economy, the family, religion, ideology, and the state tend to support the position of dominant groups. In addition, several key processes (described below) work to sustain stratification. Although those committed to equality deplore the existence of such institutional links and social processes, they would agree that it is important to understand how they operate.

INSTITUTIONAL LINKS

The Economic Roots of Stratification

Although the economic basis for stratification was discussed earlier in this chapter, it is worth repeating that every system of stratification is related to the economy. Either the original position of the dominant groups in society is rooted in economic advantages (control or ownership of productive resources) or, as in the case of priests or military leaders achieving dominant positions, powerful positions in other realms tend to be converted to economic advantage over time. The rise of educational credentials for entry to occupations is an excellent example of how privileged groups seek to reserve more desirable positions for themselves by raising the cultural and economic "capital" required for their attainment. The economic basis for stratification is very often handed down in families through the inheritance of wealth.

The Family's Role in Re-creating Stratification

In some societies (and in some communities), family name is important, usually because it alerts people to the fact that an individual is a member of a wealthy or powerful family. In many societies, but by no means all, if a family has material wealth, the laws and customs of the society allow it to pass along that wealth to its descendants (or to whomever else the family wishes). But material wealth alone (whether ownership of land, factories, money, or other resources) is rarely enough to ensure that the position of family members is maintained. New generations must be taught to think, believe, feel, and behave in ways that will be appropriate to the family's position. Families with positions or assets they wish to protect work to enhance their children's development in particular directions. An international business family, for example, may arrange for its children to live in various countries during their young adulthood so that they will learn several languages and build their own international networks.

Childrearing practices are related to social stratification and vary with parental life situations, as we saw in Chapter 6. When adults have a degree of autonomy in their work and political life, they tend to value self-reliance and try to teach it to their children. Similarly, if adults view most of the authorities in their lives with deference, they may try to teach their children the same respectful attitudes. On the other hand, if children grow up seeing their parents behave in a superior way while others respond to them with respect, they are likely to believe that is how one interacts with people. These cultural and interactional features of social life within a system of stratification enable some families to transmit cultural and social advantages to their children.

How Religion and Ideology Work to Legitimate Stratification

Virtually every stratification system is accompanied by religious or ideological beliefs that aim to legitimize the existing state of affairs. Feudal monarchies propounded the "divine right of kings"; caste societies advance the genetic and/or moral inferiority of subordinate groups; modern industrial societies rely on an ideology of equal opportunity and "merit" that claims to reward superior talent, training, and skills (rather than luck or unscrupulousness); totalitarian societies advance the claim that people are rewarded because of their "service" or loyalty to the state, or punished for its absence. Even the Afrikaaner dominance over blacks in South Africa, which is so overtly political and military, is sugar-coated with an ideology of separatism that has the approval of some religious as well as secular authorities.

Ideology is a system of ideas that reflects and justifies the interests of those who believe it. An ideology makes existing inequalities seem more "natural" or taken for granted. An important feature of ideology is that it bears some slight resemblance to reality, which makes it all the more elusive to combat. For example, the ideology of equal opportunity is just closely enough related to reality—everyone knows at least someone who has risen from poverty to prominence—that it cannot be rejected as totally false. The problem is that it is only partially true. The examples that are cited are the exceptions to the rule of unequal opportunity. Many individuals want to believe that if they work hard and do well they will achieve the rewards and satisfactions they seek. Indeed, to maximize their chances for success, individuals need to believe this. At the same time, it is easier to believe it if one's probabilities for success are relatively good. Those probabilities are influenced by one's family of birth. If individuals lack opportunities, they are more likely to reject the dominant ideologies of society.

For those lacking opportunities, then, ideology probably does little to restrain their anger, alienation, and resistance to a system that offers them little hope. Karl Marx pointed out that the dominant ideas of a society are the ideas of the ruling class and serve to justify their economic interests. As groups become aware of the legitimating role of certain ideas, they seek alternative belief systems to explain their life situations. Peasants, workers and new political parties all work to rally supporters to their cause with ideas that serve their interests and perhaps the interests of those they seek to mobilize. As a result, growing numbers of people are exposed to competing ideas. Ruling groups in various societies no longer monopolize the belief systems of society. Growing literacy, the mass media, and rapid communications have begun to broaden the spread of competing ideas.

The Role Played by Law, the State, Police, and Military

When ideology falters, any stratification system that is going to maintain itself needs to be backed by the state, law, police, and military, as the South African case shows. Without the potential for coercion, whether legal or physical, no stratification system will last for long. To functionalists, the law and legal order serve the needs of the whole society; to conflict sociologists, the legal order operates to protect and enhance the rights and property of more powerful members of society. Because the goal of the legal system is to preserve order and often to maintain the status quo, legal systems in all societies tend to operate in ways that support and maintain the advantages of more powerful members of society. In caste systems, the legal order is called upon to make caste boundaries into legal boundaries, with penalties for violations. Jobs are legally reserved for members of some castes rather than others. Intermarriage between castes is prohibited by law. Caste systems can break down only when these laws are eliminated or ignored. Totalitarian political regimes also use the law and legal machinery to legitimate their police and military actions, as in Nazi Germany.

In order to persist, dominant groups must influence the law and the legal structure of a society. One reason that ex-President Richard Nixon did not remain in office was that he could not completely dominate the law and the legal structure. There were certain procedures and processes developed by the legal system that he could not quickly change. The process of gaining influence over the legal structure of a society usually needs to be a gradual and subtle one, especially if it is to be perceived as legitimate by members of society.

What gets enacted into law, what gets defined

as a crime and what does not, and by whom, are related to the stratification system of a society. How laws are enforced and what sentences are imposed are variable and depend to some degree on a person's position in the stratification system. Sometimes interests besides those of dominant groups are also protected by law (as in laws against murder, rape, and assault) and in due process procedures. But the law will seldom contradict the interests of dominant groups for very long. This is particularly evident in the arena of regulatory and administrative law—for instance in the law pertaining to banking. The banks being regulated may have former or future employees working in the regulatory agency.

The potential for armed intervention by the state and the police underlies all legal systems. Very often the use of force is viewed as legitimate, at least by some members of society, such as when the police use force to quell an urban riot. Norms govern the conditions under which force may be used legitimately. Even when political protestors are trespassing, say, on the property of a nuclear power plant, the police are not supposed to beat them up.

The use of force and violence can backfire, particularly if it is used by authorities in ways that are seen as unjust and illegitimate by most people. Those who once believed in the legitimacy of the authorities can be "radicalized" by witnessing what seems to be an illegitimate use of force by those authorities. This happened in 1969 when Columbia University students occupied buildings in a dispute over social and political issues. Many students were opposed or indifferent to the issues until the city police were called in. When they witnessed the police beating students, dragging them downstairs by the feet with their heads banging on the stone steps, and saw their blood all over the floors and walls, many who had been indifferent came to believe that the authorities were unjust, that the demonstrating students were right, and that the armed hand of the law lay too close beneath the surface and ready to strike when dissent and conflict passed a certain point. Such incidents may also convince dominant groups that the use of police force is less effective for maintaining stratification than more subtle processes of control such as cooptation.

SOCIAL PROCESSES

Cooptation

Cooptation is one of the key social processes used to maintain any stratification system, whether societal or organizational. It refers to bringing new people into the leadership or policy-making structure of an organization or a society, specifically people who might otherwise threaten its stability or existence. The term was used by Philip Selznick (1948), who noted that the real trick for an organization or society is to share the symbols and burdens of authority without transferring real power. Stated this way, the essence of cooptation as a mechanism of control becomes apparent. For instance, granting token representation on presidential commissions or corporate boards to blacks, women, or labor unions is the first step in the process of cooptation. The second step involves making sure no major changes are made. As Selznick observes, ". . . it therefore becomes necessary to insure that the coopted elements do not get out of hand, do not take advantage of their formal position to encroach upon the actual arena of decision. Consequently, formal cooptation requires informal control over the coopted elements lest the unity of command and decision be imperiled" (1966, p. 261).

These informal controls include social favors—inviting people for lunch or dinner, playing golf or other sports with them, and so forth. During such times, newly coopted individuals are oriented to "the way things are." If new members refuse to go along with the way things have always been done, they may be socially ostracized, meetings may be set at times when they cannot attend, they may be publicly embarrassed, or other negative sanctions may be applied (Kerr, 1964). From Kerr's case study we cannot tell how widespread these sanctions are, but we can see some of the forms they take.

In short, the process of cooptation may occur when dominant groups in a society or existing leaders in an organization identify the brighter, more energetic, more vocal, and more ambitious members of subordinate groups; share with them some of the symbols and rewards of power, position, or authority; and at the same time ensure that no major changes will be made. The process of cooptation has occurred in the labor movement and in various poor people's movements (Piven and Cloward, 1977). It may be helped by the "principle of cumulative advantage," which operates in favor of dominant group members and increasingly to the benefit of individuals being coopted into the system.

The Matthew Effect or the Principle of Cumulative Advantage

"For unto every one that hath shall be given, and he shall have abundance: but from him that hath not shall be taken away even that which he hath." This passage from the Gospel of St. Matthew (13:12) has been identified by Robert K. Merton as describing the operation of the reward system in science. It takes longer for people who are relatively unknown to receive credit for their ideas, and if they collaborate with a highly esteemed scientist, the famous one tends to be credited with the work. Furthermore, recognition for excellent scientific work can be converted into improved resources and facilities for doing scientific work. Thus, concludes Merton, the operation of the reward system in science "provides a stratified distribution of chances" to scientists (1968).

The *principle of cumulative advantage,* or the *Matthew effect,* is a social process whereby one advantage an individual has is likely to lead to other advantages. An advantaged berth in the ship of life provides access to multiple resources—financial, legal, political, police, military, informational, and human. These can be applied to an individual's goals, whatever they are. Several examples illuminate the process in operation. Lawyers in large firms and officers of major corporations often receive preferential treatment from banks for loans or home mortgage money. This is one small instance of how a favorable position in one field may be converted into an asset in another. People who vacation with the rich and powerful may gain inside information, influence, or other valued resources that may heighten differences in wealth, power, or status (Domhoff, 1974).

Maintaining a system of stratification involves major social institutions such as the family and active processes, such as cooptation. It is possible, however, that these institutions and processes may contain contradictions and the potential for change.

CONFLICT, CONTRADICTIONS, AND OTHER POTENTIAL FOR CHANGE

Whenever some people have more than others, the possibility exists for conflict over those inequalities. As a result, those with more power, wealth, income, or prestige may try to control those with less and also try to reduce conflict. Those with less may resist or try to change a system that offers them less. In order to assess the amount of conflict over social stratification, we need to clarify what constitutes conflict. Certain actions are fairly clear instances—the seizure of privately held land and its redistribution among many people, or a political campaign with that aim. It is less clear whether strikes, crime rates, income tax cheating, parking violations, and vandalism may also be viewed as conflict over social stratification.

Conflict and resistance occur even in the most repressive of societies. The forms of conflict, protest, and resistance vary, depending on the society in which they occur. Reactions and efforts to control conflict and protest also differ. What forms of resistance or conflict are available, for example, in a caste and police society like

South Africa? Work stoppages are criminal offenses; weapons are prohibited to nonwhites; suspected "troublemakers" can be arrested and held indefinitely without trial; and every African must carry a "pass" that can be checked at any time. These features make resistance more difficult.

What happens? Do people passively accept their situations and go along with their oppressors? Despite all the restrictions, there *is* a tremendous amount of resistance among the black population in South Africa. Slowdowns, sit-downs, and school strikes by children are some of the forms of protest that have been used. In class societies such as that of Great Britain, conflict over inequality appears in mass demonstrations, political reforms, and labor unionization and strikes.

Some reasonably successful protest movements in the United States include the civil rights movement in the 1960s and the reawakening of the women's movement in the 1970s. Sometimes such movements benefit their leaders more than the masses. The civil rights movement, for example, may have developed a black elite with a stake in the system. On a limited basis, this strategy is being pursued by the South African government at the time of this writing. It is seeking to coopt a black elite by offering sufficient economic and social rewards to a few who will help to keep the caste system functioning. This elite minority of blacks is also meant to serve as a buffer between the dominant whites and the mass of blacks. The very process of cooptation, however, is a double-edged sword. It may be a first step toward changing the system, because efforts to contain reform-minded new leaders may fail and the process of cooptation may have unintended consequences.

Virtually all systems of stratification contain some contradictions and potential for change. Probably the most important are historical changes in the technological, economic, military, or political realms. In the United States in the 1960s and 1970s, as more women began working outside the home, their growing economic independence increased pressure for social equality. Such structural changes undercut existing ideologies (such as "a woman's place is in the home") and marshall support for alternative ideas ("equal pay for equal work"), which provide footholds for social change. There have always been ideological contradictions between democracy and capitalism, democracy and racial inequality, and democracy and sexual inequality.

Ideological tensions may appear to individuals who occupy two or more inconsistent statuses in a society. Usually the various dimensions of inequality (wealth, power, and status) are closely correlated, but sometimes an individual of relatively low social status (a minority group member or a woman, for instance) holds relatively high educational or occupational status (for example, as a doctor). Individuals occupying such inconsistent statuses may become more aware than most people of the discrepancy between their treatment in one status compared with that in another one.

Because people develop networks surrounding each of their statuses, their ideas may cross-pollinate. A member of a low status group may, by virtue of occupational position, religious group membership, or cooptation, come in contact with members of dominant groups. Depending on how willing the members of the dominant group are to include lower-status members, they may learn skills, information, or cultural styles that they can transmit to members of their own group. Again, depending on how well received they are, the lower-status members may be able to change the minds or behaviors of dominant group members to some degree.

Summary

1. Social stratification affects life chances.

2. Social inequality is less permanent than social stratification.

3. The three major sources of stratification are property, power, and prestige.

4. Class societies like Great Britain rest on economic stratification.

5. Extreme stratification by power occurs in totalitarian states such as the one Hitler built in Nazi Germany. Conformity and domination are enforced by propaganda, censorship, secret police, and force.

6. Caste refers to a permanent, hereditary, religiously sanctioned system of social ranking that affects all forms of daily interaction between differing castes. South Africa is a caste society that relies heavily upon military power and the legal system to maintain control.

7. Sociologists have offered two major answers to the question of why stratification exists. Functionalists stress that stratification is necessary to motivate people to fill important positions in society. Six major criticisms have been leveled at the functionalist view of stratification.

8. The conflict view sees stratification as growing out of the unequal power and resources of various groups in society. Marx saw stratification developing when an economic surplus was produced. When a limited number of people control the means of production and the economic surplus, classes develop. Weber suggested that stratification can also be based on political, military, or organizational power that may sometimes operate independently of economic wealth. Conflict theory has also received a number of criticisms.

9. Several efforts have been made to combine a functionalist and a conflict view of stratification. Such a synthesis suggests that stratification involves an interplay between functionalist specialization and power. Social status affects the chances people have to develop their talents. Skill and training may help people to obtain certain positions. Once there, people tend to use their positions and other resources to maintain or advance themselves.

10. Several institutional connections serve to pass on stratification from one generation to the next, including the inheritance of economic wealth, family socialization and connections, the existence of ideologies (systems of ideas) that help make existing inequalities seem more natural or taken for granted, and the use of the law and police to maintain the existing order.

11. Cooptation and the Matthew effect are social processes that tend to preserve stratification systems.

12. All systems of stratification contain conflict, contradictions, and other potential for change.

Key Terms

autocracy
caste system
class system
cooptation
ideology
legitimate
life chances
Matthew effect, or principle of cumulative advantage
power
prestige
property
social inequality
social stratification
status group
totalitarianism

Chapter 10

Social Class

Picture yourself at a beautiful beach—white sands, palm trees, turquoise sea, glorious sunshine. If you went around and talked with many different people, you would probably get a wide variety of views of that beach. The fishermen would tell you how the weather and currents affect the fish that come by; the lifeguard would be focusing on currents, undertow, small children, and perhaps bathing beauties; someone from the Environmental Protection Agency would be watching for signs of an offshore oil spill; a shell collector would be looking for special shells; and even the many people there for recreation might be looking for different things (good waves, a quiet place to read, enough people for a volleyball game), depending on their own situations. Philosophers and poets would have a different slant still. If you talked with each of them, you would come away with many different views of the beach. Does this mean that only one of them has the "right" view? Assuredly not. Each has something to tell about the beach and how it affects him or her. You can compare what each says with evidence about the beach and with your own observations. The same can be said of social class.

DEFINING AND MEASURING SOCIAL CLASS

One of the single most important ideas for understanding society is social class. *Social class* refers to a group's position in a social hierarchy based on prestige and/or property ownership. Probably no concept in social science has been used in as many different ways as has social class. Part of the reason is that individuals and groups tend to see social class in terms of their own location in the social structure. Like the people on the beach, they emphasize certain features and overlook others.

MAJOR VIEWS OF CLASS

American sociologists tend to view class in terms of social *rank,* meaning place in a social hierarchy and indicated by the willingness of various groups to interact socially with other individuals and groups. Although Warner, Meeker, and Eels (1949) mentioned occupation and wealth, their primary emphasis was on prestige, and on whether or not Americans would associate with one another as social equals. As we noted in Chapter 9, their emphasis was on shared values, life-styles, and behavior (indicated by who socialized with whom), with little attention to the social locations that shaped those behaviors. In contrast, Weber (1920) focused on the market position of individuals and groups. By this he meant how well they fared at the economic bargaining table, which was affected by their power, knowledge, skill, and scarcity. Weber's focus adds occupational position to social status.

A third theoretical approach underscores the importance of one's position in a bureaucratic structure—for example, as vice president for marketing or deputy director of the city housing agency (Dahrendorf, 1959; Lenski, 1966). Weber's view of class stresses the economic and status advantages that some groups possess; Dahrendorf's view highlights power and decision-making capacity. It suggests that position in the class structure is influenced by the significance of the decisions one makes at work. Since class is based on one's position in an organization, class would change at retirement, when one no longer possesses authority within an organization. This view stresses the growth and importance of organizations (already noted in Chapter 7) for class position, while it plays down the importance of market position and property. Weber certainly was aware of the important role played by property in social stratification, but it was Karl Marx who suggested a theory of classes based upon property ownership.

These theoretical positions may be summarized by saying they are concerned primarily with status, economic life chances, organizational position, or position in the social organization of production. These different definitions of class are important, because they influence the way class has been measured in research studies, and the concepts and measures used affect the conclusions people draw about the nature and operation of social class in the United States.

RESEARCH CONCEPTIONS OF CLASS

Most American researchers characterize someone's *socioeconomic status (SES)* by using the person's occupation, education, and income. As you can see, this index touches on several of the dimensions noted in the theoretical views of class, but it ignores distinctions based on property and position in the relations of production. (The various ways social class has been measured are summarized in Table 10.1.)

Let's look more closely at occupation and in-

Table 10.1 How Social Class Has Been Measured

Concept	Measure	Comments
"Objective" measures of socioeconomic status	Father's occupation, father's education.	Based on ranking of occupations according to their prestige.
		Treats the class structure as an unbroken band rather than viewing classes as separate groupings.
	Income (whether earned or from investments).	May classify individuals logically, but people with the same incomes may have widely different lifestyles. Difficult to distinguish groups rather than points on an unbroken band.
	Wealth (need to distinguish between productive property and personal property).	May confer control over production and may produce income without working.
Class	Position in the social relations of production.	Sees classes as distinct groups that are in relation to one another.
Subjective indicators of social class membership	An individual's subjective evaluation of the class group to which he or she belongs.	Most people end up seeing themselves as "middle class." Self-classification depends a lot on how the question is asked.

One of the indicators of socioeconomic status that sociologists use is occupation. The prestige of a particular occupation, such as machine-tool operator, production supervisor, or surgeon, is highly related to the educational background and income of people in that occupation.

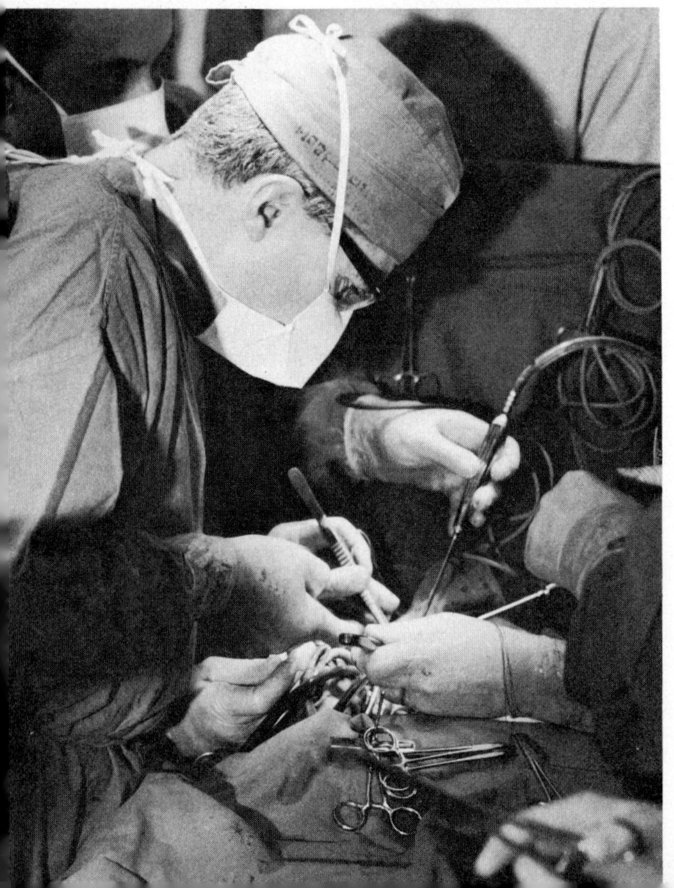

come to see if they capture the central inequalities of our society, and then consider whether adding the concept of property adds to our understanding of social class in the United States.

Occupational Rankings

How is it possible to classify the thousands of different occupations in the United States? Different scholars focus on different features of occupations. Some distinguish occupations on the basis of whether they involve mainly mental or physical work; whether people spend most of their time on the job giving orders or taking orders; in terms of access to useful knowledge and information, opportunity for advancement, degree of autonomy, or degree of exposure to occupational hazards; and finally in terms of their prestige. In all these approaches, someone assesses a particular occupation and assigns a rank to it.

In a study designed to measure occupational prestige, the National Opinion Research Center (NORC) asked a random sample of the population to give "their personal opinion of the general standing" of 90 occupations. Respondents graded each occupation on a five-point scale from "excellent" to "poor." The results of the original study in 1947 and a restudy in 1963 appear in Table 10.2. As you can see, the rankings remained quite constant from 1947 to 1963. In studying these results, Reiss et al. (1961) found that the best predictors of the rank of an occupation are the educational level and income of workers in it. Both efforts to rank occupations view the American class structure as a continuous band, rather than as composed of separate categories.

Measuring Class with Income

Income equals the sum of money wages and salaries, income from self-employment, and income other than earnings. Notice that total money income thus includes money you worked for—earnings—and income other than earnings. Income other than earnings includes money income from estates, trusts, stock divi-

Table 10.2 **Prestige Ranking of 90 Occupations in the United States**

In Table 10.2, 90 occupations in the United States have been ranked according to the scores they were given by various respondents in the United States in 1963 and 1947. The scores of the occupations in this table range from a high of 96 to a low of 33. These scores and the relative ranks of various occupations have changed little since 1963. Occupations are ranked in quite similar ways in 60 other industrial and agricultural countries as well.

Occupation	1963	1947
U.S. Supreme Court justice	94	96
Physician	93	93
Nuclear physicist	92	86
Scientist	92	89
Government scientist	91	88
State governor	91	93
Federal cabinet member	90	92
College professor	90	89
U.S. representative in Congress	90	89
Chemist	89	86
Lawyer	89	86
Diplomat in U.S. Foreign Service	89	92
Dentist	88	86
Architect	88	86
County judge	88	87
Psychologist	87	85
Minister	87	87
Member of the board of directors of a large corporation	87	86
Mayor of a large city	87	90
Priest	86	86
State gov't. department head	86	87
Civil engineer	86	84
Airline pilot	86	83
Banker	85	88
Biologist	85	81
Sociologist	83	82
Instructor in public schools	82	79
Captain in the regular army	82	80
Accountant for a large business	81	81
Public school teacher	81	78
Factory owner (about 100 people)	80	82
Building contractor	80	79
Exhibited artist	78	83
Musician in a symphony orchestra	78	81
Author of novels	78	80
Economist	78	79
International labor union official	77	75
Railroad engineer	76	76
Electrician	76	73
County agricultural agent	76	77
Owner-operator of a printing shop	75	74
Trained machinist	75	73
Farm owner and operator	74	76
Undertaker	74	72
Welfare worker for a city government	74	73
Newspaper columnist	73	74
Policeman	72	67
Reporter on a daily newspaper	71	71
Radio announcer	70	75
Bookkeeper	70	68
Tenant farmer—one who owns livestock and machinery	69	68
Insurance agent	69	68
Carpenter	68	65
Manager of a small store in a city	67	69
A local official of a labor union	67	62
Mail carrier	66	66
Railroad conductor	66	67
Traveling wholesale salesman	66	68
Plumber	65	63
Automobile repairman	64	63
Playground director	63	67
Barber	63	59
Machine operator in a factory	63	60
Owner-operator of a a lunch stand	63	62
Corporal in the regular army	62	60
Garage mechanic	62	62
Truck driver	59	54
Fisherman who owns his own boat	58	58
Clerk in a store	56	58
Milk route driver	56	54
Streetcar operator	56	58
Lumberjack	55	53
Restaurant cook	55	54
Singer in a nightclub	54	52
Filling station attendant	51	52
Dockworker	50	47
Railroad section hand	50	48
Night watchman	50	47
Coal miner	50	49
Restaurant waiter	49	48
Taxi driver	49	49
Farm hand	48	50
Janitor	48	44
Bartender	48	44
Clothes presser in a laundry	45	46
Soda fountain clerk	44	45
Share-cropper—one who owns no livestock or equipment	42	40
Garbage collector	39	35
Street sweeper	36	34
Shoe shiner	34	33

SOURCES: Hodge, Siegel, and Rossi, 1966; Treiman, 1977.

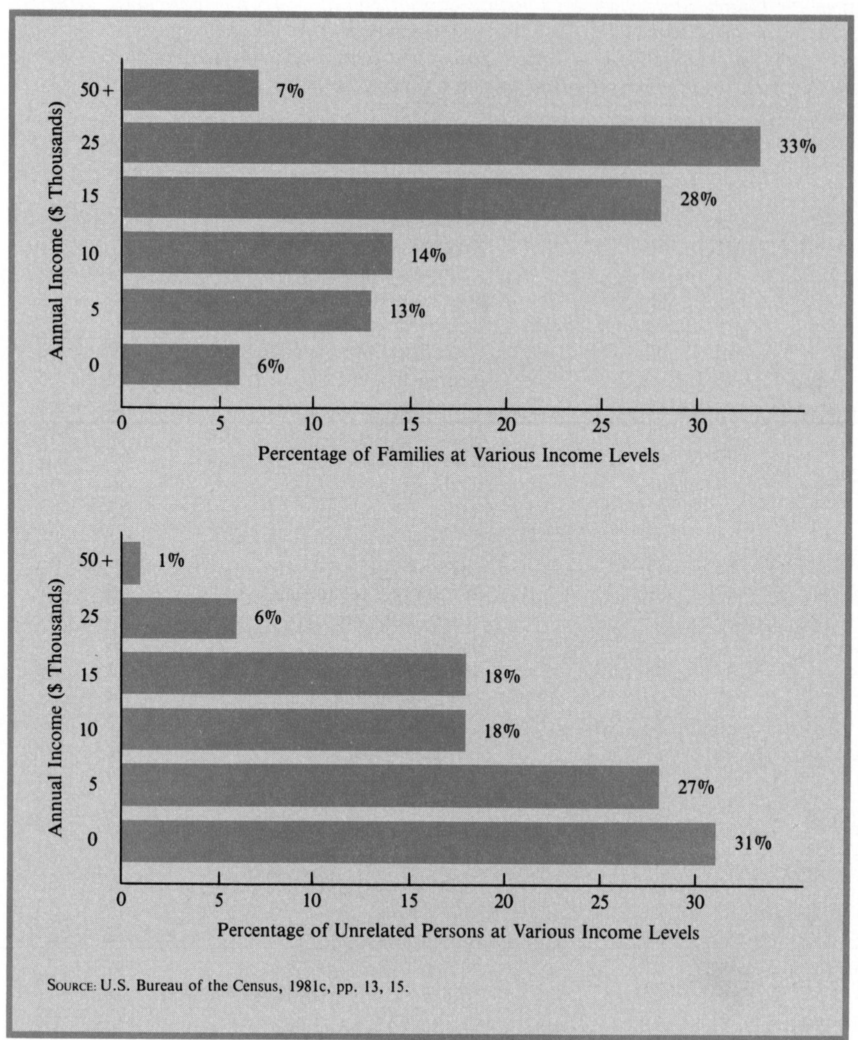

Figure 10.1 Percentage of Families and Unrelated Persons in Various Income Levels in the United States, 1980

dends, interest on savings or bonds, rental income—in short, income from money invested in your name. Families have incomes that are higher and more equally distributed than do single individuals, as Figure 10.1 indicates. This occurs because family incomes are often based on the incomes of more than one individual.

Income poses certain problems for research. People tend to be more reluctant to reveal their incomes than their occupations, and they may not always be reporting the same thing (Are they reporting gross income before taxes, or net income after taxes?) There are other problems with using income alone as an indicator of social class. The gap between manual and nonmanual workers is declining in terms of what they earn and how they spend it. Unlike Great Britain, it is difficult to judge the "social class" of a great many people in the United States based on their speech, their appearance, or the cars they drive, except at the extremes of the class structure. Both upper-class and lower-class individuals can usually be identified by appearance, but the great majority in the middle are not distinguishable by their leisure clothing.

Moreover, although income may provide a means of logically classifying individuals into different categories, those categories may have little more than numeric resemblance. The people in them may have nothing else in common. An electrician and a stockbroker may earn similar incomes in a year, but their life-styles and attitudes would probably differ widely. The use of the term social class, however, has always suggested the existence of collectivities that do actually exist in society. Thus, income may not be what distinguishes social classes. Class differences appear to be rooted in more basic underlying disparities, such as wealth.

Wealth Differences

Although occupational and income differences do exist, Marxian sociologists argue that a more fundamental cleavage underlies all capitalist industrial societies. This division is one of property, not labor. And property, or wealth, is obtained primarily through inheritance or luck rather than through occupation or income (Thurow, 1975). Wealth differs from income. Wealth is the total value (minus debts) of what a household owns. It includes consumer goods (such as houses and cars), as well as financial assets (stocks, bonds, real estate, factories).

The top fifth of the population in the United States (about 45 million people) owns or controls three-quarters of the wealth in the nation (Figure 10.2). In stark contrast, the remaining four-fifths (or about 181 million people) share the remaining one-quarter of the wealth in the nation. This vast majority owns little beyond their own personal property—clothing, furnish-

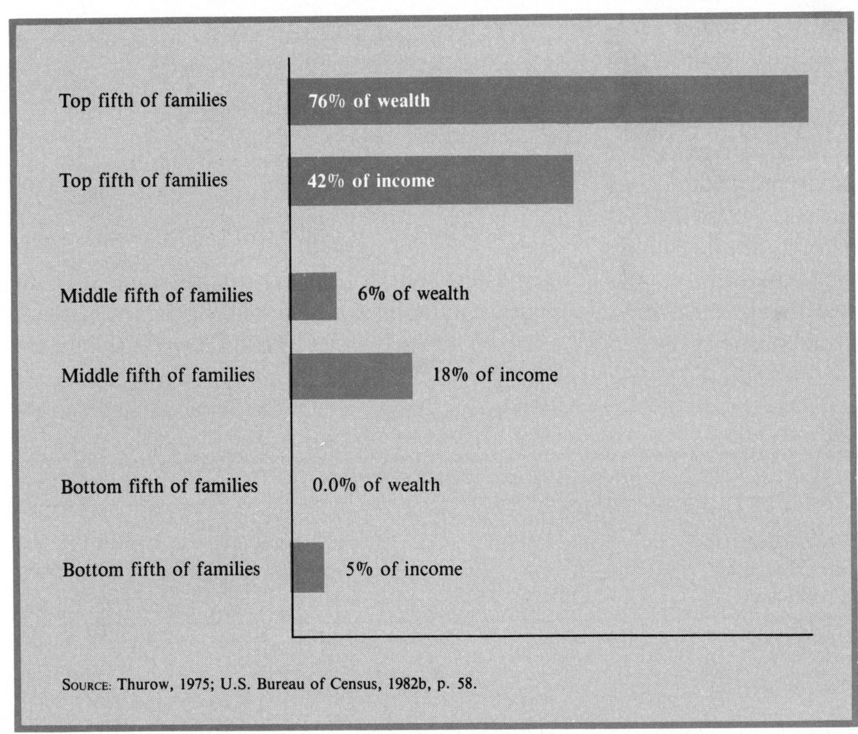

Figure 10.2 Distribution of Family Wealth and Income

ings, a car, and perhaps a house. For these people, property means something quite different from what it means for the very wealthy. It means a few possessions, many of which are still being paid for. This property does not usually produce income for the owner (except in the case of a traveling salesperson whose car may help to produce income). The bottom fifth of the nation's population owns less than 0.2 percent of the wealth in the nation (Thurow, 1975). Indeed, this group has more debts than assets.

Thus, as Figure 10.2 illustrates, the differences in the amount of wealth owned by the top and bottom fifths of the American population are enormous. A number of individuals control fortunes exceeding $500 million, while millions of people have only their debts. Income differences are considerable, but not nearly so great as wealth differences. As Figure 10.2 reveals, the top fifth of American families earned 42 percent of all the income earned in 1980, while the bottom fifth earned 5 percent—a difference of 37 percent, compared to the 76 percent difference in wealth.

The distinction between earnings and income from property holdings is crucial to understanding social class structure and to reconciling competing explanations for why social class inequality exists. Holding property is important for about 5 percent of the total American population. This 5 percent, however, represents more than 10 million people, and property is very important for them. It affects their income, power, status, self-image, and life-style. Moreover, property holding affects the social arena within which the other 95 percent of the population operates. It provides resources to the top 5 percent that are not available to the other 95 percent. These are financial resources that may be converted to power, that tend to confer status, that can command knowledge and information, and that enable them to advance ideologies consistent with their interests in the world.

Social Class as Position in the Social Relations of Production

A measure of class that is related to both wealth and income is the one used by Wright and Perrone (1977) to measure a Marxian concept of class. This conception emphasizes the position of individuals in the social relations of production. Four criteria are used to pinpoint an individual's position in the *social relations of production:*

1. The ownership of the means of production
2. The purchase of the labor power of others
3. The control of other people's labor power
4. The sale of one's own labor power

These four criteria are used in Table 10.3 to assign individuals to one of four classes. Capitalists are defined as the class that owns the means

Table 10.3 Wright's and Perrone's Expanded Marxian Criteria for Class

	Criteria for Class Position			
Class	Ownership of the Means of Production	Purchase of the Labor of Others	Control of the Labor of Others	Sale of One's Own Labor
Capitalists	Yes	Yes	Yes	No
Managers	No	No	Yes	Yes
Workers	No	No	No	Yes
Petty bourgeoisie	Yes	No	No	No

SOURCE: Wright and Perrone, 1977, p. 34.

of production, buys and controls the labor of others, and does not need to sell its own labor. Managers are considered a separate class even though they supervise others and may own some stock in the corporation. They are not capitalists unless they own a controlling interest. They also need to sell their own labor. The class position of workers is set by their situation of selling their own labor and not having any control over the labor of others. The last class, called the "petty bourgeoisie," consists of small businesspeople and shopkeepers who own their own stores but do not buy or control the labor of others in any major way.

The class categories in Table 10.3 represent an entirely different way of viewing class structure. Examining occupational differences leads to seeing classes as a ladder with many rungs. Small steps exist between positions, but it is difficult to say which rungs comprise a distinct class. The Marxian effort to measure class creates four distinct categories. These classes are in dynamic relation to one another. This means, for example, that certain people supervise others and that certain classes receive profits while others do not. There is some relationship between occupational position and class position, but it is by no means perfect. Employers are much more likely to be managers, proprietors, and officials than any other occupation, and they are much more likely to hold those occupations than are the members of other classes. Workers are likely to hold such jobs as truck drivers, clerks, or crafts workers. The total number of employers and petty bourgeoisie is rather small. The vast majority of the working population (almost 90 percent) are workers or managers. As a result, a small group occupies the dominant position in the social relations of production, a feature that is fairly invisible when we consider only occupational categories.

Some argue that class should be measured by occupation rather than by property because of the managerial revolution in American business. This has created a situation where knowledge or other technical criteria are more important than property for one's class position. It is understandable why so much stress is placed on occupation, since the majority of people in the labor force do not possess property. However, whether we want to explain variations in income or in wealth, a Marxian class analysis explains more of these differences than an occupational explanation does. Owners consistently have higher incomes than do managers and workers, even when education, occupational status, age, and length of time in job are controlled. Within the nonpropertied class, managers earn much more than workers, even when education is held constant (Wright and Perrone, 1977). This evidence is more consistent with a class analysis than with a technical skills explanation. Managerial pay scales may go up much more sharply than do worker pay scales because pay reflects not only productivity, but also the exercise of social control within businesses and bureaucracies. The promise of higher salaries may encourage individuals to control themselves and others in ways that are desired by higher-level managers and owners.

Nevertheless, Marxian class categories do not explain all the inequality in job rewards. Considerable inequalities in earnings and job fulfillment are also produced by occupational distinctions (Kalleberg and Griffin, 1980). These findings confirm once again the value of using several theoretical lenses for explaining the social world. Occupation and class together account for more inequality than does either one alone.

Subjective Indicators of Class

Assessments of occupation and productive position do not include information about individuals' perceptions of their own class positions, or the so-called *subjective dimension of social class*. Yet no consideration of social class is complete without taking into account the perceptions of individuals. It sometimes happens, for example, that Sam's neighbors consider him to be working class, while Sam considers himself to be middle class. Whose judgment do we use in such a situation? Do we follow the neighbor's (or a sociologist's) definition of Sam's social class, or do we accept Sam's self-definition? We cannot ignore Sam's ideas, because they are likely to affect his behavior. He may be more likely to have middle-class friends, to follow middle-class recreational and leisure activities, to belong to a middle-class church, and to have middle-class aspirations for his children. Although his beliefs may not coincide completely with his objective class position, they may affect his behavior. So, if we want to understand social behavior, we need to know both a person's "objective" social class and his or her subjective class identification.

In the early 1940s, pollster Elmo Roper did a nationwide survey for *Fortune* magazine in which Americans were asked whether they belonged to the "upper," "middle," or "lower" classes. When 79 percent replied that they were "middle" class, it was widely asserted that the United States was a middle-class nation. But social psychologist Richard Centers quickly challenged this interpretation. Also using a national sample, Centers added the category "working class" to the possible choices available to respondents. In his survey, half the respondents chose "working class" as their social class, and only 43 percent said they were "middle class" (Centers, 1949). Centers also found a high correlation between subjective class position and position as measured by more objective criteria, such as occupational type. The work by Centers and others who came after him suggests that Americans do not like to describe themselves as "lower class" but are quite willing to say they are "working class," which sounds honest and hard-working.

Since Centers did his study, the percentage of Americans who see themselves as working class has declined. A later national survey by Hodge and Treiman (1968) asked people: "If you were asked to use one of these names for your social class standing, which would you say you belonged to: the middle class, lower class, upper-middle class, working class, or upper class?" The replies were as follows:

Upper class	2.2%
Upper-middle class	16.6
Middle class	44.0
Working class	34.3
Lower class	2.3
Don't believe in classes	0.6

These results show the same aversion to describing oneself as lower class that Centers observed. The decline in the proportion of individuals describing themselves as working class may be due to the availability of other categories, or it may reflect the growth of the white collar sector during the time since the Centers study, since white collar workers are more likely to describe themselves as middle class. Finally, this piece of research is notable because very few people said they did not believe in classes, suggesting that nearly everyone is aware that classes exist.

A major problem with the subjective method is that it depends so heavily on how the question about class is worded. Also, some individuals may rank themselves higher than their income, occupation, property, and life-style seem to warrant. Another difficulty with using only subjective indicators of social class is that they are difficult to interpret and understand. In short, with the subjective definition we cannot tell whether it is economic or social class or some combination of the two that people are responding to.

The term *social class* may refer to property, to position in the social relations of production, to occupational category, and to income. These features affect the life chances and life-styles of individuals.

CLASS DIFFERENCES IN LIFE CHANCES AND LIFE-STYLE

Undoubtedly class location affects individuals' perceptions of their class position (including subjective definition of class). Table 10.4 pres-

Class position has a major effect on one's life-style and life chances. Some dogs owned by upper-class individuals live in greater comfort than some poor people do. The middle classes tend to think that nearly everyone in the United States is middle class.

Table 10.4 A Portrait of Class-Related Life Chances and Life Styles

	Socioeconomic Class Category (and % of total U.S. population in it)	Roots of Class Position	Occupation	Family
Property-Dominated	Upper Class (1–3%)	Ownership of productive property (usually inherited). High income (more than $150,000 per year).	Often not necessary. Managers, "public servants," philanthropists, professionals.	Dynastic alliance. Major source of identity. Modified extended family with strong kin ties. Strong elders. Age grading. Low fertility rates.
Occupation-Dominated	Upper-Middle Class (10–15%)	Occupational power and prestige. High income ($30,000 to $149,000). Some income from investments or savings.	Professionals, high-level civil servants, academics, managers. Major source of identity. Demanding of time and energy even during private time.	Generally stable. Value companionship in marriage. Isolated nuclear family. Marriage important as a rite of passage to adult responsibility and privilege. Male success traditionally requires wife serving as a helpmate.
	Lower-Middle Class (30–35%)	Lower income ($15,000 to $29,000), less property than upper-middle class.	Lower professionals, semi-professionals, sales and clerical workers, small business proprietors.	More egalitarian husband-wife relationships than working class. Increasing use of institutionalized child care. Drop in fertility rates.
	Working Class (40–45%)	Less occupational power and prestige, income and property ($5,000 to $30,000).	Skilled laborers (electricians, plumbers, machinists), truck drivers, barbers, semi-skilled laborers. Longer hours, less paid vacation.	Patriarchal, adult-centered family structure with sharply segregated sex roles. Relatives are important. Early marriage and childrearing.
Income- or Poverty-Dominated	Lower Class (20–25%)	High rates of unemployment, poverty-level income. No savings, property, or financial security (welfare–$6,000). Unemployment due to health disabilities, or lack of work opportunities.	Semi-skilled or unskilled laborers. Migrant workers. Women raised to believe they should be supported by men, untrained for work, then often deserted.	Heavy reliance on kin networks to meet daily domestic needs. Marriage not very important as an institution as it solves no economic problems and may add some. High fertility rate.

Table 10.4 *(Continued)*

	Socioeconomic Class Category	Childrearing	Education of Children	Personal Values
Property-Dominated	Upper Class	Children raised by nurses and governesses. Confers a sense of "entitlement."	Insulated from other classes at elite private schools. Attend elite colleges. Boys and girls study liberal arts.	Reveres the past, tradition. High value on "readiness," since attainment is certain but time of inheritance is not. Believe rich are rich because of self-discipline, motivation, ability, and willingness to work hard and assume responsibility.
Occupation-Dominated	Upper-Middle Class	Emphasizes development of individual autonomy. Generally more permissive than lower classes. Parents may threaten to withdraw love as punishment.	Liberal arts education at most elite schools possible. Graduate or professional schools. Increasingly comparable education for boys and girls.	Personal ambition or ambition for children. Sees high status as due to ability and achievement. Focus on careers and achievement within those careers. Value self-actualization—developing one's creativity, interpersonal sensitivity, and communication skills.
	Lower-Middle Class	Emphasizes obedience and docility, as well as sociability. More stress on discipline than higher classes.	Want schools that stress discipline and respect for adults. Parochial schools are popular with this group. More likely to attend college than working and lower classes but more likely to attend local, public institutions.	Concerned about respectability, decency, "proper" behavior, and value of hard work. Value reliability, cleanliness, personal morality, stability.
	Working Class	Stresses obedience, respect for elders. Emphasizes discipline.	Harder to plan for education. More high-school-only graduates than higher classes. Increasing college attendance at community colleges. Some preference for technical and vocational education.	Respect for authority, belief in American dream. Tend to blame themselves for lack of success and for material need.
Income- or Poverty-Dominated	Lower Class	Slightly more likely to use physical punishment on children, but much less than most people assume. Children help with necessary labor in the home.	Highest rates of illiteracy. High dropout rates. Schools in low-income areas tend to be lowest quality, with few alternatives available.	Have as strong a work motivation as any other class. Share many values with dominant strata, but accept alternatives when their situation violently contradicts those ideals.

(Continues on page 250)

Table 10.4 *(Continued)*

	Socioeconomic Class Category	Personal Style	Residence	Consumer Behavior, Leisure
Property-Dominated	Upper Class	"Good breeding," sincerity, careful personal grooming, character, graciousness, evidence of culture. Secure and favorable image.	May have more than one residence. May have long-standing family home, heirlooms, antiques. Often some joint family territory, like a summer compound or estate.	Discreet. Shun ostentatious displays of wealth, although this depends on age of family fortune.
Occupation Dominated	Upper-Middle Class	Strong favorable self-image.	Home location and furnishings are important. Considerable geographical mobility. Home ownership by 83%.	Fairly divided between the frugal and the ostentatious, depending upon situation. Value culture, books, theater, sports.
	Lower-Middle Class	Concerned with appearance of respectability. Seek to gain reputation as honest, hard-working, and responsibile members of community. Cleanliness, frugality, personal morality, and stability are valued.	Home ownership by 67%.	Frugal.
	Working Class	Strong group identity. Little social recognition for what they do. Respect their own work but know white collar work gets more public respect.	Home ownership by 61%. Highly valued and considered an achievement.	Spectator sports, hunting, fishing, boating, family gatherings, shopping expeditions, television.
Income- or Poverty-Dominated	Lower Class	Lower self-esteem. Less happy. Feel somewhat isolated socially.	Rental or other temporary lodging. Live in oldest, most deteriorated, least desirable housing and neighborhoods. Buildings in poor repair. May lack heat, plumbing; have rats, roaches, leaks. Frequent relocations.	Purchase second-hand clothing and furniture. Shop locally, pay higher prices. Spend about half of income on food, a quarter on rent.

ents a composite portrait of different classes in terms of their roots, consequences, and life-styles. Use of the term *life-style* requires some qualification, since it suggests more freedom of choice than may actually be the case. There are very real consequences of class situation that extend far beyond the style of music one prefers, the furnishings in one's home, and other superficial but highly visible features of life-style. These consequences include access to education, health, life expectancy, and general life chances, factors over which individuals have little control.

Table 10.4 *(Continued)*

	Socioeconomic Class Category	Political and Civic Behavior	Religion	Health
Property-Dominated	Upper Class	"Behind the scenes" political activity and support. Play high-prestige, often honorary roles.	Most likely to be Protestant, especially Episcopalian. Prefer subdued services.	Generally high. The best that money, education, and knowledge can buy.
Occupation-Dominated	Upper-Middle Class	High sense of civic duty. Active in community groups, political organizations, voluntary associations. Predominantly Republican.	Very likely to belong to a church. Include denominations such as Presbyterians, Quakers, Episcopalians, Unitarians, Congregationalists.	Good physical and mental health. Good health insurance plans through their jobs.
	Lower-Middle Class	May work as civil servants. Most dissatisfied with their standard of living, jobs, and family incomes.	Protestant denominations such as Baptists, Methodists, Lutherans; or Greek Orthodox or Catholic.	Longer life expectancy than lower classes. Some health insurance through their jobs.
	Working Class	Mainly Democrat. Less likely to vote than higher classes. Feels politically powerless. More than half belong to unions. Belong to churches, but two-thirds belong to no other community organizations.	More than 50% are Catholic.	More exposure to occupational health and safety hazards than higher classes. Some health insurance if a union member and regularly employed.
Income- or Poverty-Dominated	Lower Class	Less likely to vote.	More likely to belong to fundamentalist or revivalist sects.	Poorer mental and physical health. Lower life expectancy. 40% of poor have serious medical problems from malnutrition. Poorer health care. No health insurance.

SOURCES: Hacker, 1980; Huber and Form, 1973; Rossides, 1976; Vanfossen, 1979; Zablocki and Kanter, 1976.

Life-styles and life consequences are clearly influenced by one's position in the economic system. As Zablocki and Kanter (1976) suggest, these positions may be compressed into three basic categories: life-styles that are primarily property-dominated, those that are occupation-dominated, and those that are income- or poverty-dominated. Variations within these three basic categories can be illuminated by relationship to the means of production, income, authority and autonomy at work, and occupational prestige.

In Table 10.4, five socioeconomic classes are designated and their relationships to various criteria are indicated. Because multiple criteria are used, the boundaries of each category are somewhat fuzzy. The categories could be sliced somewhat thinner. The upper class, for example, could be divided into the upper-upper and the lower-upper, depending on the size of the fortune held and its age. Further divisions along occupational, income, and authority dimensions could be made within each of these class categories. The Marxian perspective is reflected in the colored rules dividing the property-holding upper class from those who must work, and separating those with fairly regular work and income from the unemployed and poor. If these cleavages are meaningful, they should be reflected in life chances and life-styles, including family, childrearing, education, personal values, personal style, residence, consumer behavior, political and civic behavior, religion, and health. Some of these consequences are summarized in the table.

DIFFERENCES IN FAMILY, CHILDREARING, AND EDUCATION

Since most property is passed down through families, the property-dominated upper class is very concerned with family identity and kin ties. Extended kin networks are important and useful to the upper class. This concern is reflected in the emphasis members of this class place on rearing and educating their children. Often nonfamily members such as nurses, governesses, and private school teachers play a large role in childrearing, but these people are paid by the families and generally perform their duties in ways the parents desire.

The upper-middle class values the companionship of marriage. Childrearing stresses the development of individual autonomy and academic and interpersonal skills, since their social position depends on education and occupation.

The lower-middle class is moving toward egalitarian relationships between husband and wife as more wives take jobs. Lower-middle-class families may keep close ties with their extended family since they are likely to live nearby. They value obedience among their children and want schools that stress discipline and respect for adults, the way parochial schools do. Lower-middle-class children are increasingly likely to attend local public college.

The working class marries earlier than any of the above groups, and its family life tends to be patriarchal, with roles segregated by sex. Wives are looking for more emotional sharing than existed in traditional working-class families (Rubin, 1976). Extended kin ties are important, and children are expected to be obedient and to respect their elders. Traditional education that stresses discipline and basic skills is preferred over educational innovations such as "open classrooms." College is more uncertain, and technical and vocational education is more likely in this group.

The lower class has less reason to value the nuclear family, since it solves few of its economic problems. Birth rates are high, however. Extended family relations are important for sharing household and childrearing work. Children are pressed into household service, caring for younger children, going to the store, or doing laundry. Parents value education, particularly that stressing basic skills in reading and arithmetic, although the parents may be illiterate or poorly educated themselves. Schools in poor areas tend to be the lowest quality in the country, with high teacher and pupil turnover. Families may have little choice about where they can send their children to school. Youths frequently drop out and seldom go to college.

DIFFERENCES IN PERSONAL VALUES, STYLE, RESIDENCE, CONSUMER BEHAVIOR, AND LEISURE

The upper class values tradition and the past and emphasizes "good breeding" (manners and personal style), graciousness, and culture. Members believe in discreet, understated public displays of wealth, emotions, personality, and leisure behavior. "Playboys" exist but tend to be frowned upon. Upper-class homes are often filled with family heirlooms and antiques, and members may vacation in a family compound at the ocean or in the mountains.

The upper-middle class values ability and achievement, as well as personal development, effort, and growth. Members of this class emphasize high culture, books, and theater, although they may also enjoy sports such as sailing, golf, tennis, football, and baseball. While they may move more often than the upper class, they value having a nice home and a "good address."

The lower-middle class seems most concerned with maintaining the appearance of respectability; hence they value cleanliness, frugality, morality, and stability. Their leisure activities are generally home-based and inexpensive. The working class may identify with other working-class people fairly strongly. They know their work does not get as much public respect as white collar work does. They value home ownership and enjoy working on their homes, cars, trucks, campers, or boats themselves. They like spectator sports, hunting, fishing, and family gatherings.

The lower class feels somewhat isolated socially. It does not participate fully in either the occupational or the consumer and leisure spheres of society, and most of its income goes for food and rent. Members of the lower class live in the poorest housing in an area, and gener-

"I read 'Art News.'"

SOURCE: Drawing by Joseph Farris, © 1982, *The New Yorker Magazine, Inc.*

ally feel more miserable than others. Leisure activities such as sports may cut across class lines. Where they do not, cultural interests may reinforce occupational differences.

DIFFERENCES IN POLITICS, RELIGION, AND HEALTH

The upper class and the upper-middle class may play an active role in political, civic, and religious activities. They are most likely to belong to Protestant denominations. They have the best health that money, education, and knowledge can obtain. The lower-middle class may be active in rank-and-file political activities, although less often in leadership positions than the upper and upper-middle classes. They live longer than the working and lower classes.

Catholics make up a larger proportion of the working class than of other classes. Traditionally members of the working class have voted for the Democratic party, although in the 1980 presidential election about 50 percent of them voted Republican. About half the working class belongs to labor unions. Their work often has health and safety hazards.

Lower-class members are less active politically than are other classes. They often belong to fundamentalist or revivalist religious groups. They have the greatest problems with mental and physical health and are least likely to have health insurance from a union or employer to help them deal with such medical problems. As a group, they have the shortest life expectancy.

Overall, then, class situation is quite strongly associated with different attitudes, behaviors, and life chances. It would be useful if these divisions of the class structure could be compared with people's subjective impressions of where they stand and whether or not they feel a sense of membership with that group. Table 10.4 reveals some of the complexity reflected in social classes and may help to explain why class consciousness is not always clearly formulated along a single dimension such as property, relation to the means of production, or income. Family life, neighborhood, residence, racial and gender differences, religion, leisure activities—all these factors and others influence individuals in the social world and shape their identities and their perceptions of the class structure and their place in it.

POVERTY

One of the starkest features of the American class structure is the widespread existence of poverty. Poverty means babies dying of lead poisoning, old people freezing to death, people eating macaroni for 30 straight days, stunted hopes, and frustrated lives. In an affluent industrial society, the existence of poverty poses sharp contradictions and challenges. Policy-makers concerned with the problem of poverty have grappled with how to define it, who is most likely to be poor, the causes of poverty, and what programs might provide relief.

DEFINITIONS OF POVERTY

Poverty has been defined in both absolute and relative terms. *Absolute poverty* refers to having too little income to buy the necessities of food, shelter, clothing, or health care. The U.S. government and other agencies use an objective standard of what a person or family needs to subsist. In 1981 the poverty level for a nonfarm family of four was $9287. The effects of poverty become apparent when we realize that such a budget allows only $200 a month for rent for a family of four.

In absolute terms, the number of people below the poverty line has declined, from 33.2 million in 1965 to 31.8 million in 1981 (Hammond Almanac 1979 for 1965; U.S. Bureau of the Census, 1982a, p. 442). Since the total population has been increasing during this time, the proportion of poor people in the population has dropped from 17.3 percent in 1965 to 14.0 percent in 1981 (U.S. Bureau of the Census, 1982a, p. 442). A major reason for this decline in the officially "poor" is the effect of entitlement programs on the elderly, which push the income of many old people just above the poverty line. What this means is that many more people are living in what the government calls "near poverty."

Relative poverty suggests that people are poor if they have much less than the average person in their society has, even if they can afford the necessities of life. Relative poverty may be more significant socially than absolute poverty. Relative poverty means that people cannot afford the material goods and life-styles that most people take for granted. Electricity, hot and cold running water, a telephone, no rats in one's home, a TV set, and shoes may not be necessary for survival, but they are considered social necessities in most parts of the United States. Some analysts suggest that relative poverty causes such antisocial behavior as delinquency, educational apathy, and attacks on the more affluent. Rainwater (1969) suggests this may occur because individuals do not feel they are part of their society.

Poverty measured in relative terms, as a percentage of all income, for example, has not diminished much over the last three decades. In 1950, the poorest 20 percent of all families earned 4.5 percent of all income, while in 1980 they earned 5 percent of all income (U.S. Bureau of the Census, 1981c, p. 15).

WHO IS POOR?

Poverty is not evenly distributed through the population. More than half the poor are under the age of 14 or over 65, and are poor because they are unable to work (Retine and Huber, 1974, p. 102). Although two-thirds of all persons below the poverty level are white, the rates of poverty are much higher for nonwhites. Only 10 percent of whites, but 33 percent of blacks, 26 percent of Hispanics, and more than 50 percent of native Americans are below the official poverty level. Poverty is most likely to be found in central cities and rural areas rather than suburbs. Families headed by women without husbands had a poverty rate of 33 percent, compared to 5 percent for husband-wife families. In short, the poor are disproportionately young, old, inner city or rural females, and members of a minority.

WHAT CAUSES POVERTY?

Poverty in the United States is not due to an overall failure to produce enough goods and services. It is, instead, a question of how wealth is distributed. To some extent the same is true on a worldwide scale. Three types of explanations of poverty have been offered: economic, political, and cultural.

Economic and Structural Explanations

A major cause of poverty is lack of jobs and low wages paid for many jobs. Half of poor families are headed by someone who works, and one-third of those family heads work full time. Someone working full time and earning the minimum wage in 1982 earned $7280, not enough to bring a family of four above the poverty line. Poverty among those who work is due to the lower pay for jobs traditionally filled by unskilled workers, minorities, and women.

The high rates of unemployment in recent years are reflected in low family incomes, particularly in one-earner families. In 1982 the United States unemployment rate was 10.8 percent (with 12 million Americans out of work). Unemployment is much higher among young people, older people, and minorities. Recent unemployment has been due to extensive layoffs, particularly in manufacturing industries such as automobiles, as well as to the limited number of new jobs. Many people listed as having jobs are actually "underemployed"—for example, people with Ph.D.s in literature who are driving cabs. Such individuals are not shown in unemployment figures.

Unemployment rates vary among industrial countries. In 1981, the rate was 7.6 percent in

Canada, 2.2 percent in Japan, 2.5 percent in Sweden, 4.2 percent in West Germany, and 10.6 percent in Britain (U.S. Bureau of the Census 1982a, p. 873). These rate differences may be partly due to economic conditions, such as rates of savings and productivity increases. Political as well as economic causes also lie behind unemployment and poverty. Rates of unemployment that are tolerated in the United States are considered politically unacceptable in Japan, Sweden, and West Germany. Their lower rates result in part from government policies to minimize unemployment.

Political Explanations

Poverty and chronic unemployment do not appear to be a major political issue in the United States. Except for President Lyndon Johnson's War on Poverty in the 1960s, recent political campaigns have focused more on cutting taxes and building military strength than on redistributing wealth and income in the United States.

The existence of poverty serves the interests of many who are more rich and powerful than the poor, suggests Herbert Gans (1971). Without poverty, much of society's dirty work would not get done; the prices of many goods and services (like housecleaning) would be much higher; many welfare workers, government bureaucrats, pawnbrokers, and police officers would be unemployed; merchants could not unload their shoddy furniture, dented canned goods, or day-old bread; and some group other than the poor would need to bear the costs of change and growth in American society—for example, relocation in the face of a new highway or cultural complex. Thus, suggests Gans, in many direct and indirect ways the existence of poor people contributes to the comfort of the middle and upper classes.[1]

[1]On the other hand, it may be argued that the costs to the middle and upper classes in terms of crime, vandalism, and loss of productive labor, as well as the costs of controlling and regulating the poor, may at some point outweigh the benefits Gans describes. At that point, a rational model would predict that social changes should occur.

Welfare programs are a major means of regulating the political and economic behavior of the poor, argue Piven and Cloward (1971). They suggest that relief programs expand in periods of mass unemployment and threats to civil disorder. When threats of civil disorder subside, welfare programs become more restrictive and aim more directly at reinforcing work norms. Piven and Cloward do not deny the value of work in all societies. Their point is, however, that welfare policies help to maintain inequities by "defining and enforcing the terms on which different classes" are made to do various kinds of work. In this way, the political and economic significance of welfare and unemployment insurance is that it makes some people "do the harshest work for the least reward" (Piven and Cloward, 1971, p. xvii). Many people in our society, however, may be unwilling to view poverty as a political and economic issue and be more likely to "blame the victims" for being poor. This approach is reflected in cultural explanations of poverty.

Cultural Explanations

Some social scientists suggest that cultural differences between the poor and others in society explain their predicament. Anthropologist Oscar Lewis (1965) suggests that a distinct *culture of poverty* develops as a reaction to political and economic exclusion in a society. This culture is characterized by the refusal to delay gratification, especially regarding sex and alcohol, a fatalistic view that one's own efforts are useless and can do nothing to change things, and a weak commitment to family and community. This culture is passed on from one generation to the next, making it difficult—if not impossible—for individuals to break out of the cycle of poverty. "Culture of poverty" explanations suggest that cultural values must change before poverty can be eliminated.

Moynihan's (1967) work on the disintegration of the black family brought about by slavery and the resulting "tangle of pathology" that passed poverty and problems from one generation of blacks to the next has striking similarities to the "culture of poverty" view. Similarly, Banfield (1968) suggests that the cause of poverty is the present rather than the future orientation of poor people. In these views, people must change their attitudes if they are to escape poverty. Other anthropologists challenge the idea that the culture of poverty is passed from one generation to the next. They argue that each generation faces the conditions of political isolation and economic deprivation that may create similar behaviors in each succeeding generation. When economic conditions improve, individuals will change their behavior and escape poverty. It is these conditions, rather than culture, they say, that explains the poverty of certain groups.

Although many academic social scientists have challenged and qualified the "culture of poverty" explanation, it appears to strike a responsive chord in Americans, who have a strong faith in an "ideology of individualism" (Feagin, 1975). The absence of an entrenched aristocracy and the existence of free land and economic opportunities in the American past generated a tremendous faith in the value of individual effort. Hard work paid off handsomely for many early settlers. In many people's minds, hard work and success were seen as going hand in hand. Therefore it was easy to conclude that the unsuccessful must be lazy, or otherwise personally responsible for their poverty.

Despite changes in the availability of free land and economic opportunities in American society and the emergence of a wealthy class, beliefs in hard work and equal opportunity persist, perhaps because they are functional for some individuals, even if they inaccurately represent society as a whole. Two studies found that Americans still tend to consider individual factors more important for explaining poverty than structural factors like chronic unemployment or fatalistic factors like poor health (Feagin, 1972; Huber and Form, 1973). Huber and Form, however, found that poor people and blacks considered personal qualities less important than did whites, the middle class, and the rich.

ANTIPOVERTY POLICIES

The most far-reaching antipoverty policy would result in full employment at a living wage. This situation has come close to being accomplished by a number of Western European countries, but has not received wide support in the United States. What we have instead is a series of welfare programs. The poor ordinarily have little influence on government. Therefore, the social welfare policies that exist cannot be assumed to serve their best interests (Piven and Cloward, 1971). Old age pensions and unemployment insurance may benefit those at the bottom of the economic order, but only certain people are eligible for those programs. You need to have worked at some point and be certified as unneeded in the labor force, either because of old age or because your job ended. Many jobs (for example, some domestic servants and agricultural workers) are denied the benefits of such insurance programs (Piven and Cloward, 1971).

Aside from these programs, the two major types of welfare are Aid to Families with Dependent Children (AFDC) and supplemental security income (SSI). About 15 million Americans receive some form of publicly labeled assistance, or welfare, each year. Nearly three-quarters of them receive AFDC; the remaining recipients comprise the aged, blind, or disabled who are eligible for supplemental security income. Only about three out of five of those below the poverty line are receiving public assistance.[2] The rest are the working poor or those on private pensions.

In the decade of the 1960s, the welfare rolls rose to 2.4 million families, an increase of 225 percent for the decade. By 1979, the figure had reached 3.6 million families. This increase, suggest Piven and Cloward, was due to the govern-

[2]The fact that about 40 percent of the poor do not receive public assistance may not be too surprising if Piven and Cloward (1971) are right in arguing that the growth of modern welfare systems may be due more to the effort to control and silence the poor than to the desire to improve their situations.

ment's anti-inflation strategy, the welfare system's high rate of accepting applications, and changing attitudes toward going on welfare. Public assistance had come increasingly to be viewed as a right rather than as something to be ashamed of. The average monthly payment to families with dependent children was $288 in 1980, or a total of $3456 per year (U.S. Bureau of the Census, 1982a, p. 340).

Many people do not regard the expansion of the welfare rolls as an acceptable antipoverty policy. After each expansion in the past, suggest Piven and Cloward, there has been a reaction aimed first at imposing work requirements and followed by the expulsion of large numbers of people from the relief rolls, pushing them into a labor market with too little work. Those who were allowed to remain on the relief rolls (some blind and aged) were treated in the punitive and degrading way that all past recipients of relief had been (Piven and Cloward, 1971).

There is, however, another form of welfare in the United States, although it is not publicly labeled and stigmatized. This form of welfare includes various market subsidies, including government contracts—for example, for computers, airplanes, tanks, or jeeps; price programs for dairy and agricultural products; and export-import policies that place tariffs on goods competing with major U.S. industries. In addition, a series of federal tax loopholes protect those who have some money to invest. These include income exclusions, such as the interest paid on municipal bonds; deductions such as the interest paid on a home mortgage or business loan; tax credits for energy-saving devices or business machinery; special tax rates on capital gains (that is, profit from selling stock or real estate); and tax shelters such as depreciation allowances for real estate, depletion allowances for oil properties, and individual retirement accounts.

Many people with modest incomes may depend on such programs or subsidies to stay afloat, and strong arguments can be made to support their economic or social value. People with more money benefit more than people with less money. It is important to realize, however, that such programs represent a form of state subsidy for investors and businesspeople and therefore resemble other social welfare programs.

The unequal effects of such policies is documented by a Brookings Institution study which found that $92 million a year in tax breaks goes to the poorest 6 million families in the United States, whereas $2.2 billion (24 times as much) flows to only 3000 families with incomes of more than $1 million per year (Stern, 1972).

Proposals to reduce absolute poverty in the United States include ideas for tax reform, job programs to reduce unemployment, more public assistance, a guaranteed annual income, and organizing the poor to demand changes. Limited efforts have been made to effect tax reform, extend public assistance, and organize the poor. The guaranteed annual income proposal has never gone beyond being discussed. The Reagan administration urged private charity rather than public efforts to overcome poverty. In such a climate, poverty is a long way from being eliminated.

The widespread persistence of poverty might be expected to increase class consciousness and militancy. Although poverty persists at the societal level, however, many individuals move in and out of poverty over the course of their lives. The existence of individual mobility, at both the poverty level and above, seems to play a major role in dampening class consciousness.

CLASS CONSCIOUSNESS AND SOCIAL MOBILITY

As we have seen, class has been defined and measured in a variety of ways, depending on whether the focus has been occupational ranking, income, wealth, or the relationship to the means of production. These measures tend to be interrelated, although their correlation is not perfect because of individual exceptions. For example, priests hold high-status occupations but seldom earn a lot of money or own much property, whereas loan sharks may be wealthy but lacking in prestige. Whatever indicators are used, however, they reveal enormous differences in wealth, income, and prestige. Why is it, then, that the United States has not witnessed the rise of a class-conscious and militant working class? Compared to other industrial nations such as France, Italy, or Great Britain, the United States has experienced much less unified social and political action directed at changing the inequalities that exist. One reason for the lack of unified opposition to the class structure may rest on the blurring of class consciousness by leisure activities and a preoccupation with social mobility.

CLASS CONSCIOUSNESS

Awareness of class differences does not necessarily create a sense of common class position and interests, called *class consciousness*. The upper class may be most aware of their common class interests and most cohesive in their actions (Baltzell, 1964; Domhoff, 1967; Useem, 1980). The working class is much less cohesive as a class than Marx predicted. Although labor unions represent class interests to a degree, there is no working-class political party in the United States, nor are class issues often expressed politically in other ways.

Why has class consciousness not developed more fully than it has among the U.S. working class? There have always been a number of factors that operate to divide the working class. These factors include racial and ethnic rivalries and gender-specific jobs and pay scales such as secretarial jobs for women. These social differences cross-cut economic similarities in the working class. The idea that ethnic diversity works to reduce class consciousness is supported by the existence of several protracted and bloody general strikes in the United States between 1870 and 1900, which certainly showed working-class consciousness. The early twentieth century was marked by waves of new immigrants of different ethnic backgrounds, as well as violent repression of the strikes that did occur.

The importance of class boundaries may be reduced by wide variations in income within the working class and considerable overlap in the incomes and consumer behaviors of the working class and middle class. While the poor are not highly visible, people know they are there, and their existence may serve to make people in the working class and lower-middle classes feel relatively better off, compared to the poor. Differences between the working class and the lower-middle class are not so great in income terms, although white collar workers tend to have more job security and benefits. Since the vast majority of the population falls into one of these two social classes and most of their contact is with members of their own or a neighboring class, they have little direct experience with vast class differences. The upper-middle class and, to an even greater extent, the upper class keep a low profile and have limited social contact with the lower-middle class and the working class. Income differences are justified on the grounds that they are earned (by superior education, experience, and talent), and property differences may be buried in corporate holdings. Exclusive residential areas, clubs, and schools further insulate the wealthy and powerful from everyone else, which keeps them from being too visible and helps ensure that other people will not make comparisons with their own economic situation.

In addition, America has been noted since its beginning as a "land of opportunity" where a person could become an *individual* success, regardless of social or economic background. So the ideology of individual success and mobility is part of the national culture and to some extent works against development of a more inclusive class consciousness. In the early years of this nation, the availability of land and rich natural resources, a shortage of labor, and a growing economy fed people's hopes that effort and opportunity could create individual progress (at least for white males). In this century, as the white collar segment of the labor force grew much faster than the blue collar portion, people had the experience of occupational mobility, if not their own at least that of their children or of people they knew. This mobility could be cited as evidence that opportunities exist for people with "ability" and the willingness to work hard. Social mobility was facilitated by geographical mobility. Individuals could move to a new region where no one knew their families or their social origins.

The development of class consciousness may be further depressed by the way Americans (more than any other nationality) seem to strive for status; that is, they seem to adopt the trappings, symbols, or other material manifestations of an affluent life-style. A blue collar worker may buy a video recording machine before a white collar worker does; a secretary may buy a fur coat, whereas a college professor probably would not. Leisure fads such as disco roller skating may sweep the country, cutting across class lines. In this way, status striving and common patterns of consumption may blur class boundaries. Status striving may reflect the ideology of upward mobility, and that ideology may reduce class consciousness and therefore fortify the class structure. Individuals preoccupied with rising or falling in the social hierarchy are not likely to challenge the existence of the class structure. The preoccupation with social mobility in American society is reflected in numerous studies of social mobility by sociologists.

SOCIAL MOBILITY

Social mobility refers to the movement from one status to another within a stratified society. Social mobility in the United States is usually examined in terms of occupation, and only occasionally in terms of income. In general terms, *vertical mobility* refers to individual or group movement upward or downward in the social hierarchy, but the possibility of downward mobility is seldom considered. *Horizontal mobility* involves moving from one social status to another of about equal rank, such as changing from one job to another similar one. Various types of mobility are summarized in Table 10.5. Most researchers focus on mobility from one generation to another, but there is also the chance of mobility within the lifetime of an individual. Someone may rise from a modest beginning to a position of high income or prestige, or aristocrats may lose their property and position in a social revolution. While infrequent, rapid shifts in social location have always captured the American imagination and are reflected in a number of novels *(Gone with the Wind)*, plays *(Death of a Salesman)*, and television series *(The Jeffersons)*. The most drastic shifts in social position occur during social revolutions when one class is deposed or foreign rulers are overthrown. This change creates opportunities for different individuals, groups, or classes to rise in the social hierarchy.

With the advent of the Industrial Revolution, upward mobility became more likely than downward mobility, because industrialization meant the expansion of higher-status and better-paid positions, while farm jobs continued to shrink. In 1900, there were 10 farm workers for every professional and technical worker (Blau and Duncan, 1967); today there are 2 professionals and technicians for every farmer. Gradual change in the occupational structure, with the expansion of clerical, technical, and professional employment and the decline of manual and farm work, explains a great deal of the upward mobility in Western industrial societies. Besides changes in the occupational structure, upward mobility has been increased by class differences in fertility rates. The upper and upper-middle classes tend to have fewer children than lower-class families, thereby possibly creating occupational vacancies that lower-status individuals can fill.

How much mobility has there traditionally been in American society? Faith in the opportunity for individual and intergenerational mobility has always fueled the hopes of Americans. In the nineteenth century, unskilled and semiskilled laborers such as factory workers and farmers did experience some mobility, but generally only a step or two up the occupational ladder (Thernstrom, 1964). In a historical study of business executives, Lipset and Bendix (1959) found that it was about as difficult to move from a working-class background to a business career in the late eighteenth century as it was early in the twentieth century.

Mobility patterns in the twentieth century are similar. In their massive study of more than 20,000 males and their fathers, Blau and Duncan (1967) found that lifetime and intergenerational mobility was frequent but limited in scope. Most people tended to move up only a step or two, and most moves occurred *within* the white collar, blue collar, or farm sectors rather than among those occupational divisions. More recent research suggests that the rates of intergenerational mobility have not changed between 1962 and 1973, but that individuals in their own lifetimes may experience more mobility between their first and their current occupations than was true in the past (Featherman and Hauser, 1978). This finding suggests that individuals now may expect more mobility within their own careers than was the case in 1962, but that rates of intergenerational mobility have changed little.

Intergenerational mobility refers to a vertical change of social status from one generation to the next. In most studies of mobility, the son's occupational status is compared with his father's. *Intragenerational mobility* refers to the vertical mobility experienced by a single individual within his or her own lifetime. The intergenerational occupational status of individuals seems to be explained by two major factors—educational level, especially higher education, and family background. By comparing the relative success of brothers, Jencks et al. found that family background explains nearly half of the difference in occupational status and about a quarter of the difference in annual earnings (1979). Educational background has a comparable effect on occupational status and earnings. Education

Table 10.5 Types of Social Mobility

	Unit Experiencing Mobility	
Type of Mobility	Individuals	Groups
Horizontal	No change in the position of the individual in the social hierarchy—a factory worker moves from one factory to another.	No change in the position of a group in the social hierarchy. A group of sales people moves from one organization to another similar one.
Vertical	Involves a change, upward, or downward, of the individual in the social hierarchy.	Involves a change in the location of a group in the social hierarchy—the prestige of scientists has risen in industrial societies, while that of the clergy has declined.
Intragenerational	Individuals are vertically mobile within their own adult lifetimes.	A group is vertically mobile within the lifetime of its members.
Intergenerational	Children of individuals are vertically mobile—the child of a truck driver becomes a business executive, the child of a doctor becomes a short-order cook.	A group is mobile from one generation to the next. The children of lower-status parents move up or the children of higher-status parents move down.
Geographical	Individuals move from one place to another.	Groups migrate from one region to another.

appears to increase earnings mainly by opening the door to high-status (and high-paying) occupations (Jencks et al., 1979).

Social mobility may have social and personal costs. Rapid changes of social circumstances were identified by Emile Durkheim as a prime basis for normlessness. Individuals who suddenly become rich and famous, such as recording artists or professional athletes in our society, may find it difficult to deal with the onslaught of people, invitations, obligations, and demands they now face. The way one was used to living no longer seems appropriate. Such individuals may feel anxiety, tension, and have difficulty adjusting (Tumin, 1967; Blau, 1956; Lipset and Bendix, 1959). Intergenerational mobility tends to widen the gulf between parents and children and to be accompanied by parent-child estrangement. Upwardly mobile men are less likely than other people to socialize with relatives or to have friends in their communities and are more likely to feel anxious and under stress (Kessin, 1971). Someone experiencing downward mobility may face similar upheavals, besides the stress of losing prestige. Downwardly mobile men, however, were more involved than average in community and family relationships and seemed to have better mental health (Kessin, 1971).

Social mobility may have mixed effects on individuals. At the societal level, however, the possibility and the ideology of social mobility encourages individual striving rather than collective action. In this way it may reduce class consciousness and lessen the chances of changing the class structure of a society.

ARE CLASSLESS INDUSTRIAL SOCIETIES POSSIBLE?

Functionalists suggest that stratification is inevitable. In contrast, conflict theorists suggest that although tendencies toward stratification exist, the range of inequality need not be as wide as it is in the United States, for instance. If this is so, what evidence is there to support it? Have any industrial societies successfully reduced, if not eliminated, stratification?

DO EASTERN EUROPE AND THE USSR HAVE CLASSLESS SOCIETIES?

In the state socialist societies of Eastern Europe and the USSR, income-producing property is not passed on by inheritance from one generation to the next one. There are income and prestige differences between occupations, however. High-level administrators in industry and the government are at the top, followed by skilled manual workers, lower-level white collar workers, and unskilled manual workers. Members of the top level, the so-called white collar intelligentsia, have joined the Communist Party in increasing numbers in recent decades. Although most of their social and economic advantage derives from occupational status, Party membership gives additional advantages—for example, the capacity to pull strings and get favored treatment with respect to placing one's child in a good school or university, obtaining the best theater tickets, or gaining a better apartment (Parkin, 1971). Persons in such high-ranking positions may be able to give their children educational advantages that serve to pass privileges from one generation to the next.

At the same time, several features suggest a less rigid system of stratification than exists in the West (Parkin, 1971): The less well born also have good chances for social advancement, and their parents have high ambitions; there is less distinction between elite culture and mass culture than in the West; and skilled workers may be taught new skills that enable them to advance. In addition to the distribution of privileges according to occupational and Party positions, state socialist societies have a totalitarian authority structure in which the Party monopolizes the decision-making processes. While such societies do not appear to have classes based on economic ownership, they do have a system of stratification based on occupational and Party positions.

COUNTRIES WITH LESS SOCIAL INEQUALITY

Although social inequalities still exist in such countries as Sweden, Denmark, and Norway, those nations do provide free medical care and free preschool care for children. Sweden has a state-controlled medical system that produces abundant numbers of doctors and dentists, with the result that they almost face an unemployment problem and are paid less well than American medics. Swedish taxpayers, however, receive extensive medical benefits (Anderson, 1974). The ample number of medical professionals notwithstanding, unemployment in general is very low. The Swedish government operates a job placement service, pays moving expenses, and provides unemployment grants until people are reemployed. Each time a child is born, the family receives a cash payment at birth, and a tax-free annual allowance until the child is 16. These allowances are designed to provide adequate support for each child in society, regardless of how much money the parents have. Roughly 90 percent of all families have similar incomes. As a result, most Scandinavians are healthy and well fed (Vanfossen, 1979). The extremes of poverty and wealth do not exist to the same extent as in the United States.

In Taiwan, conscious government planning has been aimed at reducing economic inequality. In 1953, the bottom 40 percent of Taiwan's population received only 11 percent of the country's income, while the top 20 percent got 61 percent. During the 1950s, the government instituted a free public education system through college; it also implemented land-reform programs and took control over the tobacco, oil, and liquor industries. By 1975, the bottom 40 percent of the population was receiving 22 percent of the country's income, while the top 20 percent's portion was reduced to 39 percent. These changes in the distribution of income occurred at a time when Taiwan's economy was growing rapidly, so the process may have been less painful for the privileged strata.

Not all countries with such high growth rates have managed to shift income allocations, however. In Brazil and Mexico, which have similar growth rates, the bottom 40 percent of the population earns 10 percent of the income, and the top 20 percent controls more than 60 percent. The Philippines has a similar gap (Butterfield, 1977). These examples suggest that income redistribution is a political rather than an economic question.

Wealth inequalities, however, seem even less susceptible to political reform than income inequalities. Revolution seems to be the major way that property and wealth have been redistributed, as in Cuba, China, and the Soviet Union. Such societies have reduced inequality by wealth, but they have increased the power of the state over individuals. The major base for inequality in such societies has shifted from wealth to the political, administrative, organizational, and police power of the state.

Both Cuba and China have struggled to develop participatory practices and to minimize the advantages conferred by more privileged positions. This suggests that efforts to diminish stratification require conscious analysis, planning, and practices (such as job rotations) designed to neutralize the principle of cumulative advantage. The fact that both Cuban and Chinese societies are primarily agrarian rather than industrial raises questions about whether such an approach can work in highly industrial societies. The social policies of the Scandinavian countries and Taiwan, however, suggest that many of the worst features of social inequality—grossly unequal health care and life expectancy, educational programs, and family support—can be reduced even in highly industrialized countries. It is clear that income inequality can be reduced, if not eliminated. The issue is one of political and social will, rather than sociological feasibility.

Summary

1. Social class has been defined in different ways. American sociologists tend to define class in terms of social status or honor. Weber stressed status group membership and market position, referring to how successfully one could sell his or her labor in the marketplace. A third view emphasizes position in the authority structure of an organization. Marx saw social classes as rooted in property ownership and the social organization of production.

2. Theoretical ideas of class affect how class is measured in social research. Some researchers have asked people to rank the prestige, or status, of various occupations; the best predictors of the rank of an occupation are the educational level and income of its workers.

3. Sometimes income levels are used to set up class categories, but people with similar incomes may have widely different life-styles and world views, while people with quite different incomes may be fairly similar in outlook.

4. Marxians stress that economic ownership rather than income lies behind class differences. Wealth is distributed much more unequally than is income. The top fifth of the United States population owns or controls three-quarters of the wealth in the nation, while the bottom fifth owns less than 0.2 percent of that wealth. In contrast, the top fifth earns 44 percent of all income, while the bottom fifth earns 4 percent of income.

5. When class is defined as position within the social relations of production, that definition includes aspects of ownership, authority, and market position. Defined this way, class is related to both income and power within an organization.

6. The preceding measures of class depend on so-called objective criteria, but individuals' subjective perceptions of their own class position are also important, particularly for understanding their attitudes and behaviors.

7. A number of these features of class come together when sociologists describe the life chances and life-styles of different classes. In general terms, their greater resources, including wealth, income, education, and knowledge, are reflected in the values and behaviors of the upper classes, while the lack of such resources shapes the attitudes and actions of the lower classes.

8. Although designating people as "poor" is somewhat arbitrary, the existence of large numbers of low-income people in an extremely affluent society warrants examination.

9. The poor are defined in absolute terms as anyone falling below a certain income level, and in relative terms as having much less than the average person in a society has. In the United States, poor people are more likely to be under 14 or over 65, inner city or rural, and female. The rates of poverty within groups are highest for native Americans, blacks, and Hispanics.

10. The existence of poverty in the United States is due to the way wealth and income are distributed, since enough goods and services are produced to meet the minimal needs of everyone.

11. Economic and structural explanations for poverty locate its source in the overall shortage of jobs and the existence of many low-paying jobs. Such explanations also emphasize the systematic exclusion of minorities, women, the young, and the old from better-paying and more secure jobs.

12. Political explanations focus on how powerful and privileged groups benefit from the existence of poverty in society. As a result, political pressure to eliminate poverty remains weak.

13. Cultural explanations suggest that the

poor develop a "culture of poverty" that is passed on to future generations and that makes it difficult or impossible for individuals to break out of the cycle of poverty. Critics of that view say that when economic and political conditions change, people change their cultures. Focusing on culture as a cause of poverty, however, diverts attention from its underlying structural roots.

14. The largest program for dealing with poverty is the Aid to Families with Dependent Children (AFDC) or welfare system, although only three-fifths of those below the poverty line receive public assistance. Because of a strong tradition of individualism in American society, such public assistance has been stigmatized and given reluctantly in many states.

15. Other forms of public assistance, including market subsidies, price programs, import quotas, and tax loopholes, are not stigmatized and are not called welfare, even though the amounts of money involved are very great.

16. Given the existence of poverty and of wide class inequalities, one might expect to find intense class consciousness and class conflict in the United States. Instead, class consciousness appears to be relatively low, perhaps because of leisure time diversions, styles of consumption that cross class lines, and a distinctly American ideology of upward mobility.

17. Sociologists have studied social mobility a great deal. Their focus has been on mobility in terms of occupational prestige rather than in terms of income or ownership.

18. Major studies indicate that occupational mobility both within an individual's lifetime and between generations is frequent, but limited in scope. Most people move up only a step or two with respect to occupational prestige, and most moves are within the major sectors of white collar, blue collar, or farm work rather than among those occupational divisions.

19. Most of the individual upward mobility in Western industrial societies has not been due to the replacement of people higher in the social hierarchy with those from lower backgrounds, but rather to the expansion of the professional, management, and clerical sectors. Hence, most existing mobility is due to structural changes.

20. Several industrialized countries have successfully reduced income inequalities and eliminated the extreme poverty that afflicts nearly 25 million Americans. They have done this with extensive taxation and state subsidies. In a rapidly growing economy such as that of Taiwan, the process of income redistribution may be less painful for the upper strata than it would be in a less rapidly growing economy. Stratification by wealth has been reduced mainly by social revolutions such as those in the USSR and Cuba. The result appears to have been to shift the basis for stratification from one based on wealth to one rooted in state political power.

21. Nevertheless, the social policies of the Scandinavian countries and Taiwan suggest that the worst features of social stratification (dismal poverty and greatly diminished life chances) can be reduced even in industrialized capitalist countries.

Key Terms

absolute poverty
class
class consciousness
culture of poverty
horizontal mobility
income
intergenerational mobility
intragenerational mobility
life-style
rank
relative poverty
social class
social mobility
social relations of production
socioeconomic status (SES)
subjective social class
vertical mobility

Chapter 11

Minority Groups and Age Inequality

Human beings display a wide variety of colors, shapes, and cultures. Even without traveling all over the world, we can witness this variety in any major urban center in North America—Boston, Chicago, Los Angeles, Milwaukee, New Orleans, Phoenix, New York, Mexico City, Montreal, or Toronto. Some of the observable differences between peoples are genetically linked, others are purely cultural. Even where racial differences are genetic, however, the importance attached to such differences is social rather than biological.

This chapter begins by distinguishing race and ethnicity and briefly considers the range of racial variety that exists in the world. We then turn to a descriptive account of the major racial and ethnic groups in the United States today. With this background, we examine a current major controversy—namely, whether race is declining in significance in American life. Keeping the situation of specific groups in mind, we consider the types of social relations that exist among various racial and ethnic groups. Since the United States, like many societies, has a history of racial and ethnic antagonism and conflict, it is important to consider the conditions under which racism versus peaceful, pluralistic coexistence are likely to occur.

RACE AND ETHNICITY DISTINGUISHED

RACE

The concept of *race* is used to classify *Homo sapiens* into several subdivisions based on distinguishable physical characteristics. Traditionally, physical features such as hair type (straight, curly, or woolly), skin color and the shape of the nose, lips, eyelids, or body were widely used to classify humans. Three major racial groupings were noted: Caucasian (white), Mongoloid (yellow), and Negroid (black). It has become increasingly apparent, however, that the physical traits of these groups overlap to a considerable degree. More recently, blood type has been used as a more exact measure of the genetic similarity of a particular group of people. The frequency of A, B, and O blood types, for example, as well as other blood factors, can identify genetic links between populations.[1]

The term *geographic race* refers to the large human groupings that correspond to major geographic regions such as continents. Geographic divisions such as oceans separated groupings to such an extent that they were not likely to mix. As a result, groups tended to develop genetic differences. They may also have developed genetic mutations, such as darker skin color or the capacity to store fat effectively, which were useful adaptive traits and thus tended to be preserved. Since the sixteenth century, however, there has been increasing migration and intermixing of these geographic races. As a result, there are no biologically "pure" racial forms. Moreover, within each geographic race, there

[1]Blood type A occurs most often in Western Europe, Western Asia, and among the Australian aborigines. Blood type O is more frequent in Northern and Western Europe and Southwest Africa. Isolated populations, such as the Indians of South and Central America, may be entirely of group O. The B blood type occurs with maximum frequency in Central Asia and Northern India.

are wide differences. Different cultural and physical environments have led to variations in the physical characteristics of human populations.

Because there is such variation within racial groups and because there is considerable overlap among such groups, the major significance of race is *social* rather than *biological*. Sometimes racial differences become very important in social situations; sometimes they are not relevant at all. Sometimes racial (physical) differences are also associated with cultural (ethnic) differences. When they are, that association tends to reinforce a group's identity.

ETHNICITY

An *ethnic group* is one that shares a common cultural tradition and sense of identity. It usually has its own language and religion, along with distinctive customs. These cultural differences distinguish one ethnic group from another. Often the term "ethnic group" refers only to minorities, but in societies with many culturally diverse groups, even the dominant group may be referred to as an ethnic group. Racial and ethnic identity may overlap, but frequently it does not. This is particularly true for the so-called white ethnics of the United States and Canada—for example, those with Irish or Italian backgrounds—who share a common racial background but belong to quite different ethnic groups.

WHEN DOES AN ETHNIC OR RACIAL GROUP BECOME A MINORITY GROUP?

A *minority group* is any recognizable racial, religious, ethnic, or social group in a community that suffers from some disadvantage resulting from the action of a dominant group with higher social status and greater privileges. Minority group members are excluded from full participation in the life of a society. Sometimes a minority group may even constitute a numerical majority, as is the case of blacks in South Africa or French-speaking Canadians in the province of Quebec. The critical point is not numbers, but how the group members are treated by the more powerful and dominant group or groups in society.

Not all racial and ethnic groups are treated as minority groups in society, even when they are outnumbered. Switzerland, for example, consists of a political confederation of German-speaking, French-speaking, Italian-speaking, and Romansch-speaking ethnic groups. Each has constitutionally and legally protected rights that are codified in institutional policies. No group receives unequal treatment or discrimination at the hands of any other group. Virtually everyone in the society is multilingual, so people are able to communicate with one another. It is possible to observe two Swiss people speaking, one in German, the other in French or Italian, understanding each other perfectly. The Swiss case stands in stark contrast to the situation of racial and ethnic groups in the United States.

RACIAL AND ETHNIC GROUPS IN THE UNITED STATES

WHITE ETHNICS AND WASPs

More so than a great many societies, the United States is composed of diverse ethnic and racial groups, as shown in Figure 11.1. Until about 1860, however, the United States population was relatively homogeneous, composed mainly of whites from the British Isles and the Netherlands. Even among the Irish immigrants in the United States, most were Protestants. The first large wave of immigration into the United States occurred between 1820 and 1860, when more than 5 million Europeans arrived. Nine out of ten of them were from England, Ireland, or Germany. Except for the Catholic Irish, the early immigrants were readily absorbed into the English Protestant United States. For a long time, the descendants of English Protestants

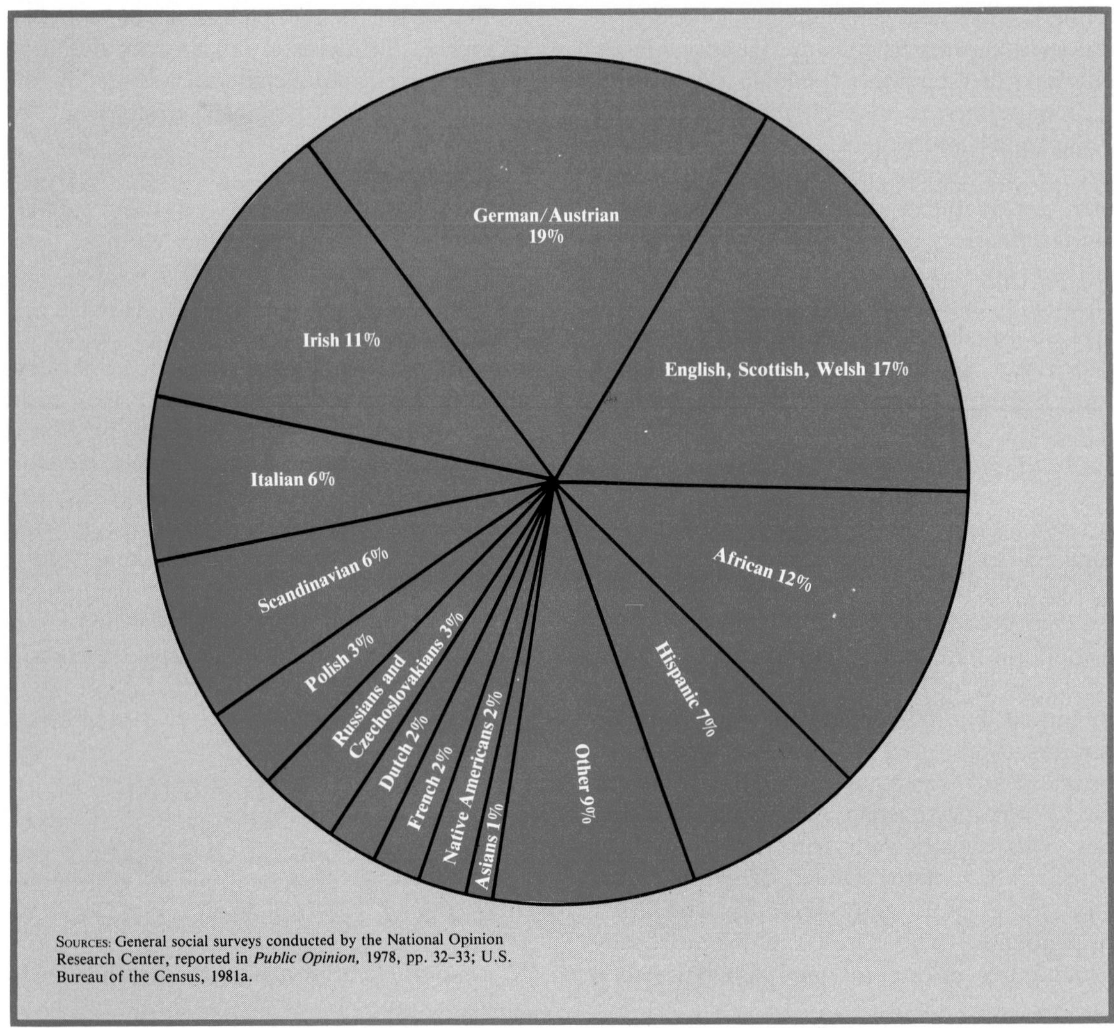

SOURCES: General social surveys conducted by the National Opinion Research Center, reported in *Public Opinion*, 1978, pp. 32–33; U.S. Bureau of the Census, 1981a.

Figure 11.1 Racial and Ethnic Composition of the United States *"Other" includes persons from Greece, Hungary, the Philippines, Switzerland, India, Portugal, Lithuania, Yugoslavia, Romania, Belgium, and Arab nations, among others. The Scandinavian category includes Danish, Finnish, Norwegian, and Swedish.*

were the dominant cultural group. The so-called WASPs (for White Anglo-Saxon Protestants) still own a great deal of property and wealth in the United States, and they tend to dominate corporate boardrooms, banks, insurance companies, law firms, and educational, cultural, and philanthropic institutions.

From 1860 to 1920, the United States received some 30 million more immigrants, mostly from central and southeastern Europe, including Italy, Poland, Russia, Greece, and the Balkans. These predominantly Catholic or Greek Orthodox immigrants settled in northern and middle-western cities. Today about 70 percent of their descendants are blue collar workers, and the rest are mainly in the lower-level white collar work force. They earn somewhat above the national average.

The term *white ethnics* was coined in the 1970s to describe people who value both their United States citizenship and their ethnic origins. Many white ethnics still live in "little Italys" or other cultural enclaves, although moves to outlying suburbs have tended to disperse some of these ethnic concentrations. Their cultural background may be shared with neighbors, friends, family members, other church members, and even co-workers. The group identity of white ethnics is based not only on a shared cultural heritage, but also on their common interests and needs in modern urban America. To the degree that they live in major cities, they are affected by high crime rates and declining municipal services. Like most Americans, they see rising prices and taxes and growing demands for employment from other minorities and women as threats to their livelihoods. At the same time, they view individual effort as the key to success and see poverty as due to the absence of individual effort. Hence they tend to be impatient with programs and groups that demand changes in the social structure.

BLACKS IN THE UNITED STATES

The first boatload of slaves was brought to the North American colonies in 1619. The shortage of labor and the economic advantages of slavery and the slave trade fueled the expansion of a practice that ultimately uprooted and enslaved millions of black Africans. Chained below deck in filthy and overcrowded ships, slaves were auctioned off like livestock at various southern port cities when they arrived. Both on the ships and at the sales, slaves from different tribes, regions, and languages were mixed together to minimize the possibility of organized revolts.

During the 250 years that slavery persisted in the United States, there were numerous slave uprisings, contradicting the myth that slaves were perfectly contented with their lot. They were brutally beaten by their masters or overseers for not working hard enough, for disobedience, or for insubordination. They were, however, almost never imprisoned for any length of time or hanged (the lynchings came later), because their labor was too valuable. Although many slaves tried to run away, the distance from their tribes and homelands made it impossible for them to return to Africa. The physical and social separation from the slaves' home societies contrasted sharply with the situation of the American Indian. Efforts to enslave individual Indians in the United States virtually always failed. Either their tribesmen came after them and rescued them, or they ran away and rejoined their people; they were much closer physically and socially to freedom. Few such options were available to Africans, although the "underground railroad" did help some escape to the North or to Canada.

Until after the Civil War, blacks had no constitutional protection for their civil rights. The Thirteenth to Fifteenth Amendments to the Constitution, passed between 1865 and 1870, provided the first promise of citizenship. The Civil Rights Act of 1875 called for equal accommodations in public facilities (except schools), but by 1883 it was voided. From 1877 on, when the last of the federal troops withdrew from the South, southern conservatives used fraud, violence, and terror to remove the voting rights of blacks and to regain control of their state governments. Secret terrorist organizations like the Ku Klux Klan and the Knights of the White Camellia flourished during this period. Shaking loose of the northern carpetbaggers and freedmen (freed slaves), southern legislatures passed a wave of Jim Crow laws segregating blacks and whites in public transportation facilities, schools, parks, cemeteries, theaters, and restaurants, and preventing blacks from voting.[2] These

[2]Jim Crow laws were laws that enforced racial segregation in the American South between the end of the formal Reconstruction period (1877) and the beginning of a strong civil rights movement in the 1960s. Jim Crow was the name of a minstrel routine performed beginning in 1828. The term came to be used as a derogatory word for blacks and as a proper noun referring to their segregated life.

In 1963 the Rev. Martin Luther King, Jr., and other black leaders led the "March on Washington" in support of civil rights for black Americans.

"separate but equal" public facilities were upheld by the United States Supreme Court in the 1896 *Plessy* v. *Ferguson* decision.

It was not until World War II that a number of economic and social changes began to affect the situation of black Americans. During the war, discrimination in defense industries was forbidden, and the armed forces were desegregated in 1945. Both the promise of employment in defense industries and the growing mechanization of southern farms spurred the migration of millions of blacks from the rural south to northern cities. Even in the North, however, segregation characterized most social relations between blacks and whites. In the epoch-making *Brown* v. *Board of Education* decision in 1954, the Supreme Court ruled that separate educational facilities were inherently unequal and therefore unconstitutional. Beginning in 1955, when Mrs. Rosa Parks refused to move to the Negro section of a bus in Montgomery, Alabama, a series of nonviolent civil rights demonstrations and protests galvanized public opinion, the mass media, and the world community. Diplomatic representatives from independent African nations had already encountered segregated facilities in the United States, creating considerable international embarrassment.

During this time, the underlying economic, legal, and political contexts of race relations were changing, resulting in a different moral and ideological climate. The tension between equal rights and segregation grew intolerable. Student sit-ins at lunch counters, "freedom riders" trying to desegregate public facilities and transportation, and voter registration drives during the early 1960s involved more than 100,000 blacks and whites. In 1963, Martin Luther King, Jr., led the March on Washington, where he proclaimed to more than 200,000 blacks and whites assembled at the Lincoln Memorial, "I have a dream . . . of an America where blacks and whites can walk together as equals." President Lyndon B. Johnson was able in 1964 to prod Congress to pass the most far-reaching civil rights bill in our nation's history. It forbade discrimination in public accommodations and threatened to withhold funds from communities that continued to operate segregated schools.

Nevertheless, years of economic frustration and police brutality led to violent reactions. An important reason was that poor black Americans no longer accepted their subordinate status as inevitable or just. Riots erupted in the black ghettoes of major United States cities, beginning in the Watts section of Los Angeles in 1965 and causing extensive property damage. The assassination of Martin Luther King, Jr., in 1967 was followed by further riots. A presidential commission investigating the events of 1967 placed most of the blame on "white racism" and declared that "our nation is moving toward two societies, one black, one white—separate and unequal." The commission urged government action at all levels to provide employment, better housing, improved education, and more adequate police protection for black ghetto residents.

Since that time, the equal rights movement has aimed for economic and social gains, and for increased political officeholding. The number of blacks in elected political offices has increased. In 1982, there were 17 blacks in the U.S. Congress and 343 in state legislatures, compared to a total of 182 in 1970, and 2863 blacks in city and county offices such as mayor, city council, and commissioner in 1981, compared to 715 in 1970. Despite these gains, however, the 5014 black elected officials still account for less than 1 percent of all U.S. public officials. Part of the reason for this is the low rate of voting among blacks. Moreover, although the election of black officials is important for symbolic reasons, they tend to lack real power. Black legislators are usually elected in decaying urban districts such as the Bedford-Stuyvesant section of Brooklyn, long-time district of former U.S. Representative Shirley Chisholm. She describes it as typical of the "shells white leaders leave behind when they abandon an area politically to blacks" (Blum, 1980 p., 1). Black mayors tend to govern cities such as Detroit, Atlanta, Washington, Newark, N.J., Oakland, Dayton, Ohio, and Gary, Indiana, which face shrinking tax bases, greater dependency on higher levels of government for aid, and large, needy populations of young and old people.

Blacks have long comprised the largest and most visible racial minority group, numbering 26.5 million (or 11.7 percent of the U.S. population) in 1980. Some population counters, however, estimate that the number of Hispanic (Spanish-speaking) Americans is rapidly approaching the number of blacks.

HISPANICS

Some Spanish settlements north of Santa Fe, New Mexico, were founded in 1598, before English settlements along the North American east coast. Only native Americans and Eskimos lived in what is now the United States before the Spanish arrived. The umbrella term "Hispanic" refers to Mexican-Americans, Puerto Ricans, and all other Spanish-speaking Americans. It is not really a single ethnic group, but a collection of many distinct ethnic groups who may share a language but differ sharply in culture and behavior. At last count (1980), the Bureau of the Census reported 14.6 million Hispanic-Americans. But if undocumented Hispanic aliens (conservatively estimated by the federal government at 7.4 million) are counted, that number raises the Hispanic population to 22 million, or 9.7 percent, of the population. Because the Hispanic population is growing faster than the black or white populations in the United States, both from higher birth rates and from higher rates of immigration, Hispanics may outnumber American blacks within the next decade.

About half of the Hispanics in the United States today are of Mexican origin, living mostly in California, Texas, Illinois, Arizona, New Mexico, and Colorado. Mexican-Americans are the largest minority group in most states in the American Southwest. More than 80 percent of the Mexican-American population lives in urban areas. It is disproportionately overrepresented in blue collar occupations and underrepresented in professional and technical fields. In 1978, the median family income for Mexican American families was $12,835, compared to $17,912 for non-Mexican-American families. The median number of years of school completed by Mexican-Americans is 9.8, lower than any other ethnic group except native Americans (Pachon and Moore, 1981, p. 117).

Several million more Hispanics are from Puerto Rico, a self-governing associated commonwealth of the United States. They live mainly in the Northeast, particularly in and around New York. In recent years, Hispanic immigration has shifted from Puerto Rico to South and Central America as the point of origin. Additionally, there are more than 700,000 Cubans who left their country because of differences with Fidel Castro and setted mainly in Florida. Besides these groups, Hispanics include Dominicans, Ecuadorians, Colombians, and natives of other Latin American countries. Although widely different in their cultural backgrounds, these groups generally share a common language and Roman Catholicism. The 1980 U.S. Census was the first to ask specifically about being of Spanish origin, so we know less historically about Hispanics than about blacks.

Hispanic-Americans include Mexican-Americans, Puerto Ricans, and all other Spanish-speaking people in the United States. Some have been in the United States for centuries and are well established, while others are more recent arrivals who face language and economic obstacles.

In some ways, Hispanics appear to face less discrimination than blacks. Their median family income was $16,401 in 1981, compared with $23,517 for whites and $13,266 for blacks. Hispanics thus earned 70 percent of what whites earned, whereas blacks earned only 56 percent of what whites earned. For any given level of education or occupation, Hispanics tend to earn less than whites but more than blacks. The span of occupations among persons of Spanish origin is enormous, ranging from migrant farm worker and unskilled laborer to bank president and business entrepreneur. There are real pockets of poverty—for example, among migrant farm workers in the Southwest or new arrivals from Puerto Rico. Hispanic households in the Northeast have a lower average income than anywhere else in the United States. Politically, Hispanics are still underrepresented at all levels of government.

ASIAN-AMERICANS

The Chinese

In the 1840s the first Chinese were brought to California to work on the railroads and in the gold mines. Between 1850 and 1882, more than 322,000 Chinese entered the United States. They worked in mines and then on the Central Pacific section of the transcontinental railroad, completed in 1869. These migrants were mostly single men who had no plans to stay forever. Their temporary status meant that they kept their Chinese language and customs. When the gold rush ended and jobs grew scarce, they were threatened, beaten, and sometimes even lynched. To protect themselves, the Chinese moved together into "Chinatown" areas where they ran restaurants, laundries, and vegetable stands. About the time of the business crash of 1876 in the United States, newspapers fanned fears of the "yellow peril." "Anti-coolie societies" were formed in a number of cities, and by 1882 the U.S. Congress had passed the Chinese Exclusion Act, which prohibited Chinese immigration for 10 years. In 1902 the act was made permanent until its repeal in 1943.

Chinese-Americans faced intense discrimination on the West Coast. Housing, schools, theaters, barbershops, hotels, and restaurants were segregated. Interracial marriage was illegal. Toward the end of the nineteenth century, the Chinese began migrating to eastern and midwestern cities to find better economic opportunities. Excluded from many occupations, they entered domestic service, and ran laundries and restaurants. Those desiring to open a business started a kind of rotating credit association. Each person paid a specific sum into a common pool. Then participants competed by bid, election, or lot to gain the right to use the entire sum. The next month members would meet again, raise another sum, and those who had not yet won would compete again. They continued until all members of the group had won a chance to use the pool. In this way, many small businesses were financed from within the community.

During World War II new job opportunities opened up, and the Chinese began to share in the postwar prosperity as well. By 1970 about 20 percent of employed Chinese men earned more than $10,000 per year, less than the 25 percent nationally who were earning that much, but more than Chinese had earned in the past. Their average income is depressed by their concentration in food and laundry service jobs (in 1970, 24 percent were in service work, more than triple the national average). Few Chinese work in the better-paying blue collar jobs, but the proportion of Chinese in professional and technical occupations increased from 3 percent in 1940 to 29 percent in 1970. This gain is more than double that made by the general population. Many Chinese have chosen careers in science, technology, engineering, education, and health.

The Chinese continue to own and operate thousands of small businesses, including laundries, restaurants, and grocery stores. In addition, the educational level of Chinese-Americans is rising. Nearly two-thirds complete high school, and more than half of those go on to college. Chinese-Americans have the highest proportion of any group with a college degree—25 percent, compared to the national average of 13 percent. One-quarter, however, have not gone beyond elementary school (Kitano, 1981, p. 130). The 1974 Supreme Court decision in the case of *Lau* v. *Nichols* stated that the failure of the San Francisco School District to provide special help to non-English-speaking Chinese students violated the Civil Rights Act of 1964. That ruling had important national implications, since it established the principle of bilingual education not only for Chinese students, but for the estimated 3.5 million other non-English-speaking minority students as well. In 1981 the U.S. Department of Education ruled that bilingual education could be handled by local districts in any way they chose.

The Immigration Act of 1965 ended the national quota system restricting the number of migrants who could come from different countries, and allowed many Chinese newcomers to enter the United States. Most of them were from Hong Kong or Taiwan. Existing Chinatowns in San Francisco, Los Angeles, and New York lacked adequate facilities for the large numbers of new arrivals, resulting in some problems of overcrowding, substandard housing, and unemployment.

Culturally, many Chinese still observe traditional practices, including the Chinese New Year, Dragon Boat, and Mid-Autumn holidays. Intermarriage with non-Chinese has increased, especially among younger people. In 1970, 30 percent of the men and 22 percent of the women in the 16- to 24-year-old age group in California had non-Chinese spouses.

The Chinese population in the United States is the largest in any nation outside Asia. Most Chinese-Americans live in urban areas. San Francisco and New York have the largest concentrations, with about 100,000 each, and Los Angeles is close behind. Despite their small numbers relative to the total population (about 0.4 percent or 806,000 in 1980), the Chinese are an identifiable group with a distinct although not completely homogeneous subculture. Their history in the United States parallels in some respects the experience of the Japanese in this country.

The Japanese

The Japanese came to the United States somewhat later than the Chinese, beginning in the 1880s and early 1900s. They found few jobs in the California cities where they landed, so many became farmers. By 1920 they owned about one-eighth of California's irrigated farmland (Lyman, 1977). Throughout the early decades that they were here, Japanese-Americans faced discrimination. To meet their financial needs, they developed mutual-aid financial systems in which individuals pooled their money into a common fund like a credit union. Individuals could earn interest on their savings and borrow money when needed. Such economic cooperation strengthened community cohesion and helped many businesses when regular banks refused to lend them money.

After Japan bombed Pearl Harbor in 1941, a wave of anti-Japanese fear swept the United States, and 120,000 Japanese-Americans on the West Coast were herded into internment camps in Arizona, Arkansas, California, Colorado, Idaho, Utah, and Wyoming. The purpose of this roundup was to avoid sabotage, spying, or collaboration with the enemy. Ethnicity was equated with nationality, an unjustified blurring of reality. Many of these Japanese were second- or third-generation Americans, and not one of them was ever brought to trial. Critics of the U.S. government's action suggest that the Japanese owned much valuable agricultural land that was then seized by white Americans and only in rare cases returned or repaid. Each Japanese family lost an average of $10,000 from this seizure of property, besides several years of their lives in prison camps (Simpson and Yinger, 1972, p. 121). The Federal Reserve Board estimated in 1942 that a total of about $400 million was lost by all Japanese residents (Masaoka, 1972).

The likelihood that this action against the Japanese was racially and economically based is suggested by the fact that similar actions were not taken against Italian-Americans or German-Americans, even though their ancestral countries were also at war with the United States. German-Americans were, however, required to register and report to government authorities periodically during the war. Along with slavery and the treatment of native Americans by the U.S. government, this internment of an ethnic group in a concentration camp represents one of the worst breaches of civil rights in American history.[3]

When finally allowed to enlist in 1943, more than 33,000 of the nisei, the second-generation Japanese-Americans, joined the armed forces and served honorably, especially in the most highly decorated all-Japanese-American 442d Regimental Combat Team. After the war, those who could returned to their lands, and many others started contract gardening businesses that flourished along with the suburban boom in California. Veterans were able to use the G.I. Bill to attend college. Today Japanese-Americans have the highest high school completion rates of any group, and their college completion rates and occupational achievement are also high. In 1940, 4 percent of Japanese males were professionals, by 1970, 31 percent were professionals.

Japanese are likely to pursue careers in the

[3]In 1980, the United States Congress established a commission to consider compensating the Japanese-Americans who spent World War II behind barbed wire. The Japanese-American community has heatedly debated this issue. Some are pressing for $25,000 for each person who was interned. Others take a "forgive and forget" stance (Kitano, 1981, p. 132; *New York Times,* 1981, p. A14).

In 1942 these and many other U.S. citizens of Japanese origin were herded into internment camps such as this one in Manzanar, California, because their ethnic origins were confused with national loyalty, an unjustified blurring of reality.

fields of medicine, pharmacy, optometry, dentistry, and engineering. Their mean family income in 1975 was $12,615, among the highest for all ethnic groups, and only 7.5 percent have incomes below the poverty level. These gains have not been offset by recent immigration, since the numbers of Japanese migrants have been small and spread out in time and space. The Japanese-American population increased only 19 percent between 1970 and 1980. As a result, community resources have not been unduly strained. Today, the 701,000 (or 0.3 percent of the population in 1980) Japanese-Americans live mostly in California and Hawaii. In Hawaii they have been a powerful political force since the 1940s, when they comprised over a third of the population.

Several explanations have been offered for the success of Japanese-Americans. These include their strong emphasis on the work ethic and their firm sense of family unity and group orientation, reflected in the polite, consensual behavior expected in social relations. Japanese moral training contains coping strategies drawn from Buddhist teachings and evident in the phrases *gaman* (meaning "don't let it bother you") and *gambatte* (meaning "don't give up"). These precepts reveal the stress placed on continuing to try even in the face of frustration and disappointment, conditions the Japanese have faced repeatedly in their time in the United States.

The Vietnamese

The most recent group of Asians to enter the United States are the Vietnamese, following the war in their country. By 1980, there were 261,714 Vietnamese in the United States. About one-third of them settled in California. Many of these families were relocated by private rather than public agencies, although the federal immigration service did modify existing quotas so that more could come into the United States. A recent survey by the U.S. Department of Health, Education, and Welfare found that 95 percent of the heads of Vietnamese refugee households are employed (McCarthy, 1980, p. 596), but other than this study we know rather little about their situation here.

Asian-Americans, especially those of Japanese ancestry, have made tremendous educational and occupational gains in recent years.

NATIVE AMERICANS

At the time of Columbus's arrival in the New World, between 1 and 2 million native Americans (whom he called "Indians," because he thought he had discovered India) lived on this continent. Their numbers steadily declined as a result of European invasion. Large numbers were destroyed by disease, warfare, massacre, and forced migrations after European settlers arrived. In 1830, for example, 70,000 Indians from five major tribes in the southeastern United States were forced to move westward. On the way, more than 20,000 died. By 1890, when the U.S. Army massacred the Sioux at Wounded Knee, South Dakota, the number of Indians had been reduced to about 300,000.

After 1890, the Bureau of Indian Affairs made native Americans wards of the federal government. It required most of them to live on reservations, which were invariably parcels of land white settlers found undesirable. An ideology of European superiority and Indian barbarism and inferiority accompanied this process of extermination and relocation. Much of this ideology persists today. In 1980 there were 1.4 million native Americans concentrated in California, Oklahoma, Arizona, New Mexico, North Carolina, Washington, South Dakota, Michigan, Texas, New York, Montana, and Minnesota, although some also live in Illinois, Wisconsin, Oregon, Alaska, and Utah. Although treated as a single ethnic group here, there are actually more than 170 Indian peoples who have different histories, cultures, and identities.

As a group, native Americans have an average annual family income of $1500, and a 45 percent unemployment rate (American Indian Fund, 1981). More than 40 percent of all native Americans still live on reservations, where most of the stores are owned by outsiders. The population suffers from high rates of disease, alcohol-

Militant native Americans seized the hamlet of Wounded Knee, South Dakota, on February 27, 1973, in an effort to have their concerns addressed. These men are patrolling the hamlet that the Sioux controlled.

ism, and suicide, and life expectancy is only 46 years (nearly 30 years less than the rest of the U.S. population). Four out of ten native Americans do not finish high school, and their median education level is 8 years (compared to a national average of 12.1 years). In 1970, about 14,000 young Indians were attending institutions of higher learning, a figure that is three times as large as the number in 1960. So although their overall educational level is relatively low, it is rising (Thernstrom, 1980, p. 65).

By 1970 the red power movement began calling for a reservation-based "tribal nationalism" (Day, 1972, p. 507). They fished in waters that were closed to them, shut down beaches, rivers, highways, and bridges on reservations; and initiated legal actions. In 1973 an angry group of 200 members of the American Indian Movement (AIM) took over the reservation town of Wounded Knee. They held the hamlet under seige for 69 days while surrounded by federal marshals. They demanded new tribal leaders, a review of Indian treaties, and a Senate inquiry into the treatment of native Americans. The occupation of Wounded Knee sparked a national movement to teach languages, crafts, tribal histories, and religious ceremonies to the new generation (Deloria, 1981, p. 148). Elsewhere a number of tribes have initiated lawsuits to reclaim illegally seized land (in Maine, for example), or to restore their fishing rights (in Alaska). A few tribes have been lucky enough to discover valuable minerals under the arid deserts where they were confined, but rich deposits of uranium, coal, or oil have helped only a relatively few tribes. Most native Americans live in abject poverty.

IS RACE DECLINING IN SIGNIFICANCE?

WILSON'S ARGUMENT

In 1978, William J. Wilson, a black sociologist, wrote a book called *The Declining Significance of Race*. In it he declared that although blacks still

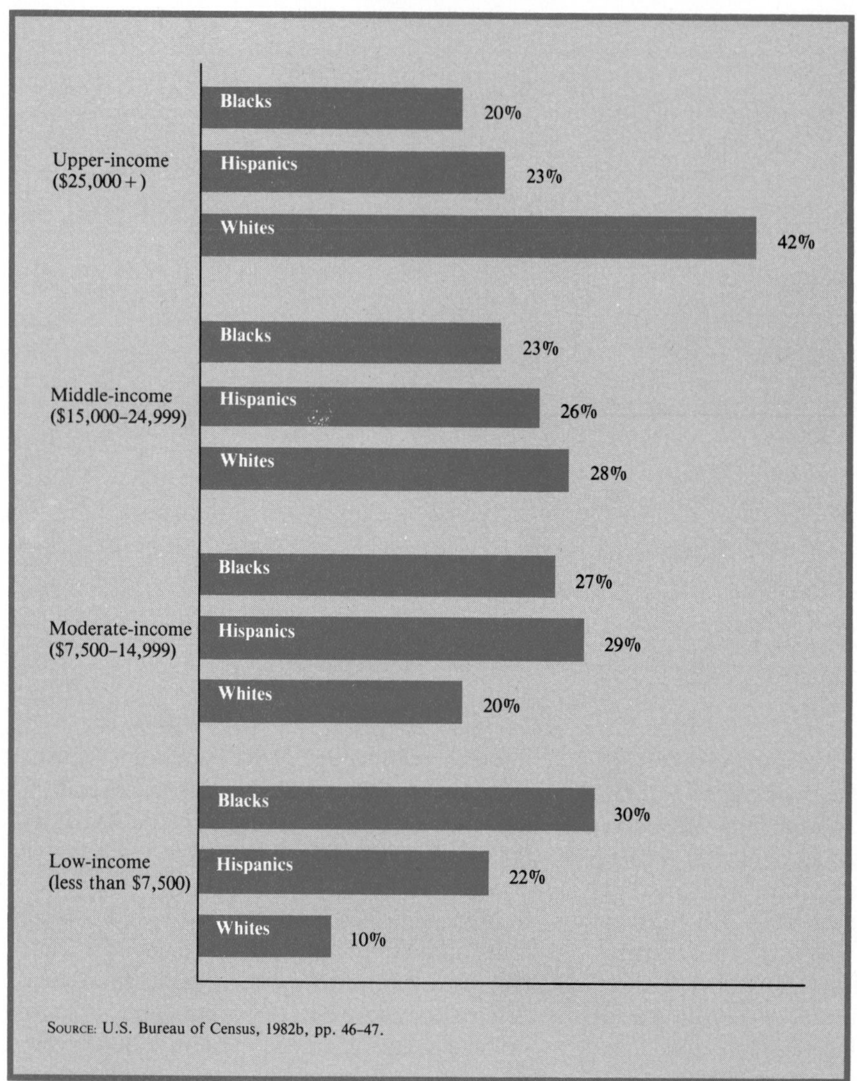

Figure 11.2 Percentage of Families at Different Income Levels, by Race, 1980

face barriers in social and institutional arrangements like housing and clubs, "in the economic sphere, class has become more important than race in determining black access to privilege and power." He continued, "it is clearly evident . . . that many talented and educated blacks are now entering positions of prestige and influence at a rate comparable to or, in some situations, exceeding that of whites with equivalent qualifications. It is equally clear that the black underclass is in a hopeless state of economic stagnation, falling further and further behind the rest of society" (1978, p. 2). Is Wilson right? Is race losing its significance? We can begin to assess his argument by considering the current situations of black, white, and Hispanic[4] families in the United States. In 1981, white households were about twice as likely as black and Hispanic ones

[4]Hispanics will be considered separately wherever existing data permit.

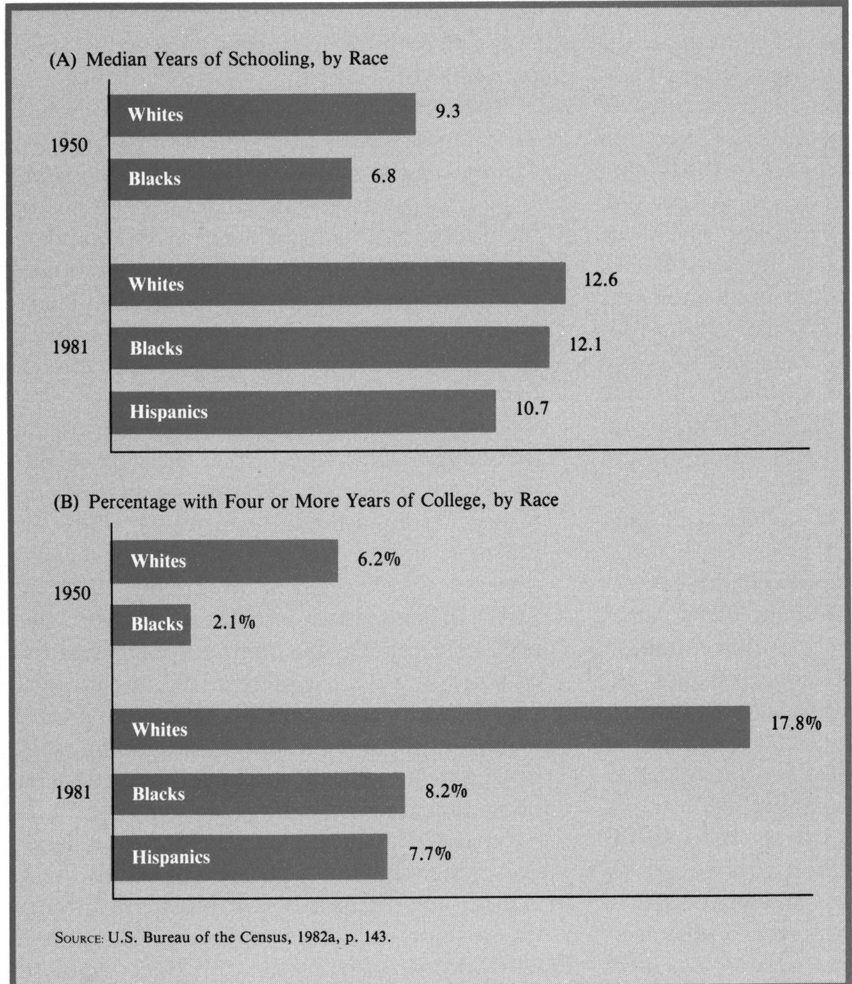

Figure 11.3 Black and White Educational Attainments, 1950 and 1981

to have incomes exceeding $25,000; black households were more than twice as likely than white ones to have low incomes (see Figure 11.2). Hispanics were more likely than blacks or whites to have moderate incomes; white households were the most likely to be in the upper income brackets.

How much of these income differences are due to what Wilson calls class (as measured by education and occupation), and how much to race? To answer this question, we can consider several types of evidence.

First, we can ask: Do blacks and whites have similar educations? In 1950, median years of schooling for blacks aged 25 and older was 6.8 years, compared to 9.3 years for all Americans in that age bracket [Figure 11.3(A)]. Thus, blacks had only 73 percent of the number of years of schooling of whites. But by 1981, blacks had 96 percent of the schooling whites had (a median of 12.1 years as compared to 12.6 years for whites), and blacks aged 25 to 29 had 98 percent of the schooling whites had (12.6 years compared to 12.9 years). In terms of median years of schooling, blacks are very close to whites. But they still lag behind in terms of the percentage who have four or more years of college [Figure 11.3(B)]. Nationally, among all U.S. residents aged 25 or older, 17.1 percent had four or more years of college in 1981, a big increase from 1950, when only 6 percent did. Only 8.2 percent of blacks had this much college in 1981, however. Although blacks still trail whites with respect to college graduation, the percentage of black college graduates among 25- to 29-year-olds increased four-fold between 1950 and 1981, while the percentage of white college graduates has tripled in that time [Figure 11.3(B)]. Thus, although blacks still lag behind whites in educational attainment, they are increasing the percentage of college graduates more rapidly than whites are.

Second, we can ask: Do blacks and Hispanics with the same amount of education earn comparable incomes? Blacks at every level of education earn less than either whites or Hispanics. Indeed, blacks with some college earn about what whites earn with some high school (Bureau of the Census, *Current Population Reports,* 1980, No. 121). So although number of years of school is related to higher average incomes for all races, it does not have as high a payoff for blacks as it does for Hispanics and whites. Blacks with higher education are younger on the average than whites with higher education. Therefore age needs to be held constant. When that is done, much of the gap between black and white earnings disappears (Freeman, 1976).

Perhaps education does not have as great a payoff for blacks because, historically, they have been denied entry to higher-paying occupations. Therefore we need to ask whether the percentages of blacks and whites in different occupations have changed over time. Between 1960 and 1981, the number of blacks doing white collar work increased dramatically, from 16 percent to 41 percent, while the percentage of white workers in such jobs increased only slightly, from 47 percent to 54 percent. Moreover, the gap between the percentage of whites and blacks in white collar jobs has declined from a 31 percent difference in 1960 to a 13 percent difference in 1981.

These are dramatic changes indeed, although their impact is reduced slightly by the realization that the biggest gains of all have occurred in clerical jobs, a category which is at the lower end of the income and prestige hierarchy. When white collar jobs are subdivided into professional/technical, managers/administrators, salesworkers, and clerical workers, the percentage of black and white clerical workers is equal. The gap between white and black professional/technical workers has shrunk to a mere 3 percent, and the percentages of black and white salesworkers differ by only 4 percent. The gap is largest among managers/administrators (6 percent), which are the most highly paid and prestigious occupations (U.S. Department of Labor, 1982, p. 164). In sum, black occupational gains have been considerable, but they do not match the educational gains. At present, the occupational gaps between blacks and whites are still greater than the gaps in educational background, suggesting that race may still have some effect on occupational placement.

Since black educational gains are not fully reflected in occupational progress, it becomes particularly important to ask if blacks performing the same occupation as whites are earning the same incomes. The closest that blacks come to whites is in blue collar jobs, where blacks earn 83 percent of what whites in blue collar jobs earn. Otherwise, blacks earn between 52 percent (among farm workers) and 81 percent (among managers/administrators) of what whites earn in the same occupational category. Furthermore, blacks earn consistently less than Hispanics in every job category except managers/administrators and blue collar workers. In the Carnegie Commission report *All Our Children* (Kenniston, 1977), Rhona Pavis presents data showing that "90 percent of the income gap between blacks and whites is the result . . . of lower pay for blacks with comparable levels of education and experience" (Willie, 1979, p. 59).

In brief, blacks are still less likely than whites to graduate from college; they are somewhat lower on the occupational scale than whites even when they have comparable educations; and they earn considerably less than whites even when they hold similar occupations. Three out of 10 black households fall below the official poverty line, whereas only 1 out of 10 white households does. Blacks also have a much higher rate of unemployment than whites. In 1981, 14 percent of blacks were unemployed, compared to 7 percent of whites. Among black teenagers aged 16 to 19 in 1983, the rate of unemployment was 45 percent, compared to 23 percent for all 16- to 19-year-olds (*New York Times,* 1983, p. A14). Finally, with respect to life itself, major differences remain in the life expectancies of blacks and whites. A black male born in 1979 had an average life expectancy of 66 years, compared to 71 years for a white male; a black female's life expectancy was 75 years, compared to 78 years for a white female.

Despite the inequalities that remain, there has been a major increase in the size of the black middle class in recent decades. If middle-class status is defined in terms of employment, education, and real income, about 2 out of 5 black Americans are now middle class, compared to 1 in 20 in 1940. While the black middle class has increased dramatically, it still lags compared to whites, since 3 out of every 5 white Americans are now middle class (Pettigrew, 1981). Race seems to be less important for determining the disadvantages of black Americans than it was in the past. Wilson does not claim that race has no importance, but he suggests that race is declining in importance. The existence of a growing black middle class and an increasing gulf between that group and a permanent underclass of poor blacks is consistent with Wilson's claim.

THE INTERACTION OF RACE AND CLASS

The increasing importance of social class does not necessarily need to imply that racial influences are therefore decreasing in importance, as Pettigrew (1981) notes. Pettigrew suggests that race and class increasingly *interact* in crucial ways in the United States. That is, being black may have different effects, depending on one's social class. For example, a 1980 study in Atlanta, Georgia, found that the political trust of white adults increased, the higher their socioeconomic level (see Figure 11.4). For black adults, however, the opposite occurred. The higher their socioeconomic level, the lower their political trust. In these and many other ways, Pettigrew says, race and class interact to produce critical effects that cannot be explained by simply adding together the separate effects of race and class.

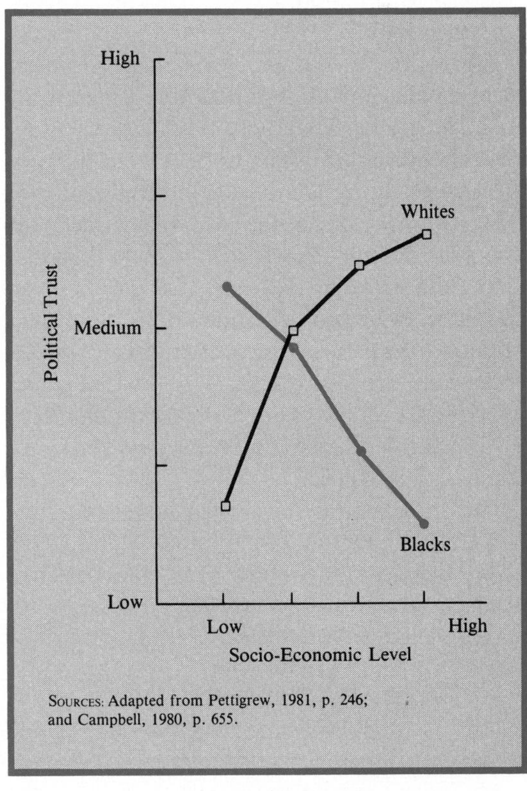

SOURCES: Adapted from Pettigrew, 1981, p. 246; and Campbell, 1980, p. 655.

Figure 11.4 Patterns of Political Trust, by Race and Class *This figure shows the interaction between adult socioeconomic level and race with respect to political trust.*

Being poor and black, for instance, is a more serious condition than the sum of its parts. Further, a black middle-class family is not in the same situation as a white middle-class family, for a number of reasons. There is the possibility of discrimination in promotion opportunities or job security (Alsop, 1980). Black middle-class families are more likely to depend on two earners; they are more likely to be first-generation middle class; and they are less likely to have any family wealth or property behind them compared to white middle-class families. For these reasons, their middle-class status may be more vulnerable than that of whites, thus revealing another way in which class and race interact.

Race and class also interact in the new forms of institutional discrimination that shape race relations. Segregation and other forms of legal discrimination have been successfully challenged in the courts. In recent years, such primary forms of discrimination have been replaced by secondary forms, which are more subtle, indirect, procedural, and claim to be nonracial. Such forms center on residential and educational patterns. Segregated schools are maintained by school district lines that follow housing segregation. Admission to colleges and professional schools relies heavily on standardized tests that produce systematic differences in the scores of blacks and whites. Professional and white collar occupations rely increasingly on educational credentials that are still not as easy for blacks to obtain as for whites.

The patterns we have been discussing are those of one nation, the United States. The United States is one instance of broader patterns of ethnic relations that have existed in various human societies.

PATTERNS OF ETHNIC RELATIONS

Patterns of ethnic relations in different societies have varied considerably, ranging from open warfare to peaceful coexistence. Because of superior power, the desires and policies of the dominant group explain a good deal of the variation in ethnic relations. Even when one group dominates another, however, the aims and desires of the minority group need to be considered. Simpson and Yinger (1972) identify six major types of policies of ethnic relations that dominant groups have developed, and they also note how minorities may respond to such policies.

1. *Assimilation* involves the merging of minority and majority groups into one group with a common culture and identity. Forced assimilation requires minority group members to give up their own religion, language, and customs and take on the culture of the dominant group. They change their ways, while the majority group makes little or no change in values and actions. This was largely the situation faced by Irish-Americans and Italian-Americans when they arrived in the United States. This model tends to assume the superiority (or at least the domination) of the majority culture. The minority group's cultural customs and language tend to be viewed as inferior and unacceptable by the dominant cultural group. If they are to gain even grudging acceptance by the dominant group, minority group members are expected to adopt the language, values, life-styles, and sometimes the religion of the dominant group. Privately they may try to retain the language, culture, and customs of their ethnic background, but publicly they try to be assimilated as much as possible.

Any ethnic group that is relatively small in numbers, is not too readily identified by its appearance, and faces a relatively intolerant "mainstream" society may find this mode of relations between groups to be the only one that is comfortable. Many white ethnics in America—Irish, Italians, Jews—have felt they had to pursue this course in relation to the dominant culture. Some individuals go so far as to change their names so that ethnic origin is not discernible; others have plastic surgery, change religions, or deny all traces of their past culture and customs. Forced assimilation such as this involves the one-way absorption of an individual or group into another group. Such changes say more about the unyielding nature of the dominant culture than they do about the individuals and groups pursuing this approach.

Robert Park (1950) advanced a theory of the "race relations cycle," suggesting that when dominant and minority groups come into contact, they go through the stages of competition, accommodation, and assimilation. Although Park never specified how movement from one stage to the next took place, the assumption that assimilation was the likely end result of ethnic diversity dominated American sociology for quite a while.

"Anglo-conformity" is the term used by Gordon (1964) to describe the most frequent form of American assimilation. The term suggests "the desirability of maintaining English institutions (as modified by the American Revolution), the English language, and English-oriented cultural patterns as dominant and standard in American life" (Gordon, 1964, p. 88). The "Anglo-conformity" model of assimilation was modified considerably by the "melting pot" vision of assimilation. In the melting pot imagery, America was described "as a totally new blend, culturally and biologically, in which the stocks and folkways of Europe were, figuratively speaking, indiscriminantly mixed in the political pot of the emerging nation and melted together by the fires of American influence and interaction into a distinctly new type" (Gordon, 1964, p. 115). Such a conception comes closer to an image of reciprocal assimilation, which involves a blending of divergent groups, with each group taking on some of the cultural practices of the others.

Amalgamation occurs when groups are assimilated biologically as well as culturally—that is, when racial or ethnic groups also intermarry. Brazil has an official policy that favors the blending of different races (except for the Indians) into a uniquely Brazilian stock.

2. *Pluralism* may occur when both majority and minority groups value their distinct cultural identities while seeking economic and political unity. Minority group members cherish their cultural heritage and do not wish to lose it, and the dominant group is willing to accept cultural variations. In such a society, groups live and let live; they respect one another's differences, but no one tries to change anyone else or make them conform to a conception of "correct" culture or life-style. Switzerland appears to exemplify pluralistic equality. As noted earlier, it has four language-ethnic groups (Germanic, French, Italian, and Romansch). Each group is represented in the formal governing structure of the country and receives equal protection under the law. Because the country was formed as a confederation of equal states, it has managed to retain proportional representation for all language-ethnic groups.

The United States and Canada do not fit completely into either the assimilation or the pluralism pattern. There has been a policy of assimilation. On the other hand, religious pluralism exists widely, and linguistic pluralism (bilingualism) has gained considerable support in American education and in Canadian national policy. Bilingualism as an educational and national policy has been hotly debated in the United States. Reasonable people differ about whether or not bilingualism and biculturalism are desirable goals. Some see the value of bilingualism in the schools as a necessary stepping stone to English fluency and proficiency in the dominant Anglo culture. Others see the goal of bilingualism as one of maintaining and advancing biculturalism at a societal level, along the lines of the French-speaking population in Canada.

3. Legal protection of minorities may occur in societies where the official policy is one of protecting minority group members, even though some groups in society may behave in a hostile way toward them. In the United States the Thirteenth, Fourteenth, and Fifteenth amendments to the Constitution aimed to protect minority rights, especially those of blacks, in situations where they were being violated. Equal opportunity legislation has the same goal.

4. Population transfer is most likely to occur when minority and majority groups are in open conflict. The dominant group often proposes "solving" the problem by removing the minority group. Fairly often, unwanted ethnic or racial groups have been transferred or removed from land that dominant groups wish to possess. This happened to many tribes of native Americans, to Japanese-Americans, to blacks in South Africa, and recently to the Chinese who were pushed out of Vietnam after the war ended there in 1975. Some people suggest that urban renewal in U.S. cities might be more appropriately called "urban removal" because it is used to remove the poor, who are often ethnic or racial minorities, from land desired by the more affluent white middle and upper classes.

Population transfer may involve the division of a nation's territory, as when the Muslim section of India was taken out of India and formed into the new state of Pakistan. In 1980, the largely French-speaking Province of Quebec had an election to decide whether or not it would remain part of the Commonwealth of Canada. (The population voted to remain Canadian.) These latter examples suggest the forms that population transfer may take when minority group members seek secession—that is, both cultural and political independence from the majority group.

5. Continued subjugation occurs when the dominant group wants to maintain its position of superiority over a minority group. South Africa's policy of apartheid is aimed directly at maintaining the domination of whites over blacks, so that black labor can be exploited to advance the prosperity of whites. Dominant groups will use whatever combination of force and ideology is necessary to maintain control.

6. The domination of one group by another may become so extreme that it leads to the extermination of a minority group by the dominant group. This may occur by cutting a group off from its food supply or by deliberate *genocide;* that is, the destruction of an entire population. Indians separated from the buffalo, Cambodians pushed off their rice fields, and other ethnic or political minorities have lost their food supply and starved in large numbers as a result. The United States destroyed perhaps two-thirds of the native American population (Simpson and Yinger, 1972). Hitler's Nazi regime in Germany tried to exterminate the Jews between 1933 and 1945. Although many fled and were concealed by non-Jewish friends, more than 6 million Jews were destroyed in concentration camps, death furnaces, and forced labor camps.

These six types of relationships may be compressed into three: assimilation, pluralism (including 2 and 3 above), and domination (4 through 6 above). Using those three, we can consider why one rather than another of these three types prevails.

WHEN DOES ONE RATHER THAN ANOTHER MODEL PREVAIL?[5]

Under what social conditions is it more likely that pluralistic equality will prevail, and when is domination more likely? First, of course, for any of these possibilities to occur, there must be contact between racial or ethnic groups. Second, the racial or ethnic groups must be identifiable by their physical traits or cultural practices, and individuals must be recognizable as belonging to one rather than another group. Besides being distinct, members of each group need a sense of ethnocentrism—that is, they need to feel that their group is the center of the social world and all others are rated and scaled in reference to it. The practice of endogamy (marrying only members of one's own group) is a good indication that ethnocentrism exists. Without ethnocentrism, groups would tend to merge, and competition would not be structured along racial or ethnic lines. By itself, however, ethnocentrism does not necessarily lead to ethnic conflict or domination of one group by another.

Instead, ethnocentrism in combination with

[5]This section draws heavily upon Noel (1968).

competition over scarce goods and resources tends to result in ethnic conflict. When there is a shortage of power, labor, land, wealth, status, or jobs, along with ethnocentrism, groups may work to enhance their own situation by exploiting other ethnically distinct groups. A double standard of morality has always tended to characterize relations betweeen in- and out-group members, with the result that different standards of morality are permitted in relation to outsiders. This double standard may take the form of exploitative labor relations, distributions of wealth, and sexual relations (since sexual relations may occur with out-group members even when marriage is rare or prohibited).

Even when ethnocentrism and competition exist between ethnic groups, it is possible for a situation of uneasy pluralistic equality or deadlocked conflict to prevail. What tips the scale from pluralism to partial or total domination of one group by another is the existence of differential power among the groups. This can take the form of superior force (weapons or armies), wealth, technology, knowledge, social organization, and the absence of legal protection for the subordinate groups. Since any initial advantage tends to magnify subsequent advantages, even a slight tilt in the scale of power can create a situation of permanent racial or ethnic domination. For example, the Dutch Boers beat the Africans in South Africa by only a small margin. Over time, however, they greatly widened the political and economic gap between themselves and the blacks. Several features are always present when such domination develops.

WHAT ACCOMPANIES RACIAL OR ETHNIC DOMINATION?

Racism refers to the institutionalized domination of one racial group by another. When domination is institutionalized, it goes beyond the practices of a single group in a single generation to pervade law, organizational rules, consistently followed social practices, and so forth. Racism is most likely to occur when there are physical or cultural differences between groups, when there is competition over scarce resources, and when one group has considerably greater power than the other.

Racism is invariably accompanied by an ideology attempting to justify the superior position of one race and the inferior position of the other race. In this sense, the ethnocentrism of the dominant group tends to become established as a social fact. In the process, a great many myths about the races, especially about the subordinate race, are circulated and tend to be believed by large numbers of people. One of the results of this myth-making process is prejudice toward the minority group(s), and usually discrimination against them. When discrimination results in less education, lower-paying jobs, and exclusion from decent housing, medical care, and other social benefits, it operates to perpetuate, and sometimes even to increase, the inequality between groups.

Every dominant group, whether its dominance is based on race, ethnicity, age, class, nationality, occupational position, or gender, always tries to legitimize its superior position with an ideology, or belief system, that portrays the status quo as a morally just system. In South Africa, an ideology of religious destiny and superiority operates to legitimize the domination of blacks by whites. In the early years of slavery in the United States, the major rationale for permitting such a condition was religious. In the colonial era, Christians were not allowed to hold other Christians as slaves; but since the Africans were "pagans" or "heathens," it was argued, it was all right to keep them as slaves. Charles Darwin's theory of evolution was used to justify the superiority of the white race, and to argue that other races stood lower on the evolutionary ladder and hence could be classified as "subhuman." This argument paralleled the religious ideology and provided a "scientific" rationale for why blacks could be enslaved.

Besides being dubbed "subhuman," blacks in the United States were also alleged to be lazy, ignorant, dirty, and unconcerned about the future. These allegations were definitely not true of most blacks. Where they may have been based on observation, such behaviors were situationally determined rather than the result of the genes or "human nature" of black people. It is hard to be energetic when you suffer from debilitating disease; it is difficult to be informed when you are denied schooling, cannot afford books, magazines, or newspapers, and the libraries are closed to you; it is difficult to bathe frequently when you have no indoor running water; and saving is impossible when there is not enough money for the basic necessities or when someone may steal any savings you have. These allegations are another example of a legitimating ideology that blames the victims for their plight, rather than seeing behavior as generated in response to certain situations (Ryan, 1971).

"Blaming the victim" can take many forms. Sometimes it appears in the way a problem is defined, as in the phrases "the black problem" or "the Jewish problem." The next step is to ask what it is about the "problem" group that might have created its inferior position in society. Two favorite—and flawed—explanations are genetic and cultural deficiencies. After religious arguments lost their potency, the "scientific" assertion that certain races or ethnic groups were genetically inferior was widely used. In the 1920s, certain Eastern and Southern European immigrants were labeled "feebleminded" because of their low scores on culturally laden IQ tests (Kamin, 1974). On the basis of these false beliefs, U.S. immigration quotas were set based on the ethnic composition of the United States in 1890.

More recently, the genetic argument for the possible inferiority of blacks compared to whites has been revived in the debate over race and IQ. Arthur Jensen (1969) noted that black Americans score an average of 10 to 15 points lower on IQ tests than whites do. From this observation, Jensen concluded that genetic factors may be strongly implicated in these differences in intelligence. Although most researchers accept that differences exist between the average black and white scores on IQ tests, they do not agree with Jensen's conclusion that these differences are due to genes rather than environment.

Jensen's interpretation is rejected for several important reasons. First, there are no genetically pure races in the United States. At least 70 percent of black Americans have some white ancestry, and perhaps 20 percent of white Americans have some black ancestry, according to Hunt and Walker (1974). Therefore, there are no pure black genes that could cause the observed differences. Second, no "IQ gene" has been identified. Instead, it is increasingly clear that IQ tests measure cultural knowledge, which is distributed unevenly in the social world. If tests measure cultural skills, it is logical that social learning and environment must contribute in a major way to test performance. Even when black and white families have similar levels of education, occupation, and income, the widespread prejudice and discrimination they face in society may create different environments (varied neighborhoods, schools, and social networks) that may affect test performance. Indeed, one study of black children who were adopted by white families showed that the IQ differences between black and white children shrank steadily the longer they had been adopted (Scarr-Salapatek and Weinberg, 1975). This evidence suggests that IQ tests reflect cultural and social advantages that are unevenly available to blacks and whites in the United States.

Although most scientists reject Jensen's suggestion that blacks are genetically inferior to whites, many have considered that cultural deficiencies may be at least partially responsible for the lower school achievement of racial minorities or lower-class children. Various explanations have been offered, including disorganized family structures, inadequate childrearing, undeveloped language use, inability to delay impulse gratification, and low self-esteem. These assumptions about serious cultural "deficiencies" in the lives of racial or ethnic minorities have been strongly refuted (Baratz and Baratz, 1970;

Labov, 1973; Ogbu, 1978; Persell, 1977, 1981). Although existing differences between racial and ethnic groups may be related to lower IQ scores on culturally loaded tests, they do not explain unequal school achievement or demonstrate cultural inferiority. Moreover, the differences that do exist appear to be rooted in the economic, political, and racial inequalities of society rather than in the failings of individuals, families, or cultures.

Defining and locating the "problem" in the individual minority group member rather than in ethnic and economic discrimination sustains the ideology of racial inferiority, thereby contributing to a situation of racial and ethnic domination of one group by another. It does so by indicating that it is the racial or ethnic minority member or group that needs to change, rather than the societal structure of domination, inequality, and discrimination.

PREJUDICE AND ITS CAUSES

Prejudice is a "prejudged" unfavorable attitude toward the members of a group who are assumed to possess negative traits. Prejudice is irrational because it is an attitude that is not based on specific experience with the people being judged. In fact, being prejudiced may seriously distort people's observations and judgments. They may presume an individual has the negative trait they expect, and be unable to tell if he or she really has it or not. Prejudice often provides the emotional support for discrimination.

Discrimination is the unequal and unfair treatment of individuals or groups on the basis of some irrelevant characteristic, such as race, ethnicity, religion, sex, or social class. Discrimination involves drawing distinctions between people in a way that violates widely accepted values and procedures—for example, by refusing to consider members of a racial minority for a job even when they have all the required formal qualifications (Simpson and Yinger, 1972). No single statement fully expresses the relationship between prejudice and discrimination. Simpson and Yinger note that all five of the following statements are true:

1. There can be prejudice without discrimination.
2. There can be discrimination without prejudice.
3. Discrimination can be among the causes of prejudice.
4. Prejudice can be among the causes of discrimination.
5. Probably most frequently prejudice and discrimination are mutually reinforcing (Simpson and Yinger, 1972, p. 29).

Discrimination is most often used to describe the action of a dominant majority in relation to a weak minority. It is the active expression of a negative prejudice toward a person or group.

Both psychological and sociological factors have been suggested as causes of prejudice. The two major psychological explanations are scapegoating and projection. In *scapegoating*, or frustration-aggression theory, people who are frustrated in achieving their social and economic goals may be unable to express their anger directly at its cause. They may be afraid (with good reason) to vent their anger against parents or a boss, for example; or they may be unable to express anger directly at such a diffuse source as inflation, war, or a natural calamity. They may, however, be able to find some weaker but innocent individual or group on whom to vent their rage. These substitute opponents are scapegoats for the real source of frustration. Sometimes people frustrated at work take out their anger on their spouses or children; sometimes they find a racial or ethnic minority to pick on.

In the process of *projection*, members of the majority group project their own unacceptable feelings or desires onto minority group members to avoid guilt or self-blame. The fear that black men lusted after white women, for example, may have arisen from the guilt white men felt for their own sexual feelings and behavior toward black women. Similarly, whites may project great anger onto every black person they see on the street because they know whites have done things that could anger blacks.

Even though these explanations appear to be purely psychological in origin, both arise from the social relations in which people are embedded. Hence, while certain psychological traits may help to explain why some people are prejudiced and others are not, there appear to be certain social conditions under which prejudice is more or less likely to emerge. The social roots of prejudice are revealed in regional variations. Middleton (1976) discovered that in the southern United States, antiblack prejudice was part of the regional subculture in certain areas but less so in others. People who moved away from those regions became less prejudiced over time, and those who moved into those regions became more prejudiced over time. This evidence supports a situational explanation for the origins of prejudice.

Whereas prejudice is an attitude held by individuals, discrimination refers to actions by individuals or institutions that disqualify or mistreat people in ways that are rationally irrelevant to the situation (Antonovsky, 1960). Over time, discrimination tends to confirm the negative vicious circle that becomes increasingly difficult for a minority group to escape. As we have seen, when relations between ethnic groups become competitive and one group seeks to dominate others, that domination is likely to become institutionalized and to be accompanied by a legitimating ideology. Institutionalized discrimination and racist ideologies fan the flames of prejudice, which reinforces discrimination, in a bitter vicious circle. Together, prejudice and discrimination may support economic and political interests. Given these tendencies, what are the prospects for racial and ethnic relations in a country like the United States?

PROSPECTS

What factors affect ethnocentrism, competition, and differential power? Ethnocentrism seems to be reduced by evidence that shatters racial myths and by greater interpersonal contact between relative equals of different groups under nonthreatening conditions. Competition between ethnic groups seems to shrink in the face of economic growth and prosperity, but tends to increase in the face of decline and scarcity. Differential power may be reduced by constitutional protection for equal rights, protective legislation, voting rights, organized political representation, a police force that upholds the law equally for all races, and allies from within the majority group. Obvious legal discrimination is no longer acceptable in American society. Furthermore, Americans increasingly reject racial injustice in principle. Racial discrimination still exists, however, in subtle forms.

Discrimination may persist because the United States has been a racially stratified society, not simply a prejudiced one. Prejudice can be overcome by better contact, communication, and understanding (Blauner, 1972, p. 28). Two decades of efforts to overcome racial stratifica-

"I'm sorry, but I can't stay long, Mrs. Breevort. I've got four more token party invitations to attend this evening."

SOURCE: Reprinted courtesy of *Penthouse Magazine*.

tion have not yet produced social and economic equality between blacks and whites. Racial stratification creates patterns that not only oppress minority group members, but preserve privileges for the dominant group. Racial stratification ensures a large group of people who have no other choice but to do the "dirty work" of society (as janitors, domestics, hospital orderlies, and morgue attendants). Such a system also preserves clean jobs with promotion opportunities for the privileged group.

Besides granting economic and occupational advantages, racial stratification confers status advantages on the dominant group. Racial stratification, in short, goes beyond prejudiced attitudes to encompass all the ways that dominant groups retain their advantages and see that minority groups do not seriously threaten those privileges. If unemployment, inflation, and limited economic growth continue to plague our economy, then scarcity rather than prosperity seems likely. When key resources are in scarce supply, sociologists predict greater rather than lesser competition between racial and ethnic groups.

The new climate of race relations in the United States is characterized by white Americans increasingly rejecting racial injustice in principle, at the same time that they are reluctant to accept the measures (such as school busing or affirmative action) necessary to eliminate that injustice. We can conclude that as of the 1980s, "America has made significant progress over the past generation, but there are still 'rivers of blood and years of darkness' to surmount" (Pettigrew, 1981, p. 252).

AGE DIFFERENTIATION

Ellen's 85-year-old grandmother, Mary Sargent, has lived alone for the last 10 years, ever since her husband died. Since she never worked, she subsists on her widow's Social Security benefits and the modest income from the savings and investments she and her husband made. She lives in a fully paid for house, but finds that rising costs are a growing burden. Her health has been good until recently, but now her family is beginning to worry about her living alone, since lately she has had several dizzy spells and falls.

In many ways, Mary Sargent reflects a significant social change. In 1900, the average life expectancy in the United States was 47, but today it is 74. Moreover, women outlive men by 8 years, on the average. In 1981, 11 percent, or 26.3 million Americans, were 65 or older, compared to 8 percent in 1950. By the year 2030, those 65 and over are expected to total 55 million persons, or nearly one-quarter of the total population.

The percentage of the American population that is 65 or older has been increasing steadily, from 8 percent in 1950 to 11 percent in 1981, to a projected 25 percent by 2030.

The enormous increase in the number and percentage of older people has led to increased interest in age as a social phenomenon. Like race, age is a biological trait that takes on social significance. In some societies, such as tribal societies in West Africa today, a person's social status increases with age. In other societies, such as the industrialized societies of North America and Europe, younger people are valued for their energy, sex appeal, and attractiveness, while middle-aged persons have the most power and status in society. How do sociologists explain these differences?

EXPLANATIONS FOR AGE DIFFERENTIATION

Functionalists suggest that in a traditional tribal society, much of the tribe's knowledge and wisdom is stored in the memories of tribal elders. They may remember which other tribes were friendly or aggressive in the past, where water was found, or how to deal with a plague of locusts. Since subsistence in such societies is drawn from the land, the elders provide a smooth and legitimate means of controlling use of the land, thereby avoiding conflict within a society. Therefore, they represent a valuable resource in the society's efforts to survive, and valuing age and elders is functional for the society. There are also fewer elders in such societies and they do not live as long.

In industrial societies, in contrast, the economic activity of most members is not centered around the land. Individuals can subsist independently of their elder kin. Moreover, the knowledge and technology that supports their activities is changing rapidly. Often the younger generations know how to do more things than do the older ones. As a result, it is not functional for such a society to rely heavily on its older generations for social and economic guidance.

The conflict perspective stresses that the way a society is arranged depends on the relative power and resources of various groups in it. In industrial societies, the elderly lose power and resources, since for many people their power and resources are rooted in jobs rather than in the land. Because there are more people who want to work than there are jobs available, the more numerous middle-aged people set age limits on who can work. As a result, both the young and the old in industrial societies tend to be squeezed out of opportunities for work, money, and status.

Symbolic interactionism approaches the issue of aging somewhat differently. One approach that interactionists might take is to examine the age of cultural heroes. When the median age of the American population was 25, in the 1960s, the cultural heroes were very young people. One of the slogans of the era was "Don't trust anyone over 30!" By the time the median age hit 30 in 1980, that slogan had disappeared and a number of important cultural heroines were over 40, for example, Jane Fonda, Meryl Streep in *Sophie's Choice,* and Ali McGraw in *The Winds of War.* Fashion magazines featured "great women over the age of 40" on their covers. Changes in the median age are correlated with changes in the social definitions of attractiveness. Although the age of cultural heroines appears to have increased in recent years, and at least one movie, *On Golden Pond,* featured older people as central characters, the question remains, how are older persons (those 65 and over) faring today?

OLDER PEOPLE IN THE UNITED STATES TODAY

To what degree does age inequality exist in contemporary industrial society? Older Americans have an average household income of $12,628, about 60 percent of the average U.S. household income of $21,036 (Gottschalk, 1983). About one-quarter of older Americans hover around the "poverty line" income of $4,000 per year. Those in the poverty category are more likely to be female, and older than those above the line. More Americans over 65 today receive Social Security benefits than ever before (92 percent), but Social Security provides only 38 percent of the total income available to older Americans (Gottschalk, 1983). Their next largest source of income was earnings from work, equal to 23 percent of total income. In 1982, however, only 18 percent of older men were working, compared to 48 percent in 1947. We do not know if this is because more are choosing retirement or because there are fewer jobs available to older workers today.

Younger workers (those 16 to 19 years old) are also much more likely to be unemployed and to earn lower wages than middle-aged workers. Some older persons are better off in one respect, namely they are more likely to own their own homes. Among older persons, 70 percent own their own homes, compared to 66 percent of the entire population. Of those, 80 percent have paid off their mortgages (Gottschalk, 1983).

ARE THE ELDERLY A "MINORITY GROUP?"

These occupational and economic inequalities by age raise the possibility that older persons resemble other minority groups. To what degree does this seem to be the case? Earlier in this chapter, a minority was defined as any recognizable group that suffers from some disadvantage as a result of the action of a dominant group. To the extent that people are excluded because of their age rather than because of their skills or ability from employment and the resultant income and status they might obtain, they may be seen as suffering from a disadvantage. They also resemble a minority group in that they are clearly identifiable, if not by appearance then by public records. A third way they resemble minority groups is in the legitimating ideologies put forward by more dominant groups in society. In the case of older persons, this includes such negative images and ideologies as poor health, senility, and social disengagement.

Among those 65 and over, however, 60 percent are generally quite well and only 40 percent suffer from some chronic mental or physical handicap (Moore, 1983). Those with health problems tend to be considerably over 65. Social disengagement may come when people are uprooted from long-term communities or retired involuntarily. When people remain in meaningful social networks, they do not seem to withdraw socially (Hochschild, 1973; Marshall, 1975). In general, older persons see themselves as better off than younger people see them, according to a 1982 national poll by Louis Harris Associates (Gottschalk, 1983). Like other negative stereotypes, these seem not to apply to large numbers of older persons. Instead, they are better understood as ideologies that try to legitimate the low power and status of older persons.

Many people over the age of 65 are much more active, healthy, and willing to try new experiences than many younger people realize.

A fourth similarity between older people and minority groups is the way they may mobilize around shared concerns and start a social movement to change their situation. Older people have become a noteworthy political presence in the United States. They have worked to obtain "senior citizen" discounts on everything from public transportation to movies and restaurant meals. Their political activity has helped to protect the Social Security system from federal budget cuts. Compared to most other age groups, proportionately more people 65 and over go to the polls. In 1980, 65 percent of those 65 and over voted, compared to only 59 percent of the whole population. Only those aged 45 to 64 voted at a higher rate (69 percent) (U.S. Bureau of the Census, 1982a). In some communities, for example, southern Florida, older voters are a particularly powerful political force. One of the political gains won was the movement in 1978 of the mandatory retirement age to 70 from 65, permitting those who wished to work longer to do so, although some observers fear this extension may hurt younger workers trying to enter the labor force.

These similarities suggest that older persons are clearly a minority group. There are some important social differences, however. All other people do not share a common ethnic or cultural heritage. They come from varied racial groups, different social classes, and they include both men and women. As a result, older people may have little in common except their chronological age. For many, that social trait may be less important than the above social characteristics. Nevertheless, the similarities and differences between age and minority group status are worth considering, particularly since age as a category of privilege or exclusion is so clearly socially and legally constructed.

Summary

1. The major significance of race is social rather than biological.

2. An ethnic group shares an identity based on a common cultural tradition.

3. A racial or ethnic group becomes a minority group when its members are singled out for unequal treatment by other groups in society.

4. The United States contains a broad mixture of racial and ethnic groups, including WASPs, white ethnics, blacks, Hispanics, Chinese, Japanese, Vietnamese, and native Americans. All of these except the white Anglo-Saxon Protestants have suffered varying degrees of discrimination and domination by others.

5. Despite the past history of domination and discrimination, there are those who argue that race is declining in significance as a cause of inequality in the United States today. The evidence on educational gains tends to support this argument, but race still appears to be related to occupation and to income, even when similarly educated whites and blacks are compared. Race and class seem to interact in significant ways.

6. Three types of social relations are possible between ethnic or racial groups in the same territory: assimilation of the subordinate group by the dominant group, pluralistic equality, and overt domination, which may result in policies of exclusion, segregation, removal, or extermination.

7. Domination and racism are most likely when members of racial or ethnic groups are clearly identifiable, when they feel a sense of ethnocentrism, when there is competition over scarce resources, and when one group has a power advantage over the other one.

8. Racism is invariably accompanied by a legitimating ideology, whether it be religious, scientific, or mythical. Frequently this ideology "blames the victims" for their situation.

9. Prejudice, or the negative judgment of an individual based on membership in a particular group, may be influenced by the psychological processes of scapegoating or projection, but it is also rooted in a social context.

10. Whereas prejudice is an attitude of individuals, discrimination refers to actions that exclude or hurt people for irrelevant racial or ethnic characteristics.

11. Although ethnocentrism and differential power between blacks and whites have been declining in the United States, the possibility of economic scarcity and greater competition along racial lines still exists.

12. Only recently have there been large numbers of older people 65 and over in the United States. Age is given quite different social meanings in different societies.

13. Functionalists, conflict theorists, and symbolic interactionists differ in the way they explain age differentiation.

14. Both older and younger people work less and earn less than middle-aged workers. Older people are somewhat more likely to own their own homes.

15. Older people resemble a minority group in that they may be excluded from jobs, income, and status because of their age, they are identifiable, and their lower status may be accompanied by negative images and legitimating ideologies. They have sometimes mobilized to change their situation. They differ from minority groups because they do not have a common ethnic or cultural heritage.

Key Terms

amalgamation
assimilation
discrimination
ethnic group
genocide
geographic race
minority group
pluralism
prejudice
projection
race
racism
scapegoating
white ethnics

RIGHT
LANE
MUST
TURN
RIGHT
WOMAN
+ MEN
WORKING

Chapter 12

Gender Roles and Inequality

The Christmas 1956 issue of *Life* magazine held up three prescriptions for women—career woman, community leader, and total housewife/mother—and clearly rejected the first two as inappropriate. The image in that magazine suggests that the social role presented to women and girls nearly three decades ago was one of passively centering one's life around a husband, children, and a home. A woman's major personal concern was to focus on being as attractive as possible for the sake of her husband and children. Men were supposed to succeed in the world outside the family and to be good providers.

Many changes in attitudes about women have occurred in the last quarter century. By 1978, a national survey showed that certain important qualities were almost as likely to be considered important in a man as in a woman (Figure 12.1). The only big difference between important qualities for men and women listed in that survey is the ability to be a good provider, a trait that is still considered more important for men than for women. The percentage of people approving of married women working has risen dramatically, from only 21 percent in 1938 to 72 percent in 1978 (Figure 12.2). In 1978 more than two-thirds of Americans questioned disagreed with the statement "Women should take care of running their homes and leave running the country to men" (NORC, 1978), while two-thirds agreed that if the husband in a family wants children but the wife decides that she does not want any children, it is all right for her to refuse to have children (*Public Opinion,* 1980, p. 34). (This figure does not suggest that two-thirds of the population does not want to have children.) From 1970 to 1979, the percentage of Americans who favor most of the efforts to strengthen and change women's status in society today rose from 42 to 65 percent (*Public Opinion,* 1980, p. 33). All these figures suggest that in less than 25 years there has been a dramatic shift in the images of ideal feminine and masculine qualities, behaviors, and attitudes toward the roles of men and women in society. One result of that shift has been a growing awareness of the distinction between sex and gender.

SEX, GENDER, AND STRATIFICATION

Sex refers to the biological distinction of being male or female. It is determined by chromosomes, reflected in genital and hormonal differences, and is difficult to change. A few successful sex-change operations have been performed. *Gender* refers to the traits and behaviors socially designated as "masculine" or "feminine" in a particular culture. These traits include styles of interaction, appearance (for example, hair styles), patterns of dress, and favored activities and behaviors.

Although in most cultures conceptions of masculinity and femininity are assumed to be

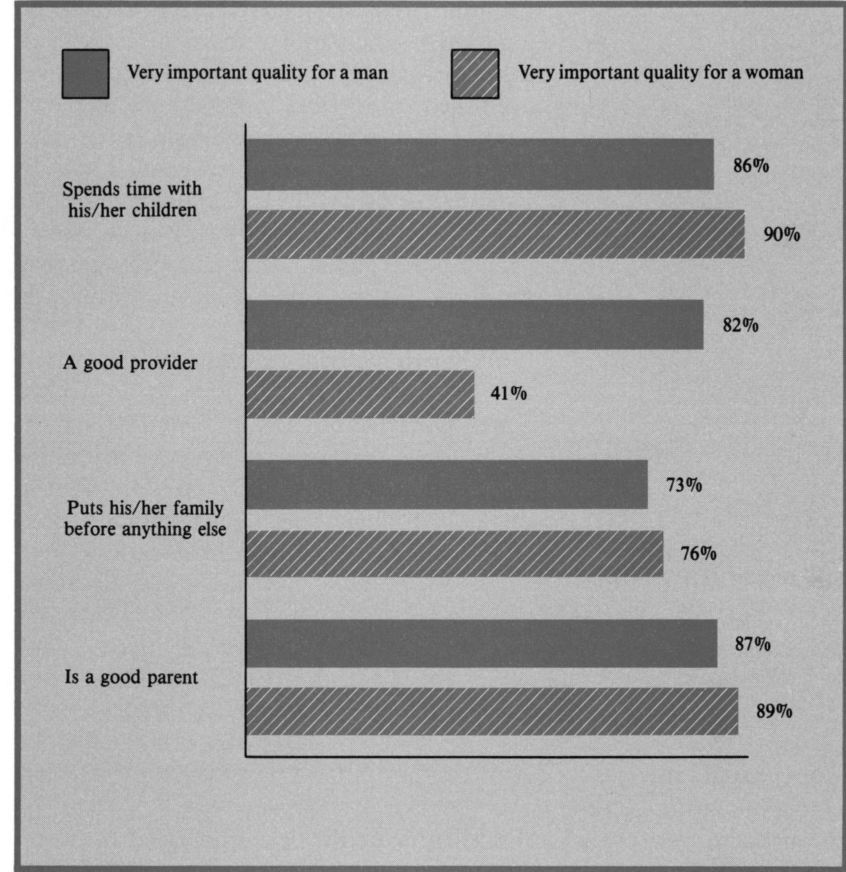

Figure 12.1 Qualities Considered Important for Men and for Women by a National Sample of Adult Men and Women

linked with biological sex differences, in fact they draw more from social assumptions and customs than from biological determinants. For example, it has been argued for many centuries in Western societies that a woman's role in giving birth to a child suits her particularly well for nurturing that child. This connection is seen as related to the greater expressiveness of women. Margaret Mead, however, studied a tribe in New Guinea, the Tchambuli, where the men reared the children, were the more expressive ones, were artistically creative, and also gossiped a great deal. The women in that tribe were the primary breadwinners; they were energetic and domineering; and they wore no jewelry or other ornaments (Mead, 1935). Similarly, in some periods of history, men's clothing was at least as elaborate as women's clothing, while at other periods, such as in the United States generally in recent decades, women's clothing was more colorful than men's. Such wide cultural variations and marked differences between historical eras suggest that expectations regarding male and female roles and characteristics do not necessarily have a biological basis.

Gender roles are the socially expected behaviors associated with being a man or a woman in a particular society. Changing gender roles have been the center of much social attention in the United States recently. Although they are of in-

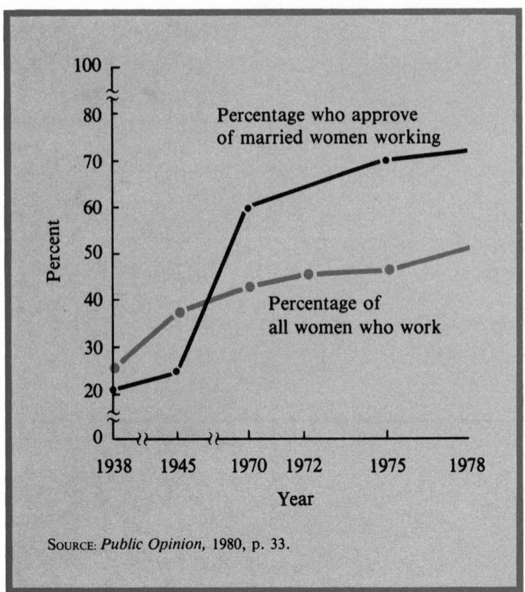

Figure 12.2 Percentage of U.S. Adults Approving of Married Women Working and Percentage of All Women Who Work, 1938–1978

terest, it is important to realize that gender roles reflect *gender differences*—variations in the social positions, roles, behaviors, attitudes, and personalities of men and women in a society. Considering gender differences does not take into account whether men are ranked more highly than women. *Sex stratification,* on the other hand, suggests that the sexes and their related gender roles are hierarchically ranked in terms of ownership, power, social control, prestige, and social rewards.

The existence of stratification by sex is revealed in the relative political, economic, and personal power exercised by men and women and in the equality or inequality of the rewards they receive. Their relative status is evident in the amount of personal and sexual freedom women have and in the extent of their informal influence. Some of these differences are summarized in Table 12.1. The relative life chances of men and women today will be discussed in the next section of this chapter.

Anthropologists suggest that sex stratification is related to inheritance patterns, rules surrounding marriage, and customs about which relatives live together. Societies in which men dominate tend to have different kinship structures from societies in which women have some power (as indicated in Table 12.1). Anthropological data indicate that societies in which women possess greater power and influence are much rarer than those in which males dominate (Murdock, 1967).

Although prescribed gender roles clearly have changed over the past 25 years in the United States, both the summary in Table 12.1 and the discussion in the next section suggest that sexual stratification still exists. The problem, then, is one of explaining why sex stratification exists and considering what its future might be.

DIFFERENCES IN THE LIFE CHANCES OF MEN AND WOMEN TODAY

Life chances are the opportunities a society offers its members. In our society, these include educational attainment, labor market participation, income and wealth, political participation, legal rights and rates of criminal victimization, health, life expectancy, and mental health. In addition, social interaction, including language, is an important interpersonal indicator of equality or inequality. In this section, the status of men and women is compared in these areas of social participation.

EDUCATIONAL ATTAINMENT

By 1989 women are projected to earn about as many bachelor's and master's degrees as men (Figure 12.3). Women's representation at the advanced degree levels is expected to continue to increase rapidly, as it has in the past decade. Even so, women are expected to earn less than

Table 12.1 Indicators of Sex Status in Various Societies

		Type of Society		
		Societies Where Males Dominate	Societies with Relative Gender Equality	Societies Where Females Have Relatively Greater Power or Influence
Kinship Structures	Kinship residence patterns	*Patrilocal:* Newly married couple lives with husband's relatives.	*Bilocal:* New couple lives with either husband's or wife's kin, depending on personal preferences and economic factors.	*Matrilocal:* Newly married couple lives with wife's kin.
	Descent system—how property is passed on	*Patrilineal:* Property is transmitted through the male line.	*Bilateral:* Property passed through both fathers and mothers.	*Matrilineal:* Property is passed through the female line.
	Rules surrounding marriage	*Polygyny:* A man may have more than one wife at a time.	*Monogamy:* Single spouse for both men and women.	*Polyandry:* A woman may have more than one husband at a time (rare).
	Personal freedom	Personal freedom of women is generally restricted. Purdah (seclusion of women) may appear in male-dominated societies.	Women have some personal freedom.	Women have considerable personal freedom.
Indicators of Sex Status	Sexual freedom of women	Sexual freedom is generally restricted. Moreover, such practices as clitoridectomy (excision of the clitoris) may appear in male-dominated societies.	Some sexual freedom for women.	Greater sexual freedom for women.
	Formal political power of women	Political power exercised entirely by men.	Political power exercised mainly by men, although women begin to gain public office.	Men may still be influential politically, often through the mother's brother.
	Informal influence of women	Women may have some informal influence [prerevolutionary Chinese women used interpersonal skills to influence their male relatives (Wolf, 1974, p. 163)]	Women may exercise influence through informal channels.	Women may have considerable informal influence.
	Economic power and rewards	Economic power controlled by men; women have little or none.	Women may have some economic power and rewards.	Women may control some economic power and resources.

SOURCE: Adapted from Nielsen, 1978, pp. 12–19.

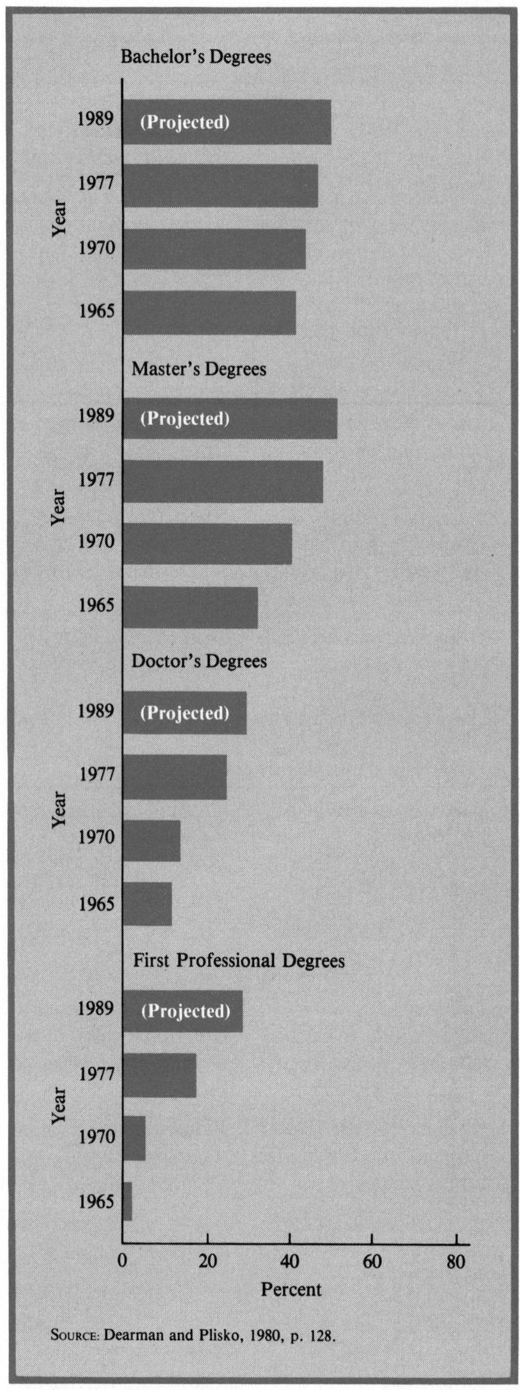

Figure 12.3 Percentage of Degrees Awarded to Females

one-third of all doctoral degrees in 1989, up from 13 percent in 1970. Women are expected to earn about 29 percent of all first professional degrees (for example, medical, law, or masters in teaching) by 1989, up from 5 percent in 1970 (Dearman and Plisko, 1980, p. 128). In recent years, women have made gains in educational attainments, but they have not yet achieved educational equality with men.

Men and women still differ somewhat in the disciplines they study, as well as in degrees they earn. In 1977, women were more likely than men to earn degrees at all levels in only three fields—home economics, library science, and foreign languages. In a few disciplines, women were more likely than men to earn bachelor's and usually master's degrees. These fields include education, fine and applied arts, the health professions, psychology, and literature. At the doctoral level in these disciplines, men still outnumbered women. In virtually all other fields surveyed—agriculture, architecture, biology, business, communications, computer science, engineering, law, mathematics, military science, physical sciences, public affairs, the social sciences, and theology—men outnumbered women at all three degree levels. Some of these fields were still studied almost exclusively by men, including agriculture, engineering, and military science (Dearman and Plisko, 1979).

To the extent that employers require degrees in certain disciplines and women lack those degrees, women are less likely to be considered for certain entry-level positions and for certain career paths. Although earning such degrees does not ensure that women will be considered or hired, not having the degree bars them from even being candidates.

LABOR MARKET PARTICIPATION

In 1981, 43 percent of the labor force 16 years old and above consisted of women, and 57 percent were men. Among the younger (under 45) segments of the population, however, an even larger proportion of women work. This shift is reflected in the fact that by 1981, 63 percent of married women with school-age children were working (U.S. Bureau of the Census, 1982a, p. 382). By the year 2000, projections suggest that 75 percent of all women will be in the labor force. This prediction represents a new script, at least for middle-class women growing up today. Gone are the days when such a woman could assume that a man would marry her and support her and their children for life. Women have both greater independence and more responsibilities. Men, in turn, have less economic power over their wives, but are spared the total responsibility of providing for their families. Most women will end up working for most of their lives, whether they had planned to or not. Working-class women have always been in the labor force in much larger proportions than their middle-class counterparts, after taking time out for childrearing. What has changed in the United States since World War II is the record level of middle-class women entering the work force.

Clearly the status of women and men as workers is converging. Since they have increasingly similar educational attainments, are they pursuing similar occupations? Women represent more than half (54 percent) of all white collar workers (Figure 12.4), but that figure needs to be broken down into various occupations within white collar work. Whereas women comprise 45 percent of all professional and technical workers, their relatively high percentage in that classification is due mainly to their overrepresentation in the now "female" occupations of nursing, library work, elementary and secondary teaching, health technology, social work, and educational and vocational counseling.

The sex composition of various occupations is not static. As the skills and rewards associated with a particular occupation are upgraded, men tend to enter it in larger numbers. This happened in the nineteenth century with respect to health care occupations, as male doctors took over more and more of the work women had been doing (as midwives, for example.) Similarly, as skills and rewards decline, the proportion of women in an occupation increases. This happened in the nineteenth century as male clerks were increasingly replaced by women and in education as female teachers took over from men (Braverman, 1974; Ehrenreich and English, 1978; Snyder, Hayward and Hudis, 1979; Tyack and Strober, 1981).

Women today are still only 6 percent of all engineers, 15 percent of lawyers and doctors, and 14 percent of all religious workers (including clergy). Within the jobs classified as professional and technical, there is a very uneven distribution by sex. Other categories of white collar work are similarly imbalanced. Women constitute 81 percent of all clerical workers, but only 28 percent of all managers and administrators and 45 percent of sales workers. Men are greatly overrepresented in blue collar work, particularly in the skilled trades such as electrical work and among farm workers, whereas most service workers are women. As long as women do not hold the same occupations as men, the chance of eliminating stratification by sex remains slim. With these major variations by sex, any comparison of the earnings of men and women clearly needs to be done *within* similar occupations.

INCOME AND WEALTH

Across the nation, women earn sixty cents for every dollar men earn (Figure 12.5). In all occupational groups, men earn more than women. In professional, technical, and kindred jobs, women earn nearly two-thirds of what men do; in sales work they earn less than half. Some of this discrepancy may be due to varied educational backgrounds and some to the greater concentration of women in lower-paying jobs within each occupational group. However, one study found that even when women were matched with men in education, work experience, occupational status, and number of weeks worked in a year, they still earned 38 percent less

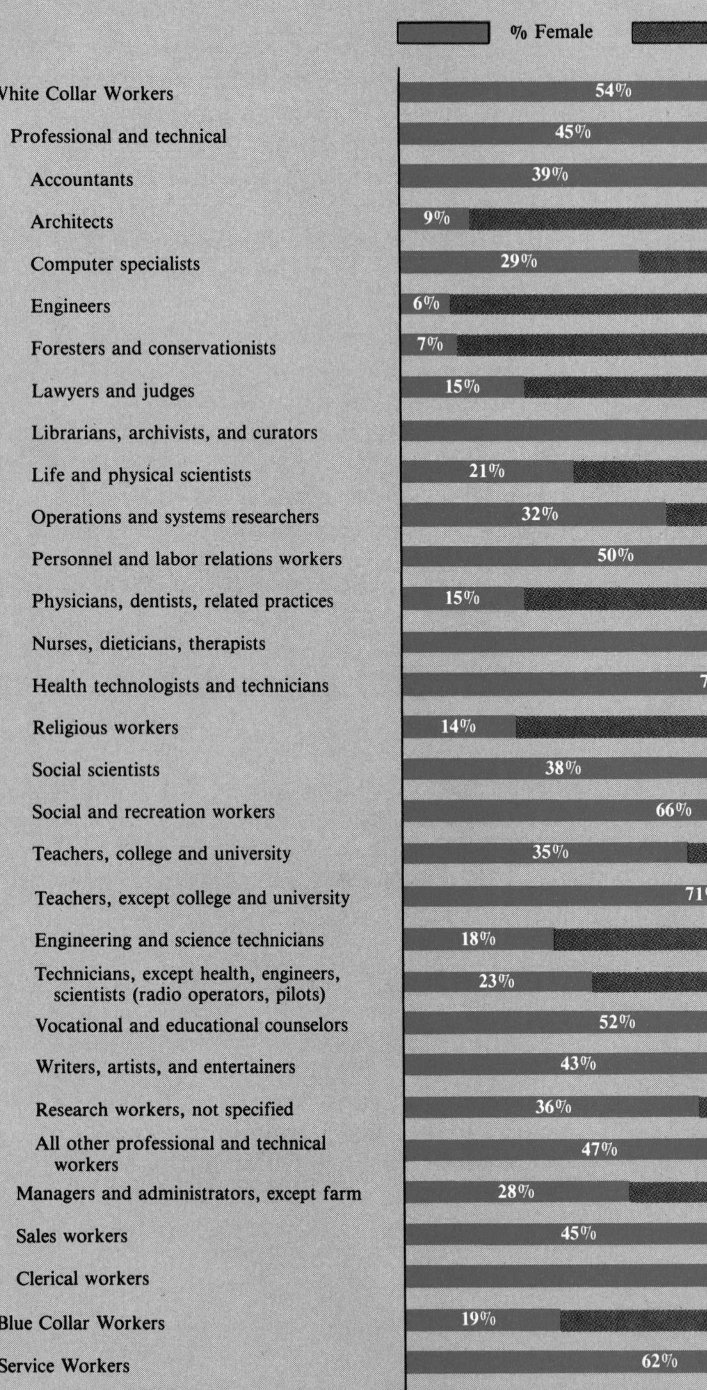

SOURCE: U.S. Department of Labor, 1983, pp. 158-159.

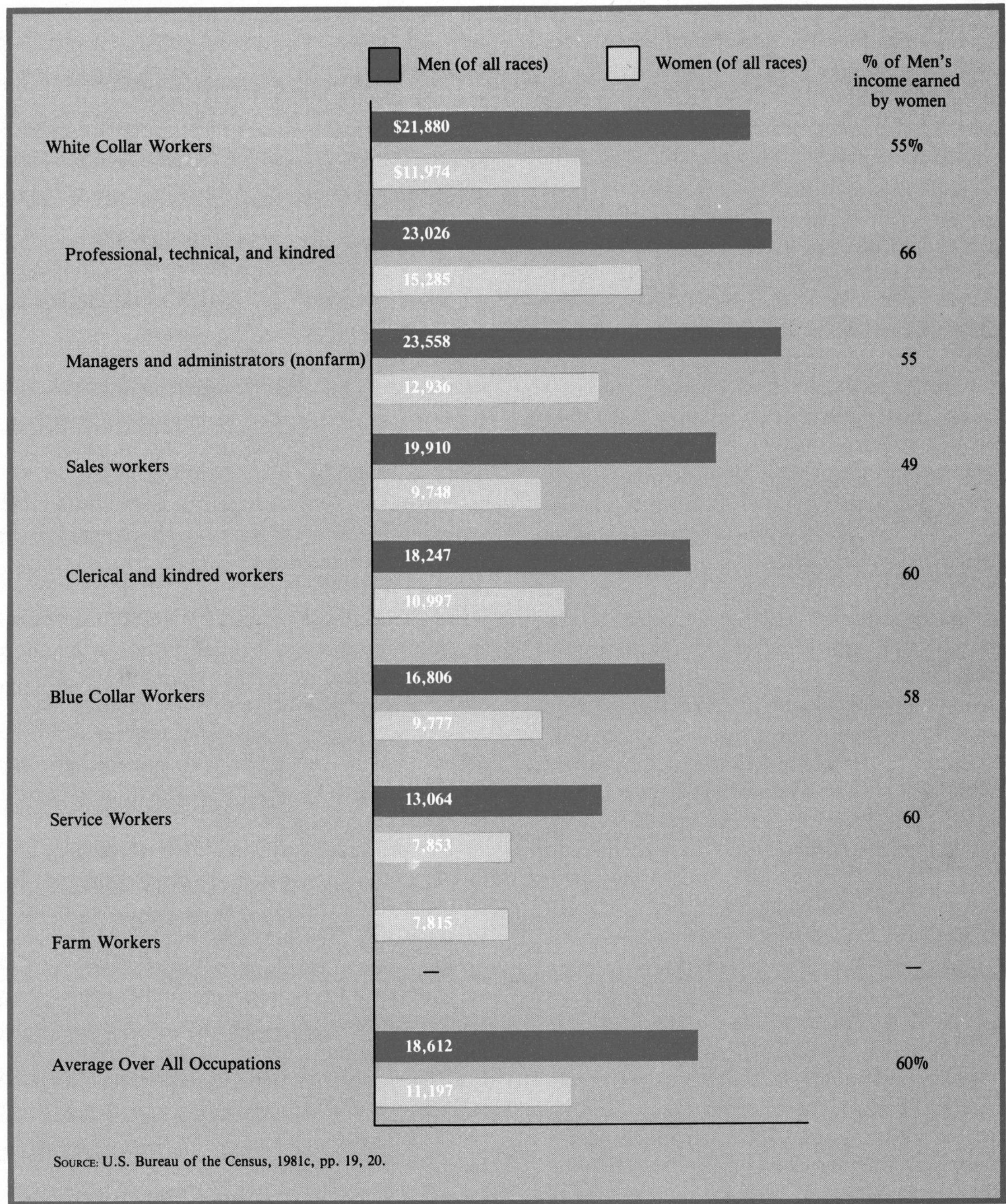

Figure 12.5 Median Income in 1980 by Occupational Group and Sex (Persons 15 years old and over, working year-round, full time)

◀ **Figure 12.4** Percentages of Men and Women in Various Occupations, 1982

(Suter and Miller, 1973). Even in medicine, where women have the same education as men, in 1978 the average income for women doctors was $39,820, compared to $67,450 for men, a gap of 41 percent (Mattera, 1980, p. 99).

Similarly, a gap of about 40 percent exists in the earnings of men and women business school graduates. Among graduates of Columbia University Graduate School of Business who had been out of school for 7 to 10 years in 1979, for example, men were earning $48,000, compared to $34,036 for women. Explanations for differences in earnings include the effect on productivity of greater job stress because one is a woman, more likelihood of holding staff rather than line positions, family duties and burdens, and (possibly) lower aspirations among women compared to men (Gallese, 1980), which may be due to how women are placed within organizations. Whatever the reasons, as long as women do not earn as much as men when they have similar educational and occupational backgrounds and achievements, sex stratification clearly exists.

Although few would disagree that women earn less than men, some assert that women own or control much of the wealth in the United States. We have already noted in Chapter 10 that the total number of wealth holders (those with estates worth more than $60,000) in the United States is relatively small. We can ask, however, whether women hold the greater share. Between 1953 and 1972, there was a slight increase in the percentage of top wealth holders who were women, from 33 percent in 1953 to 39 percent in 1972 (U.S. Bureau of the Census, 1981a, p. 454). Moreover, about half of the individuals worth $1 million or more at death were women. But 40 percent of these women were widows, most of whom, presumably, had inherited the wealth from their deceased husbands. Very often such wealth is held in trust for the children of such families, so even in this case women do not own or control an equal share of the wealth in America. Even counting those who appear to inherit their wealth relatively late in life, women only equal men; they do not surpass them (U.S. Bureau of the Census, 1978, p. 475). The figures on wealth ownership do nothing to dispel the notion that sex stratification exists in the United States.

POLITICAL PARTICIPATION

Although women have lower economic status than men, do they also have lower political status? In terms of holding elected office, the answer is "yes." In 1982, women held only 19 seats (or 4 percent of the representation) in Congress, two Senate seats, and no governorships. In 1982, 12 percent of the 7700 state legislators were women. So women are greatly underrepresented politically. They are running for political office more frequently, however. In 1980 there were 52 women candidates for the U.S. House and 1435 candidates for state legislatures. These numbers represent four times or more the number of women candidates running in 1972. Women have also increased their rates of registration and voting in national elections. Since 1978 younger groups of women were just as likely as men to be registered and to vote in national elections (*Public Opinion,* 1980).

The political participation of women is increasing, but the number of elected officials is still relatively small, suggesting significant political inequality. These formal indicators of political involvement overlook, of course, such political action as organizing community groups, the women's movement, marches, and the strikes women have participated in. Such activities are not less important than elected office; they are simply more difficult to count. Nevertheless, the participation and power of women in politics has never equaled that of men. The fact that men have dominated politics for so long is undoubtedly related to the subordinate position of women in the legal system, which has been easing only recently.

Who is this woman? In 1981, Sandra Day O'Connor was the first woman ever named to the United States Supreme Court. Her appointment symbolizes that women have made some visible gains in the occupational and political realms in recent years. At the same time, the fact that she was the first woman and remains the only woman, indicates that women still have a way to go before they achieve occupational and political equality with men.

LEGAL RIGHTS AND CRIMINAL VICTIMIZATION

Efforts to improve the legal situation of women in the United States began in 1869, when the National Woman Suffrage Association was founded and started working to get voting rights for women. An equal rights amendment to the federal Constitution was proposed as early as 1923, when it was introduced into Congress by the National Women's party. Although women were granted the vote in 1920 by the passage of the Nineteenth Amendment, wives in Alabama and Kentucky are still unable to sell or lease their own property without their husband's written approval. Only recently have certain states modified their credit regulations. Formerly, husbands were totally responsible for all bills their wives incurred, and wives had no right to obtain credit in their own names, no matter what their own incomes. Indeed, as Weitzman (1979) suggests, all states operate on an implicit, unwritten marriage contract. This contract recognizes the husband as the head of the household and holds him responsible for supporting his wife and children, and holds the wife responsible for providing domestic services and child care.

Despite the fact that an equal rights amendment was introduced into each Congress after 1923, it was not until 1972, with the support of the women's movement, that the amendment passed both houses of Congress. By January 1982, 35 states, representing 72 percent of the U.S. population, had ratified the ERA. The amendment states: "Equality of rights under the law shall not be denied or abridged by the United States or by any State on account of sex."

But later in 1982 the ERA was defeated, despite a strong last-ditch effort by women's groups. In recent years, more than half of American men and women supported the ERA, but because many state legislatures are controlled by conservative, rural males, the amendment was not ratified in 3 of the necessary 38 states.

When the Civil Rights Act of 1965 was being considered in Congress, a clause ensuring equal protection under the law regardless of sex was added by a southern Congressman as a joke in an effort to get the law defeated. The bill was passed with the clause intact, and its existence has contributed to the legal support available to women seeking equal pay for equal work. Despite the Civil Rights Act, however, women remain unequal before the law in many states.

Men and women not only have different legal rights, but they are victims of quite different kinds of crimes. Women face the risk of rape a hundred times more often than men do. In 1981 one out of every 500 women reported being raped, and the FBI estimates that probably ten times that many rapes actually occurred but were not reported. Men, on the other hand, are more likely to report being mugged, robbed, and attacked outside the home. In most states, because rape is legally defined as "an act of sexual intercourse with a female, *not one's wife,* against her will and consent" (Brownmiller, 1975), men have the legal right to rape their wives. That "right" has been challenged by several lawsuits in recent years. Additionally, a great deal of other physical abuse of women occurs in the home and is never reported to the police. "Stewart Oneglia, a female attorney who counsels victims of wife-abuse, thinks half of all American marriages may involve some physical abuse of the wife, and she doesn't mean light slaps" (Tavris and Offir, 1977, p. 20). Rather than recognizing that women are physically more vulnerable than men and trying to compensate for it, the legal system has traditionally made it difficult for women to gain legal protection or recourse—for example, from rape either in or out of marriage. As long as women are physically more vulnerable and lack adequate legal protection, equality between the sexes is in jeopardy.

HEALTH, LIFE EXPECTANCY, AND MENTAL HEALTH

Men are three times as likely as women to be murdered, and nearly three times as likely to commit suicide. The rate of violent death is much higher for men than for women, even without counting wars. Partly as a result of different rates of violent death, the average life expectancy of women born in 1979 was 77.8 years, whereas that of men was 69.9 years, a difference of nearly 8 years. Women are less likely to get serious diseases than men are. Male death rates compared to female death rates have increased for most causes of death during recent decades, including deaths from heart disease, strokes, accidents, influenza, and pneumonia. Although women have lower death rates than men, they tend to be sick more often. Between 1970 and 1980, women had 4 to 17 percent more infectious and parasitic diseases, respiratory conditions, digestive problems, and other illnesses than men did (U.S. Bureau of the Census, 1982a, p. 121).

The key question is how much these differences in life expectancy and health are caused by biological differences between the sexes and how much they are caused by social conditions that may be changing. If the fatal diseases that strike men are due in part to social stresses, then we might expect their rates to drop and the rates among women to increase as responsibilities are shared more evenly. If differential life expectancies are due to social stress factors, they may be seen as one of the costs of sex stratification borne largely by men.

Socially linked mental health problems, however, seem to bear more heavily upon women. Regardless of how mental health is defined, dozens of studies find that married women have more mental health problems than married men (Gove and Tudor, 1973; Gove, 1972). These differences do not seem to be due to biological sex differences. When Gove compared never-married men to never-married women, divorced men to divorced women, and widowed men to widowed women, the men usually had the higher rates of mental illness (Gove, 1972). Bernard (1972) found that married men were healthier both mentally and physically than single men. To control for some of the factors that may be associated with being single, researchers have compared married clergy with celibate priests and found that the married ones live longer than the single ones. Apparently, something about the structure of gender roles in marriage is helpful to men but not to women.

A wife's traditional responsibilities included living in the home established by her husband; doing the cleaning, cooking, washing; and generally caring for her husband and children. The work done in the housewife's role is generally unpaid, low in outside prestige, and involves restoring or maintaining the status quo rather than creating something new. It isolates a woman from other adults and provides little or no external recognition. Although it does provide some flexibility and autonomy during the day (much less if young children need care), it is a role that never ends. Women traditionally have little time off in the evening, on weekends, or during holidays, whereas men may sit down and relax more at home. These features of sex role behaviors have not been proved to affect the relative mental or physical health of men and women, but they do warrant further investigation. As long as the work performed by women at home has low status and few rewards, sex status will not be equal. Whenever various forms of sex stratification exist, it seems unlikely that social interaction between men and women will be equal.

SOCIAL INTERACTION AND LANGUAGE

Studies of conversations between men and women have found that women tend to be more tentative about the statements they make to men. Women often preface their remarks with qualifiers such as, "It seems to me . . . " or "Some people say . . . ." Men tend to assert: "Research shows . . . " or "Everyone knows. . . . " Even men who believe in equal rights for women frequently interrupt women when they are talking. Men, and older women for that matter, think nothing of addressing a younger to middle-aged woman as "honey" or "dear," but they never use the term when addressing men. The inappropriate use of such endearing terms tends to put down a woman's competence or authority.

As these examples illustrate, male dominance is reflected in numerous aspects of language. Within existing linguistic conventions, women lack an independent existence apart from men; their identity is presented in terms of men. Women are, it is argued, included in the generic term *man*. When two people marry, the wife has traditionally changed her name from Jane Smith to Mrs. Robert Jones. Many language practices suggest that females are immature and incompetent, whereas males are capable and complete. For example, men are seldom addressed as "boys," yet women of all ages are often called "girls" or "gals." Women still tend to be described in terms of their sexual attractiveness to men ("chick," "fox," "dog," "a ten") while men are described in terms of their sexual prowess over women ("stud," "dude," "hunk"). In a study of sexual slang, Kramer (1975) counted more than 1000 words and phrases to describe women sexually (sometimes negatively); there were many fewer words for describing men.

Thus, the language of our culture reflects many elements of the unequal status of men and women. In addition to being exposed to cultural attitudes through language, Walum (1977) argues that men and women speak differently. Consider the different impact of two reactions to an idea:

"Oh, my—such a lovely idea!"

"Damn, yes—that's a tremendous idea!"

"How come when a man does the weather forecast, he's called a 'meteorologist' . . . but when a woman does it, she's called a 'weather girl'?"

SOURCE: Used by courtesy of *New Woman*.

Walum suggests that women may be taught to appear weak, insecure, and dependent on others in the ways they express themselves. Hence language may force women to conform to the subordinate status in which society places them, therefore reaffirming in their own and others' eyes that they are indecisive or incompetent. As the next section suggests, stereotyping is not confined to language; it even appears in apparently scientific theories of the differences between men and women.

EXPLANATIONS FOR GENDER DIFFERENCES AND SEX STRATIFICATION

"Jane did that because she's a girl." "He's all boy." People operate all the time on the basis of implicit theories about why differences exist between men and women. These theories may be boiled down into those that focus on *individuals* and those that focus on *societies*. Theories about individuals attribute different status and life chances to biological differences between the sexes, or they stress the unequal socialization men and women receive. Societal theories suggest that gender roles emerge from the functions they serve in society or result from male power and domination. Considerable evidence allows us to probe both explanations.

BIOLOGICAL EXPLANATIONS

There is no denying the biological sex differences between men and women. Three factors define the sexual identity of a newborn baby: chromosomes, sex hormones, and internal sex organs and genitals. The sex of the embryo is decided by one of the 23 pairs of chromosomes (threadlike bodies that contain the genes, the determinants of heredity in all living things). In the fertilized egg cell, the mother always contributes an X chromosome; the father can provide either an X or a Y chromosome. If the father contributes an X, the child has two Xs and is a girl; if he contributes a Y, the child will have an X and a Y and be a boy. The pair of sex chromosomes determines whether the sex glands of the embryo will develop into ovaries or testes. These sex glands secrete hormones (estrogen and progesterone from the female ovaries, and testosterone and other androgens from the male testes). These hormones appear in the fetus after the twelfth week and reappear in puberty when secondary sex characteristics such as facial hair and body curves develop. In the fetus, these hormones differentiate the internal sex organs and the genitals.

In most infants, these three factors work in harmony and produce a consistent sexual identity as a male or a female. Sometimes, however, babies are born as hermaphrodites; that is, their genitals are incompletely formed or they have two sets of genitals, so their sexual identity is unclear. A child may have ovaries and a penis or be genetically male but have genitals like those of normal females. The child may be mislabeled at birth and reared as a boy or a girl, in direct contradiction to the genetic sexual identity. Such cases provide natural experiments that reveal the socially learned nature of gender identity.

In a related example, Money and Ehrhardt (1972) described a normal 7-month-old child who accidentally lost his penis during what was meant to be a routine circumcision operation. For 10 months the parents agonized over what to do. Then they decided to follow available medical advice and agree to have the boy surgically transformed into a girl. By chance, this baby boy had an identical twin brother. These two children were genetically and hormonally identical. Only their genitals and the way they were raised differed. The parents immediately began treating the new little "girl" differently. The mother let the child's hair grow longer, dressed her in pink slacks and frilly blouses, and encouraged her to wear dresses, bracelets, and hair ribbons. The mother thought the girl was much neater than her brother ("Maybe it's because I encourage it") and found her to be more willing to help with housework. Once when the young son urinated in the front yard the mother laughed, but when the daughter threw her panties over the back fence the mother gave her a little swat on the rear and told her that nice girls do not do that. For Christmas the girl wanted and received dolls, a doll house, and a doll carriage, while the boy asked for and was given a garage with cars, gas pumps, and tools. Although the girl had certain traits her mother saw as tomboyish, such as abundant physical energy, a high activity level, and bossiness among her friends, her mother thought she was not as rough as her brother.

In this and other cases of sexual reassignment, Money and Ehrhardt found that the parents reinforced different behaviors and responses in boys and girls with respect to clothing, general appearance, body movements, play, and the rehearsal of future romantic, family, academic, and vocational roles. Despite a genetic and hormonal sexual identity at odds with gender identity, these children took on the gender identities that had been socially assigned. For most people, biological and social cues interact, and the independent effect of social learning is difficult to detect because gender roles agree with sexual identities. The incongruent cases Money and Ehrhardt analyze, however, uncover the extraordinary influence of childrearing on the emergence of gender identities and behaviors. Clearly, the development of gender identity is heavily influenced by social factors. In view of this evidence, it seems unlikely that major status gaps between men and women are caused solely by biological differences.

The power of cultural rather than biological factors is heightened by considerable cross-cultural variations in what gender role behaviors are deemed appropriate for men and women. In her classic study of three New Guinea tribes, Margaret Mead (1935) found that in one, the Arapesh, both men and women were cooperative, sensitive to the needs of others, and nonaggressive—traits that are usually held to be "natural" to females. In another society, the Mundugumor, Mead found both men and women to be aggressive and unresponsive—characteristics that tend to be labeled masculine in our culture. In a third society, the Tchambuli, Mead found dominant, impersonal, and managing women living with emotionally dependent men. These cross-cultural variations suggest that cultural values and socialization rather than biological necessity are instrumental in shaping gender role behaviors and personalities. They direct our attention to the content and processes of gender role socialization.

SOCIALIZATION AS AN EXPLANATION

"Boys don't cry, girls don't swear, girls don't take their panties off, boys may (sometimes)." All children as they grow up are bombarded with directives about what they should and should not do. The directives come from parents, relatives, neighbors, friends, religious or community groups, books, television, magazines, songs, advertisements, and other aspects of culture. Many of them offer prescriptions for gender role identities.

But being *told* what boys and girls do and don't do is only one of a number of processes through which gender role expectations are conveyed. Children are praised or encouraged for what others consider to be appropriate behavior. "What a pretty, sweet little girl you are," or "My, but you're a strong young man." Besides direct verbal praise, parents and others often reward children for "being good." What they mean by "being good" varies for boys and girls, so the children must sense what is wanted and try to provide it. Acting in unacceptable ways may be ignored, discouraged, or even punished. Are girls scolded more than boys for getting their clothes dirty or for bringing their old can collections into the house? In hundreds of daily interactions, children are praised or punished for what others consider to be appropriate or inappropriate gender role behaviors.

Aside from being told what girls and boys do, and being rewarded or punished for what they do themselves, children take on gender role identities through a process called *modeling*—that is, copying the behavior of people they admire. The admired role models may be older children, adults, or even television and storybook characters. Through their own actions and attitudes, these individuals transmit messages about how members of their gender behave in particular situations.

Additionally, children may be pressured into certain kinds of role behaviors through task assignment—the jobs they are given to do around the home, in the schoolroom, or elsewhere. Girls more than boys may be asked to help their mothers with housework, whereas boys may be led by their fathers into mechanical repairs or other "masculine" chores. In a cross-cultural study of gender differences in children aged 3 through 11, Whiting and Edwards (1973) found that girls were more likely than boys to be asked to care for infants. These differences in task assignments were related to the expectation of greater nurturing behavior of girls, although when boys were also pressed into baby care, they offered as much help and support as girls did.

Task assignments can be resisted, or rebelled against, if an individual feels strongly about them, but language is a medium of socialization that saturates social life. Language tends to dissolve into our consciousness, like sugar in a cup of coffee, so it is often impossible to point to a specific word or phrase that is the offending object.

Elementary and secondary school social studies texts describe a nation created, settled, and led by men (Sadker and Sadker, 1980). In a study of children's books identified as the "very best," the books that won the coveted Caldecott Medal for the most distinguished children's picture book of the year, Weitzman et al. (1972) found females were underrepresented in titles, central roles, pictures, and stories. Most of the books were about boys, men, or animals dressed as males. For every picture of a female, there were 11 pictures of males. Such omissions may well undermine the self-esteem of girls. But the nature of socialization through language goes beyond this to include the learning of gender-specific styles of speaking.

Gender role socialization, then, operates through directives, rewards and punishment, modeling, task assignments, linguistic conventions, commissions, omissions, and styles. What are the consequences of these various forms of gender socialization?

Fear of Success?

"Anne, a medical school student, finds herself at the top of her medical school class at the end of her first semester." Ninety female undergraduates were asked to write a short story about Anne's life. The majority of women (65 percent) wrote stories with negative themes—Anne lost all her friends; she was ugly, unattractive, and lonely; and some even had her dropping out of medical school. Matina Horner, who did this research, termed these themes indicators of the "fear of success" syndrome that plagues bright women (1969). When male undergraduates were asked to complete a comparable story about John instead of Anne, they responded positively. John was portrayed as conscientious and hard-working, with a bright future. Only 9 percent of male students expressed negative themes. Horner concluded that a huge barrier of anxiety blocks the achievement of many bright women. Knowledge of Horner's research finding based on 200 undergraduates spread rapidly, and many journalists, employers, and academic administrators felt they had an explanation for why women did not achieve as well in graduate and professional school and in the world of work. The fault lay within, not outside of, women themselves.

In the years since Horner did her study, dozens of similar studies have been done in the United States and throughout the world—in Italy, Norway, the West Indies, and Yugoslavia. Criticisms of Horner have appeared, like desert flowers after a flash flood (Condry and Dyer, 1976; Hoffman, 1974; Shaver, 1976; Tresemer, 1974, 1976). Men sometimes fear success as much as women do, reported Tresemer after reviewing 67 studies. And a somewhat later study found only half as many women showing the motive to avoid success (Katz, 1972). Although "success avoidance" appears in both men and women, it seems to take different forms. Women fear social rejection if they succeed; men are more likely to question the value of success as a goal. Rather than reflecting fear of success, respondents' stories may simply reflect a realistic assessment of the results of conforming to or deviating from traditional social roles.

But it is unusual, still, for a woman to achieve Anne's level of success, and it is possible that it might elicit some negative reactions. Suppose you asked people to complete a story about an interracial couple who decided to settle in the rural South. Would everyone who predicted that bad things might happen to the couple be expressing "fear of interracial marriage," or would they simply be aware of the racist undertows in society (Condry and Dyer, 1976)? Finally, the assumption that fear of success actually affects a person's performance has been challenged. Those who were most fearful of success in Horner's group were actually honors students, suggesting that the themes in their stories did not necessarily interfere with their activities or behavior (Tresemer, 1974).

Lower Self-Esteem?

When males and females evaluate their own abilities, performances, and likelihood of future success, females tend to rank themselves lower (Crandall, 1969; Frieze, 1975; Maccoby and Jacklin, 1974; Parsons et al., 1976). Their evaluations may reflect the lower expectations of women presented in stories, on television, and in other cultural products. As in the case of the "fear of success" syndrome, however, these attitudes may not be related to actual ability, performance, or success. In addition, the somewhat lower self-esteem of women with respect to achievement does not carry over into self-esteem differences on more general measures. In global terms, self-concept refers to how one thinks about or evaluates one's self. Social psychologists try to develop scales that measure an overall feeling of satisfaction or dissatisfaction with oneself, including one's abilities, behavior, and worth. When males and females were compared on various measures of self-esteem, females were higher in 9 studies, males in 6, and there were no differences in 24 others (Maccoby and Jacklin, 1974.) Thus, with respect to overall self-esteem, girls and women do not accept for themselves the negative image society presents. Apparently differential self-esteem does not provide a full explanation for the sex differences and stratification in society.

Gender role socialization may help to explain *how* certain gender differences in behaviors or attitudes arise, but it tells us little about *why* they occur. Why did such differences in socialization arise in the first place? A major source lies in the different statuses of men and women in the adult world. Their unequal status is reflected in varied socialization experiences. To understand why unequal gender role socialization occurs, we need a societal-level explanation. Two candidates have come forward: the functional view that the existing division of labor by sex is functional for society, and the conflict view that males dominate through their superior power and control over key resources.

FUNCTIONALIST EXPLANATIONS

Functionalists argue that it was useful in traditional, tribal, and preindustrial societies for men and women to divide the work along sex lines. Mothers who bore and nursed children needed to stay near their young infants. Since they spent much of their time near home, it is likely that they took on domestic duties. The men, who tended to be physically stronger, roamed farther afield, hunting, herding, and protecting the group. In this way a division of labor developed that helped to reproduce and maintain the species.

Talcott Parsons and Robert Bales (1953) have argued that the division of labor by sex is functional for the modern family. They go on to propose that role differentiation and task specialization by sex are universal principles of family organization. They suggest that the family works best when one member, the father, assumes the *instrumental* role of supporting the family and dealing with the outside world, while the mother serves in an *expressive* role, providing the love, support, and service that sustains the family. This division of labor requires the male to be dominant and competent, and the female to be passive and nurturant.

Considerable contradictory evidence and criticism have been leveled at the functional theory. First, there are findings that challenge the universal principles of task segregation and sex role differentiation in the family. Looking at the extent to which instrumental tasks are divided in the family, in nearly half of the societies surveyed by Murdock (1978), women contributed 40 percent or more of the food supply for their society (Aronoff and Crano, 1975). Since providing food is a major instrumental task, this evidence suggests that role sharing rather than role segregation is more characteristic of the family. This undercuts the assertion that the division of labor by sex is universal and functional. If task division is not universally found and therefore not functionally necessary, it may be neither functional nor necessary in modern industrial societies. Today stength differences are irrelevant in most occupations,[1] and there are fewer families, smaller families, and many more childless families. All these factors increase opportunities for role sharing.

This argument is made by Marwell (1975), who has offered a functional explanation for the

[1]As Gloria Steinem noted, "There are really not many jobs that actually require a penis or a vagina, and all other occupations should be open to everyone."

origins of sexual differentiation. He begins by asserting that in societies where the family is assumed to be the central economic and social unit, the family must give birth to and socialize new members, produce or earn enough to support itself, and enable husbands and wives to nurture each other. These various tasks are best done by dividing the work. If tasks are assigned on the basis of sex, each family will be assured of having complementary skills. Marwell believes that in certain societies, assigning roles on the basis of sex is functional. These are societies where most people are in male-female family pairs, where the family is central for production and reproduction, and where large numbers of skills are needed to sustain the family. Nowadays, however, according to Marwell, rigid assignment to roles by sex is no longer useful. Society no longer requires that most families produce and raise many children. Economic production is highly specialized and usually occurs outside the family. Fewer skills are needed to maintain families, and therefore specialization of tasks and roles within families is no longer functional.

Finally, the rigid assignment of roles by gender may have high personal costs. Although it is unquestionably difficult for both women and men successfully to juggle a combination of career, childcare, and housework, the functional theory keeps both men and women "in their places" and denies individual preferences and options. If such a division of labor by sex was ever functional for society, its costs may have long since come to outweigh its benefits. Not all men are happy simply being providers and denying their expressiveness, and not all women are content to suppress their competence and creativity.

The functional division of labor takes a heavy toll on women. Alice Rossi (n.d.) hypothesized that women in their twenties who marry and have children will be more content initially than their agemates who are struggling through graduate school or trying to launch a new career. Sometimes beset by self-doubts, the woman who chooses a career may look longingly at her peers' cozy nests. But a decade later, when the woman hits her stride and begins to sense her own competence, the housewife feels depressed and envious. Her children are in school and she has no source of external self-esteem. Birnbaum (1975) tested Rossi's predictions with three matched samples of bright college graduates who were housewives, married professional women, and single professional women, all in their thirties. The housewives suffered from the lowest self-esteem and the most doubts about their competence, even with respect to childcare and getting along with people. They also felt the least attractive, often felt lonely, and missed the opportunity for challenge and creativity. Perhaps the saddest and most surprising finding was that the married professionals were more likely to be happy in their marriages than the housewives who devoted all their time to their families. More than half of the housewives (52 percent) saw marriage as burdensome, demanding, and restricting; only 19 percent of married professional women felt this way. This finding hardly suggests an ideal situation for those housewives or their husbands.

Although Marwell and other functionalists may explain how sex differences arose in an earlier era, they do not explain sex stratification. Specifically, they do not explain why one set of tasks is considered more valuable and important than another. The functionalist theory of stratification assumes that all societies have certain tasks to perform, and that members of society must be motivated to do those jobs. To explain sex stratification, functionalists need to assume that the tasks women do are either less important or easier than the tasks men do. Further, functionalists need to show that sex stratification somehow aids the survival, maintenance, or well-being of society. Finally, a functional explanation would need to show how even when continuously bearing and raising children was no longer needed for the biological survival of a

The rigid assignment of occupational or other roles by gender may have high personal costs. This woman construction worker and male nurse have decided to pursue their own interests despite the sexual stereotypes that surround the work they want to do.

group, it was necessary for women to remain in private roles (Nielsen, 1978). Functionalists have not been able to demonstrate these points. They have also been unable to show that the division of labor by sex is universal and therefore necessary for society. If the division of labor was ever functional, today its costs outweigh its benefits for individuals and for society. Functionalist theory may explain the origin of sex differentiation, but it fails to explain sexual stratification. Therefore, we need to look at another idea—namely, that sex stratification is explainable in terms of power and dominance.

POWER AND DOMINANCE (CONFLICT) EXPLANATIONS

Males dominate females because of their superior power and control over key resources, according to a conflict explanation of gender differences. Several theories attempting to explain the origins of male dominance have been offered. Anthropologist Levi-Strauss (1956) suggests that the inequality of women may have originated in the way they were exchanged among men to build up new families. Another anthropologist, Marvin Harris (1977), suggests that as early tribal societies expanded in size, they began to compete with neighboring tribes for hunting, herding, or growing lands. If population pressures continued to build, that competition often took the form of warfare. In the hand combat forms of warfare those tribes practiced, the greater physical strength of males became a valuable asset for the group. The greater value placed on males was reflected in female infanticide and in male supremacist values and sex roles.

Sociologist Randall Collins (1975) argues that the superior physical strength of men in relation to women is the source of their dominance. In the early years of human life, the theory goes, men dominated women through their physical stength. Women could be beaten, raped, or otherwise forced to do men's will. Once physical domination was established, men began developing ideologies to support their elevated position. These ideologies served to place mental and emotional shackles on women, with the result that they did not always need to be controlled by physical force. The possibility of force was ever-present, however, with both men and women knowing it could be activated any time. Some sociologists argue that Collins should not be taken seriously on this point, but his idea does offer one explanation for sexual stratification, since every system of domination ultimately relies on the superior force of the dominant group.

A major consequence of male domination was the exploitation of women by men. Very simply, exploitation means that men and women make unequal exchanges, with men usually getting the better deal. Unequal relations are in the interests of the dominant group, since the subordinate position of women benefits men, who retain greater economic, political, and social power and status. As long as the dominant group benefits from existing arrangements, it has little incentive to change them. In this way, gender stratification resembles stratification by class and race.

These types of stratification are also similar in that members of the subordinate group are affected by unequal control over productive resources, wealth, income, political power, and legal supports. They have unequal status compared to the dominant group in virtually all spheres of social life. Similarities also arise between race and sex when we address the question of whether the position of women and minorities has improved over the years. For both race and sex, we can ask with respect to what have conditions improved? Do we compare the past and present status of women (or minorities, in which case both appear to have made tremendous progress), or do we compare them to men (or whites, in which case they appear to have made only small gains or to have lost ground)? In a related vein, we can trace the rise of an egalitarian ideology for both minorities and women, but we can distinguish this from the condition of actual equality that may or may not have accompanied the ideology.

A final point of similarity arises in the fact that the balance of power in society, whether based on race, sex, or class, has major implications for personal interactions (Hochschild, 1973; Collins, 1975; Etheridge, 1974). Subordinates tend to be more sensitive to their superiors—students "psych out" their professors, maids know when their employers are in good moods, children learn to make requests at opportune times, and women learn to "read" the motives of husbands and bosses. Dominants are allowed certain familiarities—touching, first-naming, whistling—which subordinates are not. Dominants also maintain greater social distance and disclose less personal information (Hochschild, 1973). They might, for instance, ask about the elevator operator's children, but would not expect to be asked such a question in return. All these interpersonal differences work to maintain social inequalities by sex, race, or class. They are similar in that they affect our everyday lives and they are difficult to eliminate.

Gender stratification differs from racial stratification because women are not a numerical minority, although their lower status has sometimes been compared to that of a minority group (Hacker, 1951, p. 60–69). (Stratification by sex and race are compared in Table 12.2.) Differences also arise from the fact that women are married to men at all levels of the class system, but at any particular level they have less power and status than their male counterparts. At the same time, they may exercise some dominance over men and women in the lower classes. This exercise of dominance may reduce their dissatisfaction with gender inequality. The intimate relation between men and women in marriage may dampen sexual solidarity among women, a dam-

Table 12.2 Stratification by Sex and by Race

Similarities	Differences
Difference from the dominant group is usually evident at first sight.	Women are not a numerical minority, whereas most racial and ethnic groups are.
Unequal relations are in the interest of the dominant group, which has little incentive to change.	Women are born into, or marry into, all levels of the class structure. At any given level, however, they have less power and status than their male counterparts. Racial minorities are more likely to be in the lower social classes.
Subordinate group has unequal wealth, income, political, and legal support.	Gender solidarity may be dampened by intimate relations in marriage and by the status differences women derive from their husbands.
Inequalities are justified by myths or ideologies, such as the alleged genetic inferiority of blacks or "a woman's place is in the home."	
The gap between dominant and subordinate groups has remained fairly large over time.	
These inequalities persist despite the existence of a societal ideology of equality.	
Inequalities are reflected in personal interactions. Subordinates are more sensitive to dominants; dominants are familiar with subordinates.	

per that does not occur in attempts to change inequalities of class, race, or religion (Rossi, 1972).

EVALUATION OF THE FOUR EXPLANATIONS

Although on the face of it the biological and socialization explanations may seem contradictory and at odds with each other (another version of the old nature-nurture controversy), they actually share a number of common assumptions. They both "blame the victim" for the situation, saying that women are in the predicament because of some deficiency in their own makeup (even if it is not their fault). Furthermore, by focusing only on individuals, both explanations deflect attention from the larger social structures that may create the culture or behavior being observed.

The biological, socialization, and functional explanations all provide a seemingly scientific basis for supporting the status quo; they are legitimating ideologies that appear to be grounded in science. Conflict theory agrees with the functional and socialization theories in stressing that most important sex differences (except for size and strength) are social rather than biological in origin. The functional explanation differs sharply from the conflict theory in the way it suggests that socialization practices arise out of societal "needs" that are functional for society as a whole. The conflict view asserts that socialization practices stem from societal inequalities and the different interests of more powerful people. The theories also differ with respect to the results of socialization. Functionalists stress gender differences, but downplay the stratification that accompanies them. Conflict theorists minimize gender differences and focus on sex stratification with respect to status, power, income, and wealth.

These views are not merely topics for an academic debate; they directly affect the lives of men and women in society today. Whatever theory each of us accepts shapes our view of what needs changing and how it might be changed most effectively.

PROSPECTS FOR EQUALITY BETWEEN THE SEXES

To assess the future of gender roles in the United States, we will consider the forces that have influenced change up to the present, identify the conditions apparently necessary for achieving greater equality between the sexes, and point out possible alternatives. At the outset, we should clarify a point of confusion that frequently arises. Equality does not mean that everyone has to be exactly the *same*. It does mean that groups have equal power and resources which give them the freedom to be different. Not all differences are reflected in stratification by status, power, or wealth. For those who enjoy the variety of different people, and particularly the variety between the sexes, this may be a reassuring distinction.

FORCES THAT BROUGHT US TO WHERE WE ARE TODAY[2]

Several major factors have contributed to the changing reproductive and productive roles of women in society. These include major female life cycle changes, improved contraceptive technology, labor market demands, and social movements pressing for equality without regard to race, creed, or sex. In recent years the female life cycle and the reproductive role have been transformed. Childbearing is no longer the central fact of a woman's life. Whereas women once spent most of their adult years bearing and rearing children, they now spend less than 15 per-

[2]This section and the next have benefited greatly from Etheridge (1974) and from numerous conversations with her, and from Nielsen (1978).

cent of their lives doing so. When her youngest child starts school, the average mother still has 40 years of life left (Sullerot, 1971).

Control over Reproduction

Part, but not all, of this change is due to the nearly complete control women can exercise over their reproductive potential. They can limit and time their children (or opt not to have any, as increasing numbers of women are doing), yet need not restrict their sexual activity to do so. This reproductive control makes married women available for work. The demands of the labor market and the shortage of unmarried women workers greatly increased the number of married women who entered the work force between 1960 and 1980, gradually changing the norms surrounding the employment of married women. These changes in reproductive technology and labor market participation, along with the civil rights movement, undoubtedly influenced the women's movement.

The Women's Movement

In 1961 President John F. Kennedy appointed a National Commission on the Status of Women. This group, and similar ones at the state level, documented the current status of women in the United States and developed a network of concerned women. In 1964, Title VII of the Civil Rights Act made discrimination on the basis of sex illegal. However, the members of the Equal Employment Opportunity Commission (the EEOC), the federal agency empowered to enforce the act, did not want to extend it to include sex discrimination. The ensuing confrontation between women and EEOC officials encouraged the formation of the National Organization for Women (NOW). This group constitutes the older branch of the women's movement. It has focused on extending civil rights to all people, including women. Basically reformist in orientation, NOW has aimed at obtaining equal pay for equal work, equality before the law, credit equality, and at opening traditionally male career lines to women. In general, its strategies have included collective efforts to change existing political structures and policies through lobbying, letter writing, political marches, and media coverage.

Meanwhile, younger activist women were becoming disenchanted with the sexist attitudes and behaviors of male leaders of the political New Left. Two identifiable groups of younger feminists emerged, the radical feminists and the socialist feminists. The former see sex stratification as rooted in a man's desire to have his ego override that of a woman. They call for the elimination of all sex distinctions and especially all male privileges. The socialist feminists see sex stratification as arising from the economic system; that is, women contribute profits by serving as low-paid labor and as a reserve labor force.

Both types of younger feminists favor a complete social and political restructuring of society. In her analysis of the women's movement, Freeman (1975) suggests that the combined efforts of younger and older feminists contributed to the movement's early success. This success has begun to lay the groundwork for greater equality between men and women. At the same time, feminists have made social scientists aware of the need to identify the conditions under which equality is more or less likely to occur.

CONDITIONS NECESSARY FOR EQUALITY

A major way that social analysts work to discover conditions that are critical for a particular social state—in this case equality between the sexes—is by comparing a number of different situations that vary in at least one major respect. Etheridge (1978) used this method in examining family systems in the Oneida community (a utopian community in upstate New York begun in the mid-nineteenth century), Israeli *kibbutzim,* several U.S. mountain communes, and dual-career families in the United States and

Social analysts suggest that equality between the sexes requires economic independence for men and women, commitment to an ideology of equality, task-sharing in the public and private realms, and help with childcare.

Great Britain. From this comparative analysis, she was able to discern four conditions necessary for equality between the sexes. First, men and women need to be economically independent. This factor is a necessary but not a sufficient condition, which means that equality will not occur without it, but by itself it is not enough to ensure that equality does occur. Economic independence occurs when men and women have equal access to the productive process and receive equal shares for their contributions. Second, participants need to be committed to an ideology of equality. Without that commitment, there is no will to make the practical arrangements at home and at work that are necessary to ensure the realization of equality. The third condition is equal task allocation in public and private spheres. It flows directly from the commitment to an ideology of equality and means that men and women need to participate equally in central societal policy-making and administrative positions.

This condition is essential for gender equality because people with relatively more information, access to resources, and control over decisions feel and are, in fact, more powerful in their daily lives (Etheridge, 1978). Anyone who withdraws into the private world of the family will have less status in society than a partner who is active in the outside world. Public and private tasks need to be equally allocated between men and women; when tasks are assigned on the basis of gender, they become a major means of maintaining different and invariably unequal definitions of "masculine" and "feminine." Fourth, equal sharing of public and private tasks means that both partners will be able to work less or that some form of help with childrearing must exist. Otherwise, parents who are working, caring for children, and housekeeping are likely to become overloaded.

We can pursue this line of reasoning further. If the above four conditions are the ones necessary to achieve equality between the sexes, how can those conditions be met? In a period of rapid inflation, the two-income family is becoming a necessity in many cases.[3] In low-income homes, two incomes can ensure that the family is fed and can stay together. In higher-income families, two earners can ensure better housing, education, health care, and recreational opportunities for the family. In periods of unemployment, the two-income family has more of a cushion than the single-earner family in which the sole breadwinner may become unemployed.

Does encouraging women who want to work, and supporting equal pay for equal work (on the principle of fairness if nothing else), mean that men favor dividing the housework as well? Men and women under 45, blacks, and working women generally consider the most satisfying kind of marriage to be one where both husband and wife have jobs and both take care of the house and children (Figure 12.6). At every age group except one, women favor this arrangement somewhat more than men do. The notable exception occurs among 18- to 29-year-old men, where 73 percent prefer such a marriage compared to 62 percent of women of that age. Incidentally, men are also more likely to favor women participating in a military draft; 51 percent of men compared to 42 percent of women favor such participation.

Opinion surveys reveal what people think, like, and feel, but it is always interesting to compare such polls with what people actually do. Studies of how people spend their time show that women consistently spend more time in family care than men do. Married housewives spent the most time (more than 50 hours per week in 1975), followed by employed married women (29 hours per week), employed single women (21 hours per week), employed married men (9 hours per week), and employed single men (8 hours per week) (Robinson, 1976, in U.S. Department of Commerce, 1980, p. 559). For married working women, this time must be subtracted from time available for leisure activity. There was a slight increase in the amount of family care time men spent in 1975 compared with 1965, and a somewhat greater decrease for women during those 10 years, so perhaps some progress is being made. Despite the large differences that remain, however, only 19 percent of all women interviewed in one national study said they wanted more help from their husbands (Robinson and Robinson, 1975). It is possible that just as men may defend their occupational territories against invasions from women, many women may still want to preserve their control over the home territory (Etheridge, 1974).

A major study of how people in 12 countries[4] spend their time found remarkably similar time allocations by sex in all the countries (Szalai, 1972). What suffers most is the chance for fathers to spend time with their children. The average American father, for instance, spends only 12 minutes with his children per day (Stone, 1972). Many fathers would consider it a plus to be able to spend more time with their children.

If men assume more home responsibilities, that change may sometimes add to the demands

[3]Between 1948 and 1965, the Consumer Price Index rose at an average annual rate of about 1.7 percent. From 1970 to 1981, however, the average annual increase was 7.9 percent (U.S. Bureau of the Census, 1981, p. 467). Many single-income families are not able to keep pace with the rate of inflation.

[4]The countries studied were Belgium, Bulgaria, Czechoslovakia, East Germany, France, Hungary, Peru, Poland, the Soviet Union, the United States, West Germany, and Yugoslavia.

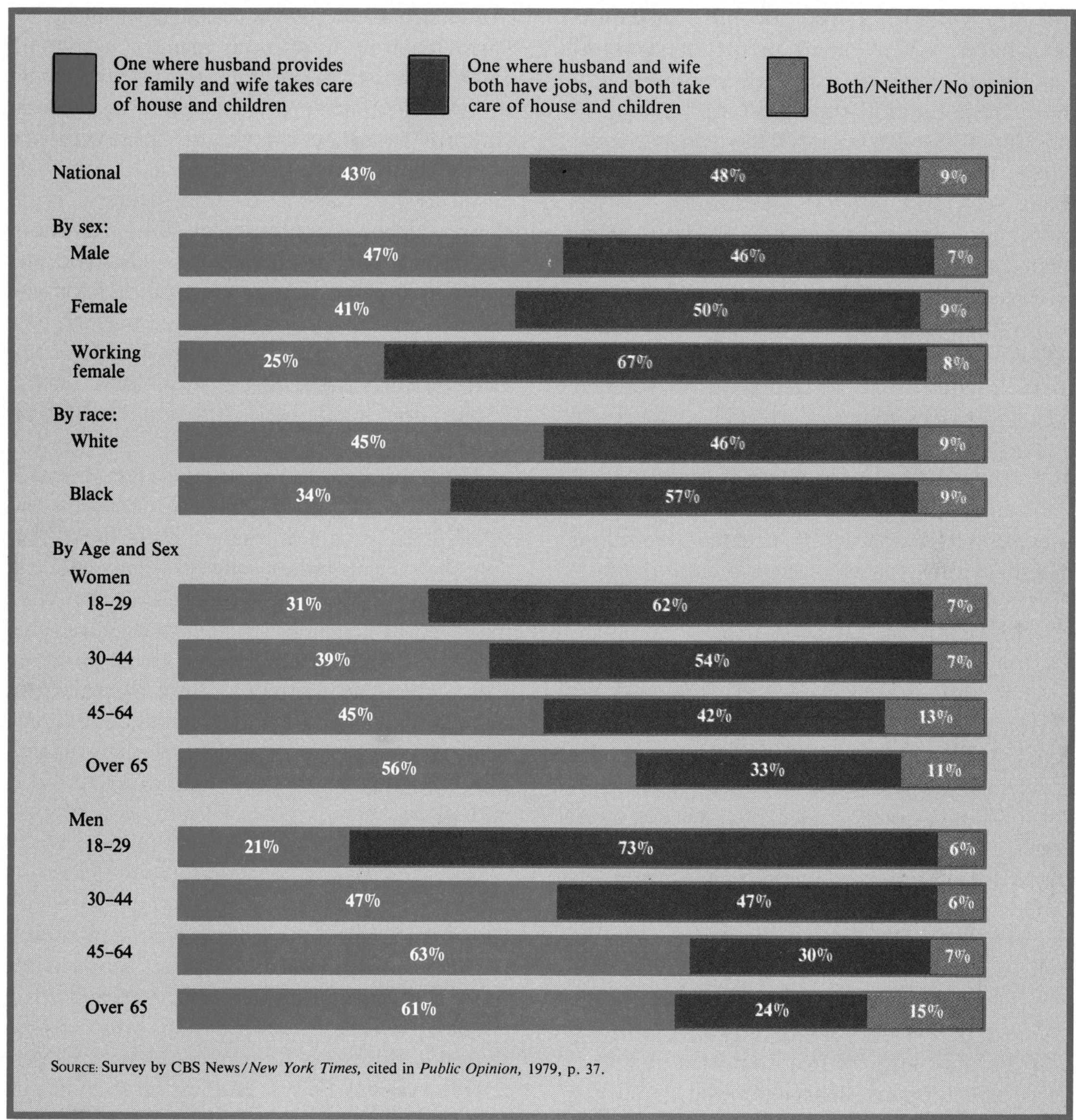

Figure 12.6 Views of What Kind of Marriage Is More Satisfying

they face but reduce them at other times. If men help with children, laundry, and cooking, women may feel free to do carpentry, electrical, and auto repairs, to rake leaves, shovel snow, or mow lawns, depending on their skills. Thus, men may no longer be held responsible for all the traditionally male activities around the home. Farrell (1976) describes other benefits that equality between the sexes may bring to men. Women who have their own lives to control may make less effort to control their husbands' lives. When a man's partner is economically independent, he may be freer to choose a more interesting low-paying position instead of a boring higher-paying job. Men may lose some of the legal burdens that discriminate against them, such as automatic responsibility for alimony, jury duty, and a mandatory later retirement age under social security.

Altogether, Farrell discusses 21 benefits men may obtain from equality between the sexes. Possibly because they are beginning to perceive these benefits, a substantial majority of younger men favor a marriage in which both husband and wife work and share the care of the house and children, as already noted in Figure 12.6. But of the three possible models for equality that exist, only one appears to meet the conditions described above. They warrant a closer look.

POSSIBLE MODELS FOR EQUALITY[5]

Sex and race share potential models for social equality. In the pluralist model, racial or gender differences are retained and valued for their diversity. But defining gender differences as equal does not eliminate structured inequalities. Moreover, pluralism suggests that existing sex differences are inevitable and permanent. Hence, the pluralist model makes true gender equality quite unlikely.

In the assimilation model, those historically excluded on the basis of race or gender are gradually brought into the mainstream as they shed their psychological, behavioral, and social distinctions and take on the language, approach, and life-styles of the dominant groups in society. In this view the way for women to achieve equality is to become more like men. This model is consistent with socialization explanations, and it assumes that the structure of American society needs no changing. It overlooks the fact that many male achievements rest heavily on the donated labor of wives who manage home and childcare duties, along with social and civic responsibilities, while the top strata of business and professional occupations are filled with men who devote nearly every ounce of their life blood to their careers. Younger feminists reject this model because they find existing institutions and practices to be oppressive, and they consider many "masculine" traits such as aggression and competitiveness to be undesirable in both men and women. Instead, they suggest the positive value of such traditionally "feminine" traits as cooperation, tenderness, and emotional sensitivity.

The hybrid model proposed by Rossi (1972) calls for a society in which both dominant and subordinate members change their lives. This approach rejects biologically fixed fates, the traditional institutional structures erected by white males, and the gender-specific socialization that accompanies them. It seeks a social order in which creativity and community are valued as much as efficiency and effectiveness, and family, fellowship, and play are on a par with work, politics, and finance for men and women, blacks and whites.

THE CASE OF SWEDEN

Clearly the hybrid model calls for a humanizing of public institutions and actions. At the same time, it may require more efficiency and effectiveness in the management of housekeeping duties. Both sexes will be called upon to perform a wide variety of tasks, ranging from child care to auto maintenance to finance. To realize this model, women and men will need to share equally in both societal and domestic policymaking and implementation. Sweden is one country that has moved in this direction. It has a national commitment to freeing women and men from traditional sex role demands. As the Swedish government stated in a report to the United Nations in 1968, the status of women

[5]This section draws heavily on Rossi (1972).

cannot be improved simply by having special measures aimed only at women. Instead, it is equally necessary to remove conditions that give men special privileges (Swedish Institute, 1979). Policy statements by political parties, government agencies, trade unions, and the news media stress that both men and women are obligated to support the family and share childrearing and homecare activities.

A major reason behind these policies has been the need for women's labor in Sweden's expanding economy (Haas, 1980). In addition, women have gained political strength—for example, doubling their representation in Parliament from 13 percent to 27 percent in the 1970s (Wistrand, 1979). Equal pay for equal work is stated in national laws, and built into labor contracts (Baude, 1979). Taxation is based on individual earnings rather than combined family income. Schools discuss the importance of equal sex roles in the family (Baude, 1979). So it may not be surprising that in 1978, nearly 71 percent of all unmarried and married Swedish women worked, compared to 88 percent of all men. Nearly half of all women work part-time (Swedish Institute, 1979).

In their attitudes, Swedes support domestic role sharing. When asked for an opinion on the statement "If the wife works outside the home, then the husband and wife should share equally in the care of the home and children," 93 percent of women and 83 percent of men surveyed by Haas (1980) agreed completely. In practice, however, sex role equality lags behind official policy and individual values. To find out about practice, Haas asked: "Who has the main responsibility for the daily care of the home?" Only 17 percent of couples said they shared the care evenly; 23 percent said it was a little more the woman's job; and 58 percent said it was mostly the woman's responsibility. Only 2 percent of the couples indicated that the man was more or mainly responsible for home care. Specific housekeeping tasks divided about the same way.

So, although Swedish policy and attitudes toward sex roles are less traditional than American ones, actual practices are somewhat traditional. Younger people are much more likely to practice role sharing, however, and this trend may increase in the future (Haas, 1980). The prestige of a woman's occupation and her income were both positively related to role sharing, suggesting that even in Sweden interpersonal gender roles are linked to resources such as income, power, and prestige.

Summary

1. In the past 25 years, life scripts for American women have changed dramatically from a passive focus on husband, children, and home to an image of active life choices involving various combinations of family and work.

2. That shift is reflected in the distinction between sex and gender. Sex indicates one's biological identity as a male or female; gender refers to the traits and behaviors culturally defined as masculine or feminine.

3. Whereas gender differences focus on variations in the social positions, roles, behaviors, and attitudes of men and women in a society, sex stratification refers to the way sex differences and gender roles are unequally ranked with respect to power and prestige.

4. Sex stratification is revealed in the relative political power, sexual freedom, and wealth available to men and women in a society.

5. Sex stratification may be affected by which relatives live together, inheritance patterns, and rules surrounding marriage.

6. Sex stratification is revealed in the dramatic differences in the life chances of men and women. Educationally, women will be earning about the same number of bachelor's degrees as men by 1985, but they still lag in advanced and professional degrees and they do not study the same fields as men.

7. Although women comprise 42 percent of the labor force, they are still overrepresented in the traditionally "female" occupations of nursing, library science, teaching, and social work, and are underrepresented in such "male" occupations as engineering, law, medicine, and the ministry. Today 80 percent of clerical jobs are held by women, compared to only 25 percent of all management and administrative jobs.

8. Women earn only sixty cents for every dollar that men earn, and major differences remain even when education, occupation, and experience are the same. Men control a larger share of wealth as well as of income.

9. Although women have stepped up their political participation in recent years, they still comprise only a small minority of elected officials. Legally men and women still do not have equal rights and responsibilities. Despite majority support among both men and women, the Equal Rights Amendment to the U.S. Constitution was not ratified.

10. Men and women face different forms of criminal victimization. Women face the risk of rape a hundred times more often than men do. Men are more likely to be robbed, mugged, attacked, and murdered. The average life expectancy for men is 69.5 years, compared to 77.2 years for women. Married women have more mental health problems than married men, but unmarried women have fewer mental health problems than unmarried men.

11. Both social interaction and language reveal differences between men and women.

12. Biological, socialization, functional, and conflict theories have been offered to explain sex differences and sex stratification. Cases of children of one biological sex who were reassigned to the other sex and reared as a member of that sex demonstrate the power of socialization in the learning of gender roles. This evidence, along with widely varied gender-linked behaviors in other cultures, suggests that cultural values and socialization rather than biological necessity are the strongest influence on gender behaviors. Socialization occurs through being told what is appropriate, modeling, task assignment, teaching materials, styles of speaking, and forms of address.

13. Some suggest that "fear of success" among women is one of the consequences of differential gender role socialization, but the evidence for this fear is mixed and less overwhelming than originally suggested. Research on self-esteem is also mixed.

14. Both functional and conflict explanations go beyond individual-level explanations to societal-level explanations and therefore can help to explain differential gender socialization. Functionalists argue that task specialization by sex is functional for the family and society, with the husband assuming the instrumental breadwinning role and the wife taking on the expressive and nurturant role. Evidence suggests that although combining work and family responsibilities is difficult, the option of doing so is more satisfying for many men and women. Functionalism helps to explain the origin of sex differentiation, but not its persistence as sex stratification.

15. The conflict and domination view of sex stratification suggests that men fare better economically and socially than women because of their superior power and resources.

16. Women share certain similarities with minority groups, but they differ in terms of numerical strength, varied class membership, and marriage ties.

17. The changing roles of men and women are related to female life cycle changes, improved contraception, labor market demands, the women's movement, and the growing economic necessity for two incomes.

18. To achieve equality between the sexes, men and women need equal access to the productive process, a commitment to an egalitarian ideology, equal participation in public and private life, and help with childcare.

19. Three models for equality exist: the pluralist, assimilation, and hybrid models. Sweden has set national policies aimed at furthering an egalitarian society that somewhat resembles the hybrid model.

Key Terms

bilateral
gender
gender differences
gender roles
matrilineal descent system
matrilocal residence pattern
monogamy
patrilineal system
patrilocal residence pattern
polyandry
polygyny
sex
sex stratification

Part Four

Social Institutions

Chapter 13

The Family

Everyone is talking about the American family. Some say it is dying, others say it is adapting to social change. Some see it as the center of meaning and intimacy in people's lives, others charge that it is a nest of emotional, social, and physical abuse. These contradictory charges clearly suggest that the family is an important institution for a lot of people and for society. Why else would so many people be giving so much thought to it?

The United States Census defines a *family* as two or more persons who are related to each other by blood, marriage, or adoption and who live together. Many people would broaden this definition to include, for example, the family units of college students who live away from home. Some people feel the definition should be widened further still to include adults who are not relatives but who have made a commitment to each other and want to live together in some sense as a family—for instance, two unrelated old people or homosexual couples. The above definition differs from a more traditional conception of the *nuclear family* which consists of a mother, a father, and their children. Sometimes sociologists and anthropologists use the term *conjugal family* instead of nuclear family to refer to the same unit.

In the conjugal family, primary emphasis is on the husband-wife relationship rather than on either of their blood relatives. The conjugal family may be far removed from its relatives, as when a husband and wife and their unmarried children move to a distant city, away from the rest of their blood relatives. An *extended family* is one in which relatives from several generations live together. These various definitions of the family reflect changing social patterns. In the United States, for example, only about a quarter of all households by 1990 are expected to consist of a married couple with one or more dependent children (Masnick and Bane, 1980). The others will consist of various combinations of individuals living together or alone. Whatever its form, the family is a unit within a larger kinship network. *Kinship* refers to socially defined family relationships, including those based on common parentage, marriage, or adoption.

In this chapter we will begin by exploring the functions the family has traditionally filled in societies, and then consider the extent to which those functions are being filled in other ways in contemporary industrial societies. Along with changes in the traditional functions, family forms and activities are changing dramatically, as we will see. Various forms of family interaction are considered next, including conflict and violence in the family, a topic that has recently received heightened attention. The final section examines the views of people who challenge the contemporary family and propose changing it in quite different ways.

THE FUNCTIONS OF THE FAMILY

Traditionally, the family as an institution has served a number of important functions in society, including sexual regulation, biological reproduction, the care and socialization of the young, the economic functions of providing food, shelter, and warmth for family members, and emotional intimacy. In most societies, few institutions could fill these functions better than the family. It is worth considering each of these functions and how they are changing.

SEXUAL REGULATION

Sex is an important drive in human beings, and it has the potential for disrupting relationships in social groups. For this reason, virtually every society has developed norms governing sexual relations. In all societies, various categories of sexual relations are possible, including marital sexual relations, incest, and homosexual relations, for example. *Marriage* is a social institution that recognizes and approves the sexual union of two or more individuals and includes a set of mutual rights and obligations. Virtually all societies encourage sex within marriage and forbid incest, but how other forms of sexual relations are regulated varies widely. Western societies, at least until recently, have generally forbidden everything except marital sexuality. In the 115 societies around the world that Murdock (1967) studied, however, only three were as strict as Western societies. About 70 percent of them allowed sexual freedom prior to marriage.

Some social analysts have suggested that sexual regulation increased when private property and a surplus of food or wealth developed, because the existence of inheritable property made it important to establish the legitimacy of heirs. The desire to regulate reproduction naturally focused on sexual relations. Since the development of effective methods of birth control, however, the societal need for regulating sexual relations may have declined, although species reproduction is still a major concern of many families.

When birth control made it possible to separate sex from reproduction, the effort to confine sex to married partners lost steam. Premarital relations are becoming increasingly acceptable in many subgroups. In 1969, only 23 percent of respondents to a Gallup poll felt that premarital sex was acceptable, compared to 59 percent in 1978 (Public Opinion, 1980b). Among college freshmen in 1981, nearly half agreed with the statement "If two people really like each other, it's all right for them to have sex even if they've known each other for only a very short time" (Astin, King, and Richardson, 1981, p. 56). Younger, more educated individuals appear to be more accepting of premarital sexual relations than do other groups in the population.

Two-thirds of all Americans say they know at least one couple living together without marriage. Young adults, the better-educated, the single, and the divorced are more likely to number such couples among their friends or acquaintances than are widowers, men over 65, and less-educated women. Just knowing such couples, however, does not mean that people approve of them. Nationally, nearly half of respondents felt that it was "morally wrong" for couples to live together without being married (Yankelovich, Skelly, and White, 1977). More than half felt that unmarried couples living together was not a moral issue. College students go even further. Two out of five in 1981 agreed with the statement "A couple should live together for some time before deciding to get married" (Astin, King, and Richardson, 1981, p. 56). Aside from not finding such behavior morally wrong, many seem to consider it socially valuable for people to live together before deciding to marry.

The growing acceptance of premarital sex has not been paralleled by a similar approval of extramarital sexual relations, however. About 80 percent of the population feels that infidelity among married men and women is morally wrong (Yankelovich, Skelly, and White, 1977).

BIOLOGICAL REPRODUCTION

All societies need to reproduce their members. The needs of societies, however, vary widely. When people had a relatively short life span and infant mortality was high, it was important that as many families as possible be formed in order to raise as many children as possible. Societies therefore placed great value on fertility and reproduction. Modern industrial societies show opposite tendencies. Life expectancy has been extended greatly, and infant mortality rates have dropped. As a result, it is no longer widely believed that people should have as many children as possible.

In recent years, biological reproduction has been increasing outside the family. In 1979, more than half a million babies were born to unmarried women, 17 percent of all live births that year. By contrast, in 1950 only 4 percent of all babies were born to unmarried women (U.S. Bureau of the Census, 1981a, p. 65). Nearly half those babies born in 1979 had mothers who were 19 years old or less, and more than half were born to black women. Adolescent parenthood is concentrated among youth of low socioeconomic status (SES) and is much rarer among high-SES youth (Haggstrom and Morrison, 1979a). These figures reflect the so-called rise in teenage pregnancy that has been so much in the news in recent years. Despite these changes, the majority (68 percent) of Americans in 1978 believed that it was "morally wrong" for people to decide "to have children even though they are not legally married and don't intend to be" (Yankelovich, Skelly, and White, March 1978).

What are the consequences of teenage pregnancy for the married or unmarried teenagers involved? Adolescent parents are more likely than married adolescent nonparents to experience marital disruption (Haggstrom and Morrison, 1979a). They are also more likely to have future children at a faster pace (Haggstrom and Morrison, 1979a; Bumpass et al., 1978; Trussell and Menken, 1978). Adolescent parents expect to get somewhat less education than nonparents (Haggstrom and Morrison, 1979a, p. 31). All these factors may hurt their prospects for caring for children.

CARE AND SOCIALIZATION OF THE YOUNG

Humans require many years of nurture and socialization before they are ready and able to become full-fledged members of their society. The care and the socialization of the young ensure that a society will have cultural as well as biological reproduction. Every effort is made to teach new members the norms, values, beliefs, and behaviors appropriate for membership in that society. In a fairly simple society, such as that of hunters and gatherers, virtually everyone of the same age and sex learned similar norms and values. In more complex societies, however, there is considerable variation in the content of social learning and teaching, in accordance with the class, ethnic group, or nationality of an individual. Such societies reproduce themselves socially, and groups within the society reproduce features of the subgroup's culture from one generation to the next. Part of the cultural content transmitted from one generation to the next may include the social relations between various groups. The family is an important means of such social and cultural reproduction.

Given the increasing numbers of children born to single parents, however, and the rising divorce rate among very young parents, how are the 12 million children of such families being cared for and socialized? Some single parents do not work, feeling that they should stay home and care for their children. Others share the responsibility for childcare with relatives, neighbors, and friends (Kamerman, 1979; Stack, 1974). More children attend preprimary programs than in the past, although higher-income

The family is a key provider of childcare and socialization of the young. In contemporary Western societies, families are also expected to offer emotional intimacy to their members.

families are more likely than lower-income families to enroll their children in such programs. Slightly more single parents report that they do not have enough time to help their children with their homework in the evenings than do individuals in two-parent families (Dearman and Plisko, 1979). The difficulties of childcare and socialization are compounded when parents are themselves very young, lack education, are unable to obtain decent jobs, and are poor.

ECONOMIC FUNCTIONS

To survive, all societies must meet the subsistence needs of their members: food, shelter, and warmth. The family has been a traditional means for seeing that the dependent members of a society were cared for by other members who were able to produce the necessary food and shelter. With the advent of industrialization, more and more individuals stopped producing food and shelter themselves and began working for others in exchange for money. The money was used to purchase economic necessities for themselves and their families.

In recent years, especially in Western societies, women have been increasingly able to work outside the home. Although they still do not earn as much as men, they are able to meet some of their subsistence needs without depending on a male earner. Some of the economic functions traditionally performed by women in the family, such as cooking, sewing, and canning, have been learned by men or are available in exchange for money. As a result of these and related changes, more and more individuals are able to sustain themselves economically without living in families.

Do family members still provide the basic economic support for their family units? It is difficult to answer this question fully, but sociologists do know that in 1975 one-quarter of U.S. households had no members who worked. By 1990, this will be true of 29 percent of households. Such households include the retired, the widowed, nonworking single parents, and handicapped or infirm single individuals. These families receive income from the government, their kin, private pension plans, and their own savings and investments. The biggest single source of government payments comes from the social security system, which makes old age, survivor's, and disability payments. That program presumes that some member of the family has worked at some earlier time.

Although the family's economic needs are currently being met by work, government programs, and kin, the growth of households without any workers may make it more difficult for such families to meet their needs for food, shelter, heat, and health care. As a result, we would expect the family's role in meeting economic needs to decrease for some people, and the role of the government and outside jobs to increase.

EMOTIONAL INTIMACY

The function of the family has varied widely in the way it meets the needs of individual members for emotional intimacy. In some societies there is little expectation that wives and husbands will be emotionally close.

Among the Nayar of India, for example, girls are married before the age of puberty to establish their place in the community. Although they and their ritual husbands are secluded together for four days, sexual relations do not necessarily occur. After that, the ritual husbands and wives have no special relationship except that the ritual wife and any children that she may have must observe rites when the husband dies. The ritual wife and husband may become lovers when they are older if both are willing, but it is not necessary. They may or may not be close sexually and emotionally.

In some societies, marriages are arranged by parents, sometimes when the partners are children, and the partners may not even know each other when they get married. More than 2000 arranged marriages occurred in the United States in 1982, when Rev. Sun Myung Moon, leader of the Unification Church, selected partners for 4150 of his young followers and then performed a massive group wedding in New York's Madison Square Garden to join them in matrimony. Many of these young people had met for the first time only days before. Some did not even speak the same language as their new spouse and could converse only through interpreters. In such situations, an individual's needs for emotional intimacy may be met by other family members, such as siblings, parents, or children.

In contemporary Western society, there is a fairly strongly and widely held expectation that husbands and wives will be intimate emotionally as well as sexually, although some variations in these expectations have been noted by social class, with members of blue collar marriages expecting less sharing and emotional intimacy than members of white collar marriages (Komarovsky, 1962). These expectations in the working class may be changing, however, Rubin (1976) suggests, as working-class wives come increasingly to look for emotional intimacy in their marriages.

Although many families fulfill the traditional functions, there has been a growth in alternatives to the family that may be providing some of the same functions. Premarital sexual relations and cohabitation, out-of-wedlock births, childcare shared by relatives, neighbors, and other institutions, and the growing capacity of women to be economically self-sufficient all tend to reduce the necessity for a two-parent, traditional family to fulfill these vital social functions. As a result, the family may be viewed more as an option than an inevitable necessity. If it works for individuals as a means of living the kind of lives they want to lead, they may choose marriage and

Table 13.1 **Major Household Configurations and Their Potential for Fulfilling Traditional Family Functions**

Major Household Forms	Sexual Intimacy	Biological Reproduction	Care of Young	Food, Shelter	Emotional Intimacy with an Adult
Two parents, one or more children	X	X	X	X	X
Childless couples	X	0	?	X	X
Single parents	?	X	X	X/?	?
Singles, no children	?	?	?	X	?

KEY:

X Means an established pattern exists so that this function may be fulfilled. It does not mean that it is always realized.

? Means that the function lacks an established and patterned basis for occurring, although the activity may happen.

0 Means the function is not being fulfilled.

family formation. If it does not, they may choose alternative arrangements. As Table 13.1 shows, most of the traditional functions the family has fulfilled can be met in other ways, although there may be no established and patterned way for them to occur. The fact that these functions can be met in other ways undoubtedly contributes to the revolution in family forms that has been occurring in the United States and other Western countries in recent years.

THE REVOLUTION IN FAMILY FORMS AND ACTIVITIES

Changing family functions are related to the changing composition of the family in Western industrialized societies. The status of individuals living together has been shifting rapidly. In fact, by 1990 most people will not be living in families as they have traditionally been defined.

MAJOR TRENDS

The family headed by a couple and having one or more children was the norm in American society as recently as 1960. At that time, three-quarters of all households contained a married couple and more than half of those couples had one or more dependent children (Figure 13.1). By 1990, only about half (55 percent) of all households will consist of a married couple, and of these only half will contain children. In one-third of the households with children, both husband and wife will work (Masnick and Bane, 1980).

The decline in the number of households headed by a married couple is mirrored by the increase in the proportion of singles, from 25 percent of households in 1960 to a projected 45 percent in 1990. Many of these men and women have been married at some time earlier in their lives. (See the box on p. 340 for more on singles and their life-styles.) In about one-quarter of households headed by women there are dependent children, and less than 10 percent of male-headed households have children. These trends are due to declining marriage rates, increasing divorce rates, and falling birth rates.

Declining Marriage Rates

The *marriage rate* per 1000 single women has declined, from 90 in 1950 to 64 in 1979 (U.S. Bureau of the Census, 1982a, p. 82). This rate may seem low. It means that in any given year,

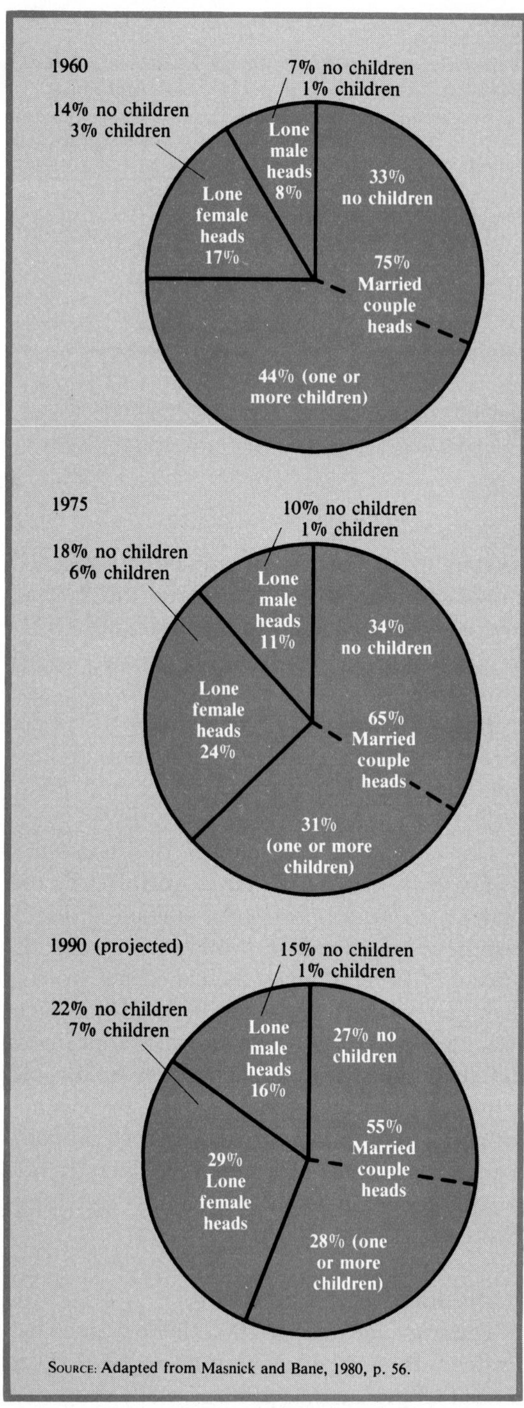

Figure 13.1 Changing Household Composition in the USA, 1960–1990

64 out of every 1000 unmarried women aged 15 and over get married that year. Those who are 15 or 16 and those over the age of 50 are less likely to marry than those between 20 and 24, the age group with the highest annual rate of marriage. The wide age span of unmarried women and taking only a single year as the basis for the measure explains why so few out of 1000 marry in a given year. Figure 13.2 shows the changes in the percentage of women who never married in various age groups over time in the United States. Some young women are simply postponing marriage while they obtain more education or get established in a career. Others will not marry at all. The national median age at first marriage reached a low of 20 for women and 23 for men in 1956. After rising steadily, it was 21.6 for women and 23.4 years for men in 1979 (U.S. Bureau of the Census, 1982a, p. 82).

Despite the rising age at which people marry and the growing number of women who have never married, most women (94 percent) favor marriage as a way of life, according to a 1980 Roper poll. The nature of the marriage relationship they desire has changed, however. A majority of women (52 percent) feel that marriage responsibilities should be shared equally by both partners, with both earning salaries and sharing family and household activities. Nearly half of men (49 percent) agree. Support for this type of relationship is greatest among younger and college-educated women. Two-thirds of them favor such a marriage (Roper Organization, 1980).

Even though women overwhelmingly favor marriage as a way of life, they continue to get married at a slower rate today than they did 20 years ago. Several reasons have been offered for this trend. First, women are more likely to pursue higher education today than in the past, a factor that is related to later marriage. Second, there has been a rise in cohabitation among unmarried couples. The number of cohabiting couples has more than doubled, from about half a million in 1970 to 1.6 million in 1980. Most of these couples are in the 25 to 34 age range, followed by those under 25; the third largest age group among cohabitors was people who were 45 to 64 years old. Despite the rapid rise in cohabiting couples, they still make up only about 3 percent of all couples living together in the United States (*The New York Times,* April 2, 1980). If other countries are any indication, however, this percentage will continue to grow in the United States. In Denmark, more than one-quarter of women 18 through 25 live with a man without being married, and in Sweden about 12 percent of all couples (aged 16 to 70) are not married (Westoff, 1978). Another indication of the trend is the attitudes of single women who were twice as likely in 1976 than they were in 1957 to view marriage primarily as a burden and restriction. In 1976, only 17 percent of single women held positive attitudes toward marriage (Bernard, 1981).

Rising Divorce Rates

If present trends continue, at least 38 percent of women who were born between 1945 and 1949 will see their first marriages end in divorce, up from 20 percent of women born from 1920 to 1924 (Glick and Norton, 1973). Women born since 1949 may experience an even higher rate of divorce, with perhaps as many as half their marriages ending in divorce. Sociologists have identified social factors that are related to divorce and suggest some of the implications of rising divorce rates.

Divorce occurs most frequently among those who have been married two or three years (DHEW, 1978, p. 1). The rate of divorce, however, is not the same for all groups in society. People who have already been divorced are more likely to divorce again, compared to people who have not been divorced. Divorce is more common among blacks than whites, among the nonreligious than the religious, and among those who marry young than among those who marry in their mid twenties. The rate of divorce for those with less than eight years of education is three times greater than for those with college educations, and it is higher among those with low earnings than those with higher incomes (Glick and Norton, 1971). Moreover, the higher a man's occupational status, the lower the divorce rate is likely to be (Cutright, 1971). Urban back-

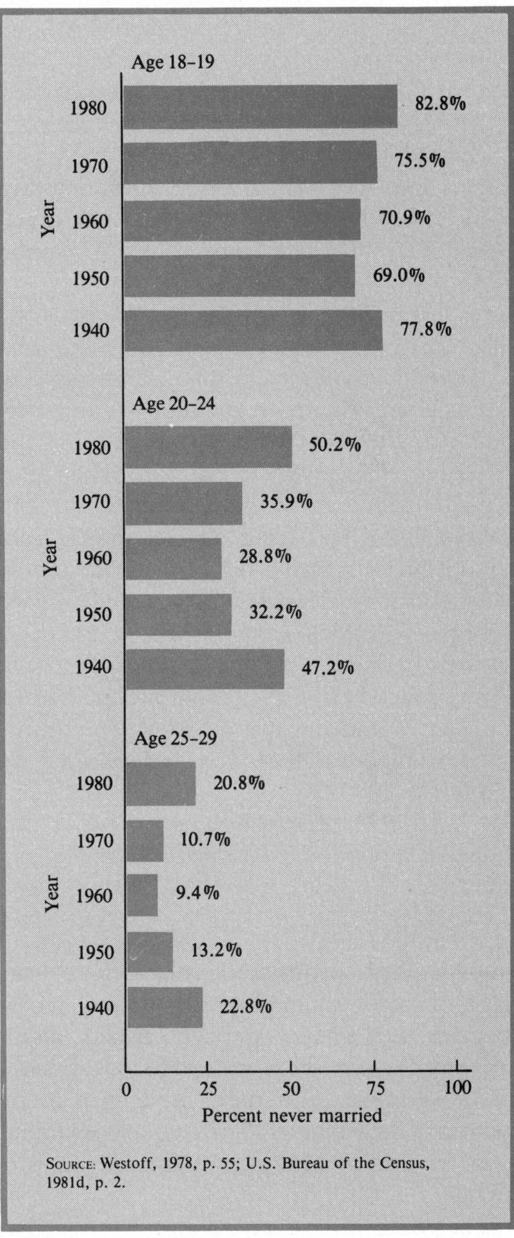

SOURCE: Westoff, 1978, p. 55; U.S. Bureau of the Census, 1981d, p. 2.

Figure 13.2 Percentage of Women Who Never Married, in Different Age Groups, 1940–1978

Singles

The number of singles—that is people over the age of 18 who are not married—has soared. In 1981, nearly 57 million Americans were single, widowed, or divorced. More than half of them had never been married. Their numbers have increased as the marriage age and divorce rate go up and as more people choose not to marry at all. Although their life situations and life-styles are quite different, they do share some common satisfactions and frustrations.

The *young singles* are in their twenties and are just out of school and into their first jobs. Although traditionally this group stayed at home with their parents until they married, in recent decades many have been able to afford their own place to live, which they often share with one or more roommates. This group may be paying off educational loans and faces the high cost of everything from rent to transportation, clothes, and furnishings. Nevertheless, they may be the most likely to live the "swinging singles" life-style characterized by lots of night life and parties. Their roommates may provide support and friendship, but they may feel pinched for privacy.

The *divorced or never-married middle-aged singles* very often live alone or cohabit with a special partner. If they are divorced, they may have financial, social, and emotional involvements with and obligations toward dependent children. They may be somewhat more established in their work than the young singles, and be earning somewhat more. They are likely to have clarified their own likes, dislikes, and interests and to have developed a good circles of friends.

The *older singles* over the age of 65 are most likely to be women because of their longer life expectancy. Many are poor and subsist on social security payments and other meager sources of income. Many never worked for income in their own lifetimes and therefore do not receive pensions from their own work. Many are involved in church or other groups that provide a sense of community and friendship.

All singles face the possibility of loneliness or the fear of loneliness. Some of the younger and middle-aged ones report the pressures of living in a "pro-marriage" environment (Stein, 1976). Many singles who are economically independent say they enjoy their freedom and find that being single provides them with greater variety and more opportunities for personal development.

---

ground, short acquaintanceship before marriage, short or no engagement period, mixed religious faith among marriage partners, disapproval of the marriage by kin and friends, dissimilar backgrounds, and different definitions by spouses of their mutual roles have all been found to be related to higher rates of divorce (Goode, 1961).

The rising divorce rate does not mean that people have stopped valuing marriage, however. It may mean the opposite—namely, that the importance of marriage as a source of emotional satisfaction has increased and that people end marriages that fail to provide such satisfaction. This interpretation is supported by the high remarriage rate for divorced persons. The remarriage rate for divorced or widowed women 14 years old and over was 40.8 per 1000 in 1979 (U.S. Bureau of the Census, 1982a, p. 82). Apparently people are not soured on marriage in general, but only on particular marriages.

Do factors other than degree of happiness influence divorce rates? A model developed by Levinger (1965) suggests an answer to this question. The model identifies three major factors affecting divorce—the attractiveness of the marriage relationship itself, the strength of barriers to marital dissolution, and the attractiveness of alternatives. His model rests on and makes sense of a great many research studies. The attractiveness of a relationship depends on whether the marriage offers emotional, social, and economic rewards to the people in it. These rewards include companionship, good communication with one's spouse, enjoyable sex, shared values, and the social and economic status obtained from a marriage. If people enter marriage largely because they feel they are experiencing a high degree of romantic love, they may find that superficial romantic love declines over time in marriage. If they do not share some common life values, companionship, or something else that makes them feel the marriage is rewarding, they may be more likely to get divorced.

Barriers to divorce—the second factor in Levinger's model—exist both within and beyond the individual. They include feelings of obligation to dependent children or of the sanctity of the marriage bond itself. Marriages between partners of the same religious faith are less likely to end in divorce, perhaps because of their shared views about marriage. Divorce is less likely in marriages where couples attend church together, where they share a common network of friends and kin, and in communities where divorce is stigmatized (Levinger, 1965). The greater the number of people in a community who are divorced, the greater the likelihood of divorce (Goode et al., 1971). When barriers to divorce are strong, divorce will be less likely; when they are weak, it will be more likely.

The third set of factors affecting divorce in a major way is the attractiveness of the alternatives to the current marriage. Is there a preferred sex partner outside the marriage? Does the wife have opportunities for independent income? Are there other individuals that one partner finds more compatible with respect to major values and goals? Are there other kin relationships that are more important to one or the other spouse and that conflict with the marriage relationship? Has superficial romantic love faded from the marriage but flamed up with someone else? Any of these possibilities might make the alternatives to a marriage more important than the marriage itself.

But none of these factors alone seems to be enough to produce the dissolution of a marriage relationship. It seems more likely that the appeal of a relationship might diminish, accompanied by relatively weak barriers to marital dissolution, combined with increasingly attractive alternatives, to increase the chances of divorce. The rising divorce rate in America (and in Western European countries as well) is probably not due to increasingly unattractive marriage relationships, but rather to the weakening of barriers to dissolving marriages and to the increasing appeal of alternatives.

Falling Birth Rates

Lower marriage rates, rising age at marriage, and higher divorce rates depress birth rates. The long-term trend in this century in the United States has been toward fewer children and smaller families, except for the post-World War II "baby boom." Figure 13.3 illustrates the rising number of births between 1945 and 1965, the declining number from 1970 to 1975, and the upturn since 1975.

Although the number of births has been rising in recent years, much of that increase reflects the large number of women of childbearing age, women who are part of the post-World War II baby boom generation. In the 1970s there were so many women of childbearing age that the absolute number of babies born rose. The actual rate of births, however, has *dropped* from 118.0 per 1000 women aged 15 to 44 years old in 1960 to 68.5 per 1000 in 1979. It is this decline in birth rates rather than the absolute number of births that sociologists and population counters have tried to explain.

Several factors seem to explain the general trend toward lower birth rates. First, work and birth rates are negatively related; as more

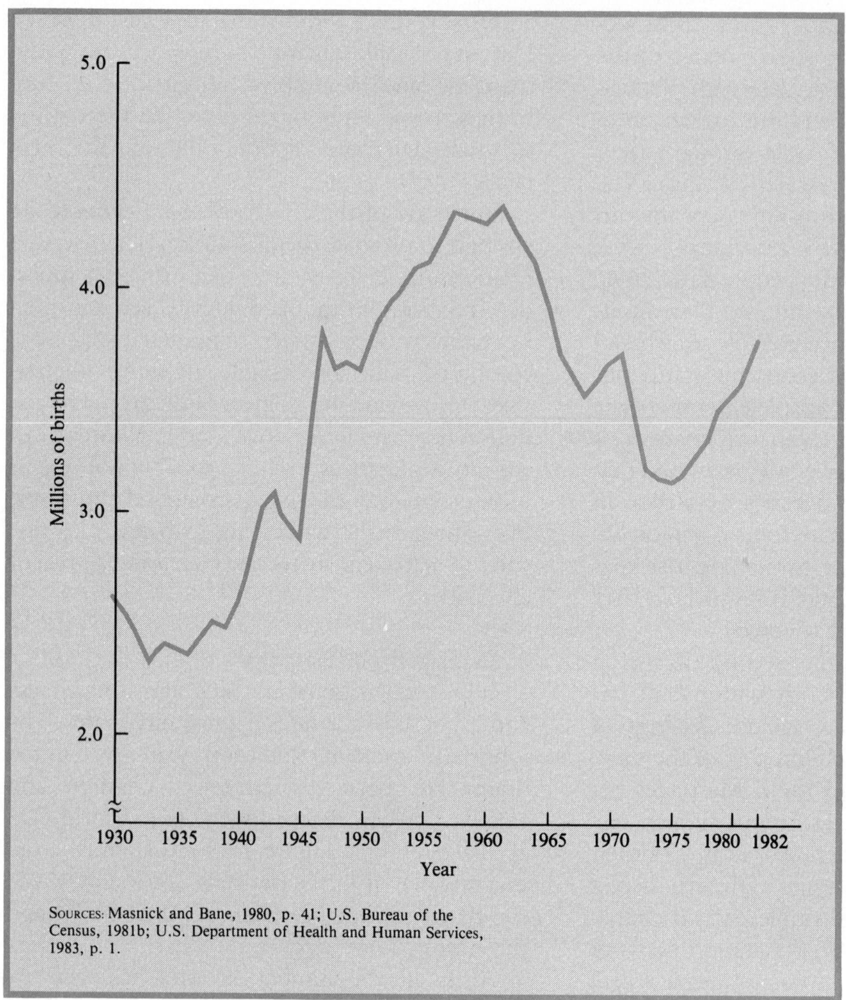

Figure 13.3 Annual Number of Births, 1929–1982

women have returned to work, the number of births has declined. Another reason for fewer births may be the emphasis on the "self." The sacrifices of childrearing seem to outweigh the pleasures for many couples in the 1970s and 1980s.

The Department of Agriculture has estimated that it will cost a total of $134,414 to raise an average child born in 1979 to his or her eighteenth birthday if the family lives in "the urban North Central region" of the United States. This estimation does not include the costs of college (Hacker, 1983, p. 166). Although everyone is not aware of these numbers, more individuals seem to be sensitive to the financial and personal costs of childrearing.

If current birth rates persist, some 30 percent of U.S. women now of childbearing age will never have children. Only once before did so few women have children, and that was during the Great Depression of the 1930s. Even then, only 22 percent of women were childless (Westoff, 1978). Westoff suggests that the decline in births can be seen as both a cause and a consequence of changes in marriage and the family.

All these trends are reflected in attitudes about ideal family size, which have changed visibly. Nearly two-thirds of all women in 1941 thought that the ideal family should include three or four children. In 1968, more than half thought that the ideal family size was two children (Roper Organization, 1980). The other spectacular shift in the 1970s is reflected in the large numbers of young women who plan to have no children at all. In 1978, 11 percent of all women aged 18 to 34 said they planned to have no children; among women 18 to 34 with postgraduate education, 21 percent expected not to have children (Bernard, 1981). The stigma and pity attached to "childless" marriages in the past has been replaced with the voluntary choice of child-free marriages for many. As a result of these tendencies, the number of children under the age of 5 dropped from 20 million to 16.9 million between 1960 and 1981 (U.S. Census, 1982a, p. 26).

Birth rates are also declining because people in the United States have been legally able to terminate unwanted pregnancies ever since the 1973 Supreme Court ruling that state laws forbidding abortion were unconstitutional. More than 4 million U.S. women, or 1 in every 11 of childbearing age, had nearly 6 million abortions between 1973 and 1978 (according to figures from the Alan Guttmacher Institute, a New York research organization). Many of these abortions terminated the pregnancies of unmarried teenagers. Nearly two-thirds of American adults believe it should be possible for a pregnant woman to obtain a legal abortion (Harris Survey, 1981, p. 2).

The right to a legal abortion has not gone unchallenged in the United States. At the time of this writing, those favoring a constitutional amendment to make abortion illegal or legislation that would designate when life begins were mounting a concerted political campaign through such organizations as the National Right to Life and the Life Amendment Political Action Committee. The pro-choice supporters include such organizations as the National Abortion Rights Action League, Planned Parenthood, the American Civil Liberties Union, the National Organization for Women, and Women USA. They maintain that the state does not have the right to control women's bodies and reproductive lives, that a woman has the right of choice over such matters, and that children have the right to be born to parents who want them and are able and willing to care for them. The right to legal abortion will unquestionably continue to be a major issue surrounding the family and fertility for many years to come.

All the changes we have been discussing in marriage, divorce, and birth rates have culminated in a number of dramatic trends in family and household composition, including the following:

1. A large decline in the proportion of households that contain husbands and wives, from 75 percent of all households in 1960 to a projected 55 percent of households in 1990 (Masnick and Bane, 1980), with an accompanying increase in the proportion of single-person households.

2. A decline in average household size, from 3.37 persons in 1950 to 2.73 persons in 1981 (U.S. Bureau of Census, 1982a). This decline has occurred despite the fact that children are staying at home longer than they did in earlier periods.

3. A rise in the proportion of female-headed households, from 17 percent in 1960 to a projected 29 percent in 1990 (Masnick and Bane, 1980). This is true of all three generations, with more widows in the oldest age group; a mixture of widows, divorced, and never-married in the middle age group; and divorced and never-married in the youngest age group.

In 1973 the Supreme Court ruled that state laws prohibiting abortion were unconstitutional. Since then, a number of abortion clinics have been established. While about two-thirds of all Americans believe that legal abortion should be available, some vocal critics challenge this position.

Working Women

Intimately linked with the revolution in household grouping is the transformation of the number of workers in each household. As more and more married women have entered the labor force, single-worker husband-wife households have plummeted, from 65 percent in 1960 to a projected 31 percent in 1990. In 1947 only one in five married women with husbands present were in the labor force; by 1981, more than half of them were (U. S. Bureau of the Census, 1982a, p. 383).

Although the revolution in labor-force participation among married women has already occurred, two other aspects of women's work have only begun to influence the family in major ways. The first of these is the degree to which women are involved in their careers. Are they intently pursuing a demanding career, working continuously and full-time over a period of years, or do they spend only minimal amounts of time and effort at work? Degree of involvement will affect how they spend their time and how their families function. (See the box on dual-career families on p. 346.) Many more women are now working full-time, year-round than were in 1960, and as women enter their thirties and forties they are more likely to work continuously for a number of years. These figures suggest that women are becoming increasingly attached to work. Many women, however, continue to work part-time or for only part of the year, from necessity or choice.

Why has the percentage of married women in the labor force increased so dramatically? The period from 1940 to 1960 was one of rising demand for workers in traditionally female occupations—clerical work and several categories of professional and service work. Moreover, the growing demand for female workers was greatest for more educated women. At the same time, there was a dramatic decline in the number of single women 18 to 34 years old. These younger single women were the ones employers had preferred during the war. As they became increasingly unavailable, employers began turning to older married women to maintain and expand the female labor force. These women, in turn, responded to the expansion of job opportunities and entered the labor force, thus producing the postwar rise in the female work rate (Oppenheimer, 1970).

IMPLICATIONS OF THESE TRENDS

All these changes—the makeup of the work force and the changes in household composition—have had profound implications for American families. As women have taken on new responsibilities as workers and breadwinners, they have often faced role overload. Help with their numerous duties has not always been forthcoming from husbands, childcare facilities, or employers. This overload has been documented in both capitalist and communist countries. In the Soviet Union, despite the deliberate

"I'm offering you marriage, Helen, and more. Much more."

SOURCE: Drawing by Saxon, © 1982, *The New Yorker Magazine, Inc.*

Dual-Career Families

Ed is a computer programmer, and his wife Cindy is a teacher. Their children are cared for by his mother three days a week and by a neighbor the other two days. Cindy generally has vacations when their children do. Ed earns about twice what she does.

Kathy earns much more in her job as a television newscaster than Mike, her bank officer husband, does. They both travel a lot, and in some ways their marriage is like the commuter marriages of couples who live apart for days or even weeks at a time for the sake of their jobs. When they had twins, Kathy took a three-month maternity leave. They have a live-in housekeeper and extra help to aid in running the household.

Orlando is a youth worker married to Jenny, who runs a gift shop. He makes dinner on the nights she works late at the store and takes the kids on Saturday outings when she works. She has Mondays off, and on that day she cooks several main dishes for the week's dinners. Orlando and Jenny spend Sundays cleaning the house, doing laundry, and grocery shopping, because they have decided they would rather save the money it would cost to pay someone to come in and do these things for them. They are hoping to save enough to buy their own home. As the children grow older, they are helping more with family chores, becoming "part of the solution rather than part of the problem," as Jenny puts it. When the children were young, they went to a day care center four days a week. Now that they are in grade school, they have after-school sports and activities until 5 o'clock.

Social scientists studying the lives of couples like these point out some of the advantages and disadvantages of dual-career families:

Advantages

1. Dual-career families generally have reasonably high incomes. Having two adults working may provide a cushion for the family if either partner is unemployed for a time.
2. Their good income may help to pay for their children's education, travel, eating out, shows, and other leisure activities.
3. Both partners often have interesting work lives, since they can afford to seek jobs they enjoy.
4. They have a lot to talk about with each other. The partners tend to have good insights into other's world.
5. The other spouse and the children may be able to go along on some business trips.
6. Both individuals tend to face challenges and keep growing, personally, socially, and intellectually.

Disadvantages

1. Role overload is possible for both husband and wife, particularly if they have children. Role overload is frequently a problem for wives. This sometimes leads to excessive fatigue and illness, although husbands do help more with children and housework than in traditional families.
2. The family needs help with childcare unless either or both partners have a relatively low-key, perhaps even part-time, career.
3. Sometimes competition flares between husbands and wives when both have careers they consider important.
4. There may be rather limited time for

housework, social life, entertaining, leisure, relaxation, volunteer activities, care of aged relatives, and other things women have traditionally done when they were not working outside the home.

5. Husbands may receive little social support for helping with childcare or household tasks.

6. Vacation times of both spouses and children may not always coincide. So even though the family may have the money to vacation together, members may not always have the time to do so.

SOURCES: Garland, 1972; Pepitone-Rockwell, 1980; Rapoport and Rapoport, 1976; Rice, 1979.

expansion of female economic and political participation, wives spend 2.5 times as many hours on housework as their husbands (Lapidus, 1978). Despite the expansion of women's participation outside the home, their home duties have often not been lightened. Childcare is the single biggest problem faced by working mothers (Kamerman, 1979).

Despite the prospects of role overload, nearly half of all the women polled by Roper in 1980 would prefer to have a job than to stay at home all the time. As recently as 1974, only about one-third of all women expressed this preference. Moreover, younger and college-educated women are even more likely to want to work. These figures suggest that women's participation in the work force will continue and perhaps increase in the future. At the same time, the majority of women and men feel strongly that more day care centers should be set up for working women.

The greater economic independence of women that has accompanied these trends has several important implications. First, fewer women need to enter or stay in marriage primarily for economic reasons. From colonial times to the present, there is evidence that whenever women had alternatives to unsatisfactory marriages they used them, as Bernard suggests (1981). Moreover, she feels that the widespread wife abuse that has begun to come to light reflects the number of women who may have felt trapped in destructive marriages because they lacked alternatives. Now more women feel they can publicly protest the abuse they are receiving. The growth of jobs for women is one such alternative, at least for some women.

The availability of alternatives to marriage can also influence the type of marriage relationship women enter into. As already noted, women and men increasingly favor more *egalitarian* marriages. For men, this means that both the burden and the social esteem that came from being the sole breadwinner and head of the household may have lessened somewhat. Some men welcome this, others do not. There is still rather limited social support for men who take on primary responsibility for housekeeping or childcare, although such support seems to be growing. In 1970, only one out of eight women and one out of five men said they would respect a male homemaker, but by 1980 two out of five women and men said that they would.

Women with higher educational levels and income were more likely to respect a male homemaker than women of lower socioeconomic status (Roper Organization, 1980). Moreover, in 1980, a significant percentage of men were quite willing to help with household chores traditionally performed by women. College-educated men are most likely to help with household tasks. Among all men, more than three-quarters help with grocery shopping and two-thirds help with housecleaning, dishwashing, and cooking. Nearly half help mind the children, while two out of five sometimes do laundry. Mending still seems to be a job men seldom do; three out of five say they never do it (Roper Organization, 1980).

Effects of Divorce on Children

How have these changes in families affected the children in them? Nearly one child in five under the age of 18 in 1980 lived with one rather than two parents. This represents 12 million children. In most instances, they live with their mothers. More than half of all black children live with one parent. The number of families with children under the age of 18 headed by women has soared in recent years, from about 1.5 million in 1960 to 5.6 million in 1981 (U.S. Bureau of the Census, 1982a, p. 51). This figure is projected to jump to 6.5 million by 1990 (Masnick and Bane, 1980). How does divorce or single parenthood affect these children? Children from single-parent families are twice as likely to do poorly in elementary school as children from two-parent families, and they are far more likely to have behavior and discipline problems. In high school, they are three times as likely to be expelled and twice as likely to drop out than their counterparts from two-parent families (Hechinger, 1980).

Are these results caused by single parenting, or are they related to some of the social conditions that accompany single parenthood? More than half the families headed by women in 1981 were poor. The economic situation of the family is more strongly correlated with learning, behavior, and discipline problems in school than is having only one parent. Studies have found that the coping strategies of single parents vary widely, but that when they work out their economic, social, and interpersonal problems, the children adjust quite well to divorce. Indeed, they are sometimes happier than they were when the parents were together and fighting all the time (Monaghan-Leckband, 1978; Weiss, 1979).

Researchers and family counselors tend to agree that a *happy* two-parent family is the best situation for children, since in such a unit the parents are able to share childcare. Furthermore, children can have close emotional relationships with an adult of each sex; there is the possibility for shared breadwinning and hence higher incomes; and each parent has adult companionship.

Not all marriage relationships are secure and happy, however, and there is a growing tendency among researchers and family counselors alike to conclude that remaining in a conflict-ridden family relationship is worse for children than divorce. The effects of divorce on children depend to a considerable degree on how the divorce is handled, whether the parents continue to fight over the custody or care of the children, whether the parents can work out amicable relationships or whether they remain embattled and bitter enemies, and the extent to which having divorced parents stigmatizes the child. Whether or not their mothers work may also affect how children adjust to divorce. The effects on children of mothers working has been the subject of considerable research.

The Effects on Children of Working Mothers

The children of working mothers have more learning and behavior problems in school and higher rates of delinquency than do children whose mothers do not work, according to some studies (Gold, 1961; Nye, 1958). Rather than jumping to the conclusion that it is harmful for mothers to work, however, subsequent researchers note that families where mothers work often have a host of additional problems which may be more strongly related to learning difficulties or delinquency than the fact that the mother works (Hoffman and Nye, 1974). Two key factors that have been identified are the family's economic situation and whether or not the working mother wanted to work. Crisis-ridden families with severe economic problems and ones where the mother neither wanted to work nor liked her job were the ones that had children with learning and behavior problems. The fact that the mother worked was not related to negative outcomes when there was less severe economic need and when the mother liked her work (Hoffman, 1963a and 1963b).

Other factors have also been identified as apparently influencing the way a mother's working affects her children. Of paramount importance is the quality of the relationship between mother and children when they are together. Can the children have fun with the mother, can they share confidences with her, do they feel she loves them and cares about them a great deal, even though they cannot be together every moment? Equally important is the quality of care children receive from other adults, whether it be from relatives, friends, neighbors, or a day care center. Are there loving, caring adults with whom the child can have fairly long-term relationships? These two conditions seem to be crucial for the healthy development of children (Bronfenbrenner, 1981).

The separation that occurs between mother and child when the mother works does not affect the personality functioning of the child (Nye et al., 1963). Children raised largely by mother substitutes in Israeli *kibbutzim* and in Communist societies have not shown negative personality effects. Several factors seem to be critical when the mother works: the extent of the mother's absence, the quality of the interaction between mother and child when she is present, and the quality of the care offered by others (Rallings and Nye, 1979). Burr (1973) reviewed the extensive literature in this area and concluded that there is no relationship between the amount of time the mother works and the personality adjustment of her children.

Not only is employment of the mother by itself not harmful to children, it appears to have some positive effects. The child of a working mother seems to see the division of household tasks as being more egalitarian (Hoffman, 1963a; Finkelman, 1966); to see maternal employment as not threatening to a marriage (King, McIntyre, and Axelson, 1968); to indicate higher esteem for his or her own sex (Vogel et al., 1970); to favor social equality for women (Meier, 1972); and to do more household chores than other children (Rallings and Nye, 1979). Overall, the children of working mothers evaluate female competence more positively, and the daughters of working mothers have higher levels of independence.

One possible negative effect was observed in the sons of working-class mothers. Maternal employment is related to a lower evaluation of their fathers by these boys, perhaps because they see their mothers as having to work and hence consider the fathers to be economically inadequate (Rallings and Nye, 1979). The sons of middle-class working mothers, however, are likely to see their fathers as more nurturant, warm, and expressive individuals (Vogel et al., 1970).

On balance, the negative effects on children of divorce or of a mother working appear to depend heavily on the social conditions surrounding the divorce or the work. When divorce results in a happier family and when a working mother is pleased with her work and with her children, the children may benefit from the situation.

FAMILY INTERACTION

Interactions between partners in a marriage begin before the marriage and undoubtedly influence the decision about whether or not to marry. One aspect of the study of family interaction is the study of the ways in which marriage partners meet and of their social characteristics. It has been suggested that courtship and marriage is a classic exchange relationship, where the attributes and resources of one partner are balanced against those of the other partner, while the process is enveloped in the glow of romantic love. An exchange view of marriage suggests that power is relevant for analyzing family interaction, including spouse, parent-child, and sibling relationships.

MATE SELECTION

As the importance of arranged marriage in a society declines, the importance of romantic love as a basis for marriage increases. Essential to the notion of romantic love is the idea that one must discover the right partner. The "right" partner is defined by shared social characteristics even in societies that permit individuals to meet and fall in love on their own. Mate selection is not left solely to chance. Instead, in the absence of parental control over mate selection, other mechanisms have evolved for matching "appropriate" young men and women, including youth groups connected with churches and synagogues, private schools, college fraternities and sororities, and computer dating services. As a result of such mechanisms, most individuals end up marrying someone who is like them with respect to age, race, religion, social background, nationality, and physical proximity. Although there are individual exceptions, the principle of social similarity prevails.

FUNCTIONALIST AND EXCHANGE VIEWS

The structural-functional view of the family suggests that it is a functional requirement in the nuclear family that final authority be assigned without ambiguity (Pitts, 1964). The usual resolution was to have the husband-father play the roles involving political and economic leadership, while women assumed responsibility for expressive, emotional relationships. This practice supports male dominance. Male superiority ensures that boys will learn to identify with their fathers rather than preserving a close relationship with their mothers and that girls will learn it is preferable to "win a man" than to stay close to their mothers.

Although functionalists are correct that the source of superior male power flows from male participation in the larger economic, political, and social order, it is not necessarily true that just because something exists it is functional. Because male and female roles were tightly prescribed by norms within the functional view, the operation of power and exchange within the family was not a significant research topic. In the nineteenth century a great many marriages may have had tightly structured normative constraints placed on them, partly because there were so few resources and alternatives available to women (Brickman, 1974; Rosaldo and Lampere, 1974; Scanzoni, 1979b).

Changes already noted in this chapter increased women's resources and alternatives to marriage, thereby increasing the possibilities for greater bargaining and exchange relationships in marriage. Considerable research has been done in the United States, France, West Germany, Yugoslavia, Turkey, Greece, Ghana, Puerto Rico, the Soviet Union, and Japan to attempt to document the relative power of husbands and wives in the marriage relationship, and the sources of that power. Most researchers have studied urban families, so we know less about conjugal power within rural families. Most research supports Blood and Wolf's classic conclusions (1960) that the power of the husband in the marriage relationship depends on his socioeconomic resources, including education, occupational prestige, and income. Spanish-speaking Americans tend to continue to favor a patriarchal ideology regardless of the husband's resources (Spiegel, 1971), but fewer women seem willing to accept the role of being bossed around by men (Murillo, 1971). Working women tend to have more egalitarian relationships with their husbands, a result that holds true cross-culturally as well as in the United States (Scanzoni, 1979a). An *egalitarian family* is one in which wife and husband share equally in family decision-making. The greater the gap between the socioeconomic resources of husband and wife, the greater the power differential between them (Blood and Wolf, 1960; Buric and Zecevic, 1967; Lupri, 1969; Michel, 1967; Oppong, 1970; Safilios-Rothschild, 1967).

The analysis of power in a marriage may seem like an empty exercise until one considers where power struggles are most likely to erupt. Conflicts occur most often over money, sex, children (whether or not to have them, how many to have, how to discipline them, how to educate them, and so forth), and where the family will live. Sociologists study such questions as these: How is the relative power of husbands and wives defined in these situations? Do they have relatively equal power? What are the implications of varying degrees of power for their relationship? The distribution of power in a marriage and the respective expectations of both partners help to explain the different types of marriage relationships couples have.

TYPES OF MARRIAGE RELATIONSHIPS

The need for intimacy, trust, acceptance, emotional support, and companionship is one of the major reasons for marriage in modern industrial society. Economic reasons are declining, sexual reproduction can be controlled and is not needed from everyone for survival of the society, so the family has fewer traditional reasons for continuing. Expectations about marriage vary, and a number of types of marriage relationships exist. In a study of 211 men and women who had been married 10 or more years and had not considered divorce, Cuber and Harroff (1972) noted five types of marriage relationships: the conflict-habituated, the devitalized, the passive-congenial, the vital, and the total.

The *conflict-habituated* relationship is continually tense and in conflict, although the conflict is kept controlled and concealed from others as much as possible. While much of the emotion in this relationship is negative, there is some emotion in it. The pair quarrels, nags, and "throws up the past" at each other. Though the partners tell interviewers their children don't know about their incompatibility, comments from the children suggest otherwise: "Oh, they're at it again—but they always are," said a teenage son. Often such couples don't know what they fight about. As one said, "You name it and we'll fight about it."

The *devitalized* relationship, by way of contrast, seems drained of any emotion, positive or negative. Partners say they were once "deeply in love," that they liked spending a great deal of time together, and that they enjoyed sex. Now they spend little pleasurable time together, except for "duty time" entertaining or doing things with their children. Sex is much less frequent and less satisfying, and the couples enjoy few common interests or activities. They do share a genuine concern for the well-being of their children and have some interest in their joint property and the husband's career, but the interest tends to be the material rather than intrinsic aspects that they share. As one wife said, "If you followed us around, you'd wonder why we ever got married. We take each other for granted. We laugh at the same things sometimes, but we don't really laugh together—the way we used to" (Cuber and Harroff, 1972, p. 278).

The *passive-congenial* relationship resembles the devitalized one, but the difference is that the passivity in the relationship has existed since the beginning; it did not develop from a previously more exciting partnership. The guiding light of passive-congenials is their practicality and sensibleness. They plan ahead carefully; they are responsible and prudent. They are not the type of people to get swept away by intense emotional involvements. They enter marriage cautiously, since as one woman said: "I wasn't just marrying him; I was choosing a father for my children. . . . I expected to perform sex in marriage, but . . . I'm willing to admit that it's a much overrated activity" (p. 280). The men in such relationships tend to see marriage as a convenient institution. As one reflected, "I don't know why everyone seems to make so much about men and women and marriage. Of course, I'm married and if anything happened to my

Devitalized marriage relationships have little or no emotional content for the partners in them.

wife, I'd get married again. I think it's the proper way to live. It's convenient, orderly, and solves a lot of problems. But there are other things in life. I spent nearly ten years preparing for the practice of my profession" (Cuber and Harroff, 1972, p. 281).

All three of these types contrast sharply with the *vital* marriage. Partners in such a marriage resemble other pairs in their concern for children, jobs, homes, and communities. They differ in their intense psychological intimacy, which provides the essence of life for both man and woman. Their greatest satisfaction in life comes from sharing time and activities with each other. As one man puts it: "I cheerfully, and that's putting it mildly, passed up two good promotions because one of them would have required some traveling and the other would have taken evenings and weekend time—and that's when Pat and I *live*. The hours with her (after 22 years of marriage) are what I live for. You should meet her . . . " (Cuber and Harroff, 1972, p. 282). Such couples realize that few of their friends have such relationships. Nevertheless, they continue "to find their central satisfaction in the life they live with and through each other" (1972, p. 283). This is not to say that they never fight or compete, because they do. Unlike the partners in the conflict-habituated marriage, however, they fight over things that are really important to them (such as where a child should go to college), and they try to avoid conflicts where possible and to settle them as quickly as they can, rather than letting them continue.

The *total* relationship resembles the vital one except that more parts of their lives are shared. Husband and wife may be business partners, collaborators, or in some other way share virtually all the important centers of their lives. One famous scientist had a wife of 30 years who was his "friend, mistress, and partner." They traveled together, and he went home for lunch with her every day. Again, as in the vital relationship, when conflicts arose the important thing was how to resolve them without destroying the relationship.

All five types of relationships have endured, so we cannot say that one or another is more or less prone to divorce. Sometimes partners who share a vital or a total relationship surprise their friends by announcing that they are getting divorced. This may happen because for them a devitalized relationship would be unendurable. They can envision marriage only in terms of a vital, meaningful, and fulfilling relationship. A decline in quality may be enough to end a vital or total relationship, while a devitalized or passive-congenial partnership may end because one person meets someone with whom he or she can have a more vital relationship.

Infidelities may occur in all these types of relationships except perhaps the total, but the reasons for them and their implications differ widely (Cuber and Harroff, 1972). The conflict-habituated pair may use infidelity as yet another expression of hostility, while passive-congenials may be unfaithful out of sheer boredom. A devitalized partner may be pursuing the lost moment of glorious romance remembered from earlier days. Adultery may occur in vital relationships as well, if the partners have agreed on an "open marriage" where they can both have sexual relationships with others. In such cases, infidelity is not seen as disloyalty, but rather as a basic human right which the loved one ought to be permitted—and which the other perhaps wants as well.

SIBLING INTERACTIONS

The marriage relationship is obviously one key type of family interaction. In any family that has children, however, there are other important interactions. These include parent-child interactions and child-child interactions (if there is more than one child in the family). Eighty percent of all children in the United States have *siblings;* that is, brothers and sisters (Mussen, Conger, and Kagan, 1974). One of the key determinants of family interaction is family size. The larger the size of the family, the fewer the number of individual parent-child interactions. On the other hand, the larger the family, the more sibling interaction.

Siblings help to socialize each other. They also increase the complexity of family interactions and conflicts. One of the ways siblings socialize each other is by performing pioneering functions for one another. Usually the older siblings blaze the trail for younger ones (Bank and Kahn, 1975), although as they get older, younger siblings sometimes take the lead. This may happen because each additional child tends to open the family more to outside influences (Schvaneveldt and Ihinger, 1979). As a result of the gradual loosening of the family system that occurs with the birth of each new member, the younger siblings tend to be more likely to break with family traditions. This phenomenon may explain why first-born siblings are more sexually conservative than later-born siblings (Reiss, 1967), and how younger siblings may pave the way for the greater experimentation of their older brothers and sisters.

In many other areas as well, siblings seem to help each other develop their individual identities, through the dual processes of identification and differentiation (Bank and Kahn, 1975). In identification, siblings may identify possibilities for themselves in the actions of their siblings and include some of these alternatives in their own repertory. Learning sexual behavior is a good example of the use of identification. Siblings also help each other to differentiate themselves, through the process of recognizing how they differ from each other ("He's that way, but I'm this way"). This helps individuals to define their own unique identities. The processes of individuation may be spurred along by sibling rivalries and conflicts.

One result of such conflict is the greater tendency to form coalitions. Siblings have more chance than only children to form alliances. They may do this to gain greater strength in relation to their parents or to forge alliances against other sibling coalitions in the family. Same-sex sibling coalitions are most common (Caplow, 1959). First-born siblings may lead a coalition against the parents because other siblings may feel that first-borns have greater power and access to the parents. Tattling, squealing, and shifting coalitions all occur in sibling coalitions.

To the degree that families represent a relatively closed and enduring social system, they need to resolve or at least stalemate the tensions and conflicts within them. Sometimes parents mediate the conflicts between competing groups of siblings; at other times the eldest child or one of the sibling coalitions may try to be the peacemaker. Sibling coalitions may produce family isolates, "black sheep," scapegoats, winners, losers, and "pets" within the family (Schvaneveldt and Ihinger, 1979). A family may also direct its unresolved hostilities between its coalitions at a scapegoat or enemy outside the family.

VIOLENCE IN THE FAMILY

Mary picked her bloodied front tooth off the shag carpet. Her face and mouth were already beginning to swell from the latest beating Tom had given her. She wondered how much longer she could put up with it. This was the fourth time since Christmas that Tom had beaten her or their 4-year-old son, Jimmy.

For a long time the social science literature on the family was filled exclusively with discussions of the functions of the family in society, with little or no attention paid to violence in the family. Those who did mention it considered only the dramatic extremes, such as homicide. Recent research is finding that physical violence and abuse between family members is statistically frequent and that it receives farily widespread cultural approval (Gelles and Strauss, 1979).

Various American and British studies reveal that about 90 percent of all parents have used physical punishment at some point in a child's life. Punishment continues into adolescence, with more than half of the student population reporting they have been hit during high school (Bachman, 1967; Steinmetz, 1971, 1974; Strauss, 1971). Physical punishment may step over the boundary into what is called child abuse. Although it is difficult to get complete figures on child abuse, conservative estimates are pegged at about half a million cases in the United States each year (Light, 1974).

Child abuse is defined differently by different people, but most would agree that broken bones, concussions, lost teeth, burns, and serious neglect constitute child abuse. Physical punishment may result in child abuse quite unintentionally when adults do not realize their own strength and hit children too hard or throw them down. Probably most adults do not set out deliberately to abuse a child. They may get so angry they lose control, they may be drunk and not fully aware of what they are doing, or they may unintentionally hit a child harder than they meant to. Because physical punishment of children receives some normative support in our society, this support may contribute to the likelihood of child abuse.

Family violence sometimes leads to murder, and 20 to 40 percent of all homicides in the United States occur between related individuals (Gelles and Strauss, 1979). Across the country, family fights are the single most frequent reason for calling the police. Physical abuse is mentioned as a complaint quite often by applicants for divorce (Levinger, 1965; O'Brien, 1971). This and other evidence suggests that violence is a major feature of family life in America and probably in most other societies as well (Strauss, 1976).

Why Does Family Violence Occur?

Why does so much violence occur in families? Is it the result of pathological individuals, or do social factors encourage the use of violence in the family? According to conflict theorists, conflict occurs in all human relationships, including the family. By its very nature, the family is a center of competing interests that result in conflicts (Sprey, 1969). Violence is one means of advancing one's interests when other methods fail (Steinmetz and Straus, 1974). In some families, violence may be the first method adopted, depending on how individual members have been taught to view violence or depending on the other resources available to individuals.

When individuals lack the resources to influence people around them, they may use violence (Goode et al., 1971). For example, a husband who receives little prestige or income from his job may resort to violence to dominate his family (Gelles and Straus, 1979). Similarly, men married to women with higher educational and occupational status than their own are more likely to use force and violence on family members than are men with higher-status occupations (O'Brien, 1971). It may be that given the cultural pressures on men to dominate in the family, men lacking the social resources for such dominance resort to superior physical strength.

This explanation stresses the use of violence as a resource for domination. Another explanation suggests that stress is a major contributor to family violence. Straus, Gelles, and Steinmetz (1980) found that low income, unemployment, part-time employment, and four or five children in the home were all related to violence toward children and violence between spouses. Each of these conditions might be considered an indicator of stress. As the number of stressful incidents faced by families increased, the frequency of family violence also increased.

A third factor associated with family violence was the concentration of family decision-making in the hands of only one person, whether husband or wife. There was less violence in families where a democratic system was used to make decisions (Gelles, 1974).

Both conflict and exchange perspectives help to illuminate aspects of family interaction such as family violence, sibling relationships, types of marriage relationships, and mate selection. In recent decades, family interactions and the family as a social institution have come under increasing scrutiny and challenge from a number of quarters.

FAMILY CHALLENGERS AND CHANGERS

The importance of the family as a social institution is indicated by the number of people who are concerned about the family in its present state and who want to change it in order to solve its problems. These challengers and changers differ widely in terms of what they see as being the root of the family's problems. As a result, the solutions they propose are extremely varied. In this section we consider the views of conservatives, Marxian and radical feminists, and moderates. For each, we examine what they see as the root causes of the family's situation, the assumptions that underlie their analyses, the solutions they propose, and the questions sociological research raises about their position.

CONSERVATIVES

Conservatives see the major source of family problems as resulting from the loss of patriarchy. They assume that a patriarchal family benefits men by bolstering their egos and making them feel strong. The traditional division of labor in the family allows men to relax at home after a hard day's work. They believe patriarchal families benefit women by giving them protection and support and benefit children by providing them with the mother's undivided attention and nurture. They also assume women are biologically and psychologically suited to rearing children.

The problems currently plaguing the family could be solved, conservatives believe, by returning to an idealized version of what existed in an earlier era—when divorce was rare, when husbands earned enough to support their wives and children in comfort, when men never drank to excess and never beat their wives or children. In this vision of what might have been, wives were always feminine, simultaneously attractive and motherly. Men worked in the outside world, women tended hearth and home. Men were the heads of the households, and their dominant position was reinforced by their economic and political roles in the outside world.

Historical and sociological research questions whether the family unit was ever as happy and well functioning as this ideal assumes. If such a family existed, did it suit the talents, interests, and skills of individuals to be assigned roles solely on the basis of sex? Could the family return to this situation today or in the future, given the economic changes and smaller families that now exist? What evidence supports the assumption that women are biologically and psychologically more suited to nurturing children than men? Is full-time mothering, to the exclusion of everything else, actually good for children? These are some of the questions recent research in the social sciences raises about the assumptions behind conservative analyses of the family.

MARXIAN AND RADICAL FEMINISTS

Marxian and radical feminists adopt a very different stance. They see the subjugation of women as the major problem, and the family as a major source of such domination. They differ among themselves with respect to how the family came to be a source of domination, with some stressing property and economic relations, others emphasizing biology, and still others stressing patriarchy.

Women lost status with the growth of private property, according to Friedrich Engels (1884). As economic surpluses were produced outside the home, household labor became less important than outside production. The traditional division of labor between men and women took on a new social meaning, and men assumed domination over women. Women became little more than servants, restricted to household and childrearing activities. Engels felt that male dominance was based on economic power and that the abolition of private property would end the oppression of women. At the same time, women would need to enter economic production in large numbers, and childrearing would need to be done on a societal rather than an individual scale. Engels has been justifiably criticized—for historical inaccuracies and because his theory fails to explain how private property and the social position of women vary in feudalism and capitalism, for example. But a major strength of his work is that it links the nature of the family and the position of women with the economic organization of a society.

In a class society, women's labor moves from a public contribution to being the private property of men. In this view, women are assumed to be dominated mainly by capitalism, in much the way that men are, with male domination over women playing a very small part (Sokoloff, 1980). Zaretsky (1976) suggests that reproduction and socialization, like food and shelter, are necessary to sustain a society. Socialist feminists like Zaretsky and Secombe (1974) argue that housewives help to produce surplus value by providing services (such as cooking, laundry, and housekeeping) to wage workers who would otherwise need to take time away from their work for capitalists if they had to perform these services for themselves.

A second group of feminists differs from Engels and socialist feminists by suggesting that the biological roots of inequality are greater than the economic ones. As a result of their childrearing function, women have always been at the "mercy of their biology," according to Shulamith Firestone in her classic work, *The Dialectic of Sex* (1970). She believes the biological family has been the cell that imprisons people in two separate classes, unequal in their social roles. As social forms became more complex, men ventured forth to organize production, politics, war, and the arts, while women remained confined within the family raising the children. Today, however, men and women have the means to end male supremacy, through the new technology of contraception and even the possibility of producing babies outside the mother's womb. In short, Firestone links the liberation of women to the destruction of the traditional family, since she sees it as irreparably bound up with the domination of women. The aim of dismantling the family has had limited appeal as the basis for a political movement, however.

A third group of critics sees patriarchy, or male dominance, as a more important source of problems than economic or biological issues. Such critics, like Cronan (1978), describe the contemporary institution of marriage as a form of slavery because the wife is obligated to provide the domestic chores to maintain the home and to care for her husband and children and is not entitled to receive any pay for the work she does. The courts do not recognize any agreement between spouses that provides for such pay (Pilpel and Zavin, 1964). Moreover, a wife is legally obligated to live where her husband decides they should live; if she refuses, she can be charged with desertion (Gallen, 1967). Finally, a wife is obligated to have sexual relations with her husband, even when she does not wish to. A husband's obligations are to provide support, protection, and maintenance to his wife and children. Thus, concludes Cronan, being a wife is a full-time job without pay, without freedom of movement, and with built-in obligations for sexual relations. In these ways, Cronan argues, the condition of marriage for a woman is as bad or worse than slavery.

Inherent in these views is the assumption that the nuclear family is the basic source of oppression for women, whether because of property, biology, or patriarchy. These critics, especially those focusing on patriarchy, seem to assume that all husbands push their rights to the legal limit, without regard for their wives' wishes, and that alternative nonslave relations are not obtainable by women in marriage.

The solutions these critics propose arise directly from their analysis of root causes. Those stressing property as the source of the problem favor having the state pay housewives a wage for their work, or they suggest that housework be socialized and collectivized (Benston, 1978). Those blaming biology and patriarchy for the subjugation of women favor abolishing the family, for example by forming all-women communes so that women can define themselves independently of their relation to men (Brown, 1978).

Questions these viewpoints raise include the following: Do men and women need and enjoy each other? How would reproduction and the socialization of infants be handled? Is there enough support in the wider society to realize these proposals? Does the lack of support represent "false consciousness" on the part of women, or do they know things about their situation these critics overlook?

MODERATES

Moderate critics of the family reject the assumptions and proposals of both conservatives and radicals, although they accept some of the ideas of both. They share the radicals' concern with the inequality of women, as reflected in low rates of participation and inequality in the political and economic realms of society and in the lack of shared childrearing and household tasks. They tend to assume, with conservatives, that women derive pleasure from nurturing and being nurtured, but they assume that men also need and enjoy giving and receiving love. They assume that traditional family forms and functions did not necessarily suit all individuals. They assume that both men and women have needs for achievement as well as nurture, and that therefore nearly everyone receives greater satisfaction when they are doing both.

Their solution is to modify the family so that men and women can experience both love and work. For example, Juliet Mitchell, in her book *Women's Estate* (1971), proposes distinguishing the various functions performed by the family so they can be dealt with individually. The oppressive weight of reproduction has been reduced somewhat for women by developments in birth control technology, but has been replaced to some degree by a psychological ideology that stresses the importance of the mother (and no one else) for early childhood socialization. Alice Rossi, in "Equality between the sexes: An immodest proposal" (1964), called for ways of easing the combination of home and work responsibilities, the rejection of psychological ideas about child development that chain women to the home, the provision of adequate care for the children of working mothers, the reconsideration of suburban patterns of living, and educational efforts to counteract outmoded or traditional images of the roles of men and women.

More recently, Friedan (1981) has called for the women's movement to recognize and support the importance of the family. If the feminine mystique tried to define women only in terms of marriage, motherhood, sexual relationships, and service of home, says Friedan, the feminist mystique runs the risk of glorifying career to the exclusion of family and parenthood. What is needed is the successful integration of the two aspects of human identity—love and work—for both men and women.

Summary

1. Traditionally, the family has been defined as two or more persons who are related by blood, marriage, or adoption, and who share a common residence.

2. Generally the traditional family fulfilled the functions of sexual regulation and expression, biological reproduction, socialization of the young, meeting economic needs, and sometimes emotional intimacy.

3. These functions have been performed increasingly outside the family, as more unmarried people live together, as the number of children born to single mothers increases, as childcare is shared by more people, and as women enter the work force in growing numbers.

4. Changing family functions have been paralleled by major changes in family forms and activities. By 1990, only about one in four households in the United States will consist of a married couple with one or more children. The number of couples without children and the number of singles is growing rapidly.

5. Changing family forms are affected by declining marriage rates, rising divorce rates, and falling birth rates.

6. Within marriages, the number of working wives has soared in the last 30 years. By 1981, one in two married women was working.

7. The changes in family forms and activities are reflected in the recognition that "the family" is no longer a single uniform institution. Instead, there are various kinds of families and households.

8. The sharing of outside roles by women has not always been accompanied by sharing roles and tasks inside the household, resulting in role overload for women. There is still a shortage of good childcare facilities. Women who work have less economic need to put up with a marriage that is unsatisfactory on other grounds.

9. Divorce appears not to affect children negatively if the single-parent family has reasonable economic and emotional supports. One-third of families headed by women have incomes below the poverty line. A *happy* two-parent family appears to reduce the stress on parents and children, but a strife-torn marriage is harder on many families than single parenthood.

10. The effects on children of their mothers working are influenced by whether the mother wants to work and likes her job and by the severity of crises in the family. When mothers work unwillingly because of numerous family problems, the children may have problems. When mothers are happy with their work, their lives, and their children, the children show no ill effects. Indeed, the employment of mothers appears to have some positive effects on children.

11. As the importance of arranged marriage in a society declines, the importance of romantic love as a basis for marriage increases. Nevertheless, people tend to marry partners who are like themselves with respect to age, race, religion, social background, nationality, and physical proximity.

12. The functionalist view that families should assign final authority without ambiguity and that males should dominate has been strongly challenged in recent years. The exchange perspective suggests that both partners bring various resources to a relationship. As the resources for women have increased, the possibilities for bargaining and exchange within marriage have increased. As a result, working women tend to have more egalitarian relationships with their husbands than do nonworking women in the United States as well as in other countries.

13. The types of marriage relationships people have depend on the relative resources of the partners and on the expectations each brings to marriage. Five types were identified by Cuber and Harroff: the conflict-habituated, the devitalized, the passive-congenial, the vital, and the total. These types help to illustrate the wide variety of interactions that occur within marriages.

14. Although not often studied by sociologists, siblings in a family may help to socialize each other. They may also develop rivalries and coalitions that families need to control.

15. Recent research suggests that violence within the family, especially against women and children, is quite frequent both in the United States and in other countries. This violence seems to be due in part to stress and in part to the use of violence as a resource in family conflicts.

16. At least three identifiable groups have challenged the present structure of the family and have tried to change it. Conservatives wish to return to a patriarchal family, with the traditional division of labor between husbands and wives. In contrast, Marxian and radical feminists seek to pay wives for their work in the home or to abolish the family altogether. Moderates aim to reduce the inequality of women within and outside the home, but they share the conservatives' desire to support the family as an important source of nurture for both men and women.

Key Terms

birth rate
conjugal family
dual-career family
egalitarian family
extended family
family
kinship
marriage
marriage rate
nuclear or conjugal family
sibling

Chapter 14

The Economy and Work

Since human life began, work has been a part of our existence. Unlike the lilies of the field or the birds of the air, the human species must work to meet basic needs for food, shelter, and water. Air and sunshine are freely available, but the other necessities for sustaining life require some effort to produce and distribute. People in all societies, from hunting and gathering tribes to complex industrial nations, participate in the activities that produce and distribute those necessities. In most individuals' lives as well, work occupies a central position. For some, work is drudgery; for others, it is a creative and satisfying process. For all of us, work significantly defines our identities in society and influences who we meet, how we relate to them, and how we see the world. The pattern of roles, norms, and activities organized around the production, distribution, and consumption of goods and services in a society is called its *economic institution*. The nature of that economic institution and the various occupations in it have a profound effect on individuals.

Economic systems differ in a variety of ways: in the amount of production (measured by gross national product, or GNP); in how that production is organized (into a capitalist, a state socialist, or mixed economy); in the mix of economic activity among agriculture and mining, manufacturing, and service spheres; in whether or not a dual economy exists; and with respect to occupational specialization. These issues are explored in the first two sections of this chapter. A society's economic system influences the nature of work, where individuals get jobs, how much they earn, the conditions of their work, their prospects for future jobs, and unemployment. These points of intersection between individual lives and economic institutions are considered in the next two sections of the chapter. Finally, natural resources, level of industrial development, the social organization of work, and world market situations all influence economic productivity. In complex societies, economic production is linked to a system of money. The nature of money and the ways in which people see it influence social behavior in important ways, as we see in the concluding section.

CAPITALIST AND STATE SOCIALIST ECONOMIES

The major economic systems of the world contain various features that can be considered aspects of Western-style capitalist market economies or centrally planned economic systems. Although neither of the two systems exists in pure form, it is instructive to know the features of an ideal version of each. All economic systems, whether capitalist or planned, must address questions concerning the kinds and quantities of goods to be produced, how to coordinate production processes, and how to distribute the fruits of economic acitivity. How much of total production, for example, will go for consumer goods and how much for research or new equipment? Although such questions deal with economic activities, in fact they are answered in social and political terms.

Economic growth is a recent concern because the idea that an entire society might grow richer within one person's lifetime was inconceivable before the Industrial Revolution transformed production. Today, economic growth is a goal in many industrialized and developing countries. Nations have political and military reasons for seeking economic growth. Politicians know that increasing the prosperity of the populace may strengthen their own positions, and national defense efforts are fortified by a healthy economy. Economic growth may be measured by assessing changes in an overall measure of economic activity, such as gross national product (GNP). When countries are compared, GNP may be divided by the total number of inhabitants in the country to arrive at a GNP per capita figure.

WESTERN CAPITALIST MARKET ECONOMIES

Capitalism is a form of economic organization in which private individuals accumulate and invest capital. They own the means of producing and distributing goods and services in a society. Owners keep a portion of the surplus generated by their activity. In capitalist private-enterprise economic systems, private investors and their hired managers decide the nature and quantity of goods to produce within a supply and demand framework. The goal in this process is to make a profit for the owners of the corporation. They try to obtain the resources, goods, and services they need for this process, and they try to manage demand through advertising and marketing. If their products are not selling, they may try to eliminate their competition (for example, through tariffs protecting against imports or through price changes) or to change their products so they will be in greater demand.

Adam Smith and Laissez-Faire Economics

The underlying philosophy of capitalism was articulated by the Englishman Adam Smith in his *Inquiry into the Nature and Causes of the Wealth of Nations* (1776). He argued that economic wealth develops best when economic actions are regulated only by the free play of market forces. That is, producers and consumers should bargain directly to decide the prices at which they are willing to exchange or buy one another's goods. The government should provide only those services for which a market price cannot be charged, such as police protection, fire fighting, or flood control. The government should not interfere with the operation of free market forces, according to Smith. A laissez-faire economic system was one completely free of governmental interference.

Smith believed that each individual, motivated by the self-interest of making a profit, is "led by an invisible hand to promote an end which was not part of his intention"—the interest of society. Until the time he wrote, the English government regulated trade very closely. Smith's work influenced a swing away from government regulation.

Keynesian Economics

By the nineteenth century, capitalism had become a highly productive economic system. Even Karl Marx, who was critical of capitalism, acknowledged that in just 100 years, capitalists had "created more massive and more colossal productive forces than have all preceding generations together." Only the Great Depression of the 1930s really challenged Adam Smith's laissez-faire economic ideology.

Keynesian economic thinking took over in Western capitalist economies after the world depression in the 1930s. In his book *The General Theory of Employment, Interest, and Money* (1936), Keynes challenged classical economic assertions that natural market forces would always produce full employment and that savings would always be invested. As monopolies, which tend to develop in capitalism, take control of production, wages and prices are not likely to decline even during economic downturns. This is because there is no competition between firms. If prices do not drop, only two other results are possible in an economic decline—inflation or unemployment. Keynes argued that vigorous government intervention through deficit spending (that is, government spending that exceeded tax revenues) was necessary to maintain high levels of employment. The government could become the employer of last resort. Many Western nations today follow policies of deficit spending and/or tax cuts in an effort to maintain consumer demand and hence high levels of employment. Such policies increase the amount of money in circulation.

Criticisms of Capitalism

Capitalism has been criticized for the way it distributes wealth and income unequally in the population, for its tendencies toward monopolies (which encourage price fixing and an end to competition), and for its periodic unemployment.

Karl Marx's criticisms of capitalism go deeper than these, however. He argued that human beings are alienated from their labor and from themselves under capitalist forms of production. People, he stated, produce goods only through their own labor, and those goods may be valued according to the amount of labor it takes to produce them. Under capitalism, the worker is not paid for part of the value of the goods produced (the "surplus value"). Instead, the surplus value is taken away from the worker and turned into a profit for the capitalist at the expense of the worker. Alienation is furthered by work in very large organizations by doing very small, specific jobs, as on an assembly line, and by never seeing how one's work helps to create the final product (for instance, a car). People may forget that these products are humanly created, and the way they are produced tends to lead to their being viewed as fetishes—that is, as objects that are viewed with awe and adoration. Through this process people lose their humanity, Marx felt.

CENTRALLY PLANNED ECONOMIES

Various centrally planned economies have tried to apply some of Marx's economic ideas. One of the major points of difference between capitalist and centrally planned economies arises from basic assumptions concerning the right to own and control productive resources and the surplus generated from them. In state *socialist societies,* productive resources are owned and controlled by the state rather than by individuals.

In its pure form, the *centrally planned economic system* includes public ownership of, or control over, all productive resources, including mines, factories, transportation, communications, and labor. The economic activity of the entire system is planned by individuals in the government. The plan allocates a fixed amount of resources to particular organizations and sets production quotas. The planners issue commands production managers must follow. The government sets prices in ways that have nothing to do with production costs. It does this as a deliberate social policy in keeping with the belief that everyone should have food, medical care, housing, and education before some people have luxury goods (for example, records or cars). For this reason, many consumer goods are extremely expensive, while essentials such as food, housing, and medical care are inexpensive by Western standards—to the degree that they are available. Two nations that practice central economic planning are the Soviet Union and the People's Republic of China.

The Soviet Economy

In the USSR, the state owns the means of production, including land, mines, and factories. The state has decided that defense and heavy industry are most important, and that consumer goods have a lower priority. So political decisions within the government and the ensuing allocation of state resources favor heavy industry, electric generating and distribution systems, transportation systems, chemical and fertilizer production, and agriculture. Such decisions do not take consumer demand into consideration, so stores will have gluts of some items while others are in short supply. When consumer goods are scarce, state officials decide how much food or clothing people need, and people must settle for whatever is available. As goods become more plentiful, consumers can become more choosy about what they want to buy.

Earning more money has limited value for workers in Soviet society. Certain key goods, like access to better housing, are determined by political influence rather than by economic market factors. Money is further devalued by the shortages of some consumer goods and the very high prices of others.

The Chinese Economy

China is a unitary state, and the state is the leading force in the national economy. It sets policies and priorities. Everyone who is able to is expected to work. Agriculture makes up one-quarter of its economic output and employed about three-quarters of its work force in 1979. China has large mineral deposits, including coal and iron ore. Since 1954, the development of the economy has been based on five-year national plans.

Under the leadership of Mao Tse-tung after the Communist Revolution, the Chinese eliminated starvation, eradicated venereal disease and drug addiction, generally improved the health of the population, and educated millions of children. The streets and sidewalks were no longer filled with multitudes of sleeping, begging, hungry human beings, as they had been in prerevolutionary days. Western observers returning from China in the 1970s were singularly impressed with how the basic needs of the population were being met, and by how happy and healthy the children seemed. They realized that such gains did not come without a price, at least by Western standards. For example, people were assigned food ration stamps for use only in a particular region, so they were able to live only in assigned area. All young people were expected to do manual labor for at least two years before applying to the university. And one criterion for admission to university was the candidate's contribution to his or her work group and community.

Despite China's progress, recessions occurred after the Great Leap Forward (1958–1960) and during the Cultural Revolution (1966–1968). In 1979, the Chinese government officially acknowledged for the first time that there were problems of unemployment, housing shortages, and hunger. As a result, several shifts in economic and social policy occurred. In 1980 it was decided to slow down the "four modernizations" in agriculture, industry, defense, and science and technology. Since the late 1970s, China has pursued a much more liberal economic policy. Joint ventures with other countries and foreign loans are now allowed. Imports more than doubled between 1977 and 1980 (*Europa Year Book,* 1982, p. 120). The Fifth National People's Congress in 1980 approved greater management autonomy for industrial enterprises; scientists were encouraged to spend less time on political activities and more international exchanges between scholars occurred; admissions tests were reinstated for university entrance; and foreign tourism began to be encouraged after years of closed borders.

There is considerably more diversity in state socialist societies than the Soviet and Chinese examples suggest. In Poland and Yugoslavia, for example, agriculture was never collectivized on the same scale as in the Soviet Union. There is a large class of small farmers in these two countries, unlike in the Soviet Union. Czechoslovakia and Hungary are fairly developed industrial countries, in contrast with Romania and Bulgaria, which are among the poorest of European countries.

Criticisms of Centrally Planned Economies

In centrally planned economies, economic and political power tend to become concentrated in the hands of one group whose authority is based on party position. Strikes, unwillingness to work overtime, or similar worker actions are considered disloyal to the state. Workers are controlled politically as well as economically. Many questions can be asked about the incentive system in state socialist economies. If essential goods or services like food and medical care are subsidized by the state and the user does not pay their full cost, will users consume more than they would if they had to pay the full costs themselves? If producers of such goods or services are protected from competition and assured of continued government subsidies, will they be blind to user needs and preferences? Critics of centrally planned economies, in short, raise questions about how much freedom individual workers have and about the effectiveness of central planning and collective rather than individual incentives.

HYBRID ECONOMIES—YUGOSLAVIA

Critics of state socialist economic systems say that centralized political planning is an inefficient way to manage a geographically dispersed economic system. Yugoslavia attempts to solve some of these problems with a hybrid economic system that blends features of both planned and market economies.

Yugoslavia broke with the Soviet Union in 1948 to follow a new path to socialism involving "self-management." In the Yugoslav system of self-management, the workers in a factory form a workers' council, and the council elects or hires its own managers. The group decides what products they will make, based on what they think will sell. They can try to borrow money from a central pool or from suppliers of raw materials, who are often located in other countries. If the organization generates a profit—that is, has money left over after paying its costs, including the wages it has agreed to pay—the workers' council decides what to do with it. The council may decide to reinvest it in the organization in order to fund research, development, and future growth. Or it may pay it out in the form of bonuses to all the members. Workers have considerable decision-making power within the limits placed on them by market influences on prices, profitability, and the incentive structure needed to motivate wage earners. The Yugoslav system of self-management relies much more on market forces than on central planning.

ARENAS OF ECONOMIC ACTIVITY

All economies, whether capitalist market systems, centrally planned ones, or hybrid economies, may be analyzed in terms of the various arenas within which economic activity occurs. Three major concepts help analyze the arenas of economic activity. First is the idea that the economy consists of primary, secondary, and tertiary sectors. The primary sector is agriculture and mining; the secondary sector is manufacturing; the tertiary sector, service activities. The United States, especially, has experienced dramatic shifts over time in the proportion of its population that is engaged in each of these sectors. Second, the concept of a dual economy sees economic work as occurring in core, periphery, and state sectors. The core or monopoly sector consists of large, profitable national or multinational firms, like the oil companies, which dominate their markets. The periphery or competitive sector consists of small, local, barely profitable firms like textile mills or restaurants. Beyond the dual realm of private economic activity, the state sector includes federal, state, and local government workers, including teachers and sanitation workers.

The third concept used to examine economic activity is the distinction between occupations and professions. An *occupation* is a position in the world of work that involves specialized technical knowledge and activities. A *profession* is a position that, in addition to specialized technical knowledge and activities, involves background and training in a body of knowledge and often some form of degree or credential. These three concepts illuminate the nature of work and the connections between individuals and the economy through jobs, income, and unemployment. Together they shape the stage on which people play their occupational roles.

PRIMARY, SECONDARY, AND TERTIARY SECTORS

In all societies, work occurs in three main sectors. In the *primary sector,* people farm, fish, fell trees, and extract ores and other resources such as coal from the ground. All the activities of this sector deal with the collection of natural resources. In the *secondary sector,* people work with the raw materials to turn them into manufactured goods. They smelt and roll steel, build cars, freeze foods, weave and sew clothing, produce chemicals, and pour concrete. This is the industrial or manufacturing sector of a society's economy. The *tertiary sector* of the economy involves services to manufacturers such as those provided by banking, transportation, insurance, and communications, as well as such social services as education, medicine, welfare, and personal services like hotels, restaurants, household service, barber and beauty shops, cleaning, laundering, and repair services. Within a given society, the proportion of people working in each sector depends on how well endowed the society is with natural resources and energy and on its level of industrial development.

In most societies, agriculture occupies most of the people working in the primary sector. The proportion of the population in agriculture is significant, because it indicates how many people remain available to produce other goods and services. A subsistence economy is one in which nearly every member of a society is engaged in gathering or producing the basic necessities of life. If the people producing food, clothing, and other essentials are able to provide such goods for more people than just themselves, it becomes possible for a society to support other activities—for example, full-time religious leaders, full-time toolmakers, storytellers, builders, and musicians. In Figure 14.1 selected nations in the world are ranked according to the proportion of their population in agriculture; their average per capita income is also indicated. In general, the smaller the proportion of the population in agriculture, the higher the per capita income.

Technology helps to explain the wide variation among nations in the size of the agricultural sector. As farming is mechanized, fewer people can produce more food. In some societies, work in the primary sector still involves very simple hand-operated technologies. Hoes, axes, picks, or fishnets owned jointly by groups of people may be used. In other societies, a great deal of expensive and elaborate farming or mining equipment is used. The mechanization of farming in the United States, for example, has led to the production of enough food for its population and the generation of a surplus for export to other nations. At the same time, the percentage of the American labor force engaged in farming has dropped dramatically, from 72 percent in 1820 to 3 percent in 1980. Food production ability, however, is not necessarily a sign of wealth. A few very rich nations (such as Kuwait) cannot produce all the food they consume, but they have other valuable resources, like oil, which they can trade for food.

The secondary, or manufacturing, sector of the U.S. economy expanded dramatically from 1820 to 1920 (as Table 14.1 shows), but has remained stable at about one-third of the labor force since 1920. As late as 1860, three out of five Americans in the labor force worked in farming. After the Civil War, however, industries that had responded to wartime needs increased their productivity. This was especially true in textiles and shoe manufacturing. The first transcontinental railroad was completed in

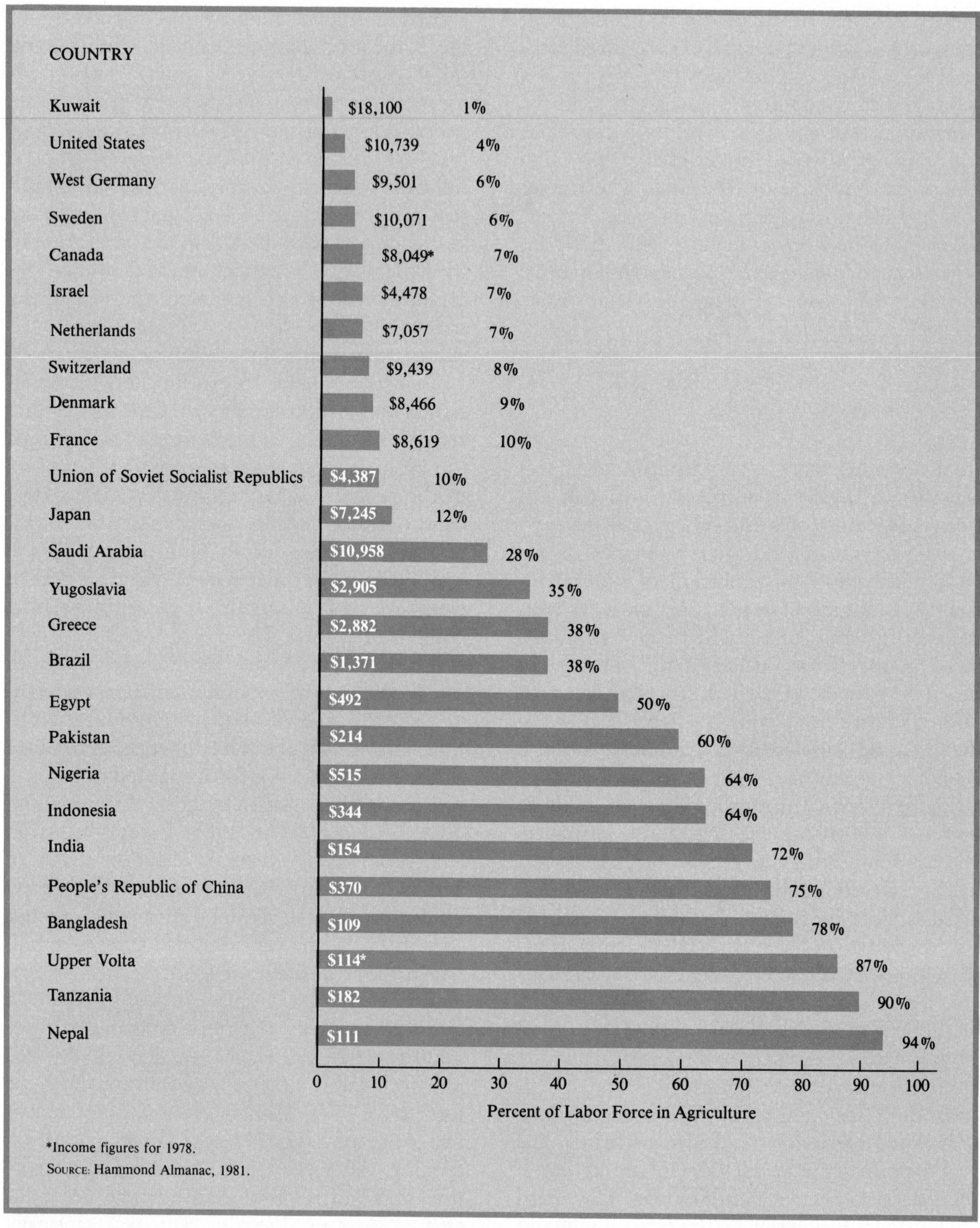

Figure 14.1 Percentage of Labor Force in Agriculture and per Capita Income, 1979

Table 14.1 **Percentage of Labor Force in Various Economic Sectors in the United States, 1820–1980**

Sector		1820	1860	1900	1920	1940	1950	1980
Primary	Agriculture, forestry, and fisheries	72	59	37	27	17	15	4
	Mining	—	1	3	3	2	2	1
		72	60	40	30	19	17	5
Secondary	Manufacturing and construction	12	18	25	31	29	33	28
	Transportation, trade, finance, real estate	—	7	17	20	24	29	33
Tertiary	Services and government	—	12	11	16	21	21	34
			19	28	36	45	50	67

SOURCE: U.S. Bureau of the Census, 1975; 1981a, p. 390.

1869, spurring the prospects for national trade. The oil and steel industries also grew tremendously in the closing decades of the nineteenth century. By 1900, the United States was the largest industrial nation in the world. The manufacturing portion of the work force continued to grow. The number of factory workers, for example, rose steadily as a percentage of the work force until 1950, when it peaked. The percentage has been declining ever since.

By 1950, half the labor force was working in the *tertiary* or *service sector* of the economy. This sector includes people who do not produce food or goods, but may aid production by providing financial, information, education, marketing, transportation, communication, or other services needed by people in the primary and secondary sectors. As machines have been developed to perform more and more agricultural and manufacturing activities, per capita productivity in those areas has increased and more people have been freed to move into the tertiary sector of the economy. As Table 14.1 shows, the tertiary sector jumped from 19 percent of the U.S. labor market in 1860 to 67 percent in 1980. This sector represents a larger percentage of the labor market in the United States than it does in Japan or West Germany (Singelmann, 1978).

THE DUAL ECONOMY: CORE, PERIPHERY, AND STATE SECTORS

Primary, secondary, and tertiary sectors of the economy refer to the types of activities people perform. Another important way of thinking about economic life is in terms of the dual economy. The *dual economy* refers to the division of the private sector of the economy into (1) a core, or monopoly, sector and (2) a periphery, or competitive, sector (Averitt, 1968; O'Connor, 1973).

Firms in the economic core have large numbers of employees, large total assets and annual sales, and generally high profits. Their operations and sales are national or international. They usually produce many different products. The major oil, automobile, chemical, steel, electronics, food, soap, tobacco, and drug companies are prime examples of core industries. The

Many people, especially women, minorities, and older and younger workers, work in the competitive, or peripheral, sector of the economy which includes textile and clothing firms, restaurants, and small general stores. This sector is highly competitive, has low profit margins, often unstable employment, and limited chances for advancement.

core sector of the economy employs about one-third of the labor force, with the largest proportion in manufacturing and mining. The markets of core firms are generally concentrated, meaning that a few very large firms sell most of what the market buys. The cash flow and credit ratings of these firms are usually very high. They tend to have more capital invested per worker than peripheral firms and to have higher productivity. Unionization is well developed in this sector, and wages are relatively high. New competitors are generally kept out through state regulations (for example, in the banking and insurance industries), by high capital requirements (as in automobile manufacturing or mining), by high overhead costs, or by heavy advertising and brand loyalty (for instance, in the soap and tobacco industries).

The people who work in the core sector of the economy constitute what has been called the primary labor market (Piore, 1975). The primary labor market contains jobs with relatively high wages, good working conditions, considerable job security, opportunities for advancement, and work rules and procedures based on due process. On-the-job training is available and may be necessary for moving up the career ladder.

In the peripheral or competitive sector of the economy, firms are relatively small. They tend to be located in one geographic region, to produce only a small line of related products, and to have markets that are normally local or regional in scope. Their cash flow is much smaller, their credit ratings are poorer, and they pay higher interest rates on borrowed funds than do core firms. Productivity is relatively low. They have less capital invested per worker, and because they are not capital-intensive, it is relatively easy for competitors to set up in business. Examples include the textile and apparel industries, meat-packing firms, restaurants, drug and grocery stores, automotive supply companies, and other small manufacturers.

Many competitive sector firms produce or sell in markets that are seasonal, subject to sudden changes in fashion or style, or are unstable for other reasons. As a result, work in these industries is seasonal and irregular, and wages are low. People who cannot find work in the core sector are more likely to accept the lower pay and poorer working conditions of the peripheral sector. Union organization is weak in this sector because of the social characteristics of the labor force and because there are large numbers of small, local firms. In addition, highly competitive markets and small profit margins make it costly for employers to recognize unions. So workers in this sector tend not to be organized, with some exceptions in the garment industry and among foundry workers (O'Connor, 1973). Competitive industries employ about one-third of the United States labor force, with the largest proportion working in services or distribution.

The competitive sector labor market differs from the core sector labor market. The more disadvantaged groups—racial minorities, women, young or old workers—are the ones most likely to end up in this market. Jobs in this sector tend to be unstable and to have short or nonexistent mobility chains. These features, combined with low wages, poor working conditions, and little job security, discourage job stability (Sokoloff, 1980). No matter how long or hard employees work at secondary labor market jobs, there are no established paths for advancing to better jobs (Gordon, 1972).

The *state sector* of the economy can be divided into goods and services produced by the state itself (for example, education, public health, welfare and other social services, and military service, excluding the production of arms), and production organized by private industries under contract with the state. The latter includes military equipment and supplies, and building and highway construction. Today nearly one-third of the U.S. labor force is employed in direct or contractual state sector activities (O'Connor, 1973).

Productivity in the state sector is relatively low and increases slowly. The demand for labor was relatively stable and increasing in the 30 years after World War II, but in the late 1970s and 1980s, public employees began being laid off. The large size of work units and relatively low turnover among employees foster the growth of labor unions in state industries, but the diversity of the work force (young, old, blacks, whites, men, women, handicapped, nonhandicapped) is an inhibiting factor. Occupational distinctions and civil service rankings also limit unionization. Because increased labor costs in the state sector tend to force up taxes, government agencies generally try to discourage the development of unions. In recent years the state sector has become more highly organized than the competitive sector, but less organized than the core sector (O'Connor, 1971). See Table 14.2 for a comparison of the three sectors.

LARGE CORPORATIONS AND MULTINATIONALS

The core or monopoly sector of economic activity consists of relatively few large corporations. Assets, sales, and jobs are concentrated in the hands of a few corporate owners and managers. In 1980, the 200 largest manufacturing corporations in the United States owned 60 percent of all corporate assets (U.S. Bureau of the Census, 1981a, p. 541). The four largest firms in the breakfast food, automobile, aluminum, and vacuum cleaner industries control 75 percent or more of the sales in those industries, not counting imports; other industries are nearly as concentrated. Moreover, the top 500 U.S. industrial firms employed 70 percent of the manufacturing labor force in 1981 (*Fortune,* May 1981, p. 323).

This tremendous concentration of economic power and resources offers financial advantages, advertising and brand-name recognition, and political power to the large corporations in the

Table 14.2 General Characteristics of Core, Periphery, and State Sectors of the Economy

	Core or Monopoly Sector	Periphery or Competitive Sector	State Sector
	(Oil, auto, chemical, and drug industries; big, prosperous multinationals)	(Textiles, auto industry suppliers, meat packing, restaurants; smaller local firms)	(Teachers, social workers, sanitation workers, federal, state, and local government workers)
Wage and salary levels	High	Low	Medium to high
Job stability	High	Low	High
Degree of labor force unionization	High	Low	Intermediate
Wages and salaries determined by	Productivity and cost of living; negotiations	Supply and demand	Political bargaining
Working conditions	Relatively good	Poor	Good
Employee benefits	Generally good	Poor	Good
Percentage of white males	High	Low	Medium
Percentage of females	Low	High	Low at upper ranks; high at lower ranks
Percentage of nonwhites	Low	High	Equals percentage of minorities in the work force

SOURCES: Averitt, 1968; Barclay, 1981; Fusfeld, 1973; O'Connor, 1973.

core sector. Such firms can limit the development of new products, resist the adoption of new technologies, and ignore new ways of organizing the work process. They are fairly effectively protected from serious competition. They may restrict the options available to consumers, keep prices high, resist new technology that is more efficient in the long run, and persist in organizing work in ways that produce boredom and alienation. The few people who own nearly 60 percent of the productive assets can decide what investments they will make, what new products or services they will develop, where they will build plants or offices, and who they will hire.

These firms do not operate in a competitive market. Instead, they constitute an *oligopoly,* a market composed of a few sellers. The products they sell are close substitutes for one another, and it is difficult for new competitors to enter the market. All firms are influenced by the pricing actions of other firms in the industry (Averitt, 1968). Because they are not operating in a competitive market, these firms can set "administered" prices, which consumers must pay unless they are willing to do without the goods or services. It is difficult, for instance, to live without home heating oil in zero-degree weather, so most consumers pay the higher administered prices oligopolies charge. (Although growing numbers of families are installing wood-burning furnaces, they still represent a small portion of the total market.)

Such firms have considerable political power not only because they can make large political contributions and have people who are well-connected politically on their boards, but also because their production, jobs, and taxes are considered valuable national resources (Evans and Schneider, 1981). Their political power is enhanced by the ability of the large firms to cooperate. Besides sharing many directors in common (Dooley, 1969; Levine, 1972; Mizruchi, 1982; Zeitlin, 1974) and having many social and intellectual ties (Domhoff, 1967, 1970; Moore, 1979; Useem, 1980, 1979, 1978), large firms are bound together by overlapping ownership. The Mellon family and bank, for example, not only have a dominant position in Gulf Oil and Alcoa Aluminum, but are also among the largest shareholders in IBM, General Electric, Atlantic Richfield, Standard Oil of California, Exxon, AT&T, Caterpillar Tractor, K Mart, Sears & Roebuck, Eastman Kodak, U.S. Steel, and Jones and Laughlin Steel. And the banking industry is itself very concentrated.

Corporations and banks are not only increasing their assets and sales and the percentage of market share they control, they are taking over other corporations to form conglomerates that operate simultaneously in many industries. ITT, for example, produces food and electrical equipment, runs hotels, and owns publishing houses. General Electric not only makes light bulbs and refrigerators, but medical systems, plastics, aircraft engines, and nuclear reactors; it also sells coal, oil, gas, and uranium.

In this process of corporate consolidation, the core sector of the U.S. economy has moved from one based on regional firms to an economy based on national firms. The process began around the turn of the century and has continued. In the latter half of this century, the core economy has been shifting from a national to a world economy. That is, the largest firms are now multinational corporations. For a time multinational corporations were overwhelmingly American, but that dominance has been waning. The proportion of the top 100 world firms that are American-based has declined from 58 percent in 1971 to 30 percent in 1982, although more remain based in the United States than in any other single country. (See Table 14.3 for a list of the top 50.)

The annual income in sales from these multinational corporations often exceeds the total gross national product of many nations. Exxon, the largest multinational corporation in the world in 1982, had sales of $108 billion that year, more than the GNP of Switzerland, Saudi Arabia, Pakistan, South Africa, and many other countries. The company employed 137,000 workers in 1982.

Committed to growth and maximizing profits, and willing to move wherever cheaper production or increased sales can be realized, the multinationals make decisions that affect whether or not people work; what they will eat, drink, and wear; and what is taught in schools (Barnet and Muller, 1974; Vernon, 1977). By pursuing a policy of mobility, they are able to play labor markets off against each other by threatening to move if labor organizes, and they can even influence national and international political relations.

Supporters of multinational firms claim that their activities result in greater efficiency, lower prices for consumers, and economic development, including the export of technologies, capital, and jobs for developing nations. Critics such as Barnet and Muller (1974) argue that multinationals are helping to create a social system that is more centralized and hierarchical than anything yet known, and that they try to substitute loyalty to the corporation for more authentic sources of community such as neighborhood, ethnic group, religion, or nation. In the process, they violate human needs for social, ecological, and psychological balance. Both critics and supporters agree that multinational corporations are playing an ever more important role in the world and have critical political, economic, and social consequences for people's daily lives.

OCCUPATIONS AND PROFESSIONS

Occupations and professions refer to the technical activities associated with particular positions in the world of work. As you can see from the two previous sections, people can have an occupation—for example, lawyer—that they per-

Table 14.3 50 Largest Multinational Corporations, 1982

Rank	Company	Total Revenues ($ millions)	Corporate Headquarters
1	EXXON	$108,108	USA
2	Royal Dutch/Shell Group	82,337	Netherlands/UK
3	Mitsui	68,709	Tokyo
4	Mitsubishi	68,271	Tokyo
5	Mobil	65,458	USA
6	General Motors	62,699	USA
7	Texaco	57,628	USA
8	British Petroleum	52,229	London
9	C. Itoh	51,502	Tokyo
10	Marubeni	47,404	Osaka
11	Sumitomo	44,931	Osaka
12	Standard Oil California	44,224	USA
13	Ford Motor	38,247	USA
14	Nissho-Iwai	32,124	Tokyo
15	Standard Oil Indiana	30,372	USA
16	Sears, Roebuck	29,260	USA
17	ENI—Ente Nazionale Indrocarburi	29,103	Rome
18	IBM	29,070	USA
19	Gulf Oil	28,252	USA
20	General Electric	27,854	USA
21	Atlantic Richfield	27,798	USA
22	IRI—Instituto Ricostruzione Industriale	26,400 (est.)	Rome
23	Phibro-Salomon	25,109	USA
24	Unilever	24,109	Netherlands/UK
25	ITT	23,197	USA
26	E I DuPont de Nemours	22,790	USA
27	TOTAL Group (Française des Pétroles)	22,654	Paris
28	VEBA Group	20,885	Dusseldorf
29	Kuwait Petroleum	19,800 (est.)	Safat, Kuwait
30	Petróleos de Venezuela SA	19,659	Caracas
31	Fiat Group	19,381	Turin
32	Elf Aquitaine Group	19,215	Paris
33	Petroleos Mexicanos	18,996	Mexico City
34	Petróleo Brasileiro SA	18,946	Rio de Janeiro
35	Citicorp	18,275	USA
36	Nippon Tel & Tel	18,192	Tokyo
37	Deutsche Bundespost	17,467	Bonn
38	Toyota Motor	17,009	Nagoya
39	NV Philips Lamp	16,997	Endhoven
40	Nissan Motor	16,794	Tokyo
41	Volkswagen Group	16,760	Wolfsburg
42	Nippon Oil	16,637	Tokyo
43	Postes et Telecommunications	16,600 (est.)	Paris
44	Safeway Stores	16,580	USA
45	The Electricity Council	16,488	London
46	Toyota Motor	16,379	Toyota City
47	Daimler-Benz Group	16,222	Stuttgart
48	Renault Group	16,137	Boul-Billancourt
49	Sun	15,967	USA
50	Phillips Petroleum	15,966	USA

SOURCE: Adapted from *Forbes,* July 5, 1982, pp. 126–130.

form in the primary, secondary, or tertiary sector of the economy. That is, a person may be a lawyer for a mining, manufacturing, or service organization. Furthermore, he or she may hold a job in the core, periphery, or state sectors of the economy. Some occupations, like lawyer, may be performed in all sectors of the economy. Others, like machine toolmaker, may be performed in only one sector, but may be located in core or periphery firms.

A study of occupations reveals the growth of occupational specialties over time and the increasing division of labor. In the last 100 years, not only have jobs shifted from the agricultural and manufacturing sectors to sales and services (as Table 14.1 shows), but the number of occupational specialties has also grown tremendously. The latest edition of the *Dictionary of Occupational Titles,* for example, lists over 17,500 occupational specialties, including air analyst, perfumer, fish culturist, tissue technician, floral designer, lease buyer, sound mixer, magazine keeper, swatch clerk, fingerprint classifier, pickler, airbrush artist, and stripper (U.S. Department of Labor, 1980d). (This government handbook lists only legitimate occupations, of course; it does not mention numbers runners, purse snatchers, pool sharks, pimps, prostitutes, drug pushers, and hired guns.)

The Division of Labor

In broad terms, the world of work is broken down by government recordkeepers into white collar, blue collar, service, and farm work (see Figure 14.2, column 2). As indicated in column 1, 43 percent of the population was working in 1981. Among those working, 53 percent were in occupations classified as white collar. The white collar category includes professional and technical workers like teachers and engineers, managers and administrators, sales workers, and clerical workers such as secretaries (column 3, Figure 14.2). Many of these occupations can be performed in the primary, secondary, or tertiary sectors. Table 14.4 shows the shift in the number of people working in white collar, blue collar, service, and farm occupations from 1900 to 1980.

Blue collar workers include skilled craft workers such as carpenters and toolmakers, operatives

Table 14.4 **Percentage of Labor Force in Various Occupations, 1900–1980**

Type of Occupation		1900	1920	1940	1970	1980
White Collar	Professional and technical	4%	5%	8%	14%	16%
	Managers, officials, and proprietors	6	7	7	11	11
	Clerical	3	8	10	17	19
	Sales	5	5	7	6	6
Blue Collar	Craftsmen and foremen	11	13	12	13	13
	Operatives	13	16	18	18	14
	Nonfarm laborers	13	12	9	5	5
Service	Service workers, except private household	4	5	7	10	13
	Private household workers	6	3	5	2	
Farm	Farmers and farm managers	20	15	10	2	3
	Farm laborers and foremen	18	12	7	2	

SOURCES: U.S. Bureau of the Census, 1970, Tables 347 and 348; 1981a, p. 401; U.S. Bureau of the Census, 1975.

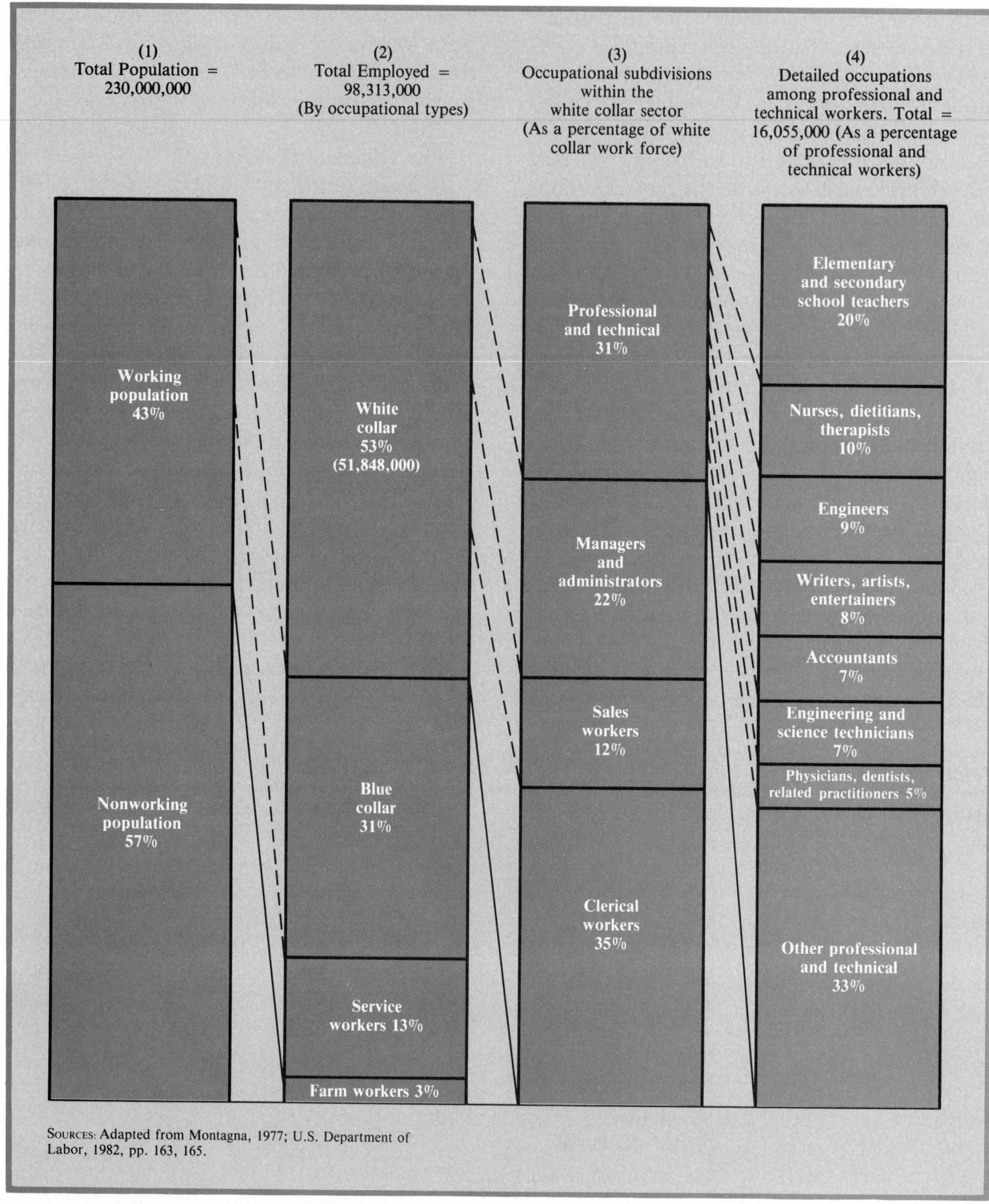

SOURCES: Adapted from Montagna, 1977; U.S. Department of Labor, 1982, pp. 163, 165.

Figure 14.2 Four Levels for Analyzing the Labor Force, 1981 such as drillers, crane operators, and assembly-line workers, and other nonfarm laborers such as garbage collectors and zookeepers. Service workers care for children, do cleaning, prepare and serve food, work as bank tellers, insurance salespersons, nursing aides or orderlies, and provide protective functions like firefighting and police protection. The final occupational type listed is that of farm workers, who may work on farms as managers or laborers. White collar occupations are broken down in Figure 14.2 into occupational subdivisions in column 3, and the professional and technical subdivision is presented in even more detail in column 4.

Professions and Professionalization

If all occupations share the interplay between knowledge and skill, nature, and other people, what is different about the professions? Sociologists such as Goode (1960) have defined the traditional professions as the ministry, law, and medicine. More recently, sociologists have included as professionals college professors, engineers, and scientific researchers. Professions are characterized as resting on a theoretical body of knowledge, not simply on the application of technical procedures. Professions, presumably, call for considerable knowledge, skill, and expertise, as well as problem-solving and decision-making abilities. Knowledge and expertise require specialized training, which is generally recognized by some form of degree or credential. Although anyone can claim to be a gardener, not everyone can claim to be a psychiatrist or a lawyer.

Professionals operate in situations where the stakes are high—salvation, jail, death. All involve considerable risks and uncertain outcomes. Therefore, not only technical knowledge and skill, but also symbolic and interpersonal skills are important. Finally, professionals claim the need for relative autonomy in the conduct of their work on the grounds that only professionals can decide the best way to perform the work, since only they have the specialized knowledge needed to make the decisions. In return for their relative autonomy, professionals claim to regulate themselves through professional associations and self-imposed ethical standards. One form this regulation takes is restricting the supply of new members in the profession so there will not be an excessive number of people competing for the available work. They also regulate and certify the training of new members, partly to restrict the number of entrants and keep their own fees high.

In recent years, workers in many occupations (for example, chiropractors, accountants, and various therapists) have tried to become more "professional" by raising educational requirements and sometimes installing state licensing procedures to certify members. This trend reflects in part the desire of clients to have "genuine" practitioners perform work for them, and in part the efforts of members of an occupation to control the number of people eligible to perform certain tasks. This effort grows out of the concern shared by many who undergo expensive training that there will be jobs available when they complete their educations.

THE NATURE OF WORK

The study of work goes well beyond a system of classification, however. Sociologists see work as consisting of human effort interacting with physical nature or with other people, or with both (Freidson, 1979). As a result, the world of physical nature, social considerations, and the state of technology all set limits on how work can be conducted and subdivided. A physician treating a patient, for example, will need to deal with the limits imposed by the patient's willingness to cooperate in the treatment, and perhaps by the cooperation and skill of X-ray technicians, nurses, or laboratory specialists. In an effort to cure a patient, the physician's knowledge and skill interacts with the physical reality of disease,

The percentage of self-employed Americans has dropped dramatically in the last two centuries. Today only about 10 percent of the labor force are independent artisans, farmers, or professionals.

with existing technology, and with other people. Manufacturing operations similarly involve an interplay between nature, knowledge, and the social coordination needed to produce something. Making a wood-burning stove, for instance, depends on natural materials such as steel, knowledge of how wood burns and how people use stoves, and coordination among metal workers, designers, marketers, and distributors.

One major factor affecting the social relations of production is the class relations of capitalist society. Ownership, or position in the authority structure of a work organization, will determine one's autonomy and power over others. Although important social relations are defined by class, the social relations of production are shaped by other factors as well. Producing a newspaper, for instance, requires various social relationships such as coordinating the work of reporters, editors, photographers, layout people, and printers in order to perform the task, whatever the class relations in the situation may be. School newspapers, for example, do not have owners who make a profit, but they must devise social relationships to produce the paper. But although the social relations of production generated by class relationships need to be considered in many spheres of work as one possible explanation for the way things are organized, they are not a sufficient explanation by themselves. Awareness of the social relations of work may occur most often among professionals, since they have the longest tradition of exercising strong control over this aspect of work.

But this is not true of most people, because in general people are no longer self-employed. In 1776, 80 percent of the American working population were independent artisans, farmers, and professionals. By 1880 this was down to 33 percent, and today it is around 10 percent. Independent artisans are not free of market pressures, of course, but they do have some flexibility with respect to when they will work and how they will do a particular job. Moreover, if they work efficiently, they benefit directly from their efforts.

What awaits the 90 percent of the work force who work for others? What is the nature of work in modern industrial and service societies today? Much has been written about the mindless monotony of assembly-line industrial production, as well as about the petty paper pushing that occurs in large-scale white collar bureaucracies. Is work as boring, repetitive, dehumanizing, dulling, alienating, fragmented, or dangerous as critics suggest? Here we consider the working situations of blue collar, white collar, and professional and managerial employees.

BLUE COLLAR WORK

Blue collar "blues" refer to the feelings of depression and unhappiness many blue collar workers feel about their work. Their dissatisfaction may be expressed in high rates of absenteeism, wildcat strikes, or sabotage of the product they are making (for example, failing to tighten an important screw or scratching the side of a new car). Because of their effects, the blue collar "blues" have been much discussed in recent years. Even adequate pay, reasonable security, safety, comfort, and convenience on the job do not protect workers against the blues, according to Seashore and Barnowe (1972). In addition, workers need a chance to perform their work well, a chance to increase their competence, to achieve, and to contribute something personal and unique to their work. Workers whose jobs measure high on variety, autonomy, and the chance to use their skills score lower on measures of political and personal alienation (Sheppard and Herrick, 1972).

Blue collar workers also complain that white collar employees have privileges they do not, such as not being required to punch a time clock, having paid vacations, sick leave, and pensions. The benefits blue collar workers receive depend largely on whether they work in the core, competitive, or state sectors of the economy. Blue collar workers may also feel that work rules are often enforced in a paramilitary fashion and that bosses often fail to listen to suggestions they have for better ways to do their jobs (Health, Education, and Welfare, 1973).

Blue collar complaints about work tend to target four major objective areas of discontent: compensation, health and safety hazards, work settings, and job security (Shostak, 1980). One's view of one's pay depends on a number of factors, including comparison with previous years. Between 1946 and 1956, the average real take-home pay of blue collar workers increased 2 percent a year; from 1956 to 1966 it increased 1.4 percent a year; and from 1966 to 1976 it increased only 0.3 percent a year, most of which went for increased local taxes. Since 1976, for blue collar workers there has been an actual drop in real, after-tax income in the face of increased inflation. Inflation brings the additional fear of rising unemployment, especially in the blue collar occupations.

Health and safety hazards are often the result of shortsighted pressures to increase productivity and profitability. U.S. Department of Labor figures suggest that each year there are 14,000 deaths from industrial accidents; 100,000 persons are permanently disabled; and about 100,000 people die from industrial diseases. An additional 300,000 may become disabled annually from occupationally related diseases. Dangerous machinery, chemicals, radiation, heat, pesticides, noise levels, and toxic fumes and dust are some of the culprits of work-related illness for blue collar workers. Since the passage in 1970 of the Occupational Safety and Health Act (OSHA), safety regulations and inspections may have provided some relief (Shostak, 1980).

Related to the health and safety of work conditions are the more general conditions under which blue collar work is done. The setting is often dirty, smelly, uncomfortable, noisy, and barren of any comfort. Outdoor workers face the harsh heat of summer and cold of winter. Blue collar workers are continually irritated by broken pay phones, coin-operated vending machines, and toilets; by filthy or nonexistent factory windows and poor ventilation systems. Work sites are seldom clean, tidy, comfortable, warm in winter or air conditioned in summer—a situation that is particularly annoying when those conditions are compared to the settings in which office workers perform their jobs.

Another negative point of comparison with white collar work hangs on the issue of job security. The general lack of growth in the blue collar occupational sector increases anxiety about being "laid off." Seniority is some defense, but even that fails to help in an economic downturn. Even when workers are reemployed elsewhere, they lose the seniority and benefits (such as more than two weeks vacation) they had slowly worked up to in another job.

Despite all the drawbacks associated with blue collar work, there are some positive features. Some workers report they are doing "real work," in contrast with paper pushing, which many of them scorn as nonwork. The results of their work are often tangible and in some way objectively measurable. For craft workers and for unionized workers in profitable industries, the pay is quite good. Overtime work results in overtime pay. Long years of education (sometimes seen as boring or expensive) are not necessary to get the job. In difficult or dangerous occupations (for example, coal mining, steel foundry work, high steel construction, or fire-fighting), strong bonds of friendship and solidarity develop between workers. Groups who face danger together seem to share a more intense capacity for laughter, living, and loving, compared to more sheltered workers (Shrank, 1978). Moreover, blue collar workers seem better at shedding their work concerns at day's end than do managers, engineers, and other white collar workers (Shrank, 1978). In his study of high steel workers, however, Cherry (1974) found that the constant danger and fear they faced tended to result in escapist activities outside work—like drinking—for at least some men.

WHITE COLLAR WORK

White collar workers are far from being satisfied with their work as well. Clerical jobs in many large organizations today are impersonal, routine, almost robotlike, and offer little prestige. Educational credentials have been raised for many jobs, but the content of the jobs, the responsibility or autonomy they afford, and their prestige and status have not increased along with the educational requirements. Workers often perform highly fragmented jobs whose connection to the larger purposes of the organization is obscure. As a result, many white collar workers feel estranged from the goals of their organization (Health, Education, Welfare, 1973).

Even middle managers have become increasingly discontented with their work. Traditionally they were strong supporters of their organizations and their policies, but there has been growing receptivity to unionization in their ranks. One in three middle managers indicates some willingness to join a union (HEW, 1973). Without unionization, many middle managers find themselves earning less than unionized blue collar workers. One compensation was that such workers always believed their jobs were secure as long as they performed them well. But in recent years large numbers of middle managers have been laid off in the auto industry, in insurance, and in publishing (Bennett, 1980). People who have invested 20 or 30 years in the same organization find themselves suddenly without a job, too young to retire and yet old enough to make moving difficult.

Many white collar workers have little influence over organizational policies and decisions. They are often called upon to implement programs they have not designed, a chore that leads to feelings of frustration or alienation. Shaping policy and making decisions is more characteristic of the work done by professionals or upper-level managers.

PROFESSIONAL AND MANAGERIAL WORK

As business and government become larger, they require more supervisors and managers to coordinate the many people in the organization. Professionals are increasingly likely to work in large organizations instead of practicing on their own. Although professional and managerial work is highly varied, it does share some common features. Much of the work involves data, information, problem-solving, and dealing with people. Lawyers need to keep abreast of the latest laws and court cases, for example, so that they can properly advise clients. Doctors and dentists want to know about new techniques, drugs, and research discoveries in order to provide the best available treatment for their patients. Sales managers need to collect and analyze sales data to see which salespeople are succeeding, to help those whose sales are lagging, or to develop new products.

Managers and professionals need to motivate and monitor the work of others. They often face conflicting demands—for example, between clients needing care and organizations short of resources, or between the personal needs of workers and the productivity demands of a firm. They may be called upon to fire people they know and like. They may face frustration because they lack the power to solve a problem, yet they are often blamed if things go wrong and seldom appreciated when things go well. Their productivity and the quality of their work may be difficult for others to assess clearly. Many work long hours, without overtime pay, and they often take problems from work home.

As managers move higher in an organization, their responsibilities increase along with the job benefits and satisfactions. Especially in the core sector, high-level managers and professionals receive high salaries, generous fringe benefits, bonuses, and stock options. Where they have some autonomy to carry out projects, they may get a sense of accomplishment and satisfaction from their work as well.

All types of work—blue collar, white collar, managerial and professional—present various frustrations and satisfactions. A key factor for all workers is whether they have the power to change the features about their work that they do not like, or whether they feel trapped and powerless. To the degree that they are able to make such changes, they may feel reasonably satisfied with their work situations.

CONNECTIONS BETWEEN INDIVIDUALS AND THE ECONOMY

GETTING JOBS

Individuals are never more directly affected by economic sectors and occupational subdivisions than when they try to find a job. On the one hand stands a job market that consists of openings in various economic and occupational sectors, and on the other hand a labor market that consists of individuals with varying experience, education, and personal qualities. The nature of these markets is shaped by structures (such as capitalism or state socialism), resources (such as mineral and energy supplies), and policy decisions. Both in the creation of job markets and in the nature of defining various "eligible" or "appropriate" labor pools, human agents and organizations make decisions and take actions that shape the opportunities open to individuals. Processes of social channeling (and excluding) send large numbers of educated white males into the core sector of the economy, which has the best wage and salary rates, the best benefits, and the best promotion opportunities. (Job prospects for college graduates in the years 1985–1990 are discussed in the box on p. 382.)

Job Prospects for College Graduates, 1985–1990

Various sectors of the economy are expected to experience different rates of growth between 1978 and 1990. The biggest percentage increases are expected in services; finance, insurance, real estate; trade; and mining. All but mining have a large number of people in them already, so the expected percentage increases represent large numbers of new jobs in those areas.

Recent college graduates have entered somewhat different types of jobs than they have in the past, and the tendency is expected to continue in the future. More graduates will go into sales, clerical, and service work, sometimes taking jobs high school graduates have filled in the past. Figure 14.3 shows the decline in the percentage of college graduates entering professional, technical, and managerial jobs between 1969 and 1980, and the increase in the proportion of more recent graduates entering sales, clerical posts, and operative work. College graduates have a lower unemployment rate than high school graduates. In 1980, the unemployment rate for all college graduates was 2 percent (up from 1.5 percent in 1970), while for college graduates who were 20 to 24 years old, it was 4.5 percent. Young high school graduates, however, had an unemployment rate of 11.4 percent in 1980 (Sargent, 1982, p. 5).

One reason for the shift in the kinds of work college graduates do is the slowing rate of growth in professional and technical jobs, including teaching positions. The trend is expected to continue. The growth rate in certain other occupations is expected to be quite a bit better, however. A large increase is projected in the number of college-educated persons working as managers and administrators and sales workers, both in percentages and in absolute numbers.

By 1990 competition for entry-level jobs will drop, as the number of workers aged 16 to 24 declines. The bulge in the labor market in 1990 will come with the workers aged 25 to 54.

The earnings advantage of college graduates over high school graduates still exists, but it has declined from the 1960s. In 1969 college graduates earned nearly 50 percent more than high school graduates, but by 1977 they earned only 32 percent more on the average. So if a high school graduate aged 25 to 34 was earning $10,000 annually in 1977, a college graduate earned $13,200 on the average.

The process of finding a job may be broken down into three parts. First, there are positions in the job market. These positions exist in the extractive, manufacturing, or service divisions and in the core, competitive, or state sectors of the economy. They may call for people with training or experience in particular occupations. Second, there are individuals in the labor market who have various qualifications for doing different types of work based on education, experience, or skills. Most economists stop analyzing the process at this point. Sociologists add the social *processes* that link individuals to particular positions. Linkages come to life immediately when we think about how people hear about positions. Less than one job in five is filled through help-wanted listings in newspapers or by employment agencies (Lathrop, 1977). Moreover, the more interesting, responsible, and higher-paying jobs with greater potential are less likely to be advertised (Becker, 1977; Bolles, 1977; Granovetter, 1974).

To understand how individuals find jobs, we need to know how they form networks and how those networks operate to provide links with jobs (see Chapter 4 for more on networks). By

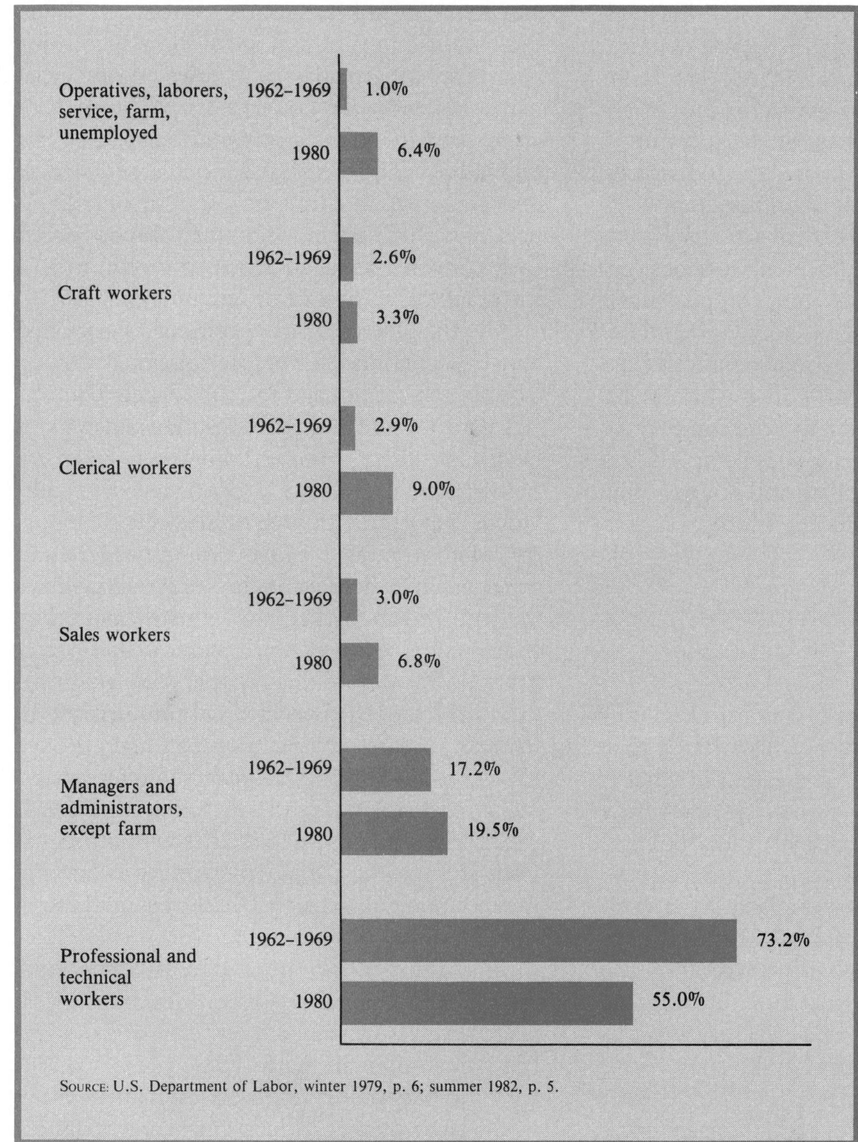

Figure 14.3 Where College Graduates Got Jobs, 1962–1969 and 1980, by Major Occupational Group

including the three elements of individual characteristics, characteristics of positions, and the links between them, sociologists are able to offer an inclusive framework for viewing how individuals actually get jobs.

In finding jobs, young people rely on the assistance of acquaintances and relatives even more than older workers do. They also find work by applying directly to employers, and this method is used in all occupations (Becker, 1977). Blacks and whites use somewhat different strategies for getting jobs, with blacks more likely to use public employment services, while whites successfully use newspaper ads and private agencies

(Becker, 1977). Whites are also more likely to hear about jobs from family or friends than are blacks. For various reasons, whites are more likely than blacks to find work in the monopoly sector. As a result, whites are likely to continue to fill many of the jobs in that sector. Individuals who find better jobs do not confine themselves to the formally listed jobs that are advertised, posted, or listed with employment agencies, because these sources exclude about 80 percent of the positions that are available at any given time. Women and minorities, who may not receive the help from informal networks that white males get, are more likely to end up in the competitive (and lower-paying) economic sector, unless their job-finding strategies are able to overcome the social channeling and discrimination that have traditionally occurred.

FACTORS AFFECTING INCOME

Some of the same features that affect how individuals get jobs also influence how much they are paid to do those jobs. The extent of what is possile depends primarily on market factors in a capitalist economy, and primarily on political factors in a state socialist economy. In capitalism, the economic rewards available for a position depend on whether it exists in the monopoly or competitive sector and on the political power of the occupation (including professional associations and unions). The total salary pool is greater in the monopoly than in the competitive sector of the economy.

Within a particular corporation, certain occupational groups have greater leverage than others. The salaries paid to lawyers, accountants, and doctors who work for an automobile company, for example, are set by the bargaining terms established by their occupational groups. Craft workers and assembly-line workers in the auto industry are represented by highly organized labor unions that have helped to negotiate what salaried workers at various levels should be paid. The pay for certain positions may depend on proximity to key resources within or outside the organization, as well as on the wage priorities set by a particular firm. Sales and financial managers, who are close to key resources, are often paid more than personnel managers, for example. Ceilings may be set on certain clerical job categories. The historical scarcity of individuals for a particular position may also be related to the income levels attached to certain jobs—for example, computer programming.

All the features of positions mentioned above—economic sector, occupational power, labor organization, and scarcity—affect the salaries paid for various positions. This analysis of positions differs from the approach taken by human capital theorists. They believe that individual characteristics such as intelligence, industry, skill, training, experience, attitudes, and other qualities determine the salaries individuals are paid in the marketplace. This is only partly true. People with greater technical skill sometimes do earn more than people with less proficiency. However, two-thirds of the variation in income occurs *within* occupational groups (Jencks et al., 1972). Differences in human capital do not explain all of that variation. Instead, much of the difference in salaries within occupations seems to be explained better by location in the monopoly or competitive sectors, and union organization.

In addition to the knowledge, skill, and experience an individual possesses, other individual characteristics influence where people work and how much they are paid. These can be considered the bargaining resources individuals bring to the labor market. Educational credentials, for example, have become increasingly important resources in the competition for certain positions. Traditionally, race, sex, socioeconomic status, attitudes, demeanor, appearance, and other personal qualities have been bargaining resources as well. Job candidates are often sorted on the basis of social traits like race and sex into lesser positions and lower incomes within the organizations where they are hired.

This discussion refers to individuals who actually reach the point of entry into particular organizations and are hired. But a series of channeling operations occurs prior to the point of entry into an organization. The channeling of individuals into positions with various incomes resembles the *linking* process in getting jobs.

What determines who gets matched with jobs that offer the possibility of high earnings? Are there institutionalized barriers to certain types of jobs (for example, their gender composition)? Who gets through such barriers, and how do they do so? What part do networks of contacts and geographic location play in that process? These are some of the questions sociologists ask about the linkages between individuals, positions, and incomes (Granovetter, 1979). They are quite different from the questions economists ask.

UNEMPLOYMENT

Perhaps the most important link between individuals and the economy is whether or not one has a job at all. The issue of unemployment has become an important one in recent years. In the United States, unemployment rates exceeded 10.8 percent in 1982, when 12 million people were out of work. These figures represent the highest rate of unemployment since the Great Depression. Because of employment shifts caused by individual illness, recent college graduations, and job changes, no society has a zero unemployment rate (although state socialist societies claim to). About 2 percent unemployment is considered nearly full employment in most industrial societies. In the United States, only people who have actively looked for work in the last four weeks and have not worked at all are defined as unemployed. People who have worked part-time or who have given up looking for work are not considered unemployed. For these reasons, official rates of unemployment understate the actual rates.

Unemployment rates are presented as a national average, although unemployment is not distributed evenly throughout the population, as Figure 14.4 shows. Teenagers and minorities are hardest hit. Although 4.6 percent of white collar employees were unemployed in the 1981–82 recession, that rate was much lower than the 18 percent rate among construction workers, or the 29 percent among auto workers (Kelly, 1982). These unemployment patterns mean that certain regions—the manufacturing Midwest, the construction-related Northwest, and urban centers with large numbers of minority teenagers—have particularly high rates of unemployment.

Unemployment occurs more often and with greater severity in the peripheral rather than the core sector of the economy. During the 1981–82 recession, for example, Marina Whitman, vice-president and chief economist at General Motors, estimated that for every one auto worker who was laid off, there were three unemployed workers in firms that supply the auto industry. Core firms are not always immune to economic recessions, but the effects of such downturns are felt much more severely in the competitive sector.

Losing a job and being unable to find a job affects individuals in negative ways. Economic hardships were cushioned in the 1973–75 recession by unemployment benefits received by more than 75 percent of the jobless. But in the 1981–82 recession, only one-third of those out of work received unemployment compensation as a result of budget cuts engineered by the Reagan administration.

> Since losing his job as a forklift driver at a mill in Molalla, Oregon, last August, James Wittig, 35, has been scrambling for a job. He applied to work as an exterminator and tried to land a job laying gravel. "I'll try anything, but there's nothing," he says. "If there's a job open in Oregon, there's at least 100 people trying to get it." Wittig's wife works as a cook for $360 a month to support him and their two children, but it is not nearly enough. Says Wittig, "I'd like to talk to the President for half an hour. I'd say, 'You're living high off the hog.

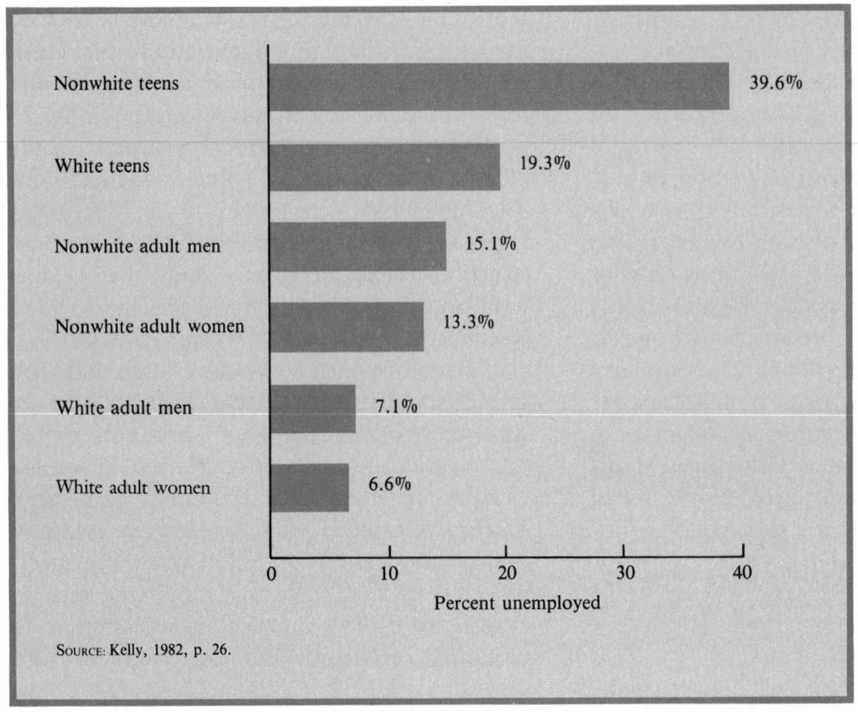

Figure 14.4 Unemployment Rates among Various Social Groups, December 1981

You're telling us how good everything's going to be in two years. But we're starving today!'" (Kelly, 1982, p. 27)

People with home mortgages and other debts to pay off are especially hard hit because they cannot subsist on a meager income. For white collar and professional workers who have never had the experience of losing their jobs, the psychological blow may be personally devastating. Virginia Hall, a job counselor for professionals in Atlanta, Georgia, observed: "All these people have mortgages and are committed to certain life-styles. . . . This is their first experience of losing a job, and they are stunned. They have no idea of how to cope" (Kelly, 1982, p. 27).

Sociological studies of the unemployed reveal a tremendous loss of self-esteem, feelings of powerlessness, and a sense of lost identity (Jahoda, Lazarsfeld, and Zeisel, 1971; Komarovsky, 1940; Maurer, 1979). These feelings may be expressed in withdrawal or depression, alcoholism, or in anger and abuse directed at family members. The personal and interpersonal costs are not captured by the statistics that make headlines. Besides affecting those without jobs, unemployment increases the anxiety and lowers the morale of those who do have jobs, making them reluctant to push for their rights on the job. High rates of unemployment are also associated with higher rates of *underemployment*—that is, people taking jobs that are not customarily filled by individuals with their level of experience or education. Drama majors waiting on tables or journalism graduates collecting trash are two examples of underemployment.

At least three sources of unemployment have been suggested by social scientists, who do not always agree on the relative importance of those causes. First, unemployment may result from inflation, reflected in higher oil and energy prices, higher wages affecting the higher prices of U.S. goods, and higher interest rates. Second, unemployment may be intensified by efforts to slow inflation, including higher interest rates and a slower growth in the supply of money in circulation. Both conditions make it difficult for consumers to finance loans to buy homes or cars, thus seriously affecting employment in the auto and construction industries.

A third source of unemployment is the globalization of the world economy. Investment capital is leaving the United States for regions where labor and raw material costs are lower and where governments offer more favorable tax treatment and less regulation (Barnet and Muller, 1974; Vernon, 1977). Some American firms have decided to compete with international firms in automobiles and steel, for example, by erecting tariff barriers against imports rather than improving productivity by adopting new production technologies (Evans and Schneider, 1981). Over time, such an emphasis on short-term rather than long-term industrial development may result in the loss of manufacturing jobs in the United States. Markets and production used to be confined within regions or within nations. Now, however, both consumers and producers have begun to look all over the world for better prices and profits. The result is that manufacturing jobs in the United States are declining. In Japan, corporations and employees are strongly bound together by mutual loyalty; employees seldom move to other firms in search of better jobs, and employers will absorb some losses rather than lay off workers. Despite rising

"There's got to be more to life than just tightening one's belt."

SOURCE: Drawing by Joe Mirachi, © 1979, *The New Yorker Magazine, Inc.*

oil and energy costs, Japan has had one of the lowest rates of unemployment during the past decade of any industrialized nation.

THE SOCIOLOGY OF MONEY

Imagine that you have just landed on the earth from the planet Mars. You see people go into a building and talk to someone who brings them a hamburger and some French fries. In return, they give the person some little pieces of paper. You find some paper on the street which you carefully cut into the same size pieces as you saw inside. You give them to the salesclerk in the hope of getting some food, but the clerk simply looks at you as if you were crazy. You are very puzzled. Why are some pieces of paper accepted in exchange for food or other goods and services, while other pieces of paper are not?

THE NATURE OF MONEY

This story illustrates the social nature of money. People accept money in various forms because they believe others will accept it from them in turn. Money is based on social conventions and on successful experience with its use. At various times and places, different items have served as money, including the wampum (beads made from shells) used by native Americans, cowries (pretty shells) in India, whales' teeth in Fiji, woven mats in the Trobriand Islands, large stone slabs on the Pacific Island of Yap, tobacco among early North American settlers and prisoners, gold and silver coins, pieces of colored paper, and small plastic rectangles also known as credit cards.

Because money is a social creation, the meaning and value people attach to it depend on their social experiences with it. The social meaning of money is apparent in two major conditions that have affected economic systems since the creation of money: inflation and depression. Each of these conditions is at least partially influenced by social factors and each has important social consequences. Both are related, in different ways, to economic growth. *Economic growth* refers to an increase in the amount of goods and services that are produced with the same amount of labor and resources. For example, when Japanese management took over an electronics plant in Chicago, it nearly doubled the plant's output and reduced quality rejects by 96 percent to a nearly zero level (Bond, 1981). The result of these efforts was economic growth.

INFLATION

Inflation is an increase in the supply of money in circulation that exceeds the rate of economic growth. When the supply of money rises relative to the available goods and services, the same amount of money will buy fewer goods or services. Consumers see the result in the form of rising prices. In sociological terms, inflation may be considered the social recognition that money is worth less in relation to various goods and services. Inflation occurs when money itself is debased, and it has occurred in situations where governments print paper money faster than economic productivity increases. We think of inflation as an economic phenomenon, but it is actually created by social and political processes, and it has major social repercussions.

Inflation does not affect all social groups in society equally. In general, inflation benefits borrowers (because they can repay their loans with "cheaper" dollars later), but hurts lenders and pinches people living on fixed incomes. People who have little discretionary income (the poor) and those who have some money but no property lose ground. Those who own property gain, since real estate and other property generally increase in value in inflationary times. As the biggest borrowers, governments benefit from inflation. Taxpayers, meanwhile, are pushed into higher tax brackets with incomes that buy fewer goods and services. The result of inflation in the United States has been a growing number of

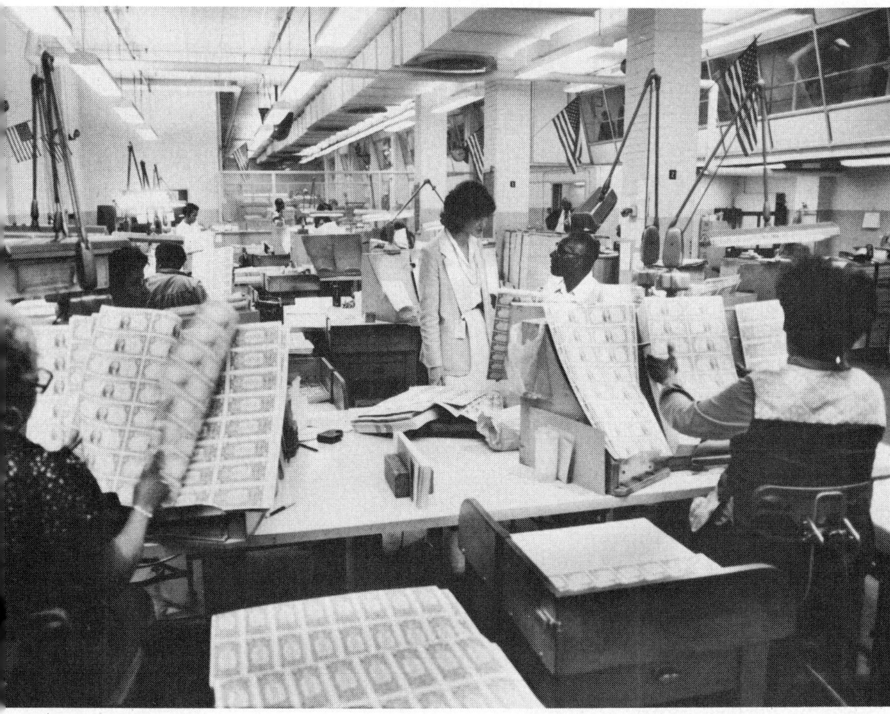

Forms of money, especially paper money, are socially created. The use of money depends on trust and confidence within a society.

taxpayer revolts designed to slash the taxes people have some control over. Another indicator of taxpayer rebellion appears in the growth of the so-called *underground economy,* which consists of exchanges in goods and services that people do not report to tax authorities. (See the box on p. 390 for more on the underground economy.) It has even been suggested that inflation undermines the traditional virtues of hard work and thrift. Certainly those virtues have less payoff in an inflationary context.

Clearly, inflation influences the attitudes and behaviors of people. During inflationary times, people save less money and tend to adopt a "spend or borrow now, repay later" approach. Such behavior reflects a response to the declining value of money and savings in an inflationary era. The scarcity and high cost of borrowing money make it difficult for people to buy homes or to start businesses.

Sociologists tend to view the market economy as constantly tending to unbalance the society in which it operates. This view has been advanced by functionalist sociologists such as Durkheim and Parsons as well as by Karl Marx and Daniel Bell (1976). The destabilizing effects of a market economy can only be offset by shared values and norms in a society, such as a belief in equal opportunity, or by some type of forced coordination ultimately backed by force, such as a military dictatorship. Economists, on the other hand, tend to view the market economy as inherently stable or at least as able to be stabilized by the skillful management of economic policies. Inflation in such a system is viewed as a problem that can be fixed, since the system itself is healthy (Goldthorpe, 1978).

Extreme inflation has severe social consequences, as can be seen in countries currently experiencing very high rates of inflation. They

The Underground Economy

> Richard Lawson is a 34-year-old financial executive with an ascending career at a big New York corporation, an Ivy League pedigree and Hollywood looks. He lives on Manhattan's West Side in a brownstone that he bought four years ago when it seemed a candidate for the wrecker's ball and has since renovated the building with his own money and toil. He is a runner, doesn't smoke, and prefers Perrier to stronger libations. A friend describes him as "upbeat, positive, a straight-arrow type." (Lohr, 1981, p. 3-1)

Even though a "straight arrow," Lawson participates in what economists and sociologists call the underground economy. He reports only two-thirds of the rental money he makes on his apartment building. The underground economy is work done or goods that are exchanged "off the books," for cash or barter, with no records kept. The underground economy exists all over the world. The French call it *travail au noir,* the Italians *lavoro nero,* the Germans *schwarzarbeiter* and the British name it *fiddling* (Malabie Jr., 1981). The phenomenon is growing in the United States, and it has important social and economic implications.

> People who don't partake tend not to notice it. But it is there, in the neighborhood laundry without a cash register, in the doctor who asks that checks be made out to cash, in the moonlighting carpenter or plumber, in the waiter or taxi driver pocketing tips, in the bar owner "skimming" cash from the till, in the dress shop that records as "inventory losses" items that it sold but didn't ring up. Then, too, there is money from criminal activity that goes unrecorded, from the drug trade in Miami to the black market for stolen art in New York. (Lohr, 1981, p. 3-1)

Several economists have come up with a way of estimating the underground economy because they realized that the official gross national product (that is, legal money transactions) is quite a bit less than the amount of money in circulation, due to underground economic activity, according to economists Peter Gutmann and Edgar Feige. In the early 1960s, the underground economy was just a few percentage points of total GNP. Today, however, it is reasonable to conclude that the underground economy may be as much as 16 percent of total GNP, or about $500 billion (MacAvoy, 1982, p. F3).

The underground economy has significant social and economic implications. From a policy point of view, "official" government figures become less and less accurate as the underground economy grows.

A major social implication of the growing underground economy is the way more and more middle-class people, who do not think of themselves as criminals, are engaging in the illegal activity of tax evasion by participating in the underground economy. This represents a shift in middle-class self-image away from a person who is law-abiding in all respects toward someone who breaks the law but still views himself or herself as respectable.

The underground economy affects the fiscal condition of the state because many nations are running major deficits in their budgets.

Leisure and sports are generally enjoyed more when they contrast with work. In recent years, the number of people working in construction and heavy manufacturing has declined, while technical, communications, financial, and service occupations have increased. These shifts are reflected in high unemployment among minorities and in the greatly increasing percent of married women who work.

Percent of single and married women in the labor force, 1940, 1960, 1981

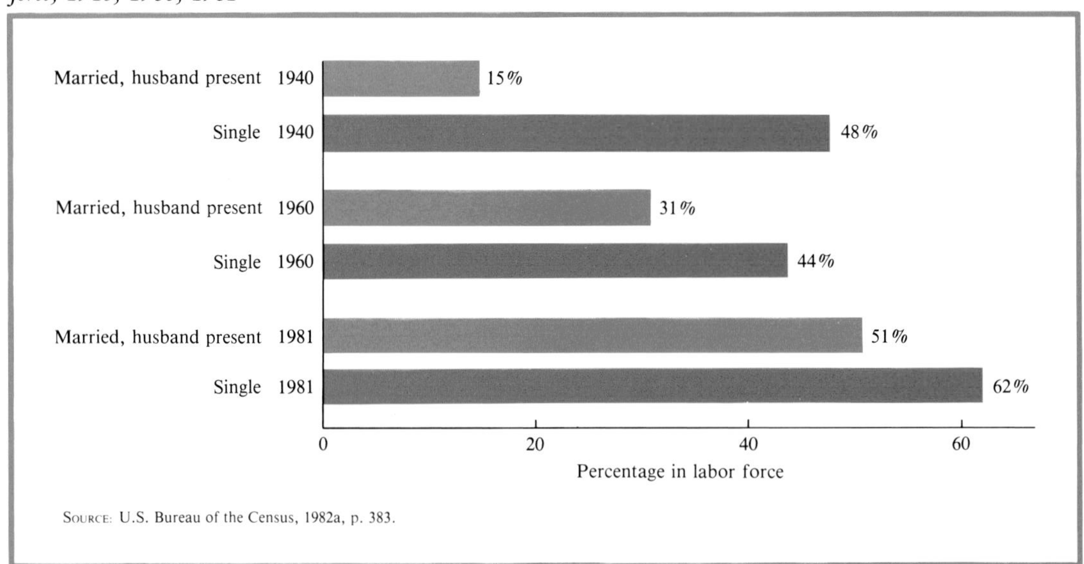

SOURCE: U.S. Bureau of the Census, 1982a, p. 383.

Unemployment rate in the United States (in percent)

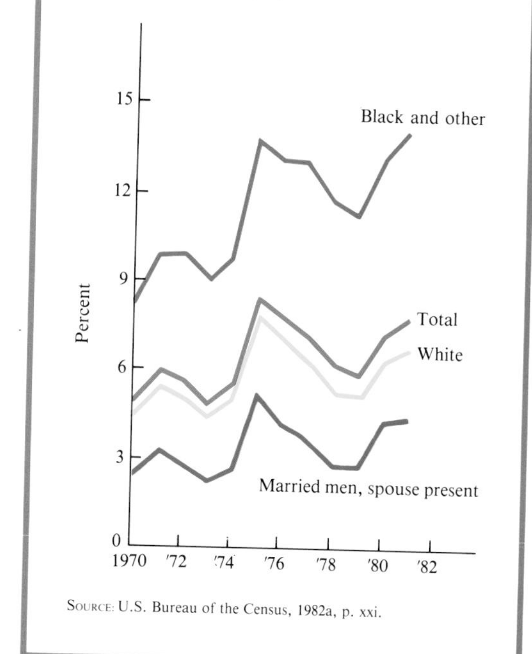

SOURCE: U.S. Bureau of the Census, 1982a, p. xxi.

padres

include Chile, Brazil, Mexico, and Argentina. Long-term lending at fixed rates of interest almost stops, and people hold little money. Rapid inflation encourages residential building, since an apartment or house is considered a good hedge against inflation. At the same time, it discourages public utility development because people are reluctant to commit their funds to long-term investments.

None of the Latin American nations has matched the hyperinflation and resulting social chaos that occurred in Germany between 1921 and 1923. In a hyperinflation—an extreme form of inflation—prices accelerate very rapidly and people resist using the currency as much as possible. In the German hyperinflation after World War I, the printing press was used on a massive scale to create money. In part this was a response to the massive reparations (war payments) Germany had to pay England, France, and the United States. People collected their wages in suitcases or wheelbarrows and rushed out to spend them immediately, before the money became totally worthless.

Hyperinflation is a good example of the limits of the social construction of reality and of the self-fulfilling prophecy in action. Once growth in the money supply loses any relation to increases in the production of goods and services, it becomes more and more difficult to sustain the socially constructed view that the money has any value. A negative self-fulfilling prophecy occurs when people lose confidence in the medium of exchange, which speeds the medium's circulation and increases the use of other forms of exchange.

THE GREAT DEPRESSION

Just as runaway inflation can have dire consequences for the social fabric, the other extreme, that of economic deflation and depression, also has severe social consequences. In a depression, economic productivity declines. The Great Depression of the 1930s was worldwide and profoundly affected the individuals who lived through it. They had quite different attitudes toward work, money, and the world than the generation that preceded or followed them. By 1933, average income in the United States had dropped to half of what it was in 1928. Ninety thousand businesses had failed, and the banking system was on the verge of collapse. Fifteen million people, or about a quarter of the working population, were unemployed.

In addition, the decade of the 1930s was a time of drought and crop failures in the Great Plains states. Farmers were uprooted from their farms and homes. In Kentucky and other Appalachian states, coal miners literally had nothing but dandelions and blackberries to eat. In major cities across the country, people stood in bread lines and went to soup kitchens, and many were malnourished (Bird, 1966). When they lost their homes or apartments, people formed "Hoovervilles," or shantytowns. There were no federal programs of unemployment insurance, bank insurance, or welfare until President Roosevelt pushed the Federal Emergency Relief Act through Congress in 1933. Private charities, churches, and city and state governments tried to keep people from starving, but their limited resources quickly proved inadequate. Most of the people who lived through those times subsequently had a terrible fear of debt, valued job security very highly, and have remained cautious and conservative in their social and economic behavior.

Summary

1. The economic institution of a society refers to the socially patterned ways that people produce and exchange goods and services.

2. Economic systems have three major social forms—Western-type capitalist market economies, centrally planned economic systems, and hybrid forms that combine features of both.

3. Capitalism draws heavily on the social and economic ideas of Adam Smith and John Maynard Keynes.

4. Critics of capitalism stress the way it exploits and alienates the individuals working in it, and the way it distributes wealth and income unequally in the population.

5. Centrally planned economies depend on state officials rather than on market factors or private ownership to decide where resources and profits should go. The Soviet Union and China are probably the purest cases of centrally planned economies.

6. Critics of planned economies question the amount of freedom workers have and whether planned economies are as efficient as capitalist ones.

7. Hybrid economies like Yugoslavia's try to decentralize power in the participatory democratic control of workers over production, and they try to have the market rather than the state determine supply and demand.

8. Economic activity has been roughly classified into three major sectors: the primary sector, where people grow or extract food and resources; the secondary sector, where raw materials are converted into products; and the tertiary sector, which provides both business and social services.

9. In the world today, most people in most societies work to produce food. In the United States, the proportion of the population in farming has declined dramatically, from 72 percent in 1820 to 3 percent in 1980. As a result, many people are free to produce other goods and services.

10. In the United States the secondary, or manufacturing, sector grew dramatically between 1820 and 1920. Since then it has remained at somewhat less than one-third of the labor force.

11. In the United States, the chief growth area has been the service sector, which has grown from 19 percent of the labor market in 1860 to 67 percent in 1980.

12. The dual economy refers to the division of the economy into a core or monopoly sector, a periphery or competitive sector, and a state sector. The core is characterized by large, oligopolistic firms that are national or multinational in operation. The periphery or competitive sector consists of small, local, barely profitable firms like textile mills and automobile suppliers. The state sector includes federal, state, and local government workers. The labor markets in these sectors differ in terms of pay scales, job security, benefits, promotion opportunities, and with respect to the social characteristics of the people in them.

13. The large national and multinational corporations that comprise the core sector of the economy control the majority of corporate assets, sales, and employees. Their annual sales exceed the GNP of many nation-states. As a result, they have a high and concentrated degree of economic, political, and social power.

14. More than 17,500 legal occupations are listed in the *Dictionary of Occupational Titles*. The type of work people do is sometimes described as blue collar, white collar, service, or farm work. White collar work in general, and the professions in particular, have expanded in recent years. Professions rest on a theoretical body of knowledge and expertise acquired through specialized training. Blue collar workers include skilled craft workers such as carpenters and toolmakers, operatives such as drillers, crane operators, and assembly-line workers, and other nonfarm laborers such as trash collectors and zookeepers. Service workers care for children, serve food, are bank tellers, salespersons, hospital orderlies, or firefighters.

15. The nature of work is affected by the type of work and by the declining number of jobs for independent artisans. Blue collar "blues" refer to the discontent blue collar workers feel because of the monotonous, boring, and non-challenging nature of their work and because of their unhappiness over the compensation, health and safety hazards, work settings, and security of their jobs.

16. White collar workers often complain that their work lacks real challenge, interest, prestige, or future prospects.

17. Professional and managerial workers are relatively well rewarded, but may face conflicting demands and frustrations.

18. Getting a job involves the characteristics of individuals and those of jobs, and the processes that link the two together. Interpersonal networks are important in that process.

19. Like jobs, income is affected by the nature of the job being done, the traits of the individuals doing it, and market and linking factors.

20. Unemployment has been a major problem in Western economies during the past decade, with rates exceeding 10 percent occurring in the United States. Unemployment has hit the hardest in the industrial Midwest and the Pacific Northwest. It has been especially hard on teenagers, minorities, and other workers in the competitive sector of the economy.

21. Money is a social invention. It survives because people accept it in exchange for goods and services. Social processes may produce situations where the money supply and economic growth are out of balance. These result in inflation, deflation, or depression, conditions that have important social implications and that affect various social groups in different ways.

Key Terms

capitalist or market economy
centrally planned economy
dual economy
economic core
economic growth
economic institution
economic periphery
hybrid economy
inflation
Keynesian economics
laissez-faire economics
occupation
oligopoly
primary economic sector
profession
secondary economic sector
socialist societies
state sector
tertiary economic sector
underemployment
underground economy

Chapter 15

Power and Politics

Power is the capacity of an individual or group to control or influence the behavior of others even in the face of opposition. A person or group is powerful in relation to someone else. For this reason, power is relational; it involves at least two parties. Possessing power is a matter of degree: Almost nobody is totally without power, although some people may be relatively powerless.

Power is considered legitimate when those who exercise it are accepted as having the right to do so. When this "rightness" is absent, power is illegitimate and may be seen as immoral, illegal, lacking popular support, or unscientific. Legitimate power is often referred to by sociologists as *authority*. In Chapter 7 we considered several types of authority, including traditional, charismatic, and rational-legal. To persist over a long period of time, the exercise of power must to some extent be legitimized. Reliance solely on force and coercion may require people to submit for a time, but it will not gain their allegiance and will break down in the long run.

When people's genuine needs and wishes are seriously taken into account and they are allowed to participate in decisions that concern them, they are more likely to accept an authority structure as legitimate. Participating in the decision-making process is sometimes referred to by applied social scientists, such as organizational consultants, as "owning the decision." In work organizations, major decisions such as the taking on of new projects, the organization of operating procedures, and the trimming of costs will be more acceptable if there is input from all levels of the work force (and perhaps compromises in the process), rather than if they are simply imposed from the top down. At the family level, parents gain more enthusiastic acceptance of plans if they involve children in making decisions rather than just telling them what to do.

Power operates at all levels of social life—in interactions between individuals, family members and friends, within organizations and institutions, at the state and national levels, and in the international arena. In this chapter we will consider the sources and expressions of power, the organization of power in the state, how functionalists and conflict theorists differ in their views of the political order, different types of state structures, how power in the United States is organized, and finally how political change occurs.

THE SOURCES AND EXPRESSIONS OF POWER

SOURCES OF POWER

The amount of power any individual has depends heavily on the resources he or she commands. These resources can be material, coercive, or normative. *Material* power accompanies such advantages as the ownership or control of property, services, and privileges. *Coercive* resources provide the ability to injure someone else physically or mentally—at the personal level, this includes verbal abuse, intimidation, and guns; at the societal level, it includes military force, police, and weaponry. *Normative* or symbolic resources confer public honor, prestige, and love (Lehman, 1977). Knowledge can also be a source of power, especially if it is used to apply other resources more effectively.

How do people acquire these resources? Most of them depend on the position of the individual in the social structure. Some of the advantages of high economic and social standing are wealth, the control of effective organizations, access to a network of people and opportunities, high moral standing, and influence over the legal structure. These advantages confer power, which in turn can be used to maintain and increase economic and social inequality. This permits the accumulation of even more power. There are other sources of power: control of or access to critical resources that are in demand, whether they be money, raw materials, supplies, information, or personnel; personal charisma or magnetism that elicits the support of others, especially important in political and religious realms; and characteristics such as charm, wit, and graciousness, which can confer power in personal relations.

Another means to power is the acquiring of a particular competence, skill, or talent. Someone who can do something extremely well will exercise power in situations where that skill or talent is useful. On the soccer field, the best players have the most power. In financial transactions, those with superior talent for investment will have the edge. Of course, acquiring competence and skills depends on having access to information and knowledge.

The different sources of power are not mutually exclusive: Any and all of them may operate in any given situation. Furthermore, power in one situation often carries over into other areas. The skilled athlete may be able to translate power on the playing field into other avenues of advancement, such as business or politics. The carryover of power poses problems for certain groups, particularly women and minorities, that have traditionally been excluded from power in any realm. The lower status generally accorded them by society may undercut their authority in organizational decision-making. High-level managers, whose primary concern is making sure their organizations run effectively and as smoothly as possible, have generally favored hiring white, educated, middle- or upper-class males in middle- and upper-management positions, in part because they already bring with them certain symbols of authority that reinforce their ability to give orders and have them accepted.

A final source of power is the desire for it, the burning ambition present in some to work their will, for good or bad, in a larger context. To what degree does the exercise of power depend upon the willingness to use any means necessary or possible? Will someone who is willing to ignore moral or legal restraints and use violence, torture, murder, or deception be able to wield more power than one who is unwilling to ignore these restraints? Under what conditions? What usually prevents power contests from going to the extremes of the use of force? Why does this work in some cases and not in others? These questions can be partially answered by examining the ways in which power is exercised.

THE EXERCISE OF POWER

We have already noted that the nature of power requires that there be at least two parties involved. It makes little sense to say that "Courtney has power," but it does make sense to say that "Courtney has power over Chris." Power is also interactional. That is, Courtney may exercise power in various ways; Chris may or may not choose to comply. Let's look more closely at the ways power is exercised and complied with (see Table 15.1).

In the first case in Table 15.1, power is exercised with "taken-for-granted" authority by

Table 15.1 Levels in the Exercise of Power and Compliance to It

After each of these actions and reactions has occurred, Chris still has the ultimate possibility of refusing to comply with Courtney's power and authority. Herein lies the ultimate limit on Courtney's power.

Courtney Can Exercise Power over Chris by:	Chris May Show Courtney Various Kinds of Compliance
1. Acting with a taken-for-granted power and authority	1. Assumed or taken-for-granted compliance
2. Stating his or her wishes or desires	2. Thought-about but willing compliance
3. Negotiating with or trying to persuade Chris	3. Negotiated or exchanged compliance
4. Exercising coercion or violence toward Chris	4. Forced or coerced compliance

Courtney when he or she has complete confidence in the right to do so. If Chris accepts this authority in an equally "taken-for-granted" manner, the operation of power in the situation may be almost invisible to the participants. This situation, where certain attitudes and behaviors are assumed and no one thinks of challenging them, occurs often in everyday life. Consider the case of a mother and child crossing the street. The mother is holding the child's hand and suddenly pulls back, saying "Wait!" because a car is approaching. The mother is exercising power and authority in the situation, but most likely neither she nor her child will think of it in these terms. They have a common interest in not being hit by the car, and the mother's experience and concern for her child makes the operation of authority in this case "taken-for-granted."

The second situation in Table 15.1 may be called "willing compliance." Here Chris may be aware that Courtney is exercising power over him or her, but for any of a number of reasons (for example, the desire to please) is willing to comply on a voluntary basis. This level of conscious, willing compliance often takes place among friends, colleagues, and family members.

At the third level in Table 15.1, Chris may resist Courtney's initial use of authority, and Courtney may then try to persuade or negotiate with Chris. Persuasion or negotiation occurs when authority is not taken for granted, there is no voluntary compliance, and coercion is inappropriate or illegitimate. Within the realm of civilized human interaction, negotiation is common and required in a broad range of situations. An important reason is that there are many sources of power among people, and even though some sources are stronger than others, even weak power sources usually cannot be completely ignored.

When Courtney tries to exercise power over Chris and fails to obtain compliance through negotiations, he or she may resort to coercion or force, the fourth case in Table 15.1. Coercion involves the application of sanctions. These may be economic, such as losing one's job, having to pay fines, or going out of business; legal, such as arrests, trials, and lawsuits; social, such as being shunned by others, solitary confinement, gossip, or nasty remarks; or physical. Violence is the most extreme form of coercion. In most societies, the state is the only entity legally empowered to use violence, and it is confined within certain limits. Still, the monopoly on violence is frequently violated.

The lower the level of legitimacy in a society, the greater the degree of coercion necessary to exercise power. If people are held back only by the threat of force, they will rebel when the opportunity presents itself. Ultimately, the use of coercion is limited. There is only so much that one person can force another to do. Courtney may kill Chris for noncompliance, but if Chris values noncompliance with Courtney's demands

The exercise of power and authority in the military is very evident, and there are serious penalties for noncompliance.

more than life, he or she can refuse to obey. Moreover, coercion is inefficient. The slave labor employed in Nazi armament plants during World War II, for example, was notoriously unproductive, and U.S. coal miners have a slogan that underscores the same point, "You can't dig coal with a bayonet."

In the final analysis, therefore, the successful exercise of power and authority requires enlisting the willing and voluntary compliance of those upon whom it is exercised. Such compliance can be of at least two different kinds. The first is called attitudinal compliance, when someone obeys because he or she accepts or "buys into" the values of the authority system. The second is behavioral conformity, in which someone obeys without necessarily believing in what is being done. In most simple cases, behavioral conformity is sufficient; in more complex situations such as political allegiance, whether or not those being ruled share the values of the rulers can be of crucial importance.

This analysis of different levels of power and compliance describes theoretical and ideal kinds of behavior. In the real world power is like an onion, with layers of habit, interpersonal social relations, and negotiation and persuasion, beneath which there is generally a capacity to reward or punish. All layers may operate at the same time in any given situation. The exercise of power at the interpersonal level is discussed by Collins, who fuses a conflict and an interactionist perspective. One indication of occupational power, Collins suggests, is the amount of talk that occurs. Manual work involves little talk, skilled labor involves somewhat more, and administrative, business, and professional work consists almost entirely of talk, especially if written communication is included. The content of talk also reflects power. People not only need to know the names of various equipment, processes, or people, but also how to use those words in appropriate ways. Third, individuals with more power have more people reporting to them and report less often to someone above them. Individuals with less power report more often (or are constantly supervised) and have few or no people reporting to them. Succeeding in one's authority relations involves understanding what forms of personal demeanor, tone, timing, and vocabulary are called for in a particular situation (Collins, 1975). These are some of the interpersonal ways in which power is reflected and exercised.

THE STATE

The clearest expression of power, authority, and force occurs in the political arena at the national and international levels. The *state* is an institutionalized way of organizing power within territorial limits. Its legal authority is backed by force, and it is accepted as legitimate, exclusive, and supreme, at least passively, by most of its citizens. The state is distinguished from government, which refers to the leaders (elected or otherwise) and bureaucracy of the state. Members of governments can and do change, but unless there is a new constitution or a revolution, the state remains the same.

THE MODERN NATION-STATE

Sovereignty is perhaps the most distinctive feature of the modern state. It is the theory by which the state legitimizes its ability to create, interpret, and enforce a legal system, use coercive power to secure obedience, and maintain its independence from other states. The concept of the state as a political unit for organizing society is relatively recent. Many date it to the writing of *The Prince* by the Italian Niccolo Machiavelli in 1513. The earlier classical Greek unit, the *polis,* was not only much smaller than the modern state, but also included in its definition a social, religious, and cultural way of life.

A *nation* is a relatively autonomous political grouping that usually shares a common language and a particular geography. The bonds of nationhood can help create a state. Despite the fact that there was no Polish state during the nineteenth century, its idea was kept alive by the Polish nation, and the state was re-created after World War I. On the other hand, the experience of being a state, including being ruled by the same authority and laws, can help instill a sense of nationhood in citizens of different cultures and language backgrounds. To varying degrees, this national identification has occurred in the United States and in Israel. The fact that diverse cultures can be melded into a state suggests how powerful the state is as a principle of social organization.

The *nation-state,* where political authority overlaps a cultural and geographic community, is a concept that goes back to the eighteenth century. It is the primary unit of organization of societies in the world today, although even in the most firmly established nation-states there will be opposition and even resistance by certain segments. For a long time, for example, the southern part of the United States defied the laws of the country against segregation until legal sanctions imposed by the federal government began to break down such resistance.

TYPES OF STATES

Not all states are alike. Even the modern state takes on a variety of forms. Considering two major dimensions helps to distinguish types of states. The first dimension is the extent of *citizen participation* in the affairs of the state. This includes such features as voting; constitutional rights to assembly, petition, free speech, a free press, and protest; access to public officials; and opportunities to render service to the state. States fall on a range along this dimension from those permitting very limited citizen participation in shaping political decisions and processes to those allowing considerably more. At the national level, there is probably no state where total participation occurs, so this dimension refers to the relative amount of participation that exists rather than to an absolute standard.

The other major dimension may be termed the *intrusiveness* of the state—that is, how much it intrudes into and influences the daily lives of its citizens. Some states try to shape everything, from education, public morality, and media to science and religion. Most states influence all these realms to some degree. This dimension refers to the degree to which it invades and restricts individual and group activities. When these two dimensions are used to make a matrix, as shown in Table 15.2, several distinctive types of states emerge. Three of these types are worth looking at in some detail.

Totalitarian States

Totalitarian states such as Nazi Germany, South Africa, or the USSR (in cell 1 of Table 15.2) allow very limited citizen participation in the operation of the state, and they intrude heavily into the daily lives of citizens. *Totalitarian* states have a number of distinctive characteristics, according to Friedrich and Brzenzinski (1965). They are usually run by a single political party that may be led by one dictator or a group of leaders. Other political parties are banned. The ruling party monopolizes positions in the government and tries to control the distribution of power, prestige, and money in the society. Totalitarian states monopolize the possession of arms and weapons, as do many nontotalitarian states, including Great Britain. Totalitarian states also use torture, interrogation, and terror to maintain control over internal as well as external enemies. Their use of force is not limited by constitutional or legal restrictions. In addition, totalitarian states may control large sectors of the economy, particularly agriculture, industry, and transportation, and may set production goals and eliminate private ownership.

While taking over all these aspects of social life, a totalitarian state also generates legitimating ideologies to justify what it is doing. One way the totalitarian state tries to maintain its ideological control is by keeping a tight hold over the mass media and education. People who challenge prevailing ideologies are not published, do not appear on television, and are not allowed to teach in schools or universities. A totalitarian regime will also try to undermine primary groups such as the family, youth groups, and churches. It does so because the existence of any strong alternative group contains the potential

Table 15.2 Types of States

		Relative Extent of Participation by Citizens	
		Narrow	Wide
Extent of State's Influence in Individual Lives	High	(1) Totalitarian states—Nazi Germany, South Africa, the USSR	(2) Some tribal societies—Nigeria
	Medium	(3) Autocratic states—Spain, Uganda, India	(4) Democratic states—United States, Great Britain
	Low	(5) Benign despots—Henry VIII of England	(6) Town meetings—Swiss cantons

for opposing it. Individuals are denied the right to reject the views and practices of a totalitarian society; even verbal opposition is prohibited.

Autocratic States

Autocratic or *authoritarian* states (cell 3 of Table 15.2) are ruled by an individual monarch or dictator who may use force and terror to stay in power and may try to control the mass media. Idi Amin in Uganda, Evita Peron of Argentina, Ferdinand Marcos of the Philippines, Francisco Franco in Spain, and Indira Gandhi in India are examples of twentieth-century autocrats. Some of them were originally elected, but they used their power and position to retain political control. Although they often curtail rights to protest and assembly, autocratic states are less involved than totalitarian regimes in controlling all aspects of their citizens' private lives. They generally refrain from tampering with the family, religion, the economy, and other traditional institutions in society. They may, however, wreck the lives and families of individuals whom they define as disloyal and proceed to torture, rape, or murder them in large numbers.

Democratic States

The word *democracy* means government of the people. Clearly, in large industrial societies not everyone can participate directly in the operation of the state. Therefore, democratic states (cell 4 of Table 15.2) are those that have a relatively greater degree of citizen participation in political affairs. The same conditions of size and complexity that preclude complete participation may also contribute to the state's intrusion into the lives of citizens. Ideology, force, and regulation of the family and economy do occur in democratic societies as well as totalitarian ones, but to a lesser extent.

Democratic states include the United States, Great Britain, most of the countries of Western Europe, and Australia. Democratic states place great importance on the protection of individual rights and on the distribution and limitation of political power. Whether through written constitutions or through unwritten bodies of well-established legal and political traditions, they set limits on the exercise of political power, particularly by the executive officer of the state. In the United States, the president, Congress, and the Supreme Court each have defined roles to play. The Founding Fathers were very concerned about building a system of checks and balances into the government because they had experienced what they felt to be a usurpation of power by the king of England.

Democratic states also assume that a legitimate government depends on the consent of the governed, not on any inherent or divine right of the ruler. Democracies that still have a monarchy, such as Great Britain and The Netherlands, grant mainly ceremonial powers to the royal family, leaving government policies to elected officials. Gaining the consent of the governed takes practical form in elective contests between more than one political party. Electoral processes and legal time in office are established by a constitution or strong traditions. Open electoral contests require mass literacy, a free press, the right to assembly, and freedom to hold differing opinions. One of the problems with single-party rule in nondemocratic states is that opposition to the party in power is easily defined as opposition to the state. In a dual-party or multiple-party system, there is an institutionalized means of differing from current practice in the form of a "loyal opposition." As this term suggests, dissent does not mean disloyalty to the state, but rather disagreement over particular policies.

Finally, democratic societies rest on the assumption that all people are entitled to the same rights under the law. Rulers are, theoretically at least, no different from any other citizens under the law. Similarly, all individuals, whatever their social class, race, or sex, are considered equal under the law. Moreover, important primary groups such as families, religions, associations,

In democracies, citizens are involved in the political affairs of the state, through contested elections, the right to assembly, and protection for people holding different opinions from the majority. Sometimes citizen participation in political decisions occurs in very concrete forms, as in this town meeting in Vermont.

and guilds are respected and protected under the law.

In some tribal societies (cell 2 of Table 15.2), such as Nigeria, the state has played a fairly strong role in regulating the lives of citizens—for instance in quelling civil war and spurring national oil production. Benign despots (cell 5) are fairly rare in today's world. Perhaps the power and resources they control makes them less willing to restrain their influence over individuals' lives.

States run primarily by town meetings (cell 6) are also rare, because of the growing size and complexity of modern states. Some Swiss cantons (roughly equivalent to one of the 50 states in the United States) do have public meetings in which all citizens may participate and vote on political decisions. Traditionally not all cantons allowed women the right to vote, but in 1981 voters approved equal legal rights for men and women. It is still the case, however, that many issues such as national defense cannot be decided at the level of the canton. The decisions made at town meetings may have limited consequences for people in their daily lives.

FUNCTIONALIST AND CONFLICT THEORIES OF POLITICAL ORDER

The state is a political, legal, and geographic entity within which power and force are organized. The *political order* is the institutionalized system of acquiring and exercising power. Sociologists are concerned with the question of when and why people accept the authority of the state as legitimate. Why a state is considered legitimate often depends on one's view of why the state is needed and how it came about. Functionalists emphasize the need for the state to maintain order and security. Conflict theorists argue that the state is used as a tool by privileged classes to support their own interests and that it emerged with the rise of private property.

FUNCTIONALIST APPROACHES TO POLITICS

The problem of social order was clearly posed by the seventeenth-century English philosopher Thomas Hobbes, who lived in England during a time of civil war and turmoil. Hobbes' view of human nature led him to believe that an absolutely powerful sovereign and state were necessary. He saw the "natural condition" of humanity as "solitary, poor, brutish and short," and humans as naturally selfish and competitive. For Hobbes, only a state ruled by someone with absolute authority could prevent the unattractive prospect of continual strife. If the sovereign, however, was unable to fulfill the function of maintaining public order and protecting subjects, then they were no longer obligated to obey.

Functionalists begin with the assumption that social order is necessary and desirable and that the state is necessary to secure this order. They focus on the positive functions the state provides for society. If it provides these functions adequately, it will most likely be perceived as being legitimate. Chief among them are the protection of life, liberty, and property; enforcement of norms in a formal way; regulation of conflict; the conduct of relations with other nations; and the planning, coordination, and regulation of activities conducted by various groups. In Western democracies certain political values, such as due process, contested elections, and human rights, must also be perceived to be functioning in everyday life.

Protecting Life, Liberty, and Property

In large industrial societies, people rely on the state to keep the peace, prevent gangs from rampaging through the streets, enforce traffic regulations, and control robbery, murder, and other crimes. The state also has the task of protecting its borders from armed invasion and illegal entry of foreigners. To perform these functions, the state sets up police forces, military services, and immigration agencies. Only the state is empowered to use force against others, although the law does allow a person to act in his or her own self-defense. Most people would agree that the state is better suited to perform these tasks than private individuals or groups. Still, certain private groups may attempt to take matters into their own hands in the name of justice, for private gain, or when state services are seen as inadequate. Most would also agree that the state should exercise its power only within the law, although again this is not always what happens.

Enforcing Norms in a Formal Way

All members of a small tribal society know the norms—the rules, values, and customs—of that society. They reinforce them by obeying them spontaneously in their daily lives. As society becomes more complex and multicultural, there is less agreement on what the norms are and therefore less willingness to enforce many of them personally. In parts of Africa today, even in cities, if a burglar is caught breaking into someone's home he will be beaten by the neighbors who apprehend him and may have to be rescued by the police to avoid being badly injured or killed. In societies like the United States, individuals who see a burglary in progress are likely to call the police rather than involve themselves in the situation.

When people are unclear about the norms operating in certain situations, the state steps in to codify behavior into formal laws. It also assumes the responsibility for enforcing these laws, although as we saw in Chapter 8, it is only partially effective in doing so.

Regulating Conflict

By writing laws to indicate which norms will prevail and when, the state sets the "rules of the game." In order to regulate and contain conflicts, it also plays the role of umpire, arbitrating disputes among individuals and groups. This role involves establishing procedures and practices for resolving disputes. The state succeeds in its role as arbitrator to the degree that it is perceived to be fair and impartial and not "in the pocket" of any particular interests.

Conducting Relations with Other Nations

If citizens independently worked out their own special agreements with foreign governments, the conduct of foreign affairs would become chaotic. Individuals with differing amounts of power would strike different bargains. The state, therefore, is empowered to work out uniform political and military relationships with other nations, which its citizens are supposed to obey, and to ensure the rights of its citizens when they travel abroad. Despite theories of free market capitalism in the United States, the power of the state also extends to regulating certain economic activities. American wheat sales to the Soviet Union depend as much on political realities at a given time as they do on market relations. OPEC nations may limit the sale of oil to the United States because of political factors. Products with strategic military importance, such as certain computers, cannot freely be sold to all countries. As nation-states throughout the world have become more interdependent economically, the power of the state to regulate the behavior of its citizens has increased.

Planning, Coordinating, and Regulating the Activities of Various Groups

The complexity of the modern world has increased the need for planning, coordination, and regulation. Air traffic, highway construction, television broadcasting, health care delivery, pension plans, environmental protection, human resource development, occupational safety, and interstate commerce are only some of the activities that would be reduced to chaos if there were not some coordination and standardization of effort to avoid duplication, omissions, conflicting operations, and harmful side effects.

Enforcing these efforts may call for a great degree of state regulation. In the United States, the number of state regulations has come under attack by those who cite the time and expense needed to comply with them. Clearly there are cases of excessive regulation that need to be brought under control. In New York City, for example, local public schools must fill out more than 125 forms annually, many of which relate to compliance with federally mandated programs and practices that are compulsory, and many of them asking for the same information. However, if industries did not bear the costs of complying with safety and pollution regulations, the costs of noncompliance would be felt in the air people breathe and the water they drink, and would be borne by innocent members of society. The state must balance the costs of enforcing regulations against the need of society for uniform, fair, and safe policies.

Newer state functions involve "social goods" that cannot be satisfied by the operation of free markets, which regulate only "individual goods"—goods individuals can produce, purchase, and enjoy. Clean air and water, for example, are social goods. From the standpoint of the market, such goods are irrational. For any firm to introduce pollution equipment without others doing likewise is unlikely, because the cost of the equipment would handicap the firm economically vis-à-vis its competitors. Only a centralized authority can make decisions regarding collective goods (Zaret, 1981).

THE CONFLICT VIEW OF THE STATE

The functionalist view of the state suggests that it is equally in everyone's interest to form a state to preserve law and order. The conflict view claims that the state was formed and continues to exist primarily to protect the positions of privileged members of society. That is, the state safeguards those who have property and position from those who do not.

Rousseau

Functionalists draw upon Hobbes and his formulation of the "problem of order." Conflict theorists are influenced by the eighteenth-century Swiss philosopher Jean-Jacques Rousseau, whose view of human nature was diametrically opposed to that of Hobbes. According to Rousseau, people in their natural state were "naturally good" and free. They pursued their own interests, primarily self-preservation, in isolation without desiring to gain unfair advantage over others. The introduction of private property, however, ended this state of tranquil equality. The existence of property stirred new conflicts and wars. Because the rich were the most concerned about protecting their property, Rousseau believed that they created the idea of a unified social state to protect life and property. He thought this development gave "new fetters to the weak and new strength to the rich, permanently destroyed natural freedom, established the law of property and inequality forever, turned adroit usurpation into an irrevocable right, and for the advantage of a few ambitious men, subjected all others to unending work, servitude, and poverty" (1750, p. 186). For Rousseau, the primary purpose of the state was thus to protect the interests of the rich.

Marx

Karl Marx also believed that the state served the interests of the privileged. He understood the state to be a part of the superstructure of society, along with religion, morality, and culture. The base of this superstructure lay in the social relationships of economic life. Marx, like Rousseau, viewed the state as an instrument of class rule that helped to rob ordinary people of their freedom. He saw the law, police, prisons, and the army as designed to maintain existing economic relationships, including control over surplus wealth.

According to Marx, throughout history different forms of social and economic organization have been accompanied by different forms of political organization. Like earlier forms of economic organization, capitalism generates internal contradictions, thereby developing the thrust for its own revolutionary overthrow. The next stage of economic development, he suggested, is the socialist revolution. Workers seize the means of production and gain economic as well as political order. Because former property owners would keep their old attitudes, this stage requires the retention of the machinery of the state, which would operate under what Engels and later Lenin called "a dictatorship of the proletariat."

In the final stage of social organization, the communist stage, there would be no need for a state or for laws, because in a free and classless society everyone voluntarily seeks the good of the entire society instead of trying to advance the interests of a narrow group of owners. Under such conditions, the state would gradually "wither away." In a communist society, persons will no longer need to be governed. Instead, services will only need to be administered and the processes of production directed. Economic life will still be organized and rules will guide social and economic life, but there will be no need for formal laws or for agents of social control like the police. Everyone will obey the rules willingly, since they will know that the rules benefit everyone equally rather than being used by one group to advance their interests at the expense of others.

In their projections about the role of the state in future societies, Marx, Engels, and Lenin departed from the role of social analysts and became social prophets. They moved from an analysis of the way the state actually operates to a prediction about its role in a different type of society.

ASSESSMENT

Marx argued that the state serves the interests of the dominant economic class in capitalist societies. Considerable evidence supports this assertion. Other conflict theorists like Max Weber (1920) and Randall Collins (1975), however, suggest that individuals and groups may gain privileges in other than simply economic ways. Groups in advantageous political or occupational positions may try to use their positions to further their own interests as well. Ownership of the means of production is one such advantage, but if ownership is shared evenly, other sources of advantage may operate, such as control over information, resources, or political decisions. Marx assumed that eliminating inequalities based on ownership would eliminate all significant inequalities among people. The possibility that political advantages might be used to advance the interests of some individuals and groups was not considered.

If the state is going to be involved in the production and the distribution of goods and services, it seems reasonable that the state will need to be more rather than less powerful than it is in capitalist societies. Existing state socialist societies such as those of the Soviet Union and China confirm this expectation. Because the state controls more areas of social life, it has more rather than less power over individuals' lives.

Marx's view also overlooks the important functions the state serves in a complex, multicultural society and world. Some of these functions, such as citizen safety, benefit all classes. The functionalist view of the state correctly points to the fulfillment of certain functions made possible by the existence of a centralized state, which Marx tended to ignore.

On the other hand, the functionalist view minimizes the possibility that the state may enhance the interests of certain economic, ethnic, and social groups in society. It is precisely this selective use of state power that is brought out by Marxian and other conflict analyses. Together, the functionalist and conflict perspectives provide a richer understanding of the social world than either of them does alone.

THE STRUCTURE OF POWER IN THE UNITED STATES

Sociological analyses of power and politics have most significance for us when we use them to understand the structure of power in our own country. How is power organized in the United States? Is there one small group of people who exercise power over all aspects of life in the society, or are there many competing groups? Do the leaders of the major institutions come together on important issues? How we, as social scientists and citizens, answer these questions goes a long way toward shaping our opinions about whether power is being exercised legitimately in society, whether we feel U.S. society is democratic, and therefore whether we feel major social and political changes are necessary or desirable. So it is not surprising that the question of how power is structured in the United States is a hotly debated issue among social scientists.

THREE COMPETING VIEWS

Sociologists tend to place themselves and others in one of three major camps on the subject—ruling class, power elite, or pluralist—depending on how they see the distribution and exercise of power in the United States.

Ruling Class View

Marxian class analysis sees a small, economically dominant *ruling class,* which controls the means of economic production. This class can and does convert its wealth and economic power into political power and social status. The ruling class view differs from the power elite view because of the relatively greater stress it places on economic class as the primary source of most power in most situations. It also tends to see the state as having relatively little independence from the economic order.

Power Elite or Ruling Elite Theories

C. Wright Mills criticized Marxian theory for failing to grant enough autonomy to the political order and for ignoring the military (Mills, 1956). Mills also questioned the Marxian belief in the inevitability of working-class opposition to a ruling class. He saw the *power elite* as a closely connected group of the corporate rich, political leaders, and military commanders who decide most key political and social issues. These leaders all operate in institutional spheres that are relatively independent at the base of their institutional pyramids, but closely interconnected at the top. Figure 15.1 illustrates this view that at the highest echelons of U.S. society, the top military men, the president, cabinet members, ranking congressional leaders, and heads of large corporations and banks confer frequently over national and international policy matters. Farther down the organizational hierarchies in each sphere, civil servants, rank-and-file military officers, and corporate staff members operate quite independently of one another.

The Pluralist View

Pluralists reject both a ruling class and a power elite view of the structure of power in the United States. Instead, they see society as composed of numerous competing interest groups that form temporary coalitions depending on the specific issues being considered. An *interest group* is a group of people that works to influence political decisions that affect its members. Farmers, for example, may join with labor unions to oppose high interest rates supported by bankers. The same farmers, however, may form a coalition with businesspeople and bankers to support investment tax credits. Given these three competing views, what evidence exists for saying that one rather than another presents a truer picture of how power is structured in the United States?

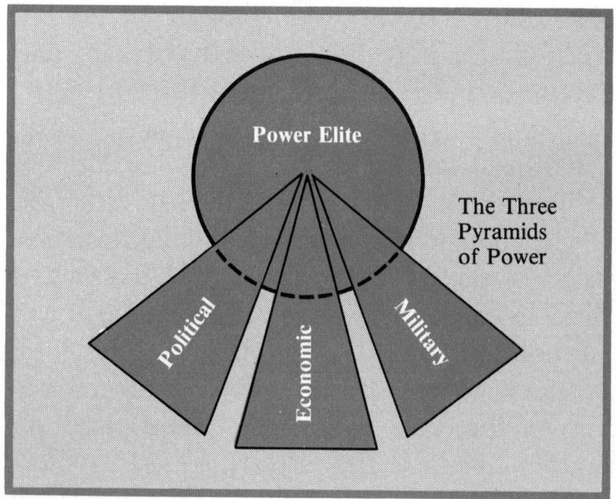

Figure 15.1 Mills' View of the Power Elite

EVIDENCE FOR HOW POWER IS DISTRIBUTED IN THE UNITED STATES

One of the first efforts to study power configurations in the United States was made by Floyd Hunter in his 1953 book, *Community Power Structure*. He asked professionals and the allegedly powerful members of one community (Atlanta, Georgia) to tell him who were the most powerful people in the city. His "reputational method" suggested that power was concentrated in the hands of relatively few corporate leaders in Atlanta. His work seemed to support a ruling class position. It is important to note, however, that his focus was regional, not national, so it may or may not describe national and international power structures.

Other social scientists severely criticized community power studies by Hunter and others for failing to study actual decision-making. Hunter studied the people reputed to have power, but he lacked proof that they actually exercised any power. Foremost among those critics was Robert Dahl, who studied New Haven, Connecticut, in a book called *Who Governs?* (1961). Dahl observed that many competing interest groups struggled to shape decisions in that city. He also asserted that the most important arena of power was political rather than economic. Inequality existed, but Dahl saw it as *dispersed* rather than *cumulative;* that is, wealth did not increase status, control over religious and educational institutions, or political influence. For a long time, Dahl's pluralist view of power in the United States prevailed.

Recently, however, William Domhoff returned to Dahl's original data and found quite a different picture. Domhoff challenged the way Dahl defined economic and social "notables" and discovered much more overlap between the two groups than Dahl reported. Domhoff found that a socially privileged class provided much of the economic leadership in New Haven society (1978). When Dahl concluded that political leaders rather than economic notables initiated important decisions such as major urban renewal plans, he suggested that the political sphere was relatively independent of the economic sphere. Looking at the same time period (1940–1960), Domhoff concluded the opposite—namely, that a cohesive power structure was operating in New Haven. Whether the focus was the origins of the local urban renewal program (in the Chamber of Commerce and Yale University) or its eventual outcome (land for the expansion of Yale, the hospital, and the downtown business community), the major actors and beneficiaries in the situation were Yale, the First New Haven National Bank, and the Chamber of Commerce (Domhoff, 1978).

Other research suggests that although representatives from a number of different groups or interests in a community may come together in certain civic organizations, it may still be possible for the more powerful economic members of such committees to pursue their own policies regardless of competing community interests. For example, one study found that bank directors who served on the "Save Saint Louis" committee with other citizens did not change their banks' policy of lending most of their money to large outside corporations instead of providing mortgages within the city limits (Ratcliff, 1980).

A major link that needs to be made concerns the connection between local power structures and national ones. In New Haven, Domhoff found that the local elite were members of interlocking directorates of national corporate boards and of such national policy-planning organizations as the Committee for Economic Development and the National Municipal League.

Recent research at the national level definitely documents the existence of an "inner group" within the capitalist class. This group has numerous contacts with leaders of government, other businesses and banks, and public institutions such as universities, hospitals, and museums (Useem, 1979; Moore, 1979). Additional evidence suggests that representatives of the capitalist class do coordinate their activities and statements in regard to public policies—for example, in first opposing and then supporting proposals for mass transportation in California from 1962 to 1974 (Whitt, 1980).

Given this evidence for the existence and relative cohesiveness of an inner group of the capitalist class, can we say that members of this group operate to benefit their own interests as a class rather than working to serve "the common good," as functionalists would suggest? At this writing, clear evidence that they operate in their own interests and to the detriment of other class groups is beginning to emerge. The possibility for such action exists, and the potential for the persistent exercise of organized power by a small group in society for its own benefit remains.

POLITICAL CHANGE

Political changes occur in a variety of different ways, depending on the structure of a particular state and on the depth and breadth of the commitment to change. Small groups of people who are highly committed to social change may use terrorism to try to change an existing situation. When a state tries to suppress efforts at peaceful political change, people sometimes accept injustice or suffering; at other times, they rebel against it. Sometimes such rebellions lead to revolutionary political changes. Political changes also occur more gradually, through a process of evolution. Sociologists want to know what conditions are associated with the various kinds of political change.

TERRORISM AS A FORM OF OPPOSITION

Some individuals and groups are so completely opposed to an existing state or society that they want nothing to do with it. They do not consider working to change the laws gradually or getting their representatives elected to be an effective or satisfying strategy. If they feel strongly enough about their cause, they may use terrorism as a strategy for trying to gain power and further their goals. Terrorism is a weapon of the politically powerless or disenfranchised. *Terrorism* refers to an attack on individuals in order to frighten society into doing one's will. It includes hijacking airplanes, planting bombs in crowded areas, kidnapping, and murder for political reasons. Sometimes political terrorists demand money to support their activities, but their avowed aims are political goals rather than personal ones. Therefore, it is particularly important to terrorists that they receive the right publicity for their actions.

Because terrorists are politically motivated, one person's terrorist is another's freedom fighter. Terrorists often have supporters within a society. They may also have foreign sympathizers, including foreign governments, who supply money, arms, and sanctuary for them. Both the Irish Republican Army (IRA) and the Palestine Liberation Organization (PLO) have international supporters—the IRA among some Irish-Americans, and the PLO within Arab nations. Support for terrorists makes it more difficult to find and stop them.

Television magnifies the impact of terrorists by personalizing their violence and bringing it into the homes of millions of people. Seeing the tearful families of victims or hostages talking to us from the screens in our homes makes it more difficult for governments to remain firm in the face of their demands. Television can also fan the fear aroused by terrorism and lead to harsh repression. Stifling dissent, however, may push more citizens toward sympathy with the terrorists and "make a society more brittle and vulnerable to attack" (Clutterbuck, 1977, p. 115). Terrorist violence is less likely to lead to revolutionary change than to repression and rigidity in a society. At times, this may be the aim of certain terrorist groups.

CONDITIONS GENERATING OBEDIENCE AND REVOLT

Strategies of peaceful protest, efforts to change the law, and even terrorism can seldom be used in a totalitarian society, where the state or an arm of the state (like a prison camp or a mental institution) may use oppression and terror to control a large population. In such a situation, when do people accept injustice and suffering, and when do they rebel against it? In situations where a cultural explanation of suffering as part of the cosmic order prevails, people may believe injustice to be inevitable and justified. Such a cultural explanation narrows human visions about how people can respond to the reality around them. This general explanation applies to experiences in Nazi concentration camps and instances where social injustice has been explained by religions that emphasize that the poor or oppressed will be reincarnated or otherwise enjoy a higher status in an afterworld.

Based on a close look at concentration camps, Moore (1978) noted four social processes that tend to suppress cooperative efforts to identify, reduce, or resist oppression. First, victims are more likely to unite against a single rebel in their midst because they observe how one defiant member can cause an entire group to be punished. Second, prior family, religious, or community ties are destroyed among sufferers, leaving individuals without social support. Cooptation is the third social process that undermines collective resistance to an oppressor. Since the dominant individuals or groups usually control vital resources, such as food, some people are willing to conform to obtain those rewards. Fourth, fragmentation occurs when an oppressed population is split into two or more competing groups, each with a distinctive way of life. Divisions may occur along religious, ethnic, national, or occupational lines. In the concentration camps, criminals were put with lawyers, Russians with Germans. Prior social antagonisms were intensified, and the result was heightened conflict between groups. These four processes tend to stifle the impulse to rebel; they create a sense of the inevitability of oppression and an aura of moral authority around the suffering. Once people see the situation in this way, resistance is unlikely.

Whereas certain social processes sap the will to resist, others fuel it. Even a small degree of social support can shatter the illusion that oppression is part of the natural order of things and nurture the development of a critical rather than an obedient response to a situation. Even one person who differs from the majority can nurture the independent judgment of others. Milgram's experiments on obedience identify some conditions that lead humans to disobey an apparently legitimate authority.

To study people's willingness to harm others while following orders, Milgrim brought 40 men from various occupations into his laboratory to participate in what he called a learning experiment. Lots were drawn, apparently, and subjects were assigned the role of teacher or pupil. The pupil was strapped into a chair, with an electrode attached to his wrists. Teachers faced an electrical control panel of dials, gauges, and switches. Switches were labeled in volts, from 15 to 315, and some had signs like "Extreme-Intensity Shock," "Danger—Severe Shock," and "XXX." The teacher read a list of word pairs to the pupil and asked him to match them up. Whenever the learner made a mistake, the experimenter instructed the teacher to throw one of the switches, beginning with the mildest, to shock the pupil. Although the teachers could not see the pupils in the next room, they could hear them through an open door.

As the experiment continued, teachers were asked to give even more severe shocks, until the pupil was screaming for mercy and begging for the experiment to end. Many teachers paused at this point, but were told by the experimenter that it was important to continue giving the shocks. After a while, the pupils began kicking the wall between the rooms while continuing to scream. Finally, when teachers read the list and asked for pupil responses, there was only silence in the other room. The experimenter said that no answer should be considered an error and that the next higher shock should be administered. This continued until the "XXX" shock at the top of the dial had been given. Of the first 40 subjects, none refused to give the shocks until the pupil began to kick the wall. Then 5 out of 40 refused. Other teachers balked between there and the end, but 26 out of 40 continued giving shocks up to the final point.

A slight change in social conditions greatly increased the resistance to authority. When two "teachers" refused to obey the experimenter's order to administer increasingly severe shocks, most other "teachers" gladly rebelled against the authority of the experimenter. Added social support effectively undercut the experimenter's authority. More subjects also refused to obey the experimenter's commands when they had to administer the punishment through direct physical contact with the "student-victim." When they had to press the victim's hand onto a shock plate, only 30 percent obeyed, compared to 65 percent who obeyed when the victim was out of sight in the next room; the size of the shock they were willing to administer was also much less under these conditions (Milgram, 1969).[1] Ap-

[1]As you may know, the shocks were fake and only the "teacher" was a real subject in the experiment. There was no actual harm done to the "pupils." The experiment was designed to test willingness to obey, even to the point of apparently injuring or killing someone.

parently, physical closeness increases identification with a victim and diminishes the willingness to obey cruel authority.

Every attempt at oppression tends to dehumanize and distance the victims of oppression. Language and beliefs paint the victim as subhuman, stupid, lazy, unfeeling, or evil, as reflected in such terms as "gooks" (to refer to the Vietnamese who fought Americans), "niggers" (to allude to American blacks), or "bitch" (to describe a woman men consider too assertive). To throw off oppression, victims must refuse to accept the labels, beliefs, and orders issued by their oppressors. To do so requires counterdefinitions and social support.

The opposition or rebellion discussed here occurs when resisters lack the power to make basic changes in the leadership structure itself. These forms of resistance or revolt differ from the broader term *revolution,* which refers to a large-scale change in the political leadership of a society and the restructuring of major features of that society. (Revolution is also used to refer to any major occurrence in society that causes basic changes—for example, industrial revolution, scientific revolution, or agricultural revolution.) While *rebellion* involves opposition to authority, it does not usually result in leadership changes. It may force an existing regime to change its policies in some way, but it is not considered a revolution unless it successfully overthrows an existing set of rulers.

REVOLUTION

When people become angry about social conditions and are organized enough to overturn existing institutions, they may create a political revolution. By comparing a number of revolutions, social thinkers have identified several common conditions that appear to precede revolutionary upheavals (Brinton, 1965; de Tocqueville, 1856; Graham, 1979; Saikal, 1980; Skocpol, 1979). Very often revolution is preceded by some improvements in social and economic conditions, as occurred before the French Revolution, the American Revolution, and the Iranian revolution of 1978. Such improvements lead to *rising expectations*—that is, a situation in which people feel that past hardships should not have to be suffered in the future. The rulers in power, however, try to control and limit the changes they allow, thus adding to the frustration of the populace. This situation is accompanied by a growing sense that the existing government is illegitimate. Power is seen as being arbitrary, and the distribution of wealth may be seen as unfair. Discontents of this kind certainly helped to fuel the American, French, Russian, and Iranian revolutions.

Existing rulers are also viewed as being weak and possibly divided internally. A crisis of confidence in the prevailing leadership builds. Many leading citizens become highly critical of the existing order. Nobles in France and Russia, just before those revolutions began, started doubting that the existing political regime would survive. Some even joined and helped to lead the revolutions. The signers of the Declaration of Independence in the United States, for example, were hardly wild-eyed rebels; many came from prominent colonial families. Given these doubts at the upper levels of society, government is often hesitant to sanction its critics strongly. Gradually the social institutions supporting the state begin to crumble, leaving only the military and the police. In the advanced stages of a revolution, members of the military often join the revolutionary forces, further weakening the government's position.

The aftermath of a revolution may also be choppy, as new political leaders try to gain power and legitimacy. Old rulers are usually executed or banished. Contending factions may fight among themselves, sometimes resulting in further executions and rapid shifts in leadership. Those who achieve power are often the ones who are most ruthless in suppressing their opposition. Revolutions are often followed by dictatorships that rule by terrorizing all who might oppose them. As they gain legitimacy, they may loosen the political reins somewhat and restore certain civil liberties.

EVOLUTION

The authors of the United States Constitution tried to build in mechanisms so that change could occur gradually, in an evolutionary rather than a revolutionary way. Some of these vehicles include the existence of more than one political party, regularly scheduled elections, and an inclusive stance toward political participation.

Political Parties

A *political party* is an organized group of people that seeks to control or influence political decisions through legal means. In some societies, political parties are active groups that individuals join and support regularly by paying dues. These parties may sponsor lectures, publications, youth groups, and other educational efforts to involve the masses in political life. The United States does not follow this pattern. The Democratic and Republican parties in the United States have few formal members. There is not one national organization for each party, but 50 or more distinct Republican and Democratic parties, since there is at least one in each state.

Most of the activity of political parties in the United States is centered around local, state, and federal election campaigns. There is a national committee for each party, but its control is loose and decentralized. There is no unified political program that everyone in a political party supports, and there are no formal ways of controlling the behavior of party officeholders once they are elected. Why, then, are political parties important at all? Their significance rests on the fact that they control the pathways to political office. Political parties determine who will be the candidates for political positions. This function gives them their political power.

Party membership in the United States is not as clearly tied to social class as it is in other countries, although the lower and working classes are more likely to vote Democratic, while upper-middle class and upper-class voters vote Republican. However, even these tendencies have weakened somewhat in recent elections. In the United States, political parties have always been less important than individual political candidates, especially at the national level. This tendency is heightened by the growing importance of the mass media. Political coverage and advertisements enable candidates to solicit contributions and votes directly from voters without depending on the party organization.

Voting Behavior

Citizens can participate in government processes in various ways. Voting in elections is often taken as an important indicator of participation. Nonvoting does not necessarily mean people are not interested in politics, however. It may be that they are interested but that they do not like the choices, or that they are reasonably satisfied with either possibility, or that they were sick, too busy, or out of town on election day. In general, younger, less educated, black, low-income, working-class voters and those with no party preference are less likely to vote in national elections. Republicans, the middle-aged, college graduates, the well-to-do, and professionals are overrepresented among voters, giving them more impact on elections (*Public Opinion*, 1980).

The first systematic research on American voting patterns was conducted by Paul F. Lazarsfeld, Bernard Berelson, and Hazel Gaudet and reported in the famous book *The People's Choice* (1944). They found that certain social statuses were closely related to political party preference and to voting behavior. Protestants, upper-class individuals, and rural dwellers were most likely to be Republicans; while Catholics, the working class, and urban dwellers were more often Democrats. People with two or three of

"You've got my vote, sir. But I'm poor, and poor people are notorious for not registering and voting."

SOURCE: Drawing by Dana Fradon, © 1982, *The New Yorker Magazine, Inc.*

these characteristics were more likely to vote for the expected party than people with mixed statuses, such as lower-class, Protestant urban dwellers. People with mixed status characteristics made up the "swing" voters who decided late in a campaign, were more likely to switch political preferences during a campaign, and were least likely to vote at all.

More recent voting studies (Berelson et al., 1954; Campbell et al., 1954) tend to confirm Lazarsfeld's original findings. The more recent research confirms one recent trend—namely, that the number of swing voters with mixed status characteristics (such as highly educated Catholics) has been growing in recent years. Seemingly as a result, we have witnessed in recent years fairly rapid shifts in political allegiances, uncertain political outcomes, and a decline in the percentage of the voting age population who are voting even in presidential elections, from 63 percent in 1960 to 53 percent in 1980 (U.S. Bureau of the Census, 1981a, p. 496). As Table 15.3 shows, voting rates are lower in the United States than in most other industrialized countries. Rates of voting are particularly low among 18- to 20-year-olds, with only 36 percent of that age group voting in 1980.

One explanation that has been offered for the declining voter turnout, especially among younger voters, is a growing sense of political alienation and apathy. Figure 15.2 reveals that between 1966 and 1977, the percentage of people who agree with a number of statements indicating political alienation has been steadily increasing. If people feel alienated from the political process, they are less likely to vote in elec-

Table 15.3 Voter Participation in Various Countries

	United States	Canada	United Kingdom	Finland	Sweden	West Germany	Australia
State-initiated or compulsory registration?	No	Yes	Yes	Yes	Yes	Yes	Yes
Compulsory voting?	No	No	No	No	No	No	No
Approximate average percentage of voting age population voting since World War II	60%	71%	74%	77%	81%	82%	87%

SOURCE: Philips and Blackman, 1975, pp. 98–99.

tions. Political apathy among many voters means that special interest groups stand a better chance of influencing the outcome of an election and that a candidate who may not have the support of the majority of the population can be elected.

The higher their social class, the more likely individuals are to participate in politics in various ways, such as working in local political organizations, campaigning for particular candidates, contacting an elected official about an issue or problem, or contributing money to a party or a candidate (Campbell et al., 1964; Verba and Nie, 1972). People are more likely to participate in various political activities when they believe they can influence politicians and political events, when they trust the political order and politicians, and when they know about political events and discuss them with others (Orum, 1978).

Lobbying Groups

One way that people influence the political process is through organized groups that represent their special interests. The American Medical Association (AMA), National Education Association, National Rifle Association (NRA), Right to Life, and United Auto Workers are among the thousands of interest groups that try to influence political decisions affecting their members. All these groups try to change the

In general, a smaller proportion of Americans vote than do citizens in other political democracies. Voting rates are particularly low among 18- to 20-year olds.

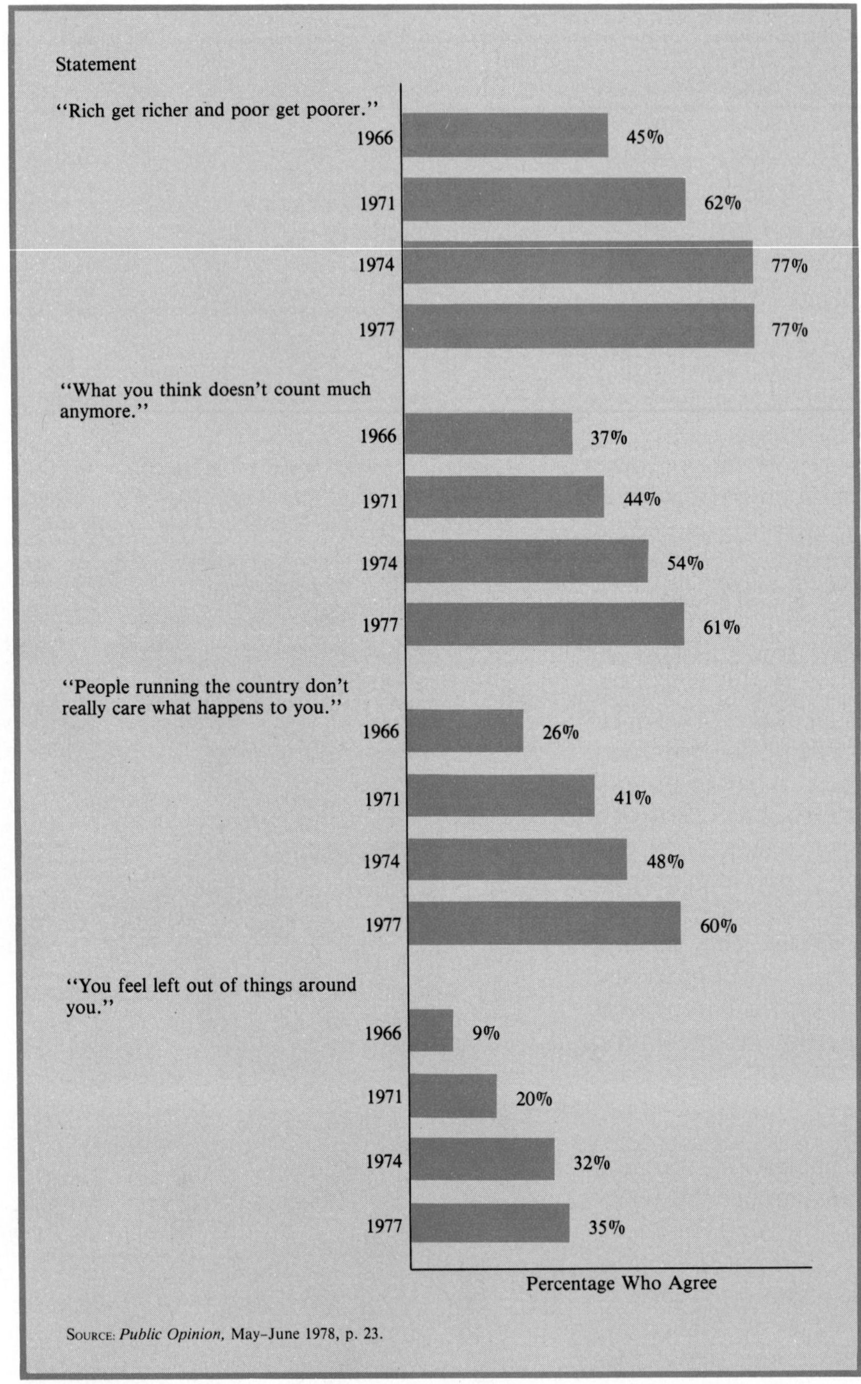

SOURCE: *Public Opinion,* May–June 1978, p. 23.

Figure 15.2 Indicators of Increasing Political Alienation in the United States

Special interest groups often try to influence legislation by hiring lobbyists, such as these from business groups pictured outside the Senate Chamber in Albany, New York.

course of state and national political events in line with their members' interests, through a process called *lobbying*. The larger and better organized their membership, and the more financial and media resources they command, the greater their influence is likely to be.

These groups hire full-time lobbyists to supply information, favors, and entertainment to lawmakers. They may offer bribes, run advertisements, pledge money and votes to candidates, threaten lawsuits, organize letter-writing campaigns, or talk directly with legislators. In recent years, right-to-life groups have been effective in using computerized national lists of voters and contributors to oppose certain political candidates whose opinions differ from their own. For years the AMA has blocked federal health insurance, and the NRA has prevented the control or registration of guns, including handguns, despite popular support for both issues.

Interest groups are especially effective in promoting issues so complex or technical that members of the general public have little knowledge about them. Specific features of the tax law, for example, may greatly benefit certain interest groups, while costing the government millions of dollars in revenues. If citizens' groups do not understand the technical details of such proposals, they are unlikely to oppose them effectively. Interest groups funnel millions of dollars each year to selected members of the Senate and Congress. Given the high costs of political campaigning and media advertising, the well-financed interest groups are likely to remain powerful forces in political life.

Summary

1. Power is the capacity of a person or group to achieve a specific goal, even in the face of opposition from others.

2. Authority is power that is accepted as legitimate; that is, the people exercising it are seen as having the right to do so.

3. The amount of power people have depends on the material, coercive, and normative resources they command. Some of these resources are inherited; others are earned.

4. Power is relational; that is, it becomes evident in relation to other people. Sometimes power differences are taken for granted; sometimes people comply willingly; sometimes they must be persuaded. If Chris does not comply with Courtney's wishes, Courtney may try to force Chris to conform. Ultimately, Chris has the option of not complying with Courtney's wishes. Therefore, Chris sets the final limits on Courtney's power.

5. Power, authority, and force appear in their most distilled form in the state. In the nation-state, political authority and sovereignty overlap with a cultural and geographic unit.

6. Totalitarian, autocratic, and democratic states differ with respect to the extent of citizen participation they allow and the degree to which they intrude into the private lives of individuals.

7. Functionalists stress the usefulness of such state roles as protection, enforcing norms, regulating conflict, dealing with other nations, and coordinating the actions of other groups. Conflict theorists, on the other hand, suggest that the state arose as a tool to serve the interests of privileged classes. Each perspective captures part of the essence of the state.

8. The structure of power in the United States has been hotly debated. The Marxian view sees a ruling class that controls the means of production. Power elite theory sees three pyramids of power—economic, political, and military—that converge at their peaks. Pluralists see society as consisting of competing interest groups, with certain ones prevailing at some times, and others at other times.

9. Research documents the existence of an "inner group" within the community of business leaders and the existence of considerable contact between business and government leaders on a wide variety of issues, thereby refuting the pluralist interpretation.

10. Terrorism is a strategy used by groups that totally reject the legal order of a society. It consists of attacking a few individuals in an effort to frighten many others and force them to meet the terrorists' demands. Television heightens the impact of terrorism.

11. Opposition of any kind is less likely to occur in societies where there is a cultural explanation of suffering and oppression. The impulse to rebel is also stifled when the whole group is punished for one defiant individual, when communal ties are torn, when certain individuals are coopted by the authorities, and when groups are split into warring factions.

12. Opposition is more likely when social supports exist and when oppressors must come into direct physical contact with their victims.

13. Revolutions involve the rapid and dramatic overthrow of political institutions. They are often preceded by some improvements in social conditions that raise peoples' expectations and fuel their discontent with the existing situation. Reigning political leadership is seen as lacking legitimacy and being weak. Prominent citizens may join and even lead the revolutionary efforts. The power of an existing government then begins to crumble, and members of the army may join the rebels. The political regime that forms after a revolution may be dictatorial and repressive until it establishes its legitimacy with the populace.

14. Constitutional democracies attempt to provide mechanisms for peaceful evolutionary change in the political order. These means include the existence of rival political parties, elections, other forms of political participation, and the operation of interest groups. All of these allow participation by some members of society in the political process, although it is sometimes questioned how open these avenues are to the general public.

Key Terms

authority
autocracy
democracy
interest group
legitimate
lobbying
nation
nation-state
political order
political party
power
power elite
rebellion
revolt
revolution
rising expectations
ruling class
sovereignty
state
terrorism
totalitarianism

Spelling
in it
pin bit
tin fit
fin hit
sin sit
tin pit
crib
bib
grab
school
hospital
hotel
HUNDREDS
TENS
ONES
DAY BY DAY CALENDAR
September

Chapter 16

Education

Remember the smell of school when it opened in the fall, the fresh paint and varnish? Remember your hopes and fears? Every September, more than 5 million American children enter school for the first time, joining 53 million more who are returning (U.S. Bureau of the Census, 1982a, p. 142). In the United States, the number and proportion of children attending school has increased dramatically. As Figure 16.1 shows, the percentage of young people (aged 14 to 17) attending high school leapt from 2 percent in 1870 to 90 percent in 1980. College attendance has increased almost as strikingly, from 2 percent in 1870 to 41 percent in 1980. More money is spent on education than on any other activity in the United States except health care, with the amount rising faster than the number of students in school. In 1981 the United States spent $140 billion (or about 7 percent of the gross national product) on all levels of public and private education. Clearly, Americans value education.

Education can be defined as the process, in school or beyond, of transmitting a society's knowledge, skills, values, and behaviors. Every society seeks to educate its young members, to prepare them for adult roles. Formal education is one way many societies prepare newcomers for membership, so education is one form of socialization. In small tribal societies, fathers taught sons how to fish or hunt; mothers taught daughters how to farm or make pottery. More specialized occupations like medicine or blacksmithing were learned from a parent or another member of the tribe. As tribal life became more complex, and especially with the growth of written language, communities began to appoint someone to teach reading and writing to a number of village children at the same time. Often such early formal education was started and supervised by religious leaders who wanted children to be able to read sacred writings. Thus began the first schools.

Especially in recent times, Americans have stressed formal education, called *schooling* by sociologists. In colonial American society, schooling was not compulsory. After 1875, states such as Massachusetts and Connecticut began to require primary education for everyone, in response to growing numbers of immigrants and a more mobile labor force. From 1918 to 1940, secondary education expanded, and the compulsory school-leaving age was raised to the teens in most states.

In the last 30 years, higher education has grown enormously. Consider the case of Charles Smith. When he graduated from high school twenty-five years ago in 1957, only about 30 percent of his age group went to college. Today more than twice as many 18-year-olds pursue some form of post-high school education. Most people have more years of schooling than they did in Charles Smith's time, and more and more employers require at least some college educa-

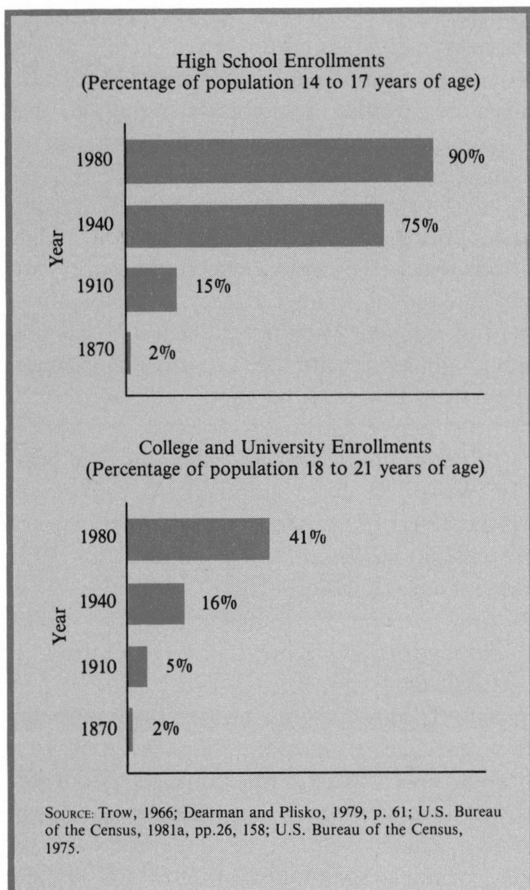

Figure 16.1 Changes in High School and College Attendance, 1870–1980

tion as a condition for employment. As a result, what happens in school takes on profound importance for a student's future, much more so than in Charlie's day. Today, students not only receive an education, they are labeled and slotted within the educational system in a way that affects their future. For these reasons, the relation between education and society, the effects of schooling, what happens inside schools, and the part schools play in reducing or enhancing inequalities have important consequences for all of us. We consider each of these issues in turn.

THE RELATION BETWEEN SCHOOLS AND SOCIETY

THE FUNCTIONS OF EDUCATION

What roles do schools serve in society? Sociologists have identified a number of their functions: (1) cultural transmission and socialization of the young; (2) selection for adult positions; and (3) support for the discovery of new knowledge, especially in higher education. Some people suggest additional latent functions of education, which will not be discussed here, such as keeping young people off the streets, providing an appropriate "marriage market" for mate selection, and serving as an agent of social reform (Goslin, 1965). Functionalist and conflict sociologists differ in the way they view these activities.

Cultural Transmission and Socialization

Education is important for passing on the social and cultural heritage of one generation to the next. The knowledge, values, beliefs, and norms that adult members of society think young members should learn are transmitted (in part) through education. Schools try to perform this task by providing experiences that instill knowledge (of history, say), skills (such as reading), attitudes (school loyalty, for example), and values (like punctuality) in their students—in other words, through *socialization*. Functionalists stress that the knowledge and skills students acquire in this process are central for obtaining and performing adult occupational roles. Functionalists tend to assume, however, that education provides the same benefits and opportunities for everyone in society. Conflict sociologists suggest that certain groups benefit more than others, partly because different social classes, races, and sexes receive different socialization in schools. They also suggest that mental skills are not as important for occupational attainment and income as functionalists claim they are.

Functionalists view education as a means of integrating society through common cultural and political socialization—for example, all children learn the pledge of allegiance in elementary school. Conflict sociologists emphasize that education is a resource used by groups competing for domination, legitimacy, power, income, or status within a society. Educational degrees may be used to exclude people from certain jobs, even when the content of the required education is unrelated to the job.

Selection and Allocation to Adult Positions

Complex societies that do not pass on adult positions by simple inheritance need a system for assigning people to various positions. Traditionally (and frequently still today), family background, race, religion, birth order, and sex determine the position an individual holds in society. In industrial societies, schools have the power to place individuals in the running for specific life positions. Schools are granted that power by state legislatures and government departments of education, which grant colleges and universities the right to award certain types of degrees. These degrees, in turn, make people eligible to be considered for certain jobs and occupations. Meyer (1977) sees schools as obtaining special *charters* to "define people as graduates and as therefore possessing distinctive rights and capacities in society." Schools therefore affect life chances through the degrees they can award.

Both functionalist and conflict sociologists agree that schools are becoming increasingly important in determining an individual's life chances. But they differ in their assessment of whether this process is fair and desirable. Functionalists argue that the growing complexity of society and the jobs in it underscore the importance of individuals occupying positions for which they are "well suited." So, to functionalists, individual ability and achievement are the most important criteria for allocating people to various curricula and occupations. Functionalists and conflict sociologists both note that schools do not always ignore the class, sex, or race of students, however.

Conflict sociologists challenge the underlying assumptions of the functionalist view. They doubt that most jobs are becoming more complex and technical; instead, they see many jobs as getting simpler. They note that test scores and school grades are unrelated to job performance, suggesting that such measures are poor indicators of "merit." Conflict sociologists see schools as allocating individuals to highly unequal positions in society and legitimizing that allocation on the basis of test scores or grades that may not be valid indicators of merit (Bourdieu, 1971; Bowles and Gintis, 1976).

Education as a Knowledge-Generating Institution

Schools also affect us through the knowledge they produce. In keeping with their view of a homogeneous society, functionalists tend to see the knowledge produced in educational institutions as equally valuable to all members of society. Conflict sociologists (such as Touraine, 1974) argue that the pursuit of knowledge in the United States has consistently been exploited by powerful elites in order to pursue the science, technology, and morality (for example, defense hardware) that benefits their position in society, often to the detriment of other groups in society. Touraine links this development to the student rebellions of the 1960s, when affluent students at some of the most selective universities in the nation began to challenge the role of the university in society.

The conflict perspective leads us to ask who supports the production of certain kinds of knowledge rather than others, and who benefits from it? For example, who supports research on missile systems, and who benefits from it? What are the consequences of some rather than other

Higher education, particularly at the community college level, has expanded considerably in recent years. Functional sociologists suggest that this expansion was a response to demands for technical skills, while conflict sociologists suggest that the expansion was a response to competition between status groups.

knowledge—for example, knowing how to treat cancer with chemicals once people have it, or knowing how to avoid getting cancer? We can ask such questions about the kinds of cancer research that are supported or the issues that get defined as "social problems."

EDUCATIONAL EXPANSION

Why has education expanded so dramatically in the United States? Functionalists argue that education expanded in response to the increasing complexity of the division of labor and the need for a more highly educated work force. Marxians such as Bowles and Gintis (1976) suggest that education expanded because of the need for capitalist owners to maintain control over an unruly labor force.

However, as Hurn (1978) points out, a need, whether of society or of a group of capitalists, does not necessarily translate directly into social practice. He believes that education expanded in the United States because people believed education would be useful to them in their own lives, and because groups were competing for status and prestige. Education was a useful symbolic resource in that competition. Hurn's position is supplemented by Collins' comparative study of the expansion of education. Collins (1977) suggests that there are three different demands for education—practical, status, and bureaucratic. These three have shaped the educational systems of various countries. The functionalist interpretation suggests that education in the United States grew to meet demands for practical or technical skills, but Collins says this was not the major reason people demanded more education. Much of modern education is not very practical; the number of years of school and grades earned are not related to work performance; and most people learn on the job much of what they need to know to do the job. Reading and writing are among the few practical skills that are taught in school. For these reasons, Collins argues that technical demands were not a major reason for expanding education.

Instead, Collins believes, American education expanded as a result of status group competition. Education motivated by the desire for status group membership is notable for ceremonies dramatizing the unity of the educated group and its status compared to that of outsiders. The content of such education reflects cultural ideals, usually impractical ones. Status group membership is defined primarily by leisure and consumption activities, not by productive work. A common culture is central for the creation of a status group community. Collins (1979) cites the great emphasis on fraternities and sororities in U.S. colleges as evidence for status group concerns in education. Historically, Collins indicates, education has been used more often to define status groups than for other purposes.

Finally, education that develops in the process of bureaucratization reflects efforts of elites to promote impersonal methods of control. The content of education is irrelevant, Collins suggests, but the central feature is the structure of grades, ranks, degrees, and formal credentials.[1] This kind of education serves some of the control purposes suggested by Bowles and Gintis (1976). Mass education, at least, may be considered an effort to ensure labor and social discipline. But, says Collins, although modern education may discipline the lower social classes, the demand for labor discipline does not explain why some industrial societies have large mass education systems while others have small ones. The United States has a very large educational system, and the Soviet Union's and Japan's are quite large, but Britain, France, and Germany all have smaller systems of higher education. These are all highly industrialized societies. Why should some have massive educational systems while others do not?

Capitalists may have pushed for mass education in some societies, as the Marxian view suggests, but compulsory education developed in Prussia and Japan prior to industrialization. Collins suggests that the expansion of education arises from the existence of a bureaucratic state. The state imposes compulsory education on groups considered threats to state control. Those economic classes, sometimes including capitalists, may influence who the state defines as needing control. So, Collins concludes, mass compulsory education was created first to impose military and political discipline. Only later, perhaps, was it adopted to further industrial discipline (1977).

In our system of higher education, elements of all three demands for education exist. We see some stress on practical skills, such as computer programming, laboratory, or business courses; we see strong residues of classical or humanistic education and ritualized ceremonies like fraternity hazing and graduation, which are the cultural aspects of attaining membership in certain status groups; and finally we see increasing specialization, stress on grades, ranks, degrees, and formal bureaucratically recognized credentials.

EFFECTS OF SCHOOLING ON INDIVIDUALS

People hope for different gains from education. Some seek to develop their minds and to learn more about their world, their culture, and them-

[1]The bureaucratic form of control that sometimes operates in education is illustrated by the World War II army experience of a German-speaking recruit. The Army gave a test to see who should become a translator. The German-speaking recruit was labeled "over qualified" based on his test performance.

selves. Others hope to get an interesting or prestigious job. Some want to make a lot of money. Probably all these motives operate in each person to varying degrees. Are people's hopes in what education can do for them justified? Does education, especially higher education, make a difference?

KNOWLEDGE AND ATTITUDES

Two major studies (Coleman et al., 1966, and Jencks et al., 1972) conclude that schools have little effect on the knowledge students possess (as measured by scores on an achievement test) that can be statistically separated from the influence of the students' homes. In other words, students who score well on an academic achievement test appear to do so because they live in socially and economically advantaged families rather than because of the schools they attend. One result of this is that academic achievement differences within the same school tend to be greater than the differences in academic achievement between schools.

Some people have interpreted these studies as saying that "schools make no difference in what students learn." One of the problems in proving that schools do make a difference is finding children who do not go to school in a society where schooling is compulsory until the age of 14 or more. One relevant example occurred in Prince Edward County in Virginia in the 1960s. Rather than integrate the public schools, the community closed them. Private schools were opened for white children, but black children were unable to attend school for four years. As a result, they knew much less than children who began first grade on schedule (Green et al., 1964). The children who had never attended school did not know who George Washington, Thomas Jefferson, or Abraham Lincoln were, how many states there are in the United States, how to do simple arithmetic, or how to read. This situation suggests that children learn a great deal from even the poorest schools in the United States.

One researcher (Wiley, 1976) suggests that the actual amount of time in school is related to the amount learned. The more hours of schooling, the more pupils learned (as measured by standardized tests). Another study (Heyns, 1978) found that sixth- and seventh-grade students who went to summer school, used the library, and read a lot in the summer made greater gains in knowledge than pupils who did not have such educational exposures during the summer. The impact of schooling was particularly dramatic for disadvantaged and minority students. These studies strongly suggest that schools do influence the knowledge and skills that pupils gain.

Education also influences the general knowledge, habits and attitudes of those who obtain it. Education is thought to prepare people for a lifetime of learning, and more educated people do indeed make greater use of printed media (newspapers, books, magazines). Better-educated individuals have wider and deeper general knowledge than those who are less educated years after they finish school (Hyman, Wright, Reed, 1975). These differences persist even when many possible confounding factors, including sex, religion, social origins, and adult social position, are controlled. Education (especially college attendance) is related to adult interest in politics and public affairs, to keeping abreast of health news, and to taking adult education courses. Moreover, education makes people more skeptical of traditional institutions and is associated with more liberal political and social attitudes (Feldman and Newcomb, 1969; Ladd, 1978). While high schools make a substantial contribution to the creation of a better-informed citizenry, college graduates know even more, read more, and have different attitudes and behaviors. In general, education is related to a greater sense of well-being and higher self-esteem (Hyman, Wright, Reed, 1975).

College students are less likely today than in the 1960s to enter professional or technical jobs, but they are still more likely than high school graduates to attain such jobs.

GETTING A JOB

Education is also the single most important factor in getting a job. As we saw earlier, theorists differ on why this is true, but they agree that for most people, at least some higher education is necessary for a professional or managerial position. Most Americans now work in large organizations (whether business, government, schools, or hospitals), and the larger and more nationally oriented these organizations are, the more they require high levels of education for white collar, managerial, or administrative jobs (Collins, 1974). About half of all college graduates hold professional or technical positions. They work as scientists, engineers, doctors, teachers, pilots, and accountants. About one in five college graduates have managerial and administrative jobs.

The percentage of recent college graduates entering professional and technical jobs is smaller than in the past, but the absolute number is larger. As Figure 14.3 shows, about 55 percent of the 8 million college graduates in 1980 entered professional and technical jobs, compared to 73 percent of the 4 million graduates who entered such jobs between 1962 and 1969. Thus, today's college graduates are less likely to obtain a professional or technical job than were their counterparts in the 1960s. A larger proportion of college graduates are now entering occupations as managers and administrators, sales workers, clerical workers and operatives, service workers, and farm workers, or are unemployed than was the case in the 1960s (Sargent, 1982). This situation has occurred because the number of college graduates has grown faster than the number of professional and technical jobs (Freeman, 1976). It still seems likely, however, that more and more of the better-paying jobs will require applicants to have attended college.

JOB PERFORMANCE

Although most social scientists concur that education is needed to help get a job, there is less agreement on whether it helps a person do that job well. No one denies that most jobs today require people to be able to read, write, and do simple arithmetic. At issue is the assumption that more education produces skills that are re-

"I said it's not often one gets one's chimney swept by a person with a B.A. from Sarah Lawrence."

SOURCE: Drawing by W. Miller, © 1982, *The New Yorker Magazine, Inc.*

quired to perform increasingly technical and complex jobs, such as those of nurses, air traffic controllers, or police officers. Research suggests that education is not related to job performance (Collins, 1974; Folger and Nam, 1967; Berg, 1970). Berg (1970), for example, studied factory workers, maintenance workers, department store clerks, technicians, secretaries, bank tellers, engineers, industrial research scientists, military personnel, and federal civil service employees and found that the more highly educated employees performed their jobs no better than less educated ones. Despite this evidence, schools are increasingly becoming the "gatekeepers" of adult positions. Whereas once people could go out and get a job "on their own," they now need a *credential* awarded by a school even to be considered. This gives the schools a much more powerful role in society.

EDUCATION AND INCOME

Do educated people earn more than less educated ones? Broadly speaking, "yes": the more education, the higher the total lifetime earnings. Figure 16.2 shows the expected lifetime earnings of men and women with different amounts of education. As you can see, those with more education are likely to earn more. The association between education and income needs further examination, however. There is a wide range of incomes for people at each level of education: Many earn less than the average and some earn more. Social factors other than educa-

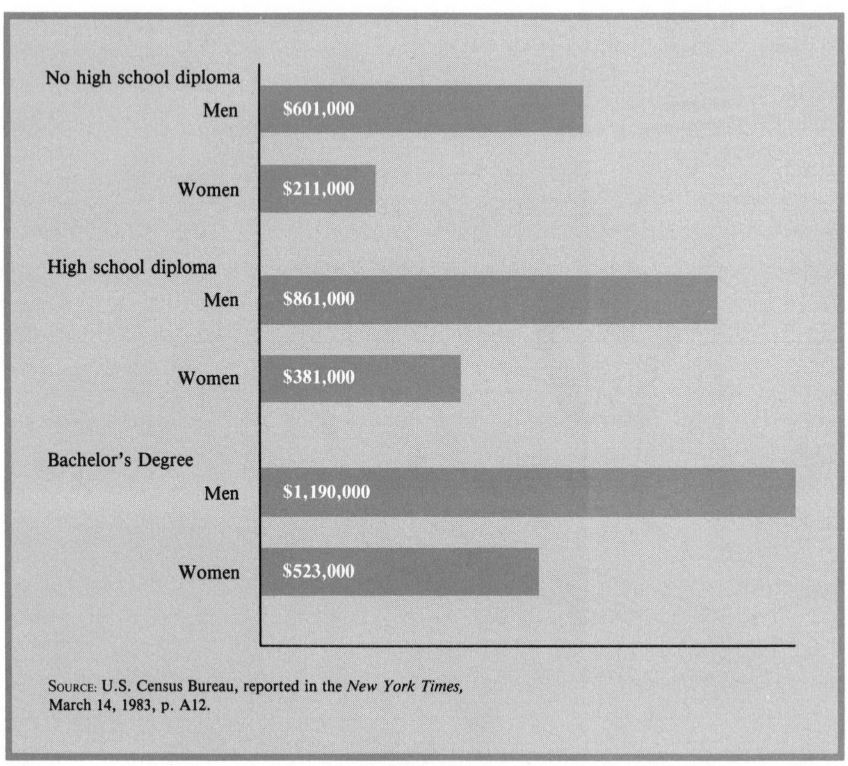

Figure 16.2 Estimated Lifetime Earnings of 1980 Male and Female College Graduates and Their Generational Peers with Less Education

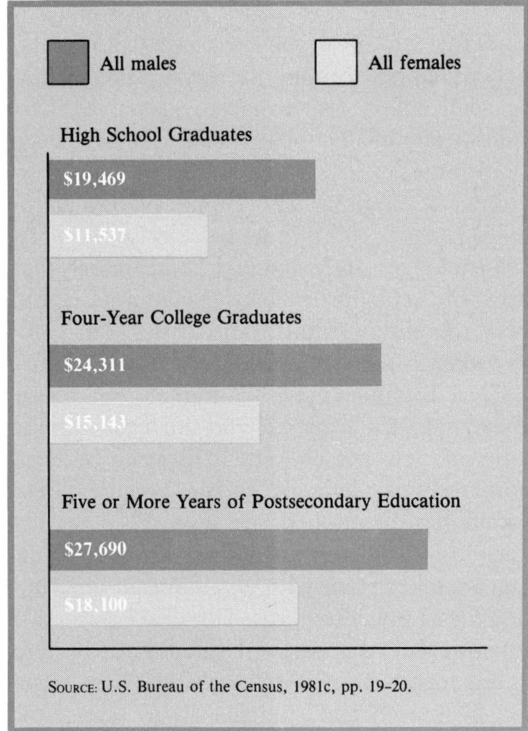

Figure 16.3 Median Income of Persons 15 Years Old and Over, Working Full Time in 1980

tion, notably race and sex, affect income. Figure 16.3 shows the income of men and women with different amounts of education who work full time. The returns on education for women are much lower than the returns for men. Females earn less than males at every level of education; indeed, female college graduates earn less than male high school graduates. The disparity is due partly to occupational segregation by sex and to employment interruptions, but pay discrimination appears to play a role as well.

Young black males who are highly educated may earn as much or more than their white male counterparts, according to some research (Freeman, 1977; Smith and Welch, 1978). Whether they continue to hold their own throughout their careers remains to be seen.

Other factors, such as type of employer, region, age, union membership, and social class background also affect how much one earns. In one analysis, Mincer (1974) concluded that level of education explained only about one-third of the variation in the earnings of white nonfarm males. Even for this group, for whom education has the greatest association with income, two-thirds of the variation in earnings was due to other factors.

The economic benefits of college have been hotly debated in recent years. Some social scientists (Freeman, 1976) argue that the cost of college plus the income lost while studying will never be earned back by graduates. Others (Witmer, 1976) counter that college definitely is worth what it costs. Most agree that the economic payoffs of college are keyed to the economy, with higher gains coming in good years and lower ones during recessions.

EDUCATION AND MOBILITY

The relationship between education and jobs and income varies by social class. Among the upper class (including owners of productive resources, high-level managers, and professionals), social origin is more important than education for achieving high position (as well as for inheriting wealth and gaining access to power). Class plays a large part in protecting the upper class from downward mobility and blocking the lower class from upward mobility (Figure 16.4). Education is used by the upper class to avoid downward mobility. Every effort is made to ensure high academic achievement and many years of school attendance. One way the upper class often does this is by sending its children to elite private schools.

Among the white middle class (which includes professionals, managers, supervisors, and some highly skilled manual workers), the education of children is related to the social positions they achieve. That is, the more education they get, the more likely they are to achieve higher status and somewhat higher paying jobs within the middle class. They have limited chances of gaining upper-class positions, however. Thus,

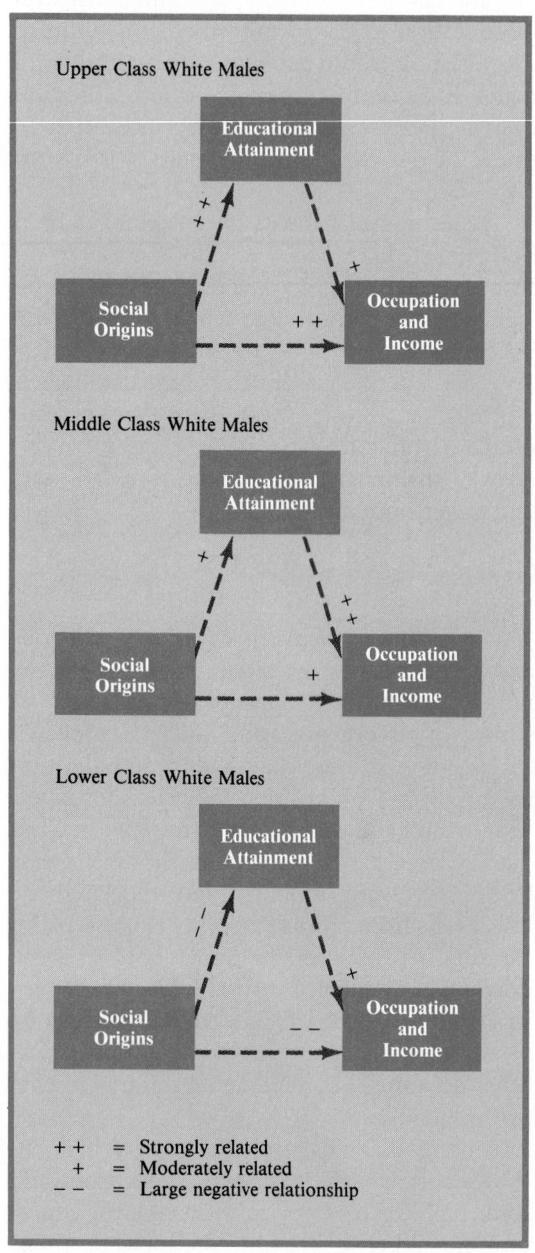

Figure 16.4 Schematic Portrayal of the Relationships Between Social Origins, Education, and Adult Occupation and Income

for white middle-class males, there is some evidence that education is related to better jobs and higher incomes. Among the lower class (including semi-skilled and unskilled manual workers and the perennially unemployed), even a college education offers poor odds for achieving a prestigious occupation (Boudon, 1973; Tinto, 1978).

Sociologists suggest at least three models that show the relationship between education and social mobility in industrial societies. The *sponsored mobility* pattern, Turner (1960) says, occurs in Great Britain. There, children are selected at an early age for academic and university education, and few get chosen. (This may be even more true of Germany today, because Great Britain has abandoned the tests given to 11-year-olds that determined their futures.) Children are selected early for elite status or are fated for a life of nonelite status. Turner contrasts this situation with that in the United States, where he sees a pattern of *contest mobility*. Here, selection is delayed and students go to school together for a long period of time. They are urged to compete with one another all along the way, in the hope that someday they may achieve a high position. A third model, presented by Rosenbaum (1976), identifies a process of *tournament selection* operating in American high schools. As in a sports playoff, you play a round, and winners have the right to go on to the next round. If you lose, you are out of the running. Unlike Turner's two theoretical models, Rosenbaum's view is based on actual practice in American society. In the tournament there is a continual process of selection, but selection works in only one direction—out. You can be eliminated, but winning one round does not make you a permanent winner.

Rosenbaum accurately describes the selection process in American society today. Competitors may be compared with the players on major league baseball teams. They are preoccupied with their standings in the league, so much so that they may mistakenly think that theirs is the "only game in town." However, perhaps unknown to them, there are sandlot players (the lower class), most of whom will never be allowed into league competition. Only one or two of their members may make it into the major leagues. Behind the scenes are the upper-class individuals who own the teams, but who do not compete themselves. Educational credentials may be likened to an invitation to try out for the teams in the league. Most lower-class members will not get those invitations. Most middle-class members will.

Within this model, it is possible for some individuals to experience occupational mobility through education, although the individual does not move upward in class. For example, the son of a pharmacist may become a dentist, thus achieving occupational mobility, but both positions are "middle class." Although individuals may move slightly up or down on the hierarchy of occupational prestige, the underlying class structure of society has not changed.[2] This helps to explain why the expansion of educational opportunity has not noticeably reduced social inequality. Social inequality is based on occupational prestige, life-style, income, and wealth ownership, and the range of inequality in society is relatively unchanged by examples of individual mobility.

Functional and conflict sociologists agree that schools have powerful socialization, allocation, and certification effects on individuals. They differ with respect to whether education promotes social opportunity via "merit" or serves to reproduce and legitimate existing inequalities in society. Part of their difference stems from functional sociologists' stress on individual mobility within the existing class structure. Conflict sociologists note that the relative positions of groups have not changed and urge the reduction of social and economic inequality within society. Both views raise questions about school organization and processes and their consequences.

[2]Recall from Chapter 10 that *class* refers to position in the system of production or to the control some positions exercise over others in the production process. *Occupation* refers to the technical division of labor in a society, and *occupational prestige* refers to the social respect given to various positions in society. Questions of occupation and occupational prestige do not tap the issues of wealth, ownership, and control.

INSIDE THE SCHOOLS

In the 1950s, the United States was surprised by the launching of the world's first space satellite by the Soviet Union. The fact that we had been "beaten" by the Soviet Union led to great agitation and to the conclusion that we had somehow fallen behind in the development of science and technology. A considerable commotion occurred in education. Leaders such as James Conant (1959), a former president of Harvard University, began to focus on what happens inside schools. Sociologists have also been interested in the organizational aspects of schools. Some features, like curriculum, teacher activities, teacher expectations, and student peer groups, may influence what individuals learn in school and how well they do. Other organizational features, including school size, governance, bureaucracy, and classroom organization, have been found to be related to how children feel about their schools, whether they feel alienated or not, and whether or not they drop out or become violent. Pupil learning, feelings, and behaviors may influence the effects of schooling on individuals and may be related to social inequalities if lower-class or minority children are more likely to attend bureaucratic or unresponsive schools or to have teachers who hold lower expectations for them. For these reasons, what occurs in schools is important to understand, both for the light it sheds on a major social institution and for its implications for the larger society.

CURRICULUM

Did you ever wonder why you study what you do in school? At one time everyone who went to school studied the same subjects. Beginning in the nineteenth century but becoming more widespread in the 1920s, students began taking different courses. Today in public secondary schools in the United States, about 36 percent of students take what is called an "academic" curriculum (college preparatory English, history, science, math, and foreign language); 20 percent take a vocational program (such as printing or auto mechanics); and 43 percent follow a general curriculum (with English, accounting, and clerical courses) (Fiske, 1983, p. C8). In private and parochial schools, nearly everyone pursues an academic curriculum (Coleman et al., 1982).

One of the curricular changes the Conant Report (1959) recommended was that students take more math, physics, and chemistry. This report is a dramatic illustration of how events outside the schools may influence what happens inside them. Once in schools that offer particular choices of curricula, students may study certain subjects because they find them socially prestigious (the classics), or because the next level of education requires them for admission (math), or because they believe they may be useful in the future (computer programming). There are patterned variations in who studies what, according to race, sex, and social class. Middle- and upper-class white pupils are more likely than lower-class and minority students to take an academic program. Females are less likely than males to study science and math, and more likely to study language and literature. These curricular choices may help to reproduce social inequalities, since high school curriculum is the single biggest determinant of college attendance (Jaffe and Adams, 1970) and influences choice of college major. College curriculum increasingly determines what graduate and professional education one may pursue, and hence to a growing degree what occupations are open to individuals.

TEACHER ACTIVITIES

Courses of study are put into practice by teachers. While the formal mandate of teachers is to teach, sociologists have observed that they spend a great deal of their time in other activities. Classrooms are crowded places, and a class is a collection of individuals who vary in background, interests, and concentration spans. There are 20 to 40 children in most classrooms, and only one or at most two teachers. Jackson (1968) found teachers had as many as a thousand interpersonal contacts each day with children in their classrooms. Because of the large number of children, teachers often function as official timekeepers, supply sergeants, traffic cops, and judges. One result is that students spend a lot of time waiting, denying their desires, being interrupted in what they are doing, and being distracted by other people (Jackson, 1968). These features of school life may resemble the adult world, but they may also make learning difficult for many children.

Teachers function as employees in a bureaucratic organization, even as they attempt to nurture young minds. Teachers are organizational spokespersons, required to take attendance, read daily announcements, collect lunch money, and administer various tests. They serve as organizational enforcers, disciplinarians, and protectors of public morality. In many schools, children are chastised for swearing or for wearing only their undershirts. In their role as evaluators, teachers continually assess the performance, character, and conformity of students (Schlechty, 1976).

TEACHER EXPECTATIONS

Teachers may lose sight of the fact that they sometimes hold unequal expectations for children. Yet one of the most dramatic ways teachers can affect students is through their own expectations of them. Many social scientists have examined whether the expectations teachers hold for children influence what they learn in school. Rosenthal and Jacobson (1968) were among the first to do so. They told teachers in an elementary school in California that certain children in their class were likely to have a mental "growth spurt" that year. Actually, the children had been given a type of intelligence test that could reveal nothing about future mental growth. The names given to the teachers had been selected randomly. At the end of the year the researchers returned to the school and gave another test to see which children had improved. All the children in the school improved somewhat, but those labeled "spurters" made greater gains than the "nonspurters," especially in the first and second grades.

The effect of the labels that had randomly been assigned is an example of the self-fulfilling prophecy. The *self-fulfilling prophecy* is a belief or prediction about a person or situation that influences that person or situation in such a way that the belief or prediction comes true. In this case, if teachers expect children to make gains and treat them accordingly, they may be more likely to make such gains, thus confirming the prophecy.

This example of "mind over matter" does not operate in all realms, but there is a growing body of data since the Rosenthal and Jacobson study that suggests how the process operates in classrooms. Although it is probably subconscious, teachers call more often on students for whom they hold high expectations. They talk to them more and tend to show more praise and acceptance of them and their ideas. Teachers may make more eye contact and show greater warmth and friendliness toward favored students. Students or classes highly esteemed by the teacher may be given more opportunities to respond, thus gaining personal confidence and reinforcing the teacher's already high expectations. Often teachers actually teach more to pupils or classes for whom they have higher expectations, and they may teach them different material as well. Not surprisingly, when teachers taught more and praised students more, the students learned more. Students also felt better about themselves and about school (Persell, 1977). Teacher expectations can be a positive or a negative force in a student's academic career, depending on what expectations teachers hold.

Teachers tend to hold lower expectations for students of ethnic minorities and lower social classes more often than the students' test scores warrant. In addition, young, minority, and lower-class students often appear more susceptible to a teacher's influence. It is possible that teachers' expectations for minority and lower-class pupils may account, in part, for their lower school achievement. We'll explore this point later in the chapter.

Some teachers hold lower expectations for the reading progress of boys, especially in the first grade (Palardy, 1969). Boys learned to read more slowly when they had teachers who expected exactly that to happen, but not when they had teachers who believed that boys and girls are equally likely to learn to read. Although we do not know how widespread different expectations by sex are, we do know that all through elementary school more boys have learning "problems" than girls.

The expectations of teachers we have been discussing are not due to personality flaws or weak character; teachers simply reflect the prevailing conditions and ideas of a society. Society often undervalues minorities or places caste barriers in their path, and underrates lower-class individuals. The lower expectations for young males may be rooted in educational literature that describes their growth cycle as somewhat behind that of female children. Educational practices may help to create and exaggerate differences between children in a teacher's mind. Finally, teachers may form expectations based on who a student's friends are.

STUDENT PEER GROUPS

Student peer group values and behaviors may be more important for explaining adolescent behavior than school or parental values, suggests Coleman in his book *The Adolescent Society* (1961). He argues that adolescents are segregated from adult society, leading to the development of a

College student subcultures are often linked to the social class backgrounds of their members. Middle-class students are more likely than college students from working-class backgrounds to join groups stressing fun, such as fraternities and sororities.

youth subculture distinct from and opposed to the culture of the adult world. Popularity among peers depends more on athletic prowess among boys and looks or personality among girls than on academic performance. Hence the student subculture may be at odds with what teachers and students are trying to do.

Other research supports Coleman's view that there is a somewhat distinct youth culture in the United States, but questions how opposed to adult society that culture is. Riley (1961), for example, found that students feel pulled between parental demands for academic success and peer pressures for engaging in social life. Most students combine elements of both into their self-images—successful students who are not "grinds," who are friendly and popular, but also realistic about the relationship between schoolwork and their adult futures.

Both visions of their adult futures and social origin seem to shape college student subcultures. Katz (1968) noted that a student might "try out" more than one subculture. Generally college students from working-class backgrounds are more likely to form subcultures valuing vocational goals, while middle-class students tend to enter groups stressing fun or favoring scholastic achievement, report Clark and Trow (1966). Another subculture observed was a nonconformist one. Today's college students are thought to be job-oriented, with other subcultures waning in importance.

Some peer groups provide social support for delinquency or violence. Stinchcombe (1964) learned that students who joined a rebellious subculture were those most pessimistic about their futures and the part school could play in brightening those futures. Whatever their social origins, students in vocational courses and those headed toward low-status jobs were most likely to join a rebellious subculture.

BUREAUCRACY IN SCHOOLS

If you attend a school of more than 500 students, you have probably encountered its bureaucratic authority system (see Chapter 7 for more discussion of bureaucracy). Bureaucracy is a type of organization with a hierarchy of offices, standardized rules and regulations to govern the conduct of affairs, and numerous records. Most public schools and universities rely on this type of organizational authority.

Advocates of bureaucracy and largeness cite several advantages. First, larger organizations with correspondingly higher budgets can provide certain facilities and programs—for example, an Olympic-size swimming pool or classes in Chinese—that would be too costly for small schools with few students. Second, teachers in one study reported a greater sense of power in schools that were more rather than less bureaucratic (Moeller and Charters, 1970). The bureaucratic schools gave teachers a sense that policies were directed and consistent rather than capricious and varied. Finally, some students say they like the feeling of anonymity they get in a large place. As long as they do what they have to do, no one bothers them. In short, some teachers and administrators find that hierarchy and standardized rules help them to run a school well. This situation may not bother some students, although other students complain that large bureaucratic schools are impersonal and alienating, and some research bears this out (Anderson, 1973).

In the public sector, smaller schools are disappearing at all levels of education. Only by sending children to private schools can parents obtain a small, intimate environment. Of course, such a course of action is generally available only to parents with the ability to pay the costs of private education.

STUDENT ALIENATION AND VIOLENCE

As schools have grown in size and in degree of bureaucratization, there also has been an increase in the number of violent incidents in schools. Such incidents have escalated sharply in the last few years. Students not only attack each other in increasing numbers, but there has been a dramatic increase in the number of serious assaults on teachers, including rapes, beatings, and even murder. The American Federation of Teachers attributes this increase to the problems underpaid teachers face in overcrowded classrooms where they cannot keep order. A hundred years ago, however, miserably paid teachers taught much larger classes of lower-class and immigrant minority pupils and maintained a high degree of order. So it seems that the decline in order in today's schools reflects a deeper problem. Students today are increasingly unwilling to accept the authority of teachers and administrators, suggests Katz (1977).

The growth of violence reflects a fundamental challenge to the legitimacy of the school as a social institution. There are other indicators of this crisis of legitimacy as well. Parents and citizens are voting down school bond issues and cutting taxes; parents are challenging the school's definition of failure as residing in the child and holding the school accountable when it fails to teach a child to read. Absenteeism and truancy are increasing. Although largeness and bureaucracy have not been proved to cause increased violence in the schools, the two trends have developed together, suggesting the possibility that they are related.

EDUCATION AND INEQUALITY

DIFFERENCES BY RACE AND CLASS

Many individual lower-class and minority children do as well or better in school than upper- and middle-class white children. But when groups are compared, socially disadvantaged children tend to get lower test scores and poorer grades and drop out sooner. Why is social background so strongly related to school achievement? Many explanations have been offered: genetic deficits, cultural gaps, inadequate schools, tracking, segregation, and societal opportunities.

Genetic Deficits

In 1969, the view that certain groups might have "inferior" genes was revived by Arthur Jensen, an educational psychologist at the University of California at Berkeley. He speculated that black children might be doing poorly in school because of their genetic backgrounds. Much of the evidence he used for his hypothesis, however, was apparently faked by Sir Cyril Burt in England. Jensen and Burt aside, the "genetic deficit" argument falters because race is a social category in the United States, not a biological one (many whites and blacks are genetically mixed). Further, no one has ever identified the specific gene or genes that transmit "intelligence." So most social scientists reject a genetic deficit explanation for racial differences in school achievement.

Sociologists also challenge how intelligence itself is measured. It is often measured by an *IQ (intelligence quotient) test,* which is a standardized paper-and-pencil test of verbal and numerical knowledge and reasoning. IQ tests do not measure originality, interpersonal sensitivity, motivation, energy, or scientific and artistic talent. In fact, no one knows exactly what they do measure. Despite the claims of some test designers that they have developed culture-free tests, most sociologists claim that IQ tests are culture-bound—that is, they require knowledge and language skills possessed by a particular cultural group. In fact, a "culture free" test is an impossibility, since every test requires background in some culture in order to take it. What thoughtful test designers mean by "culture free" is a test composed of items that are no more likely to be missed by members of one group (say, blacks) than by members of another (whites).

Members of various groups are often at a disadvantage in taking IQ tests. See, for example, the box containing the Barriology Exam. How well did you do on it? Do you consider the test a fair indication of your innate ability? If a ghetto child does not know that a cup goes on a saucer rather than on a table, how does that lack of knowledge reflect innate ability? Many IQ tests, then, measure culturally acquired knowledge and skills based on white, middle-class culture. IQ scores may be related to school success because scores are often used for tracking students (that is, grouping students by ability) into various programs, but they are not related to success in life. The way tests are used may generate self-fulfilling prophecies of academic success or failure.

Cultural Gaps

Standing in apparent opposition to the "genetic deficit" explanation of unequal school achievement is the "cultural gap" view. It suggests that poor children do badly in schools because their lives are marked by emptiness at best, or at worst by limitations in family structure, childrearing patterns, values, attitudes, or language exposure, all of which impair their intellectual development. But close studies of minority children find them to be "bathed in verbal stimulation," to be skilled users of their language (Labov, 1973), and marked by family strengths such as helpful extended family ties (Hill, 1971). The family differences that do appear are rooted in the economic, political, and racial inequalities of the society, not in the failings of individuals. Moreover, existing differences have not been pinpointed as causes of school failure. So this view does not provide a convincing explanation of unequal school achievement. Indeed, where lower-class or minority children are taught by teachers who assume they can learn and who take responsibility for teaching them, they do learn, sometimes better than white middle-class children (Brookover and Schneider, 1975).

Societal Opportunities

The generally lower school achievement of minority children has been attributed by Ogbu (1978), a social anthropologist, to the barriers they face in the larger society. He studied members of inferior castes in six societies around the world and found they all shared inferior education and a job ceiling based on caste rather than on training or ability. Children see the barriers to their full participation in adult society and become disillusioned with hard work and school success. Obgu's work is especially interesting because it attributes lower school performance to caste status rather than to race. In only three of the six societies (the United States, Britain, and New Zealand) were the minority castes racially different. In the other three societies (Japan, Israel, and India), they belonged to the same race but were stigmatized as an inferior caste by geographic origin, ancestry, or other traits. In some cases, persons facing caste barriers performed very well when they moved away from the society where they were stigmatized.

Barriology Exam

By Barriologist Emeritus Antonio Gómez

The cultural content of IQ tests may be evident in the Barriology exam based on knowledge of Mexican-American cultural mores.

1. Laurel and Hardy were popularly known in the barrio as ________

2. Duck ________ describes a hair style worn by barrio dudes in the 50's.

3. According to baby care practices of barrio women, tickling a baby will produce what defect?

4. Barrio tradition among youth has often demanded that students
- A. excel in school
- B. do poorly in school
- C. keep the group norm
- D. none of the above is applicable

5. *Pedichi* and *moocher* have what in common?

6. Eating watermelon and drinking beer simultaneously is, according to barrio lore,
- A. sexually stimulating
- B. bad for one's stomach
- C. good for hangovers
- D. not an ethnic diet

7. What slang name refers to the older barrio dudes?

8. Large brown market bags have been used in barrio households for what purpose? How about ½ gallon milk cartons?

9. Complete the following children's chant:

De tin marin
de do pinque
cucara macara
____

10. Lowered, channeled, chopped, primed all refer to what barrio art form?

Answers to Barriology Exam

1. *El gordo y el Flaco.*
2. Ducktail.
3. A speech defect.
4. C. Keep the group norm.
5. Both describe one who asks for handouts.
6. B. Bad for one's stomach.
7. *Veteranos*—adults who have been through barrio warfare and usually no longer take part in gang hassles.
8. Trash bags and garbage containers.
9. *Titere fue*—a chant used by children to select players for a game—similar to "one potato, two potato," etc.
10. A customized car.

Rate Yourself on the Con Safos Barriology Quotient Scale

Barriology Examination Questions answered correctly:

7 to 10	Chicano Barriologist, *o muy de aquellas.*
5 or 6	High Potential, *o ya casi*
3 or 4	*Vendido*, *o* culturally deprived
0 or 1	*Pendejo*

SOURCE: Ludwig and Santibanez (Eds.), *The Chicanos*, 1971, pp. 149–153.

This significant finding suggests that social rather than personal factors explain the lower school performance of some groups relative to others.

Inadequate Schools

American public schools reflect their geographic locations. In practice this would make no difference if all areas were similar, but anyone who has traveled from a downtown urban area to a suburban or rural area knows that such areas may differ immensely. Residential segregation based on income, occupation, and race abounds. Such segregation results in area schools that tend to be economically and ethnically homogeneous.

In addition to geographic distinctions, American education is divided into public and private sectors. Although only about 10 percent of the population attends private elementary and secondary schools, that group differs dramatically from the other 90 percent of the population, and their schools differ also. More than 85 percent of private and Catholic school seniors are white, compared with 78 percent of public school seniors (Coleman, Hoffer and Kilgore, 1981, p. 39). The average family income of private school students is considerably higher than that of public school families (Baird, 1977). Elite private schools spend between $10,000 and $15,000 per year on each child, compared to about $2,500 spent per child nationally in public schools. The schools also differ in goals, financial base, and size, with private schools more likely to be small and wealthy. Private school graduates overwhelmingly attend prestigious private colleges (Hammack and Cookson, 1980) and are very likely to end up in high-level business, financial, professional, or cultural positions (Armstrong, 1978). Spatial divisions, then, are one way students are separated during schooling. However, even within the same school, there are administrative devices for dividing students.

Tracking

Further segregation by race and income (and sometimes sex) occurs within most schools through the practice of tracking. *Tracking* refers to the grouping of students by ability or curriculum, often both at the same time. Students may be assigned to the academic or the vocational curriculum based on academic abilities. Once in a particular curriculum, they may be tracked further by ability into several levels within the curriculum. Test scores are a primary basis for track placement in many schools, and because test scores are highly correlated with race and social class, school classes based on such scores tend to be highly segregated by race and class. Hence, even within a mixed school, students may go to class only with students who are remarkably like themselves in important social ways. Tracking is particularly widespread in large urban school systems that are racially and economically diverse (Persell, 1977).

The results of tracking have only recently been understood. Early studies found no clear effects on the academic achievement of students. More recently, however, researchers note that upper-track students sometimes improve, but that this improvement is offset by a decline in lower-track students. When the results are averaged for an entire school, no effects are visible. The unequal results that do occur seem traceable to differences in the content, materials, and methods of teaching used, rather than to the original "ability" of the students assigned to various tracks. When children of "low" ability were placed in higher tracks they did much better than their peers in the lower track, apparently because of the educational program they received (Persell, 1977).

Desegregation

In 1954 the Supreme Court ruled in the case of *Brown* v. *Board of Education* that "separate but equal" educational facilities for black and white children are unconstitutional. Since the decision considerable attention has been devoted to the issue of desegregated education. In fact, the overwhelming majority (85 percent) of the American population believes black and white children should go to the same schools (Golladay and Noell, 1978).

What has become controversial in the past decade is the use of court-ordered busing to achieve racial balance in schools. Busing itself is not the root issue, since American children have been bused to school for generations, and many today are bused to school without regard to racial balance. The underlying concern of parents, children, and teachers is the way desegregation occurs. So it seems useful to consider what we know from social research about the conditions under which desegregation has been relatively successful.

The goals of desegregation include equal educational opportunity, equal achievement, reduced prejudice between members of different races, equal self-esteem, and increased respect among members of different races. Not all studies measure all these goals. Relatively successful desegregation (on one or more of these goals) has occurred in communities where parents, school leaders, and teachers have worked together to develop plans for desegregation, and where racial conflict has not occurred (St. John, 1975). Black students have made achievement gains in open enrollment schools, which allow students to attend schools beyond their neighborhoods, and in central schools, where attendance zones have been broadened.

In desegregation, what happens after pupils get off the bus is particularly important. Schools that show significant gains from integration are those that have good multiracial instructional materials, an experienced staff that holds favorable racial attitudes, racially mixed classrooms, work and play groups, and clearly cooperative classroom situations.

The age of the children when desegregation begins seems to affect their achievement, according to Crain and Mahard (1978). Reviewing 10 studies of desegregation among first- and second-graders, they found 8 that showed black achievement gains and 2 that showed no effect. When desegregation began in the third and fourth grades, only 9 of 21 studies reported improved black achievement. The higher the grade at which desegregation occurred, the lower the chance that academic gains would result. Whites were unaffected by the grade at which integration occurred. In short, in the middle of intense public debate about school desegregation, social researchers have begun to identify where desegregation is working more and less effectively and why.

HOW SCHOOLS AFFECT BOYS AND GIRLS

Racial differences are not the only ones that affect education. From an early age, males and females are educated somewhat differently as well. Generally, girls begin school intellectually ahead of boys. Girls tend to speak, read, and count sooner, and in the early grades of school they are better in math. Somewhere in high school, girls' performance on ability tests begins to sag, and males show greater IQ gains from youth to adulthood (Maccoby, 1966). Even so, females earn higher grades in high school than males, but they are less likely to believe they can do college work (Cross, 1968). Even when women attend prestigious colleges and earn the same grades as men, they have lower self-esteem and lower aspirations than men (*New York Times,* December 10, 1978).

Why do educational declines occur among females? Clearly, schools alone do not depress the aspirations of women. Parents, peers, the media, and general societal influences play a major part in shaping gender roles, as we saw in Chapter 12. And a number of school features may influence how girls feel about themselves and what they can do.

Sex Composition of Faculty and Staff

Although many women enter education as a career, they are not equally represented at all levels. As Figure 16.5 illustrates, the majority of elementary school teachers are female; a slight majority of secondary teachers are male. School administrators are mainly male. In 1975, 80 percent of all elementary school principals were male, as were 98 percent of all high school principals, and 99 percent of all school superintendents (Parelius and Parelius, 1978). Women who become administrators wait longer to move up than do men. School boards are also composed mainly of males. How might these figures affect school children? Two researchers, Frazier and Sadker, suggest several ways:

> Whenever an issue is too big or troublesome for the teacher (usually female) to handle, the principal (usually male) is called upon to offer the final decision, to administer the ultimate punishment or reward. And children, so alert to body cues, so sensitive to messages transmitted through the silent language, must detect the teacher's change in demeanor, the slight shift in posture that transforms confidence into deference and respect. It would be hard to misinterpret the relationship. The teacher is the boss of the class; the principal is the boss of the teacher. And the principal is a man. In the child's mind associations form. When a woman functions professionally, she takes orders from a man, and the image of female inferiority and subservience begins to come across. (Frazier and Sadker, 1973, pp. 99–100)

Hence the sex of individuals employed in the schools conveys a subtle but powerful message.

Teachers as Gender Role Socializers

Teachers may contribute to gender role stereotypes in various ways. One study asked junior high school teachers what adjectives they would use to describe good male and good female students. The teachers replied (Kemer, 1965, in Frazier and Sadker, 1973, p. 138):

Adjectives Describing Good Female Students	
appreciative	sensitive
calm	dependable
conscientious	efficient
considerate	mature
cooperative	obliging
mannerly	thorough
poised	

Adjectives Describing Good Male Students	
active	energetic
adventurous	enterprising
aggressive	frank
assertive	independent
curious	inventive

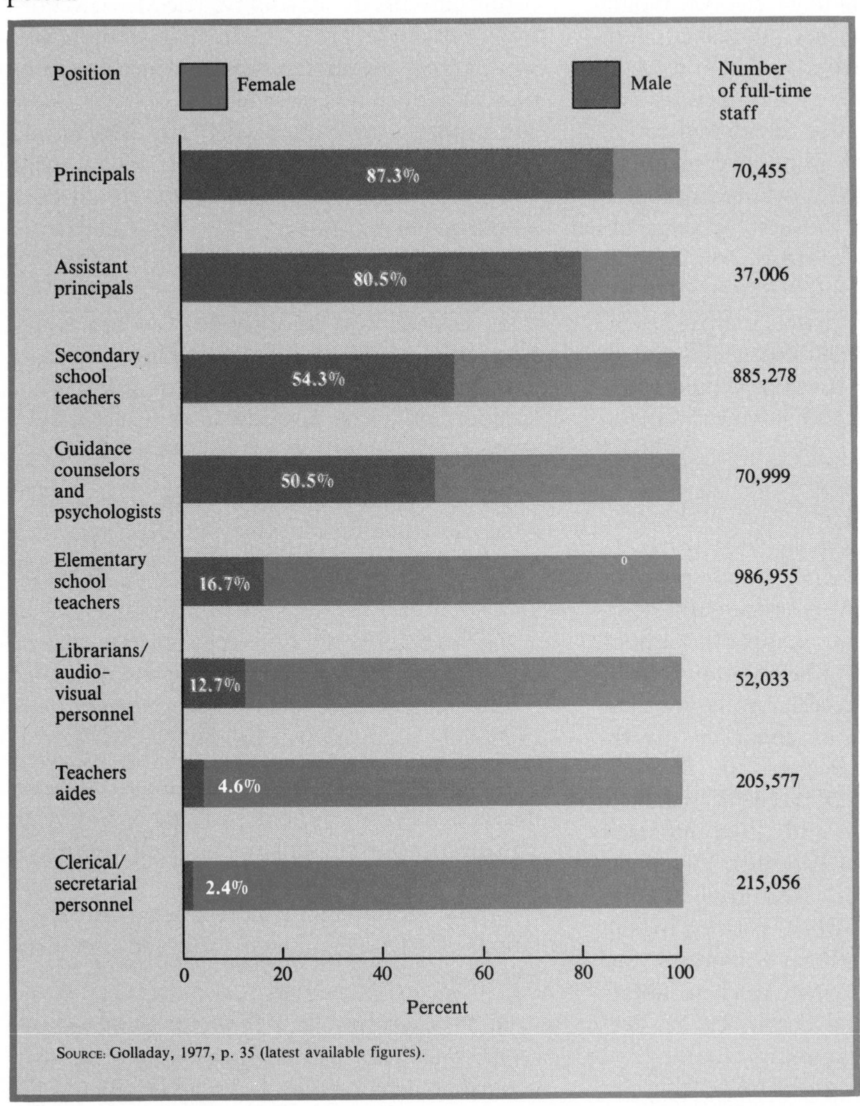

SOURCE: Golladay, 1977, p. 35 (latest available figures).

Figure 16.5 Proportion of Elementary and Secondary School Staff Who Are Male and Female

If many teachers value different traits in boys and girls, as the lists suggest, those preferences may be reflected in classroom actions and rewards. For example, several researchers find that teachers do behave differently toward boys and girls. Boys tend to receive more attention (both good and bad) than girls (Cherry, 1975; Sears and Feldman, 1966; Serbin et al., 1973). Teachers may ask boys to carry bundles and girls to pour juice, thereby adding to gender role typing in children's lives. Like teachers, guidance counselors sometimes reflect the gender role biases of their society (Pietrofessa and Schlossberg, 1974). Adolescent girls may be advised to become legal secretaries instead of lawyers, nurses rather than doctors, laboratory technologists rather than engineers. In the last few years, increasing attention has been focused on these issues, and there is hope for believing that the more obvious restrictive practices may be decreasing. Certainly as women's roles in the work force evolve, guidance counselors should begin to recognize the changes and to reflect them in their advice.

Teaching Materials as Gender Role Socializers

Teaching materials in American schools have portrayed gender roles in very limited and stereotypical ways. Children's elementary school readers surveyed in 1972 (134 books published by 14 major companies) revealed some startling trends. In these books, male characters greatly outnumbered female characters—by 5 to 2. Boys were creative, built things, and used their wits. Girls did very little and often appeared limp and dull. Clever boys appeared 131 times, clever girls only 33 times. Men lived exciting lives and did all kinds of work. Women mostly stayed home and were mothers *or* workers (but not both), and then usually only teachers, librarians, or nurses (Jacobs and Eaton, 1972). Perhaps it is not surprising that several studies show the self-esteem of girls drops the longer they are in school and as their vision of available options narrows (Minuchin, 1966).

The stories read in the early grades, the race and sex of major characters, what they do, how they live—all these aspects of school curriculum have come under increasing scrutiny as minority and feminist groups have underscored the importance of images and roles in school materials for the development of identities. There is some sense that sex role stereotypes have declined recently in curricular material. But there are competing currents in our society. The Moral Majority, for example, favors traditional gender roles, while other groups favor more equal presentation of gender role possibilities. So race, class, and gender—the major social categories of our society—seem to impinge on educational ideas and processes, and to contribute to unequal school achievement.

Summary

1. Education is an organized way of passing a society's culture to a new generation. Schools have become increasingly important gatekeepers for jobs and social rewards.

2. Education affects learning, attitudes, getting a job, and earnings, but seems to be somewhat more helpful for white middle-class males than it is for nonwhites, females, and members of the lower class.

3. Students study different subjects, even in high school, and such curricular placements determine college attendance, college major, and eventually occupational options.

4. Teachers may have a thousand or more interactions with students each day and serve as organizational representatives as well as instructors. They may be unaware of the expectations they hold for different children, but these expectations affect how students learn and how they feel about school.

5. Peer groups gain importance in adolescence. They tend to value popularity somewhat more than achievement, but may not be too far removed from adult values. Some peer groups may be rebellious or even violent.

6. The size of schools and school districts has increased greatly in the last 25 years, leading to greater bureaucracy and sometimes student alienation.

7. The roots of school violence go beyond the peer group and reflect a growing crisis in the legitimacy of the school's authority.

8. Differences in educational achievement by race are not adequately explained by genetic or cultural deficits. Instead, unequal societal opportunities, geographic and racial segregation, tracking, and teacher expectations begin to explain unequal school achievement by race and class.

9. Gender role socialization helps to explain why female educational achievement and aspirations begin to sag in high school.

Key Terms

contest mobility
education
IQ or intelligence quotient test
schooling
self-fulfilling prophecy
sponsored mobility
tournament selection
tracking

Chapter 17

Religion

WHAT IS RELIGION?
FUNCTIONALIST AND CONFLICT VIEWS
- The Functions of Religion in Society
- Conflict Views of Religion
- Evaluation

WORLD RELIGIONS
- Major World Religions
- Millennarian Movements

SECULARISM, FUNDAMENTALISM, AND EVANGELICALISM
- Secularism
- Fundamentalism
- Evangelicalism

CULTS, SECTS, DENOMINATIONS, AND CHURCHES
- Cults
- Sects
- Denominations
- Churches

RELIGION IN THE UNITED STATES
- Denominational Membership
- Characteristics of Various Denominations
- Political Participation of Denominations
- Civil Religion

SUMMARY

Religion is a major social institution in all societies because it affirms important beliefs about the nature and meaning of existence. Sociologists are especially interested in the way religious beliefs are strengthened socially and in their social consequences. Their definition of religion touches on the special content of religious beliefs and practices and on their social effects. As the French sociologist Emile Durkheim noted, "a religion is a unified system of beliefs and practices relative to sacred things, that is to say, things set apart and forbidden—beliefs and practices which unite into one single moral community called a Church, all those who adhere to them" (1915, p. 62).

WHAT IS RELIGION?

Durkheim studied religions in simple tribal societies, and his work enabled him to identify key elements that were common to all religions. He discovered three features that characterize all religions in the world. First, all religions contain a sense of the divine or holy. In many religions, this sense takes the form of a belief in one or more spiritual beings or things. However, not all religions necessarily contain such beliefs. Buddhism, for example, is a moral system that is surrounded by holiness but does not have a spiritual being at its center. Nevertheless, all religions see the world as divided into the *sacred* and the *profane*.

The sacred aspects are to be approached with respect, reverence, and awe. They are to be protected from being tarnished by everyday concerns. Christian crosses are not usually hung in kitchens or bathrooms, for example, but in church sanctuaries or chapels. Holy scriptures are handled carefully and are kept in special places. The distinction between the sacred and the profane embraces all that exists in the universe. Religious beliefs establish the sacredness of certain things and indicate what their relationship should be to profane things.

The second characteristic feature of religion is ritual. *Ritual* is one of the ways social groups maintain the identity of the sacred and mark it off from mundane activities. Durkheim observed that all religions have established rites or rules of conduct concerning how people should behave in the presence of sacred objects. The established rituals or ceremonies serve to formalize religious behaviors. On Ash Wednesday, for instance, practicing Catholics and Episcopalians may go to work wearing ashes on their foreheads as a sign of penitence. Ritual also provides a visible way to distinguish members from nonmembers. When individuals enter a church, snyagogue, or mosque at a funeral or a wedding, their familiarity or lack of familiarity with the order of service, types of prayers, and bodily movements divides members from nonmembers.

Ritual contributes to the third characteristic of religion, which is the existence of a special community of members and worshippers. Durkheim stressed that religious beliefs belong to a group. They do not exist in a vacuum, or even simply inside the heads of individuals. Individuals in the group feel united by their common faith, rituals, and the way in which they divide the world into the sacred and the profane. They put their common ideas into common practices, in what is called a church. In short, *religion* is a set of beliefs and rituals commonly shared by a special community and focusing on the sacred and supernatural.

Religion is distinguished from magic in several key ways. They are similar in that both have special appeal in situations of crisis. They both offer escape or relief from otherwise seemingly hopeless situations. They do so by offering supernatural beliefs and rituals and the hope that something miraculous may occur. Both have boundaries and taboos that separate the magical or mystical from the profane. They differ, suggests Malinowski in his classic study, *Magic, Science, and Religion,* in that *magic* is "a practical art consisting of acts which are only means to a definite end expected to follow"; religion, on the other hand, is a "body of self-contained acts being themselves the fulfillment of their purpose" (1948, p.88). Religion does not need to cause any specific result; the experience itself is sufficient. Part of what makes the experience of religion unique and satisfying, Durkheim suggests, is its shared foundation. This sharing separates it from magic. Magic does nothing to bind together those who practice it, or to forge them into a group leading a common life.

Sociology focuses on the social contexts, consequences, and meanings of religion in society. Having already examined how religion is defined by sociologists, in the remainder of this chapter we will consider how functionalist and conflict thinkers see religion as operating in society; the nature and distribution of various religions in the world; secular, fundamentalist, and evangelical trends; the difference between cults, sects, and churches; and the nature of religion in the United States.

FUNCTIONALIST AND CONFLICT VIEWS

As is true about many aspects of social life, functionalist and conflict theorists differ in their views of religion in society. Functionalists focus on the positive effects of religion for individuals and society; conflict theorists stress that religion is used by dominant groups to solidify their control over others. Each view captures part of the social significance of religion in society.

THE FUNCTIONS OF RELIGION IN SOCIETY

Humans are symbol-wielding animals who need beliefs and language systems to provide meaning in their lives. If everyone had to devise individual beliefs to comfort themselves when people get sick or die or to create totally new social practices to deal with births, weddings, or funerals, they would be under tremendous strain. For many individuals and groups, religious beliefs, practices, and communities provide an ongoing system of shared customs that offer purpose to the participants. Whether the purpose stems from a sense of shared social support and community or from a shared set of beliefs, or both, it illustrates an important function of religion in modern and simple societies.

Religion may also function to *integrate* a society. It can provide shared values and beliefs that help bind people into a community. Religious beliefs may transcend differences of economic class or ethnicity that divide a society, as the Catholic Church did in medieval Europe. But it may also be a basis for conflict in society, as has been the case in Lebanon, Northern Ireland, and Iran.

Religion often serves as an important source of *social control* by providing sacred support for

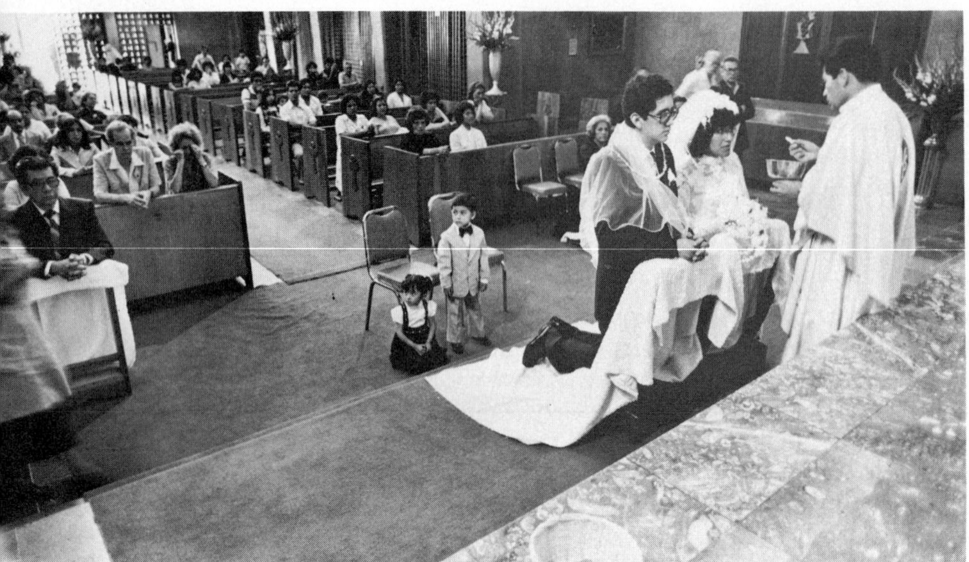

Religious ceremonies provide a way of celebrating and sanctifying major social events such as marriage. This bride and groom are receiving communion at their wedding.

many social values and norms. Relations between the sexes, races, and parents and children, for instance, are codified and reinforced by religious doctrines and practices. Biblical writings in the Old and New Testaments have supported traditional sex roles by calling for wives to submit to their husbands. Durkheim suggests that religion helps uphold the structure of society. This happens because religious practices reflect the organization of authority in a group or society. A hierarchical religious organization, for example, tends to support a ranked social structure in which authority and decision-making are concentrated at the upper levels.

Religion may also function as a *source of moral leadership* in society. Religions provide moral canons against which social realities can be compared. They often provide ideological fuel for social movements. White and black clergy provided major leadership to the civil rights movement of the 1950s and 1960s and the antinuclear protests of the 1970s and 1980s. The Moral Majority's crusade against sex and violence on television claims to be religiously inspired. These are all examples of movements pushing for social changes on the basis of religious justification.

A fifth function of religion is to provide *personal support* to individuals. Religious beliefs and rituals help to relieve anxiety, define personality, and support family and other social identities (Mol, 1976). Religion provides ceremonies to celebrate or mourn major events—birth, puberty, marriage, and death—through baptisms, bar mitzvahs, weddings, and funerals. These ceremonies provide social support and community acceptance for the individuals involved. Religion provides responses that are hallowed by tradition and by their ties with the transcendent, suggests Peter Berger (1967, 1969), thus giving individuals some meaning in an otherwise chaotic and frightening world that is being shaken by a profound crisis of belief.

CONFLICT VIEWS OF RELIGION

In contrast with the cohesive features of religion functionalism stresses, the conflict perspective emphasizes the way religion serves to protect and reinforce the position of privileged groups in society. Conflict theorists maintain that religion diverts less privileged groups from the earthly sources of their misery and directs their attention toward the promise of a better way of life in the hereafter. Karl Marx insisted that religion was an important weapon used by industrial owners to dominate the working class. He called religion the "opium of the people" and claimed that it deluded workers from perceiving their true interests and inhibited them from working for political and economic change. The Catholic Church in medieval Europe, for example, directed people's attention to rewards in the next life rather than toward inequalities in their earthly lives. In addition, it taught that one must submit to one's worldly "station" in order to obtain heavenly rewards.

In contrast to Marx, Max Weber did not view religion as an instrument of class oppression, but he did note a connection between class position and religious preference. The prosperous merchants accepted religions such as Calvinism that justified their economic success, while the working classes were more likely to adopt religions such as Methodism that met their economic necessity for orderliness and hard work.

In any society, the dominant religion will be the religion of its dominant economic and political class, according to Marx. Once a democratic, classless society is formed, there will be no need for the illusions and false promises of religion. Such reasoning has led most state socialist societies such as the Soviet Union to declare themselves atheistic and to force religion underground.

EVALUATION

The fact that religion survives in societies that have tried to substitute political systems for religious ones suggests that religion serves important functions in society, as Durkheim suggested. Moreover, these functions appear to extend beyond the efforts of a dominant class to preserve its interests. Even when a politically dominant class opposes religion, it persists.

In the Soviet Union, for example, the government has tried to abolish religion and has failed. Both Christians and Jews practice their religions despite official displeasure. Apparently people find that religion provides meaning and personal support. In Poland, the Catholic Church is so important to people that in spite of the government's attempts to abolish it, it remains a potent force in the lives of the people. The Church has been an important source of spiritual and moral leadership for Poles since the Communist takeover in the 1940s.

Societies seeking to abolish religion may try to offer "functional equivalents" to it—that is, social forms that serve some of the same functions as religion. The need for a shared set of beliefs and practices in a society may be met by alternatives such as communism, fascism, science, or the human potential movement. Communism, for example, contains a set of sacred beliefs that were expounded by revered leaders—Marx, Engels, Trotsky, and Lenin. Large-scale rituals, such as the May Day celebration, are conducted with great pomp and pageantry, and resemble religious events. The near worship of such leaders as Mao or Stalin at various times in history borders on religious behavior. With respect to shared beliefs and rituals, political philosophy and nationalism resemble religion. They differ from religion in that they have little or no relation to the divine or supernatural. As a result, these systems of belief and ritual are not totally equivalent to religion.

On the other hand, just as Marx maintained, there are many instances of grossly unequal societies in which religion has been used to reinforce the domination of one group over others. Examples of the use of religious beliefs to fortify political power include the dominant white regime in South Africa; the caste structure of Indian society that was supported by Hinduism and the religious doctrine of reincarnation which asserted that individuals were born into the caste they deserved depending on their actions in an earlier life; the Egyptian pharaohs who were considered sacred; and the European doctrine of the divine right of kings.

WORLD RELIGIONS

Nearly 60 percent of the people in the world belong to one or another of the nine major world religions (Table 17.1). These religions influence both individual lives and world events. Religious beliefs and practices are tightly interwoven with culture, with the world views that prevail in a society, with political actions, and with attitudes toward social change. Religion has influenced many of the major social movements in our society, as well as in societies around the world. Religions form the basis for many social networks that extend beyond the family (as noted in Chapter 4). Religious beliefs influence eating habits, concepts of honor and shame, business practices, and marriage relationships. Because the various religions in the world are so central to many people's social lives, it is important to know something about some of the major religions of the world, including their beliefs, rituals, the nature of their community, and where they are most widely practiced.

Table 17.1 Major Religions of the World

Religion	Number of Members (millions)
Total Christian	998.0
Roman Catholic	580.0
Protestant	342.0
Eastern Orthodox	76.0
Muslim	589.0
Hindu	478.0
Buddhist	255.0
Confucian	156.0
Shinto	57.0
Taoist	31.0
Jewish	14.0
Zoroastrian	0.3

SOURCE: Condensed and adapted from Littell, 1981, p. 604.

MAJOR WORLD RELIGIONS

Christianity

Christianity in all its forms appears to be the most widely practiced religion in the world today (see Table 17.1). Nearly one billion people are considered Christians, and more than half of them are Catholics. Christians are widely spread around the globe, with about one-third living in Europe, about one-quarter living in North America, about 15 percent in South America, 13 percent in Africa, and 10 percent in Asia.

Christianity was founded in Judea (now the modern state of Israel) about 2000 years ago around the figure of Jesus of Nazareth. Jesus's followers believed Jesus to be the Messiah or Christ, and thus called themselves Christians. Early Christians believed Christianity contained the one eternal truth and the one universal salvation. They scorned the pagan customs that were important to the Romans, whose empire at that point included Judea. However, their preaching about a "new kingdom" sounded revolutionary to some Roman officials. Together, these threats provoked considerable persecution from Roman governors. But in A.D. 312 the emperor, Constantine the Great, converted to Christianity. Although he did not make Christianity the official religion of the empire, he did found Constantinople (modern Istanbul) as a Christian city. By the fourth century, Christianity had spread throughout the empire. It spread again in the sixteenth through twentieth centuries, as missionaries followed explorers to all corners of the earth. As noted above, it is now believed to have more members than any other religion in the world. Like most major religions, it tends to assert the cultural superiority of believers over nonbelievers.

Aside from the central belief in Christ as the saviour who brings the good news of salvation after death, forms of Christian belief and practice vary widely. Individual and family prayers are important in many denominations, as are formal church services. Some stress formalized prayers designed to instill the correct doctrines, while others value spontaneous prayers created by members. Prayers generally seek to praise God, to give thanks for what has been received, or to ask God to intercede in the world to help those who need it. The Bible is the single most important document in Christianity. More copies of the Bible have been sold than of any other book in the world. It has been translated into all languages of the world, and into many remote dialects as well. The Bible is believed by Christians to contain the literal word of God or at least to be divinely inspired. The role of an ordained clergy, the organizational structure of the church, and type of church service differ widely in various forms of Christianity. But in all denominations, the major events in human experience—birth, becoming a member of the church, marriage, death—are given special significance through the meanings imposed by Christian beliefs and rituals.

Throughout its history, Christianity has been marked by doctrinal struggles and the formation of branches and sects with differing beliefs. The cleavage with the most far-reaching implications was the Protestant Reformation, which began in 1517 when Martin Luther wrote his Ninety-five Theses. The Reformation was a religious movement that attempted to purify the Christian Church morally and doctrinally. Luther denied the infallibility of the popes and attacked such moral abuses as clerical concubinage and the sale of indulgences and religious relics in churches. Jacob Burckhardt (1929), the historian of the Renaissance, saw the Reformation as forever dividing Christendom, but as reforming and saving the papacy. Western society was no longer united by the existence of a single church. On the other hand, the papacy had become a secularized Italian city-state. After the Reformation it again became a more serious religious institution under the popes of the Counterreformation.

The existence of different denominations within Christianity has probably strengthened it around the world, because in its various forms it can appeal to a wide variety of national and ethnic groups, who can find or adapt compatible beliefs. Like other major religions, Christianity often forged bonds with music (Mozart), art (Michelangelo and Leonardo da Vinci), literature (Milton's *Paradise Lost*), and more recently, television (Jerry Falwell), to reach new and existing members. Sometimes it also formed partnerships with political and secular forces, as in the Crusades conducted in the Middle Ages to recover the Holy Land.

Islam

After Christianity, Islam is the largest world religion. Muslims (believers of Islam) are heavily concentrated in North Africa, the Middle East, and parts of Asia (see Figure 17.1). The religion was founded in the seventh century by the prophet Muhammad. It emphasizes an uncompromising belief in one supreme being (monotheism) and believes in strictly following certain religious practices, such as observing five daily prayers, the profession of faith, payment of a welfare tax, fasting, and a pilgrimage to Mecca. Like Christianity, Islam has been characterized by many sects and movements, but all followers of Islam are bound by certain shared beliefs and the overarching sense of belonging to a single common community.

The Arabic word *islam* means "to surrender," and contains the fundamental religious idea of Islam—namely, that believers surrender to the will of Allah, the unique God, creator, sustainer, and restorer of the world. Allah's will is given in the book of Islamic scriptures, the Qur'an (often spelled Koran), which was revealed to Allah's

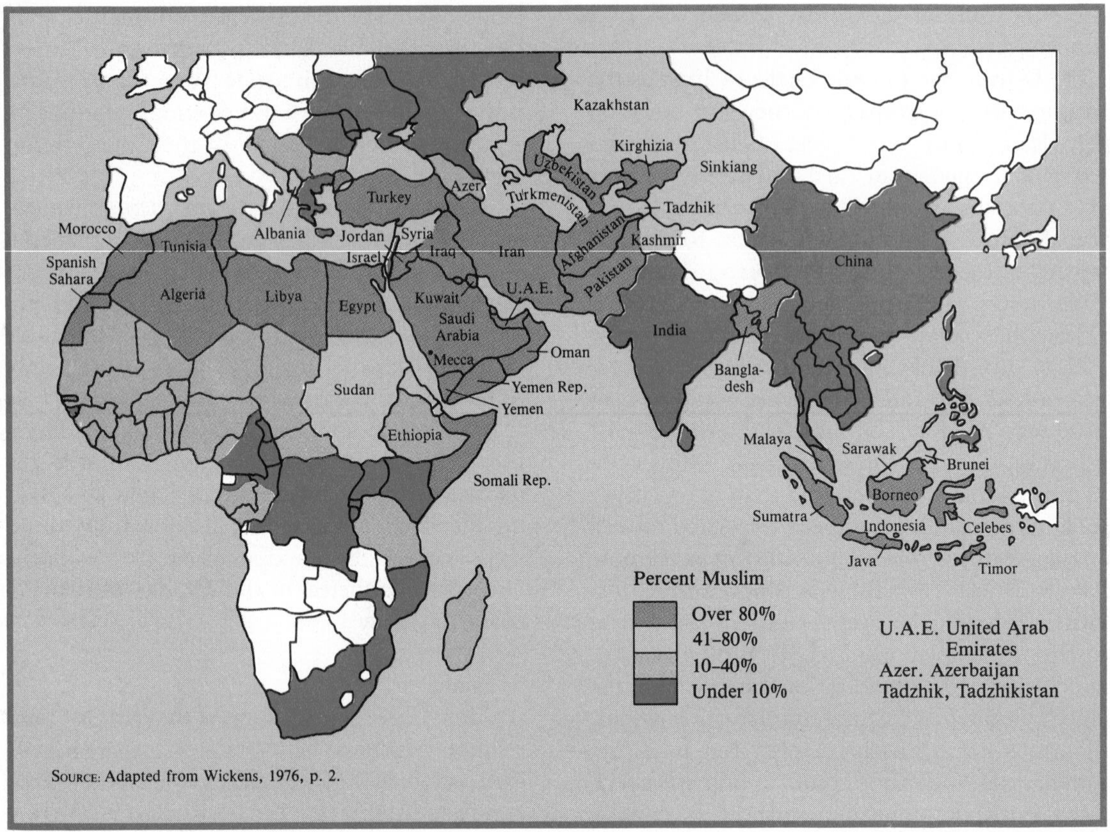

Figure 17.1 The Major Distribution of Islam in the World

messenger, Muhammad. Muhammad is believed to be the last in a long line of prophets that includes Adam, Noah, Moses, and Jesus. The Muslim confession of faith makes it clear where Muhammad stands in this procession: "There is no god but Allah and Muhammad is His Prophet."

Hinduism

Hinduism is found in India, parts of Pakistan, Sri Lanka, Nepal, and Sikkim. There are also smaller Hindu communities in parts of Southeast Asia, East and South Africa, Surinam, and on such islands as Fiji, Mauritius, and Trinidad. The umbrella community of Hindus spans a wide range of doctrines, cults, and ways of life, ranging from animal worship, magic, and worship of personal gods, to mysticism and abstract theological systems. Hinduism is a kaleidoscope of many pieces, with no single founder, central hierarchy, or final authority. Other religious doctrines, forms of worship, and gods may be considered "incomplete," but they are not considered wrong or undesirable. As a result, Hindus can follow non-Hindu religious practices without losing their Hinduism.

There are certain essential beliefs in Hinduism, including belief in an eternal, infinite, and all-embracing principle. This ultimate reality, or Brahman, is the focus of a religious search. Sometimes Brahman is seen as a personal god, called Vishnu or Shiva. There is a body of sacred

Religion and science are both major institutions in modern society. The United States is a country of many Christian denominations. Nevertheless, there are certain counties where more than 25 percent of the population belongs to one particular Christian denomination.

A Catholic church service in Austria

Both the diversity and concentration of Christian denominations are evident in this figure. Many different denominations exist around the United States, and in a number of counties more than 25 percent of the population belongs to one particular denomination. Among non-Christian religions, only Judaism has a significant concentration, in Manhattan county and Dade county, Florida.

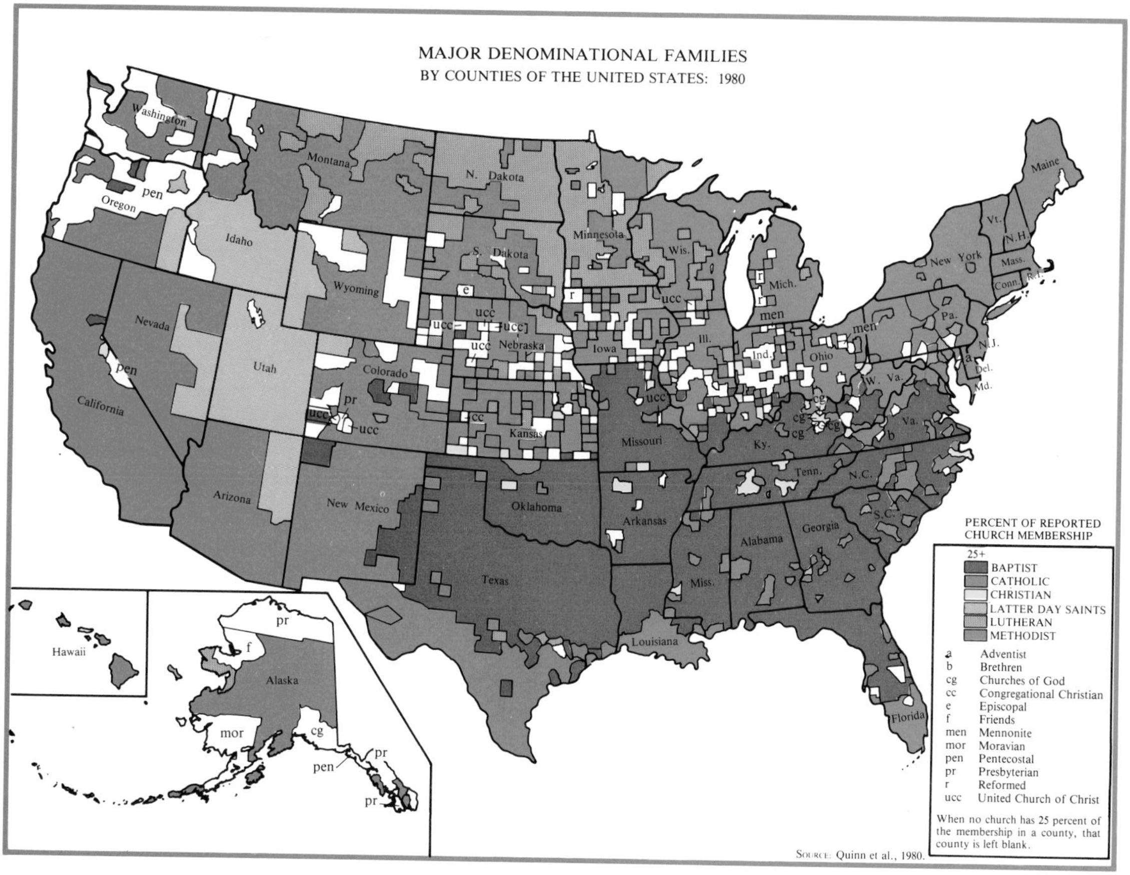

MAJOR DENOMINATIONAL FAMILIES
BY COUNTIES OF THE UNITED STATES: 1980

PERCENT OF REPORTED CHURCH MEMBERSHIP

25+
- BAPTIST
- CATHOLIC
- CHRISTIAN
- LATTER DAY SAINTS
- LUTHERAN
- METHODIST

- a Adventist
- b Brethren
- cg Churches of God
- cc Congregational Christian
- e Episcopal
- f Friends
- men Mennonite
- mor Moravian
- pen Pentecostal
- pr Presbyterian
- r Reformed
- ucc United Church of Christ

When no church has 25 percent of the membership in a county, that county is left blank.

SOURCE: Quinn et al., 1980.

Muslim worshippers

A statue of Buddha in a temple in Hawaii

Hindus bathing in the Ganges River in India

Although scientific research and development outlays have declined in recent years, tremendous scientific and technological advances have been made, from the invention of robots which can perform delicate or dangerous tasks, to breakthroughs in DNA research, computer manufacturing, and video games.

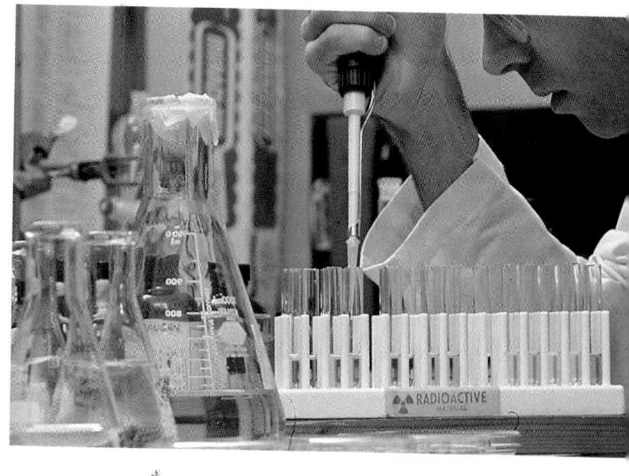

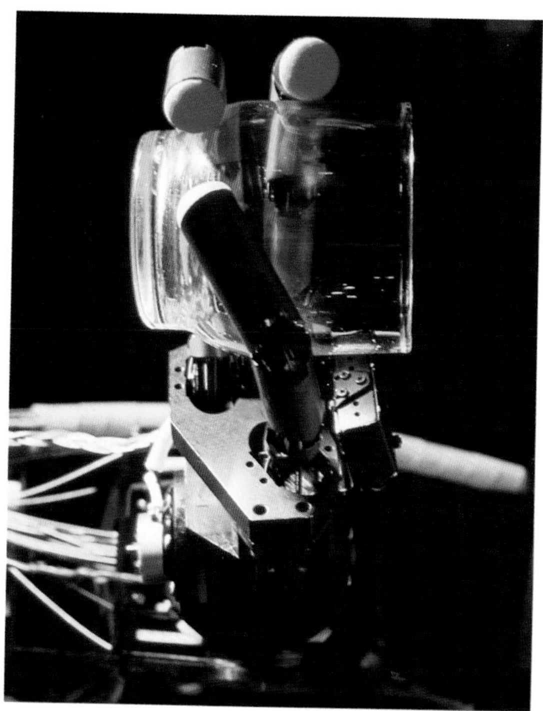

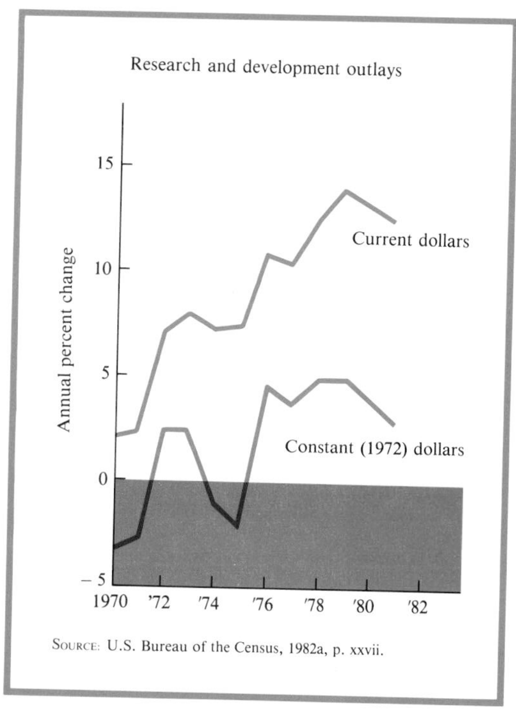

SOURCE: U.S. Bureau of the Census, 1982a, p. xxvii.

III-4

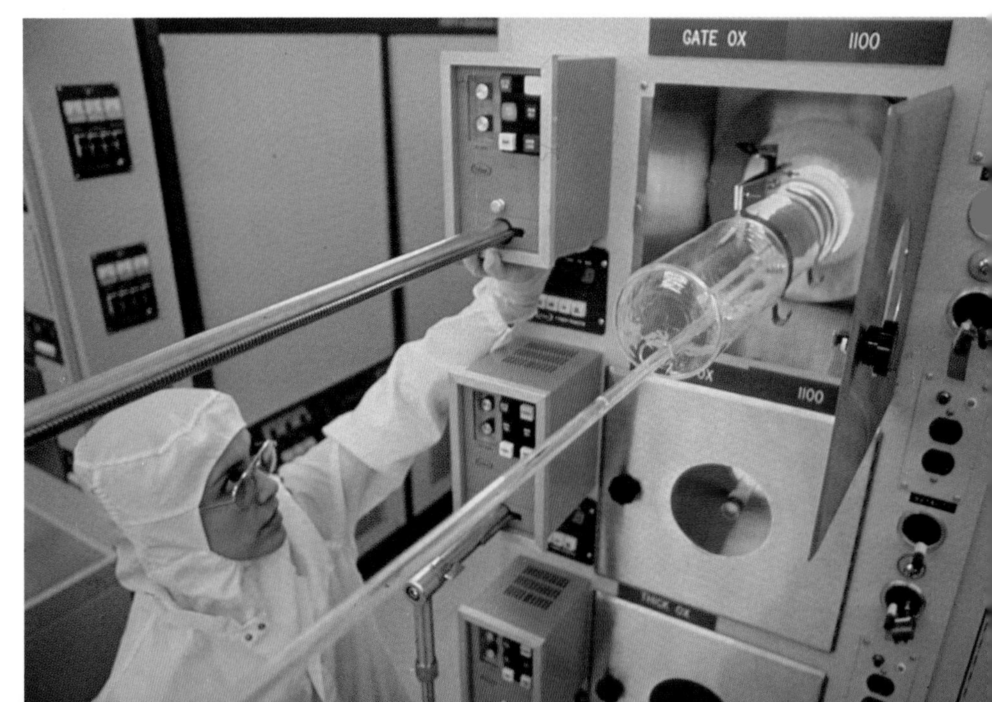

literature in Hinduism, called the Veda, which is widely accepted as important but rarely studied for religious insights.

Part of Hinduism is a belief in the spiritual and social superiority of the Brahmins, a noble class. Other members of society were ranked in prestige below Brahmins, depending on how they behaved in prior lives. Although the rigid ranking of social castes in India has been weakened in modern times, particularly in northern India, some traces remain in other arts of the country. The term Brahmin has been used widely outside Hindu society to refer to members of a social group whose moral and social superiority is widely acknowledged.

Hinduism is an all-embracing religion. It has religious, social, economic, literary, and artistic implications for a society. Its inclusiveness makes it acceptable to many who also practice their own local religions. Thus it is a religion that tends to flourish in areas of extensive migration. Its doctrine of "reincarnation," or rebirth in new bodies, tends to justify social and economic inequalities on earth as the result of one's purity or sinfulness in an earlier incarnation. Such a view deflects attention from attempting to change life on earth and directs it toward living virtuously in the hope of achieving a better situation the next time around. It borders on fatalism and may tend to depress efforts for social change.

Buddhism

Buddhism was founded in India in the sixth century B.C. by a reformer, Siddhartha Gautama, the Buddha (meaning the enlightened one). The religion spread from India to Central and Southeast Asia, China, Korea, and Japan, and has influenced the spiritual, cultural, and social life of much of Asia. Buddha stressed the impermanence of all things, and formulated the Four Noble Truths: (1) Misery is a major feature of life; (2) misery originates from within ourselves from the craving for pleasure; (3) this craving can be eliminated; and (4) this elimination can occur by diligently following a specific path. Spiritual liberation is achieved by meditation and by following the Eightfold Path, which involves right seeing, thinking, speech, action, living, effort, mindfulness, and meditation. The ultimate goal is to achieve a state of Nirvana, or salvation. Buddhism appealed to many followers of Hinduism because Buddhism was open to all regardless of caste position.

Traditional Buddhist ethics prohibit killing, stealing, sexual misconduct, lying, and drinking liquor. Despite the transitory nature of existence, Buddhism emphasizes the values of sympathy, compassion, and joyful participation in the good created by others. Buddhists promote socially useful activities such as wells, irrigation projects, bridges, hospitals, and shelters for people and animals. Moral energy and perseverance in the struggle for the common good are highly valued. Believers tend to develop a spirit of social cooperation and active participation in society. Buddhist society fosters participation by both men and women. All these features tend to strengthen the sense of human solidarity in Buddhist communities.

Buddhism has become a significant political force in efforts to establish national independence in modern Asia in such countries as Burma, Sri Lanka, Thailand, Vietnam, Cambodia, Laos, and Tibet. In South Vietnam in the 1960s and 1970s, numerous Buddhist monks committed suicide by setting themselves on fire as a protest against the war being fought there. They were dedicated to Buddha's ideal of peace, and they sacrificed themselves to stimulate resistance to the war.

Confucianism

Confucianism refers to the way of life established by the Chinese teacher and philosopher Confucius in the sixth and fifth centuries B.C. It has been followed in China for more than 2000 years. Confucianism provides a source of learning, values, and a social code. It blends religion and philosophy into a scholarly culture that influenced Taoists, Buddhists, and Christians in China. Its influence has spread to Japan, Korea, and Vietnam.

Confucianism differs from most religions in that Confucian temples stand as monuments but do not function as the site of shared religious ceremonies the way churches, synagogues, and mosques do. People can be Christians, Taoists, or Buddhists and still be Confucianists, since Confucianism is not an exclusive religion. The religious aspects of Confucianism include its reverence for heaven and for ancestors. The essential concept in Confucianism is *jen,* variously translated as "love," "virtue," and "human compassion." *Jen* refers to the ideal relationship that should prevail between people. Filial piety and ancestor worship grew out of the *jen* sentiment. Confucius also valued the cultivation of virtue and righteousness, which he believed would produce a superior person. "The superior person understands what is right," according to Confucius, "the inferior person understands what is profitable." Wisdom, virtue, reciprocity, trustworthiness, loyalty, and courage all grow out of *jen* and help to create an individual who is always calm and at ease.

Confucianism has as its ideal the development of a cultivated noble class. A nobleman is one who bears himself nobly. This quality is desirable in leaders because government consists of setting things right, and people who have not set themselves right cannot govern well. A cultivated, nonhereditary nobility would rule well and create a stable, harmonious society.

Judaism

Judaism is the religion of the Jews, who live all over the world but have a homeland in the state of Israel. Essentially, Jews believe in one deity, known as Jehovah, Yahweh, or God, who cares for the world and for His chosen people, the Jews. As a religion, Judaism focuses on a continual interaction between God and people, with God continually being unwilling to turn His back on man, despite repeated violations of the covenant by man. God reveals His divine presence through history. Despite God's actions (for example, in presenting the commandments), however, humans are constantly falling short of His expectations. As a result, prophets have appeared from time to time to bring Jews back to right practices.

The actions of God, such as leading the Israelites out of Egypt, are confirmed in the Torah, which means "to point the way," or the law. The writings of the Torah confirm the events that are acts of God. They also prescribe a series of behaviors for all aspects of social life. These include table blessings, observance of the Sabbath, celebration of the Feast of Tabernacles, the seder Passover meal, Yom Kippur, the Feast of Dedication (Hanukkah), and regular worship in the synagogue. Notable life events recognized by religious ritual include circumcision of male babies, naming of female babies in the synagogue, the Bar Mitzvahs of 13-year-old boys (some girls are beginning to have Bat Mitzvahs) symbolizing their religious coming of age, marriage, and death and burial.

Although Jews in Europe, the Middle East, and the United States have widely different racial and national origins, Judaism provides shared beliefs and practices that help to create a common culture and way of life. Moreover, Judaism is a powerful political force in the Middle East.

MILLENNARIAN MOVEMENTS

Millennarian movements are social movements based on the expectation that society will be suddenly transformed through a supernatural intervention. Movements based on a transforming vision have occurred throughout Christian history, and among the Cargo Cult believers in New Guinea and the Sioux Indians of the American plains. Millennarian movements are focused on a millennium—that is, a day when a sudden

Religious Jews celebrate the acceptance of boys into the congregation of men with a Bar Mitzvah at the age of 13.

supernatural event will radically change the lives of members of the movement.

Among Christians, such sects as Seventh Day Adventists and Jehovah's Witnesses are millennialists. They draw their inspiration from the Book of Revelation in the New Testament. In that scripture, Satan is described as bound and thrown into a bottomless pit, while Christian martyrs are raised from the dead to reign with Christ for a thousand years. It is this thousand-year period that is known as the millennium. In it, the active power of God enables individuals to realize their yearnings for peace and goodness on earth. This ideal of paradise on earth is sharply contrasted with an alternative vision of all life being destroyed in a cataclysm of fire brought on by human folly or God's judgment. Throughout history, the prophets who preach that the end of the world is at hand have received some support from the events of the time in which they were preaching.

The *cargo cults* of New Guinea were based on the expectation that great cargo ships or airplanes filled with flour, rice, cloth, tools, and weapons were created by the ancestors and piloted into New Guinea and the surrounding islands. The cargo, however, was intercepted by the European colonists. By sending in the cargo, prophets said, the ancestors were showing their support for the living. With the help of the spirits and the cargo, they could kill or drive out the European settlers and live at the same high standard the Europeans enjoyed. The cargo cults are considered millennarian movements because they expect a day when a sudden supernatural event will transform the members' lives.

These cults began to develop in the late nineteenth century and became more widespread after World War I. The prophets often claimed that crops and food should be destroyed and trading and gardening should stop, as an indication of faith. Harbors and airstrips were built so that the cargo could arrive, as were storehouses to hold it. Sometimes the prophecies appeared to be partially confirmed—for example when predicted earthquakes or epidemics of influenza occurred. In one instance, people actually believed that a ship carrying their dead ancestors had appeared in the harbor (Worsley, 1968). Events such as these tended to reinforce the credibility of the cargo cult's prophecies.

The Ghost Dance cult represented an effort by native Americans in the western United States to restore traditional cultures that had been shattered by the white conquest. Several prophets from the Northern Paiute tribe proclaimed that their dead relatives would return shortly, the whites would be pushed off their lands, and their food sources and way of life would be restored. The cult spread from Canada to Texas and as far east as the Missouri River. In 1890 it reached the Sioux at about the time of the battle of Wounded Knee in South Dakota. The cult was wrongly blamed for that uprising. The ghost shirts that the prophet had promised would protect against the army's bullets failed to protect their wearers, and many were massacred (Mooney, 1965; Utley, 1963).

These millennarian religious movements tend to arise in conditions of hardship and strain. Often members found they had lost a more favorable position in the social order, either to colonial invaders or because of the rise of new, more affluent social classes. Traditional values and norms did not help them in the new situation. Neither reasoned effort nor traditional rituals helped them to deal with the crisis (Cohn, 1957: 311). Their only hope appeared to be the intervention of a supernatural being to change the world in which they lived. If millennarian movements do not destroy their followers through some misplaced faith, they may provide hope and a sense of purpose, and serve as the basis for political organization. As a result, they may sometimes lead to dramatic social change (Cohn, 1957).

SECULARISM, FUNDAMENTALISM, AND EVANGELICALISM

One of the current major tensions in religions around the world is the pull between secularism and fundamentalism. The two tendencies work in opposite directions, and both have been increasing.

SECULARISM

Secularism includes the values of rationality, cultural and religious pluralism, tolerance of moral ambiguity, faith in education, and belief in civil rights, the rule of law, and due process. Secularism is associated with modernization and industrialization. It tends to arise in periods of rapid social change. One of the features of the Industrial Revolution has been the pushing of religion to a less central position in people's lives.

Secularism treats religion in a relativistic way by suggesting that nothing is absolutely true for all peoples, in all places, and at all times. Secularism accepts the rights of other people to pursue their own beliefs and practices and does not require others to conform to one's own beliefs and practices. Secularism also tends to see religion as one of a number of beliefs and activities that engage people, rather than an all-enveloping and dominating set of beliefs and practices that affects everything one does.

The long-term trend toward secularism began in the Renaissance as an effort to direct people toward worldly as opposed to otherworldly concerns. Religious people tended to withdraw from worldly affairs and spend their time meditating on God and the afterlife. Secularism emphasized a concern with human affairs and cultural achievements. Because of its concern with rationality and affairs of this world, over time secularism has been considered by some to be anti-Christian and antireligious. Many Christian theologians disagree, however, and suggest that secular concerns provide an opportunity for advancing Christian values.

At the institutional level, the forces of secularism tend to make religion simply one distinct institution among many in society. Other institutions, such as education, medicine, science, and the economy, take over many of the functions formerly filled by religion, and their goals may conflict with religious beliefs. Religious concerns, such as caring for the poor, are not always compatible with economic values, such as making money. Science may offer explanations for how life on earth originated that compete with religious explanations. The increasing narrowness of religion as one institution among many, along with the existence of religious pluralism, allows people to question and choose among competing beliefs. For large numbers of people, secularization has weakened religion because it undermines faith in the transcendent. As a result, Berger (1977) suggests that secularism frustrates the human desire for meaning and hope, because only a belief in the transcendent can offer such hope.

FUNDAMENTALISM

As religion has become marginal in many people's lives, the flames of fundamentalism have been fanned in a variety of religions. *Fundamentalism* is a form of religious traditionalism which insists that the faithful allow every part of their lives to be dominated by religion (Marty, 1980). Christianity, Islam, Hinduism, and Judaism have seen the growth of fundamentalism. In many areas, such as Iran and the United States, religious fundamentalism has become a force for political change. It is able to do this in part because it focuses all of a person's energies on what is considered a holy cause.

Fundamentalism is typically characterized by the literal interpretation of religious texts or teachings, by a conception of an active supernatural, and by clear-cut distinctions between sin and salvation. It is often inspired by direct religious experiences, such as those of "born again" Christians who feel that Christ has entered their lives in a very personal way and has offered them salvation. Fundamentalist churches are more likely than more liberal churches to serve as a major source of informal friendships (Glock and Stark, 1965).

One response to growing secularism has been an upsurge of social movements based on fundamentalism. Two recent forms of fundamentalism include the New Christian Right (often called the Moral Majority) and the Islamic fundamentalism in Iran. The New Christian Right includes politically organized religious groups, such as the Religious Roundtable, the Christian Voice, and the Moral Majority. Members of these groups tend to be from traditional Protestant denominations, such as Baptists, and they are often mobilized by television evangelists such as the Rev. Jerry Falwell of Virginia and the Rev. James Robison of Texas. The political groups direct their attention to working for the defeat of certain liberal candidates for Congress and the support of conservatives. They gave important support to Ronald Reagan in the 1980 presidential campaign. Organizers focus on what they see as a moral decline in national life. They feel that God has been removed from the public schools, and they want to reestablish the right to pray in public schools. They seek to remove the teaching of evolution in schools and to prevent the spread of pornography (Marty, 1981).

The New Christian Right speaks for a small minority of the population and even for a minority of the fundamentalist churches of the Middle West, South, and Southwest that supply many of its members. But although small in numbers, its highly organized and vocal approach has made its presence felt throughout the

United States. It staged a massive "Washington for Jesus" rally in 1980 at which 200,000 demonstrators turned out in support of the movement, and it has used televised appeals and sophisticated computerized direct-mail campaigns to mobilize supporters.

The movement seems to gain power from the anger people feel about the changing moral climate and those who help foster change. It offers the hope of defeating "humanists" and liberals in church and state (Marty, 1981). It is developing alternative curriculums for private fundamentalist elementary and secondary schools and trying to pressure the television networks into removing sex and violence from prime-time television.

Although some Islamic scholars deny any similarities between Islamic movements and Christian fundamentalism, the two do share some similarities. They both deplore godlessness and material concerns that push out spiritual concerns. Both seek to put religious faith into the center of people's lives, and both are relatively intolerant of those who do not share their beliefs. They also differ in a number of respects. The Islamic movements in Saudi Arabia, Libya, and Iran denounce westernization and describe the West as exploitative and imperialist. Especially in Libya, but also in Iran, the Islamic movement is advancing a form of collectivism that members say differs from Soviet forms of socialism, but advocates sharing equally the wealth generated by society. Islamic fundamentalists contrast a utopian view of life in the first century of Islam with present conditions of poverty, squalor, and oppression. That belief, together with modern methods of communication and propaganda, may move a number of Arab nations farther and farther away from effective relations with the West (Kedourie, 1980).

EVANGELICALISM

If American religious life has appeared to be torn between fundamentalism on the one hand and secularism on the other, these two tendencies may have overshadowed another very significant religious group, the evangelicals. Evangelicals see themselves as more moderate religiously and politically than either fundamentalists or secularists. They tend to see fundamentalists as narrow-minded and reactionary and to view those with secular views as beset with uncertainty and lack of faith.

Evangelicalism is a form of Protestantism that stresses the preaching of the gospel of Jesus Christ, the validity of personal conversion experiences, biblical Scripture as the basis for faith, and active preaching of the faith in one's home country and abroad. In the early part of the twentieth century they were often equated with fundamentalists, but in more recent years evangelicals have become increasingly distinct. They are more open to science, rationality, and the concerns of the Reformation. In nineteenth-century America, evangelicalism was characterized by strong support for democracy, in keeping with the Reformation doctrine that individuals did not need priests or other intermediaries between themselves and God but were equal in the eyes of God. They were optimistic that people and societies could change for the better with God's support. Today's evangelicals see themselves as part of the same tradition.

CULTS, SECTS, DENOMINATIONS, AND CHURCHES

The organized efforts of fundamentalists, liberal denominations, and evangelicals have all been challenged by the rise of a number of new religious cults in the United States in recent decades.

CULTS

A *cult* is a loosely organized group of people who together act out religious feelings, attitudes, and relationships (O'Dea, 1966). This acting out of religious feelings may not yet have

Absolutist religious cults such as the members of the Unification Church, popularly known as "Moonies," protest permissive trends in modern society. In a step that amazed many people, more than 4000 Americans agreed to marry someone chosen for them by the Rev. Sun Moon in this mass marriage ceremony in Madison Square Garden. They all wore identical suits and gowns.

the clearly defined organizational structure of a church (Greeley, 1972). Cults usually focus on an intense form of worship or an unconventional belief. They are often organized around a charismatic leader. Many of the world's great religions began as cults devoted to prophetic figures—Jesus, Buddha, and Muhammad. The rituals of a cult begin as spontaneous expression, and gradually become more patterned and standardized. Cults tend to develop rituals involving speech, gesture, songs, sacramental meals, sacrifices, and rites around the major transitions in the lives of individual members and of the group. Anywhere from 3 to 20 million people are estimated to belong to cults in the United States, and many of them are young people under the age of 25.

The "new religions" have been defined by Needleman (1970) as the non-Christian, non-Jewish faiths of Americans. They include the recent interest among a relatively small number of Americans in Hinduism, Buddhism, Sufism, the occult, Zen, Baba-lovers, Subud, transcendental meditation, Tibetan religion, astrology, reincarnation, nature religions, esotericism, and drug-associated religion. The "new religions" have been broadly classified into two types: *absolutist* movements that divide the world into two distinct camps of good and demonic forces, and *relativistic* groups that take a moral stance in the world but avoid condemning those who disagree with them (Robbins, Anthony, and Richardson, 1978).

The absolutist movements include neo-fundamentalist groups (the "Jesus movement"), neo-pentacostal groups (such as the "Children of God" and the Alamo Foundation), and the Unification Church of Reverend Sun Myung Moon ("Moonies"). These groups protest fervently against relativistic and permissive trends in

American society. They are adamantly opposed to pornography, abortion, homosexuality, and other manifestations of what they call the Anti-Christ. Some of them predict that the end of the world is at hand. These groups tend to be politically and socially conservative, and they draw their members from rural or urban lower-middle-class homes and from people with conservative-dogmatic religious backgrounds (Wuthnow, 1976a; Judah, 1974; Harder, Richardson, and Simmonds, 1972).

These groups tend to be organized as "total institutions" that seek to isolate their members from contact with outsiders, including members of their own family and friends. In doing so, they recognize a basic sociological principle that if you want to change people's attitudes and behaviors, immersion in a total environment away from competing alternatives is often an effective way to proceed. At the same time, these techniques have been criticized for breaking up families and as designed to brainwash converts (Robbins and Anthony, 1978). Such charges, and the resulting lawsuits by parents seeking to free their children from such movements, have raised serious questions about the separation of church and state, religious persecution by the state, and the rights of a young adult living with a religious cult.

In contrast to the absolutist cults, the more relativistic and mystical groups focus on metaphysical unity or "oneness" in the universe; for them, the material features of the world are, ultimately, illusory. Great stress is placed on exploring cosmic consciousness and awakening an inner spiritual life. The desired state is one of awareness or "realization" or "enlightenment." These elements appear in the new Eastern cults in America (Bellah, 1974), such as the Hare Krishna, Integral Yoga, and Nichiren Shoshu (Robbins, Anthony, and Richardson, 1978; Marin, 1975; Stone, 1976; Cox, 1977; Evans, 1973). Members of such groups are more likely to be politically liberal and reformist compared to absolutist group members (Stone, 1978; Wuthnow, 1976a). They are also more likely to be from urban, affluent, educated, and relatively sophisticated backgrounds (Wuthnow, 1976b).

The Hare Krishna cult is a closely knit and tightly regimented one. It tends to recruit young people not yet launched on their careers or in building a family (Cox, 1977; Judah, 1974; Daner, 1976; Johnson, 1976). Hare Krishna is also one of the most visible movements, since its members shave their heads and wear flowing orange robes. They sell flowers, and dance, sing, and chant in airports, in train stations, and on main streets of large cities. Members may associate only with one another; they are to follow religious disciplines, including celibacy; and they take a negative view of competition, conflict, science, rationality, and education.

Given the proliferation of various types of cults in the United States in recent years, what can we say about why they arise and why people join them? Various explanations have been offered. The rise of new cults may be an indication of the degree to which religion has become unimportant in modern society, and been reduced to simply another exotic consumer item (Wilson, 1976). Cults offer the promise of more authentic and less alienated religious experience. Others suggest that the new movements reflect a quest for community in an impersonal bureaucratic world (Richardson, Stewart, and Simmonds, 1979). Another view is that the new movements represent a search for meaning in an era of moral collapse (Glock, 1976). Science and philosophy have not provided people with values they can live by (Bellah, 1976). Most converts to new movements are seeking moral alternatives to the crumbling Protestant ethic, suggest Anthony and Robbins (1975). It is possible that each of these views explains some part of the growth of new religious sects.

SECTS

Sects resemble cults in that they consist of individuals who join the group, usually as the result of conversion. People are not usually born into membership in the group; they join because of their shared feeling of having experienced a "new birth." Sects expect a strong commitment from members, but not quite the total commitment that cults require. Sects are ascetic and austere, and seek to have members withdraw from secular life and separate themselves from others. Often this takes the form of gathering the "priesthood of believers" into an egalitarian social organization that rejects the larger society. Members are expected to participate actively, be personally committed to the group's goals, and conform closely to all instructions and teachings. Differences between clergy and laity are minimized, and often religious leaders have not been formally trained in their profession.

Sects differ from cults in that they tend to have been around longer and are more institutionalized. They do not depend on one or a few charismatic leaders to fuel religious fervor, but have established ways of passing leadership from one group to another (Troeltsch, 1929; O'Dea, 1966; 1970). Sects do tend to require a higher level of commitment and conformity than denominations or churches. Examples of sects include the Latter-Day Saints, Jehovah's Witnesses, and Seventh Day Adventists (Marty, 1982).

Sects may remain within an organized church, where members serve as agents of reform or provide a core of dedicated workers for

"You go on home without me, Irene. I'm going to join this man's cult."

charitable and missionary tasks, like the Benedictine, Dominican, Franciscan, and Jesuit religious orders in the Roman Catholic Church. Sometimes sects withdraw from the church and sometimes from the surrounding society as well. Some, such as the Amish and the Hutterites, form geographically isolated communities where they are able to establish and reproduce themselves in succeeding generations. The Jehovah's Witnesses have done this in urban areas (Wilson, 1961).

DENOMINATIONS

A *denomination* is a religious organization that emerges in a society which has no established church and permits various social or ethnic groups to practice their own religions (Greeley, 1972). Denominations are the churches of a pluralist society that has no single official religion. Some sociologists, however, describe denominations simply as sects in an advanced stage of development (O'Dea, 1970). Mormons and Quakers, for instance, may have become more like denominations than sects. Denominations tend to be more tolerant of one another than sects; they are more relaxed about the intensity of commitment required of members; and they usually have professionally trained clergy (Niebuhr, 1929).

CHURCHES

A church is more likely than a sect to accept the structure and culture of the society in which it exists. Religion and church may be separated, but an essential feature of religion in the life of many societies is the fact that it is highly organized (Greeley, 1972). Weber "distinguished a *sect* from a *church* on the grounds that the former was an elective association of adults, exclusive in terms of some selective principle, belief, or practice, while the church was inclusive" (cited in Greeley, 1972, p. 73). A church is highly integrated with the society and the economy in which it exists. At one extreme there is an official or established church, such as the Church of England, that is linked in some way with the state. Such an official church may count all citizens as members. These features tend to result in the church being socially conservative. Members are born into a church; they do not need to have a conversion experience. Churches operate on the assumption that conversion is relatively easy for all those not born into it. This contrasts sharply with the exclusive attitude of cult members, which suggests that conversion graces only the most dedicated. Religious practices are traditional and formalized in most churches. As a result, they tend to be predictable. Church clergy are almost always professionally trained and formally recognized. Churches are more likely to be hierarchically organized than are sects and to have more formal statements of beliefs and dogmas. Table 17.2 summarizes and compares the features of churches, denominations, sects, and cults presented in this section.

RELIGION IN THE UNITED STATES

The United States does not have large groups who belong to various world religions, but numerous forms of Christianity are practiced here. This variety creates unique cultural groupings, social networks, and forms of social organization.

"To find a place in American society increasingly means to place oneself in one or another of (its) religious communities," wrote the social philosopher Will Herberg (cited in Carroll et al., 1979, p. 8). This rather abstract insight takes on concrete form when one travels through the southern United States. The first question one is often asked by young people there is, "What reli-

Table 17.2 Churches, Denominations, Sects, and Cults

	Church (Church of England, Roman Catholic Church)	Denomination (Baptist, Lutheran, Methodist)	Sect (Amish, Jehovah's Witnesses, Seventh Day Adventists)	Cult (Hare Krishna, Children of God)
Relationship with society and other religions	Closely tied with the state. Tends to accept structure and culture of society. Sees itself as the only legitimate religion.	Not officially part of the state. Generally accepts structure and culture of society. Values pluralism, since it is one among many religious organizations.	Protests established authority of state and society and other religions, often claiming they are inauthentic.	Rejects other religions as well as the state and secular society.
Source of members	Most members of a society belong. Conversion experience is not needed.	Individuals are often born into a denomination, although they may switch through conversion.	Recruits new members through birth or through conversion experiences.	Recruits new members, often young people experiencing identity crises, through conversion experiences.
Organization and leadership	Hierarchically organized. Professionally trained leaders, formally recognized.	Formal organizational structures and professionally trained clergy.	May strive for egalitarian social organization. Religious leaders may have no formal training.	Strong charismatic leaders, usually without formal training.
Doctrine and beliefs	Usually has formally stated beliefs and dogma.	Some formal doctrines, but tolerates diverse views and disputes.	Emphasizes literal interpretation of scriptures, purity of doctrine, and otherworldly concerns.	Claims to offer new revelations and insights.
Involvement of members	Formal involvement, such as church attendance or baptism, is usually expected, but many members are not actively involved.	Expects formal involvement but recognizes that members have other commitments.	Expects a strong commitment from members, often reflected in life-styles that clash with secular society (Saturday Sabbath).	Requires strong involvement from members, often isolating them from nonmembers.
Religious practices	Traditional and formalized, predictable.	May vary quite widely by regions.	Tend to be ascetic and austere, and withdrawn from secular life.	Most tend to remove people from the secular world. Meditation or other practices vary widely.
Relation to fundamental, evangelical, or secular tendencies	Tends toward secularism.	Primarily reflects evangelical and secular tendencies, but may contain some fundamentalists.	Strong tendency toward fundamentalism.	Tends toward fundamentalism.

gion are you?" For them, this is a very important feature of identity. Even people who do not adhere to the beliefs and practices of a particular religion may find that their identity, their culture, and their sense of membership in a social group is shaped by religious background.

DENOMINATIONAL MEMBERSHIP

In public opinion surveys over the last three decades in the United States, between 92 and 98 percent of the population indicated a preference for some religion. This finding has remained remarkably stable for more than 30 years. Over these years the number of people indicating a preference for some form of Protestantism has declined (from 69 to 60 percent), as has a preference for Judaism (from 5 to 2 percent). The proportion of Americans with Catholic religious preferences has increased, from 20 to 27 percent. In all, only 8 percent of Americans indicate they have no religious preference. Clearly, a remarkably high proportion of the population indicates a preference for some religion. The denomination mentioned most frequently after Roman Catholicism is Baptist, about 21 percent of the population. Methodists are the third largest group (about 10 percent), followed by Presbyterians (5 percent), Lutherans (3 percent), United Church of Christ (3 percent), Episcopalians (3 percent), and all other Protestant denominations.

Although the numbers of people who indicate actual membership in various churches is smaller than the numbers indicating a preference for that denomination, the relative size of different church memberships is about the same. About one-quarter of the U.S. populaton (or 49 million people in 1973) indicated they were members of the Catholic Church. About 6 million people in the population indicated that they are members of a Jewish congregation (Carroll et al., 1979; *Public Opinion,* 1979).

Roman Catholics are the easiest religious group to count, because their highly centralized organization keeps them from splintering into competing groups. Central registration also aids in keeping count. Catholics are found in most counties of the United States, but they tend to be concentrated in the Northeast (particularly in large cities), the Great Lakes states, the Louisiana delta country, and parts of the Southwest, including southern Texas.

Although most European settlers to North America came from societies where there was little separation of church and state, many had fled to escape religious persecution. Once here, they wanted to find a way to protect various religious denominations. Even though religious diversity was valued, religious groups tended to form clusters in particular geographic regions. The most pronounced of these is the numerical dominance of the Latter-Day Saints (Mormons) in the state of Utah. Mormons have extended outward into parts of Colorado, Wyoming, Nevada, Idaho, and Arizona as well. In the southeastern United States, with the exception of the southern tips of Texas, Louisiana, and Florida, most counties are dominated by Baptists of the Southern Baptist Convention. A third concentration, of Lutherans, occurs in the upper Midwest, beginning in southern Wisconsin and curving through Minnesota, the Dakotas, and down into Iowa and Nebraska. Although Methodists are fairly widely dispersed throughout the country, they are somewhat concentrated in Pennsylvania, Delaware, Iowa, Kansas, Nebraska, and Oklahoma. As already noted, Catholics tend to be concentrated in urban white America (Carroll et al., 1979).

Although we think of the United States as the home of many religious denominations, three—Catholics, Baptists, and Methodists—account for three-fifths of the total population. The addition of Lutherans, Presbyterians, and Episcopalians includes three-fourths of the population. About 3 percent are Jewish, about 18 percent are "other Protestants," and 3 percent are "other or no religion."

CHARACTERISTICS OF VARIOUS DENOMINATIONS

The largest single denomination, Roman Catholic, has become middle class with respect to the education, occupation, and economic achievement of many of its members (Greeley, 1972). The majority of Catholics still support the Democratic party. Catholics report the highest rates of church attendance of any denomination, with more than two-thirds reporting that they attend mass weekly.

The major Protestant denominations are divided internally. The Baptist Church, for instance, has at least 16 different bodies, the largest of which is the Southern Baptists. Southern Baptists are more likely than other Baptists to be fundamentalist in their theology and conservative politically. A quarter of Baptists are blacks. Traditionally, the Baptist churches attracted the lower classes and the dispossessed, and it still ministers to many poor people in the South. In recent years, however, some Baptist churches have become prosperous as the South has become increasingly affluent. Many members follow both the otherworldly religious Gospel and an affluent personal life-style. Baptists comprise more than 50 percent of the people of many Southern counties, and it is not unusual for these communities to be dominated by a Baptist "culture."

Early Baptists believed in immersing adults in water when they were baptized and in trying to live a simple life patterned after the moral codes of early Christianity (Marty, 1976). Even today, many southern Baptists are against smoking, drinking, swearing, gambling, dancing, and card-playing. In many towns, the recreation facilities, including the swimming pool and gymnasium, are owned and operated by the church, and church youth groups provide the hub of teenage social life. Evangelistic rallies are major cultural events in many areas. In such places, non-Baptists have little chance of being elected to political office.

Methodism is in many ways a mainstream American denomination. It is fairly evenly spread throughout the United States, although in most counties members do not comprise a majority of the population. Methodism followed settlers westward, and its democratic theology (which stressed member participation and no hierarchy of church officials) appealed to frontier villages. Methodist preaching was emotional as well as intellectual, and succeeded in drawing many converts. Among workers newly arrived in the cities, Methodism appealed to those who were put off by the seemingly stodgy styles of worship practiced by Episcopalians and Congregationalists.

In the past, Methodists may have been more like Baptists in trying to fuse all aspects of members' lives with their church, but in recent years the focus on shaping the lives of members has diminished. Methodists have long been interested in bringing Christian principles into the social order, and have played an active role in public affairs. Methodists are middle class in education, occupation, and income, and average in church attendance.

Social class is correlated with denominational preferences and memberships. A number of research studies have shown that denominations are ranked according to the percentage of their members who are of higher social classes or in white collar occupations. The groups with the largest proportion of higher-class or white collar members are Jews, Episcopalians, Unitarians, Presbyterians, Christian Scientists, and Congregationalists. At the other extreme, Roman Catholics, Baptists, Mormons, Eastern Orthodox, and Fundamentalists (including Seventh Day Adventists, Pentacostals, Church of God, and Jehovah's Witnesses) have relatively more members of lower social classes (Alston, 1973; Lauer, 1975; Moberg, 1962; Nelson and Snizek, 1976; Schneider, 1952; and Warren, 1970). There are clear educational, occupational, and income differences among various religious denominations in America. It is important to realize, however, that although Episcopalians, for instance, are more likely to be more educated and have higher-status occupations, many Episcopalians are lower class. Similarly, Baptist churches may in general have large numbers of lower-class members, but they also have some wealthy members (Demerath, 1965). Denominations show a great deal of variation among their members, even though there are patterned differences among denominations on a national scale.

Within various denominations, social class is correlated with church attendance (Glock and Stark, 1965; Greeley, 1972). Those who have done better with respect to the world's ranking systems appear to be more able or willing to attend church. Certain cultural and social traits also characterize various denominations. Mormons, for example, tend to be socially and politically conservative. They do not believe in having women as religious leaders, they believe in tithing (that is, contributing one-tenth of their income to the church), and they frown on drinking and smoking. Many young people give one or two years of religious missionary service when they complete their education. They believe in self-sufficiency, and some Mormons store a year's supply of food for emergencies. They are also strong believers in helping the less fortunate members of the community. When practiced, these religious beliefs help to create a more austere life-style than that of many Americans and something of a distinct cultural community.

Like Baptists, Lutherans comprise more than 50 percent of the population in a number of counties. Lutherans have the highest rates of church membership and attendance of any Protestant denomination. They tend to be middle class with respect to education, occupation, and income. Their cultural contributions include the founding of a number of excellent colleges and the building of some architecturally distinct contemporary churches. Their representation in politics and other public spheres has been low compared to the size of their membership. Their national unity has been affected by the diverse national origins of Lutherans. Many came from Germany, but Lutheranism was also strong among Swedes, Danes, Norwegians, and Finns. Each of these groups tended to keep its own language and to be suspicious of Lutherans of other nationalities. Even today, the Lutheran Church tends to be divided by internal doctrinal and organizational battles.

In 1957, the Evangelical and Reformed churches merged with the Congregational Christian churches to form the United Church of Christ (UCC). The Congregational branch had been strong in New England in colonial times. The low-key, quiet civility of Congregational evangelism did not compete very well with the fervor of the revivalists when it came to gaining converts among frontier settlers. Although their numbers did not grow rapidly, Congregationalists did found what became excellent colleges. The UCC does not have a numerical majority in any counties in the country. As a result, it has not created a cultural style that it has imposed on nonmembers. It is well known and respected throughout the northern part of the United States, but its cultural impact is much less than that of the Roman Catholic, Baptist, and Lutheran churches around the country.

Presbyterians, Episcopalians, and Congregationalists have the highest proportion of college-educated, business, professional, and well-to-do members of any Christian denomination. Jews, however, are more highly educated and of higher occupational status and income than even Episcopalians and Presbyterians. All these religious groups have considerably more influence on American society than their numbers would suggest because of their high educational levels, their economic and social status, and their geographic locations. One indicator of their influence is extent of political participation.

POLITICAL PARTICIPATION OF DENOMINATIONS

In 1977, 77 percent of the U.S. Senate was Protestant, compared to 60 percent of the American adult population who identified themselves as Protestant (Carroll et al., 1979). Catholics, on the other hand, comprise only 13 percent of the Senate, compared to 27 percent of the population. Catholics and Protestants were represented in proportion to their numbers in the general population in the House of Representatives and in gubernatorial (governors') offices. Jews were twice as likely to hold political office than their numbers in the population would suggest.

Within the Protestant denominations, Methodists, Episcopalians, Presbyterians, United Church of Christ members, and Unitarians are overrepresented in political office relative to their size in the population. Lutherans, Baptists, and fundamentalists are underrepresented. These distributions are partially explained by the way political districts are drawn (they may include a rural Protestant area and a small piece of an urban area), and by the higher social class of most Episcopalians, UCC members, Presbyterians, and Jews. Another factor, however, appears to be related to the cultural differences between the religions. The liberal theological positions of Methodism, the UCC, Episcopalianism, and Presbyterianism promote serious attention to public as well as private moral issues (Parenti, 1967). Max Weber saw these religions as having an "inner worldly ascetic" religious orientation, meaning a system of beliefs that stresses disciplined activity within the institutions of the world but allows a challenge to them (Weber, 1922). All aspects of the world, including the economic and political arenas, are considered suitable areas in which the believer can work to glorify God.

CIVIL RELIGION

American life is notable for the way it interweaves religious and political symbols in what sociologist Robert Bellah (1967) calls a *civil religion*. We are one nation "under God," according to the pledge of allegiance. Presidents are sworn into office with their hands on the Bible. Printed on our currency are the words "In God We Trust." A major theme of public life is the vision of America as a redeemer nation and Americans as a chosen people. This vision is not rooted in any single denomination. Instead, it can embrace the pluralism of American religious life. While this tendency may seem to promote self-worship, it also operates to subject American behavior and values to moral scrutiny (Bellah, 1967).

Although the U.S. Constitution separates church and state and there is no official state religion, the political realm draws heavily on religious themes. A person who did not go to religious services would have little or no chance of being elected president, for example. Several presidents in recent years, as well as congressional leaders, have publicly proclaimed their participation in prayer groups in addition to their church attendance.

Despite the continued connection between political leaders and religious imagery, Bellah believes that in recent years American civil religion has become "an empty and broken shell" because individualism has taken over as the dominant American ethos. Individuals busily pursue private material goals. Their selfishness, suggests Bellah, may have destroyed the sense of covenant between God and a religious community. Bellah sees the present religious ferment as an effort to re-create a new moral community and to replace the decaying civil religion (1975).

Summary

1. The French sociologist Emile Durkheim noted several features that characterize all religions, including a sense of the divine or holy, the practice of established rites, and the existence of a community of worshippers.

2. Religion differs from magic in that religious rites are their own fulfillment, and they are shared.

3. Functionalists stress the integrative functions of religion in society, such as shared systems of belief, accepted moral leadership, and personal support for individuals.

4. Conflict theorists suggest that religion protects the position of privileged groups in society.

5. In societies where the state has tried to eliminate religion, it has been unsuccessful, suggesting that religion does not serve only to protect the privileged. There are societies, such as those of India or South Africa, where religion does legitimate social stratification.

6. Around the world, about 60 percent of all people belong to one of the nine largest religions: Christianity, Islam, Hinduism, Buddhism, Confucianism, Shintoism, Taoism, Judaism, and Zoroastrianism.

7. Millennarian movements that predict dramatic supernatural intervention in the world followed by a thousand years of peace have arisen throughout religious history. Some examples are the Cargo Cults of New Guinea and the Ghost Dance Cult of North American Plains Indians. Followers of these movements have often been socially displaced by newly dominant groups or classes and see little practical way of improving their plight.

8. Secular values include rationality, cultural and religious pluralism, tolerance of moral ambiguity, and faith in education, civil rights, and the rule of law. In contrast, fundamentalism calls for religion to dominate every aspect of life. Moreover, fundamentalism is often based on a literal reading of sacred texts. Both secular and fundamentalist trends have been growing in recent years. A number of fundamentalist religious movements have sprung up, including both Christian and Islamic groups.

9. Evangelicalism seeks to tread a middle ground between fundamentalism and secular, liberal denominations. It is a form of Protestantism that stresses the preaching of the gospel of Jesus Christ, the validity of personal conversion experiences, biblical Scripture as the basis for faith, and active preaching of the faith.

10. The number of religious cults seems to be growing, with estimates of membership reaching as high as 20 million in the United States. Cults are groups of people who act together out of shared religious feelings. Some cults have been criticized because they isolate members so completely from family and friends that individuals may lose the capacity for free choice.

11. Most theories explaining the growth of cults and sects emphasize the discontent people feel with modern life.

12. Sects tend to have a longer life span than cults, with some groups establishing a relatively permanent way of life and raising children within the sect.

13. Denominations are the religious organizations that emerge in a society which has no established church. Denominations and churches tend to be more integrated with the society in which they exist than cults or sects. Individuals may become members at birth, rather than needing a conversion experience to belong. Clergy are formally trained and perform functions lay members cannot. Church services tend to be more predictable than the services of cults and sects.

14. In the United States as well as around the world, an individual's religious background often affects culture, networks, and sense of membership in social groups.

15. Catholics are the largest religious denomination in the United States, with about 27 percent of the population, followed by all types of Baptists, who make up about 21 percent. Methodists number about 10 percent, and other denominations have 5 percent or less of the population as members. Catholics and Baptists tend to live in geographically concentrated areas where church membership may overlap with ethnicity. The major social and cultural activities of such areas are often run by the church of the majority.

16. Social class is related to religious denomination in the United States. Jews, Episcopalians, Unitarians, Presbyterians, Christian Scientists, and Congregationalists have a larger proportion of members with higher-status occupations and higher incomes; Roman Catholics, Baptists, Mormons, Eastern Orthodox, and fundamentalists have a larger proportion of members of lower social classes.

17. Studies of political participation by religious groups find that Methodists, Episcopalians, Presbyterians, UCC members, Unitarian-Universalists, and Jews are overrepresented in political offices relative to their numbers in the population, while Lutherans and Baptists are underrepresented. This may have to do with the stress that the former religious groups place on public as well as private morality.

18. America is considered to have a civil religion according to sociologist Robert Bellah, who pointed out how American political life is interlaced with religious symbols and rituals.

Key Terms

cargo cult
church
civil religion
cult
denomination
evangelicalism
fundamentalism
Ghost Dance cult
magic
millennarian movements
profane
religion
ritual
sacred
sect
secularism

Chapter 18

Science and Technology

We cannot go through a day without noticing the importance of science. Bridges and elevators, antibiotics and telephones, tapedecks and pacemakers, vacuum cleaners, space shuttles, jet planes, polyester, and new ways of organizing the social relations of work—all these result from the social institution we call science.

The development of science is perhaps the single most distinctive feature of modern industrial society. Here the term *science* refers to the approach used to obtain reliable knowledge about the physical and social worlds, based on systematic empirical observation. Science has helped to increase agricultural productivity, encourage economic growth, control disease, and increase life expectancy. Because it is an intense form of social discovery and invention, science is a constant source of social change both within itself and in relation to other social institutions. Science has a dark side as well. It poses major threats to life and health in the chemical, thermal, and radioactive harm it may do to us and to our environment, and it has been used to create an unsurpassed array of destructive weapons. As a result of the intense positive and negative implications of science, it is a major source of social tension and controversy.

The institution of science refers to the social communities that share certain theories and methods aimed at understanding the physical and social worlds. The word "science" may also refer to the knowledge obtained by those communities. The goal of science is to determine general principles that underlie natural and social events. It does not matter that these principles may or may not have any immediate practical utility.

Scientists are concerned with understanding the physical and social world; engineers, technologists, and managers seek to use the knowledge gathered by scientists to solve practical problems and make things work. Much of what we think of as science is actually the result of *technology,* which refers to the practical applications of scientific knowledge.

Science has flourished in only a few times and places in history. Some observers suggest that our current scientific flowering is due to the happy bonding of science and technology in our society (Sklair, 1973). Science and technology have accomplished some remarkable things in the last century. Diseases such as smallpox, diphtheria, whooping cough, scarlet fever, polio, and pneumonia have been reduced or wiped out through medical research. Crop yields have soared as the result of plant research and the development of chemical fertilizers and pesticides.

For a time, the marvels of science and technology were considered an unquestioned good, but in recent years that confident appraisal has faltered. By reducing infant mortality and extending life expectancy, the same booming crop yields and medical advances also unleashed the worst population explosion in the world's history, a slowly ticking bomb that confronts mil-

Scientific medical research has helped to eradicate or control many life-threatening diseases such as small pox. The Atlanta Center for Disease Control pictured here collects data from all over the United States and does research in an effort to understand and control dangerous outbreaks like Legionnaires' disease, toxic shock syndrome, and AIDS (acquired immune deficiency syndrome).

lions with the prospect of starvation before the century ends. The result of spraying bugs with the pesticide DDT is that the hazardous chemical has begun appearing in well water, lakes, and oceans. Changes in the production of steel and electricity produce pollutants in the American Midwest and Northeast that blow north, fall as acid rain, and kill the fish in Canadian lakes. Scandinavian countries face the same problem from industrial Europe. Einstein's theories and atom-splitting physicists have produced nuclear wastes no one knows what to do with and nuclear weapons that can destroy life on this planet.

In the first section of this chapter, we consider why and how science has become institutionalized in the modern world. We also consider the different kinds of questions functionalist and conflict sociologists raise about science as an institution. The next three sections examine the internal operations of science. Any social activity generates certain social norms that suggest how people should behave, and science is no exception. Sociologists have studied the norms of science and the conditions under which those norms may be violated.

Sociologists also study the processes of creativity and productivity within science to see how social factors affect productivity. Creative discoveries provoke change in science. Sociologists are interested in how scientists react to new discoveries and theories, particularly when they challenge existing ideas. The final section of the chapter returns to the relation between science and society to consider how science affects economic productivity, the state of science in the United States today, controversies in science policy, and issues in the democratic governance of scientific activity.

THE RISE AND INSTITUTIONALIZATION OF SCIENCE

THE RISE OF MODERN SCIENCE

Science existed in some form even in the very earliest human societies. But modern science as we know it today was inspired by the artistic Renaissance of fifteenth-century Italy, in which the classical texts of antiquity were discovered. Those texts contained Latin and Greek works on science. The invention of the printing press by Guttenberg in 1439 led to the availability of cheap books, which helped to transform learning and culture. The exploration of the world's oceans and lands placed new demands on astronomy and mathematics. Some of these developing techniques were also used by gentlemen officers, military surgeons, and engineers in the wars of Protestant reformation. These events lowered the class barriers to such applied practical knowledge.

In the seventeenth century there was a revolution in the way people thought about the natural world that did a great deal to help scientific investigation. Nature was stripped of its spiritual and human properties and became open to objective investigation. Reflected in the views of Francis Bacon in England (born 1561), René Descartes in France (born 1596), and Galileo Galilei in Italy (born 1564), this approach saw nature as something that could be explored using sensory data, disciplined observation, and reasoning. There was a growing awareness that cooperative efforts were needed to collect and test results about the natural world. The first scientific society, the Royal Society in London, was founded in 1662 to encourage the exchange of observations about the natural world and to ensure that scientists received credit for their original discoveries. These societies founded the first scientific journals to share discoveries and theories.

In this early period, science was conducted on a very small scale by gentlemen of independent means or by engineers or physicians who conducted experiments in their spare time. Benjamin Franklin, for example, carried on electrical experiments while pursuing a career as a printer, publisher, author, and statesman. Only a few universities (for example, Edinburgh in Scotland and Leiden in The Netherlands) offered serious instruction in science. The idea of a full-time career dedicated to the pursuit of scientific work or the idea of large laboratories with teams of many scientists working on projects was unknown.

The tradition of the gentleman scholar persisted longer in England then elsewhere because there were few full-time jobs for scientists there. Germany, meanwhile, was building a strong university system in the nineteenth century. At a number of different centers, research and teaching were joined; students received research training in the university laboratory. With this institutional support, and a strong system of scholarly journals and handbooks, German science took the lead in many fields between 1830 and 1880. Science in the United States during the nineteenth century was highly dependent on Europe; the major American universities were not deeply involved in basic research. Around the turn of the century, many Americans studied in Germany and returned with ideas about how to transplant features of the German system to the United States. In the 1930s, American science was greatly strengthened by the influx of refugee scholars fleeing from Nazi Germany. Many "American" Nobel prize-winning scientists were actually born and trained in Germany before moving to the United States. Since the end of World War II, there has been an unparalleled explosion of scientific achievements as nations have poured resources into the search for a deeper understanding of the physical universe.

As Price noted (1963), the growth of science has been exponential, which means that science grows at an increasingly rapid rate. One way of expressing that growth is in the number of years it takes for scientific activity to double. Whatever measure is used—for example, the number of people in science or the number of publications—it tends to double within 10 to 12 years (Price, 1963, 1975). This rate of development means that at any given time, half the scientific papers ever published have appeared in the past decade. The result is that science appears (and to some degree is) continually new (Price, 1975). Nearly 90 percent of all the scientists who ever worked are alive today. This tendency also means that most of the scientists working at any given time are quite young—that is, in the first decade of their work. So most scientific discoveries are made by young scientists, simply because there are more of them.

THE INSTITUTIONALIZATION OF SCIENCE

In order to survive and flourish in a society, science needs to be *institutionalized*—that is, careers for practicing scientists need to be established in major social institutions. This process is described by Ben-David (1971). Careers and positions in science need historical continuity and some commitment of social resources if they are to stay healthy. When such institutionalized positions exist, people can train for and pursue lifetime careers as scientists. Otherwise, the pursuit of scientific activity is restricted to the independently wealthy or to hobbyists.

Today there are nearly 3 million scientists and engineers in the United States, about one in four of whom work in research and development (U.S. Bureau of the Census, 1982a). Most research scientists work on teams in large centers connected with universities or corporations. Part of the research process consists of writing proposals to obtain funding, as well as conducting and writing up the results of the group's research. The lone scientist working in an attic or basement is rare today. The occasional one that appears (such as Stephen Jobs, who invented the Apple computer in his garage) may be given wide media coverage precisely because he or she is unusual.

Studies of occupational prestige in a number of major industrial societies show that scientific occupations are generally rated quite highly. Within the scientific community, those conducting and publishing original research are most highly esteemed (Cole and Cole, 1973). More than 70 percent of the scientists and engineers employed in research and development (R&D) worked in industry in 1982, 12 percent worked in colleges and universities, 10 percent for the federal government, and 6 percent for independent research and development centers. This is close to the proportions in 1960 (U.S. Bureau of the Census, 1982a). Within the R&D group, the highly productive units tend to be concentrated in relatively few university departments and in industrial, government, and nonprofit research laboratories.

FUNCTIONAL AND CONFLICT APPROACHES TO SCIENCE

Functionalists see science as a major source of social change in a society. Indeed, it is one of their major explanations for social change. Robert K. Merton, one of the leading sociologists of science, stresses that the relationship between science and other institutions in society does not move in only one direction. Science not only influences and changes other social institutions, such as the family (for example, through birth control technology), religion (by challenging a literal interpretation of scripture), or the economy (by enhancing economic growth), but is itself influenced by social institutions. Merton's research on science in seventeenth-century England found that there was an interplay between institutional spheres. Science was affected by industrial, trade, military, and religious concerns, as well as having powerful consequences for those institutions (1970).

The conflict perspective focuses on how the distribution of power and resources affects science—for instance, by influencing the direction scientific inquiry takes. The influence of oil and gas industries may shift scientific research toward ways of extracting oil from shale and away from exploring small-scale windmill or solar sources of energy. To the degree that large corporations shape the direction of scientific research, they are likely to sponsor work in areas that will produce the greatest profits, rather than in areas that may have social and ecological value on a large scale. Conflict theorists would therefore be likely to ask, who benefits from a particular line of research and who does not?

Some sociologists would go even further and suggest that science and the scientific method is a central part of the domination of weaker groups or nations by stronger ones (Habermas, 1970). Rationality, science, and technology have become for many Western peoples the only way of dealing with reality and other people. But although rationality may offer a valuable approach to many problems, it should not be forgotten that rationality may support the interests of certain groups (manufacturing and military interests) more than others (tribal societies, landed aristocracy, or unemployed ghetto residents), and that it may not be the best approach to all situations.

In examining the relationship between science and other institutions in society, functionalists and conflict theorists raise different types of questions. They also consider different issues within science itself. Functionalists, as we see in the next section of this chapter, examine the norms of science and how they are functional for the conduct of scientific research. Conflict theorists tend to focus on instances where those norms are violated (for example, in cases of scientific fraud), and ask whether they were violated because of the interests of one rather than another special group. Both approaches raise interesting and important questions about science as a social institution.

THE NORMS OF SCIENCE

Merton (1957) suggests that certain norms prevail in science because they are functional for science as an institution. These norms include universalism, "communism," disinterestedness, and organized skepticism. If these norms did not operate, Merton indicates, science would not survive and flourish.

Universalism suggests that scientific statements are to be evaluated in terms of already existing scientific criteria, rather than in terms of the race, sex, religion, class, or fame of the person proposing them. The importance of this norm for the health of science was revealed in Nazi Germany when it rejected non-Aryan, especially Jewish, physics. German scientists at that time did not take Einstein's theories seriously and were unable to pursue lines of development stemming from those ideas.

Communism in science refers to the joint production, ownership, and utilization of scientific ideas by the entire scientific community. Even those making major discoveries that are named after them (for example, Newton's laws, pasteurization of milk, the Salk vaccine, Einstein's theory of relativity), do not own those contributions. The ideas become part of the common property of the scientific community. One aspect of this norm is the opposition to secrecy in the conduct of scientific work. One's ideas are to be shared fully and readily with anyone who is interested.

The norm of *disinterestedness* requires scientists to put scientific truth above personal considerations. Merton suggests that the strong presence of this norm within the institution of science helps to explain "the virtual absence of fraud in the annals of science." (We consider below whether this assertion is still true.) It is permissible for scientists to be motivated by the desire for recognition for their scientific contributions or the desire to benefit humanity, but those motives must never take priority over scientific integrity.

Organized skepticism requires scientists to scrutinize all statements in terms of the evidence that supports them and their logic. No belief is too sacred not to be viewed skeptically until the evidence is in. The norm is built into the institution of science through the standards of evidence and inference that are taught to new scientists as they are trained and in the way scientific papers are reviewed before being accepted for publication by scientific journals.

Although these norms may very well reflect the beliefs, behaviors, and attitudes of most members of the scientific community, they do not give us the whole picture. We must look at actual practice in science for a complete understanding of it as a social institution. Instances abound in which these norms are violated. Famous scientists, especially Nobel prize winners, for example, are more likely to get their work accepted for publication and noticed once it is published than are little-known scientists (Zuckerman and Merton, 1971). Similarly, work by people at major research institutions may receive more attention than work by people from lesser-known places. In *The Double Helix,* James Watson (1968) tells how he visited the laboratories of other researchers to learn about the DNA research they were doing while telling them little about his own work. By using the willingness of others to share in order to advance his own work (which, with that of Francis Crick, led to the discovery in 1953 of the structure of the DNA molecule), he may have violated the norms of communism and disinterestedness.

Violations of the norms of science may come from pressures on individuals to achieve rapid research success or from strongly held personal or societal ideologies. A scientist at the Sloan-Kettering Institute, for example, painted dark patches on white mice to convince his colleagues that he had learned how to make successful skin grafts between nontwins (Rensberger, 1977). Other cases of fraudulent research have been discovered in recent years. And allegations of fraudulent or careless research by laboratories testing new drugs on animals especially concern scientists and health administrators.

Sir Cyril Burt was a British psychologist who worked from the 1930s to the 1950s on intelligence. His results showed the dominance of genetic rather than environmental influences on intelligence, and provided the "scientific" rationale for the wide use of IQ tests in the British school system. They were also the basis for Arthur Jensen's claims that the lower IQ scores of black children, compared to those of whites, may be due to genetic differences (Jensen, 1969). In recent years, Burt's studies of separated identical twins have been severely criticized. An American psychologist, Leon Kamin (1974) of Princeton University, found that Burt's work was filled with verbal contradictions and arithmetical inconsistencies, as well as failure to provide information about crucial procedural details. The medical correspondent of the London *Sunday Times* was unable to locate any evidence that the coauthors of Burt's later papers (Margaret Howard and J. Conway) had ever existed (Wade, 1976). Later the *London Times* reported that a Ms. Howard had been a faculty member at London University during the 1930s, but doubts remain about the other coauthor and about the validity of Burt's data.

Fraudulent claims waste the time and money of other scientists who try to replicate the falsified results. Careless or fraudulent research flagrantly violates the norms of disinterestedness and organized skepticism. Such violations may occur more often than people realize. One British scientist writes: "Although scientists in general are very critical of untested assumptions, the assumption of scientific impartiality is almost completely untested" (cited in Rensberger, 1977, p. 44). The pressure on young scientists for quick and successful results, rapid publication, and grant-seeking success may overpower the norm of disinterestedness. The goal of scientific discovery may be replaced by the desire for publications and grant support.

Scientists argue that cases of fraud occur infrequently and that the controls in science are good enough so that most cheaters are caught. The existence of such cases suggests that the norms are violated at least some of the time. Violations, however, do not deny the existence of norms. Indeed, the strongly stated opposition to fraudulent behavior by the scientific community suggests that the norms do operate as models of how people ought to behave. (See the box on pp. 482–483 for more on fraud in science.)

CHANGE AND RESISTANCE TO CHANGE IN SCIENCE

KUHN AND THE STRUCTURE OF SCIENTIFIC REVOLUTIONS

If the norms of science call for scientists to be open-minded and always on the lookout for evidence that seems to undermine the theories they believe, the history of science tells a different story. The stormy process whereby scientific theories are challenged, defended, and ultimately overthrown is vividly described by Kuhn (1962, 1970a). People generally believe that scientific knowledge advances like a highway being built—research experiments gradually but steadily added to the unfolding ribbon of knowledge called science. This view of how science advances is close to what Kuhn calls "normal science." However, Kuhn challenged this view with his notion of "scientific revolutions," which he saw as contrasting sharply with normal science.

By *normal science* Kuhn meant research based on one or more past scientific achievements that are accepted as a useful foundation for further practice. The achievements that form the foundation must be new enough to attract a group of scientists who want to work within it, yet open-ended enough to leave a number of unresolved problems to work on. Kuhn uses the term *paradigm* to refer to a coherent tradition of scientific laws, theory, applications, assumptions, and measurement that forms a distinct approach to problems. The paradigms we call Copernican astronomy, Newtonian physics, or Einsteinian physics have distinguishable concepts, methods, and practices. Most scientists work in "normal science," solving puzzles that can be answered within a given paradigm. When scientists are trained, they are introduced to the prevailing assumptions and practices within the dominant paradigm of their field. They do not learn all the paradigms that have been discarded throughout the history of scientific investigation, or even alternative contemporary paradigms that are regarded as "wrong." Such exposure would be considered a waste of time.

Without a guiding paradigm, researchers in a field would find it difficult to define the important problems in the field and to determine the best way of solving them. The existence of a healthy paradigm does a great deal to further the advance of knowledge through normal science. The stage becomes set for a scientific revolution when increasing numbers of problems cannot be solved by the existing paradigm and when scientific observations begin to contradict the paradigm. Called *anomalies,* such examples are set aside and ignored for a while, as long as there are other problems that can be fruitfully explored within the paradigm, and as long as no better paradigm comes along.

At such a time a scientific field may be in crisis, but scientists will not abandon their guiding paradigm until an alternative that explains more than the old one is proposed. Even when a new paradigm is offered, not all scientists will accept it immediately. Kuhn suggests that sometimes a paradigm must wait for a new generation of scientists who are not wedded to the old tradition before it is fully accepted. If a new paradigm does enable scientists to work fruitfully on more new problems, it will eventually triumph. Kuhn believes that the usual developmental pattern of mature science appears in the successive transition from one paradigm to another via revolution.

For example, in the eighteenth century the prevailing paradigm in chemistry explained fire in terms of the escape of a substance called phlogiston. But the phlogiston theory could not explain why some materials gained weight after they burned. It was in such a context that Lavoisier offered his oxygen theory of combustion, which did take into account the greater weight of some substances after they burned. Similarly, Ptolemy's theory that the earth was the center of the universe led to imprecise predictions of planetary positions and gradually gave way to the Copernican view that the sun was at the center, despite violent opposition from religious groups. In another example, the wave theory of light was challenged by the particle theory, and today a hybrid paradigm describes light as photons, entities that exhibit some characteristics of waves and some of particles (Kuhn, 1970a). These examples reveal that the development of science is not like the orderly succession of democratic governments, but instead does sometimes resemble a *scientific revolution*—that is, the dramatic overthrow of one intellectual regime (or paradigm) by another.

HOW PARADIGMS AFFECT SCIENTIFIC OBSERVATIONS

The provisional nature of science is underscored by the philosopher of science Karl Popper (1959), who suggests that science can never establish the truth of scientific laws with absolute finality. All it can do is to advance a theory as possibly true until it is demonstrated to be false. With respect to paradigm shifts, Popper's view poses problems for Kuhn. The reason is that once you step outside a theory, you lose the shared operating assumptions and accepted methods of observing and interpreting that guide the conduct of science. It then becomes

SOURCE: *The New York Times,* January 17, 1982.

Fudging Data for Fun and Profit:
The Latest Research Scandal Raises Some Ugly Questions

Fellow researchers were awed by young Mark Spector's golden touch in the lab; he could often complete in a matter of days complex experiments that took others weeks and even months to do. Shortly after he entered Cornell University in 1980 as a graduate student in biochemistry, Spector was working with some of the most eminent men in his field. Most remarkable of all, at age 24, Spector seemed on the verge of proving a bold new theory explaining how tumor-causing viruses could turn a cell cancerous. He looked like a good bet for a Nobel Prize some day.

Eighteen months later, his brilliant career was in ruins. Findings that were touted only last summer as a fundamental breakthrough in the understanding of carcinogenesis have been branded fraudulent. Colleagues discovered that his results included protein gels—isolated bits of cellular matter—that were cunningly doctored to look like something they were not. While Spector denied any wrongdoing, he was expelled from the Cornell lab, withdrew his Ph.D. thesis, even though it had already been approved, and quit the university. Important aspects of his work may yet turn out to be true, but few believe he will ever be able to return to scientific research.

Cheating, of course, is common to many professions these days, even in past bastions of integrity like science, which has traditionally placed the search for truth above all other goals. But the Spector scandal has shaken this edifice in special ways. Besides wrecking the career of a gifted young researcher, it severely damaged a major man of science, Spector's sponsor, Cornell Biochemist Efraim Racker, who was ultimately responsible for supervising the results. More important, beyond whatever personal trauma may be involved, the case has put the entire research community on trial in the public mind. Once again there are questions about how much cheating goes on in the lab and whether scientists are in fact doing enough to keep their house in order.

Last year the world of science was jolted by the public airing of four major cheating scandals, involving such prestigious institutions as Yale School of Medicine, Boston's Massachusetts General Hospital, an affiliate of Harvard, and the Boston University Medical Center, where a three-year, $1 million cancer-research project was tainted by falsified data. This year two University of California scientists have been reprimanded for a different ethical breach: violating federal guidelines governing genetic engineering. Some newspapers have begun talking about a scientific "crime wave," and though the term does not really apply, Congress took notice by holding hearings on fraud in biomedical research. One response: the National Institutes of Health, which doles out $2 billion a year for research, has threatened to cut off any

"Don't feel bad about falsifying the solution. I falsified the problem."

SOURCE: *Time*, December 7, 1981, p. 83.

institution that fails to act as a watchdog on its workers.

Many scientists are unwilling to concede any significant increase in cheating. After all, the ancient astronomer Ptolemy may have occasionally faked observations to fit his model of the universe. Isaac Newton, the father of classical physics, and the saintly monk Gregor Mendel, who founded genetics, were apparently not above fudging some of their specific data to fit a generally true theory. Defenders of present scientific procedures say the only change has been psychological: what Dr. William Raug, NIH's associate director for grants and contracts, dismisses as "a heightened consciousness and a willingness to talk" about cheating. Other observers sharply disagree. Says University of Chicago Philosopher Stephen Toulmin: "You can't change something into a highly paid, highly competitive, highly structured activity without creating occasions for people to do things they never would do in the earlier, amateur stage."

There is no doubt about the increase in pressure on researchers to produce spectacular results, especially at a time when there is a squeeze on funds for research. As Raub notes, today only 30% of the applicants for NIH grants get them, compared with up to 70% in the 1950s. Senior scientists are often so busy scrambling for funds to keep their large labs running that they rarely have the time to look as closely at what their young whizzes are doing as they would like. What was once a sportsman-like rivalry between researchers has become cutthroat competition. By publishing a paper first, even if some of the data are not quite accurate, a young scientist may beat out a rival for any number of prizes: a tenured post or promotion, a big grant from the Government, an offer from industry (especially if the researcher is working in the hot area of gene splicing), and ultimately perhaps the trip to Stockholm.

In a time of such intense competition, a researcher who happens to suspect chicanery by a rival may be only too willing to blow the whistle. Scientists also like to point out that science was long protected from fraud by a built-in safety mechanism: to be generally accepted, experiments must be repeatable by others. Indeed it was just such a failure that led to Spector's downfall. But in contemporary practice, the safeguard often does not work. So much is being done in every field that unless an experiment is really important, years may pass before anyone tries to repeat it. Especially at a time when new ideas are at a premium, there is not much profit in doing over someone else's work. Furthermore, repetition is sometimes all but impossible, as in the case of health studies involving thousands of patients.

Some scientists believe that the current flurry of cheating cases is nothing more than what they call an anomaly, a random quirk in the regular flow of events. But as canny researchers have long known, anomalies are often the first clue to some deeper discovery. For that reason alone, it may well be in the scientific community's interests to look more closely at the recent examples of ethical lapses.

SOURCE: Frederic Golden, *Time,* December 7, 1981, p. 83.

impossible to test the absolute truth or falsity of a scientific theory as Popper urges. This does not mean Kuhn believes that all theories are equally valid or that "anything goes" in science. Even though the absolute validity of a scientific theory may be impossible to determine, the relative value of one rather than another theory may be certainly judged by seeing how well the paradigm solves a number of problems in science and by considering its usefulness for suggesting further avenues of inquiry.

A strong paradigm in science may make it difficult for scientists to "see" an occurrence that is an anomaly within the paradigm. The problem partly stems from the fact that our perceptions are guided by what we believe, as demonstrated in an experiment by Bruner and Postman (1949). They asked subjects to identify a series of playing cards. Many of the cards were normal, but some had been made anomalous—for example, there was a red six of spades and a black four of hearts (in a normal deck, spades are black and hearts are red). Single cards were exposed to subjects, and after each one subjects were asked what they had seen. Even the anomalous cards were identified, without hesitation or puzzlement, as normal. The black four of hearts might, for example, be identified as a four of spades or of hearts. People were unaware that it was different and were readily able to place it in one of the categories supplied by prior experience.

If scientific theories are likened to such prior experience, the role they play in actually organizing our perceptions of the world becomes more apparent. This is why it is sometimes difficult to identify phenomena that challenge a theory. Similarly, the decision to use a certain type of apparatus or measuring instrument carries several assumptions—for example, that only certain circumstances will arise, and that the apparatus or measure being used will tap everything important about a phenomenon. If you take a thermometer to a radioactive dump, you might conclude there is nothing unusual there.

RESISTANCE TO NEW IDEAS

History is full of examples of scientific ideas being rejected by the society in which the scientist operates. Galileo was tried by the medieval Catholic Church for his heretical astronomy. Charles Darwin's ideas were strongly opposed by religious bodies in his day—and religious resistance to them persists now—on the grounds that evolutionary theory runs counter to biblical accounts of the creation. Somewhat more surprising, perhaps, is the fact that resistance to ideas occurs within the scientific community itself. Scientists, after all, strongly value open-mindedness, and view as illegitimate moral, political, or religious influences on the acceptance or rejection of a theory. But values such as open-mindedness, no matter how strongly held, do not fully explain human behavior. Cultural and social factors may reinforce or limit the expression of values in behavior (Barber, 1961). In other words, cultural blinders may operate in science as they do in other social realms.

As we noted above, theoretical ideas or methods of measuring phenomena may lead scientists to overlook or reject discoveries they or others make. Some scientists like theory; others prefer experiments or observations. Some like theories to be put into models. Some scientists want an extremely mathematical analysis, while others reject such an approach. Any of these preferences may provide a source of resistance to innovation.

A scientist's ideas may also be rejected because he or she is unknown in the community of science. A striking example was the case of the Austrian monk Gregor Mendel, whose research on inheritance of specific physical characteristics eventually created a paradigm revolution in genetics. Mendel first announced his theory in 1865, and it was published in the scientific proceedings of his time. But his discovery languished until his work was rediscovered and replicated in 1900. His work was ignored despite the fact that Mendel sent his paper to one of the most distinguished botanists of the day, Carl von Nageli of Munich. Von Nageli and other prominent scientists of the time dismissed Mendel's ideas as preposterous partly because the ideas differed from von Nageli's and partly because Mendel seemed "an insignificant provincial" to them (Barber, 1961). As science has become more organized and bureaucratized, the possibility grows that innovative ideas by unknowns will not even be published.

Professional specialization among scientists may lead to the rejection of new ideas that come from people outside a particular specialty. An interesting example comes from the history of medicine. Pasteur's germ theory of disease generated violent resistance from the medical men of his time. They continued to operate with dirty hands and instruments, causing countless patients to die of infection.

SOCIAL PROCESSES AFFECTING SCIENTIFIC PRODUCTIVITY

Despite the resistance to ideas, a great deal of innovation does occur within science. *Innovation* refers to the discovery or invention of new ideas, things, or methods. Innovation tends to stimulate further innovation. Besides sometimes blocking scientific developments, social processes may also encourage and increase innovation, leading to greater productivity.

Numbers of scientists and funds are important for scientific productivity (Price, 1971). By themselves, however, they do not seem to ensure success. Sociologists studying science have tried to identify what social features of scientific groups contribute to their greater or lesser productivity. *Scientific productivity* means making new discoveries, confirming or disconfirming theoretical hypotheses through experimentation and other types of research, and publishing the results of that research. At the national level, the relatively small British, German, and Swiss scientific communities have won Nobel prizes and produced scientific papers at a disproportionately high rate for their numbers and financing since 1950 (Collins, 1975). There are many cases of one research laboratory, with financial and staff resources similar to another, producing many more inventions and discoveries than others. Such occurrences suggest that although adequate resources are necessary for scientific and technological advances, they do not guarantee results.

Several other factors seem to enhance productivity. Where there is maximum competition between research centers innovation will be greater, assuming that all rewards are not controlled by a single organization (Collins, 1975). This permits a number of alternative approaches to be pursued. Innovations are also more likely to occur where independent disciplines come into contact or where an individual is trained in one field but takes a job teaching or doing research in a different but related field. This has happened when people trained in biology moved into psychology and when mathematicians shifted into sociology. Laboratories that are organized in a hierarchical rather than a decentralized democratic way limit scientific productivity in a field by crimping the career chances of younger scientists (Ben-David and Zloczower, 1962) or by inducing premature conformity to ways of solving problems.

Young people are the source of many new ideas and innovations in science because they are not wedded to already established ways of doing things. The ease with which many young people have accepted computers is a good example of their openness to technological changes.

These general principles are illustrated by the case of the University of California at Berkeley's work in microelectronics. The founders of that program established a situation in which experimental facilities and equipment are shared among faculty people, a setup that is uncommon in American universities and virtually unknown in other countries. Not only does the arrangement mean that together the researchers have better facilities than any one of them could have singly, it also means that the researchers communicate and learn from one another as they pursue their own work. These factors appear to have contributed to the worldwide leadership of that department in microelectronics (Hodges, 1979).

In an industrial setting, technological innovations are encouraged by companies that not only reward successful new ideas, but also avoid punishing failures. Innovation flourishes when the producer of an unsuccessful idea is encouraged to try a second and often even a third time to come up with something new. In addition, scientific productivity is high in organizations in which ideas are solicited from everyone from top executives to middle managers to customers—without regard to the rank of the originator (Ingrassia, 1980).

Certain patterns run through a number of major industrial innovations, including the development of the IBM 360 computer, the introduction of the Xerox 914, the development of synthetic rubber by the petrochemical industry during World War II, and Data General's creation of the MV/8000 computer introduced in 1980 (Kidder, 1981; Quinn, 1979). The facilitating conditions in all those situations include these:

1. Strong incentives for successful development at the corporate level, whether from gains in market share or increased profits.
2. For those doing the work, the goals of the project needed to be clear to all and to inspire fervent commitment. Making more money rarely brings this level of commitment, but creating a significant technical advance can spur people to new efforts.
3. While the goal needed to be clearly defined by management, the people working on the project needed to have important roles in finding the particular technologies or solutions for meeting those needs.
4. These firms encouraged multiple competing approaches at both the basic research and the development stages. J. Thomas West of Data General heightened a dispute among engineers into almost a blood feud, but in the process raised performance to new peaks.
5. The companies also involved the people who would eventually use, make, install, or service the product or system they were designing.
6. At the corporate level, there was a longer than usual time horizon on the major innovation (10 to 20 years or longer). Data General was an exception in that an unusually short time (18 months) was available. In that case, the time limit was part of the challenge.
7. There was support for risky projects from top management.

One problem with technological innovation in organizations is the concern for profits. Many companies purposely keep research expenditures low so that they will not eat into profits. Such corporate behavior may keep profits sound in the short run but hurt them in later years, when the lack of research results in fewer new products to sell. One solution is for organizations to mix short-range and long-range projects. One company expects to get 25 percent of its total sales each year from products that did not exist five years earlier. Other companies have a special fund to finance long-shot projects. At Texas Instruments, which has such a fund, about half of the projects fail, a record that leaves the company unperturbed. Another company offers cash incentives to inventors and enables top scientists to earn more than the managers to whom they report. The incentives show that technical creativity is highly valued and will be rewarded (Ingrassia, 1980).

In one study, creative ability, as measured by social researchers, was not necessarily related to scientific productivity (Pelz and Andrews, 1966). Instead, the study showed the significance of the delicate interplay between personal characteristics and the social organization of scientific work. Several work situations seemed to encourage high levels of productivity from the scientists' creative abilities, including working on a project or specializing in an area for a relatively short time, working on a team that was not too tightly coordinated, having the opportunity to influence important decisions, and having the facilities to communicate new ideas to others (Pelz and Andrews, 1966). Highly creative scientists who worked in environments where new ideas were not valued tended to become frustrated and to produce less than moderately creative scientists in better settings.

Scientific productivity has important implications for economic development, controversies over science policies, and the democratic governance of science. In other words, the relationship between science and society affects and is affected by scientific productivity.

SCIENCE AND SOCIETY

Factors within as well as outside science may influence its direction. Wars and revolutions, famine and plague, sea exploration, economic booms and busts, religious revivals, and secular ideologies will affect staffing, social support for science, the material apparatus, and even the areas considered important for research. Just as events and institutions outside science may affect what happens within it, so also may science influence the position of one nation relative to others—for example by accelerating the economic growth of a society or by increasing its military prowess. Within a society, controversies over the safety and desirability of various science policies may provoke public debate and protest. Such controversies raise serious issues about the place of knowledge and participation in the creation of science policy in a democracy.

SCIENCE AND ECONOMIC PRODUCTIVITY

Like a robust worker in the prime of life, American productivity seemed healthy for nearly 20 years after World War II. The annual rate of increase in labor productivity (output per hour) averaged 3.2 percent in the period from 1948 to 1965, slowed to 2.3 percent in the 1965 to 1973 period, and tumbled to only 1.2 percent in the 1973 to 1978 period (Federal Reserve Bank of San Francisco, 1980). By 1978 the rate had dropped to 0.5 percent, and in the second quarter of 1981, American productivity *declined* 2.4 percent (Stockton, 1981, p. 16).

The past economic productivity in the United States may have drawn heavily on scientific and technological innovation. Some economists estimate that nearly half of the economic growth of the United States between 1929 and 1969 was due to technical innovation (Tesar, 1978). Can this trend continue? The possibilities for scientific advances include computers that think like humans and mechanical robots that work better than humans. Gene-splicing techniques for recombining the DNA building blocks of cells are creating new organisms that can fight diseases like hoof and mouth, which afflicts cattle. Soon it may be possible to isolate the genes of molds that produce the nitrates in soil needed by plants and splice them into the genetic structure of the plants, eliminating the need for chemical fertilizers. Tiny manmade organisms may be able to digest oil spills, thus minimizing damage to

Technical innovations, such as these robotic welders in automobile manufacturing, often increase economic productivity.

the environment. The energy crisis may be partially solved by technologies such as silicon photovoltaic cells that can convert sunlight directly into electricity. Such discoveries suggest that we stand on the brink of a great technological transformation.

Which societies are in the best position to capitalize on these tremendous scientific developments? Japan, Germany, and Great Britain, at least, are making a concerted effort to capture some of the new electronic developments. A five-year program is under way in Japan, financed by $250 million in government and industrial money, to develop microelectronic technologies and production equipment. The British government has invested at least $90 million in a new company to develop and manufacture large-scale integrated circuits used in computers and other electronic devices. The Japanese, the Germans, and the Russians have increased the proportion of GNP earmarked for research and development. The United States has been reducing its investment. The development and application of science requires resources and supportive settings. The basic research support that the U.S. government has been providing in recent years has not kept pace with inflation. Although business support for basic research has been increasing, it has not been rising fast enough to close the gap.

An estimated $77 billion of federal and private money was spent on research and development in the United States in 1982. This represents 2 percent of the total gross national product, and is down from 3 percent of GNP in 1964 (U.S. Bureau of the Census, 1982a, p. 593). One consequence of this decline in funding may be the 25 percent decrease in the number of patents issued to Americans for new inventions since 1971. At the same time, the number issued to foreigners has risen 14 percent. Since 1975, noncitizens have received more than one-third of all patents issued by the Patent Office, compared with one-fifth 10 years ago. This is just one symptom which suggests that American innovation may be declining. No one knows how much money for research and development is enough. Furthermore, legislators, members of the public, and business leaders need to believe that more money spent on research and development will result in a stronger economy and more jobs.

THE STATE OF SCIENCE IN THE UNITED STATES

Sociologists have offered several explanations for the declining rate of scientific development in the United States. These include a shortage of faculty to teach science and engineering, the rapid exportation of new technological breakthroughs by multinational corporations, and the diversion of existing scientific and technological personnel into military research and development.

Japan, with half the population of the United States, graduated 19,257 electrical engineers with bachelor's and master's degrees or doctorates in 1977, while the United States produced a total of 14,290. An estimated one-third to one-half of engineering doctoral students in the United States are from foreign countries. High salaries for students graduating with a bachelor's degree in engineering serve to diminish the number who are interested in pursuing graduate degrees. The result is a major shortage of faculty to teach engineering students, making it difficult to expand research and the training of new engineers. Countries that are able to expand their training programs (or send their students to the United States for training) will be in a better position to maximize technological developments.

In addition to not keeping pace with the demand for well-trained scientific personnel, the United States has changed its policy about exporting technology. As recently as the late 1960s, firms in the United States would not sell their most advanced (called "front-end") technology to other countries because they would lose their competitive advantage by doing so. Now many U.S. firms have overseas subsidiaries that are using the newest technologies. Sometimes the latest technology is licensed to a foreign company, as when the Amdahl Corporation licensed its state-of-the-art computer technology to Fujitsu, a Japanese computer maker (Blumberg, 1980). Well-developed foreign firms are then able to save the research and development costs that went into producing a given level of technology and to use that technology as a springboard for further advances. Such a step may accelerate the research and development of foreign technology, but it does nothing for the state of science and technology in the United States. (Such sales or licensing agreements do a great deal for the short-term balance sheets of multinational corporations, however.)

The third, and perhaps most significant, explanation for the slowing growth of American science and technology is the $2000 billion the United States has spent on military activities since 1946. Since World War II ended, the United States has spent a larger share of its gross national product on the military than any other advanced capitalist nation. (This does not include the Soviet Union.) The United States has spent about 9 percent of its GNP on the military, compared to less than 1 percent in Japan (Symanski, 1973). Some of these expenditures have been directed at scientific research and development, but usually they tend to be quite specifically applied to military or space efforts and do not support basic research in a broad variety of fields. Considerable scientific talent and resources have been devoted to research on nerve gas, but rather little to sickle cell anemia.

A permanent military economy not only soaks up large numbers of scientists and technologists, drawing them away from other forms of research, but the products of their research tend to be unproductive for improving human life or enhancing economic prosperity (Melman, 1974; Blumberg, 1980). This is not to say that life-enhancing scientific or technical breakthroughs never occur as the result of military research and development, but simply that the same amount of money spent on a more general range of scientific investigation would have many more productive and useful results.

A number of social analysts suggest that one reason American science and technology has declined is because so much of it has been applied to military efforts such as the development of these MX Intercontinental Missiles rather than to more broadly useful scientific research.

CONTROVERSIAL ISSUES IN SCIENCE POLICY

A number of controversies have swirled around science policy in the United States in recent years, but most of them have not dealt with how much money should be spent on the military compared to basic scientific research or training. Instead, the public has tended to become concerned about close-to-home issues like gene-splicing and the disposal of radioactive and poisonous waste products. These issues affect people in their own backyards, and they have generated considerable public discussion and protest.

Gene-Splicing

Critics of gene-splicing say scientists should abandon their belief that they can pursue new knowledge, regardless of the possible consequences to society. Gene-splicing, or recombinant DNA experiments, consists of cutting up the long, threadlike molecules of DNA (the substance that carries genetic instructions to cells) from several different organisms, combining them, and inserting them into a hospitable cell where they can grow. Although DNA mutations have occurred in nature for years, producing new traits in animals and plants, the splices done by scientists permit combinations that would not occur in nature because the organisms involved would not normally interbreed. Right now, for example, insulin for diabetics can be produced only by the pancreas of cattle or pigs, but new ways of producing insulin may be possible through recombinant DNA.

The risk involved in this new procedure is that the DNA pieces will combine in new, unforeseen ways, possibly producing a dangerous bacteria strain harmful to life that could rapidly reproduce itself and could not be stopped by any known methods. Recognizing this risk, scientists themselves sounded the alarm in 1973. A group of scientists wrote an open letter in the journal *Science* in 1974, asking the National

Academy of Sciences (NAS) to establish a committee to consider various problems of recombinant DNA. The committee formed by NAS responded with a recommendation for a moratorium on certain types of gene-splicing research and asked the National Institutes of Health to establish guidelines. The guidelines set four levels of risk and prescribed containment conditions for each level. These steps heightened public fear of recombinant DNA research.

A question arose regarding whether molecular biologists should be allowed to police themselves, or whether the public had a legal right to restrict their research. Public hearings in the city council in Cambridge, Massachusetts, led to a two-year moratorium on research at Harvard University and the Massachusetts Institute of Technology that was lifted in 1977. Other cities also held hearings, and the debate carried over in the U.S. Congress, which drew up federal legislative proposals. Many scientists feared that the laws would be too restrictive. They pointed out that humanity faces problems of disease, malnutrition, and pollution, all of which might be helped by research into gene-splicing, and that to allow fears of unknown hazards to interfere with promising solutions to existing problems seemed short-sighted.

Nuclear Waste Disposal

Difficulties also surround the problem of nuclear wastes, since a safe and permanent way to dispose of them remains to be found. To some observers, this problem represents the greatest obstacle in the way of extended use of atomic power (Tinker, 1979). Societies utilizing atomic power have to face the problem of what to do with certain kinds of highly radioactive waste produced in nuclear reactors. One highly radioactive substance, plutonium-239, takes 488,000 years to drop to a radioactive level of less than one-millionth of its initial levels. No method of containment has ever been tested for that long, nor has a solution been found for where to place such wastes so they will not escape into the air or water (Tinker, 1979, p. 366). When the future of humanity on this planet is conceived of in terms of hundreds of thousands or millions of years, it is possible to imagine the extent of the problem of protecting future generations from accidentally finding and irrecoverably releasing nuclear wastes into the earth's ecosystem.

IMPLICATIONS FOR DEMOCRATIC GOVERNANCE

These examples show that the practice of science and public policy are coming together at increasingly important decision points. Any society with great scientific capabilities faces the problem of how to regulate and control scientific and technological innovations. Unlike many other social institutions, science is one social institution we cannot ignore. If people do not like the institution of the family, they can choose not to re-create it in their adult lives. If they dislike the institutional forms of religion, they can remain unaffiliated. If they dislike the political institutions of a given state, they can move to another nation or work to elect another party. The institution of science, however, may affect us in ways that we cannot escape. If the water or air becomes polluted, there may be no alternatives available. If a deadly virus escapes and ravages the world, there may be no safe haven. If the temperature of the earth is raised and more of the polar ice caps melt, the east and west coasts of the United States may be under 30 feet of water. A small drop in the earth's temperature could set the world on a path to another ice age. Unleashing even a small percentage of the world's nuclear weapon arsenal could destroy life as we know it.

These examples illustrate how powerfully science may affect our lives. In many ways, scientific and technological developments have outrun the forms of social organization we have for creating an orderly and democratic means to debate and decide what policies to pursue. The people who will be affected have little chance to learn about, discuss, and decide what to do about a particular development.

Public forums in which policies regarding the applications of scientific and technical developments and perhaps the allocation of resources into various areas of research and development can be discussed require that several conditions be met. People need to be educated and informed about scientific issues. Laypersons, including leaders of public agencies and elected officials, are often unable to assess the scientific evidence and arguments advanced on both sides of a policy issue. Such a situation poses serious problems for governance and decision-making in a democracy: How can participatory democracy be maintained when people do not understand the scientific principles on which a debate hinges? At the very least, nonscientists need to receive a good science education in school and have continuing education in science through books, magazines, television, and other media. They need to be willing to take the time and trouble to educate themselves about the key issues that need to be decided.

Scientists themselves are frequently divided on the risks involved in various procedures and how they evaluate those dangers. These scientists need to be able to explain in language that is understandable to nonscientists what the issues and what the benefits and dangers of various courses of action are. Scientists and nonscientists together need to discuss and decide issues of science policy. As things stand presently, laypersons can only protest or obstruct already decided policy, such as decisions to build a nuclear power plant or an industrial waste dump. There is no social mechanism for debating and voting on policies before they are decided.

The scientific community is understandably wary about the possible tyranny of ignorance that might result from debating science issues in a political arena. The dangers of unbridled political control over scientific thought are well documented. In the Soviet Union, for instance, Lysenkoism was the only form of genetics that could be taught in universities or used in agricultural experiments. This body of doctrine denied the existence of genes and believed that an organism could be changed by its environment and that those changes could be passed on to its offspring. This politically determined genetic position dominated Soviet agriculture and education from the 1930s to the 1960s, when it was discredited. Another example occurred in Nazi Germany, where the state declared the genetic superiority of the Aryan race in an effort to provide some scientific legitimacy for the persecution of Jews.

These examples show what happens when scientific evidence is overruled by political power. Clearly, scientific theories and research results cannot be determined by popular vote. What is done with those theories and research findings, however, may affect many people in a society. Science policies are more likely to be viewed as legitimate and science more likely to receive public support if the people who will be affected have a voice in forming the policies. Without such participation, a society runs the risk that certain avenues of scientific research and development (nuclear power and weapons or sugar-coated cereals) are vigorously pursued, while others (soil erosion or preventive medicine) are neglected. The lack of citizen participation in issues of science policy also runs the risk of developing a technocratic elite that loses touch with the concerns of the general population and is no longer able to weigh those concerns when making decisions.

Summary

1. The results of scientific activities affect us on a daily basis. The institution of science refers to the community devoted to developing theories and methods for understanding the physical and social world. The term "science" is also used to refer to the knowledge produced by that community.

2. Technology refers to the practical applications of scientific knowledge. Science applications have produced far-reaching benefits, but they have also raised concerns about possible negative effects.

3. The rise of modern science as we know it began in the fifteenth century. Scientific development was spurred on by the printing press, the lowering of class barriers between theoretical and practical knowledge, and new approaches to understanding the physical world. The start of scientific societies and journals, and subsequent development of university instruction in science, all contributed to the institutional support for science as an activity.

4. Today nearly 3 million scientists and engineers work in the United States, and about one-quarter of them are doing research and development work.

5. In order to flourish in a society, science needs to have continuity and commitment within that society. Resources need to be allocated on a predictable basis, so that people can develop careers in science.

6. The functionalist approach to science emphasizes the interdependence of science with various other institutions in society, stresses that science is a major source of social change, and realizes that there may be positive as well as negative consequences of scientific activity.

7. The conflict approach stresses how the unequal distribution of power and resources in society or within science may shape the direction scientific development takes. It asks which specific groups do and do not benefit from particular policies and practices.

8. Science as a social activity is governed by the norms of universalism, communism, disinterestedness, and organized skepticism. Although sometimes violated in practice, the strong reaction among scientists to such violations suggests the existence of the norms Merton identified.

9. Sociologists have studied productivity within the scientific community and identified a number of conditions that enhance it, including competition between universities, cooperation within organizations, a "safe" environment for innovation, and the chance to influence decisions.

10. Kuhn's work on the nature of scientific revolutions suggests that major scientific paradigms do not change gradually in an evolutionary fashion, but abruptly in a revolutionary way.

11. Popper suggests that scientific views may be tentatively considered true until proved false, but Kuhn indicates that the paradigm guiding a scientist's work may make it difficult to see contradictory evidence. Laypersons and scientists alike may resist new discoveries for a variety of social reasons.

12. Scientific productivity has contributed to the economic development of industrialized countries. Flagging economic productivity in the United States in recent years has generated new concerns about scientific research and development.

13. Sociologists suggest that the declining rate of scientific development in the United States is due to a shortage of science and engineering faculty, the rapid exportation of new technologies, and the diversion of scientific personnel and resources into military research and development.

14. Controversial science policies are often ones that endanger individuals in their own neighborhoods. Gene-splicing and nuclear waste disposal are two issues of science policy that have aroused considerable public controversy.

Key Terms

anomalies
innovation
normal science
paradigm
science
scientific revolution
technology

Part Five

Social Changes and Issues

IF THE FAMILY FARM
GOES
AMERICA'S ECONOMY
IS GONE!
NEW MEXICO

Chapter 19

Social Change, Collective Behavior, and Social Movements

As you read this chapter, social changes are happening all around us: the shrinking size of the American family, soaring rates of divorce, more single parents, a growing "underground" economy, increases in violent and white collar crime, and changing premarital sexual attitudes. *Social change* is a modification or transformation of the way a society is organized. It includes changes in social institutions such as the economy or the family, changes in social stratification, changes in social roles (for example, the relations between blacks and whites or men and women), and social or political revolutions. Social change refers to significant and major changes in patterned social behaviors at the institutional or societal level, rather than to little changes within a small group. This chapter considers social changes both within industrialized nations and in the developing areas of the world. It begins by calling attention to social changes that are currently unfolding and suggests some of their implications for the future. Then we consider major social changes and theories that try to explain them. The second section highlights the close interplay between social change and changes in the physical world, population, economic and agricultural production, scientific and technological development.

Collective behavior includes spontaneous social behavior and more organized social movements. Social movements are often the mechanism by which people work together to guide or suppress particular social changes. The third and fourth sections in the chapter examine the nature of collective behavior and social movements, why they occur, why they take the forms they do, and why they succeed or fail.

One of the major sources of social change in many nations of the world today is the press toward modernization. Theorists have differing views about changes in developing nations and about what should be done to encourage their development. These issues are explored in the final section of the chapter.

MAJOR SOCIAL CHANGES IN OUR TIME

There undoubtedly have been times in human history when the children of one generation grew up and lived a life very similar to that of their grandparents. Today, however, we cannot assume that our lives will be lived in a world that does not change socially or physically. A major series of social changes accompanied the transformation of agricultural societies into industrial societies. That transition was marked by a declining proportion of people who were needed in agriculture, by the growth of railroads, and by the rise of such industries as steelmaking, oil refining, chemical production, and manufacturing. This process was accompanied by the growth of monopoly capitalism, the rise of nation-states and political centralization within them, and demands for expanded political participation. A demographic transition also occurred: societies moved from high birth and death rates to high birth rates and low death rates, and then to a condition of both low birth and death rates. (These social changes are described in Chapter 3; the changes in where people work are shown in Table 14.1; and the demographic transition will be discussed in Chapter 20.)

Today we are living through another series of massive social changes, including shifts within national societies, the globalization of the world economy, the emergence of a world system, and the ever-increasing importance of money, knowledge, and information as sources of power and control on a worldwide basis.

CHANGES WITHIN NATIONAL SOCIETIES

The Western industrial world may be on the brink of a third revolution in productive activity. The first occurred with the transformation of agriculture from sticks and hoes to massive mechanized farming, a process that took many centuries, and the second was the Industrial Revolution of the nineteenth century. The one we are now poised on has been variously called the "post-industrial society" by Daniel Bell (1973), the "third wave" by futurologist Alvin Toffler (1980), and the "micro millennium" by Christopher Evans (1979). Bell suggests that the *post-industrial society* is notable for the greater importance of intellectual rather than manufacturing technology. Knowledge and planning are the key to organized action in modern societies, according to Bell (1973).

All these terms suggest the growing importance of information in our society. The exchange and control of information is now possible on a worldwide basis, due to the rise of jet transportation, worldwide telephone communications, computerized systems that can process large amounts of information from all over the world rapidly, and television satellites. Messages can be beamed throughout the world, distributing news, culture, and advertisements to remote areas. World power and influence still depend to a considerable degree on industrial and military might, but the form in which control is exercised is moving in new directions, shaped by new capacities for data collection, analysis, and transmission.

The potential for such developments is enhanced by the recent growth in the use of microcomputers. They are small and relatively inexpensive and can store and process more information than the room-sized, expensive computers of a decade ago. In the words of microcomputing expert Jim Eldin: "The microcomputer is a watershed technology—like the electric light, the automobile, and the telephone it stands to change our everyday lives more than we can know" (Cornish, 1981, p. 18). Microcomputers play an increasingly important part in inventory control, budgeting, word processing, payroll operations, mailings, and cost calculations. I wrote parts of this book, for example, on a computer with a word-processing program, which means I could store, edit, and print material electronically. In schools and homes, computers are being used to give students individual practice in arithmetic, grammar, geography, spelling, and many other subjects.

Computers, telephones, and satellites allow data to be sent rapidly from one part of the world to another. People or goods can also move quickly around the globe. Video games and videotape machines are booming entertainment industries. These technological developments are changing the nature of work, leisure, and the distribution of people in various parts of the labor market.

In industrial societies, access to capital is a major determinant of power and influence. Some observers, for example Daniel Bell (1973), see the shift from an industrial to a post-industrial society as creating a more open society, since a person's power does not need to depend on inherited wealth, but can be based on skill in analyzing information. Support for this position comes from the increase in the number of new companies started each year. At the height of industrial society in 1950 (when more people worked in manufacturing in the United States than ever before or since), 93,000 new companies were being created annually. Today, more than 450,000 firms are starting up each year. Most of these are information companies, such as computer hardware or software firms. At the same time, however, the very largest companies in the country are controlling more resources than ever before. What Bell overlooks is that access to information is still heavily dependent on the control of capital. As a result, inequalities of wealth and power may become even greater in the future that they have been in the past.

GROWING SPECIALIZATION

The technological developments that are fueling the transformation from an industrial to an information society call for large numbers of scientists, engineers, and technicians. Such people have highly specialized skills. The education and training of these information workers may be related to the expansion and lengthening of educational programs, as well as their specialization. A major result of specialization is the growing need for new mechanisms of integration, and the capacity to link information from a variety of specialties into a coherent frame for decision-making. For instance, information on various diseases around the United States is pulled together in Atlanta, Georgia, at the Center for Disease Control. Individuals who can figure out how an organization can solve important problems using existing computer hardware and software, and who can communicate with both the people who run the organizations and those who run the machines, provide very important bridging functions in our society.

The trend toward greater specialization is reflected in leisure as well as in occupations. The great general interest magazines of the 1940s to 1960s, such as *Look, Life,* and *The Saturday Evening Post,* with circulations exceeding 10 million, have folded. In their place have come more than 4000 special interest magazines, such as *Working Woman, Architectural Digest, Cycle, Runner, Home Video,* and *Stereo Review.* The three big national television networks—ABC, CBS, and NBC—are the *Look, Life,* and *Post* of the 1980s, according to Naisbitt (1981). These general networks are losing viewers to more specialized programs. Their gradual slide from prominence is due to cable television and growing room for choice in home entertainment through VCRs and videodisc players. But at the same time that interests and tastes are becoming more fragmented, economic life is becoming more interdependent.

THE ACCELERATING SHIFT TO A GLOBAL ECONOMY

A *global economy* is one in which the economic life and health of one nation depends on what happens in the other nations around the world. Four illustrations of the trend toward an increasingly global rather than a national economy are the declining capacity of any single nation to dominate the world economy, the growing importance of multinational rather than national corporations, the growth of world trade, and the increase in international banking.

In the post-World War II era, the United States dominated the world economy as Great Britain had in the nineteenth century. But the dominant single country is being replaced by a number of strong industrial nations. In 1971, the United States accounted for 58 of the 100 largest corporations in the world; by 1982, that figure was down to only 30 of the world's 100 largest corporations (Conference Board, 1981, and *Forbes,* July 1982). Right now, Japan is the world's leading industrial power. In 1980 it produced 2 million more cars than any other country, and it had already passed the United States as the world's leading steelmaker.

Part of this growth of multiple rather than solo economic power has occurred because of the expansion of multinational corporations. Multinationals have work forces, sales, and income from a number of nations rather than primarily from one country. In the 1950s, for example, most automobiles were made and sold in the same country by a corporation that tended to be confined to that nation. Now the auto industry is in the process of becoming the first major global industry. By the end of the 1980s, the 30 world auto companies will, as a result of failures or mergers, have consolidated into about 7 or 8 companies that manufacture and sell parts and cars all around the world.

The growth of international manufacturing and marketing is reflected in the skyrocketing volume of world trade. Tape decks from Hong Kong, Japanese cars, running shoes from Korea, Swiss cheese, Danish beer—you no doubt can add some examples of your own to the list—all illustrate the growth of world trade in recent years. The total volume of exports and imports around the world soared from $50 billion in 1965 to more than $500 billion in 1981 (U.S. Bureau of the Census, 1982a), an increase of 1000 percent in 16 years.

A fourth indicator of the growing global economy is the accelerating speed with which money moves around the world. One day in 1974 at the New York Clearinghouse Interbank Payments System (CHIPS), nearly $43 billion was transferred among banks all over the world (Mayer, 1974). By 1982, $200 billion was being shifted on an average day. On its busiest day in 1982, the CHIPS system cleared $389 billion throughout the world, which was more than all the demand deposits in all the commercial banks in the United States that day (Huffell, 1982). Ninety percent of all international payments go through this clearinghouse, so these figures provide a reasonable measure of the magnitude of international banking transactions.

Together these four indicators suggest that the processes affecting the economy of a single nation are no longer totally within its borders. This means that financial and manufacturing decisions made far away may have major economic and social consequences for individuals. Decisions determining interest rates, locations of plants, and layoffs will tend to be influenced by events farther and farther away from the people being affected.

THE GROWING GAP BETWEEN RICH AND POOR NATIONS

Cheap energy and labor were the twin pillars supporting the rapid industrial expansion of Western Europe and especially the United States. Although some developing nations still supply cheap labor, the disappearance of cheap energy in the world today affects agricultural, industrial, and transportation development in all nations. The gradual depletion of fossil fuels, the intensifying problem of producing enough food for the growing world population, more competitive world markets, growing water shortages, and the pollution of air and water supplies all suggest that developing nations of the world will have greater difficulty raising their standard of living than did the early industrializers.

As industries, information systems, banking, energy sources, and nuclear capabilities become increasingly concentrated, and as technology becomes increasingly sophisticated, the power and wealth of nations that control major nuclear, industrial, and information resources will intensify, while nations without such resources will have less food, industry, information, and world power.

As Figure 19.1 shows, this gap is reflected in the income levels, life expectancies, and illiteracy rates of highly industrialized compared to developing nations. People living in Switzerland have a per capita share of their nation's gross national

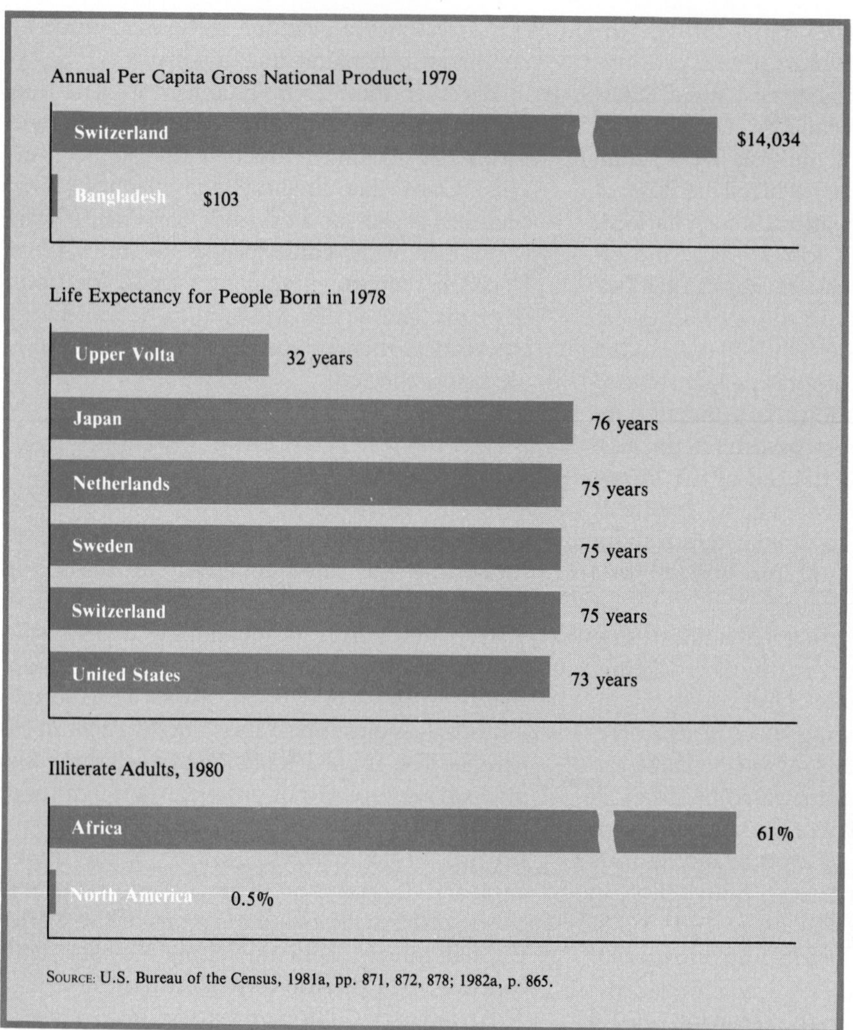

Figure 19.1 Life Chances in Developing and Industrialized Countries

product that is 136 times more than that of individuals in the poor country of Bangladesh. People in the industrialized countries of Japan, the Netherlands, Sweden, and Switzerland live more than twice as long, on the average, than people in an impoverished country like Upper Volta. While exact rates of illiteracy are difficult to obtain, many more people in Africa are unable to read compared to the number in North America. And the enormous gap between largely agricultural nations and highly industrialized nations appears to be growing rather than shrinking.

ESCALATING DESTRUCTIVE POSSIBILITIES

The social changes described here are insignificant when compared to the possibility of the total ruin that could result from a nuclear attack. The experience of several individuals who lived during the two atomic bombs dropped on Japan in 1945 is portrayed in the box on pp. 504–505. The pain, suffering, and death of millions of innocent civilians that may be caused by a warring nation in a nuclear attack far exceeds the destruc-

Living Beneath the Atomic Cloud

Michiko Ogino, 10 years old, was left in charge of his younger sisters when his mother went out to the fields to pick eggplants. The bomb brought the house down on them all, leaving his 2-year-old sister with her legs pinned under a cross-beam:

Mamma was bombed at noon
When getting eggplants in the field,
Short, red and crisp her hair stood,
Tender and red her skin was all over.

So Mrs. Ogino, although the clothes were burned from her body and she had received a fatal dose of radiation, could still run back from the fields to succor her children. One after another, passing sailors and neighbors heaved at the beam to release the trapped 2-year-old, failed, and, bowing with Japanese courtesy, went on their way to help others.

Mother was looking down at my little sister. Tiny eyes looked up from below. Mother looked around, studying the way the beams were piled up. Then she got into an opening under the beam, and putting her right shoulder under a portion of it, she strained with all her might. We heard a cracking sound and the beams were lifted a little. My little sister's legs were freed.

Peeled off was the skin
  over her shoulder
That once lifted the beam
  off my sister.
Constant blood was spurting
From the sore flesh appearing. . . .

Mrs. Ogino died that night. Fujio Tsujimoto, who was 5 years old, was in the playground of Yamazato Primary School, Nagasaki, just before the bomb dropped. Hearing the sound of a plane, he grabbed his grandmother's hand and they were the first into the deepest part of the air-raid shelter. The entrance to the shelter, as well as the playground, was covered with the dying. "My brothers and sisters didn't get to the shelter in time, they were burnt and crying. Half an hour later, my mother appeared. She was covered with blood. She had been making lunch at home when the bomb was dropped."

"My younger sisters died the next day. My mother—she also died the next day. And then my older brother died. . . .

The survivors made a pile of wood on the playground and began to cremate the corpses. My brother was burned. Mother also was burned and quickly turned to white bones which dropped down among the live coals. I cried as I looked on the scene. Grandmother was also watching, praying with a rosary. . . .

I am now in the fourth grade at Yamazato Primary School. That playground of terrible memories is now completely cleared and my friends play there happily. I play with my friends there too, but sometimes I suddenly remember that awful day. When I do, I squat down on the spot where we cremated our mother and touch the earth with my fingers. When I dig deep in the ground with a piece of bamboo, several pieces of charcoal appear. Looking at the spot for a while, I can dimly see my mother's image in the earth. So when I see someone else walking on that place, it makes me very angry."

The quoted material is testimony of the children of Nagasaki that appears in *Living Beneath the Atomic Cloud.* What it makes clear is that the "instant" of detonation was protracted over days and weeks, and was full, not only of physical misery but of unutterable yearning and suffering.. . . .

Tens of thousands have died subsequently from the aftereffects of that day—chiefly leukemia, and various cancers and diseases of the blood and digestive organs.

One remarkable consequence of those two detonations is that the survivors in those two cities, and the descendants of the sufferers, were transformed into advocates, not of revenge but of international understanding and peace. To this day, work for peace is regarded as a civic duty, and the mayors of Nagasaki and Hiroshima regard this work as the principal obligation of their offices.

SOURCE: Adapted from E. P. Thompson, "A Letter to America." *The Nation,* January 24, 1981, pp. 80–81.

tive potential previously available to any society on earth.

The nuclear bombs that now exist are many times more powerful than those used by the United States in Japan. The United States and the Soviet Union together have more than 10,000 nuclear warheads. If only 1 percent of nuclear weapons survived a nuclear exchange, the Soviets would still have enough warheads left to destroy more than 50 of the largest cities in the United States—each to a far greater extent than Hiroshima (Thompson, 1981). Such realizations have led many observers to conclude that no one can "win" a nuclear exchange.

Because nuclear weapons have transformed the means of waging war, a number of religious leaders have spoken out against them. In 1981, for example, the senior Anglican bishops declared that the Christian concept of a "just war" did not apply in a nuclear age, and they called for multilateral nuclear disarmament. Other religious leaders played an active role in the march for disarmament in New York City in 1982, when more than 750,000 people assembled in Central Park.

SOURCES AND THEORIES OF SOCIAL CHANGE

"Vancouver! Vancouver! This is it. . . ." With those words—tinged with excitement rather than panic, hearers said—David Johnston, geologist for the United States Geological Survey, announced the end of calm and the start of cataclysm. Thirty-year-old blond-bearded David was stationed at a USGS camp called Coldwater II, six miles from [the top of Mount St. Helens on May 18, 1980] to monitor eruptions.

Those words were his last. The eruption he reported was powerful and unexpectedly lateral. Much of the initial blast was nozzled horizontally, fanning out northwest and northeast, its hurricane wave of scalding gases and fire-hot debris traveling at 200 miles an hour. Its force catapulted the geologist and the house trailer that sheltered him off a high ridge and into space above Coldwater Creek. His body has yet to be found. . . . North and west of the mountain top, 150-foot Douglas firs were uprooted or broken like brittle straws for distances as far as 17 miles from the mountain. . . . A roiling pillar of ash plumed eastward into a widening dark cloud that would give Yakima, 85 miles distant, midnight blackness at 9:30 A.M. and would last the day. Much of eastern Washington, northern Idaho, and western Montana would be brought to a halt by the ashfall. Within days the silt from the mountain would reach the Pacific, after causing destructive floods . . . and closing the busy Columbia River to deep-draft ships. (Findley, 1981, pp. 17–18)

The blast from Mount St. Helens was the first volcanic event in the contiguous 48 states in 63 years. It devastated an area of more than 200 square miles, killed at least 34 people, imperiled thousands of others, and triggered destructive floods and mudflows. At least 32 more persons were listed as missing. Forestry, farming, and tourism were all gravely affected by the heat, ash, floods, and mudflows created by the blast. The damage was estimated as being in excess of $2 billion.

Most social changes do not occur as cataclysmically as those following the eruption of Mount St. Helens. Usually, no single factor accounts for all the social changes that occur in the world, although the major civilization of Pompeii was destroyed suddenly when Mt. Vesuvius erupted in Italy in A.D. 79. Some of the notable factors that cause social change are changes in the physical environment, including shifting energy sources; population changes; scientific and technological developments; ideas and ideologies; and cultural innovation and diffusion.

CHANGES IN THE PHYSICAL ENVIRONMENT

No one can predict precisely how a particular change in the physical environment will affect social life, but we do know that major physical changes such as a volcano or earthquake may produce certain short- and long-term social changes. Floods, typhoons, hurricanes, earthquakes, volcanic eruptions, and coal mine cave-ins all tend to produce a concerted social effort against a common threat in the physical environment. People cooperate, and groups form to rescue individuals who are trapped and to dig out survivors and property.

About 13,000 years ago, the temperature of the world gradually increased and the thick glaciers that had covered much of North America and Northern Europe began melting away. As the ice receded, forests gradually took over most of the grassy plains, where large animals such as the woolly mammoth, woolly rhinoceros, steppe bison, and giant elk, and numerous types of goats had grazed. The reduction of grasslands combined with a steady growth in the human population produced a crisis. Many large animals were hunted into extinction. By 7000 B.C., 32 genera of large animals became extinct in North America, including horses, oxen, elephants, camels, ground sloths, and giant rodents. Gradually, the various tribes began to rely on plants for ever-greater amounts of their food. The extinction of large meat animals triggered the shift to an agricultural form of food production in both the Old and the New Worlds (Harris, 1977). Changes in the physical world gradually transformed social life. Agricultural communities were much more permanent than nomadic groups.

The physical environment of a society may also influence the rate of social change by the way geography encourages or discourages contact between societies. Countries such as Yugoslavia, which have been invaded and occupied by various different tribes, reflect such social encounters in their language, customs, and cooking. Relatively isolated societies, protected by oceans or mountains from other social groups, over time develop their own language and customs that tend to distinguish them from other societies. Such societies are not exposed to new ways, so they have little chance for change as a result of cultural diffusion from other societies. Physically isolated societies are likely to experience social change from dramatic physical events, such as an earthquake or volcano, or through their own invention and discovery. Unless they face major new problems needing solution, however, their rate of invention may be slow. Invention is encouraged by other inventions and by new needs.

POPULATION CHANGES

The total number of people in a society, birth and death rates, the relative size of different age groups, and patterns of migration and settlement within their geographic territory all influence social changes.

When adequate food is available, populations tend to increase in size. As they grow, they need to find better ways to produce more food to feed ever-larger numbers of people. This need may produce agricultural innovations, which in turn may require new forms of social organization. Large-scale farming such as that practiced on the American Plains requires considerable technology and planning both for producing food and for distributing it.

If existing land and technology are unable to support the population, one of three social changes will almost certainly occur. People will starve in large numbers; there will be struggle and conflict and perhaps even war in order to obtain food; or large numbers of people will migrate to what they hope will be more hospitable areas. In the last decade we have witnessed all three of these responses to hunger in places as far afield as Southeast Asia, East Africa, and Haiti.

The social changes wrought by large-scale migrations are evident in the history of the United States. The early waves of immigrants in the nineteenth century included Germans, Scandinavians, large numbers of Irish, and then Italians. They were followed by Eastern Europeans. In 1903, more than 800,000 people came to the United States, and about 1,000,000 came in each of the next 10 years. Of the 13 million or so immigrants to the United States between 1897 and 1914, fully 10 million were from Southern and Eastern Europe. One of the results of this tide of new arrivals was the passage in 1924 of restrictive legislation virtually closing the nation's doors to further immigration from those regions for decades to come. Each new group brought cultural ideas and practices that aroused various responses among the existing population. For example, the Prohibition Amendment to the U.S. Constitution forbidding the sale of alcoholic beverages for anything but medicinal purposes has been attributed to a reaction against heavy drinking by urban immigrants.

Selective loosening of immigration quotas in recent years has led to the effects of migration continuing today. In recent years Miami, Florida, has become 36 percent Hispanic, and San Antonio, Texas, 45 percent Hispanic, according to the 1980 census. Although the percentage of Hispanics in Los Angeles–Long Beach is only 28 percent, in absolute numbers that means more than 2 million people. Such an influx of migrants with a different language and culture invariably stirs social changes in language, food, music, and family size. Some observers suggest that the riots by black Americans in Miami in 1980 were a reaction to their feeling of being squeezed out of jobs by new immigrants.

Gradual physical changes, like prolonged droughts, may also generate changes. The great drought in the American Plains in the 1930s drove thousands of farmers off the land. Oklahoma was especially badly hit. Crops never came up or shriveled on the stalk. Farmers couldn't pay their mortgages, and many lost their homes and their land. Nearly half a million migrated to California, where they eked out livings as migrant laborers. Their arrival on the West Coast produced a series of social conflicts and changes. Homeless people without jobs drifted from place to place, putting up shantytowns wherever they could, to the distress of existing residents. Local wages sagged below their already low rates. This example shows how two separate sources of social change—environmental changes and population shifts—interact to produce marked social changes.

Another major migration that caused social changes in the United States was the exodus of rural blacks from southern farms in the 1940s. Between 1940 and 1966, 3.7 million blacks moved from the southern states to the largest northern cities (Piven and Cloward, 1971). As

Major migrations often cause significant social changes, as in the Cuban migrations to southern Florida. This banker of Cuban origin has moved into a key financial position.

the farms became mechanized the workers lost their jobs, and southern blacks migrated to major industrial cities such as Chicago, Detroit, Cleveland, St. Louis, New York, and Cincinnati. Rural blacks were exposed to drugs, gambling, thievery, prostitution, youth gangs, economic hardship, and racism. In recent years reverse migration has occurred, as some blacks have returned to southern cities (Herbers, 1981).

American society faces the prospect of yet another major wave of internal migration as business, industry, and population move from the North, for instance out of New York and Rhode Island, to the South and the Southwest, especially to California, Texas, Arizona, and Florida. More of the population of the United States now lives in the South and West than in the North, for the first time in the nation's history, according to the 1980 census. In the 1970s, 90 percent of the country's growth occurred in the South and West, while such symbols of northern industrialism as Chicago, Cleveland, Detroit, and Pittsburgh lost up to 26 percent of their populations (Naisbitt, 1981). During the decade of the 1970s, the South gained 3433 people per day while the Northeast gained only 21 people per day, on the average (Russell and Robey, 1981). The South and West's gains in people, jobs, money, and political power have meant a tilting of influence and opportunity away from the traditionally powerful industrial heartland and Northeast toward a new geographic area of the United States. A new financial empire is rising in Los Angeles and Houston.

Social changes are also spurred by changes in the age distribution within a population. In the United States, the "baby boom" after World War II produced a bulge of young people who needed schools and colleges. In the 1980s that generation is storming the market for jobs, houses, and consumer goods. As they age, the "graying" of the population will continue, with a growing group of retired people needing health care and other social programs. As the baby boom members pass through each stage of the life cycle, their disproportionately large number means that they create a ripple of social changes all around them, including the scarcity of teachers, housing, and jobs. The "birth dearth" (shortage of births in recent decades) that has followed in their wake has created equally profound, if opposite, changes. Schools are closing because there are fewer children to attend them; colleges and universities are worried they will have too few students in the future; and some far-sighted employers are realizing that there may be labor shortages in the 1990s.

SCIENTIFIC AND TECHNOLOGICAL DEVELOPMENTS

Many of the agricultural and industrial transformations noted earlier, along with the profound social changes they triggered, have been caused by scientific or technological breakthroughs. There is always an interplay between technical and social changes. Without a social and cultural climate that permits change, the pace of technical change slows. Once technological developments occur, their potential for social change is enormous. The jet engine, for example, underwent a long development from 1930, when the first patent was filed by the British engineer Frank Whittle, to 1942, when the first usable engine was built (Ziman, 1976). Spurred by the war effort, Britain raced to build a jet fighter plane. In Germany, meanwhile, engineers were working on a jet plane as well, but the German Air Ministry was committed to piston airplanes and failed to support the effort adequately. The German Air Ministry was able to resist technical changes. As a result, Germany was unable to gain air superiority with a fast jet fighter during World War II (Ziman, 1976).

History is filled with instances of social changes set in motion by technological changes. The European conquest of the world in the sixteenth to eighteenth centuries, for instance, was made possible by the three-masted sea-going galleons and the use of cannons. Several technical developments in agriculture, including the horseshoe, the shoulder harness, the iron-tipped plow, and a system of three-crop rotation, produced widespread social changes. The increased crop yields resulting from these developments raised the peasants' standard of living and allowed them to buy manufactured goods. The production of surplus food allowed the growth of cities. The rise of cities created a new social class—merchants and skilled artisans—who helped to create capitalism. The invention of the steam engine and the development of ways of using it to power spinning and weaving operations enabled the Industrial Revolution to occur when and where it did (White, 1962).

More recently, the development of jet aircraft broke down the social isolation of many regions in the world, accelerating exposure to new peoples and ideas, just as years earlier the automobile did the same for many regions in the United States. Movies and television have spread certain cultural ideas around the world by making people aware of lives and experiences far different from their own.

The scientific development with the greatest potential for social change is the emergence of nuclear weaponry. It contains the frightening possibility of destroying civilization unless social and political restraints are exercised. If civilization is not destroyed by nuclear weapons, another response to their existence might be the formation of a powerful world government that could regulate their use. Such a prospect seems dim at the moment, given the general levels of distrust among nations and their unwillingness to give up any national sovereignty. The likelihood of such a change depends on how serious a threat to survival nuclear weaponry is perceived to be by government leaders.

In medicine, technical advances have changed the definition of death. In the past, someone who had stopped breathing and whose heart had ceased to beat was considered dead. Now, with ways of stimulating the heart to resume beating and respirators to aid breathing, the medical definition of death has been changed to the cessation of brain waves. This has resulted in a number of cases of individuals who were "dead" with respect to everything except their brain waves. Serious ethical controversies swirl around the issue of whether their respirators should be disconnected and who has the authority to make such a decision. Furthermore, who should bear the tremendous expense of sustaining life in such a form? As these issues are resolved, they will lead to further social changes arising from various medical technologies. Beyond sustaining life on a mechanical basis, technical medical developments have lengthened life expectancy and cut the death rates in industrial socieities, resulting in much older populations.

Technological Determinism?

Technological developments unquestionably cause social changes. Some sociologists go so far as to argue that there is a kind of *technological determinism* that shapes social life in rather fixed ways. Such a view of word processing on computers, for instance, suggests that technology will inevitably lead to certain social arrangements, such as the greater independence of machine operators. In fact, however, work involving such technology may be socially organized in various ways, only some of which result in greater worker autonomy. Thus, while technical developments undoubtedly influence social life, it is not possible to predict exactly what form the social changes will take. As the American automobile was rising in importance, a social observer might have predicted that cars would influence culture and be used to express social status, but could not have said exactly how this would occur. Most forms of technological development allow for several possible forms of social response.

Culture Lag

Cultural values and practices change more slowly than technical developments. Humans tend to accept new tools and technological inventions more rapidly than they embrace cultural changes and new ideas. William Ogburn (1922) called this process *culture lag* between material innovations and cultural practices. For example, rapidly growing rates of population growth in early stages of modernization reflect a cultural lag. The ideal of large families persists even though changing economic conditions make children an economic liability rather than an asset.

Some observers suggest that for each technical advance, there is a compensatory cultural development. Naisbitt (1981) calls this the "high tech/high touch" syndrome. He believes that when any major technology is introduced into a society, there is a counterbalancing human response, or else the technology is rejected. Television, for example, has been accompanied by the growth of the group therapy, personal growth, and human potential movements. In medicine, the expansion of new life-sustaining equipment has heightened interest in the human quality of death and the hospice movement. Personal family doctors are increasingly valued at the same time that heart transplants and brain scanners have emerged. The growth of computerized word processing has enhanced the value of handwritten notes and letters.

Although communication satellites, long-distance telephone connections, and home computer terminals mean that people could stay home and do almost all their work and shopping from there, they are not going to want to, suggests Naisbitt. The increasing development and use of non-face-to-face communication will mean that more and more people are going to want to talk and meet directly together. The increased use of the telephone and the jet plane has

One source of social change is people's ideas about the way things are or should be, for example their ideas about what kinds of dolls should be manufactured and bought.

been accompanied by more conferences and meetings.

IDEAS AND IDEOLOGY AS SOURCES OF CHANGE

There are times when ideas or ideologies seem to be a major force behind social change. For example, in writing about the French Revolution, de Tocqueville (1856) observed a revolution of rising expectations that he saw as a major force pushing for revolution. People whose lives had been unchanged for generations suddenly witnessed major social upheavals and reacted by thinking, "Why not me? Why can't I make my life different?" The resulting image of a possible alternative did much to fuel the French Revolution and uprisings in other European countries in the nineteenth century.

A major recent change in our ideological and political environment was the race of oil prices, from $2 a barrel to more than $40 in 1981, and the attendant rise in the price of natural gas and coal, because of the political and economic agreement of the OPEC nations. For Americans, this was a particularly dramatic change. Europeans have been used to expensive fuel for a long time. They drive smaller cars, live in attached rather than free-standing homes near major urban centers, and use bicycles more. For Americans, the sudden increase in the price of fuel led to some rapid changes. Fewer people could afford large cars or homes. People began conserving energy, insulating their homes, driving less, buying smaller cars, and exploring alternative energy sources like wood, solar heat, and windmills. There was a rise in the number of bicycles and mopeds in our cities, more people roller skating, and a growth in the sale of long underwear. Some observers suggest that shared forms of social life centering around churches, schools, or communities will grow in importance as a result of the energy crisis, while the distant single-family vacation home and cross-country family automobile trips will decline.

The so-called oil glut of 1983 seems to have dampened these trends. Some observers feel that lower oil prices are only temporary, however.

SOURCES OF CULTURAL CHANGE

Culture, as we saw in Chapter 3, consists of customs, values, ideas, and artifacts, including language, religion, strategies for obtaining food, and the tools that are used. *Cultural change* refers to modifications in any of these aspects of a culture. Such cultural changes may produce social changes—that is, changes in the way a society is organized. Cultural changes can occur in several ways. *Innovations* refer to new ways of doing something. They may result from the *discovery* of something that already exists, like uranium, or the *invention* of something new, like plastic. *Diffusion* refers to the spread of a cultural innovation to other people or even to another society. Discoveries or inventions produce social change only when they are widely used in a society.

Invention, discovery, and diffusion may all influence the course of a cultural innovation. Penicillin, for instance, was discovered by Alexander Fleming in 1928, and his findings were published in a scientific journal. The quiet Fleming was unable to secure the financial and biochemical resources that were needed to isolate and purify the substance in any quantity, so the discovery slept for 10 years. Then a team of scientists at Oxford, England, began refining penicillin. Considerable invention was required to find ways to produce the drug in useful amounts. The team took the idea to the United States in 1941 to get the backing of the American pharmaceutical industry. In the beginning, it took six months of laboratory work to get enough active penicillin to treat one case (Ziman, 1976). The diffusion of the initial ideas encouraged further invention, which increased diffusion, and so on. As a cure for pneumonia and other life-threatening diseases, penicillin did much to lower death rates. Its strength against venereal disease helped to pave the way for the sexual revolution of this century. Thus, the discovery, invention, and diffusion of a single cultural innovation—penicillin—has facilitated far-reaching social changes.

THEORIES OF SOCIAL CHANGE

The discussion of sources of social change has focused on identifying a series of triggering events that may set off change processes. Some sociologists have tried to go beyond such specific events, however, to describe and explain social changes in more general theoretical terms. Evolutionary theories, functionalist theories, cyclical theories, and conflict theories of social change have been advanced. Each of these is worth considering briefly, because they help us to think about social changes more broadly.

Evolutionary Theories

Evolutionary theories begin with the observation that some societies are simple, while others are more complex. They suggest that societies have a tendency to become more complex because of innovation or diffusion as they learn more elaborate subsistence strategies. Although they do not argue that social change will occur in the same way in every society, they do see a tendency for societies to evolve from simpler forms to more complex ones. This perspective risks an implicit bias that more complex societies are superior to less complex ones—that is, that they represent a higher order of development in some sense. Such a belief may be used to justify the domination of simpler societies by more complex ones.

Functionalist Theories

Functionalists see society as a stable and balanced collection of interdependent parts, like an organism in that it tries to reestablish its equilibrium, or balance, after an unsettling event occurs. In 1982, tornadoes ravaged the Great Plains of the United States and floods rampaged through southern Connecticut. In 1983, floods devastated Louisiana. Lives and homes were lost, but people quickly tried to get their lives back to normal. Functionalism has been criticized because it has difficulty explaining *why* social changes occur if the social order is basically balanced. When pressed by critics, Parsons (1937, 1951) and other functionalists stress that no one or two single sources of change are primary in social systems. Instead, several sources of social change are possible.

First, changes can occur from strains within a society—for example when young people do not see society the same way their parents do. Social changes can also originate from the outside, through cultural diffusion, physical events, or military invasion. Examples of the first two sources of change from the outside were presented earlier in this section. With respect to military action, it is safe to say that major social changes have occurred in the Falkland Islands as a result of the British and Argentine war there. A third way that functionalists explain social change is in terms of the ever-increasing differentiation of social institutions as societies become more complex. Gradually, for instance, schools have taken over many of the socialization functions once performed by the family. Now within schools more specialization is occurring as schools provide learning specialists, psychologists, career counselors, health aides, and nutritionists.

Functionalism seems to be best suited for explaining evolutionary social changes within institutions, and is less able to explain massive social changes such as social movements or revolutions.

Cyclical Theories

Cyclical theories such as those of Spengler (1945) and Toynbee (1947) suggest that societies, or civilizations, follow a certain life course. According to Spengler, they are vigorous, innovative, and idealistic in youth. In middle age, the rate of innovation declines and they become more materialistic. As they reach full maturity, their capacities decline more severely. Toynbee holds out the hope that civilizations can learn from the errors of earlier societies and thus be able to mount an effective response to the challenges they face, whether from the environment or from internal or external opponents.

Although both Spengler's and Toynbee's theories bear some resemblance to the rise and fall of various civilizations in history, neither of them identifies the social processes that help or limit the rise or decline of a civilization. Their ideas present broad descriptive patterns and are elegant in their formulation, but they do little to explain why social changes occur when and where they do.

Social Conflict Theories

Social conflict theories do not explain social change so much as they expect change as an integral part of social life. The tendency of individuals and social groups to compete for scarce resources or for prestige may be a major source of social change, suggest Lenski (1966) and Collins (1975). Competing groups may be formed with ethnic, national, cultural, or religious bonds. For Marx, *class conflict* was the most important source of cleavage and conflict in society—that is, conflict between those who own the means of production and those who have nothing to exchange with owners except their labor power.

The potential for class conflict exists in any society with an unequal class structure, but that conflict is not always expressed, nor does it always lead to social change. The same is true among ethnic or religious groups. Although they may be competing for scarce resources, their competition may or may not erupt into open conflict and may or may not lead to social change. Thus, social conflict theories, like other theories of social change, do not fully explain why social changes occur when and where they do. Instead, they suggest conditions that may contribute to change. Sometimes social changes emerge from collective behavior or social movements.

COLLECTIVE BEHAVIOR

Fads such as "Pet Rocks" and riots are both examples of what sociologists call collective behavior. Views about collective behavior have changed over time. At the beginning of this century, prominent social theorists felt threatened by social change and their ideas about collective behavior reflected their unease. They tended to define collective behavior as the relatively spontaneous and unstructured behavior of unorganized collections of people who are responding to a common influence. In the 1950s, researchers tried to take a more detached view of collective behavior. Today, a number of activist researchers study collective behavior with an eye to encouraging social change. One result of this shift has been more emphasis on the study of social movements than on less organized forms of collective behavior such as fads, fashions, rumors, mass hysteria, and riots (Marx and Wood, 1975). In this section we consider the more spontaneous forms of collective behavior, and the following section treats social movements.

SPONTANEOUS FORMS OF COLLECTIVE BEHAVIOR

Fads

Fads are striking behaviors that spread rapidly, are embraced enthusiastically, yet remain popular for only a short time. Examples include M.A.S.H. t-shirts, "punk" hairstyles, and "streaking" (running naked in public as occurred in the late 1960s).

Fashion

Fashion is a socially approved but temporary style of appearance or behavior such as wearing cowboy boots in cities, drinking white wine or Perrier water rather than beer or hard liquor. Commercial interests support fashion changes through advertising and media coverage. Following fashions of various kinds can be a form of *"conspicuous consumption,"* that is, the consumption of resources, goods, or services primarily for display purposes with the aid of enhancing one's social status (Veblen, 1899). By following fashions one shows that he or she can afford to stay current (Blumer, 1968, 1969).

Rumor

Rumors are reports that are passed informally from one person to another without firm evidence. Rumors often develop in highly charged social situations where accurate information is absent or lacks credibility. Any account that seems plausible or fits the prejudices of the people involved may be seized upon and passed along to others. For example, the Watts riots in 1965 were fueled in part by the rumor that white police officers had beaten a pregnant black woman.

Panics and Mass Hysteria

Panics refer to a frightened response to an immediate threat by an aggregate of people. They become irrational and may act in uncooperative ways that increase their risk. Panics may occur when there is a fire in a theater or a hotel and people trample each other in their haste to escape. Panics also occur in financial markets, for example, in the stock market crash of 1929 and the sudden fall in stock prices in 1980.

Mass hysteria involves widely felt fear and anxiety, often based on some erroneous belief or information. In 1938 H.G. Wells' novel, *The*

War of the Worlds, was broadcast over a New York radio station. Although the program began with an announcement that the program was a fictional dramatization, some people tuned in late and others were fooled by an announcer who interrupted the music to say that strange disturbances had been observed in New Jersey. Soon the music was again interrupted by an apparent eye-witness account of a strange meteorite that had landed and from which a monster emerged. Various "experts," "scientists," and "public officials" made comments. Then the station announced that the Martian invaders had destroyed an army unit and moved on to New York City where it had overcome the population with poison gas. By the time of the half-hour station break, panic had struck. Phone lines were swamped, crowds swarmed into bus and train stations, people hid in cellars or jumped into their cars and drove away.

The dramatization was so vivid that people did not search for additional evidence, for example, by turning their radio dial to another station. The level of anxiety in this period of depression just prior to World War II was sufficiently high that mass hysteria flourished (Cantril, 1940; Herzog, 1955; Houseman, 1948).

In 1983 a similar incident occurred. A TV movie, "Special Bulletin," showed an unnervingly realistic account of terrorists staging a nuclear attack on Charleston, S.C. The two-hour drama was presented as a network television news special that had interrupted regular programming. Aware of the panic that followed *War of the Worlds* in 1938, NBC ran notices reminding viewers that they were watching a movie. In addition, during the climactic explosion, they flashed the word, "DRAMATIZATION" on the screen. Nevertheless, the network heard from panic-stricken callers who feared that Charleston was being destroyed. Many viewers who knew it was fictional still felt terrified, perhaps because the movie showed something that could really happen.

Riots

Riots are destructive and sometimes violent collective outbursts. Antidraft riots occurred in New York City in 1893 when white laborers protested efforts to draft them into the Union army. (More affluent whites could buy their way out of the draft.) Race riots in which whites rampaged through the black sections of Chicago took place in 1919 and in Detroit in 1943. The black ghetto riots of the mid-1960s in Cleveland, Detroit, the Watts section of Los Angeles, and Rochester, New York, were aimed not at people so much as at the stores and businesses owned by whites from outside the ghetto.

Riots differ from mass movements because they are more likely to be violent, they may be relatively more spontaneous, and they may be aimed less at attaining a particular goal. One way of including both riots and social movements in

Table 19.1 Types of Riots

		Goal Oriented?	
		Yes	No
Unifying Belief?	Yes	A Change-oriented riots: draft riots, food riots, revolutionary mobs.	B Hate and/or destruction riots: lynching parties, cross-burnings.
	No	C Situational riots: prison riots, looting.	D Issueless riots: at sports events or rock concerts.

SOURCE: Marx (1970)

a common frame for analysis would be to focus more on the larger context in which the behavior occurs and to examine meanings and symbols that participants share.

Riots might be classified in terms of two dimensions, suggests Gary Marx (1970): Does the riot have a specific goal or not, and does it have a unifying belief or not? (See Table 19.1.) The riots in cell A of Table 19.1 may come very close to revolutions or social movements. Because these types of collective behavior are relatively enduring and may have far-reaching consequences for the social order, they are treated in more detail in the next section.

THEORIES OF COLLECTIVE BEHAVIOR

Theories of collective behavior seek to explain all forms of such behavior, from social movements to revolutions to panics and fads. These theories try to address the questions: Why does collective behavior occur and what direction will it take? At least four major theories have been offered.

Le Bon's "Contagion" Theory

The French thinker, Gustave Le Bon, was one of the early theorists who were alarmed by collective behavior. In his classic book, *The Crowd,* written in 1895, he suggested that people turn from rational individuals into violent, crazed animals when they are part of a crowd. This happens because the anonymity people feel in a crowd gives them a sense of power. Emotions sweep through a crowd like a contagious virus (hence the name of his theory). As a result, people become more susceptible to the suggestions of fanatical leaders. Le Bon's work has been criticized for its aristocratic bias, for its failure to explain calm collective behavior such as peace vigils, and for its inability to explain why contagion may or may not spread through a crowd. Not everyone accepts Le Bon's view that joining a crowd infects a person with irrational desires.

Convergence Theory

Convergence theory suggests that certain crowds attract particular people, who may be inclined toward behaving in specific irrational ways. This theory helps to explain lynch mobs and rock star fans who crowd into concerts. The theory does not explain shifts in the middle of a collective action, for example, when a mob calms down or when it decides to loot rather than to burn.

Emergent-Norm Theory

Emergent-norm theory offers a more sociological explanation for collective behavior. Rather than suggesting, as Le Bon does, that collective behavior is due to some contagious irrationality in a crowd or to the emotional predispositions the way convergence theory does, emergent-norm theory suggests that collective behavior develops in a situation that may be ambiguous, for example, some people in a crowd start to push or the lights go out all over New York City. In such a relatively normless situation, some people step forward to try to forge a shared definition of the situation. In this process, common norms of behavior emerge. Rumors may circulate, for example, that "there aren't enough tickets" or "it's the incompetent power company again" which contribute to the emerging definitions and norms. Others in the crowd may conform to the emergent norms or resist them. Hence pushing in a crowd may lead to people being suffocated or trampled to death, as happened to eleven people at a concert given by The Who in Cincinnati, Ohio in 1979, or it may lead to others stepping forward and getting the crowd to "stay cool."

In the first major New York City blackout in 1965, the emergent norms were constructive and helpful ones. Some people helped direct traffic, since the traffic lights were out. Others brought candles, flashlights, or food to shut-ins. A general festival atmosphere prevailed. In the second major blackout in 1977, some parts of the city experienced a new set of emergent norms—looting stores under cover of darkness.

Thus, emergent-norm theory helps to explain why crowd behavior may take different forms at different times, depending on what definitions and norms emerge. It is somewhat less helpful in explaining whether or not collective behavior will occur in the first place.

Value-added theory

Smelser's value-added theory (1963) suggests that many instances of collective behavior represent efforts to change the social environment. Collective behavior develops through six stages, each one of which contributes to the process:

1. *Structural conduciveness* refers to the social conditions that allow collective behavior to occur. In the *Invasion from Mars* incident, people were anxious about the war scare in Europe (Herzog, 1955). They were also accustomed to having radio programs interrupted with real news bulletins.
2. *Structural strains* are social conditions that fail to fit people's expectations about how things should be. Hence there are discrepancies, conflicts, or ambiguities in the social order. When people think their social and economic conditions should be improving, but they are not, there is a structural strain that may lead to collective behavior. The theory is weak on indicating when strain leads to collective behavior and when it does not.
3. *Generalized belief* refers to a shared definition of a situation and what needs to be done about it. Injustice and indignity alone do not lead to collective behavior, unless they are defined as unacceptable and worthy of resistance. Not everyone involved may share exactly the same beliefs. Also, beliefs may be more or less important in some collective behaviors than in others, for example, less important in panics and more important in social movements.
4. *Precipitating factors* are dramatic incidents or behaviors that give the generalized beliefs concrete substance. When Mrs. Rosa Parks refused to move to the back of the bus, that action was a significant precipitating factor in the Birmingham Bus Boycott that helped to focus the Civil Rights Movement.
5. *Mobilization for action* refers to the way participants in collective behavior become organized for further action. For Mrs. Parks' gesture to be a precipitating factor, it had to be used as a rallying cry for further action.
6. *Social control* may limit the emergence of collective behavior. Even when these five stages have been experienced, collective behavior may or may not occur because of the amount of social control that is exercised. The actions of the police, national guard, mass media, institutional authorities, and others may serve to weaken or magnify a collective behavior. Sometimes police action contains a riot while other times it fires it up. When collective behavior is focused, sustained, and is aimed at social changes it takes the form of social movements.

SOCIAL MOVEMENTS

Cultural innovations may be started by a single individual, but they depend on larger social groups or organizations to be diffused and to create social changes. Many social changes are due to organized, collective efforts by groups of people consciously committed to making changes in society. Such efforts are *social movements*. These movements are not simply temporary "flashes in the pan" but have some permanence—they develop leaders and followers, and they involve deliberate planning to mobilize more members, public opinion, and other resources.

WHY SOCIAL MOVEMENTS OCCUR

From slave revolts in ancient Egypt and Rome through the French Revolution and contemporary antinuclear protests, people have joined forces throughout history to try to shape the direction of their lives and societies. Ground Zero, Right to Life, the Moonies, the Grey Panthers—these are just a few of the many social movements that exist in American society today. Sociologists try to explain why social movements occur, why they take the forms that they do, and why they succeed or fail.

Social movements are a bit like volcanos in that they do not usually erupt without giving warning rumbles. The first step is the growing feeling among individuals or groups that something is wrong with the social order. The feeling of discontent or deprivation usually has two parts, an objective basis and subjective perceptions of that reality (Lauer, 1976). Take the nuclear arms freeze—disarmament movement, for instance. In Pella, Iowa, "the movement" began in February 1982 with an advertisement in the local paper that read: "Wanted: People Who Don't Want to Die in a Nuclear Holocaust." As Fialka reports:

> There were already isolated pockets of nuclear angst growing in this rural, conservative and stubbornly prosperous town of 8,000 people in central Iowa. What that ad provided was the spark, the catalyst that brought parishioners out of some of the local churches, teachers from the town's two high schools, and students and faculty from Central College. Together, they sat down to map out a week of activism designed to teach people about the horrors of nuclear war. (1982a, p. 1)

People may endure horrible conditions for centuries because they consider them to be inevitable. Their perceptions influence their feelings about the correctness of existing conditions and about whether they can or should be changed. But once perceptions shift and the conditions begin to seem unjust or the possibility of change occurs, social movements may arise.

As we have said, one of the roots of mobilization is a rising sense of injustice: Existing conditions begin to seem wrong to growing numbers of people; social arrangements are seen to violate the norms and values of a society; and people begin to have an alternative vision of how things might be. Then the possibility of organizing into a social movement arises.

NECESSARY CONDITIONS FOR A SOCIAL MOVEMENT

To emerge as a social movement, an issue or group needs leadership, members, and the mobilization of resources.

Leadership

To be successful, social movements need effective leaders who can create shared visions of what people are working for and mobilize the resources needed to accomplish their common goals. The Ground Zero group, one example of an antinuclear organization, was started by Roger C. Molander, a 41-year-old physicist who had been advising the White House on nuclear targeting strategies. Mr. Molander and his brother Earl, a Harvard Business School professor, decided in 1981 to establish a new organization aimed at people who had not been in movements before. "We wanted to be in the mainstream," says Roger Molander (Fialka, 1982a, p. 1). Since he and his brother were so established in the mainstream of society themselves, they were well suited to lead a mainstream movement.

Leaders help with the symbolic task of redefining a situation as unjust, identifying the

One way that social movements marshal resources and gain converts is by proclaiming their message for others to see.

source of the problem, and proposing solutions to it. Early demonstrators in the Ground Zero Movement carried signs that read, "If This Were Ground Zero, a One Megaton Nuclear Explosion Would Totally Destroy Virtually Everything within Two Miles of This Spot—Instantly." Signs such as that one began to rouse people's awareness of the issue.

Leaders perform other functions for a social movement as well: they help to formulate a movement's ideology; they arouse the commitment of members and potential members; they articulate the movement's position to the larger society; and they decide the strategies to pursue. Often there is more than one leader in a movement, because no single person has all the skills such a movement needs. As a movement develops, different leadership needs may arise. The early stages seem to call for agitators who stir things up and prophets who spread the news and generate enthusiasm. As a social movement becomes more formally organized, its need for administrators increases, as does the need for strong leadership in the larger community (Spector and Kitsuse, 1973, 1977). The civil rights movement illustrates all these types of leadership. In 1961, the Congress of Racial Equality sent "Freedom Riders" of both races through the South on public buses to challenge segregation laws in interstate transportation. These Freedom Riders were perceived by some to be agitators. The Student Nonviolent Coordinating Committee helped to fill the role of prophet by spreading word of the movement across college campuses and by generating support from people of all ages who were pleased to see students involved. Efforts at voter registration throughout the South called for administrative leadership. Getting the civil rights bill through Congress in 1964 required strong leadership within the larger society from President Lyndon B. Johnson.

Outside leadership may be particularly important in getting a social movement started (McCarthy and Zald, 1977; Zald and McCarthy, 1979). The civil rights movement, for example, was greatly helped by the leadership of Martin Luther King, Jr. What might have been a single incident, the arrest of Mrs. Rosa Parks for refusing to move to the Negro section of a bus in Montgomery, Alabama, on December 5, 1955, was transformed by Martin Luther King, Jr., into a major resistance movement. A boycott staged against the bus company resulted in the desegregation of its facilities. After that success, the methods of picketting and boycotting spread rapidly to other southern communities. The Rev. King's Southern Christian Leadership

Conference provided moral and practical support for the protest movement. In addition to being a powerful preacher and speaker who could rally people around a shared vision (for example, with his "I have a dream" speech at the 1963 Civil Rights March on Washington, D.C.), the Rev. King was adept at building bridges with other church leaders and with leaders in labor, government, and education.

The antinuclear movement was also supplemented by significant outside support. A growing number of Catholic bishops began pushing the church to take a pro-freeze stance, and many church leaders spoke about the topic from the pulpit. The drive also picked up substantial strength in Congress, where Democratic Senator Edward Kennedy of Massachusetts and Republican Senator Mark Hatfield of Oregon led a bipartisan effort. They introduced a resolution in Congress calling for a freeze on the testing, production, and further deployment of nuclear weapons by both the United States and the Soviet Union. Considerable financial support was donated by younger members of the Rockefeller family (Fialka, 1982a; Fialka, 1982b). It is important to realize, however, that outside agitators can do little to mobilize a social movement if conditions do not need improvement and if people have not already begun to perceive the need for a change. Outside leadership may be helpful in the beginning stages of a social movement, but few movements can flourish without strong local leaders and members.

Membership

Any significant social movement needs to recruit large numbers of committed members. Support for a nuclear freeze swelled in 1982. Citizens in more than 400 American towns and numerous state legislatures passed resolutions endorsing a nuclear weapons freeze. Activists in California collected some 500,000 signatures to put the issue on the state ballot in November (Fialka, 1982a, p. 1).

For a long time, sociological research on social movements focused on the values, attitudes, and grievances of participants in an effort to explain why people did or did not join particular movements. The individual social psychology of participants is one aspect of the phenomenon, but more recent analyses of social movements have emphasized political, sociological, and economic theories more than social psychological ones (Gamson, 1975; McCarthy and Zald, 1977). This shift has resulted from research suggesting little or no relationship between personal deprivation and willingness to participate in social movements (Snyder and Tilly, 1972; Mueller, 1972; Bowen et al., 1968; Crawford and Naditch, 1970). Mobilization theory views members as one of several key resources needed for a social movement to succeed. Rapid mobilization of members does not occur by recruiting large numbers of solitary individuals, but by tying in with existing groups of people who are already organized (Oberschall, 1973). A major way that a movement gains strength is by forming organizational networks. (This presumes, of course, that the organizations share common goals.)

Mobilization of Resources

The *resource mobilization theory* of social movements considers how a social movement seeks to marshal key resources, how it tries to establish connections with other groups, what outside support it needs, and how external authorities may try to control or coopt it (McCarthy and Zald, 1977; Tilly, 1975; Tilly, Tilly, and Tilly, 1975). The resources available to social movements include the number of people committed to a movement's goals and the intensity of their commitment; the verbal and visual communications skills of leaders and members, including their access to mimeographing machines, printing presses, photographs, audio and videotapes, music, and the mass media; the organizational skills of leaders or the services of professional organizers; the legal and financial skills of members; and the ability to tap millions of dollars in contributions to support their goals.

Resource mobilization theory suggests that social movements are affected by the total amount of discretionary resources available, by the way social movements are organized (for example, having many isolated supporters or a series of local chapters), and by the number of social organizations competing for the total resources available to social movements (McCarthy and Zald, 1977). The antinuclear movement, including Ground Zero, has been extremely effective in tapping significant financial, organizational, and communications resources. Many major religious denominations and large donors have given important support. Numerous effective teaching devices, including films such as *The Last Epidemic, Eight Days to Zero, Atomic Café,* and *War Without Winners* have been developed and shown on national television and at hundreds of church and community rallies around the United States. Jonathan Schell's book, *The Fate of the World* (1982), has had a powerful impact, with its suggestion that a nuclear war would destroy life on earth.

SUCCESS OR FAILURE OF SOCIAL MOVEMENTS

When social movements are able to mobilize many members as well as considerable resources, and when they have effective leaders, they have the potential for success. Success, however, ultimately depends on wise strategy decisions and the effective use of the resources members have been able to mobilize. At the time of this writing, the antinuclear movement has been very successful in terms of leadership, mobilizing resources, and membership. It was able to mount the largest disarmament demonstration in U.S. history on June 12, 1982, in New York City, consisting of more than 750,000 people who traveled from all over the world in support of the United Nations second special session on disarmament. The ultimate test of any movement, of course, is whether or not it can make the social changes it desires. The goal of the antinuclear movement is to educate the public to the true horrors of nuclear war and to put pressure on the president and Congress to negotiate a cutback in nuclear arms with the Soviet Union.

Unsuccessful movements begin the same way as successful ones, with members trying to gain public support for their aims. What happens, however, is that their appeals may fall on deaf ears; they may make claims that others do not believe; they may be powerless members of society to whom others will not listen; or their strategies may alienate rather than enlist supporters.

TYPES OF SOCIAL MOVEMENTS

The strategies and tactics selected by various social movements depend to a considerable degree on their goals. *Revolutionary movements* are so dissatisfied with society that they want to overhaul it completely and replace present social forms with ones of their own design. When a revolutionary movement succeeds, as those in China and Cuba did, they create widespread social changes. Because they feel no allegiance to the existing social system, members may be willing to use warfare, murder, bombings, ambushes, or other violence to advance their goals. They differ markedly from *reform movements,* which basically accept the status quo but seek certain specific changes. The antidraft movement, the antinuclear movement, and the gay rights movement are all examples of reform movements. Tactically they tend not to favor the use of violence or of strategies that might alienate the mainstream institutions of society, since they continue to hope for support from other social groups. Instead, they favor public demonstrations and marches, efforts to change legislation, and educational strategies.

Regressive movements, such as the Islamic resurgence in the Middle East in recent years or the Moral Majority in the United States, aim to move the social world back to where they perceive it to have been at an earlier time. Islamic fundamentalists drove the shah of Iran from political power and tried to restore religious rule in the person of the Ayatollah. Such social movements may use both violence and persuasion to gain control.

MODERNIZATION

A major source of social change in a number of developing nations in recent years has been the push toward industrialization and development. *Industrialization* refers to the shift within a nation's economy from a primarily agricultural base to steel production and oil refining. The transformation from an agricultural to an industrial society is accompanied by more productive agriculture, more specialized division of labor, greater urbanization, higher rates of literacy, and improved systems of transportation (such as railroads, highways, or canals) and communication (such as postal service, telephone and telegraph networks, radio and television broadcasting). Today, countries such as India, South Korea, and Mexico are struggling to make the transition from an agricultural to an industrial society.

Some sociologists use the term *modernization* to describe the major shift from a traditional agricultural society to a highly industrialized society. Modernization affects many areas of social life, undermining traditional religious systems, family ties, village loyalties, and customs. Some traditionalists and nationalists in modernizing countries equate modern practices with Western domination. But even they realize that feeding and educating their populations and keeping them healthy and housed requires some industrialization. Their hope is to try to control the process of development so that traditional values are not destroyed by it.

Modernization has a number of interrelated social consequences, including the transfer of culture through television and films from one society to another (Barnett and Muller, 1974; Smith, 1980); the possibility of permanent personality change (Inkeles and Smith, 1974); the growing importance of large bureaucratic organizations such as the army or the national government rather than family, village, or ethnic groups; and declining death rates.

Considerable research has been done to investigate how modernization may change personalities. Inkeles and Smith (1974) surveyed 6000 men from six developing countries and found that some of them had what they called a "modern personality," characterized by a strong future orientation, confidence in the effectiveness of human action in the world, and an openness to new ideas. Such "modern" attitudes were more likely to be found in educated men who had worked in a factory-type setting than in farmers, other nonfactory workers, or those with little education, suggesting that "modern" attitudes grow out of a person's educational and work experiences.

Social thinkers hold competing views of the dynamics behind economic development, and those views have important social consequences in the world. United States foreign policy with regard to Vietnam and other developing countries has been guided by what American policymakers assume about the way development occurs. For these reasons, it is important to consider briefly two different views of modernization—convergence theory and dependency theory.

CONVERGENCE THEORY

Convergence theory suggests that modernizing nations come to resemble one another more and more closely over time (their individual characteristics *converge*). They shed their unique cultural traditions and begin thinking and acting more like one another and more like already developed societies (Lerner, 1968).

Stage theories of economic development are

considered one form of convergence theory. Stage theories, proposed by such economic thinkers as W. W. Rostow (1960), view nations as going through various stages on the path to development. One of these stages is called the *takeoff,* suggesting that economic development occurs only after a critical level of economic activity has been reached. The stages are assumed to be somewhat similiar in all developing societies.

Convergence theory suggests that developing nations desire to become more like Western nations in every respect and ignores the role Western nations may play in pushing them in this direction in order to exploit their natural resources, labor, or potential markets. Such criticisms of convergence theory have led to alternative theories about the place of developing nations in the world economy. Two of these theories include dependency theory and its extension, world systems analysis.

DEPENDENCY THEORY

Developing nations do not operate in a world vacuum. Other, more powerful, and highly developed nations have a stake in how they develop. An early proponent of *dependency theory,* André Gunder Frank (1966), challenged the stage theory of economic development advanced by convergence theorists. He saw the major industrial nations as the "metropolitan centers" of a world in which developing nations were the rural hinterlands. The center takes advantage of the cheap labor and raw materials of the outer regions to produce a surplus controlled by the center. Such an arrangement makes the center reluctant to encourage industrial development in outer areas because not only would the center not control it, but the outer areas might end up competing with the center's production. In Frank's view, those nations that are least involved with the major industrial powers have the greatest chance of becoming industrialized.

Many developing nations have a single major cash crop or raw material, such as sugar, coffee, copper, or bananas, that they export to industrialized nations. Local leaders who want to encourage the industrial development of their countries need advanced technologies, people who can run them, and money to invest. Where can they get these resources? Major sources are the already-strong multinational corporations, the international banking community (dominated by American and Western European banks), the International Monetary Fund, private (generally Western) investors, or the World Bank. Although many of these sources are eager to lend money to developing nations, they do so on terms favorable to themselves. Not only are their interest rates high, but they often demand a voice in national policies dealing with taxation, military spending, and other internal affairs. As a result, the developing nations lose some control over the direction of their development. Western backers may be concerned that the country be an open market for their own manufactured goods, including such consumer items as toasters and cars. Industrialized nations do not want other nations to become self-sufficient with respect to such goods, because they want to control the market. Nor do they want such goods banned or highly taxed (Frank, 1967, 1969, 1980; Magdoff, 1978; Mytelka, 1979; Rodney, 1974).

The control of Namibia (also called South-West Africa) by the Republic of South Africa illustrates dependency theory very clearly. After a long history of domination by Portuguese, Dutch, British, and German colonists, followed by occupation by South Africa, the territory of Namibia was placed under United Nations control in 1969. That UN resolution also called for the withdrawal of South Africa from Namibia and for the eventual independence of Namibia. South Africa has refused to surrender its claim. Besides keeping Namibia politically dependent, South Africa controls most of the mining, fishing, beef, and fur industries that comprise the territory's primary sources of wealth (Crocker and Hartland-Thunberg, 1978; German Development Institute, 1978; Green, 1978; Hodgson, 1982; May, 1982). Although it is a somewhat extreme example because it lacks formal independence, the case of Namibia reveals the degree to which nations beyond the borders of a particular territory may control social and economic activities within a country.

Dependency theory questions convergence theory's assumption that developing nations are simply at an earlier stage of development and will eventually reach the same "advanced" stage as industrial capitalist countries. Instead, dependency theory suggests that the needs of developing nations for external financing, technology, and personnel, and their history of domination by colonial powers makes their prospects for development quite different from those of already industrialized nations.

WORLD SYSTEMS ANALYSIS

World systems anaylsis extends dependency theory by taking into account current and historical relationships between nations and societies. For example, Immanuel Wallerstein (1974) considers a social system as largely self-contained, with the dynamics of development stemming mainly from internal sources. Given this definition, he sees only two genuine types of social systems in the world: small, self-contained tribes, and world systems.

World systems consist of sets of interconnected societies, and they contain many diverse cultures and a highly refined division of labor. Wallerstein believes that only two types of world systems have ever existed, world empires and world economies. In a world empire there is a single political and military system controlling the physical area of the system. Charlemagne's Europe, the Roman Empire, and the British Empire are all examples of world empires. World economies incorporate a wide variety of cultures and lands into a trading network, but they are not bound by a common political and military authority. The modern world economy, based on a capitalist form of economic organization, has prevailed for the last 400 years without becoming a world empire. Modern capitalism has taken advantage of the absence of a single system of political control to maneuver the system advantageously. Different sets of political boundaries and rules mean, for example, that the cheap labor of one area may be combined with the favorable tax situation in another area to maximize profits, as noted in our earlier discussion of multinational corporations.

Wallerstein sees world economies as divided into core states and peripheral areas. The core states consist of the advantaged areas of the world economy, which have strong, integrated state machinery and national cultures. In the twentieth century these are the highly industrialized, militarily powerful nations, such as the United States and the Soviet Union. These nations tend to dominate peripheral areas, which have weak state machinery, weaker economic activities, and less cultural consistency. These include developing nations in Africa, Central America, and countries such as Afghanistan. Semiperipheral areas operate as buffers and traders between core and periphery areas. They are trying to industrialize and diversify their economies. They are less likely than peripheral areas to be manipulated by core states. Countries like Iran or Spain might be considered semiperipheral. As such, they mute some of the political opposition that might otherwise be directed at the core.

Wallerstein's ideas suggest that the more powerful positions of core states will enable them to shape the direction of social change in the future. As much as they might like to change, peripheral areas will find it difficult to do so. The rise of OPEC, however, suggests that when peripheral areas become socially and politically organized, they may create considerable social change in the core states.

Summary

1. Social change is a change in the way a society is organized, and it is one of the striking features of the era in which we live.

2. Some of the many social changes we face include the transformation of our economy from a manufacturing to an information and service base, growing occupational specialization, the shift from a national to a global economy, a growing gap between rich and poor nations, and intensifying potential for nuclear destruction.

3. Some of these changes are fueled by the growth of microcomputers, the use of robots in manufacturing, and the development of communication satellites.

4. Social changes have many sources, including shifts in the physical environment (such as volcanic eruptions or droughts), population shifts (such as dropping birth and death rates or migrations), scientific and technological developments, and changing ideas.

5. Culture lag refers to the fact that tools and technology are changed more rapidly and easily than cultural practices.

6. Cultural changes may involve discoveries or inventions of technology or cultural practices. Unless they are diffused to other people, such innovations do not lead to social changes.

7. At least four theoretical efforts have been made to explain social change in general terms. These include evolutionary, functionalist, cyclical, and conflict theories. Each offers some insight into the nature of social change, but no one alone explains why social changes occur when or where they do.

8. Collective behavior refers to relatively spontaneous behavior by collections of people who may be more or less organized. The types of behavior studied range from fads and fashions through rumors, panics, mass hysteria, riots, and social movements.

9. Four major theories of collective behavior are considered—Le Bon's "contagion" theory, convergence theory, emergent-norm theory, and Smelser's value-added theory.

10. Smelser's theory suggests that collective behavior develops through six stages, each of which contributes to the process. The stages are: structural conduciveness, structural strains, generalized belief, precipitating factors, mobilization for action, and social control.

11. Social movements represent organized efforts to promote or retard social changes. Realizing they can do more together than alone, people have come together in social movements all through history.

12. Conditions necessary for the growth of social movements are a sense of injustice over current conditions, good leadership, and the mobilization of resources, such as members, money, and media. Success or failure depends on all these factors. The process is illustrated by the current antinuclear movement in the United States.

13. Revolutionary, reform, and regressive movements differ in their goals and their tactics.

14. Modernization is one form of social change that is brewing in many areas of the world. Convergence theory sees this process as gradual and evolutionary; developing nations steadily become more like contemporary industrial ones.

15. Dependency theory and world systems analysis stress the historical relations between dominant and developing nations and argue that the latter cannot simply follow the path trod by early industrializers. They may need new models if they are to break away from their dependence on dominant world states.

Key Terms

class conflict
convergence theory

cultural change
culture lag
cyclical theories
dependency theory
diffusion
discovery
evolutionary theories
fads
fashion
global economy
innovation
invention
mass hysteria
modernization
panics
post-industrial society
reform movement
regressive movement
resource mobilization theory
revolutionary movement
riots
rumors
social change
social movement
stage theory
technological determinism
world systems analysis

Chapter 20

Population and Health

The number of people who can survive in a given physical environment depends on the complex interaction of food production, birth rates, and death rates. All three processes have social causes and social consequences. Birth and death rates are influenced by social customs and the social organization of medical care, as well as more directly by nutrition and disease control. The health and fertility of a population may also be influenced by the ecological balance within a particular physical environment. People living or working in environments with chemical or radioactive pollutants in them, for example, have had higher rates of sterility, birth defects, and illness than people living in less polluted areas. Health and population are integrally related to the ecological balance within a particular physical environment. In this chapter each of these vital issues—population, ecology, and health—is considered in turn. Although these concerns are treated separately, their interdependence will become apparent.

WORLD POPULATION CHANGES

In early human history, in fact for the first 99 percent of the time humans have been on the earth, population growth was very slow, as Figure 20.1 shows. *Population* refers to all the people living in a given geographic area. Death rates, particularly among infants and young children, were so high that even high birth rates led to only a gradual increase in the population. With the agricultural revolution beginning about 8000 B.C., the population gradually increased. Initially, death rates probably increased in agricultural societies because of sanitation and disease problems in the growing urban areas. Fertility rates also rose, however, because the improved diet increased the ability of women to conceive and bear children.

The rate of population growth accelerated after 1750. With the onset of the Industrial Revolution, death rates dropped dramatically because of increased food production, better transportation (which improved the distribution of food), and improved sanitation. Since the time of the Industrial Revolution, Western Europe and North America have undergone what has been called a ***demographic transition:*** The birth rate has declined so that it is about equal to the death rate. The three stages in the demographic transition are first, the stage of high birth and high death rates, especially among children. Before the Industrial Revolution, this was the stage most societies were in. In the second stage, improved food production and distribution and medical care produce a sharp drop in death rates, but birth rates remain high. The second stage occurred in the early stages of industrialization and is happening in many developing nations today. In the third stage, birth rates drop so they are once again in balance with death rates.

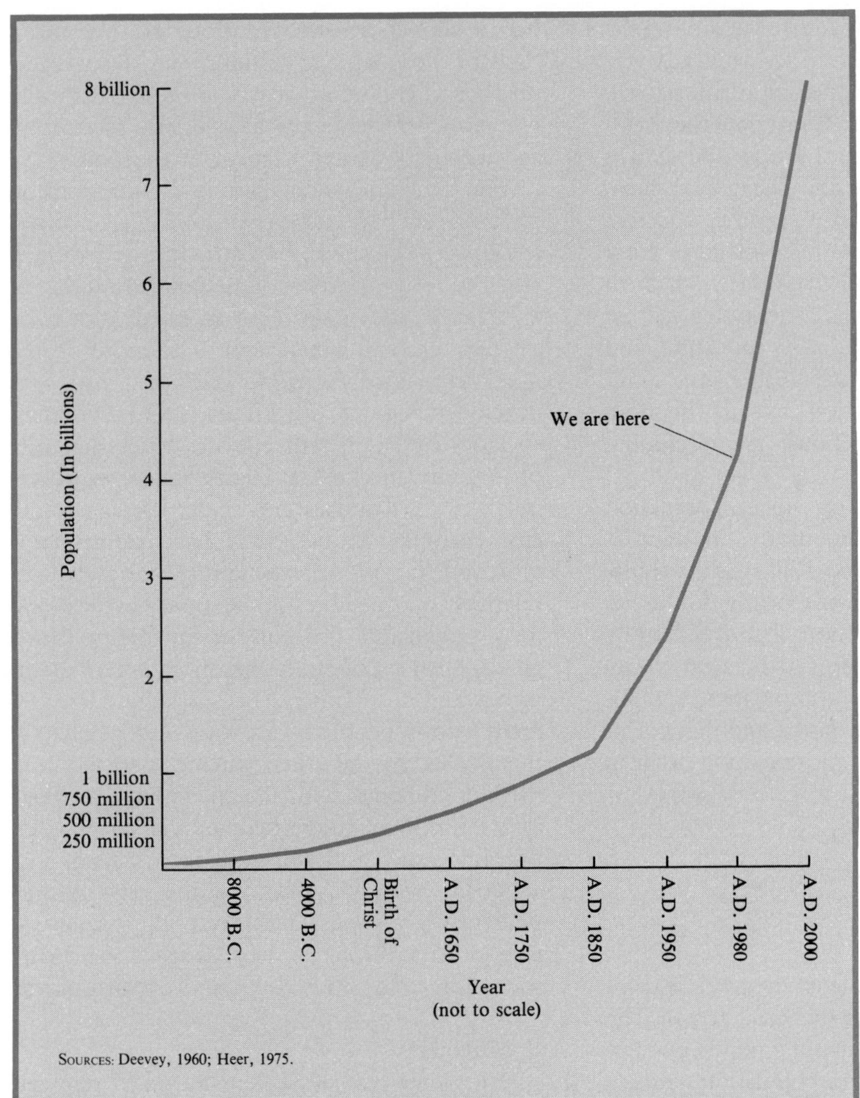

Figure 20.1 World Population Explosion

Why does this happen? *Demography* (the study of population trends) suggests that in an agrarian society, children are an economic advantage. There is plenty of work for children to do on a farm, and there is usually enough to feed them. They also represent old-age insurance for their parents, since they are expected to care for their elders in later life. Industrialization changes children from income producers to income consumers. As a result, industrial families tend to have fewer children. This has been the trend for the past 200 years, since well before foolproof methods of contraception were developed.

In the late nineteenth century, breakthroughs in germ theory and vaccination against infectious diseases lowered mortality rates still further. At first these developments lowered mortality only in Europe and the United States, but after World War II (1945), medical and public health advances spread all over the world, lowering death rates in many other countries as well. Within one or two generations after the death rate began to decline in Europe and North America, the fertility rate also began to decline, but more slowly. Although the physical factors that reduce death rates may change fairly quickly, the social norms that value high birth rates change more slowly. The result is that births increase until gradually industrial and urban life weakens the pressure for large families. Total world population growth therefore slowed, but growth continues in developing nations.

This capsule history of world population changes leads to one of the most important issues facing the human race: Will world population continue to explode, and nearly double, as some experts suggest, to more than 8 billion by 2000? Or will the rate of growth begin to decline, possibly leading to a population equilibrium between number of deaths and number of births? Will the demographic transition occur in the developing world and if so, how soon?

A POPULATION VOCABULARY

Growth

In order to study population issues, it is helpful to understand several technical terms. The *crude birth rate* refers to the total number of live births per 1000 persons in a population within a particular year. People who think about how the birth rate is calculated often come up with an objection: "Suppose one society had lots of women of childbearing age and another society had relatively few women in that age bracket, shouldn't that difference somehow be reflected in the statistics?" If you were thinking along those lines, you are absolutely right, and demographers agree with you. They have developed what they call a *total fertility rate,* which relates the birth rate to the number of women of childbearing age. It uses information about the number of women in each age group and the birth rates of those women to figure out the average number of children that would be born to each woman over her reproductive life, if current age-specific birth rates remained constant.

The total fertility rate permits comparisons of societies that may have very different age and sex structures. The age and sex structure of a society refers to the proportion of the population that is a particular age or sex. (For an example of contrasting age and sex structures in more developed regions of the world compared with less developed regions, see Figure 20.2.) Different societies have different age structures that can profoundly affect social life. A society in which much of the population is under the age of 20 (for example, Mexico) will have tremendous food and educational expenditures and will have relatively few members of the society in the work force to generate a surplus for supporting those needs. Such a society also has more potential for increasing in numbers, because there are so many young people to grow up and reproduce themselves. At the other extreme, a society like the United States, with a relatively large proportion of retirement-age people, will have other problems, such as health care for the elderly and adequate pensions. Knowing the existing age structure of a society and projecting that structure into the future can help us make successful social forecasts about issues and opportunities.

Mortality

The other critical element in world population growth is the death, or *mortality,* rate. Like fertility rates, there are several ways mortality rates can be calculated. The *crude death rate* is the number of deaths per 1000 persons occurring within a one-year period in a particular population. Crude death rates tell us little about the probability of death at any given age, however, since the age structure of a population can dramatically influence the crude death rate. In 1967, the crude death rate in West Berlin was 18 while in West Germany it was 11, suggesting that mortality was much higher in West Berlin.

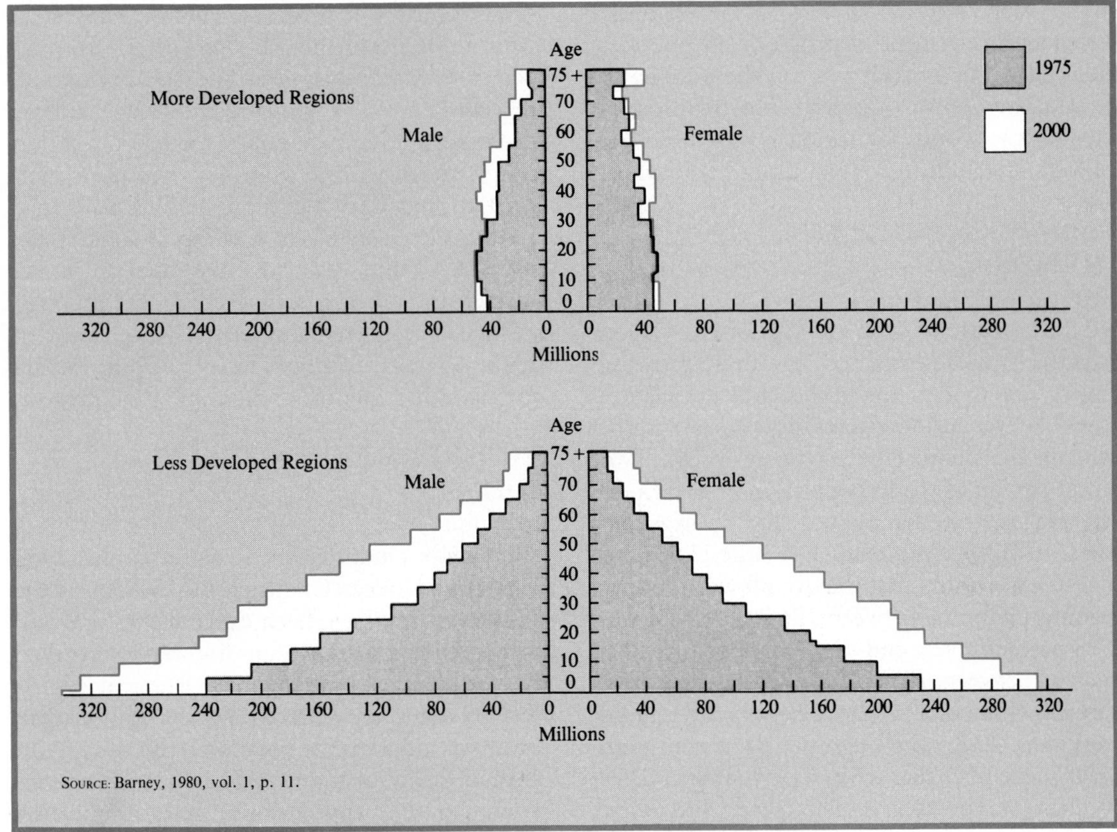

Figure 20.2 Age and Sex Composition of the World's Population in More and Less Developed Regions, 1975 and 2000

Yet a female baby had nearly a 90 percent chance of surviving to be 55 in both places. Mortality probabilities were the same, despite different crude death rates; the difference in the crude death rates was undoubtedly affected by the fact that 21 percent of West Berliners were 65 or older (and therefore more likely to die), compared to only 12 percent of West Germans (Weeks, 1981).

To capture the essence of a society's mortality experience while considering the age and sex structure of that society, we can compute a *life expectancy index,* which gives the average age at death for a group of people born in a particular year. Such an index is derived from a *life table.* Life tables require a system of registering vital statistics, especially deaths by age and sex, and an accurate census showing the number of people in each age and sex category. They summarize the mortality experience of a particular population. Insurance companies use life tables to compute life insurance premiums. Life expectancy indexes are good summary statistics for comparing societies or subgroups within a society. As noted in earlier chapters, the life expectancy of blacks and whites in the United States is quite different, as is that of males and females.

Another important measure used by population experts is the *growth rate,* which is the difference between birth and death rates, excluding immigration. *Migration* refers to the relatively permanent movement of people from one area to another. The growth rate and the total fertility rate are used to consider the question of whether the world population is continuing to explode, is stabilizing, or may ultimately decline.

WORLD POPULATION TRENDS

We are at a critical time in terms of population growth. World population has been growing rapidly, and there is now such a large population base that even a slow rate of growth can rapidly increase the number of people on earth. Two recent studies of world population growth indicate that the rate has slowed slightly in recent years. In *World Population: 1977,* the U.S. Census Bureau reports that the overall world population growth rate between 1965 and 1970 was 1.98 percent a year and that it dropped to 1.88 percent between 1975 and 1977, a drop of 5 percent. (For some of the variations by region, see Figure 20.3.) Although this drop may seem small, remember that when a percentage relates to a base of more than 4 billion, every little digit counts.

The Census Bureau's report is consistent with the World Fertility Survey of 41 developing and 20 developed countries. So far, data have been analyzed for 15 of the developing countries and 4 of the developed countries. These preliminary findings indicate how rapidly the birth rate is declining. In all but 3 of the 15 countries, the birth rate declined dramatically. For example, in Costa Rica, married women age 45 to 49 have had an average of 7.2 children, but younger women are expected to have only 3.8 children on the average by the time they reach that age (*The New York Times,* 1979).

Why is the birth rate declining so rapidly? Women increasingly indicate that they do not desire any more children than the number they currently have. This finding is true for all socioeconomic groups, including less educated and rural women. The percentage of married women who desire no further children ranges from 61 percent in Colombia, Peru, and Sri Lanka, to 30 percent in Nepal. Increasing knowledge and use of contraceptive techniques around the world enable many women who want no more children to avoid having more. Additionally, the average age at marriage is rising in some Asian countries (thus delaying the age at which women there begin having children), although the marriage age remains relatively unchanged in Latin America. All these factors help to explain the declining rate of world population growth.

TRENDS IN INDUSTRIAL NATIONS

The more industrialized nations, including Western European countries, the USSR, and the United States, have been experiencing dramatically declining fertility rates for even longer than have the developing nations. These declining fertility rates are reflected in the low growth rates in industrialized nations (Figure 20.3). Indeed, many of the world's developed nations seem to be approaching zero population growth.

Zero population growth (ZPG) occurs when the population of a nation or the world remains the same from one year to the next. That is, the number of people remains stable. It does not mean that no new babies are born, but only that the number of births does not exceed the number of deaths. Austria, East and West Germany, and Luxembourg already have more deaths than births each year, resulting in a declining population. The United Kingdom is approaching equilibrium; that is, births and deaths are about equal. Noted demographer Charles Westoff suggests that if current fertility trends continue, Belgium, Czechoslovakia, Denmark, Hungary, Norway, and Sweden will reach zero growth in a few years, followed by Bulgaria, Finland, Greece, Italy, and Switzerland by about 1990 (Westoff, 1978). If present trends persist be-

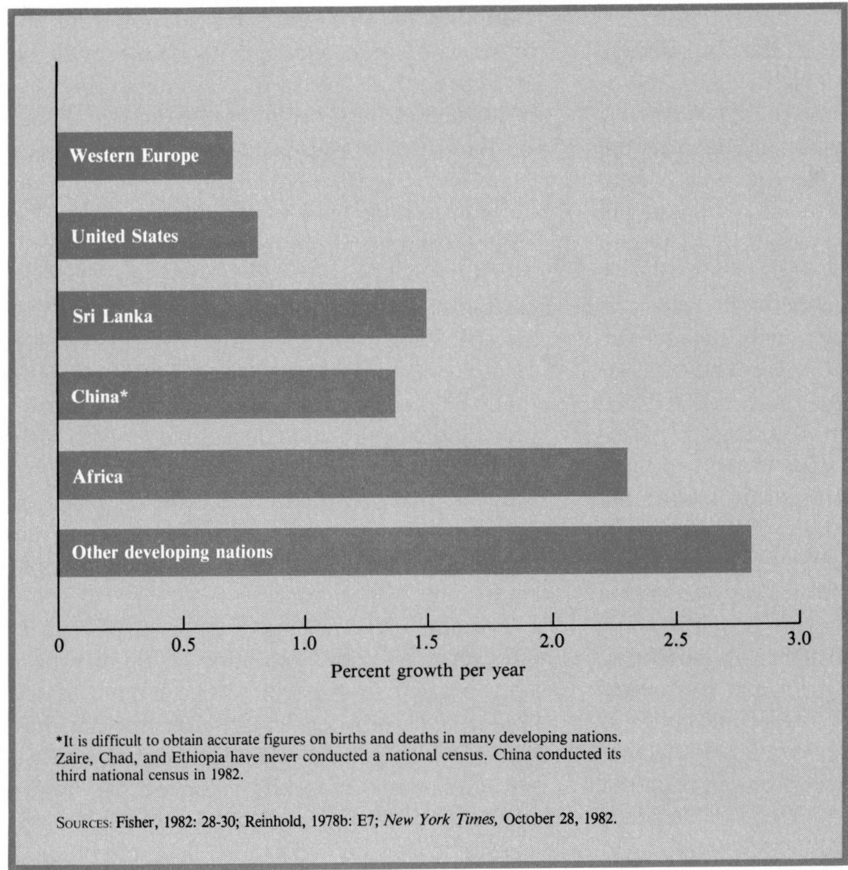

Figure 20.3 Variations in Growth Rates by Country

yond that time, the population of Europe and the USSR would begin to decline by the year 2000, and the United States population would stop growing in about 2015. Westoff argues that declining fertility is part of a long-term trend, and that a number of factors favor the continuation of that trend.

The two biggest reasons for the decline in fertility in industrialized nations are interrelated. First, more women are in the labor force. This means that the economic costs of having children are magnified. The second reason for the fertility decline is the decreasing frequency of marriage. Women who work are less tied to having their economic needs met through marriage. Birth rates are also reduced by the rising divorce rates among those who do marry and by the declining rate of remarriage among divorced persons.

CONSEQUENCES OF TRENDS

Although prior efforts to predict future population trends have not been very successful, it seems reasonable to expect that populations in the United States and Western Europe *will* stop growing in the next 30 years. Meanwhile, the world population will continue to grow, although at a slower rate than in the past. If these predictions come true, what are the likely consequences?

In the United States, especially, there is the possibility of a "top-heavy" age structure by about 2030. Most college students of today will be in their late sixties or seventies by then, and they will be affected by changes in the elderly dependency ratio expected between now and then. The *elderly dependency ratio* relates the size of the elderly population (65 years and over) to the working-age population (ages 18 to 64). Unless another baby boom or a surge of immigration occurs, the elderly dependency ratio will rise steadily and then climb sharply around the year 2010, as shown in Figure 20.4. In 1970, there were 17 elderly per 100 working-age people. By the year 2030, there are expected to be 32 elderly per 100 working-age people.

Since social security payments, in particular, are financed out of the payments of *current* workers, this shift in the dependency ratio means that many more people will be collecting benefits and many fewer will be supporting the system. An increase in the elderly dependency ratio undoubtedly places a heavier burden on those who are working. This burden will be eased to some degree by the growing proportion of women in the work force. By the year 2000, 75 percent of working-age females are expected to be in the labor force.

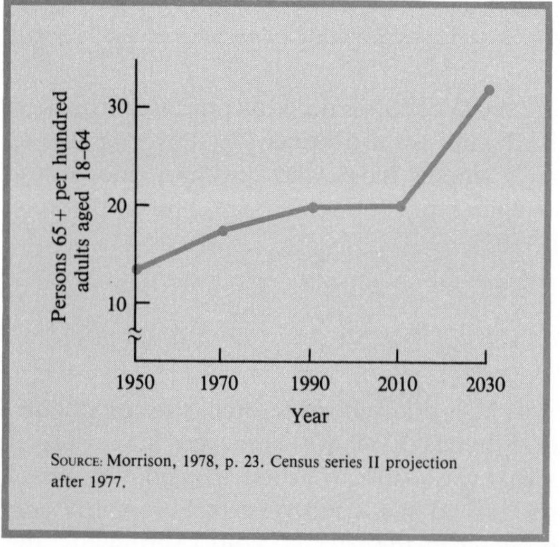

Source: Morrison, 1978, p. 23. Census series II projection after 1977.

Figure 20.4 Elderly Dependency Ratio, 1950–2030

Approaching zero population growth in the United States will affect more than the elderly dependency ratio. Assuming that regional migrations continue, some areas will experience growth, while others will lose residents. If, for example, cities retain large numbers of dependent elderly and children, they will be strained to provide the health and educational services such populations require. Other areas, such as sunbelt suburbs, may experience the growing pains of traffic congestion and inadequate sewers even though they are gaining relatively affluent workers in their prime years.

Societies experiencing low or zero growth rates may be more receptive to immigration from beyond their borders. The United States has a long history of immigration that has dramatically changed its population size, age structure, and ethnic composition. Since 1924, immigration has been restricted considerably by legislation, but immigration policies can be used to affect overall population size. Gaining population through immigration may lead to other problems, however. Westoff, for example, feels that countries with major immigrations seem to experience problems sooner or later due to differences in language, customs, religion, or race (1978). Some Northern European countries have admitted workers from other countries for limited stays by issuing work permits or temporary visas. The practice has supplied labor to industrial societies and provided work (usually of a menial kind) to unemployed laborers from more populous countries. In periods of economic contraction, however, workers are sent home, placing the burden of unemployment on them and their home countries rather than on the countries that received the benefit of their labor. International migration probably cannot fully counteract the effects of a stationary or declining national growth rate (Westoff, 1978). So the likely issues stemming from current population trends need to be addressed.

Most of the rest of the world is in a situation exactly opposite that of the United States and Western Europe. Even with declining rates of growth, world population is expected to continue growing for the foreseeable future. What are the implications of this growth for the globe? Does the world have enough food, air, water, energy, and other resources to support nearly twice as many people as now live here, or will overpopulation lead to wars, massive migrations, or more millions dying of starvation within our lifetime?

MALTHUS AND MARX ON POPULATION PRESSURES

The consequences of population growth have been hotly debated since an English clergyman and professor, Thomas Robert Malthus, published his now famous *An Essay on Population* in 1798. Malthus believed that humans, like plants and animals, were "impelled" to reproduce and that they would multiply to an "incalculable" number in the future if there were no checks on population growth. The ultimate check was the lack of food, and Malthus saw population growing more rapidly than the food supply could expand. The result of these two tendencies would be poverty and eventual starvation, unless people took action. Malthus personally approved of only one way of limiting population growth, and that was use of "moral restraint." People were to remain chaste until they could support a family, and only then were they to marry. He considered contraception, abortion, and sterilization "improper means" of birth control. Malthus practiced what he preached (as far as we know). He waited to marry and have his children until he had obtained a secure job as a college professor, even though it meant putting off marriage until he was 39. Although people have given him "bad press" by suggesting that he had 11 children, he actually had only 3 (Nickerson, 1975).

Germany was one state that took Malthus's advice in the nineteenth century by legislating against marriages in which the father could not guarantee that his family would avoid welfare (Glass, 1953). As a result, many out-of-wedlock children were born in Germany at the time. Growing up in Germany then, Karl Marx and Frederich Engels were strongly influenced by the effects of Malthus's ideas, particularly the way they increased the number of children on welfare. Marx and Engels saw this trend as an outrage against humanity (Weeks, 1981). In particular, they rejected Malthus's view that poverty was the fault of the poor. Instead, they saw poverty as due to the capitalist organization of production. They viewed the human condition as a result of social and economic arrangements. In the kind of society they envisioned, population growth would lead to greater economic production and well-being. Science and technology could enhance food production to keep pace with population expansion.

The Malthusian perspective remains alive today and shapes much of the debate and action over world population. Malthus's ideas have been developed and modified by Paul Ehrlich in his book *The Population Bomb* (1968), and in the so-called Club of Rome's Report, *The Limits to Growth* (Meadows et al., 1972).[1] These books have helped to raise public consciousness in the United States and Western Europe about the negative effects of recent population growth. Ehrlich advocates all methods of birth control, since he foresees a calamitous war, famine, or other dire consequence if something is not done quickly.

The Marxian perspective has been modified

[1]The Club of Rome is an informal international association of economists, industrialists, academics, and scientists devoted to studying the interdependent economic, political, natural, and social elements of the global system. It first met in 1968 in Rome. Members share the conviction that the major problems facing the world are so complex and interrelated that traditional institutions and policies are no longer able to deal with them.

in recent decades, but it continues to place the locus of the population issue in a different place than does the Malthusian view. Prior to the 1960s, Marxians tended to take the ideological position that a well-organized society should be able to handle any population growth that occurs (Sauvy, 1969). More recently, Marxians have tempered this position. Both the Soviet Union and China, countries whose social philosophy draws on Marxist principles, permit contraception and abortion. In addition, in China a couple generally cannot marry until their combined ages total 50, a requirement that reduces fertility. Moreover, families with several children are "counseled" by members of their communities about the virtues of smaller families. Families having fewer children may receive certain preferential treatment—for example, larger apartments, having school fees paid for their children, and other benefits (Sullivan, 1979).

Despite the modifications of the Marxian perspective in practice, a tug of war between the Malthusian and Marxist positions still rends public policy debates over population growth and economic development. At the 1974 World Population Conference in Bucharest, the United States and Western Europe stressed that developing nations would never break out of poverty unless they controlled their populations. Socialist countries challenged the Western world's efforts to define population growth as the single most important problem facing developing nations. Marxians see the single-minded focus on the population issue as diverting attention from the more fundamental issues of the economic exploitation and political domination of developing nations by more powerful nations and multinational corporations. They stress that starvation, for instance, is not so much a matter of inadequate food production and overpopulation as it is a question of the distribution of existing food. Multinational corporations buy land in developing nations and use it to produce cash crops for export rather than for food to feed the local population (Barnet and Muller, 1974).

In terms of emphasis, then, the Marxian position remains quite distinct from the Malthusian approach. The result at the World Population Conference was that an unlikely coalition of Catholic and socialist countries rejected a proposal to give family planning programs top priority. The World Population Plan of Action finally adopted did not stress that population growth handicapped social and economic development. Despite this lack of a clear statement, it is interesting that the rate of population growth appears to have dropped dramatically since then. But even so, the number of people inhabiting the globe continues to grow.

WORLD FOOD PRODUCTION

Every second of every day there are 2½ babies born somewhere in the world, on the average. If it took you 4 seconds to read these sentences, 10 new lives appeared on earth during that time. This means almost 220,000 per day and 80,000,000 per year. One reason for this growth, despite the declining rate of fertility, is the very young age structure of most developing nations in the world, as is evident in Figure 20.2. Even with major declines in fertility, the large numbers of young people reaching childbearing age means the world will soon need to provide food for at least another 2 *billion* people in the foreseeable future. Can the world produce enough food to meet this demand?

One of the factors affecting the amount of food that can be produced is the amount of land available for growing crops. About 11 percent of the world's land surface lends itself well to farm production, and most of it is already in use (Weeks, 1981). No major untapped areas comparable to the Great Plains of North America lie awaiting the plow. The Amazon Basin and other jungle areas appear to have rather shallow layers of topsoil, so they provide little hope. Also, like other areas that are not now under cultivation, they would require massive effort and expense to clear and make usable.

Not only is it unlikely that we can use much more of the world's land for growing crops, but we are actually losing some of the suitable land to erosion, urbanization, and desertification—the gradual transformation of farm land into desert. It follows that if our usable land base is shrinking, the only hope is to raise the yield per acre on the land that is available.

THE GREEN REVOLUTION

The development and use of new forms of grain to improve crop yields led to the so-called *green revolution*. Hybrid wheat and rice with shorter stems but more grain-producing stalks were developed by agricultural scientists in the 1940s and 1950s. By 1971, about 50 million acres were sown with high-yield varieties (HYV) of wheat (Brown, 1973). When these seeds were planted, harvests soared. In Mexico, for instance, wheat production jumped from 3 metric tons per hectare to 6 or 8 tons (Chandler, 1971). Similar gains in rice production were obtained in India, Pakistan, the Philippines, Indonesia, and South Vietnam. This transformation of agricultural productivity has been called the "green revolution."

In order to produce, these seeds need much more water, fertilizer, and pesticides than did existing varieties. Fertilizers and pesticides are usually petroleum-based, and irrigation systems need to be pumped by fuel, usually oil. So the potential of these new seeds was much greater in the 1960s, when the price of oil was lower than it is today. The green revolution and other forms of intensive agriculture have other costs. Many pesticides and fertilizers are either poisonous or carcinogenic (cancer-producing). They not only contaminate the produce and the soil, but they are washed by the rain into rivers and lakes, where they affect drinking water supplies and build up as concentrated residues in the bodies of fish, farm animals, and people. Over time, the pressure to increase crop yields may seriously (and permanently) affect the quality of farmland and water supplies.

Extensive irrigation may deplete underground water supplies more rapidly than they can be replenished. In the long run, overusing those areas may cause them to dry up and become unfit for farming. On balance, while the green revolution has led to dramatic gains in productivity, it does not seem to offer an easy solution to the problems of world food production.

THE SEAS

What about the food potential of the sea? Can we catch more fish or grow and harvest kelp, algae, plankton, or other sea life to enhance our food supply? From 1950 to 1970, the annual catch of fish grew from 22 to 70 million tons (Brown, 1975),and it seemed as if the supply of fish was endless. Since 1970, however, the amount of fish caught has declined, perhaps due to overfishing. Also, since the sea is the ultimate repository of all pollutants, dangerous quantities of DDT, mercury, and radioactive particles have begun to appear in some seafood. As a result, the oceans no longer appear to offer a major source of food for a growing world population.

STEMMING WASTE

At this point in history, technology seems unable to raise food production in substantial ways. This limitation suggests the vital importance of conservation and the changing of eating habits. It has been estimated that people in wealthy nations discard as much as 25 percent of the food they buy (*Newsweek*, 1974). People in certain nations tend to overeat, and suffer from obesity and diseases related to obesity. Certain types of food, especially beef, require more acres to produce a pound of protein than do other kinds of food, such as grains and poultry. It takes several pounds of grain to produce one pound of beef, whereas the same amount of protein can be produced much more efficiently in peanuts, peas, soybeans, and beans. If Americans and Western Europeans reduce their intake of red meat protein and increase their intake of more efficient forms of protein, they will stretch the world's food supplies. Food patterns and preferences are deeply rooted cultural features, however, and usually change quite slowly, although changes along these lines have begun, apparently in response to both price and health concerns.

FOOD DISTRIBUTION

About half of the world's food is based on grain (rice, wheat, and corn). In the 1970s, only the United States, Canada, Argentina, Australia, and New Zealand had enough grain to be able to export some. Most other areas in the world had to import grain. Though Americans represent only 4 percent of the world's population and American farmers comprised only 3 percent of the American labor force in 1980, they produced 42 percent of the world's corn and 15 percent of the world's wheat (U.S. Bureau of the Census, 1982a, p. 678). American farmers are by far the most effective in the world; each one can feed 59 people, on the average, a much higher ratio than occurs in other countries (see Figure 20.5). In the last two decades, the rest of the world has become increasingly dependent on American exports to feed people. Rich nations, such as Kuwait, import food to improve or vary their diets; poorer, faster-growing nations such as India and Bangladesh require imported food to avoid massive starvation. The latter countries, which also may lack valuable natural resources such as oil or copper, are the very ones that find it most difficult to pay for the food they so desperately need.

The issue of whether food is a commodity to be bought and sold or traded for, or whether food is a human right more important than economic or political concerns, came to be more than simply an academic debate in the 1970s and 1980s, when millions of people began starving to death in the Sahel (the region south of the Sahara Desert in Africa), Bangladesh, Cambo-

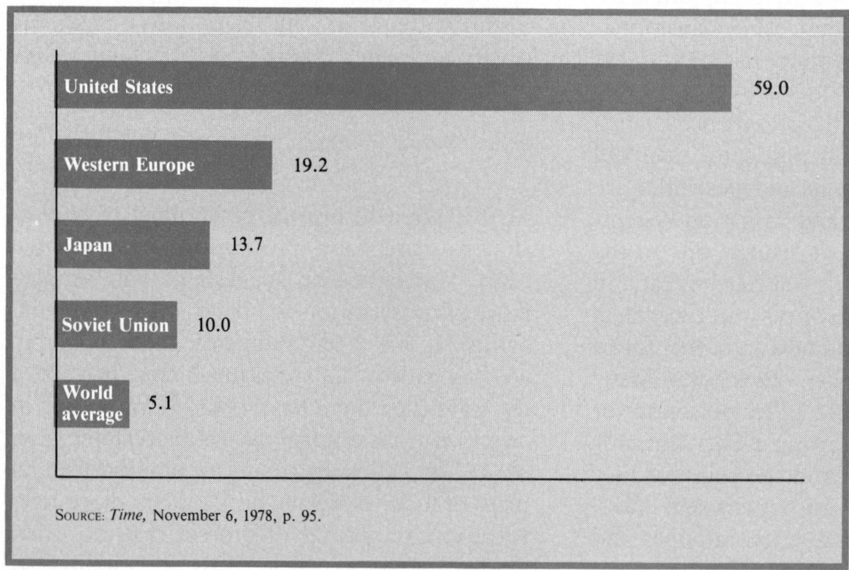

SOURCE: *Time*, November 6, 1978, p. 95.

Figure 20.5 Number of People Fed per Farmer

dia, Ethiopia, and Somalia. The world is facing the moral, social, and political question of whose responsibility it is to feed people. Do those with control over large food surpluses have the right to withhold food from people who need it because they cannot pay for it?

There are strong feelings on both sides of this question. The Environmental Fund, a research center and "think-tank" in Washington, D.C., takes one stance toward the problem of world hunger. It argues, for example, that American aid merely encourages less-developed nations to "have as many children as they please," while "others have the responsibility to feed them" (Environmental Fund, 1976, p. 2). In their view, the real crisis is population growth. They are staunchly in the neo-Malthusian camp, and demand that less-developed nations cut their birth rates in response to food shortages.

Other groups, such as Bread for the World, adopt a position of moral responsibility. They believe that as long as nations that have been blessed by nature and location have a food surplus, they have an obligation to share that food with others. The only way for individuals in poorer nations to limit family size voluntarily is for them to see that the children they do have will survive and grow up. In agricultural societies, children are still the only form of old-age insurance people have. This being the case, they will not limit their childrearing unless they can be sure their children will not die of starvation or nutrition-related diseases. This position stresses the point that the present hunger problem is a distribution problem, rather than a production problem.

A third and more drastic position is called *triage*. The term triage is taken from wartime medical work, where the wounded were classified into those who would definitely benefit from medical attention, those who might, and those who were too badly injured to gain from care. In responding to world hunger, a triage approach involves the determination, by nations with surplus food, of those needy nations that are most likely to survive, and concentrating existing food surpluses on them while ignoring the others (Environmental Fund, 1976).

Whatever the short-term actions nations take to deal with the world population and hunger problem, in the not too distant future the only immediately visible way to avert world starvation on a major scale seems to be population control. With the reduction of death rates on a worldwide basis, the growth of population has far exceeded gains in agricultural productivity. We are staring at a crisis of global proportions. Unless technology produces some dramatic and rapid changes, we appear to be approaching the limits of existing subsistence strategies.

Starvation is a very real prospect for millions of people each year. Many public and private agencies have set up camps for refugees fleeing from droughts or political persecution, such as this Cambodian mother and child in a Thai refugee camp. Groups urging moral responsibility for the world's hungry stress that hunger today results from the way food is distributed rather than from problems of food production.

Food production and distribution are important, but other factors also affect birth and death rates. Chief among them are ecology and health care delivery.

ECOLOGY

Ecology is the study of how organisms relate to one another and to their environments. The *ecosystem* refers to the system formed by the interaction of a community of organisms with their environment. In the broadest sense, the human ecosystem is the planet earth. The study of ecology has become increasingly important in recent years as people have begun to feel the effects of a century of industrialization on the environment, and as they realize they may be doing irreversible damage to that environment and to themselves.

Attitudes toward the natural environment have varied widely through time. Many preliterate tribal societies have a religious attitude toward nature, and treat everything in it with respect. To native Americans, for example, plants, animals, and even rocks were seen as containing spirits as vital as the human spirit. As a result, they did not feel they could impose their wishes on nature. They could take what they needed, in an attitude of respectful gratitude, but were not to waste anything they took or in any way spoil nature.

The attitude of native Americans contrasts sharply with that held by Western industrializers, who tend to see themselves as apart from nature and to view nature as a collection of resources to be exploited. Such a view sees nature as existing to meet human needs and desires. Short-term profit and productivity are the only things to consider. Long-term consequences are ignored, or it is assumed that technology can be developed to deal with them. Human desires are seen as the only important force in determining how the environment is shaped. Ponds may be drained for housing, rivers dammed, and highways carved into the sides of mountains. People even try to turn away the tides in an effort to keep shorefront property from eroding.

The more nature is manipulated, the more technology and human intervention is needed to sustain the results. New breeds of animals need constant human attention to survive. New hybrid grains that produced the green revolution require irrigation, chemical fertilizers, and pesticides to flourish. The more the environment is exploited, the more intensified become the two major threats faced by our ecological system: pollution and depletion of natural resources.

THE ENVIRONMENTAL MOVEMENT

In recent years, environmental exploitation has been challenged by many people, including Barry Commoner, an economist and ecological crusader (1971). He offers four principles of ecology. First, everything is related to everything else. Because all organisms are interconnected, if even one gets out of balance, it will affect the balance of the others. Second, everything must go somewhere, meaning that there is no safe place to hide poisons. If they go into the air, they will be brought down to earth by rain and snow, picked up by plants and animals, and eventually reach humans. One dramatic illustration of this principle is that today mother's milk contains ten times more of the insecticide DDT than is permitted in dairy milk sold in stores.

Third, "nature knows best." This means that whenever people try to change or "improve" a natural system, they will harm that system. Every organic substance produced by a living organism has a counterpart somewhere in nature that can break it down. This principle ensures that recycling occurs. In nature, there is no such thing as waste. People and animals, for example, exhale carbon dioxide, plants use it as nourishment. Plants in turn give off oxygen, which is needed by animals and humans. Organisms or enzymes break down decaying organic matter into simpler elements that further the growth of other things. But the synthetic fibers and plastics we have invented in recent years cannot be broken down by nature into reusable forms. This is what it means when we say something is not biodegradable. If it does not break down naturally, it must be burned, thereby creating pollution, or it piles up. Heavily populated areas are running out of space to dump their styrofoam cups, plastic tampon applicators, and polyester fabrics.

Fourth, "there is no such thing as a free lunch." In ecology, every gain has some cost. Because everything is interdependent, that cost can be delayed, but it cannot be avoided. We are reaching the point where soon we can no longer avoid beginning to pay those costs.

POLLUTION

The air, water, and soil are seriously polluted in many areas of the world. The air in urban and industrial areas stings people's eyes, burns their lungs, and strains their hearts. Fumes from auto exhaust, steel and paper mills, oil refineries, incinerators, and electric generating plants are affected by sunlight and form smog, a substance that not only clouds landscapes but shortens lives. Chemically created fertilizers are applied in heavy doses to raise crop yields on American farms. What growing plants do not consume does not break down into simpler compounds. Instead, it runs off into local streams, rivers, and lakes. There the chemicals promote the growth of so much algae that fish cannot survive. The result is that the balance of nature is upset.

We have already mentioned that certain pesticides like DDT do not break down into simpler, safe compounds. Fertilizers and pesticides represent a small fraction of some 50,000 chemical compounds that have been created and marketed in the United States in the past generation. About three-quarters of these are considered by the Environmental Protection Agency to be surely or possibly harmful to human health. Many contribute to the increase in the number of cancer cases in this country. The rate at which these hazardous compounds are produced has soared. In 1941, the American petrochemical industry produced 1 billion pounds of synthetic chemicals. By 1977, production had skyrocketed to 350 billion pounds. Many of these chemicals are useful and even vital in our daily lives, but they have heavy ecological costs.

One of the major causes for concern is that chemical wastes are seeping into groundwater that has been stored slowly over the centuries in porous places underground, threatening to contaminate the water supplies of more than half the nation's population. Millions of barrels of chemical waste have been disposed of, often in the dark of night, in unmarked and unsafe containers. These barrels are ticking time bombs. Nobody knows where all the "skeletons" are buried. The EPA estimates that there are about 231,000 sites and "lagoons" where chemicals have been dumped, and as many as 2,000 of these dumps may pose serious risks. The nation had a glimpse of the problem in 1980, when it was discovered that a chemical landfill in the Love Canal near Niagara Falls, New York, had begun to contaminate the surrounding area. Residents were plagued by high rates of cancer, birth defects, and respiratory and neurological problems.

In addition to calling attention to the health risks related to the things people pour into the air, water, and soil, the study of ecology also draws attention to the use of nonrenewable resources. Some sources of energy like sunlight, windpower, and hydroelectric power are constantly renewing themselves. Other resources are part of an ever-dwindling supply.

RESOURCE DEPLETION

Until the Middle Eastern oil crises in 1973–74 and 1979, most people had never thought that the world might run out of certain resources. The world's supply of clean air and water, oil, iron, aluminum, natural gas, gold, silver, and copper somehow seemed limitless. Those crises, and the gas station lines that accompanied them, showed that the supply of natural resources had

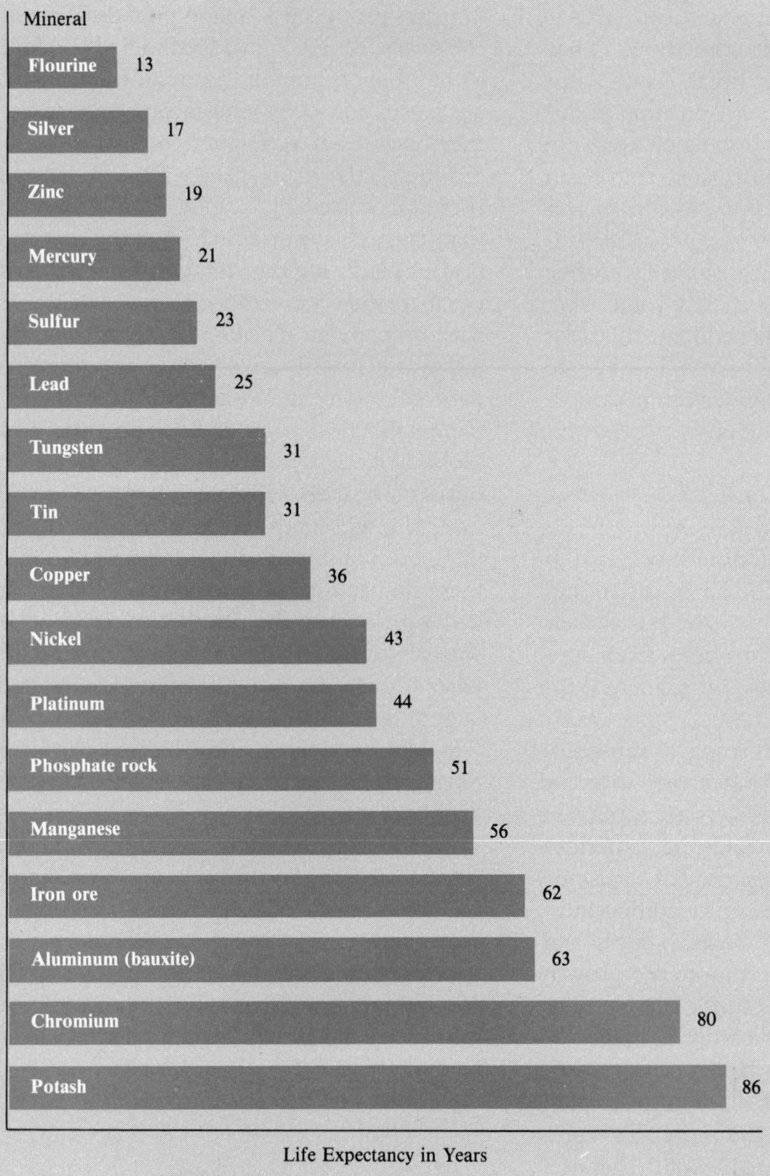

Mineral	Life Expectancy in Years
Flourine	13
Silver	17
Zinc	19
Mercury	21
Sulfur	23
Lead	25
Tungsten	31
Tin	31
Copper	36
Nickel	43
Platinum	44
Phosphate rock	51
Manganese	56
Iron ore	62
Aluminum (bauxite)	63
Chromium	80
Potash	86

SOURCE: Barney, 1980, p. 29.

Figure 20.6 Life Expectancies of 1976 World Reserves of Selected Minerals*

*Assumes no increase in 1976 reserves and assumes that usage increases at the amount projected in the Global 2000 Technical Report, Table 12–2.

physical and political limitations. As Figure 20.6 indicates, many key resources are expected to last only a few more years at current projected rates of consumption.

Energy production throughout the world consumes a great deal of oil, coal, and natural gas, all of which are nonrenewable resources. Optimists argue that new supplies of resources will be discovered or that substitutes will be invented. More pessimistic forecasts like the *Limits to Growth* report by Meadows et al. (1972) suggest that resource depletion, pollution, population growth, food production, and industrial growth are headed for collision and ultimate collapse, if present trends continue. Although the assumptions and computations in that report have been questioned, it is becoming increasingly apparent that the planet has limited resources and that only so much pollution can be tolerated. Such realizations have prompted people to begin exploring alternative patterns of resource use.

ALTERNATIVES TO DEPLETION

Conservation, changed patterns of consumption, home production of simple foods, and recycling are some of the strategies individuals are exploring to cut costs and avoid resource depletion. As the costs of oil and natural gas have skyrocketed, people have tried to find ways to conserve energy. Many people are driving less, using more fuel-efficient vehicles, turning down their thermostats, adding insulation and storm windows to apartments or homes, exploring solar sources of energy, building "earth houses" partially underground, and constructing smaller dwellings. Smaller homes and cars also take fewer natural resources to build.

Conservation of resources seems to be encouraged when individuals benefit directly from the consequences of their efforts. When tenants pay their own utility bills, they use less gas and electricity than when landlords pay the utilities and simply pass along the costs in higher rents. There is renewed interest in the quality and durability of products, which means that fewer resources are consumed through constant replacement of consumer goods. Recycling centers are also on the increase. New forms of recycling are being explored, including ways of turning garbage into energy. Some of these alternatives are discussed by Schumacher (1973) in his book *Small Is Beautiful.*

The so-called natural foods movement stresses growing crops by using organic fertilizers and natural pest repellents, and it encourages people to produce more of their own food. Home gardening is on the increase, and even city dwellers are more and more likely to have a tub of tomatoes in a sunny window or to make their own alfalfa or mung bean sprouts.

Values, norms, and social and economic interests all contribute to the ecological crisis the world now faces. One source of ecological problems is the powerful and profitable petrochemical industry. But people who eagerly purchase their products are responsible as well. Our culture is part of the problem, and people need to change their values and attitudes if they are going to become part of the solution. These solutions lie beyond the power of technical innovations. They require changes in underlying attitudes and behaviors, tax structures, and the social organization of agriculture and industry. Existing institutions must change so that they support the ecosystem rather than undermine it. We face a race against time to see whether we can change our attitudes and institutions before we destroy our ecological support system.

HEALTH AND SOCIETY

Life expectancy and illness are strongly influenced by ecological and social factors. The way people respond to and treat different illnesses also varies across cultures. The same physical ailment may be treated by witchcraft, prayer, the laying on of hands, or radiation and chemotherapy, depending on the culture in which the illness occurs.

In addition, people in different societies around the world die of very different causes. In preindustrial and developing societies, people may weaken and die of infections such as pneumonia, starvation, and parasites such as tapeworms. Many young children die of malnourishment, typhoid, or diphtheria. In industrial societies, most of these causes of death have been eliminated. Moreover, previously stubborn diseases such as smallpox, polio, German measles, tetanus, diphtheria, mumps, and measles have been controlled or eliminated.

Given the control modern medicine has over many life-threatening diseases, the recent outbreak of a mysterious illness known as AIDS (or acquired immune deficiency syndrome) has been particularly frightening. AIDS results in the breakdown of the body's mechanisms for resisting disease. Of the 1,450 AIDS cases reported between June 1981 and May 1983, 38.5 percent resulted in death. Of the cases diagnosed two or more years before, the fatality rate was 82 percent (Pear, 1983). In May 1983 the U.S. Public Health Service declared AIDS its "No. 1 priority," but some people faulted the Service for neglecting the disease because its major victims have been homosexual or bisexual men, drug users, Haitian immigrants, or hemophiliacs. Recent research, however, suggests that AIDS may be sexually transmitted from men to women (Altman, 1983). Aside from these clues, very little is known about the cause of AIDS or how to treat it. One consequence of the outbreak of AIDS has been a reexamination of gay life-styles, much as the increased prevalence of herpes led to a reexamination of heterosexual relationships. The difference is that while herpes may be uncomfortable or embarrassing, AIDS is often fatal.

If they do not get AIDS, people in industrial societies generally live to be much older, and die of quite different causes than people in preindustrial societies. Some of the causes include diet, smoking, and lack of exercise. Americans, for example, love juicy hamburgers, steaks, and bacon and eggs. Such a cholesterol-rich diet combined with no exercise and smoking results in high mortality rates from heart disease, cancer, and strokes. Americans also drink and drive and do not regulate handguns in most areas, with the result that accidents, including numerous ones caused by alcohol, cars, and guns, are the fourth leading cause of death in the United States.

Within the United States there are wide differences in death rates and types of illness according to social class, race, and sex. (There also are cultural differences in reaction to pain, as the box indicates.) As noted in Chapters 11 and 12, whites have a longer life expectancy than blacks, and women live longer than men. Moreover, the higher one's social class, the healthier one tends to be. This phenomenon seems to be due to better nutrition, lower exposure to health hazards and stressful situations, more knowledge about health, and greater access to superior health care (Kitagawa, 1972; Syme and Berkman, 1981).

Why do women live longer than men? The life expectancy of women has increased dramatically in the last 60 years. In 1920, the life expectancy for women was 56, only two years longer than that for men. By 1980, it was 78, about eight years longer than men's (U.S. Bureau of the Census, 1982a). Among young adults, males are more likely to succumb to accidents. At older ages, heart and kidney diseases and lung cancer contribute to the higher mortality of men. Women, in turn, have become less likely to die in childbirth or of uterine cancer in recent years (Waldron, 1981). Cultural factors play a role in the lower mortality rates among married rather than single or widowed males, particularly from such causes as cirrhosis of the liver (associated with heavy drinking). Gove (1973) argues that married men receive better physical care than single ones and have a greater sense of psychological well-being. See the box on "Not So Merry Widowers," pp. 548–549.

OCCUPATIONS AND CANCER

Between 1960 and 1978 in the United States, deaths due to stroke, hypertension, arteriosclerosis, and accidents declined. Deaths from heart disease remained constant in that period, while deaths from cancer increased from 16 percent of all deaths to 21 percent (U.S. Bureau of the Census, 1981a). Only two other causes of death have increased as significantly in recent years: homicide and cirrhosis of the liver.

More than 53 million people in the United States—more than one-quarter of the population—will develop some form of cancer. Why, in the face of improved techniques of identifying and treating cancer, has the rate of death due to this disease increased? Some argue that the increases are associated with the growth of industrial chemicals in our environment and the exposure of large numbers of people to those chemicals over the last four decades (Epstein, 1981). Experts suggest that up to 90 percent of human cancers are environmentally induced.

This conclusion is supported by evidence showing how the incidence of cancer varies geographically (Epstein, 1981). It is already known that about 50 percent of longtime asbestos-insulation workers die of cancer; the rates of bladder cancer are very high in dye and rubber industry workers; lung cancer is up in uranium miners of Colorado and coke oven workers. Other cancers are associated with certain occupations: skin cancer in shale oil workers; nasal sinus cancer in woodworkers; liver cancer in workers making polyvinyl chloride; leukemia in benzene workers; and cancer of the pancreas in organic chemists. Lung cancer is demonstrably higher in smokers than in nonsmokers, and possibly in their spouses and children as well.

Such cancers are ultimately preventable if the specific causes can be pinpointed. Spotting cancer-causing agents is sometimes difficult because cancers crop up 15 or 20 years after workers or residents are exposed to the agents (Selikoff, 1980). Not only are workers exposed, but vast areas of the world are in danger of contamination from the chemical wastes produced by many manufacturing processes (Magnuson, 1980).

Despite overwhelming hints that environmental causes of cancer might be a fruitful area for further investigation, the National Cancer Institute's expenditures on environmental cancer agents has been estimated at only 5 to 20 percent of the total (Epstein, 1981). Industry seems unconcerned with the issue. When additional regulatory standards limiting environmental and occupational exposure to toxic agents are proposed, industries often respond by forecasting major economic distress and unemployment as a result of the regulations. Such calculations overlook the fact that the economic (not to mention the human) costs of cancer are at least $15 billion a year (Epstein, 1981). The scourge of cancer calls for major social, economic, and political solutions at least as much as medical ones.

HEALTH CARE ORGANIZATION AND DELIVERY

The manner in which health care is organized and delivered in different societies is influenced by many social factors. Perhaps the most striking feature of health care organization in the United States is the way it is financed. Medical care is considered a service that is available to those who can pay for it—just as, say, the services of an interior decorator are available to people who can afford one. The price of medical care is based on the free play of market forces. This free market model of medical care stands in sharp contrast to the way medical services are organized elsewhere. In virtually all other industrial countries, medical care is viewed more as a right than a service to be purchased. Health care systems receive subsidies from the state, so that the kind and quality of the medical care received depends on the nature of the illness, not on a person's income (Freidson, 1978).

The organization of American health care is also characterized by the monopolistic control physicians have over medical practice. Doctors

Cultural Differences in Reactions to Pain

Medical practitioners have noticed for some time that members of different cultural groups have different reactions to pain, illness, and medical treatment. Understanding these differences is important not only for the individuals who provide health services to different people, but also for what they show about the importance of culture for shaping something as seemingly physical as the perception of pain.

In interviews with patients, physicians, nurses, and family members, Zborowski (1981) found wide variations in the way pain was perceived and reacted to by male patients of Jewish, Italian, and "old American" (that is, Anglo-Saxon) origin. All the patients were in a veterans hospital, and all had some type of back ailment.

Both Jews and Italians were described by medical staff as very sensitive to pain. Some doctors thought they had a lower threshold of pain than members of so-called Nordic groups. Since the threshold of pain is physiological and is similar for all human beings regardless of nationality (Hardy, Wolff, and Goodell, 1952), these behavioral differences in response must be cultural in origin.

Both Italians and Jews were described as very emotional in their responses to pain, but they also had some differences in their attitudes toward pain. Members of both groups felt free to speak about their pain, complain about it, and groan, moan, or cry. They did not like to be alone, and expected sympathy and assistance from their families and friends. Italians seemed more concerned about the immediacy of the pain experience, while Jews were concerned about the significance of the pain for their general health and its implications for the welfare of their families.

The patients' feelings were reflected in their attitudes toward drugs. Italians wanted effective pain relief. If a drug provided that, patients forgot their suffering and became cheerful. Jewish patients were often reluctant to accept drugs, for fear they might harm their health in the long run. Italian patients tended to show greater confidence in their doctors, while Jewish patients were more skeptical. For Italians, this confidence was enhanced if the doctors could relieve their pain. On the other hand, even if their pain was eased, Jews wondered whether the doctor could help the underlying illness.

Patients of "old American" origin saw no point in emotionally laden complaints about pain. They tended instead to "report" the nature of the pain experienced, where it was, and how often it occurred. They tended to seek approval from hospital personnel, and did not want to be seen as a nuisance to the staff. Limiting their emotional reactions to pain was a major way they tried to find approval. This reaction on the part of "old Americans" seemed to be an accurate interpretation of what American or Americanized medical people desired. Doctors tended to describe the behavior of Italian and Jewish patients as exaggerated and overemotional. As a result, doctors minimized the pain experiences of such patients or, even more strongly, labeled them as deviants, hypochondriacs, and neurotics (Zborowski, 1981).

Like Jewish patients, "old American" patients shared a concern with the significance of pain as a symptom of deeper-seated illness. The latter group felt, much as the Italians did, that suffering pain is unnecessary when something can be done to relieve it. Also, while Jewish patients were anxious and pessimistic about their futures, "old Americans" were much more optimistic that the source of their pain could be "fixed." Their anxieties were relieved when they believed that as much as possible was being done to treat their pain. They liked an interventionist attitude on the part of attending health professionals. Being in the hospital was a part of treatment that they expected, and therefore they seemed less disturbed by hospital treatment than Italian or Jewish patients. "Old Americans" also differed from Jewish and Italian patients in that they preferred to be alone when their pain was severe and not to be surrounded by family and friends at that time.

Finally, individuals' reactions to pain differed depending on their occupations. Manual workers with ruptured spinal discs were much more upset by their pain than were professional workers with the same ailment, probably because of its effect on their livelihoods (Zborowski, 1981).

Pain, like illness and cause of death, is closely related to social factors. Knowing something about the social origins and social consequences of people's reactions to pain can be very helpful to health professionals and to the people experiencing the pain.

have an exclusive state-supported right, apparent in the licensing of physicians, to practice medicine. They are the only ones who are legally entitled to prescribe restricted drugs, cut into the human body, and sign a certificate giving the cause of death.

Although it is very much taken for granted today, M.D.s have not always had an exclusive monopoly on medicine. Until the latter part of the nineteenth century, various groups, including midwives, shared medical practice with doctors. But by the 1920s, virtually only M.D. physicians had the legal right to practice medicine in the United States (Conrad and Kern, 1981). Their monopoly extends over the right to define illness and how to treat it, the right to limit and evaluate other medical care workers, and the supervision of childbirth. It also includes a very

This exercise class for expectant mothers reflects changing conceptions of pregnancy and childbirth.

Not So Merry Widowers: *The Stresses of Survival Can Be a Mortal Blow*

Social scientists have long recognized that few traumas are as hard to bear as the death of a spouse. For the survivor, the intense distress can lead to serious psychological and physical ailments. Now, a new study of survivors shows that widowhood dramatically raises the chances of death for some survivors—men. The death of a husband has almost no effect on women's mortality rates.

The study, published in the current issue of the *American Journal of Public Health,* was conducted by three researchers from the John Hopkins University School of Hygiene and Public Health. Knud J. Helsing, Moyses Szklo and George W. Comstock followed the lives of 1,204 men and 2,828 women in semi-rural Washington County, Md., who were widowed between 1963 and 1974. With each spouse's death, the survivor was matched with a still married person, cross-referenced for comparison not only by race, sex and age, but also by such factors as years of schooling, age at first marriage, frequency of church attendance, whether the person smoked cigarettes, and the number of bathrooms and number of animals on the premises.

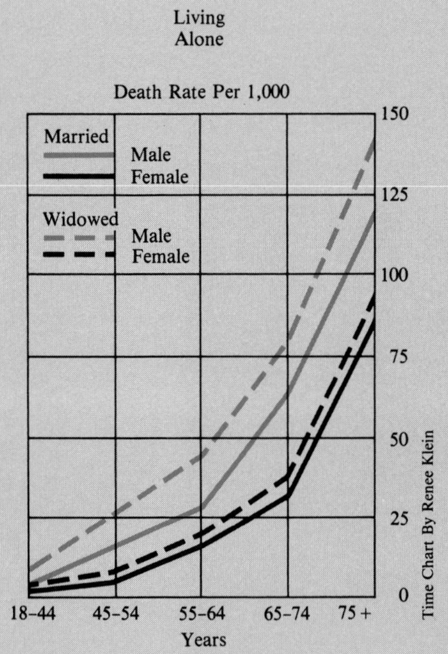

The study's most unexpected finding was negative: there was no evidence that either men or women were significantly more likely to die in the early months after bereavement. "That was the big surprise," Helsing, the principal investigator, told TIME last week. "Our original premise was that the stress of the loss of a spouse would show up in mortality very quickly, and then the person would get over it. Instead, it is the stressful life situation of the widowed that seems to be hard on people." A great deal harder on men than on women, it appears. The overall mortality rate was 26% higher for widowers than for married men, compared with only a 3.8% difference in the rate between widows and married women. For widowers aged 55 to 64, the mortality rate was almost 61% higher than for married men in the same age group.

The researchers do not know why wives are less affected by the loss of a spouse than husbands, except to suggest in their paper that "the same physiologic and psychologic differences that give females greater longevity than males also act to make females more resistant to the stress of widowhood." Says Helsing: "Women may be more adaptable. They may have more of a sense of survivability."

One of the study's most important findings was that remarriage by widowers dramatically lowered their mortality rates. In men under 55 who remarried—and at least half of them did—the death rate was at least

Living Alone

Death Rate Per 1,000

Married: Male, Female

Widowed: Male, Female

150, 125, 100, 75, 50, 25, 0

18–44, 45–54, 55–64, 65–74, 75+

Years

Time Chart By Renee Klein

SOURCE: *American Journal of Public Health* and *Time,* August 10, 1981, p. 45

70% lower than for those who did not; in men aged 55 to 64, it was 50% lower. In fact, death rates for widowers who remarried were even lower than for men in the same age groups who were married throughout the period of study.

One finding was equally devastating for both widowed men and women: a dramatic rise in mortality—by three or four times—if a widowed person moved into a retirement or nursing home because of illness or inability to live with other family members. And there is no consolation in living alone: this too contributes to higher mortality rates. Even allowing for the fact that it may be the less healthy widowed who fail to remarry, the researchers feel it is fair to ask whether it may be marriage—or remarriage—that "provides the care and social support that tends to reduce mortality." If a causal connection between remarriage and reduced mortality can be established, they observe, "changes in Social Security and income tax laws to encourage remarriage of the widowed would be justified as public health measures."

SOURCE: *Time*, August 10, 1981, p. 45.

strong influence over the financing and planning of health services.

The way medicine is socially organized in the United States has resulted in professional autonomy for physicians, a hierarchical social organization of health care delivery personnel, the high cost of medical care, limited national health care planning, and more emphasis on the treatment of illness than on its prevention. People who can get into medical school and who can afford to attend end up as doctors with a great deal of independence. They decide where they want to practice, in what they would like to specialize, whom they will treat, and what they will charge for their services.

One result of this free market model and the relatively great autonomy of doctors has been the increasing specialization of modern medicine. Until World War II, most physicians were family doctors, practicing general medicine and making house calls. Now, all but 13 percent of the nation's doctors are specialists (U.S. Bureau of the Census, 1982a). This specialization may lead to higher costs, loss of perspective on a whole human being, and lack of continuity of treatment. Physicians are also very unevenly distributed throughout the nation. In 1979, Washington, D.C., had 552 active physicians per 100,000 population, compared to 107 per 100,000 in Mississippi (U.S. Bureau of the Census, 1982a). Thousands of towns and counties in America have no doctor at all.

The lines of authority within the health professions are sharply drawn by occupational rank. In hospitals all doctors, even inexperienced beginning ones, have authority over all nurses, no matter how experienced they are. This means, for instance, that when a new doctor prescribes the wrong drug dosage, a nurse has no formal authority to change the prescription. An experienced nurse might say, "Did you say 200 mg of ______ drug, which is the usual dosage?" (when the doctor said 2000 mg), and hope that the doctor picks up on the face-saving cue that is offered.

A third critical consequence of the organization of medical care in the United States is its high cost compared to other countries. Health care costs increased more than 20 times between 1950 and 1981, as Figure 20.7 shows. Some $287 billion (or 9.8 percent of GNP) was spent on health expenditures in 1981. This was up from $13 billion, or 4.5 percent of GNP, in 1950 (U.S. Bureau of the Census, 1982a).

Although three quarters of the population had some kind of private health insurance in 1979, that still left a quarter of Americans without any coverage at all (U.S. Bureau of the Census, 1982a). Moreover, many who have coverage find that it is limited as to the kind and

These young doctors must deal with a trend in American medicine toward greater specialization and away from general practice. In recent years more women are becoming physicians than was true in the past, but certain specialities, such as surgery, still have very few women in them.

amount of payment. The result is that some people can pay high prices to see private physicians, while many have only crowded public clinics and hospital outpatient facilities available to them. And some cannot afford any medical or dental care at all. As long as health care is conceived of as a consumer good to be purchased by private individuals rather than as a social good that should be available to everyone, there will be a limited amount of political attention devoted to national health care planning. This is likely to result in the absence of any coherent planning and protection for all the members of a society.

Another major consequence of the current organization of health care is the relatively greater emphasis on the treatment rather than the prevention of illness. Yet some contexts and activities actively create illness and injury—for example, occupations such as logging, mining, chemical handling, or professional football have much higher rates of illness or injury than do many other occupations. Certain behaviors such as being competitive, aggressive, and impatient may be encouraged and rewarded in our society and yet be linked to higher rates of heart attacks and high blood pressure. Various foods and drugs are widely advertised around the world (for instance, sugar-filled soft drinks, coffee, cigarettes, and tranquilizers), despite the growing evidence that they may be harmful to health.

One attempt individuals have made to maintain or improve their own health is evident in the so-called physical fitness craze. In recent years, many people living in industrial societies, especially in the United States, have joined health clubs, taken up jogging, or tried to play

The communities in which people live are influenced by food production, trade, technology, and occupational activities. A highly productive farm economy in the United States allows very densely populated cities to exist.

American farmlands

Houston, Texas

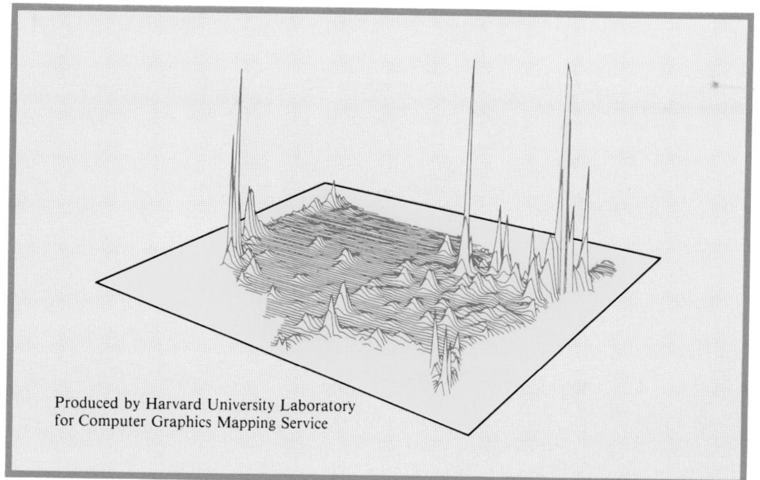

Population density in the United States, 1979

In the last decade population growth has been greater in the west and south of the United States than in the north central and northeast. In the 1970s, for the first time in more than a century, nonmetropolitan areas grew faster than metropolitan areas did.

Population changes in the United States, 1970 to 1980 (in percent)

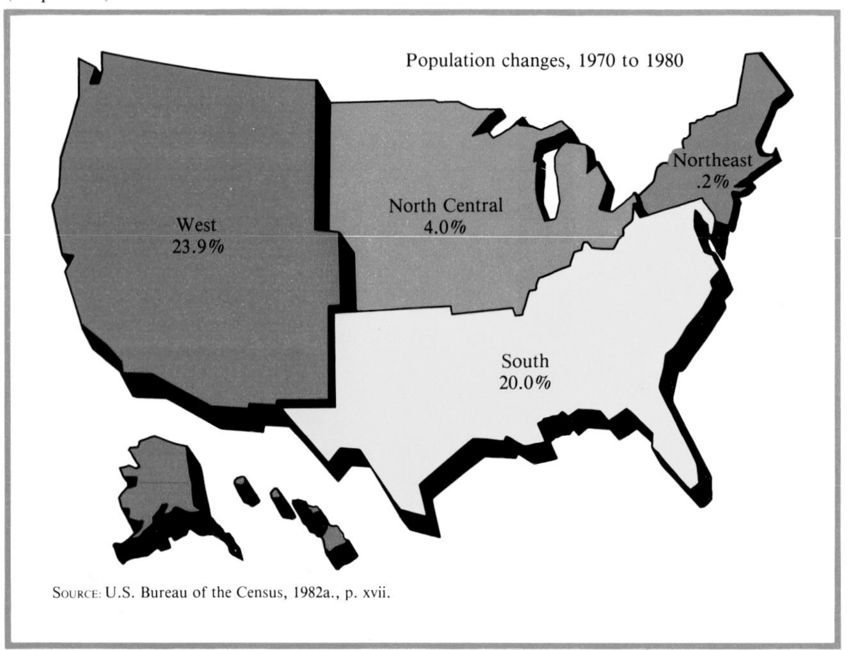

SOURCE: U.S. Bureau of the Census, 1982a., p. xvii.

The expansion of suburbs was fueled in part by the post-World War II "baby boom."

The "baby boom" in the United States in 1960, 1990, and 2025 (projected)

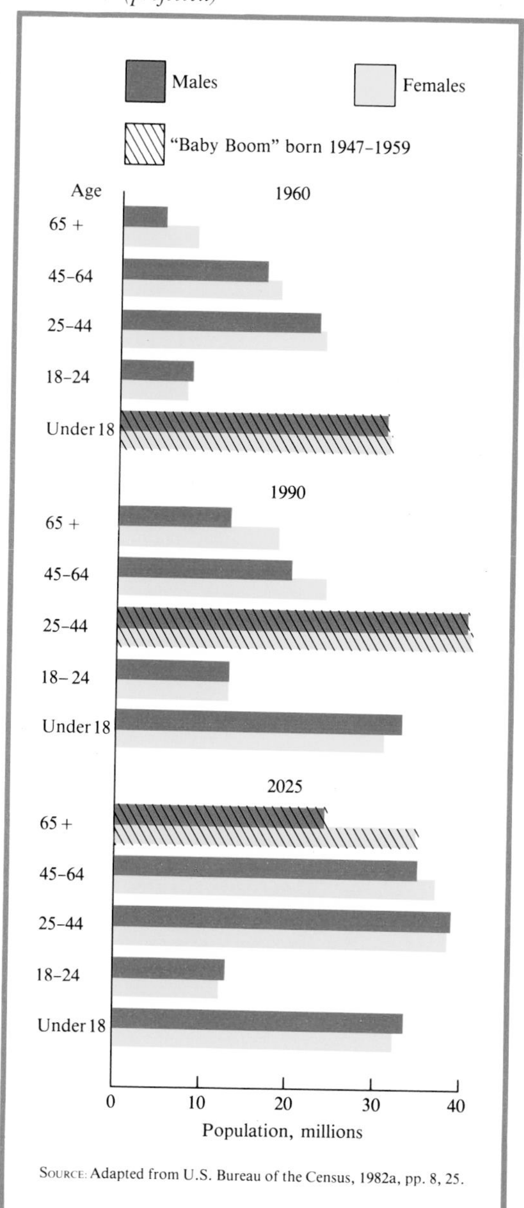

SOURCE: Adapted from U.S. Bureau of the Census, 1982a, pp. 8, 25.

The nature and growth of cities as diverse as Baltimore and Toronto has been influenced by population changes including immigration from other lands.

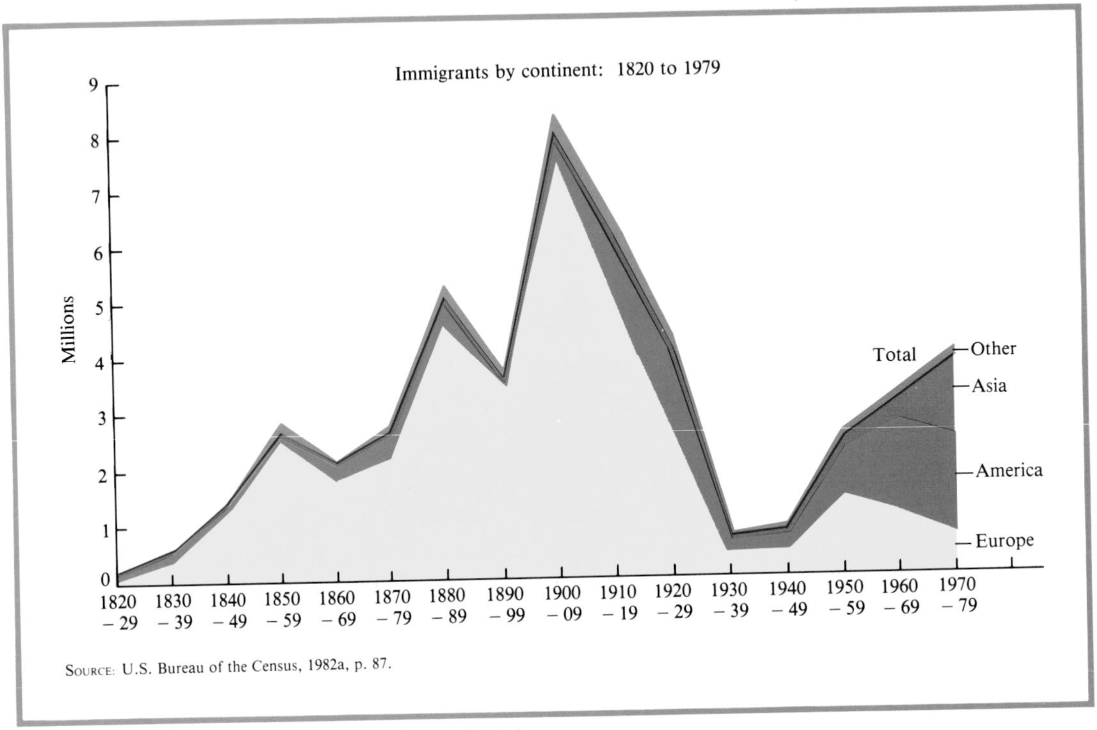
Immigrants by continent: 1820 to 1979
Millions
9
8
7
6
5
4
3
2
1
0
1820 – 29
1830 – 39
1840 – 49
1850 – 59
1860 – 69
1870 – 79
1880 – 89
1890 – 99
1900 – 09
1910 – 19
1920 – 29
1930 – 39
1940 – 49
1950 – 59
1960 – 69
1970 – 79
Total
Other
Asia
America
Europe
SOURCE: U.S. Bureau of the Census, 1982a, p. 87.

Immigrants to the United States by continent of origin, 1820–1979.

LIGHT
STREET
PAVILION

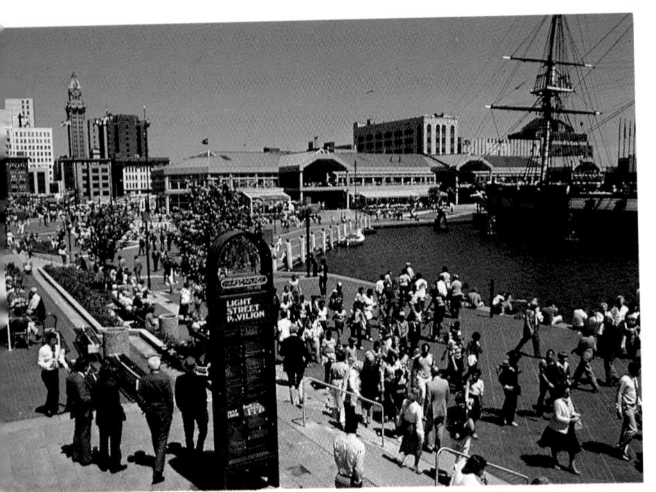

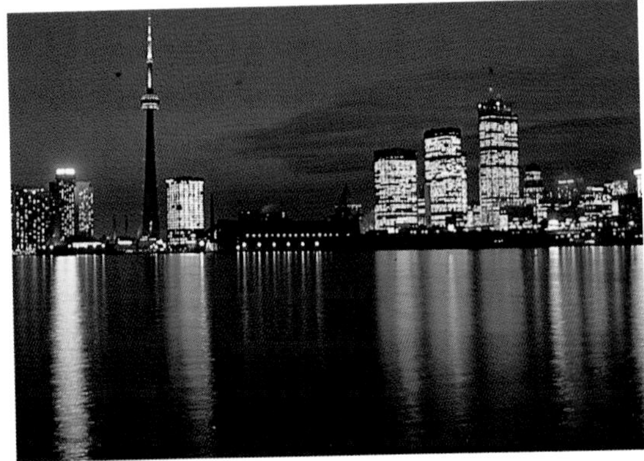

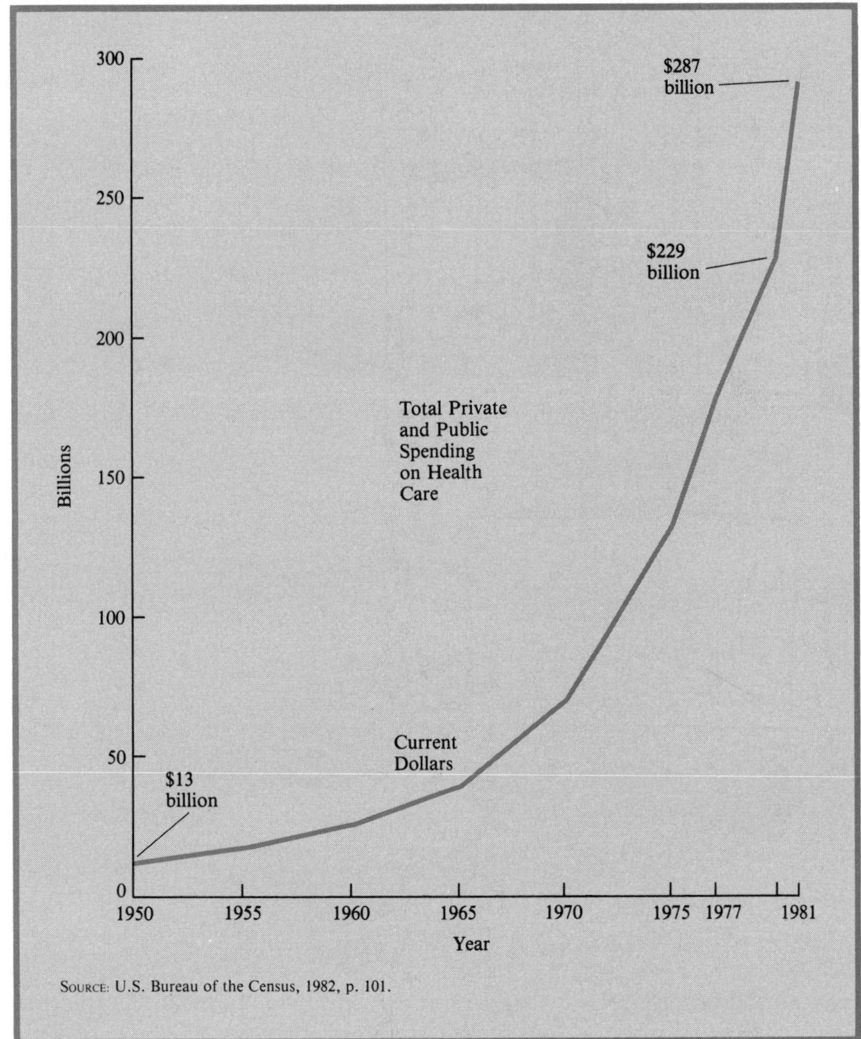

Figure 20.7 Rising Costs of Medical Care, 1950–1981

some sport regularly. But almost no one is examining the social sources of illness and death. The process requires a quite different kind of analysis and intervention than what is generally practiced by the health profession. It involves efforts to change the ecological, political, and social sources of illness in our society. Medical treatment, on the other hand, is more appropriate for acute infectious diseases such as pneumonia, which lend themselves well to treatment with antibiotics, than for long-term chronic diseases such as heart disease, cancer, and stroke, which are more likely to afflict people in industrial societies (Torrens, 1978).

Summary

1. For a long time in human history, population growth (birth rates minus death rates) remained constant at a steady replacement level. The demographic transition occurred in three

"Well, Mr. Fensterwold, are we ready to go home?"

SOURCE: Drawing by P. Steiner, © 1982, *The New Yorker Magazine, Inc.*

stages. First, with the agricultural revolution, birth rates rose sharply, probably from improved nutrition, while death rates remained constant or rose only slightly. Population size began to increase.

2. Second, with the advent of the Industrial Revolution, death rates dropped sharply in Western Europe, while birth rates remained high for a while. As a result, the population began to increase noticeably.

3. Within two generations, the fertility rate also began declining in Europe and North America. At the same time, disease control reduced mortality in the rest of the world, resulting in a major worldwide population explosion. The big question for the future of our planet is whether birth rates will drop in the rest of the world the way they have in Western Europe and North America. There are some signs that the rate of growth in world population is declining, but with more than 4 billion people already living on earth, an even greater decline is needed if the population is to be stabilized.

4. With current knowledge, there is little that can be done to improve food production markedly. Some steps can be taken to minimize waste, change habits to eat more efficient forms of protein, and improve distribution. Since the time of the great agricultural empires, however, the control of a food surplus has tended to mean other forms of control and subordination as well. How surplus world food is managed will be one of the great social, moral, and political issues of our era.

5. Ecology focuses on our social and physical environment in the broadest sense. Simple tribal societies tend to accept nature as they find it; Western industrializers view nature as something to be dominated and changed. Ecologists suggest that all organisms on earth are interdependent, that nature knows best, and that everything taken from nature has some cost.

6. Two major ecological problems are pollution of air, water, and earth and depletion of key natural resources.

7. Alternatives to resource depletion involve changing the way people view the world, conserving energy and resource consumption, and modifying eating habits.

8. Ecological and social factors influence life expectancy and the types of illnesses people contract. Developing nations have high death rates from starvation, infection, and parasites, whereas industrial nations have eliminated many infectious diseases. Environmental substances and dietary habits contribute to high mortality from heart disease, cancer, and strokes in industrialized societies.

9. More than one American in four will develop some form of cancer. Some experts believe that as much as 90 percent of human cancer is environmentally induced. This underscores the importance of investigating the social and occupational factors related to high incidence of cancer if the disease is to be controlled.

10. Health care systems are organized differently in various societies. The United States contrasts with other industrial societies because medical care delivery is based on a free market model. This means that health care is considered a service available to those who can pay for it. Most other industrial societies view medical care as a right rather than a service. One result is the high cost of health care in the United States.

11. Health care emphasizes the treatment rather than the prevention of illness. Treatment involves medical intervention, while prevention involves changing the social and economic contexts that help to create illness and injuries.

Key Terms

crude birth rate
crude death rate
demographic transition
demography
ecology
ecosystem
elderly dependency ratio
green revolution
growth rate
life expectancy index
life table
migration
mortality rate
population
total fertility rate
zero population growth (ZPG)

Chapter 21

Urbanization and Suburbanization

One of the first questions people often ask someone they've just met is "Where are you from?" Geographic origin helps us understand people, because the places where people live influence what they know, the experiences they have, and to some degree the way they see the world. In large areas of the world today, including North and South America, Europe, Australia–New Zealand, and the Soviet Union, more than half the population lives in urban centers. Only in Africa and parts of Asia and Oceania does less than half the population live in cities. The growth of cities, or *urbanization* as it is called, is one of the largest changes in the organization of human society.

For most of human history, people lived in small clusters, bands, or communities that were often temporary. They hunted, gathered, or raised their own food. A city contrasts sharply with such an arrangement, since a *city* is a relatively permanent settlement of large numbers of people who do not grow or gather their own food. Within the last several centuries, human society has shifted from a small community base to being urban-centered.

Cities are important for a number of reasons. First, they affect how people live and behave. This difference was described in Chapter 3 as the shift from community to society, with all the shifts from personal to more impersonal relations that such a trend involves. Cities affect the growth of institutions in a society. In more diverse and anonymous cities, the family is less able to enforce the kind of behavior wanted from family members. As a result, more formal political, legal, and economic organizations are required to exercise social control.

By bringing together large numbers of people, cities promote the development of specialized occupations. If you are a hat maker, for example, you need to be in a settlement large enough to supply a steady stream of buyers for your hats. So a hat maker might thrive in a city but not in a village.

Economic and political power tends to be concentrated in urban areas. This was as true of the cities of ancient Egypt, or the Rome of the Roman Empire, as of the investment and banking centers in New York and Switzerland, and the political centers of Washington, D.C., or Ottawa, Canada, today. National cities like Paris reveal the political, cultural, and economic concentration of urban life in its most intense form. In France, for example, virtually all cities have a rail link to Paris, but many of those cities have no rail connections with each other. Cultural and political activities are similarly concentrated in the national city.

Because cities concentrate power, people, and other resources, they increase the chances of communication, stimulation, and exchange among city-dwellers. Cities bring people into face-to-face contact, enabling them to think, discuss, and act together. Such contact and communication is important for decision-making and the exercise of power. Such exposure may lead to further opportunities and may increase the power of the people there. Because of their central locations, urbanites may also have superior communication and transportation links with people in other cities within a country or around the world. Urban centers have always served as the hubs of major transportation networks—first as seaports and rail centers, and now as centers for air transport. Most of the major urban centers around the world are linked by nonstop jet plane connections. The concentration of power, people, and resources in cities, along with increased communication and transportation facilities, may stimulate ideas and projects, increase the power of people there, and lead to more opportunities in the arts, politics, business, or finance.

As a result, cities act as a magnet, drawing ambitious and talented people, especially people involved in finance, law, politics, communications, and the arts. Cities are the source of much of a society's "high culture," as well as popular music, records, tapes, movies, books, and big-time sports. Today, with television and other forms of mass media also concentrated in cities, these cultural products are beamed all through a society, reaching even very remote areas.

Older urban centers offer, in concentrated form, a taste of the ills that afflict industrial societies around the world: crime, violence, vandalism, arson, homeless people, congestion, pollution, the threat of fiscal insolvency, and decay of the infrastructure (highways, bridges, water mains, sewers, housing, public transportation systems). As such, their problems may foretell the future for suburbs as well. At the same time, the efforts of many urban residents to stop the decay of their cities provide hopeful examples of the ways in which people can tackle difficult social problems.

THE GROWTH OF CITIES

Although we tend to take cities for granted, they did not always exist. Sociologists have considered why cities developed in the places and times that they did. Three major factors have contributed to the rise of cities in various parts of the world: agricultural importance, trade, and industrialization.

Cities developed first in areas that were favorable to agriculture. Rich agricultural areas were able to produce a surplus of food that could support some nonfarmers. Since transporting large quantities of food very far was difficult in earlier times, settlements tended to grow up near agricultural areas. The first cities developed about 5000 years ago in the Middle Eastern valley of the Tigris-Euphrates Rivers, in Egypt along the Nile, along the Yellow River Valley in China, and the Indus River Valley in Pakistan. All these areas had rich soil, a favorable climate, and plenty of water. The rivers provided transport routes for trade, and many cities grew larger because of their roles as trading centers.

As cities grow, they require increasingly complex systems of social organization and control. Such systems must extend to the surrounding agricultural areas in order to draw in the agricultural surplus. This requires religious, political, and military organizations to extract taxes or tribute from the food-producing areas and transfer them to the central power in cities. The importance of political and military organization was particularly apparent in the way the Roman Empire used agricultural surpluses to build cities. As the Roman legions conquered new lands, they set up systems of tax collection which they used to build aqueducts, sewer systems, and public buildings in their cities. These cities would probably not have been built without political and social systems for extracting or exchanging surpluses from agricultural areas.

World trade was a second major impetus to the development of cities. In the sixteenth and seventeenth centuries, many new port cities sprang up, including New York and Boston in North America, Capetown in South Africa, Bombay in India, and Rio de Janeiro in Brazil. All these cities were centers of trade and colonial rule.

Industrialization was a third major source of

urbanization, along with agricultural and trading importance. As factories expanded in Great Britain, people migrated to cities in search of work. British cities such as Birmingham, Leeds, and Manchester, and younger American cities including Rochester, Detroit, Minneapolis–St. Paul, and Chicago, all grew in response to industrialization.

In many Third World countries today, large numbers of rural people migrate from the farms and villages to the cities, pursuing the dream of a better life. Mexico City, for example, has experienced a major population explosion in recent years, due to the migration of the landless farm workers. For many, however, there are no jobs, and they end up living in makeshift shanties or tents around the fringes of the urban center. As a result, some developing nations are labeled "overurbanized" by sociologists.

THE URBAN ENVIRONMENT IN THE UNITED STATES

In the United States, both trade and industrialization contributed to the rise of cities. Between 1850 and 1970, urbanization increased, first in the Northeast, then in the South, and most recently in the West and Southwest. One way the urban areas handled their increasing populations was by expanding outward from their centers, in what has been called urban sprawl or suburbanization. This tendency began around 1900 in older cities like New York and Philadelphia, and became very pronounced all over the country after World War II ended in 1945—for instance, north of Chicago, in Houston, Texas, and in California's Orange County. In the 1970s these trends of more than a century appeared to be reversing slightly. The 50 largest metropolitan areas in the United States grew only 7 percent in that decade, compared to the 9 percent growth in all metropolitan areas and a 15 percent growth in nonmetropolitan areas (Russell, 1981). Apparently the trend of more than a century toward urban concentration has begun to reverse itself. People are moving in greater numbers to small towns and rural areas.

In the United States, most people live in metropolitan areas. The term *metropolitan area* refers to the central city and its surrounding suburbs. Sociologists and demographers use the term *Standard Metropolitan Statistical Area (SMSA)* to refer to a county or a group of counties including at least one city with a population of 50,000 or more. On the basis of the 1980 census, there were 318 SMSAs in the United States, and 75 percent of the entire population lived in those 318 SMSAs. SMSAs that run together are called *Standard Consolidated Statistical Areas (SCSAs)*. There were 13 of these in the 1980 census. The largest of these consists of the New York, Newark, and Jersey City SCSA. As Figure 21.1 shows, 44 percent of the people of the United

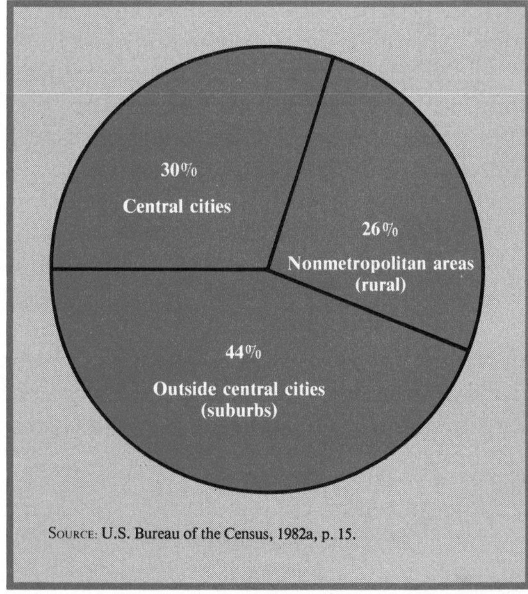

Figure 21.1 Proportion of Total U.S. Population in Central Cities, Suburbs, and Nonmetropolitan Areas, 1980

States lived in suburbs in 1980, whereas only 30 percent lived in central cities. Smaller cities (those with populations under 500,000) grew during the 1970s as part of the general spread of the population away from larger urban centers. The remaining 26 percent of the U.S. population lived in nonmetropolitan or rural areas.

LIFE IN CENTRAL CITIES

American literature and art has traditionally found value in rural life and has viewed city life as corrupt, evil, crowded, unhealthy, and dirty. Gallup polls within the past decade suggest that many Americans still hold these views. At least three features of urban life seem to have produced negative reactions in people: the physical congestion, noise, and dirt of city life; suspicion of the minorities and different cultures that live in cities; and the excessive social stimulation and isolation that cities create in individuals.

Central cities have attracted large numbers of immigrants, beginning with Europeans and continuing more recently with blacks from the southern United States and Hispanics from the Caribbean and Mexico. Most of these immigrants were poor, and when they arrived many affluent and educated residents moved to larger homes in less crowded areas on the outer rims of cities. Nationally, three-quarters of the people who now live in central cities are white and about one-quarter are black (Long and DeAre, 1981). In 1980, 56 percent of all blacks in the United States lived in central cities. Other ethnic groups such as Hispanics, Chinese, and Japanese comprise significant percentages in certain cities as well.

Some city-dwellers who move out cite the attractions of newer homes with yards and driveways as pulling them away from the city, while others mention noise, dirty streets, crime, or crowding inside and outside their homes as negative features pushing them out. Respondents to surveys do not necessarily say they left a neighborhood because its racial or ethnic composition was changing, although they may say that other people move for those reasons. So-called white flight from cities or at least from urban schools because of school integration has been a hotly debated issue among sociologists, with some (for example, Coleman, Kelly, and Moore, 1975) saying that whites leave urban schools when large-scale school desegregation occurs. Others (for example, Farley, Richards, and Wurdock, 1980) argue that whites leave even in districts that do not desegregate. This finding suggests that whites may be leaving for better housing or more space, rather than because of racial integration in the schools.

Whatever the reasons that Americans in general have often viewed life in central cities with distaste, sociologists writing about urban life have sometimes tended to see cities as having a negative effect on the social life of their inhabitants. A number of critical studies of cities were done by American sociologists at the University of Chicago. Many of the ideas found in these studies are distilled in a well-known paper by Louis Wirth entitled "Urbanism as a Way of Life" (1938). Wirth emphasized the size, density, and diversity of urban populations and suggested that they bombard individuals with more stimuli than they can handle. As a result, people escape into an impersonal, unfriendly, and distant style of relating to other people.

Such defenses are only partly effective, and people become tense and anxious as a result of the people and events impinging on them. City life, Wirth said, also results in people relating to each other only in terms of some specific task or role—as a newspaper vendor, bank teller, dry cleaner, or grocery clerk—rather than as more complete human beings. Most of these roles deal with economic relationships, so that rules of the marketplace rather than of friendship and community prevail. This means, according to Wirth, that city-dwellers have few true friends who can help them in times of personal need.

City life also promotes highly specialized activities that are distinctly separate. As a result,

Urban congestion is a drawback of city life for many people. Despite such limitations, these youngsters have found a space in which to play their own games.

people belong to many groups, and no single group has the undivided allegiance of the individual. This situation, according to Wirth, weakens primary groups like the family. This weakening results in individual behavior that is less controlled by membership in any single social group and is less predictable. The close concentration of different individuals in cities tends to make them more tolerant of others who think and behave differently from the way they do. By promoting diversity rather than solidarity, cities permit more individual freedom. But that very freedom may lead to a condition of *anomie,* or normlessness, which individuals find very difficult to tolerate.

Different groups may demand conflicting behaviors or values of individuals. One group of friends, for example, may expect an individual to stay out late drinking on a Saturday night, while another group may expect to see the same individual ushering at an early church service the next morning. These different and even competing demands may cause individuals to feel inner turmoil. The existence of a wide variety of subgroups may even lead individuals into forming bonds with a deviant group that commits illegal activities, suggests Wirth.

Not every sociologist accepts Wirth's description and analysis of urban life. One critic, Herbert Gans (1962a), suggests that Wirth was contrasting urban life to a folk society, rather than to rural life in an industrial society. As we saw in Chapter 3, individuals in a folk or tribal society have strong primary bonds with virtually everyone in their group or community. Most individuals are tightly integrated into such societies, and informal social controls operate effectively in such a situation. Even in rural areas of large-scale industrial societies, many of these strong primary group ties are weakened or broken.

Gans goes further and states it is unreasonable to suggest that people behave the way they do because of where they *live,* rather than because of other features of their social life. He argues that there are at least five types of urban residents, each of whom follows a different life-style. They do not all behave in the way that Wirth described as typical of city-dwellers.

THE MAKEUP OF URBAN POPULATIONS

The five types of urban residents that Gans (1962a) describes are the cosmopolites, the unmarried or childless, the ethnic villagers, the deprived, and the trapped. The *cosmopolites* are artists, writers, musicians, students, intellectuals, and professionals. They live in the city to be near cultural facilities only a city can support. Many are unmarried or childless. If they are affluent, they may have children and hire servants or governesses to help with their care. This group normally includes some of the richest and most powerful city residents.

The *unmarried or childless* may be temporarily or permanently in that status. Those who are temporary may come to the city as young adults and share an apartment with friends until they marry and have children. Then they may leave the city for the suburbs. The ones who never marry or have children frequently stay in the city permanently.

The *ethnic villagers* live in such ethnic enclaves as Little Italy in New York, Chinatown in many cities, or Koreatown in Los Angeles. Their lives center around primary groups such as their families. Except on their jobs, they have little to do with the life of the city around them. Their lives are very different from those described by Wirth, because they live what resembles a village life set within the borders of large cities. Secondary groups and formal organizations such as political clubs tend to be weak within their communities, and they are suspicious of anything and anyone from outside the neighborhood.

The three groups just discussed are likely to have chosen to live in the city; the final two types described by Gans have no choice. The *deprived* include the very poor, the physically or mentally handicapped, victims of racial prejudice, and people lacking assistance from their families. The *trapped* are unable to move when a neighborhood changes. Many of these people are old and live in rent-controlled or low-rent apartments or in homes purchased many years ago. Most lack the money or the energy to move.

Gans suggests that Wirth's characterization of city life as the same for everyone is too simple. Instead, Gans indicates that the social structures and cultural patterns people like the ethnic villagers bring with them to the city or the cosmopolites develop by living in the city protect individuals from the feeling of not belonging anywhere that Wirth described.

SOCIAL NETWORKS IN CITIES

A third student of urban life, Claude Fischer (1976), uses features of the work of Gans and Wirth to illuminate the ways in which urbanism influences personal lives. Like Wirth, he believes that population size does affect social life, but in a positive way by creating and strengthening social groups. In a large aggregate of people as found in a city, individuals are more likely to find others like themselves with whom they can form a subculture centered around their special interests. Where else but in a large city could, for example, bassoonists, hot air balloonists, tap dancers, Ukrainian nationalists, sadomasochists, and diamond dealers form common groups? Cities provide the numerical and financial base to support such specialization and to allow individuals to form networks with others who share their own special interests. As noted in Chapter 4, a social network refers to a specific set of relationships among individuals (Fischer et al., 1977). Some of these networks may seem "devi-

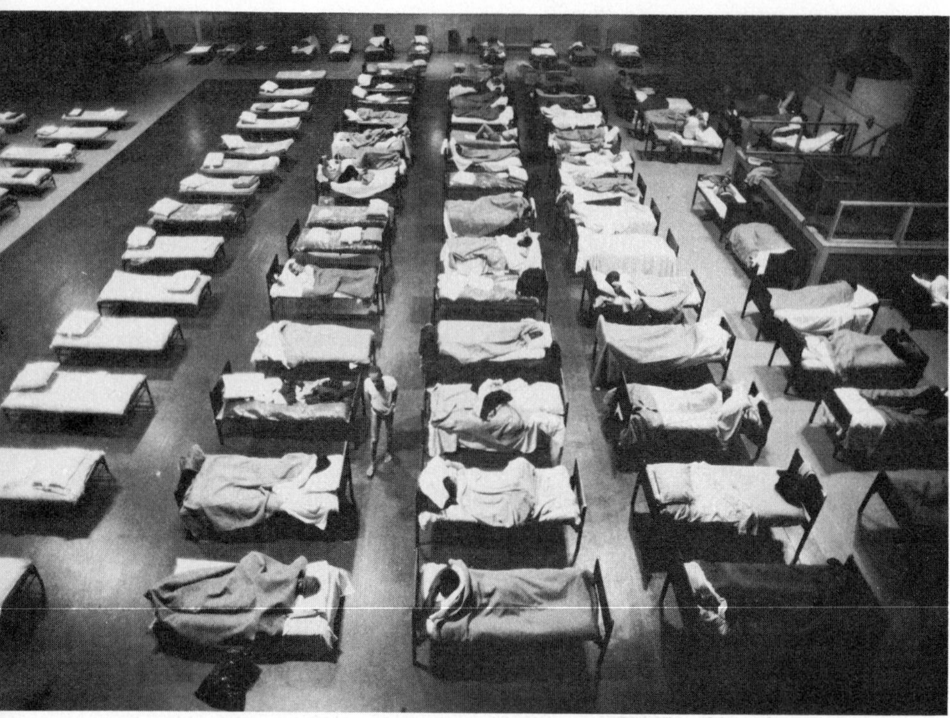

Many cities contain growing numbers of homeless people, as a result of evicting people when low-cost housing is converted into more expensive apartments or condominiums and as a result of mental patients being released from institutions. Some private and city agencies have set up shelters for these homeless people, but often there are not enough places for everyone.

ant" in the eyes of other groups, but the diversity of city life enhances the tolerance for networks that differ from one's own.

Cities, then, promote diversity, individuality, and freedom. But cities also have some social costs, including chaos, crime, noise, pollution, congestion, and corruption (Lapham, 1980). Sennett (1970) notes additional sources of chaos in city life, including the potential conflict arising from close contact between diverse groups. He stresses, however, that such chaos promotes individuality, greater self-control, and more awareness of others.

These features of city living have been suggested as major sources of creativity and innovation. Organizations that move out to their own private enclaves in the suburbs lose a major source of stimulation and new ideas. It becomes much more difficult for their members to meet friends or acquaintances for lunch, a drink, or dinner, or to meet them by chance on the street or while waiting in line at the bank. The casual exchanges that occur constantly in city life have to be arranged when an organization is located outside the city. In the city, people do not spend their time talking only with other people in their organization. They also have chances to meet people from other organizations and occupations. It is precisely these informal or easily arranged exchanges among diverse people that may promote creativity and innovation in urban dwellers.

THEORIES OF URBAN DEVELOPMENT

Sociologists have developed three different models to describe the spatial development of cities. The concentric-zone theory was developed by Park, Burgess, and McKenzie (1925) based on their study of Chicago. It seemed at first that the pattern might be universal, and indeed it did fit St. Louis, Missouri, and some other cities. Hoyt (1939) later realized that a different model—the sector model—fit the development of such cities as Minneapolis, San Francisco, and Richmond, Virginia, better than the concentric-zone model did. In the 1940s, a more refined multiple-nuclei model was developed to fit the growth of cities like Boston. All three models are portrayed graphically in Figure 21.2.

THE CONCENTRIC ZONE THEORY

Park, Burgess, and McKenzie (1925) suggested that a "modern" city consists of a series of *concentric zones*. These zones grow out from the center, like the rings formed by a pebble dropped into a pond. In each zone, land is used in a different way. The innermost zone is the *central business district,* which contains department stores, banks, hotels, theaters, business offices, rail and bus centers, and government buildings. The next concentric circle forms the *zone in transition,* which represents mixed residential and commercial land use. Often, this zone is where earlier residents of a city once lived. As commercial activities began to spread, newly arrived immigrants settled there in crowded dwellings that often became slums. If groups stay in such areas long enough, they often develop cohesive social networks. Little Italys and Chinatowns may develop in such areas.

Third is the *zone of workers' homes,* consisting of aging but often quite stable residential areas, where workers' families can afford to live and may do so for several generations. The fourth circle makes up the *middle-class residential zone* and contains many single-family dwellings where white collar workers and professionals live. Fifth is a band of upper-class residences. Sixth is the *commuter zone,* where upper-middle and upper-class administrators, executives, and professionals live. In most places, this zone consists of suburban areas.

Some concentric zone theorists include outlying agricultural areas: first, those that produce milk, eggs, and butter; second, even farther afield, areas that provide produce and meat. Although useful for describing urban development, the concentric zone theory does not explain why some cities simply do not correspond to zones. Nor does it explain why growth patterns vary over time.

THE SECTOR THEORY

The *sector theory* helps to deal with changes in the way cities develop. Hoyt (1939) described urban growth as following major trolley lines or waterways, and expanding away from overcrowded areas. According to this theory, cities will not develop in full rings, but in wedge-shaped patterns that follow transport systems. This pattern explains how some downtown areas, such as Boston's Beacon Hill or Manhattan's Park and Fifth Avenues, remain fashionable and vital, regardless of what else happens around them. The theory fails to recognize, however, that not all development occurs in areas that are adjacent to similar ones.

THE MULTIPLE-NUCLEI THEORY

Not all cities have a central downtown area or core in relation to which zones or sectors grow. Many cities in the United States have a number of business centers, as well as residential and industrial sections. The *multiple-nuclei theory,* proposed by Harris and Ullman (1945), takes into

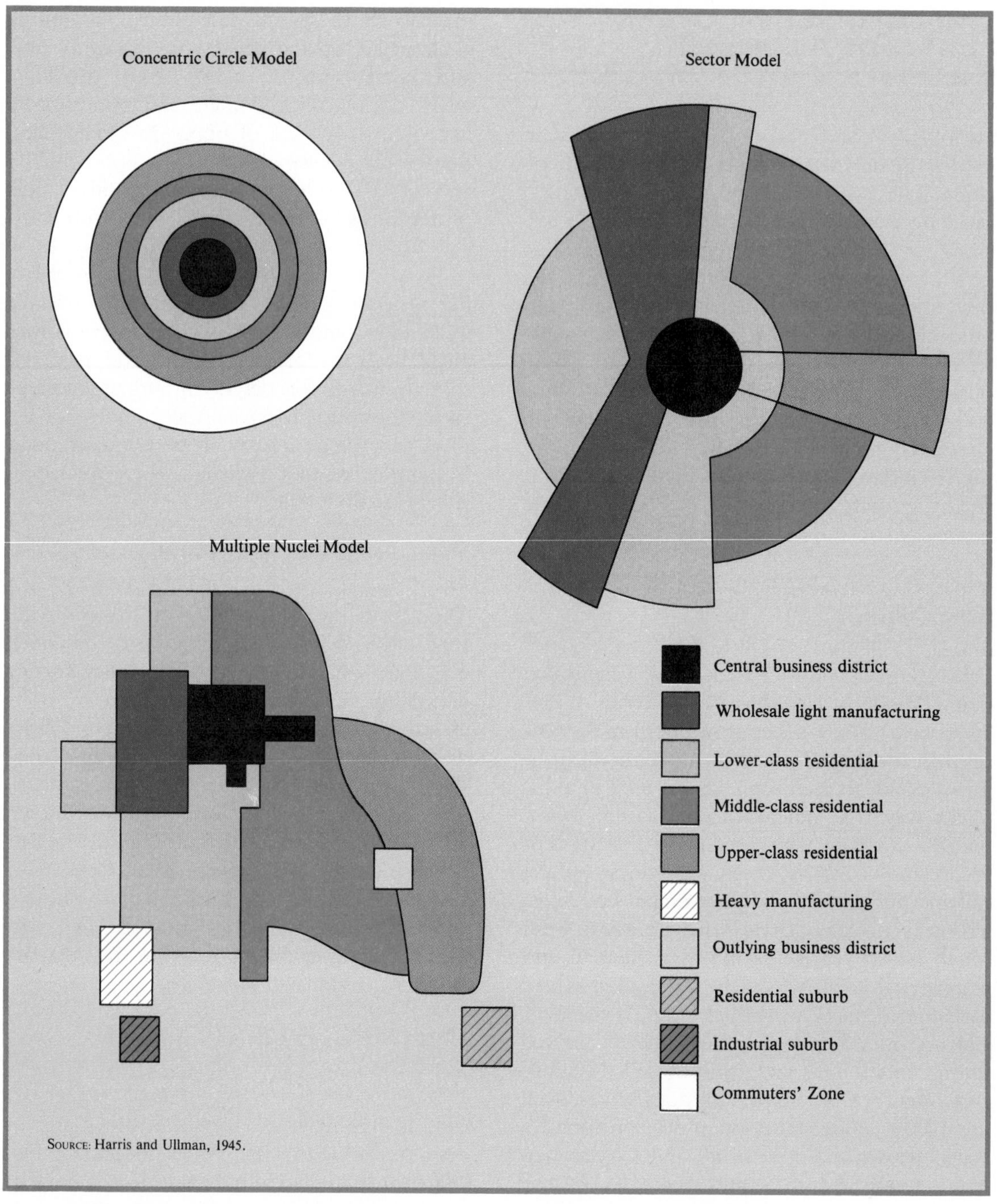

Figure 21.2 Three Theories of Urban Development

account the way land use tends to become specialized around certain functions—an area of artists' galleries and lofts, a meat-cutting center, the so-called tenderloin section with its sex shops, pornographic movies, and vice operations, a printing area, and a financial center, for instance. Different activities thus cluster around different nuclei within a city; they are not all concentrated in one downtown area.

EXPLAINING DIFFERENT URBAN FORMS

None of the three theories we have just discussed offers a single explanation of why different cities take the particular forms they do. More recently, Gordon (1977) has advanced a comprehensive theory that links the development of cities with the stage of economic production they are experiencing at the time of their major growth. He suggests that there are three types of cities: commercial, industrial, and corporate. The form they take depends on the process of capital accumulation that was dominant at the time the cities developed to maturity.

Commercial Cities

Commercial cities developed as merchant capitalists bought and sold commodities. From the outset in the American colonies, political controls were placed on where ships could land and unload. In the North, only Boston, New York, Philadelphia, and later Baltimore were officially sanctioned commercial ports where British merchants could unload. These limits benefited political authorities by requiring fewer customs stations, and aided merchants who faced limited competition as a result.

In the early commercial cities, most people owned their own property. Many worked in the same building where they lived, since most businesses were small. The hub of commercial cities was the wharf. People of many different backgrounds and occupations lived and worked in close quarters in central city districts. There was an active neighborhood street life (Warner, 1968). Streets in the wharf area were narrow, and zigged and zagged in unexpected patterns. The outer ring of these cities consisted of the transient poor, who stayed in temporary shanties or roominghouses (Gordon, 1977). When urban land speculation boomed, new streets and buildings were mapped out in regular rectangles (Mumford, 1961). This pattern of development is evident in Manhattan above Houston Street, and contrasts sharply with the irregular streets in lower Manhattan and the Wall Street area. Philadelphia shows a similar pattern.

Industrial Cities

The industrial city was exemplified by Chicago. Early factories were built along river banks because waterpower was their source of energy. Once coal replaced water as the major energy source, factories could be built anywhere. Economists suggest that large cities were chosen as the sites for major factories because they offered: (1) large numbers of workers, (2) markets for their goods, (3) major rail and water transportation, and (4) other factories that produced needed supplies. Gordon feels that large cities also offered desirable conditions for controlling labor (1977).

The growth of the industrial city changed the commercial urban forms. Huge factories were built downtown near rail or water transportation centers, and segregated, working-class housing was built nearby. The middle and upper classes began moving out of the center of town, although major shopping districts were still located downtown. These developments led to major residential segregation by economic class, and the separation of jobs and residences.

In his analysis of why cities developed the way they did, Gordon adds the dimension of social class, a factor that was not included in the three ecological models of how cities develop. Economic and class considerations also help to explain the rise of cities consisting of corporate headquarters.

Corporate Cities

The corporate city is characterized by towering skyscrapers housing corporate headquarters and banking and legal services. In such cities, industrial activity has moved rapidly away from the center of the city, sometimes outside the city altogether. The corporate cities include some older industrial cities like New York that have shifted away from manufacturing activity toward the financial, communications, and business services needed by corporate headquarters. They also include some newer cities such as Houston, San Diego, and Denver, which have grown up as the centers of energy, electronics, and defense corporations.

The growth of corporate cities may have been spurred by efforts to control labor more effectively, suggests Gordon (1977). If labor became too militant in a particular region, an industry could simply move to a different location out of the city or often out of the state. Increasingly, manufacturing and administrative functions were separated, with plant managers handling manufacturing at regionally dispersed plants while central corporate headquarters were built downtown. This division of corporate functions increased the growth of corporate cities.

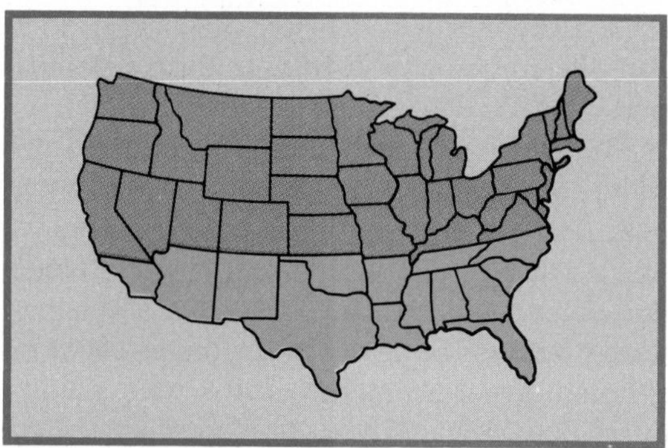

Figure 21.3 The American Sunbelt *A useful definition of* sunbelt *is to follow the 37th parallel across the United States, from southern California to North Carolina. Clark county in Nevada, which contains Las Vegas, should be included as well. In California, the upper boundaries of the sunbelt are formed by San Bernardino, Kern, and San Louis Obispo counties, according to Rice (1981).*

The political boundaries of cities and how they changed over time are also related to capitalist development. While manufacturing concerns were operating in center cities, industry favored annexing outlying regions as people moved out to them to spread the tax base. (The *tax base* refers to the boundaries within which a political unit has the power to tax.) But when manufacturing began to move out, the trend toward annexation ended abruptly, since industries wanted to be outside the taxing authority of central cities, suggests Gordon (1977). One result is that today's city is politically fragmented, with hundreds of distinct urban and suburban jurisdictions trying to tax and govern single metropolitan areas. Whereas older industrial cities had been dominated by shopping areas downtown, corporate headquarters now began to dominate some cities. The new corporate cities were described as the "fragmented metropolis" (Fogelson, 1967), since they have no center at all. They are one step beyond the multiple-nuclei city, which consisted of a number of clusters around various centers.

Several other developments contributed to the recent growth of new corporate cities. Cold War fears pumped billions of dollars of military money into southern, southwestern, and western Sunbelt cities.[1] The auto, oil, and highway construction industries promoted automobile transportation and the sprawling development so characteristic of new cities like San Diego, Los Angeles, and Houston, as their development has been fueled by military spending on missiles, space shuttles, jet aircraft, and weapons. When cars are the major means of transportation, housing can be built anywhere people can drive, rather than growing out along existing rail lines, for instance.

[1]The *Sunbelt* does not always refer to the same states when it is used by different writers, but a useful definition is suggested in Figure 21.3.

No single theory of urban development seems to explain the development of all cities. Instead, the types of economic activity that prevail when a city is developing, the geographic constraints (water or mountains for instance), and the political decisions of urban governments all appear to play a role. A few cities, such as New York, appear to be able to shift from one form of economic activity to another, and in the process alter the way space is used within the city limits.

URBAN PROBLEMS

As much of the new development money leaves non-Sunbelt, inner-city areas, poor urban dwellers face a number of interconnected problems: crumbling, rat-infested dwellings; the lack of decent jobs; drug addiction; high crime rates; garbage; prostitution; and brutality from the environment or from relatives. These problems have their causes in societal-level forces and changes, including the migration of rural minorities into large urban areas in pursuit of jobs, the movement of industry out of central cities, "redlining,"[2] the decline of urban schools, and the profit in selling illegal drugs. Addressing these problems at a societal level is not likely until the fiscal crisis of the cities is squarely faced.

FISCAL CRISIS

Middle-class city dwellers, retailers, and businesses have moved in increasing numbers to the suburbs or to the Sunbelt. Some of the reasons they cite for their moves are the availability of land, fewer zoning restrictions, lower taxes, less congestion, and lower energy costs. Once they move, individuals and businesses stop paying the heavy taxes imposed by the central cities. Those who remain in central cities are increasingly the young, the old, the poor, the uneducated, and the handicapped. Their needs for certain services—education, health care, subsidized housing, transportation, welfare, police and fire protection—place a heavy strain on municipalities, which have a dwindling capacity for financing those services. When cities are forced to raise taxes to meet the costs of such services, they risk driving out still more middle-class residents and businesses.

Commuters from the suburbs continue to use city transportation, water, sanitation, and other services, although they often pay no taxes. As a result, some cities and states, such as New York City and New York state, have implemented a small tax on income earned in New York, regardless of where the person earning it lives.

Balancing individual and organizational rights and freedoms while at the same time considering larger societal needs is one of the most vexing political, social, and economic issues facing our society today. Nowhere is it more apparent than in urban centers. The departure of productive economic enterprises and of the middle class occurs because of decisions by corporate decision-makers, suggests Gordon (1977) and others. When corporate leaders feel that central city locations are no longer profitable centers for their activities, they are likely to relocate. Then all the individuals associated with these activities must make decisions about relocating.

In the United States, business executives usually see their enterprises as quite distinct from society and from the geographic areas in which those enterprises are located. If a greater profit can be made by locating elsewhere, this line of reasoning goes, then the firm should pick up and move to some other location. The fact that a move will contribute to the unemployment of an area, to the shrinking tax base of a city, and therefore to the failure to provide human and social services, is not usually one of the criteria used in making corporate decisions. The burden

[2]*Redlining* refers to the practice by banks of refusing to lend money for mortgages and home improvements in certain neighborhoods, sometimes indicated by a red line around an area on the map.

of the costs of city services is borne by the shrinking numbers of taxpayers left. Often services must also be reduced. As the weight of the burden mounts, more people and organizations depart. Some of the costs and consequences of private corporate decisions could be dealt with by public services if the national treasury spent more on social services and less on military expenditures, suggests Sennett (1970).

INDIVIDUAL RESPONSES

Individuals do not respond in identical ways to large-scale urban problems. Some people degenerate in the face of the problems and pressures of the city, while others fasten like bulldogs on slender threads of hope. (See the box, "Life in an Urban Ghetto Bar."). The latter group struggles to find some social structural supports like a steady job or a good school to reinforce their own efforts. They see the nearly overwhelming social forces working against them, but they still try to influence their own fates. The more social, political, and economic resources groups can bring to this effort, the more likely they are to create social changes that go beyond their own lives and begin to alter their environment.

Impoverished urban residents have the fewest resources, yet thousands of them are refusing to be destroyed by conditions that might discourage anyone. Neighborhood groups have mobilized to support local hospitals and schools that were threatened with being closed down; block associations are planting trees, flowers, and mounting crime patrols; urban homesteaders in Baltimore and elsewhere are rebuilding crumbling row houses; religious communities are operating ambulance corps; various community groups are sponsoring hot lunch programs for senior citizens; and some urban school principals and teachers have created schools that are havens of hope and successful learning.

Groups with more resources can make even bigger changes. The New York City banking community (which held large numbers of city bonds) rushed around to see that the city did not go bankrupt in 1976 (Silk and Silk, 1980). The Minneapolis–St. Paul business community constructed a new orchestra hall, built a pedestrian mall, and contributed more than a million dollars to a community association that is rehabilitating a 95-square-block residential area (Teltsch, 1981; Moskal, 1981). Urban developer James Rouse has created a number of new urban market centers in Boston, Philadelphia, Baltimore, Santa Monica, New York, St. Louis, and San Francisco. He suggests that cities can be revitalized by creating a marketplace festival in the downtown areas (*Time,* August 24, 1981).

Recently the growth of two-earner households, more than half of which have no children, has renewed interest in urban rather than suburban living. The upper-middle class has been rediscovering the desirability of certain central city neighborhoods—for example, Park Slope in Brooklyn, New York; Alexandria, Virginia; San Francisco's Alamo Square; Capitol Hill in Washington, D.C.; Chicago's Near North Side; Boston's Prudential Center area; Baltimore's Harborplace; and Philadelphia's Society Hill. Termed *gentrification,* the resettlement of previously working-class or manufacturing areas creates additional tax sources for cities. The new inhabitants of these areas (the "gentry") need fewer health and welfare services but may demand more sanitation, transportation, police, recreation, and other services. The interests of all members of a community may not be equally served by such resettlements, however. The high rents and high selling prices that result from such urban renewal may lead to the displacement of the poor who had been living in the area.

All these efforts reveal certain common sociological principles. Rather than throwing up their hands in despair over the destructive social forces around them, groups of individuals decided to "do something" about the urban problems they faced. They did not work alone, however, but through their families, friends, tenant associations, churches, business contacts, or

Life in an Urban Ghetto Bar

Elijah Anderson, a social anthropologist, hung out for several years in an urban ghetto bar and learned a great deal about the social mores of the people who came to the bar. Some were permanent winos or hoodlums, but others had found a precarious toehold on which to balance their lives. One such person was Pee Wee.

> Pee Wee is a brown-skinned, thirty-four-year-old employed printer's aid. He is five feet eleven inches tall and weighs about 160 pounds. Pee Wee is happily married and has three daughters. Very proud of his family, he balances his time between Jelly's [the bar where the study took place] and home. Pee Wee says he got married "to try to have something." He grew up about a mile from Jelly's among the street gangs that dominated the area at that time. He highly values the "education I got out in these streets." After graduating from high school, a rare achievement for anyone hanging around the streets, the alley, and the corner near Jelly's, Pee Wee joined the army paratroopers and served in the Dominican Republic. He was a "good soldier" and received an honorable discharge from the army, which distinguishes him still further. This background gives Pee Wee a certain amount of esteem both among the more street-oriented members in the peer group, many of whom regard toughness as a primary virtue, and among the regulars, who value formal education and decency. Pee Wee's posture in the group is that of a quiet but tough person. He "never bothers nobody" and "nobody never bothers him." From his posture and reputation, group members generally like and respect Pee Wee.
>
> For the regulars, "strong character," being of "some 'count," and "decency" are the very important values. Regulars gravitate toward those who demonstrate decency through their actions and attempt, not always successfully, to avoid those who do not. They like to be around those who "treat other people right." They admire and trust those who can demonstrate a "visible means of support," which they often consider one of the primary characteristics of a decent person, particularly if the person is friendly and amiable with them. The people they consider "low class" and "no 'count"—wineheads and hoodlums—generally cannot offer evidence of a job or a secure place in the wider society, and thus they "bear watching."
>
> The most impressive evidence of this secure place in the wider society is the nature of a person's visible means of support. Occupations that give the regulars their special relationship to the wider society range from factory work to janitorial service to truck driving. A few men work two jobs. The most important characteristic of a job is its regularity, but also important is the amount of money it pays and the status and identity it confers on the person as "a hard-working man." Just having a job lends the jobholder an aura of reliability among the fellows at Jelly's. Before group members are willing to grant their trust, they usually want to know if a man works. Hence, types of jobs regarded as worthwhile and decent can range across a broad spectrum, owing in large part to the men's appreciation of what limited types of occupations historically have been and still are available to lowly-educated black men. At Jelly's a large variety of work tasks can contribute to a respectable identity. The basic status issue is usually whether or not the man works.

SOURCE: Anderson, 1978, pp. 58–60.

other groups. What they decided to do depended on their perspective on the situation—how they viewed it and what they saw as being in their own best interests. How much they could do depended to a considerable degree on their economic, social, and political resources. These examples drive home the idea that while it is important to analyze the structural forces that create urban problems, those forces need not discourage people from taking action. In families, neighborhoods, churches, schools, block associations, unions, and co-ops, people can forge social bonds to improve their lives as urban dwellers.

Increased use of cars, federal highway systems, and tax deductions for interest payments on home mortgages all contributed to the growth of suburbs, especially since World War II.

SUBURBANIZATION

Suburbs began developing in the United States around 1900. They may be small villages or good-sized towns, but all suburbs have in common that they are within commuting range of the central city in their Standard Metropolitan Statistical Area (SMSA). In fact, suburbs include all the localities in an SMSA that are not central cities. In this section we trace the history of their growth, and then examine how suburbs are physically different from central cities, how the people who live in them may differ from urban dwellers, how suburban living may affect people in a number of ways, and how suburbs appear to affect special populations, including women, the aged, and minorities.

THE RISE OF SUBURBS

There has been a steady increase in the suburban population since 1900. *Suburbs* are fairly small communities that develop near central cities. As streetcar lines were built, people gradually moved farther away from where they worked. By 1920, already about 17 percent of the population lived in suburbs. The rise in automobile use in the 1920s contributed greatly to the continued growth of suburbs. During the Depression and World War II suburban growth slowed, but it leapt upward after the war, as tract homes began to be produced on a mass scale. By 1980, 44 percent of the population lived in suburbs, and businesses had begun to move there as well. The trend toward suburbanization was encouraged by several federal programs, including cheaper land, fewer zoning restrictions, and the economies of mass production. Federal programs such as low-interest Federal Housing Authority and GI mortgages, federally financed highways, and the deductibility of home mortgage interest on income taxes encouraged the development of suburbs. Room to build developments on low-cost land spurred the process of suburbanization.

The biggest growth areas in the 1970s were the suburbs around large southern metropolitan areas, particularly Fort Lauderdale–Hollywood in Florida, Houston, Texas, and Tampa–St. Petersburg, Florida. The suburbs of Phoenix, Denver–Boulder, and Salt Lake City–Ogden also grew rapidly in the 1970s (Russell, 1981).

The recent growth of suburbs and even small towns has been facilitated by technological developments, especially in the areas of transportation and communications. The development of highways, cars, and trucks along with the telephone, radio, television, and even cable TV meant that people could live farther away from where they worked and still keep in touch and get to work. The possibilities of earning a living in small towns are enhanced by emerging computer technologies that permit the collection and analysis of data far away from their sources and the electronic transfer of messages. In addition, the shift in the economy away from heavy manufacturing toward service, communications, and information "industries" increases the possibilities for ever greater decentralization. Suburban borders of urban centers continue to expand as people search for desirable or affordable property.

CHARACTERISTICS OF SUBURBAN LIFE

Suburbs look different from most central cities. They have fewer high rise buildings; they are less densely built and populated; they usually have

SOURCE: Drawing by H. Martin, © 1982, *The New Yorker Magazine, Inc.*

more lawns, trees, and flowers and many more single-family and free-standing houses. There are fewer apartment buildings in suburbs than central cities, although there may be some. The suburb is not unique, however. Outer urban areas often resemble suburbs with their lawns, patios, driveways, and less dense housing.

People who live in the suburbs are more likely to be married couples between the ages of 30 and 50 with children, and less likely to be single, divorced, or retired persons than are people who live in cities. They are also likely to be more homogeneous with respect to race, occupation, education, income, recreational activities, and perhaps with respect to social and political views compared to city dwellers. As a general rule, then, suburbs tend to bring together people who share many social and behavioral traits, and to do this in smaller and somewhat more self-contained social communities. These differences between urban and suburban dwellers are intensified among higher-status residents. Educated suburbanites are much more likely than educated urban dwellers to own a house, have children, or be housewives (if they are women), as well as to live in an economically and racially homogeneous neighborhood (Fischer and Jackson, 1977).

HOW SUBURBAN LIVING AFFECTS PEOPLE

Suburbanites are more locally oriented than city-dwellers. This means that in their leisure activities, suburbanites tend to be more involved in home pursuits, such as gardening and entertaining. People living in town tend to go out more often to theaters and museums. Suburbanites also talk more frequently on a casual basis with their neighbors, visit in one another's homes, and participate in neighborhood organizations (Lopata, 1972). Finally, suburbanites are more likely to draw their friends from among their neighbors than are urban dwellers (Fischer et al., 1977). These features are considered indicators of *localism,* or interest in one's neighbors.

Differences between urban and suburban residents remain when such personal characteristics as having children, social class, employment status of women in the household, and years of residence are controlled (Fischer and Jackson, 1977). If these differences do not seem to be due to personal factors, what is it about suburbs that might encourage localism? Both single-family homes and compatible neighbors appear to encourage the greater localism of suburbanites. Homeowners spend more time around their homes than apartment dwellers do, which may lead to greater localism. Being around other people who are locally oriented seems to encourage people who move to the suburbs to become more involved locally, and even to act together—for example, by forming a neighborhood association (Fischer and Jackson, 1977).

HOW SUBURBS AFFECT SPECIAL POPULATIONS

Immobile or special populations appear to be more isolated in suburbs than their neighbors or people like them who live in cities (Gans, 1967; Tomeh, 1964; Abu-Lughod and Foley, 1960). Considerable research has been done on this issue with respect to women, the aged, and minorities, three groups that may face isolation in the suburbs.

Suburbs and Women

Suburbs affect women differently than they do men (Fava, 1978). Wives are more likely than their husbands to feel isolated from relatives and friends. Quite often they can overcome their feelings of isolation by becoming socially involved with their neighbors, but if they do not find compatible neighbors, they may be lonely (Fava, 1975; Fisher et al., 1977).

The growth of suburbs after World War II paralleled the return of women to full-time domesticity. Some might argue that such a result was another instance of what Rose Coser calls using physical space to regulate social relations (1975). The geographic dispersion and low population density of suburban areas seem designed to support women playing the role of full-time housewife and mother. Because of the high time and travel costs, suburban life makes it more difficult for women to form support groups, to find stimulating activities, and to get rewarding jobs. The extensive needs of the home, yard, and cars, dispersed shopping, and the chauffeuring of children to various activities all make it more difficult for women in the suburbs to be anything but housewives and mothers. It may be no accident that the return of many wives and mothers to the labor force has coincided with the resettlement of many urban areas.

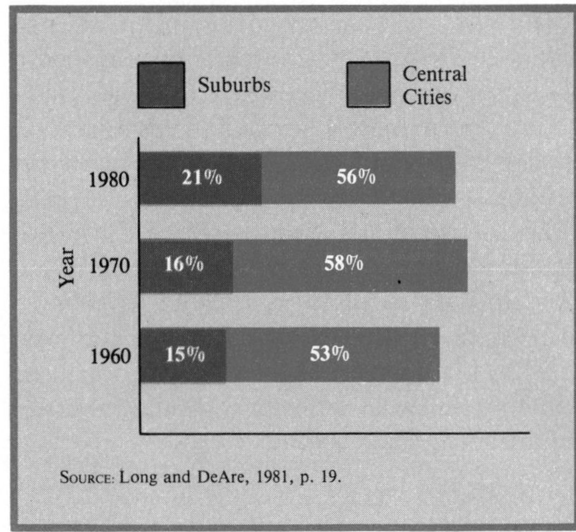

Figure 21.4 Percentage of Blacks Who Live in Central Cities and Suburbs, 1960–1980

Suburbs and the Aged

For the population over 65, 60 percent of whom were women in 1980, the suburbs may offer greater physical safety from crime, but automobile transportation—a necessity in most suburbs—becomes increasingly difficult for the elderly to manage. Suburbs may be removed from specialized health care facilities, and much of the housing may be too large, too expensive, or require too much care. Because many suburbs have zoning restrictions on renting out rooms or subdividing homes into apartments, that source of income is not usually available to elderly people in the suburbs. Although walking would enhance the health of many older people, the opportunity in suburbs to walk to shops, parks, and social events is limited.

The financial and physical problems of the elderly make them relatively immobile. Several studies have found that the farther from the center of town elderly people lived, the fewer friends they had, the less socially active they were, and the lonelier they said they were (Carp, 1975; Bourg, 1975; Cantor, 1975).

Suburbs and Minorities

Besides having some negative features for women and the elderly, suburbs also affect minorities differently than they affect whites. Traditionally, blacks were largely excluded from the suburbs by real estate covenants, although that picture has begun to change in the last decade. As shown in Figure 21.4, the 1980 Census revealed that the percentage of blacks living in central cities declined for the first time in many decades, while the percentage of blacks living in the suburbs has increased from 15 percent in 1960 to 21 percent in 1980 (Long and DeAre, 1981). The proportion of Hispanics living in suburbs is also up, to 37 percent in 1980 (Herbers, 1981a). We still know little about the suburbs in which minorities live, and whether or not minorities are segregated within suburbs. Nor do we know what the impact of suburbanization will be on black women, who have traditionally been more likely to work than have white women.

One in five blacks now lives in the suburbs. This trend suggests that some blacks have made economic gains and have been able to buy or rent homes on a nondiscriminatory basis in some suburbs. At the same time, the percentage of the population in central cities who are black has been increasing. These seemingly contradictory trends have occurred because whites have left central cities at a faster rate than blacks and because of the generally higher birth rates of blacks. In the past, the growth of the black population in cities was due largely to black migration to northern urban areas. But this migration appears to have stopped. Instead, blacks are beginning to migrate to the suburbs.

Social or cultural minorities and those isolated for various reasons, such as the elderly and women, tend to be more isolated in suburbs than in cities. Because suburbs are relatively small and homogeneous, it is difficult for those who are somewhat different to find compatible companions (Gans, 1967).

Summary

1. Urbanization represents one of the biggest changes in the way human society has been organized over time. A city is a large, long-term settlement of people who do not produce their own food.

2. Cities are important for the occupational specialization they permit, for the political and economic power concentrated in them, and for their cultural creations. They also provide concentrated doses of such social ills as crime, decay, and fiscal insolvency.

3. The first cities in favorable agricultural and trading centers. The rise of cities is accompanied by an increasingly complex system of social organization and control.

4. In the United States, urbanization continued to spread after 1850 up until the 1970s, when small towns and rural areas began to grow faster than urban areas for the first time. Among Americans, 44 percent live in suburbs, 26 percent in small towns or rural areas, and 30 percent in central cities.

5. The city has been viewed negatively in American culture. Wirth felt that cities produced distant, impersonal, and unfriendly personal relationships. Gans challenged Wirth's view and suggested there were at least five types of urban life-styles: cosmopolites, the childless and single, the ethnic villagers, the deprived, and the trapped. Fischer feels that urban density creates and strengthens social networks, which in turn enrich the lives of urban residents.

6. Three major theories of urban development have been offered. The concentric zone theory suggests that cities grow out from their center like the rings of a tree trunk. The sector theory indicates that cities grow in specialized districts following transportation systems. The multiple-nuclei theory recognizes that not all cities have a single center. Instead, there may be various nuclei, depending on the function being served.

7. Gordon suggests that cities develop according to the stage of economic production they are in when they do most of their growing. Commercial, industrial, and corporate cities each take different forms.

8. Decaying housing, too few jobs, drug addiction, and crime are some of the problems urban dwellers face. These problems are fanned by urban fiscal crises. As affluent urban residents and businesses move outside the boundaries of many cities, the social service needs of the remaining population increase while the tax revenues to support them decline.

9. Despite the massive problems urban residents face, many have found ways of adapting to or improving their environments. In many places, families, block associations, churches, and other groups are forging social bonds to improve urban life.

10. In the United States urbanization was followed by suburbanization, especially after World War II ended. More Americans now live in suburbs than in either urban or rural areas. Technological developments in transportation and communications, as well as federal tax policies, have spurred the growth of suburbs.

11. Suburban residents are more homogeneous than urban dwellers with respect to race, occupation, education, income, and recreational activities. They are also more likely to socialize with their neighbors than are city residents.

12. The physical setting of suburbs seems to influence women, whose social and occupational opportunities may be limited by the low density of suburbs, and the elderly, who may not be able to drive or to find compact housing.

13. Minorities have begun moving to suburbs in greater numbers in the past decade, but so far we know little about the consequences of this migration.

Key Terms

city
concentric-zone theory
gentrification
metropolitan area
multiple-nuclei theory
sector theory
Standard Consolidated Statistical Area (SCSA)
Standard Metropolitan Statistical Area (SMSA)
suburb
urbanization

107

Part Six

Contemporary Areas of Sociological Inquiry

Chapter 22

Sex and Sexuality

Sexuality is a term that encompasses the biology of intercourse and reproduction as well as the values, feelings, and human relationships that surround those biological processes. Sexuality is very important to individuals, since the biological drive that develops with maturity is a strong one. Sexuality is tied in with people's personalities, their images of themselves, and their responses to others. Sexual feelings, fantasies, and behaviors occupy large spaces in people's personal and leisure lives. Relationships with others may be highly charged with sexual overtones. Even when a person is trying to do something else—perhaps study in the library—sexual feelings and thoughts may creep into awareness.

Individuals are not left to decide on their own how they will express their sexuality. Instead, all societies actively regulate, direct, and shape the sexuality of their members. Society sets limits on when, how, and with whom sexual relations can occur. The social aspects of sexuality are at least as important as the biological ones. Sexuality finds expression through and is shaped by social relationships. Sexuality involves erotic needs and attachments, emotional needs and involvements, and sexual behavior, all of which find expression through, are shaped by, or are frustrated by social relationships.

Even the biological expression of sexual behavior is influenced by social relationships and cultural values and norms. The forms and sources of sexual gratification, the meanings given to various kinds of sexual relationships, and the significance and desirability of sex are shaped by the customs and meanings of the culture or subculture to which an individual belongs and by the way those cultural features interact with an individual's particular social experiences. Sexual behavior may involve physiological release, emotional relationships and satisfactions, reproduction, and economic exchange. In some times and some settings, it may have political or religious overtones as well.

One universal form sexual expression has taken has been its institutionalization within marriage. In virtually all societies, marriage includes the sexual union of husband and wife, with the full blessing and support of religious and political institutions. This sexual and social bond forms the bedrock on which the institution of the family is built, and the family is the basic unit of all societies. Most families seek to create the next generation, produce legitimate heirs, and provide care and socialization for the young. Further, families desire to pass on the family name and other ascribed characteristics such as nationality, and to transmit whatever property the family owns from one generation to the next. Since a sexual relationship underlies this vital institution, it is not surprising that society takes such a deep interest in the sexual activities of individual members.

SOCIAL ASPECTS OF HUMAN SEXUALITY

Although a biological sex drive is innate in humans, sexual feelings and behaviors are socially

In every society sexual expression is shaped by social values and norms.

learned. Society defines for us what it considers to be normal and acceptable with respect to sexuality. Its definitions and rules vary over time, by place, and with changes in political and social power. Chapter 5 noted how the rules governing sexual behavior in restrictive and permissive societies differ. Yet the influence of society and culture extends beyond such rules, to the point of coloring what we consider to be sexually attractive or stimulating and our capacity to express our sexuality.

The social molding of sexual expression is apparent in the reports on feral children who were reared by animals. Such children show little focused interest in others. Zingg reviewed some three dozen cases of children who lived in extreme isolation or with animal companions in the wild. He notes that the children's sexual impulses were inhibited, an observation that stands in sharp contrast to their gross and vigorous expression of other drives, such as hunger (Zingg, 1940). Itard reported that Victor (the "wild boy of Aveyron") felt a certain uneasiness in the company of women, but did not have any socially learned ways of expressing his sexual feelings. Sometimes he would gently pinch the hand, arms, or knees of women; finding no satisfaction from such activities, he would usually end up pushing a woman away in annoyance (Itard, quoted in Lane, 1976, p. 158). Children raised in extreme isolation tend to masturbate a great deal, suggesting that they had not learned any way of expressing their sexuality through interactions with other people.

The social nature of sexuality is visible in the variation of sexual practices and feelings across cultures and over time within the same culture. Every child is taught about sex, whether directly or indirectly, but each culture teaches different lessons. It is the social patterning of sexuality that makes sex a concern of sociological inquiry.

The definition of what is considered attractive varies widely from one society to another and within subcultures of a particular society.

SEXUALITY THROUGHOUT THE WORLD

Much of what is known about sexuality in other societies throughout the world is based on Ford and Beach's extensive review (1951) of anthropological reports of 190 societies whose locations range from the edge of the Arctic Circle to the southern tip of Australia. Their work showed them, for example, that physical appearance is an important aspect of sexual attractiveness in all societies. Male attractiveness, however, tends to be based more on the man's skills and prowess than on his facial appearance, while physical beauty seems to be a more important consideration in female attractiveness in most societies. The idea of physical beauty varies widely, however. More cultures consider a plump woman more attractive than a slim one, and many prefer women with a broad pelvis and wide hips. In a few cultures, breasts are important criteria of sexual attractiveness, but sometimes small upright breasts are preferred, and sometimes long pendulous ones. The shape of the nose, mouth, eyes, or ears may be particularly important in determining sexual attractiveness in different cultures. In addition, personal cleanliness is stressed as a necessary element of attractiveness in many cultures, as is youthfulness.

Once an attractive partner has been found, cultures teach widely differing ways to stimulate that person sexually. In many societies, kissing precedes and accompanies sexual intercourse. But among some peoples kissing appears to be unknown, as is the case with the Siriono of Eastern Bolivia. The Tinguian of the Phillippine Islands place their lips near their partner's face and then suddenly inhale.

In general, cultures differ greatly with respect to the amount and kinds of sexual foreplay practiced. Even within some cultures, such as ours, couples vary greatly in their use of foreplay. Some engage in extensive genital stimulation prior to intercourse, while others move immediately to coitus itself.

Handling, stroking, and rubbing one's partner's genitals is practiced in many cultures, with both manual and oral stimulation widely used. Such contact is forbidden in a few cultures such as the Tikopia on a Pacific island east of the Solomons and the Wogeo off New Guinea. In some societies sexual excitement is expressed or enhanced by scratching, biting, hairpulling, and other behaviors that cause pain. Bruises or red marks may be signs of sexual status or may arouse jest among one's peers in certain cultures, such as the Toda of India. In other cultures there is no association of pain with sexual arousal and satisfaction. In such cultures, the experience of pain in a sexual context will detract from sexual activity and enjoyment.

Humans in a wide variety of cultures seem to prefer privacy for sexual intercourse. In some, suitable privacy is found indoors, so that is where sexual behavior occurs. In others, dwellings are crowded places, and couples prefer finding a secluded outdoor spot. Some peoples, including such native American tribes as the Kwakiutl, Hopi, and the Crow, consider night and darkness to be the only proper time for sexual relations. Where there is no cultural prescription, either night or day may be chosen. Some peoples, such as the Rucuyen in the mountains of Brazil and the Yapese in the Caroline Islands in the Pacific, have a definite preference for daylight, and the Chenchu of India believe that children conceived in the dark will be blind.

Many cultures place limitations on when intercourse can occur, even within marriage. Menstruating, pregnant, or lactating women are not considered appropriate sexual partners among a number of peoples. In some cultures, anyone who is ill is forbidden to have intercourse, and sometimes, as with the Chewa of Central Africa, this prohibition extends to all the relatives of a sick person. In many cultures widows are ex-

While youthfulness is an element of sexual attractiveness in many cultures, older people often enjoy caring and sexually active relationships as well.

pected to abstain from sexual relationships for longer than widowers. Religious celebrations may be accompanied by sexual restraints. Hunting, gardening, and warfare are sometimes surrounded with sexual taboos at certain critical times. Some coaches still urge players to abstain from sexual relations for a day or two before big games, in the belief that sexual denial will sharpen their prowess on the field.

Relatively few social customs restrict marital coitus in the United States. Frequency of sexual relations may be determined by the desire, health, and availability of both partners. However, although there are relatively few customs applying to all social groups in industrial societies, some customs and practices have been found to vary by social class and educational levels. Lower- and working-class partners are more likely to prefer having intercourse with the lights off, while upper-middle and upper-class couples prefer some illumination in the room. How much clothing people wear while engaged in sexual activities also seems to vary by social class, with higher-class couples preferring more nudity than lower-class couples, in general.

Similarly, oral-genital sexual stimulation appears to vary with the educational level of couples, with more educated persons more likely to report experiencing or performing such behaviors than less educated ones (Hunt, 1974). Because oral-genital sexual stimulation has been defined by some as an act performed by homosexuals, it, along with other sexual acts performed by homosexuals, are illegal in all but 13 states in the United States, even if performed privately by heterosexual married couples (DeLora and Warren, 1977). Few, if any, heterosexuals have been arrested for performing oral sex, but legislation prohibiting what many people do in their own homes does exist.

SEXUALITY IN WESTERN SOCIETIES

Attitudes toward sexuality have changed dramatically over the last several hundred years, moving from the view of sex as sin to sex as acceptable pleasure, and everywhere in between. Whenever major changes in attitudes occur, it is likely that some groups will retain the values of an earlier era. This is clearly the case today with respect to sexuality.

Sex and Religion

Since its early years, the Christian church tried to control sexual behavior. Christianity, along with a number of other religions, tended to divide the world into the godly, spiritual portion and the carnal, material world. This division was captured by the struggle between the spirit which aspired to escape the world and the flesh which bound one to the world. Sex epitomized the flesh and was thus considered the enemy of the spirit. While Judaism accepted this dual vision of the world, it excluded marital sexual union from the antisexual restrictions. The Mosaic law is a clear instance of the way both Judaism and Christianity attempted to regulate sexuality by injecting sex with a strong moral dimension. Six of the Ten Commandments, for example, deal with human relationships, and two of these address sex directly ("Thou shalt not commit adultery" and "Thou shalt not covet thy neighbor's wife"). These commandments firmly forbid extramarital relationships.

The early religious teachings did not stop there. Even within marriage, sex was viewed as an unfortunate necessity for reproduction but not as a pleasure to be enjoyed. Sex as basically a sinful activity is reflected in St. Paul's statement that it was "better to marry than to burn." By saying this he was indicating that sexual activity outside of marriage was grounds for eternal damnation, so it was better to get married to avoid helfire. He felt that it was better still to remain celibate if a person could.

For centuries, the official Christian doctrine on sex was that it was a necessary evil, to be permitted for purposes of procreation within marriage, but not an experience to be celebrated or enjoyed for its own sake. In the early centuries of Christianity, women were viewed as spiritually weak creatures, quick to yield to fleshly impulses. Much of the blame for sexual weakness was placed on women. Like Eve, women were cast as evil temptresses who seduced men to sin.

Even in the nineteenth century, reproduction was the major religiously legitimate purpose of sex, although religious support for this purpose was sometimes supplemented by appeals to the need to increase the population of the nation, society, or species (Rosow and Persell, 1980). A different view of women and sexuality gradually emerged. Increasingly women were portrayed as essentially without sexual feelings.

Changes in sexual values and practices in recent years have not gone unnoticed by religious authorities. Today, there is less unity among religious leaders over issues of sexuality than there was in the past. Some leaders reaffirm traditional values, while others seek to open themselves to new directions. In 1976, the Vatican issued its Declaration on Certain Questions Concerning Sexual Ethics, which reaffirmed traditional teachings condemning premarital sex, homosexuality, and masturbation. In 1980, the Fifth World Synod of Roman Catholic Bishops issued A Message to Christian Families in the Modern World in which the bishops vehemently opposed contraception, sterilization, abortion, and euthanasia and reaffirmed that the bond of marriage must be both permanent and indissoluble (*The New York Times,* October 26, 1980, p. 18). In both these statements, the Catholic Church continues to uphold a view of sexuality and marriage as religiously imbued and subject to religious authority.

A somewhat different perspective was presented in 1977, when the Catholic Theological Society of America published a book entitled *Human Sexuality*. In it, theologians suggested the need for pastoral guidelines that emphasize the goodness and sacredness of human sexuality as a creative and integrative force. They seem to be suggesting that sexuality can be a positive force in individual lives and can encourage the building of good relationships between people. The differences between the two schools of thought is evident in their treatment of masturbation. The Vatican declared "masturbation is an intrinsically and seriously disordered act" (1976). In contrast, the American theologians stressed the complex meaning of masturbation, and deplored extreme views that either condemned masturbation as immoral or treated it very casually, thereby failing to do justice to its complex nature and significance.

Religious authorities face the difficulty of maintaining moral leadership over a diverse body of members in the face of growing secularization. These competing positions indicate that some leaders are trying to be the source of norms and values even in the face of challenges from their members, and others are responding to the changing norms, values, and behaviors of their members.

Sex as Recreation

The recommendations of religious leaders no doubt reflect a trend that has been noted by such sociologists as John Gagnon. He suggests that as our society has moved from a religious to an individual justification for much of what we do, there has been a movement away from the social justifications of sexual conduct to more personal ones (1977). He believes that sexuality has come increasingly to be defined in terms of individual desires and preferences. As a result, the importance of sexuality as love, play, and joy has received more emphasis. (Witness the popularity of the book *The Joy of Sex* by Alex Comfort.) The purpose of sexuality in our society, now, Gagnon suggests, is essentially for recreation rather than procreation. This trend has encouraged much greater tolerance of birth control, abortion, premarital sexual relationships, and homosexuality.

Sex and the Law

Religion was the original source of customs and laws governing sexuality, and some religious views were gradually incorporated into state codes. The Napoleonic Code broke with some religious traditions and permitted somewhat greater sexual tolerance than earlier laws. Laws against homosexual behavior between consenting adults in private, for example, were dropped. No such break occurred in English and American sex laws. Most sex laws differ from other laws in that they are aimed directly at maintaining morality, rather than at preserving and protecting individual or property rights.

Some sex laws do seek to protect individuals; they deal with the notion of consent in sexual relations. Sex without consent is considered rape. In addition, individuals who are deemed unable to give consent, including minors, mental retardates, and the insane, are legally protected. This means that the law assumes they are unable to give "consent" in a legally binding way because they are under age or mentally incompetent and are considered to lack the right or the ability to give such consent. There is considerable consensus in many societies against sexual conduct involving force and violence and against the sexual exploitation of children. Beyond that, there is less agreement about what the law should or should not prohibit (MacNamara and Sagarin, 1977).

Despite the lack of consensus about how the law should regulate sexual behavior, another kind of sex law aims at preventing offense to public sensibilities. Laws, for example, prohibit public sexual actions, exhibitionism, and offensive sexual solicitations. Other sex laws seek to maintain sexual morality as defined by state legislators. The United States, in sharp contrast to Western Europe, has extensive laws relating to sexual conduct and morality. Communist countries in Europe and the Soviet Union, some but not all countries where the Catholic Church is strong, and the Islamic world all tend to have sex laws and punishments as severe as those in the United States (MacNamara and Sagarin, 1977).

Laws in the United States prohibit premarital intercourse, extramarital intercourse, homosexuality, *prostitution* (the selling of sexual favors), incest, peeping, intercourse with animals, and even specific sexual acts such as oral or anal intercourse, depending on the state. Some states go so far as to prohibit everything except face-to-face intercourse, even among married couples. Laws that attempt to maintain morality are extemely difficult to enforce, particularly when the behavior being legislated occurs in the privacy of one's marriage and home.

Rape

Rape is a crime of violence, not a crime of sexual passion. In most penal codes, rape is defined as a completed sexual assault by a male upon a female (MacNamara and Sagarin, 1977), although males may also rape other males, as has often occurred within the U.S. prison system (Davis, 1970). Rape represents "a sexual invasion of the body by force, an incursion into the private, personal inner space without consent—in short, an internal assault from one of several avenues and by one of several methods [that] constitutes a deliberate violation of emotional, physical and rational integrity and is a hostile, degrading act of violence. . . ." (Brownmiller, 1975, p. 422).

Rape is a particularly repugnant crime because it uses an organ of sexual intimacy as a weapon to inflict injury and degradation on another person. While it is a terrible thing to be stabbed or shot, knives or guns are not used on other occasions as instruments of lovemaking. As a result, someone who is raped is not only injured (and quite often killed as well), but also traumatized. In many cultures, the victim of rape is also shamed. Her defilement is used to stigmatize her, in a classic instance of blaming the victim. Even if the culture does not stigmatize a woman for being raped, she has to rid herself of the terrible memories of being violated and hurt and somehow come around to a state where she can interact sexually with a man in a joyful way.

Sociologists have tried to understand the causes of rape, the frequency of it, how it is reacted to by society, and what the consequences of it are. In a forceful analysis, the writer Susan Brownmiller (1975) suggests that rape reflects more than an assault of one individual on another; it represents an extension of the general subjugation of women in society. In many subtle and not-so-subtle ways, men exercise their domination over women. Males make the laws and rules that govern the lives of men and women; men head the major institutions of society—the state, religion, business and finance, medicine, media, and education. They may not always be aware of the negative ways in which the rules and customs they establish or maintain may affect women. Men are also the principle enforcers of the rules, filling the ranks of the army, national guard, and police forces.

Another feature of our society is the attitude that women are "fair game" sexually for men. There is a tendency in the media and other features of our culture to portray women as sex objects that exist for the purpose of gratifying men. A climate that supports the sexual exploitation and conquest of women by men is fed by the availability of pornography and prostitution in society. Such a climate contributes to the incidence of rape, argues Brownmiller (1975).

The rate of forcible rape cases has increased steadily since 1967 (see Figure 22.1). Moreover, the rate of forcible rape has been increasing at a faster rate than any other violent crime (U.S. Bureau of the Census, 1982a). It is impossible to tell how much of this increase is due to an increasing willingness of victims to report what has happened to them and how much is due to an actual increase in the number of rapes committed. Rape is probably "the most underreported crime" (U.S. Department of Justice, 1981, p. 15). Nevertheless, some portion of the increase may well reflect growing numbers of forcible rapes.

What constitutes force is a debatable issue in our society. Is someone like an employer, professor, or doctor who uses his position of authority to sway a woman to have intercourse with him using force? Is a male who forcibly undresses a woman on a date and makes her submit to sexual intercourse committing forcible rape? Since some women are taught to "play hard to get" even when they are willing to have intercourse with a man, and some men are taught to be insistent in pushing themselves on a woman, there is room for ambiguity and misunderstanding in such a situation.

The frequency of rape is not reflected in the way society reacts to rape victims. Often male police officers, judges, and juries doubt a rape victim's claims. One study found that juries were less likely to convict accused rapists than were judges (Kalven and Zeisel, 1966). Months after

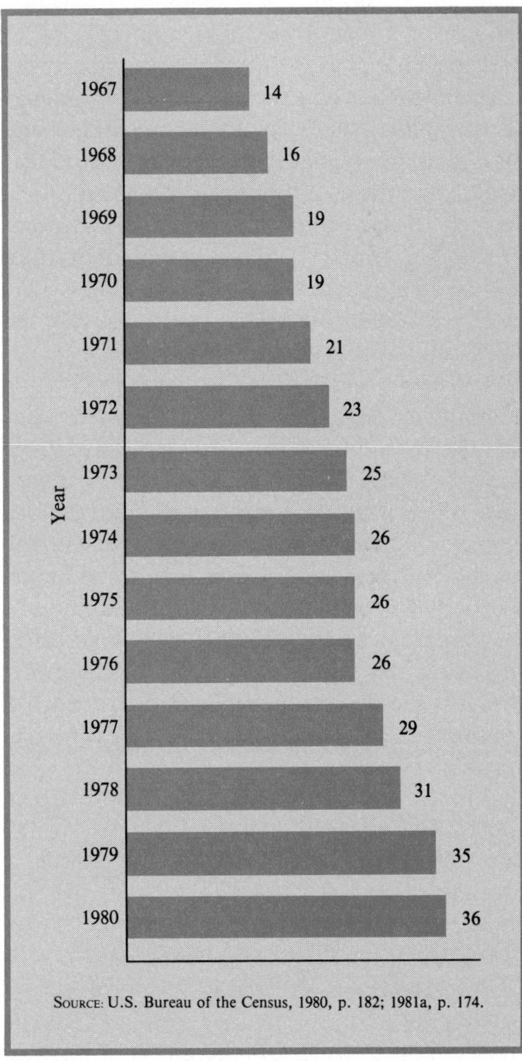

SOURCE: U.S. Bureau of the Census, 1980, p. 182; 1981a, p. 174.

Figure 22.1 Rate of Forcible Rape per 100,000 Inhabitants a rape has occurred, a victim has to re-live the trauma by appearing in court and being cross-examined by the defense attorney for the alleged rapist, who may try to argue that the victim is a prostitute or did something to encourage the rapist.

Few rapists actually reach jail, and for those who do the average time spent in jail is only four years (Brownmiller, 1975). This evidence suggests that many still view rape as an act of passion rather than an act of anger and violence. Because of women's "structural vulnerability" to rape, rape serves as a "process of intimidation by which all men keep all women in a state of fear" (Brownmiller, 1975, p. 5). Brownmiller suggests that rape serves to perpetuate male domination over women by force because rape is to women what lynching was to blacks—a means of keeping "uppity" individuals in their place and serving as an object lesson to others who might consider becoming psychologically or physically independent (1975).

The significance of rape is that it captures in a single act an underlying and pervasive view of male-female relations (Brownmiller, 1975). Rape becomes the means by which men reveal their superior power and strength in relation to women. A physical act comes to represent the psychological and social domination men exercise over women in society. Rape does not occur in animal societies, reports Brownmiller after reviewing the zoological evidence, suggesting that it is the desire for domination in the social realm that leads to rape occurring in the human species.

TEENAGE SEXUAL ACTIVITY

CHANGES IN TEENAGE SEXUAL BEHAVIOR

In the 1940s, about 20 percent of American women reported that they had had premarital intercourse before the age of 19 (Kinsey et al., 1953). By 1979, about half of all teenage girls had experienced premarital intercourse (Haas, 1979; Zelnik and Kanter, 1980). These figures indicate a dramatic change in the teenage premarital sexual activity of women over the last 40 years. At the same time, the sexual behavior of male American teenagers has remained constant, with nearly three-quarters experiencing coitus before the age of 19 (Kinsey et al., 1948; Zelnik and Kanter, 1980).

The relative constancy of male sexual activity, combined with increased female premarital sexual experience, has several implications. Apparently in the late 1940s and early 1950s, quite a large number of males were having sexual intercourse with relatively few females. Such a pattern of sexual relations magnified the great divide in the social landscape between those few girls who engaged in sexual intercourse and the overwhelming majority of girls with whom a male could not have sexual relations before marriage. Such a social division intensified the ***double standard*** of sexual conduct for males and females, a standard that considered premarital sex to be acceptable for men but not for women. As more women have become involved in sexual relationships, often with the person whom they expect to marry, the negative view of such behavior in women has declined.

Only a small percentage of boys or girls now feel that it is desirable for either men or women to be virgins when they marry. Among 17- and 18-year-old boys, 17 percent agreed that a girl should be a virgin when she marries and less than one in ten felt that a boy should be. Among girls of the same age, one-quarter felt that a girl should be a virgin, while one in six felt a boy should be (Hass, 1979). This evidence suggests that attitudes have changed more than behaviors, since the percentages of males and females who are still virgins is higher than the percentage who think it is important to be a virgin. The evidence also suggests that lingering traces remain of the double standard of normative conduct governing the sexual behavior of males and females. Although the numbers are small, both males and females are more likely to think females rather than males should be virgins at marriage.

These trends in sexual values and activity have personal and social meanings for the individuals involved. Sorenson (1973) studied the personal values and sexual behavior of 13- to 19-year-olds in the United States and found that the great majority of adolescents receive a great deal of satisfaction from their sex lives. A majority of boys and girls claims that they do what they want to do, regardless of what society thinks. The majority disagree that the most important aspect of their sexual relationships is the physical pleasure it provides. Instead, they suggest that they value sex because it is something in their lives that they make decisions about; it makes a relationship with someone else seem more important than a mere friendship; it enhances communication with members of the opposite sex; and it may compensate for the painful, irrational, or unnecessary aspects of life such as parents who fight, racial injustice, or world conflict (Sorenson, 1973). The personal meanings and satisfactions teenagers gain from their sexual experiences provide a better context for understanding the large-scale social trends described above.

MASTURBATION AS SOCIAL BEHAVIOR

The social context and meanings of sexual behaviors shape the significance of the behavior. The social importance of sex and sexuality is evident even in such a seemingly solitary and individual act as masturbation, or self-stimulation. While masturbating is no longer considered dangerous to one's health (it is no longer purported to cause blindness or to make one's hand fall off), it is still the cause of some embarrassment. One study of teenage sexuality found that young people (like adults) were more reluctant to discuss masturbation than most other forms of sexual activity. So, there does seem to be some residual social stigma attached to the act of masturbating. Despite lingering embarrassment about the subject, most 17- to 18-year-olds think it is all right for a boy or a girl their age to masturbate, with 85 percent of the boys and 72 percent of the girls expressing this belief. Moreover, they are also quite likely to practice it themselves, with 80 percent of males and 59 percent of females indicating that they do masturbate.

In their interviews with teenagers, Hass and his associates (1979) found instances where masturbation served as a physical release while enabling individuals to behave socially in ways that met their own expectations. For example, one 17-year-old girl reported, "After I lost my virginity I read the *Hite Report* and I found there were other ways of releasing my sexual emotions through masturbation without jumping into bed with every guy I meet. Now I do it when my desire is great and so I won't become promiscuous" (1979, p. 91). Another comment suggests that masturbation represents a form of social-sexual learning that will prepare one for sexual relations with others in the future, as in the remark by an 18-year-old boy who said: "I wondered what happened during intercourse so I tried to reenact what happens in order to find out" (Hass, 1979, p. 90).

The socially conditioned nature of sexual feelings, responses, and behaviors is revealed in the seemingly solitary practice of masturbation. Teenagers report having social and interpersonal fantasies while they are masturbating. Physical satisfaction is tied in with social relationships and meanings, whether real or imagined. Sometimes sexual fantasies allow individuals to think about situations that would be unacceptable for them to carry out socially, such as incestuous relations, prostitution, "kinky" sex, sexual relations with movie stars, or with someone admired from a distance. Freedom in their mental images of what they can do sexually enables individuals to behave socially in the more restrained ways they may feel are necessary. In this way, sexual fantasies and solitary behaviors may offer a way for individuals to reconcile personal feelings and desires with social expectations and conventions.

TEENAGE PREGNANCY

Not all teenage sexual activity remains in the realm of fantasy or masturbation, however, as the soaring rate of teenage pregnancy makes clear. Social policy-makers and sociologists alike have pondered the issue of why teenage pregnancy is rising, and their research provides a number of insights.

The increase in premarital sexual activity among teenagers has been accompanied by an increasing number of premarital pregnancies. In the three years between 1975 and 1978, more than 60 percent of the first births to white teenagers and 90 percent of the first births to black teenagers were premaritally conceived (O'Connell and Moore, 1980). The high premarital conception rate among teenagers is highlighted by a comparison with women aged 20 to 24. In that same time period (1975 to 1978), only 17 percent of the first births to whites and 56 percent of those to blacks were premaritally conceived. In the last 20 years, the proportion of first births premaritally conceived has risen nearly 100 percent for white teenagers and 50 percent for blacks (O'Connell and Moore, 1980). For all ages, the percentage of births to unmarried women increased from 4 percent in 1950 to 17 percent in 1979 (U.S. Bureau of the Census, 1972a, p. 66).

Teenage sexual activity and pregnancy has increased dramatically in the last two decades, particularly among white teenagers.

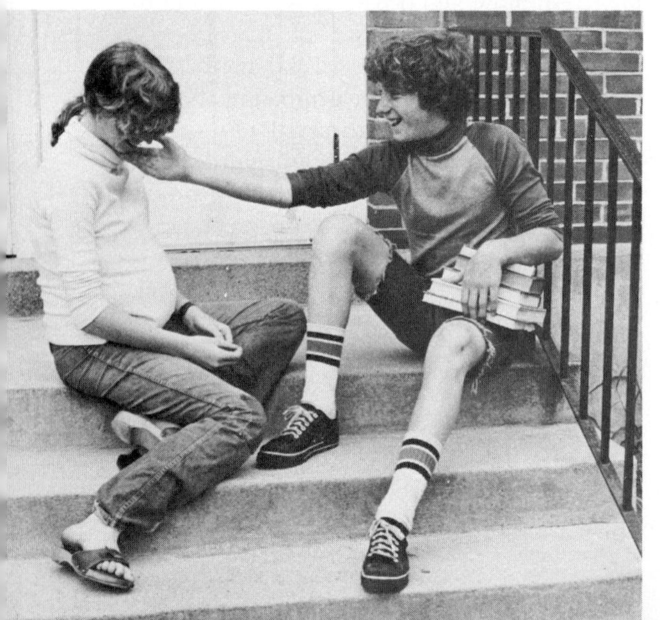

Why has the percentage of teenage out-of-wedlock pregnancies increased? At least one possible explanation can be ruled out, and that is the age when women first have intercourse. Women are not more likely to begin having intercourse at a younger age than they were in 1971. The average age is 16.4 years for white women and 15.5 years for black women (Zelnik and Kanter, 1980). While the age of teenagers having sexual relations has not dropped, the number of teenagers, especially white teenagers, who are sexually active has increased from one in four in 1971 to nearly one in two in 1979 (Zelnik and Kanter, 1980). The rate of sexual activity among black teenagers has not increased significantly in this time period. As a result, the racial differential in premarital sexual activity that existed in the past has rapidly narrowed.

Although the number of sexually active teenage girls has increased, the percentage among them who say that they want to get pregnant has declined from 25 percent in 1971 to 18 percent in 1979.[1] At the same time, those indicating they do not want to get pregnant are more likely to say they use contraceptives (9 percent in 1971 compared to 32 percent in 1979). Why, then, has the percentage of premarital pregnancies increased so dramatically? Several reasons seem likely.

Of all teenagers who do not want to get pregnant, less than one-third ever use contraceptives, meaning that more than two-thirds risk becom-

[1]Reasons unmarried teenagers give for wanting to get pregnant include wanting to get out of their parents' house, having a baby to love, getting welfare, and being like their friends or relatives.

ing pregnant. One reason for not using contraceptives may be the fact that more than half of the pregnancies among unwed teenagers occur within six months of their first intercourse, and one in five occur within the first month of sexual activity (Zabin, 1981). Among teenagers who never used contraceptives, the pregnancy rate jumped, perhaps because they were having intercourse more frequently. But pregnancies were also up among teenagers who said they always used contraceptives. This increase may be due to the declining use of the pill or the IUD, and the rise in the use of less effective methods of contraception, especially withdrawal before ejaculation, a decidedly risky method (Zelnik and Kanter, 1980).

Having sexual relations without using contraception, even though one does not want to get pregnant, may be explained by several factors. Teenagers may lack knowledge about how one does and does not get pregnant. They may lack access to effective methods of contraception, most of which require medical examinations and prescriptions to procure. Such a requirement may be too expensive or difficult for teenagers to manage. In certain areas, the availability of contraceptive information and materials, especially to teenagers, is limited by law.

The beliefs of teenagers themselves may also contribute to high pregnancy rates. One survey revealed that nearly one-third of all adolescents believed that "If a girl truly doesn't want to have a baby, she won't get pregnant, even though she may have sex without taking any birth-control precautions" (Sorenson, 1973). The inability of this belief to affect the outcome is vividly revealed in the soaring numbers of premarital pregnancies and births among unmarried teenagers (see Figure 22.2). In an age of economic uncertainty, high technology, and increasingly stringent educational requirements for jobs, early parenthood places significant social, educational, and economic strains on teenagers. Teenage mothers are also more likely to have miscarriages, stillborn babies, or babies with birth defects than are mothers in their twenties.

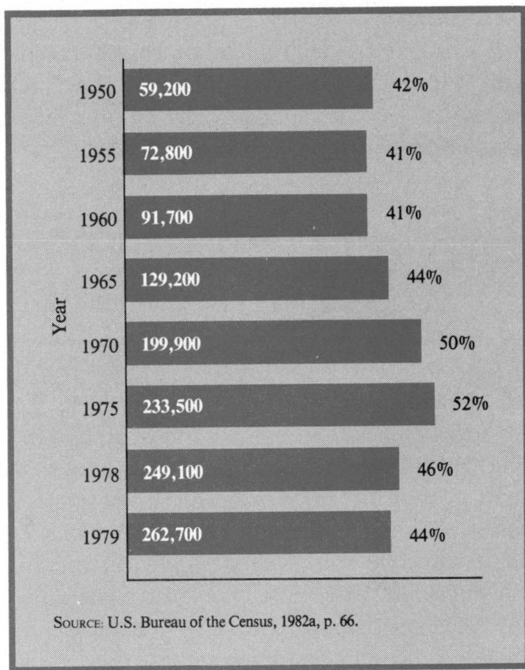

Figure 22.2 Number of Babies Born to Unwed Mothers 19 Years of Age or Younger, 1950–1979 *The number of babies born to young unwed mothers has soared in recent years, from nearly 60,000 in 1950 to more than 250,000 in 1979. On the right is the percent of live births that are out-of-wedlock among mothers aged 19 or younger. Fewer babies are put up for adoption today, so many more unwed teenagers have babies to raise.*

The educational attainments and aspirations of teenage mothers and fathers suffer as a result of early marriage and early parenthood (Haggstrom et al., 1981). Youths (and their parents) may be increasingly aware of how teenage parenthood jeopardizes educational and career plans. Premaritally pregnant teenagers are less likely to get married than ever before, and those who do not marry are increasingly likely to terminate their pregnancies with induced abortions. More than 31 percent of all abortions performed in the United States are performed for teenage women. Another three out of ten teenagers indicated that they wanted and needed abortions but were unable to obtain them. The 160,000 teenagers who indicated this represented about 60 percent of all unintended births among teenagers (Alan Guttmacher Institute, 1981).[2]

THE GAY WORLD—HOMOSEXUALITY AND LESBIANISM

Understanding the gay world requires us to define several terms. "Straight" is the word used to refer to *heterosexual* individuals whose preferred partner for erotic, emotional, and sexual interaction is someone of the opposite sex. A *homosexual* is someone who is emotionally, erotically, and physically attracted to persons of the same sex. Some people are exclusively attracted to people of the same sex, some are exclusively heterosexual, and many have mixed same-sex and heterosexual experiences (see Figure 22.3).

Lesbians are women who are attracted to women; *homosexuals* are men who are drawn to men. Some people use the term "homosexual" to include both men and women who are attracted to same-sex individuals. Some lesbians, however, wish to distinguish themselves from men and therefore prefer the term lesbian to homosexual. The term *gay* refers to both men and women. A gay identity goes one step farther in a social sense, to include cultural and social affiliation with a homosexual or lesbian community (Warren, 1974). Being a member of the gay community helps to neutralize the stigma the larger society may attach to homosexuality, because that community does not accept the negatively stigmatizing social definitions of homosexuality as sick, sinful, or wierd. Instead, the gay community helps individuals to accept a homosexual identity as positive and good.

Within the gay community, two major strategies for dealing with gayness in relation to the outside world have developed. *Secret gays* segregate their lives by time, place, and relationships into gay and straight activities. When operating in the straight world, they try to conceal their sexual identity from the people around them. *Gay liberationists,* in contrast, actively bring their gay identity into all aspects of their life experiences. The liberationists tend to be politically radical and in sympathy with oppressed groups, while the secret community is more likely to be apolitical or conservative politically (Warren, 1974). Secret gays seek to evade the efforts of straight society to stigmatize them, while gay liberationists try to confront and transform the stigma (Humphreys, 1972).

Gay people face at least three types of oppression in our society: legal-physical, in which certain kinds of behavior practiced by a stigmatized group are declared illegal and people practicing them are subject to arrest; occupational-financial, in which opportunities for jobs, advancement, and income are limited for gay people;

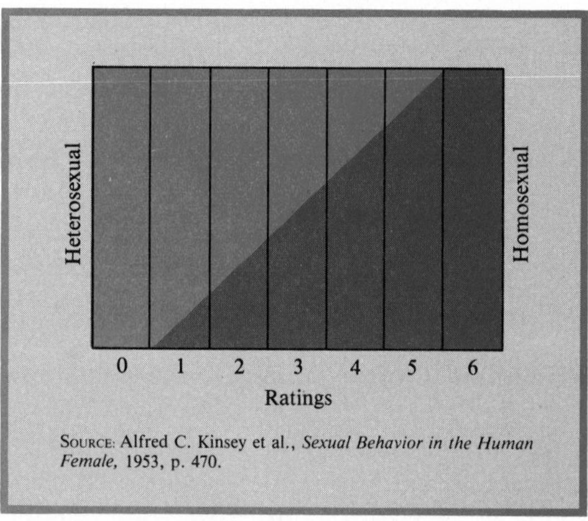

SOURCE: Alfred C. Kinsey et al., *Sexual Behavior in the Human Female,* 1953, p. 470.

Figure 22.3 Kinsey's Heterosexual–Homosexual Rating Scale *Some people have completely heterosexual histories (the left-most column in the diagram); others have exclusively same-sex histories; and a great many people are in between, with some mixture of heterosexual and same-sex experiences.*

[2]This means that if abortion is declared illegal again in many states, the likelihood of out-of-wedlock teenage pregnancies increasing is very great.

and ego-destructive, in which stigmatized individuals are made to feel sick, sinful, or otherwise despicable (Humphreys, 1972).

The negative effects of such social stigmatization are apparent in the cases of people who have attempted to change their homosexual orientation by aversive behavior modification—for example, by getting electric shocks while viewing erotic pictures of same-sex individuals (Riordon, 1979). The results of such "treatment" seem to be influenced by how strongly an individual wants to change, by how long he or she has been a homosexual, and by the nature of the heterosexual experiences the individual has had. Other gays sought less drastic "cures" through psychotherapy. With the advent of gay liberation and intensive debates within the American Psychiatric Association, there seems to be increasing rejection of aversive therapies and a growing sense among both gays and psychiatrists that changing one's sexual orientation is unnecessary, difficult, and undesirable. Instead, therapy should be directed at helping individuals accept themselves and function well as they are (Katchadourian and Lunde, 1972).

Whether individual gays choose an openly gay life-style and a gay liberationist stance or pursue a secret gay life-style may depend to a considerable degree on occupation and where one works. Some occupations and organizations practice overt discrimination against gays, refusing to hire or promote them or firing them when their identities are discovered (Levine, 1979). Until such discriminatory practices are eliminated, gay people working in such situations seem to be faced with the difficult choice of keeping their gay identities secret or endangering their careers.

Similar life-style distinctions exist within the lesbian community. What Wolf (1979) calls the "old gay life" centered around lesbian bars, which were the only public places where a woman could go to meet other lesbians. Yet the bars represented a kind of social ghetto, "a place where the stigmatized were hemmed in and allowed to socialize" (Wolf, 1979, p. 46). The social life that centered around bars was often superficial, based on role playing and encouraging its own form of depression and isolation. This depression may have resulted in large part from the fact that participants tended to accept the negative stereotype of lesbianism held by the larger society. They tended to accept a stigmatized identity and to feel they did not deserve any better.

Wolf sees a second socio-historical era in lesbian life emerging with the rise of homophile organizations in the 1950s. Such groups include the Daughters of Bilitis for women and the Mattachine Society for men. They serve as civil rights and educational organizations for gays working within the norms of the larger society. They do research, try to change the attitudes of society and gay people about their identities, sponsor consciousness-raising groups, and form political coalitions with other groups to achieve common goals.

The third historical development Wolf notes is the rise of militant lesbian feminism, which had its counterpart in the more militant male gay liberationists. This approach aimed to transform society rather than to work for moderate change within it. Lesbian feminism, for instance, proudly defines lesbianism in positive terms and sees it as leading the way toward a feminist future in which both selves and society would be redesigned (Wolf, 1979). In the male gay community, one manifestation of gay liberation takes a form called "radical drag," in which a man wears an evening dress and gloves with boots, a beard, and a hairy chest (Warren, 1974). Such a display is designed to shock the straight world and to challenge conventional definitions of sexuality and appearance.

The goal of gay liberation movements is to change an oppressive system, thereby destroying old patterns of dominance and exploitation (Wolf, 1979). One result has been that the self-esteem of gays has increased tremendously. Another result is that in some areas such as in San Francisco, California, and Greenwich Village, New York, gay rights are taken seriously by politicians. In brief, social roles both within and beyond the gay community are beginning to be redefined as a result of the gay rights and liberation movements (Wolf, 1979).

HISTORICAL VIEWS OF HOMOSEXUALITY AND LESBIANISM

Although opponents of homosexuality consider it "contrary to nature," and hence always repellent, social history suggests otherwise. In classical Greece, male homosexual love was widely portrayed in literature and art, and was often valued more than heterosexual love (Dover, 1978). The usually temporary sexual relationships between youths and older men played an important role in the education of the youths. In Mesopotamia during the Sumerian period (2250 B.C.), homosexual intercourse played a significant part in religious ceremonies (Bullough, 1976). Among the 76 tribal societies surveyed by Ford and Beach (1951), about one-third disapproved of homosexual activities, while two-thirds approved of some forms of homosexuality.

In the very early Christian church, homosexual behavior was not visibly opposed. But from the third through the sixth centuries, as the Roman Empire began to dissolve, government regulation of personal morality and general sexual asceticism increased and was marked by growing hostility to homosexuality. In Visigothic Spain between the sixth and the eighth centuries A.D., for example, homosexuals and Jews were sometimes singled out as scapegoats for the social tensions caused by ethnic and religious conflicts in the population. In the early Middle Ages, moral theology was generally silent on the issue of homosexuality, or at worst viewed it as in a class with heterosexual fornication.

In eleventh-century Europe, homosexual literature and culture reappeared and faced little public hostility. By the thirteenth and fourteenth centuries, however, there was increasing intolerance for deviation from the majority in many areas, including homosexuality. This was the era in which Jews were expelled from many areas of Europe, the Inquisition was underway, and witches were being burned at the stake. The general intolerance was reflected in theological, moral, and legal writings of the age (Boswell, 1980).

In Europe and the United States in the eighteenth century, sexuality was increasingly seen as within the medical realm as well as subject to theological judgments. In the nineteenth century, sexual intercourse was viewed as consuming vital bodily energies. Excessive sexual activity was considered debilitating. All nonprocreative instances of sexual expression were viewed as wasteful. Achieving orgasm was considered equal to losing several ounces of blood and was thought to lower the life force. All nonreproductive sex, including masturbation and homosexuality, was considered pathological (Bullough, 1976). The reproductive value of sex within marriage justified such relations, but even married couples were urged by clergy and hygiene textbooks of the time to exercise sexual restraint. Couples who wanted to use contraceptives were considered pathological cases for quite a while (Bullough, 1976).

By the middle of the twentieth century, the reproductive value of sex was increasingly downplayed, but homosexuality was considered taboo in many social circles. Some people considered it "unnatural"; others felt it was repulsive. In general, known homosexuals or lesbians were socially stigmatized. In the 1970s, several trends contributed to a growing tolerance of homosexuality in certain segments of the population. Postwar prosperity encouraged consumer expenditures and self-expression rather than the self-denial, austerity, and production stressed in an earlier era. The growth of female exployment, a growing concern about overpopulation, and improved birth control techniques all helped to separate the procreational from the recreational functions of sexuality. More educated, affluent youth increasingly rejected legal restrictions based on sexual orientation. They were willing to support, or at least did not oppose, the gay liberation movement.

In recent years there has been a backlash against the liberalized attitude toward homosexuality, which has been reflected in public referendums aimed at repealing or rejecting legislation protecting the civil rights of homosexuals. The social root of this backlash lies in lower-middle-class people who work in bureaucratic organizations or in highly competitive small businesses, suggest Greenberg and Bystryn (1982). Opposition to homosexuality also arises among rural white people (Levitt and Klassen, 1979). These are the same people who oppose abortion, contraception, and the women's movement. Their own social, economic, and religious positions may encourage more restrictive sexual attitudes and behaviors.

FREQUENCY OF HOMOSEXUALITY AND LESBIANISM

The research of Kinsey and his associates in the 1940s suggests that sexuality cannot always be neatly categorized as heterosexual or homosexual. Instead, sexual behavior should be thought of as a wide range of behaviors from exclusively homosexual to exclusively heterosexual, as Figure 22.3 shows. Most people are not at the extremes, but somewhere in between. In addition, many people have experienced a variety of feelings and behaviors along the range.

When Kinsey set out to determine the number of people with same-sex experiences, he excluded any such behavior that occurred before puberty. Even with this limitation, he learned that by the time they were 45 years old, 37 percent of males had experienced at least one homosexual contact leading to orgasm. Among women, this was true of 13 percent. Single people were more likely to report such contact, with 50 percent of single males and 26 percent of single females indicating such experience by age 45. Another 13 percent of males had felt homosexual desires or attractions but had not acted on them. Other studies in the United States, as well as research in Germany and Sweden, confirm the Kinsey figures that about 4 percent of the white, college-educated adult male population is predominantly homosexual (Gebhard, 1972). This represents about 4 million American males over the age of 21 who are predominantly homosexual in attitudes and behaviors. About 1 percent of women are predominantly same-sex in their preferences and behaviors (Gebhard, 1972). This suggests that at least 1 million women are interested primarily in other women.

More recent studies by Kinsey's Institute for Sex Research suggest that the earlier figures still hold. Laypersons and sex researchers, both assuming a gradual loosening of sexual mores, had quite different expectations concerning the effects on same-sex behavior. Many people feared that the greater visibility of same-sex relations in our society would increase such contacts. Sex researchers, in contrast, expected that the general loosening of mores would reduce same-sex relations because heterosexual experiences could be obtained earlier and more easily. Neither expectation has been supported, and the rates of same-sex contact have remained quite constant over the years (Tripp, 1979).

EXPLANATIONS OF SAME-SEX ORIENTATION

Biological, psychological, and sociological explanations have been offered to explain why some individuals are attracted to others of the same sex. Few research studies, however, have attempted to analyze all three types of explanations together. One major study based on about 1500 heterosexual and homosexual individuals attempted to do precisely that. Bell, Weinberg, and Hammersmith (1981) of the Institute for Sex Research at Indiana University were startled to find that many traditional notions about the causes and development of same-sex orientation were not supported by their research.

The widely accepted psychological theories

suggesting that homosexuality is due to certain parental behaviors, such as dominant mothers, and weak fathers, was not supported. Lack of acceptance by one's peers while growing up seems to be an unimportant factor in homosexual development. The sociological theory that homosexuality results from being labeled as sexually different is not supported, because such labels appear to be the result of a developing homosexual orientation rather than a cause of it. Frightening experiences such as being raped by someone of the opposite sex do not seem to direct women toward lesbianism, nor does being seduced by an older person of one's own sex cause someone to become a homosexual. Although homosexuals sometimes have experiences such as those noted above, they are no more likely to have them than are heterosexuals. How then is sexual orientation determined?

Bell and his associates suggest that sexual orientation is likely to be already determined before boys and girls reach adolescence, even though they have not yet been active sexually. People experience homosexual feelings about three years before they experience any homosexual activity. The existence of these feelings was more importantly related to adult sexual orientation than prior homosexual behaviors. The feelings were experienced by males around the age of 13 and by females about the age of 16. Participation in homosexual activities occurred several years later and grew out of the homosexual feelings they had, rather than being the source of such feelings. Homosexuals had about as many heterosexual experiences while growing up as did heterosexuals, but they differed in that they did not find such experiences gratifying.

Gender nonconformity during childhood and adolescence is related to a homosexual orientation, but only about half of the homosexual respondents showed atypical gender traits while growing up. A person's childhood and adolescent sexual feelings (and to a lesser extent behaviors) continue in that person's adult sexual orientation. The continuity may reflect either very strong conditioning situations that teach boys and girls how to respond homosexually, or the emergence of a deep-seated propensity toward either homosexuality or heterosexuality that begins in childhood and continues into adulthood. In sum, Bell, Weinberg, and Hammersmith feel they have identified "a pattern of feelings and reactions within the child that cannot be traced back to a single social or psychological root" (1981, pp. 183–192). Furthermore, they suggest that their findings are not inconsistent with what they would expect to find if there were a biological basis for sexual preference.

The nature of a society may affect the frequency of same-sex orientations of its members. Societies that applaud bravery and courage tend to idealize and eroticize male attributes. Such societies, like the Tanganyikan Nayakyusa, the warrior Mohave Indians of the Southwest, or the Algerian Kabyles, tend to involve most males in some forms of homosexual activity (Katchadourian and Lunde, 1972; Tripp, 1979). When heterosexuality and homosexuality are defined by a culture as mutually exclusive identities, people seem to be less willing to define themselves as homosexuals if they also experience heterosexual attractions and behaviors (Duberman, 1974). Other societies, such as certain contemporary Arab states, offer the possibility of bisexuality, enabling people to form a self-identity that recognizes their multifaceted sexuality.

The social creation of homosexual identities is apparent in the lives of individuals who occasionally engage in homosexual activity yet also lead conventional working- or middle-class lives that include marriage and parenthood. They see themselves as "not really homosexual" (Miller, 1979). Young male prostitutes who allow older male homosexuals to fellate them in exchange for money do not define themselves as homosexuals, either. Instead, they consider what they do as simply a way of making money (Reiss, 1961; Hoffman, 1979). Studies of homosexuality in prisons suggest that not all the participants are considered homosexuals by their peers. Only those who take the role of the other sex are viewed as homosexuals. The sexual aggressors, considered to be "voluntary aggressors," are tagged "wolves" or "jockers." They are seen as playing the conventional masculine role, and thus may often be defined by their peers as heterosexuals even when their aim is sexual gratification through homosexual acts. The submissive partners, or involuntary recruits, are dubbed "fags," "fairies," "effeminates," "queens," or "punks." They are thought to have lost their masculinity, even if they are raped (Kirkham, 1971; Lindner, 1951; Lockwood, 1979; Sagarin, 1976; Sykes, 1958).

SAME-SEX BEHAVIORS AND LIFE-STYLES

Much of our knowledge about same-sex behaviors is based on research by Bell and Weinberg (1978) of the Institute for Sex Research. They conducted extensive interviews with nearly 5000 black and white males and females who engage in same-sex behavior. While their research suffers from the same problems that all studies of sexual behavior have—namely, the use of nonrandom samples that may not be typical of an entire population—nevertheless they have made a significant effort toward describing and analyzing same-sex behavior in the United States.

The single most striking result of their research is the diversity of behaviors that exist. The range of behaviors is extensive and shows the degree to which generally held stereotypical views of homosexual behavior are mistaken. There is no single life-style, set of sexual behaviors, or type of relationship that appears among all homosexuals and lesbians.

Both men and women who engage in same-sex relations tend not to adopt a single role, such as that of being the active or the passive partner in the sex act. Unlike prison studies, where such role typing frequently occurs, in the sample interviewed by Bell and Weinberg individuals alternated between initiating and receiving overtures. Individuals do not limit themselves to a single sexual technique or practice, but tend to experience a variety of forms of sexual contact. Younger people tend to have more varied sexual repertoires than older people. Some of the variation in sexual techniques may result from the lack of cultural approval for homosexual and lesbian behavior in general (Tripp, 1979). Tripp suggests that since no forms of sexual behavior are especially prescribed, individuals are freer to experiment and devise their own.

As is true among heterosexuals, sexual behaviors and preferences are correlated with race, social class, and sex. Fellatio (oral sexual contact) was the most frequently reported technique among black and white homosexuals. Among white males, mutual masturbation was the technique next most frequently used, while black males were more likely to engage in anal intercourse (Bell and Weinberg, 1978). Body rubbing to orgasm was used by only a few, and was more commonly reported by lower-status men. The most desired activities were receiving fellatio (27 percent) and performing anal intercourse (26 percent).

Among women, mutual masturbation was the most frequently used technique (40 percent), with cunnilingus (oral sexual contact) next. About 25 percent of white lesbians and 50 percent of black lesbians performed cunnilingus one time a week or more. Such activity was more frequent among younger women. About 20 percent of white lesbians and 40 percent of black ones achieved orgasm through body rubbing. As with males, this practice was more frequent among members of lower-status occupations. Cunnilingus was the sexual activity most preferred by lesbians.

Just as the roles and techniques experienced in same-sex relations vary considerably, the appearance of the participants is quite diverse. Many people tend to assume they can detect a homosexual or lesbian by the way he or she looks. However, even the trained sex researchers in the Kinsey group could recognize only 15 percent of homosexuals and 5 percent of lesbians, despite the cues they had based on dress and whether a known homosexual or lesbian had referred the respondent to them. Many masculine-looking males are gay, as are a number of feminine-looking females. Similarly, not all effeminate-appearing males or masculine-appearing females are attracted to members of their own sex.

Another important area of variation in same-sex life-styles occurs with respect to the types of relationships that are formed. In their research, Bell and Weinberg (1978) found five types which they termed close-coupled, open-coupled, functional, dysfunctional, and asexual. Close-coupled individuals had long-term, marriagelike relationships with a single partner. Men and women in this group had fewer sexual problems and did much less cruising (that is, visiting bars to meet other gays) than the other people interviewed. Females in this group had less regret over being lesbians, were more active sexually, and used more sexual techniques than other female respondents. The open-coupled people had regular same-sex partners, but they had more sexual problems, spent more time cruising, or had more outside relationships than did the close-coupleds. Women showed these characteristics to a lesser extent than did men.

The functional gays were not coupled, but they were sexually active and had little regret over their same-sex preferences. None of the dysfunctionals were coupled. Although most of them were sexually active with numerous partners, they had more regrets about their sexual preferences and reported more sexual problems. Not many women were classified as dysfunctional, but those who were tended to be younger than the men and to think of themselves as lacking in sex appeal to other women. The asexuals were low in level of sexual activity, number of partners, amount of cruising, and reported relatively more sexual problems. Both male and female asexuals were older, on the average, than other respondents.

Some gay men and lesbian women may follow life-styles that differ from those of heterosexuals. But there is no single life-style that everyone follows. For many, it may be that a preference for one sex or another as an object of emotional and erotic choice is the only major difference between homosexuals and heterosexuals. Beyond that preference, gays and lesbians may show the same range of behaviors that heterosexuals do with respect to life-styles and emotional commitments.

Summary

1. Sexuality is important to both individuals and societies.

2. Social norms and structures influence what sexual behavior is considered acceptable and what individuals find attractive. Societies place limits on when and with whom sexual relations can occur.

3. For centuries, Judaism and Christianity were antisexual, accepting sex only for its role in procreation. In recent decades, the joyous aspects of sexuality have been more widely affirmed.

4. Rape is a crime of violence, not an act of passion. It may be encouraged by a society and culture in which women are dominated by men and the sexual exploitation of women is taken for granted. Rape is the most underreported violent crime. Accused rapists who are caught are seldom convicted, and the few rapists who go to jail serve an average sentence of only four years. These features suggest that rape is not treated as a form of physical assault by society and the legal system.

5. Sexual activity among teenagers, especially white teenagers, has increased dramatically in the last 40 years. About half of American teenage girls have experienced premarital intercourse, as have about three-quarters of American teenage boys. The double standard of sexual morality for boys and girls seems to be declining, but it is not completely gone. The social meaning of sexuality is evident even in solitary behaviors like masturbation.

6. Premarital pregnancies are on the increase. Teenagers are not beginning sexual relations at an earlier age, on the average, but they are having them more frequently. Half of premarital teenage pregnancies occur within six months of first intercourse. While more teenagers say they do not want to get pregnant now compared to earlier years, their use of the relatively more effective methods of birth control has declined. In 1979, more than 250,000 babies were born to unmarried teenagers. Early parenthood depresses the educational and occupational aspirations and attainments of teenage boys and girls.

7. In the gay world, the term "straight" refers to heterosexuals. Homosexuals are emotionally, erotically, and physically attracted to persons of the same sex. Homosexual men are drawn to other men, lesbians are women attracted to other women. A gay identity includes membership in a social community of homosexuals or lesbians. Secret gays feel they must not divulge their gay identity to the straight world, while gay liberationist males and lesbian feminists seek to change the oppressive straight society.

8. Same-sex behaviors have been widely practiced in different societies, and viewed in varied ways in those societies. General attitudes in Western society toward sexuality have been reflected in social mores regarding homosexuality and lesbianism. In the eighteenth and nineteenth centuries, homosexuality was treated harshly. By the 1970s, sexual orientation was increasingly viewed as a matter of individual choice, although rural and lower-middle-class groups in the population have reacted to the moral permissiveness they see around them and have tried to enforce more restrictive sexual values and laws on heterosexual and same-sex relationships.

9. Despite these shifts in societal reactions to same-sex behavior, its frequency seems to have remained stable over the last 40 years, with about 4 percent of the male population and about 1 percent of the female population being exclusively interested in same-sex relationships. One of Kinsey's major findings was that most people are not exclusively homosexual or lesbian, but experience some mixture of same- and opposite-sex attractions and behaviors.

10. Recent research suggests that sexual orientation is determined early in life, but existing evidence does not support sociological labeling theory explanations of homosexuality or psychological theories of family interaction.

11. Sociological explanations for the frequency of same-sex behavior stress two features of a society. The degree to which masculinity is idealized in a society is related to how eroticized maleness becomes, and hence to the frequency of homosexual relations between males. Cultural definitions and group memberships influence how sexual behaviors are linked to particular sexual identities.

12. Same-sex behaviors are not all alike. Homosexuals and lesbians vary considerably with respect to taking the passive or active role with a sexual partner, sexual techniques, appearance and mannerisms, and types of relationships they form.

Key Terms

double standard
heterosexual
homosexual
lesbian
prostitution

N653

Chapter 23

Sport and Leisure

Leisure and sport may seem to be less weighty subjects than some of the other social processes and institutions discussed in this book. However, sport and leisure activities excite human interest and passions, and people spend a lot of time and money on them. So, while they may seem less significant, sport and leisure engage the hearts of millions of people. In addition, they illustrate important sociological and societal features, including the ways in which various angles of sociological vision—functionalism, conflict theory, and symbolic interactionism—raise different questions about the world. Finally, they provide new insights into social life.

In this chapter we examine some of the questions sociologists have raised about leisure and sport, consider the tremendous growth of leisure time that has occurred in Western societies in the past two decades, and examine sport in relation to society generally and as it reflects social stratification.

THE RELATION BETWEEN LEISURE AND SOCIAL LIFE

As is the case with individual tastes and preferences, leisure and sport activities are influenced by social values, norms, culture, and social structure. At the same time, leisure and sport reveal self-aware individuals who carve out some areas of choice for themselves. In this way, leisure and sport bring into sharp relief the dual elements of social forces and individual will. Yes, we are influenced by social forces outside ourselves, but we also select and choose from among those forces what we will affirm, reject, or modify.

THE INTERPLAY BETWEEN LIFE AND LEISURE

Sociologists differ in the ways they see sport and leisure. Some see them as an extension of the values and skills people use in their occupations (Parker and Smith, 1976). Others suggest that how people experience their everyday world influences the leisure activities they pursue. People select activities that contrast with or complement their regular affairs, suggest Mitchell (1983) and Ball (1972). When everyday life is routine, limiting, and tightly structured, people seek variety and personal challenge in recreation. They hunger for situations where the results depend on their own choices (Mitchell, 1983). In mountain climbing, for example, people use their own skills and strategies to influence such outcomes as falling or staying alive. Ball (1972) calls this *control-oriented* action.

Controlled risk taking, reflected in activities such as skiing, scuba diving, skydiving, hang-gliding, and mountain climbing, is more likely to occur in societies whose routine affairs are marked by safety and stability. Numerous mountaineers, for example, come from Britain, France, Germany, Switzerland, Japan, and the United States; relatively few are from Uganda, Ethiopia, Turkey, Peru, Pakistan, Nepal, Vietnam, or Cambodia. Their origins do not depend totally on the availability of mountains or of wealth (Mitchell, 1983). Within the United States, mountaineers are well-educated, secure, middle- and upper-class individuals, many of whom are engineers and applied scientists (Mitchell, 1983).

Acceptance-oriented action differs from control-oriented action, and is reflected in such activities as "fair" dice games or watching TV, suggests Ball (1972). An individual's skill does not affect the result of acceptance-oriented action. Social groups that regularly cope with risks and uncertainties in their daily lives, people with hazardous or insecure jobs, with little education or political influence, and with relatively little control over their own lives and experience, do not usually seek to exercise control in the face of uncertainty. Instead, they seek leisure activities that require no effort on their part but only the acceptance of their fate. They escape responsibility and blame, yet still have the chance to win against the odds or to relax from grueling daily activities. Ball's theory helps to explain why different activities may be more popular in some societies than others and why various social groups within a society may be more or less likely to participate in various types of leisure.

THE CONCEPT OF FLOW

Successful leisure is characterized by *flow,* an experience of total involvement in one's activities. In flow experiences, people do not feel the need to consciously intervene. Instead, the action of one moment flows smoothly into the next action (Csikszentmihalyi, 1974; Mitchell, 1983). Action characterized by flow is freely chosen, self-rewarding, and contains an uncertainty of outcomes that allows for creativity.

In activities characterized by flow, the self does not need to function in its role as negotiator. In much of social life the self serves to negotiate and reconcile the needs of individuals, on the one hand, and the demands of social groups and society, on the other hand. Flow experiences differ from other social life because the self can go "off-duty" for a time. As a result, experiences of flow are immensely rewarding and restorative in and of themselves, without regard to any objective accomplishment they produce. While the condition of flow may be most purely experienced in something like mountaineering or soccer, it is possible that flow experiences may occur in everyday life—for example, in conversation, lovemaking, cake baking, gardening, carpentry, dancing, choir practice, or other satisfying efforts in school or on the job (Mitchell, 1983).

Although individuals experience flow as a psychological condition, it is also possible to describe the social conditions under which flow experiences can occur. Mitchell defines flow as occurring in the middle ground between alienation and anomie. He sees anomie and alienation as opposite poles on a spectrum ranging from certainty to uncertainty in the way social life is experienced by individuals. People experience alienation when they can predict how they will behave based on the social world they inhabit. Every possibility for creativity or spontaneity is stifled by social rules and regulations. Life in prisons, concentration camps, military academies, or on the assembly line may provide so much certainty that it is viewed as alienating by individuals. Individuals may feel powerless and unable to do anything they find personally rewarding (Mitchell, 1983).

Anomie stands at the other extreme. Individuals feel anomie when they do not know what to expect in most or all their social interactions—for example, when a social encounter differs from anything previously experienced and when known rules do not help to predict how others will behave. The lives of secret agents, homeless urban dwellers, confidence-game artists, or lone shipwreck victims in foreign lands may contain considerable uncertainty about the results of their actions and produce anomie in individuals, suggests Mitchell (1983).

Flow occurs at a point of balance between the extremes of anomie and alienation. "Flow emerges in circumstances which are perceived as both problematic and soluble" (Mitchell, 1983, p. 188). Certain social conditions reduce the chances that flow will occur. These include the overrationalization of life, leisure, and sport. Examples might be white-water rafting trips where people become passengers rather than participants in the situation, or professional sports where winning, records, and standings become much more important than the process itself. The more rationalized play becomes, the more self-conscious the participants are and the less the chances of having a flow experience (Mitchell, 1983).

THE GROWTH OF LEISURE

THE INCREASING LEISURE IN INDUSTRIAL SOCIETIES

The number of hours worked in nonagricultural pursuits has declined from about 60 hours per week at the beginning of the century to 38.6 hours in 1960, and to 34.8 hours in 1982 (U.S. Bureau of the Census, 1982a, p. 394). Between 1965 and 1975, the average number of hours devoted to free-time activities increased, while the amount of time spent on family care and work decreased (U.S. Department of Commerce, 1980, p. 528). Indeed, as Figure 23.1 shows, people now spend more time on leisure pursuits than on any other social activity, including family, personal care, and employment. As Mitchell (1983) notes, in the past two decades life expectancy has increased, retirement age has decreased, health has improved, and paid vacations for plant and office workers have doubled in number and increased in length. People now have more time, energy, money, and inclination to participate in leisure activities than ever before.

People are also spending more money on their leisure pursuits. As Figure 23.2 reveals, personal expenditures on leisure activities have been increasing since 1960, both in terms of the absolute dollar amounts and as a percentage of gross national product (except for a slight dip in 1978). Such spending totaled $18 billion in 1960. By 1978, it had soared to $91 billion, more than a fivefold increase. The amount comes close to the $105 billion spent on national defense in 1978. When social observers speak of the "leisure explosion," they are referring to the expansion of nonwork time and to growing expenditures on leisure activities.

HOW PEOPLE SPEND THEIR LEISURE

How do you like to spend your leisure time? Do you enjoy sitting around doing nothing, going to a friend's house, playing a sport or watching one, playing music or listening to it, walking in the park, swimming, or climbing a mountain? If you ask your classmates what their preferred leisure activities are, you will probably get many different kinds of answers. This is not to say that there are no patterns to people's preferred leisure activities. Many of the leisure activities people enjoy are socially learned. If you took a group of bushpersons from Southwest Africa to a baseball game, they might not enjoy it very much. Nor would everyone necessarily like opera the first time they attended one.

The problems social scientists have dealing with a world that is both objectively present yet subjectively defined and interpreted is evident in the phenomenon of leisure. Some social scientists deal with this problem by focusing only on an effort to measure leisure objectively. Thus, for example, some define leisure as free or unobligated time. Thus leisure is simply the residual time left over after required activities have

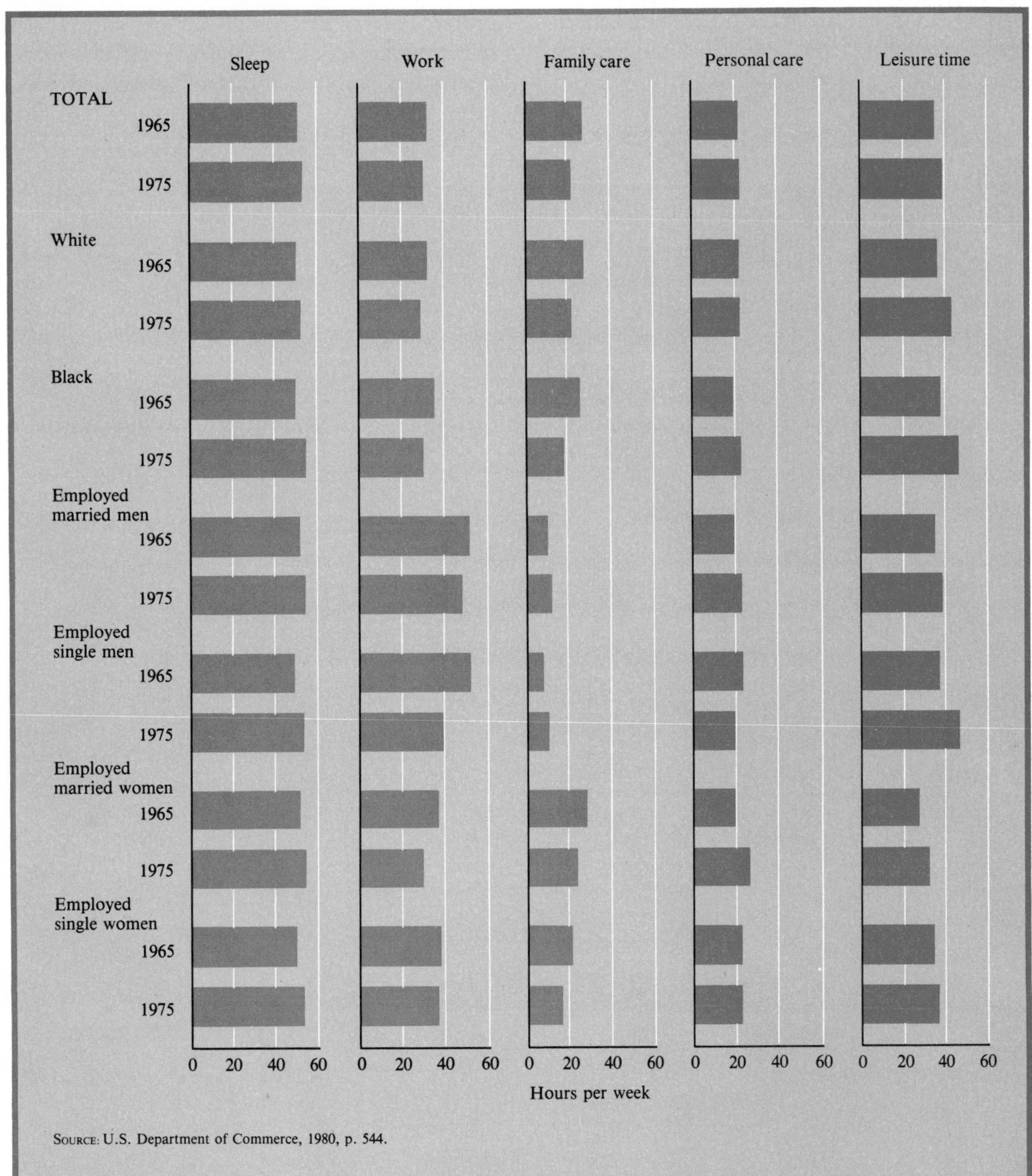

Figure 23.1 Average Hours per Week Spent in Major Types of Activities by Selected Urban Population Groups, 1965 and 1975

been attended to—work, housekeeping, childcare, shopping, personal care (including eating and sleeping), study, participation in various organizations, and the travel associated with all these activities (Robinson, 1977). This approach reflects an attitude among some social scientists that leisure is neither as relevant nor as interesting as other forms of social activities. How about you? Are your leisure activities simply the residual of time allotted to more impor-

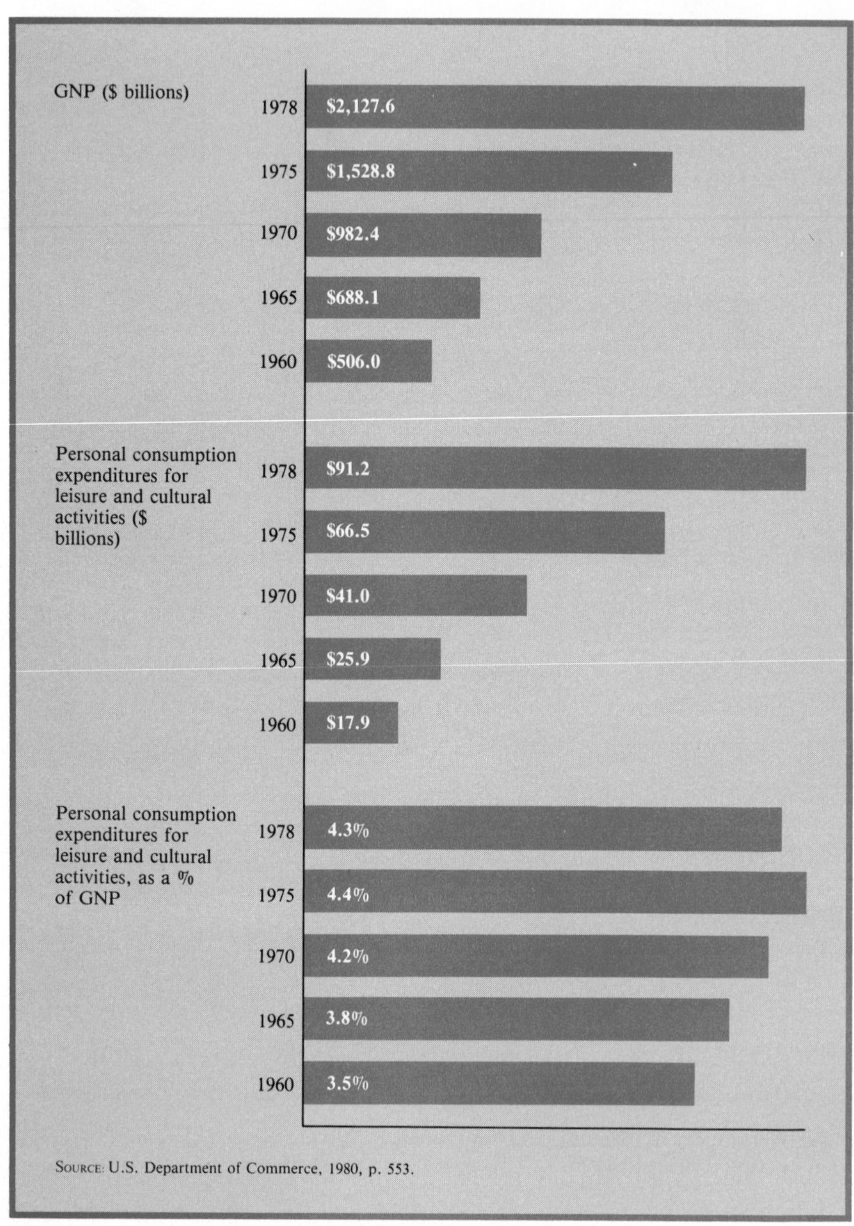

Figure 23.2 Gross National Product and Personal Consumption Expenditures for Leisure and Cultural Activities, Selected Years, 1960–1978

tant tasks? Or are they of major importance to you?

Aside from the fact that not everyone accepts the notion of certain activities being "required," there is the further problem that some people consider them quite pleasurable "leisure" activities, even though they may have to be done in some form. Some individuals, for example, enjoy playing with their children, even though that may be tagged by a social researcher as a necessary activity—childcare. Others may enjoy using their "leisure" time to wash their cars or the windows of their homes.

The various meanings of time and the activities that fill it make a tidy sociological study of leisure very difficult. Nevertheless, in order to understand more fully why people in a society do certain things they consider leisure activities, we need to know both the meaning of the activity for the individual participant and the significance attributed to the activity by sociologists. The study of the ways in which people spend their leisure time is of interest to sociologists who view leisure activities as an indicator of cultural values and possibly even "national character." It is also of interest to government policymakers, social planners, and businesspeople.

One "objective" approach to the study of leisure is simply to ask people what kinds of leisure activities they frequently engage in. As Figure 23.3 indicates, the activity mentioned by the largest percentage (54 percent) was eating, followed by watching television, listening to the radio, reading books, listening to music at home, and fixing things around the house (ABC News-Harris Survey, 1979). Social activities like parties, eating out, or dancing were mentioned by one-quarter of respondents, as was having sex. Fewer than a quarter mentioned participating in church or club activities, outdoor activities such as hiking, fishing, hunting or boating, or participation in sports like swimming, tennis, and golf. The activities most often reported as being done frequently require little effort, and most can be done at home.

When people were asked in another survey, "What is your *favorite* leisure activity?" television finished first (with 30 percent of the population mentioning it), followed by reading (15 percent), and staying home with family (11 percent). (Sex was not listed as a choice.) These activities need not exclude each other, since you can stay home with your family and watch televi-

People spend their leisure time in many different activities, virtually all of which are socially learned.

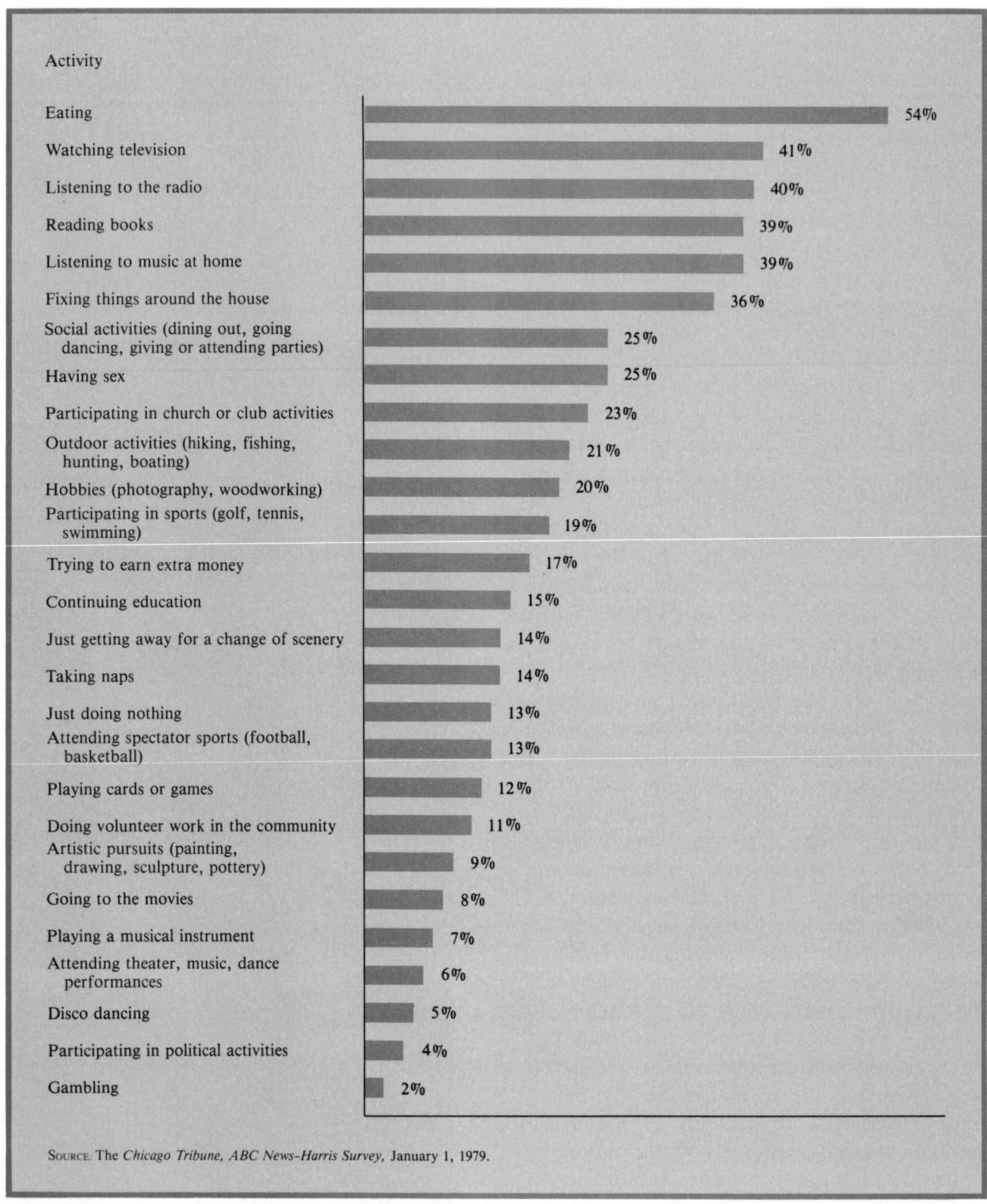

Figure 23.3 Leisure Activities of Americans

sion at the same time. Less than 4 percent indicated participating in sports or indoor hobbies as their favorite activity (Gallup Poll, 1977, in U.S. Department of Commerce, 1980, p. 556). Interestingly, most of the indicated activities require little active participation. Despite the much-touted fitness boom in this country, more than four out of five Americans do not participate in sports according to one survey, and less than 4 percent do according to another survey. The increase in sports and fitness activities (or at least the surging sales of running shoes), may be due to the growing number of young adults aged 18 to 35.

Given all the talk about the "fitness craze," it is surprising to hear what people consider to be "outdoor or physical activities." Most frequently mentioned, as being done five or more times a year, are driving for pleasure and walking or jogging (57 percent each), followed by swimming or sunbathing at a pool and picnicking (40 percent each), and attending a sports event (44 percent). Even in the realm of outdoor activity, a clear picture comes forward: Americans are not engaged in strenuous outdoor physical activity with great frequency or in great numbers. They appear much more likely to spend their leisure time in relatively quiet and passive activities such as watching television. Some sociologists suggest that despite the pervasive emphasis on physical fitness in our culture, people are actually getting less exercise than they did 50 years ago. Instead of walking half an hour daily as many people used to, a small number go jogging for seven minutes once or twice a week. The rest have cut down their walking time without sub-

These skaters and bikers are involved in relatively active leisure activities. Many inhabitants of industrialized societies spend their leisure in less vigorous activities than these.

stituting other physical activities. Auto use per capita, for instance, has more than doubled in the last 30 years (Mitchell, 1981).

FUNCTIONALIST VIEWS OF LEISURE

Functionalist views raise questions about an activity's significance for major social institutions such as the family or for societal integration. In families, shared leisure is associated with open communication and with higher marital satisfaction scores (Orthner, 1976; Presvelou, 1971; West and Mirriam, 1970). Research in this vein emphasizes the positive or negative functions of leisure for other institutions in society, or for society itself. Functionalist theory suggests that leisure helps to hold societies together by motivating individuals to fill their social roles. They may work so that they can afford to go to the big game on the weekend, or they may work overtime to purchase a desired recreational vehicle. Certain other leisure activities may serve to promote societal cohesiveness. Examples are the bicentennial celebration of American Independence, Thanksgiving, Bastille Day celebrations in France, May Day in the Soviet Union, or special parades celebrating the heritage of a particular ethnic group, like St. Patrick's Day or Columbus Day parades. Such leisure activities may mute the degree of class conflict within a society. In shared leisure activities, such as company picnics or softball games, owners and workers may develop a sense of unity that seems to transcend their economic differences.

Although functionalist and conflict sociologists might agree that economic differences may sometimes be overcome, they evaluate that result differently. On the other hand, recreational pursuits sometimes openly conflict with work. In certain parts of the country, absenteeism from work runs high when the hunting or fishing season opens. And the major cause of absenteeism from work is alcohol consumption, which is another form of leisure activity (Mitchell, 1981).

LEISURE AS CULTURAL COMPETITION

Conflict theorists focus on leisure activities as resources in the cultural competition between groups. Leisure activities may be indicators of cultural membership or nonmembership. If someone plays *bocce* (the Italian bowling game) or squash, or rides horseback, or collects pre-Colombian art or early American antiques, such activities or souvenirs serve as a set of cultural badges that may be revealed at appropriate times to verify membership in a particular group (Burdge, 1969; Clark, 1956; White, 1956). Because leisure activities are not necessarily prescribed by occupational demands, they are more open-ended, and they are expected to reflect one's "true personality" more fully. Since part of one's personality is tastes and pleasures cultivated through childhood and family exposure, they are presumably a significant indicator of class and status background.

Cultural differences arise among various users of the outdoors and national parks (DeVall and Harry, 1978). Backpackers and wilderness buffs differ from people who stay in heated cabins, and both groups see themselves as different from people who drive up to a campsite in their RVs (recreational vehicles), plug into running water, gas, and electricity, and turn on their television sets. All of them may go to a national park for the same general purpose, to enjoy the outdoors in some form, but how they become involved with nature reflects cultural differences among various groups. Picnics may have similar cultural content, depending on whether the fare is hot dogs, potato chips, and beer or French paté, strawberries, and white wine. The meaning that different cultural groups attach to various menus varies widely. The conflict perspective goes beyond simply noticing individual or group differences in cultural style to suggest that sometimes such variations become resources in status competitions between groups.

Sometimes leisure competition moves out of

the realm of cultural tastes and into direct competition over scarce resources such as land in national parks or recreational waters. At any given moment, the existence of limited facilities means that people will compete for their use. Ethnic groups may compete over city basketball courts, and social classes may compete over how park lands are allocated among wilderness areas, developed campgrounds, RV stations, or concessions. Are resources allocated in a way everyone considers fair, or do some groups get special access? Access to publicly supported national parks is supposedly allocated on a first-come, first-served basis, but there is evidence that socially or politically powerful people have easier access (Langley, 1981). The worlds of leisure and recreation are not insulated from the realities of stratification.

SPORT AND SOCIETY

The sports a society glorifies may be an important indicator of that society's structure and essence. With this in mind, we will discuss the historical changes sports have undergone in England and the United States and will compare American sports to those played by other societies. We will also examine the ways in which sports reflect the inequalities that exist within a society, whether those inequalities are based on race, gender, or social class.

DEFINITIONS OF SPORT

Play, games, and sport sound like the same activities to most of us, but sociologists of sport use those terms for different and specific activities. *Play* refers to spontaneous activity, undertaken freely for its own enjoyment, not designed to accomplish any productive end, yet governed by rules and often characterized by an element of make-believe. *Games* are one form of play, although not all forms of play are games. Games involve competitive or cooperative interaction in which the outcome is determined by physical skill, strength, strategy, or chance. *Sport* is a form of game in which the outcome is affected by physical skill and prowess (Loy, 1968; Loy, McPherson, and Kenyon, 1978). Chess, for example, is a game but not a sport, while kite flying may be considered a sport.

Athletics, by way of contrast, is associated with occupations, and is part work. When sports are performed for pay, elements of work are likely to be more important than the playful aspects of the activity. College players on athletic scholarships often mention that in high school they played ball for fun, but in college it is work. The links among these aspects of sport are portrayed schematically in Figure 23.4. Modern sport may be seen as being at the center of a band between work and play. At the same time, the dotted lines in Figure 23.4 suggest that work may have elements of play within it, just as play may have some elements of work in it.

The interconnection between sport and society is revealed in three kinds of evidence: first, how sports evolved historically in the United States and England; second, sport in the United States compared with sport in other societies; and third, views of sport as reflecting a larger debate about the nature of American society and how it is studied and evaluated.

THE HISTORICAL EVOLUTION OF SPORT IN ENGLAND AND THE UNITED STATES

American attitudes toward sport and games were influenced by two trends: the English royalist tradition that favored sports and gaming on the one hand, and the Puritan tradition that actively opposed play, sport, and all forms of "frivolous" activity (Dulles, 1965). The English aristocracy always enjoyed gaming and sports, but the middle-class Puritan leaders of the American colonies in their early years stood in opposition

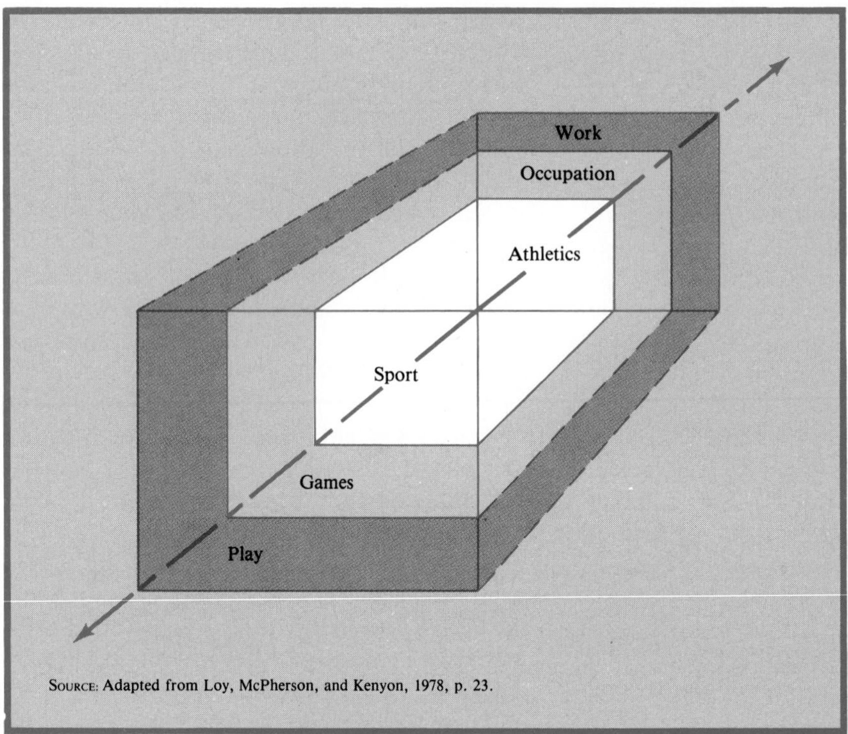

SOURCE: Adapted from Loy, McPherson, and Kenyon, 1978, p. 23.

Figure 23.4 Sport on a Play-Work Band

to the worldliness of the established Church of England and the pleasures of the rich, landed nobility. They detested idleness and saw pleasure as sinful (Dulles, 1965). In 1611, Sir Thomas Dale forbade bowling on the green in Jamestown, Virginia. About the same time, Governor Endicott of the Massachusetts Bay Colony cut down the Maypole at Merry Mount. The early settlers did have a practical need to promote industry and frugality, but the Puritan leaders went far beyond those practical needs in their efforts to stifle play.

The publication in England of *Tom Brown's Schooldays* in 1857 by Thomas Hughes may have helped to provide a moral justification for sport even to Puritans. That author praised games for the way they built character (Goodhart and Chataway, 1973). The claim that sport enhanced virtue gave it new respectability in the eyes of the Puritan middle classes, who could use their capacity to rationalize activities to develop organized sport. Shortly thereafter, the modern forms of rugby, football, hockey, and swimming contests were developed. Lawn tennis began spreading around the world, polo staged a comeback, and golf competitions began. Various other sports such as badminton, court tennis, squash, and croquet were all newly organized (Goodhart and Chataway, 1973).

Along with changing attitudes toward sport, attitudes toward work were also easing somewhat. By the mid-nineteenth century, many English workers had Saturday afternoons free from work. The shift in the moral conception of sport and the organizational efforts of the middle class, along with improved communications, more leisure, and growing urbanization, all contributed to the growth of mass spectator sports.

Similar transformations occurred in the United States.

In eighteenth- and nineteenth-century American society, sporting events consisted of foot, boat, and horse races, log splitting, shooting, horse pulling, and plowing contests, and sometimes cockfighting. Except for the last activity, these sports involve skills that were functionally related to the challenges of a rural environment. They generally had an individual rather than a team winner. Such events were often staged at county fairs or local gatherings, with some spectators watching. There was nothing akin to the large masses of spectators who today crowd gigantic sports stadiums or follow sport through the mass media. Sport in that earlier era was neither highly organized nor centralized.

Major demographic, economic, and technological changes that occurred in the United States transformed the social context of sport. Huge waves of immigration and growing American industry greatly increased the number of urban dwellers. The invention of lightbulbs in 1897 and the development of railroads meant that teams could travel to other cities to play and that athletic contests could be held at night. Stadiums—ever larger—were built. Baseball's National League was founded in 1876, the Na-

"Have a pious, thrifty, hardworking day."

SOURCE: Drawing by Ed Fisher, © 1979, *The New Yorker Magazine, Inc.*

tional Hockey League in 1917, the National Football League in 1922, and the National Basketball Association in 1946. Newspapers began adding sport coverage in the late 1890s. The growth of radio after 1900 meant that even people who could not attend could follow the games.

More recently, the advent of jet planes and television has intensified this growth. Television really fueled the expansion of professional sport because it provides huge TV audiences, high advertising fees, gigantic profits for the networks, and huge revenues to the leagues. In 1960 there were 42 professional sport franchises; by 1970 there were 87 franchises. Television has affected the content as well as the expansion of sport. Some rules have been changed—for example, the use of tie-breakers in tennis so that a set cannot drag on endlessly; there are commercial timeouts; and games are scheduled to fill prime-time hours.

All these developments enhanced the growth of professional athletics, spurred the rise of sport figures as cultural heroes, and shaped the direction of professional sport organizations. Today's athletic teams are organized as large-scale monopoly organizations involved in regional rivalries that sometimes become quite intense. Big-time professional football, baseball, basketball, and hockey are large-scale business operations.

COMPARISONS WITH OTHER SOCIETIES

The sports that are popular in a society seem to reflect the values that predominate in a particular society, and those values in turn may reflect underlying economic and cultural practices. Sport in the United States is characterized by competition rather than cooperation, high levels of violence, and spectatorship rather than participation on the part of most adults. If we considered only the United States, it would be easy to assume that all sport is competitively organized with the goal of producing winners and losers. The sport of other societies reflects some of the different values of those societies, however.

The Tangu people of Oceania play a game called *taketak*. Two opposing teams try to throw a spinning top made from a dried fruit rind and touch a group of palm branches that have been driven into the ground. Each team tries to hit exactly the same number of stakes as the other team. The object of the game is to demonstrate the similarity of the teams, not the superiority of one team over another one. In this way, the game reflects the cultural message that people are morally equivalent. This value is also reflected in the fact that the Tangu exchange food and other essentials (Burridge, 1957).

In another society, sport is used as a substitute for warfare. In the Gahaku tribe of New Guinea, a sporting contest is set up to redress a grievance one tribe has against another. The team from the tribe believed to have committed an offense enters the contest with a score of one. The object of the encounter is to "even the score." When that has been done, the game is over and the grievance is settled (Read, 1965). Competition is not considered an end in itself, but a means for resolving preexisting conflicts between groups.

In Switzerland, a society characterized by decentralized economic production and diverse cultural groups, large-scale national sport competitions are less popular than family outings that involve hiking, skiing, or swimming (Clinard, 1978). Rather than stressing competitive games among professional teams, the Swiss place relatively greater stress on sharing their enjoyment of nature and maintaining good health.

Americans and Europeans seem to value spectator sports with distinctly different characteristics. Americans value skill and teamwork in situations that are tightly bound by space and time limitations, as reflected in football, baseball, basketball, and hockey. Europeans place greater value on individual exploits in the face of exhaustion, danger, or suffering, such as occurs in the 22-day, 2600-mile Tour de France bicycle race, speed skiing, and car racing (Daley, 1963). Why these different preferences exist is explained by sociologists such as Ball (1972) and Mitchell (1983) in terms of the way they complement the everyday lives of participants and spectators.

Europeans in general may feel less opportunity to take risks and find challenges as individuals, while many Americans may find daily challenges but have little chance to experience the fruitful combination of teamwork and skill within a finite time and space. Sport also reflects the amount of violence in a society and how violence is viewed. The United States, with the highest per capita homicide rate in the world, also exhibits a high degree of violence in sport, especially among players. Other Western countries are less likely to experience violence among players, but more likely to have violent episodes among spectators.

How do we explain different levels of violence in sport, and what are their consequences for society? Some sport clearly encourages violent behavior among the players. Football, for example, encourages violence. Indeed, physical contests and violence are part of the game, whether in tackling, blocking, or protecting the quarterback. As a result, many players are injured. The National Football League found that each season the 1040 players in the league suffered an average of 1101 injuries so severe that they were unable to return to the game or to a subsequent game or practice. Each year about 13 percent of all players undergo surgery (Surface, 1974).

Canadian and American ice hockey, too, is especially known for the physical abuse of players and numerous fights. Aggressive body checking and physical domination are considered necessary for winning. As a result, a "subculture of violence" develops, even among young amateur players (Smith, 1979). Fans realize the place of violence in the game, and often favor more aggressive players over more skillful ones. While player attitudes and values supportive of violence are related to violent behavior in the game, Smith found that they were poor predictors of how often these same players got into fights in their private lives. In the USSR, ice hockey players are valued more for their skating ability and their good passing than for their prowess as fighters, suggesting that even in the same sport cultural factors influence which aspects are emphasized.

Why do violent sports thrive in some societies but not in others? Some theories suggest that sport serves as a form of social safety valve, allowing individuals to vent their seething aggressions, and thereby lowering the chances of war or other forms of violence. The theory seems to rest on the assumption that some degree of aggression is innate and that frustration produces further aggressive feelings, which somehow accumulate in individuals or societies until released. It is argued that when too much aggressive tension is bottled up inside individuals or societies, interpersonal conflict or war results.

A competing theory termed the culture pattern theory suggests that sport does not provide an emotional release from aggression. The theory further suggests that aggression and violence are learned—not innate—behaviors. Societies that are already strongly aggressive will promote competitive and aggressive sport, while those that are more cooperative will promote peaceful or cooperative sport. Exposure to one kind of sport or the other will increase the violent or peaceful tendencies that already exist in a society.

A direct test of these competing theories was made by Sipes (1973), who randomly selected 20 tribal societies to see if warlike societies had combative sport. Nine out of ten warlike societies had combative sport, while only two out of ten peaceful societies had combative sport. These findings provide strong support for the culture pattern model. Sipes also examined the relative popularity of combative sport in the United States between 1920 and 1970 and found that combative sports such as football and hunting were more popular in times of war, while baseball, a sport without violence, was less popular during wartime. This analysis also tends to support the culture pattern model, Sipes suggests. Perhaps during wartime the levels of aggression in an entire society are raised, yet most of the population cannot engage in actual warfare. This excessive aggression might need some tension release through violent sport. Although Sipe's analysis supports the culture pattern theory, it does not fully refute the competing tension release model. Combative sport, whatever its cause, may still serve as a safety valve or release for the members of a particular society (Eitzen, 1979b).

Further support for the learned nature of violence, however, is found by researchers who examine the effects on spectators of watching violent sports (Goldstein and Arms, 1971; Green and Berkowitz, 1966; Turner, 1968). Several kinds of violence occur among spectators at sporting events. *Rowdyism* refers to generalized interpersonal violence or property destruction. It appears to be unrelated to what is happening on the playing field, but reflects instead the anger of people who come to games with the idea of having a good fight or destroying the place.

In England, rowdy behavior is a growing problem at soccer matches (Taylor, 1972). Incidents are also increasing in the United States. Spectators may run onto the playing field, throw beer or solid objects at players, set off firecrackers, or rip out the seats. Fimrite (1974) suggests both societal and sport-related reasons for the growing frequency of such behavior, including increased drinking at games, greater permissiveness in raising the young, who feel they can vent their emotions however they like, growing contempt for established institutions, and a widening breach between fans and players as professional athletes command ever-higher salaries and are willing to strike or move to another city when it suits them.

Sport riots may occur as a new form of victory celebration. A *riot* is a destructive and sometimes violent collective outburst. Quite often the spectators on the winning side tear down the opponents' goal posts (Klein, 1981). In a somewhat more extreme example, when the New York Mets won the World Series in 1969, the fans stripped the stadium of anything they could break loose and carry away, including signs, bases, grass, seats, and wood. Other sport riots reflect hostility rather than jubilation. Societies with major ethnic, class, religious, political, or economic cleavages are likely to have riots when the members of groups already at odds meet in a sports contest. Riots have erupted, for example, when black lower-class high schools have played affluent white schools in football playoffs or when countries that are having border skirmishes meet in a soccer contest.

Riots do not always occur under such conditions, however, and sociologists try to analyze what makes riots more or less likely to occur. One factor is the absence of other avenues for expressing grievances. In societies that lack effective means of political protest, violence associated with sporting events may be more severe. This interpretation is supported by the violent riots that occur in Latin American countries. A soccer riot in Lima, Peru, resulted in the death of 293 fans and the injury of more than 500 others. Fans in relatively poor countries may identify strongly with players who come from humble backgrounds similar to their own. Such identification seems greatly to intensify the feelings of the fans. Under such conditions, riots may occur if there is a precipitating event, such as a fight between spectators, a contested call by officials, or violence or injury among the players (Eitzen, 1979b). The severity of the riot may be affected by the importance of the contest, the intensity of the traditional rivalry between competing teams, and the violence of the sport being watched, suggests Lewis (1975).

THEORETICAL VIEWS OF SPORT AND SOCIETY

Large numbers of people in the United States seem to believe that sport contributes to the well-being of society and the individuals in it. In fact, 75 percent of the respondents in a midwestern urban area agreed that sport is "particularly important for the well-being of our society," and 71 percent agreed that "sports are valuable because they help youngsters to become good citizens" (Spreitzer and Snyder, 1975). General Douglas MacArthur felt that sport stimulated the pride and genius of the American people and renewed their national spirit.

In one sense, the way people view sport reflects the way they view and evaluate American society. Those who are basically satisfied with the nature and structure of American society will be similarly uncritical of sport. They will see sport as compatible with the basic values of society and as contributing to social stability. Those who are critical of the structure of American society are more likely to see sport as a means of diverting the masses from their frustrations and a way of making a profit from the efforts of athletes. Each of these views is limited, but both direct our attention to important questions about sport and society.

THE FUNCTIONALIST VIEW OF SPORT

Functionalist sociologists have considered how sport helps a society to meet the functional needs of pattern maintenance and tension management, integration, goal attainment, and adaptation. We will define these terms and explain the ways in which sport promotes them—in the view of functionalists.

Social patterns are *maintained* when individuals become motivated to support the structures and values of a particular society. If sport teaches loyalty to a team, unselfishness to teammates, and the desire to work hard, achieve, and win, all within a rule-bound structure, those values and motives and the willingness to accept the existing structure all contribute to the maintenance of the existing social structure. Furthermore, players learn limits on ways they can express anger or disappointment within a particular social setting, thus learning ways of managing tension.

Compared to nonathletes, students who participate in high school sport are more likely to accept school norms and traditions (Schafer and Phillips, 1970) and are more conservative in their political attitudes (Rehberg and Cohen, 1976). There is no evidence, however, that such values result directly from participation in sport, or that such values are the most functional ones for young people to learn. Regarding the motivations sport is supposed to teach, it may be that more people are discouraged from working hard and achieving as a result of their experiences than are encouraged. Since the structure of sport allows for few winners, those who do not make the team or who regularly lose despite their best efforts may end up believing that hard work and effort are not enough to win. Instead, they may come to feel that people need to be exceptional in order to be successful—for example, very tall (as in basketball) or very large (in football). Most people may conclude that their own efforts cannot influence the outcome or that illicit means are justified—cheating, use of drugs, or injuring other players. Such a result would not be functional for a society.

Integration involves the acceptance of certain common values and motives. It also involves the effective coordination and communication of various members of society, even if they belong to different racial, religious, or social class groups. With its emphasis on coordinated teamwork, sport is presumed to develop interpersonal skills in individuals, which will help achieve integration. Business organizations often sponsor company teams on the assumption that people who play together will work together better in the office. At a community level, sport has been suggested as a major means of integrating members of a town, city, or region without regard to the class, racial, or religious divisions that might otherwise be prominent.

International competitions are stressed as a mechanism for enhancing national solidarity or promoting mutually beneficial relationships between countries. The same might be true within a nation as well. Interscholastic sports or regional competitions might promote travel, exchange, contacts, and other forms of communication among schools or regions that could provide a basis for greater integration. Whether or not sport will serve to achieve such results probably depends on the severity of other social cleavages—political, racial, or economic—between competing groups. Sport may enhance integration, but it may also heighten conflicts and rivalries. It is not always clear why sport sometimes fosters social cohesiveness and at other times does not.

All societies need to know how to attain goals such as producing food in order to survive. In a general way, *goal attainment* in a society is helped by sport, functionalists suggest, because sport stresses a goal-oriented model of behavior; it develops mental and physical fitness and encourages self-discipline. These experiences are considered useful for the various goal-attainment activities of a society. No studies have proved that sport helps a society to attain its goals, however, so this assertion should be considered an idea to be tested rather than a statement of fact.

All social systems need to adapt to their ecological and social space on earth, and sport is seen as fulfilling this need for *adaptation* in several ways. In simple societies, sport stresses the physical skills and dexterities that are directly useful in hunting or in battle. By publicly displaying and valuing such skills through sport, a society can encourage their development. In modern industrial societies, it is less clear how sport may help a society adapt to its environment, although it may contribute to the general level of health in a society. In his extensive study, the writer James Michener suggests that sport has two major justifications: improving the overall physical health of the individuals in a society throughout their lifetime, and providing entertainment to players and spectators (1976). The former may be considered a form of physical adaptation, while the latter may improve the mental health of individuals.

Even in industrial societies, several sociologists have suggested that sport can serve as preparation for combat readiness (Wohl, 1970). State laws making physical education programs in American schools mandatory grew out of the increased pressure to be prepared militarily after World War I. World War II gave physical education and organized sports a similar boost (Cozens and Stumpf, 1953). It is not apparent that the Korean or Vietnamese wars had the same results, however. Within a competitive society, sports programs may teach people how to manage losing and failure, since most people and teams do not win. The idea that sport helps societies adapt can also be considered a hunch to be tested with careful research.

CONFLICT PERSPECTIVES ON SPORT

Although sport may under certain conditions promote the social functions functionalists claim it does, it may also have dysfunctional consequences. Because conflict theorists stress the unequal power and resources of various groups in society, they raise questions about whether sport might serve the interests of some groups more than others. Big-time athletics, for example, may benefit a few individuals in society while actually exploiting many others, including players and spectators. Within a society, critics contend, sport may serve as an *opiate*—that is, as something that takes people's minds off problems but does nothing to solve those problems (Hoch, 1972). In this view, sport is the great distractor. Sport keeps workers, for example, from realizing how boring and alienating their jobs are. Besides distracting people, sport operates in ways that fortify the position of the powerful elite groups of society. Specifically, popular violent sports like football, hockey, and boxing make official, rule-governed violence appear acceptable and even part of a package of idealized masculinity. Seeing that violence is acceptable within the world of sport helps to make it seem more acceptable in other realms.

Sport, according to conflict theorists, also encourages the belief that hard work is a necessary and a sufficient cause of success. Such a belief tends to legitimate the positions of people who control more resources in society, since it suggests that people occupy positions on the basis of their own talents and efforts.

Conflict theorists also suggest that the nature of sport has shifted away from being an activity to be enjoyed for its own sake to a product to be consumed. This means that instead of going out and having a good time playing a sport with one's friends, sport has become an important commodity that is promoted, marketed, and sold so that certain groups can make a profit. Team owners promote a phony loyalty to their teams in an effort to fill the stands with supporters. What was fun when played by amateurs loses its enjoyment, and winning becomes much more important than having a good time.

In such a situation, the intrinsic satisfactions that are derived from flow experiences are replaced by the pursuit of external goals such as prestige or profits. "The purpose of play shifts from the achievement of immediate enjoyment to earning ultimate successes, from means to ends" (Mitchell, 1983, pp. 13–38). Fewer people become active participants who freely choose their own actions, decisions, and risks. Individuals become spectators and critics of sport, but no longer participants.

A Marxian conflict analysis of sport tends to lump all forms of sporting activity into the same category. Little League baseball and professional boxing tend to be treated similarly in that they are seen as serving the same interests. Such treatment is clearly an oversimplification. Another problem is that Hoch's analysis of sport as an opiate assumes that the people who are involved in sports as players or spectators would be involved in critically analyzing and reforming American social structure if it were not for their involvement in sports.

Given the composition and attitudes of those people who are sports fans—namely, solid middle-class, working-class, and some upper-middle-class people, all of whom tend to support the political, economic, and social status quo—it seems unlikely that most of them would be involved in challenging the system in any case. We do not know if the existence of sports increases their general level of satisfaction with the status quo or whether people who pursue occupations in which goal attainment and achievement are important are drawn to sports. Without studies of the long-term effects of sports involvement on one's political and social behavior and beliefs, we cannot tell whether or not Hoch's view is supported.

AN INTERACTIONIST VIEW OF SPORT

We have already seen sport as viewed by conflict and functionalist analysts. We can also consider it from an interactionist perspective. This approach places greater emphasis on the meanings attached to sport by interacting individuals. The perspective stresses the active role of players and spectators in shaping the social organization, conduct, and interpretation of sport.

Mountain climbing clearly reveals the importance of human agency and social definitions in the conduct and interpretation of sport. Take the issue of accidents, which can fatally affect a climber. When a slip occurs, mountaineers spend hours discussing it, trying to figure out what happened and why. The mountains are not dangerous places, they say, and events are controllable by human agents. If something goes wrong in the mountains, it is because people failed to follow the clear rules climbers are supposed to obey. Determining the degree to which a seasoned climber should know something and seeing whether or not proper procedures were followed enables other climbers to define an event as an avoidable accident. Thus, people remain the masters of their fates (Mitchell, 1981, 1983). In these ways mountain climbing illustrates features of all sports—namely, that events by themselves have no set meaning until the participants and spectators define and interpret those events. People define a "good sport," a "good player," or an "avoidable accident."

By drawing on both an interactionist and a Marxian perspective, we may raise some questions. Who has relatively greater power and resources in a particular sport? Who is therefore able to have their definitions and rules prevail? In privately owned professional sports leagues, the owners, the media, and the spectators are influential in creating or modifying the rules and definitions. In a sport such as mountain climbing, there are no owners and there is little media intrusion. Under such conditions, the definitions of participants and their peers prevail. Even in rigid traditional sports, however, there may be borderline rules or definitions that are open to negotiation, depending on how strongly various participants feel about changing them.

SPORT AND STRATIFICATION

Do sports provide upward mobility for talented youngsters regardless of race, sex, or social class? This is a controversial question in professional sports in the United States. Supporters of the American social structure stress the openness of the system to talent and effort. They extoll the opportunities sport offers to proficient youngsters, however humble their backgrounds. Black athletes are highly visible in basketball, football, and baseball. As a result, the belief that sport provides blacks with "a ladder to success and a passport to a better life" is widely held (Miller and Russell, 1971). The widespread assertion that sport is "color blind," however, needs closer examination to see if it fits social facts.

RACE AND SPORT

Critical commentators suggest that the visibility of blacks in a few sports actually masks the racial cleavages that exist within the institution. They note that blacks are involved in only a few sports—football, basketball, baseball, boxing, and track. There are many other sports with few or no black participants, including hockey, tennis, golf, swimming, polo, mountain climbing, skiing, car racing, horse racing, sailing, figure skating, and gymnastics. It seems unlikely that the absence of blacks from these sports is due to lack of athletic ability so much as to lack of opportunity to learn and practice a particular sport. Mitchell goes even further than this to suggest that the absence of blacks and other minorities from certain sports is a commentary on their perception of their own position in society, not just an indication of their access to tools, techniques, and resources (Mitchell, 1982).

In those sports that do have a high proportion of blacks, critical commentators focus on three examples of discrimination within them: the assignment of playing positions, rewards and promotions within sports, and performance standards (Eitzen and Yetman, 1979). Black players tend to be assigned by professional coaches and managers to particular positions, such as outfielders in baseball (see Figure 23.5). In that way, they do not compete against whites in all positions, including pitcher. Position assignment has been explained by the importance of a position for social interaction on a team. Sociologists suggest that the more central the position, the greater the chance that it will be filled by whites (Loy and McElvogue, 1970). In

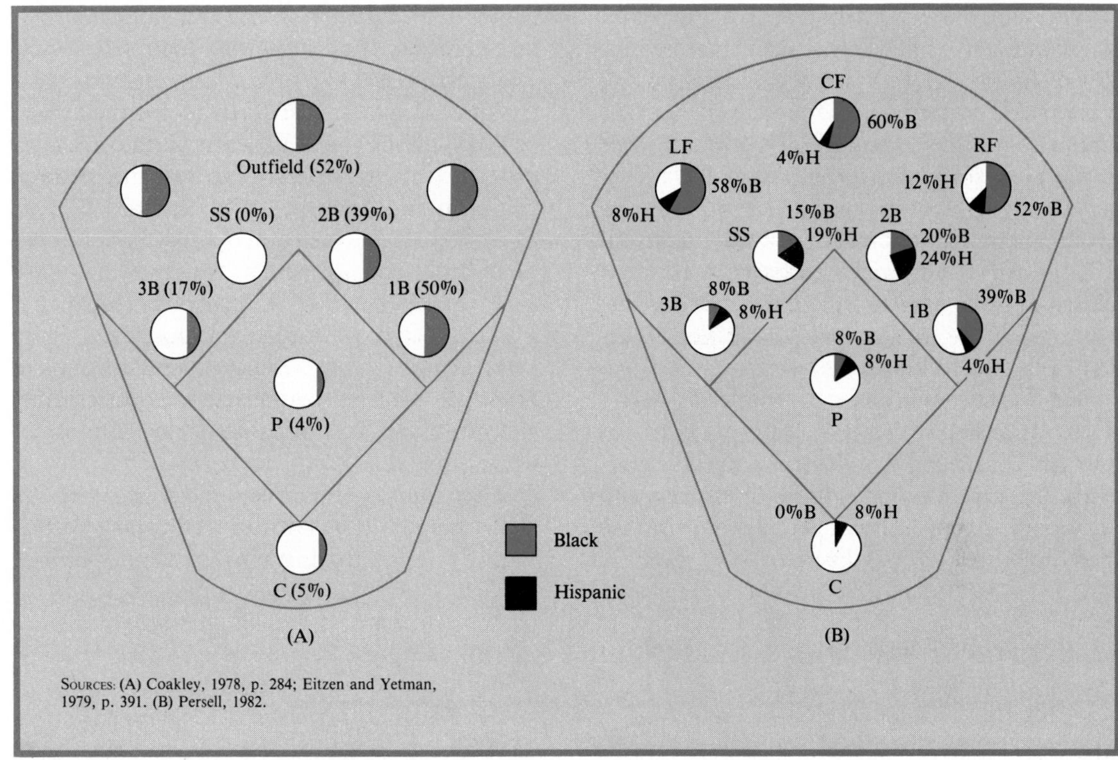

SOURCES: (A) Coakley, 1978, p. 284; Eitzen and Yetman, 1979, p. 391. (B) Persell, 1982.

Figure 23.5 (A) Percentage of Black Players in Major League Baseball Starting Positions in 1975 (B) Percentage of Black and Hispanic Players in Major League Baseball Starting Lineups in 1982 *Between 1975 and 1982, the percentage of black players in the outfield increased slightly, as did the percentage of black players at shortstop and pitcher. The percentage of black players declined, however, in the positions of first, second, and third bases, and catcher. Black players remain much more likely to play outfield positions than to play infield positions. In 1982 there were no black catchers, a position that has often led to future coaching jobs. Although these figures do not prove that racial discrimination exists in baseball, they do raise interesting questions about why blacks are more or less likely to play some positions rather than others.*

football, the central positions are quarterback, center, offensive guard, and linebacker; in baseball they are pitcher, catcher, and infielders. These are the positions that are filled by whites rather than blacks. Between 1960 and 1975, the proportion of blacks in baseball increased dramatically, but almost all their gains were in the noncentral positions (Eitzen and Yetman, 1979). This was true between 1975 and 1982 as well, when shortstop and second base were the only positions to gain significantly more minority representation (as shown in Figure 23.5).

Others suggest that the spatial centrality of the position is less important than the degree of leadership responsibility and the chance to influence the outcome of the game that the position represents (Brower, 1973; Edwards, 1969). This assertion is supported by the small number of blacks in the key positions of quarterback, placekick holder, and kicker (Eitzen and Yetman, 1979). In baseball this is reflected in the small proportion of minorities who play catcher (see Figure 23.5). Edwards suggests that the absence of blacks in leadership positions is due to the persistence of negative stereotypes in the sports world about black intellectual and leadership abilities. Although racial "stacking" by position existed in college basketball in 1972, it had disappeared in both college and professional basketball by 1974 (Eitzen and Yetman, 1979).

Position assignment by race affects the rewards blacks and whites receive in sports. About one-third of the most highly paid baseball players in 1982 were either pitchers or catchers and one-quarter played one of the bases, positions that minorities are less likely to play than are whites (see Table 23.1 and Figure 23.5). Although black superstars with high salaries are frequently in the sports news and the mean salaries of black players often equal or exceed those of white players, the salaries of black players do not match their exemplary performance records (Eitzman and Yetman, 1979; Scully, 1971). If all black players were paid in a way that reflected their achievements, and if blacks were more likely to play the more lucrative positions, then it is likely that they would earn more than white players in general. Also, the off-field earnings of black players from commercials, endorsements, and off-season jobs often do not equal those of white players.

After their sports careers end, blacks are less likely than whites to obtain well-paying sportscasting jobs. Coaching jobs are disproportion-

Table 23.1 Most Highly Paid Baseball Players by Position and Race, 1982

Name	Team	Race	Position	Annual Earnings (in millions)
Gary Carter	Montreal	W	Catcher	$2.0
George Foster	New York Mets	B	Left field	2.0
Mike Schmidt	Philadelphia	W	Third base	1.8
Dave Winfield	New York Yankees	B	Left field	1.5
Fred Lynn	California	W	Center field	1.3
Jack Clark	San Francisco	W	Right field	1.1
George Brett	Kansas City	W	Third base	1.0
Andre Dawson	Montreal	B	Center field	1.0
Nolan Ryan	Houston	W	Pitcher	1.0
Dave Parker	Pittsburgh	B	Right field	1.0
Phil Niekro	Atlanta	W	Pitcher	1.0
Ken Griffey	New York Yankees	B	Right field	1.0
Eddie Murray	Baltimore	B	First base	1.0
Baseball Players with Contracts Valued at Slightly Less Than $1 Million Annually in 1982				
Rod Carew	California	B	First base	
Reggie Jackson	California	B	Right field	
Pete Rose	Philadelphia	W	First base	
Ron Guidry	New York Yankees	W	Pitcher	
J. R. Richard	Houston	B	Pitcher	
Dennis Leonard	Kansas City	W	Pitcher	

SOURCE: Klein, 1982, p. 1.

ately held by white rather than black former athletes. Part of the reason for few black coaches at all levels may rest on the positions they held while players. In baseball between 1968 and 1971, 68 percent of all managers were former infielders (Eitzen and Yetman, 1979). Because blacks have traditionally lacked the leadership experience of these positions, they may have been hindered in their chances of becoming coaches right from the start.

The blacks who do play professional sports seem to have higher performance records than whites, at least in baseball and football (Pascal and Rapping, 1970). In baseball, black batting averages are 20 points higher than those of whites (Eitzen and Yetman, 1979; Rosenblatt, 1967). Blacks are more likely than whites to be on the starting teams in football and basketball, although basketball players on all teams are increasingly black. This evidence suggests that to play professional sports, blacks need to be good enough to make the starting team, while there are many more jobs for whites as average players who may spend part of their time "sitting on the bench."

This evidence suggests that sport is not color-blind, that discrimination against black athletes exists with respect to their assignment to positions and to the rewards they receive. If racial discrimination exists in sports, where clearly measurable performance is presumably the only criterion for advancement and reward, then no arena of American life can be assumed to be free of discrimination, suggest Eitzen and Yetman (1979). Sport, then, becomes a crucial test of whether a society treats all members fairly.

GENDER AND SPORT

Women, like blacks, have been stereotyped in sport. Women have been barred by law or social custom at least since the Olympic Games began in 776 B.C. in ancient Greece. For some time, a series of myths about the physical nature of women suggested that women would endanger their childbearing capacity if they played sports. More recently, biological research shows that those myths are just that, and are quite unfounded in fact. Another restraint on the participation of women in sport has been the social definitions of masculinity and femininity that prevailed in American society, and in industrial societies generally. Women were supposed to be passive rather than active. Certain forms of activity were considered appropriate for females: figure skating, dance, diving, horseback riding, skiing, golf, archery, bowling, badminton, and volleyball. Some of these activities, such as riding and skiing, are restricted to women of sufficient economic resources. In others, the degree of face-to-face competition is limited, as is the size of the physical object that needs to be moved by the application of force (Metheny, 1965).

Until recently, both the extent and the type of sports participation available to women have been limited by legal or social sanctions. It was always acceptable, however, for women to be active supporters and spectators of vigorous male sports activities—for example, by being cheerleaders. The struggle to redefine and reassign power in sport reflects an underlying struggle to redefine gender rules and relationships in all areas of society (Heide, 1978). At the high school and college level, if sport develops the self-confidence, teamwork, perseverance, strength, and physical health that its supporters claim, why should girls and women be denied these positive outcomes? Leadership at the national level, combined with pressure from the women's movement, has led to a shift in the view of sport as training for masculinity to sport as training for achievement by either sex.

The push for sexual equality in sport received major support from the passage of the so-called Title IX legislation of 1972, which reads: "No person in the United States shall, on the basis of sex, be excluded from participation in, be denied the benefits of, or be subjected to discrimination under any education program or activity receiving Federal financial assistance." Title IX seems to have influenced the participation of women in sport. In 1970–71 (before Title IX) high school girls were 7 percent of all high school athletes; by 1976–77, they were 28 percent (Grett, 1978). Moreover, in 1974, 60 colleges offered athletic scholarships to women; by 1978, 500 colleges offered them (Pogge, 1978).

SOCIAL CLASS AND SPORT

Ever since Veblen declared that sport and leisure are used by their participants to proclaim economic and cultural distinctiveness (1899), the possible link between social class and sport has been suggested. Generally, sociologists have analyzed two types of issues: First, how is social class related to the sports that people play? Second, does sports participation affect an individual's chances for social mobility?

The sports played by individuals are clearly related to social class background. The higher classes are much more likely to participate in sailing, riding, skiing, golf, racquet games, swimming, crew, and fencing. Members of the lower social classes are much more likely to be involved in boxing, wrestling, football, and baseball (Loy, 1969). Class differences are fairly easily explained in terms of what sports are taught in schools, the availability of public recreational facilities, and the need for expensive equipment and professional instructors.

Leaving aside for the moment the class-linked nature of participation in many sports, let us examine whether participation in the relatively open sports of boxing, basketball, football, and baseball increases an individual's chances of upward social mobility. The rags to riches tales of some players, such as Babe Ruth, O. J. Simpson, Muhammad Ali, and Fernando Valenzuela, suggest this possibility. Moreover, the highly publicized second careers of sports heroes as movie stars (Jimmy Brown), sports commentators (Frank Gifford), or politicians (Bill Bradley and Jack Kemp) support the view of sports as a social aid. Most of these stories overlook three things. The rags to riches stories describe players at the peaks of their careers. They do not always show them in their retirement or describe how far their sport celebrity carries them in later life. They do not indicate how many hopefuls there are for every successful star. Finally, most of the success stories fail to spell out how these people used their sports fame to achieve success.

Four ways that participation in sport might help upward social mobility are suggested by Loy (1969). We will mention each of them and then consider the relevant evidence. First, sports skills may help a player to enter professional sports. But what are the odds of this happening? For every 200,000 high school seniors who play basketball, there are only 5,700 college seniors who play. Of those, 211 are drafted by the pros, and only 55 are actually signed (Durso, 1975). This means that most young players will be disappointed. These odds are seldom perceived by lower-class or minority youngsters and their parents. For these reasons, black leaders like Roscoe C. Brown, president of Bronx Community College, and the tennis player Arthur Ashe urge young people to spend two hours in the library for every one hour they spend on the athletic field.

Second, Loy suggests that sports may enhance an individual's educational aspirations and attainment. When compared to nonathletes, high school athletes are likely to get slightly better grades (especially if they have blue collar parents), are less likely to become delinquents, and are more likely to be upwardly mobile (Phillips and Schafer, 1971). Athletics may raise the aspirations for kids who would not otherwise go to college (Snyder and Spreitzer, 1978). This assertion is confirmed by a study of former Notre Dame college football players. Members of the team were more likely to be from lower-status backgrounds than the regular college students (Sack and Thiel, 1979). The relatively small numbers of athletic scholarships compared to the number of hopefuls means that not everyone

Sociologists are interested in understanding all types of human behavior, from leisure and sport to family formation, childrearing, and power and inequality.

will get one, but the existence of such scholarships may raise the educational aspirations of some students and actually help a few to go to college who might not otherwise have gone.

Third, success in college or professional sports may result in a former athlete being sought after and sponsored for a position in business. One's fame as a starring college or professional ballplayer is traded for a high-paying job in business. But although fame may open doors, education and socioeconomic background is related to subsequent advancement on the job (Haerle, 1975), suggesting that the convertibility of sports fame for lower-class or minority players might be somewhat limited. A study of Notre Dame football players found that 41 percent of former first-team football players were making $50,000 or more annually 14 to 34 years after graduation from college, compared to 30 percent of second-team players, 24 percent of nonteam members, and 13 percent of reserve players (Sack and Thiel, 1979). This finding is consistent with the sponsorship view of sport and mobility.

The fourth way sports may help individuals achieve social mobility is by teaching attitudes and behaviors that have value off the field. This interpretation is also consistent with the Notre Dame study, which suggests that the interpersonal skills and character traits that produce successful athletes may be precisely the same ones that make successful entrepreneurs. "Athletes who rise to the top in the often brutal competition of big time college football may be best suited for careers in business" (Sack and Thiel, 1979, p. 65). This suggests that individuals who perform well under stress and who are strivers and achievers in sport may perform the same way in business situations. Sack and Thiel did not measure the personality characteristics of team members compared to regular graduates, so this interpretation cannot be tested definitively with the available data.

One somewhat disturbing finding they do report is the fact that football players are more likely to report that they cheated on their schoolwork while in college than are regular students—69 percent of ballplayers reported cheating, compared to 43 percent of regular students (Sack and Thiel, 1979). The possibility also exists that players learn attitudes and behaviors that are not particularly helpful for social mobility. Total devotion to their sport may not help them if they are cut from the team or if they must face the prospect of an early retirement. (All athletes face early retirement; the only question is how early.) Players devoted to sports may face a major identity crisis when they are cut. As Wayne Embry, the former general manager of the Milwaukee Bucks basketball team noted, "I see that every year—the guys who have gone to school and never thought of having a vocation to fall back on. You tell them they have been cut and they can't believe you" (quoted in Snyder and Spreitzer, 1978, p. 84). This may be a problem for members of all social classes, as Page notes former Ivy League athletes who never go beyond their days of glory as gridiron heroes (1969).

Summary

1. Leisure and sport illustrate a number of sociological and societal features. They may extend or complement the values and skills people use in their daily occupations.

2. Successful leisure is characterized by flow. A flow experience is freely chosen; it totally involves the self; it is self-rewarding; and it contains an uncertainty of outcomes that allows for creativity. Flow experiences are inhibited by self-consciousness and overrationalization.

3. Leisure time has increased dramatically for Americans over the last 20 years, and now exceeds the amount of time people spend working or with their families. Leisure expenditures have increased fivefold in the last two decades. Watching television is the leisure activity people mention most frequently. Despite the much-publicized "fitness craze," Americans do not appear to be spending a great deal of time on strenuous physical activity.

4. Functionalist views of leisure stress the consequences of leisure activities for family or societal cohesiveness.

5. Conflict theorists suggest that leisure activities and resources may be used by groups in cultural competition with one another.

6. Sport is a form of game in which the outcome is affected by physical skill and prowess. Sport in America has been influenced by English royalty, which loved games, and by the Puritans, who frowned on idle pleasures.

7. Early sport in the United States represented individual competitions in some skill that was useful for dealing with the environment.

8. Urbanization, immigration, and industrialization swelled the populations in a given city or region who could cheer a sports team. Demographic and technological changes encouraged the growth of big-time sports beginning in the early twentieth century and continuing to the present.

9. Some societies favor less competitive or less violent sport than does the United States. Two competing theories have been offered to explain why violent sport thrives in some societies but not in others, the culture pattern theory and the tension release theory. Sipes's analysis supports the former interpretation, but the existence of violent sport in a violent society does not prove that one causes the other.

10. Violence among spectators has also increased in recent years, and several sociological explanations have been offered to explain its incidence, including greater societal permissiveness, growing contempt for social institutions, and a widening gap between fans and highly paid athletes.

11. People's views of sport tend to mirror their views of American society in general. Some see sport as positive and functional for the maintenance, integration, goal attainment, and adaptation of society. Others argue that sport distracts people from examining the social roots of their problems. Sport also tends to justify the use of violence as an acceptable means of attaining certain ends and to legitimate the existence of large-scale inequalities of wealth and power. Functionalist and Marxian analyses of sport both direct our attention to interesting questions about sport.

12. Symbolic interactionists add a new dimension to the understanding of sport, specifically the insight that events and rules in sport, as in all forms of social life, are socially created by the various participants in the situation. Some participants in that process may control greater power and resources than others, however.

13. Racial inequalities occur within sport with respect to the sports played by blacks and whites, the stacking of blacks into particular positions in baseball and football, and the relative rewards blacks and whites receive in sports.

14. Like blacks, women have been excluded and stereotyped in sports. In recent years Title IX has provided some impetus for more opportunities for women athletes.

15. The sports individuals play are related to class backgrounds. Sport has been touted as an avenue of upward mobility for talented members of the lower classes. Rags to riches tales of superstars neglect to mention the thousands of hopefuls who do not achieve stardom; they do not follow the stars beyond their short-lived careers; and they fail to indicate how sport may help social mobility. Four ways that sport may aid mobility include using one's skills to become a professional player; the possibility that sports success might increase educational aspirations and attainment through athletic scholarships; the sponsorship of a former athlete in business; and the learning of attitudes and behaviors through sport that are useful in later life.

Key Terms

athletics
culture pattern theory
flow
game
play
riot
rowdyism
sport
tension release theory

Glossary

Absolute poverty The condition of having too little income to buy the neccessities—food, shelter, clothing, health care.

Achieved status A social position (status) obtained through an individual's own talents and efforts.

Aggregate A collection of unrelated people who do not know one another but who may occupy a common space—for example, a crowd of people crossing a city street.

Agrarian societies Societies in which large-scale cultivation, using plows and draft animals, is the primary means of subsistence.

Alienation The process whereby something that people have created escapes their control and takes on a form that is hostile and oppressive to them. Leads to a sense of helplessness, powerlessness, and meaninglessness in the people who experience it.

Amalgamation The biological as well as cultural assimilation (merging) of racial or ethnic groups.

Anomalies In science, an observation or problem that cannot be explained or solved in terms of a prevailing paradigm.

Anomie A breakdown or confusion in the norms, values, and culture of a group or a society. A condition of relative normlessness.

Anomie theory The theory which suggests that deviance and crime occur when there is an acute gap between cultural norms and goals and the socially structured opportunities for individuals to achieve those goals.

Anticipatory socialization The process of taking on the attitudes, values, and behaviors of a status or role one expects to occupy in the future.

Ascribed status A social position (status), such as sex, race, and social class, that a person acquires at birth.

Assimilation The merging of minority and majority groups into one group with a common culture and identity.

Athletics A form of sport that is closer to work than to play.

Attributes The categories of a variable; in the United States, the variable political party includes the attributes Democratic and Republican.

Authority Power regarded as legitimate.

Autocracy Rule or government concentrated in a single ruler or group of leaders who are willing to use force to maintain control.

Behavior modification A deliberate effort to change behavior by praising or otherwise rewarding desired behavior and ignoring or otherwise failing to reward undesirable behavior.

Behaviorism An approach in psychology, based on the study of observable behavior, which rejects the scientific validity of concepts referring to mental states, such as "value" or "attitude."

Bias The influence of a scientist's personal values and attitudes on scientific observation and conclusions.

Bicultural The capacity to understand and function well in more than one cultural group.

Bilateral A society in which descent and inheritance are counted through both mother's and father's families.

Birth rate Number of births per year per 1000 women 15 to 44 years old.

Bureaucracy A large-scale, formal organization with centralized authority, a hierarchical chain of command, explicit rules and procedures, and an emphasis on formal positions rather than persons.

Capitalism A form of economic organization in which private individuals accumulate and invest capital, and own the means of production and control profits.

Cargo cult A millennarian movement in the South Pacific based on the expectation that cargo ships filled with food and other goods were being sent by ancestors to show support for the living.

Caste system A closed system of social stratification in which prestige and social relationships are based on hereditary position at birth.

Centrally planned economy An economic system that includes public ownership of or control over all productive resources and whose activity is planned by the government.

Charisma The exceptional mystical or even supernatural quality of personality attributed to a person by others. Literally, "the gift of grace."

Charismatic leader Individual who enlists the strong emotional support of followers through personal and seemingly supernatural qualities.

Church A formally organized, institutionalized religious organization with formal and traditional religious doctrine, beliefs, and practices.

City A relatively permanent settlement of large numbers of people who do not grow or gather their own food.

Civil law The branch of law that deals largely with wrongs against the individual.

Civil religion The interweaving of religious and political symbols in public life.

Class Position in a social hierarchy based on prestige and/or property ownership.

Class conflict The struggle between competing classes, specifically between the class that owns the means of production and the class or classes that do not.

Class consciousness The sense of common class position and shared interests held by members of a social class.

Class system A system of stratification based primarily on the unequal ownership and control of economic resources.

Coercion A form of social interaction in which one is made to do something through the use of social pressure, threats, or force.

Cognitive development The systematic improvement of intellectual ability through a series of stages.

Commitment Willingness of members of a group to do what is needed to maintain the group.

Community A settled group of people with a shared identity and interdependent relationships.

Competition A goal-directed form of social interaction in which the goals or objects pursued are limited, so not all competitors can attain them. Competitive behavior is governed by rules and limitations (restraints).

Concentric-zone theory A theory of urban development which holds that cities grow around a central business district in concentric zones, with each zone devoted to a different land use.

Concept A word or set of words that aim to describe a phenomenon or process in the world.

Concrete operations stage The stage of cognitive development, identified by Piaget, at which children learn rules and relationships about the physical world; occurs from ages 7 to 12.

Conditioning The effort to shape behavior by rewarding (reinforcing) desired actions; actions not reinforced tend to disappear.

Conflict A form of social interaction involving direct struggle between individuals or groups over commonly valued resources or goals. Differs from competition because individuals are more interested in defeating an opponent than in achieving a goal.

Conflict perspective One of the major theoretical perspectives in sociology: emphasizes the importance of unequal power and conflict in society. *Weberian conflict theorists* stress inequality and conflict based on class, status, and power; *Marxian theorists* emphasize conflict and inequality based on ownership of the means of production.

Conjugal family A form of family organization centered around the husband-wife relationship rather than around blood relationships.

Conformity Going along with the norms or behaviors of a group.

Content analysis A research method used to describe and analyze in an objective and systematic way the content of literature, speeches, or other media presentations. The method helps to identify cultural themes or trends.

Contest mobility The educational pattern in which selection for academic and university education is delayed, and children compete throughout their schooling for high position.

Control group A group which is not exposed to the independent variable of interest to a researcher, but whose members' background and experience are otherwise like those of the experimental group which is exposed to the independent variable.

Controlling for In research, the effort to hold constant factors that might be influencing observed changes in the dependent variable.

Convergence theory A theory which suggests that modernizing nations come to resemble one another over time.

Cooperation A form of social interaction involving collaborative effort among people to achieve a common goal.

Cooptation A social process by which people who might otherwise threaten the stability or existence of an organization are brought into the leadership or policy-making structure of that organization.

Correlation An observed association between a change in the value of one variable and a change in the value of another variable.

Counterculture A subculture whose norms and values sharply contradict the dominant norms and values of the society in which it occurs.

Crime A behavior prohibited by law.

Criminal law Law enacted by recognized political authorities that prohibits or requires certain behaviors.

Criteria for inferring causality Evidence that two variables are correlated, that the hypothesized cause preceded the hypothesized effect in time, and evidence eliminating rival hypotheses.

Crude birth rate The total number of live births per 1000 persons in a population within a particular year.

Crude death rate The number of deaths per 1000 persons occurring within a one-year period in a particular population.

Cult A loosely organized group of people who together act out religious feelings, attitudes, and relationships; may focus on an unusual form of worship or belief.

Cultural change Modifications or transformations of a culture's customs, values, ideas, or artifacts.

Cultural determinism The view that the nature of a society is shaped primarily by the ideas and values of the people living in it.

Cultural relativism The view that the customs and ideas of a society must be viewed within the context of that society.

Cultural universals Cultural features, such as the use of language, shared by all human societies.

Culture The common heritage shared by the people of a society, consisting of customs, values, ideas, and artifacts.

Culture lag The time difference between the introduction of material innovations and resulting changes in cultural practices.

Culture pattern theory In the sociology of sport, a theory that explains aggression and violence in sport as learned behavior which mirrors the degree of aggression and violence in the society.

Culture of poverty A distinctive culture, thought to develop among poor people, and characterized by failure to delay gratification, fatalism, and weak family and community ties.

Cyclical theories Theories of social change which suggest that societies follow a certain life course, from vigorous and innovative youth to more materialistic maturity, and then to decline.

Democracy A form of political organization in which power resides with the people and is exercised by them.

Democratic-collective organization An organization in which authority is placed in the group as a whole, rules are minimized, members have considerable control over their work, and job differentiation is minimized.

Demographic transition The demographic change experienced in Western Europe and North America since the Industrial Revolution in which the birth rate has declined so that it is about equal to the death rate.

Demography The scientific study of population size, composition, and distribution, and patterns of change in those features.

Denomination One of a number of religious organizations in a society with no official state church. Has some formal doctrines, beliefs, and practices, but tolerates diverse religious views.

Dependency theory A theory about the place of developing nations in the world economy which suggests that major industrial nations take advantage of the cheap labor and raw materials of developing nations and hence are reluctant to see them become industrialized.

Dependent variable The variable that occurs or changes in a patterned way due to the presence of, or changes in, another variable or variables.

Descriptive study A research study whose goal is to describe the social phenomena being studied.

Deviance Behaviors or characteristics that violate important social norms.

Deviant career The regular pursuit of activities regarded by the individual and by others as deviant.

Differential association A theory that attributes the existence of deviant behavior to learning from friends or associates.

Differentiation, functional The division of labor or of social roles within a society or an organization.

Differentiation, rank The unequal evaluation of various social positions.

Diffusion The spread of inventions and discoveries from one group or culture to another on a voluntary basis; a source of cultural change.

Discovery The uncovering of something that existed but was unknown; a source of cultural change.

Discrimination The unequal and unfair treatment of individuals or groups on the basis of some irrelevant characteristic, such as race, ethnicity, religion, sex, or social class.

Division of labor The specialization of economic activities, and the tendency for people to become more specialized in what they do.

Dominant status One social position that overshadows the other social positions an individual occupies.

Double standard A set of social norms that allows males greater freedom of sexual expression, particularly before marriage, than females.

Dramaturgical analysis An approach to social situations developed by Erving Goffman in which they are examined as though they were a theatrical production.

Dual-career family A family form in which both husband and wife have careers.

Dual economy The division of the private sector of the economy into monopoly (core) and competitive (periphery) sectors.

Dyad A group composed of two people.

Dysfunction Any consequence of a social system that disturbs or hinders the integration, adjustment, or stability of the system.

Ecological view An approach to the study of culture or other social phenomena that emphasizes the importance of examining climate, food and water supplies, and existing enemies in the environment.

Ecology The scientific study of how organisms relate to one another and to their environments.

Economic core The sector of the economy characterized by large, generally very profitable, oligopolistic firms that are national or multinational in scope of operation; also called the monopoly sector.

Economic growth An increase in the amount of goods and services produced with the same amount of labor and resources.

Economic institution The pattern of roles, norms, and activities organized around the production, distribution, and consumption of goods and services in a society.

Economic periphery The sector of the economy characterized by small, local, barely profitable firms; also called the competitive sector.

Ecosystem A system formed by the interaction of a community of organisms with their environment.

Education The process, in school or beyond, of transmitting a society's knowledge, skills, values, and behaviors.

Egalitarian family A family in which husband and wife share equally in family decision-making.

Ego In Freudian theory, a concept referring to the conscious, rational part of the personality structure, which mediates between the impulses of the id and the rules of society.

Elderly dependency ratio The ratio between the number of the elderly (65 and over) and the number of working-age people (ages 18 to 64).

Equilibrium In functionalist theory, the view that the parts of a society fit together into a balanced whole.

Ethnic group A group that shares a common cultural tradition and sense of identity.

Ethnocentrism The tendency to see one's own culture as superior to all others.

Ethnography A detailed study based on actual observation of the way of life of a human group or society.

Ethnomethodology The study of the methods used by individuals to communicate and make sense of their everyday lives as members of society. Many ethnomethodologists focus on the study of language and everyday conversation.

Evangelicalism A form of Protestantism that stresses the preaching of the gospel of Jesus Christ, the validity of personal conversion, the Bible as the basis for belief, and active preaching of the faith.

Evolutionary theory In sociology, the theory that societies tend gradually to become more complex because of innovation or diffusion. In biology, the theory that living organisms develop new traits that may aid their adaptation or survival, and the development of these traits is encouraged.

Exchange A form of social interaction involving trade of tangibles (objects) or intangibles (sentiments) between individuals.

Exchange theory An interpretive perspective that explains social interaction on the basis of the exchange of various tangible or intangible social rewards.

Experimental group In research, a group of individuals exposed to the independent variable being introduced by the experimentor.

Explanatory study A research study with the goal of explaining how or why things happen the way they do in the social world.

Expressive leader A group leader whose role in the group is to help maintain stability through joking, mediating conflicts, and otherwise reducing tension.

Extended family A family in which relatives from several generations live together.

Face-work A term used by Goffman to refer to the actions taken by individuals to make their behavior appear consistent with the image they want to present.

Family Two or more persons who are related by blood, marriage, or adoption and who live together. They usually form an economic unit, and adult members care for the dependent children.

Flow An experience of total involvement in one's present activity.

Folkways Social norms to which people generally conform, although they receive little pressure to do so.

Formal operations stage The stage of cognitive development, identified by Piaget, at which young people can isolate the elements of a problem and systematically consider a variety of solutions; occurs around age 12.

Formal organization A social group deliberately formed to pursue certain goals.

Formal sanction A social reward or punishment that is administered in an organized, systematic way, such as receiving a diploma or getting a fine.

Functions The consequences of social phenomena for other parts of society or for society as a whole.

Functional differentiation. See *Differentiation, functional.*

Functional equivalent A feature or process in society that has the same function (consequence) as some other feature or process.

Functional perspective A theoretical approach that analyses social phenomena in terms of their functions in a social system.

Functional prerequisites The needs a society must meet in order to survive, including subsistence, distribution, biological reproduction, cultural transmission, safety, and communication.

Fundamentalism A form of religious traditionalism characterized by the literal interpretation of religious texts, a conception of an active supernatural, and clear distinctions between sin and salvation.

Game A form of play involving competitive or cooperative interaction in which the outcome is determined by physical skill, strength, strategy, or chance.

Gemeinschaft A term used by Tönnies to describe a small, traditional, community-centered society in which people have close, personal, face-to-face relationships and value social relationships as ends in themselves.

Gender The traits and behaviors socially designated as "masculine" or "feminine" in a particular society.

Gender differences Variations in the social positions, roles, behaviors, attitudes, and personalities of men and women in a society.

Gender roles The socially expected behaviors associated with being a man or a woman in a particular society.

Generalized other A general idea of the expectations, attitudes, and values of a group or community.

Genocide The destruction of an entire population.

Gentrification The resettlement of upper-middle class people in working-class or manufacturing areas of a city.

Geographic race Any of a number of large human groupings that correspond to major geographic regions such as continents.

Gesellschaft A term used by Tönnies to describe urban industrial society, in which people have impersonal, formal, contractual, and specialized relationships and tend to use social relationships as a means to an end.

Ghost Dance cult A form of millennarian movement among native Americans in the 1890s based on the prophecy that their dead relatives would return, push the whites off tribal lands, and restore traditional ways of life.

Global economy An economy in which the economic life and health of one nation depends on what happens in other nations.

Green revolution The improvement in agricultural production based on higher-yielding grains, and increased use of fertilizers, pesticides, and irrigation.

Group A collection of people who know one another and interact on the basis of common expectations.

Groupthink The tendency of individuals to follow the ideas or actions of a group.

Growth rate In demography, the difference between birth and death rates, excluding immigration.

Heterosexual A person whose preferred partner for erotic, emotional, and sexual interaction is someone of the opposite sex.

Homosexual Someone who is emotionally, erotically, and physically attracted to persons of his or her own sex.

Horizontal mobility Movement from one social status to another of about equal rank in the social hierarchy.

Horticultural societies Societies in which the cultivation of plants with hoes is the primary means of subsistence.

Hunting and gathering societies Societies that obtain food by hunting animals, fishing, and gathering fruits, nuts, and grains. These societies do not plant crops or have domesticated animals.

Hybrid economy An economic system that blends features of both centrally planned and capitalist (market) economies.

Hypothesis A tentative statement asserting a relationship between one factor and something else (based on theory, prior research, or general observation).

Id In Freudian theory, a concept referring to the unconscious instinctual impulses—for instance, sexual or aggressive impulses.

Ideal values Values that people say are important to them, whether or not their behavior supports them.

Ideology A system of ideas that reflects, rationalizes, and defends the interests of those who believe in it.

Impression management A term used by Goffman to describe the efforts of individuals to influence how others perceive them.

Incest Sexual intercourse with close family members; widely forbidden by strong social norms.

Incest taboo The prohibition of sexual intercourse between fathers and daughters, mothers and sons, and brothers and sisters.

Income The sum of money wages and salaries (earnings) plus income other than earnings.

Independent variable The variable whose occurrence or change results in the occurrence or change of another variable; the hypothesized cause of something else.

Industrialized societies Societies that rely on mechanized production, rather than human or animal labor, as the primary means of subsistence.

Inflation An increase in the supply of money in circulation that exceeds the rate of economic growth, making money worth less in relation to the goods and services it can buy.

Informal sanction A social reward or punishment that is given informally through social interaction, such as an approving smile or a disapproving frown.

Innovation The discovery or invention of new ideas, things, or methods; a source of cultural change.

Instinct A genetically determined behavior triggered by specific conditions or events.

Institutions The patterned and enduring roles, statuses, and norms that have formed around successful strategies for meeting basic social needs.

Institutionalized Social practices that have become established, patterned, and predictable, and that are supported by custom, tradition, and/or law.

Instrumental leader A group leader whose role is to keep the group's attention directed to the task at hand.

Intelligence quotient test (IQ) A standardized set of questions or problems designed to measure verbal and numerical knowledge and reasoning.

Interactionist perspective A theoretical approach to studying the social world that focuses on how individuals interact and create social definitions of events.

Interest group A group that works to influence political decisions that affect its members.

Intergenerational mobility A vertical change of social status from one generation to the next.

Interlocking directorates The practice of overlapping memberships on corporate boards of directors.

Intermittent reinforcement In learning theory, the provision of a reward sometimes but not always when a desired behavior is shown.

Internalization The process of taking social norms, roles, and values into one's own mind.

Interpretive perspective One of the major theoretical perspectives in sociology: focuses on how individuals make sense of the world and react to the symbolic meanings attached to social life.

Intragenerational mobility A vertical change of social status experienced by an individual within his or her own lifetime.

Invention An innovation in material or nonmaterial culture, often produced by combining existing cultural elements in new ways; a source of cultural change.

Keynesian economics The economic theory, advanced by John Maynard Keynes, which holds that government intervention, through deficit spending, may be necessary to maintain high levels of employment.

Kinship Socially defined family relationships, including those based on common parentage, marriage, or adoption.

Labeling theory A theory of deviance that focuses on the process by which some people are labeled deviant by other people (and thus take on deviant identities), rather than on the nature of the behavior itself.

Laissez-faire economics An economic theory, advanced by Adam Smith, which holds that the economic system develops and functions best when left to market forces, without government intervention.

Language Spoken or written symbols combined into a system and governed by rules.

Latent function The unintended and/or unrecognized function or consequence of some thing or process in a social system.

Law The system of formalized rules established by political authorities and backed by the power of the state for the purpose of controlling or regulating social behavior.

Learning theory In psychology, the theory that specific human behaviors are acquired or forgotten as a result of the rewards or punishments associated with them.

Legitimate In reference to power, the sense by people in a situation that those who are exercising power have the right to do so.

Lesbian A woman who is emotionally, erotically, and physically attracted to other women.

Life chances The probabilities of an individual having access to or failing to have access to various opportunities in society.

Life course The biological and social sequence of birth, growing up, maturity, aging, and death.

Life expectancy index The average age at death for a group of people born in a particular year.

Life-style Family, childrearing, and educational attitudes and practices; personal values; type of residence; consumer, political, and civic behavior; religion.

Life table A statistical table that presents the death rate and life expectancy of each of a series of age-sex categories for a particular population.

Line job A job that is part of the central operations of an organization, rather than one that provides support services for the operating structure.

Lobbying The process of trying to influence political decisions so they will be favorable to one's interests and goals.

Looking-glass self The sense of one's self an individual gets from the way others view and treat him or her.

Macro level An analysis of societies that focuses on large-scale institutions, structures, and processes.

Magic According to Malinowski, "a practical art consisting of acts which are only means to a definite end expected to follow."

Manifest function The intended function or consequence of some thing or process in a social system.

Marriage A social institution that recognizes and approves the sexual union of two or more individuals and includes a set of mutual rights and obligations.

Marriage rate Number of marriages in a year per 1000 single women 15 to 44 years old.

Marxian conflict theory Conflict theory that uses the ideas of Karl Marx and stresses the importance of class struggle centered around the social relations of economic production.

Mass media Widely disseminated forms of communication, such as books, magazines, radio, television, and movies.

Matrilineal descent system Descent and inheritance traced solely through the mother and her family.

Matrilocal residence pattern A married couple living with the wife's family or in the wife's community.

Matthew effect The social process whereby one advantage an individual has is likely to lead to additional advantages.

Mean, arithmetic The sum of a set of mathematical values divided by the number of values; a measure of central tendency in a series of data.

Median The number that cuts a distribution of figures in half; a positional measure of central tendency in a series of data.

Method of comparison An approach that compares one subgroup or society with another one for the purpose of understanding social differences.

Methodology The rules, principles, and practices that guide the collection of evidence and the conclusions drawn from it.

Metropolitan area A central city and the suburbs surrounding it.

Micro level An analysis of societies that focuses on small-scale processes, such as how individuals interact and how they attach meanings to the social actions of others.

Migration The relatively permanent movement of people from one area to another.

Millennarian movements Social movements based on the expectation that society will be suddenly transformed through supernatural intervention.

Minority group Any recognizable racial, religious, ethnic, or social group that suffers from some disadvantage resulting from the action of a dominant group with higher social status and greater privileges.

Mode The value that occurs most often in a series of mathematical values.

Modernization The economic and social transformation that occurs when a traditional agricultural society becomes highly industrialized.

Monogamy A family form in which both men and women have a single spouse.

Monopoly The exclusive control of a particular industry, market, service, or commodity by a single organization.

Mores Strongly held social norms, a violation of which causes a sense of moral outrage.

Mortality rate The rate of deaths in a population.

Multinational corporation A corporation that locates its operations in a number of nations.

Multiple-nuclei theory A theory of urban development which holds that cities develop around a number of different centers, each with its own special activities.

Nation A relatively autonomous political grouping that usually shares a common language and a particular geography.

Nation-state A social organization in which political authority overlaps a cultural and geographical community.

Negative sanctions Actions intended to deter or punish unwanted social behaviors.

Negotiation A form of social interaction in which two or more parties in conflict or competition arrive at a mutually satisfactory agreement.

Network See *Social network.*

Nomadic Societies that move their residences from place to place.

Nonverbal communication Visual and other meaningful symbols that do not use language.

Norm A shared rule about acceptable or unacceptable social behavior.

Normal science Used by Kuhn to describe research based on one or more past scientific achievements that are accepted as a useful foundation for further study.

Nuclear family A family form consisting of a married couple and their children.

Objectivity Procedures researchers follow to minimize distortions in observation or interpretation due to personal or social values.

Occupation A position in the world of work that involves specialized knowledge and activities.

Oligarchy The rule of the many by the few.

Oligopoly The control of a particular industry, market, service, or commodity by a few large organizations.

Open system In organizational theory, the degree to which an organization is open to and dependent on its environment.

Operationalization In research, the actual procedures or operations conducted to measure a variable.

Organization Social group deliberately formed to pursue certain values and goals.

Organizational ritualism A form of behavior in organizations, particularly in bureaucracies, in which people follow the rules and regulations so closely that they forget the purpose of those rules and regulations.

Paradigm In the sociology of science, a coherent tradition of scientific law, theory, and assumptions that forms a distinct approach to problems.

Parkinson's law Work expands to fill the available time.

Participant observation A research method in which the researcher does observation while taking part in the activities of the social group being studied.

Pastoral societies Societies in which the raising and herding of animals such as sheep, goats, and cows is the primary means of subsistence.

Patriarchal family A form of family organization in which the father is the formal head of the family.

Patrilineal descent system Descent and inheritance traced solely through the father and his family.

Patrilocal residence pattern A married couple living with the husband's family or in the husband's community.

Peer group Friends and associates of about the same age and social status.

Peter principle A phenomenon, observed by Lawrence Peter, that people in organizations tend to get promoted for competent performance until they ultimately reach their level of incompetence.

Play Spontaneous activity undertaken freely for its own enjoyment, yet governed by rules and often characterized by an element of make-believe.

Pluralism In ethnic relations, the condition that exists when both majority and minority groups value their distinct cultural identities while at the same time seeking economic and political unity. In political sociology, the view that society is composed of competing interest groups, with power diffused among them.

Political order The institutionalized system of acquiring and exercising power.

Political party An organized group of people that seeks to control or influence political decisions through legal means.

Polyandry A form of marriage in which one woman may be married to more than one man at the same time.

Polygyny A form of marriage in which a man may be married to more than one woman at the same time.

Population In demography, all the people living in a given geographic area. In research, the total number of cases with a particular characteristic.

Positive sanctions Rewards for socially desired behavior.

Post-industrial society A term used by Bell (1973) to refer to societies organized around knowledge and planning rather than industrial production.

Power The capacity of an individual or group to control or influence the behavior of others, even in the face of opposition.

Power elite According to Mills, a closely connected group of the corporate rich, political leaders, and military commanders who decide most key social and political issues.

Prejudice A "prejudged" unfavorable attitude toward the members of a particular group, who are assumed to possess negative traits.

Preoperational stage The stage of cognitive development, identified by Piaget, at which children begin to use language and to treat objects as symbols of other things; occurs from 1½ to 7 years of age.

Prestige The social recognition, respect, and deference accorded individuals or groups based on their social status.

Primary deviance Deviant behavior that is invisible to others, is short-lived, or is unimportant, and does not therefore contribute to being publicly labeled as deviant.

Primary economic sector The sector of an economy in which natural resources are gathered or extracted.

Primary group A social group characterized by frequent face-to-face interaction, by the commitment and emotional ties members feel for one another, and by relative permanence.

Principle of cumulative advantage See *Matthew effect.*

Profane In the sociology of religion, that which is not considered sacred or holy.

Profession An occupation that rests on a theoretical body of knowledge and thus requires specialized training usually recognized by the granting of a degree or credential.

Projection A psychological process of attributing one's own unacceptable feelings or desires to other people to avoid guilt and self-blame.

Property The rights and obligations a group or individual has in relation to an object, resource, or activity.

Prostitution The selling of sexual favors.

Race A classification of humans into groups based on distinguishable physical characteristics that may form the basis for significant social identities.

Racism The institutionalized domination of one racial group by another.

Random sample A sample of units drawn from a larger population in such a way that every unit has a known and equal chance of being selected.

Range The total spread of values in a set of figures.

Rank Place in a social hierarchy.

Rank differentiation See *Differentiation, rank.*

Real values The values people consider truly important, as evident in their behavior and how they spend their time and money.

Rebellion In anomie theory, a form of deviance that occurs when individuals reject culturally valued means and goals and substitute new means and goals. In political sociology, the expression of opposition to an established authority.

Reference group A social group whose standards and opinions are used by an individual to help define or evaluate beliefs, values, and behaviors.

Reform movement A type of social movement that accepts the status quo but seeks certain specific social reforms.

Regressive movement A type of social movement whose aim is to move the social world back to where members believe it to have been at an earlier time.

Relative poverty The condition of having much less income than the average person in society, even if one can afford the necessities of life.

Religion A set of shared beliefs and rituals common to a special community and focusing on the sacred and supernatural.

Research design The specific plan for conducting a research study, including sampling, measurement, and data analysis.

Resocialization The process of socializing people away from a group or activity in which they are involved.

Resource mobilization theory The theory that social movements are affected by their ability to marshal various key resources.

Retreatism In anomie theory, a form of deviance that occurs when individuals abandon culturally valued means and goals.

Revolt An uprising against the leadership of an organization which, unlike revolution, does not result in the overthrow of existing leadership.

Revolution A large-scale change in the political leadership of a society and the restructuring of major features of that society.

Revolutionary movement A type of social movement whose aim is to completely reorganize existing society.

Riot A destructive and sometimes violent collective outburst.

Rising expectations A situation in which people feel that past hardships should not have to be suffered in the future.

Ritual In the sociology of religion, the rules of conduct concerning behavior in the presence of the sacred. Intended to produce feelings of reverence, awe, and group identity.

Ritualism In anomie theory, a form of deviance in which individuals lose sight of socially valued goals but conform closely to socially prescribed means.

Rival hypothesis An explanation that competes with the original hypothesis in a study.

Role To functionalists, the culturally prescribed and socially patterned behaviors associated with particular social positions. For interactionists, the effort to mesh the demands of a social position with one's own identity.

Role accumulation Adding more statuses and roles to the ones an individual already has.

Role conflict A situation in which two or more social roles make incompatible demands on a person.

Role expectations Commonly shared norms

about how a person is supposed to behave in a particular role.

Role performance The behaviors of a person performing a certain social role.

Role set The cluster of roles that accompanies a particular status.

Role strain The feeling that the demands made by one's social positions are more than that person can handle; also called role overload.

Rowdyism Generalized interpersonal violence or property destruction occurring at spectator events.

Ruling class A small class that controls the means of economic production and dominates political decisions.

Sacred In the sociology of religion, anything that is perceived as divine or holy and engenders feelings of respect, reverence, and awe.

Sanction A social reward or punishment for approved or disapproved behavior; can be positive or negative, formal or informal.

Scapegoating Blaming a convenient but innocent person or group for one's trouble or guilt.

Schooling Formal education.

Science An approach used to obtain reliable knowledge about the physical and social worlds, based on systematic empirical observations; the knowledge so obtained.

Scientific revolution The dramatic overthrow of one intellectual paradigm by another.

Secondary deviance Behavior discovered by others and publicly labeled by them as deviant.

Secondary economic sector The sector of an economy in which raw materials are turned into manufactured goods.

Secondary group A social group bound together for the accomplishment of common tasks, with few emotional ties among members.

Sect An exclusive, highly cohesive group of ascetic religious believers. Sects usually last longer and are more institutionalized than cults.

Sector theory A theory of urban development which explains that cities develop in wedge-shaped patterns following transportation systems.

Secularism A perspective on the world that includes the values of rationality, cultural and religious pluralism, tolerance of moral ambiguity, faith in education, and belief in civil rights, the rule of law, and due process.

Self-fulfilling prophecy A belief or prediction about a person or situation that influences that person or situation in such a way that the belief or prediction comes true.

Sensorimotor stage The stage of cognitive development, identified by Piaget, when children begin to use their senses and muscles; occurs from birth to about 18 months of age.

Sex The biological distinction of being male or female.

Sex stratification The hierarchical ranking of men and women and their gender roles in terms of unequal ownership, power, social control, prestige, and social rewards.

Sibling A brother or sister.

Social change A modification or transformation in the way society is organized.

Social class A group's position in a social hierarchy based on prestige and/or property ownership.

Social construction of reality The process of socially creating definitions of situations and having them appear to be natural.

Social control The relatively patterned and systematic ways in which society guides and restrains individual behaviors so that people act in predictable and desired ways.

Social forces The social structures and culture individuals face in a society.

Social inequality The existence of unequal opportunities or rewards for people in different social positions.

Social interaction The ways people behave in

relation to one another by means of language, gestures, and symbols.

Social learning theory A form of learning theory which suggests that people learn through observation and imitation, even though they are not rewarded or punished for certain behaviors.

Social mobility The movement from one status to another within a stratified society.

Social movement A group of people who work together to guide or suppress particular changes in the way society is organized.

Social network A set of interdependent relations or links between individuals.

Social psychology The scientific study of how individual behavior is socially influenced.

Social relations of production The organization of economic life, based on owning or not owning the means of production, purchasing or selling labor power, and controlling or not controlling other people's labor power.

Social sciences Related disciplines that study human activity and communication.

Social stratification The fairly permanent ranking of positions in a society, in terms of unequal power, prestige, or privilege.

Social structure The patterned and interrelated statuses and roles in a particular society.

Socialist societies Societies in which productive resources are owned and controlled by the state rather than by individuals.

Socialization The process of preparing newcomers to become members of an existing social group.

Society A group of people with a shared and somewhat distinct culture, who live in a defined territory, feel some unity as a group, and see themselves as distinct from other peoples.

Sociobiology The scientific study of the biological basis for human behavior.

Socioeconomic status (SES) An index of social status that considers a person's occupation, education, and income as measures of social status.

Sociology The scientific study of human social behavior; includes the study of social contexts and social processes.

Sovereignty The authority claimed by a state to maintain a legal system, use coercive power to secure obedience, and maintain its independence from other states.

Sponsored mobility The pattern in which certain children are selected at an early age for academic and university education, and are thus helped to achieve higher social status.

Sport A form of game in which the outcome is affected by physical skill.

Staff job In an organization, an advisory or administrative job that supports the manufacturing, production, selling, or other primary activities of the organization.

Stage theory A theory which suggests that nations go through various systematic stages of development.

Standard consolidated statistical area (SCSA) The area formed by two or more standard metropolitan statistical areas that run together.

Standard metropolitan statistical area (SMSA) A county or group of counties including at least one city with a population of 50,000 or more. In the New England states, SMSAs consist of towns and cities instead of counties.

State The institutionalized, legal organization of power within territorial limits.

State sector The sector of the economy controlled by local, state, or federal governments that supplies goods and services under direct contract to the state.

Status A socially defined position in society, which carries with it certain prescribed rights, obligations, and expected behaviors.

Status group People who share a social identity based on similar values and life-styles.

Stigmatization The process of spoiling a person's identity by labeling him or her in a negative way.

Structural-functional perspective One of the major theoretical perspectives in sociology, developed by Talcott Parsons: focuses on how the various parts of society fit together or adjust to maintain the equilibrium of the whole.

Subculture A distinguishable group that shares a number of features with the dominant culture within which it exists, as well as having unique features, such as language, customs, or values.

Subjective meanings The values and interpretations individuals place on their life situations and experiences; may vary from person to person.

Subjective social class A person's own perception of his or her class position.

Suburb A fairly small community within an urban area that includes a central city.

Superego In Freudian theory, the part of the personality structure that upholds the norms of society.

Symbol Any object or sign that evokes a shared social response.

Symbolic interaction Interaction that relies on shared symbols such as language.

Symbolic interactionism An interpretive perspective, inspired by the work of George Herbert Mead, which says that individuals learn meanings through interaction with others and then organize their lives around these socially created meanings.

Taboo A strongly prohibited social practice; the strongest form of social norm.

Technological determinism The belief that technological development shapes social life in rather fixed ways.

Technology The practical applications of scientific knowledge.

Terrorism An attack on people designed to frighten society and force it to meet the terrorists' demands.

Tertiary economic sector The sector of an economy that offers services to individuals as well as to business.

Theory A system of orienting ideas, concepts, and their relationships that provides a way of organizing the observable world.

Theory X A view of organizational behavior which suggests that people hate their jobs, want to avoid responsibility, resist change, and do not care about organizational needs.

Theory Y A view of organizational behavior which suggests that people have the desire to work, to be creative, and to take responsibility for their jobs and for the organization.

Total fertility rate An estimate of the average number of children that would be born to each woman over her reproductive life if current age-specific birth rates remained constant.

Total institution A place where people spend 24 hours of every day for an extended part of their lives, cut off from the rest of society and tightly controlled by the people in charge.

Totalitarianism A form of autocracy that involves the use of state power to control and regulate all phases of life.

Tournament selection The educational pattern in which a continual process of selection serves to weed out candidates; winners move on to the next round of selection, and losers are eliminated from the competition.

Tracking The practice of grouping students by ability or curriculum or both.

Triad A group composed of three people.

Underemployment The hiring of people in jobs that are not customarily filled by individuals with their relatively high levels of experience or education.

Underground economy Exchanges of goods and services that people do not report to tax authorities.

Unit of analysis Who or what is being studied in a piece of social research.

Urbanization The growth of cities.

Value-oriented action A term used by Weber to refer to action that is valued for its own sake, regardless of its chance for success.

Values Strongly held general ideas that people

share about what is good and bad, desirable or undesirable; values provide yardsticks for judging specific acts and goals.

Variable A logical set of attributes with different degrees of magnitude, or different categories. For example, age is a variable on which people can be classified according to the number of years they have lived.

Vertical integration A form of business organization that attempts to control the business environment by assuming control of one or more of its resources or business outlets.

Vertical mobility Movement of an individual or a group, upward or downward, from one social status to another.

Weberian conflict theorists Conflict theorists who, using the ideas of Max Weber, stress the significance of conflict in social life, especially conflict among status groups such as those based on occupation, ethnic background, or religion.

White collar crime Crimes committed by "respectable" individuals, often while they practice their occupations—for example, embezzling money or stealing computer time.

White ethnics White Americans who value and preserve aspects of their ethnic heritage.

World systems analysis A form of sociological anaylsis that stresses understanding national behavior in terms of historical and contemporary relationships among nations and societies.

Zero population growth (ZPG) The situation that occurs when the population of a nation or the world remains stable from one year to the next.

References

ABC News–Harris Survey
1979 "Leisure time activities." New York: Chicago Tribune–New York News Syndicate, Inc. (January 1).

Abu-Lughod, J., and M. M. Foley
1960 "The consumer votes by moving." and "Consumer preferences: The city versus the suburb." Pp. 134–214 in N. N. Foote et al. (eds.), *Choices and Housing Constraints.* New York: McGraw-Hill.

Akers, Ronald L.
1964 "Socio-economic status and delinquent behavior: A retest." *Journal of Research in Crime and Delinquency* 1: 38–46.

Alan Guttmacher Institute
1981 *Teenage Pregnancy: The Problem That Hasn't Gone Away*. New York: Alan Guttmacher Institute.

Alsop, Ronald
1980 "Minority report: Middle-class blacks worry about slipping, still face racial bias: despite gains, many homes need 2 jobs to prosper; work is often insecure." *Wall Street Journal* (November 3): 1, 28.

Alston, Jon P.
1973 "Aggregate social mobility among major Protestant denominations and major religious groups, 1939–1969." *Sociological Analysis* 34 (fall): 230–235.

Altman, Lawrence K.
1983 "Research traces AIDS in 6 of 7 female partners." *New York Times,* May 19: B4.

American Demographics
1981 "Demographic forecasts: Labor force." 3: 46–47.

American Indian Fund
1981 "How about 'human rights' for this American, too?" Letter to potential contributors. New York: Association on American Indian Affairs, Inc.

Anderson, Barry D.
1973 "School bureaucratization and alienation from high school." *Sociology of Education* 46: 315–334.

Anderson, Charles H.
1974 *Political Economy of Social Class.* Englewood Cliffs, NJ: Prentice-Hall.

Anderson, Elijah
1978 *A Place on the Corner.* Chicago: University of Chicago Press.

Anthony, Dick, and Thomas Robbins
1975 "Youth culture, spiritual ferment and the confusion of moral meanings." Paper presented to the Society for the Scientific Study of Religion.

Antonovsky, Aaron
1960 "The social meaning of discrimination." *Phylon* 21: 13–19.

Armstrong, Christopher F.
1978 "Private education and the persistence of privilege: The case of two New England schools." Paper presented at the Eastern Sociological Society meeting, Philadelphia.

Aronoff, Joel, and William D. Crano
1975 "A re-examination of the cross-cultural principles of task segregation and sex role differentiation in the family." *American Sociological Review* 40 (February): 12–20.

Asch, Solomon E.
1952 *Social Psychology*. Englewood Cliffs, NJ: Prentice-Hall.

Astin, Alexander W., Margo R. King, and Gerald T. Richardson
1981 *The American Freshman: National Norms for Fall 1981*. University of California, Los Angeles: Cooperative Institutional Research Program, Laboratory for Research in Higher Education, Graduate School of Education.

Astin, Helen S.
forthcoming "Academic scholarship and its rewards." In M. L. Maehr and M. W. Steinkamp (eds.), *Women in Science*. Greenwich, CT: JAI Press.

Austin, Charles
1982 "Study of day care in U.S. finds churches are the main suppliers." *New York Times* (November 6): 14.

Averitt, Robert
1968 *The Dual Economy*. New York: Norton.

Bachman, J. G.
1967 *Youth in Transition*. Ann Arbor: Institute for Social Research, University of Michigan.

Bair, Lowell (tr.)
1974 *The Essential Rousseau*. New York: Mentor.

Baird, Leonard L.
1977 *The Elite Schools*. Lexington, MA: Lexington Books.

Bales, Robert F., and Philip E. Slater
1954 "Role differentiation in small decision making groups." Pp. 259–306 in Talcott Parsons and Robert F. Bales (eds.), *Family Socialization and Interaction Process Analysis*. New York: Free Press.

Bales, Robert F., and Fred L. Strodbeck
1951 "Phases in group problem solving." *Journal of Abnormal and Social Psychology* 46: 485–495.

Ball, Donald
1972 "What the action is: A cross-cultural approach." *Journal for the Theory of Social Behavior* 2 (October): 121–143.

Baltzell, E. Digby
1979 *Puritan Boston and Quaker Philadelphia*. New York: Free Press.

Baltzell, E. Digby
1964 *The Protestant Establishment: Aristocracy and Caste in America*. New York: Random House.

Bandura, Albert
1977 *Social Learning Theory*. Englewood Cliffs, NJ: Prentice-Hall.

Bandura, Albert
1969 "Social-learning theory of identificatory processes." Pp. 213–262 in David A. Goslin (ed.), *Handbook of Socialization Theory and Research*. Chicago: Rand McNally.

Bandura, Albert
1969 *Principles of Behavior Modification*. New York: Holt, Rinehart and Winston.

Bandura, Albert, and Richard H. Walters
1963 *Social Learning and Personality Development*. New York: Holt, Rinehart and Winston.

Banfield, Edward
1960 *The Unheavenly City*. Boston: Little, Brown.

Bank, S., and M. D. Kahn
1979 "Sisterhood-brotherhood is powerful: Sibling subsystems and family therapy." *Family Process* 14: 311–337.

Barash, David P.
1977 *Sociobiology and Behavior*. New York: Elsevier.

Baratz, Joan, and Stephen Baratz
1970 "Early childhood intervention: The social scientific basis of institutionalized racism." *Harvard Educational Review* 39: 29–50.

Barber, Bernard
1961 "Resistance by scientists to scientific discovery." *Science* 134 (September 1): 596–602.

Barclay, Bill
1981 "The economy: Who benefits?" Pp. 189–216 in Scott G. McNall (ed.), *Political Economy*. Glenview, IL: Scott, Foresman.

Barnet, Richard, and Ronald Muller
1975 *Global Reach: The Power of the Multinational Corporations*. New York: Simon and Schuster.

Barney, Gerald O.
1980 *The Global 2000 Report to the President*. Volume 1. Washington, D.C.: U.S. Government Printing Office.

Barry, Herbert III, Irvin Child, and Margaret Bacon
1959 "Relation of child training to subsistence economy." *American Anthropologist* 61: 51–63.

Barry, Herbert III, Lili Josephson, Edith Lauer, and Catherine Marshall
1976 "Traits inculcated in childhood: Cross-

cultural codes." *Ethnology* 15 (January): 83–114.

Barton, Allen H., and Bo Anderson
1966 "Change in an organizational system: Formalization of a qualitative study." Pp. 400–418 in Amitai Etzioni (ed.), *Complex Organizations.* New York: Holt, Rinehart and Winston.

Baude, Annika
1979 "Public policy and changing family patterns in Sweden: 1930–1977." Pp. 145–176 in Jean Lipman-Bluman and Jessie Bernard (eds.), *Sex Roles and Social Policy.* Beverly Hills, CA: Sage.

Becker, Ernest
1973 *The Denial of Death.* New York: Free Press.

Becker, Gary
1968 "Crime and punishment: An economic approach." *Journal of Political Economy* 75: 169–217.

Becker, Henry Jay
1977 "How young people find career-entry jobs: A review of the literature." Report No. 241, Center for Social Organization of Schools, Johns Hopkins University.

Becker, Howard S.
1973 "Labeling theory reconsidered." In *Outsiders,* revised edition. New York: Free Press.

Becker, Howard S.
1963 *Outsiders.* New York: Free Press

Becker, Howard S.
1956 *Man in Reciprocity: Introductory Lectures on Culture, Society, and Personality.* New York: Praeger.

Bell, Alan P., and Martin S. Weinberg
1978 *Homosexualities: A Study of Diversities among Men and Women.* New York: Touchstone.

Bell, Alan P., Martin S. Weinberg, and Sue Kiefer Hammersmith
1981 *Sexual Preference.* Bloomington, IN: Indiana University Press.

Bell, Daniel
1976 *The Cultural Contradictions of Capitalism.* New York: Harper & Row.

Bell, Daniel
1973 *The Coming of Post-Industrial Society.* New York: Basic Books.

Bellah, Robert
1975 *The Broken Covenant.* New York: Seabury.

Bellah, Robert N.
1974 "New religious consciousness." *New Republic* 171: 33–41.

Bellah, Robert N.
1967 "Civil religion in America." *Daedalus* 96 (winter): 1–21.

Ben-David, Joseph
1971 *The Scientist's Role in Society.* Englewood Cliffs, NJ: Prentice-Hall.

Ben-David, Joseph, and A. Zloczower
1962 "Universities and academic systems in modern societies." *European Journal of Sociology* 3: 45–85.

Benedict, Ruth
1934 *Patterns of Culture.* Boston: Houghton Mifflin.

Bennett, Amanda
1980 "Detroit distress: White-collar workers are singing the blues in the auto industry." *Wall Street Journal* (May 1): 1, 35.

Benston, Margaret
1978 "The political economy of women's liberation." Pp. 176–184 in Alison M. Jagger and Paula Rothenberg Struhl (eds.), *Feminist Frameworks.* New York: McGraw-Hill.

Berelson, Bernard, Paul Lazarsfeld, and William McPhee
1954 *Voting: A Study of Opinion Formation in a Presidential Campaign.* Chicago: University of Chicago Press.

Berg, Ivar E.
1970 *Education and Jobs: The Great Training Robbery.* New York: Praeger.

Berger, Peter L.
1977 *Facing Up to Modernity: Excursions in Society, Politics, and Religion. New York: Basic Books.*

Berger, Peter L.
1969 *Rumor of Angels: Modern Society and the Rediscovery of the Supernatural. Garden City, NY: Doubleday.*

Berger, Peter L.
1967 *The Sacred Canopy: Elements of a Sociological Theory of Religion.* Garden City, NY: Doubleday.

Berger, Peter L. and Thomas Luckmann
1966 *The Social Construction of Reality.* Garden City, NY: Doubleday & Company, Inc.

Bernard, J.
1981 "Facing the future." *Transaction* 18: 53–59.

Bernard, Jessie
1972 *The Future of Marriage.* New York: Bantam.

Bernstein, Basil
1977 "Class and pedagogies: Visible and invisible." Pp. 116—156 in Basil Bernstein (ed.), *Class, Codes and Control.* Volume 3. Second edition. Boston: Routledge & Kegan Paul.

Bernstein, Paul
1976 *The Dynamics of Bureaucracy.* Chicago: University of Chicago Press.

Bettleheim, Bruno

1971 *The Informed Heart.* New York: Avon.

Bird, Caroline
1966 *The Invisible Scar.* New York: David McKay.

Birket-Smith, Kaj
1935 *The Eskimos.* New York: Dutton.

Birnbaum, Judith Abelew
1975 Life patterns and self-esteem in gifted family-oriented and career-committed women. Pp. 396–419 in Martha T. Shuch Mednick, Sandra Schwartz Tangri, and Lois Wladis Hoffman (eds.), *Women and Achievement: Social and Motivational Analyses.* New York: Halsted Press.

Blackburn, Robert T., Charles E. Behymer, and David E. Hall
1978 "Correlates of faculty publications." *Sociology of Education* 51: 132–141.

Blau, Peter
1968 "Interaction, IV: Social exchange." In David L. Sills (ed.), *International Encyclopedia of the Social Sciences* 7. New York: Free Press.

Blau, Peter M.
1956 "Social mobility and interpersonal relaions." *American Journal of Sociology* 21: 290–295.

Blau, Peter M.
1955 *The Dynamics of Bureaucracy.* Chicago: University of Chicago Press.

Blau, Peter M., and Otis Dudley Duncan
1967 *The American Occupational Structure.* New York: Wiley.

Blauner, Robert
1972 *Racial Oppression in America.* New York: Harper & Row.

Blood, R. O., and D. M. Wolfe
1960 *Husbands and Wives.* New York: Free Press.

Blum, David J.
1980 "Black politicians fear they can't do much to help their people." *Wall Street Journal* (October 29): 1, 18.

Blumberg, Paul
1980 *Inequality in an Age of Decline.* New York: Oxford University Press.

Blumer, Herbert
1968 "Fashion." Pp. 341–345 in David V. Sills (ed.), *International Encyclopedia of the Social Sciences 5.* New York: Macmillan.

Blumer, Herbert
1969 "Fashion: From class differentiation to collective behavior." *Sociological Quarterly* 10 (winter): 275–291.

Blumstein, Philip W., and Pepper Schwartz
in progress Study of sexuality among homosexual and heterosexual men and women.

Boland, Walter R.
1973 "Size, external relations, and the distribution of power: A study of colleges and universities." Pp. 428–441 in Wolf V. Heydebrand (ed.), *Comparative Organizations.* Englewood Cliffs, NJ: Prentice-Hall.

Bolles, Richard Nelson
1977 *What Color Is Your Parachute?* Revised edition. Berkeley, CA: Ten Speed Press.

Bond, Nicholas A. Jr.
1981 "The psychological component in productivity." *Wall Street Journal* (March 10): 35.

Bourdieu, Pierre
1971 "Systems of education and systems of thought." Pp. 189–207 in M. F. D. Young (ed.), *Knowledge and Control.* London: Collier-Macmillan.

Boswell, John
1980 *Christianity, Social Tolerance and Homosexuality.* Chicago: University of Chicago Press.

Boucher, J. D., and P. Ekman
1975 "Facial areas of emotional information." *Journal of Communication* 25: 21–29

Boudon, Raymond
1973 *Education, Opportunity, and Social Inequality.* New York: Wiley.

Bourg, C. J.
1975 "Elderly in a southern metropolitan area." *The Gerontologist* 15 (February): 15–22.

Bowen, D., E. Bowen, S. Gawiser, and L. Masotti
1968 "Deprivation, mobility, and orientation toward protest of the urban poor." Pp. 187–200 in L. Mascotti and D. Bowen (ed.), *Riots and Rebellion: Civil Violence in the Urban Community.* Beverly Hills, CA: Sage.

Bowles, Samuel, and Herbert Gintis
1976 *Schooling in Capitalist America.* New York: Basic Books.

Bracy, Terrence
1979 "Car Ind 4 Sale. Orig. Own." *New York Times* (August 20): A21.

Braithwaite, John
1981 "The myth of social class and criminality reconsidered." *American Sociological Review* 46: 36–57.

Braithwaite, John
1979 *Inequality, Crime, and Public Policy.* London and Boston: Routledge and Kegan Paul.

Braithwaite, J., and V. Braithwaite
1978 "Unpublished cross-tabulations from data reported in 'An exploratory study of delinquency and the nature of schooling.'" *Australian and New Zealand Journal of Sociology* 14: 25–32.

Braverman, Harry
1974 *Labor and Monopoly Capital.* New York: Monthly Review Press.
Brenner, M. Harvey
1973 *Mental Illness and the Economy.* Cambridge, MA: Harvard University Press.
Brickman, P.
1974 *Social Conflict.* Lexington, MA: Heath.
Briggs, Kenneth A.
1982 "Mainstream U.S. evangelicals surge in Protestant influence." *New York Times* (March 14): 1, 50.
Brinton, Crane
1965 *The Anatomy of Revolution.* Revised and expanded edition. New York: Random House.
Brofenbrenner, Urie
1981 "Children and families: 1984?" *Transaction* 18: 38–41.
Brofenbrenner, Urie
1970 *Two Worlds of Childhood: U.S. and U.S.S.R.* New York: Basic Books–Russell Sage Foundation.
Brookover, Wilbur B., and Jeffrey M. Schneider
1975 "Academic environments and elementary school achievement." *Journal of Research and Development in Education* 9: 82–91.
Brower, J. J.
1973 "The black side of football: The salience of race." Unpublished doctoral dissertation. Santa Barbara: University of California.
Brown, G.
1976 "The social causes of disease." In D. Tuckett (ed.), *An Introduction to Medical Sociology.* London: Tavistock.
Brown, Lester R.
1975 "The world food prospect." *Science* 190: 1053–59.
Brown, Lester R.
1973 "Population and affluence: Growing pressures on world food resources." *Population Bulletin* 29: 1–31.
Brown, Rita Mae
1978 "Living with other women." Pp. 245–247 in Alison M. Jagger and Paula Rothenberg Struhl (eds.), *Feminist Frameworks.* New York: McGraw-Hill.
Brownmiller, Susan
1975 *Against Our Will: Men, Women and Rape.* New York: Bantam Books.
Bruner, Jerome S., and Leo Postman
1949 "On the perception of incongruity: A paradigm." *Journal of Personality* 18: 206–223.
Bullough, Vern L.
1976 *Sexual Variance in Society and History.* New York: Wiley.
Bumpass, Larry L., Ronald R. Rindfuss, and Richard B. Janosik
1978 "Age and marital status at first birth and the pace of subsequent fertility." *Demography* 15: 75–86.
Burckhardt, Jacob
1929/1958 *The Civilization of the Renaissance in Italy.* New York: Harper Torchbooks.
Burdge, Rabel J.
1969 "Levels of occupational prestige and leisure activity." *Journal of Leisure Research* 3: 262–274.
Buric, O., and A. Zecevic
1967 "Family authority, marital satisfaction, and the social network in Yugoslavia." *Journal of Marriage and the Family* 29: 225–236.
Burr, Wesley R.
1973 *Theory Construction and the Sociology of the Family.* New York: Wiley-Interscience.
Burridge, K. O. L.
1957 "Disputing in Tangu." *American Anthropologist* 56: 143–146.
Butterfield, Fox
1977 "Taiwan bridges the income gap while maintaining high growth." *New York Times* (April 12): 25, 26.
Butz, William P., and Michael P. Ward
1979 "Baby boom and baby bust: A new view." *American Demographics* 1: 11–17.

Campbell, Angus, Philip E. Converse, Warren E. Miller, and Donald D. Stokes
1964 *The American Voter—An Abridgement.* New York: Wiley.
Campbell, Angus, Gerald Gurin, and W. E. Miller
1954 *The Voter Decides.* Evanston, IL: Row, Peterson.
Campbell, Bruce A.
1980 "The interaction of race and socioeconomic status in the development of political attitudes." *Social Science Quarterly* 60 (March): 651–658.
Cantor, M. H.
1975 "Life space and the social support system of the inner city elderly of New York." *The Gerontologist* 15 (February): 23–26.
Cantril, Hadley, Herta Herzog, and Hazel Gaudet
1940 *The Invasion from Mars.* Princeton, NJ: Princeton University Press.
Caplow, Theodore
1959 "Further development of a theory of coalitions in the triad." *American Journal of Sociology* 64 (March): 488–493.
Caplow, Theodore, and Howard M. Bahr
1979 "Half a century of change in adolescent

attitudes: Replication of a Middletown Survey by the Lynds." *Public Opinion Quarterly* 43: 1–17.

Carp, F. M.
1975 "Life-style and location within the city." *The Gerontologist* 15 (February): 27–33

Carroll, Jackson W., Douglas W. Johnson, and Martin E. Marty
1979 *Religion in America: 1950 to the Present.* New York: Harper & Row.

Centers, Richard
1949 *The Psychology of Social Classes.* Princeton, NJ: Princeton University Press.

Centra, John A., and Nancy M. Kuykendall
1975 *Women, Men and the Doctorate.* Princeton, NJ: Educational Testing Service.

Chagnon, N. A.
1968 *Yanomamö The Fierce People.* New York: Holt, Rinehart and Winston.

Chambliss, William J.
1969 *Crime and the Legal Process.* New York: McGraw-Hill.

Chandler, Robert F.
1971 "The scientific basis for the increased yield capacity of rice and wheat and its present and potential impact on food production in the developing countries." Pp. 25–43 in Thomas T. Poleman and Donald K. Freebain (eds.), *Food, Population and Employment: The Impact of the Green Revolution.* New York: Praeger.

Charters, W. W. Jr.
1974 "Social class analysis and the control of public education." Pp. 98–113 in Elizabeth L. Useem and Michael Useem (eds.), *The Education Establishment.* Englewood Cliffs, NJ: Prentice-Hall.

Cherry, L.
1975 "Teacher-child verbal interaction: An approach to the study of sex differences." Pp. 172–183 in B. Thorne and N. Henley (eds.), *Language and Sex: Difference and Dominance.* Rowley, MA: Newbury House.

Cherry, Mike
1974 *On High Steel.* New York: Ballantine.

Childe, V. Gordon
1964 *What Happened in History.* Baltimore: Penguin.

Cicourel, Aaron V.
1968 *The Social Organization of Juvenile Justice.* New York: Wiley.

Clark, Alfred C.
1956 "The use of leisure and its relation to occupational prestige." *American Sociological Review* 21: 301–307.

Clark, Burton R., and Martin Trow
1966 "The organizational context." Pp. 17–70 in Theodore M. Newcomb and Everett K. Wilson (eds.), *College Peer Groups: Problems and Prospects for Research.* Chicago: Aldine.

Clark, Lindley H. Jr.
1980 "Analysts debate how to slow the economy to curb rising prices." *Wall Street Journal* (April 24): 1, 39.

Clark, R. W.
1971 *Einstein: The Life and Times.* New York: World.

Clinard, Marshall B.
1978 *Cities with Little Crime: The Case of Switzerland.* Cambridge, Eng.: Cambridge University Press.

Clutterbuck, Richard Lewis
1977 *Guerrilas and Terrorists.* London: Faber and Faber.

Cohen, Albert K.
1966 *Deviance and Control.* Englewood Cliffs, NJ: Prentice-Hall.

Cohen, Albert K.
1965 "Sociology of the deviant act: Anomie theory and beyond." *American Sociological Review* 30 (February): 5–14.

Cohn, Norman
1957 *The Pursuit of the Millennium.* Fairlawn, NJ: Essential Books.

Cole, Jonathan
1979 *Fair Science.* New York: Free Press.

Cole, Jonathan R., and Stephen Cole
1973 *Social Stratification in Science.* Chicago: University of Chicago Press.

Coleman, James
1961 *The Adolescent Society.* New York: Free Press,

Coleman, James S., Ernest Q. Campbell, Carol J. Hobson, James McPartland, Alexander M. Mood, Frederic D. Weinfeld, and Robert L. York
1966 *Equality of Educational Opportunity.* Washington, D.C.: U.S. Government Printing Office.

Coleman, James, Thomas Hoffer, and Sally Kilgore
1981 *Public and Private Schools.* Washington, D.C.: National Center for Education Statistics.

Coleman, James S., Sara D. Kelly, and John A. Moore
1975 *Trends in School Segregation, 1968–73.* Washington: The Urban Institute.

Coleman, James S., and Carol B. Stocking
in progress High school and beyond study.

Coles, Robert
1977 *Privileged Ones.* Volume V of *Children of Crisis.* Boston: Little, Brown.

Coles, Robert

1967 *Migrants, Sharecroppers, Mountaineers.* Volume II of *Children of Crisis.* Boston: Little, Brown.

Collins, Randall
1979 *The Credential Society.* New York: Academic Press.

Collins, Randall
1977 "Some Comparative Principles of Educational Stratification." *Harvard Educational Review* 47: 1–27.

Collins, Randall
1975 *Conflict Sociology.* New York: Academic Press.

Collins, Randall
1974 "Where are educational requirements for employment highest?" *Sociology of Education* 47: 419–442.

Collins, Randall
1971 "Functional and conflict theories of educational stratification." *American Sociological Review* 36: 1002–1019.

Comfort, Alex
1972 *The Joy of Sex.* New York: Simon and Schuster.

Comstock, George, Steven Chaffee, Natan Katzman, Maxwell McCombs, and Donald Roberts
1978 *Television and Human Behavior.* New York: Columbia University Press.

Conant, James B.
1959 *The American High School Today: A First Report to Interested Citizens.* New York: McGraw-Hill.

Condry, John, and Sharon Dyer
1976 "Fear of success: Attribution of cause to the victim." *Journal of Social Issues* 32: 63–83.

Conference Board
1979 *The World's Multinationals: A Global Challenge.* Information Bulletin No. 84. New York: The Conference Board.

Connecticut Mutual Life Insurance Company
1980 *Connecticut Mutual Life Report on American Values in the 80s: The Impact of Belief* (September–December). Survey by Research and Forecasts, Inc.

Conrad, Peter, and Rochelle Kern (eds.)
1981 *The Sociology of Health and Illness.* New York: St. Martin's Press.

Conrad, Peter, and Joseph W. Schneider
1980 *Deviance and Medicalization: From Badness to Sickness.* St. Louis, MO: C. V. Mosby.

Cooley, Charles Horton
1902/1922 *Human Nature and the Social Order.* New York: Scribner's.

Coombs, R. H., and P. S. Powers
1975 "Socialization for death: The physician's role." *Urban Life* 4: 250–271.

Cornish, Edward
1981 "The information society: Communications and computers." Pp. 9–35 in Martin A. Bacheller (ed.), *The Hammond Almanac.* Maplewood, NJ: Hammond.

Coser, Lewis A.
1967 *Continuities in the Study of Social Conflict.* New York: Free Press.

Coser, Lewis A.
1956 *The Functions of Social Conflict.* New York: Free Press.

Coser, Rose Laub
1975 "Stay home Little Sheba: On placement, displacement and social change." *Social Problems* 22 (April): 470–480.

Cottle, Thomas J.
1974 "What tracking did to Ollie Taylor." *Social Policy* 5: 21–24.

Covello, Vincent T.
1979 "Inequality and opportunity: Occupational mobility and educational attainment in five nations." Unpublished paper, National Science Foundation.

Cox, Harvey
1977 *Turning East.* New York: Simon and Schuster.

Cozens, F., and F. Stumpf
1953 *Sports in American Life.* Chicago: University of Chicago Press.

Crain, Robert L., and Rita E. Mahard
1978 "Desegregation and black achievement: A case-survey of the literature." *Law and Contemporary Problems* 42 (summer): 17–56.

Crandall, Virginia C.
1969 "Sex differences in expectancy of intellectual and academic reinforcement." Pp. 11–45 in Charles P. Smith (ed.), *Achievement-Related Motives in Children.* New York: Russell Sage Foundation.

Crawford, T. J., and M. Naditch
1970 "Relative deprivation, powerlessness and militancy: The psychology of social protest." *Psychiatry* 33 (May): 208–223.

Crocker, C. A., and P. Hartland-Thunberg
1978 *Namibia at the Crossroads: Economic and Political Prospects.* Washington, D.C.: Georgetown University, Center for Strategic and International Studies.

Cronan, Sheila
1978 "Marriage." Pp. 240–245 in Alison M. Jagger and Paula Rothenberg Struhl (eds.), *Feminist Frameworks.* New York: McGraw-Hill.

Cross, Patricia
1968 "College women: A research descrip-

tion." *Journal of the National Association of Women Deans and Counselors* 32: 12–21.

Crystal, John C., and Richard N. Bolles
1974 *Where Do I Go from Here with My Life?* New York: Seabury.

Csikszentmihalyi, Mihaly
1974 *Flow: Studies of Enjoyment.* Chicago: University of Chicago Press.

Cuber, John F., and Peggy B. Harroff
1972 "Five kinds of relationships." Pp. 276–287 in Ira L. Reiss (ed.), *Readings on the Family System.* New York: Holt, Rinehart and Winston.

Cummings, Scott, and Del Taebel
1978 "The economic socialization of children: A neo-Marxist analysis." *Social Problems* 26: 198–210.

Currie, Ian D.
1966 "The Sapir-Whorf hypothesis." *Berkeley Journal of Sociology* 11: 14–31.

Curtiss, Susan
1977 *Genie.* New York: Academic Press.

Cutright, P.
1971 "Income and family events: Marital stability." *Journal of Marriage and the Family* 33 (April): 291–306.

Dahl, Robert A.
1961 *Who Governs?* New Haven, CT: Yale University Press.

Dahrendorf, Ralf
1959 *Class and Class Conflict in Industrial Society.* Stanford, CA: Stanford University Press.

Dahrendorf, Ralf
1958 "Out of utopia: Toward a reorientation of sociological analysis." *American Journal of Sociology* 64: 115–127.

Daley, Robert
1963 *The Bizarre World of European Sports.* New York: William Morrow.

Daner, Francine
1976 *The American Children of Krsna: A Study of the Hare Krsna Movement.* New York: Holt, Rinehart and Winston.

Darwin, Charles
1859/1958 *The Origin of Species.* New York: Mentor.

Davis, Alan J.
1970 "Sexual assaults in the Philadelphia prison system." Pp. 107–124 in John H. Gagnon and William Simon (eds.), *The Sexual Scene.* Chicago: Transaction/Aldine.

Davis, Kingsley
1947 "Final note on a case of extreme isolation." *American Journal of Sociology* 50 (March): 432–437.

Davis, Kingsley, and Wilbert E. Moore
1945 "Some principles of stratification." *American Sociological Review* 10: 242–249.

Davis, Nanette J.
1972 "Labeling theory in deviance research: A critique and evaluation." *The Sociological Quarterly* 13 (fall): 447–474.

Day, Robert C.
1972 "The Emergence of Activism as a Social Movement." Pp. 506–532 in Howard M. Bahr, Bruce A. Chadwick, and Robert C. Day (eds.), *Native Americans Today: Sociological Perspectives.* New York: Harper & Row.

Dearman, Nancy B., and Valena White Plisko
1980 *The Condition of Education.* Washington, D.C.: National Center for Education Statistics.

Dearman, Nancy B., and Valena White Plisko
1979 *The Condition of Education.* 1979 edition. Washington, D.C.: National Center for Education Statistics, U.S. Department of Health, Education and Welfare.

Deevey, Edward S. Jr.
1960 "The human population." *Scientific American* 203: 195–204.

DeLora, Joann S., and Carol A. B. Warren
1977 *Understanding Sexual Interaction.* Boston: Houghton Mifflin.

Deloria, Vine Jr.
1981 "Native Americans: The American Indian today." *The Annals of the American Academy of Political and Social Science* 454 (March): 125–138.

Demerath, N. J. III
1966 *Social Class in American Protestantism.* Chicago: Rand McNally.

DeVall, Bill, and Joseph Harry
1978 "Who hates whom in the great outdoors: Recreation equipment and the microecology of leisure settings." Paper presented at the annual meeting of the American Sociological Association, San Francisco.

Dickson, Paul
1975 *The Future of the Workplace.* New York: Weybright and Tally.

Domhoff, G. William
1978 *Who Really Rules? New Haven and Community Power Reexamined.* New Brunswick, NJ: Transaction Books.

Domhoff, G. William
1974 *The Bohemian Grove and Other Retreats.* New York: Harper & Row.

Domhoff, G. William
1970 *The Higher Circles.* New York: Vintage.

Domhoff, G. William

1967 *Who Rules America?* Englewood Cliffs, NJ: Prentice-Hall.

Dooley, P. C.
1969 "The interlocking directorate." *American Economic Review* 59: 314–323.

Dover, K. J.
1978 *Greek Homosexuality*. Cambridge, MA: Harvard University Press.

Duberman, Martin
1974 "The bisexual debate." *New Times* 2: 34–41.

Dulles, F. R.
1965 *A History of Recreation*. Englewood Cliffs, NJ: Prentice-Hall.

Durkheim, Emile
1915 *The Elementary Forms of the Religious Life*. Glencoe, IL: Free Press.

Durkheim, Emile
1897/1951 *Suicide*. Glencoe, IL: Free Press.

Durkheim, Emile
1893/1933 *The Division of Labor in Society*. Glencoe, IL: Free Press.

Durso, Joseph
1971 *The Sports Factory: An Investigation into College Sports*. New York: Quadrangle.

Edwards, Harry
1969 *The Revolt of the Black Athlete*. New York: Free Press.

Ehrenreich, Barbara, and Deirdre English
1978 *For Her Own Good: 150 Years of the Experts' Advice to Women*. Garden City, NY: Anchor.

Ehrlich, Issac
1977 "Capital punishment and deterrence: Some further thoughts and additional evidence." *Journal of Political Economy* 85: 741–788.

Ehrlich, Issac
1975 "The deterrent effect of capital punishment: A question of life and death." *American Economic Review* 65 (June): 397–417.

Ehrlich, Issac
1974 "Participation in illegitimate activities: An economic analysis." Pp. 68–134 in G. S. Becker and W. M. Landes (eds.), *Essays in the Economics of Crime and Punishment*. New York: Columbia University Press.

Ehrlich, Paul
1968 *The Population Bomb*. New York: Ballantine Books.

Eitzen, D. Stanley
1979a "Sport and Deviance." Pp. 73–87 in D. Stanley Eitzen (ed.), *Sport in Contemporary Society*. New York, St. Martin's Press.

Eitzen, D. Stanley
1979b "The structure of sport and society." Pp. 41–46 in D. Stanley Eitzen (ed.), *Sport in Contemporary Society*. New York, St. Martin's Press.

Eitzen, D. Stanley, and Norman R. Yetman
1979c "Immune from racism?" Pp. 388–408 in D. Stanley (ed.), *Sport in Contemporary Society*. New York, St. Martin's Press.

Ekman, P., and W. V. Friesen
1969 "The repetoire of nonverbal behavior: Categories, origins, usage, and coding." *Semiotica* 1: 49–98.

Elder, Glen H. Jr.
1974 *Children of the Great Depression*. Chicago: University of Chicago Press.

Elkin, A. P.
1954 *The Australian Aborigines*. Third edition. Sydney: Angus and Robertson.

Elliott, Delbert S., and Suzanne S. Ageton
1980 "Reconciling race and class differences in self-reported and official estimates of delinquency." *American Sociological Review* 45 (February): 95–110.

Ellis, Godfrey J., Gary R. Lee, and Larry R. Petersen
1978 "Supervision and conformity: A cross-cultural analysis of parental socialization values." *American Journal of Sociology* 84: 386–403.

Emerson, Joan P.
1970 "Behavior in private places: Sustaining definitions of reality in gynecological examinations." Pp. 74–97 in Hans Peter Dreitzel (ed.), *Recent Sociology* No. 2. New York: Macmillan.

Empey, LaMar Taylor
1978 *American Delinquency*. Homewood, IL: Dorsey Press.

Engels, Frederick
1884/1972 *The Origin of the Family, Private Property, and the State*. New York: Pathfinder Press.

Ennis, Philip H.
1967 "Criminal victimization in the U.S.: A report of a national survey." *Field Survey II, President's Commission on Law Enforcement and Administration of Justice*. Washington, D.C.: U.S. Government Printing Office.

Environmental Fund
1976 *World Hunger: Too Little Food or Too Many People?* Washington, D.C.: Environmental Fund.

Epstein, Samuel S.
1981 "The political and economic basis of cancer." Pp. 75–82 in Peter Conrad and Rochelle Kern (eds.), *The Sociology of Health and Illness*. New York: St. Martin's Press.

Erikson, Kai T.

1966 *Wayward Puritans: A Study in the Sociology of Deviance*. New York: Wiley.

Erikson, Erik H.
1950/1963 *Childhood and Society*. Second edition. New York: Norton.

Etheridge, Carolyn F.
1978 "Equality in the family: Comparative analysis and theoretical model." *International Journal of Women's Studies* 1: 50–63.

Etheridge, Carolyn F.
1974 "The dynamics of changing sex-roles: An integrating theoretical analysis." Paper presented at the annual meeting of the American Sociological Association, Montreal.

Etzioni, Amitai
1965 "Dual leadership in complex organizations." *American Sociological Review* 30: 688–698.

Etzioni, Amitai
1964 *Modern Organizations*. Englewood Cliffs, NJ: Prentice-Hall.

Europa Year Book
1982 *A World Survey*. London: Europa Publications.

Evans, Christopher
1979 *The Micro Millennium*. New York: Washington Square Press.

Evans, Christopher
1973 *Cults of Unreason*. New York: Spectrum.

Evans, Peter B., and Steven A. Schneider
1981 "The political economy of the corporation." Pp. 216–241 in Scott G. McNall (ed.), *Political Economy: A Critique of American Society*. Glenview, IL: Scott, Foresman.

Farley, Reynolds, Toni Richards, and Clarence Wurdock
1980 "School desegregation and white flight: An investigation of competing models and their discrepant findings." *Sociology of Education* 53 (July): 123–139.

Farrell, Warren
1976 "Women's liberation as men's liberation: Twenty-one examples." Pp. 278–290 in Deborah S. David and Robert Brannon (eds.), *The Forty-Nine Percent Majority: The Male Sex Role*. Reading, MA: Addison-Wesley.

Fava, Sylvia F.
1978 "Women's place in the new suburbia." Paper presented at the annual meeting of the American Sociological Association, San Francisco.

Fava, Sylvia F.
1975 "Beyond suburbia." *Annals of the American Academy* 422 (November): 10–24.

Feagin, Joe R.
1975 *Subordinating the Poor: Welfare and American Beliefs*. Englewood Cliffs, NJ: Prentice-Hall.

Featherman, David L., and Robert M. Hauser
1978 *Opportunity and Change*. New York: Academic Press.

Federal Reserve Bank of San Francisco
1980 "Documenting the productivity lag." *Weekly Letter*. November 7 and 14.

Feldman, Kenneth A., and Theodore M. Newcomb
1969 *The Impact of College upon Students*. San Francisco: Jossey-Bass.

Felson, Marcus
1978 "Individious distinctions among cars, clothes and suburbs." *Public Opinion Quarterly 42*: 49–58.

Fialka, John J.
1982a "Ground Zero: Town of Pella, Iowa, talks of little other than nuclear attack." *Wall Street Journal* (April 16): 1, 22.

Fialka, John J.
1982b "Atom-weapons issue stirs divisive debate in the Catholic Church." *Wall Street Journal* (June 9): 1, 20.

Fimrite, Ron
1974 "Take me out to the brawl game." *Sports Illustrated* (June 17): 10–13.

Findley, Rowe
1981 "St. Helens: Mountain with a death wish." *National Geographic,* 159: 3–65.

Finkelman, J. J.
1966 "Maternal employment, family relationships and parental role perception." Unpublished doctoral dissertation, Yeshiva University, Israel.

Firestone, Shulamith
1970 *The Dialectic of Sex*. New York: Morrow.

Fischer, Claude S.
1976 *The Urban Experience*. New York: Harcourt Brace Jovanovich.

Fischer, Claude S., and Robert Max Jackson
1977 "Suburbanism and localism." Pp. 117–138 in Claude S. Fischer et al., *Networks and Places*. New York: Free Press.

Fischer, Claude S., Robert Max Jackson, C. Ann Stueve, Kathleen Gerson, Lynn McCallister Jones, with Mark Baldassare
1977 *Networks and Places: Social Relations in the Urban Setting*. New York: Free Press.

Fisher, M. F. K.
1982 "Big numbers." *The New Yorker* (July 12): 28–30.

Fiske, Edward B.
1983 "Academic courses lose favor." *New York Times* (April 26): C1, C8.

Flanagan, Timothy J., David J. van Alstyne, and

Michael R. Gottfredson (eds.)
1982 *Sourcebook of Criminal Justice Statistics—1981.* U.S. Department of Justice, Bureau of Justice Statistics. Washington, D.C.: U.S. Government Printing Office.

Fogelson, Robert
1967 *The Fragmented Metropolis: Los Angeles, 1850–1930.* Cambridge, MA: Harvard University Press.

Folger, John D., and Charles B. Nam
1967 *Education of the American Population.* Washington, D.C.: U.S. Bureau of the Census, U.S. Government Printing Office.

Forbes
1982 "The 100 largest U.S. multinationals" and "The 100 largest foreign companies." July 5: 126–130.

Ford, Clellan S., and Frank A. Beach
1951 *Patterns of Sexual Behavior.* New York: Harper Torchbooks.

Fox, Mary Frank
1981 "Sex, salary, and achievement: Reward-dualism in academia." *Sociology of Education* 54: 71–84.

Frank, André Gunder
1980 *Crisis in the World Economy.* New York: Holmes & Meier.

Frank, André Gunder
1979 *Dependent Accumulation and Underdevelopment.* New York: Monthly Review Press.

Frank, André Gunder
1967 *Capitalism and Underdevelopment in Latin America.* New York: Monthly Review Press.

Frank, André Gunder
1966 "The development of underdevelopment." *Monthly Review* 18 (September): 3–17.

Frazier, Nancy, and Myra Sadker
1973 *Sexism in School and Society.* New York: Harper & Row.

Freedman, Daniel G.
1974 *Human Infancy: An Evolutionary Perspective.* Hillsdale, NJ: Lawrence Erlbaum Associates.

Freeman, Jo
1975 *The Politics of Women's Liberation.* New York: David McKay.

Freeman, Richard B.
1977 *Black Elite: The New Market for Highly Educated Black Americans.* New York: McGraw-Hill.

Freeman, Richard B.
1976 *The Over-Educated American.* New York: Academic Press.

Freidson, Eliot
1980 "Conceiving of divisions of labor." Paper presented at the annual meeting of the American Sociological Association, New York.

Freidson, Eliot
1978 "The prospects for health services in the United States." *Medical Care* 16: 971–983.

Friedan, Betty
1981 *The Second Stage.* New York: Summit Books.

Friedan, Betty
1963 *The Feminine Mystique.* New York: Dell.

Friedrich, Carl Joachim, and Zbigniew K. Brzezinski
1965 *Totalitarian Dictatorship and Autocracy.* Second edition. Cambridge, MA: Harvard University Press.

Frieze, Irene H.
1975 "Women's expectations for and causal attributions of success and failure." Pp. 158–171 in Martha T. S. Mednick, Sandra Schwartz Tangri, and Lois Wladis Hoffman (eds.), *Women and Achievement: Social and Motivational Analyses.* Washington, D.C.: Hemisphere.

Fusfeld, Daniel
1973 *The Basic Economics of the Urban Racial Crisis.* New York: Holt, Rinehart and Winston.

Gagnon, John H.
1977 *Human Sexualities.* Glenview, IL: Scott, Foresman.

Gallen, Richard T.
1967 *Wives' Legal Rights.* New York: Dell.

Gallese, Liz Roman
1980 "Women and the race up the company ladder." *Wall Street Journal* (November 3): 30.

Gallup, George H.
1979 *The Gallup Poll.* Chicago: Field Enterprises, Inc.

Gamson, William A.
1975 *The Strategy of Protest.* Homewood, IL: Dorsey Press.

Gans, Herbert J.
1971 "The uses of poverty: The poor pay all." *Social Policy* 2: 21–23.

Gans, Herbert J.
1967 *The Levittowners.* New York: Free Press.

Gans, Herbert J.
1962a "Urbanism and suburbanism as ways of life: A re-evaluation of definitions." Pp. 625–648 in Arnold Rose (ed.), *Human Behavior and Social Processes.* Boston: Houghton Mifflin.

Gans, Herbert J.
1962b *The Urban Villagers.* New York: Free Press.

Garabedian, Peter G.
1963 "Social roles and processes of socialization in the prison community." *Social Problems*

11: 139–152.

Garfinkel, Harold
1967 *Studies in Ethnomethodology*. Englewood Cliffs, NJ: Prentice-Hall.

Garfinkel, Harold
1956 "Conditions of successful degradation ceremonies." *American Journal of Sociology* 61: 420–424.

Garland, T. Neal
1972 "The better half? The male in the dual profession family." Pp. 199–215 in Constantina Safilios-Rothschild (ed.), *Toward a Sociology of Women*. Lexington, MA: Xerox College Publishing.

Garn, Stanley M.
1971 *Human Races*. Third edition. Springfield, IL: Charles C. Thomas.

Gathorne-Hardy, Jonathan
1977 *The Old School Tie*. New York: Viking.

Gebhard, Paul H.
1972 "Incidence of overt homosexuality in the United States and Western Europe." Pp. 22–29 in John M. Livingood (ed.), *National Institute of Mental Health Task Force on Homosexuality: Final Report and Background Papers*. Washington, D.C.: U.S. Government Printing Office.

Gecas, Viktor
1979 "The influence of social class on socialization." Pp. 365–404 in Wesley R. Burr, Reuben Hill, F. Ivan Nye, and Ira L. Reiss (eds.), *Contemporary Theories about the Family*. New York: Free Press.

Gelles, Richard J.
1974 *The Violent Home: A Study of Physical Aggression between Husbands and Wives*. Beverly Hills, CA: Sage.

Gelles, Richard J., and Murray A. Straus
1979 "Determinants of violence in the family: Toward a theoretical integration." Pp. 549–581 in Wesley R. Burr et al. (eds.), *Contemporary Theories about the Family*. Volume I. New York: Free Press.

German Development Institute
1978 *Multi-Sectorial Study on Namibia*. Berlin, West Germany.

Giaquinta, Joe, and Carole Kazlow
1981 "The endurance of the traditional classroom in American elementary schools: Some social and economic considerations." Paper presented at the annual meeting of the Society for the Study of Social Problems, Toronto.

Gilligan, Carol
1977 "In a different voice: Women's conception of the self and of morality." *Harvard Educational Review* 47: 481–517.

Gilmartin, Brian G.
1979 "The case against spanking." *Human Behavior* (February): 18–23.

Glass, D. V. (ed.)
1953 *Introduction to Malthus*. New York: Wiley.

Glick, Paul C., and Arthur J. Norton
1973 "Perspectives on the recent upturn in divorce and remarriage." *Demography* 10: 301–314.

Glick, Paul C., and Arthur J. Norton
1971 "Frequency, duration and probability of marriage and divorce." *Journal of Marriage and the Family* 33 (May): 307–317.

Glock, Charles
1976 "Consciousness among contemporary youth: An interpretation." Pp. 353–366 in C. Glock and R. Bellah (eds.), *The New Religious Consciousness*. Berkeley: University of California Press.

Glock, Charles, and Rodney Stark
1965 *Religion and Society in Tension*. Chicago: Rand McNally.

Goffman, Erving
1974 *Frame Analysis*. Cambridge, MA: Harvard University Press.

Goffman, Erving
1971 *Relations in Public*. New York: Basic Books.

Goffman, Erving
1967 *Interaction Ritual: Essays on Face-to-Face Behavior*. Garden City, NY: Doubleday.

Goffman, Erving
1963a *Behavior in Public Places*. New York: Free Press.

Goffman, Erving
1963b *Stigma: Notes on the Management of Spoiled Identity*. Englewood Cliffs, NJ: Prentice-Hall.

Goffman, Erving
1961 *Asylums*. Garden City, NY: Doubleday.

Goffman, Erving
1959 *The Presentation of Self in Everyday Life*. Garden City, NY: Doubleday-Anchor.

Gold, Martin
1970 *Delinquent Behavior in an American City*. Belmont, CA: Brooks/Cole.

Gold, Martin
1963 *Status Forces in Delinquent Boys*. Ann Arbor, MI: Institute for Social Research.

Gold, Martin, and Donald J. Reimer
1974 "Changing patterns of delinquent behavior among Americans 13–16 years old: 1967–1972." *National Survey of Youth, Report No. 1*. Ann Arbor: University of Michigan Institute for Social Research (mimeo).

Goldstein, Jeffrey H., and Robert L. Arms

1971 "Effects of observing athletic contests on hostility." *Sociometry* 34 (March): 83–90.

Goldthorpe, John H.
1978 "The current inflation: Towards a sociological account." Pp. 186–214 in Fred Hirsch and John H. Goldthorpe (eds.), *The Political Economy of Inflation*. London: Martin Robertson.

Golladay, Mary A.
1977 *The Condition of Education*. Washington, D.C.: National Center for Education Statistics.

Golladay, Mary A., and Jay Noell (eds.)
1978 *The Condition of Education*. Washington, D.C.: National Center for Education Statistics.

Goode, William J.
1977 *Principles of Sociology*. New York: McGraw-Hill.

Goode, William J.
1976 "Family disorganization." Pp. 511–554 in Robert K. Merton and Robert A. Nisbet (eds.), *Contemporary Social Problems*. Fourth edition. New York: Harcourt Brace Jovanovich.

Goode, William J.
1960 "Encroachment, charlatanism, and the emerging profession: Psychology, medicine, and sociology." *American Sociological Review* 25: 902–914.

Goode, William J., Elizabeth Hopkins, and Helen M. McClure
1971 *Social Systems and Family Patterns: A Propositional Inventory*. New York: Bobbs-Merrill.

Goodhart, Philip, and Christopher Chataway
1973 "The rise of sports." Pp. 211–217 in Peter N. Stearus (ed.), *The Other Side of Western Civilization: Readings in Everyday Life*. Volume II: *The Sixteenth Century to the Present*. New York: Harcourt Brace Jovanovich.

Gordon, David M.
1977 "Capitalism and the roots of urban crisis." Pp. 82–112 in Roger E. Alcaly and David Mermelstein (eds.), *The Fiscal Crisis of American Cities*. New York: Vintage.

Gordon, David M.
1972 *Theories of Poverty and Unemployment: Orthodox, Radical, and Dual Labor Market Perspectives*. Lexington, MA: Lexington Books.

Gordon, Loraine, Suzanne Blignaut, Carole Cooper, and Linda Ensor
1979 *Survey of Race Relations in South Africa 1978*. Johannesburg: South African Institute of Race Relations.

Gordon, Milton
1964 *Assimilation in American Life*. New York: Oxford University Press.

Goring, Charles
1913 *The English Convict*. London: His Majesty's Stationery Office.

Goslin, David A.
1965 *The School in Contemporary Society*. Glenview, IL: Scott, Foresman.

Gottschalk, Earl C., Jr.
1983 "Older Americans: The Aging Made Gains in the 1970s, Outpacing Rest of the Population." *Wall Street Journal* (February 17): 1, 24.

Gould, Stephen Jay
1976 "Biological potential vs. biological determinism." Pp. 343–351 in Arthur L. Caplan (ed.), *The Sociobiology Debate*. New York: Harper & Row.

Gove, Walter R.
1973 "Sex, marital status, and mortality." *American Journal of Sociology* 79: 45–67.

Gove, Walter R.
1972 "The relationship between sex roles, marital status, and mental illness." *Social Forces* 51: 34–44.

Gove, Walter R., and Jeanette F. Tudor
1973 "Adult sex roles and mental illness." *American Journal of Sociology* 78: 812–832.

Graham, Robert
1979 *Iran: The Illusion of Power*. New York: St. Martin's Press.

Granovetter, Mark
1979 "Toward a sociological theory of income differences." Paper presented at the annual meeting of the American Sociological Association, Boston.

Granovetter, Mark S.
1974 *Getting a Job: A study of contacts and careers*. Cambridge, MA: Harvard University Press.

Greeley, Andrew
1972 *The Denominational Society*. Glenview, IL: Scott, Foresman.

Green, R. H.
1979 *Namibia in Transition: Towards a Political Economy of Liberation*. Sussex, England: Institute of Development Studies.

Green, Russell, and Leonard Berkowitz
1966 "Name-mediated aggressive cue properties." *Journal of Personality* 34: 456–465.

Green, Robert L., Louis J. Hoffmann, Richard J. Morse, Marilyn E. Hayes, and Robert F. Morgan
1964 "The educational status of children in a district without public schools." Cooperative Research Project 2321. Washington, D.C.: U.S. Office of Education.

Greenberg, B. S., and B. Dervin
1970 *Use of the Mass Media by the Urban Poor*. New York: Praeger.

Greenberg, David
1981 Personal communication.

Greenberg, David F. (ed.)
1981 *Crime and Capitalism.* Palo Alto, CA: Mayfield.

Greenberg, David F.
1977a "Delinquency and the age structure of society." *Contemporary Crises* 1: 189–223.

Greenberg, David F.
1977b "The dynamics of oscillatory punishment processes." *Journal of Criminal Law and Criminology* 68: 643–651.

Greenberg, David F.
1977c "The correctional effects of corrections: A survey of evaluations." Pp. 111–148 in David F. Greenberg (ed.), *Corrections and Punishment.* Beverly Hills, CA: Sage.

Greenberg, David F.
1976 "On one-dimensional Marxist criminology." *Theory and Society* 3: 610–621.

Greenberg, David F., and Marcia H. Bystryn
1982 "Christian intolerance of homosexuality." *American Journal of Sociology* 88: 515–548.

Greenberg, David F., and Marcia H. Bystryn
1978 "Social sources of the prohibition against male homosexuality." Paper presented at the annual meeting of the Society for the Study of Social Problems.

Greenberg, David F., Ronald C. Kessler, and Charles H. Logan
1977 "Crime rates and arrest rates: A casual analysis." *American Sociological Review* 44: 843–850.

Grett, Wayne
1978 "More sports." *Des Moines Tribune* (April 5): 34.

Haas, Linda
1980 "Domestic role-sharing in Sweden." Paper presented at the annual meeting of the American Sociological Association, New York.

Habermas, Jürgen
1970 *Toward a Rational Society.* Boston: Beacon.

Hacker, Andrew (ed.)
1983 *U/S: A Statistical Portrait of the American People.* New York: Viking.

Hacker, Andrew
1980 "Creating inequality in America." *New York Review of Books* (March 20): 20–27.

Hacker, Helen
1951 "Women as a minority group." *Social Forces* 30: 60–69.

Haerle, Rudolph D. Jr.
1975 "Education, athletic scholarships, and the occupational career of the professional athlete." *Sociology of Work and Occupations* 2 (November): 373–403.

Hagen, John
1975 "The social and legal construction of criminal justice: A study of the presentencing process." *Social Problems* 22: 620–637.

Hagen, John
1974 "Extra-legal attributes and criminal sentencing: An assessment of a sociological viewpoint." *Law and Society Review* 8: 357–383.

Haggstrom, Gus W., Thomas J. Blaschke, David E. Kanouse, William Lisowski, and Peter A. Morrison
1981 *Teenage Parents: Their Ambitions and Attainments.* Santa Monica, CA: RAND.

Hall, Edward T.
1966 *The Hidden Dimension.* Garden City, NY: Doubleday-Anchor.

Hammack, Floyd Morgan, and Peter W. Cookson Jr.
1980 "Colleges attended by graduates of elite secondary schools." *The Educational Forum* 44 (May): 483–490.

The Hammond Almanac
1979 Maplewood, NJ: Hammond Almanac, Inc.

Hannan, Michael T., and John Freeman
1977 "The population ecology of organizations." *American Journal of Sociology* 82: 929–966.

Harder, Mary W., J. T. Richardson, and R. B. Simmonds
1972 "The Jesus people." *Psychology Today* 6: 45ff.

Hardt, R. H.
1968 "Delinquency and social class: Bad kids or good cops?" Pp. 132–145 in I. Deutscher and E. Thompson (eds.), *Among the People: Encounters with the Poor.* New York: Basic Books.

Hardy, James D., Harold G. Wolff, and Helen Goodell
1952 *Pain Sensations and Reactions.* Baltimore: Williams and Wilkins.

Hare, A. Paul
1976 *Handbook of Small Group Research.* Second edition. New York: Free Press.

Harlow, Harry F.
1963 The maternal affectional system. Pp. 3–33 in B. M. Foss (ed.), *The Determinants of Infant Behavior.* New York: Wiley.

Harlow, H. F., and M. K. Harlow
1965 "The affectional systems." Pp. 287–334 in S. Schrier, H. F. Harlow, and F. Stollnitz (eds), *Behavior of Nonhuman Primates.* Volume II. New York: Academic Press.

Harper, Robert G., Arthur N. Wiens, and Joseph D. Matarazzo
1978 *Nonverbal Communication: The State of the Art.* New York: Wiley.

Harris, Chauncey D., and Edward L. Ullman
1945 "The nature of cities." *The Annals of the American Academy of Political and Social Science* 242: 7–17.

Harris, Marvin
1979 *Cultural Materialism: The Struggle for a Science of Culture*. New York: Random House.

Harris, Marvin
1977 *Cannibals and Kings: The Origins of Cultures*. New York: Vintage.

Harris, Marvin
1974 *Cows, Pigs, Wars and Witches: The Riddles of Culture*. New York: Random House.

Harris Survey
1981 "Legalized abortion supported by majority of Americans." (June 4). New York: Chicago Tribune-New York News Syndicate, Inc.

Hartley, Wynona S.
1968 "Self-conception and organizational adaptation." Paper presented at the annual meeting of the Midwest Sociological Association.

Hass, Aaron
1979 *Teenage Sexuality*. New York: Macmillan.

Hatt, Paul K., and Cecil C. North
1947 "Jobs and occupations: A popular evaluation." *Opinion News* 9 (September): 1–13.

Health, Education and Welfare
1973 *Work in America*. Cambridge, MA: MIT Press.

Hechinger, Fred M.
1980 "Is one-parent household a handicap for pupils?" *New York Times* (September 30): C1, C5.

Heer, David M.
1975 *Society and Population*. Second edition. Englewood Cliffs, NJ: Prentice-Hall.

Heide, Wilma
1978 "Feminism for a sporting future." In Carole A. Oglesby (ed.), *Women and Sport: From Myth to Reality*. Philadelphia: Lea and Febiger.

Henslin, James, and Mae A. Briggs
1971 "Dramaturgical desexualization: The sociology of the vaginal examination." In James M. Henslin (ed.), *Studies in the Sociology of Sex*. New York: Appleton-Century-Crofts.

Herbers, John
1981a "Hispanic gains in suburbs found." *New York Times* (June 28): 1, 36.

Herbers, John
1981b "Blacks returning to southern cities." *New York Times* (July 5): 1, 9.

Herzog, Herta
1955 "Why did people believe in the 'Invasion from Mars'?" Pp. 420–428 in Paul F. Lazarsfeld and Morris Rosenberg (eds.), *The Language of Social Research*. New York: Free Press.

Hess, Robert D., and Torney, Judith V.
1967 *The Development of Political Attitudes in Children*. Chicago: Aldine.

Heyns, Barbara
1978 *Summer Learning and the Effects of Schooling*. New York: Academic Press.

Hill, Robert
1971 *The Strengths of Black Families*. New York: Emerson Hall.

Hindelang, Michael J.
1976 *An Analysis of Victimization Survey Results from the Eight Impact Cities*. U.S. Department of Justice, Law Enforcement Assistance Administration. Washington, D.C.: U.S. Government Printing Office.

Hindelang, Michael J., Michael R. Gottfredson, and Timothy J. Flanagan (eds.)
1981 *Sourcebook of Criminal Justice Statistics—1980*. U.S. Department of Justice, Bureau of Justice Statistics. Washington, D.C.: U.S. Government Printing Office.

Hindelang, Michael J., Travis Hirschi, and Joseph C. Weis
1979 "Correlates of delinquency: The illusion of discrepancy between self-report and official measures." *American Sociological Review* 44: 995–1014.

Hirschi, Travis
1969 *Causes of Delinquency*. Berkeley: University of California Press.

Hobbes, Thomas
1651/1962 *Leviathan*. Michael Oakeshott (ed.). New York: Macmillan.

Hoch, Paul
1972 *Rip Off the Big Game*. Garden City, NY: Doubleday.

Hochschild, Arlie
1983 *The Managed Heart*. Berkeley: University of California Press.

Hochschild, Arlie
1978 "Conventionalizing feeling, putting it on the market, and looking for 'authenticity.'" Paper presented at the International Sociological Association meeting.

Hochschild, Arlie
1973a "A review of sex role research." *American Journal of Sociology* 78: 249–267.

Hochschild, Arlie
1973b *The Unexpected Community*. Englewood Cliffs, NJ: Prentice-Hall.

Hodge, Robert W., and Donald J. Treiman
1968 "Class identification in the United States." *American Journal of Sociology* 73: 535–547.

Hodge, Robert W., Paul M. Siegel, and Peter H. Rossi

1966 "Occupational prestige in the United States: 1925–1963." Pp. 322–334 in Reinhard Bendix and Seymour Martin Lipset (eds.), *Class, Status, and Power.* Second edition. New York: Free Press.

Hodge, Robert W., Donald J. Treiman, and Peter H. Rossi

1966 "A comparative study of occupational prestige." Pp. 309–321 in Reinhard Bendix and Seymour Martin Lipset (eds.), *Class, Status, and Power.* Second edition. New York: Free Press.

Hodges, David A.

1979 "The microelectronics revolution." Testimony before the University of California Board of Regents.

Hodgson, Bryan

1982 "Namibia: Nearly a Nation?" *National Geographic* 161: 754–797.

Hoffman, Lois W.

1974 "Fear of success in males and females: 1965 and 1971." *Journal of Consulting and Clinical Psychology* 42: 353–358.

Hoffman, Lois W.

1963 "Effects on children: Summary and discussion." In F. I. Nye and L. W. Hoffman (eds.), *The Employed Mother in America.* Chicago: Rand McNally.

Hoffman, Lois W., and F. I. Nye (eds.)

1974 *Working Mothers.* San Francisco: Jossey-Bass.

Hoffman, Martin

1979 "The male prostitute." Pp. 275–284 in Martin P. Levine (ed.), *Gay Men.* New York: Harper & Row.

Hohenstein, William F.

1969 "Factors influencing the police disposition of juvenile offenders." Pp. 138–149 in Thorsten Sellin and Marvin E. Wolfgang (eds.), *Delinquency: Selected Studies.* New York: Wiley.

Holland, Judith R., and Carole Oglesby

1979 "Women in sport: The synthesis begins." *The Annals of the American Academy of Political and Social Science* 445 (September): 80–90.

Hollander v. *Connecticut Interstate Athletic Conference*

1971 Superior Court of New Haven, County Court (March 29).

Homans, George

1961 *Social Behavior: Its Elementary Forms.* New York: Harcourt Brace Jovanovich.

Homans, George C.

1950 *The Human Group.* New York: Harcourt Brace Jovanovich.

Horowitz, Irving Louis

1962 "Consensus, conflict, and cooperation." *Social Forces* 41: 177–188.

Houseman, John

1948 "The Men from Mars." *Harper's Magazine* 197 (December): 78–82.

Hoyt, Homer

1939 *The Structure and Growth of Residential Neighborhoods in American Cities.* Washington, D.C.: Federal Housing Authority.

Huber, Joan, and William H. Form

1973 *Income and Ideology: An Analysis of the American Political Formula.* New York: Free Press.

Huffell, Walter

1982 Personal telephone communication (June 4).

Hughes, Everett C.

1945 "Dilemmas and contradictions of status." *American Journal of Sociology* (March) 50: 353–359.

Humphreys, Laud

1972 *Out of the Closets: The Sociology of Homosexual Liberation.* Englewood Cliffs, NJ: Prentice-Hall.

Humphreys, Laud

1970 *Tearoom Trade: Impersonal Sex in Public Places.* Chicago: Aldine.

Hunt, Chester L., and Lewis Walker

1974 *Ethnic Diversity.* Homewood, IL: Dorsey Press.

Hunt, Morton M.

1974 *Sexual Behavior in the 1970s.* Chicago: Playboy Press.

Hunter, Floyd

1953 *Community Power Structure.* Chapel Hill: University of North Carolina Press.

Hurn, Christopher J.

1978 *The Limits and Possibilities of Schooling.* Boston: Allyn and Bacon.

Hyman, Herbert H., Charles R. Wright, and John Shelton Reed

1975 *The Enduring Effects of Education.* Chicago: University of Chicago Press.

Illinois Institute for Juvenile Research

1972 *Juvenile Delinquency in Illinois.* Chicago: Illinois Department of Mental Health.

Ingrassia, Lawrence

1980 "Taking chances: How four companies spawn new projects by encouraging risks." *Wall Street Journal* (September 18): 1, 19.

Inkeles, Alex, and David H. Smith

1974 *Becoming Modern.* Cambridge, MA: Harvard University Press.

Jackson, Philip W.
1968 *Life in Classrooms*. New York: Holt, Rinehart, and Winston.

Jacobs, Carol, and Cynthia Eaton
1972 "Sexism in the elementary school." *Today's Education* 61: 20–22.

Jaffe, A. J., and W. Adams
1970 "Academic and social factors related to entrance and retention at two- and four-year colleges in the late 1960's." New York: Bureau of Applied Social Research, Columbia University.

Jahoda, Marie, Paul Lazarsfeld, and Hans Zeisel
1971 *Marienthal: The Sociology of an Unemployed Community*. Chicago: Aldine/Atherton.

Janis, Irving L.
1973 *Victims of Groupthink*. Boston: Houghton Mifflin.

Janis, Irving L., and Leon Mann
1979 *Decision Making: A Psychological Analysis of Conflict, Choice, and Commitment*. New York: Free Press.

Jencks, Christopher, Susan Bartlett, Mary Corcoran, James Crouse, David Eaglesfield, Gregory Jackson, Kent McClelland, Peter Mueser, Michael Olneck, Joseph Schwartz, Sherry Ward, and Jill Williams
1979 *Who Gets Ahead? The Determinants of Economic Success in America*. New York: Basic Books.

Jencks, Christopher, Marshall Smith, Henry Acland, Mary Jo Bane, David Cohen, Herbert Gintis, Barbara Heyns, and Stephan Michelson
1972 *Inequality: A Reassessment of the Effect of Family and Schooling in America*. New York: Basic Books.

Jennings, M. Kent, and Richard G. Niemi
1968 "Patterns of political learning." *Harvard Educational Review* 38 (summer): 443–467.

Jensen, Arthur R.
1969 "How much can we boost I.Q. and scholastic achievement?" *Harvard Educational Review* 39: 1–123.

Jensen, Gary, and Raymond Eve
1976 "Sex differences in delinquency." *Criminology* 13 (February): 427–448.

Joffe, Carole
1979 "Symbolic interactionism and the study of social services." Pp. 235–256 in Norman K. Denzin (ed.), *Studies in Symbolic Interaction*. Volume 2. Greenwich, CT: JAI Press.

Johnson, Douglas W., Paul R. Picard, and Bernard Quinn
1974 *Churches and Church Membership in the United States*. Washington, D.C.: Glenmary Research Center.

Johnson, Gregory
1976 "The Hare Krishna in San Francisco." Pp. 31–51 in C. Glock and R. Bellah (eds.), *The New Religious Consciousness*. Berkeley: University of California Press.

Johnson, Kirk
1982 "The executives who are hooked on squash." *New York Times* (March 21): 9.

Johnson, Sheila K.
1971 "Sociology of Christmas cards." *Society* 8: 27–29.

Judah, J. Stillson
1974 "The Hare Krishna in San Fancisco." Pp. 31–51 in C. Glock and R. Bellah (eds.), *The New Religious Consciousness*. Berkeley: University of California Press.

Kalleberg, Arne L., and Larry J. Griffin
1980 "Class, occupation, and inequality in job rewards." *American Journal of Sociology* 85: 731–768.

Kalven, Harry, and Hans Zeisel
1966 *The American Jury*. Boston: Little Brown.

Kamerman, Sheila B.
1979 "Parenting in an unresponsive society." Notes: Program in Sex Roles and Social Change, Center for the Social Sciences, Columbia University (spring): 1–2.

Kamin, Leon J.
1974 *The Science and Politics of I.Q.* Hillsdale, NJ: Erlbaum.

Kanter, Rosabeth Moss
1979 "Complex organizations." Paper presented at the annual meeting of the American Sociological Association, Boston.

Kanter, Rosabeth Moss
1977 *Men and Women of the Corporation*. New York: Basic Books.

Kanter, Rosabeth Moss
1972 *Commitment and Community: Communes and Utopias in Sociological Perspective*. Cambridge, MA: Harvard University Press.

Karier, Clarence J.
1973 "Testing for order and control in the corporate liberal state." Pp. 108–137 in Clarence J. Karier, Paul Violas, and Joel Spring (eds.), *Roots of Crisis: American Education in the Twentieth Century*. Chicago: Rand McNally.

Katchadourian, Herant A., and Donald T. Lunde
1972 *Fundamentals of Human Sexuality*. New York: Holt, Rinehart and Winston.

Katz, Joseph, et al.
1968 *No Time for Youth: Growth and Constraint in College Students*. San Francisco: Jossey-Bass.

Katz, Marlaine L.

1972 "Female motive to avoid success: A psychological barrier or a response to deviance?" Unpublished manuscript, School of Education, Stanford University.

Katz, Michael B.
1977 "Education and inequality: An historical perspective." Paper presented for Russell Sage Foundation project on history and social policy. New York.

Kedourie, Elie
1980 "Islam resurgent." Pp. 58–63 in *Britannica Book of the Year.* Chicago: Encyclopaedia Britannica.

Kelly, James
1982 "Unemployment on the rise." *Time* (February 8): 22–29.

Kemer, B. J.
1965 "A study of the relationship between the sex of the student and the assignment of marks by secondary school teachers." Ph.D. dissertation, Michigan State University.

Keniston, Kenneth, and Carnegie Council on Children
1977 *All Our Children.* New York: Harcourt Brace Jovanovich.

Kephart, William M.
1950 "A quantitative analysis of intragroup relationships." *American Journal of Sociology* 60: 544–549.

Kerr, Norman D.
1973 "The school board as an agency of legitimation." Pp. 380–400 in Sam Sieber and David Wilder, *The School in Society.* New York: Free Press.

Kerr, Norman D.
1964 "The school board as an agency of legitimation." *Sociology of Education* 38: 34–59.

Kessin, Kenneth
1971 "Social and psychological consequences of intergenerational occupational mobility." *American Journal of Sociology* 77: 1–18.

Keynes, John Maynard
1936/1973 *The General Theory of Employment, Interest and Money.* New York: Cambridge University Press.

Kidder, Tracy
1981 *The Soul of a New Machine.* Boston: Atlantic/Little, Brown.

King, K., J. McIntyre, and L. J. Axelson
1968 "Adolescent views of maternal employment as a threat to the marital relationship." *Journal of Marriage and the Family* 30: 633–637.

Kinsey, Alfred C., Wardell B. Pomeroy, Clyde E. Martin, and Paul H. Gebhard
1953 *Sexual Behavior in the Human Female.* Philadelphia: Saunders.

Kinsey, Alfred C., Wardell B. Pomeroy, and Clyde E. Martin
1948 *Sexual Behavior in the Human Male.* Philadelphia: Saunders.

Kirkham, George Lester
1971 "Homosexuality in prison." Pp. 325–349 in James M. Henslin (ed.), *Studies in the Sociology of Sex.* New York: Appleton-Century-Crofts.

Kitagawa, Evelyn M.
1972 "Socioeconomic differences in mortality in the United States and some implications for population policy." In Charles F. Westoff and Robert Parke Jr., (eds.), *Demographic and Social Aspects of Population Growth and the American Future.* Volume 1. Washington, D.C.: Commission on Population Growth and the American Future.

Kitano, Harry H. L.
1981 "Asian-Americans: The Chinese, Japanese, Koreans, Filipinos, and Southeast Asians." *The Annals of the American Academy of Political and Social Science* 454 (March): 125–138.

Kleck, Gary
1981 "Racial discrimination in criminal sentencing: A critical evaluation of the evidence with additional evidence on the death penalty." *American Sociological Review* 46 (December): 783–805.

Klein, Frederick C.
1982 "The Richest Oriole: A millionaire slugger, Eddie Murray keeps his eye on 'real life.'" *Wall Street Journal* (April 5): 1, 18.

Klein, Heywood
1981 "Goal posts tumble like tackled backs at college stadiums." *Wall Street Journal* (November 3): 1, 23.

Kluckhohn, Clyde
1954 *Mirror for Man.* New York: McGraw-Hill.

Kohlberg, Lawrence
1981 *The Philosophy of Moral Development: Essays in Moral Development.* New York: Harper & Row.

Kohlberg, Lawrence
1976 "Moral stages and moralization: The cognitive-developmental approach." Pp. 31–53 in Thomas Lickona (ed.), *Moral Development and Behavior: Theory, Research, and Social Issues.* New York: Holt, Rinehart and Winston.

Kohlberg, Lawrence
1969 "Stage and sequence: The cognitive-developmental approach to socialization." Pp.

347–480 in D. A. Goslin (ed.), *Handbook of Socialization Theory and Research*. Chicago: Rand McNally.

Kohlberg, Lawrence
1963 "The development of children's orientation toward a moral order. Sequence in the development of moral thought." *Vita Humana* 6: 11–33.

Kohn, Melvin
1969 *Class and Conformity*. Homewood, IL: Dorsey Press.

Komarovsky, Mirra
1962 *Blue-Collar Marriage*. New York: Vintage.

Komarovsky, Mirra
1940/1971 *The Unemployed Man and His Family*. New York: Octagon Books.

Korte, Charles, and Stanley Milgram
1970 "Acquaintance links between white and Negro populations: Applications of the small world method." *Journal of Personality and Social Psychology* 15: 101–108.

Kramer, Cheris
1975 "Women's speech: Separate but unequal?" Pp. 43–56 in Barrie Thorne and Nancy Henley (eds.), *Language and Sex: Difference and Dominance*. Rowley, MA: Newbury House.

Kubler-Ross, Elisabeth
1969 *On Death and Dying*. New York: Macmillan.

Kuhn, Manford H., and Thomas S. McPartland
1954 "An empirical investigation of self-attitudes." *American Sociological Review* 19 (February): 68–76.

Kuhn, Thomas S.
1970a *The Structure of Scientific Revolutions*. Second edition, enlarged. Chicago: University of Chicago Press.

Kuhn, Thomas S.
1970b "Reflections on my critics." Pp. 231–278 in I. Lakatos and A. Musgrave (eds.), *Criticism and the Growth of Knowledge*. New York: Cambridge University Press.

Kuhn, Thomas S.
1962 *The Structure of Scientific Revolutions*. Chicago: University of Chicago Press.

Labov, William
1973 "The logic of nonstandard English." Pp. 21–66 in N. Keddie (ed.), *The Myth of Cultural Deprivation*. Harmondsworth, Eng.: Penguin.

Ladd, Everett Jr.
1978 "The new lines are drawn: Class and ideology in America." *Public Opinion* (July–August): 48–53.

Lane, Harlan
1976 *The Wild Boy of Aveyron*. Cambridge, MA: Harvard University Press.

Lapham, Lewis
1980 *Fortune's Child*. Garden City, NY: Doubleday.

Lapidus, Gail Warshofsky
1978 *Women in Soviet Society*. Berkeley: University of California Press.

Langley, Monica
1981 "Perks at parks help perk up vacations of federal VIPs." *Wall Street Journal* (June 14): 1, 16.

Lasch, Christopher
1979 *The Culture of Narcissism*. New York: Norton.

Latané, Bibb, and John M. Darley
1970 *The Unresponsive Bystander: Why Doesn't He Help?* Englewood Cliffs, NJ: Prentice-Hall.

Lathrop, Richard
1977 *Who's Hiring Who*. Berkeley, CA: Ten Speed Press.

Lauer, Robert H.
1976 "Afterword: Summary and directions for the future." Pp. 259–264 in Robert H. Lauer (ed.), *Social Movements and Social Change*. Carbondale: Southern Illinois University Press.

Lauer, Robert H.
1975 "Occupational and religious mobility in a small city." *Sociological Quarterly* 16: 380–392.

Lawrence, Paul, and Jay Lorsch
1967 *Organization and Environment*. Cambridge, MA: Harvard University Press.

Lazarsfeld, Paul, Bernard Berelson, and Hazel Gaudet
1944 *The People's Choice*. New York: Columbia University Press.

Le Bon, Gustav
1960 *The Crowd*. New York: Viking Press. First published in 1895.

Leavitt, H. J.
1964 *Managerial Psychology*. Chicago: University of Chicago press.

Lehman, Edward W.
1977 *Political Society: A Macrosociology of Politics*. New York: Columbia University Press.

Lemert, Edwin M.
1951 *Social pathology*. New York: McGraw-Hill.

Lenski, Gerhard
1979 "Marxist experiments in destratification: An appraisal." *Social Forces* 57: 364–383.

Lenski, Gerhard E.
1966 *Power and Privilege: A Theory of Social Stratification*. New York: McGraw-Hill.

Lenski, Gerhard, and Jean Lenski
1978 *Human Societies: An Introduction to Macrosociology*. Third edition. New York: McGraw-Hill.

Lerner, Daniel
1968 "Modernization: Social Aspects." In D. L. Sills (ed.), *International Encyclopedia of the Social Sciences*. Volume 10. New York: Free Press.

Lerner, I. M.
1968 *Heredity, Evolution, and Society*. San Francisco: Freeman.

Levine, Joel H.
1972 "The sphere of influence." *American Sociological Review* 37 (February): 14–27.

Levine, Martin P. (ed.)
1979 *Gay Men*. New York: Harper & Row.

LeVine, Robert A., and Donald T. Campbell
1972 *Ethnocentrism: Theories of Conflict, Ethnic Attitudes, and Group Behavior*. New York: Wiley.

Levinger, George
1965 "Marital cohesiveness and dissolution: An integrative review." *Journal of Marriage and the Family* 27: 19–28.

Levinson, Daniel J., with Charlotte N. Darrow, Edward B. Klein, Maria H. Levinson, and Braxton McKee
1978 *The Seasons of a Man's Life*. New York: Knopf.

Lévi-Strauss, Claude
1956 "The Family." Pp. 142–170 in Harry L. Shapiro (ed.), *Man, Culture, and Society*. New York: Oxford University Press.

Levitt, Eugene E., and Albert D. Klassen Jr.
1979 "Public attitudes toward homosexuality." Pp. 19–35 in Martin P. Levine (ed.), *Gay Men*. New York: Harper & Row.

Lewis, Gordon H.
1972 "Role differentiation." *American Sociological Review* 37: 424–434.

Lewis, Jerry M.
1975 "Sports riots: Some research questions." Paper presented at the annual meeting of the American Sociological Association, San Francisco.

Lewis, Oscar
1965 *La Vida*. New York: Random House.

Light, Richard J.
1974 "Abused and neglected children in America: A study of alternative policies." *Harvard Educational Review* 43 (November): 556–598.

Lin, Nan, Walter M. Ensel, and John C. Vaughn
1981 "Social resources and strength of ties: Structural factors in occupational status attainment." *American Sociological Review* 46 (August): 393–405.

Lindner, Robert
1951 "Sex in prison." *Complex* 6: 5–20.

Lipset, Seymour Martin, and Reinhard Bendix
1959 *Social Mobility in Industrial Society*. Berkeley: University of California Press.

Lipton, Douglass, Robert Martinson, and Judith Wilks
1975 *The Effectiveness of Correctional Treatment: A Survey of Treatment Evaluation Studies*. New York: Praeger.

Liska, A. E., and M. Tausig
1979 "Theoretical interpretations of social class and racial differentials in legal decision-making for juveniles." *The Sociological Quarterly* 20: 197–207.

Littell, Franklin H.
1981 "World church membership." P. 604 in *Britannica Book of the Year*. Chicago: Encyclopaedia Britannica.

Lizotte, Alan J.
1978 "Extra-legal factors in Chicago's criminal courts: Testing the conflict model of criminal justice." *Social Problems* 25: 564–580.

Lockwood, Daniel
1979 *Prison Sexual Violence*. New York: Elsevier.

Lombroso, Cesare
1911/1968 *Crime: Its Causes and Remedies*. Henry P. Horton, tr. Montclair, NJ: Patterson Smith.

Lopata, Helena Z.
1972 *Occupation: Housewife*. New York: Oxford University Press.

Lohr, Steve
1981 "How tax evasion has grown." *New York Times* (March 15): 3: 1, 15.

Long, Larry, and Diana DeAre
1981 "The suburbanization of blacks." *American Demographics* 3: 16–21, 44.

Lorenz, Konrad Z.
1952 *King Solomon's Ring*. London: Methuen.

Loy, John W. Jr.
1969 "The study of sport and social mobility." Pp. 101–119 in G. S. Kenyon (ed.), *Aspects of Contemporary Sport Sociology*. Chicago: The Athletic Institute.

Loy, John W. Jr.
1968 "The nature of sport: A definitional effort." *Quest,* Monograph 10 (May): 1–15.

Loy, John W., and J. F. McElvogue
1970 "Racial segregation in American sport." *The International Review of Sport Sociology* 5: 5–23.

Loy, John W., Barry D. McPherson, and Gerald

Kenyon
1978 *Sport and Social Systems.* Reading, MA: Addison-Wesley.

Ludwig, Ed, and James Santibanez (eds.)
1971 *The Chicanos: Mexican American Voices.* Baltimore: Penguin.

Lupri, E.
1969 "Contemporary authority patterns in the West German family: A study in cross-national validation." *Journal of Marriage and the Family* 31: 134–144.

Lyle, J., and H. R. Hoffman
1972 "Children's use of television and other media." Pp. 129–256 in E. A. Rubinstein, G. A. Comstock, and J. P. Murray (eds.), *Television and Social Behavior.* Volume 4: *Television in Day-to-Day Life: Patterns of Use.* Washington, D.C.: U. S. Government Printing Office.

Lyman, Stanford M.
1977 *The Asian in North America.* Santa Barbara, CA: American Bibliographical Center–Clio Press.

Lynd, Robert S., and Helen Merrell Lynd
1929 *Middletown: A Study in American Culture.* New York: Harcourt Brace Jovanovich.

McCall, George J., and J. L. Simmons
1969 *Issues in Participant Observation: A Text and Reader.* Reading, MA: Addison-Wesley.

McCall, George J., and J. L. Simmons
1966 *Identities and Interactions.* New York: Free Press.

McCarthy, John D., and Mayer N. Zald
1977 "Resource mobilization and social movements: A partial theory." *American Journal of Sociology* 82: 1212–1241.

McCarthy, John E.
1980 "The boat people." Pp. 594–596 in *Britannica Book of the Year.* Chicago: Encyclopaedia Britannica.

McCleery, Richard H.
1966 "Policy change in prison management." Pp. 376–400 in Amitai Etzioni (ed.), *Complex Organizations: A Reader.* New York: Holt, Rinehart and Winston.

McDowell, Edwin
1979 "Imports and trucks aid dealers." *New York Times* (August 20): D1, D6.

McGregor, Douglas
1960 *The Human Side of Enterprise.* New York: McGraw-Hill.

McKinlay, John B.
1981 "A case for refocusing upstream: The political economy of illness." Pp. 613–633 in Peter Conrad and Rochelle Kern (eds.), *The Sociology of Health and Illness.* New York: St. Martin's Press.

MacAvoy, Paul W.
1982 "The underground—no recession there." *New York Times* (July 4): F3.

Maccoby, Eleanor
1966 "Sex differences in intellectual functioning." Pp. 25–55 in Eleanor Maccoby (ed.), *The Development of Sex Differences.* Stanford, CA: Stanford University Press.

Maccoby, Eleanor E., and Carol N. Jacklin
1974 *The Psychology of Sex Differences.* Stanford, CA: Stanford University Press.

MacLeish, Kenneth
1972 "Stone age men of the Philippines." *National Geographic* 142: 218–249.

Machiavelli, Niccolo
1513/1900 *The Prince.* New York: New American Library.

MacNamara, Donal E. J., and Edward Sagarin
1977 *Sex, Crime, and the Law.* New York: Free Press.

Magnuson, Ed
1980 "The poisoning of America." *Time* (September 22): 58–69.

Magdoff, H.
1978 *Imperialism: From the Colonial Era to the Present.* New York: Monthly Review Press.

Malabie, Alfred L. Jr.
1981 "Off-the-books business booms in Europe." *Wall Street Journal* (August 24): 1.

Malinowski, Bronislaw
1948 *Magic, Science and Religion.* Garden City, NY: Doubleday-Anchor.

Malinowski, B.
1926 "Anthropology." *Encyclopaedia Britannica.* Pp. 132–133, first supplementary volume. London and New York: Encyclopaedia Britannica.

Malson, Lucien
1972 *Wolf Children and the Problem of Human Nature.* New York: New Left Books.

Malthus, Thomas R.
1798/1965 *An Essay on Population.* New York: Augustus Kelley, Bookseller.

Manis, Jerome G., and Bernard N. Meltzer
1978 *Symbolic Interaction: A Reader in Social Psychology.* Boston: Allyn and Bacon.

Marin, Peter
1975 "The new narcissism: The trouble with the human potential movement." *Harpers* 251: 45–56.

Marshall, Victor W.
1975 "Socialization for impending death in a retirement village." *American Journal of Sociology*

80: 1124–1144.

Martin, Susan E.
1982 Personal communication (February 1).

Martin, Susan E.
1980 *Breaking and Entering: Policewomen on Patrol*. Berkeley: University of California Press.

Martinson, Robert
1974 "What works? Questions and answers about prison reform." *Public Interest* 10: 22–54.

Marty, Martin E.
1982 "Religion in America since mid-century." *Daedalus* 3: 149–163.

Marty, Martin E.
1981 "The new Christian right." Pp. 605–606 in *Britannica Book of the Year*. Chicago: Encyclopaedia Britannica.

Marty, Martin E.
1980 "Resurgent fundamentalism." Pp. 606–607 in *Britannica Book of the Year*. Chicago: Encyclopaedia Britannica.

Marty, Martin E.
1976 *A Nation of Behavers*. Chicago: University of Chicago Press.

Marwell, Gerald
1975 "Why ascription? Parts of a more or less formal theory of the functions and dysfunctions of sex roles." *American Sociological Review* 40: 445–455.

Marx, Gary T.
1970 "Issueless riots." *Annals of the American Academy of Political and Social Science* 391 (September): 12–33.

Marx, Gary T. and James L. Wood
1975 "Strands of theory and research in collective behavior." Pp. 363–428 in Alex Inkeles, James Coleman, and Neil Smelser (eds.), *Annual Review of Sociology*, volume 1. Palo Alto, CA: Annual Reviews Inc.

Marx, Karl
1867–1895/1967 *Capital*. New York: International.

Marx, Karl, and Engels, Frederick
1846/1947 *The German Ideology*. Parts I and II. R. Pascal (ed.). New York: International.

Masaoka, Mike
1972 "The evacuation of the Japanese Americans and its aftermath." Pp. 186–195 in Arnold Rose and Caroline Rose (eds.), *Minority Problems*. New York: Harper & Row.

Masnick, George, and Mary Jo Bane
1980 The Nation's Families: 1960–1990. Cambridge, MA: Joint Center for Urban Studies, MIT and Harvard University.

Masters, William Howell, and Virginia Johnson
1979 *Homosexuality in Perspective*. Boston: Little, Brown.

Mattera, Marianne Dekker
1980 "Female doctors: Why they're on an economic treadmill." *Medical Economics* 57 (February 18): 98–110.

Matza, David
1969 *Becoming Deviant*. Englewood Cliffs, NJ: Prentice-Hall.

Maurer, Harry
1979 *Not Working: An Oral History of the Unemployed*. New York: Holt, Rinehart and Winston.

Mauss, Marcel
1954 *The Gift*. New York: Free Press.

May, Edward
1982 "Impasse in Namibia." *Christianity and Crisis* 42 (June 7): 159–164.

Mayer, Martin
1974 *The Bankers*. New York: Ballantine.

Mead, George Herbert
1934 *Mind, Self, and Society*. Chicago: University of Chicago Press.

Mead, Margaret
1935 *Sex and Temperament in Three Primitive Societies*. New York: Morrow.

Meadows, D. H., D. L. Meadows, J. Randers, and W. Behrens, III
1972 *The Limits to Growth*. New York: New American Library.

Mehan, Hugh
1978 "Structuring school structure." *Harvard Educational Review* 48: 32–64.

Mehan, Hugh
1974 "Ethnomethodology and education." Pp. 141–198 in David W. O'Shea (ed.), *Sociology of the School and Schooling*. Washington, D.C.: National Institute of Education.

Meier, H. C.
1972 "Mother-centeredness and college youth's attitudes toward social equality for women: Some empirical findings." *Journal of Marriage and the Family* 34: 115–121.

Melbin, Murray
1979 "Settling the frontier of night." *Psychology Today* (June): 40–41, 43, 45, 47, 51, 94, 96, 97.

Melman, Seymour
1974 *The Permanent War Economy: American Capitalism in Decline*. New York: Simon and Schuster.

Merton, Robert K.
1970 "Social and cultural contexts of science." Originally published as "Preface: 1970," in Robert K. Merton, *Science, Technology and Society in Seventeenth-Century England*. New York: Howard Fertig, Inc., and Harper & Row.

Merton, Robert K.
1968 "The Matthew effect in science." *Science* 159 (January 5): 56–63.

Merton, Robert K.
1957 "Science and democratic social structure." In *Social Theory and Social Structure*. New York: Free Press.

Merton, Robert K.
1957 *Social Theory and Social Structure*. New York: Free Press.

Messner, Steven F.
1980 "Income inequality and murder rates: Some cross-national findings." Pp. 185–198 in Richard Tomasson (ed.), *Comparative Social Research*. Volume 3. Greenwich, CT: JAI Press.

Messner, Steven F.
1978 "Income inequality and murder rates: Some cross-national findings." Paper presented at the annual meeting of the American Sociological Association.

Metheny, Eleanor
1965 "Symbolic forms of movement: The feminine image in sports." Pp. 289–301 in *Sport and American Society*. Reading, MA: Addison-Wesley.

Meyer, John
1977 "Education as an institution." *American Journal of Sociology* 83 (July): 55–77.

Michel, A.
1967 "Comparative data concerning the interaction in French and American families." *Journal of Marriage and the Family* 29: 337–344.

Michels, Robert
1911/1967 *Political Parties*. New York: Free Press.

Michener, James A.
1976 *Sports in America*. New York: Fawcett Crest.

Middleton, Russell
1976 "Regional differences in prejudice." *American Sociological Review* 41: 94–117.

Milgram, Stanley
1969 *Obedience to Authority*. New York: Harper & Row.

Milgram, Stanley, and John Sabini
1978 "On maintaining urban norms: A field experiment in the subway." Pp. 31–40 in A. Baum, J. Singer, and S. Valins (eds.), *Advances in Environmental Psychology*. Volume 1: *The Urban Environment*. Hillsdale, NJ: Erlbaum.

Miller, Ann R.
1978 "Changing work life patterns: A twenty-five year review." *Annals of the American Academy of Political and Social Science* 435: 83–101.

Miller, Brian
1979 "Unpromised paternity: Life styles of gay fathers." Pp. 239–252 in Martin P. Levine (ed.), *Gay Men*. New York: Harper & Row.

Miller, D. M., and K. R. E. Russell
1971 *Sport: A Contemporary View*. Philadelphia: Lea and Febiger.

Miller, Rita Sieden
1978 "The social construction and reconstruction of physiological events: Acquiring the pregnancy identity." Pp. 181–204 in Norman K. Denzin (ed.), *Studies in Symbolic Interaction*. Volume 2. Greenwich, CT: JAI Press.

Mills, C. Wright
1956 *The Power Elite*. New York: Oxford University Press.

Mincer, Jacob
1974 *Schooling, Experience and Earnings*. New York: Columbia University Press.

Minsky, Terri
1981 "Gripes of Rath: Workers who bought Iowa slaughterhouse regret that they did." *Wall Street Journal* (December 2): 1, 23.

Minuchin, Patricia
1966 "Sex differences in children: Research findings in an educational context." *National Elementary Principal* 46: 45–58.

Mitchell, Juliet
1971 *Woman's Estate*. New York: Vintage.

Mitchell, Richard G. Jr.
1983 *Mountaineering: A Sociologist's Perspective*. Chicago: University of Chicago Press.

Mitchell, Richard G. Jr.
1982 Personal communication (January 12).

Mitchell, Richard G. Jr.
1981 Personal communication.

Mizruchi, Mark S.
1982 *The American Corporate Network: 1904–1974*. Beverly Hills, CA: Sage.

Moberg, David O.
1962 *The Church as a Social Institution*. Englewood Cliffs, NJ: Prentice-Hall.

Moeller, G. H., and W. W. Charters Jr.
1970 "Relation of bureaucratization to sense of power among teachers." Pp. 638–655 in Matthew W. Miles and W. W. Charters Jr. (eds.), *Learning in Social Settings*. Boston: Allyn and Bacon.

Mol, Hans J.
1976 *Identity and the Sacred*. New York: Free Press.

Monaghan-Leckband, Kathleen
1978 "Role adaptations of single parents: A challenge of the pathological view of male and female single parents." Unpublished doctoral

dissertation, New York University.

Money, John, and Anke A. Ehrhardt
1972 *Man and Woman: Boy and Girl.* New York: Mentor.

Montagna, Paul D.
1977 *Occupations and Society: Toward a Sociology of the Labor Market.* New York: Wiley.

Moodie, T. Dunbar
1975 *The Rise of Afrikanerdom: Power, Apartheid, and the Africaner Civil Religion.* Berkeley: University of California Press.

Mooney, James
1965 *The Ghost-Dance Religion and Sioux Outbreak of 1890.* Chicago: University of Chicago Press.

Moore, Barrington Jr.
1978 *Injustice: The Social Bases of Obedience and Revolt.* White Plains, NY: M. E. Sharpe.

Moore, Didi
1983 "America's Neglected Elderly." *New York Times Magazine* (January 30): 30–32, ff.

Moore, Gwen
1979 "The structure of a national elite network." *American Sociological Review* 44: 673–692.

Morrison, Peter A.
1978 "Overview of demographic trends shaping the nation's future." Testimony before the Joint Economic Committee, U.S. Congress, May 31.

Moskal, Brian S.
1981 "The Minneapolis story: A primer on social concern." *Industry Week* (August 10): 59–61.

Moynihan, Daniel Patrick
1967 *The Negro Family: The Case for National Action.* In Lee Rainwater and William L. Yancey (eds.), *The Moynihan Report and the Politics of Controversy.* Cambridge, MA: MIT Press.

Mueller, E.
1972 "A test of a partial theory of potential for political violence." *American Political Science Review* 66 (September): 928–959.

Mumford, Lewis
1961 *The City in History.* New York: Harcourt, Brace and World.

Murdock, George
1967 *Ethnographic Atlas.* Pittsburgh, PA: University of Pittsburgh Press.

Murdock, George P.
1945 "The common denominator of cultures." Pp. 123–142 in Ralph Linton (ed.), *The Science of Man and the World Crisis.* New York: Columbia University Press.

Murillo, N.
1971 "The Mexican-American family." In N. N. Wagner and M. J. Haug (eds.), *Chicanos: Social and Psychological Perspectives.* St. Louis, MO: C. V. Mosby.

Mussen, P. H., J. J. Conger, and J. Kagan
1974 *Child Development and Personality.* New York: Harper & Row.

Mytelka, L. K.
1979 *Regional Development in a Global Economy.* New Haven, CT: Yale University Press.

Naisbitt, John
1981 "The bottom-up society: America between eras." *Public Opinion* (April–May): 18–19, 54–57.

Nance, John
1975 *The Gentle Tasaday.* New York: Harcourt Brace Jovanovich.

Needleman, Jacob
1970 *The New Religions.* Garden City, NY: Doubleday.

Nelsen, Hart M., and William E. Snizek
1976 "Musical pews: Rural and urban modes of occupational and religious mobility." *Sociology and Social Research* 60: 279–289.

Newsweek
1981 "Why public schools fail." April 20: 62–73.

Newsweek
1974 "The world food crisis: Bumper crop to empty bowls: How to ease the hunger pangs." November 11: 56–61, 67.

New York Times
1983 "B.A. degree worth $329,000 in earnings." March 14: A12.

New York Times
1983 "Job plight of young blacks tied to despair, skills lack." April 19: A14.

New York Times
1982 "China, pop. 1,008, 175, 288: One-fourth of the world." October 28.

New York Times
1982 "Nation's prisoner population rose 6.9% in first half of '82." November 8: A12.

New York Times
1981 "An apology to the internees." August 4: A14.

New York Times
1980 "Fifth World Synod of Roman Catholic bishops: Excerpts from bishops' 'message to Christian families in the modern world.'" October 26: 18.

New York Times
1980 "Marriage age is up, census data show." April 2: C17.

New York Times

1979 "Survey reports fertility levels plummet in developing nations." August 10: A8.

New York Times
1978 "College women and self-esteem." December 10: 85.

Nickerson, J.
1975 *Homage to Malthus.* Port Washington, NY: National University Publications.

Niebuhr, H. Richard
1929 *The Social Sources of Denominationalism.* New York: Holt.

Nielsen, Joyce McCarl
1978 *Sex in Society: Perspectives on Stratification.* Belmont, CA: Wadsworth.

Nielsen Television Index
n.d. *Report on Television Usage.* Hackensack, NJ: A. C. Nielsen Co.

Nisbet, Robert A.
1966 *The Sociological Tradition,* New York: Basic Books.

Noel, Donald L.
1968 "How ethnic inequality begins." *Social Problems* 16: 157–172.

NORC
1978 "General Social Survey." National Opinion Research Center, University of Chicago. Cited in *Public Opinion,* 1980.

Nye, F. Ivan
1958 *Family Relationships and Delinquent Behavior.* New York: Wiley.

Nye, F. Ivan, Joseph B. Perry Jr., and Richard H. Ogles
1963 "Anxiety and anti-social behavior in preschool children." Pp. 82–94 in F. I. Nye and L. W. Hoffman (eds.), *The Employed Mother in America.* Chicago: Rand McNally.

Nye, F. Ivan, James F. Short Jr., and Virgil J. Olson
1958 "Socioeconomic status and delinquent behavior." *American Journal of Sociology* 63: 381–389.

Oberschall, Anthony
1973 *Social Conflict and Social Movements.* Englewood Cliffs, NJ: Prentice-Hall.

O'Brien, John E.
1971 "Violence in divorce prone families." *Journal of Marriage and the Family* 33 (November): 692–698.

O'Connell, Martin, and Maurice J. Moore
1980 "The legitimacy status of first births to U.S. women aged 15–24, 1939–1978." *Family Planning Perspectives* 12: 16–23, 25.

O'Connor, James
1973 *The Fiscal Crisis of the State.* New York: St. Martin's Press.

O'Dea, Thomas F.
1970 *Sociology and the Study of Religion.* New York: Basic Books.

O'Dea, Thomas F.
1966 *The Sociology of Religion.* Englewood Cliffs, NJ: Prentice-Hall.

Ogbu, John U.
1978 *Minority Education and Caste.* New York: Academic Press.

Ogburn, William F.
1922 *Social Change: With Respect to Culture and Original Nature.* New York: B. W. Huebsch.

Oppenheimer, Valerie Kincade
1970 *The Female Labor Force in the United States.* Westport, CT: Greenwood Press.

Oppong, C.
1970 "Conjugal power and resources: An urban African example." *Journal of Marriage and the Family* 32: 676–691.

Orthner, D.
1976 "Patterns of leisure and marital interaction." *Journal of Leisure Research* 8: 98–111.

Orum, Anthony M.
1978 *Introduction to Political Sociology: The Anatomy of the Body Politic.* Englewood Cliffs, NJ: Prentice-Hall.

Orwell, George
1949 *1984.* New York: New American Library.

Ossowski, S.
1963 *Class Structure in the Social Consciousness.* Sheila Patterson, tr. New York: Free Press.

Ouchi, William G.
1981 *Theory Z: How American Business Can Meet the Japanese Challenge.* New York: Avon.

Pachon, Harry P., and Joan W. Moore
1981 "Mexican Americans." *The Annals of the American Academy of Political and Social Science* 454 (March): 111–124.

Page, Charles H.
1969 "Symposium summary, with reflections upon the sociology of sport as a research field." Pp. 189–209 in Gerald S. Kenyon (ed.), *Aspects of Contemporary Sport Sociology.* Chicago: The Athletic Institute.

Palardy, J. Michael
1969 "What teachers believe–what children achieve." *Elementary School Journal* 69: 370–374.

Parelius, Ann Parker, and Robert J. Parelius
1978 *The Sociology of Education.* Englewood Cliffs, NJ: Prentice-Hall.

Parenti, Michael
1967 "Political values and religious culture: Jews, Catholics, and Protestants." *Journal for the*

Scientific Study of Religion 7 (fall): 259–269.

Park, Robert E.
1950 *Race and Culture*. New York: Free Press.

Park, Robert E., Ernest W. Burgess, and Roderick D. McKenzie
1925 *The City*. Chicago: University of Chicago Press.

Parker, Stanley R., and Michael A. Smith
1976 "Work and leisure." Pp. 37–64 in Robert Dubin (ed.), *Handbook of Work Organization and Society*. Chicago: Rand McNally.

Parkin, Frank
1971 *Class Inequality and Political Order*. New York: Praeger.

Parsons, J. E., D. N. Ruble, K. L. Hodges, and A. W. Small
1976 "Cognitive-developmental factors in emerging sex differences in achievement-related expectancies." *Journal of Social Issues* 32: 47–61.

Parsons, P. A.
1967 *The Genetic Analysis of Behavior*. London: Methuen.

Parsons, Talcott
1966 *Societies: Evolutionary and Comparative Perspectives*. Englewood Cliffs, NJ: Prentice-Hall.

Parsons, Talcott
1951 *The Social System*. Glencoe, IL: Free Press.

Parsons, Talcott
1937/1949 *The Structure of Social Action*. Glencoe, IL: Free Press.

Parsons, Talcott, and Robert F. Bales
1953 *Family, Socialization and Interaction Process*. Glencoe, IL: Free Press.

Pascal, A. H., and L. A. Rapping
1970 *Racial Discrimination in Organized Baseball*. Santa Monica, CA: RAND.

Pear, Robert
1983 "Health chief calls AIDS battle 'No. 1 priority'." *New York Times*, May 25: A1.

Pearlin, Leonard I.
1971 *Class Context and Family Relations: A Cross-National Study*. Boston: Little, Brown.

Pelz, Donald C., and Frank M. Andrews
1966 *Scientists in Organizations*. New York: Wiley.

Pepitone-Rockwell, Fran (ed.)
1980 *Dual-Career Couples*. Beverly Hills, CA: Sage.

Perrow, Charles
1981 "Normal accident at three mile island." *Society* 18: 17–26.

Perrow, Charles
1979a *Complex Organizations: A Critical Essay*. Second edition. Glenview, IL: Scott, Foresman.

Perrow, Charles
1979b "Organizational theory in a society of organizations." Paper presented at the annual meeting of the American Sociological Association.

Perrow, Charles
1976 "Control in organizations: The centralized-decentralized bureaucracy." Paper presented at the annual meeting of the American Sociological Association, New York.

Perry, Stewart E.
1978 *San Francisco Scavengers*. Berkeley: University of California Press.

Persell, Caroline Hodges
in press "Gender, rewards and research in education." *Psychology of Women Quarterly*.

Persell, Caroline Hodges
1982 "Percentage of blacks and Hispanics in 1982 baseball starting lineup." Unpublished study.

Persell, Caroline Hodges
1981 "Genetic and cultural deficit theories." *Journal of Black Studies* 12: 19–37.

Persell, Caroline Hodges
1977 *Education and Inequality*. New York: Free Press.

Peter, Laurence J.
1969 *The Peter Principle: Why Things Always Go Wrong*. New York: Bantam.

Pettigrew, Tom
1981 "Race and class: An interactive view." *Daedalus* 110: 233–255.

Petzinger, Thomas Jr.
1980 "Come to Pittsburgh, where life's shocks are soon forgotten." *Wall Street Journal* (January 17): 1.

Philips, Kevin P., and Paul H. Blackman
1975 *Electoral Reform and Voter Participation*. Washington, D.C.: American Enterprise Institute for Public Policy Research.

Phillips, John C., and Walter E. Schafer
1971 "Consequences of participation in interscholastic sports: A prospectus and review." *Pacific Sociological Review* (July): 328–338.

Piaget, Jean
1954 *The Construction of Reality in the Child*. New York: Basic Books.

Piaget, Jean
1950 *The Psychology of Intelligence*. London: Routledge and Kegan Paul.

Piaget, Jean
1932 *The Moral Judgment of the Child*. New York: Harcourt Brace Jovanovich.

Pietrofesa, John J., and Nancy K. Schlossberg
1974 "Counselor bias and the female occupa-

tional role." Pp. 148–150 in William M. Cave and Mark A. Chesler (eds.), *Sociology of Education*. New York: Macmillan.

Pilpel, Harriet F., and Theodore Zavin
1964 *Your Marriage and the Law*. New York: Collier.

Pines, Maya
1981 "The civilizing of Genie." *Psychology Today* 15: 28–34.

Piore, Michael J.
1975 "Notes for a theory of labor market stratification." Pp. 125–150 in R. C. Edwards, M. Reich, and D. M. Gordon (eds.), *Labor Market Segmentation*. Lexington, MA: D. C. Heath.

Pitts, J. R.
1964 "The structural-functional approach." Pp. 51–124 in H. T. Christensen (ed.), *Handbook of Marriage and the Family*. Chicago: Rand McNally.

Piven, Frances Fox, and Richard A. Cloward
1977 *Poor People's Movements: Why They Succeed, How They Fail*. New York: Vintage.

Piven, Frances Fox, and Richard A. Cloward
1971 *Regulating the Poor: The Functions of Public Welfare*. New York: Vintage.

Pogge, Mariann
1978 "From cheerleader to competitor." *Update* (fall): 18.

Popper, Karl
1959 *The Logic of Scientific Discovery*. New York: Basic Books.

Presthus, Robert
1962 *The Organizational Society*. New York: Vintage.

Presvelou, C.
1971 "Impact of differential leisure activities in intra-spousal dynamics." *Human Relations* 24: 565–574.

Price, Derek de Solla
1975 "The productivity of research scientists." Pp. 408–421 in *Yearbook of Science and the Future*. Chicago: Encyclopaedia Britannica.

Price, Derek J. de Solla
1971 "Measuring the size of science." Cited in Joseph Ben-David, *The Scientist's Role in Society*.

Price, Derek J. de Solla
1963 *Little Science Big Science*. New York: Columbia University Press.

Public Opinion
1980 "Psephological psouffle." April–May: 34.

Public Opinion
1980 "Premarital sex gains acceptance, extramarital doesn't." December–January: 28.

Public Opinion
1980 "The 70's: Decade of second thoughts." December–January: 19–42.

Public Opinion
1979 "The modern woman: How far has she come?" January–February: 35–39.

Public Opinion
1979 "Religious preference." March–May: 34.

Public Opinion
1978 "American ethnic and religious groups." November–December: 32–33.

Putnam, R. D.
1976 *The Comparative Study of Political Elites*. Englewood Cliffs, NJ: Prentice-Hall.

Quinn, Bernard, Herman Anderson, Martin Bradley, Paul Goetting, and Peggy Shriver
1982 *Churches and Church Membership in the United States: 1980*. Atlanta, Ga.: Glenmary Research Center.

Quinn, James Brian
1979 "Technological innovation, entrepreneurship, and strategy." *Sloan Management Review* (spring): 19–30.

Quinney, Richard
1974 *Critique of Legal Order: Crime Control in Capitalist Society*. Boston: Little, Brown.

Quinney, Richard
1970 *The Social Reality of Crime*. Boston: Little, Brown.

Rainwater, Lee
1969 "The problem of lower-class culture and poverty-war strategy." In Daniel Moynihan (ed.), *On Understanding Poverty*. New York: Basic Books.

Rallings, E. M., and F. I. Nye
1979 "Wife-mother employment, family, and society." Pp. 203–226 in W. R. Burr, R. Hill, F. I. Nye, and I. L. Riess (eds.), *Contemporary Theories about the Family*. Volume 1: *Research-Based Theories*. New York: Free Press.

Rapoport, Robert, and Rhona Rapoport
1976 *Dual-Career Families Reexamined: New Integrations of Work and Family*. New York: Harper & Row.

Ratcliff, Richard E.
1980 "Banks and corporate lending: An analysis of the impact of the internal structure of the capitalist class on the lending behavior of banks." *American Sociological Review* 45: 553–570.

Read, Kenneth
1965 *The High Valley*. New York: Scribner's.

Rees, C. Roger, and Mady Wechsler Segal
1980 "Role differentiation in groups: The rela-

tionship between instrumental and expressive leadership in two college football teams." Paper presented at the annual meeting of the American Sociological Association, New York.

Rehberg, R. A., and M. Cohen
1976 "Political attitudes and participation in extracurricular activities." In Daniel M. Landers (ed.), *Social Problems in Athletics*. Urbana: University of Illinois Press.

Reinhold, Robert
1978a "World population growth slows." *New York Times* (November 20): 1, A32.

Reinhold, Robert
1978b "China's millions are still hard to count." *New York Times* (November 26): E7.

Reiss, Albert J. Jr.
1961 "The social integration of peers and queers." *Social Problems* 9: 102–120.

Reiss, Albert J. Jr., Otis D. Duncan, Paul K. Hatt, and Cecil C. North
1961 *Occupational and Social Status*. New York: Free Press.

Reiss, Ira L.
1967 *The Social Context of Premarital Sexual Permissiveness*. New York: Holt, Rinehart and Winston.

Rensberger, Boyce
1977 "Fraud in research is a rising problem in science." *New York Times* (January 23): 1, 44.

Reskin, Barbara F.
1978 "Scientific productivity, sex, and location in the institution of science." *American Journal of Sociology* 83: 1235–1243.

Retine, Nancy, and Joan Huber
1974 "The demography of poverty: Trends in the sixties." In Joan Huber and Peter Chalfant (eds.), *The Sociology of American Poverty*. Cambridge, MA: Schenkman.

Reynolds, Morgan O.
1971 "Crime for profit: The economics of theft." Ph.D. dissertation, University of Wisconsin.

Rice, Bradley R.
1981 "Searching for the sunbelt." *American Demographics* 3: 22–23.

Rice, David G.
1979 *The Dual-Career Marriage*. New York: Free Press.

Richardson, James T., M. Stewart, and R. B. Simmonds
1979 *Organized Miracles: A Study of a Contemporary Youth, Communal, Fundamentalist Organization*. New Brunswick, NJ: Transaction Books.

Riley, Matilda et al.
1961 "Adolescent values and the Reisman typology: An empirical analysis." In Seymour Lipset and Leo Lowenthal (eds.), *Culture and Social Character*. New York: Free Press.

Riordon, Michael
1979 "Notes of a willing victim." Pp. 78–99 in Martin P. Levine (ed.), *Gay Men*. New York: Harper & Row.

Robbins, Thomas, and Dick Anthony
1978 "New religions, families and brainwashing." *Society* 15 (May–June): 77–83.

Robbins, Thomas, Dick Anthony, and James Richardson
1978 "Theory and research on today's 'new religions.'" *Sociological Analysis* 39: 95–122.

Robinson, John P.
1977 *How Americans Use Their Time: A Social-Psychological Analysis of Everyday Behavior*. New York: Praeger.

Robinson, John P.
1976 "Changes in America's use of time, 1965–1975." Report of Communication Center, Cleveland State University.

Robinson, Nancy H., and John P. Robinson
1975 "Sex roles and the territoriality of everyday behavior." Unpublished ms. Ann Arbor: Survey Research Center, University of Michigan.

Rodney, W.
1974 *How Europe Underdeveloped Africa*. Washington, D.C.: Howard University Press.

Roethlisberger, Fritz J., and William J. Dickson
1939 *Management and the Worker*. Cambridge, MA: Harvard University Press.

Roper Organization
1980 *The 1980 Virginia Slims American Women's Opinion Poll*. New York.

Rosaldo, M. Z., and L. Lamphere
1974 *Woman, Culture and Society*. Stanford, CA: Stanford University Press.

Rosen, Hugh
1980 *The Development of Socio-Moral Knowledge: A Cognitive-Structural Approach*. New York: Columbia University Press.

Rosenbaum, James E.
1976 *Making Inequality*. New York: Wiley.

Rosenblatt, A.
1967 "Negroes in baseball: The failure of success." *Trans-action* 4: 51–53.

Rosenhan, D. L.
1973 "On being sane in insane places." *Science* 179: 1–9.

Rosenthal, Robert, and Lenore Jacobson
1968 *Pygmalion in the Classroom*. New York: Holt, Rinehart and Winston.

Rosow, Kenneth, and Caroline Hodges Persell

1980 "Sex education from 1900 to 1920: A study of ideological social control." *Qualitative Sociology* 3: 186–203.

Ross, Heather L., and Isabel V. Sawhill
1975 *Time of Transition: The Growth of Families Headed by Women.* Washington, D.C.: The Urban Institute.

Ross, James B., and Mary M. McLaughlin (eds.)
1949 *The Portable Medieval Reader.* New York: Viking.

Rossi, Alice S.
1972 "Sex equality: The beginnings of ideology." Pp. 344–353 in Constantina Safilios-Rothschild (ed.), *Toward a Sociology of Women.* Lexington, MA: Xerox College Publishing.

Rossi, Alice S.
1964 "Equality between the sexes: An immodest proposal." *Daedalus* (spring): 607–652.

Rossi, Alice S.
n.d. "The roots of ambivalence in American women." Unpublished manuscript.

Rossides, Daniel
1976 *The American Class System.* Boston: Houghton Mifflin.

Rostow, W. W.
1960 *The Stages of Economic Growth: A Non-Communist Manifesto.* New York: Cambridge University Press.

Rothschild-Whitt, Joyce
1979 "The collectivist oranization: An alternative to rational-bureaucratic models." *American Sociological Review* 44 (August): 509–527.

Rothschild-Whitt, Joyce
1976 "Conditions facilitating participatory-democratic organizations." *Sociological Inquiry* 46: 75–86.

Rousseau, Jean-Jacques
1750/1974 *Discourse on the Origin of Inequality.* Lowell Bair, tr. New York: New American Library.

Rowes, Barbara
1979 *The Book of Quotes.* New York: Dutton.

Royal Commission on the Distribution of Income and Wealth
1980 *An A to Z of Income and Wealth.* London: Her Majesty's Stationery Office.

Rubin, Lillian Breslow
1976 *Worlds of Pain: Life in the Working-Class Family.* New York: Basic Books.

Russell, Cheryl
1981 "A tale of fifty cities." *American Demographics* 3: 24–27.

Russell, Cheryl, and Bryant Robey
1981 "Follow the sun: Census shifts explained." *American Demographics* 3: 18–21.

Russell, Josian Cox
1972 *Medieval Regions and their Cities.* Bloomington: Indiana University Press.

Russell, Raymond
1982 "Rewards of participation in the worker-owned firm." In F. Lindenfeld and J. Rothschild-Whitt (eds.), *Workplace Democracy and Social Change.* Boston: Porter Sargent.

Ryan, William
1971 *Blaming the Victim.* New York: Random House.

Sack, Allen L., and Robert Thiel
1979 "College football and social mobility: A case study of Notre Dame football players." *Sociology of Education* 52 (January): 60–66.

Sadker, Myra Pollack, and David Miller Sadker
1980 "Sexism in teacher-education texts." *Harvard Educational Review* 50: 36–46.

Safilios-Rothschild, Constantina
1967 "A comparison of power structure and marital satisfaction in urban Greek and French families." *Journal of Marriage and the Family* 29: 345–352.

Sagarin, Edward
1976 "Prison homosexuality and its effects on post-prison sexual behavior." *Psychiatry* 39: 245–257.

Saikal, Amin
1980 *The Rise and Fall of the Shah.* Princeton, NJ: Princeton University Press.

St. John, Nancy Hoyt
1975 *School Desegregation.* New York: Wiley.

Samuelson, Paul A.
1980 *Economics.* Eleventh edition. New York: McGraw-Hill.

Sargent, Jon
1982 "The job outlook for college graduates during the 1980s." *Occupational Outlook Quarterly* 26 (summer): 2–7.

Sauvy, A.
1969 *General Theory of Population.* New York: Basic Books.

Scanzoni, John
1972 *Sexual Bargaining: Power Politics in American Marriage.* Englewood Cliffs, NJ: Prentice-Hall.

Scarr-Salapatek, Sandra, and Richard A. Weinberg
1975 "When black children grow up in white homes." *Psychology Today* 9:80–82.

Schafer, W. E., and J. C. Phillips
1970 "The athletic subculture: A preliminary study." Paper presented at the American Sociological Association meetings, Washington, D.C.

Schell, Jonathan
1982 *The Fate of the World.* New York: Knopf.

Schlechty, Phillip C.
1976 *Teaching and Social Behavior: Toward an Organizational Theory of Instruction.* Boston: Allyn and Bacon.

Schneider, Herbert
1952 *Religion in 20th Century America.* Cambridge, MA: Harvard University Press.

Schrank, Robert
1978 *Ten Thousand Working Days.* Cambridge, MA: MIT Press.

Schumacher, E. F.
1973 *Small is Beautiful.* New York: Harper & Row.

Schur, Edwin M.
1982 Personal communication.

Schur, Edwin M.
1980 *The Politics of Deviance: Stigma Contests and the Uses of Power.* Englewood Cliffs, NJ: Prentice-Hall.

Schur, Edwin M.
1979 *Interpreting Deviance: A Sociological Introduction.* New York: Harper & Row.

Schur, Edwin M.
1971 *Labeling Deviant Behavior: Its Sociological Implications.* New York: Harper & Row.

Schur, Edwin M.
1968 *Law and Society: A Sociological View.* New York: Random House.

Schur, Edwin M.
1965 *Crimes without Victims.* Englewood Cliffs, NJ: Prentice-Hall.

Schvaneveldt, Jay D., and Marilyn Ihinger
1979 "Sibling relationships in the family." Pp. 453–467 in Wesley R. Burr et al., *Contemporary Theories about the Family.* Volume I. New York: Free Press.

Schwartz, Barry
1975 *Queuing and Waiting.* Chicago: University of Chicago Press.

Scully, G. W.
1979 "Discrimination: The case of baseball." Pp. 365–387 in D. Stanley Eitzen (ed.), *Sport in Contemporary Society.* New York: St. Martin's Press.

Sears, Pauline, and David Feldman
1966 "Teacher interactions with boys and girls." *National Elementary Principal* 46: 30–35.

Seashore, Stanley E., and J. Thad Barnowe
1972 "Demographic and job factors associated with the 'blue collar blues.'" Mimeo.

Seay, B., B. K. Alexander, and H. F. Harlow
1964 "Maternal behavior of socially deprived rhesus monkeys." *Journal of Abnormal and Social Psychology* 69: 345–354.

Secombe, Wally
1974 "The housewife and her labor under capitalism." *New Left Review* 83 January–February: 3–24.

Selikoff, Irving
1980 "The toxicity connection." *Time* (September 22): 63.

Selznick, Philip
1966 *TVA and the Grass Roots.* New York: Harper Torchbooks.

Selznick, Philip
1948 "Foundations of the theory of organizations." *American Sociological Review* 13: 25–35.

Sennett, Richard
1974 *The Fall of Public Man.* New York: Vintage.

Sennett, Richard
1970 *The Uses of Disorder.* New York: Vintage.

Sennett, Richard, and Jonathan Cobb
1973 *The Hidden Injuries of Class.* New York: Vintage.

Serbin, L. A., K. D. O'Leary, R. N. Kent, and I. J. Tonick
1973 "A comparison of teacher response to the pre-academic and problem behavior of boys and girls." *Child Development* 44: 796–804.

Serrin, William
1981 "After 34 years jobs declining in government." *New York Times* (December 27): 1, 44.

Shaver, Phillip
1976 "Questions concerning fear of success and its conceptual relatives." *Sex Roles* 2: 305–320.

Shaw, Clifford
190 *The Jack-Roller.* Chicago: University of Chicago Press.

Sheppard, Harold L., and Neal Q. Merrick
1972 *Where Have All the Robots Gone? Worker Dissent in the Seventies.* New York: Free Press.

Shostak, Arthur B.
1980 *Blue-Collar Stress.* Reading, MA: Addison-Wesley.

Sieber, Sam D.
1974 "Toward a theory of role accumulation." *American Sociological Review* 39 (August): 567–578.

Silk, Leonard, and Mark Silk
1980 *The American Establishment.* New York: Basic Books.

Sills, David L.
1957 *The Volunteers.* New York: Free Press.

Simmel, Georg
1956 *Conflict and the Web of Group Affiliation.* Kurt H. Wolff, tr. Glencoe, IL: Free Press.

Simmel, Georg
1905/1955 *Conflict and the Web of Group Affiliations.* Kurt H. Wolff and Reinhard Bendix (eds.). New York: Free Press.

Simmel, Georg
1950 *The Sociology of Georg Simmel.* Kurt J. Wolff (ed.) Glencoe, IL: Free Press.

Simmons, Jerry L.
1969 *Deviants.* Berkeley, CA: Glendessary Press.

Simon, Herbert A.
1957 *Models of Men, Social and Rational.* New York: Wiley.

Simon, Rita James
1979 "Arrest statistics." Pp. 101–113 in Freda Adler and Rita James Simon (eds.), *The Criminology of Deviant Women.* Boston: Houghton Mifflin.

Simpson, George E., and J. Milton Yinger
1972 *Racial and Cultural Minorities: An Analysis of Prejudice and Discrimination.* Fourth edition. New York: Harper & Row.

Simpson, R.
1956 "A modification of the functional theory of stratification." *Social Forces* 35: 132–137.

Singelmann, Joachim
1978 *From Agriculture to Services: The Transformation of Industrial Employment.* Beverly Hills, CA: Sage.

Sipes, Richard G.
1973 "War, sports and aggression: An empirical test of two rival theories." *American Anthropologist* 75 (January): 64–86.

Sjoquist, David
1971 "Property Crime as an Economic Phenomenon." Ph.D. dissertation, University of Minnesota.

Skelly, Florence R.
1978 "Emerging values of the young worker." Talk given at the 28th annual meeting, La Costa Hotel, California, April 4.

Sklair, Leslie
1973 *Organized Knowledge.* St. Albans, Herts: Paladin.

Skocpol, Theda
1979 *States and Social Revolutions.* New York: Cambridge University Press.

Smelser, Neil J.
1963 *Theory of Collective Behavior.* New York: Free Press. Originally published 1962.

Smith, Adam
1776/1976 *The Wealth of Nations.* New York: Oxford University Press.

Smith, Anthony
1980 *The Geopolitics of Information: How Western Culture Dominates the World.* New York: Oxford University Press.

Smith, G.
1975 "Leisure, recreation and delinquency." Master's thesis, Department of Anthropology and Sociology, University of Queensland.

Smith, James P., and Finis Welch
1978 *Race Differences in Earnings: A Survey and New Evidence.* Santa Monica, CA: RAND.

Smith, Jerome F.
1980 *The Coming Currency Collapse.* New York: Books in Focus.

Smith, Michael D.
1979 "Hockey violence: A test of the violent subculture hypothesis." *Social Problems* 27 (December): 235–247.

Smith, T. Lynn, and Paul E. Zopf Jr.
1976 *Demography: Principles and Methods.* Port Washington, NY: Alfred.

Snyder, David, Mark D. Hayward, and Paula M. Hudis
1979 "The location of change in the sexual structure of occupations, 1950–1970: Insights from labor market segmentation theory." *American Journal of Sociology* 84: 706–717.

Snyder, D., and Charles Tilly
1972 "Hardship and collective violence in France." *American Sociological Review* 37 (October): 520–532.

Snyder, Eldon E., and Elmer Spreitzer
1978 *Social Aspects of Sport.* Englewood Cliffs, NJ: Prentice-Hall.

Sociobiology Study Group of Science for the People
1976 "Sociobiology—Another biological determinism." Pp. 280–290 in Arthur L. Caplan (ed.), *The Sociobiology Debate.* New York: Harper & Row.

Sokoloff, Natalie
1980 *Between Money and Love: The Dialectics of Women, Home and Market Work.* New York: Praeger.

Sorenson, Robert C.
1973 *Adolescent Sexuality in Contemporary America.* New York: World.

Spector, Malcolm
1977 "Legitimizing homosexuality." *Society* 14: 52–56.

Spector, Malcolm, and John I. Kitsuse
1977 *Constructing Social Problems.* Menlo Park, CA: Cummings.

Spector, Malcolm, and John I. Kitsuse
1973 "Social problems: A re-formulation." *Social Problems* 21: 145–159.

Speiglman, Richard
1977 "Prison drugs, psychiatry, and the state."

Pp. 149–171 in David F. Greenberg (ed.), *Corrections and Punishment*. Beverly Hills, CA: Sage.

Spengler, Oswald
1945 *The Decline of the West,* 2 vols. New York: Knopf.

Spiegel, J.
1971 *Transactions*. New York: Science House.

Spitz, Rene A.
1972 "Hospitalism: An inquiry into the genesis of psychiatric conditions in early childhood." (Originally copyrighted 1945 and 1946). Pp. 202–223 in Urie Bronfenbrenner (ed.), *Influences on Human Development*. Hinsdale, IL: Dryden Press.

Spreitzer, Elmer, and Eldon E. Snyder
1975 "The psychosocial functions of sport as perceived by the general population." *International Review of Sport Sociology* 3–4: 87–93.

Sprey, Jetse
1979 "Conflict theory and the study of marriage and the family." Pp. 130–159 in Wesley R. Burr et al., *Contemporary Theories about the Family*. Volume II. New York: Free Press.

Sprey, Jetse
1969 "The family as a system in conflict." *Journal of Marriage and the Family* 31 (November): 722–731.

Stack, Carol B.
1974 *All Our Kin: Strategies for Survival in a Black Community*. New York: Harper Colophon.

Starr, Bernard D., and Marcella Bakur Weiner
1980 *The Starr and Weiner Report on Sex and Sexuality in the Mature Years*. New York: Paddington.

Stein, Peter J.
1976 *Single*. Englewood Cliffs, NJ: Prentice-Hall.

Steinmetz, Suzanne K.
1979 "Disciplinary techniques and their relationship to aggressiveness, dependency, and conscience." Pp. 405–438 in Wesley R. Burr et al., *Contemporary Theories about the Family*. Volume I. New York: Free Press.

Steinmetz, Suzanne K.
1974 "Occupational environment in relation to physical punishment and dogmatism." Pp. 166–179 in Suzanne K. Steinmetz and Murray A. Straus (eds.), *Violence in the Family*. New York: Dodd, Mead.

Steinmetz, Suzanne K.
1971 "Occupation and physical punishment: A response to Straus." *Journal of Marriage and the Family* 33 (November): 664–666.

Steinmetz, Suzanne K., and Murray A. Straus (eds.)
1974 *Violence in the Family*. New York: Harper & Row. (Originally published by Dodd, Mead, 1974.)

Stephens, William N.
1963 *The Family in Cross-cultural Perspective*. New York: Holt, Rinehart and Winston.

Stern, Daniel
1977 *The First Relationship: Infant and Mother*. Cambridge, MA: Harvard University Press.

Stern, Philip M.
1972 "Uncle Sam's welfare program for the rich." *New York Times Magazine*. April 16.

Stinchcombe, Arthur L.
1969 "Some empirical consequences of the Davis-Moore theory of stratification." Pp. 50–55 in Jack L. Roach, Llewellyn Gross, and Orville Gursslin (eds.), *Social Stratification in the United States*. Englewood Cliffs, NJ: Prentice-Hall.

Stinchcombe, Arthur L.
1964 *Rebellion in a High School*. Chicago: Quadrangle.

Stockton, William
1981 "The technology race: America's struggle to stay ahead." *New York Times Magazine* (June 26): 14–19ff.

Stone, Donald
1978 "The human potential movement." *Society* 15: 66–71.

Stone, Donald
1976 "The human potential movement." Pp. 93–115 in C. Glock and R. Bellah (eds.), *The New Religious Consciousness*. Berkeley: University of California Press.

Stone, Philip J.
1972 "Child care in twelve countries." Pp. 249–264 in Alexander Szalai (ed.), *The Use of Time*. The Hague: Mouton.

Stouffer, Samuel, et al.
1949 *The American Soldier*. Volume 1. Princeton, NJ: Princeton University Press.

Straus, Murray A.
1976 "Sexual inequality, cultural norms, and wife-beating." *Victimology* 1: 54–76.

Straus, Murray A.
1971 "Some social antecedents of physical punishment: A linkage theory interpretation." *Journal of Marriage and the Family* 33 (November): 658–663.

Straus, Murray A., Richard J. Gelles, and Suzanne K. Steinmetz
1979 *Behind Closed Doors: Violence in the American Family*. Garden City, NY: Doubleday-Anchor.

Sudnow, David

1967 *Passing On: The Social Organization of Dying*. Englewood Cliffs, NJ: Prentice-Hall.

Sullerot, Evelyn
1971 *Woman, Society and Change*. New York: World University Library.

Sullivan, Walter
1979 "A tough new drive on births in China." *New York Times* (October 10): C1.

Surface, Bill
1974 "Pro football: Is it getting too dirty?" *Reader's Digest* (November): 151–154.

Suter, Larry E., and Herman P. Miller
1973 "Income differences between men and career women." *American Journal of Sociology* 78:962–974.

Sutherland, Edwin H.
1937 *The Professional Thief.* Chicago: University of Chicago Press.

Sutherland, Edwin H., and Donald R. Cressey
1978 *Criminology*. New York: Lippincott.

Swedish Institute
1979 "Equality between women and men in Sweden." *Fact Sheet on Sweden*. Stockholm: Swedish Institute.

Swidler, Ann
1979 *Organization without Authority*. Cambridge, MA: Harvard University Press.

Sykes, Gresham M.
1958 *The Society of Captives: A Study of a Maximum Security Prison*. Princeton, NJ: Princeton University Press.

Syme, S. Leonard, and Lisa F. Berkman
1981 "Social class, susceptibility, and sickness." Pp. 35–44 in Peter Conrad and Rochelle Kern (eds.), *The Sociology of Health and Illness*. New York: St. Martin's Press.

Szalai, Alexander (ed.)
1972 *The Use of Time*. The Hague, Netherlands: Mouton.

Szymanski, Albert
1973 "Military spending and economic stagnation." *American Journal of Sociology* 79 (July): 1–14.

Tavris, Carol, and Carole Offir
1977 *The Longest War: Sex Differences in Perspective*. New York: Harcourt Brace Jovanovich.

Taylor, Ian
1972 "'Football mad': A speculative sociology of football hooliganism." Pp. 352–377 in Eric Dunning (ed.) *Sport: Readings from a Sociological Perspective*. Toronto: University of Toronto Press.

Taylor, Ian, Paul Walton, and Jock Young
1973 *The New Criminology: For a Social Theory of Deviance*. New York: Harper & Row.

Teal, D.
1971 *The Gay Militants*. New York: Stein and Day.

Teltsch, Kathleen
1981 "Corporate aid helping twin cities to thrive." *New York Times* (August 27): A1, A11.

Temin, Carolyn Engel
1979 "Discriminatory sentencing of women offenders." Pp. 273–286 in Freda Adler and Rita James Simon (eds.), *The Criminology of Deviant Women*. Boston: Houghton Mifflin.

Terry, R. M.
1967 "Discrimination in the handling of juvenile offenders by social-control agencies." *Journal of Research in Crime and Delinquency* 4: 218–230.

Tesar, Delbert
1978 "Mission-oriented research for light machinery." *Science* 201 (September): 880–887.

Thernstrom, Stephan
1964 *Poverty and Progress: Social Mobility in a Nineteenth-Century City*. Cambridge, MA: Harvard University Press.

Thernstrom, Stephan, Ann Orlov, and Oscar Handlin (eds.)
1980 *Harvard Encyclopedia of American Ethnic Groups*. Cambridge, MA: Harvard University Press.

Thoits, Peggy A.
1983 "Multiple identities and psychological well-being: A reformulation and test of the social isolation hypothesis." *American Sociological Review* 48 (April): 174–187

Thompson, E. P.
1981 "A Letter to America." *The Nation* (January 24): 68–93.

Thompson, E. P.
1967 "Time, work-discipline, and industrial capitalism." *Past and Present* 38 (December): 56–97.

Thurow, Lester
1975 *Generating Inequality*. New York: Basic Books.

Tilly, Charles
1975 "Revolution and collective violence." Pp. 483–555 in F. Greenstein and N. Polsky (eds.), *Handbook of Political Science*. Volume 3: *Macro Political Theory*. Reading, MA: Addison-Wesley

Tilly, Charles, L. Tilly, and R. Tilly
1975 *The Rebellious Century: 1830–1930*. Cambridge, MA: Harvard University Press.

Time
1982 "Soaring costs: U.S. health bill jumps 15.1%." August 9.

Time
1981 "He digs downtown." August 24: 42–48.

Time
1981 "Not so merry widowers." August 10: 45.

Time
1978 "The American farmer." November 6: 95.

Time
1978 "Women talk but men cut in." September 25: 82.

Tinker, Jon
1979 "The indestructible garbage." Pp. 365–367 in *Britannica Book of the Year.* Chicago: Encyclopaedia Britannica.

Tinto, Vincent
1978 "Does schooling matter? A retrospective assessment." Pp. 201–235 in Lee S. Shulman (ed.), *Review of Research in Education* 5, 1977. Itasca, IL: Peacock.

Tittle, Charles R., and Wayne J. Villemez
1977 "Social class and criminality." *Social Forces* 56: 475–502.

Tittle, Charles R., Wayne J. Villemez, and Douglas A. Smith
1978 "The myth of social class and criminality." *American Sociological Review* 43: 643–656.

Titmuss, Richard M.
1971 *The Gift Relationship.* New York: Random House.

Toby, Jackson
1981 "Deterrence without punishment." *Criminology* 19: 195–209.

de Tocqueville, Alexis
1856/1955 *The Old Regime and the French Revolution.* Stuart Gilbert, tr. Garden City, NY: Doubleday.

de Tocqueville, Alexis
1835/1954 *Democracy in America.* Volumes 1 and 2. New York: Vintage Books.

Toffler, Alvin
1980 *The Third Wave.* New York: Bantam.

Tomeh, A. K.
1964 "Informal group participation and residential pattern." *American Journal of Sociology* 70 (July): 28–35.

Tönnies, Ferdinand
1887/1957 *Community and Society.* New York: Harper Torchbooks.

Torrens, Paul R.
1978 *The American Health Care System: Issues and Problems.* St. Louis, MO: C. V. Mosby.

Touraine, Alain
1974 *The Academic System in American Society.* New York: McGraw-Hill.

Toynbee, Arnold J.
1947 *A Study of History,* 10 vols. Oxford, Eng.: Oxford University Press.

Travers, Jeffrey, and Stanley Milgram
1969 "An experimental study of the small world problem." *Sociometry* 32: 425–443.

Treiman, Donald J.
1977 *Occupational Prestige in Comparative Perspective.* New York: Academic Press.

Treiman, Donald J., and Kermit Terrell
1975 "The process of status attainment in the United States and Great Britain." *American Journal of Sociology* 81 (November): 563–583.

Tresemer, David
1976 "Do women fear success?" *Signs* 1 (summer): 863–874.

Tresemer, David
1974 "Fear of success: Popular, but unproven." *Psychology Today* (March): 82–85.

Tripp, Clarence A.
1979 "An interview by Philip Nobile." *New York Magazine* (June 25): 36–41.

Troeltsch, Ernst
1929 *The Social Teachings of the Christian Churches.* Volume I. Olive Wyon, tr. New York: Macmillan.

Trow, Martin
1966 "The second transformation of American secondary education." Pp. 437–449 in Reinhard Bendix and Seymour M. Lipset (eds.), *Class, Status and Power.* New York: Free Press.

Trussell, James, and Jane Menken
1978 "Early childbearing and subsequent fertility." *Family Planning Perspectives* 10: 209–218.

Tuckett, David (ed.)
1976 *An Introduction to Medical Sociology.* London: Tavistock.

Tullock, Gordon
1974 "Does punishment deter crime?" *The Public Interest* 36: 103–111.

Tumin, Melvin M.
1967 *Social Stratification: The Forms and Functions of Inequality.* Englewood Cliffs, NJ: Prentice-Hall.

Tumin, Melvin M.
1953 "Some principles of stratification: A critical analysis." *American Sociological Review* 18: 387–394.

Turnbull, Colin M.
1972 *The Mountain People.* New York: Simon and Schuster.

Turner, Edward T.
1968 "The effects of viewing college football, basketball and wrestling on the elicited aggressive responses of male spectators." Pp. 325–328

in Gerald Kenyon (ed.), *Contemporary Psychology of Sport.* Chicago: The Athletic Institute.

Turner, Jonathan
1978 *The Structure of Sociological Theory.* Revised edition. Homewood, IL: Dorsey Press.

Turner, Ralph H.
1976 "The real self: From institution to impulse." *American Journal of Sociology* 81: 989–1016.

Turner, Ralph H.
1960 "Modes of social ascent through education: Sponsored and contest mobility." *American Sociological Review* 25: 121–139.

Tyack, David B., and Myra H. Strober
1981 "Women and men in the schools: A history of the sexual structuring of educational employment." Report presented to the National Institute of Education, Washington, D.C.

Underwood, J.
1969 "The desperate coach." *Sports Illustrated* 31: 66–76.

U.S. Bureau of the Census
1982a *Statistical Abstract of the United States: 1982–83.* Washington, D.C.: U.S. Government Printing Office.

U.S. Bureau of the Census
1982b *Current Population Reports,* Series P-60, No. 132; Money Income of Households, Families and Persons in the United States: 1980. Washington, D.C.: U.S. Government Printing office.

U.S. Bureau of the Census
1981a *Statistical Abstract of the United States: 1981.* Washington, D.C.: U.S. Government Printing Office.

U.S. Bureau of the Census
1981b *USA Statistics in Brief 1981.* Washington, D.C.: U.S. Government Printing Office.

U.S. Bureau of the Census
1981c *Current Population Reports,* Series P-60, No. 127; Money Income and Poverty Status of Families and Persons in the United States: 1980 (Advance data from the March 1981 Current Population Survey). Washington, D.C.: U.S. Government Printing Office.

U.S. Bureau of the Census
1981d *Current Population Reports,* Series P-20, No.365, Marital Status and Living Arrangements: March 1980. Washington, D.C.: U.S. Government Printing Office.

U.S. Bureau of the Census
1980 *Statistical Abstract of the United States: 1980.* Washington, D.C.: U.S. Government Printing Office.

U.S. Bureau of the Census
1979a *Statistical Abstract of the United States: 1979.* Washington, D.C.: U.S. Government Printing Office.

U.S. Bureau of the Census
1979b Money Income and Poverty Status of Families and Persons in the United States: 1978 (Advance Report). *Current Population Reports, Consumer Income,* Series P-60, No.120, November.

U.S. Bureau of the Census
1978 *Statistical Abstract of the United States: 1978.* Washington, D.C.: U.S. Government Printing Office.

U.S. Bureau of the Census
1977 *Census of Manufacturers.* Volume I. Washington, D.C.: U.S. Government Printing Office.

U.S. Bureau of the Census
1975 *Historical Statistics of the United States, Colonial Times to 1970.* Bicentennial edition, Part 2. Washington, D.C.: U.S. Government Printing Office.

U.S. Department of Commerce
1980 *Social Indicators III: Selected Data on Social Conditions and Trends in the United States.* Washington, D.C.: U.S. Government Printing Office.

U.S. Department of Commerce
1977 *Social Indicators 1976.* Washington, D.C.: U.S. Government Printing Office.

U.S. Department of Health and Human Services
1982 "Births, marriages, divorces, and deaths for 1981." *Monthly Vital Statistics Report* 30 (March 18). Washington D.C.: National Center for Health Statistics.

U.S. Department of Health and Human Services
1983 "Births, marriages, divorces, and deaths for 1982." *Monthly Vital Statistics Report* 31 (March 14).

U.S. Department of Justice
1981 *Uniform Crime Reports: Crime in the United States, 1980.* Washington, D.C.: U.S. Government Printing Office.

U.S. Department of Justice
1979 *FBI Uniform Crime Reports: Crime in the United States.* Washington, D.C.: U.S. Government Printing Office.

U.S. Department of Labor, Bureau of Labor Statistics
1983 *Employment and Earnings* 30 (January). Washington, D.C.: U.S. Government Printing Office.

U.S. Department of Labor, Bureau of Labor Statistics

1982 *Employment and Earnings* 29 (January). Washington, D.C.: U.S. Government Printing Office.

U.S. Department of Labor, Bureau of Labor Statistics
1980 *Employment and Earnings* 27 (January): 174–175. Washington, D.C.: U.S. Government Printing Office.

U.S. Department of Labor, Bureau of Labor Statistics
1980 *Occupational Outlook for College Graduates,* 1980–81 edition. Bulletin 2076. Washington, D.C.: U.S. Government Printing Office.

U.S. Department of Labor
1977 *Dictionary of Occupational Titles.* Washington, D.C.: U.S. Government Printing Office.

U.S. National Science Foundation
1980 *National Patterns of Science and Technology Resources.* Washington, D.C.: U.S. Government Printing Office.

U.S. News and World Report
1979 "Why $1 out of $11 goes for health." March 5: 40.

Useem, Michael
1980 "Corporations and the corporate elite." Pp. 41–77 in Alex Inkeles, Neil J. Smelser, and Ralph H. Turner (eds.), *Annual Review of Sociology.* Palo Alto, CA: Annual Reviews, Inc.

Useem, Michael
1979 "The social organization of the American business elite and participation of corporation directors in the governance of American institutions." *American Sociological Review* 44 (August): 553–572.

Useem, Michael
1978 "Inner group of the American capitalist class." *Social Problems* 25 (February) 225–240.

Utley, Robert M.
1963 *The Last Days of the Sioux Nation.* New Haven, CT: Yale University Press.

Valentine, Charles A.
1971 "Deficit, difference, and bicultural models of Afro-American behavior." *Harvard Educational Review* 41: 137–157.

Van den Berghe, Peter
1963 "Dialectic and functionalism: Toward a theoretical synthesis." *American Sociological Review* 28: 695–705.

Van den Haag, Ernest
1975 *On Punishing Criminals: Concerning an Old and Very Painful Question.* New York: Basic Books.

Vanfossen, Beth E.
1979 *The Structure of Social Inequality.* Boston: Little, Brown.

Veblen, Thorstein
1899/1967 *The Theory of the Leisure Class.* New York: Penguin.

Veevers, Jean E.
1980 *Childless by Choice.* Toronto: Butterworths.

Verba, Sidney, and Norman Nie
1972 *Participation in America: Political Democracy and Social Equality.* New York: Harper & Row.

Vernon, Raymond
1977 *Storm over the Multinationals: The Real Issues.* Cambridge, MA: Harvard University Press.

Vogel, S. R., I. K. Broverman, D. M. Broverman, F. E. Clarkson, and P. S. Rosenkrantz
1970 "Maternal employment and perception of sex roles among college students." *Developmental Psychology* 3: 384–391.

Voss, Harwin L.
1966 "Socioeconomic status and reported delinquent behavior." *Social Problems* 13: 314–324.

Wade, Nicholas
1976 "IQ and heredity: Suspicion of fraud beclouds classic experiment." *Science* 194 (November 26): 916–919.

Waldron, Ingrid
1981 "Why do women live longer than men?" Pp. 45–66 in Peter Conrad and Rochelle Kern (eds.), *The Sociology of Health and Illness.* New York: St. Martin's Press.

Wallace, Ruth A., and Alison Wolf
1980 *Contemporary Sociological Theory.* Englewood Cliffs, NJ: Prentice-Hall.

Wallace, Walter L.
1971 *The Logic of Science in Sociology.* Chicago: Aldine/Atherton.

Wallerstein, Immanuel
1974 *The Modern World-System.* New York: Academic Press.

Walum, Laurel Richardson
1977 *The Dynamics of Sex and Gender: A Sociological Perspective.* Chicago: Rand NcNally.

Warner, Sam Bass
1968 *The Private City.* Philadelphia: University of Pennsylvania Press.

Warner, W. Lloyd, Marchia Meeker, and Kenneth Eels
1949 *Social Class in America.* Chicago: Science Research Associates.

Warren, Bruce L.
1970 "Socioeconomic achievement and reli-

gion: The American case." Pp. 130–155 in Edward O. Laumann (ed.), *Social Stratification*. Indianapolis: Bobbs-Merrill.

Warren, Carol A.
1974 *Identity and Community in the Gay World*. New York: Wiley.

Watson, James D.
1968 *The Double Helix*. New York: Atheneum.

Wax, Murray L., and Rosalie Wax
1971 "Cultural deprivation as an educational ideology." Pp. 127–139 in Eleanor B. Leacock (ed.), *The Culture of Poverty: A Critique*. New York: Simon and Schuster.

Webb, Eugene J., Donald T. Campbell, Richard D. Schwartz, and Lee Sechrest
1966 *Unobtrusive Measures: Nonreactive Research in the Social Sciences*. Chicago: Rand McNally.

Weber, Max
1925/1958 *From Max Weber: Essays in Sociology*. Hans Gerth and C. Wright Mills (eds.). New York: Oxford University Press.

Weber, Max
1925/1947 *The Theory of Social and Economic Organization*. Glencoe, IL: Free Press.

Weber, Max
1922/1963 *The Sociology of Religion*. Boston: Beacon.

Weber, Max
1920/1968 *Economy and Society*. Gunther Ross (ed.). New York: Bedminster.

Weber, Max
1904/1958 *The Protestant Ethic and the Spirit of Capitalism*. New York: Scribner's.

Weiss, Robert S.
1979 *Going It Alone: The Family Life and Social Situation of the Single Parent*. New York: Basic Books.

Weitzman, Lenore J.
1979 *Sex Role Socialization*. Palo Alto, CA: Mayfield.

Weitzman, Lenore J., Deborah Eifler, Elizabeth Hokada, and Catherine Ross
1972 "Sex role socialization in picture books for pre-school children." *American Journal of Sociology* 77: 1125–1150.

Weeks, John R.
1981 *Population: An Introduction to Concepts and Issues*. Second edition. Belmont, CA: Wadsworth.

Wentworth, William M.
1980 *Context and Understanding: An Inquiry into Socialization Theory*. New York: Elsevier.

West, P., and L. C. Merriam Jr.
1970 "Outdoor recreation and family cohesiveness: A research proposal." *Journal of Leisure Research* 2: 251–259.

Westoff, Charles F.
1978 "Marriage and fertility in the developed countries." *Scientific American 239: 51–57.*

White, Lynn Jr.
1964 *Medieval Technology and Social Change*. New York: Oxford University Press.

White, R. Clyde
1955 "Social class differences in the use of leisure." *American Journal of Sociology* 61: 145–150.

Whiting, Beatrice, and Carolyn Pope Edwards
1973 "A cross-cultural analysis of sex differences in the behavior of children aged 3 through 11." *Journal of Social Psychology* 91: 171–188.

Whitt, J. Allen
1980 "Can capitalists organize themselves?" *Insurgent Sociologist* 9: 51–59.

Wickens, G. M.
1976 "Introduction to the Middle East." Pp. 1–14 in R. M. Savory (ed.), *Introduction to Islamic Civilization*. Cambridge, Eng.: Cambridge University Press.

Wiley, D. E.
1976 "Another hour, another day: Quantity of schooling, a potent path for policy." Pp. 225–265 in W. H. Sewell et al. (eds.), *Schooling and Achievement in American Society*. New York: Academic Press.

Williams, Jay R., and Martin Gold
1972 "From delinquent behavior to official delinquency." *Social Problems* 20 (fall): 209–229.

Williams, Raymond
1976 *Keywords: A Vocabulary of Culture and Society*. New York: Oxford University Press.

Williams, Raymond
1976 "Developments in the Sociology of Culture." *Sociology* 10: 497–506.

Williams, Robin M. Jr.
1966 "Some further comments on chronic controversies." *American Journal of Sociology* 71: 717–721.

Williams, Robin M. Jr.
1960 *American Society: A Sociological Interpretation*. New York: Knopf.

Willie, Charles V.
1979 *Caste and Class Controversy*. New York: General Hall.

Wilson, Bryan R.
1976 *Contemporary Transformations of Religion*. Oxford, Eng.: Oxford University Press.

Wilson, Bryan R.
1961 *Sects and Society*. Berkeley: University of California Press.

Wilson, Edward O.
1975a *Sociobiology: The New Synthesis*. Cam-

bridge, MA: Harvard University Press.

Wilson, Edward O.
1975b "Human decency is animal." *New York Times Magazine* (October 12): 38–50.

Wilson, Harriett
1980 "Parents can cut the crime rate." *New Society* 54 (December 4): 456–458.

Wilson, William Julius
1978 *The Declining Significance of Race*. Chicago: University of Chicago Press.

Winn, Marie
1977 *The Plug-In Drug: Television, Children and the Family*. New York: Viking Press.

Wirth, Louis
1938 "Urbanism as a way of life." *American Journal of Sociology* 44 (July): 3–24.

Wise, Nancy B.
1967 "Juvenile delinquency among middle-class girls." Pp. 179–188 in Edmund W. Vaz (ed.), *Middle-Class Juvenile Delinquency*. New York: Harper & Row.

Wistrand, Birgitta
1979 "Women, demand real political power!" *Dagens Nyheter* (Stockholm daily newspaper), October 28, p.2, cited in Haas.

Witkin, Herman A., et al.
1976 "Criminality in XYY and XXY men." *Science* 193: 547–555.

Witmer, David R.
1976 Is the value of college-going really declining? *Change* 8 (December): 46–47, 60–61.

Wohl, Andrzej
1970 "Competitive sport and its social functions." *International Review of Sport Sociology* 5: 117–124.

Wolf, Deborah Coleman
1979 *The Lesbian Community*. Berkeley: University of California Press.

Wolfgang, Marvin E., et al.
1972 *Delinquency in a Birth Cohort*. Chicago: University of Chicago Press.

Worsley, Peter
1968 *The Trumpet Shall Sound*. Second edition. New York: Schocken Books.

Wright, Erik Olin, and Luca Perrone
1977 "Marxist class categories and income inequality." *American Sociological Review* 42 (February): 32–55.

Wrong, Dennis
1961 "The oversocialized conception of man in modern sociology." *American Sociological Review* 26: 183–193.

Wuthnow, Robert
1976a "The new religions in social context." Pp. 267–293 in C. Glock and R. Bellah (eds.), *The New Religious Consciousness*. Berkeley: University of California Press.

Wuthnow, Robert
1976b *The Consciousness Reformation*. Berkeley: University of California Press.

Yaeger, Matthew G.
1979 "Unemployment and imprisonment." *Journal of Criminal Law and Criminology* 70: 586–588.

Yankelovich, Daniel
1978 "The new psychological contracts at work." *Psychology Today* (May): 46, 47, 49.

Yankelovich, Skelly, and White Survey
1978 "Views on morality." *Public Opinion* (December–January): 27.

Yankelovich, Skelly, and White Survey
1977 "Views on morality." *Public Opinion* (December–January): 27.

Yarrow, Marian Radke, Charlotte Green Schwartz, Harriet S. Murphy, and Leila Calhoun Deasy
1955 "The psychological meaning of mental illness in the family." *Journal of Social Issues* 11: 12–24.

Yinger, J. Milton
1977 "Counterculture and social change." *American Sociological Review* 42: 833–853.

Zabin, Laurie Schwab
1981 "The impact of early use of prescription contraceptives on reducing premarital teenage pregnancies." *Family Planning Perspectives* 13: 72–74.

Zablocki, Benjamin D., and Rosabeth Moss Kanter
1976 "The differentiation of life-styles." Pp. 269–298 in Alex Inkeles, James Coleman, and Neil Smelser (eds.), *Annual Review of Sociology*. Palo Alto, CA: Annual Reviews, Inc.

Zald, Mayer N., and John D. McCarthy (eds.)
1979 *The Dynamics of Social Movements*. Cambridge, MA: Winthrop.

Zaret, David
1981 Review of *Understanding Society* manuscript for Harper & Row.

Zaretsky, Eli
1978 "The effects of the economic crisis on the family." Pp. 209–218 in *U.S. Capitalism in Crisis*. New York: Union for Radical Political Economics.

Zaretsky, Eli
1976 *Capitalism, the Family, and Personal Life*. New York: Harper & Row.

Zatz, Marjorie
1982 Personal communication.

Zborowski, Mark

1981 "Cultural components in responses to pain." Pp. 126–138 in Peter Conrad and Rochelle Kern (eds.), *The Sociology of Health and Illness*. New York: St. Martin's Press.

Zeitlin, Irving M.
1967 *Marxism: A Reexamination*. New York: Van Nostrand.

Zeitlin, Maurice
1974 "Corporate ownership and control: The large corporation and the capitalist class." *American Journal of Sociology* 79: 1073–1119.

Zelditch, Morris Jr.
1955 "Role differentiation in the nuclear family: A comparative study." Chapter 2 in Talcott Parsons and Robert F. Bales (eds.), *Family, Socialization and Interaction Process Analysis*. New York: Free Press.

Zelnik, Melvin, and John F. Kanter
1980 "Sexual activity, contraceptive use and pregnancy among metropolitan-area teenagers: 1971–1979." *Family Planning Perspectives* 12: 230–231, 233–237.

Ziman, John
1976 *The Force of Knowledge*. New York: Cambridge University Press.

Zimbardo, Philip G.
1972 "Pathology of imprisonment." *Society* 9 (April): 4–8.

Zimmerman, Don H., and D. Lawrence Wieder
1970 "Ethnomethodology and the problem of order: Comments on Denzin." Pp. 287–295 in Jack Douglas (ed.), *Understanding Everyday Life*. Chicago: Aldine.

Zingg, Robert M.
1942 "Feral man and cases of extreme isolation of individuals." Pp. 131–365 in J. M. L. Singh and Robert M. Zingg, *Wolf-Children and Feral Man*. New York: Harper & Brothers.

Zuckerman, Harriet, and Robert K. Merton
1971 "Patterns of evaluation in science: Institutionalisation, structure and functions of the referee system." *Minerva* 9: 66–100.

Zurcher, Louis A. Jr.
1977 *The Mutable Self: A Self-Concept for Social Change*. Beverly Hills, CA: Sage.

Zwerdling, Daniel
1980 *Workplace Democracy*. New York: Harper & Row.

Index

F

S

83 84 85 86 87 9 8 7 6 5 4 3 2 1